Employment Law for Business

Fifth Edition

Dawn D. Bennett-Alexander
University of Georgia

Laura P. Hartman
DePaul University

McGraw-Hill Irwin

Boston   Burr Ridge, IL   Dubuque, IA   Madison, WI   New York   San Francisco   St. Louis
Bangkok   Bogotá   Caracas   Kuala Lumpur   Lisbon   London   Madrid   Mexico City
Milan   Montreal   New Delhi   Santiago   Seoul   Singapore   Sydney   Taipei   Toronto

**McGraw-Hill
Irwin**

EMPLOYMENT LAW FOR BUSINESS
Published by McGraw-Hill/Irwin, a business unit of The McGraw-Hill Companies, Inc., 1221
Avenue of the Americas, New York, NY, 10020. Copyright © 2007 by The McGraw-Hill Companies, Inc.
All rights reserved. No part of this publication may be reproduced or distributed in any form or by
any means, or stored in a database or retrieval system, without the prior written consent of The McGraw-
Hill Companies, Inc., including, but not limited to, in any network or other electronic storage
or transmission, or broadcast for distance learning.

Some ancillaries, including electronic and print components, may not be available to customers
outside the United States.

This book is printed on acid-free paper.

1 2 3 4 5 6 7 8 9 0 DOC/DOC 0 9 8 7 6 5

ISBN-13: 978-0-07-302895-8
ISBN-10: 0-07-302895-9

Editorial director: *John E. Biernat*
Senior sponsoring editor: *Kelly H. Lowery*
Editorial assistant: *Kirsten Guidero*
Senior marketing manager: *Lisa Nicks*
Media producer: *Benjamin Curless*
Project manager: *Bruce Gin*
Senior production supervisor: *Rose Hepburn*
Designer: *Kami Carter*
Senior media project manager: *Lynn M. Bluhm*
Cover design: *Kami Carter*
Interior design: *Kami Carter*
Typeface: *10.5/12 Times New Roman*
Compositor: *Cenveo*
Printer: *R. R. Donnelley*

Library of Congress Cataloging-in-Publication Data

Bennett-Alexander, Dawn.
    Employment law for business / Dawn D. Bennett-Alexander, Laura P. Hartman.—5th ed.
        p. cm.
    Includes index.
    ISBN-13: 978-0-07-302895-8 (alk. paper)
    ISBN-10: 0-07-302895-9 (alk. paper)
    1. Labor laws and legislation—United States. 2. Discrimination in employment—Law and
legislation—United States. I. Hartman, Laura Pincus. II. Title.
    KF3455.B46 2007
    344.7301—dc22   2005049646

www.mhhe.com

My Habeebee

and

My very first Grandchild
Can't wait to see you!!

and

Dr. Patricia Del Rey
Bet you never dreamed this would come out of the course you
asked for ☺—thanx!

D D B-A

With my love, to my wondrous and wonderful children, Emma
and Rachel.

L P H

About the Authors

Dawn D. Bennett-Alexander *University of Georgia*

Dawn D. Bennett-Alexander, Esq., is an award-winning tenured associate professor of employment law and legal studies at the University of Georgia's Terry College of Business and an attorney admitted to practice in the District of Columbia and six federal jurisdictions. She is a cum laude graduate of the Howard University School of Law and a magna cum laude graduate of the Federal City College, now the University of the District of Columbia. She was cofounder and cochair, with her coauthor, of the Employment and Labor Law Section of the Academy of Legal Studies in Business and coeditor of the section's *Employment and Labor Law Quarterly;* past coeditor of the section's newsletter; and past president of the Southeastern Academy of Legal Studies in Business. Bennett-Alexander taught employment law in the University of North Florida's MBA program from 1982 to 1987 and has been conducting employment law seminars for managers and supervisors since 1985. Prior to teaching, Bennett-Alexander worked at the Federal Labor Relations Authority, the White House Domestic Council, the U.S. Federal Trade Commission, Antioch School of Law, and as law clerk to the Honorable Julia Cooper Mack at the highest court in the District of Columbia, the D.C. Court of Appeals. Bennett-Alexander publishes widely in the employment law area, is a noted expert on employment law and diversity issues, was asked to write the first-ever sexual harassment entry for *Grolier Encyclopedia,* edited the National Employee Rights Institute's definitive book on federal employment, has been widely quoted on TV, radio, and in the print press, including *USA Today, The Wall Street Journal,* and *Fortune* magazine, and is founder of Practical Diversity, consultants on diversity and employment law issues. Bennett-Alexander was a 2000–2001 recipient of the Fulbright Senior Scholar Fellowship under which she taught at the Ghana School of Law in Ghana, West Africa, and conducted research on race and gender in employment. She dedicates all her research and writing in this area to her three daughters and will be a proud Grandma for the first time on March 13, 2006! ☺

Laura P. Hartman *DePaul University*

Laura Hartman is Associate Vice President for Academic Affairs at DePaul University, where she is responsible for coordinating the development of new academic programs. She is also a Professor of Business Ethics and Legal Studies in the Management Department in DePaul's College of Commerce.

Hartman's scholarship focuses on the ethics of the employment relationship with a primary emphasis in the areas of global labor conditions and standards, and the impact of technology on the employment relationship. Her research and consulting efforts have garnered national media attention by publications such as *Fortune Small Business* where she was named one of the "Top 10 Minds for Small Business," as well as *The Wall Street Journal, BusinessWeek,* and the *New York Times.* She has written several texts, including *Rising Above Sweatshops: Innovative Management Approaches to Global Labor Challenges, Employment Law for Business, and Perspectives in Business Ethics.*

She serves on several editorial boards including that of the predominant academic journal in business ethics, *Business Ethics Quarterly.*

Professor Hartman has engaged in ethics training workshops and presentations for a number of local and international companies and professional associations at the employee, executive, and board levels. Her ability to appropriately translate the ethics training for each of these levels is one of her noteworthy strengths. Previously, Hartman held the Grainger Chair of Business Ethics at the University of Wisconsin–Madison School of Business. She has also served as an adjunct professor of business law and ethics at Northwestern's Kellogg Graduate School of Management.

In 2003, Hartman was awarded the First Annual Vincentian Ethics Award. She currently serves on the Board of Directors of DePaul's Institute for Business & Professional Ethics, previously held DePaul's Wicklander Chair in Professional Ethics, and served as chair of the University's Public Service Council. She was president of the Society for Business Ethics and cofounder and cochair of the Employment and Labor Law Section of the Academy of Legal Studies in Business. In addition, she was coeditor of the section's Employment and Labor Law Quarterly, and served as president of the Midwest Academy of Legal Studies in Business for the 1994–1995 term.

Hartman graduated magna cum laude from Tufts University and received her law degree from the University of Chicago Law School. She currently serves as vice president of the Francis W. Parker School Alumni Board. She lives in Chicago with her two daughters, Emma and Rachel.

Preface to the First Edition

- If a disabled employee could perform the job requirements when hired, but the job has progressed and the employee is no longer able to perform, must the employer keep her on?
- Is an employer liable when a supervisor sexually harasses an employee, but the employer knew nothing of it?
- Is an employer liable for racial discrimination because she terminates a black male who refuses to abide by the "no-beard" rule?
- Can an employer be successfully sued for "reverse discrimination" by an employee who feels harmed by the employer's affirmative action plan?
- How far can an employer go in instituting a dress code?
- If an employer has two equally qualified applicants from which to choose and prefers the white one to the black one, is it illegal discrimination for the employer to hire the white applicant, or must the employer hire the black one?
- Must an employer send to training the employee who is in line to attend, if that employee will retire shortly?
- Must an employer keep an employee known to be HIV-positive when other employees fear for their own health because of their exposure to the HIV-positive employee?
- Is it a violation of wage and hour laws for an employer to hire his 13-year-old daughter to pick strawberries during the summer?
- Is an ex-employer liable for defamation if he gives a negative recommendation about an ex-employee to a potential employer who inquires?
- Must an employer disclose to employees that chemicals with which they work are potentially harmful?
- Can an employer stop employees from forming a union?

These types of questions, which are routinely decided in workplaces everyday, can have devastating financial and productivity consequences if mishandled by the employer. Yet few employers or their managers and supervisors are equipped to handle them well. That is why this textbook was created.

Between fiscal years 1970 when newly enacted job discrimination legislation cases started to rise and 1983, the number of federal discrimination suits grew from fewer than 350 per year to around 9,000 per year. This is an astonishing 2,166 percent growth in the volume of discrimination suits, compared with only 125 percent growth in general federal civil cases for the same period. A major factor in this statistic is that the groups protected by Title VII of the Civil Rights Act of 1964 and similar legislation, including minorities, women, and white males over 40, now constitute over 70 percent of the total workforce. Add to that number those protected by laws addressing disability, wages and hours, and unions, workplace environmental right-to-know laws, tort laws, and occupational safety and health laws, and the percentage increases even more. There was a 95.7 percent increase from 1969's 45.84 million such employees to 1989's 89.70 million employees.

It is good that employers and employees alike are now getting the benefits derived from having a safer, fairer workplace and one more reflective of the population's diversity. However, this is not without its attendant challenges. One of those challenges is reflected in the statistics given above. With the advent of workplace regulation by the government, particularly the Civil Rights Act of 1964, there is more of an expectation by employees of certain basic rights in the workplace. When these expectations are not met, and the affected population comprises more than 70 percent of the workforce, problems and their attendant litigation will be high.

Plaintiffs won 57 percent of lawsuits brought for wrongful termination based on race, gender, and disability discrimination in the seven-year period between 1988 and 1995. The median compensatory damage award was more than $100,000. Much of the litigation and liability arising in the area covered by these statistics is avoidable. Many times the only difference between an employer being sued or not is a manager or supervisor who recognizes that the decision being made may lead to unnecessary litigation and thus avoids it.

We have seen what types of employment law problems are most prevalent in the workplace from our extensive experience in the classroom, in our research and writing, as well as in conducting over the years many employment seminars for managers, supervisors, business owners, equal employment opportunity officers, human resources personnel, general counsels, and others. We have seen how management most often strays from appropriate considerations and treads on thin legal ice, exposing it to potential increased liability. We came to realize that many of the mistakes were based on ignorance rather than malice. Often it was simply not knowing that a decision was being handled incorrectly.

Becoming more aware of potential liability does not mean the employer is not free to make legitimate workplace decisions. It simply means that those decisions are handled appropriately in ways that lessen or avoid liability. The problem does not lie in not being able to terminate the female who is chronically late for work because the employer thinks she will sue for gender discrimination. Rather, the challenge lies in doing it in a way that precludes her from being able to file a successful claim. It does not mean the employer must retain her, despite her failure to adequately meet workplace expectations and requirements. It means simply that the employer must make certain the termination is beyond reproach. If the employee has performed in a way that results in termination, this should be documentable and, therefore, defensible.

Termination of the employee under such circumstances should present no problem, assuming similarly situated employees have been treated consistently in the same manner. The employer is free to make the management decisions necessary to run the business, but she or he simply does so correctly.

Knowing how to do so correctly doesn't just happen. It must be learned. We set out to create a textbook aimed at anyone who would, or presently does, manage people. Knowing what is in this book is a necessity. For those already in the workplace, your day is filled with one awkward situation after another—for which you wish you had the answers. For those in school, you will soon be in the workplace, and in the not-too-distant future you will likely be in a position managing others. We cannot promise answers to every one of your questions, but we can promise that we will provide the information and basic considerations in most areas that will help you arrive at an informed, reasonable, and defensible answer about which you can feel more comfortable. You will not walk away feeling as if you rolled the dice when you made a workplace decision, and then wait with anxiety to see if the decision will backfire in some way.

In an effort to best inform employers of the reasoning behind legal requirements and to provide a basis for making decisions in "gray areas," we often provide background in relevant social or political movements, or both, as well as in legislative history and other relevant considerations. Law is not created in a vacuum, and this information gives the law context so the purpose is more easily understood. Often understanding why a law exists can help an employer make the correct choices in interpreting the law when making workplace decisions with no clear-cut answers.

Legal cases are used to illustrate important concepts; however, we realize that it is the managerial aspects of the concepts with which you must deal. Therefore, we took great pains to try to rid the cases of unnecessary "legalese" and procedural matters that would be more relevant to a lawyer or law student. We also follow each case with questions designed to aid in thinking critically about the issues involved from an employer's standpoint, rather than from a purely legal standpoint. We understand that *how* employers make their decisions has a great impact on the decisions made. Therefore, our case-end questions are designed as critical-thinking questions to get the student to go beyond the legal concepts and think critically about management issues. This process of learning to analyze and think critically about issues from different points of view will greatly enhance student decision-making abilities as future managers or business owners. Addressing the issues in the way they are likely to arise in life greatly enhances that ability.

It is one thing to know that the law prohibits gender discrimination in employment. It is quite another to recognize such discrimination when it occurs and govern oneself accordingly. For instance, a female employee says she cannot use a "filthy" toilet, which is the only one at the work site. The employer can dismiss the complaint and tell the employee she must use the toilet, and perhaps later be held liable for gender discrimination. Or the employer can think of what implications this may have, given that this is a female employee essentially being denied a right that male employees have in access to a usable toilet. The employer then realizes there may be a problem and is more likely to make the better decision.

This seemingly unlikely scenario is based on an actual case, which you will later read. It is a great example of how simple but unexpected decisions can create liability in surprising ways. Knowing the background and intent of a law often can help in situations where the answer to the problem may not be readily apparent. Including the law in your thinking can help the thought process for making well-founded decisions.

We also have included boxed items from easily accessible media sources that you come across every day, such as *People* magazine and the *USA Today* newspaper. The intent is to demonstrate how the matters discussed are interesting and integrated into everyday life, yet they can have serious repercussions for employers.

Much of today's litigation results from workplace decisions arising from unfortunate ideas about various groups and from lack of awareness about what may result in litigation. We do not want to take away anyone's right to think whatever he or she wants about whomever he or she wants, but we do want to teach that those thoughts may result in legal trouble when they are acted on.

Something new and innovative must be done if we are to break the cycle of insensitivity and myopia that results in spiraling numbers of unnecessary lawsuits. Part of breaking this cycle is language and using terminology that more accurately reflects those considerations. We have, therefore, in a rather unorthodox move, taken the offensive and created a path, rather than followed one.

For instance, the term "sex" is used in this text to mean sex only in a purely sexual sense. The term "gender" is used to distinguish males from females. With the increasing use of sexual harassment as a cause of action, it became confusing to continue to speak of "sex" as meaning gender, particularly when it adds to the confusion to understand that sex need *not* be present in a sexual harassment claim but gender differences *are* required. For instance, to say that a claim must be based on "a difference in treatment based on sex" leaves it unclear as to whether it means gender or sexual activity. Since it actually means gender, we have made such clarifications. Also, use of the term "sex" in connection with gender discrimination cases, the majority of which are brought by women, continues to inject sexuality into the equation of women and work. This, in turn, contributes to keeping women and sexuality connected in an inappropriate setting (employment). Further, it does so at a time when there is an attempt to decrease such connections and, instead, concentrate on the applicant's qualifications for the job.

So, too, with the term "homosexuality." In this text, the term "affinity orientation" is used instead. The traditional term emphasizes, for one group and not others, the highly personal yet generally irrelevant issue of the employee's sexuality. The use of the term sets up those within that group for consideration as different (usually interpreted to be "less than"), when they may well be qualified for the job and otherwise acceptable. With sexuality being highlighted in referring to them, it becomes difficult to think of them in any other light. The term also continues to pander to the historically more sensational or titillating aspects of the applicant's personal life and uses it to color her or his entire life when all that should be of interest is ability to do the job. Using more appropriate terminology will hopefully keep the focus on that ability.

The term "disabled" is used, rather than "handicapped," to conform to the more enlightened view taken by the Americans with Disabilities Act of 1990. It gets away from the old notion that those who were differently abled went "cap in hand" looking for handouts. Rather, it recognizes the importance of including in employment these 43 million Americans who can contribute to the workplace.

There is also a diligent effort to use gender-inclusive or neutral terminology—for example, police officers, rather than policemen; firefighters, rather than firemen; servers, rather than waiters or waitresses; flight attendants, rather than stewards or stewardesses. We urge you to add to the list and use such language in your conversations. To use different terminology for males and females performing the same job reflects a gender difference when there is no need to do so. If, as the law requires, it is irrelevant because it is the job itself on which we wish to focus, then our language should reflect this.

It is not simply a matter of terminology. Terminology is powerful. It conveys ideas to us about the matter spoken of. To the extent we change our language to be more neutral when referring to employees, it will be easier to change our ingrained notions of the "appropriateness" of traditional employment roles based on gender, sexuality, or other largely irrelevant criteria and make employment discrimination laws more effective.

This conscious choice of language also is not a reflection of temporal "political correctness" considerations. It goes far beyond what terming something "politically correct" tends to do. These changes in terminology are substantive and nontrivial changes that attempt to have language reflect reality, rather than have our reality shaped and limited by the language we use. Being sensitive to the matter of language can help make us more sensitive to what stands behind the words. That is an important aid in avoiding liability and obeying the law.

The best way to determine what an employer must do to avoid liability for employment decisions is to look at cases to see what courts have used to determine previous liability. This is why we have provided many and varied cases for you to consider. Much care has been taken to make the cases not only relevant, informative, and illustrative but also interesting, up to date, and easy to read. There is a good mix of new cases, along with the old "standards" that still define an area. We have assiduously tried to avoid legalese and intricate legal consideration. Instead, we emphasize the legal managerial aspects of cases—that is, what does the case mean that management should or should not do to be best protected from violating the law?

We wanted the textbook to be informative, readable, and a resource, to encourage critical and creative thinking about workplace problems, and to sensitize you to the need for effective workplace management. We think we have accomplished our goal. We hope the text is as interesting and informative for you to read and use as it was exciting and challenging for us to write.

We *sincerely* would like to know what you think. We urge you to write and let us know—good or bad—your thoughts.

Dawn D. Bennett-Alexander
Terry College of Business
University of Georgia
202 Brooks Hall
Athens, GA 30602-6255
(706) 542-4290
E-mail: dawndba@uga.edu

Laura P. Hartman
Executive Offices
DePaul University
1 E. Jackson Blvd.
Chicago, IL 60604-2787
(312) 362-6569
E-mail: lhartman@depaul.edu

Preface to the Fifth Edition

Wow! If you only *knew!* The **Fifth** Edition! A-mazing. When we first began this venture more than 10 years ago, we didn't know if we'd be able to sell enough copies of the textbook to justify even having a *second* edition!

Luckily, we had a publisher who understood the situation and made a commitment to hang in there with us. The problem was that there was no established market for this textbook. There were so few classes in this area that they didn't even show up as a blip on the radar screen. Actually, we only knew of two! But having worked in this area for years, we knew the need was there, even if the students, faculty, and even employers weren't aware of it yet. You can imagine that a publisher would not want to take on the risk of publishing a textbook that was only going to sit on the shelves because there were no classes providing a market of students!

We convinced the publishers that "if you publish it, they will come."

And come they did. From the minute the book was first released, it was embraced. And just as we thought, classes were developed, students flooded in, and by the time the smoke cleared, the first edition had exceeded all the publisher's forecasts and expectations. The need that we knew was there really was there, and an entire discipline was created. The project has never looked back since. The textbook remains the leading textbook of its kind in the country and is still outselling its projections!

We can't thank the publishers enough for being so committed to this textbook. Without their commitment, none of this would have happened. And we can't thank professors and students enough for being there for us, supporting us, believing in the textbook and our voices, and trusting that we will honor the law and our commitment to bring the best to faculty and students.

As we have done with other editions, in this fifth edition, we have continued to make updates and improvements that we think will help students understand better. We have included new cases, updated text, added new boxed information, added up-to-the-minute legal issues, more insights, and a modified structure. We have kept the things you tell us you love, and even added to them.

As always, we *truly* welcome your feedback. We are the only textbook we know of that actually gets fan letters! Keep them coming! ☺ We urge you to e-mail us about any thoughts you have about the text, good or bad, as well as suggestions, unclear items you don't understand, errata, or anything else you think would be helpful. And again as always, we hope you have as much fun reading the book as we did writing it. It really is a pleasure. Enjoy!

Dawn D. Bennett-Alexander, Esq.

Athens, GA

August 20, 2005

Acknowledgments

The authors would like to honor and thank the following individuals, without whose assistance and support this text would never have been written: McGraw-Hill Higher Education editorial support, including Craig Beytien, for having the insight and courage to sign the first employment law text of its kind before many others were able to see the vast but undeniable merit of doing so; Kelly H. Lowery, editor; and Kirsten Guidero, editorial assistant. Finally, for their contributions to our fifth edition revisions, we would like to thank the scholars who have class tested and reviewed this manuscript, including the following:

Margaret Leibowitz
Cornell University; New York Law School

Mike Kendrich
Lipscomb University (TN)

Nancy Boyd-Lillie
University of North Texas

Curt Behrens
Northern Illinois University

Lisa Hubacek
University of Texas

Dana Richardson
Northwest Louisiana Tech College

Susan Gardner
California State University–Chico

Elizabeth Wilson
Georgia Southwestern State University

Charles Hollon
Shippensburg University of Pennsylvania

David Hames
University of Nevada–Las Vegas

Steven L. Popejoy
Central Mission State University

Bennett-Alexander: I would like to thank (1) my coauthor, Laura Pincus Hartman, one of my very favorite people in the whole world, for her wonderful enthusiasm, intellect, energy, support, and hard work; (2) our publishers, editors and other support staff who love this project as much as we do—Kelly Lowery, you're the best!; (3) my daughters Jenniffer Dawn Bennett Alexander Jones, Anne Alexis Bennett-Alexander, and Tess Alexandra-Bennett Harrison for being my special gifts from above and for knowing that my very favorite thing in the whole world is being their Mama—even though they drive me crazy ☺; (4) Saeid El Manglify, my precious Egyptian habeebee, for finding me in the Sahara and convincing me I must listen to him—he was right; (5) my sisters, Brenda Bennett Watkins and Dr. Gale C. Bennett Harris for their unwavering confidence, love, support, and laughs; (6) Edward Demont Jones (my Ed), for loving my Jen so, treating us both like queens, and being so very, very funny; (7) Ray Gant (my Ray Ray), #90 Georgia Bulldog Defensive Lineman, for the laughs, lessons, laundry, and football info ☺; (8) my department chair, Dr. Rob Hoyt, who is supportive in so many ways; (9) the thousands of managers, supervisors, employers, and employees who have shared their experiences and insights over the years; (10) my colleagues from across the country who have been so very supportive of this text; and, last but *certainly* not least, (11) my favorites, my students, who are a never-ending source of utter wonder, insight, and fun for me. Do we have a good time, *or what?*

This text is *immeasurably* richer for having the contributions of *each* of you.

DDB-A

Hartman: I am grateful for the assistance of so many individuals who have helped to bring this fifth edition to press. First, I am always and eternally grateful for the existence on this earth of my coauthor, Dawn (and her willingness to continue to work alongside me). I would never have the interest in continuing if I did not have the warmth, compassion, and acceptance on which I have learned to rely from Dawn. We are both grateful for the continued support of our editor, Kelly Lowery (and Andy Winston before her) and their staff.

Second, I am grateful to Shannon Shumpert, former Associate General Counsel at DePaul, for drafting the section on HIPAA, and to my friend and colleague Robin Struve for making sure my ERISA chapter was up to speed and for adding her own sophisticated legal expertise through significant modifications. Any mistakes in either area are completely my own!

Finally, I owe peace in my life to those who are responsible for creating it in my heart—my daughters Emma and Rachel.

LPH

Text Organization

Part 1 gives the foundations for employment law, covering introductory topics and cases to set the stage for later coverage. This initial section now includes more material to give students a more thorough grounding.

Chapter 1 now includes more coverage of topics essential to understanding the employer–employee relationship, such as testing, assessments, and discussion of basic terms and situations. The material in this chapter has been reorganized so that it now has a more intuitive flow.

Chapter 2 now covers Title VII of the Civil Rights Act in order to illustrate the foundational nature this groundbreaking legislation has for employment law.

Chapter 3 now encompasses the legal structure that defines the employment relationship and the evolution of that relationship, including how the law governs recruitment, selection, hiring, testing, appraisals, and other connected issues. This chapter has been expanded to reflect recent changes.

Part 2 covers various types of discrimination in employment, with each chapter revised to reflect recent changes.

Chapter 4 includes the recent case upholding affirmative action, *Grutter* v. *Bollinger,* recent revisions to affirmative action regulations, and misuse of affirmative action.

Chapter 5 has been expanded with a historical overview of racism in the United States, giving students a deeper understanding of how prevalent racial discrimination still is.

Chapter 6 features updates to gender discrimination issues and case outcomes, including coverage of pregnancy discrimination, gender stereotypes, employer grooming codes, and how the FMLA affects the employment relationship.

Chapter 7 clearly explains the difference between quid pro quo and hostile environment sexual harassment as well as how to avoid employer liability in this important area.

xiv

Employment Law for Business, 5e has been significantly revised and updated to reflect the latest developments in a wide spectrum of case law and regulatory legislation, giving students and instructors the most thorough yet accessible coverage available. Part 1 of this edition has also been reorganized so that the presentation of topics follows a more intuitive ordering. In addition, essential pedagogical tools have been strengthened to better facilitate learning, including changes to the chapter-opening scenarios, expansions in the end-of-chapter questions, and updates to the key terms with definitions. Take a look at the new organization and key features that will help anchor your understanding of employment law.

Chapter 8 discusses developments in affinity orientation discrimination issues and offers management tips on how to handle this fast-evolving topic.

Chapter 9 gives students up-to-date considerations on the many aspects of religious discrimination, including explanations of the legal definition of religion, points on the employer's duty to reasonably accommodate employees, and information on the correct usage of religion as a BFOQ.

A new section in Chapter 10 covers harassment based on national origin, including case coverage and updates on post–September 11, 2001, developments.

Chapter 11 incorporates brand-new coverage of age discrimination, including the landmark 2005 case, *Smith* v. *City of Jackson.*

Chapter 12 explores the complex world of disability discrimination, featuring discussion on intellectual disabilities and five new cases.

Part 3 lays out additional regulatory processes and dilemmas in employment.

Chapter 13 covers right to privacy issues, with updates on post–September 11, 2001 regulations.

Chapter 14 includes material on the Fair Labor Standards Act (FLSA) guidelines and the major overhaul of overtime regulations.

Chapter 15 includes material on new OSHA standards, penalties for violations, and new statistics in occupational health and safety.

Chapter 16 discusses new ERISA regulations and their implications, including coverage of HIPAA and related materials.

Chapter 17 discusses labor law history and considerations.

Key Features for the Fifth Edition

Chapter Outlines

Each chapter begins with an outline of topics covered, giving students a bird's-eye view of the material and making it easy to jump directly to particular subjects within a chapter. Use the outline to refresh your memory of key chapter subjects, as a quick reference point, and as an overview demonstrating how chapter topics are linked together.

Opening Scenarios

Based on real cases and situations, chapter-opening scenarios introduce topics and material that illustrate the need for chapter concepts. Scenarios are then revisited throughout the chapter text as material pertinent to the opening scenario is discussed. When you encounter the scenario icon in the chapter body, return to the corresponding opening scenario to see if you can now articulate the correct way to solve the problem.

Opening Scenarios

SCENARIO 1

Emma Bina is working as a research scientist at a laboratory when she is approached with an employment offer from a competing laboratory. The competing lab director offers Emma nearly double her present salary and superior research equipment and opportunities. The lab director tells Emma that she can remain employed with the new company as long as she does satisfactory work. Emma accepts the offer, sells her house, takes her dog and cats and moves to the new state, buys a new house, and settles in. Emma's first two evaluations are superior. Then, six months after arriving, Emma is terminated and...

SCENARIO 2

Mark Richter is about to retire as a candy salesperson when he closes on a deal the candy company has been trying to land for a long time. Just before Mark is to collect his substantial commission, he is terminated. Does Mark have a basis on which to sue for unlawful termination?

SCENARIO 3

Jenna Zitron informs her employer that she has been summoned to serve jury duty for a week. Though rescheduling her duties is not a problem, Jenna is told by her employer that, if she serves jury duty over the protest of the employer...

ex-employee must show that the employer's actions were motivated by *bad faith, malice, or retaliation.* At least 44 states allow this exception. Violations of public policy usually arise from the employee being terminated for acts such as refusing to violate a criminal statute on behalf of the employer or at the employer's request, exercising a statutory right, fulfilling a statutory duty, or disclosing violations of statutes by an employer.

For instance, a state may have a law that says that qualified citizens must serve jury duty unless they come within one of the statutory exceptions. The employer does not want the employee to miss work by serving jury duty. The employee serves jury duty and is terminated by the employer. The employee sues the employer for unjust dismissal. The employer counters with the at-will doctrine, which states that the employer can terminate the employee for any reason the employer wishes to use. The Jury System Improvements Act prohibits employers from discriminating based on jury service in federal courts. States vary in terms of their protection for state and local jury service. Even in states where the protection is less clear, many courts have then held that the employer's termination of the employee under these circumstances constitutes a violation of public policy. That is, by

Management Tips

These boxes, included near the conclusion of each chapter, encapsulate how key concepts relate to managerial concerns. The authors offer concise tips on how to put chapter material into practice in the real world.

Management Tips

- Always evaluate the status of your workers; don't assume employee or independent-contractor status for any worker.
- Employment status is relevant to employer payroll and other financial issues; therefore, misclassification may be costly to the employer.
- While an employer is not liable to independent contractors for discrimination based on Title VII, the independent contractor may have other causes of action. Therefore, hiring an independent contractor is not a safe harbor from liability.

- other factors, the worker has complete control over the manner in which the work will be done, uses her or his own supplies, is paid by the project rather than by the hour, and sets her or his own hours to complete the project.
- Monitor staffing firms with which you contract for temporary or other contingent workers to ensure that the workers are being properly paid and that the firm provides workers' compensation coverage.[1]

Key Terms

Key terms are indicated in boldface and defined in the margin the first time the term is used. The terms are also listed in the glossary at the end of the book for quick reference.

Figures and Exhibits

Numerous exhibits and figures are included throughout the text to reinforce concepts visually and to provide students with essential background information.

Chapter Summaries

Each chapter closes with a summary section, giving students and instructors a tool for checking comprehension. Use this bulleted list as an aide in retaining key chapter points.

Summary

- Why is the definition of "employee" important? The distinction between employees and independent contractors is crucial from a financial perspective. Because many regulations require different responsibilities from employers of employees and independent contractors, it is imperative that an employer be confident of the classification of its employees.
- How does an employer make the distinction between employees and independent contractors? The classification of employees may vary depending on the statute that is to be applied or on the court in which a given case is scheduled to be heard. However, the common thread is generally the right of the employer to control the actions of the worker. Where this is present, the worker is likely to be considered an employee. Other factors to be considered include those that are part of the economic realities test, which evaluates the economics of the employment situation. Finally, some workers may be classified statutorily as employees, making the distinction all the easier.
- Who is an "employer"? The definition of employer is generally agreed on. An employer is usually thought to be one who employs or uses others (either employees or independent contractors, or both) to do its work, or to work on its behalf.
- When an employer decides to terminate an employee, there is always a reason for the termination. The reason need not be fair or even justified; only tricky is that it would not

Guide to Reading Cases

This guide gives succinct direction on how get the most out of text cases. Terminology definitions, case citation explanations, and a walkthrough of the trial process are all included to help facilitate student comprehension.

Guide to Reading Cases

Thank you very much to the several students who have contacted us and asked that we improve your understanding by including a guide to reading and understanding the cases. We consider the cases an important and integral part of the chapters. By viewing the court decisions included in the text, you get to see for yourself what the court considers important when deciding a given issue. This in turn gives you as a decision maker insight into what you need to keep in mind when making decisions on similar issues in the workplace. The more you know about how a court thinks about issues that may end up in litigation, the better you can avoid it.

We provide the following in order to help you better understand the cases so that you can use them to their fullest. In order to tell you about how to view the cases, we have

Cases with Discussion Questions

Multiple cases are embedded within each chapter to illustrate main points. Cases include background information and excerpts from court proceedings so students get a snapshot of how issues play out in real-life litigations. Cases also include questions prompting students to synthesize case details with chapter coverage by using critical thinking.

Palmateer v. International Harvester Company *85 Ill.2d 124, 421 N.E.2d 876 (1981)*

Ray Palmateer had worked for International Harvester (IH) for 16 years at the time of his discharge. Palmateer sued IH for retaliatory discharge, claiming that he was terminated because he supplied information to local law enforcement authorities regarding a co-worker's criminal activities and for offering to assist in the investigation and trial of the co-worker if necessary.

Simon, J.

[The court discusses the history of the tort of retaliatory discharge in Illinois and explains that the law will not support the termination of an at-will employment relationship where the termination would contravene public policy.] But the Achilles heel of the principle lies in the definition of public policy. When a discharge contravenes public policy in any way, the employer has committed a legal wrong. However, the employer re-

one favoring the effective protection of the lives and property of citizens.

No specific constitutional or statutory provision requires a citizen to take an active part in the ferreting out and the prosecution of crime, but public policy nevertheless favors citizen crime-fighters. Public policy favors Palmateer's conduct in volunteering information to the law enforcement agency. Palmateer was under a statutory duty to further assist officials when requested to do so.

The foundation of the tort of retaliatory discharge

contravenes public policy in any way, the employer has committed a legal wrong. However, the employer retains the right to fire workers at will in cases "where no clear mandate of public policy is involved."

There is no precise definition of the term. In general, it can be said that public policy concerns what is right and just and what affects the citizens of the State collectively. It is to be found in the State's constitution and statutes and, when they are silent, in its judicial decisions. Although there is no precise line of demarcation dividing matters that are the subject of public policies from matters purely personal, a survey of cases in other States involving retaliatory discharge shows that a matter must strike at the heart of a citizen's social rights, duties, and responsibilities before the tort will be allowed.

It is clear that Palmateer has here alleged that he was fired in violation of an established public policy. There is no public policy more basic, nothing more implicit in the concept of ordered liberty than the enforcement of a State's criminal code. There is no public

duty to further assist officials when requested to do so.

The foundation of the tort of retaliatory discharge lies in the protection of public policy, and there is a clear public policy favoring investigation and prosecution of criminal offenses. Palmateer has stated a cause of action for retaliatory discharge.

Case Questions

1. Is there a difference between the court's protection of an employee who reports a rape by a co-worker or the theft of a car, and an employee who is constantly reporting the theft of the company's paper clips and pens?
2. Should the latter employee in the above question be protected? Consider that the court in *Palmateer* remarked that "the magnitude of the crime is not the issue here. It was the General Assembly who decided that the theft of a $2 screwdriver was a problem that should be resolved by resort to the criminal justice system."
3. What are other areas of public policy that might

End of Chapter Material

Included at the end of each chapter is a complete set of questions incorporating chapter concepts. Use these as tools to assess your understanding of chapter material.

Chapter-End Questions

1. Holtzman began working for World Book as a part-time sales representative in 1983. Her position required selling World Book's educational products. Until 1995, she worked as a part-time sales representative and then a district manager for World Book. In 1995, World Book decided to separate the parent division from the school and library division and reorganize its sales force by outsourcing: contracting with individual "regional directors" who would in turn contract with individual sales representatives. The same people who had worked for World Book under the previous arrangement filled many of the positions under the new structure, in which branch managers became separately incorporated regional directors and district managers while sales representatives took positions with the newly formed companies.

Holtzman signed a contract with Lee, a former World Book branch manager who had formed her own corporation and gathered a sales force consisting largely of former World Book sales representatives. Holtzman eventually became a territory coordinator, a position

Instructor's Resource CD

Complementary for instructors, this CD-Rom includes teaching notes, class discussion starters, PowerPoint presentations, solutions to chapter-end questions, and a comprehensive Test Bank in document and computerized formats. Instructors also benefit from online access to all these IRCD components through the text's Online Learning Center.

You Be the Judge Case Videos

With these unscripted videos of typical employment law case examples, students can watch as plaintiff and defendant present arguments before a real judge, explain their rationales, and hear the judge's verdict. Also available is the full set of You Be the Judge cases—this interactive DVD covers the full range of Business Law topics and is formatted for easy use in personal computers. Students view background material in addition to hearing the courtroom argument, then must weigh in with their own rulings before hearing the judge's verdict. View the You Be the Judge demo at this book's Online Learning Center, and ask your sales representative how to package the DVD set, ISBN 0073275018, with this book for a discount.

Online Learning Center with PowerWeb

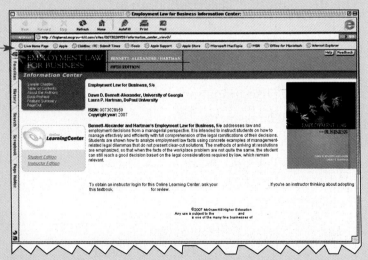

The Online Learning Center for this text gives a complete overview of its organization, features, and supplements. Students can study chapter objectives, view the Guide to Reading Cases, access the book's Glossary, and assess their learning with new, expanded chapter quizzes. The Power-Web function offers students the ability to do research on current events, access live news feeds, and review more course concepts. Register using the passcodes from the book's insert card to take advantage of this comprehensive online supplement! Instructors using the OLC can view all student materials as well as gain access to exclusive instructor resources, including the online version of the Instructor's Resource CD-ROM, with teaching notes and discussion suggestions. Jump start your learning now by visiting *www.mhhe.com/emplaw5e*.

Brief Contents

Table of Contents

Guide to Reading Cases

Thank you very much to the several students who have contacted us and asked that we improve your understanding by including a guide to reading and understanding the cases. We consider the cases an important and integral part of the chapters. By viewing the court decisions included in the text, you get to see for yourself what the court considers important when deciding a given issue. This in turn gives you as a decision maker insight into what you need to keep in mind when making decisions on similar issues in the workplace. The more you know about how a court thinks about issues that may end up in litigation, the better you can avoid it.

We provide the following in order to help you better understand the cases so that you can use them to their fullest. In order to tell you about how to view the cases, we have to give you a little background on the legal system. Hopefully, it will only be a refresher of your previous law or civics courses.

STARE DECISIS AND PRECEDENT

The American legal system is based on *stare decisis,* a system of using legal precedent. Once a judge renders a decision in a case, the decision is generally written and placed in a *law reporter* and must be followed in that jurisdiction when other similar cases arise. The case thus becomes precedent for future cases.

Most of the decisions in the chapters are from federal courts since most of the topics we discuss are based on federal law. Federal courts consist of trial courts (called the "U.S. District Court" for a particular district), courts of appeal (called the "U.S. Circuit Court" for a particular circuit) and the U.S. Supreme Court. U.S. Supreme Court decisions apply to all jurisdictions, and once there is a U.S. Supreme Court decision, all courts must follow the precedent. Circuit court decisions are mandatory precedent only for the circuit in which the decision is issued. All courts in that circuit must follow the U.S. Circuit Court precedents. District court decisions (precedent) are applicable only to the district in which they were made. When courts that are not in the jurisdiction are faced with a novel issue they have not decided before, they can look to other jurisdictions to see how they handled the issue. If such a court likes the other jurisdiction's decision, it can use the approach taken by that jurisdiction's court. However, it is not bound to follow the other court's decision if that court is not in its jurisdiction.

UNDERSTANDING THE CASE INFORMATION

With this in mind, let's take a look at a typical case included in this book. Each of the cases is an actual law case written by a judge. The first thing you will see is the *case name.* This is derived from the parties involved—the one suing (called "plaintiff" at the district court level) and the one being sued (called "defendant" at the district court level). At the court of appeals or Supreme Court level, the first name generally reflects who appealed the case to that court. It may or may not be the party who initially brought the case at the district court level. At the court of appeals level the person who appealed the case to the court of appeals is known as the appellant and the other party is known as the appeller. At the Supreme Court level they are known as the petitioner and the respondent.

Under the case name, the next line will have several numbers and a few letters. This is called a *case citation*. A case citation is the means by which the full case can be located in a law reporter if you want to find the case for yourself in a law library or a legal database such as LEXIS/NEXIS. Reporters are books in which judges' case decisions are kept for later retrieval by lawyers, law students, judges, and others. Law reporters can be found in any law library, and many cases can be found on the Internet.

Take a minute and turn to one of the cases in the text. Any case will do. A typical citation would be "72 U.S. 544 (2002)." This means that you can find the decision in volume 72 of the *U.S. Supreme Court Reporter* at page 544 and that it is a 2002 decision. The U.S. reporters contain U.S. Supreme Court decisions. Reporters have different names based on the court decisions contained in them; thus their citations are different.

The citation "43 F.3d 762 (9th Cir. 2002)" means that you can find the case decision in volume 43 of the *Federal Reporter,* third series, at page 762 and that the decision came out of the U.S. Circuit Court of Appeals for the Ninth Circuit in the year 2002. The *Federal Reporters* contain the cases of the U.S. Circuit Courts of Appeal from across the country.

Similarly, the citation "750 F. Supp. 234 (S.D.N.Y. 2002)" means that you can find the case decision in volume 750 of the *Federal Supplement Reporters,* which contain U.S. District Court cases, at page 234. The case was decided in the year 2002 by the U.S. District Court in the Southern District of New York.

In looking at the chapter cases, after the citation we include a short blurb on the case to let you know before you read it what the case is about, what the main issues are, and what the court decided. This is designed to give you a "heads up," rather than just dumping you into the case cold, with no background on what you are about to read.

The next line you see will have a name and then a comma followed by "J." This is the name of the judge who wrote the decision you are reading. The "J" stands for "judge" or "justice." Judges oversee lower courts, while the term for them used in higher courts is "justices." "CJ" stands for "chief justice."

The next thing you see in looking at the chapter case is the body of the decision. Judges write for lawyers and judges, not for the public at large. As such, they use a lot of legal terms (which we call "legalese") that can make the decisions difficult for a nonlawyer to read. There are also many procedural issues included in cases, which have little or nothing to do with the issues we are providing the case to illustrate. There may also be many other issues in the case that are not relevant for our purposes. Therefore, rather than give you the entire decision of the court, we instead usually give you a shortened, excerpted version of the case containing only the information relevant for the issue being discussed. If you want to see the entire case for yourself, you can find it by using the citation provided just below the name of the case, as explained above. By not bogging you down in legalese, procedural matters and other issues irrelevant to our point, we make the cases more accessible and understandable and much less confusing, while still giving you all you need to illustrate our point.

The last thing you will see in the chapter cases is the final decision of the court itself. If the case is a trial court decision by the district court, it will provide relief either for the plaintiff bringing the case or for the defendant against whom the case is brought.

If a defendant makes a *motion to dismiss,* the court will decide that issue and say either that the motion to dismiss is *granted* or that it is *denied.* A defendant will make a motion to dismiss when he or she thinks there is not enough evidence to constitute a violation of law. If the motion to dismiss is granted, the decision favors the defendant in that the court throws the case out. If the motion to dismiss is denied, it means the plaintiff's case can proceed to trial.

The parties may also ask the court to grant a *motion for summary judgment.* This essentially requests that the court take a look at the documentary information submitted by the parties and make a judgment based on that, as there is allegedly no issue that needs to be determined by a jury. Again, the court will either grant the motion for summary judgment or deny it. If the court grants a motion for summary judgment, it will also determine the issues and grant a judgment in favor of one of the parties. If the court dismisses a motion for summary judgment, the case proceeds to trial.

If the case is in the appellate court, it means that one of the parties did not like the trial court's decision. This party appeals the case to the appellate court, seeking to overturn the decision based on what it alleges are errors of law committed by the court below. Cases can't be appealed simply because one of the parties did not like the facts found by the lower court. After the appellate court reviews the lower court's decision, the court of appeals will either *affirm* the lower court's decision, which means the decision is allowed to stand, or it will *reverse* the lower court's decision, which means the lower court's decision is overturned. If there is work still to be done on the case, the court will also order *remand.* Remand is an order by the court to the lower court telling it to take the case back and do what needs to be done based on the court's decision.

It is also possible that the appellate court will issue a *per curiam* decision. This is merely a brief decision by the court, rather than a long one.

Following the court's decision is a set of questions that are intended to translate what you have read in the case into issues that you would be likely to have to think about as a business owner, manager, or supervisor. The questions generally are included to make you think about what you read in the case and how it would impact your decisions as a manager. They are provided as a way to make you think critically and learn how to ask yourself the important questions that you will need to deal with each time you make an employment decision.

The chapter cases and the case-end questions are important tools for you to use to learn to think like a manager or supervisor. Reading the courts' language and thinking about the issues in the case-end questions will greatly assist you in making solid, defensible workplace decisions as a manager or supervisor.

Part **One**

The Regulation of the Employment Relationship

Chapter One

The Regulation of Employment

Chapter Outline

Opening Scenarios

SCENARIO 1

1 *Scenario*

Emma Bina is working as a research scientist at a laboratory when she is approached with an employment offer from a competing laboratory. The competing lab director offers Emma nearly double her present salary and superior research equipment and opportunities. The lab director tells Emma that she can remain employed with the new company as long as she does satisfactory work. Emma accepts the offer, sells her house, takes her dog and cats and moves to the new state, buys a new house, and settles in. Emma's first two evaluations are superior. Then, six months after arriving, Emma is terminated and the employer offers no explanation. Emma sues for unlawful termination. Does she win? Why or why not?

SCENARIO 2

2 *Scenario*

Mark Richter is about to retire as a candy salesperson when he closes on a deal the candy company has been trying to land for a long time. Just before Mark is to collect his substantial commission, he is terminated. Does Mark have a basis on which to sue for unlawful termination?

SCENARIO 3

3 *Scenario*

Jenna Zitron informs her employer that she has been summoned to serve jury duty for a week. Though rescheduling her duties is not a problem, Jenna is told by her employer that, if she serves jury duty rather than trying to be relieved of it, she will be terminated. Jenna refuses to lie to be relieved of jury duty. Does Jenna have a basis on which to sue for unlawful termination?

INTRODUCTION TO THE REGULATORY ENVIRONMENT

How is the employer regulated? How much can Congress or the courts tell an employer how to run its business, whom it should hire or fire, or how it should treat its employees?

If an employer wants to hire someone to work every other hour every other week, it should be free to do so as long as it can locate an employee who is willing to enter into such an agreement. Or, if an employer requires that all employees wear a purple chicken costume throughout the workday, there is no reason why that requirement could not be enforced if the employer can find employees to accept the agreement.

The freedom to contract is crucial to freedom of the market; an employee may choose to work or not to work for a given employer, and an employer may choose to hire or not to hire a given applicant.

As a result, though the employment relationship is regulated in some important ways, Congress tries to avoid telling employers how to manage their employees or dictating whom the employer should or should not hire. It is unlikely that Congress would enact legislation that would require employers to hire certain individuals or groups of individuals (like a pure quota system) or that would prevent employers and employees from freely negotiating the responsibilities of a given job. (See Exhibit 1.1.) For example, employers historically have had the right to discharge an employee whenever they wished to do so.

However, Congress has passed employment-related laws when it believes that the employee is not on equal footing with the employer. For example, Congress has passed laws that require employers to pay minimum wages and to refrain from using certain criteria, such as race or gender, in arriving at specific employment decisions. These laws reflect the reality that employers stand in a position of power in the employment relationship. Legal protections granted to employees seek to make the "power relationship" between employer and employee one that is fair and equitable.

Exhibit 1.1   Myths about the Regulation of Employment

1. You have a right to your job.
2. Once you're hired, your employer may not fire you unless if there's a good reason.
3. As an employer, you may not terminate someone unless that worker does something "bad."
4. You have someone working for you whom you really do not get along with; you may not fire that person for that reason alone.
5. As an employer, you may have a rule that, if any employee reports the wrongdoings of the firm to the government, she or he will be terminated.

Is Regulation Necessary?

There are those scholars, however, who do not believe that regulation of discrimination and other areas of the employment relationship is necessary. President Ronald Reagan acknowledged this general philosophy when he enacted Executive Order 12291 in 1981. That order provided that no regulatory action be undertaken *unless the potential benefits to society outweigh the potential costs.* Proponents of this view believe that the market will work to encourage employers' rational, nonbiased behavior.

For example, Title VII of the Civil Rights Act of 1964 ("Title VII") prohibits discrimination based on race and gender, among other characteristics. (For detailed discussion of Title VII, see Chapter 3.) Some economists have argued that rational individuals interested in profit maximization will never hesitate to hire the most qualified applicants, regardless of their race. Status-dependent decisions are inefficient, since they are generally based on the incorrect and naive belief that members of one class are less meritorious than others. These employers understand that if they were to allow their prejudices to govern or influence their employment decisions, they may overlook the most qualified applicant because that applicant was black or a woman. Therefore, they will not let prejudices cause them to hire less-qualified individuals and employ a less-efficient workforce.

However, opponents of this position contend that discrimination continues because often employers are faced with the choice of two *equally* qualified applicants for a position. In that case, the prejudiced employer suffers no decrease in efficiency of her or his firm as a result of choosing the white or male applicant over the minority or female applicant. Therefore, economic forces do not afford absolute protection against employment discrimination where the discrimination is based on race, gender, national origin, or other protected categories.

WHO IS SUBJECT TO REGULATION?

The issue of whether someone is an employer or employee is a critical one when it comes to regulation and one that depends on a variety of factors. (See Exhibit 1.2.) Business decisions made in one context, for instance, may give rise to liability when there may no liability in another (depending on factors such as the size of the business organization). In addition, defining an individual as an employee allows that person causes of action that an independent contractor might not have.

Exhibit 1.2   Myths about Who Is an Employee and Who Is Not

1. An employee is anyone who is paid to work.
2. As long as a person chooses how she will perform her job, she is an independent contractor and not an employee.
3. The one who hires the worker is liable for anything that the employee does in the course of his or her employment.
4. If someone is an employee under one statute, that person is considered an employee under all employment-related statutes.
5. If someone is considered an employer for purposes of one statute, he or she is considered an employer for all statutes.
6. It is always better to hire someone as an independent contractor, rather than as an employee.
7. If a mistake is made in categorizing one's workers, it's no big deal.

In this section, we will examine who is an employer and an employee and how it is decided.

These legal entities are not just the concern of the employer's lawyer and accountant. Temporary help, leased workers, independent contractors, vendors, "outsourcing," and staffing firms have become common elements of the employment landscape. While contingent workers are not "employees," mere labels will not stop a court or administrative agency from determining that the worker has been misclassified, that an employment relationship exists.[1]

Origins in Agency Law

The law relating to the employment relationship is based on the traditional law of master and servant, which evolved into the law of agency. It may be helpful to briefly review the fundamentals of the law of agency in order to gain a better perspective on the legal regulation of the employment relationship that follows.

In an agency relationship, the party for whom another acts and from whom she or he derives authority to act is known and referred to as a "principal," while the one who represents the principal is known as an "agent." The agent is like a substitute appointed by the principal with power to do certain things. The agent is considered as the representative of the principal and acts for, in the place of, the principal. Similarly, an employee is the agent of the employer, the principal. The employee is the representative of the employer and acts in its place. For example, if Alex hires Emma to sell his painting on his behalf, agreeing to pay her a commission if she does so, Alex would be the principal and Emma would be his agent.

In an employment agency relationship, the employee–agent is under a specific duty to the principal to act only as *authorized*. As a rule, if an agent exceeds her authority or places the property of the principal at risk without authority, the principal is now responsible to the third party for all loss or damage naturally resulting from the agent's unauthorized acts

---

[1] Kenneth J. Turnbull, "Using Contingent Workers Can Create Complications," *New York Law Journal,* Jan. 12, 2001.

(while the agent remains liable to the principal for the same amount). In other words, if Alex told Emma to sell the painting for any price above $100, and she sells it instead for $80, she would be acting without authority. Emma would be liable to Alex for his losses up to the amount authorized, $20, and Alex would be required to sell the painting for the lower price. An agent is subject to a duty to properly conduct himself in the discharge of the agency transaction, and he is liable for injuries resulting to the principal from his unwarranted misconduct. So if Emma misses an appointment at which someone intended to purchase the painting because she overslept, again she would be liable.

Accordingly, if an employee acts in a way that exceeds her authority, the employer may still be liable to a third party (though the employee would then be liable back to the employer because she exceeded her authority). For instance, assume an employee of a construction company has the authority to charge building supplies at the local hardware store for use in the firm's projects. If that employee went into the hardware store and charged supplies to the firm but then later used those supplies to build her daughter's clubhouse, the construction company (the principal) would still owe the hardware store (the third party) for the supplies since the employee (the agent) represented the company in the purchase, though the employee (the agent) would be liable to the company for the price of the inappropriately purchased supplies.

Throughout the entire relationship, the principal has the obligation toward the agent to exercise good faith in their relationship, and the principal has to use care to prevent the agent from coming to any harm during the agency relationship. This requirement translates into the employer's responsibility to provide a safe and healthy working environment for the workers.

In addition to creating these implied duties for the employment relationship, the principal–agent characterization is important to the working relationship for other reasons, explained in the next section.

Why Is It Important to Determine Whether a Worker Is an Employee?

independent contractor
Generally, a person who contracts with a principal to perform a task according to her or his own methods, and who is not under the principal's control regarding the physical details of the work.

You are hired by a company to do a job. Are you its employee or an **independent contractor**? While most workers may have no doubt about which they are, the actual answer may vary, depending on the statute, case law, or other analysis to be applied. The courts, employers, and the government are unable to agree on one definition of "employee" and "employer," so it varies, depending on the situation and the law being used. In addition, some statutes do not give effective guidance. For instance, the Employee Retirement Income Security Act (ERISA) defines employee as "any individual employed by an employer." As one court said, this nominal definition is "completely circular and explains nothing." The distinction is significant for tax law compliance and categorization, for benefit plans, for cost reduction plans, and for discrimination claims. For instance, Title VII applies to employers and prohibits them from discriminating against employees. It does not, however, cover discrimination against independent contractors. In addition, employers will not be liable for most torts committed by an independent contractor within the scope of the working relationship.

The definition of employee is all the more important as companies hire supplemental or contingent workers on an independent-contractor basis to cut costs. An employer's responsibilities generally increase when someone is an employee. This section of the chapter will discuss the implications of this characterization and why it is important to determine whether a worker is an employee. A later section, "How Do You Determine Whether a Worker Is an Employee?," will present the different ways to determine employment status.

Employer Payroll Deductions

Recall that an independent contractor is someone who performs work for the principal in a relationship where the principal does not control how the job is done. The principal does not oversee the independent contractor or give orders, other than what the final product is to be and what the principal wants. The independent contractor is then free to perform the requested service or act as he or she sees fit. This is in contrast to an employee over whom the employer has much more control about how the job is executed.

Also, an employer paying an employee is subject to different requirements than when paying an independent contractor. In general, for employees it is the employer's duty to pay Social Security (FICA), the FICA excise tax, Railroad Retirement Tax Act (RRTA) withholding amounts, federal unemployment compensation (FUTA), IRS federal income tax withholdings, Medicare, and state taxes. In addition, it is the employer's responsibility to withhold a certain percentage of the employee's wages for federal income tax purposes.

On the other hand, an independent contractor must be responsible for the payment of such taxes on his or her own. The principal merely pays the fee to the contractor, and the contractor then pays the taxes at a later date, usually through four estimated payments per year. Thus, the principal is able to avoid the tax expenses and bookkeeping costs associated with such withholdings.

Benefits

When you have taken jobs in the past, were you offered a certain number of paid vacation or sick days, a retirement plan, a parking spot, a medical or dental plan? These are known as *benefits,* and they cost the employer money outside of the wages the employer must pay the employee. In an effort to attract and retain superior personnel, employers offer employees a range of benefits that generally are not required to be offered, such as dental, medical, pension, and profit-sharing plans. Independent contractors have no access to these benefits.

The Employee Retirement Income Security Act of 1974 (ERISA) was enacted to protect employee benefit plan participants from retirement plan abuses by administrators; and the Fair Labor Standards Act of 1938 (FLSA) was enacted to establish standards for minimum wages, overtime pay, employer recordkeeping, and child labor. Where a worker is considered an employee, ERISA protects the employee's benefits, while the FLSA regulates the amount of money an employee must be paid per hour and overtime compensation. A willful misclassification under FLSA may result in imprisonment and up to a $10,000 fine, imposed by the Department of Labor.

Discrimination and Affirmative Action

Can an independent contractor hold the employer liable for gender discrimination? No, Title VII and other related antidiscrimination statutes only protect *employees* from discrimination by employers. Employers are able to avoid discrimination and wrongful discharge claims where the worker is an independent contractor. (See below for discussion on coverage of employers by various statutes.)

However, as will be explored throughout this chapter, merely labeling a worker as an "independent contractor" does not protect against liability under federal antidiscrimination statutes such as Title VII. Courts and the EEOC will examine a variety of factors to determine the true meaning of the relationship between the worker and the organization. If the worker is more appropriately classified as an employee, then the label will be peeled off, allowing for antidiscrimination statutes to apply.

Additionally, the National Labor Relations Act protects only employees and not independent contractors from unfair labor practices. Note, however, that independent contractors may be considered to be *employers,* so they may be subject to these regulations from the other side of the fence.

Cost Reductions

It would seem to be a safe statement that an objective of most employers is to reduce cost and to increase profit. Employees are more expensive to employ, due to the above regulations that require greater expenditures on behalf of employees, as well as the fact that others must be hired to maintain records of the employees. In addition, by hiring independent contractors, the cost of overtime is eliminated (the federal wage and hour laws do not apply to independent contractors) and the employer is able to avoid any work-related expenses, such as tools, training, or traveling. The employer is also guaranteed satisfactory performance of the job for which the contractor was hired because it is the contractor's contractual obligation to adequately perform the contract with the employer, while the employee is generally able to quit without incurring liability (the at-will doctrine). If there is a breach of the agreement between the employer and the independent contractor, the independent contractor not only stands to lose the job but may also be liable for resulting damages. An employee is usually compensated for work completed with less liability for failure to perfectly perform.

vicarious liability
The imposition of liability on one party for the wrongs of another. Liability may extend from an employee to the employer on this basis if the employee is acting within the scope of her or his employment at the time the liability arose.

In addition, the employee may actually cause the employer to have greater liability exposure. An employer is **vicariously liable** if the employee causes harm to a third party while the employee is in the course of employment. For instance, if an employee is driving a company car from one company plant to another and, in the course of that trip, sideswipes another vehicle, the employer may be liable to the owner of the other vehicle. While the employee may be required to indemnify or reimburse the employer for any liability incurred as a result of the negligence, generally the third party goes after the employer because the employee does not have the funds to pay the liability. The employer could sue the employee for this reimbursement but, more likely, will write it off as an expense of doing business.

Finally, some managers contend that independent contractors are more motivated and, as a result, have a higher level of performance as a consequence of their freedom to control their own work and futures.

On the other hand, there may be situations where, notwithstanding the decrease in the amount of benefits that the employer must provide, independent contractors may still be more expensive to employ. This situation may exist where the employer finds that it is cheaper to have its employees perform certain types of work that are characteristically expensive to contract. Often a large firm will find it more profitable to employ a legal staff, and pay their benefits and salaries, than to employ a law firm every time a legal question arises. Or a school may find it less expensive to maintain a full janitorial staff than to employ a professional cleaning crew whenever something needs to be taken care of at the school.

The Cost of Mistakes

Workers and employers alike make mistakes about whether a worker is an independent contractor or an employee. If a worker is classified as an independent contractor but later found to constitute an employee, the punishment by the IRS is harsh. The employer is not only liable for its share of FICA and FUTA but is also subject to an additional penalty equal to 20 percent of the FICA that should have been withheld. In addition, the employer is liable for 1.5 percent of the wages received by the employee. These penalty charges apply if 1099 forms (records of payments to independent contractors) have been compiled for the worker. If, on the other hand, the forms have not been completed, the penalties increase to 40 percent of FICA and 3 percent of wages. Where the IRS determines that the worker was *deliberately* classified as an independent contractor to avoid paying taxes, the fines and penalties can easily run into six figures for even the smallest business.

In addition to potential IRS violations, the employer may be liable for violations of the National Labor Relations Act of 1935 (NLRA). Liability may include reinstatement and back pay to employees fired in violation of the NLRA under the mistaken belief that they were independent contractors. The employer may also be liable under the Fair Labor Standards Act of 1938 (FLSA) for amounts of unpaid wages or overtime compensation and for attorneys' fees and costs. Under the Employee Retirement Income Security Act of 1974 (ERISA) an employer may be liable for accrued but unpaid benefits. In addition, there is possible liability under the Social Security Act of 1935 and under state workers' compensation and unemployment compensation laws.

The fines for each violation are substantial. For example, any person who willfully violates the FLSA is subject to a fine of $10,000 and six months' imprisonment. Additionally, the tax advantages of a qualified retirement or fringe benefit plan to employers or employees may be lost as a result of misclassification.

Why is the IRS so intent on ensuring that improper classification does not occur? The IRS estimates that it loses over $2 billion a year in uncollected taxes that should have been paid by employers or the independent contractors whom they have hired. In 1989 alone, 76,000 workers were reclassified from independent contractors to employees; in some fields, misclassification rates run as high as 92 percent. As one scholar has written, IRS agents are told, "Go forth and find employees!" The IRS will generally attempt to "match" workers who claim to be independent contractors with their companies. If an independent contractor earned more than $10,000 from one source during a one-year period, the independent status of that individual is suspect.

The IRS is particularly interested in situations where a company is forced by rising costs to downsize. In doing so, many of its older workers choose to accept early retirement. Older workers, however, are often those who are more experienced and who have developed expertise in various areas of the company. Companies search for ways to use these "experts" without violating pension plan restrictions regarding recalling employees. Hiring them as independent contractors appears to be an efficient, cost-saving mechanism. Nevertheless, the IRS has successfully challenged the employment of these workers as independent contractors where they are hired to perform services *substantially similar* to those they rendered as employees of the firm. In an analogous situation, any individual who is hired as an independent contractor to perform in a capacity substantially similar to that performed by a company's own employees will be subject to IRS challenge.

But there is hope for correct classification: the 1978 Revenue Act forms a safe harbor for employers who have consistently classified a class of workers as independent contractors. Section 530 cites four criteria required to claim a worker as an independent contractor.

First, the business must have never treated the worker as an employee for the purposes of employment taxes for any period (e.g., the company has never withheld income or FICA tax from its payments). Second, all federal tax returns with respect to this worker were filed consistent with the worker being an independent contractor. Third, the company has treated all those in positions substantially similar to that of this worker as independent contractors. And fourth, the company has a reasonable basis for treating the worker as an independent contractor. Such a reasonable basis may include a judicial precedent or published IRS ruling, a past IRS audit of the company, or long-standing industry practices, as will be discussed in greater detail later in this chapter. Where these conditions have been satisfied, the employer is not liable for misclassification.

WHO CONSTITUTES AN EMPLOYER?

Courts and regulatory agencies have not experienced great difficulty in defining the term "employer." Depending on the applicable statute or provision, an *employer* is one who employs or uses others to do his or her work, or to work on his or her behalf. Most statutes specifically include in this definition employment agencies, labor organizations, and joint labor–management committees. Issues may arise where an entity claims to be a private membership club (exempt from Title VII prohibitions) or a multinational company that may or may not be subject to application of various U.S. laws. Or, a determination must be made whether the employer receives federal funds or maintains federal contracts for coverage under the Rehabilitation Act of 1973, among others. The most exacting issue is usually how many employees an employer must have in order to be subject to a given statute. However, it is crucial for employers to be familiar with those statutes to which it is subject and those from which it is immune.

The Civil Rights Act of 1866

The Civil Rights Act (CRA) of 1866 regulates the actions of all individuals or entities that enter into a contract to employ another. An employer under the CRA of 1866 is one with 15 or more employees.

Title VII of the Civil Rights Act of 1964

Title VII applies to all firms or their agents engaged in an industry affecting commerce that employ 15 or more employees for each working day in each of 20 or more weeks in the current or preceding calendar year. Title VII exempts from its regulation government-owned corporations, Indian tribes, and bona fide private membership clubs. "Commerce," in this context, is defined as trade, traffic, transportation, transmission, or communication among the states, between a state and any other place, within the District of Columbia, or within a possession of the United States. "Industry affecting commerce" means any activity, business, or industry in commerce or in which a labor dispute would hinder or obstruct commerce or the free flow of commerce. Lack of *intent* to affect commerce is no defense to coverage.

"Working day" is generally computed by counting the number of employees maintained on the payroll in a given week, as opposed to the number of employees who work on any one day. This calculation provides for a more expansive definition of "employer" since it includes hourly and part-time workers.[2]

Note, however, that this form of calculation is merely the majority approach; other courts have found that part-time employees who work for any part of each day of the workweek should be counted, while part-time employees who work full days for only a portion of the workweek should not be counted.

Title VI of the Civil Rights Act of 1964

Title VI applies the race, color, and national origin proscriptions of Title VII to any program or activity that receives federal financial assistance. States and state agencies are also covered under the Civil Rights Restoration Act of 1987. Title VI applies where the financial assistance to the program or activity has as its primary objective the provision of employment.

The Department of Education, one of the larger federal funding agencies, cites four categories of programs that will be covered by Title VI: projects under the Public Works Acceleration Act; work-study programs under the Vocational Education Act of 1963; programs under other funding statutes that are limited to, or in which a preference is given to, students or others training for employment; and assistance to rehabilitation facilities under the Vocational Rehabilitation Act.

Unless it falls within one of the five exemptions, a government contractor is also prohibited from discriminating on the bases of race, color, religion, gender, or national origin by Executive Order 11246. The order exempts (1) employers with contracts of less than $10,000 from the requirement to include an equal employment opportunity clause in each of their contracts; (2) contracts for work performed outside the United States by employees not recruited within the United States; (3) contracts with state and local governments by providing that the EEO requirements do not apply to any agency of that government that is not participating in the work of the contract; (4) religious educational institutions that hire only people of that religion; (5) preferences offered to Native Americans living on or near a reservation in connection with employment on or near the reservation; and (6) certain contracts on the basis of national interest or security reasons.

Age Discrimination in Employment Act of 1967

The Age Discrimination in Employment Act (ADEA) applies to all entities or their agents that employ 20 or more employees on each working day for 20 or more weeks during the current or preceding calendar year (using the same definition of "employ"

---

[2] *Walters v. Metropolitan Educational Enterprises, Inc.,* 72 FEP Cases (BNA) 1211 (1997).

as Title VII, that is, maintained on the payroll). In addition to an exemption similar to that of Title VII for government-owned corporations, the ADEA also exempts American employers who control foreign firms where compliance with the ADEA in connection with an American employee would cause the foreign firm to violate the laws of the country in which it is located. Title VII, unlike the ADEA, does *not* exempt Indian tribes or private membership clubs.

The Americans with Disabilities Act

The Americans with Disabilities Act (ADA) applies to all employers with 15 or more workers, including state and local government employers through its Title II (a), employment agencies, labor unions, and joint labor-management committees. It is similar to Title VII and computes number of employees in the same manner as described previously in regard to that act. The definition of "employer" also includes persons who are "agents" of the employer, such as managers, supervisors, foremen, or others who act for the employer, such as agencies used to conduct background checks on candidates. Executive agencies of the U.S. government are exempt from the ADA, but these agencies are covered instead by similar nondiscrimination requirements and additional affirmative employment requirements under Section 501 of the Rehabilitation Act of 1973 (see below). Also exempted from the ADA, similar to Title VII, are corporations fully owned by the U.S. government, Indian tribes, and bona fide private membership clubs that are not labor organizations and that are exempt from taxation under the Internal Revenue Code. Religious organizations are covered by the ADA, but they may give employment preference to people of their own religion or religious organization.

The Fair Labor Standards Act

The Fair Labor Standards Act (FLSA) offers coverage to workers not necessarily based on a particular definition of "employer" but on two distinct forms of coverage: "enterprise coverage" and "individual coverage." Enterprise coverage refers to the protections offered to employees who work for certain businesses or organizations (i.e., "enterprises") that have at least two employees and do at least $500,000 a year in business, or that are involved in certain specified industries such as hospitals, businesses providing medical or nursing care for residents, schools and preschools, and government agencies. Individual coverage refers to the protections offered to employees if their work regularly involves them in commerce between states ("interstate commerce"). The FLSA provides coverage, even when there is no enterprise coverage, to workers who are "engaged in commerce or in the production of goods for commerce." This coverage may include workers who produce goods that will be sent out of state, who regularly make telephone calls as part of their job to persons located in other states, or who travel to other states for their jobs. Also, domestic service workers (such as housekeepers, full-time babysitters, and cooks) are normally covered by the law. There are several exemptions based on the work that the individual conducts; those will be discussed later in this text.

Rehabilitation Act of 1973

The Rehabilitation Act provides that covered agencies may not discriminate against otherwise qualified disabled individuals, and it applies not only to all entities, programs, and activities that receive federal funds and to government contractors, but also to all programs and activities of any executive agency as well as the U.S. Postal Service. Federal funding may include grants, loans, contracts, provision of personnel, or real or personal property. A covered federal contractor is one who maintains a contract with the federal government in excess of $10,000 annually for the provision of personal property or nonpersonal services. A contract may include any agreement between any department, agency, establishment, or instrumentality of the federal government and any person. It does not include employment contracts where the parties to the agreement are employer and employee. There is no requirement similar to that of Title VI that the assistance must be for the provision of employment.

HOW DO YOU DETERMINE WHETHER A WORKER IS AN EMPLOYEE?

Courts have offered varied interpretations of whether someone is an employee. Generally, which interpretation is used depends on the factual circumstances presented by each case, as well as which law is at issue.

A consistently cited case that illustrates the effect of the difference between classification as an independent contractor and as an employee is *Lemmerman* v. *A.T. Williams Oil Co.,* in which an eight-year-old boy frequently performed odd jobs for the Wilco Service Station at which his mother was employed. He was paid $1 a day to perform such services as stocking shelves and sweeping up. One day the boy fell and cut his hand. The boy sought damages in the form of lost wages, pain, and suffering. The main issue in this case was whether he was an employee. If he was an employee, then his sole remedy was in the form of workers' compensation; however, if he was, instead, an independent contractor, Wilco would lose the protection of the workers' compensation limits and would be liable in tort for additional amounts. Over a strong dissenting opinion, the court in *Lemmerman* determined that the boy was actually an employee of the defendant and, therefore, could not recover beyond a standard workers' compensation claim.

While many laws refer to similar definitions of "employee" or "independent contractor," other laws or regulations may rely on an entirely different test to answer the issue. Congress has responded by stating that employees are those not classified as independent contractors. The House has further explained that an employee is "one who works for another." The National Labor Relations Act states that "the term 'employee' shall not include . . . any individual having the status of an independent contractor" but does not define independent contractor.

Several tests have been developed and are commonly used by courts to classify employees and independent contractors. These tests include the common-law test of agency, which focuses on the right of control, the Internal Revenue Service (IRS) 20-factor analysis, and the economic realities analysis. Several courts also use a hybrid approach, using one test that combines factors from other tests.

Under the **common-law agency test**, a persuasive indicator of independent-contractor status is the ability to control the manner in which the work is performed. This test was derived from the law involving domestic relations of the "master and servant." Where the master had control over the servant, the worker was considered the master's servant, employed by and connected to that master, more similar to common-law property rights than contract rights. Today, the contract or agency principles apply rather than property principles. The element of control has persisted in today's interpretation of who constitutes an employee and who is an independent contractor. The right to control remains the predominant factor.

Under the common-law agency approach, the employer need not actually control the work, but must merely *have the right or ability* to control the work for a worker to be classified an employee. Although this is a strong indication that the worker is an employee, other factors usually are considered. For example, it has been held that an employee is one who works for wages or salary and is under direct supervision. An independent contractor has benefited as one who does a "job for a price, decides how the work will be done, usually hires others to do the work, and depends for their income not upon wages, but upon the difference between what they pay for goods, materials and labor and what they receive for the end result, that is upon profits."

The common-law test is specifically and consistently used to determine employee status in connection with FUTA and FICA taxes, in determining whether an employee is a statutory employee (discussed later in this chapter), as well as in federal income tax withholding.

IRS test
List of 20 factors to which the IRS looks to determine whether someone is an employee or an independent contractor. The IRS compiled this list from the results of judgments of the courts relating to this issue.

Under the **IRS 20-factor analysis**, the IRS, in training material issued in July 1996, explained that "this Twenty Factor Test is an analytical tool and *not* the legal test used for determining worker status. The legal test is whether there is a right to direct and control the means and details of the work" (emphasis in original).[3]

EEOC guidance on application of EEO laws to contingent workers provides similar guidelines for determining whether working conditions are controlled by the business, thus placing the worker within the protection of the federal antidiscrimination statutes. However, the following 20 factors have been consistently and continually articulated by courts, regulatory agencies, commentators, and scholars as critical to the determination of the status of an individual worker. When these factors are satisfied, courts are more likely to find "employee" status. In addition, the IRS stated that these 20 factors are not inclusive but that "every piece of information that helps determine the extent to which the business retains the right to control the worker is important." (See Exhibit 1.3.)

1. *Instructions.* A worker who is required to comply with other persons' instructions about when, where, and how to perform the work is ordinarily considered to be an employee.
2. *Training.* Training a worker indicates that the employer exercises control over the means by which the result is accomplished.
3. *Integration.* When the success or continuation of a business depends on the performance of certain services, the worker performing those services is subject to a certain amount of control by the owner of the business.
4. *Services rendered personally.* If the services must be rendered personally, the employer controls both the means and the results of the work.
5. *Hiring, supervising, and paying assistants.* Control is exercised if the employer hires, supervises, and pays assistants.

[3] Department of Treasury, Internal Revenue Service, "Employee or Independent Contractor?" Training 3320-102 (July 1996).

Exhibit 1.3

Employee or Independent Contractor?

The IRS, in its training materials, offers this case study on the question of whether someone is an employee or an independent contractor:

A computer programmer is laid off when company X downsizes. Company X agrees to pay the programmer $10,000 to complete a one-time project to create a certain product. It is not clear how long it will take to complete the project, and the programmer is not guaranteed any minimum payment for the hours spent on the project. The programmer does the work on a new high-end computer, which was purchased by the company. The programmer works at home, but may attend meetings of the software development group at the firm. Company X provides the programmer with no instructions beyond the specifications for the product itself. The programmer and company X have a written contract, which provides that the programmer is considered to be an independent contractor, is required to pay her own taxes, and receives no benefits from company X.

Is she an employee?

Source: Internal Revenue Service; case modified slightly by the author.

6. *Continuing relationships.* The existence of a continuing relationship between the worker and the employer indicates an employer–employee relationship.

7. *Set hours of work.* The establishment of hours of work by the employer indicates control.

8. *Full time required.* If the worker must devote full time to the employer's business, the employer has control over the worker's time. An independent contractor is free to work when and for whom she or he chooses.

9. *Doing work on the employer's premises.* Control is indicated if the work is performed on the employer's premises.

10. *Order or sequence set.* Control is indicated if a worker is not free to choose his or her own pattern of work but must perform services in the sequence set by the employer.

11. *Oral or written reports.* Control is indicated if the worker must submit regular oral or written reports to the employer.

12. *Furnishing tools and materials.* If the employer furnishes significant tools, materials, and other equipment, an employer–employee relationship usually exists.

13. *Payment by hour, week, or month.* Payment by the hour, week, or month points to an employer–employee relationship, provided that this method of payment is just not a convenient way of paying a lump sum agreed on as a cost of a job. However, hourly pay may not be evidence that a worker is an employee if it is customary to pay an independent contractor by the hour (an attorney, for example). An independent contractor usually is paid by the job or on a straight commission.

14. *Payment of business or traveling expenses.* Payment of the worker's business or traveling expenses, or both, is indicative of an employer–employee relationship. However, this factor is less important because companies do reimburse independent contractors.

15. *Significant investment.* A worker is an independent contractor if she or he invests in facilities that are not typically maintained by employees, such as the maintenance of an office rented at fair value from an unrelated party. An employee depends on the employer for such facilities.

16. *Realization of profit or loss.* A worker who can realize a profit or loss (in addition to the profit or loss ordinarily realized by employees) through management of resources is an independent contractor. The worker who cannot is generally an employee.

17. *Working for more than one firm at a time.* If a worker performs more than *de minimis* services for a number of unrelated persons at the same time, she or he is usually considered an independent contractor.

18. *Making service available to the general public.* A worker is usually an independent contractor if the services are made available to the general public on a regular or consistent basis.

19. *Right to discharge.* The right of the employer to discharge a worker indicates that he or she is an employee.

20. *Right to terminate.* A worker is an employee if the right to end the relationship with the principal is available at any time he or she wishes without incurring liability.

In addition to the basic analysis under the IRS test, attorney Christina Morfeld provides the following helpful analysis to consider when determining whether an individual is more appropriately classified as an employee or independent contractor (IC) (see also Exhibit 1.4):

	Yes	No
1. Is the individual's work vital to the company's core business?	**Employee** activities are integrated with the organization's business operations.	**IC** services are typically limited to nonessential business activities.
2. Did you train the individual to perform tasks in a specific way?	**Employees** are usually taught the specific work procedures that they are expected to follow and must comply with any other employer requirements with regard to these activities.	**ICs** are generally considered "experts" in their field and, as such, can determine which work methods are most appropriate. Additionally, they are typically held accountable only for outcomes, not the means with which they are achieved.
3. Do you (or can you) instruct the individual as to when, where, and how the work is performed?		
4. Do you (or can you) control the sequence or order the work performed?		
5. Do you (or can you) set the hours of work for the individual?	**Employees** generally work on a schedule determined by their employer.	**ICs** can work whatever hours they choose, provided that agreed-upon deadlines are met.
6. Do you (or can you) require the individual to perform the work personally?	**Employees** must do the tasks for which they were hired themselves.	**ICs** are free to delegate to their own staff or subcontract the work to others.
7. Do you (or can you) prohibit the individual from hiring, supervising, and paying assistants?		

8. Does the individual perform regular and continuous services for you?	**Employees** typically have an open-ended relationship with a company, even if the work is performed at irregular intervals.	**ICs** work on a project-by-project basis, each time with a new contract.
9. Does the individual provide services on a substantially full-time basis to your company?	**Employees** are usually expected to devote all working hours to their employer.	**ICs** do not spend so much time with any one company that they are restricted from doing projects for others and, in fact, generally work for multiple clients concurrently.
10. Is your company the sole o major source of income for the individual?		
11. Is the work performed on your premises?	**Employees** are ordinarily required to work on-site.	**ICs** are free to work off-site, such as in a home office.
12. Do you (or can you) require the individual to submit regular reports, either written or oral?	**Employees** may be asked to provide status or activity reports on a regular basis.	**ICs** are responsible for producing a final deliverable and are not, therefore, required to provide interim reports.
13. Do you pay the individual by the hour, week, or month?	**Employees** are usually paid at fixed intervals.	**ICs** are generally paid for their results, not the amount of time worked.
14. Do you pay the individual's travel and business expenses?	**Employees** who incur work-related expenses are typically reimbursed by their employer.	**ICs** are usually expected to incorporate out-of-pocket expenses into their project fee rather than be directly reimbursed for them.
15. Do you furnish tools or equipment for the individual?	**Employees** generally use company provided supplies.	**ICs** are expected to own and use their own supplies.
16. Does the individual have a significant investment in facilities, tools, or equipment?	**ICs** incur expenses related to work space, equipment, etc., like any other business owner.	**Employees** typically use their company's facilities, tools and equipment.
17. Can the individual realize a profit or loss from his or her services to your company?	**ICs** run the risk of nonpayment if a project is not completed according to the specifications detailed in the contract.	**Employees** can usually expect steady paychecks.
18. Does the individual make his or her services available to the general public?	**ICs** publicize their services to a wide range of potential clients via direct mail, advertising, etc.	**Employees** do not typically position and market themselves as services providers.
19. Can the individual terminate the relationship without liability?	**Employees** can quit at any time and can typically be released "at will" by their employers.	**ICs** are legally obligated to complete projects according to contract provisions and can only be dismissed if they fail to do so.
20. Do you have the right to discharge the individual at any time?		

Reprinted from Christina Morfeld, "Employee vs. Independent Contractor: A Game of 20 Questions," http://affinitybizcomm.com/EEvsIC.htm, with permission of the author, Christina Morfeld.

Finally, under the *economic realities test,* courts consider whether the worker is economically dependent on the business or, as a matter of economic fact, is in business for himself or herself. In applying the economic realities test, courts look to the degree of control exerted by the alleged employer over the worker, the worker's opportunity for profit or loss, the worker's investment in the business, the permanence of the working relationship, the degree of skill required by the worker, and the extent the work is an integral part of the alleged employer's business. Typically, all of these factors are considered as a whole with none of the factors being determinative.

In the following case, the point at issue concerned whether four physicians in a medical practice could be counted as "employees" of the practice. The Supreme Court applied the common-law standard of control found in the Restatement (Second) of Agency and Equal Employment Opportunity Commission (EEOC) guidelines, whereas the District Court originally relied on the economic realities test. The workers believed they were employees rather than independent contractors and thus entitled to overtime compensation. The court used the economic realities test in determining the classification of the workers.

Clackamas Gastroenterology Associates, P. C. v. Wells,
123 S.Ct. 1673 (2003)

Wells sued Clackamas, a medical clinic, alleging disability discrimination in violation of the Americans with Disabilities Act (ADA). However, since the Americans with Disabilities Act of 1990 (ADA) only applies to businesses whose workforce included "15 or more employees for each working day in each of 20 or more calendar weeks in the current or preceding calendar year," a question arose as to whether four physicians actively engaged in medical practice as shareholders and directors of a professional corporation should be counted as "employees." The United States District Court for the District of Oregon granted the clinic's motion for summary judgment and Wells appealed. The Ninth Circuit reversed and remanded.

Stevens, J.

Petitioner, Clackamas Gastroenterology Associates, P. C., is a medical clinic in Oregon. It employed respondent, Deborah Anne Wells, as a bookkeeper from 1986 until 1997. After her termination, she brought this action against the clinic alleging unlawful discrimination on the basis of disability under the ADA. Petitioner denied that it was covered by the Act and moved for summary judgment, asserting that it did not have 15 or more employees for the 20 weeks required by the statute. It is undisputed that the accuracy of that assertion depends on whether the four physician–shareholders who own the professional corporation and constitute its board of directors are counted as employees.

The District Court . . . granted the motion. Relying on an "economic realities" test adopted by the Seventh Circuit in *EEOC v. Dowd & Dowd, Ltd.,* the District Court concluded that the four doctors were "more analogous to partners in a partnership than to shareholders in a general corporation" and therefore were "not employees for purposes of the federal antidiscrimination laws."

A divided panel of the Court of Appeals for the Ninth Circuit reversed. Noting that the Second Circuit had rejected the economic realities approach, the majority held that the use of any corporation, including a professional corporation, "precludes any examination designed to determine whether the entity is in fact a partnership." It saw "no reason to permit a professional corporation to secure the 'best of both possible worlds' by allowing it both to assert its corporate status in order to reap the tax and civil liability advantages and to argue that it is like a partnership in order to avoid liability for unlawful employment discrimination." The dissenting judge stressed the differences between an Oregon physicians' professional corporation and an ordinary business corporation, and argued that Congress' reasons for exempting small employers from the coverage of the Act should apply to petitioner.

We granted certiorari to resolve the conflict in the Circuits, which extends beyond the Seventh and the Second Circuits.

II

"We have often been asked to construe the meaning of 'employee' where the statute containing the term does not helpfully define it." *Nationwide Mut. Ins. Co.* v. *Darden.* The definition of the term in the ADA simply states that an "employee" is "an individual employed by an employer." That surely qualifies as a mere "nominal definition" that is "completely circular and explains nothing." As we explained in Darden, our cases construing similar language give us guidance on how best to fill the gap in the statutory text.

* * *

Rather than looking to the common law, petitioner argues that courts should determine whether a shareholder–director of a professional corporation is an "employee" by asking whether the shareholder–director is, in reality, a "partner." . . . The question whether a shareholder–director is an employee, however, cannot be answered by asking whether the shareholder–director appears to be the functional equivalent of a partner. Today there are partnerships that include hundreds of members, some of whom may well qualify as "employees" because control is concentrated in a small number of managing partners. Thus, asking whether shareholder–directors are partners—rather than asking whether they are employees—simply begs the question.

Nor does the approach adopted by the Court of Appeals in this case fare any better. The majority's approach, which paid particular attention to "the broad purpose of the ADA," is consistent with the statutory purpose of ridding the Nation of the evil of discrimination. Nevertheless, two countervailing considerations must be weighed in the balance. First, as the dissenting judge noted below, the congressional decision to limit the coverage of the legislation to firms with 15 or more employees has its own justification that must be respected—namely, easing entry into the market and preserving the competitive position of smaller firms.

Second, as *Darden* reminds us, congressional silence often reflects an expectation that courts will look to the common law to fill gaps in statutory text, particularly when an undefined term has a settled meaning at common law. Congress has overridden judicial decisions that went beyond the common law in an effort to correct "the mischief" at which a statute was aimed.

. . . The common law's definition of the master–servant relationship does provide helpful guidance. At common law the relevant factors defining the master–servant relationship focus on the master's control over the servant. The general definition of the term "servant" in the Restatement (Second) of Agency, for example, refers to a person whose work is "controlled or is subject to the right to control by the master." In addition, the Restatement's more specific definition of the term "servant" lists factors to be considered when distinguishing between servants and independent contractors, the first of which is "the extent of control" that one may exercise over the details of the work of the other. We think that the common-law element of control is the principal guidepost that should be followed in this case.

This is the position that is advocated by the Equal Employment Opportunity Commission (EEOC), the agency that has special enforcement responsibilities under the ADA and other federal statutes containing similar threshold issues for determining coverage. It argues that a court should examine "whether shareholder–directors operate independently and manage the business or instead are subject to the firm's control." According to the EEOC's view, "[i]f the shareholder–directors operate independently and manage the business, they are proprietors and not employees; if they are subject to the firm's control, they are employees."

Specific EEOC guidelines discuss both the broad question of who is an "employee" and the narrower question of when partners, officers, members of boards of directors, and major shareholders qualify as employees. With respect to the broad question, the guidelines list 16 factors—taken from *Darden*—that may be relevant to "whether the employer controls the means and manner of the worker's work performance." The guidelines list six factors to be considered in answering the narrower question, which they frame as "whether the individual acts independently and participates in managing the organization, or whether the individual is subject to the organization's control."

We are persuaded by the EEOC's focus on the common-law touchstone of control and specifically by its submission that each of the following six factors is relevant to the inquiry whether a shareholder–director is an employee:

- "Whether the organization can hire or fire the individual or set the rules and regulations of the individual's work
- "Whether and, if so, to what extent the organization supervises the individual's work
- "Whether the individual reports to someone higher in the organization
- "Whether and, if so, to what extent the individual is able to influence the organization
- "Whether the parties intended that the individual be an employee, as expressed in written agreements or contracts
- "Whether the individual shares in the profits, losses, and liabilities of the organization."

As the EEOC's standard reflects, an employer is the person, or group of persons, who owns and manages the enterprise. The employer can hire and fire employees, can assign tasks to employees and supervise their performance, and can decide how the profits and losses of the business are to be distributed. The mere fact that a person has a particular title—such as partner, director, or vice president—should not necessarily be used to determine whether he or she is an employee or a proprietor. Nor should the mere existence of a document styled "employment agreement" lead inexorably to the conclusion that either party is an employee. Rather, as was true in applying common law rules to the independent-contractor-versus-employee issue confronted in *Darden,* the answer to whether a shareholder–director is an employee depends on "'all of the incidents of the relationship . . . with no one factor being decisive.'"

III

Some of the District Court's findings—when considered in light of the EEOC's standard—appear to weigh in favor of a conclusion that the four director–shareholder physicians in this case are not employees of the clinic. For example, they apparently control the operation of their clinic, they share the profits, and they are personally liable for malpractice claims. There may, however, be evidence in the record that would contradict those findings or support a contrary conclusion under the EEOC's standard that we endorse today. Accordingly, as we did in Darden, we reverse the judgment of the Court of Appeals and remand the case to that court for further proceedings consistent with this opinion.

It is so ordered.

Justice GINSBURG, with whom Justice BREYER joins, dissenting.

"There is nothing inherently inconsistent between the coexistence of a proprietary and an employment relationship." As doctors performing the everyday work of petitioner Clackamas Gastroenterology Associates, P. C., the physician–shareholders function in several respects as common-law employees, a designation they embrace for various purposes under federal and state law. Classifying as employees all doctors daily engaged as caregivers on Clackamas' premises, moreover, serves the animating purpose of the Americans with Disabilities Act of 1990 (ADA or Act). Seeing no cause to shelter Clackamas from the governance of the ADA, I would affirm the judgment of the Court of Appeals.

An "employee," the ADA provides, is "an individual employed by an employer." Where, as here, a federal statute uses the word "employee" without explaining the term's intended scope, we ordinarily presume "Congress intended to describe the conventional master–servant relationship as understood by common-law agency doctrine." The Court today selects one of the common-law indicia of a master–servant relationship—control over the work of others engaged in the business of the enterprise—and accords that factor overriding significance. I would not so shrink the inquiry.

Are the physician–shareholders "servants" of Clackamas for the purpose relevant here? The Restatement defines "servant" to mean "an agent employed by a master to perform service in his affairs whose physical conduct in the performance of the service is controlled or is subject to the right to control by the master." When acting as clinic doctors, the physician–shareholders appear to fit the Restatement definition. The doctors provide services on behalf of the corporation, in whose name the practice is conducted. The doctors have employment contracts with Clackamas under which they receive salaries and yearly bonuses, and they work at facilities owned or leased by the corporation. In performing their duties, the doctors must "compl[y] with . . . standards [the organization has] established."

The physician–shareholders, it bears emphasis, invite the designation "employee" for various purposes under federal and state law. The Employee Retirement Income Security Act of 1974 (ERISA), much like the ADA, defines "employee" as "any individual employed by an employer." Clackamas readily acknowledges that the physician–shareholders are "employees" for ERISA purposes. Indeed, gaining qualification as "employees" under ERISA was the prime reason the physician–shareholders chose the corporate form instead of a partnership. Further, Clackamas agrees, the physician–shareholders are covered by Oregon's workers' compensation law, a statute applicable to "person[s] . . . who . . . furnish services for a remuneration, subject to the direction and control of an employer." Finally, by electing to organize their practice as a corporation, the physician–shareholders created an entity separate and distinct from themselves, one that would afford them limited liability for the debts of the enterprise. I see no reason to allow the doctors to escape from their choice of corporate form when the question becomes whether they are employees for purposes of federal antidiscrimination statutes.

Nothing in or about the ADA counsels otherwise. As the Court observes, the reason for exempting businesses with fewer than 15 employees from the Act, was "to spare very small firms from the potentially crushing expense of mastering the intricacies of the antidiscrimination laws, establishing procedures to assure compliance, and defending against suits when efforts at compliance fail." The inquiry the Court endorses to determine the physician–shareholders' qualification as employees asks whether they "ac[t] independently and participat[e] in managing the organization, or . . . [are] subject to the organization's control." Under the Court's approach, a firm's coverage by the ADA might sometimes turn on variations in ownership structure unrelated to the magnitude of the company's business or its capacity for complying with federal prescriptions.

This case is illustrative. In 1996, Clackamas had 4 physician–shareholders and at least 14 other employees for 28 full weeks; in 1997, it had 4 physician–shareholders and at least 14 other employees for 37 full weeks. Beyond question, the corporation would have been covered by the ADA had one of the physician–shareholders sold his stake in the business and become a "mere" employee. Yet such a change in ownership arrangements would not alter the magnitude of Clackamas' operation: In both circumstances, the corporation would have had at least 18 people on site doing the everyday work of the clinic for the requisite number of weeks.

The Equal Employment Opportunity Commission's approach, which the Court endorses, it is true, "excludes from protection those who are most able to control the firm's practices and who, as a consequence, are least vulnerable to the discriminatory treatment prohibited by the Act." As this dispute demonstrates, however, the determination whether the physician–shareholders are employees of Clackamas affects not only whether they may sue under the ADA, but also—and of far greater practical import—whether employees like bookkeeper Deborah Anne Wells are covered by the Act. Because the character of the relationship between Clackamas and the doctors supplies no justification for withholding from clerical worker Wells federal protection against discrimination in the workplace, I would affirm the judgment of the Court of Appeals.

Case Questions

1. Are you more persuaded by the District Court's analysis (applying the economic realities test), the ninth Circuit's analysis (reviewing the distinction between a corporation and a partnership), or the Supreme Court's analysis (relying on the common-law element of control)?

2. Do you believe that *Clackamas* will make it easier or more difficult to classify individuals as employees? No matter what your answer to this above question, do you believe the *Clackamas* decision will lead to the fairest results?

3. Are you persuaded more by the majority or dissent? Is it relevant to your decision that the physicians are classified as employees under another act (ERISA)? Which answer best seems to serve the objectives of the ADA?

Contingent or Temporary Workers

A *contingent worker* is one whose job with an employer is temporary, is sporadic, or differs in any way from the norm of full-time employment. As used by the EEOC, the term "contingent worker" includes those who are hired by an employer through a staffing firm, as well as temporary, seasonal, and part-time workers, and those considered to be independent contractors rather than employees.[4] (See Exhibit 1.5.)

[4] See "EEOC Enforcement Guidance on Application of EEO Laws to Contingent Workers Placed by Temporary Employment Agencies and Other Staffing Firms," *EEOC Enforcement Guidance,* December 1997.

INDEPENDENT CONTRACTOR OR EMPLOYEE

Which are you?

For federal tax purposes, this is an important distinction. Worker classification affects how you pay your federal income tax, social security and Medicare taxes, and how you file your tax return. Classification affects your eligibility for employer and social security and Medicare benefits and your tax responsibilities. If you aren't sure of your work status, you should find out now. This brochure can help you.

The courts have considered many facts in deciding whether a worker is an **independent contractor** or an **employee**. These relevant facts fall into three main categories: *behavioral control*; *financial control*; and *relationship of the parties*. In each case, it is very important to consider all the facts – no single fact provides the answer. Carefully review the following definitions.

BEHAVIORAL CONTROL

These facts show whether there is a right to direct or control how the worker does the work. A worker is an employee when the business has the right to direct and control the worker. The business does not have to actually direct or control the way the work is done – as long as the employer has the right to direct and control the work. For example:

- **Instructions** – if you receive extensive instructions on how work is to be done, this suggests that you are an **employee.** Instructions can cover a wide range of topics, for example:

  - how, when, or where to do the work

  - what tools or equipment to use

  - what assistants to hire to help with the work

  - where to purchase supplies and services

  If you receive less extensive instructions about what should be done, but not how it should be done, you may be an **independent contractor.** For instance, instructions about time and place may be less important than directions on how the work is performed.

- **Training** – if the business provides you with training about required procedures and methods, this indicates that the business wants the work done in a certain way, and this suggests that you may be an **employee.**

FINANCIAL CONTROL

These facts show whether there is a right to direct or control the business part of the work. For example:

- **Significant Investment** – if you have a significant investment in your work, you may be an **independent contractor.** While there is no precise dollar test, the investment must have substance. However, a significant investment is not necessary to be an **independent contractor.**

- **Expenses** – if you are not reimbursed for some or all business expenses, then you may be an **independent contractor,** especially if your unreimbursed business expenses are high.

- **Opportunity for Profit or Loss** – if you can realize a profit or incur a loss, this suggests that you are in business for yourself and that you may be an **independent contractor.**

RELATIONSHIP OF THE PARTIES

These are facts that illustrate how the business and the worker perceive their relationship. For example:

- **Employee Benefits** – if you receive benefits, such as insurance, pension, or paid leave, this is an indication that you may be an **employee.** If you do not receive benefits, however, you could be either an **employee** or an **independent contractor.**

- **Written Contracts** – a written contract may show what both you and the business intend. This may be very significant if it is difficult, if not impossible, to determine status based on other facts.

When You Are an *Employee*

- Your employer must withhold income tax and your portion of social security and Medicare taxes. Also, your employer is responsible for paying social security, Medicare, and unemployment (FUTA) taxes on your wages. Your employer must give you a Form W-2, *Wage and Tax Statement,* showing the amount of taxes withheld from your pay.

- You may deduct unreimbursed employee business expenses on Schedule A of your income tax return, but only if you itemize deductions and they total more than two percent of your adjusted gross income.

When You Are an *Independent Contractor*

- The business may be required to give you Form 1099-MISC, *Miscellaneous Income,* to report what it has paid to you.

- You are responsible for paying your own income tax and self-employment tax (Self-Employment Contributions Act – SECA). The business does not withhold taxes from your pay. You may need to make estimated tax payments during the year to cover your tax liabilities.

- You may deduct business expenses on Schedule C of your income tax return.

Source: Internal Revenue Service Publication 1779 (Rev. 12-99), Catalog No. 16134L.

Exhibit 1.5

Contingent Workers

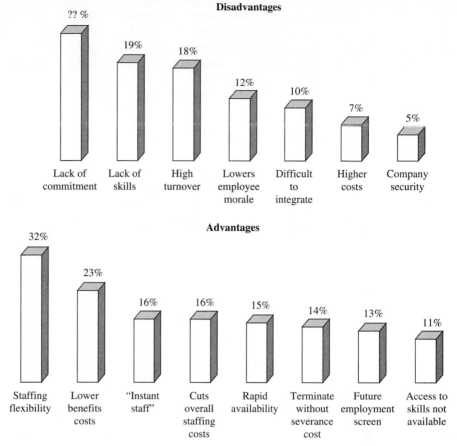

Disadvantages

??%	19%	18%	12%	10%	7%	5%
Lack of commitment	Lack of skills	High turnover	Lowers employee morale	Difficult to integrate	Higher costs	Company security

Advantages

32%	23%	16%	16%	15%	14%	13%	11%
Staffing flexibility	Lower benefits costs	"Instant staff"	Cuts overall staffing costs	Rapid availability	Terminate without severance cost	Future employment screen	Access to skills not available

Source: Reprinted with the permission of *HR Magazine,* published by the Society for Human Resource Management, Alexandria, Va.

When utilizing contingent and temporary workers, an employer must be cognizant of the advantages and disadvantages. (See Exhibit 1.5.) Although contingent or temporary workers provide a cost savings as a short-term benefit, depending on their classification they could be entitled to protection under the employment laws. It is important to be sure the classification given is the true classification.

The Joint Employer

Whether a contingent worker who is placed by a staffing firm with the firm's clients is an employee depends on a number of factors, including whether the staffing firm or the client retains the right to control when, where, and how the worker performs the job and whether there is a continuing relationship with the worker, among other factors. What is unique about the worker placed by a staffing firm is the potential for joint liability between the staffing firm and the client.

Similarly, in a case that sought to determine liability for wage and hour violations, the Second Circuit Court of Appeals considered whether the right to control is necessary to create liability based on joint employment. In *Zheng* v. *Liberty Apparel Co.,* 355 F.3d 61 (2d Cir. 2003), Liberty was a clothing manufacturer that subcontracted with a garment factory to produce its clothing. In finding liability based on the joint employer concept, the court held that all relevant factors should be considered including (but not limited to):

1. Whether the manufacturer/contractor employer's premises and equipment were used for the subcontractor's work.
2. Whether the subcontractor had a business that could or did shift as a unit from one putative joint employer to another.
3. The extent to which the subcontractor performed a discrete line-job that was integral to the contractor's process of production.
4. Whether responsibility under the contracts could pass from one subcontractor to another without material change.
5. The degree to which the contractors or their agents supervised the subcontractor's work.
6. Whether the subcontractors worked exclusively or predominantly for the contractors.[5]

The court specifically warned that not all outsourcing relationships would be classified as "joint employers," only those that "lack a substantial economic purpose, but it is manifestly not intended to bring normal, strategically oriented contracting schemes within the ambit of the FLSA."

Title VII prohibits staffing firms from illegally discriminating against workers in assignments and opportunities for employment. Staffing firms may qualify as the employer of the placed worker, as well. For example, if the staffing firm pays the worker and provides training and workers' compensation coverage, it may create an employment relationship with the worker.

If a client of a staffing firm supervises, trains, and otherwise directs the worker with whom it has a continuing relationship, then perhaps the client will become an employer of the worker. Could both the staffing firm and the client be considered the worker's employer? The answer is yes: The staffing firm and client may share liability as employers of the worker.

This raises concerns regarding liability under wage and hour laws, workers' compensation, and federal antidiscrimination statutes such as Title VII. Federal courts have recognized "joint and several" liability between staffing firm and client. The worker may collect compensatory damages from either one or both of the entities combined.

Further, employers may be held liable as "third-party interferers" under Title VII. For example, if an employer decides to ask its staffing firm to replace the temporary receptionist with one of another race, the receptionist could proceed with a Title VII claim against the employer because it improperly interfered with her employment opportunities with the staffing firm. Therefore, an employer using a staffing firm cannot avoid liability for discriminating against a temporary worker merely because it did not "employ" the worker.

---

[5] Ibid. at 72.

Defining "Applicant"

Since federal regulations often require employers to track applicants on the basis of race, gender, and ethnicity, it is important to have a clear and consistent definition of who is an "applicant." Moreover, in this electronic age, technology has altered the way that people apply for jobs. As a result, the Uniform Guidelines on Employee Selection Procedures were modified to include the following, expanded definition of applicant in the context of the Internet and related electronic data processing technologies: An "applicant" exists when three conditions have been met:

1. The employer has acted to fill a particular position.
2. The individual has followed the employer's standard procedures for submitting applications.
3. The individual has indicated an interest in the particular position. Where the applicant is instead a traditional job seeker, the original definition still applies—an applicant is someone who has "indicated an interest in being considered" for employment. The impact of this change is that an e-mail inquiry about a job does not qualify the sender as an applicant, nor does the posting of a résumé on a third party job board.

BACKGROUND—THE EMPLOYMENT-AT-WILL DOCTRINE

at-will employment
An employment relationship where there is no contractual obligation to remain in the relationship; either party may terminate the relationship at any time, for any reason, as long as the reason is not prohibited by law, such as for discriminatory purposes.

Initially, the theoretical underpinnings of the American employer–employee relationship was one based on the English feudal system. When employers were the wealthy landowners who owned the land on which "serfs" (workers) toiled, employers supplied virtually all the workers' needs, took care of disputes that arose, and allowed the workers to live out their lives on the land after they could no longer be the productive serfs they once were. The employer took care of the employees as parents would their children.

When we moved from an agrarian society toward a more industrialized one, the employee–employer relationship became further removed than before, but the underlying theory was still maintained: The employee could work for the employer as long as the employee wished, and leave when the employee no longer wished to work for the employer (therefore, the employees worked at their own will). The reverse was also true: The employer employed the employee for as long as the employer wished, and, when the employer no longer wished to have the employee in his or her employ, the employee had to leave.

Both parties were free to leave at virtually any time for any reason. Of course, if there was a contract between the parties, either as a collective bargaining agreement or an individual contract, the relationship was not governed by the will of the parties, but rather by the contract. Further, government employees generally were not considered at-will employees: Limitations were imposed on the government employer through rules governing the terms and termination of the federal employment relationship.

When "equal employment opportunity" legislation entered the equation, the employer's rights to hire and fire were circumscribed to a great extent. While an employer was free to terminate an employee for no particular reason, it could not terminate a worker based on race, gender, religion, national origin, age, or disability. Providing protection for members of historically discriminated-against groups through such laws as Title VII, the Age Discrimination in Employment Act, and the Americans with

Disabilities Act also had the predictable effect of making all employees feel more empowered in their employment relationships. While virtually no employees sued employers before such legislation, subsequently employees were willing to challenge employers' decisions in legal actions.

With women, minorities, older employees, disabled employees, and veterans given protected status under the laws, it was not long before those who were not afforded specific protection began to sue employers, based on their perception that it "just wasn't right" for an employer to be able to terminate them for any reason of the employer, regardless of whether the reason was in violation of antidiscrimination statutes. To them it was beside the point that they did not fit neatly into a protected category. They had been "wronged" and they wanted their just due. An employee could be fired if the employer didn't like the employee's green socks, or the way the employee wore his hair, or because the employee "blew it" on attempting to get his first account after being hired. There was no recourse because, since the relationship was at will, the employer could fire the employee for whatever reason the employer wished, as long as it was not a violation of the law.

Visualize a whole luscious, delectable pie of your favorite type. That pie represents the employer's rights in the workplace. At first, virtually the whole pie belonged to the employer. The employer could do practically anything the employer wished to do regarding the right to hire, fire, pay, or legislate employee activities in the workplace. Then Congress began passing laws that limited in some way the employer's prerogatives. The pie gets smaller and smaller as more and more of the pie is "eaten away" by laws. There are both state and federal laws governing wages and hours, child labor laws, equal employment laws, equal pay laws—all of which govern such areas as wages the employer will pay, time limits on how long employees can work, limits on the age employees must be, and prohibitions on reasons the employer can refuse to hire or terminate or discipline employees. If an employer was unionized, there was even less pie left. Employers who had their mouths set on having the whole pie ended up with much less than they envisioned. Then along comes the weakening of the employment-at-will concept, and much of the pie the employer thought was left is taken away. The amount of pie left to the employer is enough to be a filling portion, but much less than the employer initially thought he or she would have for disposal.

Regardless of whether a terminated employee is a member of a group protected from discrimination, the employee may bring suit on the basis of unjust dismissal or wrongful termination. The employee believes that there is an unjust reason for his or her dismissal and brings suit against the employer, seeking reinstatement or compensatory and punitive damages for the losses suffered in being unjustly dismissed.

Unjust dismissal cases have been brought alleging termination for signing a union card, filing workers' compensation claims, refusing to assist the employer in committing a crime, refusing to commit a crime on the employer's behalf, refusing to forgo suit against the employer for a valid legal claim against the employer, refusal to avoid jury duty, refusal to falsify records, refusal to lie in testifying in a case involving the employer, reporting wrongdoing or illegal activity by the employer, and termination at a time when the employee was about to receive a substantial bonus from the employer.

Probably because the law also began to recognize certain basic rights in its concept of the employment relationship, and because of the basic unfairness involved in some of the cases that the courts were asked to decide, courts all over the country began making exceptions to the at-will doctrine. The at-will doctrine is developed on a state-by-state basis because each state is free to make law governing the at-will doctrine. Therefore, the changes in the at-will doctrine vary from state to state. Congress has entertained proposals to deal with the at-will doctrine on the federal level, but, as of yet, none has been successful. In August 1991, the Commission on Uniform State Laws issued a model termination act that states may use. The intent is to make terminations so uniform across the country that there will be some predictability and consistency where now there is only a patchwork of laws and case law. This model act, and its status, will be discussed later in the chapter.

The state-by-state approach to addressing the exceptions to the at-will doctrine has created a crazy quilt of laws across the country. In some states the at-will doctrine has virtually no exceptions and, therefore, remains virtually intact as it always was. In other states the courts have created judicial exceptions to the at-will doctrine that apply in certain limited circumstances. In still other states, the state legislature has passed laws providing legislative exceptions to the at-will doctrine.

EXCEPTIONS TO THE AT-WILL DOCTRINE

Employment at will is still the basic law in many states. However, the employment-at-will doctrine several years ago began to erode. There have been several judicial exceptions to the rule created by courts. The result is that, even though an employer can terminate an employee for any legal reason, if the reason is one that is determined to fall within an exception to the at-will doctrine, the employee can assert a claim for wrongful termination or discharge, for which the employee can receive damages or reinstatement.

Though difficult cases for employees to prove, courts and state legislation have been fairly consistent in holding that exceptions will be permitted where the employer breaches an implied covenant of good faith and fair dealing, where an implied promise to the employee was breached, or where breach of an implied contract with the employee or the discharge is in violation of some recognized public policy. Keep in mind that if the employee and employer have an individual contract or a collective bargaining agreement, then the employment relationship is governed by the agreement. If the employer is the government, then the employment relationship regarding dismissals is governed by appropriate government regulations. It is the other 65 percent of the workforce that is covered by the employment-at-will doctrine.

The Worker Adjustment and Retraining Notification Act

The Worker Adjustment and Retraining Notification (WARN) Act generally requires that 60 days' advance notice of a "plant closing" or "mass layoff" be given to affected employees. A plant closing triggers a notice requirement if it would result in employment loss for 50 or more workers during a 30-day period. "Mass layoff" is defined as employment losses at one location during any 30-day period of 500 or more workers, or of 50–499 workers if they comprise at least one-third of the active workforce. Employees who have worked less than 6 months of the prior 12 or who work less than 20 hours a week are excluded from both computations. If an employer does not comply with the requirements of the WARN Act notices, employees can recover pay and benefits for the period for which notice was not given, up to a maximum of 60 days. All but small employers and public employers are required to provide written notice of a "plant closing" or "mass layoff" no less than 60 days in advance.

Exceptions to the Doctrine of Employment-at-Will

States vary in terms of their recognition of the following exceptions to the doctrine of employment-at-will. Some states recognize one or more exceptions while others might recognize none at all. In addition, the definition of these exceptions may also vary from state to state.

- Bad faith, malicious or retaliatory termination in violation of **public policy**.
- Termination in breach of the **implied covenant of good faith and fair dealing**.
- Termination in breach of some other **implied contract term**, such as those that might be created by employee handbook provisions (in certain jurisdictions).
- Termination in violation of the doctrine of **promissory estoppel** (where the employee reasonably relied on an employer's promise, to the employee's detriment).
- Other exceptions as determined by **statutes** (such as WARN).

The number of employees is a key factor in determining whether the WARN Act is applicable. Only an employer who has 100 or more full-time employees or has 100 or more employees who, in the aggregate, work at least 4,000 hours per week are covered by the WARN Act. In counting the number of employees, U.S. citizens working at foreign sites, temporary employees, and employees working for a subsidiary as part of the parent company must be considered in the calculation.

There are three exceptions to the 60-day notice requirements. The first, referred to as the "faltering company" exception, involves an employer who is actively seeking capital and who in good faith believes that giving notice to the employees will preclude the employer from obtaining the needed capital. The second exception occurs when the required notice is not given due to a "sudden, dramatic, and unexpected" business circumstance not reasonably foreseen and outside the employers' control. The last exception is for actions arising out of a "natural disaster" such as a flood, earthquake, or drought.

Violation of Public Policy

One of the most visible exceptions that states are fairly consistent in recognizing, either through legislation or court cases, has been based on a violation of public policy. For a terminated employee to sustain a cause of action against her or his employer on this basis, the ex-employee must show that the employer's actions were motivated by *bad faith, malice, or retaliation*. At least 44 states allow this exception. Violations of public policy usually arise from the employee being terminated for acts such as refusing to violate a criminal statute on behalf of the employer or at the employer's request, exercising a statutory right, fulfilling a statutory duty, or disclosing violations of statutes by an employer.

Scenario

For instance, a state may have a law that says that qualified citizens must serve jury duty unless they come within one of the statutory exceptions. The employer does not want the employee to miss work by serving jury duty. The employee serves jury duty and is terminated by the employer. The employee sues the employer for unjust dismissal. The employer counters with the at-will doctrine, which states that the employer can terminate the employee for any reason the employer wishes to use. The Jury System Improvements Act prohibits employers from discriminating based on jury service in federal courts. States vary in terms of their protection for state and local jury service. Even in states where the protection is less clear, many courts have then held that the employer's termination of the employee under these circumstances constitutes a violation of public policy. That is, by

State Rulings Chart

Availability of common-law exceptions to the employment-at-will doctrine on state-by-state basis. Implied contract includes implications through employer policies, handbooks, promises, or other representations.

	Implied Contract	Public Policy	Good Faith and Fair Dealing
Alabama	Yes	No	No
Alaska	Yes	Yes	Yes
Arizona	Yes	Yes	Yes
Arkansas	No	Yes	No
California	Yes	Yes	Yes
Colorado	Yes	Yes	No
Connecticut	Yes	Yes	Yes
Delaware	Yes	Yes	Yes
District of Columbia	Yes	Yes	No
Florida	No	No	No
Georgia	No	No	No
Hawaii	Yes	Yes	No
Idaho	Yes	Yes	Yes
Illinois	Yes	Yes	No
Indiana	Yes	Yes	No
Iowa	Yes	Yes	No
Kansas	Yes	Yes	No
Kentucky	Yes	Yes	No
Louisiana	No	No	No
Maine	Yes	No	No
Maryland	Yes	Yes	No
Massachusetts	Yes	Yes	Yes
Michigan	Yes	Yes	No
Minnesota	Yes	Yes	No
Mississippi	No	Yes	No
Missouri	No	Yes	No
Montana	Yes	Yes	Yes
Nebraska	Yes	Yes	No
Nevada	Yes	Yes	No
New Hampshire	Yes	Yes	Yes
New Jersey	Yes	Yes	Yes
New Mexico	Yes	Yes	No
New York	Yes	No	No
North Carolina	Yes	Yes	No
North Dakota	Yes	Yes	No
Ohio	Yes	Yes	No
Oklahoma	Yes	Yes	No
Oregon	Yes	Yes	No
Pennsylvania	Yes	Yes	No
Rhode Island	NC	No	NC
South Carolina	Yes	Yes	No
South Dakota	Yes	Yes	No

(continued)

State Rulings Chart (continued)

	Implied Contract	Public Policy	Good Faith and Fair Dealing
Tennessee	Yes	Yes	No
Texas	Yes	Yes	No
Utah	Yes	Yes	Yes
Vermont	Yes	Yes	No
Washington	Yes	Yes	No
West Virginia	Yes	Yes	No
Wisconsin	Yes	Yes	No
Wyoming	Yes	Yes	Yes

NC: No case or no clear expression.

Reproduced with permission from BNA's Labor & Employment Law Library, IERM 505:51, http://www.bna.com/products/labor/lelw.htm (June 2004). Copyright © 2004 by the Bureau of National Affairs, Inc. (800-372-1033), http://www.bna.com.

the legislature passing such a law requiring jury duty service, it thus has been legislatively determined that serving jury duty is a public policy that should be upheld. Thus, terminating the employee for fulfilling that statutory duty is a violation of public policy by the employer. For the court to allow an employer to terminate an employee who upholds this public policy would be inconsistent with the public policy exhibited by the statute; therefore, the employer's termination of the employee will not be upheld.

In one Washington State Supreme Court case, *Gardner* v. *Loomis Armored, Inc.,* the court ruled that an employer violated public policy when it fired an armored-truck driver after the driver left the vehicle in order to rescue a robbery hostage. In that case, the driver was making a routine stop at a bank. When he saw the bank's manager running from the bank followed by a man wielding a knife, he locked the truck's door and ran to her rescue. While the woman was saved, the driver was fired for violating his employer's policy prohibiting him from leaving his vehicle. The court held that his termination violated the public policy encouraging such "heroic conduct." Understanding the confusion sometimes left in the wake of decisions surrounding public policy, the court noted that "this holding does not create an affirmative legal duty requiring citizens to intervene in dangerous life threatening situations. We simply observe that society values and encourages voluntary rescuers when a life is in danger. Additionally, our adherence to this public policy does nothing to invalidate [the firm's] work rule regarding drivers' leaving the trucks. The rule's importance cannot be understated, and drivers do subject themselves to a great risk of harm by leaving the driver's compartment. Our holding merely forbids [the firm] from firing [the driver] when he broke the rule because he saw a woman who faced imminent life-threatening harm, and he reasonably believed his intervention was necessary to save her life. Finally, by focusing on the narrow public policy encouraging citizens to save human lives from life threatening situations, we continue to protect employers from frivolous lawsuits."[6]

On the other hand, while courts often strive to be sensitive to family obligations, a refusal to work overtime in consideration of those obligations was deemed a legal

---

[6] *Gardner* v. *Loomis Armored, Inc.,* 128 Wash. 2d 931, 913 P.2d 377 (1996).

basis for termination. In other words, such termination of an at-will employee did not violate a public policy or any legally recognized right or duty of the employee.[7] While the courts that have adopted the exception agree that the competing interests of employers and society require that the exception be recognized, as evidenced by the *Gardner* case, above, there is considerable disagreement in connection with what is the public policy and what constitutes a violation of the policy. In one of the leading cases in this area, the Illinois court stated that "the Achilles heel of the principle lies in the definition of public policy."

Whistle-Blowing

Some states have included "whistle-blowing" under the public policy exception. *Whistle-blowing* refers to an employee's reporting of the employer's wrongdoings. In a typical case involving whistle-blowing, the employee is fired for reporting the employer's wrongdoings. You may recall one of the most infamous cases of whistle-blowing is recent decades, Sherron Watkins' actions in connection with Enron's accounting malfeasance.

In 1982, Congress enacted the Federal Whistleblower Statute, which prohibits retaliatory action specifically against defense contractor employees who disclose information pertaining to a violation of the law governing defense contracts. The statute is administered by the Department of Defense and is enforced solely by that department; that is, an individual who suffers retaliatory action under this statute may not bring a private suit (common-law recovery in certain states continues to exist and is the subject of this section). The statute states specifically:

> An employee of a defense contractor may not be discharged, demoted, or otherwise discriminated against as a reprisal for disclosing to a Member of Congress or an authorized official of the Department of Defense or of Justice information relating to a substantial violation of law related to a defense contract (including the competition for or negotiation of a defense contract).

Additionally, in 1989 Congress amended the Civil Service Reform Act of 1978 to include the Whistleblowers Protection Act, which expands the protection afforded to federal employees who report government fraud, waste, and abuse. The act applies to all employees appointed in the civil service who are engaged in the performance of a federal function and are supervised by a federal official. Employees of federal contractors, therefore, are not covered by the act since they are hired by the contractor and not the government itself.

At least 39 states, including California, Florida, New York, and Texas, also provide some form of legislative protection for whistle-blowers. Almost half of these state whistle-blower protection statutes protect both public and private sector employees who report wrongdoings of their employer. Some states limit protection to the reporting of violation of federal, state, or local laws. However, an increasing number of states, including California, Colorado, and Illinois, protect the reporting of mismanagement or gross waste of public funds or of a substantial and specific danger to public health and safety. A few states,

---

[7] *Upton v. JWP Businessland,* 682 N.E.2d 1357 (Mass. 1997).

Exhibit 1.6

States with Whistle-Blower Protection Statutes

STATES WITH ONLY PUBLIC SECTOR WHISTLE-BLOWER PROTECTION STATUTES

Alaska, Arizona, Colorado, Delaware, Georgia,[2] Indiana, Kansas, Kentucky, Maryland,[1] Missouri, Oklahoma, Oregon, Pennsylvania,[3] South Carolina, South Dakota, Texas, Utah, Washington,[4] West Virginia, Wisconsin[2]

[1] Maryland restricts coverage to employees and classified-service applicants within the executive branch of state government.

[2] Georgia and Wisconsin exclude employees of the office of the governor, the legislature, and the courts.

[3] Pennsylvania's law excludes teachers, although school administrators are covered. Pennsylvania also has a separate law governing public utility employees.

[4] Washington has separate laws covering state employees and local government employees.

STATES WITH BOTH PRIVATE AND PUBLIC SECTOR WHISTLE-BLOWER PROTECTION

California, Connecticut,[2] Florida, Hawaii, Illinois, Iowa, Louisiana, Maine, Michigan, Minnesota,[1] New Hampshire,[1] New Jersey, New York, North Carolina, North Dakota, Ohio, Rhode Island, Tennessee[3]

[1] The laws in Minnesota and New Hampshire specifically exclude independent contractors.

[2] Connecticut has separate laws extending whistle-blower protection to public service, nuclear-power, and state and local employees who report hazardous conditions.

[3] Tennessee has two whistle-blower laws, one that covers only local school-system employees, and the other covering any employee who reports, or refuses to participate in, illegal activities.

— Separate laws in Nevada cover state employees and peace officers.

— Montana also protects public and private-sector whistle-blowers through its Wrongful Discharge from Employment Act.

Source: Bureau of National Affairs, Inc., *Individual Employment Rights Manual,* No. 133, 505:28–29 (July 2001).

such as Alaska, Maine, Louisiana, and Pennsylvania, require that whistle-blowing reports be made in "good faith." (See Exhibit 1.6.)

If there is a statute permitting an employee to take certain action or to pursue certain rights, the employer is prohibited from terminating employees for engaging in such activity. Examples of this type of legislation include state statutes permitting the employee to file a workers' compensation claim for on-the-job injuries sustained by the employee. Assume the employee files the claim and is terminated by the employer for doing so. If the employee sues for wrongful termination or retaliatory discharge, and the state is one that recognizes the public policy exception to the at-will doctrine, the employee will most likely win. Another example of legislation protecting whistle-blowers is the Sarbanes-Oxley Act, which primarily addresses issues relating to accountability and transparency in corporate governance (such as the issues that arose during the infamous Enron debacle). The act specifically provides protection to employees of publicly traded companies who disclose corporate misbehavior, even if the disclosure was made only internally to management or to the board of directors and not necessarily to relevant government authorities. The following case is a seminal one in this area, exploring whether assisting law enforcement agencies should be protected by public policy. Following *Palmateer,* the *Green* case involves an employee who continually reported inspection flaws and was fired.

Palmateer v. International Harvester Company *85 Ill.2d 124, 421 N.E.2d 876 (1981)*

Ray Palmateer had worked for International Harvester (IH) for 16 years at the time of his discharge. Palmateer sued IH for retaliatory discharge, claiming that he was terminated because he supplied information to local law enforcement authorities regarding a co-worker's criminal activities and for offering to assist in the investigation and trial of the co-worker if necessary.

Simon, J.

[The court discusses the history of the tort of retaliatory discharge in Illinois and explains that the law will not support the termination of an at-will employment relationship where the termination would contravene public policy.] But the Achilles heel of the principle lies in the definition of public policy. When a discharge contravenes public policy in any way, the employer has committed a legal wrong. However, the employer retains the right to fire workers at will in cases "where no clear mandate of public policy is involved."

There is no precise definition of the term. In general, it can be said that public policy concerns what is right and just and what affects the citizens of the State collectively. It is to be found in the State's constitution and statutes and, when they are silent, in its judicial decisions. Although there is no precise line of demarcation dividing matters that are the subject of public policies from matters purely personal, a survey of cases in other States involving retaliatory discharge shows that a matter must strike at the heart of a citizen's social rights, duties, and responsibilities before the tort will be allowed.

It is clear that Palmateer has here alleged that he was fired in violation of an established public policy. There is no public policy more basic, nothing more implicit in the concept of ordered liberty than the enforcement of a State's criminal code. There is no public policy more important or more fundamental than the one favoring the effective protection of the lives and property of citizens.

No specific constitutional or statutory provision requires a citizen to take an active part in the ferreting out and the prosecution of crime, but public policy nevertheless favors citizen crime-fighters. Public policy favors Palmateer's conduct in volunteering information to the law enforcement agency. Palmateer was under a statutory duty to further assist officials when requested to do so.

The foundation of the tort of retaliatory discharge lies in the protection of public policy, and there is a clear public policy favoring investigation and prosecution of criminal offenses. Palmateer has stated a cause of action for retaliatory discharge.

Case Questions

1. Is there a difference between the court's protection of an employee who reports a rape by a co-worker or the theft of a car, and an employee who is constantly reporting the theft of the company's paper clips and pens?

2. Should the latter employee in the above question be protected? Consider that the court in *Palmateer* remarked that "the magnitude of the crime is not the issue here. It was the General Assembly who decided that the theft of a $2 screwdriver was a problem that should be resolved by resort to the criminal justice system."

3. What are other areas of public policy that might offer protection to terminated workers?

Green v. Ralee Engineering Company *78 Cal.Rptr.2d 16 (CA. 1998)*

An employee was terminated after calling attention to the fact that parts that had failed inspection were still being shipped to purchasers. He sued for wrongful discharge, asserting a public policy exception to the at-will employment rule. The court agreed that the termination violated public policy.

Chin, J.

Richard Green was a quality control inspector for Ralee Engineering Company, a fuselage and wing component manufacturer who supplied parts to airplane assembly companies. One of Green's responsibilities included inspecting parts before they were shipped to the assembly companies. Green noticed that Ralee Engineering was shipping parts to assembly companies even when those parts failed the inspections his team had performed. During a two-year period, Green called this practice to the attention of his immediate superiors and various management personnel, including the company president. Citing a lack of business, Green was dismissed from Ralee in 1991 after serving the company for 23 years. Green admitted he was an at-will employee but filed a wrongful discharge suit for alleging that a number of less-experienced inspectors than Green were retained and that the real reason for his dismissal was retaliation for his objections to the defective parts. Green argued that the discharge fell within the nationally well-recognized exception to the at-will employment providing tort damages where an employee was discharged for a reason that violated an important public policy.

May administrative regulations be a source of fundamental public policy that limits an employer's right to discharge an otherwise at-will employee? Although our legislature has determined that an employment contract is generally terminable at either party's will, we have created a narrow exception to this rule by recognizing that an employer's right to discharge an at-will employee is subject to limits that fundamental public policy imposes. At-will employees may recover tort damages from their employers if they can show they were discharged in contravention of fundamental public policy.

Employees who assert wrongful discharge claims must show that the important public interests they seek to protect are "tethered to fundamental policies that are delineated in constitutional or statutory provisions." Here, we address a related, albeit narrow issue. We must decide whether particular administrative regulations implementing the Federal Aviation Act of 1958, a public safety statute that created the Federal Aviation Administration (FAA), should be included as a source of fundamental public policy that limits an employer's right to discharge an at-will employee. Like the Court of Appeal, we conclude they should.

We continue to believe that, aside from constitutional policy, the legislature, and not the courts, is vested with the responsibility to declare the public policy of the state. Recognizing this important distinction, however, does not allow us to ignore the fact that statutorily authorized regulations that effectuate the legislature's purpose to ensure commercial airline safety are "tethered to" statutory provisions. . . .

* * *

Defendant argues principally that, even if we assume it did everything plaintiff claimed, its conduct violated no public policy embodied in a constitutional or statutory provision. Consequently, defendant argues, plaintiff's discharge fails to qualify as a wrongful discharge.

As we explain, we agree with the Court of Appeal in concluding that the federal safety regulations promulgated to address important public safety concerns may serve as a source of fundamental public policy. The regulations satisfy our requirement that the action be tethered to fundamental policies delineated in a statutory or constitutional provision. . . .

* * *

Public policy cases fall into one of four categories: the employee (1) refused to violate a statute; (2) performed a statutory obligation; (3) exercised a constitutional or statutory right or privilege; or (4) reported a statutory violation for the public's benefit. . . . In order to provide an exception to the at-will mandate, the policy must be "public" in that it "affects society at large" rather than the individual, must have been articulated at the time of discharge, and must be "fundamental" and "substantial."

The limitation on public policy sources (that they must be supported by either constitutional or statutory provisions) grew from our belief that "public policy as a concept is notoriously resistant to precise definition, and that courts should venture into this area, if at all, with great care and due deference to the judgment of the legislative branch" in order to avoid judicial policymaking. . . .

* * *

. . . The question we now address is whether important public safety regulations governing commercial airline safety may provide a basis for declaring a public policy in the context of a retaliatory discharge action.

Federal regulations promoting the proper manufacture and inspection of component airline parts advance the important public policy objectives. In the Federal Aviation Act of 1958 Congress declared the public interest in commercial air safety. . . .

* * *

Plaintiff performed the FAA-required inspections on the parts intended for use in Boeing aircraft to further a fundamental policy: "to ensure that each article produced conforms to the type design and is in a condition for safe operation." Therefore, this regulation-based fundamental public policy may serve as the foundation for plaintiff's claim. It furthers important safety policies affecting the public at large and does not merely serve either the employee's or employer's personal or proprietary interest. As we noted, "[t]here is no public policy more important or more fundamental than the one favoring the effective protection of the lives and property of citizens."

* * *

We emphasize that not all administrative regulations can support such claims, but only those that implicate substantial public policies. It is insufficient for employees to allege that they were discharged for refusing to violate a statute or follow a statutory duty; they must also allege that the statute in question was designed to protect the public or advance some substantial public policy goal. Employees must do the same when alleging a discharge for refusing to follow administrative regulations that implement an important statutory objective. In the case of both statutes and regulations based on statutes, courts must distinguish between those that promote a "clearly mandated public policy" and those that do not. . . .

We conclude that the public policy behind federal regulations concerning airline safety has a basis in statutory provisions, consistent with our rule that the public policy giving rise to a wrongful termination action have a basis in a constitutional or statutory provision. Congress has specifically directed the FAA to assign, maintain, and enhance safety and security as the highest priorities in air commerce and to regulate air commerce "in a way that best promotes its safety." Our judicial decisions favor protecting employees who vindicate important public policy interests. Allowing defendant to discharge plaintiff with impunity after he sought to halt or eliminate its alleged inspection practices would only undermine the important and fundamental public policy favoring safe air travel. By including significant administrative safety regulations promulgated to serve important FAA mandates as a source of fundamental public policy limiting an employer's right to discharge an otherwise at-will employee, we effectively guarantee that employers do not exercise their right to terminate their employees at will in a way that undermines more important public safety objectives. AFFIRMED and REMANDED.

Case Questions

1. Not all the justices agreed with this opinion. Do you agree with the majority's opinion? Why or why not?
2. Do you think an important factor in this case was the airline industry and the fact that safety of air travel was an issue?
3. The court notes that it should determine what policy should be considered "public policies" in relation to these types of causes of action. Do you agree? Who do you think should determine such public policies—the courts, the legislature (state or federal), employers, or employees?

public policy
A legal concept intended to ensure that no individual lawfully do that which has a tendency to be injurious to the public or against the public good. Public policy is undermined by anything that harms a sense of individual rights.

In determining what exactly constitutes **public policy**, one should consider two factors: *clarity and impact.* In evaluating the clarity, or substantiality, of the policy, the employer should look to both the definiteness and weight of the policy. For instance, a statute that specifically protects individuals from discharge if they leave work to tend to a family emergency clearly articulates a public policy in that regard. On the other hand, if the basis for the employee's claim of public policy is one line in the legislative history of the statute, which was not later incorporated into the statute, such a public concern may lack the needed clarity to support the claim.

Generally, courts require that the statement of public policy be rooted in a statutory or constitutional provision. In that way, courts are able to maintain some type of consistency among cases. This allows managers some degree of predictability in terms of the consequences of their employment decisions.

In evaluating the impact of the public policy, the employer should look to the impact of the discharge on the public interest served by the policy. For instance, will this discharge discourage others from exercising their rights or discourage compliance with that policy, and, therefore, frustrate the policy itself? Further, is the satisfaction of that policy dependent on the cooperation of the employees, and would such cooperation also be impacted? Accordingly, the focus in the latter inquiry is not on the effect of the discharge on this individual employee but on society as a whole and the future impact of the policy. As noted by one scholar in this area, the burden on the individual discharged employee is insufficient to support a cause of action because it is offset by the employer's legitimate interests in maximizing employee control, efficiency, and productivity.

Other reasons for termination that, at first blush, appear to be solid bases for claims of wrongful termination may not be protected. For example, where an employee was discharged for seeking the assistance of an attorney after receiving a poor evaluation, the Seventh Circuit Court of Appeals held that the termination was proper. An employee's discharge for performing acts that one would like to believe society should encourage is not necessarily protected. The outcome in a particular case will depend on the precedent of the jurisdiction in which the termination occurs.

While some states allow these exceptions articulated above, but do not allow for an extension of the doctrine beyond that, other states remain reticent in their denial of the public policy exception to at-will employment. For instance, though it seems counterintuitive, the appellate court in New York held that an employee who was terminated for refusing to participate in illegal schemes designed to defraud the IRS, and for reporting these activities to a supervisor, could not maintain an action for wrongful discharge.

Supporting this line of court decisions is the principle that any modification to at-will employment should come from the legislature, either state or federal. Where there is a clear statement of public policy from the legislature, these courts are more likely to allow the public policy exception. However, where no clear mandate exists, the courts posit that any declaration of public policy would entail stepping over the line that divides the formation of law and the application of law.

Breach of Implied Covenant of Good Faith and Fair Dealing

Another exception to the at-will employment presumption is the implied duty of good faith and fair dealing in the performance and enforcement of every contract. This requirement should not be confused with a contractual requirement of "good cause" prior to termination; an employer can terminate a worker for good cause under a contract. A New York court defined the duty as follows:

covenant of good faith and fair dealing
Implied contractual obligation to act in good faith in the fulfillment of each party's contractual duties.

> In every contract there is an implied covenant that neither party shall do anything which will have the effect of destroying or injuring the right of the other party to receive the fruits of the contract, which means that in every contract there exists an implied covenant of good faith and fair dealing. While the public policy exception to the at-will doctrine looks to the law to judge the employer's actions and deems them violations of public policy or not, the breach of implied covenant of good faith looks instead to the actions between the parties to do so.

Where the implied **covenant of good faith and fair dealing** is recognized as an exception to the at-will doctrine, courts have implied that any agreement between the employer has inherent in it, unless specifically excluded, a promise that the parties will deal with each other fairly and in good faith. Consider the situation where the employer and employee may have entered into a contract of employment, but the particulars of why and when an employee could be terminated were not specifically addressed in the parties' contractual agreements. Assume the employee is then terminated for what the employee believes is an unwarranted reason, but the court looks to the contract and finds that the matter is not covered by the contract. The court will then look to the facts to see whether the termination is valid under the contract or in breach of the implied covenant of good faith and fair dealing.

Only 13 states recognize this covenant as an exception to at-will employment: Some states allow the cause of action but limit the damages awarded to those that would be awarded under a breach of contract claim, while other states allow the terminated employee to recover higher tort damages.

Scenario

In connection with scenario 2, discussed at the beginning of the chapter, Mark Richter may have a claim against his employer for breach of the covenant of good faith and fair dealing. Mark's employer is, in effect, denying Mark the fruits of his labor.

Critics of this implied agreement argue that, where an agreement is specifically nondurational, there should be no expectation of guaranteed employment of any length. As long as both parties are aware that the relationship may be terminated at any time, it would be extremely difficult to prove that either party acted in bad faith in terminating the relationship. Courts have supported this contention in holding that the implied covenant does not recognize the balance between the employee's interest in maintaining her or his employment and the employer's interest in running its business as it sees fit. "The absence of good cause to discharge an employee does not alone give rise to an enforceable claim for breach of a condition of good faith and fair dealing." To the contrary, employers may terminate an individual for any reason, as long as the true reason is not contradictory to public policy, against the law, and in contravention of another agreement. The case below seeks to clarify this distinction.

Guz v. Bechtel Nat. Inc. *100 Cal.Rptr.2d 352 (Ca. 2000)*

Plaintiff John Guz, a longtime employee of Bechtel National, Inc. (BNI), was terminated at age 49 when his work unit was eliminated as a way to reduce costs. At the time he was hired and at his termination, Bechtel maintained Personnel Policy 1101 on the subject of termination of employment which stated that "Bechtel employees have no employment agreements guaranteeing continuous service and may resign at their option or be terminated at the option of Bechtel." Guz sued BNI and its parent, Bechtel Corporation, alleging age discrimination, breach of an implied contract to be terminated only for good cause, and breach of the implied covenant of good faith and fair dealing. The trial court granted Bechtel's motion for summary judgment and dismissed the action. In a split decision, the Court of Appeal reversed. The majority found that Bechtel had demonstrated no grounds to foreclose a trial on any of the claims asserted in the complaint. The Supreme Court of California reverses the judgment of the Court of Appeals and remands.

* * *

Baxter, J.

III. Implied covenant claim

Bechtel next urges that the trial court properly dismissed Guz's separate claim for breach of the implied covenant of good faith and fair dealing because, on the facts and arguments presented, this theory of recovery is either inapplicable or superfluous. We agree.

The sole asserted basis for Guz's implied covenant claim is that Bechtel violated its established personnel policies when it terminated him without a prior opportunity to improve his "unsatisfactory" performance, used no force ranking or other objective criteria when selecting him for layoff, and omitted to consider him for other positions for which he was qualified. Guz urges that *even if his contract was for employment at will,* the implied covenant of good faith and fair dealing precluded Bechtel from "unfairly" denying him the contract's benefits by failing to follow its own termination policies.

Thus, Guz argues, in effect, that the implied covenant can impose substantive terms and conditions beyond those to which the contract parties actually agreed. However, as indicated above, such a theory directly contradicts our conclusions in *Foley* v. *Interactive Data Corp.* (1988). The covenant of good faith and fair dealing, implied by law in every contract, exists merely to prevent one contracting party from unfairly frustrating the other party's right to receive the *benefits of the agreement actually made.* The covenant thus cannot "be endowed with an existence independent of its contractual underpinnings." It cannot impose substantive duties or limits on the contracting parties beyond those incorporated in the specific terms of their agreement.

. . . The mere existence of an employment relationship affords no expectation, protectible by law, that employment will continue, or will end only on certain conditions, unless the parties have actually adopted such terms. Thus if the employer's termination decisions, however arbitrary, do not breach such a substantive contract provision, they are not precluded by the covenant.

This logic led us to emphasize in *Foley* that "breach of the implied covenant cannot logically be based on a claim that [the] discharge [of an at-will employee] was made without good cause." As we noted, "[b]ecause the implied covenant protects only the parties' right to receive the benefit of their agreement, and, in an at-will relationship there is no agreement to terminate only for good cause, the implied covenant standing alone cannot be read to impose such a duty."

The same reasoning applies to any case where an employee argues that even if his employment was at will, his arbitrary dismissal frustrated his contract benefits and thus violated the implied covenant of good faith and fair dealing. Precisely because employment at will *allows* the employer freedom to terminate the relationship as it chooses, the employer does not frustrate the employee's contractual rights merely by doing so.

In such a case, "the employee cannot complain about a deprivation of the benefits of continued employment, for the agreement never provided for a continuation of its benefits in the first instance."

Guz cites several decisions suggesting that the implied covenant precludes an employer from terminating even an at-will employee unfairly, such as by refusing to follow its own established policies and practices. (*Rulon-Miller* v. *International Business Machines Corp.* (1984) [employer's duty of fair dealing requires that "like cases be treated alike"; thus, employer's termination rules and regulations, if any, must be followed]; see *Gray* v. *Superior Court* (1988) [long service plus violation of employer policies may establish breach of covenant of "fair treatment"]; *Pugh* v. *See's Candies, Inc.* (1981) [termination after long service, in violation of employer policies, may breach implied covenant to refrain from arbitrary treatment]; see also *Kern* v. *Levolor Lorentzen, Inc.* (1990) [covenant requires "cooperation in carrying out the contract and honesty in creating or settling disputes"; breach of covenant may thus be shown where employee establishes lengthy satisfactory service and violation of employer's termination policies].) But insofar as these authorities suggest that the implied covenant may impose limits on an employer's termination rights beyond those either expressed or implied in fact in the employment contract itself, they contravene the persuasive reasoning of *Foley,* and are therefore disapproved.

Similarly at odds with *Foley* are suggestions that independent recovery for breach of the implied covenant may be available if the employer terminated the employee in "bad faith" or "without probable cause," i.e., without determining "honestly and in good faith that good cause for discharge existed." Where the employment contract itself allows the employer to terminate at will, its motive and lack of care in doing so are, in most cases at least, irrelevant.

A number of Court of Appeal decisions since *Foley* have recognized that the implied covenant of good faith and fair dealing imposes no independent limits on an employer's prerogative to dismiss employees. (E.g., *Camp* v. *Jeffer, Mangels, Butler & Marmaro* (1995) [implied covenant did not preclude unfair termination where there was no express or implied-in-fact contract limiting employer's termination rights]; *Flait* v. *North American Watch Corp.* (1992) [employment contract contained express at-will term; because employee thus could not show her termination broke any "contractual covenant or promise," implied covenant claim must fail]; *Slivinsky* v. *Watkins-Johnson Co.* (1990) [where contract contained express at-will clause, implied covenant claim must fail because employee could not show her termination without good cause frustrated "the [parties'] intentions and reasonable expectations . . . within the contract"].) We affirm that this is the law.

Of course, as we have indicated above, the employer's personnel policies and practices may become *implied-in-fact terms* of the contract between employer and employee. If that has occurred, the employer's failure to follow such policies when terminating an employee is a breach of the contract itself.

A breach of the contract may also constitute a breach of the implied covenant of good faith and fair dealing. But insofar as the employer's acts are directly actionable as a breach of an implied-in-fact contract term, a claim that merely realleges that breach as a violation of the covenant is superfluous. This is because, as we explained at length in *Foley,* the remedy for breach of an employment agreement, including the covenant of good faith and fair dealing implied by law therein, is *solely contractual.* In the employment context, an implied covenant theory affords no separate *measure of recovery,* such as tort damages. Allegations that the breach was wrongful, in bad faith, arbitrary, and unfair are unavailing; there is no tort of "bad faith breach" of an employment contract.

We adhere to these principles here. To the extent Guz's implied covenant cause of action seeks to impose limits on Bechtel's termination rights *beyond* those to which the parties actually agreed, the claim is invalid. To the extent the implied covenant claim seeks simply to invoke terms to which the parties *did* agree, it is superfluous. Guz's remedy, if any, for Bechtel's alleged violation of its personnel policies depends on proof that they were contract terms to which the parties actually agreed. The trial court thus properly dismissed the implied covenant cause of action.[8]

Case Questions

1. Based on *Guz,* can the implied covenant of good faith and fair dealing apply to any conditions not actually stated in a contract? In other words, can the covenant apply to anything beyond that which is actually stated in an employment contract, if any? If not, is there no implied covenant as long as someone is at-will without a contract?

2. Are you more persuaded by the cases cited by the court in favor of a holding that the implied covenant precludes an employer from terminating even an at-will employee unfairly, or the *Foley* decision which held that the covenant "cannot impose substantive duties or limits on the contracting parties beyond those incorporated in the specific terms of their agreement"?

3. Explain the distinction between the court's discussion of the covenant of good faith and fair dealing and the possibility of an implied contract term (see also the next section in this chapter).

---

[8] We do not suggest the covenant of good faith and fair dealing has no function whatever in the interpretation and enforcement of employment contracts. As indicated above, the covenant prevents a party from acting in bad faith to frustrate the contract's *actual* benefits. Thus, for example, the covenant might be violated if termination of an at-will employee was a mere pretext to cheat the worker out of another contract benefit to which the employee was clearly entitled, such as compensation already earned. We confront no such claim here.

Breach of Implied Contract

implied contract
A contract that is not expressed, but, instead, is created by other words or conduct of the parties involved.

What happens when the employer is not violating an express contractual agreement, yet there seems to be an injustice done? That is where the theory of **implied contracts** comes in. The court finds such contracts from several different sources. Primarily, an implied contract arises from the acts of the parties; the acts leading to the creation of an implied contract vary from situation to situation.

Employers should be aware of the implied contract. In recent years, courts have been willing to find contracts implied from statements made during preemployment interviews about the candidate becoming a "permanent" employee or from conversations quoting yearly or other periodic salaries. In such cases, when the employee has been terminated in less than the time quoted in the salary (e.g., telling the employee the job pays $50,000 per year), then the employee has been able to maintain an action for the remainder of the salary on the theory that there was an implied contract created of a year's duration. If the employee is released before the end of that year, for other than good cause, the termination may result in liability for the salary remaining on the year's contract. The court considers what implied contract obligations an employer may have created in the following case.

Torosyan v. Boehringer Ingelheim Pharmaceuticals, Inc.
662 A.2d 89 (Conn. 1995)

After being given assurances of job security, an applicant was hired, then later terminated. The employee sued for a breach of an implied contract, using statements made by the employer as the basis of his claim. The court permitted the cause of action to survive a motion to dismiss.

Peters, C. J.

At the outset, we note that all employer–employee relationships not governed by express contracts involve some type of implied "contract" of employment. "There cannot be any serious dispute that there is a bargain of some kind; otherwise, the employee would not be working." To determine the contents of any particular implied contract of employment, the factual circumstances of the parties' relationship must be examined in light of legal rules governing unilateral contracts.

Pursuant to the legal principles governing such contracts, in order to find that an implied contract of employment incorporates specific representations orally made by the employer or contained in provisions in an employee manual, the trier of fact is required to find the following subordinate facts. Initially, the trier of fact is required to find that the employer's oral representations or issuance of a handbook to the employee was an "offer"—i.e., that it was a promise to the employee that, if the employee worked for the company, his or her employment would thereafter be governed by those oral or written statements, or both. If the oral representations and/or the handbook constitute an "offer," the trier of fact then is required to find that the employee accepted that offer. Subsequent oral representations or the issuance of subsequent handbooks must be evaluated by the same criteria. To be incorporated into

the implied contract of employment, any such representation or handbook must constitute an offer to modify the preexisting terms of employment by substituting a new implied contract for the old. Furthermore, the proposed modifications, like the original offers, must be accepted.

Typically, an implied contract of employment does not limit the terminability of an employee's employment but merely includes terms specifying wages, working hours, job responsibilities, and the like. Thus "[a]s a general rule, contracts of permanent employment, or for an indefinite term, are terminable at will."

* * *

. . . The plaintiff testified that certain statements were made to him in the context of an employment interview in direct response to his inquiries about job security. One of those statements was that if the plaintiff did a good job, the defendant would take care of him. Another statement was that the plaintiff's employment would be governed by an employment manual. The offer letter sent to the plaintiff neither stated that it contained the entire terms of the employment offer nor disclaimed any guarantees of job security. The defendant's oral representations were material to the plaintiff's decision to move from California and accept employment with the defendant. The employee manual was provided to the plaintiff on the first day of work, and he immediately proceeded to read it to ensure that it was consistent with the defendant's representations. The manual explicitly qualified the defendant's right to discharge with the words "for cause." The manual also stated that every employee could speak to an executive officer about "job-related problems which [he or she] may feel cannot be worked out successfully with [his or her] immediate supervisor or manager." Finally, after reading the manual, the plaintiff continued to work for the defendant for several years.

* * *

Because the defendant does not allege that there was "just cause" for the discharge in the absence of actual falsification of documents by the plaintiff, we AFFIRM the trial court's determination in this case that there was no cause for the plaintiff's discharge.

Case Questions

1. Do you agree with the court's decision? Why or why not?

2. If the employer had later distributed a new manual that specifically stated that all workers were subject to "at-will" employment, would this case have been decided differently?

3. What can companies do to avoid liability like that found in the above case?

Notwithstanding some of the court's comments in the above case, the Supreme Court in North Carolina held to the contrary:

> This court has repeatedly held that in the absence of a contractual agreement between an employer and an employee establishing a definite term of employment, the relationship is presumed to be terminable at the will of either party, without regard to the quality of performance of either party . . . "If you do your job, you'll have a job," is not sufficient to make this indefinite hiring terminable only for cause. *Kurtzman* v. *Applied Analytical Inds., Inc.,* 493 S.E.2d 420 (N.C. 1997).

In addition, the court noted that there should be no exception based on an employee's decision to move her or his residence or other burdens that the new position might have placed on the employee.

Scenario

Regarding scenario 1, Emma Bina may have a claim against her new employer based on a breach of an implied employment contract. Emma accepted her position with the understanding that, in exchange for sacrificing her previous position and the sale of her house, and so on, she would be employed as long as she performed satisfactory work. Her work was more than satisfactory, yet she still lost her job. If this could have been avoided (i.e., the company did not go bankrupt or something similar), she might have a claim. (The majority of courts would agree with the *Torosyan* decision.)

Implied Contract Based on Employment Policy Manuals and Handbooks

Employment policy manuals may, in fact, form an implied contract. Employers use policy manuals as a means of organizing workplace policies and communicating them to employees. Employment policy manuals are the most logical way to handle the matter of workplace policies, because they present the employee, manager, and supervisor with one central place to search for policies when issues arise. However, employment policy manuals may present problems by unwittingly creating contracts of employment that limit the at-will nature of the employment relationship in which the employer maintains such a modicum of control over the duration of the employment relationship. Instead, the employee may have an implied contract, which may not be to the employer's advantage. Nobody wants to become bound to a contract when they are not even aware that they are doing so.

Many state courts have held that the rules and regulations set forth in an employee handbook or policy manual may form a contract between the employer and employee. The employee, by accepting the employment, becomes bound by the policies, as does the employer. As discussed in the *Guz* case earlier, the employer's failure to then abide by the policies may be cause of subsequent litigation and liability toward an employee harmed by the employee's failure to do so. Employers should be careful when creating an employment policy manual that includes a statement that employees will only be terminated for good cause, or that employees become "permanent" employees once the successfully complete their probationary period. These have been held to create binding agreements between the employer and employee, and the employer's later termination of the employee, inconsistent with those statements, has resulted in liability.

Some employers have tried to avoid the characterization of their employment policies or handbooks as potential contract terms by including in those documents a disclaimer such as the following:

> Our employment relationship is to be considered "at-will" as that term is defined in this state. Nothing in this policy [or handbook] shall be construed as a modification to that characterization and, where there is an apparent conflict between the statements in this policy [or handbook], the policy [or handbook] shall be construed to support a determination of an at-will relationship or shall become null.

Some states have statutorily addressed this issue by delineating the type of disclaimer that will be accepted in that state. For instance, in South Carolina, a disclaimer in a handbook or personnel manual to be valid must be underlined and in capital letters on the first page of the document and the document must be signed by the employee verifying that the employee has read and understood that statement. Disclaimers in other employment-related documents must satisfy the other requirements but need not be signed.

More often, states have addressed this issue in their courts rather than by specific statute. Courts regularly require that the disclaimers be clear, prominent, conspicuous, unambiguous, and an employee signature is often required. Notwithstanding the language above, disclaimers that conflict with other language in that document or in employee handbooks or policies may be rendered null by the courts.

In one case, *Steve Hicks* v. *Methodist Medical Center,*[9] plaintiff Steven Hicks was terminated in violation of his employee handbook. The defendant Methodist Medical Center claimed that it was allowed to modify the handbook at any time pursuant to a disclaimer found in the book. The court held that, in order to negate any promises made in contract provisions, a disclaimer must be "conspicuous." Since the disclaimer was located at page 38 of the handbook, was not highlighted, printed in capital letters, or in any way prominently displayed, the disclaimer was not conspicuous and so did not negate the promises made in the handbook's provisions. The court therefore found that a contract existed.

Exception Based on Promissory Estoppel

Promissory estoppel is another form of exception to the at-will rule. Promissory estoppel is similar to the implied contract claim except that the promise, implied or express, does not rise to the level of a contract. Perhaps there is no mutual consideration or some

---

[9] 593 N.E.2d 119 (Ill. App. 3d 1992).

other flaw; however, a plaintiff filing a claim based on promissory estoppel may still be able to refute an employer's contention of an at-will environment. For estoppel to attach, the plaintiff must show that the employer or prospective employer made a promise upon which the work reasonably relied to her or his detriment. Often the case turns on whether it was reasonable for the worker to rely on the employer's promise without an underlying contract. In addition, it is critical to have a clear and unambiguous promise. In a 2004 case, the worker believed that he had a position at DaimlerChrysler until he retired. He based his belief on exchanges during interviews for a position in which he told interviewers that he expected to hold the new position for another 12 to 15 years. In reviewing the facts of the case, the court held that, though promissory estoppel is a perfectly acceptable basis on which to find an at-will exception, "there is no evidence that Gunthorpe was promised continued employment" in his new position. "His subjective expectations are irrelevant."[10]

INTRODUCTION TO WRONGFUL DISCHARGE

compensatory damages
Money damages given to a party to compensate for direct losses due to an injury suffered.

punitive damages
Money damages designed to punish flagrant wrongdoers and to deter them and others from engaging in similar conduct in the future.

In November 2001, a Texas jury awarded a former employee who was wrongfully terminated $30.5 million in damages. In March 2000, a federal jury in California deliberated just half a day before awarding more than $500,000 to a scientist who claimed she had been fired from Stanford University Medical School for complaining about sexual discrimination. Do these sound like judgments you want to have to pay to employees or ex-employees out of the coffers of your business? Probably not. You can think of far better ways to spend your money. After all, you're in business to *make* money, not to hand it away. But such judgments, rather than becoming less frequent, are becoming more so. Risk managers should also be aware that under Title VII, claims of discriminatory termination may result not only in reinstatement but in **compensatory** and **punitive damages** awards. While these statutory damages are "capped" at amounts dependent on the size of the employer, judges are allowed to, for example, award attorney's fees to the prevailing party in successful Title VII actions, sending the total judgment well into six or seven figures.

As discussed above, if there is no express agreement or contract to the contrary, employment is considered to be at will; that is, either the employer or the employee may terminate the relationship at their will. Nevertheless, even where a discharge involves no statutory discrimination, breach of contract, or traditional exception to the at-will doctrine discussed above, the termination may still be considered wrongful and the employer may be liable for "wrongful discharge," "wrongful termination," or "unjust dismissal." Therefore, in addition to ensuring that workplace policies do not wrongfully discriminate against employees, and do not fall under other exceptions, the employer must also beware of situations in which the employer's policy or action in a particular termination can form the basis for unjust dismissal. Since such bases can be so diverse, the employer must be vigilant in watching this area, and employees must be fully aware of their rights, even though the relationship may be considered at will.

---

[10] *Gunthorpe v. DaimlerChrysler Corp.*, 90 Fed. App. 877 (6th Cir. 2004).

Constructive Discharge

constructive discharge
Occurs when the employee is given no reasonable alternative but to terminate the employment relationship; considered an involuntary act on the part of the employee.

The "discharge" addressed in this chapter may refer either to "firing" or to an employee's decision to leave under certain circumstances. **Constructive discharge** exists where the employee is given no alternative but to quit her or his position; that is, the act of leaving was not truly voluntary. Therefore, while the employer did not actually fire the employee, it was the actions of the employer that *caused* the employee to leave. Constructive discharge usually evolves from circumstances where an employer knows that it cannot really terminate an employee for one reason or another. So, to avoid being sued for wrongful termination, the employer creates an environment where the employee has no choice but to leave. If courts were to allow this type of treatment, those laws that restrict employers' actions from wrongful termination, such as Title VII, would have no effect.

The test for constructive discharge is whether the employer made the working conditions *so intolerable that no reasonable employee should be expected to endure.* A 2004 opinion further explained that "an employee's work environment need not be literally unbearable in order to effect a constructive discharge. It is enough that the employee has no recourse within the employer's organization or reasonably believes there is no chance for fair treatment."[11] A minority of courts hold that the former employee must also show that the employer created the intolerable working conditions *with the specific intent of forcing the employee to quit.* However, this intent can be inferred where the employee's departure is a reasonably foreseeable consequence of the employer's actions.[12] Finally, to find constructive discharge, the circumstances complained of must be aggravated, which may occur where there is one horrible event or a number of minor instances of hostile behavior. Consider whether the following case satisfies this definition.

[11] *Van Meter Industries* v. *Mason City Human Rights Commission,* No. 107/02-1161 (Ind. 2004).
[12] *Martin v. Cavalier Hotel Corp.,* 67 FEP Cases 300 (4th Cir. 1995).

Pennsylvania State Police v. Suders *Dkt. No. 03-95, — S.Ct. —, 2004 WL 1300153 (2004)*

In March 1998, the Pennsylvania State Police (PSP) hired plaintiff–respondent Suders to work as a police communications operator for the McConnellsburg barracks, where her male supervisors subjected her to a continuous barrage of sexual harassment. In June 1998, Suders told the PSP's Equal Employment Opportunity Officer, Virginia Smith-Elliott, that she might need help, but neither woman followed up on the conversation. Two months later, Suders contacted Smith-Elliott again, this time reporting that she was being harassed and was afraid. Smith-Elliott told Suders to file a complaint, but did not tell her how to obtain the necessary form. Two days later, Suders' supervisors arrested her for theft of her own computer-skills exam papers. Suders had removed the papers after concluding that the supervisors had falsely reported that she had repeatedly failed, when in fact, the exams were never forwarded for grading. Suders then resigned from the force and sued the PSP, claiming sexual harassment and constructive discharge, in violation of Title VII.

The District Court granted the PSP's motion for summary judgment, finding that the PSP was not vicariously liable for the supervisors' conduct. In support of its decision, the District Court referred to *Faragher* v. *Boca Raton* and *Burlington Industries, Inc.* v. *Ellerth* (see also Chapter 7), where the Supreme Court held that an employer is only liable for supervisor harassment where there is a "tangible employment action, such as discharge, demotion, or undesirable reassignment." Where there is no tangible action, the employer may raise an affirmative defense to liability. To prevail on the basis of that defense, the employer must prove that (1) it exercised reasonable care to prevent and correct promptly any sexually harassing behavior, and that (2) the employee unreasonably failed to take advantage of any preventive or corrective opportunities provided by the employer or to avoid harm otherwise. Suders' hostile work environment [suit] failed according to the District Court because she unreasonably failed to avail herself of the PSP's internal anti-harassment procedures.

The Third Circuit reversed and remanded the case for trial, disagreeing with the District Court in two key respects: First, even with an affirmative defense, there remained genuine issues of material fact about the effectiveness of the PSP's program to address sexual harassment claims; second, Suders had stated a claim of constructive discharge due to hostile work environment that the lower court failed to address. The appeals court ruled that a constructive discharge, if proved, constitutes a tangible employment action that renders an employer strictly liable and precludes recourse to the Ellerth/Faragher affirmative defense.

The Supreme Court reviewed and identifies the prima facie case of constructive discharge using harassment as a basis. The court concludes that there is a difference between those cases where there is an official act of a supervisor that constitutes the adverse employment action, and those cases where the discharge itself is intended to constitute the adverse employment action. It concludes that an employer does not have recourse to the Ellerth/Faragher affirmative defense in the former case, but that the defense is available to the employer whose supervisors are charged with harassment without an additional precipitating act. It therefore vacates the Third Circuit's judgment and remands the case for further proceedings.

Ginsburg delivered the opinion of the Court, in which Rehnquist, and Stevens, O'Connor, Scalia, Kennedy, Souter, and Breyer joined. Thomas filed a dissenting opinion.

Plaintiff–respondent Nancy Drew Suders alleged sexually harassing conduct by her supervisors, officers of the Pennsylvania State Police (PSP), of such severity she was forced to resign. The question presented concerns the proof burdens parties bear when a sexual harassment/constructive discharge claim of that character is asserted under Title VII of the Civil Rights Act of 1964.

To establish hostile work environment, plaintiffs. like Suders must show harassing behavior "sufficiently severe or pervasive to alter the conditions of [their] employment." *Meritor Savmgs Bank, FSB* v. *Vinson.* . . Beyond that, we hold, to establish "constructive discharge," the plaintiff must make a further showing: She must show that the abusive working environment became so intolerable that her resignation qualified as a fitting response. An employer may defend against such a claim by showing both (1) that it had installed a readily accessible and effective policy for reporting and resolving complaints of sexual harassment, and (2) that the plaintiff unreasonably failed to avail herself of that employer-provided preventive or remedial apparatus. This affirmative defense will

not be available to the employer, however, if the plaintiff quits in reasonable response to an employer-sanctioned adverse action officially changing her employment status or situation, for example, a humiliating demotion, extreme cut in pay, or transfer to a position in which she would face unbearable working conditions. In so ruling today, we follow the path marked by our 1998 decisions in *Burlington Industries, Inc.* v. *Ellerth,* and *Faragher* v. *Boca Raton.*

I

***

The Court of Appeals then made the ruling challenged here: It held that "a constructive discharge, when proved, constitutes a tangible employment action." Under *Ellerth* and *Faragher,* the court observed, such an action renders an employer strictly liable and precludes employer recourse to the affirmative defense announced in those decisions. The Third Circuit recognized that the Courts of Appeals for the Second and Sixth Circuits had ruled otherwise. A constructive discharge resulting from a supervisor-created hostile work environment, both Circuits had held, does not qualify as a tangible employment action, and therefore does not stop an employer from invoking the *Ellerth/Faragher* affirmative defense. The Third Circuit, however, reasoned that a constructive discharge "'constitutes a significant change in employment status' by ending the employer–employee relationship" and "also inflicts the same type of 'direct economic harm'" as the tangible employment actions *Ellerth* and *Faragher* offered by way of example (discharge, demotion, undesirable reassignment). Satisfied that Suders had "raised genuine issues of material fact as to her claim of constructive discharge," and that the PSP was "precluded from asserting the affirmative defense to liability advanced in support of its motion for summary judgment," the Court of Appeals remanded Suders' Title VII claim for trial.

***

II

A

Under the constructive discharge doctrine, an employee's reasonable decision to resign because of unendurable working conditions is assimilated to a formal discharge for remedial purposes. The inquiry is objective: Did working conditions become so intolerable that a reasonable person in the employee's position would have felt compelled to resign?

***

B

This case concerns an employer's liability for one subset of Title VII constructive discharge claims: constructive discharge resulting from sexual harassment, or "hostile work environment," attributable to a supervisor. Our starting point is the framework *Ellerth* and *Faragher* established to govern employer liability for sexual harassment by supervisors. As earlier noted, those decisions delineate two categories of hostile work environment claims: (1) harassment that "culminates in a tangible employment action," for which employers are strictly liable, and (2) harassment that takes place in the absence of a tangible employment action, to which employers may assert an affirmative defense. With the background set out above in mind, we turn to the key issues here at stake: Into which *Ellerth/Faragher* category do hostile-environment constructive discharge claims fall—and what proof burdens do the parties bear in such cases? In *Ellerth* and *Faragher,* the plaintiffs–employees sought to hold their employers vicariously liable for sexual harassment by their supervisors, even though the plaintiffs "suffer[ed] no adverse, tangible job consequences.". . .

. . . [W]e held that when no tangible employment action is taken, the employer may defeat vicarious liability for supervisor harassment by establishing, as an affirmative defense, both that "the employer exercised reasonable care to prevent and correct promptly any sexually harassing behavior," and that "the plaintiff employee unreasonably failed to take advantage of any preventive or corrective opportunities provided by the employer or to avoid harm otherwise."

***

1

. . . A hostile-environment constructive discharge claim entails something more: A plaintiff who advances such a compound claim must show working conditions so intolerable that a reasonable person would have felt compelled to resign.

Suders' claim is of the same genre as the hostile work environment claims the Court analyzed in *Ellerth* and *Faragher*. Essentially, Suders presents a "worse case" harassment scenario, harassment ratcheted up to the breaking point. Like the harassment considered in our pathmaking decisions, harassment so intolerable as to cause a resignation may be effected through co-worker conduct, unofficial supervisory conduct, or official company acts. Unlike an actual termination, which is *always* effected through an official act of the company, a constructive discharge need not be. A constructive discharge involves both an employee's decision to leave and precipitating conduct: The former involves no official action; the latter, like a harassment claim without any constructive discharge assertion, may or may not involve official action.

***

2

***

Following *Ellerth* and *Faragher*, the plaintiff who alleges no tangible employment action has the duty to mitigate harm, but the defendant bears the burden to allege and prove that the plaintiff failed in that regard. The plaintiff might elect to allege facts relevant to mitigation in her pleading or to present those facts in her case in chief, but she would do so in anticipation of the employer's affirmative defense, not as a legal requirement.

We agree with the Third Circuit that the case, in its current posture, presents genuine issues of material fact concerning Suders' hostile work environment and constructive discharge claims. We hold, however, that the

Court of Appeals erred in declaring the affirmative defense described in *Ellerth* and *Faragher* never available in constructive discharge cases. Accordingly, we vacate the Third Circuit's judgment and remand the case for further proceedings consistent with this opinion.

It is so ordered.

DISSENT

Justice Thomas, dissenting

. . . [T]he National Labor Relations Board (NLRB) developed the concept of constructive discharge to address situations in which employers coerced employees into resigning because of the employees' involvement in union activities. In light of this specific focus, the NLRB requires employees to establish two elements to prove a constructive discharge. First, the employer must impose burdens upon the employee that "cause, and [are] intended to cause, a change in his working conditions so difficult or unpleasant as to force him to resign. Second, it must be shown that those burdens were imposed because of the employee's union activities."

When the constructive discharge concept was first imported into Title VII of the Civil Rights Act of 1964, some courts imposed similar requirements. Moreover, because the Court had not yet recognized the hostile work environment cause of action, the first successful Title VII constructive discharge claims typically involved adverse employment actions. If, in order to establish a constructive discharge, an employee must prove that his employer subjected him to an adverse employment action with the specific intent of forcing the employee to quit, it makes sense to attach the same legal consequences to a constructive discharge as to an actual discharge.

The Court has now adopted a definition of constructive discharge, however, that does not in the least resemble actual discharge. The Court holds that to establish "constructive discharge," a plaintiff must "show that the abusive working environment became so intolerable that [the employee's] resignation qualified as a fitting response." Under this rule, it is possible to allege a constructive discharge absent any adverse employment action. Moreover, a majority of Courts of Appeals have declined to impose a specific intent or reasonable foreseeability requirement.

Thus, as it is currently conceived, a "constructive" discharge does not require a "company act[] that can be performed only by the exercise of specific authority granted by the employer," nor does it require that the act be undertaken with the same purpose as an actual discharge. Under these circumstances, it no longer makes sense to view a constructive discharge as equivalent to an actual discharge. Instead, as the Court points out, a constructive discharge is more akin to "an aggravated case of . . . sexual harassment or hostile work environment." And under this "hostile work environment plus" framework, the proper standard for determining employer liability is the same standard for hostile work environment claims that I articulated in *Burlington Industries., Inc.* "An employer should be liable if, and only if, the plaintiff proves that the employer was negligent in permitting the supervisor's conduct to occur." If a supervisor takes an adverse employment action because of sex that directly results in the constructive discharge, the employer is vicariously liable. But, where the alleged constructive discharge results only from a hostile work environment, an employer is liable if negligent. Because respondent has not adduced sufficient evidence of an adverse employment action taken because of her sex, nor has she proffered any evidence that petitioner knew or should have known of the alleged harassment, I would reverse the judgment of the Court of Appeals.

Case Questions

1. Do you agree with Justice Thomas' dissenting assessment of the distinction between proving constructive discharge and proving actual discharge?

2. Do you agree that an adverse employment action is so critical to a claim of constructive discharge?

3. What do you expect to be the enduring impact of this decision?

Retaliatory Discharge

Retaliatory discharge is another constraint on employment at-will. Though discharge in retaliation for exercising specific rights was discussed previously in this chapter in connection with public policy, it will also be addressed in later chapters with regard to discharges in connection with various specific statutes, such as termination for filing an ADA complaint, ADEA complaint, or other charge with the EEOC. Title VII specifically prohibits adverse employment actions based on the fact that an employee or former employee has "made a charge, testified, assisted or participated in any manner in an investigation, proceeding or hearing under this [Act]." Note that retaliatory discharge claims are somewhat distinct from discharge based on whistle-blowing (even though the discharge might be in retaliation for the whistle-blowing) since the former is prohibited by Title VII while employees are protected from the latter by a number of different statutes. Since retaliatory discharge claims can be brought based simply on one's participation in a protected activity such as a colleague's Title VII complaint or one's opposition to a wrongful employer practice, it is not necessary for the claimant to actually be a member of a protected group or to have suffered discrimination herself.

The prima facie case for retaliatory discharge includes evidence of

1. Protected activity—opposition to discrimination or participation in the statutory complaint process.
2. Adverse action.
3. Causal connection between the protected activity and the adverse action.[13]

To determine whether the employee has satisfied the prima facie case, the EEOC's compliance manual suggests the following questions:[14]

1. Did the charging party (CP/employee) oppose discrimination?
    a. Did the charging party explicitly or implicitly communicate to the respondent (R/employer) or another covered entity a belief that its activity constituted unlawful discrimination under Title VII, the ADA, the ADEA, or the EPA?
        i. If the protest was broad or ambiguous, would CP's protest reasonably have been interpreted as opposition to such unlawful discrimination?
        ii. Did someone closely associated with CP oppose discrimination?
    b. Was the manner of opposition reasonable? Was the manner of opposition so disruptive that it significantly interfered with R's legitimate business concerns?
        i. If the manner of opposition was not reasonable, CP is not protected under the antiretaliation clauses.
    c. Did CP have a reasonable and good faith belief that the opposed practice violated the antidiscrimination laws?
        i. If so, CP is protected against retaliation, even if s/he was mistaken about the unlawfulness of the challenged practices.
        ii. If not, CP is not protected under the antiretaliation clauses.
2. Did CP participate in the statutory complaint process?
    a. Did CP or someone closely associated with CP file a charge, or testify, assist, or participate in any manner in an investigation, proceeding, hearing, or lawsuit under the statutes enforced by the EEOC?
        i. If so, CP is protected against retaliation regardless of the validity or reasonableness of the original allegation of discrimination.
        ii. CP is protected against retaliation by a respondent for participating in statutory complaint proceedings even if that complaint involved a different covered entity.

---

[13] EEOC Compliance Manual, "Guidance and Instructions for Investigating and Analyzing Claims of Retaliation," http://www.eeoc.gov/policy/docs/retal.html (5/20/98).

[14] Ibid.

3. Did R subject CP to any kind of adverse treatment?
   a. Adverse actions undertaken after CP's employment relationship with R ended, such as negative job references, can be challenged.
   b. Although trivial annoyances are not actionable, more significant retaliatory treatment that is reasonably likely to deter protected activity is unlawful. There is no requirement that the adverse action materially affect the terms, conditions, or privileges of employment.
4. Causal connection—Is there direct evidence that retaliation was a motive for the adverse action?
   a. Did R official admit that it undertook the adverse action because of the protected activity?
   b. Did R official express bias against CP based on the protected activity? If so, is there evidence linking that statement of bias to the adverse action?
   c. Such a link would be established if, for example, the statement was made by the decision maker at the time of the challenged action.
   d. If there is direct evidence that retaliation was a motive for the adverse action, "cause" should be found. Evidence as to any additional legitimate motive would be relevant only to relief, under a mixed-motives analysis.
5. Is there circumstantial evidence that retaliation was the true reason for the adverse action?
   a. Is there evidence raising an inference that retaliation was the cause of the adverse action?
      i. Such an inference is raised if the adverse action took place shortly after the protected activity and if the decision maker was aware of the protected activity before undertaking the adverse action.
      ii. If there was a long period of time between the protected activity and the adverse action, determine whether there is other evidence raising an inference that the cause of the adverse action was retaliation.
   b. Has R produced evidence of a legitimate, nondiscriminatory reason for the adverse action?
   c. Is R's explanation a pretext designed to hide retaliation?
      i. Did R treat similarly situated employees who did not engage in protected activity differently from CP?
      ii. Did R subject CP to heightened scrutiny after she or he engaged in protected activity?
      iii. If, on the basis of all of the evidence, the investigator is persuaded that retaliation was the true reason for the adverse action, then "cause" should be found.[15]

EEOC guidance expands the interpretation of this provision, explaining that an adverse employment action need not actually be termination, nor must it materially affect the terms, conditions, or privileges of the employment relationship. In fact, an employee is still protected even if he or she participates in an investigation that eventually uncovers no wrongdoing. However, where an employee merely protests or opposes illegal

---

[15] Ibid. (adapted).

discrimination and does not file a formal charge, the worker is afforded slightly less protection. To be covered, the worker must have a reasonable belief in the illegality of the practice. A belief that wouldn't be held by another reasonable person could preclude a plaintiff's claim. For instance, in *Clark County School District* v. *Breeden,* 85 FEP Cases 730 (2001), the Supreme Court held that a plaintiff's belief that she was protesting unlawful sexual harassment was not reasonable. "No one could reasonably believe that this incident [alleged by the plaintiff] violated Title VII."

Courts are sensitive to claims of retaliation in order to protect an employee's right to protest wrongful employment or other actions. If workers were not protected against retaliation, there would be a strong deterrent to asserting one's rights. On the other hand, if the employer's action is legitimately based in law or on legitimate, nondiscriminatory reason (LNDR), the employer's actions are protected.[16] EEOC guidance recommends that evidence of retaliation is sufficient to support a claim as long as it played any role in the employer's decision. The courts, however, don't necessarily agree, concluding instead that an employer's decision is insulated if it would have made the same decision notwithstanding the retaliatory motive.[17]

Constitutional Protections

Though perhaps it goes without saying, under certain circumstances an employer may not take an adverse employment action against a worker for exercising constitutional rights. However, this applies only where the employer is a public entity since constitutional rights exist against state action rather than action by private employers. For instance, a public employer may not terminate a worker for the exercise of free speech (including whistle-blowing under most circumstances) or based on a particular political affiliation. These same protections may apply in connection with private employers where the adverse actions violate some recognized expression of public policy, even without state action. Examples of this application include protection of an employee who refused to participate in an employer's public lobbying campaign but no protection for an employee who chooses to become a candidate in a campaign.

Military Leave

Under the Uniformed Services Employment and Reemployment Rights Act (USERRA), workers who enter military service and receive an honorable discharge are guaranteed reemployment protected against discrimination and retaliation on the basis of their service or time in service (see Exhibit 1.7). USERRA provides protection to all workers who perform service in the uniformed services. Though the act specifically does not apply to temporary workers, it does apply to anyone with a realistic expectation of ongoing employment such as a seasonal worker who returns on a recurring basis or part-time workers who work on a continued basis. The service covered may be voluntary or conscripted and any type of duty, including training and/or examinations.

To take advantage of USERRA, an employee must provide advance written or verbal notice to the employer (unless is unreasonable or unable to do so by military necessity),

---

[16] *Sahli* v. *Bull HN Information Systems Inc.,* No. SJC-08697 (Mass. D.Ct. 2002).

[17] *McNutt* v. *Board of Trustees of the University of Illinois,* 76 FEP Cases 989 (7th Cir. 1998).

Exhibit 1.7 — Employee Rights under USERRA

YOUR RIGHTS UNDER USERRA
THE UNIFORMED SERVICES EMPLOYMENT AND REEMPLOYMENT RIGHTS ACT

USERRA protects the job rights of individuals who voluntarily or involuntarily leave employment positions to undertake military service. USERRA also prohibits employers from discriminating against past and present members of the uniformed services, and applicants to the uniformed services.

REEMPLOYMENT RIGHTS

You have the right to be reemployed in your civilian job if you leave that job to perform service in the uniformed service and:

☆ you ensure that your employer receives advance written or verbal notice of your service;

☆ you have five years or less of cumulative service in the uniformed services while with that particular employer;

☆ you return to work or apply for reemployment in a timely manner after conclusion of service; and

☆ you have not been separated from service with a disqualifying discharge or under other than honorable conditions.

If you are eligible to be reemployed, you must be restored to the job and benefits you would have attained if you had not been absent due to military service or, in some cases, a comparable job.

RIGHT TO BE FREE FROM DISCRIMINATION AND RETALIATION

If you:

☆ are a past or present member of the uniformed service;

☆ have applied for membership in the uniformed service; or

☆ are obligated to serve in the uniformed service;

then an employer may not deny you any of the following because of this status:

☆ initial employment;

☆ reemployment;

☆ retention in employment;

☆ promotion; or

☆ any benefit of employment.

In addition, an employer may not retaliate against anyone assisting in the enforcement of USERRA rights, including testifying or making a statement in connection with a proceeding under USERRA, even if that person has no service connection.

HEALTH INSURANCE PROTECTION

☆ If you leave your job to perform military service, you have the right to elect to continue your existing employer-based health plan coverage for you and your dependents for up to 24 months while in the military.

☆ Even if you don't elect to continue coverage during your military service, you have the right to be reinstated in your employer's health plan when you are reemployed, generally without any waiting periods or exclusions (e.g., pre-existing condition exclusions) except for service-connected illnesses or injuries.

ENFORCEMENT

☆ The U.S. Department of Labor, Veterans Employment and Training Service (VETS) is authorized to investigate and resolve complaints of USERRA violations.

☆ For assistance in filing a complaint, or for any other information on USERRA, contact VETS at 1-866-4-USA-DOL or visit its website at http://www.dol.gov/vets. An interactive online USERRA Advisor can be viewed at http://www.dol.gov/elaws/userra.htm.

☆ If you file a complaint with VETS and VETS is unable to resolve it, you may request that your case be referred to the Department of Justice or the Office of Special Counsel, depending on the employer, for representation.

☆ You may also bypass the VETS process and bring a civil action against an employer for violations of USERRA.

The rights listed here may vary depending on the circumstances. This notice was prepared by VETS, and may be viewed on the internet at this address: http://www.dol.gov/vets/programs/userra/poster.pdf. Federal law requires employers to notify employees of their rights under USERRA, and employers may meet this requirement by displaying this notice where they customarily place notices for employees.

U.S. Department of Labor
1-866-487-2365

ESGR
EMPLOYER SUPPORT OF THE GUARD AND RESERVE
1-800-336-4590
Publication Date—February 2005

must take a leave from this particular employer of no more than a cumulative of five years, and must submit an application for reemployment within the required time period (which depends on the length of the individual's service). If these requisites are satisfied, the employee must be allowed to return to the position in which she or he would have found themselves if they had remained with the employer, or a position of equivalent rank, pay, and seniority. However, an employer is relieved of the obligation to reemploy under USERRA if its circumstances have changed so reemployment is impossible (such as a reduction in force that eliminated the position), or if it would impose an undue burden on the employer (such as the case of a returning worker disabled in service who cannot be reasonably accommodated; see Chapter 12).

An employer is not required to pay the worker during the leave unless, of course, the worker chooses to use accrued allowable paid leave (though they are not required to use that leave). The act also contains provisions for the continuation of medical coverage and pension benefits (for which military leave constitutes standard work time with the employer).

Wrongful Discharge Based on Other Tort Liability

A *tort* is a violation of a duty, other than one owed when the parties have a contract. Where a termination happens because of intentional and outrageous conduct on the part of the employer and causes emotional distress to the employee, the employee may have a tort claim for a wrongful discharge in approximately half of the United States. For example, in one case, an employee was terminated because she was having a relationship with a competitor's employee. The court determined that forcing the employee to choose between her position at the company and her relationship with a male companion constituted outrageous conduct.

One problem exists in connection with a claim for physical or emotional damages under tort theories. In many states, an employee's damages are limited by workers' compensation laws. Where an injury is work related, such as emotional distress as a result of discharge, these statutes provide that the workers' compensation process is a worker's exclusive remedy. An exception exists where a claim of injury is based solely on emotional distress; in that situation, many times workers' compensation will be denied. Therefore, in those cases, the employee may proceed against the employer under a tort claim. To avoid liability for this tort, the employer should ensure that the process by which an employee is terminated is respectful of the employee as well as mindful of the interests of the employer.

Where a discharge acts to defame the employee, there may be sufficient basis for a tort action for defamation. To sustain a claim for defamation, the employee must be able to show that (1) the employer made a false and defamatory statement about the employee, (2) the statement was communicated to a third party without the employee's consent, and (3) the communication caused harm to the employee. Claims of defamation usually arise where an employer makes statements about the employee to other employees or her or his prospective employers. This issue is covered in Chapter 13 relating to the employee's privacy rights and employer references.

Finally, where the termination results from a wrongful invasion of privacy, an employee may collect damages. For instance, where the employer wrongfully invades the employee's privacy, searches her purse, and consequently terminates her, the termination may be wrongful.

Management Tips

- No matter the size of your organization, as long as you have hired one individual to work for you, you are considered an employer and potentially subject to numerous federal and other regulations, as well as to wrongful termination liability.

- You are always allowed to hire the best person for a job; the law merely states that you may not make this decision based on prejudice or stereotypes. In order to avoid a wrongful discharge suit and, more importantly, to ensure the ethical quality of your decisions, don't fire someone for some reason that violates basic principles of dignity, respect, or social justice.

- You have the right to fire an employee for *any* reason as long as it is not for one of the specific reasons prohibited by law. On the other hand, if you don't have sufficient documentation or other evidence of the appropriate reason for your decision, a court might infer that your basis is wrongful.

- While it is inconvenient, to say the least, when an employee reports wrongdoing occurring at your firm, under most circumstances, you may not retaliate against that person. Be sure to avoid even the *appearance* of retaliation, as the actual motivation for employment decisions is often difficult to prove.

- Since statements in an employment policy manual may be construed in some circumstances as contractual promises, review all documentation *as if* you will be bound to it as a contract.

- Have sufficient training for all employees who will conduct interviews, since the firm may be bound by promises made to applicants during interviews if the applicant relies on the promise in accepting a position.

- Review arbitration agreements to ensure fairness.

- Review noncompete agreements, if valid and enforceable under applicable state law, to ensure that the restrictions placed on employees are reasonable.

- Have termination decisions be subject to internal review. Unilateral decisions to fire an employee may lead to emotion rather than reason being used to determine terminations.

- In the event of a layoff:

— Clearly explain to employees the reasons for the actions taken: Document all efforts to communicate with employees.

— Prepare the managers who will deliver the message.

— Speak plainly and don't make promises.

— Avoid euphemisms such as "We are all family and we will be together again someday."

— Emphasize that it's not personal.

— Know how layoffs will affect the demographic breakdown of the staff.*

*Matthew Boyle, "The Not-So-Fine Art of the Layoff," *Fortune,* Mar. 19, 2001, pp. 209–210.

THE "FREEDOM" TO CONTRACT IN THE REGULATORY EMPLOYMENT ENVIRONMENT

In the age of increasingly complex regulations governing the workplace, the relationship between employer and employee is still essentially contractual. As you have seen throughout this chapter, terms and conditions of employment may be expressed or implied. Though an employer is generally free to design contract terms of any kind, the terms and conditions set by an employer cannot violate the letter or the spirit of applicable laws. In addition, courts and legislatures may determine that certain types of agreements between employer and employee are unenforceable, given other competing interests at stake. The focus of this chapter, therefore, is the manner in which the employment relationship is regulated in general. These regulations, as mentioned, tend to restrict what an employer can do. Accordingly, though this is the first chapter in the text, you will find discussions throughout with regard to all employment decisions, including terminations.

Covenants Not to Compete ("Noncompete Agreements")

One employment constraint that has received varying degrees of acceptance by different states is the so-called noncompete agreement. While individuals in positions of trust and confidence already owe a duty of loyalty to their employers during employment, even without a noncompete agreement, a **noncompete agreement** usually requires that the employee not disclose trade secrets, solicit other employees or customers, or enter into competition with the employer upon termination of the employment relationship. All states allow employers to control what information a former worker can use or disclose in a competing business and whether a former worker can encourage clients, customers, and former co-workers to leave the employer.

However, not all states allow employers to prevent former workers from competing with them. These covenants are specifically permitted in Hawaii, South Dakota, Texas, and Wisconsin. In Nevada, Montana, North Dakota, and Oklahoma, an agreement limiting for whom a former employee can work and where he or she can work will not be enforced. In several other states, such as Alabama, Colorado, Florida, Oregon, Louisiana, California, and Texas, an employer may only keep a worker from competing under certain circumstances. For example, in Colorado, "management personnel" may have noncompete agreements enforced against them while others may not. In all other states, an employer may restrict where, when, and what type of work an employee may engage in at the end of the employment relationship, as long as the restrictions are reasonable.[18]

But what are "reasonable" restrictions on an employee's ability to enter into competition with the employer after the employment relationship has ended? The Restatement (Second) of Contracts explains that common law generally prohibits the restriction "if it is greater than necessary to protect the employer's legitimate interests or if the promisee's need is outweighed by the hardship to the promisor and likely injury to the public." In determining what is reasonable, courts look to the geographical and time limitations placed on the employee's ability to engage in competition. The definition of "competition" under the noncompete agreement is also relevant: Is the employee prohibited from working in any capacity with a competitor or merely restricted from entering into direct competition with the employer? Restrictions that are for an indefinite period of time, or that prohibit the employee from working "anywhere in the United States," may be considered unreasonable. However, as an example, restricting an employee from engaging in direct competition with the employer for one year from the end of their employment relationship within the same county may be considered reasonable. Generally, in order to be

noncompete agreement
An agreement signed by the employee agreeing not to disclose the employer's confidential information or enter into competition with the employer for a specified period of time and/or within a specified region.

[18] Shannon Miehe, *How to Create a Noncompete Agreement* (Berkeley, CA: Nolo Press, 2001), pp. 1/3, 1/4.

considered reasonable, the restrictive covenant should not prevent the employee from earning a living of any sort under its terms.

It is generally accepted that a valid restrictive covenant will meet the following qualifications:

1. It protects a legitimate business interest.
2. It is ancillary to a legitimate business relationship.
3. It provides a benefit to both the employee and employer.
4. It is reasonable in scope and duration.
5. It is not contrary to the public interest.[19]

In *EarthWeb* v. *Schlack*,[20] a federal judge was asked to enforce a covenant not to compete that would have prohibited a Web site content manager from working for a new employer in "direct competition" with EarthWeb for one year. The new employer, International Data Group, planned to launch a Web site, Itworld.com. The judge considered one year in "Internet time" to be too burdensome. In arriving at this conclusion, the judge assessed the characteristics of the Internet industry, which is dynamic, constantly evolving, and lacking geographical borders. Further, Schlack's former position with EarthWeb was "cutting-edge" and "depended on keeping abreast of the daily changes in content on the Internet."

A lesson learned from *EarthWeb* applies to all employers considering the use of noncompete agreements: Reasonableness is measured by the realities of the industry and the nature of the employee's occupation.

As mentioned above, covenants not to compete sometimes also include provisions with regard to trade secrets or confidentiality with regard to employer intellectual property. The issue often depends on what an employer considers to be trade secrets versus information in the public domain or commonly known in an industry. Confidential customer lists or customer preferences are often the source of trouble since they are usually maintained by individual workers based on professional relationships; however, most courts deem them property of the employer. Pricing, revenue, and other projections and marketing strategies are also commonly considered to be trade secrets. On the other hand, processes that are known by many in a particular industry or other information that is otherwise available through external sources are not considered to be company property. Note that customer lists, if accessible through public means, would therefore no longer fall under the rubric of trade secrets.

The Uniform Trade Secrets Act is a model act that 45 states have adopted. It provides relief in the form of monetary damages, attorney's fees, and injunctive relief for misappropriation of trade secrets and includes a provision for "inevitable disclosure." Under this doctrine, courts have found that employees may be in violation of a confidentiality agreement if they accept a new position with a different employer that will necessarily require the employee to divulge or otherwise use the prior employer's trade secrets.

---

[19] W. Martucci and J. Place, "Covenants Not to Compete," *Employment Relations Today* 21 (1998), pp. 77–83.

[20] 171 F. Supp. 2d 299 (S.D.N.Y. 1999).

Keeping Trade Secrets "Secret"[1]

An essential element in obtaining relief under the Uniform Trade Secrets Act is to show that the trade secret is, in fact, treated as secret—that is, that the company that owns the trade secret takes reasonable precautions to prevent disclosure to anyone other than an intended recipient. In making this determination, courts look to a number of factors. A company wishing to maintain its trade secrets as "secret" should consider these same factors. The following checklist, although not all-inclusive, provides guidance on maintaining the secret status of trade secrets:

TRADE SECRET CHECKLIST

- Are employees and third parties with access to trade secrets required to sign confidentiality agreements?
- Are employees and third parties with access to trade secrets alerted to their confidential and proprietary nature, for example, through personnel manuals, reminder memoranda, posted warnings, appropriate labels on the data, and the like?
- Is sensitive data kept under lock and key?
- Is access to sensitive data limited to those with a particular need for the information?
- Is the information maintained in an area with a photocopying machine?
- Are documents containing sensitive data kept by people at their own desks? If so, is it necessary?
- Are desks containing sensitive data locked and is access limited only to those with need to that data?
- Is the data marked plainly and obviously as "Secret," "Confidential," "Restricted Access," or with a similar identifier? If documents containing confidential or trade secret data must be shared with third parties, do you have comprehensive, written confidentiality agreements with those third parties and provisions that such data is to be returned or destroyed once there is no further need for the data?
- If confidential documents are given to certain employees, are they serially numbered? Is a log of such documents kept by a company official?
- Are the documents containing confidential data ever left unattended on desks or in a lunchroom or conference room where personnel unauthorized to see such information could come in contact with the documents?

- Are visitors, guests, and nonessential personnel restricted from areas in which secret processes or machines are developed, operated, or displayed in a way that could be considered revealing to a knowledgeable observer?
- Are visitors and guests allowed to visit factories or facilities where secret processes or machines are in use or operation?
- Is there a company policy limiting or prohibiting the use of cameras by visitors?
- Are all visitors, including suppliers, vendors, and maintenance persons, required to sign in, state the nature of their visit, indicate with whom they are visiting, and sign out?
- Are special internal procedures in place to verify the service calls of repair and service personnel including verifying the service person's credentials and the purpose of the visit?
- Are doors and entryways leading to areas where secret processes are maintained or performed or where machinery is operated kept locked?
- Are keys issued only to those employees who need them?
- If security and alarm systems are required to protect a secret process effectively, are they installed?
- Are security guards used when necessary?
- Are all document control systems, such as those described above, periodically reviewed and revised?
- Is disclosure of a substantial portion of trade secret information through display, publication, or advertising prohibited?
- Are employees instructed not to discuss secret company projects in the presence of visitors, especially suppliers and vendors?
- Are federal copyright laws used to protect documents?

COMMENT

As a final point, courts will generally help those who can demonstrate that they have acted prudently to protect themselves. Be ready to show the efforts and especially the money used to produce trade secrets and the steps taken to preserve their secrecy.

[1] Reprinted with permission from Smith, Currie & Hancock, LLP, http://www.smithcurrie.com/fall-2003-7.htm.

Arbitration Agreements in Employment Contracts

Another covenant included in some employment contracts today is an agreement regarding arbitration. A *typical arbitration agreement* provides that "any dispute or claim concerning Employee's employment with [Employer] or the terms, conditions, or benefits of such employment, will be settled by binding arbitration." This agreement is usually entered into at the beginning of the employment relationship or as part of the preemployment process. **Arbitration** involves selecting a neutral party to consider evidence and arguments presented by the parties and arriving at a decision. Under "binding" arbitration, the parties are held to the decision of the arbitrator and cannot file a lawsuit in court.

arbitration
The selection of a neutral or third party to consider a dispute and to deliver a binding or nonbinding decision.

As a form of alternate dispute resolution (ADR), arbitration serves as an efficient mechanism for avoiding lengthy and costly litigation. Further, it may avoid the embarrassment potentially generated by a public proceeding. These advantages to arbitration in business are reflected in a federal policy strongly favoring this form of dispute resolution. The Federal Arbitration Act of 1925 (FAA) declared that arbitration provisions in contracts involving commerce "shall be valid, irrevocable, and enforceable," unless the contract is invalid for other reasons applicable to any kind of contract. State statutes, such as the California Arbitration Act (CAA), codified the strong policy favoring resolution of commercial disputes with arbitration.

Whether the FAA applied to employment contracts was a question left to the federal courts. In *Circuit City Stores, Inc.* v. *Adams,*[21] the U.S. Supreme Court considered an arbitration agreement entered into by Adams in an employment application with Circuit City in 1995 in Santa Rosa, California. In 1997, Adams filed an employment discrimination lawsuit against Circuit City in state court, alleging that he had resigned as a sales counselor because he was subjected to sexual orientation harassment by coworkers and a manager in violation of California law. Circuit City asked a federal court to enforce the arbitration agreement pursuant to the FAA. The Court held that employment arbitration agreements, except for those covering workers engaged in transportation, are covered by the FAA.

Questions still remain about the enforceability of arbitration agreements: Can employers enforce arbitration agreements that place an undue burden on employees seeking to vindicate their rights, such as requiring them to pay all arbitration costs? Also, may an administrative agency such as the Equal Employment Opportunity Commission, which enforces federal antidiscrimination protections, exercise its power to seek judicial relief on behalf of an employee who has signed an arbitration agreement?

The answer to the second question was given by the U.S. Supreme Court in *EEOC* v. *Waffle House.*[22] In his application for employment with Waffle House, Eric Baker entered into an arbitration agreement with the prospective employer. After he began working as a grill operator at a South Carolina Waffle House, Baker suffered a seizure at work and was soon discharged. He filed a charge of discrimination against his former employer with the EEOC. The EEOC filed an enforcement action against Waffle House in federal court on Baker's behalf, seeking compensatory and punitive damages.

[21] 532 U.S. 105 (2001).
[22] 122 S. Ct. 754 (2002)..

The EEOC also sought an order to stop Waffle House from continuing its unlawful employment practices.

The U.S. Supreme Court considered whether the arbitration agreement that Baker had entered into with Waffle House barred the EEOC from intervening in this manner. The Court held that the EEOC was not barred by the arbitration agreement, as it was not a party to the agreement. Therefore, public agencies are not limited by the existence of an arbitration agreement between employers and employees.

Courts have struggled with the issue of fairness in deciding whether certain mandatory arbitration agreements are enforceable against employees seeking to vindicate their rights. Employees may not understand what they have agreed to, or they may understand but feel they have no choice but to agree. Court are concerned in part because the rights that an employee gives up are so critical to fairness—a jury trial, full discovery, judicial review, and certain statutory remedies, among others. In *Armendariz* v. *Foundation Health Psychcare Services, Inc.,*[23] the California Supreme Court set forth minimum requirements for enforcement of a mandatory employment arbitration agreement:

1. The agreement cannot exclude relief that would otherwise be available in court (e.g., punitive damages).
2. The parties must be allowed to conduct discovery sufficient to allow them to adequately arbitrate claims.
3. Employers cannot require employees to pay unreasonable costs or arbitrator's fees, as this unduly adds to the burden of bringing a claim.
4. The arbitrator must be neutral and issue a written award.
5. The arbitration agreement must be mutual: Employers should also be bound to arbitration of employment-related disputes.

In *Labor Ready Central* v. *Gonzalez,*[24] a state appellate court in Texas concluded that an employment arbitration agreement was not enforceable because the employer was not required to arbitrate claims it may assert against Gonzalez. The lack of mutuality of obligation made the agreement unenforceable.

Thus, express agreements entered into between employers and employees may still be subject to regulatory and judicial oversight to ensure fairness and equity in the employment relationship.

MANAGEMENT CONSIDERATIONS

For reasons cited earlier in this chapter, an employer may hire someone with the intent of establishing an employment relationship or an independent-contractor relationship. A variety of protections available to the employer allows the employer some measure of control over this seemingly arbitrary categorization process. However, none will guarantee a court determination of employee or independent-contractor status.

[23] 24 Cal. 4th 83 (2000).
[24] 2001 Tex. App. LEXIS 7995 (Tex. App. 2001).

Management Tips

- Always evaluate the status of your workers; don't assume employee or independent-contractor status for any worker.
- Employment status is relevant to employer payroll and other financial issues; therefore, misclassification may be costly to the employer.
- While an employer is not liable to independent contractors for discrimination based on Title VII, the independent contractor may have other causes of action. Therefore, hiring an independent contractor is not a safe harbor from liability.
- If your intent is to hire an individual as an independent contractor, ensure that, among other factors, the worker has complete control over the manner in which the work will be done, uses her or his own supplies, is paid by the project rather than by the hour, and sets her or his own hours to complete the project.
- Monitor staffing firms with which you contract for temporary or other contingent workers to ensure that the workers are being properly paid and that the firm provides workers' compensation coverage.[1]

[1] See Kenneth J. Turnbull, "Using Contingent Workers Can Create Complications," *New York Law Journal*, Jan. 12, 2001.

First, as in most relationships, a written document will help to identify the nature of the association between the parties and their rights and obligations, provided that the role of the worker is consistent with the duties of an employee or independent contractor. While the classification made in this document is not binding in any way on the courts or the IRS, it may serve as persuasive evidence about the parties' intentions.

If the person is hired as an employee, and it is so stipulated in the document, the written agreement may be considered an employment agreement. The employer should be careful to discuss whether the employment duration will remain at will or for a specified time period.

If the employer intends to hire the worker as an independent contractor, the agreement should articulate the extent of the worker's control over her or his performance and the outcome to be produced pursuant to the contract. Further, where the agreement recites particular hours to be worked, rather than a deadline for completion, it is more likely that the worker will be considered an employee.

Included in the written agreement should be a discussion of who is responsible for the payment of income taxes and benefits and for the division of responsibility for office expenses and overhead, such as tools, supplies, and office rent.

Second, the independent contractor should be paid on the basis of the nature of the job completed, rather than the hours worked to complete it.

Third, no training should be offered to an independent contractor; courts hypothesize that the reason an employer would hire outside help is to reduce these costs. On the other hand, where an employer provides extensive training and support, it is likely that the employer seeks to reap a benefit from this investment in the long run through continued service of its employee.

Fourth, where additional assistance is required, an independent contractor will be made to supply that extra assistance, while an employer would be the party to provide the aid if the worker is an employee. The employer may offer to guarantee a loan to the contractor to allow her or him to obtain the assistance, or new tools, or other equipment if necessary without threatening the independent-contractor status.

Finally, where the risk of misclassification is great—for instance, where the failure to correctly categorize the worker may result in large financial penalties—the employer may choose to obtain an advance ruling from the IRS regarding the nature of the relationship. This is accomplished through the filing of IRS Form SS-8 (see Exhibit 1.8).

Given the possibility of unlimited compensatory and punitive damage awards in wrongful discharge actions, employers are cautioned regarding their interpretation and implementation of the at-will employment arrangement. Employees' protections from unjust dismissal are not limited to statutes prohibiting employment discrimination based on certain factors. Increasingly, employees are able to rely on promises made by the employer through, for example, the employment policy manual. Further, public policy considerations beyond antidiscrimination protections also place limits on the manner in which an employer may terminate an employment relationship. An employer is prohibited from acting in a manner that undermines public policy, however defined.

When an employee is terminated for exercising a protected right, for performing a public duty, for refusing to commit a crime or an immoral or unethical act, or for exposing the employer's or a co-worker's wrongdoings, the termination may be wrongful, and the employer may be liable for the payment of economic damages, as well as compensation for emotional distress and suffering.

In order to limit liability for wrongful termination, employers should strive to make honesty and fairness core values of the organization that are reflected in their employment practices. Employees' exercise of their protected rights and performance of their public duties should be supported but employers should inform workers pre-employment that employment is at-will, if applicable. Evaluations should be forthcoming in good-faith critique related to job performance. Overstatements regarding the employee's prospects for advancement, perhaps made to maintain employee retention, should be avoided. False information about the health and future of the organization should also not be made, even if for the purpose of heightening employee morale. Arbitration and noncompete agreements should conform with legal requirements for enforceability and should enter the employment relationship only as good-faith measures to further the organization's risk management efforts.

Be careful of statements made to interviewees regarding promises of why an employee will be dismissed or regarding salary or permanent status. Ensure that contracts for dismissed employees cannot be implied from acts the employer has done, like setting up the expectation of permanent employment by longevity, consistently great evaluation, and the like. It may mean, for the employer, that the employer has even less flexibility than desirable in this area. However, the employer's ability to control is most conclusive in determining liability.

Exhibit 1.8   IRS Form SS-8

Form **SS-8**
(Rev. June 2003)
Department of the Treasury
Internal Revenue Service

**Determination of Worker Status
for Purposes of Federal Employment Taxes
and Income Tax Withholding**

OMB No. 1545-0004

Name of firm (or person) for whom the worker performed services	Worker's name

Firm's address (include street address, apt. or suite no., city, state, and ZIP code)	Worker's address (include street address, apt. or suite no., city, state, and ZIP code)

Trade name	Telephone number (include area code) ( )	Worker's social security number

Telephone number (include area code) ( )	Firm's employer identification number	Worker's employer identification number (if any)

If the worker is paid by a firm other than the one listed on this form for these services, enter the name, address, and employer identification number of the payer.

Important Information Needed To Process Your Request

We must have your permission to disclose your name and the information on this form and any attachments to other parties involved with this request. **Do we have your permission to disclose this information?** . . . . ☐ **Yes**   ☐ **No**
If you answered "No" or did not mark a box, we will not process your request and will not issue a determination.

You must answer ALL items OR mark them "Unknown" or "Does not apply." If you need more space, attach another sheet.

A This form is being completed by: ☐ Firm ☐ Worker; for services performed _____ to _____ .
(beginning date)   (ending date)

B Explain your reason(s) for filing this form (e.g., you received a bill from the IRS, you believe you received a Form 1099 or Form W-2 erroneously, you are unable to get worker's compensation benefits, you were audited or are being audited by the IRS). ------------------------------------
----

C Total number of workers who performed or are performing the same or similar services _____ .

D How did the worker obtain the job? ☐ Application ☐ Bid ☐ Employment Agency ☐ Other (specify) _____ .

E Attach copies of all supporting documentation (contracts, invoices, memos, Forms W-2, Forms 1099, IRS closing agreements, IRS rulings, etc.). In addition, please inform us of any current or past litigation concerning the worker's status. If no income reporting forms (Form 1099-MISC or W-2) were furnished to the worker, enter the amount of income earned for the year(s) at issue $ _____ .

F Describe the firm's business. --

G Describe the work done by the worker and provide the worker's job title. -----------------------------
----

H Explain why you believe the worker is an employee or an independent contractor. --------------------
----

I Did the worker perform services for the firm before getting this position? . . . . ☐ **Yes** ☐ **No** ☐ **N/A**
If "Yes," what were the dates of the prior service? ---
If "Yes," explain the differences, if any, between the current and prior service. ----------------------
----

J If the work is done under a written agreement between the firm and the worker, attach a copy (preferably signed by both parties). Describe the terms and conditions of the work arrangement. --
----

For Privacy Act and Paperwork Reduction Act Notice, see page 5.   Cat. No. 16106T   Form **SS-8** (Rev. 6-2003)

Exhibit 1.8 (continued)

Part I   Behavioral Control

1   What specific training and/or instruction is the worker given by the firm? ---------------------------------------

2   How does the worker receive work assignments? ---

3   Who determines the methods by which the assignments are performed? --

4   Who is the worker required to contact if problems or complaints arise and who is responsible for their resolution? -----------------------

5   What types of reports are required from the worker? Attach examples. ---

6   Describe the worker's daily routine (i.e., schedule, hours, etc.). --

7   At what location(s) does the worker perform services (e.g., firm's premises, own shop or office, home, customer's location, etc.)? ---------

8   Describe any meetings the worker is required to attend and any penalties for not attending (e.g., sales meetings, monthly meetings, staff meetings, etc.). --------------------------------

9   Is the worker required to provide the services personally? . . . . ☐ **Yes** ☐ **No**

10 If substitutes or helpers are needed, who hires them? ---

11 If the worker hires the substitutes or helpers, is approval required? . . . . ☐ **Yes** ☐ **No**
    If "Yes," by whom? --

12 Who pays the substitutes or helpers? --

13 Is the worker reimbursed if the worker pays the substitutes or helpers? . . . . ☐ **Yes** ☐ **No**
    If "Yes," by whom?

Part II   Financial Control

1   List the supplies, equipment, materials, and property provided by each party:
    The firm --
    The worker --
    Other party ---

2   Does the worker lease equipment? . . . . ☐ **Yes** ☐ **No**
    If "Yes," what are the terms of the lease? (Attach a copy or explanatory statement.) -----------------------------

3   What expenses are incurred by the worker in the performance of services for the firm? ---------------------------

4   Specify which, if any, expenses are reimbursed by:
    The firm --
    Other party ---

5   Type of pay the worker receives: ☐ Salary   ☐ Commission   ☐ Hourly Wage   ☐ Piece Work
    ☐ Lump Sum   ☐ Other (specify) ---
    If type of pay is commission, and the firm guarantees a minimum amount of pay, specify amount $ _____ .

llowed a drawing account for advances? . . . . ☐ Yes ☐ No   6   Is the worker a
often? --   If "Yes," how c
strictions. --   Specify any re:

e customer pay? . . . . ☐ Firm   ☐ Worker   7   Whom does th
; the worker pay the total amount to the firm? ☐ Yes ☐ No   If "No," explain. -----------------   If worker, does

:arry worker's compensation insurance on the worker? . . . . ☐ Yes ☐ No   8   Does the firm c
: loss or financial risk, if any, can the worker incur beyond the normal loss of salary (e.g., loss or damage of equipment,   9   What economi:
   material, etc.)?

Form **SS-8** (Rev. 6-2003)

Exhibit 1.8 (continued)

Part III   Relationship of the Worker and Firm

1   List the benefits available to the worker (e.g., paid vacations, sick pay, pensions, bonuses). ---

2   Can the relationship be terminated by either party without incurring liability or penalty? . . . .   ☐ **Yes**   ☐ **No**
If "No," explain your answer. ---

3   Does the worker perform similar services for others?   . . . .   ☐ **Yes**   ☐ **No**
If "Yes," is the worker required to get approval from the firm? . . . .   ☐ **Yes**   ☐ **No**

4   Describe any agreements prohibiting competition between the worker and the firm while the worker is performing services or during any later period. Attach any available documentation. ---

5   Is the worker a member of a union? . . . .   ☐ **Yes**   ☐ **No**

6   What type of advertising, if any, does the worker do (e.g., a business listing in a directory, business cards, etc.)? Provide copies, if applicable.

7   If the worker assembles or processes a product at home, who provides the materials and instructions or pattern? ----------------------

8   What does the worker do with the finished product (e.g., return it to the firm, provide it to another party, or sell it)? --------------------

9   How does the firm represent the worker to its customers (e.g., employee, partner, representative, or contractor)? -----------------------

10 If the worker no longer performs services for the firm, how did the relationship end? --

Part IV   For Service Providers or Salespersons—Complete this part if the worker provided a service directly to customers or is a salesperson.

1   What are the worker's responsibilities in soliciting new customers? ---

2   Who provides the worker with leads to prospective customers? --

3   Describe any reporting requirements pertaining to the leads. ---

4   What terms and conditions of sale, if any, are required by the firm? --

5   Are orders submitted to and subject to approval by the firm? . . . .   ☐ **Yes**   ☐ **No**

6   Who determines the worker's territory? --

7   Did the worker pay for the privilege of serving customers on the route or in the territory? . . . .   ☐ **Yes**   ☐ **No**
If "Yes," whom did the worker pay? ---
If "Yes," how much did the worker pay? . . . . $ _____ .

8   Where does the worker sell the product (e.g., in a home, retail establishment, etc.)? --

9   List the product and/or services distributed by the worker (e.g., meat, vegetables, fruit, bakery products, beverages, or laundry or dry cleaning services). If more than one type of product and/or service is distributed, specify the principal one. -----------------------------------

10 Does the worker sell life insurance full time? . . . .   ☐ **Yes**   ☐ **No**

11 Does the worker sell other types of insurance for the firm? . . . .   ☐ **Yes**   ☐ **No**
If "Yes," enter the percentage of the worker's total working time spent in selling other types of insurance.   . . .   _____%

12 If the worker solicits orders from wholesalers, retailers, contractors, or operators of hotels, restaurants, or other similar establishments, enter the percentage of the worker's time spent in the solicitation.   . . . .   _____%

13 Is the merchandise purchased by the customers for resale or use in their business operations? . . . .   ☐ **Yes**   ☐ **No**
Describe the merchandise and state whether it is equipment installed on the customers' premises. --------------------------------

Part V   Signature (see page 4)

Under penalties of perjury, I declare that I have examined this request, including accompanying documents, and to the best of my knowledge and belief, the facts presented are true, correct, and complete.

Signature ▶ _____   Title ▶ _____   Date ▶ _____
(Type or print name below)

Form **SS-8** (Rev. 6-2003)

Summary

- Why is the definition of "employee" important? The distinction between employees and independent contractors is crucial from a financial perspective. Because many regulations require different responsibilities from employers of employees and independent contractors, it is imperative that an employer be confident of the classification of its employees.

- How does an employer make the distinction between employees and independent contractors? The classification of employees may vary depending on the statute that is to be applied or on the court in which a given case is scheduled to be heard. However, the common thread is generally the right of the employer to control the actions of the worker. Where this is present, the worker is likely to be considered an employee. Other factors to be considered include those that are part of the economic realities test, which evaluates the economics of the employment situation. Finally, some workers may be classified statutorily as employees, making the distinction all the easier.

- Who is an "employer"? The definition of employer is generally agreed on. An employer is usually thought to be one who employs or uses others (either employees or independent contractors, or both) to do its work, or to work on its behalf.

- When an employer decides to terminate an employee, there is always a reason for the termination. That reason need not be fair, or even justified; the only restriction is that it should not be made on *improper* bases.

- To ensure that the discharge decision is not wrongful and to protect against a claim of wrongful discharge, employers should establish a discharge procedure to be followed in the course of every termination.

  1. The supervisor with the authority to make the termination decision should draft written responses to the following questions:
     —What is the nature of the action to be taken?
     —What is the factual basis for this action?
     —Is there any evidence of this factual basis, oral or written?
     —If this action is based on the employee's behavior, did the employee obtain permission or give notice of her or his intent to engage in this behavior prior to doing so? (For instance, if the employee needed to take time off for a stated purpose, did she or he first receive permission to do so? [If permission has been granted, termination based on this behavior may constitute outrageous conduct.])
     —If this action is based on the employee's behavior, is this behavior of the type in which she or he has a right or obligation to engage by law (such as jury duty, testifying pursuant to a subpoena, etc.)?
     —If this action is based on the employee's behavior, is this a type of behavior that an employer ought to encourage (such as assisting in the investigation of a crime)?
     —If this action is based on the employee's behavior, did this behavior harm us, as an organization? [Termination would be subject to greater scrutiny.]
     —Is this action based on an omission or refusal to act on the part of the employee? If so, did the employee refuse to act in such a manner that could be construed as unethical, immoral, illegal, or humiliating?

  2. Once the supervisor has responded to the above questions, the supervisor and an individual specifically chosen to review discharge decisions should review the responses to address whether they may give rise to liability. Where the potential exists, the employer is now better equipped to determine the costs and benefits of the anticipated action.

  3. After a review of the facts and the supervisor's responses, it is in the employer's best interests to investigate the events leading to the discharge and to solicit a response from the employee relating to the possibility of termination. It allows the employee to feel as if she or he has had the opportunity to be heard. It also ensures that all of the relevant facts have been brought to the surface.

4. After the hearing, the supervisor and the termination "specialist" should review the information in light of earlier decisions and appropriate business judgment; consistency is crucial and the best defense.

Chapter End Questions

1. Holtzman began working for World Book as a part-time sales representative in 1983. Her position required selling World Book's educational products. Until 1995, she worked as a part-time sales representative and then a district manager for World Book. In 1995, World Book decided to separate the parent division from the school and library division and reorganize its sales force by outsourcing: contracting with individual "regional directors" who would in turn contract with individual sales representatives. The same people who had worked for World Book under the previous arrangement filled many of the positions under the new structure, in which branch managers became separately incorporated regional directors and district managers while sales representatives took positions with the newly formed companies.

   Holtzman signed a contract with Lee, a former World Book branch manager who had formed her own corporation and gathered a sales force consisting largely of former World Book sales representatives. Holtzman eventually became a territory coordinator, a position slightly above sales representative but still reporting to Lee. In 1998, Holtzman was told that she was losing her territory and would no longer be selling World Book products. Holtzman sued World Book, claiming that the loss of her territory was effectively a termination. What is the result of her lawsuit? [*Holtzman* v. *The World Book Company, Inc.*, 2001 U.S. Dist. LEXIS 18531 (E.D. Pa. Nov. 13, 2001).]

2. Think about the following questions from the point of view of violation of public policy or breach of a covenant of good faith and fair dealing, and see what the outcome would be.

   a. An employee was suspended pending discharge for sleeping and "loafing" on the job. The employer offered to change the penalty to suspension without pay if the plaintiff would sign a "last-chance agreement" under which he waived and released "any claims, suits, or causes of action" against the defendant. The employee refused to sign because he was unwilling to waive his rights to state unemployment benefits or workers' compensation. Under state statute, agreements to waive such rights are invalid. The employee is discharged. [*Edelberg* v. *Leco Corp.*, 236 Mich. App. 177 (1999).]

   b. A nurse is asked by her employer to sign a backdated Medicare form. She refuses, and is terminated that day. As a health care provider, she is required to complete that particular form. [*Callantine* v. *Staff Builders, Inc.*, 271 F.3d 1124 (8th Cir. 2001).]

   c. A legal secretary to a county commissioner is terminated because of her political beliefs. [*Armour* v. *County of Beaver*, 271 F.3d 417 (3d Cir. 2001).]

   d. A company's lawyer is terminated when he refuses to remove, from the company's files, documents that would be harmful to the company if they were given to opposing counsel under a discovery order in litigation the company is involved in. [*Herbster* v. *Northern American Co. for Life and Health Ins.*, 501 N.E.2d 343 (Ill. App. Ct. 1986), cert. denied, 484 U.S. 850 (1987).]

   e. Employee is terminated because she married a co-worker. [*McCluskey* v. *Clark Oil & Refining Corp.*, 498 N.E.2d 559 (Ill. App. Ct. 1986).]

   f. Employee discovers that his supervisor is involved in a wrongdoing. The supervisor terminates the employee to prevent the employee from disclosing her wrongdoing to higher-level management. [*Adler* v. *American Standard Corp.*, 830 F.2d 1303 (4th Cir. 1987).]

g. A legal secretary is hired by a law firm. The Letter of Employment stated, "In the event of any dispute or claim between you and the firm . . . including, but not limited to claims arising from or related to your employment or the termination of your employment, we jointly agree to submit all such disputes or claims to confidential binding arbitration, under the Federal Arbitration Act." On his third day of work, the employee informs his superiors that he would not agree to arbitrate disputes. He was told that the arbitration provision was "not negotiable" and that his continued employment was contingent upon signing the agreement. The employee declined to sign the agreement and was discharged [*Lagatree* v. *Luce, Forward, Hamilton & Scripps,* 74 Cal. App. 4th 1005 (Cal. App. 2d Div. 1 1999).]

h. Employee is licensed to perform certain medical procedures, but he is terminated for refusing to perform a procedure he is not licensed to perform. [*O'Sullivan* v. *Mallon,* 390 A.2d 149 (N.J. Super. Ct. Law Div. 1978).]

i. An employee was fired from his job as security manager for a medical center because he was suspected of making an obscene phone call to another employee and refused to submit to voice print analysis to confirm or refute the accusation. He sued the employer for wrongful discharge, claiming that the employer's request violated public policy. A state statute prohibits an employer from requiring an employee to submit to a polygraph examination as a condition or precondition of employment. [*Theisen* v. *Covenant Medical Center,* 636 N.W.2d 74 (Iowa 2001).]

3. Is a covenant not to compete enforceable when it prohibits a doctor from practicing medicine for two years from the date of his employment termination within a 10-mile radius of hospitals to which his former practice provides services? [*Medical Specialists* v. *Sleweon,* 652 N.W.2d 517 (Ind. 1995).]

4. Mariani was a licensed CPA who worked for Colorado Blue Cross and Blue Shield as manager of general accounting for human resources. She complained to her supervisors about questionable accounting practices on a number of occasions and was fired. She claims that her termination was in violation of public policy in favor of accurate reporting, as found in the Board of Accountancy Rules of Professional Conduct. BCBS claims that the rules are not an arbiter of public policy as ethics codes are too variable. Who is correct? [*Rocky Mountain Hospital* v. *Mariani,* 916 P.2d 519 (Colo. 1996).]

5. An employee receives a letter of reprimand that goes in his personnel file but is not demoted and does not suffer any other action. Does the letter constitute an adverse employment action? [*Krause* v. *LaCross,* 87 FEP Cases 1475 (7th Cir. 2001).]

6. A staffing firm provides landscaping services for clients on an ongoing basis. The staffing firm selects and pays the workers, provides health insurance, and withholds taxes. The firm provides the equipment and supplies necessary to do the work. It also supervises the workers on the clients' premises. Client A reserves the right to direct the staffing-firm workers to perform particular tasks at particular times or in a specified manner, although it does not generally exercise that authority. Client A evaluates the quality of the workers' performance and regularly reports its findings to the firm. It can require the firm to remove a worker from the job assignment if it is dissatisfied. Who is the employer of the workers?

7. The Duprees, Terry and Jerry, are former employees of UPS. They both started working for UPS as hourly union employees and were protected by union laws against being fired except "for cause." They were both promoted to managerial positions, which they accepted on the representation that they would retain job security since managerial positions were not provided with union protection. Soon after her promotion, Terry Dupree alleged that a senior manager, Pepper Simmons, was sexually harassing her. A few months after Terry Dupree's allegation, Simmons allegedly discovered that Terry was dating Jerry, who was in

the same managerial level as Terry. Simmons, according to the Duprees, vowed to "get his job," and Jerry Dupree was soon fired for violating the UPS fraternization policy. The Duprees say that it was their understanding that this policy only governed relations between supervisors and hourly employees, not relations between two supervisors. Terry Dupree filed a sexual harassment complaint against Simmons, on which UPS took no disciplinary action. After Terry filed this complaint, her supervisors began "writing her up" for infractions of company policy. After several infractions, the UPS management offered her $12,000 to resign. She refused and was fired. Oklahoma recognizes a cause of action arising from the termination of an at-will employee against an employer in "cases in which the discharge is contrary to a clear mandate of public policy as articulated by constitutional, statutory or decisional law." What result? [*Dupree* v. *United Parcel Service, Inc.,* 956 F.2d 219 (10th Cir. 1992).]

8. Alberto Camargo was killed when his tractor rolled over as he was driving over a large mound of manure in a corral belonging to Tjaarda Dairy. Camargo was an employee of Golden Cal Trucking, and Golden Cal Trucking was an independent contractor that Tjaarda Dairy had hired to scrape the manure out of its corrals and to haul it away in exchange for the right to purchase the manure at a discount. Plaintiffs, Camargo's wife and five children, sued defendants Tjaarda Dairy and Perry Tjaarda on the theory, among others, that they were *negligent in hiring* Golden Cal Trucking because they failed to determine whether Camargo was qualified to operate the tractor safely. Is Tjaarda Dairy liable for Camargo's death? [*Camargo* v. *Tjaarda Dairy,* 25 Cal. 4th 1235 (2001).]

9. Patricia Meleen, a chemical dependency counselor, brought charges alleging wrongful discharge, defamation, and emotional distress against the Hazelden Foundation, a chemical dependency clinic, in regard to her discharge due to her alleged sexual relations with a former patient. Hazelden's written employment policies prohibited unprofessional and unethical conduct, including sexual contact between patients and counselors. A former patient alleged that Meleen had initiated a social and sexual relationship with him within one year of his discharge. A committee appointed by Hazelden told Meleen of the allegation against her and suspended her with pay in spite of Meleen's denial that she was involved in any improper relations or sexual contact with the former patient. Hazelden offered Meleen a nonclinical position, and, when she refused, she was dismissed. Is the dismissal wrongful? [*Meleen* v. *Hazelden Foundation,* 928 F.2d 795 (8th Cir. 1991).]

10. Farlow graduated from law school in 1988 and was employed by Wachovia Bank of North Carolina to represent it. In 1993, Wachovia discussed the possibility of Farlow's working as in-house counsel for Wachovia to handle recovery and bankruptcy cases. On her employment application, Farlow disclosed that she had been convicted of two counts of misdemeanor larceny in 1982. Those convictions made it unlawful for her to become an employee of Wachovia without FDIC approval. Wachovia proceeded with its working relationship with Farlow, who closed her private practice and moved on site with Wachovia. The parties executed a written contract under which Farlow would provide legal services as an independent contractor. Both parties intended that Farlow would not be considered an employee unless the FDIC waiver was obtained. Such a waiver was never sought for Farlow.

Farlow was considered an independent contractor for tax purposes and was never paid a salary by Wachovia but, instead, was paid for the bills she submitted. She received no benefits or compensation for business travel. She used letterhead that designated her simply as an attorney-at-law and did not receive business cards. However, she was provided with on-site office space, support, staff, equipment, and the use of company vehicles. She was paid for continuing education. Wachovia exercised control over the hours in which she had access to her office.

After complaining about a sexually and racially hostile work environment. Farlow was terminated. She filed several claims under Title VII. Was Wachovia Farlow's employer? [*Farlow* v. *Wachovia Bank of North Carolina,* 259 F.R.D. 309 (4th Cir. 2001).]

11. Max Huber was the agency manager at Standard Insurance's Los Angeles office. He was employed as an at-will employee, and his contract did not specify any fixed duration of guaranteed employment. Huber was discharged by the company after eight years because of his alleged negative attitude, the company's increasing expense ratio, and the agency's decreasing recruiting. Huber provided evidence that he had never received negative criticism in any of his evaluations, and that his recruiting had been successful. Huber demonstrated that, even though the company had a decrease in recruitment during his employment, he himself had a net increase of contracted agents of 1,100 percent. Huber claims that he was discharged because he was asked to write a letter of recommendation about his supervisor, Canfield, whose termination was being considered. Johnson, Canfield's supervisor, was disappointed with the positive recommendation that Huber wrote because it made Canfield's termination difficult to execute. Johnson is alleged to have transferred Huber to expedite Canfield's termination, and he eventually discharged Huber in retaliation for the positive letter of recommendation. If Huber files suit, what result? [*Huber* v. *Standard Insurance Co.,* 841 F.2d 980 (9th Cir. 1988).]

Chapter **Two**

Title VII of the Civil Rights Act of 1964

STATUTORY BASIS

Title VII of the Civil Rights Act of 1964

(a) It shall be an unlawful employment practice for an employer—

(1) to fail or refuse to hire or to discharge any individual, or otherwise to discriminate against any individual with respect to his compensation, terms, conditions, or privileges of employment, because of such individual's race, color, religion, sex, or national origin; or

(2) to limit, segregate, or classify his employees or applicants for employment in any way which would deprive or tend to deprive any individual of employment opportunities or otherwise adversely affect his status as an employee, because of such individual's race, color, religion, sex, or national origin. Title VII of the Civil Rights Act of 1964, as amended, 42 U.S.C.A. sec. 2000e et seq., sec. 703 (a).

A HISTORIC RIGHTS ACT

Title VII of the Civil Rights Act of 1964 is the single most important piece of legislation that has helped to shape and define employment law rights in this country. It was an ambitious piece of social legislation, the likes of which had never been attempted here, so passage of the law was not an easy task.

The Civil Rights Act of 1964 prohibits discrimination in voting, education, employment, public accommodations, and the receipt of federal funds on the basis of race, color, gender, national origin, or religion. Although five categories of discrimination are included in the law, it was racial discrimination that was truly the moving force for its enactment. Blacks had been brought to America from Africa to be slaves, period. No other role was envisioned for them. It was thus not surprising that when slavery ended 246 years later, the country struggled to forge a new relationship with blacks with whom they had no legal or social relationship other than ownership or blacks serving their needs in the most menial ways. Ninety-nine years later, when the civil rights legislation was debated in Congress and eventually passed in 1964, the country was

Exhibit 2.1   June 1961 (Pre–Title VII) Newspaper Want Ad

INDEX TO WANT ADS

ANNOUNCEMENTS

1—Funeral Notices
2—Funeral Notices, Colored

MALE EMPLOYMENT

14—Male Help Wanted
15—Male Employment Agencies
16—Situations Wanted, Male
17—Male, Female Help Wanted

FEMALE EMPLOYMENT

22—Female Help Wanted
23—Female Employment Agencies
24—Situations Wanted, Female

COLORED EMPLOYMENT

26—Help Wanted Male, Colored
27—Employment Agency Male, Colored
28—Situations Wanted Male, Colored
29—Help Wanted Female, Colored
30—Employment Agency Female, Colored
31—Situations Wanted Female, Colored

This exhibit, taken from an actual newspaper, is typical of the index to want ads from the classified section found in newspapers in the United States before Title VII was passed in 1964. Note the separate categories based on race and gender. This is no longer legal under Title VII.

deeply divided in trying to move away from its post–Civil War history of its treatment of blacks—a history that included everything from benign neglect to lynchings to legally sanctioned discrimination, called "Jim Crow" laws. There were laws regulating the separation of blacks and whites in every facet of life from birth to death. Laws prohibited blacks and whites from marrying, going to school together, and working together. Every facility imaginable was segregated, including movies, restaurants, hospitals, cemeteries, libraries, funeral homes, doctors' waiting rooms, swimming pools, taxicabs, churches, housing developments, parks, water fountains, colleges, public transportation, recreational facilities, toilets, social organizations, and stores. Blacks could not vote, sue whites, testify against them, raise their voice to them, or even look them in the eye or stay on the sidewalk if they passed by. If a black wanted to buy shoes he or she had to bring a paper cutout of the foot, rather than try the shoe on in the store. If they wanted food from a restaurant, they had to go to the back door and order it to be taken away. Separation of the races was complete under Jim Crow and Jim Crow was only outlawed in 1964. (See Exhibit 2.1.)

The doctrine of separate but equal educational facilities had fallen 10 years before passage of the Civil Rights Act, in 1954, with the U.S. Supreme Court's decision in

Brown v. *Topeka Board of Education.*[1] Citizens were challenging infringements upon the right of blacks to vote. There were boycotts, "freedom rides," and sit-in demonstrations for the right to nonsegregated public accommodations, transportation, municipal parks, swimming pools, libraries, and lunch counters. There was racial unrest, strife, marches, and civil disobedience on as close to a mass scale as this country has ever experienced. Something had to give.

In an impressive show of how important societal considerations can be in shaping law, the 1964 Civil Rights Act was passed the year after the historic March on Washington in August 1963. It was at this march that the late Rev. Dr. Martin Luther King, Jr., gave his famous "I Have a Dream" speech on the steps of the Lincoln Memorial. In the largest march of its kind ever held in this country until then, hundreds of thousands of people of all races, creeds, colors, and walks of life traveled from around the world to show legislators that legalized racism was no longer tolerable in a society that considered itself to be civilized.

Title VII of the Civil Rights Act of 1964 is the employment section of the act, but it is only one title of a much larger piece of legislation. The Civil Rights Act of 1964 also created the legal basis for nondiscrimination in voting, education, public accommodations, and federally assisted programs. Since employment in large measure defines the availability of the other matters, the case law in Title VII of the Civil Rights Act quickly became the most important arbiter of rights under the new law. In President John F. Kennedy's original message to Congress upon introducing the act in 1963, he stated: "There is little value in a Negro's obtaining the right to be admitted to hotels and restaurants if he has no cash in his pocket and no job."

The face of the workplace has changed dramatically since the passage of the act. More women and minorities than ever before are engaged in meaningful employment. While Title VII applies equally to everyone, because of the particular history behind the law it gave new rights to women and minorities, who had only limited legal recourse available for job discrimination before the act. With the passage of Title VII, the door was opened to prohibiting job discrimination and creating expectations of fairness in employment. It was not long before additional federal legislation followed providing similar protection from discrimination in the workplace based on age, Vietnam veteran status, and disability. State and local governments passed laws paralleling Title VII and the other protective legislation. Some laws added categories, such as marital status, affinity orientation, receipt of public benefits, or others as prohibited categories of discrimination. For instance, California prohibits discrimination on the basis of being a victim of domestic violence and imposed personal liability on co-workers regardless of whether the employer knew or should have known of the conduct and failed to take immediate corrective action. Washington, D.C., added personal appearance to its list of prohibited categories. The new expectations did not stop there. As we saw in the chapter on employment-at-will, others not included in the coverage of the statutes came to have heightened expectations about the workplace and their role within it and were willing to pressure legislators and sue employers in pursuit of these perceived rights. The exceptions created in the take-no-prisoners employment-at-will doctrine largely owe

---

[1] 347 U.S. 483 (1954).

their existence to the expectations caused by Title VII. Once protection from unjust dismissal was provided on the basis of race, gender, and so on, it made it easier for judges and legislatures to take the step of extending it to other wrongful terminations.

For employers, Title VII meant that the workplace was no longer a place in which decisions regarding hiring, promotion, and the like could go unchallenged. Now there were prohibitions on some of the factors that had previously been a part of many employers' considerations (see, e.g. Exhibit 2.1 showing an actual newspaper classified ad categorized by race). Employers had been feeling the effects of federal regulation in the workplace for some time. Among others, there were wage and hour and child labor laws regulating minimum ages, wages, and permissible work hours that employers could impose, and there were labor laws protecting collective bargaining. Now came Title VII, regulating to some extent the bases an employer could use to hire or promote employees.

After enactment, Title VII was amended several times to further strengthen it. There were amendments in 1972 and 1978, with the passage of the Equal Employment Opportunity Act of 1972 and the Pregnancy Discrimination Act of 1978. The 1972 amendment expanded Title VII's coverage to include government employees and to strengthen the enforcement powers of the enforcing agency created by the law, the Equal Employment Opportunity Commission (EEOC). The 1978 amendment added discrimination on the basis of pregnancy as a type of gender discrimination.

In its most far-reaching overhaul since its passage, the act was also amended by the Civil Rights Act of 1991. This amendment added jury trials, compensatory and punitive damages (where appropriate), and several other provisions, further strengthening the law. (See Exhibit 2.2.)

The EEOC is now the lead agency for handling issues of job discrimination and deals with most matters of employment discrimination arising under federal laws, including age and disability. The U.S. Department of Justice handles cases involving most government agencies such as police and fire departments. The Office of Federal Contract Compliance Programs (OFCCP) enforces Executive Order 11246 concerning affirmative action in government contracting. The EEOC has implemented regulations that govern agency procedures and requirements under the law, and it provides guidelines to employers for dealing with employment discrimination laws. The EEOC's regulations can be found in the Code of Federal Regulations (e.g., 29 CFR Part 1604.1-9, Guidelines on Discrimination Because of Sex; 29 CFR Part 1604.10, Guidelines on Discrimination Because of Sex, Pregnancy and Childbirth; 29 CFR Part 1606, Guidelines on Discrimination Because of National Origin; 29 CFR Part 1607, Employee Selection Procedures; 29 CFR Part 1613.701-707, Guidelines on Discrimination Because of Disability; 45 CFR Part 90, Guidelines on Discrimination Because of Age).

Most employers have come to accept the reality of Title VII. Some have gone beyond acceptance and grown to appreciate the diversity and breadth of the workplace that the law engenders. EEOC has changed also. Forty years after the effective date of the 1964 Civil Rights Act in 2005, it is clear that the agency has maintained its mission to eradicate workplace discrimination, but changed some of its tactics as it has gained experience. While its mission has always been conciliation based, it did not always seem that way. In carving out its new, untrod territory, it aggressively went after employers in order to establish its presence and place in the law (which, along with being

Exhibit 2.2   Civil Rights Act of 1991

When the Civil Rights Act of 1991 was signed into law by President George Bush on November 21, 1991, it was the end of a fierce battle that had raged for several years over the increasingly conservative decisions of the U.S. Supreme Court in civil rights cases. The new law was a major overhaul for Title VII. The law's nearly 30-year history was scrutinized. It is significant for employers that, when presented the opportunity, Congress chose to strengthen the law in many ways, rather than lessen its effectiveness. Among other things, the new law for the first time in Title VII cases:

- Permitted:
  —Jury trials where compensatory or punitive damages are sought.
  —Compensatory damages in religious, gender, and disability cases (such damages were already allowed for race and national origin under related legislation).
  —Punitive damages for the same (except against governmental agencies).
  —Unlimited medical expenses.
- Limited the extent to which "reverse discrimination" suits could be brought.
- Authorized expert witness fees to successful plaintiffs.
- Codified the disparate impact theory.
- Broadened protections against private race discrimination in 42 USC section 1981 cases.
- Expanded the right to bring actions challenging discriminatory seniority systems.
- Extended extraterritorial coverage of Title VII to U.S. citizens working for U.S. companies outside the United States, except where it would violate the laws of the country.
- Extended coverage and established procedures for Senate employees.
- Established the Glass Ceiling Commission.
- Established the National Award for Diversity and Excellence in American Executive Management (known as the Frances Perkins–Elizabeth Hanford Dole National Award for Diversity and Excellence in American Executive Management) for businesses who "have made substantial efforts to promote the opportunities and development experiences of women and minorities and foster advancement to management and decision-making positions within the business."

"the feds," caused more than a little employer resentment). Once that was established, it began living up to its conciliation mission. It now prefers to be proactive and have employers avoid litigation by thoroughly understanding the law and its requirements. EEOC has sponsored thousands of outreach programs to teach employers and employees, alike, about the law, and has initiated extensive mediation programs to try to handle discrimination claims quickly, efficiently, and without litigation.

As the demographics and the workplace change, EEOC has incorporated these changes into its mission, for instance, by forming the TIGAAR (the Information Group for Asian-American Rights) initiative to promote voluntary compliance with employment laws by Asian-American employers and to educate Asian-American employees about their workplace rights; through programs with Sikh and Muslim communities in response to post-9/11 religious and national origin discrimination; or by working with Native Americans through the Council of Tribal Employment Rights (CTER) to

Exhibit 2.3   Cages

Cages. Consider a birdcage. If you look very closely at just one wire in the cage, you cannot see the other wires. If your conception of what is before you is determined by this myopic focus, you could look at that one wire, up and down the length of it, and be unable to see why a bird would not just fly around the wire any time it wanted to go somewhere. Furthermore, even if, one day at a time, you myopically inspected each wire, you still could not see why a bird would have trouble going past the wires to get anywhere. There is no physical property of any one wire, nothing that the closest scrutiny could discover, that will reveal how a bird could be inhibited or harmed by it except in the most accidental way. It is only when you step back, stop looking at the wires one by one, microscopically, and take a macroscopic view of the whole cage, that you can see why the bird does not go anywhere; and then you will see it in a moment. It will require no great subtlety of mental powers. It is perfectly obvious that the bird is surrounded by a network of systematically related barriers, no one of which would be the least hindrance to its flight, but which, by their relations to each other, are as confining as the solid walls of a dungeon.

Source: From "Oppression," by Marilyn Frye, *The Politics of Reality,* reprinted in *Race, Class and Gender: An Anthology,* Margaret L. Anderson and Patricia Hill Collins, 1992, Wadsworth Press. Used by permission.

---

eliminate workplace discrimination on or near Native American reservations, secure Native American preference agreements with employers operating on or near reservations, and process employment discrimination complaints.

Much work, however, remains. EEOC still receives discrimination charges in record numbers. For instance, charges of race discrimination have increased every decade since the inception of Title VII. Retaliation charges and "egregious discrimination" charges are increasing. While it prefers conciliation, EEOC will still aggressively pursue employers when conciliation does not work to its satisfaction. The best way to avoid violations of employment discrimination laws is to know and understand their requirements. That is what the following sections and chapters will help you do.

Keep Exhibit 2.3, "Cages," in mind as you go through this section of the text. Most of us look at things microscopically. That is, we tend to see only the situation in front of us, and don't give much thought to the larger picture into which it fits. But it is this larger picture within which we actually operate. It is the one the law considers when enacting legislation, the courts consider in deciding cases, and thus the one an employer should consider when developing workplace policies or responding to workplace situations. Often, a situation, in and of itself, may seem to us to have little or no significance. "Why are they whining about this?" we say; "Why can't they just go along?" "Why are they being so sensitive?" But we are often missing the larger picture and how this situation may fit into it. Like the birdcage in Exhibit 2.3, each thing, in and of itself, may not be a big deal, but put each of these things together, and a picture is revealed of a very different reality for those who must deal with the "wires."

Many of the situations you see in the following chapters are "wires" that Title VII and other protective legislation try to eradicate in an effort to break down the seemingly impenetrable invisible barriers we have erected around issues of race, gender, disabilities, ethnicity, religion, age, and affinity orientation. As you go through the cases and

75

information, think not only about the micro picture of what is going on in front of you but also about the larger macro picture that it fits into. Sometimes what makes little sense in one setting, makes all the sense in the world in the other.

Another way to look at it is as if it is one of those repeating-pattern "Magic Eye" pictures so popular a few years ago. If you stare at one the correct way, you get to see the detailed 3-D picture you'd never see by just glancing at the surface picture. The picture hasn't changed, but you've looked at it in a way that now lets you see another, richly detailed picture you didn't even know was there. Learning about employment discrimination will not change the reality you already know (the repeating-pattern picture you see at a glance), but will instead help you to see another, richer picture inside this one—one that will greatly assist you in being an effective manager who is less likely to be responsible for workplace discrimination.

What does this all mean? Let's look at an example. A female who works in a garage comes in one day and there are photos of nude females all around the shop. She complains to the supervisor and he tells her that the men like the photos and if she doesn't like it, just don't look at them. The guys she works with begin to rib her about complaining. They tell her she's a "wuss," "can't cut the mustard" and "can't hang with the big boys." "What's the big deal?" you say. "Why didn't she just shut up and ignore the photos?"

Well, in and of itself the photos may not seem like much. But when you look at the issue in context, it looks quite different. Research shows that in workplaces in which nude photos, adult language, sexual teasing, jokes, and so on, are present, women tend to be paid less and receive fewer and less significant raises, promotions, and training. It is not unlikely that the environment that supports such photos doesn't clearly draw lines between the people in the photos and females at work. Case after case bears it out. So the photos themselves aren't really the whole issue. It's the micro picture, the repeating-pattern picture you see at a glance. But the macro picture, the 3-D picture, is the objectification of women and what contributes to women being viewed as less than and not as capable in a workplace in which they may well be just as capable as anyone else. What might have seemed like harmless joking or photos in the micro view takes on much more significance in the macro view and has much more of a potential negative impact on the work experience of the female employee.

Again, as you go through the following chapters, try to look at the micro as well as the macro picture—the repeating-pattern surface picture as well as the 3-D picture inside. You will get also benefit from the case questions, which help you view what you have read in a larger context. Again, it is this context that will be under scrutiny when the policies of a workplace form the basis of a lawsuit. Thinking about that context beforehand and making policies consistent with it will give the employer a much greater chance of avoiding embarrassing and costly litigation.

THE STRUCTURE OF TITLE VII

What Is Prohibited under Title VII

Title VII prohibits discrimination in hiring, firing, training, promotion, discipline, or other workplace decisions on the basis of an employee or applicant's race, color, gender, national origin, or religion. Included in the prohibitions are discrimination in pay,

Exhibit 2.4

Title VII Provisions

An employer cannot discriminate on the basis of:

- Race
- Color
- Gender
- Religion
- National origin

In making decisions regarding:

- Hiring
- Firing
- Training
- Discipline
- Compensation
- Benefits
- Classification
- Or other terms or conditions of employment

---

terms and conditions of employment, training, layoffs, and benefits. Virtually any workplace decision can be challenged by an applicant or employee who falls within the Title VII categories. (See Exhibit 2.4.)

Who Must Comply

Title VII applies to employers, unions, and joint labor and management committees making admission, referral, training, and other decisions, and to employment agencies and other similar hiring entities making referrals for employment. It applies to all private employers employing 15 or more employees, and to federal, state, and local governments. (See Exhibit 2.5.)

Who Is Covered

Title VII applies to public (governmental) and private (nongovernmental) employees alike. Unlike labor laws that do not apply to managerial employees or wage and hour laws that exempt certain types of employees, Title VII covers all levels and types of employees. The Civil Rights Act of 1991 further extended Title VII's coverage to U.S. citizens employed by American employers outside the United States. Non-U.S. citizens are protected in the United States but not outside the United States.

 Undocumented workers are also covered by the law, but after the U.S. Supreme Court's recent ruling in *Hoffman Plastic Compounds, Inc.* v. *NLRB,*[2] the EEOC reexamined its position on remedies for undocumented workers. In *Hoffman,* the Court said that U.S. immigration laws outweighed the employer's labor violations; therefore, the employee could not recover back pay for violations of the labor law. The EEOC had been treating undocumented worker claims of employment discrimination under Title

[2] 122 S.Ct. 1275 (2002).

Exhibit 2.5

Who Must Comply

- Employers engaged in interstate commerce if they have:
  —Fifteen or more employees for each working day in each of 20 or more calendar weeks in the current or preceding calendar year.
- Labor organizations of any kind that exist to deal with employers concerning labor issues, engaged in an industry affecting commerce.
- Employment agencies that, with or without compensation, procure employees for employers or opportunities to work for employees.

VII like violations against any other worker. After *Hoffman*, EEOC said that employment discrimination against undocumented workers is still illegal, and they will not ask their status in handling their discrimination claims, but *Hoffman* affected the availability of some forms of relief, such as reinstatement and back pay for periods after discharge or failure to hire.

Who Is Not Covered

Exemptions under Title VII are limited. Title VII permits businesses operated on or around Native American Indian reservations to give preferential treatment to Native Americans. The act specifically states that it does not apply to actions taken with respect to someone who is a member of the Communist party or other organization required to register as a Communist-action or Communist-front organization. The law permits religious institutions and associations to discriminate when performing their activities. For instance, a Catholic priest could not successfully sue under Title VII alleging religious discrimination for not being hired to lead a Jewish synagogue. (See Exhibit 2.6.) In the case below, the employee was not able to effectively bring her claim for gender discrimination because of this limitation on religious claims.

Petruska v. Gannon University *350 F. Supp. 2d 666*
(W.D. Pa. 2004)

Employee, the chaplain of a Catholic university, sued for gender-based employment discrimination in violation of, among other things, Title VII. The court dismissed the action, saying that the university, as a religious institution, was not subject to Title VII.

McLaughlin, J.

MEMORANDUM OPINION

Gannon University is a private, Catholic, diocesan college established under the laws of the Commonwealth of Pennsylvania and located in Erie, Pennsylvania.

Plaintiff employee was initially hired by Gannon as Director for the University's Center for Social Concerns and commenced her employment on July 16,

1997. In considering and accepting this position, employee relied upon Gannon's self-representation as an equal opportunity employer that does not discriminate on the basis of, among other things, gender.

Rubino subsequently took a leave of absence as Gannon's President after allegations surfaced that he had had a sexual affair with a subordinate at the University. Shortly after Rubino's departure, another female employee at the University came forward with accusations that Rubino had sexually harassed her for a number of years. Employee was instrumental in bringing this claim to the attention of Trautman, the Bishop of the Roman Catholic Diocese of Erie and, pursuant to Gannon's by-laws, Chair of the Gannon Board of Trustees, having certain extraordinary powers reserved to him by the Board, and Dr. Thomas Ostrowski, then Provost of Gannon.

Following Rubino's resignation in May of 2000, Gannon engaged in a campaign to cover up Rubino's sexual misconduct at the insistence of Trautman. Employee was vocal in opposing this and other of the Administration's policies and procedures, which she viewed as discriminatory toward females. One such policy was Trautman's willingness to allow allegedly abusive clergy to remain on campus, including at least one former Gannon priest who had been removed because of sexual misconduct directed at students. Employee also strongly opposed the University's efforts, during the time that Rubino was coming under investigation for alleged sexual harassment of females, to limit the time frame within which victims of sexual harassment could file grievances. Moreover, as Chair of the University's Institutional Integrity Committee, employee was instrumental in submitting a Middle States accreditation report which raised issues of gender-based inequality in the pay of Gannon's female employees and which was critical of the University's policies and procedures for addressing complaints of sexual harassment and other forms of discrimination. Despite pressure from the University's administration, employee refused to change those portions of the report which were critical of the University.

Employee contends that, in retaliation for the foregoing conduct and because of her gender, she was discriminated against in the terms and conditions of her employment. Believing that she was about to be fired, employee served Gannon with two weeks notice of her resignation on October 14, 2002. Employee was advised the following day that her resignation was accepted effective immediately and that she was to pack her belongings and leave the campus. Her access to the campus and to students was strictly limited thereafter. Following employee's departure, Rouch, her supervisor, stated on several occasions to both students and staff that a female would not be considered to replace employee as Chaplain.

The University has moved to dismiss all claims on the ground that they are barred by the so-called "ministerial exception," which is frequently applied in employment discrimination cases involving religious institutions.

The ministerial exception is rooted in the First Amendment which provides that "Congress shall make no law respecting an establishment of religion, or prohibiting the free exercise thereof . . ." U.S. Const. Amend I. Among the prerogatives protected by the Free Exercise Clause is the right of religious institutions to manage their internal affairs.

The Establishment Clause prohibits laws "respecting an establishment of religion." U.S. Const. Amend. I. The Supreme Court held that a statute comports with the Establishment Clause if it has a secular legislative purpose, if its principal or primary effect neither advances nor inhibits religion, and if it does not foster an "excessive government entanglement with religion." Unconstitutional entanglement with religion may arise in situations "where a 'protracted legal process pit(s) church and state as adversaries,' . . . and where the Government is placed in a position of choosing among 'competing religious visions.'"

Consistent with these principles, a number of circuit courts of appeals have held that the First Amendment precludes courts from adjudicating employment discrimination suits between church and minister. Among the first decisions involving Title VII was *McClure* v. *The Salvation Army,* 460 F.2d 553 (5th Cir. 1972), in which the court observed that it is only in the rarest of occasions—e.g., where there is a need to prevent the "gravest abuses, endangering paramount [state] interest"—that government-imposed limitations on the free exercise of religion can be upheld.

Regarding matters of employment, the court noted that the relationship between an organized church and its ministers is its lifeblood. The minister is the chief instrument by which the church seeks to fulfill its purpose. Matters touching this relationship must necessarily be recognized as of prime ecclesiastical concern. Just as the initial function of selecting a minister is a matter of church administration and government, so are the functions which accompany such a selection.

The church's practices relative to its ministers' assignments, salaries, and duties, the court concluded, were "matters of church administration and government and thus, purely of ecclesiastical cognizance." The court found that application of Title VII to McClure's case would necessarily involve an investigation and review of these practices which, in turn, would result in state interference in matters of church administration and government—"matters of a singular ecclesiastical concern"—and threaten the separation of church and state contemplated by the Establishment Clause. The court determined it need not rule on this constitutional issue because, it held, Congress did not intend the statute to regulate the employment relationship between church and minister.

The ministerial exception "does not apply solely to the hiring and firing of ministers, but also relates to the broader relationship between an organized religious institution and its clergy." In fact, *any matters* "touching this relationship" are necessarily considered "as of prime ecclesiastical concern." Issues such as a minister's salary, place of assignment, and the duty he is to perform in furtherance of the religious mission of the church are all matters "touching" the church–minister relationship.

[It is not] significant that Gannon has not asserted a religious basis for the challenged employment actions, for "the focus under the ministerial exception is on the action taken [by the employer], not possible motives." Indeed, "the exception precludes any inquiry whatsoever into the reasons behind a church's ministerial employment decision." "The church need not, for example, proffer any religious justification for its decision, for the Free Exercise Clause 'protects the act of a decision rather than a motivation behind it.'"

We acknowledge employee's concerns that discrimination, in any form, should not be tolerated in civilized society. Employee passionately argues that tolerance of gender-based discrimination in the workplace has led to sexual exploitation and harassment, which turns women into objects. To allow these behaviors to go unregulated simply because they [sic] employer is a religious entity and the employee is claimed to be a minister is unjustified and perpetuates the very evils Congress sought to eliminate. It is hard to argue that certain conduct is even wrong when churches freely engage in it. This has a tremendous impact on establishing social norms. . . .

In rendering this decision, this Court, like others, is "mindful of the potential for abuse" which application

of the ministerial exception can invite, "namely, the use of the First Amendment as a pretextual shield to protect otherwise prohibited employment decisions." But it bears reiterating that the ministerial exception, though "robust where it applies," Roman Catholic Diocese, is not without limits and therefore "does not insulate wholesale the religious employer from the operation of federal anti-discrimination statutes." For one, the exception does not apply to employment decisions concerning individuals with purely custodial or administrative functions. It has also been found inapplicable in the context of Title VII sexual harassment claims. The "saving grace," as one court has noted, "lies in the recognition that courts consistently have subjected the personnel decisions of various religious organizations to statutory scrutiny where the duties of the employees were not of a religious nature." Moreover, the existence of the ministerial exception does not derogate the profound state interest in "assuring equal employment opportunities for all, regardless of race, sex, or national origin." Rather, the exception simply recognizes that the "introduction of government standards to the selection of spiritual leaders would significantly, and perniciously, rearrange the relationship between church and state.'" Application of the exception thus manifests no more than the reality that a constitutional command cannot yield to even the noblest and most exigent of statutory mandates.

Based upon the foregoing reasons, the Court Defendants' motions to dismiss is GRANTED.

Case Questions

1. Do you agree with the court's decision? Explain.
2. As a manager in this situation, how do you think you would have handled the chaplain's complaints?
3. Given the power that religious organizations have under Title VII, how do you think employment discrimination concerns can be addressed in the religious workplace?

claimant or **charging party**
The person who brings an action alleging violation of Title VII.

Filing Claims under Title VII

Nonfederal employees who feel they have experienced employment discrimination may file a charge or claim with the EEOC. An employee filing such a claim is called a **claimant** or a **charging party**. Employers should be aware that it costs an employee only time and energy to go to the nearest EEOC office and file a claim. By law, the EEOC must in some way handle every claim it receives. To discourage claims and

Exhibit 2.6   Employees Who Are Not Covered by Title VII

- Employees of employers having less than 15 employees.
- Employees whose employers are not engaged in interstate commerce.
- Non-U.S. citizens employed outside the United States.
- Employees of religious institutions, associations, or corporations hired to perform work connected with carrying on religious activities.
- Members of Communist organizations.
- Employers employing Native Americans living in or around Native American reservations.
- Employers who are engaged in interstate commerce but do not employ 15 or more employees for each of 20 or more calendar weeks in the current or preceding a calendar year.

ensure the best defense when they arise, employers should ensure that their policies and procedures are legal, fair, and consistently applied.

Regarding the ease of bringing EEO claims, there is good news and bad news for employers. The good news is that the vast majority of charges are sifted out of the system for one reason or another. For instance, in fiscal year 2004, of the 58,328 charges filed with the EEOC, 10.4 percent were settled, 16.7 percent had administrative closures (failure of the claimant to pursue the claim, loss of contact with the claimant, etc.), 63.6 percent resulted in findings of no reasonable cause, and reasonable cause was found in only 5.1 percent of the charges.

The bad news is that the EEOC's success rate is pretty high. An August 13, 2002, report on a five-year litigation study released by the EEOC (covering fiscal years 1997–2001) reported that approximately 91 percent of the EEOC's suits are successfully resolved through consent decrees, settlement agreements, and favorable court orders. The success rate for trials is 60.24 percent (compared to a success rate of 26.8 percent for private plaintiffs in workplace bias suits). This percentage goes up to 80 percent in trial appeals (compared to 16 percent success rate for private attorneys). Those are not good numbers for employers tangling with the EEOC. The best defense is a good offense. Avoiding trouble in the first place lessens the chances of having to deal with the EEOC and therefore the chances of probably losing.

Nonfederal government employee claims must be filed within 180 days of the discriminatory event except as noted in the next section involving 706 agencies. For federal employees, claims must be filed with their employing agency within 45 days of the event. In a very significant U.S. Supreme Court case, *National Railroad Passenger Corp. (Amtrak) v. Morgan,*[3] these deadlines were made a bit more flexible by the Court for harassment cases. In the *Morgan* case the Supreme Court said that since on-the-job harassment is part of a pattern of behavior, if a charge is filed with the EEOC within the statutory period, a jury can consider actions that occurred outside the statutory period. That is, the violation is considered to be a continuing one, so the claimant is not limited to only evidence relating to the specific event resulting in the lawsuit.

[3] 536 U.S. 101 (2002).

The reason for the fairly short statute of limitations is an attempt to ensure that the necessary parties and witnesses are still available and that events are not too remote to recollect accurately. Violations of Title VII may also be brought to the EEOC's attention because of its own investigation or by information provided by employers meeting their **recordkeeping and reporting requirements** under the law.

recordkeeping and reporting requirements
Title VII requires that certain documents must be maintained and periodically reported to the EEOC.

You should be aware that the filing process is different for federal employees, although the EEOC is seeking to make it conform more closely to the nonfederal employee regulations. Federal employees are protected by Title VII, but the procedures for handling their claims simply follow a different path.

State Law Interface in the Filing Process

706 agency
State agency that handles EEOC claims on the basis of a work-sharing agreement with the EEOC.

Since most states have their own fair employment practice laws, they also have their own state and local enforcement agencies for employment discrimination claims. Most of these agencies contract with the EEOC to be what is called a **"706" agency** (named for section 706 of the act). These agencies receive and process claims of discrimination for the EEOC in addition to carrying on their own state business on the basis of a work-sharing agreement with the EEOC.

conciliation
Attempting to reach agreement on a claim through discussion, without resort to litigation.

Title VII's intent is that claims be **conciliated** if possible. Local agencies serve as a type of screening process for the more serious cases. If the complaint is not satisfactorily disposed at this level, it may eventually be taken by the EEOC and, if necessary, litigated. State and local agencies have their own procedures, which are similar to those of the EEOC.

If there is a 706 agency in the employee's jurisdiction and the employee goes there to file a claim, the employee has 300 days rather than 180 days within which to do so. In essence, filing with a 706 agency expands the filing time an employee has to bring a claim. If an employee files his or her claim with the EEOC when there is a 706 agency in the jurisdiction, the EEOC defers the complaint to the 706 agency for 60 days before investigating. The employee can file the complaint with the EEOC, but the EEOC sends it to the 706 agency, and EEOC will not move on the claim for 60 days.

respondent or **responding party**
Person to whom an EEOC claim is directed, usually the employer.

In further explaining the process, reference will only be made to the EEOC as the enforcing agency involved.

Proceeding through the EEOC

antiretaliation provisions
Provisions making it illegal to treat an employee adversely because the employee pursued his or her rights under Title VII.

Within 10 days of the employee filing a claim with the EEOC, the EEOC serves notice of the charge to the employer (called **respondent** or **responding party**). Title VII also includes **antiretaliation provisions**. It is a separate offense for an employer to retaliate against an employee for pursuing rights under Title VII. Noting that retaliation claims had doubled since 1991, in late 1998 the EEOC issued retaliation guidelines to make clear its view on what constitutes retaliation for pursuing Title VII rights and how it will view such claims by employees. In fiscal year 2004, retaliation claims were, by far, the third largest percentage of claims filed under Title VII, with race at 34.9 percent, gender at 30.5 percent, and retaliation at 25.5 percent.

Mediation

Hot. That is the best way to describe EEOC's approach to mediation. In response to complaints of a tremendous backlog of cases and claims that went on for years, in recent years the EEOC has adopted several important steps to try to streamline its case-handling process and make it more efficient, effective, and less time-consuming for employees filing claims. Primary among the steps is its adoption of mediation as an alternative to a full-blown EEOC investigation. In furtherance of this, EEOC has begun several different programs involving mediation. In 1999 it launched the expanded mediation program discussed in the next paragraph. In 2003, in recognition that many private sector employers already have extensive mediation programs set up to handle workplace issues, the EEOC began a "referral-back" program. Private sector employment discrimination claims are referred back to participating employers for mediation by the employer's own mediation program to see if they can be resolved without going any further. The same year, the EEOC ushered in a pilot program to have local fair employment practice offices mediate claims on the EEOC's behalf. In addition, in response to the EEOC's finding that there were more employees willing to mediate than there were employers willing to do so, the EEOC instituted "universal mediation agreements," under which employers agree to have their claims mediated by the EEOC when discrimination charges are filed. As of the end of fiscal year 2004, the EEOC had signed universal agreements to mediate with 71 large corporations and 637 local employers. National universal mediation agreements have been signed with such employers as Ford Motor Company, Huddle House, Inc., Ryan's Restaurant Group, Inc., and Southern Company.

Generally, the way mediation works is that after a discrimination charge is filed by the employee and notice of the charge is given to the employer, the EEOC screens the charge to see if it is one that is appropriate for mediation. If it is appropriate for mediation, EEOC will offer that option to the parties. Complex and weak cases are not offered mediation. The agency estimates that it offers mediation to 60 to 70 percent of its incoming workload of 80,000 cases per year. Of those, about 15 percent are actually mediated. Both parties are sent letters offering mediation, and the decision to participate is voluntary for both parties. Each side has 10 days to respond to the offer to mediate. If both parties elect mediation, the charge must be mediated within 60 days for in-house mediation or 45 days for external mediation.

If the parties choose to mediate, then during mediation they will have the opportunity to present their positions, express their opinions, provide information, and express their request for relief. Any information disclosed during this process is not to be revealed to anyone, including EEOC employees. If the parties reach agreement, that agreement is as binding as any other settlement agreement.

EEOC Investigation

If the parties choose not to mediate the charge or if the mediation is not successful, the charge is referred back to the EEOC for handling. The EEOC investigates the complaint by talking with the employer and employee and any other necessary witnesses as well as viewing any documents or even visiting the workplace.

Exhibit 2.7   The Procedure for Bringing a Claim within the EEOC

- Employee goes to EEOC office and files EEOC complaint.
- Agency sends notice to employer responding party accused of discrimination.
- Parties receive referral to mediation (if appropriate).
- If both elect mediation, charge is mediated.
- If parties agree in mediation, the negotiated settlement is binding. Complaint is resolved and closed.
- If mediation is not successful or parties choose not to mediate, EEOC investigates the claim.
- Parties meet and try to conciliate.
- If agreement is reached, claim is resolved and closed.
- If no agreement is reached, EEOC makes determination of reasonable cause or no reasonable cause.
- If no reasonable cause, employee is notified and given right-to-sue letter.
- If reasonable cause is found, agency notifies employer of proposed remedy.
- If employer disagrees, he or she appeals decision to next agency level.

EEOC's Determination

reasonable cause
EEOC finding that basis for illegal discrimination exists.

After appropriate investigation, the EEOC makes a determination as to whether there is **reasonable cause** or no reasonable cause for the employee to charge the employer with violating Title VII. Once there has been an investigation and a cause or no-cause finding, either party can ask for reconsideration of the EEOC's decision.

No-Reasonable-Cause Finding

no reasonable cause
EEOC finding that no reasonable basis for illegal discrimination exists.

After investigation, if the EEOC finds there is **no reasonable cause** for the employee's discrimination complaint, the employee is notified by an EEOC **right-to-sue letter**. If the employee wants to pursue the matter further despite EEOC's conclusion that Title VII has not been violated, the employee is now free to do so, having **exhausted the administrative remedies**. The employee can then bring suit against the employer in federal court within 90 days of receiving the right-to-sue letter. (See Exhibit 2.7.)

Reasonable-Cause-Finding

right-to-sue letter
Letter given by EEOC to claimants, permitting them to pursue their claim in court.

If the EEOC finds there is reasonable cause for the employee to charge the employer with discrimination, it will attempt to have the parties meet together and conciliate the matter. That is, the EEOC will bring the parties together in a fairly informal setting with an **EEO investigator**.

The EEO investigator sets forth what has been found during the investigation and discusses with the parties the ways the matter can be resolved. Often the employee is satisfied if the employer simply agrees to provide a favorable letter of recommendation. The majority of claims filed with the EEOC are adequately disposed of at this stage of the proceedings. If the claim is not adequately disposed of, the EEOC can take the matter further and eventually file suit against the employer in federal district court.

exhaustion of administrative remedies
Going through the established EEOC administrative procedure before being permitted to seek judicial review of an agency decision.

Scenario

EEO investigator
Employee of EEOC who reviews complaints for merit.

judicial review
Court review of an agency's decision.

de novo review
Complete new look at administrative case by the reviewing court.

mandatory arbitration agreements
Agreement an employee signs as a condition of employment, requiring that any workplace disputes be arbitrated rather than litigated.

Judicial Review

If no conciliation is reached, the EEOC may eventually file a civil action in federal district court. As we have seen, if the EEOC originally found no cause and issued the complaining party a right-to-sue letter, the employee can take the case to court, seeking **judicial review**. Title VII requires that courts give EEOC decisions *de novo review*. A court can only take a Title VII discrimination case for judicial review after the EEOC has first disposed of the claim. Thus, in opening scenario 1, Jack cannot immediately file a discrimination lawsuit against his employer because Jack has not yet gone through the EEOC's administrative process and exhausted his administrative remedies.

Upon going to court, the case is handled entirely new, as if there had not already been a finding by the EEOC. Employees proceeding with a no-reasonable-cause letter are also free to develop the case however they wish without being bound by the EEOC's determination. If a party is not satisfied with the court's decision and has a basis upon which to appeal, the case can be appealed up to, and including, the U.S. Supreme Court, if it agrees to hear the case.

Before we leave the area of judicial review, we need to discuss a matter that has become important in the area of employees' pursuing their rights under Title VII and having the right to judicial review of the EEOC's decisions.

In recent years, **mandatory arbitration agreements** have gained tremendously in popularity. Previously confined almost exclusively to unions and the securities industry, these agreements are entered into by employees with their employers when they are hired and stipulate that any workplace disputes will be disposed of by submitting them to arbitration rather than to EEOC or the courts.

The appeal of mandatory arbitration clauses is that they greatly decrease the time and resources parties would spend by fighting workplace legal battles in court. There are at least two major drawbacks for employees: (1) When they are trying to obtain employment, potential employees generally feel they have little choice about signing away their rights to go to court, and (2) once a case goes to arbitration, the arbitrator's decision is not subject to judicial review by the courts unless the decision can be shown to be the result of fraud or collusion, is unconstitutional, or suffers some similar malady. This means that the vast majority of arbitration awards, many rendered by arbitrators with no legal background or grounding in Title VII issues, remain intact, free from review by the courts. It also means that while employers gain the advantage of having fewer cases in court, employees have the disadvantage of essentially having the courts closed to them in Title VII cases, even though Title VII provides for both an administrative process and judicial review.

With few downsides for employers, mandatory arbitration agreements have become so popular with employers that they are now fairly routine. Employees who come to the EEOC intending to file claims of employment discrimination are told that they cannot do so because they have entered into a mandatory arbitration agreement with their employer, which requires them to seek redress through arbitration, *not* EEOC or the courts.

Two recent U.S. Supreme Court cases have decided important issues in this area. In *Circuit City* v. *Adams*,[4] the Supreme Court held that mandatory arbitration clauses requiring arbitration of workplace claims, including those under Title VII, are enforceable under the Federal Arbitration Act. In *EEOC* v. *Waffle House, Inc.*,[5] the Court held that even though an employee is subject to a mandatory arbitration agreement, since the EEOC is not a party to the agreement, the agreement does not prevent the EEOC from pursuing victim-specific relief such as back pay, reinstatement, and damages as part of an enforcement action.

So, EEOC claims clearly can now be the subject of mandatory arbitration, but this does not prevent the EEOC from bringing its own enforcement action against the employer and even asking for victim-specific relief for the employee. An employer can avoid a Title VII court case by requiring mandatory arbitration of workplace claims, but may then have to contend with the EEOC bringing suit on its own.

Legislation to overturn *Circuit City* and only permit voluntary arbitration agreements was introduced in both the House and Senate shortly after the decision, but did not pass. Perhaps this was, at least in part, because the Supreme Court gave further indication of how it will view mandatory arbitration agreements in a later *Circuit City* case. In its initial decision, the Supreme Court required the *Circuit City* case to be remanded to the lower court for actions not inconsistent with its ruling. On remand, the Court of Appeals applied the Federal Arbitration Act and ruled that the employer's mandatory arbitration agreement was unconscionable and unenforceable because it was offered on a take-it-or-leave-it basis, did not require the company to arbitrate claims, limited the relief available to employees, and required employees to pay half of the arbitration costs. When the Court of Appeals' decision came back to the Supreme Court for review, the Court declined to hear it, leaving the Court of Appeals' refusal to enforce the mandatory arbitration agreement intact.[6]

Perhaps also, at least in part in response to mandatory arbitration agreements, EEOC stepped up its mediation programs in order to provide employers with an alternative between litigation and mandatory arbitration. The EEOC had, since 1991, been moving in the direction of mediation, but it heated up after the Supreme Court decisions on mandatory arbitration. Its subsequent litigation alternatives heavily favoring mediation included plans aimed squarely at employers, with its adoption of the national uniform mediation agreements (NUMAs) and referral-back programs. As discussed earlier, the NUMAs specifically commit employers to mediation of Title VII claims, while the referral-back programs allow employers to use their own in-house ADR programs to attempt to settle such claims.

back pay
Money awarded for time employee was not working (usually due to termination) because of illegal discrimination.

front pay
Money awarded for time a claimant would have been in a job had illegal discrimination not occurred to keep him or her out.

Remedies

If the employee wins the case, the employer may be liable for **back pay** of up to two years before the filing of the charge with the EEOC, for **front pay** for future earnings that the employee would have received absent discrimination, for reinstatement of the employee to

---

[4] 532 U.S. 105 (2001).

[5] 534 U.S. 279 (2002).

[6] *Circuit City Stores, Inc.* v. *Adams*, 535 U.S. 1112 (2002).

Exhibit 2.8

Remedies under Title VII

- Back pay   *2 yrs* [handwritten]
- Front pay — *future earn* [handwritten]
- Reinstatement
- Seniority
- Retroactive seniority

- Injunctive relief
- Compensatory damages
- Punitive damages
- Attorney fees
- Medical costs

retroactive seniority
Seniority that dates back to the time the claimant was treated illegally.

make-whole relief
Attempts to put claimant in position he or she would have been in had there been no discrimination.

compensatory damages
Money awarded to compensate the injured party for direct losses.

punitive damages
Money over and above compensatory damages, imposed by court to punish defendant and to act as a deterrent.

disparate/ adverse impact
Effect of facially neutral policy is deleterious for Title VII group.

his or her position, for **retroactive seniority,** for injunctive relief, if applicable, and for attorney's fees. Until passage of the Civil Rights Act of 1991, remedies for discrimination under Title VII were limited to **make-whole relief** and injunctive relief.

The Civil Rights Act of 1991 added **compensatory damages** and **punitive damages** as available remedies. Punitive damages are permitted when it is shown that the employer's action was malicious or was done with reckless indifference to federally protected rights of the employee. They are not allowed under the **disparate/adverse impact** or unintentional theory of discrimination (to be discussed shortly) and may not be recovered from governmental employers. Compensatory damages may include future pecuniary loss, emotional pain, suffering, inconvenience, mental anguish, loss of enjoyment of life, and other nonpecuniary losses. (See Exhibit 2.8.)   *Key* [handwritten]

There are certain limitations on the damages under the law. Gender discrimination (including sexual harassment) and religious discrimination have a $300,000 cap total on nonpecuniary (pain and suffering) compensatory and punitive damages. There is no limitation on medical compensatory damages. The cap depends on the number of employees the employer has (see Exhibit 2.9). Juries may not be told of the caps on liability. Since race and national origin discrimination cases can also be brought under 42 USC section 1981, which permits unlimited compensatory damages, the caps do not apply to these categories. In 2001, the U.S. Supreme Court ruled that though compensatory damages are capped by the law, the limitations do not apply to front pay.[7] Also, as previously discussed, the U.S. Supreme Court's *Hoffman* decision[8] foreclosed the ability of undocumented workers to receive post-discharge back pay, and the EEOC rescinded its policy guidance suggesting otherwise.

With the addition of compensatory and punitive damages possible in Title VII cases, litigation has dramatically increased. It is now more worthwhile for employees to sue and for lawyers to take the cases. The possibility of money damages also makes it more likely that employers will settle more suits rather than risk large damage awards. Again, the best defense to costly litigation and liability is solid, consistently applied workplace policies.

Jury Trials

The Civil Rights Act of 1991 also added jury trials to Title VII. From the creation of Title VII in 1964 until passage of the 1991 Civil Rights Act 27 years later, jury trials

[7] *Pollard* v. *E.I. duPont de Nemours & Co.,* 532 U.S. 843 (2001).
[8] *Hoffman Plastic Compounds, Inc.* v. *NLRB,* 535 U.S. 137 (2002).

For employers with:

- 15 to 100 employees, there is a cap of $50,000.
- 101 to 200 employees, there is a cap of $100,000.
- 201 to 500 employees, there is a cap of $200,000.
- More than 500 employees, there is a cap of $300,000.

were not permitted under Title VII. Jury trials are now permitted under Title VII at the request of either party when compensatory and punitive damages are sought.

There is always less predictability about case outcomes when juries are involved. Arguing one's cause to a judge who is a trained member of the legal profession is quite different from arguing to a jury of 6 to 12 jurors, all of whom come with their own backgrounds, prejudices, and predilections. Employers now have even more incentive to ensure that their policies and actions are well reasoned, business-related, and justifiable—especially since employees have even more incentive to sue.

THEORETICAL BASES FOR TITLE VII LAWSUITS

plaintiff
One who brings a civil action.

OK, so we get past the agency procedures and go to court for our discrimination claim. In alleging discrimination, an employee **plaintiff** may use either of two theories to bring suit under Title VII: disparate treatment or disparate impact. The suit must fit into one theory or the other to be recognized under Title VII. A thorough understanding of each will help employers to make sounder policies that avoid litigation in the first place and enhance the workplace. Since cases will be our vehicle for viewing Title VII, we will speak of the parties as plaintiff and **defendant**. Since it is necessary to exhaust administrative remedies before going to court in virtually all situations, the employee has first filed a claim with the EEOC, and the case has eventually been taken to court by the employee plaintiff with or without EEOC representing him or her.

defendant
One against whom a case is brought.

Disparate Treatment ~ Dísera

disparate treatment
Treating similarly situated employee differently because of prohibited Title VII factors.

Disparate treatment is the Title VII theory used in cases of individual discrimination. The plaintiff employee (or applicant) bringing suit alleges that the defendant employer treats the employee differently than other similarly situated employees. Further, the employee alleges that the reason for the difference is the employees' race, religion, gender, color, or national origin. Disparate treatment is considered intentional discrimination, but the plaintiff need not actually know that unlawful discrimination is the reason for the difference. That is, the employee need not prove that the employer actually said that race, gender, and so on was the reason for the decision. As you will see in the following case, the U.S. Supreme Court has come up with a set of indicators that leaves discrimination as the only plausible explanation when all other possibilities are eliminated. (See Exhibit 2.8.) In disparate treatment cases, the employer's policy is discriminatory on its face.

McDonnell Douglas Corp. v. Green *411 U.S. 792 (1973)*

Green, an employee of McDonnell Douglas and a black civil rights activist, engaged with others in "disruptive and illegal activity" against his employer in the form of a traffic stall-in. The activity was done as part of Green's protest that his discharge from McDonnell Douglas was racially motivated, as were the firm's general hiring practices. McDonnell Douglas later rejected Green's reemployment application on the ground of the illegal conduct. Green sued, alleging race discrimination. The case is important because it is the first time the U.S. Supreme Court set forth how to prove a disparate treatment case under Title VII. In such cases the employee can use an inference of discrimination drawn from a set of inquiries the Court set forth.

Powell, J.

The critical issue before us concerns the order and allocation of proof in a private, nonclass action challenging employment discrimination. The language of Title VII makes plain the purpose of Congress to assure equality of employment opportunities and to eliminate those discriminatory practices and devices which have fostered racially stratified job environments to the disadvantage of minority citizens.

The complainant in a Title VII trial must carry the initial burden under the statute of establishing a **prima facie case** of racial discrimination. This may be done by showing (i) that he belongs to a racial minority; (ii) that he applied and was qualified for a job for which the employer was seeking applicants; (iii) that, despite his qualifications, he was rejected; and (iv) that, after his rejection, the position remained open and the employer continued to seek applicants from persons of complainant's qualifications. The facts necessarily will vary in Title VII cases, and the specification of the prima facie proof required from Green is not necessarily applicable in every respect to differing factual situations.

In the instant case, Green proved a prima facie case. McDonnell Douglas sought mechanics, Green's trade, and continued to do so after Green's rejection. McDonnell Douglas, moreover, does not dispute Green's qualifications and acknowledges that his past work performance in McDonnell Douglas' employ was "satisfactory."

The burden then must shift to the employer to articulate some legitimate, nondiscriminatory reason for the employee's rejection. We need not attempt to detail every matter which fairly could be recognized as a reasonable basis for a refusal to hire. Here McDonnell Douglas has assigned Green's participation in unlawful conduct against it as the cause for his rejection. We think that this suffices to discharge McDonnell Douglas' burden of proof at this stage and to meet Green's prima facie case of discrimination.

But the inquiry must not end here. While Title VII does not, without more, compel the rehiring of Green, neither does it permit McDonnell Douglas to use Green's conduct as a pretext for the sort of discrimination prohibited by Title VII. On remand, Green must be afforded a fair opportunity to show that McDonnell Douglas's stated reason for Green's rejection was in fact pretext. Especially relevant to such a showing would be evidence that white employees involved in acts against McDonnell Douglas of comparable seriousness to the "stall-in" were nevertheless retained or rehired.

McDonnell Douglas may justifiably refuse to rehire one who was engaged in unlawful, disruptive acts against it, but only if this criterion is applied alike to members of all races. Other evidence that may be relevant to any showing of pretext includes facts as to McDonnell Douglas' treatment of Green during his prior term of employment; McDonnell Douglas' reaction, if any, to Green's legitimate civil rights activities; and McDonnell Douglas' general policy and practice with respect to minority employment.

On the latter point, statistics as to McDonnell Douglas' employment policy and practice may be helpful to a determination of whether McDonnell Douglas' refusal to rehire Green in this case conformed to a general pattern of discrimination against blacks. The District Court may, for example, determine, after reasonable discovery that "the [racial] composition of defendant's labor force is itself reflective of restrictive or exclusionary practices." We caution that such general determinations, while helpful, may not be in and of themselves controlling as to an individualized hiring decision, particularly in the presence of an otherwise justifiable reason for refusing to rehire. In short, on the retrial Green must be

a facie

ging facts it each rement of a of action.

given a full and fair opportunity to demonstrate by competent evidence that the presumptively valid reasons for his rejection were in fact a cover up for a racially discriminatory decision. VACATED and REMANDED.

Case Questions

1. Do you think the Court should require actual evidence of discrimination in disparate treatment cases rather than permitting an inference? What are the advantages? Disadvantages?

2. Practically speaking, is an employer's burden really met after the employer "articulates" a legitimate nondiscriminatory reason for rejecting the employee? Explain.

3. Does the Court say that Green must be kept on in spite of his illegal activities? Discuss.

The effect of the *McDonnell Douglas* inquiries is to set up a legal test of all relevant factors that are generally taken into consideration in making employment decisions. Once those considerations have been ruled out as the reason for failure to hire the applicant, the only factor left to consider is the applicant's membership in one of Title VII's prohibited categories (i.e., race, color, gender, religion, or national origin).

The *McDonnell Douglas* Court recognized that there would be scenarios under Title VII other than failure to rehire (i.e., failure to promote or train, discriminatory discipline, and so on) and its test would not be directly transferrable to them, but it could be modified accordingly. For instance, the issue may not be a refusal to rehire; it may, instead, be a dismissal. In such a case, the employee would show the factors as they relate to dismissal.

If an employer makes decisions in accordance with these requirements, it is less likely that the decisions will later be successfully challenged by the employee in court. Disparate treatment cases involve an employer's variance from the normal scheme of things, to which the employee can point to show he or she was treated differently. Employers should therefore consistently treat similarly situated employees similarly. If there are differences, ensure that they are justifiable.

Think carefully before deciding to single out an employee for a workplace action. Is the reason for the action clear? Can it be articulated? Based on the information the employer used to make the decision, is it reasonable? Rational? Is the information serving as the basis for the decision reliable? Balanced? Is the justification job related? If the employer is satisfied with the answers to these questions, the decision is probably defensible. If not, reexamine the considerations for the decision, find its weakness, and determine what can be done to address the weakness. The employer will then be in a much better position to defend the decision and show it is supported by legitimate, nondiscriminatory reasons.

Legitimate, Nondiscriminatory Reason Defense

Even if the employee establishes all four of the elements of the prima facie case of disparate treatment, it is only a rebuttable presumption. That is, that, alone, does not establish that the employer discriminated against the employee. There may be some other explanation for what the employer did. As the Court stated in *McDonnell Douglas,* the employer may defend against the prima facie case of disparate treatment by showing that there was a legitimate, nondiscriminatory reason for the decision involving the employee. That reason may be virtually anything that makes sense and is not related to Title VII criteria. It is only discrimination on the basis of Title VII that is protected. For instance, Title VII does not protect the category of jerks. If it can legitimately be shown that the action was taken because the employee was acting like a jerk, then regardless of Title VII, there is no

Exhibit 2-10   Disparate Treatment

Employee's Prima Facie Case Requirements *(meet reqmts [enough] to have a case)*

- Employee belongs to a group protected by Title VII.
- Employee applied and was qualified for a job for which the employer was seeking applicants.
- Despite his or her qualifications, employee was rejected for the job.
- After employee's rejection, the position remained open and employer continued to seek applicants with employee's qualifications.

This is modified to conform to the situation forming the basis of the suit, as appropriate. For instance, if it was termination rather than hiring, or discipline rather than hiring, the requirements would be adjusted accordingly.

Employer's Defense: Employer can defend by showing that the action was taken for a legitimate, nondiscriminatory reason.

Employee's Counter: Employee can counter with evidence that the legitimate, nondiscriminatory reason was actually a mere pretext for the employer to discriminate.

---

protection. However, if it turns out that the only jerks terminated are those of a particular race, gender, ethnicity, and the like, then the employer is still violating Title VII.

But even if the employer can show a legitimate, nondiscriminatory reason for the action toward the employee, the analysis does not end there. The employee can then counter the employer's defense by showing that the legitimate, nondiscriminatory reason being shown by the employer is a mere pretext for discrimination. That is, that while on its face the reason may appear legitimate, there is actually something discriminatory going on. For instance, in *McDonnell Douglas,* the employer said it would not rehire Green because he engaged in unlawful activity. If Green could show that the employer had rehired white employees who had engaged in similar unlawful activities, then McDonnell Douglas' legitimate, nondiscriminatory reason for the treatment of Green would appear to be a mere pretext for discrimination, since white employees who engaged in similar activities had been rehired despite their activity, but Green, black, had not.

The BFOQ Defense

bona fide
occupational
qualification
(BFOQ)
Permissible dis-
crimination if
legally neces-
sary for
employer's par-
ticular business.

Employers may also defend against disparate treatment cases by showing that the basis for the employer's intentional discrimination is a **bona fide occupational qualification (BFOQ)** reasonably necessary to the employer's particular business. This is available only for disparate treatment cases involving gender, religion, and national origin, and is not available for race or color. BFOQ is legalized discrimination and, therefore, very narrowly construed by the courts.

To have a successful BFOQ defense, the employer must be able to show that the basis for preferring one group over another goes to the essence of what the employer is in business to do, and that predominant attributes of the group discriminated against are at odds with that business. For instance, it has been held that, because bus companies and airlines are in the business of safely transporting passengers from one place to another, and driving and piloting skills begin to deteriorate at a certain age, a maximum age requirement for hiring is an appropriate BFOQ for bus drivers and pilots. The evidence supporting the qualification must be credible, and not just the employer's opinion. The employer must also be able to show it would be impractical to determine if each individual member of the group who is discriminated against could qualify for the position.

As you can see from the following case, not every attempt to show a BFOQ is successful. Weigh the business considerations in the following case against the dictates of Title VII, and think about how you would decide the issue.

Wilson v. Southwest Airlines Company *517 F. Supp. 292* (N.D. Tex. Dallas Div. 1981)

A male sued Southwest Airlines after he was not hired as a flight attendant because he was male. The airline argued that being female was a BFOQ for being a flight attendant. The court disagreed.

MEMORANDUM OPINION

Southwest conceded that its refusal to hire males was intentional. The airline also conceded that its height–weight restrictions would have an adverse impact on male applicants, if actually applied. Southwest contends, however, that the BFOQ exception to Title VII's ban on gender discrimination justifies its hiring only females for the public contact positions of flight attendant and ticket agent. The BFOQ window through which Southwest attempts to fly permits gender discrimination in situations where the employer can prove that gender is a "bona fide occupational qualification reasonably necessary to the normal operation of that particular business or enterprise." Southwest reasons it may discriminate against males because its attractive female flight attendants and ticket agents personify the airline's sexy image and fulfill its public promise to take passengers skyward with "love." The airline claims maintenance of its females-only hiring policy is crucial to its continued financial success.

Since it has been admitted that Southwest discriminates on the basis of gender, the only issue to decide is whether Southwest has proved that being female is a BFOQ reasonably necessary to the normal operation of its particular business.

As an integral part of its youthful, feminine image, Southwest has employed only females in the high customer contact positions of ticket agent and flight attendant. From the start, Southwest's attractive personnel, dressed in high boots and hot-pants, generated public interest and "free ink." Their sex appeal has been used to attract male customers to the airline. Southwest's

flight attendants, and to a lesser degree its ticket agents, have been featured in newspaper, magazine, billboard, and television advertisements during the past 10 years. According to Southwest, its female flight attendants have come to "personify" Southwest's public image.

Southwest has enjoyed enormous success in recent years. From 1979 to 1980, the company's earnings rose from $17 million to $28 million when most other airlines suffered heavy losses.

The broad scope of Title VII's coverage is qualified by Section 703(e), the BFOQ exception Section 703(e) states:

(e) Notwithstanding any other provision of this subchapter,

(1) It shall not be an unlawful employment practice for an employer to hire . . . on the basis of his religion, gender, or national origin in those certain instances where religion, gender, or national origin is a bona fide occupational qualification reasonably necessary to the normal operation of that particular business or enterprise.

The BFOQ defense is not to be confused with the doctrine of "business necessity" which operates only in cases involving unintentional discrimination, when job criteria which are "fair in form, but discriminatory in operation" are shown to be "related to" job performance.

This Circuit's decisions have given rise to a two step BFOQ test: (1) does the particular job under consideration require that the worker be of one gender only; and if so, (2) is that requirement reasonably necessary to the "essence" of the employer's business. The first level of inquiry is designed to test whether gender is so essential to job performance that a member of the opposite gender simply could not do the same job.

To rely on the bona fide occupational qualification exception, an employer has the burden of proving that he had reasonable cause to believe, that is a factual basis for believing, that all or substantially all women would be unable to perform safely and efficiently the duties of the job involved. The second level is designed to assure that the qualification being scrutinized is one so important to the operation of the business that the business would be undermined if employees of the "wrong" gender were hired. . . . The use of the word "necessary" in section 703(e) requires that we apply a business necessity test, not a business convenience test. That is to say, discrimination based on gender is valid only when the essence of the business operation would be undermined by not hiring members of one gender exclusively.

Applying the first level test for a BFOQ to Southwest's particular operations results in the conclusion that being female is not a qualification required to perform successfully the jobs of flight attendant and ticket agent with Southwest. Like any other airline, Southwest's primary function is to transport passengers safely and quickly from one point to another. To do this, Southwest employs ticket agents whose primary job duties are to ticket passengers and check baggage, and flight attendants, whose primary duties are to assist passengers during boarding and deboarding, to instruct passengers in the location and use of aircraft safety equipment, and to serve passengers cocktails and snacks during the airline's short commuter flights. Mechanical, nongender-linked duties dominate both these occupations. Indeed, on Southwest's short-haul commuter flights there is time for little else. That Southwest's female personnel may perform their mechanical duties "with love" does not change the result. "Love" is the manner of job performance, not the job performed.

Southwest's argument that its primary function is "to make a profit," not to transport passengers, must be rejected. Without doubt the goal of every business is to make a profit. For purposes of BFOQ analysis, however, the business "essence" inquiry focuses on the particular service provided and the job tasks and functions involved, not the business goal. If an employer could justify employment discrimination merely on the grounds that it is necessary to make a profit, Title VII would be nullified in short order.

In order not to undermine Congress' purpose to prevent employers from "refusing to hire an individual based on stereotyped characterizations of the genders," a BFOQ for gender must be denied where gender is merely useful for attracting customers of the opposite gender, but where hiring both genders will not alter or undermine the essential function of the employer's business. Rejecting a wider BFOQ for gender does not eliminate the commercial exploitation of sex appeal. It only requires, consistent with the purposes of Title VII, that employers exploit the attractiveness and allure of a gender-integrated workforce. Neither Southwest, nor the traveling public, will suffer from such a rule. More to the point, it is my judgment that this is what Congress intended.

Case Questions

1. What should be done if, as here, the public likes the employer's marketing scheme?

2. Do you think the standards for BFOQs are too strict? Explain.

3. Should a commercial success argument be given more weight by the courts? How should that be balanced with concern for Congress' position on discrimination?

Make sure that you understand the distinction the court made in *Southwest Airlines* between the essence of *what* an employer is in business to do and *how* the employer chooses to do it. People often neglect this distinction and cannot understand why business owners cannot simply hire whomever they want (or not, as the case may be) if it has a marketing scheme it wants to pursue. Marketing schemes go to the "how" of the employer's business, as in how an employer chooses to conduct his or her business or attract people to it, rather than the "what" of the business, which is the actual business itself. Getting passengers safely from one point to another is the "what," in *Southwest*. How the airline chose to market that business of safely transporting customers is another matter and has little to do with the actual conduct of the business itself. Perhaps the Playboy Club bunnies will make it clearer.

Key

After the success of *Playboy* magazine, Playboy opened several Playboy clubs in which the servers were dressed as Playboy bunnies. The purpose of the clubs was not to serve drinks as much as it was to extend *Playboy* magazine and its theme of beautiful women dressed in bunny costumes into another form for public consumption. *Playboy* magazine and its concept was purely for the purpose of adult male entertainment. The bunnies serving drinks were not so much drink servers as they were Playboy bunnies in the flesh rather than on a magazine page. That is what the business of the clubs was all about. Though it later chose to open up its policies to include male bunnies, being female was a defensible BFOQ for being a bunny server in a Playboy club because having female bunnies was what the club was in business to do.

Hooters

Contrast this with Hooters restaurants, where Hooters asserted that its business is serving spicy chicken wings. Since males can serve chicken wings just as well as females, being female is not a BFOQ for being a Hooters server. However, if Hooters had said the purpose of its business is to provide males with scantily clad female servers for entertainment purposes, as it was with the Playboy clubs, then being female would be a BFOQ.

Disparate Impact

facially neutral policy
Workplace policy applies equally to all appropriate employees.

3
Scenario

While disparate treatment is based on an employee's allegations that she or he is treated differently as an individual based on a policy that is discriminatory on its face, disparate impact cases are generally statistically based group cases alleging that the employer's policy, while neutral on its face (**facially neutral**), has a disparate or adverse impact on a protected Title VII group. If such a policy impacts protected groups more harshly than majority groups, illegal discrimination may be found. This is the basis for why the police department's policy fails in opening scenario 3. The 5-foot-4, 130-pound policy would screen out many more females than males and would therefore have to be shown to be job-related in order to stand. Females are, as a group, slighter and shorter than males, so the policy has a disparate impact on women and could be gender discrimination in violation of Title VII. Actually, this has been found to be true of males in certain ethnic groups, too.

The disparate impact theory was established by the Supreme Court in 1971 in the *Griggs* case, below. *Griggs* is generally recognized as the first important case under Title VII, setting forth how Title VII was to be interpreted by courts. Even though the law became effective in 1965, it was not until *Griggs* in 1971 that it was taken seriously by most employers. *Griggs* has since been codified into law by the Civil Rights Act of 1991. Notice the difference between the theories in the decision of the case below involving disparate impact and the previous case involving disparate treatment.

Key

Griggs v. Duke Power Co. *401 U.S. 424 (1971)*

Until the day Title VII became effective, it was the policy of Duke Power Co. that blacks be employed in only one of its five departments: the Labor Department. The highest paid black employee in the Labor Department made less than the lowest paid white employee in any other department. Blacks could not transfer out of the Labor Department into any other department. The day Title VII became effective, Duke instituted a policy requiring new hires to have a high school diploma and passing scores on two general intelligence tests in order to be placed in any department other than Labor and a high school diploma to transfer to other departments from Labor. Two months later, Duke required that transferees from the Labor or Coal Handling Departments who had no high school diploma pass two general intelligence tests. White employees already in other departments were grandfathered in under the new policy and the high school diploma and intelligence test requirements did not apply to them. Black employees brought this action under Title VII of the Civil Rights Act of 1964, challenging the employer's requirement of a high school diploma and the passing of intelligence tests as a condition of employment in or transfer to jobs at the power plant. They alleged the requirements are not job related and have the effect of disqualifying blacks from employment or transfer at a higher rate than whites. The U.S. Supreme Court held that the act dictated that job requirements which have a disproportionate impact on groups protected by Title VII be shown to be job related.

Burger, J.

We granted the writ in this case to resolve the question of whether an employer is prohibited by Title VII of the Civil Rights Act of 1964 from requiring a high school education or passing of a standardized general intelligence test as a condition of employment in or transfer to jobs when *(a)* neither standard is shown to be significantly related to successful job performance, *(b)* both requirements operate to disqualify Negroes at a substantially higher rate than white applicants, and *(c)* the jobs in question formerly had been filled only by white employees as part of a longstanding practice of giving preference to whites.

What is required by Congress [under Title VII] is the removal of artificial, arbitrary, and unnecessary barriers to employment when the barriers operate invidiously to discriminate on the basis of racial or other impermissible classifications.

The act proscribes not only overt discrimination but also practices that are fair in form, but discriminatory in operation. The touchstone is business necessity. If an employment practice which operates to exclude Negroes cannot be shown to be related to job performance, the practice is prohibited.

On the record before us, neither the high school completion requirement nor the general intelligence test is shown to bear a demonstrable relationship to successful performance of the jobs for which it was used. Both were adopted without meaningful study of their relationship to job performance ability.

The evidence shows that employees who have not completed high school or taken the tests have continued to perform satisfactorily and make progress in departments for which the high school and test criteria are now used.

Good intent or absence of discriminatory intent does not redeem employment procedures or testing mechanisms that operate as "built-in head winds" for minority groups and are unrelated to measuring job capability.

The facts of this case demonstrate the inadequacy of broad and general testing devices as well as the infirmity of using diplomas or degrees as general measures of capability. History is filled with examples of men and women who rendered highly effective performance without the conventional badges of accomplishment in terms of certificates, diplomas, or degrees. Diplomas and tests are useful servants, but Congress has mandated the commonsense proposition that they are not to become masters of reality.

Nothing in the act precludes the use of testing or measuring procedures; obviously they are useful. What Congress has forbidden is giving these devices and mechanisms controlling force unless they are demonstrably a reasonable measure of job performance. Congress has not commanded that the less qualified be measured or preferred over the better qualified simply because of minority origins. Far from disparaging job qualifications as such, Congress has made such qualifications the controlling factor, so that race, religion, nationality, and sex become irrelevant. What Congress has commanded is that any tests used must measure the person for the job and not the person in the abstract. REVERSED.

Case Questions

1. Does this case make sense to you? Why? Why not?
2. The Court said the employer's intent does not matter here. Should it? Explain.
3. What would be your biggest concern as an employer who read this decision?

Court cases have determined the following screening devices have a disparate impact:

- Credit status—gender, race.
- Arrest record—race.
- Unwed pregnancy—gender, race.
- Height and weight requirements—gender, national origin.
- Educational requirements—race.
- Marital status—gender.
- Conviction of crime unrelated to job performance—race.

screening device
Factor used to weed out applicants from the pool of candidates.

Griggs stood as good law until 1989 when the U.S. Supreme Court decided *Wards Cove Packing Co.* v. *Atonio.*[9] In that case the Court held that the burden was on the employee to show that the employer's policy was *not* job related. In *Griggs* the burden was on the *employer* to show that the policy *was* job related. This increase in the employee's burden was taken as a setback in what was considered to be settled civil rights law. It moved Congress to immediately call for *Griggs* and its 18-year progeny to be enacted into law so it would no longer be subject to the vagaries of whoever was sitting on the U.S. Supreme Court. The Civil Rights Act of 1991 did this.

Disparate impact cases can be an employer's nightmare. No matter how careful an employer tries to be, a policy, procedure, or **screening device** may serve as the basis of a disparate impact claim if the employer is not vigilant in watching for its indefensible disparate impact. Even the most seemingly innocuous policies can turn up unexpected cases of disparate impact. (See Exhibit 2.11.) Employers must guard against analyzing policies or actions for signs of intentional discrimination, yet missing those with a disparate impact. Ensure that any screening device is explainable and justifiable as job related if it has a disparate impact on Title VII groups.

What Constitutes a Disparate Impact?

We have talked about disparate impact in general, but we have not yet discussed what actually constitutes a disparate impact. Any time an employer uses a factor as a screening device to decide who receives the benefit of any type of employment decision—from hiring to termination, from promotion to training, from raises to employee benefit packages—it can be the basis for disparate impact analysis.

four-fifths rule
Minority must do at least 80 percent or four-fifths as well as majority on screening device or presumption of disparate impact arises, and device must then be shown to be job related.

Recall that Title VII does not mention disparate impact. On August 25, 1978, several federal agencies, including the EEOC and the Departments of Justice and Labor, adopted a set of uniform guidelines to provide standards for ruling on the legality of employee selection procedures. The Uniform Guidelines on Employee Selection Procedures takes the position that there is a 20 percent margin permissible between the outcome of the majority and the minority under a given screening device. This is known as the **four-fifths rule**. Disparate impact is statistically demonstrated when the selection rate for groups protected by Title VII is less than 80 percent or four-fifths that of the higher scoring majority group.

[9] 490 U.S. 642 (1989).

Key

For example, 100 women and 100 men take a promotion examination. One hundred percent of the women and 50 percent of the men pass the exam. The men have only performed 50 percent as well as the women. Since the men did not pass at a rate of at least 80 percent of the women's passage rate, the exam has a disparate impact on the men. The employer would now be required to show that the exam is job related. If this can be shown to the satisfaction of the court, then the job requirement will be permitted even though it has a disparate impact. Even then the policy may still be struck down if the men can show there is a way to accomplish the employer's legitimate goal in using the exam, without it having such a harsh impact on them.

For example, suppose a store like Sears has a 75-pound lifting requirement for applicants who apply to work as mechanics in their car repair facilities. A woman sues for gender discrimination, saying the lifting requirement has a disparate impact on women because they generally cannot lift that much weight. The store is able to show that employees who work in the car repair facilities move heavy tools from place to place in the garage. That is a legitimate justification. Though the lifting policy screens out women applying for jobs as mechanics at a higher rate than it does men, and for argument's sake, let's say women only do 20 percent as well as men on the lifting requirement, thus not meeting the four-fifths rule, the employer has provided a legitimate, nondiscriminatory reason for the lifting policy. But suppose the applicant can counter that if the employer used a rolling tool cart (which is actually sold by Sears) then the policy would not have such a harmful impact on women and would still allow Sears what it needs. Even though Sears has given a legitimate, nondiscriminatory reason for its policy, it has been demonstrated that the policy can be made less harsh by using the cart.

The four-fifths rule guideline is only a rule of thumb. The U.S. Supreme Court stated in *Watson* v. *Ft. Worth Bank and Trust*[10] that it has never used mathematical precision to determine disparate impact. What is clear is that the employee is required to show that the statistical evidence is significant and has the effect of selecting applicants for hiring and promotion in ways adversely affecting groups protected by Title VII.

The terminology regarding scoring is intentionally imprecise, because the "outcome" depends on the nature of the screening device. The screening device can be anything that distinguishes one employee from another for workplace decision purposes. It may be a policy of hiring only ex-football players as barroom bouncers (most females would be precluded from consideration since most of them have not played football); requiring a minimum passing score on a written or other examination; physical attributes such as height and weight requirements; or of another type of differentiating factor. Disparate impact's coverage is very broad and virtually any policy may be challenged.

If the device is a written examination, then the outcomes compared will be test scores of one group (usually whites) versus another (usually blacks). If the screening device is a no-beard policy, then the outcome will be the percentage of black males affected by the medical condition, which is exacerbated if they shave, versus the percentage of white males so affected. If it is a height and weight requirement, it will be the percentage of females or members of traditionally shorter and slighter ethnic groups who can meet that requirement versus the percentage of males or majority members

[10] 487 U.S. 997 (1988).

who can do so. The hallmark of these devices is that they appear neutral on their face. That is, they apply equally to everyone. Yet on closer examination, there is a harsher impact on a group with Title VII protection.

Disparate Impact and Subjective Criteria

When addressing the issue of the disparate impact of screening devices, subjective and objective criteria are a concern. *Objective criteria* are factors that are able to be quantified by anyone, such as whether the employee made a certain score on a written exam. *Subjective criteria* are, instead, factors based on someone's personal thoughts or ideas (i.e., a supervisor's opinion as to whether the employee being considered for promotion is "compatible" with the workplace).

Initially it was suspected that subjective criteria could not be the basis for disparate impact claims since the Supreme Court cases had involved only objective factors, such as height and weight, educational requirements, test scores, and the like. In *Watson* v. *Fort Worth Bank,* the Supreme Court, for the first time, determined that subjective criteria could also be the basis for a disparate impact claim.

In *Watson,* a black employee had worked for the bank for years and was constantly passed over for promotion in favor of white employees. She eventually brought suit, alleging racial discrimination in that the bank's subjective promotion policy had a disparate impact upon black employees. The bank's policy was to promote employees based on the recommendation of the supervisor (all of whom were white). The Supreme Court held that the disparate impact analysis could indeed be used in determining illegal discrimination in subjective criteria cases.

Disparate Impact of Preemployment Interviews and Employment Applications

Quite often questions asked during idle conversational chat during preemployment interviews or included on job applications may unwittingly be the basis for Title VII claims. Such questions or discussions should therefore be scrutinized for their potential impact, and interviewers should be trained in potential trouble areas to be avoided. If the premise is that the purpose of questions is to elicit information to be used in the evaluation process, then it makes sense to the applicant that if the question is asked, the employer must plan to use the information. It may seem like innocent conversation to the interviewer, but if the applicant is rejected, then whether or not the information was gathered for discriminatory purposes, the applicant has the foundation for alleging that it illegally impacted the decision-making process. (See Exhibit 2.11.) Only questions relevant to legal considerations for evaluating the applicant should be asked. There is virtually always a way to elicit legal, necessary information without violating the law or exposing the employer to potential liability.

For example, applications often ask the marital status of the applicant. Since there is often discrimination against married women holding certain jobs, this question has a potential disparate impact on married female applicants (but not married male applicants). If the married female applicant is not hired, she can allege that it was because she was a married female. This may have nothing whatsoever to do with the actual reason for her rejection, but since the employer asked the question, the argument can be made that it did. In truth, employers often ask this question because they want to know whom to contact in case of an emergency should the applicant be hired and suffer an on-the-job emergency. Simply asking who should be contacted in case of emergency, or not soliciting such information until after the applicant is hired, gives the employer exactly what the employer needs without risking potential liability by asking questions about gender or marital status that pose a risk. That is why in opening scenario 2, Jill, as one who interviews applicants, is in need of training, just like those who actually hire applicants.

Scenario

The Business Necessity Defense

In a disparate impact claim, the employer can use the defense that the challenged policy, neutral on its face, that has a disparate impact on a group protected by Title VII is actually job related and consistent with **business necessity**. For instance, an employee challenges the employer's policy of requesting credit information and demonstrates that, because of shorter credit histories, fewer women are hired than men. The employer can show that it needs the policy because it is in the business of handling large sums of money and that hiring only those people with good and stable credit histories is a business necessity. Business necessity may not be used as a defense to a disparate treatment claim.

business necessity
Defense to a disparate impact case based on the employer's need for the policy as a legitimate requirement for the job.

In a disparate impact case, once the employer provides evidence rebutting the employee's prima facie case by showing business necessity or other means of rebuttal, the employee can show that there is a means of addressing the issue that has less of an adverse impact than the challenged policy. If this is shown to the court's satisfaction, then the employee will prevail and the policy will be struck down.

Knowing these requirements provides the employer with valuable insight into what is necessary to protect itself from liability. Even though disparate impact claims can be difficult to detect beforehand, once they are brought to the employer's attention by the employee, they can be used as an opportunity to revisit the policy. With flexible, creative, and innovative approaches, the employer is able to avoid many problems in this area.

Other Defenses to Title VII Claims

Once an employee provides prima facie evidence that the employer has discriminated, in addition to the BFOQ and business necessity defenses discussed, the employer may perhaps present evidence of other defenses:

- That the employee's evidence is not true—that is, this is not the employer's policy as alleged or that it was not applied as the employee alleges, employee's statistics regarding the policy's disparate impact are incorrect and there is no disparate impact, or the treatment employee says she or he received did not occur.

- That the employer's "bottom line" comes out correctly. We initially said that disparate impact is a statistical theory. Employers have tried to avoid litigation under this theory by taking measures to ensure that the relevant statistics will not exhibit a disparate impact. In an area in which they feel they may be vulnerable, such as in minorities' passing scores on a written examination, they may make decisions to use criteria that make it appear as if minorities do at least 80 percent as well as the majority so the prima facie elements for a disparate impact case are not met. This attempt at an end run around Title VII was soundly rejected by the U.S. Supreme Court in *Connecticut* v. *Teal,* below. Note that this is also very often the reason you hear someone say there are "quotas" in a workplace. They are there *not* because the law requires them—it doesn't—but rather because the employer has self-imposed them to try to avoid liability. *Not* a good idea. The best policy is to have an open, fair employment process. Manipulating statistics to reach a "suitable" bottom-line outcome is *not* permitted, as shown in *Connecticut* v. *Teal,* below.

Connecticut v. Teal *457 U.S. 440 (1982)*

Unsuccessful black promotion candidates sued the employer for race discrimination. The employees alleged that even though the employer's final promotion figures showed no disparate impact, the employer's process of arriving at the bottom-line figures should be subject to scrutiny for disparate impact. The Supreme Court agreed.

Brennan, J.

Black employees of a Connecticut state agency were promoted provisionally to supervisors. To attain permanent status as supervisors, they were first required to receive a passing score on a written examination. There was a disparate impact, in that blacks passed at a rate of approximately 68 percent of the passing rate for whites. The black employees who failed the examination were thus excluded from further consideration for permanent supervisory positions. They then brought an action against the state of Connecticut and certain state agencies and officials, alleging violation of Title VII of the Civil Rights Act of 1964 by requiring, as an absolute condition for consideration for promotion, that applicants pass a written test that disproportionately excluded blacks and was not job related. Before trial, Connecticut made promotions from the eligibility list, with an overall result that 22.9 percent of the black candidates were promoted but only 13.5 percent of the white candidates—thus no disparate impact resulted from the final promotions.

We consider here whether an employer sued for violation of Title VII of the Civil Rights Act of 1964 may assert a "bottom-line" theory of defense. Under that theory, as asserted in this case, an employer's acts of racial discrimination in promotions effected by an examination having disparate impact would not render the employer liable for the racial discrimination suffered by employees barred from promotion if the "bottom-line" result of the promotional process was an appropriate racial balance. We hold that the "bottom line" does not preclude employees from establishing a prima facie case, nor does it provide the employer with a defense to such a case.

A nonjob-related test that has a disparate racial impact, and is used to "limit" or "classify" employees, is "used to discriminate" within the meaning of Title VII, whether or not it was "designed or intended" to have this effect and despite an employer's efforts to compensate for its discriminatory effect.

Employer's claim of disparate impact from the examination, a pass-fail barrier to employment opportunity, states a prima facie case of employment discrimination under Title VII despite their employer's nondiscriminatory "bottom line," and that "bottom line" is no defense to this prima facie case.

Having determined that employees' claim comes within the terms of Title VII, we must address the suggestion of the employer and some *amici curiae* ["friends of the court"—nonparties who wish to have their positions considered by the Supreme Court in its deliberation of an issue] that we recognize an exception, either in the nature of an additional burden on employees seeking to establish a prima facie case or in the nature of an affirmative defense, for cases in which an employer has compensated for a discriminatory pass-fail barrier by hiring or promoting a sufficient number of black employees to reach a nondiscriminatory "bottom line." We reject this suggestion, which is in essence nothing more than a request that we redefine the protections guaranteed by Title VII.

Section 703(a)(2) prohibits practices that would deprive or tend to deprive "any individual of employment opportunities." The principal focus of the statute is the protection of the individual employee, rather than the protection of the minority group as a whole.

The Court has stated that a nondiscriminatory "bottom line" and an employer's good-faith efforts to achieve a nondiscriminatory workforce might in some cases assist an employer in rebutting the inference that particular action had been intentionally discriminatory: Proof that a workforce was racially balanced or that it contained a disproportionately high percentage of minority employees is not wholly irrelevant on the issue of intent when that issue is yet to be decided. But resolution of the factual question of intent is not what is at issue in this case. Rather, employer seeks simply to justify discrimination against the employees on the basis of their favorable treatment of other members of the employees' racial group. Under Title VII, a racially balanced workforce cannot immunize an employer from liability for specific acts of discrimination.

It is clear beyond cavil that the obligation imposed by Title VII is to provide an equal opportunity for each applicant regardless of race, without regard to whether members of the applicant's race are already proportionately represented in the workforce.

Congress never intended to give an employer license to discriminate against some employees on the basis of race or gender merely because he favorably treats other members of the employees' group. In sum, the employer's nondiscriminatory "bottom line" is no answer, under the terms of Title VII, to the employees' prima facie claim of employment discrimination. AFFIRMED and REMANDED.

Case Questions

1. After being sued but before trial, why do you think that the agency promoted a larger percentage of blacks than whites when a larger percentage of whites actually passed the exam?

2. Should the employees have been allowed to sue if the bottom line showed no discrimination?

3. How could the employer here have avoided liability?

Teal demonstrates that Title VII requires equal employment *opportunity,* not simply equal *employment.* This is *extremely* important to keep in mind. It is *not* purely a "numbers game" as many employers, including the state of Connecticut, have interpreted the law. Under the Civil Rights Act of 1991, it is an unfair employment practice for an employer to adjust the scores of, or to use different cutoff scores for, or to otherwise alter the results of, an employment-related test on the basis of a prohibited category as was done in *Teal.*

Employers' policies should ensure that everyone has an equal chance at the job, based on qualifications. The *Teal* employees had been in their positions on a provisional basis for nearly two years before taking the examination. The employer therefore had nearly two years of actual job performance that it could consider to determine the applicant's promotability. Instead, an exam was administered, requiring a certain score, which exam the employer could not show to be related to the job. Of course, the logical question is, "Then why give it?" Make sure you ask yourself that question before using screening devices that may operate to exclude certain groups on a disproportional basis. If you cannot justify the device, you take an unnecessary risk by using it.

AN IMPORTANT NOTE

One of the prevalent misconceptions about Title VII is that all an employee must do is file a claim and the employer is automatically deemed to be liable for discrimination. This is not true. Discrimination claims under Title VII and other employment discrimination legislation must be proved just as any other lawsuits. It is not enough for an employee to allege he or she is being discriminated against. The employee must offer evidence to support the claim. As shown in *Ali,* below, not doing so has predictable results.

Many times managers do not discipline or even terminate employees with Title VII protection for fear of being sued. This should not be the approach. Rather, simply treat them and their actions as you would those of any other similarly situated employee and be consistent. There is no need to walk on eggshells. If an employee is not performing as he or she should, Title VII affords them no protection whatsoever just because they are in a protected class based on race, gender, national origin, and so forth. Title VII is not a job guarantee for women and minorities. Instead, it requires employers to provide them with equal employment opportunity, including termination if it is called for. No one can stop the employee from suing. The best an employer can do is engage in consistency and even-handedness that makes for a less desirable target, and to have justifiable decisions to defend once sued.

As you read *Ali,* take note of the inadvisability of the questionable parts of the encounter between the employer and the employee.

Ali v. Mount Sinai Hospital *68 Empl. Prac. Dec. (CCH) P44,188, 1996 U.S. Dist. Lexis 8079 (S.D.N.Y. 1996)*

An employee sued the employer for racial discrimination in violation of Title VII, for discriminatory enforcement of the employer's dress code. She alleged she was disciplined for violating the code but whites were not. The court found that the employee had offered no evidence of discriminatory enforcement, so the court had no choice but to find in favor of the employer.

Gershon, J.

It is undisputed that, at all relevant times, the Hospital had a detailed three-page dress code for all of its nursing department staff, including unit clerks. It expressly provided that "the style chosen be conservative and in keeping with the professional image in nursing" and that the "Unit clerks wear the blue smock provided by the Hospital with conservative street clothes." The wearing of boots, among other items of dress, was expressly prohibited. With regard to hair, the dress code provided that "it should be clean and neatly groomed to prevent interference with patient care" and only "plain" hair barrettes and hairpins should be worn. As plaintiff acknowledges, "The hallmark of said code was that the staff had to dress and groom themselves in a conservative manner."

It is also undisputed that Ms. Ali violated the dress code. Ms. Ali reported to work at the CSICU wearing a red, three-quarter length, cowl-necked dress and red boots made of lycra fabric which went over her knees. Over her dress, Ms. Ali wore the regulation smock provided by the Hospital. She wore her hair in what she says she then called a "punk" style. She now calls it a "fade"

style, which she describes as an "Afro hairstyle." It was shorter on the sides than on the top and was in its natural color, black. According to Dr. Shields, Ms. Ali's hair was not conservative because it "was so high" and "you noticed it right away because it was high and back behind the ears and down. It certainly caused you to look at her. It caused attention." Deposition of Dr. Elizabeth Shields: Her hair "had to be at least three to five inches high down behind her ears." This description by Dr. Shields has not been disputed.

According to the employee, Dr. Shields approached her and asked her to look in the mirror and see what looks back at her. Ali responded that she looked beautiful. Ms. Ali testified that Dr. Shields told her that "I belong in a zoo, and then the last thing she said was I look like I [am] . . . going to a disco or belong in a disco or something to that effect." Dr. Shields testified: "I told her about the whole outfit. She had red boots, red dress, in the unit. This is the post open heart unit. People come out of here after just having cracked their chest. We were expected to be conservative."

Title VII makes it an unlawful employment practice for an employer "to fail or refuse to hire or to discharge any individual, or otherwise to discriminate against any individual with respect to his compensation, terms, conditions, or privileges of employment, because of such individual's race, color, religion, sex, or national origin. . . ." Defendants seek summary judgment dismissing the complaint on the ground that plaintiff cannot make a prima facie showing that they engaged in discriminatory conduct.

To establish a prima facie case of individualized disparate treatment from an alleged discriminatory enforcement of the dress code, plaintiff must show that she is a member of a protected class and that, at the time of the alleged discriminatory treatment, she was satisfactorily performing the duties of her position. This she has done. However, her prima facie showing must also include a showing that Mount Sinai Hospital had a dress code and that it was applied to her under circumstances giving rise to an inference of discrimination.

Reviewing all of the evidence submitted on the motion, employee does not raise an issue of fact as to whether the enforcement of the code against her was discriminatory. There is no dispute that employee was in violation of the dress code. Her claim is that the dress code was enforced against her but not against others, who also violated its requirements, but were not black. The problem is the utter lack of evidence supporting this position.

Employee offers no evidence that the dress code was not enforced against other Hospital employees as it was against her. Dr. Shields' testimony that the dress code had been enforced against other nurses was not disputed. Although Ms. Ali identified certain caucasian women whom she believed were in violation of the code, she failed to set forth any evidence to show a lack of enforcement.

All that employee's testimony establishes is that she was unaware of the enforcement of the dress code against others. Following a full opportunity for discovery, employee has not proffered any additional evidence to support her claim of disparate treatment. On this record, there is no reason to believe that she will be able to offer at trial evidence from which a jury could reasonably conclude that there was racially discriminatory enforcement of the dress code.

It is not enough that Ms. Ali sincerely believes that she was the subject of discrimination; "[a] plaintiff is not entitled to a trial based on pure speculation, no matter how earnestly held." Summary judgment is appropriate here because employee has failed to raise an issue of fact as to whether the dress code was enforced against her under circumstances giving rise to an inference of discrimination. Motion to dismiss GRANTED.

Case Questions

1. What do you think of the way in which Ali was approached by Dr. Shields about her violation of the dress code? Does this seem advisable to you?

2. How much of a role do you think different cultural values played in this situation? Explain.

3. What can the employer do to avoid even the appearance of unfair enforcement of its dress policy in the future?

Management Tips

Since potentially all employees can bind the employer by their discriminatory actions, it is important for all employees to understand the law. This not only will greatly aid them in avoiding acts that may cause the employer liability, but it will also go far in creating a work environment in which discrimination is less likely to occur. Through training, make sure that all employees understand:

- What Title VII is.
- What Title VII requires.

- Who Title VII applies to.
- How the employees' actions can bring about liability for the employer.
- What kinds of actions will be looked at in a Title VII proceeding.
- That the employer will not allow Title VII to be violated.
- That all employees have a right to a workplace free of illegal discrimination.

Summary

- Title VII prohibits employers, unions, joint labor–management committees, and employment agencies from discriminating in any aspect of employment on the basis of race, color, religion, gender, or national origin.
- Title VII addresses subtle as well as overt discrimination; disparate treatment as well as disparate impact; and discrimination that is intentional as well as unintentional.
- The law allows for compensatory and punitive damages, where appropriate, as well as jury trials.
- The employer's best defense is a good offense. A strong, top-down policy of nondiscrimination can be effective in setting the right tone and getting the message to managers and employees alike that discrimination in employment will not be tolerated.
- Strong policies, consistently and appropriately enforced, as well as periodic training and updating as issues emerge, and even as a means of review, are most helpful.
- To the extent that an employer complies with Title VII, it can safely be said that workplace productivity will benefit, as will the employer's coffers, because unlawful employment discrimination can be costly to the employer in more ways than one.

Chapter-End Questions

1. While reviewing preemployment reports as part of her job, the claimant read a report in which an applicant admitted commenting to an employee at a prior job that "making love to you is like making love to the Grand Canyon." Later, at a meeting convened by her supervisor, the supervisor read the quote and said he didn't understand it. A male subordinate said he would explain it to him later, and both chuckled. The claimant interpreted the exchange as sexual harassment and reported it internally. The claimant alleges that nearly every action after the incident constituted retaliation for her complaint, including a lateral transfer. Will the court agree? [*Clark County School District* v. *Breeden,* 121 S.Ct. 1508 (2001).]

2. How long does a private employee have to file a claim with the EEOC or be barred from doing so?

3. Lin Teung files a complaint with the EEOC for national origin discrimination. His jurisdiction has a 706 agency. When Teung calls up the EEOC after 45 days to see how his case is progressing, he learns that the EEOC has not yet moved on it. Teung feels the EEOC is violating its own rules. Is it?

4. Althea, black, has been a deejay for a local Christian music station for several years. The station gets a new general manager and within a month he terminates Althea. The reason he gave was that it was inappropriate for a black deejay to play music on a white Christian music station. Althea sues the station. What is her best theory for proceeding?

5. Melinda wants to file a sexual harassment claim against her employer but feels she cannot do so because he would retaliate against her by firing her. She also has no money to sue him. Any advice for Melinda?

6. Saeid, a Muslim, alleges that his supervisor made numerous remarks belittling his Muslim religion, Arabs generally, and him specifically. The comments were not made in the context of a specific employment decision affecting Saeid. Is this sufficient for the court to find discriminatory ill will? [*Maarouf* v. *Walker Manufacturing Co.,* 210 F.3d 750 (7th Cir. 2000).]

7. A construction company was sued for harassment when it failed to take seriously the complaints about offensive graffiti scrawled on rented portable toilets. The employer defended

by saying (1) employees should be used to such rude and crude behavior, (2) the employer did not own or maintain the equipment, which came with graffiti already on it, (3) it took action after a formal employee complaint, and (4) the graffiti insulted everyone. Will the defenses be successful? [*Malone* v. *Foster-Wheeler Constructors,* 21 Fed. Appx. 470 (Westlaw) (7th Cir. 2001) (unpub. opinion).]

8. An employee files a race discrimination claim against the employer under Title VII. The employee alleges that after filing a claim with the EEOC, her ratings went from outstanding to satisfactory and she was excluded from meetings and important workplace communications, which made it impossible for her to satisfactorily perform her job. The court denied the race discrimination claim. Must it also deny the retaliation claim? [*Lafate* v. *Chase Manhattan Bank,* 123 F. Supp.2d 773 (D.DE 2000).]

9. Day Care Center has a policy stating that no employee can be over 5 feet 4 inches, because the employer thinks children feel more comfortable with people who are closer to them in size. Does Tiffany, who is 5 feet 7 inches, have a claim? If so, under what theory could she proceed?

10. During the interview Gale had with Leslie Accounting Firm, Gale was asked whether she had any children, whether she planned to have any more children, to what church she belonged, and what her husband did for a living. Are these questions illegal? Explain.

Chapter **Three**

Legal Construction of the Employment Environment

Chapter Outline

Opening Scenarios

SCENARIO 1

1 Scenario

Wendy Swan is asked to fill two new positions at her company. The first requires complicated engineering knowledge; the second has no prerequisites and no opportunity for advancement without a college degree. Wendy wants to hire younger workers so they will be more likely to have a long tenure at the firm. The advertisement for the positions placed in a newspaper of general circulation requests résumés from "recent college graduates," engineering degrees preferred. Is Wendy's firm subject to any liability based on this advertisement?

SCENARIO 2

2 Scenario

Shefali Trivedi is the manager at a large food store and has hired many young employees to work for her on a part-time basis. During the past few weeks, she has noticed that she is missing a sizable amount of her stock in many different areas. She has no idea where to begin a search for suspects but is convinced that it is an "inside" job, because her security during nonworking hours is excellent. Can she simply notify each of her employees that they will all be required to submit to a polygraph test to determine who is involved, or should she perform additional investigation and use the polygraph test only as a means of confirmation of suspicion?

In addition, Shefali has not yet purchased computerized checkout scanners, and therefore all of the product prices must be input by hand to the store registers. Shefali has found in the past that certain employees are able to perform this task at a much more rapid pace than others. To maintain store efficiency, she decides to test all applicants relating to their ability to input prices into the register. After administering an on-site timed test, she finds that 12 white applicants, 2 black applicants, and 1 Hispanic applicant are represented among the top 15 performers, in that order of performance. Shefali has five positions available. Will she be subject to liability for disparate impact discrimination if she proceeds to hire the five top performers, all of whom are white?

SCENARIO 3

3 Scenario

Mark-Jonathan is the supervisor of 12 employees, most of whom generally perform adequate work in conformance with company job descriptions and standards. However, he has had problems in completing the performance appraisals of two employees.

The first employee is Gordy, a young man who went through a divorce during the past year. He was awarded custody of his children and has had a difficult time throughout this past year balancing his increased familial responsibilities with his job requirements. He has missed several important meetings as a result. Gordy has received two written warnings about his inadequate performance, and a poor year-end performance appraisal would mean an automatic dismissal. However, Mark-Jonathan is confident that Gordy will be able to successfully manage these two priorities in the coming year, if only given the chance. Does Mark-Jonathan draft an honest appraisal of his past performance with the knowledge that it would mean Gordy would lose his job according to company policy, or does he decide to use his discretion and offer a less than truthful assessment, knowing that it is in the company's best interest to retain this employee?

Mark-Jonathan's dilemma is accentuated by the fact that he is to review Julio, an Argentinean worker who holds a position similar to Gordy's. Julio is consistently late for work and has also received two written warnings about his inadequate performance. Mark-Jonathan has no idea why Julio arrives late, and, when asked, Julio offers no sufficient justification. If Mark-Jonathan writes a performance evaluation that highlights this poor behavior, similar to Gordy's, and terminates Julio but not Gordy (a white male), Mark-Jonathan is concerned about the potential for discrimination implications.

EVOLUTION OF THE EMPLOYMENT RELATIONSHIP

The human resources of a firm are among its most valuable assets; consequently, the utmost discretion must be used in their selection process. The law recognizes this and permits employers much leeway in choosing, managing, and terminating employees. Virtually the only restrictions on the employment relationship are the laws that protect

Exhibit 3.1   Myths about Hiring Your Employee or Getting Your Job

1. The best way to promote workplace unity is to get hiring suggestions only from those who already work there.
2. As long as an advertisement is placed somewhere in the city where hiring is to be done, an employer cannot be accused of selective recruiting.
3. The purpose of this interview is for the employer to find out information about the employee. The employer can hide information about itself.
4. There's nothing wrong with promoting only from within; after all, it raises employee morale and encourages devotion.
5. The only problem with nepotism (favoring family members in hiring decisions) is that present employees may resent the hired family member and believe he or she got the job because of the familial connection.

certain groups from employment discrimination (as will be discussed). History has demonstrated a need for such protection. As we will see, discrimination in employment, whether intentional or unintentional, is allowed unless it is based on or has a different impact on individuals from an impermissible category, such as gender, race, and the like. Employers looking for a salesperson may discriminate against applicants who cannot get along well with others; employers hiring computer technicians may discriminate on the basis of computer training; and other individuals may be discriminated against for equally permissible reasons. (See Exhibit 3.1.)

The focus of this chapter will be on the evolution of the employment relationship, from recruitment of appropriate candidates, through hiring, testing, and performance appraisals. Though the chapter will not reiterate completely the nature of Title VII regulation discussed in Chapter 2, it is difficult to discuss the regulation of this evolution without heavily drawing on those parameters. Accordingly, we will briefly mention appropriate and applicable laws as they arise, though fuller coverage will be given to these issues in the chapters that follow.

Establishing the employment relationship begins with recruitment. Employers use a variety of techniques to locate suitable applicants. Once the employer has a group from which to choose, information gathering begins. This stage consists of soliciting information from the applicant through forms, interviews, references, and testing. Targeting recruitment and selection has been found to be the most effective way to reduce employment discrimination charges. While testing will be addressed in the following chapter, this chapter will discuss regulation of the means by which employers establish the employment relationship.

RECRUITMENT

The first step in the evolution of the employment relationship is the employer's recruitment of the worker. Recruitment practices are particularly susceptible to claims of discrimination as barriers to equal opportunity. If applicants are denied access to employment opportunities on the basis of membership in a protected class, they may have a claim against the potential employer for discriminatory practice. Recruitment, as with every other phase of the employment process, is subject to government regulation, including Title VII of the Civil Rights Act of 1964, the Rehabilitation Act of 1973 (if a federal agency, employer, or contractor), the Americans with Disabilities Act of 1990 (if a private sector employer), the Age Discrimination in Employment Act of 1967, the Immigration Reform and Control Act of 1986, and various state laws relating to fair employment practices.

In part, these statutes require that an employer not only recruit from a diverse audience but also design employment announcements that will encourage a diverse group of applicants. How does the employer obtain its applicant pool? Does it place an advertisement in a local newspaper, advertise on the radio in a given neighborhood, ask certain people to submit résumés, ask current employees for suggestions? Does the advertisement contain gender-specific language that would discourage certain groups from applying for the position? Each of these possibilities has potential hazards. When the employer utilizes recruitment practices that result in an adverse impact on a group protected by antidiscrimination statutes, that practice may be wrongful even if the employer had no intent to discriminate.

Federal Statutory Regulation of Recruitment

As mentioned, to prevent liability, employers must be aware of several laws when recruiting employees (see Exhibit 3.2).

Additionally, the EEOC has offered important guidance on disability-related inquiries of applicants as well as employees under the Americans with Disabilities Act, which is covered in Chapter 12. Prior to an offer of employment, an employer may not ask disability-related questions or require any medical examinations, even if they are related to the job. However, the EEOC's Enforcement Guidances offer that an employer may ask whether an applicant will need a "reasonable accommodation" during the hiring process (e.g., interview, written test, job demonstration). The employer may also inquire whether the applicant will need a reasonable accommodation for the job if the employer knows that an applicant has a disability. If an employer cannot inquire about an applicant's disability, then how would the employer know? Either the disability is obvious or the applicant has voluntarily disclosed the information, and the employer reasonably believes that the applicant will need a reasonable accommodation.

The employer must provide a reasonable accommodation to a qualified applicant with a disability even if it believes that it will be unable to provide this individual with a reasonable accommodation on the job. According to the EEOC, in many instances, employers will be unable to determine whether an individual needs reasonable accommodation to perform the job based solely on a request for accommodation during the application process, or whether the same type or degree of accommodation will be needed on the job as was required for the application process.

State Employment Law Regulation

Many states have enacted legislation specifically aimed at expansion of the federal statutes above. For instance, many states have human rights acts that include in their protections the prohibitions against discrimination based on marital status or affinity orientation. The statutes generally establish a state human rights commission, which

Exhibit 3.2   Federal Laws Regulating Recruitment

TITLE VII OF THE CIVIL RIGHTS ACT OF 1964

Section 703(a)(1)   It shall be an unlawful employment practice for an employer to fail or refuse to hire . . . any individual or otherwise to discriminate against any individual with respect to his [sic] compensation, terms, conditions, or privileges of employment, because of such individual's race, color, religion, sex, or national origin.

Section 704(b)   It shall be an unlawful employment practice for an employer, . . . to print or cause to be printed or published any notice or advertisement relating to employment by such an employer indicating any preference, limitation, specification, or discrimination based on race, color, religion, sex, or national origin, except that such a notice or advertisement may indicate a preference, limitation, specification, or discrimination based on religion, sex, or national origin when religion, sex, or national origin is a bona fide occupational qualification for employment.

VOCATIONAL REHABILITATION ACT OF 1973 AND THE AMERICANS WITH DISABILITIES ACT OF 1990

The Rehabilitation Act and the Americans with Disabilities Act, which will be covered in depth in Chapter 12, protect otherwise qualified individuals with disabilities. The former regulates the employment practices of federal contractors, agencies, and employers, while the latter act applies similar standards to private sector employers of 25 (15, effective July 1993) employees or more.

The Rehabilitation Act specifically provides that, in connection with recruitment, contractors and their subcontractors who have contracts with the government in excess of $10,000 must design and commit to an affirmative action program with the purpose of providing employment opportunities to disabled applicants. Affirmative action recruitment programs may include specific recruitment plans for universities for the disabled, designing positions that will easily accommodate a disabled employee, and adjusting work schedules to conform to the needs of certain applicants.

AGE DISCRIMINATION IN EMPLOYMENT ACT OF 1967

All employers of 20 or more employees are subject to the act, which prohibits discrimination against an individual 40 years of age or older, unless age is a bona fide occupational qualification. In addition, the act states:

Section 4(e)   It shall be unlawful for an employer . . . to print or publish, or cause to be printed or published, any notice or advertisement relating to employment . . . indicating any preference, limitation, specification or discrimination based on age.

IMMIGRATION REFORM AND CONTROL ACT OF 1986

IRCA is slightly different in its regulation of recruitment. IRCA applies to all employers. IRCA's purpose is to eliminate work opportunities that attract illegal aliens to the United States. With regard to discrimination based on national origin, the act provides that all employers must determine the eligibility of each individual they intend to hire, prior to the commencement of employment. In this way, IRCA condones discrimination against illegal aliens in recruitment. Note that while IRCA applies to all employers, its discrimination provisions apply only to those with four employees or more.

Exhibit 3.3   Common-Law Recruitment Violations

FRAUD

1. Misrepresentation
2. Of a material fact
3. With the intent to deceive or recklessness about truth or falsity
4. On which the applicant reasonably relies
5. To her or his detriment

MISREPRESENTATION

1. False statement.
2. True statement creating a false impression.
3. Silence where:
   - It is necessary to correct applicant's mistaken belief about material facts.
   - There is active concealment of material facts.
   - It is necessary to correct an employer's statement that was true at the time made but subsequently became false.

MATERIAL FACTS

1. Statement of fact
2. Which will influence
3. A reasonable person
4. Regarding whether to enter into a contract

Note that opinions are not material facts because it would be generally unreasonable to rely fully on the opinion of another in arriving at a decision.

---

hears claims brought under the state act. Several other states have enacted legislation that closely mirrors Title VII but covers a larger number of employers. In the case below, the court addresses the marital status provision of the Minnesota statute.

Common Law: Misrepresentations and Fraud

Employers should be careful of statements and promises made during the recruitment process. A company representative who makes an intentional or negligent misrepresentation that encourages an applicant to take a job may be liable to that applicant for harm that results. Misrepresentations may include claims regarding the terms of the job offer, including the type of position available, the salary to be paid, the job requirements, and other matters directly relating to the representation of the offer.

To be successful in a misrepresentation action, the applicant must show that the employer misrepresented a material fact, either intentionally or with recklessness about its truth or falsity, that the applicant reasonably relied on this representation in arriving at the decision to accept the offer, and that she or he was damaged by this reliance. (See Exhibit 3.3.)

For example, assume an applicant is told by her employer at the time when she is hired that she will automatically receive a raise at her six-month review. Based on this representation, the applicant accepts an offer. Six months pass and she does not receive the promised raise. She would be able to sue her employer for the misrepresentation that induced her to take the job.

Additionally, the misrepresentation need not actually be a false statement: Where a statement creates a false impression, the employer may also be liable for fraud. Or, where the employer is aware that the applicant is under a mistaken belief about the position or the company, the employer's silence may constitute misrepresentation.

Where the employer hides certain bits of information, the employer's silence may again be considered misrepresentation. For instance, suppose an employer needs someone to serve as an assistant to the president of the company. The president has a reputation for being unpleasant to his assistants and for constantly firing them. The employer, therefore, solicits applications for a general administrative position, "with specific duties to be assigned later," knowing the hiree will spend the majority of time working for the president.

Someone applies for the job and states during his interview that he would like the position and says he is glad that it is not the assistant-to-the-president position for which they were interviewing last month. He is hired, and, even though he has an excellent offer from another company for more money, decides to take the job because he likes the work environment. Later he is told that he will be spending a large part of his workday with the president. The employee could sue the employer for misrepresentation, even though the employer did not respond to his statement about the president during the interview.

Employers may also be liable for fraud in recruitment when misstatements are used to discourage potential applicants from pursuing positions. For instance, an employer who wishes to maintain a male-dominated workforce may intentionally present an excessively negative image of the position or the company in an effort to persuade females not to apply. If all candidates are offered the same information, there may be no basis for a discrimination claim. However, if only the female applicants receive this discouraging outlook, the practice presents to the female applicants a "chilling" effect and the employer may be subject to claims of gender discrimination.

Application of Regulation to Recruitment Practices

Advertisements

Statutes and the common-law claim of fraud protect applicants from discriminatory recruitment practices, ranging from a refusal to interview Latinos to a job notice that is posted only in the executive suite where it will be seen primarily by white males. Assume, for instance, that an employer advertises in a newspaper that is circulated in a neighborhood that has an extremely high Asian population with very few other minorities represented; also, that the employer can expect to see almost all of its applications from Asians and few, if any, applications from other groups. While there may be no intent to discriminate, the effect of the practice is an unbalanced workforce with a disparate impact on non-Asians.

In connection with scenario 1, recall that Wendy is concerned about placing an advertisement requesting résumés from "recent college grads." Older workers may claim that they are discouraged from applying due to the language—they are less likely to be "recent" college grads. On the other hand, language such as this does not constitute a *per se* violation. Instead, the applicant would have to establish a prima facie case of age discrimination. Though terminology such as this seems to be a minor concern to some, courts have found that it may lead to a belief that stereotyping or pigeonholing of one gender or a certain age group in certain positions is condoned by the law. Consider Dominick's supermarket's experience when it named the second-in-command of its deli section the "Second Deli Man," notwithstanding whether the person was male or female. Maybe someone at Dominick's noticed the inconsistency this might create, but probably no one expected a class-action suit by 1,500 women alleging gender discrimination! While this was only one of numerous pieces of evidence, it may have made a difference in encouraging a settlement.

Word-of-Mouth Recruiting

The same discriminatory effect may occur where an employer obtains its new employees from referrals from within its own workforce, or "word-of-mouth" recruiting. Generally most people know and recommend others similar to themselves. Word-of-mouth recruiting generally results in a homogeneous workplace.

This type of recruiting is not necessarily harmful where precautions are taken to ensure a balanced applicant pool or where it is necessary for ensuring hire of the safest and most competent workers. Benefits to this type of recruitment include the preliminary screening accomplished by the current employees before they even recommend the applicant for the position, and the propensity for long-term service and loyalty among the new hires. Since they already have bonds to the company, a family attitude toward the firm, resulting in increased productivity, is more easily developed. In fact, a 2001 survey by the Society for Human Resource Management found that almost 70 percent of respondents considered employee referral programs more cost-effective than other recruiting methods.[1] But, consider how this might lead to liability under Title VII.

The following two cases present the court's analysis of word-of-mouth recruiting efforts. Consider the distinction between *disparate impact* and *disparate treatment* in the context of word-of-mouth recruiting. What are the questions a court must answer to determine if word-of-mouth recruiting results in disparate treatment? Could word-of-mouth recruiting ever lead to liability for disparate impact?

[1] "Word of Mouth Is Best Recruiting Method," http://www.relojournal.com/july2001/referral.htm.

Equal Employment Opportunity Commission v. Chicago Miniature Lamp Works *947 F.2d 292 (7th Cir. 1991)*

The employer hired employees for entry-level positions through word of mouth. There were only one or two black employees in entry-level positions and there were very few black applicants.

The EEOC claimed that Chicago Miniature Lamp Works (Miniature) discriminated against blacks in its recruitment and hiring of its entry-level workers. Miniature's principal method of obtaining new entry-level workers was almost exclusively based on word of mouth in order to fill its entry-level job openings. Employees would simply tell their relatives and friends about the nature of the job—if interested, these persons then would come to Miniature's office and complete an application form. Miniature did not tell or encourage its employees to recruit in this manner. The evidence indicates that the only time Miniature initiated this word-of-mouth process was when it adopted an affirmative action plan. At that time, Miniature asked one or two black employees to recruit black applicants from among their relatives and friends. Evidence indicated that 1 person was hired for every 15 who applied. Because of the success of this process, Miniature never advertised for these jobs, and only rarely used the State of Illinois unemployment referral service.

Between 1978 and 1981, Miniature hired 146 entry-level workers. Nine of these workers (6 percent) were black. The trial court concluded that "the statistical probability of Chicago Miniature's hiring so few blacks in the 1978–81 period, in the absence of racial bias against blacks in recruitment and hiring, is virtually zero." The trial court also concluded that racial bias was the reason for the disparities between the percentage of blacks in Miniature's entry-level workforce for the years 1970–1981 and the percentage of black entry-level workers in Chicago. However, the court of appeals reversed.

Cummings, J.

***

. . . Congress intended a delicate balance, strongly condemning discrimination on account of a protected characteristic, yet recognizing that racial imbalances in the workforce may result from legitimate, nondiscriminatory factors. A recognition of this tension informs our analysis in this case.

The district court found Miniature liable based on both a disparate treatment and a disparate impact model. Although it is clear that the same set of facts can support both theories of liability, it is important to treat each model separately because each has its own theoretical underpinnings. The disparate treatment model is based most directly on Title VII's statutory language and requires an inquiry into the defendant's state of mind. The defendant is liable under this model when the plaintiff can prove that the defendant subjectively intended to discriminate against the plaintiff on account of a protected trait.

In a disparate impact case, however, motive is irrelevant. "Under the Act, practices . . . neutral on their face, and even neutral in terms of intent, cannot be maintained if they operate to 'freeze' the status quo of prior discriminatory employment practices." The line between disparate impact and disparate treatment cases is most blurred in "pattern and practice" cases such as this one, because statistics can be used to prove both disparate treatment and disparate impact.

A. DISPARATE TREATMENT

A prima facie case for a pattern or practice of disparate treatment can be established by "statistical evidence demonstrating substantial disparities in the application of employment actions as to minorities . . . buttressed by evidence of general policies or specific instances of discrimination." The plaintiff must prove "more than the mere occurrence of isolated or 'accidental' or sporadic discriminatory acts." Instead, the plaintiff must show that racial discrimination was the "standard operating procedure—the regular rather than the unusual practice."

As part of its attempt to separate its recruiting and hiring practices, Miniature argues that it did not recruit and therefore, as a matter of logic, it could not have recruited discriminatorily. We reject this simplistic syllogism. . . .

***

. . . Miniature has recruited; it made an intentional decision to rely on word of mouth to attract applicants for its entry-level openings. Miniature knew how workers were learning of its employment opportunities. When it adopted an affirmative action plan in 1977, it made an effort to tell its black employees to contact their friends and relatives in order to increase the effectiveness of its word-of-mouth network in the black community. Miniature also used other recruiting procedures at times. It used newspaper advertisements to attract clerical and secretarial applicants. On occasion it used a job referral service. But Miniature obviously intentionally chose not to use these two forms of recruiting for its entry-level workers.

***

We reject defendant's claim that "Miniature cannot be held liable because it did not commit any act." It was the trial court's finding that Miniature's overall entry-level hiring decisions were made with racial animus. It is true that the trial court focused on Miniature's reliance on word of mouth as evidence of its discriminatory intent. . . . Miniature's passive reliance on word of mouth to generate applicants must be given minimal weight because it involved no affirmative act by Miniature. Drawing the inference of intent from "nonaction" is necessarily more difficult than drawing the inference of intent from particular actions. This is especially true since intent means more than knowledge that a certain action (or nonaction) will cause certain discriminatory results. Intent means a subjective desire or wish for these discriminatory results to occur.

A pattern or practice of disparate treatment is shown through a combination of "statistical evidence demonstrating substantial disparities . . . buttressed by evidence of general policies or specific instances of discrimination." . . .

Miniature argues that the EEOC's statistics are clearly erroneous because they do not include the following considerations: relative commuting distance, shift preference, and lack of an English fluency requirement. The EEOC responds that any attack on its statistical evidence should be precluded, since Miniature did not include these variables in its own statistical analysis.

***

It is clear that Miniature was held liable because there were relatively few blacks in its applicant pool as compared to the number of entry-level black workers in Chicago. The EEOC's statistical expert used a very simple demographic model. The applicant's race was the only variable considered in the model, and Miniature's racial composition was compared with the racial composition of Chicago as a whole.

***

The trial court erred in concluding that Miniature was liable under Title VII for disparate treatment of blacks. This is one of those rare cases where the statistical evidence credited by the lower court does not support liability. Anecdotal evidence of intentional discrimination, only tangentially relied upon by the lower court, also fails to carry the day for the EEOC.

B. DISPARATE IMPACT

When conducting its disparate impact analysis, the trial court again focused on the statistics put forward by the EEOC's expert and on Miniature's reliance on word-of-mouth recruiting. Underscoring the basic similarity in the two approaches, the court began by stating that the "EEOC's statistics are not open to rebuttal under the disparate-impact model any more than under the

disparate-treatment model." The district court recognized that under a disparate-impact approach a plaintiff must identify a particular practice that caused the disparate impact. In this case, the district court considered the "particular practice" to be reliance on word-of-mouth recruiting. Since "Chicago Miniature has not even sought to offer any evidence tending to show its reliance on word-of-mouth recruiting is business-related," the court concluded that the EEOC's disparate impact case was established and unrebutted.

We concluded above that it was clearly erroneous for the trial court to rely on the statistical evidence put forward by the EEOC. Since the EEOC relied on the same evidence to uphold liability under its disparate impact claim that it relied upon for its disparate treatment claim, it was also clearly erroneous for the trial court to support its findings of disparate impact with this statistical evidence.

There is another reason that the holding of disparate impact liability against Miniature cannot stand. In a disparate impact case, "plaintiff is . . . responsible for isolating and identifying the specific employment practices that are allegedly responsible for any observed statistical disparities." The EEOC does not allege that Miniature affirmatively engaged in word-of-mouth recruitment of the kind where it told or encouraged its employees to refer applicants for entry-level jobs. Instead, it is uncontested that Miniature passively waited for applicants who typically learned of opportunities from current Miniature employees. The court erred in considering passive reliance on employee word-of-mouth recruiting as a particular employment practice for the purposes of disparate impact. The practices here are undertaken solely by employees. Therefore, disparate impact liability against Miniature must be reversed.

As stated above, the reliance on word of mouth to obtain applicants for jobs does not insulate an employer from a finding of disparate treatment of minorities. However, for the purposes of disparate impact, a more affirmative act by the employer must be shown in order to establish causation. "[A] Title VII plaintiff does not make out a case of disparate impact simply by showing that, 'at the bottom line,' there is a racial imbalance in the work force." The EEOC here, in essence, is attacking Miniature's overall hiring procedure by pointing to the "bottom line" results; it has not made the more focused allegation required by *Wards Cove* that a specific, affirmative employment practice caused the disparity between entry-level workers at Miniature and entry-level workers throughout Chicago.

There is no doubt that racial discrimination in employment remains widespread in Chicago. Without probative evidence of discriminatory intent, however, Miniature is not liable when it passively relies on the natural flow of applicants for its entry-level positions. Miniature's entry-level hiring practices were straightforward, simple, and effective. The EEOC's misspecified statistical model that ignored commuting distance and language fluency requirements, when unaccompanied by more probative anecdotal testimony, cannot support a ruling that Miniature violated Title VII by discriminating against blacks. Therefore, the trial court erred in finding Miniature liable under Title VII. Its disparate treatment and disparate impact findings were clearly erroneous because they credited statistics that did not take into account applicant preference and because the anecdotal evidence presented at trial was not sufficiently probative. In addition, the EEOC's disparate impact theory fails because the EEOC did not specifically identify a particular practice by the employer that caused any disparity. REVERSED.

Case Questions

1. Would an unbalanced workforce due to word-of-mouth recruiting alone ever constitute disparate treatment?

2. Consider your and the court's response to the above question. Would your decision be different if it could be shown that, in a certain small, all-white firm, recruiting was done only using word of mouth and this effort resulted in only white applicants?

3. How would you balance the advantages of word-of-mouth recruiting against the possibility of discriminatory impact?

EEOC v. Consolidated Service System　*989 F.2d 233 (7th Cir. 1993)*

Defendant is a small janitorial firm in Chicago owned by Mr. Hwang, a Korean immigrant, and staffed mostly by Koreans. The firm relied mainly on word-of-mouth recruiting. Between 1983 and 1987, 73 percent of the applicants for jobs and 81 percent of the hires were Korean, while less than 1 percent of the workforce in the Chicago area is Korean. The district court found that these discrepancies were not due to discrimination.

Posner, J.

We said that Consolidated is a small company. The EEOC's lawyer told us at argument that the company's annual sales are only $400,000. We mention this fact not to remind the reader of David and Goliath, or to suggest that Consolidated is exempt from Title VII (it is not), or to express wonderment that a firm of this size could litigate in federal court for seven years (and counting) with a federal agency, but to explain why Mr. Hwang relies on word of mouth to obtain employees rather than reaching out to a broader community less heavily Korean. It is the cheapest method of recruitment. Indeed, it is practically costless. Persons approach Hwang or his employees—most of whom are Korean too—at work or at social events, and once or twice Hwang has asked employees whether they know anyone who wants a job. At argument the EEOC's lawyer conceded, perhaps improvidently but if so only slightly so, the Hwang's recruitment posture could be described as totally passive. Hwang did buy newspaper advertisements on three occasions—once in a Korean-language newspaper and twice in the *Chicago Tribune*—but as these ads resulted in zero hires, the experience doubtless only confirmed him in the passive posture. The EEOC argues that the single Korean newspaper ad, which ran for only three days and yielded not a single hire, is evidence of discrimination. If so, it is very weak evidence. The Commission points to the fact that Hwang could have obtained job applicants at no expense from the Illinois Job Service as further evidence of discrimination. But he testified that he had never heard of the Illinois Job Service and the district judge believed him.

If an employer can obtain all the competent workers he wants, at wages no higher than the minimum that he expects to have to pay, without beating the bushes for workers—without in fact spending a cent on recruitment—he can reduce his costs of doing business by adopting just the stance of Mr. Hwang. And this is no mean consideration to a firm whose annual revenues in a highly competitive business are those of a mom and pop grocery store. Of course if the employer is a member of an ethnic community, especially an immigrant one, this stance is likely to result in the perpetuation of an ethnically imbalanced workforce. Members of these communities tend to work and to socialize with each other rather than with people in the larger community. The social and business network of an immigrant community racially and culturally distinct from the majority of Americans is bound to be largely confined to that community, making it inevitable that when the network is used for job recruitment the recruits will be drawn disproportionately from the community.

No inference of *intentional* discrimination can be drawn from the pattern we have described, even if the employer would prefer to employ people drawn predominantly or even entirely from his own ethnic or, here, national-origin community. Discrimination is not preference or aversion; it is acting on the preference or aversion. If the most efficient method of hiring adopted *because* it is the most efficient (not defended because it is efficient—the statute does not allow an employer to justify intentional discrimination by reference to efficiency) just happens to produce a workforce whose racial or religious or ethnic or national-origin or gender composition pleases the employer, this is not intentional discrimination. The motive is not a discriminatory one. "Knowledge of a disparity is not the same thing as an intent to cause or maintain it." Or if, though the motives behind adoption of the method were a mixture of discrimination and efficiency, Mr. Hwang would have adopted the identical method of recruitment even if he had no interest in the national origin of his employees, the fact that he had such an interest would not be a "but for" cause of the discriminatory outcome and again there would be no liability. There is no evidence that Hwang is biased in favor of Koreans or prejudiced against any group underrepresented in his workforce, except what the Commission asks us to infer from the imbalance in that force and Hwang's passive stance.

If this were a disparate-impact case (as it was once, but the Commission has abandoned its claim of disparate impact), and, if, contrary to *EEOC* v. *Chicago Miniature Lamp Works,* word of mouth recruitment were deemed an employment practice and hence was subject to review for disparate impact, as assumed in *Clark* v. *Chrysler Corp.,* then the advantages of word-of-mouth recruitment would have to be balanced against its possibly discriminatory effect when the employer's current workforce is already skewed along racial or other disfavored lines. But in a case of disparate treatment, the question is different. It is whether word-of-mouth recruitment gives rise to an inference of intentional discrimination. Unlike an explicit racial or ethnic criterion or, what we may assume without deciding amounts to the same thing, a rule confining hiring to relatives of existing employees in a racially or ethnically skewed workforce, as in *Thomas* v. *Washington County School Board,* word-of-mouth recruiting does not compel an inference of intentional discrimination. At least it does not do so where, as in the case of Consolidated Services Systems, it is clearly, as we have been at pains to emphasize, the cheapest and most efficient method of recruitment, notwithstanding its discriminatory impact. Of course, Consolidated had some non-Korean applicants for employment, and if it had never hired any this would support, perhaps decisively, as inference of discrimination. Although the respective percentages of Korean and of non-Korean applicants hired were clearly favorable to Koreans (33 percent to 20 percent), the EEOC was unable to find a single person out of the 99 rejected non-Koreans who could show that he or she was interested in a job that Mr. Hwang ever hired for. Many, perhaps most, of these were persons who responded to the ad he placed in the *Chicago Tribune* for a contract that he never got, hence never hired for.

The Commission cites the statement of Consolidated's lawyer that his client took advantage of the fact that the Korean immigrant community offered a ready market of cheap labor as an admission of "active" discrimination on the basis of national origin. It is not discrimination, and it is certainly not active discrimination, for an employer to sit back and wait for people willing to work for low wages to apply to him. The fact that they are ethnically or racially uniform does not impose upon him a duty to spend money advertising in the help-wanted columns of the *Chicago Tribune*. The Commission deemed Consolidated's "admission" corroborated by the testimony of the sociologist William Liu, Consolidated's own expert witness, who explained that it was natural for a recent Korean immigrant such as Hwang to hire other recent Korean immigrants, with whom he shared a common culture, and that the consequence would be a workforce disproportionately Korean. Well, of course. People who share a common culture tend to work together as well as marry together and socialize together. That is not evidence of illegal discrimination.

In a nation of immigrants, this must be reckoned an ominous case despite its outcome. The United States has many recent immigrants, and today as historically they tend to cluster in their own communities, united by ties of language, culture, and background. Often they form small businesses composed largely of relatives, friends, and other members of their community, and they obtain new employees by word of mouth. These small businesses—grocery stores, furniture stores, clothing stores, cleaning services, restaurants, gas stations—have been for many immigrant groups, and continue to be, the first rung on the ladder of American success. Derided as clannish, resented for their ambition and hard work, hated or despised for their otherness, recent immigrants are frequent targets of discrimination, some of it violent. It would be a bitter irony if the federal agency dedicated to enforcing the antidiscrimination laws succeeded in using those laws to kick these people off the ladder by compelling them to institute costly systems of hiring. There is equal danger to small black-run businesses in our central cities. Must such businesses undertake in the name of nondiscrimination costly measures to recruit non-black employees?

Although Consolidated has been dragged through seven years of federal litigation at outrageous expense for a firm of its size, we agree with the Commission that this suit was not frivolous. The statistical disparity gave the Commission a leg up, and it might conceivably have succeeded in its disparate-impact claim but for our intervening decision in *EEOC* v. *Chicago Miniature Lamp Works,* supra. Had the judge believed the Commission's witnesses, the outcome even of the disparate-treatment claim might have been different. The Equal Access to Justice Act was intended, one might have thought, for just such a case as this, where a groundless but not frivolous suit is brought by the mighty federal government against a tiny firm; but Consolidated concedes its inapplicability. We do not know on what the concession is based—possibly on cases like *Escobar Ruiz* v. *INS,* on rehearing, holding the Act inapplicable to statutes that have their own fee-shifting statutes—but other cases, such as *Gavette* v. *Office of Personnel Management,* are contra. It may not be too late for Consolidated to reconsider its concession in light of our holding in *McDonald* v. *Schweiker,* supra, regarding the deadline for seeking fees under the Act.

AFFIRMED.

Case Questions

1. If the court in *Consolidated* ruled that, even though the statistics told another story, there was no evidence of "intentional" discrimination, would an unbalanced workforce due to word-of-mouth recruiting alone ever constitute disparate treatment?

2. Consider your and the court's response to the above question. Would your decision be different if it could be shown that, in a certain small, all-white firm, recruiting was done only using word of mouth and this effort resulted in only white applicants. Would your decision remain the same?

3. If this case were tried as a disparate impact case, as discussed by the court, how would you balance the advantages of word-of-mouth recruiting against the possibility of a discriminatory impact?

Nepotism

Nepotism is the practice of hiring members of the same family, and some employers rely on this to locate the most appropriate candidates. Such employers theorize that, if the mother and the firm are a "good fit," then the daughter may also work out well. Therefore, the least costly method of locating additional employees may be to ask current employees whether their family members may be interested in a position. This practice also results in homogeneity, as the company becomes a conglomerate of a number of homogeneous families, with greatest likelihood of discrimination resulting from a disparate impact.

Nepotism policies are not, per se, illegal. When an employee or applicant challenges the policy, the court will determine whether it has an adverse impact on a protected class. If so, it will be found illegal unless the employer has a strong justification in favor of its business necessity.

An antinepotism policy (one stating that the company will *not* hire family members) may also be discriminatory where it is not applied across the board. For example, if the antinepotism policy provides that a wife may not be hired if her husband is a current employee, but does not provide the parallel provision prohibiting the hiring of husbands of current employees, the policy may be discriminatory. Similar problems exist where the policy is enforced only at one level of the company. Where the line workers in a firm are primarily Hispanic and management is primarily white, an antinepotism policy for line workers that does not apply to management would result in disparate impact.

Courts have consistently upheld general antinepotism policies that provide that the company will not hire the *spouse* of a current employee, as long as there is no evidence of disparate impact or the policy applies to employees at all levels of employment.

Promoting from Within

While promoting from within the company is not in and of itself illegal, it also has the potential for discriminatory results, depending on the process used and the makeup of the workforce. Some employers use a secretive process, quietly soliciting interest in a position from a few upper-level employees selected on recommendations from their supervisors. The employer then conducts interviews with the candidates and extends an offer. After the employee accepts the offer, a notice is posted announcing the promotion. If women and minorities are not well represented in a firm, such a process may result in a disparate impact against them, even where the purpose of the employer is merely to locate and promote the most qualified candidate.

Employers are more likely to post a notice of position availability in which all employees are offered the opportunity to compete for open positions. The employer is less vulnerable to attack for discriminatory policies as long as the workforce is relatively balanced so there is equal employment opportunity.

Venue Recruiting

Employers may decide to conduct recruiting at a university or high school. Similar precautions must be taken to attract diverse applicants in a locale that may be either purposefully or unintentionally uniform. The same effect may result when an employer recruits with a preference for experienced applicants for entry-level jobs—for instance, recruiting firefighters and specifying a preference for applicants with experience in volunteer fire departments. The court held that this recruitment practice was wrongful, because volunteer fire departments tended to be hostile to minorities and to women as firefighters. Preference for firefighters with this experience, therefore, would lead to few, if any, women and minorities being hired. Employers should be aware of the effects of the composition of their workforce on women and minorities and the effects of the sources of their recruitment.

Walk-In Applicants

Recruiting may not be necessary where the company is constantly receiving unsolicited applications. Depending on the professional, potential employees may send their résumés to prospective employers in hopes of locating an open position, or of persuading them to create one. While this strategy may be effective in locating employees and reducing costs of actual formal recruiting, the company may find that its reputation attracts only one type of employee, while others are intimidated by, are unaware of, or are uninterested in the firm. Equal employment opportunity is again lost.

Neutral Solicitation

While selecting an appropriate source from which to choose applicants is crucial, it is also important to fashion the process to encourage diverse applicants. For instance, an advertisement that requests "recent college grads" may discourage older workers from applying and result in an adverse impact on them. Or a job announcement that states the employer is looking for "busboys" or "servicemen" may deter females from applying. Other terms that at first appear innocuous are discouraging to one group or another as well, including "draftsman," "saleswoman," "repairman," "waiter," "host," and "maid." The announcement or solicitation should invite applications from all groups and should not suggest a preference for any one class of individual.

Résumé Collection Concerns

Since applicants acquire certain rights simply by virtue of being applicants (such as the right under Title VII to sue for discrimination if rejected for inappropriate reasons), it is critical to control the processing of applications. If, for instance, you receive an inquiry by e-mail from the daughter of one of your friends, does this constitute an application? Is this woman an applicant? If you are not involved in this hiring process, the best response may be simply to leave the e-mail or attached résumé unopened (if possible!) and to forward it to the appropriate human resources individual.

Once an application is received, federal employers or contractors have a duty to keep records and collect information regarding compliance with selection or affirmative action requirements and other obligations. Other employers should retain this information as well, since (1) some statutes have record-keeping requirements, such as the Age Discrimination in Employment Act, and (2) one of the ways to refute an applicant's claim of discrimination is through statistical analysis of the applicant pool.

Since "applicant" is not defined by any of the enforcement bodies such as the EEOC or Department of Justice, it is a good idea for employers to do so for themselves. This definition could be useful in later litigation, if the situation arises. One example of a definition of an applicant is anyone who fills out one of the company's application forms. Those who do not fill out the prescribed form are *not* considered applicants. In this way, the firm has greater control over this pool and, therefore, over its obligations.

PREFERENTIAL TREATMENT

Preferential treatment, or more generally affirmative action, may be required by federal law depending on the employer, on the number of employees, and on the type of position available. This chapter will introduce the regulation of preferential treatment under various statutes, while the later chapter on affirmative action will address the substantive questions surrounding the extent to which employers have satisfied the requirements discussed here.

The difference between *preferential treatment* and affirmative action, as those terms are used in this section, is that preferential treatment means simply a preference offered to members of a certain class that is not offered to members of other classes; *affirmative action* provides for the most equal opportunity possible to members of various groups historically not having been provided equal opportunity, and may include preferential treatment, education programs, referral services, or preemployment preparation or training for certain groups.

Title VII does not require that preferential treatment be given to any specific protected class. In fact, the statute states that preferential treatment cannot be used to remedy the existing number or percentage imbalance of a protected group. However, if a protected group has been discriminated against by the employer, the employer can consider this as a *factor* in its hiring decision. Title VII states:

> Nothing in this title shall be interpreted to require any employer . . . to grant preferential treatment to any individual or to any group because of the race, color, religion, sex, or national origin of such individual or group on account of an imbalance which may exist with respect to the total number or percentage of persons of any race, color, religion, sex or national origin employed . . . in comparison with the total number or percentage of any persons of such race, color, religion, sex or national origin in any community. [Section 703(j).]

The Rehabilitation Act requires affirmative action programs for the employment of disabled employees, though not specifically preferential treatment. The act distinguishes between small contractors, those with contracts between $2,500 and $50,000, and large contractors, those with contracts of $50,000 or more. The action required of the smaller employer is limited to posting notices of the obligation to be nondiscriminatory in its hiring practices. The larger employer must maintain a more specific written action plan, including a review of job requirements to confirm that those requirements acting as barriers to disabled applications are actually job-related; a commitment to making reasonable accommodations for those employees who require them; recruitment at institutions that train disabled individuals; and other activities that, collectively, demonstrate the employer's commitment to hiring disabled employees.

The Vietnam Era Veterans' Readjustment Assistance Act of 1974 provides that government contractors with contracts of $10,000 or more must undertake affirmative action programs for the purpose of employing and advancing disabled and qualified veterans who were on active duty between August 5, 1964, and May 7, 1975. Similar to the Rehabilitation Act, those contractors who have contracts of $50,000 or more must design and maintain a written affirmative action program.

Executive Order 11246, as amended, regulates the activities of those who have contracts of $10,000 or more with the federal government. The order was signed before Title VII was enacted and requires similar employment actions (i.e., the order prohibits a covered employer from basing any employment decision on race, color, religion, sex, or national origin). Contractors with contracts of over $50,000 must design and implement affirmative action programs whenever women or minorities are "underutilized," or underrepresented, in the workforce. *Underutilization* is defined by Revised Order No. 4 as "having fewer minorities or women in a particular job group than would reasonably be expected by their availability." The plan must also establish timetables for elimination of the disparity and address the satisfaction of these goals in the program.

Finally, the Civil Service Reform Act of 1978 provides that all federal government agencies implement programs designed to create "a federal workforce reflective of the Nation's diversity." This general statement of intent provides the basis for involuntary affirmative action programs, discussed in the affirmative action chapter.

The Office of Federal Contract Compliance Programs (OFCCP), which administers the Executive Order, offers several recruitment suggestions to ensure that an affirmative action program does not unduly discriminate in reverse (i.e., discriminate against white males in favor of minorities and women). For instance, the OFCCP recommends that the employer obtain applicant referrals from a medley of organizations that would likely be able to refer minorities or women, such as the Job Corps, the Urban League, the National Organization for Women, and the Professional Women's Caucus. It is further recommended that the organization invite a representative of these groups to the place of employment and instruct the representatives regarding the necessary requirements for each available position, as well as the formal recruiting and referral procedures. Women and minorities within the company may also be a valuable source of applicant referrals, and such referrals should be encouraged. Finally, inclusion of current female and minority employees in the recruitment process is essential.

INFORMATION GATHERING AND SELECTION

Once the employer has recruited a group of applicants, on what basis does the employer reach a final conclusion regarding the employment of any given applicant? The next step is for the employer to weigh the appropriateness of the applicant—given her or his experience, education, fit with the company, and other information gained through interviews, reference checks, testing, and application forms—with the needs of the company and any negative information on the candidate discovered in the course of the information gathering. Gathering this information is a timely, yet important, process that is subject to suspicion by applicants as a result of its potential for the invasion of privacy and discriminatory treatment. While the extent to which an employer is prohibited from delving into private information about an employee on the basis of invasion of privacy is discussed in the chapter on privacy, this section will examine the information that the employer may or may not obtain based on a potential for discrimination.

The Application Process

The hiring process usually begins with an application for employment. Most of us at some point have filled out an employment application. Did you ever stop to think about whether the employer actually had a right to ask these questions? Under most circumstances, the application requests information that will serve as the basis for screening out applicants because of education or experience requirements. Questions that are business related and used for a nondiscriminatory purpose are appropriate. The form will generally ask for name, address, educational background, work experience, and other qualifications for the position; but it may additionally request your date of birth, nationality, religion, marital status, children, or ethnicity.

There are only a few questions that are strictly prohibited by federal law from being asked on an application and during the interview process. Any questions concerning disability, specific health inquiries, and workers' compensation history are prohibited by the Americans with Disabilities Act of 1990. Other questions regarding age, sex, religion, marital status, nationality, and ethnicity are not prohibited by federal law but they are dangerous. Questions relating to these areas must be related to the position for which the applicant applies in order for an employer to be able to ask such questions. If they are not related and it can be shown these inquiries are being made to discriminate against applicants, the employers could be facing liability. Furthermore, even if the employer does not base its employment decision on the responses of these inquiries, where the selection process results in a disparate impact against a protected group, the employer could also be liable.

Nevertheless, research has shown that companies frequently violate guidelines promulgated by the EEOC regarding appropriate application and interview questions. You may even be thinking right now that you have answered these questions on some form in the past. The areas of inquiry that are most often violated include education (where not business justified and where questions relate to religious affiliation of the school, and so on), arrest records, physical disabilities, and age. Even the most innocuous remark may be inappropriate. For instance, an employer is advised not to ask questions regarding the name of the applicant, other than what it is (it may be perceived as national origin discrimination). Questions relating to other names by which the applicant may be known are proper, while questions regarding the origins of an interesting surname or whether it is a maiden name are improper (it may be perceived as marital status discrimination).

Moreover, while most applicants are used to filling in the response to a question regarding gender on an application, an employer actually has no right to that knowledge unless gender is a bona fide occupational qualification. As hair and eye color may lead to an inference regarding the applicant's race or color, these questions, too, may be inappropriate, but not *per se* illegal if it is a bona fide qualification.

The Interview

The second step in the process is usually an interview with a representative of the employer. Discrimination may occur during the interview in the same manner in which it is present on application forms. If it would be improper to ask a question on the application, it is just as improper to ask for the same information in an interview.

Questions are not the only source of discrimination during an interview. In a recent study conducted by the Urban Institute, researchers found that black applicants were treated more harshly during interviews than white applicants with identical qualifications. Researchers submitted pairs of applications of black and white applicants for available positions. The researchers found that blacks were treated more favorably than whites in 27 percent of the interview situations, while they were treated less favorably than whites in half of the interviews. Black applicants suffered greater abuses, including longer waiting times, shorter interviews, and being interviewed by a greater number of individuals. White applicants were found to be more likely to receive a job offer. All of this occurred under controlled circumstances where the applications of the pairs were kept equal in terms of qualifications and experience. An interview must, therefore, not only be nondiscriminatory in terms of the information solicited but also in terms of the process in which it is conducted.

Acceptable	Subject	Unacceptable
"Have you ever used another name?"	Name	"What is your maiden name?"
"Can you, after employment, submit verification of your legal authorization to work in the United States?" or statement that such proof may be required after a decision is made to hire the candidate	Citizenship	"Are you a U.S. citizen?"; citizenship of spouse, parents, or other relative; birthplace of applicant, applicant's parents, spouse, or other relative; requirements that applicant produce naturalization papers, alien card, etc., prior to decision to hire applicant.
Questions as to languages applicant reads, speaks, or writes, if use of a language other than English is relevant to the job for which applicant is applying	National origin	Questions as to nationality, lineage, ancestry, national origin, descent, or parentage of applicant, applicant's parents, or spouse; "What is your native language?"; "What language do you use most?"; "How did you acquire the ability to speak [language other than English]?"
Statement of company policy regarding work assignment of employees who are related.	Sex, Family	Number and/or ages of children or dependents; provisions for child care; "Are you pregnant?"; "Are you using birth control?"; spouse's name or contact information.
"Can you perform [specific job-related tasks]?"	Physical or mental disability	"Are you in good health?"; "Have you ever received workers' compensation?"; "Do you have any disabilities?"
Statement by employer of regular days, hours, or shifts to be worked	Religion	Religious days observed; "Does your religion prohibit you from working weekends or holidays?"

Source: Adapted from State of California Department of Fair Employment and Housing DFEH-161 (rev. 12/93).

There are four areas of potential problems in connection with the interview. First, the employer must ensure that the interview procedures do not discourage women, minorities, or other protected groups from continuing the process. Second, employers should be aware that all-white or all-male interviewers, or interviewers who are not well trained, may subject the employer to liability. Third, the training of the interviewers is crucial to avoid biased questions, gender-based remarks, and unbalanced interviews. Fourth, the evaluation of the applicant subsequent to the interview should follow a consistent and evaluative process rather than reflect arbitrary and subjective opinions.

Exhibit 3.4 offers guidance on developing acceptable questions for an interview. Questions should be uniformly applied to all applicants.

Background or Reference Check, Negligent Hiring

Once the applicant has successfully completed the interview process, the next step for the employer is to check the applicant's background and references. This is how the employer discovers whether what is contained in the application and what is said during the interview are true, and whether there is any additional information that might be relevant to the person's employment. The *Small Business Report* found that 80 percent of job applications contain false information regarding prior work history, while 30 percent of the information related to educational background is false. On the other hand, as job responsibilities decrease, the employer is less likely to verify all of the information provided by the applicant. A check, therefore, is crucial to verify the information given on the application and in the interview. (See Exhibit 3.5.)

It is important, as well, to ensure that no undiscovered information would disqualify the applicant from employment or may subject other employees, clients, or customers to a dangerous situation and the employer to a claim of negligent hiring. For these reasons, employers may verify not only education and experience, but also driving records, credit verification, refusals of bonds, or exclusion from government programs. An employer is liable for negligent hiring where an employee causes harm that could have been prevented if the employer had conducted a reasonable and responsible background check on the employee; in other words, when the employer knew or should have known that the worker was not fit for the job. The person injured may claim that the **negligence** of the employer placed the employee in a position where harm could result, and, therefore, the employer contributed to that harm (see Exhibit 3.6). Though it may shock you to consider, 20 workers are murdered at work each week in America, while 1,800 suffer same type of assault.[2] Since 30 percent of workplace attacks are committed by co-workers or ex-co-workers, this is a critical area of caution.[3]

For instance, in one case an applicant for an over-the-road truck driving position had a criminal record for rape and sexual misconduct, but no driving violations. However, the applicant stated on his application that he had no prior criminal convictions or traffic offenses. The employer verified the statement regarding traffic offenses and found it to be true, but did not investigate the statement regarding criminal convictions. The applicant was hired by the employer. While on a scheduled work route for the employer, he picked up a hitchhiker and raped her. The victim sued the employer for negligent hiring, since the employer was shown to be aware that truck drivers pick up hitchhikers but neglected to ensure that its truck drivers were harmless.

In another case, VIP Companion Care reached a settlement with the New York Attorney General after it was found to have hired workers with criminal histories to provide companion care in the homes of aged and infirm clients. One of these workers later stole the credit card of an elderly woman for whom she was caring. As part of its settlement, VIP was required to conduct criminal background checks of all of its employees, as well as pay restitution, fines, and penalties. An additional wrinkle is added in the case of temporary or contingent workers. Employers often hire their workforce from temp agencies, which have engaged in background screening of the worker on

negligence
The failure to do something in such a way or manner as a reasonable person would have done the same thing; or doing something that a reasonable person would not do. Failing to raise one's standard of care to the level of care that a reasonable person would use in a given situation.

[2] Kerry Parker, "Workplace Violence Considerations for Employers," *New Jersey Lawyer,* April 1999, p. 18.
[3] Dawn Anfunso, "Deflecting Workplace Violence," *Personnel Journal* 73, no. 10 (October 1994), pp. 66–67.

Exhibit 3.5   Tips for Tracing Lies

20 TIPS FOR CATCHING RÉSUMÉ FRAUD

1. Carefully note the order of the material given on the résumé. What's given up front is generally what the applicant wishes to emphasize. But what's hidden below may well be more revealing.

2. Concentrate on the most important points in the applicant's résumé. Diverting attention to too many insignificant details draws focus away from key areas.

3. Does the applicant's history follow a logical sequence? For example, has there been a consistent upward progression during the career? Or has there been a downward trend? People don't tend to leave better jobs for poorer ones.

4. Look for conflicting details or overlapping dates.

5. Look for gaps in dates. It's common for applicants who wish to cover something up to try to omit it.

6. Look for omissions of any kind.

7. Pay attention to what the applicant doesn't say as much as to what he or she does say. You'll probably find the most valuable information in those areas your applicant doesn't want to discuss.

8. Get particulars about various subjects. For example, if the applicant says he or she studied business at Harvard, find out what courses he or she took. Casually ask some questions about the campus or physical environment—just to determine if he or she really was there. People who are dishonest will probably stumble on questions like those.

9. Be sure to discuss all key points.

10. Question the applicant about details as you review the résumé. It will be much harder for him or her to remember false information.

11. Probe the applicant's reasons for leaving past jobs, or for jumping from school to school.

12. How quick and sharp are the applicant's answers? Do they sound rehearsed? An honest person has no need to hesitate or rehearse.

13. Does the applicant look you in the eye? Notice body language.

14. Ask the applicant if he or she minds if you verify information. Then assure him or her that you will need to verify every detail. Imposters likely will drop out at that point.

15. Ask colleagues to sit in on your interview. Your associates may catch vital signs or details that you might miss. They might also think of revealing questions to ask.

16. When confirming information by phone, begin by asking for the company operator. That will help you be sure that the place you're calling is a genuine company. Then move on to the personnel department, and then to the particular manager indicated.

17. Send something in the mail. That will enable you to determine if the address given is genuine.

18. Ask references you're given for other references. The applicant is bound to provide only favorable references. But those sources may be aware of others.

19. If the applicant sought the help of a résumé service or other career placement service, ask him or her why. The reasons may be legitimate. But they may also be revealing.

20. If the résumé isn't very clear, or if it has been produced by a professional service, consider asking the applicant to redo it in his or her own way.

Source: Workforce online, reprinted from Christopher J. Bachler, *Personnel Journal* 74, no. 6 (June 1995), p. 55.

Exhibit 3.6   Grounds for Negligent Hiring Claim

To state a claim for **negligent hiring,** the plaintiff must show:

1. The existence of an employer–employee relationship.
2. The employee's incompetence or inappropriateness for the position assumed.
3. The employer's actual or constructive knowledge of such incompetence or inappropriateness, or the employer's ability.
4. That the employee's act or omission caused the plaintiff's injuries.
5. That the employer's negligence in hiring or retaining the employee was the proximate cause of the plaintiff's injuries (i.e., on investigation, the employer could have discovered the relevant information and prevented the incident from occurring).

their own. It is arguable that an employer must ensure the reasonableness and diligence of these third party checks to be sufficiently insulated from liability for negligently hiring these workers, though the court's decisions are not uniform. Unfortunately, research suggests that screening of temporary workers by agencies is inconsistent and not reliable.[4]

To carefully and adequately check on an applicant's references, the employer has several options. First, the employer may contact the reference in person, by telephone, or by letter and request a general statement about whether the information stated in the application and interview is correct. For example, the employer may contact a prior employer of the applicant to confirm that the applicant actually worked there during the time period stated on the application, in the position identified, and at the salary named. Second, the contact might be much more specific, posing questions about the applicant's abilities and qualifications for the available position. Third, the employer may undertake an independent check of credit standing through a credit reporting agency, military service and discharge status, driving record, criminal record, or other public information to obtain the most complete information on the applicant.

There are problems inherent in each form of query.

- Most employers are willing to verify the employment of past employees, but obtaining this limited information may not necessarily satisfy the standard of care required to avoid a claim of negligent hiring.
- Certain information is not available to employers and is protected by state law. For instance, if an employer asks about the applicant's prior criminal arrest record, or even certain convictions, in one of several states that statutorily protect disclosure of this type of information, the employer may be subject to a claim of invasion of privacy or other statutory violations.
- There may also be the basis for a claim of disparate impact where it can be shown that those of one protected class are arrested more often than others. In that case, asking about an arrest record where the offense is not necessarily related to job performance may result in adverse impact. Note that arrests and convictions are not

[4] Charles White and Joanie Sompayrac, "Employee Screening Practices and the Temporary Help Industry," unpublished manuscript.

Exhibit 3.7 Obtaining Information from Prior Employers

Where an employer is having a difficult time obtaining information from a prior employer of an applicant for a position, author Edward Andler offers the following advice:

Introduce yourself:

If Reference Answers

- Mr/Ms/ _____, my name is _____ with the XYZ Company.
- We are in the process of hiring _____. Before we will extend an offer, we need to verify her/his background. She/he has asked that we contact you as her/his personal/employment reference.
- I would like to spend a few minutes with you. Is this a convenient time to talk? When would be the best time/day? At work/home?
- Everything we talk about is confidential and will be treated that way.

If Reference Will Not Cooperate

- Ask if she/he would like a personal call from the candidate authorizing her/him to speak with you.

Fallback (Comment)

- I cannot understand why we're having a problem getting you to talk with us, because we're just trying to help _____ get a new job. Who can I talk with to clear this matter up?

Source: E. C. Andler, *Winning the Hiring Game* (Traverse City, MI: Smith Collins, 1992).

---

the same. Employers are more limited in inquiring about arrest records than about convictions relevant to the job.

- The Fair Credit Reporting Act requires that an employer notify the applicant in writing of its intention to conduct an investigative consumer report, and that it inform the applicant of the information it seeks. It further requires the employee to obtain written authorization to obtain the report. In addition, if the employer plans to take an adverse employment action based on the report, it must notify the employee of the reporting agency and give notice that he or she can get a free copy of the report and that he or she can dispute its contents.

- The reference and background information gathering process is a lengthy one and may be unmanageable, given the employer's position requirements.

- Employers may not be willing to offer any further information than that the applicant worked at that company for a time. Employers have cause for concern, given the large number of defamation actions filed against employers based on references. (See Exhibit 3.7; see also Chapter 13.)

The most effective means by which to avoid this potential stumbling block is to request that the applicant sign a statement on the application form, which states that former employers are released from liability for offering references on her or his behalf. In the course of making a request for a reference from those former employers, the release should be sent to the former employer along with a copy of the applicant's entire application.

The amount of background and reference checking necessary to be shielded from a claim of negligent hiring varies from situation to situation. A position that provides for absolutely no contact with clients, customers, or other employees may necessitate a quick check of the information contained on the application, while a position that requires a great deal of personal contact would require an investigation into the applicants prior experiences and background. An employer must exercise reasonable care in hiring applicants who may pose a risk to others as a result of their employment and the employer's negligent failure to obtain more complete information. The standard of care to be met is what would be exercised by a reasonable employer in similar circumstances. If an employer had no means by which to learn of a dangerous propensity, or if discovery of this information would place a great burden on the employer, a court is more likely to deny a claim for negligent hiring.

Reference Checks: Potential Liability for Providing References?

About half the states have recently enacted Employment Record Disclosure Acts, which insulate an employer from liability as a result of offering a good faith reference for a previous employee. In other words, an employer who provides information to a new employer about a previous employee may not be sued for defamation as long as there is a good-faith belief in the truth of the statement made. The impact of the act is to allow employers who previously offered only neutral references (i.e., verification of employment, title, and pay) to provide an actual evaluation of the worker's performance, without fear of liability as long as there is a good faith belief in its veracity. Of course, the evaluation should be job related and should not violate a worker's civil rights. While the restrictions on what information may be lawfully transmitted vary from state to state, this legislation will allow previous employers to be more free about their concerns regarding past employees.

However, this protection does not go so far as to protect an employer who issues a negative reference in retaliation for a Title VII claim by a former employee. For example, in *Robinson* v. *Shell Oil Company,* a former employee claimed that his employer had given a negative reference to a prospective employer *because* he had filed a charge of race discrimination with the EEOC after he was terminated. The court ruled that former employees have the same right as current employees to sue on grounds that they were retaliated against for exercising their Title VII rights.

Due to an increasing risk of lawsuits as a result of reference checks, many employers have adopted an official policy of providing only name, position held, and salary, or simply saying "No comment." (See Paul Barada's "When References Won't Talk," which follows after the next Exhibit.) However, employers should be aware that, should an employer choose not to provide reference information on prior employees, it could face liability for injuries to the prospective employer who sought the reference, or even third parties. In one case, a former employer settled for an undisclosed amount after allegedly sending an incomplete referral letter that neglected to mention that the former employee had been fired for bringing a gun to work. The employee was subsequently hired by an insurance company and went on

Former Employees

Strategy	Considerations

Examine state law to determine whether statutory protection is available for employers giving references.

- If yes, conform reference policy for former employees to state law.
- If no, develop a policy that balances the potential legal costs with the future employers' need for information regarding the former employee.

- Possible protection under General Liability Policy.
- Require form signed by former employee authorizing release of information.

Current and Future Employees

Strategy	Considerations

Preemployment:
For each new hire or position change, review position to determine risk factors. Based on assessment, determine scope of necessary applicant investigation.

Employment application should include:

- Statement that any misrepresentation is grounds for dismissal, no matter when discovered.
- Inquiry as to any criminal convictions.
- Signed permission for all former employers to release reference information, including reason for separation and eligibility for rehire.
- Data on all education, certifications, and experience relevant to position.

If applicant is deemed to be qualified via personal interviews, skills, or other preemployment tests, begin background check commensurate with prior review of position and risk factors. In particular, the employer should:

- Verify all claimed credentials and certifications.
  Instigate any necessary criminal background checks.
- Send signed consent form to past employers requesting appropriate information.
- Request any other pertinent information, given job duties/responsibilities.

Risk factors include:

- Contact with the public/children/ infirm.
- Access to employer property.
- Operation of motor vehicles/dangerous equipment.

If applicant discloses a criminal conviction, determine the nature of the crime and whether it is within the scope of job requirements or job related.

Where former employer does not respond, employer will need to follow up and document due diligence. Where former employer has a "no comment" reference policy, depending on position's risk factors, remind former employer of potential negligent reference issues and allow former employer opportunity to reconsider. Document due diligence.

Where negative information is received, consider risk factors, consider investigating further, or seek applicant's rebuttal to information received, and make best decision possible for all concerned.

Exhibit 3.8   (continued)

During Employment:
If an employee exhibits any display of greater than ordinary temper or violent behavior:

- Remove employee from potentially hazardous duties (i.e., working closely with public, children, or the infirm.
- Require anger management or similar counseling before reinstatement to prior duties.

Postemployment:
When employee is terminating employment, present Reference Permission Form for employee to sign during exit interview and inform employee that factual information will be provided to future employers.

    If contacted for reference of past employee:

- Provide data as prescribed by Reference Permission Form.

Consider potential position risk factors, including risk to third parties, when deciding whether to release additional relevant factual information.

Source: S. Arsenault, D. Jessup, M. Hass, and J. Philbrick, "The Legal Implications of Workplace Violence: Negligent References, Negligent Hiring, and Negligent Supervision and Retention," *Journal of Legal Studies in Business* 9 (2002), pp. 31–63. Reprinted by permission of the authors and *Journal of Legal Studies in Business.*

a rampage, killing three and wounding two of his co-workers, before killing himself.[5]

While employers may not have an affirmative duty to respond to a reference inquiry, those who choose to respond may be held liable for negligent misrepresentation based on misleading statements made in employment references. Therefore, while there is no affirmative duty to respond, once an employer opts to do so, some courts have held that it creates a duty to respond fully and honestly, to avoid foreseeable harm.[6]

One possible safeguard an employer can utilize is requiring written release from former employees before any information is released. However, the written release should be voluntary, should allow the former employee to discuss the waiver with an attorney, and should include the employee's agreement not to contest his or her termination or the contents of the personnel file. For additional guidance, see Exhibit 3.8 and Exhibit 3.9.

[5] 17 Daily Lab. Rep. No. 193 (Oct. 5, 1995).
[6] *Randi W. v. Muroc Joint Unified School Dist.,* 14 Cal. 4th 1066 (1997).

Exhibit 3.9

Tips for Employer Protection

So how does the employer protect itself? Precaution.

During the Interview Process

- Obtain releases from all applicants allowing the employer to check on previous employment.
- Request that all applicants obtain copies of their personnel files from previous employers.

Before a Position Is Offered to the Candidate

- Investigate the employment record, including all gaps, missing data, and positions held.
- Review educational records carefully. Contact the institutions listed to verify their existence, the years attended, the course of study, and, most importantly, actual graduation with degree.
- Check references, especially when several are reluctant to speak. This may be viewed as a warning beacon that they do not have much good to say or have no desire to support the candidate. (On the other hand, ensure that this unwillingness is not the result of a bad relationship with the person. Allow the candidate the opportunity to explain.)

After the Candidate Is Hired

- Maintain clear, consistent policies relating to employment decisions.
- Follow up on the implementation and enforcement of these policies.

---

compelled self-publication
Occurs when an ex-employee is forced to repeat the reason for her or his termination and thereby makes a claim for defamation.

Employer liability in connection with reference checks can also arise in an unexpected manner—from an ex-employee's own mouth through **compelled self-publication**. Compelled self-publication occurs when an ex-employee is forced to repeat the reason for her or his termination. When the reason for the termination is allegedly defamatory (for instance, termination based on false accusations of insubordination or theft), then courts have held that self-publication can satisfy the prima facie requirements of defamation since the employee was compelled to publish the defamatory statement to a third person (the potential new employer), and since it was foreseeable to the employer that the employee would be so compelled to repeat the basis for termination. "The concept of compelled self-publication does no more than hold the originator of the defamatory statement liable for damages caused by the statement where the originator knows, or should know, of circumstances whereby the defamed person has no reasonable means of avoiding publication of the statement or avoiding the resulting damages; in other words, in cases where the defamed person was compelled to publish the statement."[7] The tort of compelled self-publication, however, is recognized in a minority of states.[8]

[7] *Lewis* v. *Equitable Life Assur. Soc'y,* 389 N.W.2d 876, 888 (Minn.1986).

[8] See review of caselaw in *Cweklinsky* v. *Mobil Chemical Co.,* 837 A.2d 759, 765 (Conn. 2004). States include Colorado, Iowa, Minnesota, Connecticut, and California.

When References Won't Talk[1]

The question employers most frequently ask is, "What do I do when references won't talk?" While at first it might seem like an unsolvable problem, there actually is an easy answer.

The first thing to realize is that the prospective employer is in charge of the hiring process, not the candidate. Employers have every right to ask candidates for the types of references they want, not necessarily the references the candidate wants to give them. Employers can tell the job seeker, "We check references, and we'd like you to provide the names of a superior (someone for whom you worked directly), a peer (someone with whom you worked) and a subordinate (someone who reported directly to you)." Not every candidate can come up with exactly that mix of references, but the point is that any employer can specify the types of references they want to contact. References should be people with whom the candidate has actually worked on a daily basis within the last five to seven years. If a candidate can't provide those types of references, no matter how well he/she interviews or looks on paper, my advice would be to look for someone else to fill the vacancy.

I'm reminded of a company in Ohio that wanted to hire a new plant manager. They identified their first choice. He interviewed well, knew all the right answers, and appeared to be technically competent, they said. They asked me to check references, almost as an afterthought. The very first reference with whom I spoke said when they hired the candidate, he had interviewed well, knew all the right answers, and appeared to be technically competent. "It took us about six months to discover that he could only do about a third of what he claimed he could." I asked, "What do you think his main strength was?" The reply: "interviewing." The previous employer hadn't bothered to check any references at all.

The prospective employer should also make sure the candidate gives the company express permission to contact references, which means having the candidate sign a release giving the prospective employer, or its agents, specific permission to talk to the references provided.

This increases the likelihood that references will talk in detail and at length because the candidate will have to ask superiors, peers, and subordinates to serve as references. The references should expect a call and should be willing to freely and honestly discuss the candidate's job performance.

But what do you do if an important reference still refuses to comment about the candidate? People seeking employment have a responsibility in the hiring process, so put the burden right back on the candidate to contact any reluctant references and urge them to respond to calls from the prospective employer. If the reference still refuses to comment, even after being asked again, tell the candidate to come up with another appropriate reference who will. If the candidate can't do that, my advice, again, is to look for someone else to fill the job. Why would a candidate give a prospective employer the name of a reference who wouldn't talk In the first place?

Someone who agrees to serve as a reference, but adamantly refuses to say anything about the candidate when the prospective employer calls, sends up a red flag of major proportions that should not be ignored. But what about the reference who is simply following a company policy that only permits disclosure of the old "name, rank, and serial number"? Again, why would the candidate ask a co-worker who wouldn't violate that policy to be a reference? Job seekers need to remember that a prospective employer isn't asking references to speak on behalf of the company, but to simply offer honestly held opinions or documented facts. Sometimes calling a reluctant reference at home is another way to obtain necessary information about the candidate.

The responsibility for providing references that are familiar with past job performance and willing to talk about it rests squarely on the candidate's shoulders.

[1]Reprinted with permission of Paul W. Barada and Barada Associates, Inc., Rushville, IN (www.baradainc.com).

Exhibit 3.10

Reasons for Not Hiring

Possible lawful reasons for choosing to reject a candidate:

1. No positions available.
2. Not interested in positions available.
3. Not qualified for positions available.
4. Not qualified for position being sought.
5. Better qualified persons were hired instead.
6. Cannot work hours offered.
7. Rejected our job offer.
8. Unable to communicate effectively in the English language (if required for position).
9. Obviously under the influence of drugs or alcohol during the employment interview.
10. Did not return for follow-up interview or otherwise failed to complete the preemployment process.
11. Employment interview revealed no interest in type of work.

"After-Acquired Evidence" Defense in Wrongful Termination Suits

While the previous discussion has focused on potential for employer wrongdoing, what happens when an applicant includes misstatements on her or his application? According to a 1995 Supreme Court decision, *McKennon* v. *Nashville Banner Publ. Co.,*[9] an employer need not hire someone once the misstatement or misconduct has been discovered, or may fire someone for that reason. Often, this situation will come up after someone has been fired for another, allegedly wrongful reason. The "after-acquired evidence" of the misstatements is admissible to show the court that, whether or not the employer had unlawful reasons for the action, it also had this legal justification for the action. In *McKennon,* the court held that a discharge in violation of the ADEA was acceptable where the employer would have terminated the employment anyway because of a breach of confidentiality.

Documentation of Failure to Hire

No federal statute or guideline requires that employers document the reasons for failing to hire any specific applicant. However, it may be in the best interests of the employer to articulate the reasons in order to avoid the presumption of inappropriate reasons. (See Exhibit 3.10.) In addition, since a claim under Title VII or other statutes may come long after the decision was made, documentation will help an employer recall the particular reasons why a certain applicant was rejected so that she or he is not left, perhaps on the witness stand, to say "I don't remember!"

---

[9] 115 S.Ct. 879 (1995).

Moreover, the individuals who originally made the decision about this candidate may no longer be with the firm. Finally, a firm may choose to document in order to supplement statistical data proving a lack of discrimination. This paper trail may serve to prove that others who were similarly situated were treated the same way, not differently. For instance, in a gender discrimination action, the documentation may demonstrate that no one with a certain low level of experience was hired, male or female.

On the other hand, documentation may also serve to demonstrate facts to which the employer does not want to be bound. Once the reason for failing to hire is on paper, the employer is now bound to use that, alone, as the reason for the decision. Further, while any one decision may seem appropriate, systematic documentation of these decisions may demonstrate a pattern of adverse impact that one might not notice if nothing is ever recorded.

The decision about whether to put on paper reasons for failing to hire is best left to individual employers who may choose to record this information, while instituting a monitoring system that will catch any areas of potential vulnerability. This is not to say that employers should use paper or choose not to use it as a form of "cover-up"; instead, employers may discover problem areas and respond appropriately and lawfully to them once observed. As long as an employer's policies about hiring are consistently applied and are reasonable, there should be no problems—whether recorded in writing or not.

TESTING IN THE EMPLOYMENT ENVIRONMENT

preemployment testing
Testing that takes place before hiring, or sometimes after hiring but before employment, in connection with such qualities as integrity, honesty, drug and alcohol use, HIV, or other characteristics.

The third step beyond recruitment and information gathering is to hone in on the particular information that would tell the employer if this is the right worker to satisfy the job's essential requirements. Testing may allow the employer to do so. However, while preemployment testing can help locate ideal employees, it may also land the employer in court. Managing the risk created by use of preemployment tests requires an understanding of the types of preemployment tests used, the benefits they offer, and their possible costs, beyond the monetary expenditures involved in testing. This balance is critical, given the high incident rate of résumé fraud (a recent survey by Colorado-based Avert, Inc., of 2.6 million job applications revealed that 44 percent of the résumés contained lies).[10]

Preemployment testing began in the 1950s as a response to the inefficiencies that were purportedly present in American business. Since that time, preemployment testing has been considered a necessity to the selection process. The majority of selection tests originally given were conducted as a means of bettering the company's position in a competitive market. Testing was seen as the answer to workplace personnel problems, ineffective hiring programs, and the inappropriate job placement of hirees. Employers believed they would be more competitive if they could test applicants to

---

[10] See Jeffrey Kluger, "Pumping Up Your Past," *Time,* June 10, 2002, p. 41.

Management Tips   The Employment Relationship

- If you are looking for the most qualified candidate, make sure that you are advertising in *all* of the places where that candidate might look for employment—not just the obvious places where you are sure to find the same type of workers as those that already work for you.

- Be wary of representations about the firm that are made during recruitment interviews. While, of course, you want to encourage the best candidates to work for your firm, sometimes glowing accounts of life at the firm might cross the line to misrepresentations. Also, be cautious about promises made to prospective employees as these might be construed as part of the individual's contract with the firm.

- While word-of-mouth recruiting, nepotism, and promoting from within may seem to be the easiest methods for locating a new employee, these methods are also likely to produce new employees quite similar to your present employees. Make sure that you employ additional methods to ensure diversity in the applicant pool.

- Take a look at your written applicant form. Does it ask for any information that is not relevant to the candidate's potential ability to do the job? Is there any information upon which you are prohibited from basing an employment decision, such as age?

- Background checks are relevant to most positions. If you fail to conduct a check, you might be liable for any actions that you would have learned about in the check, such as previous workplace violence. From a cost-benefit perspective, conducting the check usually wins.

"weed out" those who failed the tests. These tests became the wave of the future. However, many managers administered tests that had never been validated as indicators of performance or were not specifically job-related in any way. (See Exhibits 3.11 and 3.12.)

In 1990, former U.S. Surgeon General C. Everett Koop estimated that between 14 and 25 percent of employees between the ages of 18 and 40 would test positive for illegal substances on any given day. At that time, the estimated cost of substance abuse in the workplace in the form of lost productivity, medical claims, and accidents amounted to $142 billion per year. Since that time, cost estimates have risen sharply, with the Department of Labor estimating that alcohol and drug abuse cost the economy $246 billion in 1992, with alcoholism specifically being responsible for at least 500 million lost workdays each year.[11] The enormity of this figure is one of the reasons why approximately 22 million employees were tested in 1992 alone.

Testing in the workplace has taken two forms: tests for the purpose of finding the best individual for a position and tests to ensure that the individual is free of problems that would prevent her or him from performing the position's functions. Examples of the former include achievement tests and personality indicators. The problem with this

---

[11] Department of Labor, www.dol.gov/elaws/asp/drugfree/benefits.htm (accessed 6/28/04).

Exhibit 3.11

Myths about Testing in Employment

1. The Constitution will always protect an employee against unreasonable searches.
2. In the private employment sector, employers can pretty much do what they want in terms of testing.
3. Polygraphs are reliable.
4. If you test positive for drug or alcohol on an employment test, you will be terminated.
5. HIV testing is relevant to job performance.

type of eligibility test is that, while it may appear facially neutral, it may have a disparate impact on a protected class. Pursuant to Title VII of the Civil Rights Act of 1964, where adverse impact has been shown, the test may still be used if it has been professionally developed and validated (discussed later in this chapter). If used properly, however, a validated test will not only determine for the employer the most appropriate applicant for the position but may also reduce the chance for discriminatory choices based on conscious or subconscious employer bias.

The latter form of examination refers to tests for ineligibility, such as for drug and alcohol abuse, and other impairments that may limit an applicant's ability to perform. Drug and alcohol addictions have become pervasive issues in our society. Highly publicized mishaps, such as the alcohol-related Exxon *Valdez* disaster and drug-related railway incidents, have added to our consternation. The problem of addiction has permeated almost every facet of our lives, including the workplace. Employers have institutionalized prevention programs, not only for the safety of their workers but also in an effort to ensure high productivity and quality output. As technology has improved, impairment tests have become more efficient, less expensive, and therefore more prevalent.

In an effort to protect individual employee rights, courts do a balancing test to determine the legality of ineligibility testing. "At some point, an individual's privacy interests trump an employer's efficiency concerns. That point is when the invasion of privacy is 'substantially and highly offensive to the reasonable person,'" one judge stated. The courts accordingly weigh the conflicting interest of the employer in securing a problem-free or substance-free workplace against the privacy rights of the employee and protections against self-incrimination.

As many of the protections afforded to the employee derive from the Constitution (4th Amendment protection against unreasonable searches and seizures, 5th Amendment right against self-incrimination, and 5th and 14th Amendments' protections of due process), government employees and contractors generally receive greater protection in these areas than do employees in the private sector. However, state constitutions can be a source of protection in the private sector as well. The issue of privacy rights is more completely discussed in Chapter 13. This discussion, instead, will be concerned with the potential for discrimination in the course of testing procedures and requirements, and the various statutes that protect against related discrimination.

Employer's interest in securing a problem-free or substance-free workplace

versus

Employee's privacy rights and protections against self-incrimination

Legality of Eligibility Testing

eligibility testing
Tests an employer administers to ensure that the potential employee is capable and qualified to perform the requirements of the position.

What do we mean by "eligibility testing"? **Eligibility testing** comprises those tests an employer administers to ensure that the potential employee is capable and qualified to perform the requirements of the position. Some tests are also used to determine who is most capable among applicants. These tests may include intelligence tests, tests of physical stamina, eye exams, tests for levels of achievement or aptitude, or tests for the presence of certain personality traits. Tests for ineligibility, on the other hand, test for disqualifying factors, such as drug and alcohol tests, polygraphs, and HIV testing.

Of course, a test may cross the line between the two. For instance, an employer may administer a preemployment, postoffer medical exam to determine whether the applicant is sufficiently healthy to perform the job requirements. If the individual fails the medical examination, the test has determined that she or he is not qualified for the position and, therefore, is ineligible.

Employers may conduct eligibility tests for a variety of reasons. For example, the position may require a unique skill for which the employer wishes to test the applicants. Those applicants who possess that skill will continue in the application process. Or perhaps the employer may need to ensure that the applicants meet minimum standards to satisfy requirements of the position. For instance, an eye exam may be required for all potential bus drivers, or an English language competency examination for all applicants for customer relations positions. These tests, however, may in their implementation have a disparate impact on members of a protected class. To illustrate, the employer's test for English language competency would have an adverse impact on individuals of non-English-speaking origin. Where discrimination on the basis of national origin has been shown, the employer may continue to use the test only where it can establish that the requirement is a bona fide occupational qualification.

business necessity
A character trait that is necessary for the essence of the business.

Title VII specifically exempts professionally developed employment tests of eligibility from disparate impact claims of discrimination, as long as the test is not designed, intended, or used to discriminate on the basis of membership in a protected class. Therefore, if a test has been validated according to strict validation standards, Title VII does not prohibit its use, even where a disparate impact is present. For an eligibility test to be legally validated as an effective gauge of performance, an employer must show that the test is job-related and consistent with **business necessity**. In other words, providing evidence of validity involves showing that test scores can be used to determine appropriate and meaningful inferences about probable job-related behavior.

job analysis
Information
regarding the
nature of the
work associated
with a job and
the knowledge,
skills, and abilities required to
perform that
work.

For example, most people would agree a test of general math is probably related to successful performance as a cashier. Thus, even if this type of test had disparate impact against a particular group, it would be allowable if the employer provided **job analysis** data supporting its claim that math skills were required to perform the job. Suppose that a greeting card company found through various job analytic techniques that creativity is necessary for someone who designs greeting cards. Based on the job analysis data, this company most likely would be permitted to use an instrument that tests for creativity, even if it has adverse impact against a certain group. An employer should, however, be prepared to offer evidence that the test instrument really does measure creativity. In general, the more abstract the trait the instrument purports to test, the more difficult it becomes to establish evidence of validity. Different approaches for establishing the validity of a test instrument are available and are discussed later. Note that a test still may be challenged if there exists a less discriminatory alternative.

The Seventh Circuit held in *Melendez* v. *Illinois Bell Telephone Co.*[12] that the employer's aptitude test had a disparate impact on Hispanic job applicants because there was no significant correlation between an applicant's test score and his or her ability to perform the duties of an entry-level manager. The plaintiff's expert testified that the aptitude tests could "predict a person's job performance only 3 percent better than chance alone."

A job applicant or employees can show adverse affects by different methods but the most common approach is the "applicants-statistics" approach. The approach compares the percentage of minority applicants successfully passing a personality or aptitude test to the percentage of majority applicants.

Test Validity

In 1975, the Supreme Court decided *Albemarle Paper Co.* v. *Moody,*[13] a seminal case with regard to test validation. In that case, Albemarle Paper imposed a requirement for skilled labor positions of a high school diploma and two tests. The court found it critical that Albemarle Paper made no attempt to validate the tests for job relatedness and simply adopted a national norm score as a cut-off point for new applicants. The court held that "discriminatory tests are impermissible unless shown, by professionally acceptable methods, to be predictive of or significantly correlated with important elements of work behavior which comprise or are relevant to the job or jobs for which employees are being evaluated." Because of defects in the validation process, the court found that Albemarle was liable for discrimination for failure to evidence job relatedness of a discriminatory test process.

In 1978, the EEOC, with the assistance of several other government agencies, developed the Uniform Guidelines on Employee Selection Procedures as a framework for employers in connection with the determination of the proper use of tests and other selection procedures. Where a selection test has been shown to have an adverse impact on a protected class, the guidelines identify three approaches to gathering evidence of

[12] 79 F.3d 661, 665–669 (7th Cir. 1996).
[13] 422 U.S. 405 (1975).

validation
Evidence that shows a test evaluates what it says it evaluates.

validity; the choice of **validation** strategy depends on the type of inference the user wishes to draw from the test scores. The guidelines define an adverse impact on a protected class as any procedure that has a selection rate for any group of less than 80 percent of the selection rate of the group with the highest rate.

Criterion-Related Validation

The most traditional type of validating a test is criterion-related/empirical statistical validity. The test must be shown to accurately predict job performance as evidenced by the ability to do the job. This form of validation collects data relating to job performance from a simulated exercise or other on-the-job measures of performance. This data is known as the criterion, or criteria if more than one measure of job performance is used. Once the test in question has been administered, and criterion measures have been taken, statistical relationships between the criteria and test scores are examined. Evidence of validity is obtained if there exists a systematic relationship between the criteria and the test scores. The strength of the relationship helps to determine how accurately performance can be predicted from test scores. The guidelines explain that the criterion on which the test is based may include other measures than work proficiency, such as training time, supervisory ratings, regularity of attendance, and tenure. Whatever criteria are used, they must represent major or critical work behaviors as revealed by careful job analyses. In connection with criterion-based validation, it is important that the employer identify the proper criteria to be measured, identify the proper measurement, and establish a significant level of correlation between criterion measurement and job performance. Evidence for criterion-related validity can be obtained by one of two methods: predictive or concurrent. Predictive validity studies administer the test first and later collect criterion data. Concurrent studies collect both test and criterion data at the same time. Both types of studies then examine the statistical relationships between the two data sets. Concurrent studies are often used because predictive studies frequently prove to be less feasible.

Content Validation

A test that demonstrates content validity is one that has sufficiently sampled the knowledge and/or skills required by the specific position for job performance. To ensure content validity, the job domain must first be defined based on careful job analysis. This definition should identify important tasks, behaviors, and the knowledge the job requires. The test must then be judged against a representative sample of these tasks, behaviors, and knowledge. Employers should be particularly concerned with this type of validity during test construction, as it is easiest to ensure representativeness at this stage. In determining representativeness, it is also important to consider the format and response properties of test items: a test measuring a skill or ability should either closely approximate an observable work behavior or its product should closely approximate an observable work product. The closer the content and context of the test are to work samples or behaviors, the stronger the basis for content validity. Contrary to criterion validity, which attempts to predict performance, a test that demonstrates content validity specifically measures performance of certain position requirements.

Construct Validation

Evidence of construct validity is generally most useful when test scores are considered measures of a psychological characteristic such as reasoning ability, introversion (a personality characteristic), leadership behaviors, and others. These characteristics are theoretical constructions about behavior, and in an employment setting are about job-related behavior. Several issues must be considered when gathering evidence for construct validity. First, the construct must be shown to be important for job performance. As with content validity, this is done through the use of careful job analysis. In addition, the construct should be well defined, distinguished from other constructs, and should specify how the construct relates to other variables. Construct validity is determined by examining the intercorrelation of test items (i.e., ensuring the internal consistency of the test) and examining relationships with other measures of the same construct and with measures of different constructs. These relationships should be strong for measures of the same construct and weak for measures of distinct constructs.

Subgroup Norming

Traditionally, the EEOC has considered evidence of differential validation. In other words, a test not only must be valid for the overall population to be tested (i.e., be differentially valid) but also must be valid for each separate minority subgroup. In the past, this goal was achieved by making adjustments within a particular subgroup population to make scores equivalent across subgroup populations. However, this practice of subgroup norming, or "race norming" as it is sometimes called, was made illegal by the Civil Rights Act of 1991. The ban on subgroup norming is not limited to race as the means of defining subgroups; subgroups may also no longer be defined in terms of gender, religion, or national origin. Critics of subgroup norming say the practice is unfair because it essentially amounts to using different standards or cutoff scores for different groups. Advocates claimed the practice "leveled the playing field" and increased the employment opportunities of minorities and females.

The Uniform Guidelines on Employee Selection Procedures also require that, where there is evidence of an adverse impact, employers of 100 or more employees must maintain specific records in order to ascertain the validity of tests and their impact on various populations. The type of documentation required varies depending on the type of validity test required. (See Exhibit 3.13.)

Job-Related Requirement

In addition to ascertaining test validation, an employer must show that the specific trait for which the applicant is being tested is job-related. For instance, in *Evans* v. *City of Evanston,* female applicants for firefighter positions claimed that the physical agility tests for the positions had a disparate impact on women. The defendant, however, presented evidence that the examination was rationally related to a legitimate purpose of the city. The court stated that, as long as the scoring system was fair, the test was acceptable, even if it did in fact impact women differently than men.

Griggs v. *Duke Power Co.,* discussed previously, is illustrative of the court's response to issues relating to testing and is one of the seminal cases in the area. As you may recall, on the day that Title VII became effective, Duke Power began to require that all employees have either a high school diploma or pass an intelligence test in order to continue employment or to transfer positions at the company. Previously, the highest paid black at Duke Power's labor department (the only positions originally available to blacks) was paid lower than any of the white employees in other departments. The new

Criterion Validation	Content Validation	Construct Validation
User, location, and date(s) of studies	User, location, and date(s) of studies	User, location, and date(s) of studies
Problem and setting	Problem and setting	Problem and setting
Job analysis or review of job information	Job analysis, content of the job	Construct definition
Job titles and codes	Selection procedure and its content	Job analysis
Criterion measures	Relationship between the selection procedure and the job	Job titles and codes
Sample description		Description of selection procedure
Description of selection procedure	Alternative procedures investigated	Relationship between the selection procedure and job performance
Techniques and results	Uses and applications	Alternative procedures investigated
Alternative procedures investigated	Contact person	Uses and applications
Uses and applications	Steps taken to ensure accuracy and completeness	Steps taken to ensure accuracy and completeness
Source data		Source data
Contact person		Contact person
Steps taken to ensure accuracy and completeness		

requirement effectively excluded blacks from positions at Duke Power. The court found that, if an employment practice that has a disparate impact on a protected class cannot be shown to be related to job performance, the practice is prohibited, even if the employer did not intend to discriminate. As the court said in the excerpt provided earlier, "good intent or absence of discriminatory intent does not redeem employment practices or testing mechanisms that operate as 'built-in headwinds' for minority groups and are unrelated to measuring job capability."

Preparing selection testing programs that will be acceptable to the courts can become a complex and labor-intensive process. The comprehensive inquiry exercised by many courts suggests several issues that employers should be aware of in developing or using an employment-related testing program. First, employers must carefully conduct job analyses, ensuring adequate representation of minority groups when collecting data concerning jobs. Second, a specific strategy for validation is necessary, and adequate support must be obtained in order to be acceptable to the courts. Clear links between the information necessary to answer test questions and work performance should be shown. Third, attention to test administration and security can also be relevant, particularly if there is any chance that someone may cheat. Fourth, if there is more than one section or part to a test (i.e., using a test battery), the weighting of those parts in making the employment decision will also be taken into account by the courts. A specific rationale for the weights applied should be logical and based on job analysis data rather than an arbitrary assignment of weights. Finally, the test itself should be systematically developed using job analysis data and representative groups of job incumbents.

Integrity and Personality Tests

Because employers have been restricted in their use of polygraph tests (to be discussed in the next section), many have resorted to subjective tests that purport to measure honesty or integrity through analysis of written or oral answers to numerous questions.

Integrity tests are believed to measure a wide variety of constructs, such as honesty, integrity, propensity to steal, attitudes, and counterproductivity. There is general agreement among experts that integrity tests can predict a number of outcomes of interest to employers and that they have validity levels comparable to many other kinds of tests used in employment settings. In addition, the tests have not been shown to have a consistently adverse impact on any one protected group. However, like the polygraph, integrity tests are likely to have many false positives, and are difficult to validate (e.g., some have used polygraph tests or past criminal behavior).

While the validity of such tests in discovering useful employment-related information remains at issue, the tests have not been shown to have a consistently adverse impact on any one protected group.

Personality tests have also become a viable option in preemployment selection screening. As with other nontraditional selection strategies, these tests have proved to be free from discriminatory selection results. Personality tests should not be confused with intelligence tests, which have suffered a great deal of criticism in connection with their potential for disparate impact discrimination against various minority groups. It is generally agreed that a basic intelligence test is too blunt an instrument with which to determine any specific employment-related results.

Personality tests have recently been shown to reasonably predict job performance behaviors across a variety of jobs (for example, service jobs and military personnel) using various criteria of performance (e.g., tenure and supervisory performance ratings). However, employers must be sure their tests cover relevant dimensions of personality using a reliable and valid instrument. Some employers have resorted to dubious measures, such as handwriting analysis and other nontraditional forms of employee selection. Because of the use of these methods, several states severely restrict or prohibit various personality tests.

Soroka v. Dayton Hudson Corp. *235 Cal. App. 3d 654 (1991)*

Appellants Sibi Soroka, Sue Urry, and William D'Arcangelo sued Dayton Hudson claiming that its practice of requiring Target Store security officer applicants to pass a psychological screening (called the "Psychoscreen") discriminated on the basis of race, gender, religion, and physical handicap. The appellants took the test. Soroka was hired; Urry, a Mormon, and D'Arcangelo were not hired. The main functions of the store security officers (SSO) are to observe, apprehend, and arrest shoplifters. The SSOs carry handcuffs and are allowed to use force against a suspect in self-defense. Target contends that good judgment and emotional stability are important skills for the SSOs. The purpose of the Psychoscreen, Target argues, is to screen out applicants who are emotionally unstable, who may put customers or employees in jeopardy, or who will not take direction or follow store procedures.

The test used is a combination of two different accepted psychological tests. The resulting test includes questions about the applicant's religious attitudes, such as "my soul sometimes leaves my body. . . . I have no patience with people who believe there is only one true religion. . . . Everything is turning out just like the prophets of the Bible said it would." The test also includes questions regarding the applicant's sexual preference, such as "I have been in trouble one or more times because of my sex behavior. . . . I am very attracted to members of my own sex. . . . I like to talk about sex . . . Many of my dreams are about sex matters." Although the tests are scored by outside consultants and applicants are rated as to emotional stability, interpersonal style, addiction potential, dependability and reliability, and socialization, Target does not receive individual responses to the questions. Hiring decisions may be made on the basis of these recommendations, although the recommendations may be overridden.

Reardon, J.

Soroka . . . argues that Target has not demonstrated that its Psychoscreen questions are job-related, that is, that they provide information relevant to the emotional stability of its SSO applicants. Having considered the religious belief and sexual orientation questions carefully, we find this contention . . . persuasive.

Although the state right of privacy is broader than the federal right, California courts construing article I, section I of the California constitution have looked to federal precedents for guidance. Under the lower federal standard, employees may not be compelled to submit to a violation of their right to privacy unless a clear, direct nexus exists between the nature of the employee's duty and the nature of the violation. We are satisfied that this nexus requirement applies with even greater force under article I, section I.

. . . we turn to the voter's interpretation of article I, section I. The ballot argument, the only legislative history for the privacy amendment, specifically states that one purpose of the constitutional right of privacy is to prevent businesses from "collecting unnecessary information about us." It also asserts that the right to privacy would "preclude the collection of *extraneous or frivolous* information." Thus, the ballot language requires that the information collected be necessary to achieve the purpose for which the information has been gathered.

The California Supreme Court has also recognized this nexus requirement. When it found that public employees could not be compelled to take a polygraph test, it criticized the questions asked as both highly personal and unrelated to any employment duties. It found that a public employer may require its workers to answer some questions but only those that specifically, directly, and narrowly relate to the performance of the employee's official duties.

While Target unquestionably has an interest in employing emotionally stable persons to be SSOs, testing applicants about their religious beliefs and sexual orientation does not further this interest. To justify the invasion of privacy resulting from the use of the Psychoscreen, Target must demonstrate a compelling interest and must establish that the test serves a job-related interest. [The court found that Target did not do so.]

Case Questions

1. Why do you think Target administered this test? What did it learn about each applicant as a result of the test?

2. Is there any relevance between the responses to the questions asked and the individual's ability to perform the job?

3. If Target's main purpose was to determine emotional stability, what other method could it have used to obtain this information about its applicants?

face validity
A test that looks well suited to its purpose.

One of the difficulties in using personality or other less objective testing techniques for employment purposes is the concept of **face validity**. Face validity is concerned with whether a test appears to measure what it is supposed to measure. No statistical properties are involved. While not a technical or legally recognized form of validity, face validity can often be important in avoiding legal action based solely on the test taker's perception of what the test assesses. As in *Soroka* above, even if the questions in the Psychoscreen had not invaded the privacy of the test takers, the appellants might still have brought legal action based on the apparent lack of relationship to the job.

Simply because a test is an accepted psychological measure does not make that test relevant to a particular job, nor does it validate its use in any situation.

Currently there are reliable personality measures available that avoid using the type of items used in the Psychoscreen that seem a particular invasion of privacy. Employers must be aware of the types of items used on any tests and their relationship to the job in order to shield themselves from legal liability.

Physical Ability Tests

Whereas tests of general skills are often used to find out whether job applicants have the mental ability to perform a certain job, and integrity tests are used as an indicator of whether an applicant will engage in counterproductive behaviors such as theft, physical ability tests are administered to applicants seeking particularly physically demanding jobs. This type of test is used to increase the likelihood that candidates will be able to perform the essential physical functions of the job in question. Because the ADA calls for the testing of essential functions, general tests of fitness may no longer be an appropriate means of testing for physical fitness. For instance, physical ability tests in the past might have required applicants to perform sit-ups, lift weights, and run certain distances. The logic of this test approach is that those who do better on these events are more physically fit and thus better able to perform the physical tasks of the job in question.

This approach is problematic under the ADA, however, because an employer can only test for an applicant's ability to perform the essential functions of the job and most jobs do not directly require employees to do sit-ups or lift weights. Under current laws, physical ability testing usually results in some type of job simulation. For example, a physical ability exam for entry-level firefighters might require applicants to drag hoses, open fire hydrants, or climb ladders. Job simulations imply a content approach to test validation because the test components are direct samples of the job domain. This approach to physical ability testing is used extensively in the public sector.

Medical Tests

Many employers require preemployment, postoffer medical tests to ensure that the applicant is physically capable of performing the requirements of the position. Medical examinations are prohibited only prior to the offer to protect against wrongful discrimination based on a discovered disability. Pursuant to the Americans with Disabilities Act and the Vocational Rehabilitation Act, an employer may not reach an employment determination on the basis of a disability, where the applicant (or employee) is otherwise qualified for the position, with or without reasonable accommodation. (For more on disability discrimination, see Chapter 13.)

Medical examinations subsequent to the offer of employment but prior to the actual employment are allowed under the acts for the purpose of determining whether an employee is able to perform the job for which she or he has been hired. The acts require, however, that all employees within the same job category be subject to the medical examination requirement; individual applicants may not be singled out. In addition, all information generated through the examination process must be maintained in confidential files, separate from other general personnel-related information.

Subsequent to the applicant's employment, no medical examination may be required unless the test is job-related and justified by business necessity.

Legality of Ineligibility Testing

A variety of reasons encourages workplace testing for ineligibility. First, the employer may wish to reduce workplace injury or to provide a safer working environment. Drug testing has been shown to drastically reduce the number of workplace injuries and personal injury claims. A number of workplace studies measuring the accident rates of companies before and after implementing drug testing indicate that drug testing is indeed an important safety factor.[14] Second, an employer may use drug tests to predict employee performance or to deter poor performance; in addition to a reduction in accident rates, research has shown that "absenteeism, tardiness, employee theft and behavioral problems typically decrease with the implementation and maintenance of drug testing. Productivity and employee morale rise with improved attendance, attention to work and improved performance."[15] Third, testing can reduce the employer's financial responsibility to the state workers' compensation system. The use of an illegal substance, which contributes to the claimant's injury, may serve as a defense to the employer's liability.

Despite the fact that the Constitution only protects employees from invasive or wrongful state action, an employee may make a number of possible claims against testing. Portions of the constitutions or state statutes of certain states establish private sector requirements for workplace testing. For example, San Francisco has enacted an ordinance that requires reasonable suspicion based on evidence of job impairment or danger to others before testing is deemed appropriate. Mandatory or random testing would not be allowed in this jurisdiction.

There is also some support for a claim of common-law invasion of privacy in connection to private sector testing, under certain circumstances.[16] In order to support a claim of invasion of privacy, the individual must show that her or his privacy was invaded by (1) unreasonable intrusion upon her or his seclusion; (2) appropriation of her or his name or likeness; (3) unreasonable publicity of her or his private facts; and (4) publicity that unreasonably places the individual in a false light before the public. Of these causes of action, the ones most likely to arise in the employment context are intrusion and public disclosure of private facts. Some courts have adopted some or all of these causes of action while others have not.

Workers have also found support for claims based on reckless or negligent infliction of emotional distress. This would occur where the employee can show that the employer's intrusion into the employee's private affairs constitutes intentional (and in some states, even reckless or negligent) extreme and outrageous conduct, and would cause mental suffering, shame, or humiliation (be highly offensive) to a reasonable individual under similar circumstances. In determining the offensiveness or reasonableness of the invasion, courts will balance the employer's reason for the test with the extent or intrusiveness of the invasion of privacy.

---

[14] William F. Current, "Drug Testing: How Both Employers and Employees Benefit," *Occupational Hazards, December 12, 2002,* http://www.occupationalhazards.com/safety_zones/44/article.php?id=5282, referring to Robert Taggert, "Results of the Drug Testing Program at Southern Pacific Railroad," *Drugs in the Workplace: Research and Evaluation Data.* Research Monograph 91, National Institute on Drug Abuse (1989).

[15] Ibid.

[16] *Baughman v. Wal-Mart Stores, Inc.,* 592 S.E.2d 824 (W.Va. 2003); *Twigg v. Hercules Corporation,* 406 S.E.2d 52 (W.Va. 1990).

defamation
An intentional tort involving the publication of false statements about another.

In addition to a common-law invasion of privacy argument, an employee may be able to state a claim for **defamation**. The employee must be able to show that the employer disseminated his or her intimate information to the public and that disclosure was not reasonably necessary to serve the employer's legitimate business interest in the fitness of the employee to perform her or his job. This latter requirement would allow dissemination of the information to those people who have a "need to know" the information to adequately perform their jobs. The exception is lost where the employer disclosed the information on the basis of its malice against the employee. Once the test has been administered, whether it is a physical, drug test, or polygraph, it is advisable for the employer to secure the chain of custody of any data, samples, or both and to confirm the results with other examinations.

Finally, the employee may have a common-law cause of action for wrongful discharge in violation of public policy. An employee may base his or her claim on the argument that the court should not condone certain employer activities because those activities would directly contravene some clear public policy. In *Twigg* v. *Hercules Corporation,* the West Virginia Supreme Court held that, even though there was no state statute against drug testing, a strong public policy exists against testing. Therefore, since it was unclear whether the employee's job actually brought him into close physical contact with the explosive fuels produced by the employer, there was insufficient support for the testing. The court instead held there were only two exceptions to the policy against testing: (1) where conducted by an employer based on a reasonable good-faith suspicion of an employee's drug usage and (2) where an employee's job responsibility involves public safety or the safety of others.

Generally, congruent with fundamental theories of employment law, a discharge resulting from an employee's failure to take a test for ineligibility is protected under the employment-at-will doctrine. The employment relationship is based on consent of both parties; if the employee does not wish to be subject to various requirements or conditions of employment, the employee may refuse and leave. If the employee, for instance, is uncomfortable with the idea of random drug testing, that employee may quit and work in an environment in which she or he is more comfortable.

Polygraphs

polygraph
A lie-detecting device that measures biological reactions to individuals when questioned.

One of the most newsworthy areas of testing is the **polygraph** or lie detector. In each year during the past decade, more than 2 million private sector employees were asked to take a lie detector test. While the actual number of polygraph tests administered is unknown, it is probative to learn that there are between 2,000 and 3,500 polygraphers practicing in the United States. There are at least nine schools of polygraph analysis that graduate hundreds more each year.

A polygraph test measures three physiological indicators of arousal: rate and depth of respiration, cardiovascular activity, and perspiration. The examiner asks a structured set of questions, and the subject is evaluated as honest or deceitful based on the pattern of arousal responses. The test has been criticized, however, because other catalysts than dishonesty may produce similar effects in an individual subject. For instance, if an individual is aware that the basis for the test is a concern regarding theft, she or he may become innocently aroused when asked questions relating to the theft. On the other hand, the individual who has actually committed the theft may not be concerned at all; if the person was capable of theft, she or he may be just as comfortable with deceit.

The desire of employers to use polygraphs is perplexing when one considers the reliability of these tests (or lack thereof). In 1983, the Congressional Office of Technology Assessment conducted a study of polygraph reliability. The office found there is a dearth of research or scientific evidence to prove the polygraph is valid for screening purposes. In fact, it has been found that accuracy rates range from 90 to 50 percent.

Because of the large number of false positives and inaccuracies of the polygraph test, a loud outcry from those wrongly accused of improper behavior has resulted in the enactment of the Federal Employee Polygraph Protection Act of 1988. This act, to a great extent, puts an end to polygraph use in selection and greatly restricts its use in many other employment situations. The act provides that an employer may not:

1. Directly or indirectly require, request, suggest, or cause any employee to take or submit to any lie detector test (e.g., a polygraph, deceptograph, voice-stress analyzer, psychological-stress evaluator, and any similar mechanical or electrical device used to render a diagnostic opinion about the honesty of an individual).

2. Use, accept, refer to, or inquire about the results of any lie detector test of any job applicant or current employee.

3. Discharge, discipline, discriminate against, or deny employment or promotion to (or threaten to take such adverse action against) any prospective or current employee who refuses, declines, or fails to take or submit to a lie detector test or who fails such a test.

However, certain employers are exempt from these regulations. These employers include:

1. Private employers whose primary business purpose is to provide security services. Prospective employees may be tested if the positions to which they are applying involve the protection of nuclear power facilities; shipments or storage of radioactive or other toxic waste materials; public transportation of currency, negotiable securities, precious commodities, or proprietary information.

2. Employers involved in the manufacture, distribution, or dispensing of controlled substances. Employers may administer polygraph tests to applicants for positions that would provide direct access to the manufacture, storage, distribution, or sale of a controlled substance.

3. Federal, state, and local government employers. The federal government may also test private consultants or experts under contract to the Defense Department, the National Security Agency, the Defense Intelligence Agency, the Central Intelligence Agency, and the Federal Bureau of Investigation.

Scenario

According to the act, a private employer may also test current employees if the following four conditions exist: First, the test must be administered in connection with a workplace theft or incident investigation. Second, the employee must have had reasonable access to the missing property or loss incurred. Third, the employer must have reasonable suspicion that this particular employee was involved. Fourth, the employee must have been given written information regarding the basis for the investigation and for the suspicion that she or he is involved. Furthermore, an employer cannot discharge, discipline, or otherwise discriminate against the test taker in any manner on the basis of the polygraph test results or refusal to take a polygraph test, without additional supporting evidence. This is called the *investigation exemption*. (See Exhibit 3.14.)

Exhibit 3.14   Employee Rights under Polygraph Protection Act

Employers are required by the Act to offer certain information to all individuals who may be subject to a polygraph. The information required is as follows:

Sample Notice to Examinee

Section 8(b) of the Employee Polygraph Protection Act, and Department of Labor regulations (29 CFR 801.22) require that you be given the following information before taking a polygraph examination:

1.(a) The polygraph examination area [does] [does not] contain a two-way mirror, a camera, or other device through which you may be observed.

(b) Another device, such as those used in conversation or recording, [will] [will not] by used during the examination.

(c) Both you and the employer have the right, with the other's knowledge, to record electronically the entire examination.

2.(a) You have the right to terminate the test at any time.

(b) You have the right, and will be given the opportunity, to review all questions to be asked during the test.

(c) You may not be asked questions in a manner which degrades, or needlessly intrudes.

(d) You may not be asked any questions concerning: Religious beliefs or opinions; beliefs regarding racial matters; political beliefs or affiliations; matters relating to sexual behavior; beliefs, affiliations, opinions, or lawful activities regarding unions or labor organizations.

(e) The test may not be conducted if there is sufficient written evidence by a physician that you are suffering from a medical or psychological condition or undergoing treatment that might cause abnormal responses during the examination.

3.(a) The test is not and cannot be required as a condition of employment.

(b) The employer may not discharge, dismiss, discipline, deny employment or promotion, or otherwise discriminate against you based on the analysis of a polygraph test, or based on your refusal to take such a test without additional evidence which would support such action.

(c)(1) In connection with an ongoing investigation, the additional evidence required for an employer to take adverse action against you, including termination, may be (A) evidence that you had access to the property that is the subject of investigation, together with (B) the evidence supporting the employer's reasonable suspicion that you were involved in the incident or activity under investigation.

(2) Any statement made by you before or during the test may serve as additional supporting evidence for an adverse employment action, as described in 3(b) above, and any admission of criminal conduct by you may be transmitted to an appropriate government law enforcement agency.

4.(a) Information acquired from a polygraph test may be disclosed by the examiner or by the employer only:

(1) To you or any other person specifically designated in writing by you to receive such information:

(2) To the employer that requested the test:

(3) To a court, governmental agency, arbitrator, or mediator that obtains a court order:

(continued)

Exhibit 3.14 (continued)

(4) To a U.S. Department of Labor official when specifically designated in writing by you to receive such information.

(b) Information acquired from a polygraph test may be disclosed by the employer to an appropriate governmental agency without a court order where, and only insofar as, the information disclosed is an admission of criminal conduct.

5. If any of your rights or protections under the law are violated, you have the right to file a complaint with the Wage and Hour Division of the U.S. Department of Labor, or to take action in court against the employer. Employers who violate this law are liable to the affected examinee, who may recover such legal or equitable relief as may be appropriate, including employment, reinstatement, and promotion, payment of lost wages and benefits, and reasonable costs, including attorney's fees. The Secretary of Labor may also bring action to restrain violations of the Act, or may assess civil money penalties against the employer.

6. Your rights under the Act may not be waived, either voluntarily or involuntarily, by contract or otherwise, except as part of a written settlement to a pending action or complaint under the Act and agreed to and signed by the parties.

I acknowledge that I have received a copy of the above notice and that it has been read to me.

_____
(Date)

_____
(Signature)

Source: Reprinted from 53 Fed. Reg. 204 (Oct. 21, 1988).

The Federal Employee Polygraph Protection Act also provides that, except in limited settlement-related circumstances, employees may not waive their rights under the act, nor is an employer allowed to offer financial incentives to employees to take the test or to waive their rights.

Violations of the act are subject to fines as high as $10,000 per violation, as well as reinstatement, employment, or promotion, and the payment of back wages and benefits to the adversely affected individual. The Wage and Hour Division of the Employment Standards Administration of the Department of Labor has the authority to administer the Employee Polygraph Protection Act.

In addition to the regulations promulgated by Congress, 33 states have statutes that either prohibit or restrict the use of polygraph examinations for use in employment decisions. Where a state law is more restrictive than the federal act, the act does not preempt the statute.

A recently patented test, the *digital video functional capacity assessment (DV-FCA)*, may evaluate whether an individual is falsely claiming an injury or impairment that isn't revealed by an X-ray or other medical tests. The test involves videotaping the individual while he or she performs a series of 20 motions, including repetitive movements, walking, bending, and lifting. The filmed movements are then analyzed by a computer program, which generates graphs that allegedly show the individual's ability to perform each task. The biggest customers of DV-FCA are insurance companies. One

I, Ronald Reagan, President of the United States of America, find that:

Drug use is having serious adverse effects upon a significant proportion of the national work force and results in billions of dollars of lost productivity each year;

The Federal government, as an employer, is concerned with the well-being of its employees, the successful accomplishment of agency missions, and the need to maintain employee productivity;

The Federal government, as the largest employer in the nation, can and should show the way towards achieving drug-free work places through a program designed to offer drug users a helping hand and, at the same time, demonstrating to drug users and potential drug users that drugs will not be tolerated in the Federal work place.

---

customer stated that in approximately 100 uses, DV-FCA results were consistent with other tests physicians might use.[17]

Drug and Alcohol Tests

In response to the growing problem of drugs in the workplace (70 percent of all illegal drug users are employed) and related injuries and accidents, former President George Bush enacted a Drug-Free Workplace Act in 1988, which authorized the drug testing (or "biochemical surveillance") of federal employees under certain circumstances. Widely publicized estimates suggest that illegal drug use costs American businesses more than $60 billion annually. The cost impacts to businesses of drug use in the workplace based on congressional findings include a 66 percent higher absenteeism rate among drug users, 300 percent higher rate of health benefit utilization, and 90 percent higher rate of disciplinary actions, as well as findings that 47 percent of workplace accidents are drug-related and that employee turnover is significantly higher. (See Exhibits 3.15 and 3.16.) However, testing is not without costs. In 2004, approximately 35 million workplace drug tests were performed at a cost of more than $1 billion.[18]

Preemployment screening of job applicants and testing as a part of a rehabilitation program are allowed by the act. In addition, the act requires that federal contractors and grant recipients satisfy certain requirements designed to eliminate the effects of elicit drugs from the workplace. In response to the act, all federal agencies established individual drug-use testing programs designed to ensure the safety and security of the government and the public. For example, the Department of Defense has instituted an employee assistance program that focuses on counseling and rehabilitation, in addition to self and supervisory referrals to substance abuse treatment clinics.

---

[17] See Mary P. Gallagher, "A Verbal Threshold Lie Detector?" *New Jersey Law Journal,* Oct. 31, 2000.

[18] Paul v. Rountree, "Drug Testing and Workplace Accidents," http://www.aiha.org/aihce04/handouts/pt227rountree1.pdf.

The Benefits

- Ridding the workplace of substance abuse can improve morale, increase productivity and create a competitive advantage.
- A comprehensive program may qualify an employer for discounts on workers' compensation and other insurance premiums.
- The prevention of a single accident or injury may pay for the entire program costs for several years.
- Some contractors may need to have a DFWP to be eligible for business.
- Many employers have successfully formulated policies which deal with ethical and privacy issues, and have successfully controlled their responsibility for, and the costs associated with, treatment and rehabilitation benefits.
- Unions have initiated DFWPs with employers to promote good public relations and recapture work for their members.
- Having a DFWP sends a very clear message to employees, their families and the community as to the company's position on illegal drug use.

The Drawbacks

- A DFWP can increase distrust between management and workers, and degrade morale and productivity in some workplaces.
- A comprehensive DFWP could add significantly to the cost of doing business.
- False accusations, misidentification of employees as drug users, unjustified dismissals and violation of confidentiality obligations could prompt burdensome litigation.
- Identifying substance users may entail an obligation to provide costly counseling and treatment for a relapsing condition. It is not always easy to contain the financial drain, and health insurance premiums could rise.
- A DFWP, particularly one that features drug testing, can raise serious ethical and privacy issues.
- Where the workplace is organized, the employer faces additional negotiations with the union.

Drug-Free Workplace Policy Checklist

1. What is our current company policy regarding the use of alcohol and other drugs?
2. How much of a drug or alcohol problem does our company have at the present time?
3. What is the nature of the problem (absenteeism, quality, productivity, safety, etc.)?
4. How much does this problem cost the company?
5. What type of DFWP would be most likely to improve the situation?
   a. urine testing
   b. impairment testing
   c. under the influence testing
   d. better supervision and quality control
   e. Employee Assistance Plan
   f. a combination of the above

Exhibit 3.16 (continued)

6. If testing is involved, who will be tested?
   a. applicants
   b. employees in safety sensitive positions
   c. all employees
7. Under what circumstances will testing be done?
   a. preemployment
   b. for cause
   c. random
   d. combination
8. What will be done with those who fail the test?
9. What action will be taken regarding those who refuse to be tested?
10. What would be the costs of such a program?
11. What would be the benefits? How much would the problems described in 3 & 4 above be reduced by the program? How great is the financial benefit of the reduction?
12. Do the projected benefits justify the costs?
13. Which proposed components of the DFWP are cost effective?
14. How do the company's employees feel about the proposed DFWP? Would they be more supportive of another option? Have we sought their input?
15. (If the company is organized) Has the proposed DFWP been negotiated with the union?
16. Is the proposed DFWP consistent with company values?
17. Is the proposed DFWP legal in the jurisdictions where it will be implemented?

Choosing a Policy

The first step in developing a policy is to decide whether to have a DFWP. Some employers may choose instead to judge employees simply on the basis of performance. Once a company has made a basic policy choice, it can consider in more detail the objectives it intends to achieve. There are a variety of possible motivations for pursuing such a program:

1. *Complying with legal requirements.* Under federal law, some employers are required to establish DFWPs, including engaging in drug (and possibly alcohol) testing.
2. *Reducing liability risks.* Having a DFWP may be viewed as assisting in the defense against certain legal actions, although DFWPs may also generate other kinds of claims.
3. *Reducing business costs due to accidents, absenteeism and ill health.* Eliminating drug use is seen as a way to promote safety and efficiency, improve the health of the workforce and curtail use of sick leave, medical benefits and workers' compensation.
4. *Ensuring the integrity of employees.* A potential cause of theft, pilferage and blackmail is removed, and workers' confidence in each other is enhanced.

(continued)

Exhibit 3.16 (continued)

5. *Determining fitness for duty and corroborating evidence of misconduct.* A DFWP may help establish uniformity in standards of behavior and in discipline imposed. To establish the DFWP the employer must determine the proper balance between punitive and rehabilitative elements of the program. Being identified as substance abuser may lead to discharge, but there may also be an attempt at rehabilitating employees and returning them to duty.

6. *Assuring public confidence in the business.* The employer prevents embarrassment by taking genuine steps to deal with employees who are affected by substance abuse.

7. *Promoting a "drug-free" society.* Many employers, seeing themselves as responsible members of society, sense a moral obligation to support law enforcement efforts against illicit drugs. NIDA has stated its "belief that the fight against illegal drugs in the workplace is critical to the nation's war against drug use." It has encouraged private employers to adopt DFWPs.

Source: ABA Section of Labor and Employment Law, *Attorney's Guide to Drugs in the Workplace* (1996). Reprinted with permission.

The act also provides that, for a drug-use testing program to be legal, the covered employers must post and distribute a policy statement explaining the unlawful manufacture, distribution, dispensation, possession, or use of controlled substances is prohibited. Discipline or sanctions against the offending employee are left to the employer's discretion. However, if a criminal conviction arises from a workplace substance abuse offense, the employer is required to administer an employment sanction or to advise and direct the employee to an approved substance abuse treatment program. To protect the employee's right to due process, the employer must educate the workforce of any drug/alcohol policy and testing procedures. In addition, laboratory and screening procedures must meet certain standards. In one case, *Fraternal Order of Police* v. *Tucker,* the court concluded that the employees were denied due process because they were not informed of the basis of the employer's suspicion and because they were not offered the opportunity to rebut the employer's claims.

National Treasury Employees Union v. Von Raab
489 U.S. 656 (1989)

The U.S. Customs Service implemented a drug screening program which required urinalysis tests of service employees who wanted to be transferred or promoted to positions where there might be some contact with drugs, such as confiscation, or where the employee might have to carry a firearm or handle classified material. The program provides that the results of the test may not be turned over to any other agency without the employee's written consent. The petitioners, a federal employees' union and one of its officials, sued claiming a violation of the Fourth Amendment. The district court agreed and enjoined the program because the plan was overly intrusive without probable cause or reasonable suspicion. The court of appeals vacated the injunction, holding that this type of search was reasonable in light of its limited scope and the service's strong interest in detecting drug use among employees in certain positions. The Supreme Court affirmed in connection with positions involving contact with drugs and/or firearms but vacated and remanded the decision in regards to those positions which require handling of classified materials.

Kennedy, J.

In *Skinner* v. *Railway Labor Executives Assn.,* decided today, we held that federal regulations requiring employees of private railroads to produce urine samples for chemical testing implicate the Fourth Amendment, as those tests invade reasonable expectations of privacy. Our earlier cases have settled that the Fourth Amendment protects individuals from unreasonable searches conducted by the Government, even when the Government acts as an employer and, in view of our holding in *Railway Labor* that urine tests are searches, it follows that the Customs Service's drug testing program must meet the reasonableness requirement of the Fourth Amendment.

While we have often emphasized and reiterate today that a search must be supported, as a general matter, by warrant issued upon probable cause, our decision in *Railway Labor* reaffirms the longstanding principle that neither a warrant nor probable cause, nor, indeed, any measure of individualized suspicion, is an indispensable component of reasonableness in every circumstance. As we note in *Railway Labor,* our cases establish that where a Fourth Amendment intrusion serves special governmental needs, beyond the normal need for law enforcement, it is necessary to balance the individual's privacy expectations against the Government's interests to determine whether it is impractical to require a warrant or some level of individualized suspicion in the particular context.

It is clear that the Customs Service's drug testing program is not designed to serve the ordinary needs of law enforcement. Test results may not be used in criminal prosecution of the employee without the employee's consent. The purposes of the program are to deter drug use among those eligible for promotion to sensitive positions within the Service and to prevent the promotion of drug users to those positions. These substantial interests, no less than the Government's concern for safe rail transportation at issue in *Railway Labor,* present a special need that may justify departure from the ordinary warrant and probable cause requirements.

Petitioners do not contend that a warrant is required by the balance of privacy and governmental interests in this context, nor could any such contention withstand scrutiny. We have recognized that requiring the Government to procure a warrant for every work-related intrusion "would conflict with 'the common sense realization that government offices could not function if every employment decision became a constitutional matter.'"

Even where it is reasonable to dispense with the warrant requirement in the particular circumstances, a search ordinarily must be based on probable cause. . . . We think Customs employees who are directly involved in the interdiction of illegal drugs or who are required to carry firearms in the line of duty likewise have a diminished expectation of privacy in respect to intrusions occasioned by a urine test. Because successful performance of their duties depends uniquely on their judgment and dexterity, these employees cannot reasonably expect to keep from the Service personal information that bears directly on their fitness.

In sum, we believe that the Government has demonstrated that its compelling interests in safeguarding our borders and the public safety outweigh the privacy expectations of employees who seek to be promoted to positions that directly involve the interdiction of illegal drugs or who are required to carry a firearm. We hold that the testing of these employees is reasonable under the Fourth Amendment.

Case Questions

1. An approved drug use test must be conducted within reasonable parameters. In *Capua,* the court determined that a urine collection process may not be reasonable if "done under close surveillance of a government representative [as it] is likely to be a very embarrassing and humiliating experience." Courts will generally balance the employee's rights against the employer's stated basis for the test and determine whether the cause of the test is reasonable and substantial. For instance, in *Skinner* v. *Railway Labor Executives Assn.,* the Supreme Court stated that the railway employees had a reduced expectation of privacy due to the highly regulated nature of the industry. In addition, societal interests, such as safety and security of the railways, may outweigh the individual employee's privacy interests. When might this be the case?

2. Why do you think the Court made a distinction between positions involving contact with drugs and firearms and positions that require handling of classified materials?

As discussed in other contexts in this chapter, the legality of drug testing relies, in part, on the reliability and effectiveness of the testing procedure itself. The most common form of employee drug-use screening test is an *immunoassay test.* The typical test kit will include a number of solutions (reagents) that are added to a urine sample. When the reagent containing a drug antibody is mixed with the urine, any drug-infected urine will become more dense. When the change in density is visible, the test result is positive. Confirmatory tests should then be administered. The test costs between $4.50 and $25.00 depending on the number of drugs that the employer wants to test.

The immunoassay test has several limitations. First, the test is subject to cross-reactivity, where the test detects small amounts of similarly structured drugs, some of which are not illegal. Second, the test does not evidence the time or quantity of ingestion, or the effects of the impairment on job performance. In addition, the test only investigates the presence of one drug at a time.

A second form of drug testing, testing hair follicles (*radioimmunoassay of hair*), has therefore become more popular among employers. This test works on the theory that substances are absorbed into the bloodstream and incorporated into the hair as it grows. A hair follicle test can purportedly determine the chronology and degree of the subject's drug use by reporting what was in the body at the time the hair was formed in the follicle. Any positive response is confirmed by a more sensitive gas chromatography/ mass spectrometry test. The procedure involves cutting a small amount of hair from the subject, approximately $1\frac{1}{2}$ inches in length from the back of the head so as to remain physically unnoticed. The sample is placed in a collection envelope, which is immediately sealed and transported to a testing facility.

Because of the sampling technique, hair follicle testing is slightly less intrusive than are urinalyses. Many urinalysis examinations are monitored to prevent tampering or contamination; this type of intrusion into personal activities would not be required in a follicle exam. In addition, the window of detection opened by a follicle test is much greater than that of a urinalysis. The follicle test is reliable up to a period of approximately three months, compared with the one- to three-day window of reliability for urinalysis.

On the other hand, many of the arguments that arise in connection with urinalysis drug testing can be repeated here. Hair follicle testing provides much quantifiable information regarding the amount of drugs ingested, and the time over which the drugs were taken. Given its ability to reveal extensive information, follicle testing has been attacked as an unreasonable intrusion into the subject's private life in connection with unregulated and unrelated off-work activities. Decision makers should keep in mind the decision of the Sixth Circuit Court in *Baggs* v. *Eagle-Picher Industries, Inc.,* that represents a somewhat minority perspective on the issue of testing. In applying Michigan law, the court held that an employer can use "intrusive and even objectionable means to obtain employment-related information about an employee."

In a recent study performed by Steelcase Corporation, the firm found that the overall positive response rate jumped from 2.7 percent, when urinalyses were used to detect marijuana and cocaine usage, to 18.0 percent, when hair follicle testing was used. In follow-up interviews, individuals who tested negative for substance usage, according to the urinalysis, but positive, according to the follicle test, reported that they did actually use illegal substances some time within the three months prior to the examination.

As a result of these criticisms of urinalyses, federal workers may soon be subject to more invasive procedures in the coming years. In an effort to deter and to detect illegal drug use by the 1.6 million federal civilian workers, the Bush administration through its Substance Abuse and Mental Health Services Administration (SAMHSA) suggested that federal agencies should have the option of using alternative tests, in addition to the traditional urine sampling, in testing for abuse. As mentioned above, SAMHSA specifically points to the inaccuracy of urine tests because of their vulnerability to masking agents and their short testing window after use of the substance. Instead, federal workers would be tested using their saliva, sweat, and hair samples. This proposal is currently open for public opinion before Congress.

One additional issue raised by drug and alcohol testing involves the Americans with Disabilities Act. The act, which applies to private sector employers, provides that individuals who currently use illegal drugs are not considered individuals with disabilities. However, if an employee or applicant is pursuing or has successfully completed a rehabilitation program, and demonstrates that they have a disability based on prior use, she or he is covered by the act and therefore entitled to reasonable accommodation. (See Chapter 13 regarding the ADA.)

The Drug-Free Workplace Act does not apply to private sector employers. An increasing number of private employers have implemented drug programs for their employees. According to congressional testimony given by Lawrence Bennett, a spokesperson for the Coalition for a Drug Free Greater Cincinnati, 98 percent of Fortune 200 companies have drug-free workplace programs in place. Private employers have generally followed the guidelines set forth in the act of 1989 in the institution of their own programs, and such programs have generally been upheld where reasonable procedures are followed. There do exist several occupation-specific regulations that restrict or require drug testing of employees. Where the government requires or actively encourages testing by the private sector, the testing may be subject to constitutional scrutiny. For instance, the Department of Transportation (DOT) requires private sector transportation employers to randomly drug test employees in safety or security-related positions. In addition, under certain circumstances, DOT requires preemployment and periodic testing, testing where reasonable cause exists, and subsequent to any accidents. An employee who tests positive is removed from her or his position and can only return after successful completion of a rehabilitation program. These requirements must meet constitutional requirements of privacy and due process, even though the testing is actually carried out by private employers.

On June 23, 1998, the House of Representatives passed the Drug-Free Workplace Act of 1998, aimed at providing small businesses—who often lack the resources and infrastructure to conduct employee drug tests—with financial resources and technical assistance for implementing drug testing programs. The three purposes of the act are to (1) educate small business concerns about the advantages of a drug-free workplace; (2) provide financial incentives and technical assistance to enable small business concerns to create a drug-free workplace; and (3) assist working parents in keeping their children drug free. The Drug-Free Workplace Act of 1998 provides a $10 million grant program for nonprofit organizations that have the ability to provide technical assistance to small businesses in establishing drug-free policies.

Additionally, 23 states have enacted legislation designed to protect the privacy of private sector employees. These state laws vary in their approach; some states offer a great deal of protection for employees and may be classified as pro-employee (such as Connecticut, California, and Minnesota), while other states allow testing after satisfaction of only modest burdens and are classified as pro-employer (such as Utah).

It should be noted that some legal scholars do not believe there is a connection between the recreational use of drugs and low productivity. Some researchers have been shocked by low levels of drug-related absenteeism and terminations in their studies. Others have found no effect from drug use on worksite performance and have criticized misleading characteristics of pro-drug testing data. Instead, they contend that, even if the data were supportive of testing, drug testing ignores the presumption of innocence guaranteed to each individual. In many situations, a refusal to submit to a drug test is treated as an admission of drug usage.

Genetic Tests

genetic testing
Investigation and evaluation of an individual's biological predispositions based on the presence of a specific disease-associated gene on an individual's chromosomes.

Genetic testing is a scientific development that involves the use of laser and computer technology. Scientists make diagnostic predictions by locating a specific disease-associated gene on an individual's chromosomes. This type of testing evolved in the 1960s in connection with research regarding individuals who were "hypersusceptible" to certain chemicals used in certain workplaces. By testing an applicant's genes, the researchers were able to ascertain which applicants would be expected to experience negative reactions to various chemicals. Two decades later, Congress asked the Office of Technology Assessment (OTA) to conduct a study in the area. The OTA concluded in 1983 that "none of the genetic tests evaluated by the OTA meets established scientific criteria for routine use in an occupational setting. However, there is enough suggestive evidence to merit further research."

Today, with the tremendous advances in medicine and technology, employers who choose to use genetic testing would have tremendous amounts of information at their fingertips. Governments and private sector firms are rushing to map the entire human genome for the purposes of preventing and treating countless health problems. However, though the Genetic Non-Discrimination Act is currently before Congress, no federal legislation or regulations restrict the use of this personal, private, and potentially volatile information. (See Chapter 12 for additional discussion of how this issue relates to disability discrimination.) The fear includes the concern that an employer might discover something about an individual's genetic makeup that points to the *potential* for a debilitating disease and therefore may choose not to hire the individual based on that potential, even though the person may never develop that disease. In addition, the individual might have no previous knowledge of her disposition toward the disease and, in fact, might not want to know. Should the employer let that person know the reasons for their failure to get the job? Taken to an extreme, genetic testing might allow society to separate individuals on the basis of their potential for disease—a result that should not be taken lightly. Simply because we have the ability to test for something, does that mean that we should?

Moreover, genetic testing is far from perfect. Researchers have discovered that some of the genetic differences found in the test might be due to damage to the genes from the test itself. Similarly, the tests (in their present technological state) evidence only the response of the sample to the presence of a certain toxic agent. The results show merely that the subject is more susceptible to that toxic agent than someone else. Only infrequently can the test show more than this mere susceptibility or potentiality.

One additional issue raised by genetic testing is based on the fact that the genetic irregularities that may substantially impair a major life activity may be considered protected disabilities under the Americans with Disabilities and Vocational Rehabilitation Acts. A genetic test may encourage discrimination based on myths, fears, and stereotypes about genetic differences.

In addition, at least 26 states prohibit or limit genetic testing as a matter of law. Except to determine an employee's susceptibility or level of exposure to potentially toxic chemicals in the workplace, employers in several states, including New Hampshire, Illinois, North Carolina, Rhode Island, Vermont, and Wisconsin, are prohibited from using genetic testing as a condition of employment. Many states also prohibit discrimination and employment decisions made on the basis of genetic information.

Unique Considerations of HIV/AIDS Testing

HIV
Human immuno-deficiency virus, the virus that causes AIDS.

AIDS
Acquired immune deficiency syndrome, a syndrome in which the individual's immune system ceases to function properly and during which the individual is susceptible, in most cases fatally, to opportunistic diseases. AIDS is not transmitted through casual contact; to transmit the disease, there must be an exchange of fluids. The disease may be transmitted through sexual contact, during which there is an exchange of bodily fluids; needle sharing; or an exchange of blood.

Employers unreasonably fearful about the onslaught of **HIV** in the workplace and the effect it will have on their workforces are anxious to test their employees or applicants for the presence of HIV. However, the HIV test in the workplace is inappropriate for two reasons. First, for the test to be justified, it must serve a legitimate business purpose. Because HIV is not transmitted by casual contact of the sort that takes place in a work environment, an HIV test is improper for most positions. Second, the test reports only the subject's status as of several weeks, if not months, in the past. The test does not determine the HIV status of the individual as of the day of the examination. Therefore, unless the employer monitors and restricts the employee's off-work activities prior to the test and between testing, the inquiry is inefficient and ineffective.

In addition, an employer may not take an adverse employment action against an employee merely based on the knowledge that the individual is HIV-positive. That employee or applicant is protected by both the federal Vocational Rehabilitation Act and the Americans with Disabilities Act. These acts provide that an employer may not make an employment decision based on the individual's HIV status, where the person is otherwise qualified to perform the essential requirements of the position.

Frequently called the "AIDS Test," the HIV test does not actually test for **AIDS**. Instead, it tests for the presence of antibodies to HIV in the blood. If the first test performed—called the *ELISA (Enzyme Linked Immunosorbent Assay)*—is positive, a second ELISA test is performed to confirm the results. If that is positive, an additional test, the *Western Blot,* is conducted. One's body may take as long as six months to produce the HIV antibodies. A negative test result may be irrelevant if taken less than six months since the subject's last transmissive activity.

One area of HIV testing that has received a great deal of attention is the testing of health care workers (HCW) and the disclosure of their results. Several arguments can be made against mandatory testing of HCWs, but proponents of testing have a response for each. The first argument is that it is a waste of time and money to test workers, because the actual risk of HIV transmission is so small. In fact the chances of HIV transmission to a patient have been compared to the chances of a fatal accident occurring on the way to the hospital.

Proponents of testing argue that the justification lies in the certainty that surgeons do cut themselves in surgery. In fact, a surgeon cuts a glove in approximately one out of every four cases and sustains a significant skin cut in 1 out of every 40 cases.

The second argument against testing is that the expense of testing these workers not only would take away from available funds for researching an HIV cure but would be excessive and unnecessary, due to the frequency of testing that would be necessary. Frequent testing is necessary, due to the test's inability to verify HIV status up to the date of the test. In fact, if an HCW were tested today, that test would evidence his or her condition as of six months prior to today. Because no one has yet suggested that the HCW disclose all transmissive activities since a time six months prior to testing, and because hospitals have not yet proposed testing on a daily basis (to prevent transmission as a result of the previous night's activities), testing appears to be a worthy cause but a futile effort.

Yet proponents question whether it is possible there is a way of testing that is both efficient and economical. Drug and HIV testing in the military is evidence that a mass mandatory testing program is possible. In fact, the military is able to test for HIV at a cost of less than $3 per test, with a false-positive rate of close to zero. Timely, inexpensive, and accurate tests are available; it is unlikely that their costs will exhaust research funds.

The third argument against testing is that, if testing becomes mandatory, it would act as a declaration our society has no faith or trust in HCWs. In effect, society would be testing the Hippocratic oath by which each HCW is required to abide every time an HIV test is administered. Many patients would refuse to see their doctor unless the results of the doctor's HIV test were available.

Proponents would respond, however, that even now many patients do not merely rely on the doctor's oath to make sure that they will receive professional treatment. News stories abound regarding unnecessary tests given to patients who have the money, and the failure to give certain tests or treatment to those who do not have the money. By making testing mandatory, society and lawmakers are recognizing that the health care industry should take affirmative steps to protect the public from sickness. A fundamental part of the Hippocratic oath is that a physician should cause no harm. Mandatory testing is one manner by which to guarantee this oath to the public.

An additional societal cost is the investment that society has made in training thousands of HCWs. This investment would be lost, causing a need to train replacements and to retrain the infected HCWs to preclude their burden on America's welfare system. The economic costs would be devastating to society in the additional form of increased health care costs. Moreover, the basic rights of all HCWs would be undermined. The right to privacy is a fundamental right, one that should not be revoked. Once the door to testing employees is opened for HIV testing, the borderline that protects employees and applicants from discriminatory tests will become blurred. If mandatory testing is invoked, the government will in effect be undermining its own efforts to stem discrimination against disabled employees and to ground policies in fact, rather than in fear.

Finally, the lives of thousands of HCWs and their loved ones will be shattered. The problems these people will face range from loss of friends to loss of employment to loss of insurance to loss of self-esteem. It is clear that the problem facing this industry comprises not only whether to implement mandatory testing but what to do if an HCW finds he or she is HIV-positive. The options facing the employee are few, at best.

Exhibit 3.17 — Establishing Drug Testing in the Workplace

The U.S. Department of Health and Human Services prescribes the following process by which to establish drug testing in a workplace:

1. Determine the need for drug testing in your work setting.
   - Examine the employee assistance program utilization.
   - Administer a confidential survey.
   - Conduct a cost–benefit analysis. (Costs: initial screen plus confirmation tests, staffing and training. Benefits: potential savings from reduced sick leave, absenteeism, health benefits utilization.)
   - Assess health insurance utilization, accidents, safety complaints.
2. Develop a drug testing policy.
   - Consult legal resources.
   - Develop goal, rationale, limitations of drug testing.
   - Specific drugs to test. (Marijuana, cocaine, amphetamines, opiates, and phencyclidine [PCP] are those for which employees are most often tested.)
   - Set up disciplinary process and employee assistance program (EAP) referral process.
   - Specify details of collection, lab testing procedures, including chain of custody.
   - Set up conditions for designating sensitive positions where random testing.

MANAGEMENT CONSIDERATIONS: TESTING

A workplace substance abuse program should incorporate (1) a written abuse policy that has been drafted after input from employees, (2) a supervisory training program, (3) an employee education and awareness program, (4) access to an employee assistance program, and (5) a drug testing program, where appropriate.

There are three possible corporate approaches for testing employees for ineligibility. First, the employer may establish mandatory testing, which requires that all employees be tested for drug or alcohol use or some other form of ineligibility when they enter a specific program or at the time of their annual physical. Second, an employer may implement "probable cause" testing, where an employer tests employees only if there is suspicion of ineligibility, and testing is implemented for the purpose of discovering a safety, conduct, or performance problem. Third, employers may implement random testing.

The decision about what method to use for testing will depend on the goals of the employer. Does it want to test its entire workforce? Or merely potential problem employees? In any case, an employer should, first, look carefully at state and local laws in connection with specific test-related legislation, as well as at statutes regarding privacy and so on. Second, the employer should clearly articulate its policy regarding substance use, lie detectors, and other tests, as well as its purpose, the procedure by which this policy is enforced, and the appeals process. Third, the policy must be consistently implemented and diligently documented. Possible human and laboratory errors must be minimized. Fourth, all positive results should be confirmed with additional tests. (See Exhibit 3.17.)

Management Tips   Testing

- Private sector employers are *not* generally restricted by the Fourth Amendment protection against unreasonable searches. Therefore, as a private employer, you are allowed to conduct searches under a lower standard. On the other hand, common-law protections against invasions of privacy do apply in the private sector.
- You have an absolute right to determine whether someone is sufficiently healthy to do a job. The problem arises where your tests don't quite tell you that information or where you are testing for eligibility beyond the job's requirements. Make sure that your test will yield results that are relevant to the job in question.
- Health or eligibility testing should be conducted postoffer, preemployment.

- All tests should be validated; that is, they should be shown to test what they intend to test. Using an invalid test might subject you to liability.
- Restrict access to the information gained during testing. If you disclose the information to individuals who don't have a need to know it, you may be liable for an invasion of privacy or for defamation should the information turn out to be false.
- If you choose to try a polygraph test on workers, be wary of the restrictions imposed by the Employee Polygraph Protection Act.
- Since being HIV-free or AIDS-free is seldom (if ever) a BFOQ, testing for HIV is most likely to be unwarranted and a wrongful invasion of privacy.

PERFORMANCE APPRAISALS, EVALUATION, AND DISCIPLINE SCHEMES

performance appraisal
A periodic assessment of an employee's performance, usually completed by her or his immediate supervisor and reviewed, at times, by others in the company.

Once a worker is chosen and hired, the next step in the evolution of the employment relationship encompasses the management of that relationship, which should also allow for the employee's professional development. The balance should not necessarily be in opposition. Workplaces bring together employers and employees. Generally, employees wish to come into an organization and rise as high as they can go. Generally, an employer wishes to have qualified employees who can handle what must be done to accomplish the job. An employee who wants to progress within her or his employment organization does so by meeting the employer's expectations and doing so in an exemplary way. Employees hope to document support for their progression through **performance appraisals (PAs)**. Employers wishing to have employees best suited for the job at hand must identify the best employee for promotion, demotion, retention, transfers, training, and raises. They hope to obtain the necessary information to do so through the periodic evaluation of employees. Disputes arise when an employer's expectations of the employee do not meet with the employee's understanding of the performance expected. These disputes are most often brought to light through the evaluation system.

Above all, the purpose of the performance appraisal should be to identify those characteristics the employer hopes the employee will accentuate and to dissuade the employee from exhibiting characteristics not in keeping with the organization's objectives.

1. An employer can't be liable for giving a negative reference as long as it is based on a poor performance evaluation.
2. To accommodate individual employees' or applicants' needs (such as a disability), the employer must lower its standards or qualifications.
3. If the jobs of minority workers are dependent on their evaluation by other workers, bias cannot be eliminated.
4. As long as the employer believes that the employee understands the requirements or bases for the performance evaluation, the employer is not obligated to do anything further or to allow leeway in compliance.

Performance appraisals have the potential for discriminatory effect, because discrimination may exist in the way the employer utilizes the evaluations as well as in the manner the appraisal is conducted.

Employers are not required to maintain poor performers. Termination as a result of inadequate work performance is justified by business considerations. It is the measure of adequacy that often results in an adverse impact or is the consequence of adverse treatment, which must be avoided by employers. (See Exhibit 3.18.)

Of the many ways in which an employer may assess employees' performance levels, the most efficient and effective methods are those that utilize a variety of schemes to obtain the most complete job-related information.

Methods available include *management by objective (MBO),* which requires the manager and the employee to jointly set objectives that must be met within a specified time period. If the goal is not reached by the deadline as agreed, the employee's performance is deemed unsatisfactory. Another example of a performance appraisal system is the *checklist system* (weighted or nonweighted), which evaluates each employee according to a list of behaviors found to be related to job performance. In advance, the checklist is prepared (and weighted, if necessary) based on the effectiveness by job experts. A third approach is called the *summated scale,* which requires supervisors to indicate how often the employee satisfies (how much the employee agrees, how strong the employee represents, and so on) each of several behavior-based statements, both desirable and undesirable.

The key points in creating a performance appraisal system are summarized in Exhibit 3.19.

Legal Implications of Performance Appraisal Systems

Given their potential for inherent subjectivity, as well as biased or skewed results, performance appraisal schemes are prone to abuse and criticism. It is undeniable that it is integral to the proper management of any workplace to have the ability to evaluate the performance of its employees, but concerns remain regarding the efficacy and propriety of the evaluation systems available. The area of performance appraisal systems has been compared to a fire truck that is able to put out a fire only because its faulty brakes failed to stop the truck outside of the burning building. The truck instead roars directly into the building, dousing the flames as it goes. "We, too, suffer from faulty equipment that may or may not help put out any 'fires.'"

Exhibit 3.19   Creating a Legal and Effective Performance
Appraisal System

1. *Define your objectives.* What is the desired outcome from the evaluation—communication of supervisors' opinions, determination of compensation and bonus allotments, employees' professional development, etc.?

2. *Assess the current system.* Gather feedback from those who have reviewed or been reviewed under the current system to evaluate how your employees' needs fit with your objectives.

3. *Consider available options.* Perhaps a competency-based evaluation system that features different levels of expectations depending on years of experience would better fit your objectives as an employer.

4. *Determine a system of measurement.* Consider replacing numerical values that are prone to "grade inflation" with commentary.

5. *Decide how the system will work.* Who will evaluate whom? How often? Should employees give self-evaluations? How will the information collected from the evaluations be used?

6. *Implement the new system.* Orientations, training seminars, etc., will help ensure that all employees understand their roles and how the system works.

Source: Susan Manch, "Re-Evaluating Evaluations," *Legal Times*, June 7, 2001.

Moreover, courts differ greatly in their decisions regarding similar performance appraisal methods; therefore, a rational and predictable conclusion is almost impossible about the propriety of any single method. What one is left with is merely direction.

Disparate Impact

The legal implications of performance appraisals become relevant when their information is used as the basis for any employment-related decision. The Uniform Guidelines on Employee Selection Procedures apply to "tests and other selection procedures which are used as the basis for any employment decision"; therefore, the guidelines regulate the design and use of performance appraisals. Improper performance appraisal systems are those that do not fairly or adequately evaluate performance but, instead, perpetuate stereotypes that have an adverse impact on protected classes.

For example, the Supreme Court, in *Albemarle Paper Company v. Moody,* discussed earlier, held that the paired-comparison standards (selecting the "better" of two employees) used by the employer as the basis for an empirical validation study were vague, prone to subjective interpretations, and thus discriminatory and unacceptable. Where a performance appraisal system has a disparate impact on a protected class, it is subject to high scrutiny by the courts.

Disparate impact may be determined by a number of methods, the most common of which is described in the guidelines as the "four-fifths rule" (discussed in Chapter 3). Recall that under the rule there is a presumption of discrimination where the selection rate (for any employment decision) of the protected group is less than 80 percent of the selection rate of the nonminority group. For example, if the number of males and females at a firm is equal, but the performance evaluation system results in promotions of 85 percent of the males and only 3 percent of the females, a court will presume discrimination, which may then be rebutted by the employer.

As with other areas in which disparate impact is shown, the employer may still defend the system used if the performance appraisal was sufficiently job related. There must be some reasonable need for it, and some means by which to ensure its objectivity and fairness. If, for example, a checklist system is instituted, the employer must show that the person doing the checking is reasonably free of bias, and that the list itself is a fair representation of what is to be expected of the reasonable or "common" employee. This is called *validation* and is strictly regulated by the guidelines.

Disparate Treatment

A performance appraisal may also result in disparate *treatment,* such as where a female employee is rated subject to different criteria than are the male employees. An example of this type of sexual stereotyping was at issue in the *Hopkins* v. *Price Waterhouse* case. In that case, a female accounting executive did not receive a promotion to partner based on her performance evaluation. During the evaluation, the plaintiff had been told that she needed to take a charm school course, maintain more social grace, walk, talk, and dress more like a woman, use less profanity, and act less "macho." The Supreme Court ruled in favor of the employee, even though the employer offered evidence of various nondiscriminatory bases for the denial of the partnership. The Court found that, as long as the sexual stereotype and discriminatory appraisal were "motivating factors" in the employer's denial, the motive was illegitimate. This was incorporated into Title VII in the Civil Rights Act of 1991 amending Title VII.

While most of us would claim that we rate people based on equivalent factors, research has shown in fact that we do not. Raters are often influenced by physical or other traits or attributes such as national origin, age, accent, and so on. Research has also shown that raters can be swayed by physical attractiveness or body type, as well.[19] People perceived as more attractive, for example, may be viewed as more intelligent and more competent, which could certainly have an impact on appraisers and their treatment of certain groups. Employers can guard against this type of influence through objective and/or practical assessments.

An employee disputing the performance appraisal may also prove a case using the disparate treatment analysis first articulated in *McDonnell Douglas* v. *Green.* The employee must show that he or she (1) is a member of a protected class, (2) suffered an adverse employment decision as a result of a performance evaluation, (3) was actually qualified to perform the responsibilities of the position, and (4) was replaced by someone with similar qualifications who is not a member of a protected class.

In connection with scenario 3, where Mark-Jonathan is considering his alternatives with regard to his evaluation of Gordy, Mark-Jonathan must consider the disparate treatment implications of his decision. If Mark-Jonathan bends the rules a bit

Scenario

---

[19] K. Dion, E. Berscheild, and E. Walster, "What Is Beautiful Is Good," *Journal of Personality and Social Psychology* 24 (1986), pp. 285–90; D. Landy and H. Sigall, "Beauty Is Talent: Task Evaluation as a Function of the Performer's Physical Attractiveness," *Journal of Personality and Social Psychology* 29 (1974), pp. 299–304, in R. Brown, *Social Psychology,* 2nd ed. (New York: Free Press, 1986), pp. 393–94.

for Gordy, in consideration of his recent divorce and other life-changing events, he may get into trouble unless he evaluates the life-changing events that take place in the lives of *each* of his subordinates. Failure to do so would result in him treating Gordy differently, simply because he knows about Gordy's situation. While this might be fine in Gordy's mind, the next person to come along might not be so happy about it. In scenario 3, that is just what happens. Julio has a record similar to Gordy's. Suppose that he, too, has some difficulties in his life that have had an impact on his work performance. If Mark-Jonathan does not consider these difficulties, he would be treating Julio differently than he treated Gordy, resulting in disparate treatment.

It is important to be aware of these issues, even where the difference in treatment is not the result of any intentional wrongful discrimination. If Mark-Jonathan cannot show why there was a difference in the way he treated Gordy and Julio, it may be difficult to prove that it was not the result of discrimination.

Defamation

If you recall, we discussed earlier the potential for defamation through compelled self-publication of an allegedly incorrect basis for termination. Defamation can also occur in connection with the publication of performance appraisals and employers should take similar precautions to avoid liability. In this situation, faulty performance appraisals are not only subject to claims of discrimination, but also wrongful discharge or negligent evaluation. Defamation may exist where the employer:

- States false and defamatory words concerning the employee.
- Negligently or intentionally communicates these statements to a third party without the employee's consent.
- Thereby subjects the employee to harm or loss of reputation.

In other words, if the employer makes a false statement during the course of an employee evaluation, and that evaluation is transmitted to a third party (such as a future employer), the employee may have a claim for defamation. A false evaluation does not necessarily contain false information, but it may evaluate the employee on improper criteria (data on which the employee was told she or he would not be rated).

An evaluation may also be considered false where the rater does not include information that would explain or justify a poor appraisal, such as the fact that the employee's poor task completion rate was due to a sight disorder, which has since been corrected. Finally, a false evaluation may exist where a rater revises a prior evaluation in an attempt to justify subsequent adverse action taken against the employee. Truth is a complete defense to defamation, and truth and honesty by raters should be ensured throughout the appraisal process.

One troublesome aspect of defamation in connection with the publication of performance reviews exists where a firm chooses to share the results of an internal investigation of performance with an enforcement entity. For example, E.F. Hutton conducted an internal investigation after it pleaded guilty in 1985 to 2,000 counts of mail and wire fraud. The firm found (and shared with the public) that, while the top officials of the

Procedural Recommendations for Legally Sound Performance Appraisals

Appraisal procedures:

1. Should be standardized and uniform for all employees within a job group.
2. Should be formally communicated to employees.
3. Should provide notice of performance deficiencies and opportunities to correct them.
4. Should provide access for employees to review appraisal results.
5. Should provide formal appeal mechanisms that allow for employee input.
6. Should use multiple, diverse, and unbiased raters.

7. Should provide written instructions and training for raters.
8. Should require thorough and consistent documentation across raters that includes specific examples of performance based on personal knowledge.
9. Should establish a system to detect potentially discriminatory effects or abuses of the system overall.

Reprinted with permission from Stanley B. Malos and Wiley & Sons, "Current Legal Issues in Performance Appraisal," in James Smither, *Performance Appraisal: State of the Art Methods for Performance Management* (Hoboken, NJ: Wiley & Sons, 1998), pp. 49–94.

firm were not involved in the wrongdoing, certain midlevel managers had improperly used their positions for personal profit.

One of these managers decided to sue the firm for $10 million on the basis of defamation. Though Hutton prevailed, the suit cost the firm enormous amounts of money in defense costs. As mentioned above, this manager was required to show that Hutton negligently published false statements about him. Hutton also argued that it had a qualified privilege to publish the results of internal investigations, so the standard was elevated to one including malice (plaintiff must show that the statement was made with actual knowledge of or reckless disregard as to its falsity).

Negligent Performance Evaluations

negligence
The omission to do something a reasonable person would do, when guided by those considerations that ordinarily regulate human affairs, or something that a prudent and reasonable person would not do.

An employee may have a claim against an employer for the employer's **negligence** in conducting a performance evaluation. The employee must be able to show a contract existed that provided for a performance evaluation. This may either be in the form of a formal employment contract or merely an agreement to include an evaluation in the criteria for promotion or merit salary increase. The liability of the employer stems from the common law doctrine that, where a party to a contract undertakes an obligation to perform certain obligations, the party becomes liable for any wrongdoing that results from the performance of that obligation.

The employee in *Schipani* v. *Ford Motor Co.*[20] claimed that Ford Motor Company breached its contractual duty to evaluate in an objective manner. The court in *Schipani* held that an employer has a duty to exercise reasonable care in the course of employee evaluations. Failure to do so may give rise to a cause of action in tort for negligence.

A unique legal issue arises in connection with performance appraisals of individuals with disabilities. An employer is not required to lower quality or quality standards to

[20] 102 Mich. App. 606 (1980).

accommodate a disabled employee, but it must do what is possible to enable the employee to perform her or his essential responsibilities, while not subjecting itself to an undue burden or hardship. The otherwise qualified employee who has a disability must be evaluated on reasonable job-related performance standards for the duties assigned to that position.

Jensen v. Hewlett-Packard Company *18 Cal.Rptr.2d 83* (Cal. Ct. App. 1993)

An employee who did not agree with his performance evaluation filed suit against the employer for defamation.

Sonenshine, J.

Sean Jensen seeks reversal of a judgment in his defamation action against his former employer, Hewlett-Packard Company, and one of its supervisors, Rod Smith. The lawsuit involves a difference of opinion between the employer and employee about the quality of the employee's work. A supervisor, Hank Phelps, evaluated the employee, Jensen, as needing to improve his on-the-job performance in certain respects. Jensen took offense at the evaluation, claimed it was false, and accused Phelps of trying to hide his own incompetence. He demanded the evaluation be removed from his personnel file and challenged Phelps "to prove his various allegations to an impartial factfinder." Hewlett-Packard investigated the matter and sided with Phelps.

***

As a prelude to our holding, we express our strong judicial disfavor for libel suits based on communications in employment performance reviews, particularly when, as here, the tort claim appears to be an attempted end run around the law. In light of the multitude of laws designed to protect the employee from oppressive employment practices, evaluations serve the important business purpose of documenting the employer's hiring, promotion, discipline and firing practices. Moreover, the laudable practice of evaluating employees is to be encouraged for other important reasons. The performance review is a vehicle for informing the employee of what management expects, how the employee measures up, and what he or she needs to do to obtain wage increases, promotions or other recognition. Thus, the primary recipient and beneficiary of the communication is the employee. Tangential beneficiaries are ordinarily, as in the case here, all part of a management group with a common interest, i.e., the efficient running of the business.

Clearly, there is a legitimate raison d'etre for such records, and management has an unquestioned obligation to keep them. We would therefore be loathe to subject an employer to the threat of a libel suit in which a jury might decide, for instance, that the employee should have been given a rating of "average," rather than "needs improvement," or that the employee had an ability, unrecognized and unappreciated by a foolish supervisor, to get along with and lead others.

Yet that result is exactly what Jensen intended to accomplish with his libel action against Hewlett-Packard: to have an "impartial fact-finder" judge whether Phelps was "right" or "wrong" in his criticisms of Jensen, which is to say whether Jensen was more valuable to Hewlett-Packard than the employer was willing to acknowledge.

Based on the facts here, we hold that unless an employer's performance evaluation falsely accuses an employee of criminal conduct, lack of integrity, dishonesty, incompetence or reprehensible personal characteristics or behavior, it cannot support a cause of action for libel. This is true even when the employer's perceptions about an employee's efforts, attitude, performance, potential or worth to the enterprise are objectively wrong and cannot be supported by reference to concrete, provable facts. Moreover, where an employee alleges the employer's negative evaluations are feigned, the only potentially available remedy lies in contract, for breach of the implied covenant of good faith and fair dealing.

***

The first ground raised by Hewlett-Packard was Jensen's failure to present facts demonstrating the evaluation statement was libelous. In defamation actions, it is entirely appropriate for the court to determine in the first instance "whether the publication could reasonably have been understood to have a libelous meaning."

"Libel is a false and unprivileged publication by writing . . . which exposes any person to hatred, contempt, ridicule, or obloquy, or which causes him [or her] to be shunned or avoided, or which has a tendency to injure him [or her] in his [or her] occupation." A publication "must contain a false statement of fact" to give rise to liability for defamation. A statement of opinion "cannot be false and is outside the meaning of libel." "[T]he dispositive question . . . is 'whether a reasonable fact finder could conclude that the published statements imply a probably false factual assertion.'" The court examines the communication in light of the context in which it was published. The communication's meaning must be considered in reference to relevant factors, such as the occasion of the utterance, the persons addressed, the purpose to be served, and "all of the circumstances attending the publication."

Under the above standards, could any of the comments in Phelps's evaluation reasonably be interpreted as false statements of fact? No. First, we note the context: The communication was a 14-page evaluation of Jensen's performance, prepared by Phelps in the course of his designated duties as Jensen's manager. It was one of a series of evaluations, less favorable than those that preceded or followed it. It documented one manager's assessment of Jensen's work habits, interpersonal skills and level of effort, and it outlined the employer's expectations with regard to Jensen's improvement. It was presented to Jensen for his review and its contents were seen by or made known to a number of management people who participated in periodic employee-ranking sessions. Jensen was given the opportunity to respond to the evaluation, which he did. There is absolutely nothing in the attendant circumstances tending to show the document constituted anything but business-as-usual.

Next, the word "evaluation" denotes opinion, not fact. "Evaluation" is defined in Webster's Third New International Dictionary as ". . . the act or result of evaluating: JUDGMENT APPRAISAL, RATING, INTERPRETATION." To "evaluate" is ". . . to examine and judge concerning the worth, quality, signifi-

cance, amount, degree, or condition of." The dictionary definition is not necessarily dispositive of the fact/opinion issue, but it certainly implies the defendants' intended legitimate purpose of the document, i.e., its use as a management tool for examining, appraising, judging and documenting the employee's performance.

Finally, we turn to the contents of the evaluation, none of which suggests Jensen lacked honesty, integrity or the inherent competence, qualification, capability or fitness to do his job, or that he had reprehensible personal characteristics. Three categories of comments are involved: ratings by which Phelps expressed a value judgment, such as "good," "acceptable" or "unacceptable," about Jensen's comparative level of skills, performance or attitude; directions in which Phelps advised Jensen that he was expected to develop or improve in various areas; and general remarks about Jensen's attitude toward his job responsibilities and his co-workers.

But even if the comments were objectively unjustified or made in bad faith, they could not provide a legitimate basis for Jensen's libel claim because they were statements of opinion, not false statements of fact. . . .

. . . It is poor policy to create an atmosphere of fear of liability which stifles management from exercising its "fundamental prerogatives . . . to control the workplace and to retain only the best-qualified employees." Here, there is no claim that the negative evaluation was fabricated as a pretext for prohibited discrimination; rather there is only Jensen's unsubstantiated charge his supervisor's opinion was objectively wrong and subjectively feigned. We are compelled to conclude the court is an inappropriate forum for resolution of this grievance. No matter the denomination of the cause of action, employers should neither be required to justify performance evaluations by reference to objectively provable facts, nor subjected to fear of liability for good faith, but mistaken, judgments about the value of an individual employee to the business enterprise.

Case Questions

1. Would an employer be able to say anything on an evaluation and not be held liable?
2. Do you agree with this opinion? Why or why not?
3. What can a company do to protect itself from such libel suits?

Rowe v. General Motors Corp. *457 F.2d 348 (5th Cir. 1972)*

General Motors employees Jake Rowe, Willie Williams, and Clarence Williams brought a charge of racial discrimination based on GM's practice of reaching promotion decisions by relying on the recommendations of foremen. This practice operated to discriminate against African-Americans and was held to be unlawful, even though the practice appeared to be fair on its face and General Motors had no intention to discriminate.

Henderson, J.

Until 1962, GMAD [GM's Atlanta plant] was wholly segregated with Blacks being limited to the few custodial jobs. In 1962, GM opened up all jobs to Blacks. Each of the three plaintiff employees sought promotion/transfer from their hourly jobs on the production lines to salaried jobs by using the "employee initiated" method [where employee makes an application directly to the personnel administrator]. Among other things, they base their charge of racial discrimination on the foreman referral system and claim that because they are Blacks, they have been hindered in obtaining the required recommendation of their immediate foreman and have therefore been unable to secure promotion.

It is clearly not enough under Title VII that the procedures utilized by employers are fair in form. These procedures must be fair in operation. Likewise, the intent of employers who utilize such discriminatory procedures is not controlling since "Congress directed the thrust of the Act to the *consequences* of employment practices, not simply the motivation."

We think it clear that the promotion/transfer procedures as applied violate Title VII in several particulars which can be briefly capsulated:

(i) The foreman's recommendation is the indispensable single most important factor in the promotion process.

(ii) Foremen are given no written instructions pertaining to the qualifications necessary for promotion. (They are given nothing in writing telling them what to look for in making their recommendations.)

(iii) Those standards which were determined to be controlling are vague and subjective.

(iv) Hourly employees are not notified of promotion opportunities nor are they notified of the qualifications necessary to get jobs.

(v) There are no safeguards in the procedures designed to avert discriminatory practices.

A brief consideration of some of the testimony of employees strengthens these conclusions. For example, Mr. Griswold, a foreman at GMAD, testified that he did not know what management was looking for in candidates for salaried jobs other than the job of foreman. Mr. Farnim, the GMAD Salaried Personnel Administrator, had to acknowledge that the methods for promotion/transfer at GMAD would enable an individual foreman, if he were so inclined, to exercise racial discrimination in his selection of candidates for promotion/transfer, and that, under the social structure of the time and place, Blacks may very well have been hindered in obtaining recommendations from their foremen since there is no familial or social association between these two groups. All we do today is recognize that promotion/transfer procedures which depend almost entirely upon the subjective evaluation and favorable recommendation of the immediate foreman are a ready mechanism for discrimination against Blacks, much of which can be covertly concealed and, for that matter, not really known to management. We and others have expressed a skepticism that Black persons whose positions are dependent directly on decisive recommendations from Whites can expect nondiscriminatory action.

Case Questions

1. Is there any way to incorporate recommendations as a significant part of an employment evaluation scheme without suffering the same result as GM?

2. How can an employer ensure that its evaluation scheme is fair in operation, not just fair in form?

3. Do you agree with the skepticism expressed in the last sentence of the decision? Do you think things are significantly different than when the case was decided in 1972? That is, would the same language be appropriate in a decision today?

DISCIPLINE

As with any other area that involves actions taken toward employees, employee discipline is a sensitive domain, which must be approached with a critical eye. Regulation of employment decisions applies to any decision, whether involving retention, promotion, and raises, or demotion, termination, or other forms of discipline. All discipline decisions must be nondiscriminatorily applied and objectively administered. Discipline systems that have the purpose of educating the employee who is found to be in violation are generally considered by employees to be more fair and less arbitrary than traditional punishment systems of disciplinary action.

In general, a system that maintains consistency in application, that provides specific guidelines for attaining the varying levels of performance, and that communicates this information to employees is one likely to be deemed "fair." The fairer the system, the less likely it will come under attack from disgruntled employees.

Furthermore, the most effective and efficient method by which to ensure appropriate treatment of disciplinary action is to factually and completely document each action taken (whether such action was written or oral) and its background support. This assures employees of adequate feedback, and lawsuits will not hinge on the vagaries of a particular supervisor's memory. Where no documentation is maintained, there is no evidence that the employee was given the opportunity to redress the infraction or poor performance.

Progressive discipline involves a set of steps before a challenging employee will be terminated for poor performance. In other words, the employee is given a standardized and articulated set of "chances" to improve behavior or performance before discharge occurs. Though tailored to the needs of the workplace, these steps may begin with an oral warning, followed by a written warning, light punishment, and so on until reaching a determination of discharge. Positive discipline refers to a progressive discipline process that involves counseling or other interventions that increase in severity or demands, rather than punishments. Where either process is in place, it is critical that the process be implemented across the board and in a nonarbitrary manner in order to ensure fair treatment to all workers. Failure to impose progressive discipline systems in a standard format for all covered workers may result in potential liability for disparate treatment.[21] Where the employer does follow this process in a committed way, the process itself may be protection against liability through its consistent application to all workers.[22]

An employee who is subject to discipline has a right to request that a co-worker be present as a witness during an investigatory interview. This right is not limited to the union employee: Nonunion employees have a right to representation under *Epilepsy Foundation of Northeast Ohio* v. *NLRB,* 268 F.3d 1095 (D.C. Cir. 2001), cert. denied 122 S.Ct. 2356 (2002).

Documentation of discipline, as well as of appraisals, warnings, and commendations, should be retained in each employee's file and should be given to the employee to provide her or him with the opportunity to appeal the action.

[21] *Chertkova* v. *Connecticut General Life Insurance,* 71 FEP Cases 1006 (2d Cir. 1996).

[22] See *Hanchard* v. *Facilities Development Corporation,* 10 IER Cases 1004 (N.Y. App. 1995); *Gipson* v. *KAS Snacktime Company,* 71 FEP Cases 1677 (E.D. Mo. 1994).

Management Tips   Performance Management and Evaluation

- Documentation such as written performance appraisals can be your protection against wrongful lawsuits charging discrimination. As mentioned before, you are allowed to terminate someone for any reason *except* for certain prohibited reasons. As long as you document poor or deteriorating performance, you may generally terminate an individual on that basis and have protection against claims of discrimination.

- On the other hand, if you do conduct written performance appraisals but treat workers with similar appraisals differently, you may be subject to charges of discrimination.

- Where performance appraisals are conducted by a manager on the basis of stereotypes or prejudice, you are subject to claims of either disparate treatment or disparate impact. Therefore, make sure that all supervisors undergo training in connection with nonbiased reporting and evaluations that are free from prejudgments.

- Make sure that there are precautions against inappropriate disclosures. An employer may be subject to claims of privacy invasions or defamation under certain circumstances.

- If your employee manual or other materials state that you will conduct appraisals, failure to conduct them may be a problem. Make sure that you are willing to live with the claims you make regarding the regularity of appraisals and other promises.

Summary

- Employers believe that freedom of contract should permit them to hire whom they please. However, such statutes as Title VII and IRCA require the employer to ensure that all qualified employees are provided with equal employment opportunity and that decisions to hire are based solely on appropriate concerns and not on prejudice or bias that is neither supported nor relevant to business necessities.

- An ethic of nondiscrimination must permeate the hiring process from advertising the position to drafting the application form to making the decision to hire.

- One of the most effective means by which an employer can protect itself from claims of discrimination in the recruitment/application process is to have a clear view of the job to be filled and who is the best person to fill that job (i.e., an adequate, specific job description for each position within the company).

- After the employer has conducted the analysis, it should implement those results by reviewing the written job descriptions to ensure that they are clear and specific in line with the analysis; all nonessential job requirements should be deleted or defined as nonessential, and minimum requirements should be listed.

- Employers are cautioned, however, that the court or enforcement agency will look first to the actual job performance, then only to the description to the extent that it accurately reflects what the employee really does in that position. If the employer fails to include a function in the description, that may be used as an admission that the function is nonessential. If the function is nonessential, it is likely that an employment decision made on that basis will be suspect.

- Employers should ensure that recruitment procedures seek not only to obtain the most diversified applicant pool by reaching diverse communities but also encourage diverse applicants through the language used and the presentation of the firm.

- Employers should establish efficient, effective procedures to guarantee that they know *who* they are hiring. If an employer wants a certain type of person to fill a position, ensure that the one hired is such a person. Failure to do so may result in liability under a theory of negligent hiring.

- Employers should review their applications to ensure they are asking only for information that is defensibly job-related or necessary to make a decision about whether to hire the candidate.
- Since employers are liable for negligent hiring based on what they knew or should have known, it is critical to do a thorough background check on each new hire. This may include new hires through employment agencies, as well, since those agencies do not always conduct background checks sufficient to insulate the ultimate employer.
- Though prior employers are not obligated to provide references beyond the individual's position, salary, and dates of work, if the employer chooses to do so beyond that basic level, the reference must be complete and honest to prevent foreseeable harm.
- Testing for eligibility and ineligibility is a necessary component of the selection procedure. No employer would hire an unqualified employee if it knew the qualifications of the employee in advance of the hiring determination.
- Designing the appropriate preemployment tests in order to ensure applicants can perform the functions of the job is critical, not only to effective selection procedures but also to the prevention of liability for disparate results of your procedure.
- To keep an employer's evaluation techniques within parameters that are relatively safe from criticism, the employer should first describe precisely what is required of each position to be evaluated. An adequate description will include the following:
  1. Position title.
  2. Department or division in which the position is located.
  3. Title of supervisor (not name, as the individual may change while the supervisory position would not).
  4. Function or purpose of position.
  5. Scope of responsibility for accomplishing that purpose.
  6. Specific duties and responsibilities.
  7. Knowledge, experience, or qualifications necessary for performance of the above duties and responsibilities (the connection should be apparent or explained).
  8. Organizational relationship, persons to whom the employee should report, those employees who report to this supervisor, and those employees over whom the supervisor has direct supervisory responsibilities.
- No "unwritten" qualifications should exist. These may have a disparate impact against those employees outside the "loop" of information, pursuant to which employees learn of the "real" way of obtaining promotions and other workplace benefits.
- The employer should communicate to its employees the nature, content, timing, and weight of the performance appraisal and ensure that the employees understand each of the standards pursuant to which they will be evaluated.
- The bases for the evaluation should be specific and job- or task-defined, rather than subjective, global measures of job performance. For example, a performance measure, such as "ability to finish tasks within specified time period," is preferable to "timeliness." "Suggests new approaches" would be preferable to "industrious." This is because the supervisor evaluating the individual is given baselines and vantage points, such as the schedules that she or he has given the employee, rather than being forced to reach a conclusion about the employee's timeliness in general.
- The employer should request justifications of ratings wherever possible. Some researchers have suggested that documentation should be required only where a rating is extreme;

however, this may be construed by the court as bending over backward only in those circumstances where the rating may be questioned. To the contrary, where an employer maintains a policy that each evaluation should be documented, the consistency of treatment is a defense in itself.

- In addition to affording the employee the opportunity to be heard during the process, the employer should establish a formal appeals process, which the employee may follow subsequent to receipt of the final appraisal. This process may be implemented by the employer through its supervisors, a committee comprised of representatives from all levels of the company, or a committee comprised of the employee's peers. Under most circumstances, appeals processes act as a means to air differences and to explain misunderstandings, deterring later litigation.

Chapter-End Questions

1. In the process of its recruitment of Peters, Security Pacific informed Peters that the company was doing "just fine" and Peters would have "a long tenure" at Security Pacific, should he accept the position offered. In doing so, Security Pacific concealed its financial losses and the substantial, known risk that the project on which Peters was hired to work might soon be abandoned and Peters laid off. Peters accepts the position and moves from New Orleans to Denver to begin his new job. Two months later, Peters is laid off as a result of Security Pacific's poor financial condition. Does Peters have a cause of action?

2. A school district performs standard teacher evaluations including unannounced visits to classrooms, and messages are often delivered to the classroom throughout the day. It is discovered that a teacher engaged in intimate sexual contact with a student during the school day. Is the school district liable for negligent hiring? Should the employer have known that this could happen? [*P. L.* v. *Aubert,* 545 N.W.2d 666 (Minn. 1996).]

3. Can an employer automatically exclude all applicants with conviction records? What if the policy was limited to felony convictions?

4. A group home for individuals with developmental disabilities hires a single, sexually active male with no evidence of dangerous tendencies. The home used to have a policy against allowing male staff members to be alone with female residents, but the policy is no longer in effect. Is the home liable when the male staff member sexually assaults a female resident? [*Niece* v. *Elmview Group Home,* 904 P.2d 784 (Wash. App. 1995).]

5. Phillips, an African-American woman, applied for a position as secretary at the Mississippi legislature as a "walk-in" applicant. Phillips worked in the same building, which was made up of approximately 80 percent African-American employees. She stopped by the office one day to ask if the office was hiring clerical help. She was told that the office was and she was given an application to fill out. After not hearing a response from the office regarding the position, she called and learned that a white woman with similar qualifications had filled the position, even though Phillips applied before this woman. The office defended itself, claiming only that it has a practice of not contacting walk-in applicants for positions. Phillips claims that this policy disfavors African-American applicants who work in the building and is, therefore, illegal based on disparate impact. What result?

6. Eule Ford was a police officer with the city of Pagedale, Missouri, police department. After working there for four years, he was appointed Pagedale's acting chief of police. One year later, Leatrice Dowd was appointed mayor and Alvin Wilson succeeded Ford as permanent chief of police. Ford and Dowd did not have a good relationship; Dowd instituted disciplinary proceedings against him and fired him on several occasions (but the Pagedale

board overturned the decisions each time). After Dowd heard a rumor that Ford was associating with a reputed drug dealer, she ordered that Ford undergo urinalysis testing and told him that failure to comply would result in serious disciplinary actions. The order requiring the testing stated that Dowd understood this rumor to mean that Ford was involved in "some type of illegal drug use and/or abuse." Ford complied with her order and all tests were found to be negative. However, Dowd's order remained in Ford's personnel file. When he later left the department and sought work elsewhere, he was unable to find employment as a result of this order in his file. Ford filed suit, claiming damages as a result of the city's wrongful and vengeful testing program. [*Ford* v. *Dowd,* 931 F.2d 1286 (8th Cir. 1991).]

7. Herman Smith was employed by Greyhound Lines for approximately 13 years as a clerk and was subject to the collective bargaining agreement of the union. He was responsible for receiving packages to be shipped from customers and either accepting cash or charging the transaction to the customer. On one occasion, Smith accepted two packages from a salesman and marked the receipt "charge." The salesman's company later claimed that the salesman had paid cash. Smith's terminal manager, Howard Kratovel, conducted an investigation, which seemed to show that the cash discrepancy was indeed Smith's fault. Smith was given a notice for discharge; but he was told that, if he took a polygraph test and passed, he would be reinstated with back pay. Smith signed a release, took the test, and failed it. Smith filed a complaint against the company, alleging wrongful discharge, defamation, and invasion of privacy. [*Smith* v. *Greyhound Lines, Inc.,* 614 F. Supp. 558 (D.C. Pa. 1984).]

8. In response to the Drug-Free Workplace Act, the Department of Labor (DOL) instituted its Drug-Free Workplace Plan, which designated certain DOL positions as sensitive in regard to public health and safety or national security. Employees in these positions, called "testing-designated positions," could be subject to drug testing, including testing based on a reasonable suspicion of on-duty or off-duty drug use. The American Federation of Government Employees sought to enjoin this type of testing. Will the DOL's plan hold up in court? [*AFGE* v. *Martin,* 969 F.2d 788 (9th Cir. 1992).]

9. An individual contacts you in connection with a reference for one of your worst employees, who was just recently terminated for poor performance. This individual asks whether you believe the former employee will perform well in a similar position at a new company. How do you respond? Is your response different if the former employee was terminated for stealing, and the individual asks whether this employee can be trusted?

10. Which of the following statements would be acceptable in a performance evaluation?

   - "Even though Jacquie was out on a few religious retreats, she exceeded June sales goals by 10 percent."

   - "Although a new, young college graduate, Spiro was very capable in leading the sales meeting."

   - "Despite time off for medical leaves, Renee was able to surpass productivity of many of her colleagues."

   - "Though a bit tough to understand, Margeaux has received excellent reviews for her customer service."

Part **Two**

Regulation of Discrimination in Employment

Hi. Yes, we're speaking to you. Yes, we actually *do* know you're there! We think about you all the time. With each and every word we write. From the very beginning of this textbook, more than 10 years ago, our *constant* thought in writing this text for you has always been: How can we say this so they "get it"? What information do they need to know in order to prevent liability? What interesting cases can we choose that will best illustrate what we are saying? What cases can we choose that will not only give them insight into how the court thinks so they will know what to consider when making workplace decisions, but also that will demonstrate how a manager or supervisor should act in this situation, so they will not cause liability for the employer? All for you.

We have read thousands of cases, hundreds of studies, and zillions of journal, newspaper, and magazine articles, and perhaps just as important, we have spoken with thousands of employers, managers, supervisors, employees, and students. We do this all with an eye toward how we can better tell you what you need to know to avoid unnecessary and preventable workplace liability.

What we've found over the years is that when it comes to the subject matter covered in this section, telling you the law is simply not enough. The subject matter of this section is much more personal than just the laws, per se. It calls upon you as managers and supervisors to make decisions that call into play your own personal narratives. As such, we would be remiss if we did not approach this area a bit differently—a way that is not geared to giving you all you need to make defensible workplace decisions. We have found through our extensive experience that it is necessary to not only give you the law, but also a solid grounding in the background and history of certain areas so you will understand the area better and better inform your own personal narrative so you will make better, more informed workplace decisions to avoid liability.

For over 20 years we have been on a quest to deconstruct how workplace managers make the decisions they do that cause liability for the employer so that we can share that information with you and prevent you from being in the same position. We **HATE** seeing employers pay out money for unnecessary, avoidable liability! We **CAN'T STAND** the thought of our students or our readers being the cause of actions in the workplace that result in liability for the employer, when it all could have been so easily avoided!

The things you see in these chapters reflect that. However, we understand that in choosing to do this, we may come off as being "preachy." What we are **actually** doing is stepping outside of the pure law to give you better information and more context because we know from our extensive experience that that is how the decisions are made and how the courts will judge them. You can bet on it (but only if it's legal in your state ☺).

So, as you read the chapters in this section, keep in mind that what appears to be outside of the pure law is included in order to give you what you need to be able to make better decisions in the workplace. If it seems like we're preaching, maybe we are. We are **passionate** about teaching you what you need to know to avoid workplace liability. If it takes sounding preachy, we'll own it. Just so you understand that the preaching comes straight from the law and research and is put there to help you do your job better. This is such interesting stuff. Have fun!

Chapter **Four**

Affirmative Action

SCENARIO 1

Scenario

Employer is concerned that her workplace has only a few blacks, Hispanics, and women in upper-level management and skilled labor jobs. Most unskilled labor and clerical positions are held by women and minorities. Employer decides to institute a program that will increase the numbers of minorities and women in management and skilled labor positions. Is this permissible? Do you have all relevant facts needed to decide? Explain.

SCENARIO 2

Scenario

Union has not permitted blacks to become a part of its ranks because of opposition from union members. Black employees win when they sue to join. The court orders appropriate remedies. The union still resists blacks as members. Eventually the court orders that the union admit a certain number of blacks by a certain time or be held in contempt of court. Is this a permissible remedy under Title VII?

SCENARIO 3

Scenario

An employer is found by a court to have discriminated. As part of an appropriate remedy, employer is ordered to promote one female for every male that is promoted, until the desired goal is met. Male employees who were next in line for promotions sue the employer, alleging reverse discrimination in that the new promotees are being hired on the basis of gender, and the suing employees are being harmed because of their gender. Who wins and why?

STATUTORY BASIS

Except in the contracts exempted in accordance with Section 204 of this Order, all Government contracting agencies shall include in every Government contract hereafter entered into the following provisions:

During the performance of this contract, the contractor agrees as follows:

(1) The contractor will not discriminate against any employee or applicant for employment because of race, color, religion, sex, or national origin. The contractor will take affirmative action to ensure that applicants are employed, and that employees are treated during employment, without regard to their race, color, religion, sex, or national origin. Such action shall include, but not be limited to, the following: employment, upgrading, demotion, or transfer; recruitment or recruitment advertising; layoff or termination; rates of pay or other forms of compensation; and selection for training, including apprenticeship. [202, Executive Order 11246.]

If the court finds that respondent has intentionally engaged in or is intentionally engaging in an unlawful employment practice charged in the complaint, the court may enjoin the respondent from engaging in such unlawful employment practice, and order such affirmative action as may be appropriate, which may include, but is not limited to, reinstatement or hiring of employees . . . or any other equitable relief as the court deems appropriate. [Section 706(g) of Title VII of the Civil Rights Act of 1964, 42 USC 2000e, sec. 706(g).]

Several other pieces of more limited protective employment legislation, such as the Rehabilitation Act and the Vietnam Era Veterans' Readjustment Assistance Act, also contain affirmative action provisions.

THE DESIGN AND UNSTABLE HISTORY

Introduction

affirmative action
Intentional inclusion of women and minorities in the workplace based on a finding of their previous exclusion.

Noise. There is a lot of it around the concept of **affirmative action**. It can be difficult to turn off the noise and determine what is real and what is not. Did you ever hear someone say, "We *have* to hire a black" or "We *have* to hire a woman"? Such a statement is likely rooted somewhere in the concept of affirmative action. While there may be truth somewhere in the statement, it is probably far from what it appears to be. Many, mistakenly, think affirmative action is a law that takes qualified whites or males out of their jobs and gives the jobs to unqualified minorities or females, or that affirmative action is an entitlement program that provides unqualified women or minorities with jobs while qualified whites or males, or both, are shut out of the workplace.

Imagine sitting at a nice upscale restaurant enjoying a great meal. At the table next to yours is what appears to be a mother and a daughter in her early twenties. Suddenly the mother raises her hand and slaps the daughter hard across the face. Everything stops. Everyone in the restaurant is shocked. You are appalled. You think the mother must be crazy for doing such a thing and you find yourself being angry at the mother for such a violent, heartless, embarrassing spectacle.

Imagine your surprise when you learn that from birth, the daughter has suffered violent seizures from time to time. She has managed to live a fairly normal life, and is an honor student in her senior year of college, but occasionally, for no particular reason that doctors can discern, she will have a seizure. She gets a certain look in her eyes when the seizure is about to occur, and the only way it can be prevented is to immediately slap her hard across the face.

What a difference knowledge and context makes. What may appear as one thing without knowing the context can seem quite different if you do. We find that our students, and most employees we meet, dislike affirmative action. However, they rarely know what it actually is, and they know even less about its context. Seen from their experience of living in a post–Title VII world, and not having given a lot of thought to discrimination, it makes no sense at all to have race or gender play any part whatsoever in an employment or any other decision. However, once they learn what it is and why it was created, they have a better foundation upon which to base their opinion. Whether it changes their opinion is up to them, but at least now they are basing that opinion on fact rather than misconceptions. This is extremely important for making workplace decisions.

Most of the anger around affirmative action comes from the issue of race. Despite the fact that white women have made the most gains under affirmative action, there is still the basic view that blacks are getting something others are not, just because they are black, and this makes people angry. Perhaps, as with our students and employees, viewing affirmative action in the context of a rough racial timeline will give you more information and a context for the law and thus a clearer view. It puts what nowadays appears to be a ridiculously unfair legal requirement into its proper context, thus making it more understandable.

1619—First slaves arrive in America. Slavery is a way of life for blacks who have virtually no other role in American society. They are considered as property and necessary for the economic development of the South, in particular. Like a cow or chicken, they have no rights, including the right to read or write, marry, keep their children, or even their own life. Many places have more slaves than whites (for instance, at one point, South Carolina was 80 percent slaves), and the safety of whites who fear slave revolts is a constant concern. Personnel are not available to constantly watch them, so methods are developed to keep them in line without constant supervision. Slave Codes, policies and actions that make them aware of their subjugation every minute of every day, accomplish this mental and physical enslavement. This approach continues for the next 246 years.

1865—The Civil War ends. The war had begun four years earlier in 1861 to prevent the South from leaving the United States and establishing its own country in which it could have slaves.

1865—The 13th Amendment to the Constitution abolishes slavery. Slave Codes are replaced by Black Codes. After federal troops, which had come to the South to make sure slavery actually ended, leave 11 years later (the period called Reconstruction), the Ku Klux Klan (KKK) rises and, through violence and intimidation, enforces Jim Crow laws codifying racial segregation. Jim Crow is in force by law or social custom to some degree virtually everywhere in the country. Under Jim Crow laws blacks are segregated from whites in every aspect of their lives, and under the policy of "separate but equal" are relegated to segregated and inferior housing, education, transportation, public accommodations, and the like. While the Constitution guarantees them the right to vote, blacks are not permitted to do so, and job discrimination, housing discrimination, and education discrimination is legal. Lynching blacks to maintain control is common and the federal government refuses to intervene despite repeated requests to do so. This continues for the next 100 years, except for public school segregation, which is outlawed by the U.S. Supreme Court in 1954 in the case of *Brown* v. *Topeka Board of Education.*[1] Most schools are not completely desegregated, however, until well into the 1960s, and not without significant resistance and rioting by whites, including shutting down entire public school systems rather than integrate them. Two people are killed and 150 troops injured when the first blacks show up to attend the University of Alabama. Segregation is so strict and insinuated into every aspect of society that, in 1959, Alabama state librarian Emily Reed is fired for refusing to remove the children's book, *A Rabbit's Wedding,* from her library, despite demands of state senators who say it (and other books like it) should be removed and burned because the groom was a black bunny and the bride was a white bunny.

1965—Civil Rights Act of 1964 becomes effective. The country is to go from 346 years of treating blacks as inferior in every way to treating them as equals in education, housing, employment, public accommodations, and receipt of federal funds. To put this in perspective, 1964 is the year the Beatles burst onto the U.S. music scene.

1971—First important Title VII case decided by the U.S. Supreme Court, Griggs v. Duke Power Co.[2] The case is significant because since blacks have never been equal in the United States, and have always been treated as inferior, few know

---

[1] 347 U.S. 483 (1954).
[2] 401 U.S. 424 (1971).

what this picture of equality under Title VII was actually supposed to look like. Is it enough to simply take down the "Colored" and "White" signs? The Supreme Court decision made it clear that equality meant equality in every way. Now the country understands that it must take Title VII seriously. For perspective, the Rolling Stones' "Brown Sugar" is a top hit for the year.

1979—First workplace affirmative action case decided by the U.S. Supreme Court. The Court determines that affirmative action is a viable means of effectuating the law and addressing present-day vestiges of the 346-year system that kept blacks subjugated. Perspective: The Village People's hit single, "Y.M.C.A.*,"* sweeps the country.

1980s—Affirmative action is hotly debated between the presidents, who are opposed, and federal agencies responsible for enforcement of the laws, some of which oppose the law and others of which do not. Employers, seeing these very public disagreements, were confused about what they were required to do, but knew they were supposed to do something and that affirmative action meant they were supposed to have blacks and women. So, they often simply did what they thought they needed to do to try to protect themselves from violating the law. They often determined how many minorities and women they needed to prevent a disparate impact, and hired that number. This became transformed into the idea of a quota in society's eyes. Note that this was not imposed by the government, but came about as a result of employers trying to protect themselves and thinking this was the right way to do it. At the same time, politicians took advantage of the situation by using depictions of whites being fired from jobs in order to hire blacks—something that was always illegal under the law, but that fed into constituents' worst fears. This is the time of Madonna's "Like A Virgin," Michael Jackson's "Thriller," and Cindy Lauper's "Girls Just Wanna Have Fun." (See Exhibit 4.2.)

2004—The last Civil War widow dies.

Two things should become apparent in viewing this timeline: (1) affirmative action has not been around for as long as we may think, and (2) the 25 years or so it has been on the country's radar screen is not a very long time compared to the 346-year history that created the *present-day* vestiges of race that the concept seeks to remedy. Many people *hate* affirmative action. Most who do generally make that determination based on misconceptions about what it is. (See Exhibit 4.1.) You get to keep your feelings about it, whatever they are, but (l) you need to know what it actually is, rather than what you may have been told or gathered here and there, and (2) you need to know how and why it applies to the workplace. In this chapter we'll clear up the misconceptions. We'll learn what affirmative action is, what it is not, what the law requires, and whom it affects.

From the outset, you should realize that affirmative action does not apply to all employers. For the most part it applies to those with 50 or more employees who have contracts with the federal government to provide the government with goods or services worth $50,000 or more. As a part of that contract the government requires the employer to agree not to discriminate in the workplace and further, to engage in affirmative action if it is found to be needed (discussed later in the chapter). Contracts are completely voluntary agreements that we can choose to enter or not. Just as each of us has the choice to contract or not, or to support businesses whose policies we like or don't like with our

Exhibit 4.1 — Affirmative Action Myths

Here are some common misconceptions about affirmative action gathered from students, employees, managers, supervisors, and business owners over the years. See if you recognize any of them.

- Affirmative action requires employers to remove qualified whites and males from their jobs and give these jobs to minorities and women whether they are qualified or not.
- Affirmative action prevents employers from hiring white males who are more qualified for the job.
- Under affirmative action, all an employee must be is a female or a minority to be placed in a job.
- Most employees who obtain jobs under affirmative action plans are unqualified for the job.
- Workplace productivity and efficiency always suffer under affirmative action plans.
- There should be no affirmative action because the best person is always the one who gets the job.

money or not, so too does the federal government. It has decided that it does not want to contract with businesses that discriminate against employees in violation of Title VII.

Keep in mind that *affirmative action regulations do not apply to everyone, but only to just over 20 percent of the workforce.* Despite what you think or may have heard, it is not a law that affects everyone, and it certainly does not require anyone to give up his or her job to someone who is not even qualified to hold it. And, are you ready for this? *It also doesn't require quotas.* In fact, they are, for the most part, actually illegal! Bet this goes against everything you've ever heard. Amazing, isn't it?

At its simplest, affirmative action involves the employer bringing qualified women and minorities (or others statutorily mandated groups) into a workplace *from which it has been determined that they are excluded* in order to make the workplace more reflective of the population from which the employees are drawn. This would ordinarily happen on its own in the absence of discrimination or its vestiges. This intentional inclusion must be premised on one of several bases we will discuss. Initiating an effort to intentionally include employees previously excluded is quite different from saying that workplace discrimination is prohibited. The former is the active approach required by Executive Order 11246; the latter, Title VII's passive approach.

Efforts to eliminate affirmative action in employment, government contracts, university admissions, and other areas come primarily from those who feel it has outlived its usefulness and causes only ill will among majority employees. Many think of it as "punishment" to redress slavery and feel they should not have to bear the burden of something for which they had no responsibility. And whites are not the only ones who complain about affirmative action. Black University of California regent and outspoken affirmative action critic Ward Connerly suggested in a *60 Minutes* interview that "Black Americans are not hobbled by chains any longer. We're free to compete. We're capable of competing. It is an absolute insult to suggest that we can't."

Before deciding if affirmative action has outlived its usefulness, keep in mind the timeline discussed earlier. The first workplace affirmative action case did not reach the

Exhibit 4.2   1980s Media Statements Regarding Affirmative Action

After the seminal U.S. Supreme Court cases on affirmative action in 1978 and 1979, the concept was really shaped and molded by fallout from the Court's decisions in the 1980s. You can gather from the statements below how incredibly divisive the issue was, even for the federal administrators and others with responsibility in the area. Think about how recent this was—there are reruns on TV that go back much further!

3/4/85. "Department of Justice is asking public sector employers to change their negotiated consent decrees [which DOJ had previously pressed for] to eliminate preferential treatment to nonvictims of discrimination." (*BNA Daily Labor Report,* No. 42.)

4/4/05. "[Dept. of] Justice moves to eliminate quotas called 'betrayal' by Birmingham mayor, in testimony before the Subcommittee on Civil and Constitutional Rights of the House Judiciary Committee. Cites 'remarkable progress' made in bringing blacks into the city's fire and police departments." (*BNA Daily Labor Report,* No. 74.)

5/6/85. "Challenges Mount to Department of Justice's Anti-Quota Moves." (*BNA Daily Labor Report,* No. 87.)

9/16/85. "Congress recently ordered an audit of the U.S. Civil Rights Commission and the EEOC, headed by Clarence Pendleton, Jr., and Clarence Thomas, respectively, to find out if financial and personnel troubles are hurting the way both federal panels are enforcing civil rights laws." (*Jet* magazine, p. 16.)

10/17/85. "Attorney General Meese acknowledges that review of Executive Order 11246 is proceeding at Cabinet level, but dismisses charges that Administration officials are at odds over question of affirmative action." (*BNA Daily Labor Report,* No. 201.)

11/29/85. "Majority of Senate is on record as opposing efforts by Attorney General Meese and others in Administration to alter Executive Order 11246 to prohibit goals and timetables for minority hiring." (*BNA Daily Labor Report,* No. 230.)

5/12/86. "Business Applauded for Opposing Changes in Affirmative Action Order." (*BNA Daily Labor Report,* No. 91.)

7/7/86. "Civil Rights Groups Applaud Supreme Court [for *Cleveland Firefighters and Sheet Metal Workers* decisions upholding affirmative action]; Department of Justice Vows to Continue Bid to Revise Executive Order 11246." (*BNA Daily Labor Report,* No. 129.)

7/7/86. "Labor Department says 'we don't see anything in these cases to suggest a legal necessity to change either the executive order or the OFCCP program.'" (*BNA Daily Labor Report,* No. 129.)

6/4/87. "OFCCP Enforcement Activity Scored by House Labor Staff: Alleged Lack of OFCCP Enforcement Activity Criticized by House Labor Staff." (*BNA Daily Labor Report,* No. 106.)

6/5/87. "DOL Official Defends OFCCP's Performance Against Charges of Declining Enforcement." (*BNA Daily Labor Report,* No. 107.)

7/2/89. "Civil Rights: Is Era Coming to an End? Decades of Change Called into Question by [Supreme Court] Rulings." (*Atlanta Journal and Constitution,* A–1.)

U.S. Supreme Court until 1979. Throughout the 1980s government agencies and officials argued about it, and employers were confused. Note too that while many changes have come about since the passage of Title VII, statistics still show blacks and other minorities lagging behind in jobs, and even farther behind in promotions and pay. Do the tidbits given in Exhibit 4.3 seem to you like everything is now equal?

Exhibit 4.3

Affirmative Action Tidbits

Take a look at the items below and think about whether research indicates that affirmative action has outlived its usefulness.

- According to the U.S. Census, 23 percent of the workforce is minority, up from 10.7 percent in 1964.

- In 2003, white women's median weekly earnings were 76 percent those of white men. Black women's earnings were 66 percent of the earnings of white men, and Latina women's earnings were 55 percent of white men's earnings.

- Black women with bachelor's degrees make only $1,545 more per year than white males who have only completed high school.

- In an important longitudinal study of black and white women ages 34 to 44, only one-fifth of the gap between their wages could be explained by education and experience. The study found that while women are segregated into lower-paying jobs, the impact is greater on black women than white women.

- Research indicates that as the percentage of females and the percentage of minorities in a job increases, average pay falls, even when all other factors are held steady.

- Black men with professional degrees receive 79 percent of the salary paid to white men with the same degrees and comparable jobs. Black women earn 60 percent.

- A study conducted by the U.S. Department of Labor found that women and minorities have made more progress breaking through the glass ceiling at smaller companies. Women comprise 25 percent of the managers and corporate officers in smaller establishments, while minorities represent 10 percent. But among Fortune 500 companies, women held 18 percent of the managerial jobs, with minorities holding 7 percent.

- The federal Glass Ceiling Commission found that white women made up close to half the workforce, but held only 5 percent of the senior level jobs in corporations. Blacks and other minorities account for less than 3 percent of top jobs (vice president and above).

- The Glass Ceiling Commission found that a majority of chief executives acknowledge that the federal guidelines have been crucial in maintaining their commitment to a diverse workforce. It is estimated that only 30 to 40 percent of American companies are committed to affirmative action programs purely for business reasons, without any federal pressure. Most medium-size and small companies, where job growth is greatest and affirmative action gains biggest, have adopted affirmative action only grudgingly, and without guidelines, they are most likely to toss it overboard.

- Studies show that there is little correlation between what black and white workers score on employment tests and how they perform in the workplace.

- A Census Bureau survey of 3,000 businesses asked them to list the things they consider most important when hiring workers. The employers ranked test scores as 8th on a list of 11 factors. Job testing did not come into wide usage in the United States until after Title VII.

- The Glass Ceiling Commission research reported that stereotyping and prejudice still rule many executive suites. Women and minorities are frequently routed into career paths like customer relations and human resources, which usually do not lead to the top jobs.

Exhibit 4.3 (continued)

- Cecelia Conrad, associate professor of economics at Barnard College in New York, examined whether affirmative action plans had hurt worker productivity. She found "no evidence that there has been any decline in productivity due to affirmative action." She also found no evidence of improved productivity due to affirmative action.
- A study of Standard and Poor's 500 companies found firms that broke barriers for women and minorities reported stock market records nearly 2.5 times better than comparable companies that took no action.

As you will see, however, affirmative action is used only when there is a *demonstrated* underrepresentation or a finding of discrimination. It is designed to remedy *present-day* employment inequities based on race or gender. A seven-volume study released on October 1, 1999, by Harvard University and the Russell Sage Foundation found that racial stereotypes and attitudes "heavily influence the labor market, with blacks landing at the very bottom." The researchers found that "race is deeply entrenched in the country's cultural landscape—perhaps even more than many Americans realize or are willing to admit." Attitudes such as those found by the Harvard study find their way into the workplace and affect minority and female employees working there. That, in turn, leads to the need for assistance such as affirmative action to remedy the situation.

If we could think of one thing that bothers us the most about affirmative action, it is that we view our country as based on fairness and our achievement as based on the effort we put forth. Affirmative action seems to fly in the face of this because it appears that women and blacks or other minorities get something without any effort. All they have to do is be born female or black and show up and they get the job or get into schools or are granted contracts. Based on this premise, it makes absolutely perfect sense to greatly resent affirmative action. However, as we have seen, research demonstrates this is far from reality.

Throughout the chapter, keep this thought in mind: If Alaska is 99 percent Inuit (Eskimo), then, all things being equal, that will be reflected at all or most levels of their employment spectrum. All things being equal, it would look odd if Alaska is 99 percent Inuit and there are only 5 percent Inuits holding managerial-level jobs but 100 percent of the unskilled labor jobs. Of course, the reality is that it is rare to have a workforce that has so little diversity. Among other things, there will also be differing skill levels and interests within the workforce from which the employees are drawn. However, the example is instructive for purposes of illustrating how a workplace should reflect the available workforce from which its employees are drawn. If there is a significant difference, which cannot be accounted for otherwise, the difference between availability and representation in the workplace should be addressed. In essence, this is affirmative action. We believe that the more you understand what affirmative action actually is and what it is used for, the more likely you are to help your employer more effectively meet affirmative action obligations.

Affirmative action also arises in other contexts such as college admissions, granting government contracts, and set-asides. However, except in limited cases, these are beyond the scope of this text, which only addresses the employment setting.

AFFIRMATIVE ACTION UNDER EXECUTIVE ORDER 11246

Though people tend to think of affirmative action as a part of Title VII, and, in fact, Title VII has an affirmative action component as part of its statutory remedies, affirmative action actually stems from a requirement imposed by Executive Order 11246 and its amendments. Under the executive order, those employers who contract to furnish the federal government with goods and services (called federal contractors) must agree not to discriminate in the hiring, termination, promotion, pay, and so on of employees on the basis of race, color, religion, gender, or national origin.

The first forerunner to E.O. 11246 was Executive Order 8802, signed by President Franklin D. Roosevelt on June 25, 1941. It applied only to defense contracts and was issued to combat discrimination during World War II "as a prerequisite to the successful conduct of our national defense production effort." This executive order underwent several changes before the present version was signed into law by President Lyndon B. Johnson on September 24, 1965.

E.O. 11246 Provisions

In addition to prohibiting discrimination in employment, for certain contracts the executive order requires that contractors who have underrepresentations of women minorities in their workplace agree to take steps to ensure adequate representation. In cases where the employer refuses to remedy disparities found, he or she is **debarred** from further participation in government contracts. This is a rare occurrence, since most employers eventually comply with OFCCP's suggestions for remedying disparities.

The executive order is enforced by the Office of Federal Contract Compliance Programs (OFCCP) in the U.S. Department of Labor, which issues extensive regulations implementing the executive order (41 CFR 60). OFCCP's enforcement addresses only the employer's participation in federal government contracts and contains no provisions for private lawsuits by employees. Employees seeking redress must do so through their state's fair employment practice laws, Title VII, or similar legislation previously discussed. However, employees may file complaints with OFCCP, which the Secretary of Labor is authorized to receive and investigate, and may sue the secretary to compel performance of executive order requirements.

Title VII prohibits discrimination in employment, but it does not impose affirmative duties on the employer. However, as a part of the remedies provided under Title VII, courts may order affirmative action.

Employers who contract with the federal government to provide goods and services of $10,000 or more must agree to comply with the executive order. In addition, contractors and subcontractors agree to:

- Post in conspicuous places, available to employees and applicants, notices provided by the contracting officer setting forth the provisions of the nondiscrimination clause. You may have seen these in your workplace or university/college.
- Include in all the contractor's solicitations or advertisements for employees a statement that all qualified applicants will receive consideration for employment without regard to race, color, religion, gender, or national origin.

debar
Prohibit a federal contractor from further participation in government contracts.

- Include a statement of these obligations in all subcontracts or purchase orders, unless exempted, which will be binding on each subcontractor or vendor.
- Furnish all information and reports required by the executive order and the implementing regulations, and permit access to the contractor's or subcontractor's books, records, and accounts by the contracting agency and the Secretary of Labor for purposes of investigation to ascertain compliance with the executive order and its regulations.

Under the implementing regulations, Executive Order 11246 increases compliance requirements based on the amount of the contract. For the smallest contracts the employer agrees that, in addition to not discriminating in employment, it will post notices that it is an equal opportunity employer. If a contractor or subcontractor has 50 or more employees and a nonconstruction contract of $50,000 or more, the contractor must develop a written **affirmative action plan** for each of his or her establishments within 120 days of the beginning of the contract.

Affirmative Action Plans

Affirmative action plans must be developed according to the rules set forth in the Code of Federal Regulations (CFR) Part 60-2 that effectuates the Executive Order. According to the regulations, "an affirmative action plan should be considered a management tool—an integral part of the way a corporation conducts its business . . . to encourage self-evaluation in every aspect of an employment by establishing systems to monitor and examine the contractor's employment decisions and compensation systems to ensure that they are free of discrimination." (See Exhibit 4.4, "More Than a 'Numbers Game.'")

Affirmative action plans have both quantitative and qualitative aspects. The quantitative part of the plan examines the contractor's workplace to get a snapshot, of sorts, of who works there and in what capacity, as relates to minorities and women. Minority categories include Black, Hispanic, Asian/Pacific Islander, and American Indians/Alaskan Natives. The qualitative part of the plan sets out a plan of action for how to address any **underrepresentation, underutilization**, or other problems found.

In order to get the snapshot of what the contractor's workplace looks like as it relates to minorities and/or females, employers must prepare an **organizational profile**. An organizational profile shows staffing patterns within a workplace, much like an organizational chart, showing each of the organizational units, their relationship to one another, and the gender, race, and ethnic composition of each unit. It is "one method contractors use to determine whether barriers to equal employment opportunity exist in their organization."

Another part of the snapshot is the contractor's **job group analysis**. Job group analysis combines job titles at the contractor's workplace that have similar content, wage rates, and opportunities. The job group analysis must include a list of the job titles for each job group and the percentage of minorities and the percentage of women it employs in each job group. This analysis is then compared to the availability of women and/or minorities for these job groups.

Now that the contractor has this snapshot of the workplace, the foundation of the affirmative action plan is laid. The purpose of the snapshot is to see if there is an underrepresentation of women and/or minorities based on the difference between their

---

affirmative action plan
A government contractor's plan containing placement goals for inclusion of women and minorities in the workplace and timetables for accomplishing the goals.

underrepresentation or **underutilization**
Significantly fewer minorities or women in the workplace than relevant statistics indicate are available.

organizational profile
Staffing patterns showing organizational units, relationship to each other, and gender, race, and ethnic composition.

job group analysis
Combines job titles with similar content, wage rates, and opportunities.

availability
Minorities and women in a geographic area who are qualified for a particular position.

availability in the workforce from which employees are hired and their presence in the workplace. Availability is important in order to "establish a benchmark against which the demographic composition of the contractor's employees can be compared in order to determine whether barriers to equal employment opportunity may exist within particular job groups."

Availability is not based on the mere presence of women and minorities in a given geographic area. Rather, it is based on the availability of women and minorities qualified for the particular job. Simply because women are 35 percent of the general population for a particular geographic area does not mean that they are all qualified to be doctors, professors, skilled craft workers, or managers. Availability for jobs as, for instance, managers, would only consider those qualified to fill the position of managers, rather than all women in the geographic area. The regulations contain resources for finding out availability for various jobs in a given geographic area.

The two factors to be used in determining availability of employees (separately for minorities and women for each job group) are: (1) the percentage of minorities or women with requisite skills in the reasonable recruitment area, defined as the geographical areas from which the contractor usually seeks or reasonably could seek workers to fill the positions in question, and (2) the percentage of minorities or women among those promotable, transferable, and trainable within the contractor's organization.

If the percentage of women and/or minorities employed in a job group is less than would reasonably be expected based on their availability in the area from which employees are drawn, the contractor must establish a **placement goal** that reflects the reasonable availability of women and/or minorities in the geographic area.

placement goal
Percentage of women and/or minorities to be hired to correct underrepresentation, based on availability in the geographic area.

By regulation, placement goals, which serve as objectives "reasonably attainable by means of applying every "good faith effort" to make all aspects of the entire affirmative action program work," do not mean that the underrepresentation is an admission or a finding of discrimination. They are designed to measure progress toward achieving equal employment opportunity and "may not be rigid and inflexible quotas which must be met," nor a ceiling or floor for employing certain groups. "*Quotas are expressly forbidden*" (Sec. 60-2.16(e)(1)). In making decisions, employers are expressly *not* required "to hire a person who lacks qualifications to perform the job successfully, or hire a less qualified person in preference to a more qualified one" (Sec. 60-2.16(e)(4)). In all employment decisions, the contractor must make selections in a nondiscriminatory manner (Sec. 60-2.16(e)(2)).

Once this quantitative part of the affirmative action plan is in place, if an underrepresentation or other problem has been found, the contractor must then develop and execute "action-oriented" programs designed to correct them. OFCCP believes that in order for the programs to be effective, they must be more than the contractor's "business as usual," which, of course, led to the underrepresentation in the first place. (See Exhibit 4.6.)

OFCCP may perform audits of contractors to determine if they are complying with the regulations and providing equal employment opportunity. To withstand an OFCCP audit, contractors must show that they have made good faith efforts to remove any identified barriers to equal employment opportunity, expand employment opportunities, and produce measurable results. As part of its action program, contractors must:

- Develop and implement internal auditing systems that periodically measure the effectiveness of their affirmative action plans, including monitoring records of all personnel activity to ensure that the contractor's nondiscriminatory policy is being carried out.
- Require internal reporting on a scheduled basis as to the degree to which equal employment opportunity and organizational objectives are attained.
- Review report results with all levels of management.
- Advise top management of the program's effectiveness and submit recommendations for improvement, where necessary.

corporate management compliance evaluation
Evaluations of mid- and senior-level employee advancement.

In an effort to combat the glass ceiling, the regulations also require **corporate management compliance evaluations** designed to determine whether employees are encountering artificial barriers to advancement to mid- and senior-level corporate management. During such evaluations, special attention is given to those components of the employment process that affect advancement into these upper-level positions.

Each year, OFCCP conducts an Equal Opportunity Survey to provide the agency with compliance data early in the evaluation process so that it can more effectively and efficiently identify contractors for further evaluation, as well as acting as a self-evaluation tool for contractors. The survey requests brief information that will allow OFCCP to have an accurate assessment of contractor personnel activities, pay practices, and affirmative action performance. Employers are required to submit data on applicants, hires, promotions, terminations, compensation, and tenure by race and gender. (See Exhibit 4.8.)

Again, there is no requirement of quotas under Executive Order 11246 or under Title VII. In fact, as we saw previously, the law specifically says it is not to be interpreted as such. Virtually the only time quotas are permitted is when there has been a long-standing violation of the law and there is little other recourse. The *Sheet Metal Workers* case, later in the chapter, demonstrated this with the union's resistance over an 18-year period, resulting in the imposition of quotas.

Placement goals to remedy underrepresentation should not be confused with quotas. As long as an employer can show a legitimate, good faith effort to reach affirmative action placement goals, quotas are not required and will not be imposed as a remedy for underrepresentation.

Penalties for Noncompliance

The Secretary of Labor or the appropriate contracting agency can impose on the employer a number of penalties for noncompliance, including:

- Publishing the names of nonconforming contractors or labor unions.
- Recommending to the EEOC or the Department of Justice that proceedings be instituted under Title VII.
- Requesting that the Attorney General bring suit to enforce the executive order in cases of actual or threatened substantial violations of the contractual EEO clause.

- Recommending to the Department of Justice that criminal proceedings be initiated for furnishing false information to a contracting agency or the Secretary of Labor.
- Canceling, terminating, or suspending the contract, or any portion thereof, for failure of the contractor or subcontractor to comply with the nondiscrimination provisions of the contract (this may be done absolutely, or continuance may be conditioned on a program for future compliance approved by the contracting agency).
- Debarring the noncomplying contractor from entering into further government contracts until the contractor has satisfied the secretary that it will abide by the provisions of the order.

The Secretary of Labor must make reasonable efforts to secure compliance by conference, conciliation, mediation, and persuasion before requesting the U.S. Attorney General to act or before canceling or surrendering a contract. While a hearing is required before the secretary can debar a contractor, it may be granted before any other sanction is imposed, if appropriate. As a practical matter, the more severe penalties are rarely used, because contractors are generally not so recalcitrant toward OFCCP orders.

In making its compliance determinations for contractors' affirmative action plans, OFCCP will not make the judgment solely on whether the contractor's affirmative action goals are met, that is, "the numbers game." (See Exhibit 4.4.) That alone will not serve as a basis for sanctions under the Executive Order. What is important to OFCCP is the nature and extent of the contractor's good faith affirmative action activities and the appropriateness of those activities to the problems the contractor has identified in the workplace. An assessment of compliance will be made on both statistical and nonstatistical information indicating whether employees and applicants are being treated without regard to the prohibited categories of the Executive Order.

The affirmative action plan regulations clearly state that they prefer to have contractors perform ongoing monitoring of their workplaces to ensure that their policies and practices are consistent with nondiscriminatory hiring, termination, pay, and other workplace considerations. An employer would do well to heed that advice and catch any small problems before they become larger ones. Careful monitoring will address this quite well.

JUDICIAL AFFIRMATIVE ACTION

judicial affirmative action
Affirmative action ordered by a court, rather than arising from Executive Order 11246.

Rather than an affirmative action plan imposed by Executive Order 11246, an employee may sue for violation of Title VII and the affirmative action arises in response to a finding of workplace discrimination that must be remedied now that a court has found that discrimination does, in fact, exist and because of the nature of the violation, an affirmative action plan is the appropriate means to remedy the violation. Title VII gives courts fairly wide latitude in redressing wrongs. The courts' imposition of affirmative action as the means of redress is known as **judicial affirmative action**.

Courts have played an important role in shaping the concept of affirmative action. While there are no specific requirements as to what form an affirmative action plan must take (see Exhibit 4.5), if the plan is in keeping with the requirements set forth below, the employer has little to fear from such suits—although the monetary and energy costs in dealing with them are great.

Exhibit 4.4

More Than a "Numbers Game"—Major Affirmative
Action Regulation Overhaul: The Dog Now Wags
the Tail, Rather Than Vice Versa

Most people tend to think of affirmative action as a "numbers game" in which an employer tries to hire a certain magic number of minorities and women in order to avoid running into trouble with the "feds." That is *so* not the case. Actually, there may have been some basis for that view when set against the background of the 1980s discussed earlier. When much of the policy was hammered out, OFCCP may have seemed more interested in the bottom line figures. But as affirmative action evolved, it became clear that numbers, alone, were not sufficient. After all, it is equal employment *opportunity* that the law wanted to ensure, confident that if the opportunities were equal, that would be reflected in the bottom line figures. With the numbers approach, OFCCP obviously found the managerial policies suffered at the hands of trying to achieve numbers and the intent of the law was not being met. The tail was wagging the dog, rather than vice versa.

In 2000, OFCCP issued the most comprehensive set of changes to its regulations since the 1970s. Not only did the new regulations make changes in a few significant ways affirmative action plans are to be developed, such as decreasing the number of availability factors it will consider from eight to two and permitting employers to replace the previously required workforce analysis with an organization profile that is usually simpler, but it also clarified and reaffirmed basic foundations of affirmative action. In recognizing this more balanced approach, OFCCP said that "Affirmative action programs contain a diagnostic component which includes a number of quantitative analyses designed to evaluate the composition of the workforce of the contractor and compare it to the composition of the relevant labor pools. Affirmative action programs also include action-oriented programs."

Probably most importantly, it was clear that OFCCP was moving from an approach that was perceived as being interested primarily in the mechanics of affirmative action plans submitted by employers, to one in which the plan is viewed as "a management tool to ensure equal employment opportunity." The agency said that "A central premise underlying affirmative action is that, absent discrimination, over time a contractor's workforce, generally, will reflect the gender, racial and ethnic profile of the labor pools from which the contractor recruits and selects. If women and minorities are not being employed at a rate to be expected given their availability in the relevant labor pool, the contractor's affirmative action program includes specific practical steps designed to address this underutilization. Effective affirmative action programs also include internal auditing and reporting systems as a means of measuring the contractor's progress toward achieving the workforce that would be expected in the absence of discrimination."

Rather than being a numbers game, OFCCP envisions affirmative action plans as a way for contractors to take the opportunity to look at their workforces and see if they are reflective of the relevant population they are drawn from and if they see they are not, to make a plan to work toward making that happen. This reflects the understanding that given the country's racial, ethnic, and gender history, without taking the time and opportunity to actually step back and take a view of the larger picture, employers may not be aware of the underrepresentation, and thus it will continue. In addressing its preferred approach, OFCCP noted that this analysis should not just be done in anticipation of reporting to OFCCP, but on a regular basis as part of its management of the workplace in all aspects. "An affirmative action program also ensures equal employment opportunity by institutionalizing the contractor's commitment to equality in

(continued)

Exhibit 4.4 (continued)

every aspect of the employment process. Therefore, as part of its affirmative action program, a contractor monitors and examines its employment decisions and compensation systems to evaluate the impact of those systems on women and minorities."

In this more holistic view OFCCP pronounced in its regulatory revisions, it said that "An affirmative action program is, thus, more than a paperwork exercise. An affirmative action program includes those policies, practices, and procedures that the contractor implements to ensure that all qualified applicants and employees are receiving an equal opportunity for recruitment, selection, advancement, and every other term and privilege associated with employment. Affirmative action, ideally, is a part of the way the contractor regularly conducts its business. OFCCP has found that when an affirmative action program is approached from this perspective, as a powerful management tool, there is a positive correlation between the presence of affirmative action and the absence of discrimination.

"Pursuant to these regulatory changes, OFCCP will focus its resources on the action undertaken to promote equal employment opportunity, rather than on the technical compliance."

Source: *Government Contractors Affirmative Action Requirements: Final Rule.* Volume 165, Number 219, pages 68021–47, 41 CFR Parts 60-1 and 60-2, effective 12/13/2000, http://www.dol.gov/esa/regs/fedreg/final/2000028693.htm.

The first affirmative action case to reach the U.S. Supreme Court, *Regents of the University of California* v. *Bakke*[3], involved affirmative action in medical school admissions, rather than employment; however, the case is viewed as the one that opened the affirmative action debate, and much of its reasoning was used in subsequent employment cases. While endorsing the concept of affirmative action to further the educational goal of a diverse student body, the Court struck down the University of California's affirmative action plan because it set aside a certain number of places for "disadvantaged students," who could also compete for the other spaces. The Court said it was not fair to have the disadvantaged group have additional spaces open to them that were not available to others.

In *Local 28, Sheet Metal Workers* v. *EEOC,* the Court imposed one of the stiffer judicial affirmative action plans ever developed, but only after the Court's orders had repeatedly been ignored by the union. In the case, the question arose as to who can receive the benefit of affirmative action plans. Can the plan benefit individuals who were not the actual victims of the employer's discriminatory practices? The Supreme Court held that there need not be a showing of discrimination against the particular individual (employee, applicant, promotion candidate, and the like) as long as the affirmative action plan meets appropriate requirements (see Exhibit 4.5) and the individual fits into the category of employees the plan was designed to benefit. This approach recognizes that the employer's policy may result in discouraging certain people from ever even applying for a job because they know it would be futile, given the employer's history.

While the notion of providing relief for nonspecific victims of discrimination may appear somewhat questionable, the *Sheet Metal Workers* is the type of situation that justifies such action. As you read the case, in addition to thinking about what the union

[3] 438 U.S. 265 (1978).

Exhibit 4.5

Affirmative Actions

While there are guidelines as to what may or may not be legally acceptable as affirmative action designed to intentionally include women and minorities in the workplace, there are no specific requirements about what affirmative action must be taken. As a result, employers' means of addressing affirmative action have varied greatly. Keep in mind the Supreme Court's characterization of plans that are acceptable when viewing the following ideas employers have used. Just because employers have used these methods does not mean they are always legal. Sometimes they may simply be convenient.

- *Advertising for applicants in nontraditional sources.* Employers solicit minority and female applicants through resources such as historically black colleges and universities, women's colleges, minority and female civic, educational, religious, and social organizations, including the NAACP, National Urban League, La Raza, American Indian Movement, National Organization for Women, and other such groups.

- *One-for-one hiring, training, or promotion programs.* One minority or female is hired, trained, or promoted for every white or male until a certain desired goal is reached. This is usually only used in long-standing, resistant cases of underrepresentation, and is rarely used anymore.

- *Preferential layoff provisions.* As in *Wygant,* in recognition of the reality that recently hired female and minority employees would be lost if layoffs are conducted based on seniority and, thereby, affirmative action gains lost, employers institute plans that are designed to prevent the percentage of minorities and women from falling below a certain point. Some minorities and women with less seniority may be retained, while those with more are laid off. While the U.S. Supreme Court did not prohibit this approach, it did indicate an employer would have to overcome a very rigorous analysis to ensure protection of the adversely impacted employees.

- *Extra consideration.* Women and minorities are considered along with all other candidates, but extra consideration is paid to their status as women and minorities, and, all other factors being equal, they may be chosen for the job.

- *Lower standards.* Women and minorities may be taken out of the regular pool of candidates and given different, usually less stringent, standards for qualifying for the position. Natural questions are why the higher standards are imposed if the job can be performed with lesser qualifications and why someone who is not qualified under the higher, "normal" standards should be given the job? This is *not* a good approach, and would probably *not* pass judicial muster.

- *Added points.* Much like with a veteran's preference, the employer has a rating system giving points for various criteria, and women and minorities receive extra points because they are women or minorities. This was not permitted by the U.S. Supreme Court in the undergraduate admission program at the University of Michigan.

- *Minority or female "positions."* In an effort to meet affirmative action goals, employers create and fund positions that are designed to be filled only by women or minorities. These positions may or may not be needed by the employer. This is not a smart approach for an employer and would not stand up in court.

Some of the approaches are more desirable than others because they are less likely to result in "reverse discrimination" suits or more likely to result in qualified minority or

(continued)

Exhibit 4.5   (continued)

female employees. Affirmative action plans walk a fine line between not holding women and minorities to lower standards than other employees, while, at the same time, not permitting the standards to be arbitrary and likely to unnecessarily or unwittingly screen out female or minority candidates. The 1991 Civil Rights Act made it unlawful to "adjust the scores of, use different cutoff scores for, or otherwise alter the results of, employment related tests" on the basis of race, color, religion, gender, or national origin. Since there are few rules, employers can be creative, within the guidelines provided by law. Now that you have seen some of the affirmative action schemes employers have used, which seem most suited to accomplish the goals of affirmative action, while having the least adverse impact on other employees? How would you design an affirmative action plan?

Scenario

or employer should have done, think of how you would have handled the situation if you were the court imposing the remedy. Also think of whether you would have allowed the situation to go on for so long if you were the court. This case is the basis for opening scenario 2.

Local 28, Sheet Metal Workers v. EEOC *478 U.S. 421 (1986)*

The union and its apprenticeship committee were found guilty of discrimination against Hispanics and blacks and were ordered to remedy the violations. They were found numerous times to be in contempt of the court's order and after 18 years the court eventually imposed fines and an affirmative action plan as a remedy. The plan included benefits to persons not members of the union. The Supreme Court held the remedies to be appropriate under the circumstances.

Brennan, J.

Local 28 represents sheet metal workers employed by contractors in the New York City metropolitan area. The Local 28 Joint Apprenticeship Committee (JAC) is a labor–management committee which operates a 4-year apprenticeship training program designed to teach sheet metal skills. Apprentices enrolled in the program receive training both from classes and from on-the-job work experience. Upon completing the program, apprentices become journeyman members of Local 28. Successful completion of the program is the principal means of attaining union membership.

In 1964, the New York State Commission for Human Rights determined that the union and JAC had excluded blacks from the union and apprenticeship program in violation of state law. The Commission, among other things, found that the union had never had any black members or apprentices, and that "admission to apprenticeship is conducted largely on a nepot[is]tic

basis involving sponsorship by incumbent union members," creating an impenetrable barrier for nonwhite applicants. The union and JAC were ordered to "cease and desist" their racially discriminatory practices. Over the next 18 years and innumerable trips to court, the union did not remedy the discrimination.

To remedy the contempt and the union's refusal to comply with court orders, the court imposed a 29 percent nonwhite membership goal to be met by a certain date, and a $150,000 fine to be placed in a fund designed to increase nonwhite membership in the apprenticeship program and the union. The fund was used for a variety of purposes, including:

- Providing counseling and tutorial services to nonwhite apprentices, giving them benefits that had traditionally been available to white apprentices from family and friends.
- Providing financial support to employers otherwise unable to hire a sufficient number of apprentices.

- Providing matching funds to attract additional funding for job-training programs.
- Creating part-time and summer sheet metal jobs for qualified nonwhite youths.
- Extending financial assistance to needy apprentices.
- Paying for nonwhite union members to serve as liaisons to vocational and technical schools with sheet metal programs in order to increase the pool of qualified nonwhite applicants for the apprenticeship program.

The union appealed the remedy. Principally, the parties maintain that the Fund and goal exceeds the scope of remedies available under Title VII because it extends race-conscious preferences to individuals who are not the identified victims of their unlawful discrimination. They argue that section 706(g) authorizes a district court to award preferential relief only to actual victims of unlawful discrimination. They maintain that the goal and Fund violates this provision since it requires them to extend benefits to black and Hispanic individuals who are not the identified victims of unlawful discrimination. We reject this argument and hold that section 706(g) does not prohibit a court from ordering, in appropriate circumstances, affirmative race-conscious relief as a remedy for past discrimination. Specifically, we hold that such relief may be appropriate where an employer or a labor union has engaged in persistent or egregious discrimination, or where necessary to dissipate the lingering effects of pervasive discrimination.

The availability of race-conscious affirmative relief under section 706(g) as a remedy for a violation of Title VII furthers the broad purposes underlying the statute. Congress enacted Title VII based on its determination that racial minorities were subject to pervasive and systematic discrimination in employment. It was clear to Congress that the crux of the problem was "to open employment opportunities for Negroes in occupations which have been traditionally closed to them and it was to this problem that Title VII's prohibition against racial discrimination was primarily addressed." Title VII was designed to achieve equality of employment opportunities and remove barriers that have operated in the past to favor an identifiable group of white employees over other employees. In order to foster equal employment opportunities, Congress gave the lower courts broad power under section 706(g) to

fashion the most complete relief possible to remedy past discrimination.

In most cases, the court need only order the employer or union to cease engaging in discriminatory practices, and award make-whole relief to the individuals victimized by those practices. In some instances, however, it may be necessary to require the employer or union to take affirmative steps to end discrimination effectively to enforce Title VII. Where an employer or union has engaged in particularly longstanding or egregious discrimination, an injunction simply reiterating Title VII's prohibition against discrimination will often prove useless and will only result in endless enforcement litigation. In such cases, requiring a recalcitrant employer or unions to hire and to admit qualified minorities roughly in proportion to the number of qualified minorities in the workforce may be the only effective way to ensure the full enjoyment of the rights protected by Title VII.

Further, even where the employer or union formally ceases to engage in discrimination, informal mechanisms may obstruct equal employment opportunities. An employer's reputation for discrimination may discourage minorities from seeking available employment. In these circumstances, affirmative race-conscious relief may be the only means available to assure equality of employment opportunities and to eliminate those discriminatory practices and devices which have fostered racially stratified job environments to the disadvantage of minority citizens. Affirmative action promptly operates to change the outward and visible signs of yesterday's racial distinctions and thus, to provide an impetus to the process of dismantling the barriers, psychological or otherwise, erected by past practices.

Finally, a district court may find it necessary to order interim hiring or promotional goals pending the development of nondiscriminatory hiring or promotion procedures. In these cases, the use of numerical goals provides a compromise between two unacceptable alternatives: an outright ban on hiring or promotions, or continued use of a discriminatory selection procedure.

We have previously suggested that courts may utilize certain kinds of racial preferences to remedy past discrimination under Title VII. The Courts of Appeals have unanimously agreed that racial preferences may be used, in appropriate cases, to remedy past discrimination under Title VII. The extensive legislative history of the Act supports this view. Many opponents of Title VII argued that an employer could be found guilty of discrimination under the statute simply because of a racial imbalance in his workforce, and would be compelled to implement racial "quotas" to avoid being charged with liability. At the same time, supporters of the bill insisted that employers would not violate Title VII simply because of racial imbalance, and emphasized that neither the EEOC nor the courts could compel employers to adopt quotas solely to facilitate racial balancing. The debate concerning what Title VII did and did not require culminated in the adoption of section 703(j), which stated expressly that the statute did not require an employer or labor union to adopt quotas or preferences simply because of a racial imbalance.

Although we conclude that section 706(g) does not foreclose a court from instituting some sort of racial preferences where necessary to remedy past discrimination, we do not mean to suggest such relief is always proper. The court should exercise its discretion with an eye towards Congress' concern that the measures not be invoked simply to create a racially balanced workforce. In the majority of cases the court will not have to impose affirmative action as a remedy for past discrimination, but need only order the employer or union to cease engaging in discriminatory practices. However, in some cases, affirmative action may be necessary in order effectively to enforce Title VII, such as with persistent or egregious discrimination or to dissipate the effects of pervasive discrimination. The court should also take care to tailor its orders to fit the nature of the violation it seeks to correct.

Here, the membership goal and Fund were necessary to remedy the union and JAC's pervasive and egregious discrimination and its lingering effects. The goal was flexible and thus gives a strong indication that it was not being used simply to achieve and maintain racial balance, but rather as a benchmark against which the court could gauge the union's efforts. Twice the court adjusted the deadline for the goal and has continually approved changes in the size of apprenticeship classes to account for economic conditions preventing the union from meeting its targets. And it is temporary in that it will end as soon as the percentage of minority union members approximates the percentage of minorities in the local labor force. Similarly the fund is scheduled to terminate when the union achieves its membership goal and the court determines it is no longer needed to remedy past discrimination. Also, neither the goal nor the fund unnecessarily trammels the interests of white employees. They do not require any union members to be laid off, and do not discriminate against existing union members. While whites seeking admission into the union may be denied benefits extended to nonwhite counterparts, the court's orders do not stand as an absolute bar to such individuals; indeed a majority of new union members have been white. Many of the provisions of the orders are race-neutral (such as the requirement that the JAC assign one apprenticeship for every four journeymen workers) and the union and JAC remain free to adopt the provisions of the order for the benefit of white members and applicants. Accordingly, we AFFIRM.

Case Questions

1. Is it clear to you why a court would be able to include in its remedies those who are not directly discriminated against by an employer? Explain.

2. If you were the court and were still trying to get the union to comply with your order 18 years after the fact, what would you have done?

3. As an employer, how could you avoid such a result?

VOLUNTARY AFFIRMATIVE ACTION

After the Court for the first time dealt with the issue of affirmative action in the *Bakke* case, the next big questions were whether a similar analysis applied (1) if the affirmative action plan involved private rather than state action, (2) if the plan involved a workplace rather than a university admissions program, and (3) whether voluntary affirmative action plans are permissible rather than only those required by Executive Order 11246 or imposed by a court to remedy prior discrimination found to have existed. The opportunity to have those important Title VII developmental questions answered came the year after *Bakke,* in the *United Steelworkers of America, AFL-CIO* v. *Weber* case on page 200. As you will see in *Weber,* the answer to all three questions was yes.

According to the federal regulations governing voluntary affirmative action plans:

Affirmative action to improve opportunities for minorities and women must be encouraged and protected in order to carry out the Congressional intent embodied in Title VII. Affirmative action under these principles means those actions appropriate to overcome the effects of past or present practices, policies, or other barriers to equal employment opportunity. Such voluntary affirmative action cannot be measured by the standard of whether it would have been required had there been litigation, for this standard would undermine the legislative purpose of first encouraging voluntary action without litigation. Rather, persons subject to Title VII must be allowed flexibility in modifying employment systems and practices to comport with the purposes of Title VII. Correspondingly, Title VII must be construed to permit such voluntary action, and those taking such action should be afforded the protection against Title VII liability which the Commission is authorized to provide under section 713(b)(1) [providing that no person shall be subject to any liability or punishment for or on account of (1) the commission by such person of an unlawful employment practice if he pleads and proves that the act or omission complained of was in good faith, in conformity with, and in reliance on any written interpretation or opinion of the Commission.]

Employers, labor organizations, and other persons subject to Title VII may, and are encouraged to take affirmative action in such circumstances, including, but not limited to, the following:

(1) Training plans and programs, including on-the-job training, which emphasize providing minorities and women with the opportunity, skill, and experience necessary to perform the functions of skilled trades, crafts, or professions;

(2) Extensive and focused recruiting activity;

(3) Elimination of the adverse impact caused by unvalidated selection criteria (see Sections 3 and 6, Uniform Guidelines on Employee Selection Procedures (1978), 43 FR 30290; 38297; 38299 (August 25, 1978));

(4) Modification through collective bargaining where a labor organization represents employees, or unilaterally where one does not, of promotion and layoff procedures.

Source: 29 CFR Ch. XIV (7-1-03 Edition) § 1608.4, http://a257.g.akamaitech.net/7/257/2422/ 08aug20031600/edocket.access.gpo.gov/cfr_2003/julqtr/pdf/29cfr1608.3.pdf.

Based on *Weber*, in addition to affirmative action plans required by Executive Order 11246 and those imposed by a court to remedy discrimination found in the workplace pursuant to a Title VII claim, there is also the possibility of voluntary affirmative action. Here, the employer decides to institute an affirmative action plan on his or her own, regardless of whether the employer is required to do so under the Executive Order, and despite the fact that no one has brought a Title VII case. Employers generally engage in voluntary affirmative action as a proactive measure to avoid discrimination claims after making a determination that there is an underrepresentation of minorities and women in the workplace. However, an employer cannot simply unilaterally decide to institute a plan out of the goodness of his or her heart and run with it. Based on *Weber* there are strict guidelines that must be followed if the plan is to withstand a reverse discrimination challenge by an affected employee alleging discrimination because of the plan's implementation. (See Exhibit 4.6.)

United Steelworkers of America, AFL-CIO v. Weber

443 U.S. 193 (1979)

A white employee sued under Title VII alleging race discrimination, in that the union and employer adopted a voluntary affirmative action plan reserving for black employees 50 percent of the openings in a training program until the percentage of black craft workers in the plant approximated the percentage of blacks in the local labor force. The Supreme Court held that the program was permissible, in that Title VII did not prohibit voluntary race-conscious affirmative action plans undertaken to eliminate a manifest racial imbalance, the measure is only temporary, and it did not unnecessarily trample the rights of white employees.

Brennan, J.

In 1974, the union and Kaiser entered into a master collective bargaining agreement covering terms and conditions of employment at 15 Kaiser plants. The agreement included an affirmative action plan designed to eliminate conspicuous racial imbalances in Kaiser's craftwork force, which was almost exclusively white. The plan was to eliminate this racial imbalance by reserving for black employees 50 percent of the openings in in-plant craft-training programs until the percentage of black craftworkers in a plant is commensurate with the percentage of blacks in the local labor force.

This litigation arose from the operation of the affirmative action plan at Kaiser's Gramercy plant where, prior to 1974, only 1.83 percent of the skilled craftworkers were black, even though the local workforce was approximately 39 percent black. Pursuant to the national agreement, rather than continue its practice of hiring trained outsiders, Kaiser established a training program to train its production workers to fill craft openings. Pursuant to the master collective bargaining agreement, trainees were selected on the basis of seniority, with the proviso that at least 50 percent of the trainees were to be black until the percentage of black skilled craftworkers in the Gramercy plant approximated the percentage of blacks in the local labor force. During the first year of the plan, seven black and six white craft trainees were selected, with the most senior black trainee having less seniority than several white production workers whose bids for admission to the program were rejected. Weber was one of those workers.

After being turned down for the training program when blacks with less seniority were admitted, Weber

sued, alleging that, because the affirmative action program had resulted in junior black employees receiving training in preference to more senior white employees, Weber, and others similarly situated, had been discriminated against in violation of sections 703(a) and (d) of Title VII of the Civil Rights Act of 1964 which made it unlawful to discriminate on the basis of race in the hiring and selection of apprentices for training programs.

The question is whether Congress, in Title VII, left employers and unions in the private sector free to take such race-conscious steps to eliminate manifest racial imbalances in traditionally segregated job categories. We hold that Title VII does not prohibit such race-conscious affirmative action plans.

Weber argues that since *McDonald* [see Chapter 5] settled that Title VII forbids discrimination against whites as well as blacks, and since the affirmative action plan here discriminates against whites solely because they are white, the plan therefore violates Title VII.

Weber's argument is not without force. But it overlooks the significance of the fact that the plan is an affirmative action plan voluntarily adopted by private parties to eliminate traditional patterns of racial segregation. In this context, Weber's reliance upon a literal construction of sections 703(a) and (d) and *McDonald* is misplaced. It is a familiar rule that a thing may be within the letter of the statute and yet not within the statute, because not within its spirit nor within the intention of its makers. The prohibition against racial discrimination in sections 703(a) and (d) of Title VII must therefore be read against the background of the legislative history of Title VII and the historical context from which the Act arose. Examination of those sources makes clear that an interpretation of the sections that forbade all race-conscious affirmative action would "bring about an end completely at variance with the purpose of the statute" and must be rejected.

Congress's primary concern in enacting the prohibition against racial discrimination in Title VII of the Civil Rights Act of 1964 was with "the plight of the Negro in our economy." Before 1964 blacks were largely relegated to "unskilled and semi-skilled jobs." Because of automation the number of such jobs was rapidly decreasing. As a consequence, "the relative position of the Negro worker [was] steadily worsening. In 1947 the nonwhite employment rate was only 64 percent higher than the white race; in 1962 it was 124 percent." Congress considered this a serious social problem and feared that the goal of the Civil Rights Act—the integration of blacks into the mainstream of society—could not be achieved unless the trend were reversed. It further recognized that this would not be possible unless blacks were able to secure jobs "which have a future."

Accordingly, it was clear to Congress that "[t]he crux of the problem [was] to open employment opportunities for Negroes in occupations which have been traditionally closed to them," and it was to this problem that Title VII's prohibition against racial discrimination in employment was primarily addressed.

It plainly appears from the House Report accompanying the Civil Rights Act that Congress did not intend wholly to prohibit private and voluntary affirmative action efforts as one method of solving this problem. The Report provides: "No bill can or should lay claim to eliminating all of the causes and consequences of racial and other types of discrimination against minorities. There is reason to believe, however, that national leadership provided by the enactment of Federal legislation dealing with the most troublesome problems *will create an atmosphere conducive to voluntary or local resolution of other forms of discrimination.*" H.R. Rep. No. 914, 88th Cong., 1st Sess., pt. 1, p. 18 (1963); U.S. Code Cong. & Admin. News 1964, pp. 2355, 2393. (Emphasis supplied.)

Given this legislative history, we cannot agree with Weber that Congress intended to prohibit the private sector from taking effective steps to accomplish the goal that Congress designed Title VII to achieve. The very statutory words intended as a spur or catalyst to cause "employers and unions to self-examine and to self-evaluate their employment practices and to endeavor to eliminate, so far as possible, the last vestiges of an unfortunate and ignominious page in this country's history," cannot be interpreted as an absolute

prohibition against all private, voluntary, race-conscious affirmative action efforts to hasten the elimination of such vestiges. It would be ironic if a law triggered by a Nation's concern over centuries of racial injustice and intended to improve the lot of those who had "been excluded from the American dream for so long," constituted the first legislative prohibition of all voluntary, private, race-conscious efforts to abolish traditional patterns of racial segregation and hierarchy.

The purposes of the plan mirror those of the statute. Both were designed to break down old patterns of racial segregation and hierarchy. Both were structured to "open employment opportunities for Negroes in occupations which have been traditionally closed to them."

At the same time, the plan does not unnecessarily trammel the interests of the white employees. The plan does not require the discharge of white workers and their replacement with new black hirees. Nor does the plan create an absolute bar to the advancement of white employees; half of those trained in the program will be white. Moreover, the plan is a temporary measure; it is not intended to maintain racial balance, but simply to eliminate a manifest racial imbalance. Preferential selection of craft trainees at the Gramercy plant will end as soon as the percentage of black skilled craftworkers in the Gramercy plant approximates the percentage of blacks in the local labor force.

We conclude, therefore, that the adoption of the Kaiser–USWA plan for the Gramercy plant falls within the area of discretion left by Title VII to the private sector voluntarily to adopt affirmative action plans designed to eliminate conspicuous racial imbalance in traditionally segregated job categories. Accordingly, the judgment of the Fifth Circuit is REVERSED.

Case Questions

1. Does this decision make sense to you? Why? Why not?

2. If, because of discrimination, blacks were not in a workplace for as long as whites and, therefore, did not have as much seniority as whites, does it seem reasonable to allow blacks with less seniority than whites to join the training program? If not, can you think of an alternative?

3. As a manager in a firm that is thinking of instituting a voluntary affirmative action plan, what factors would you consider?

Many employers were surprised by *Weber,* since the year before the Court struck down a voluntary affirmative action plan in *Bakke.* While both concerned affirmative action plans, there were considerable differences, beyond even public versus private employers. Some of these differences and the Court's reasoning got lost in news coverage. Both decisions endorsed the concept of affirmative action, but the requirements were not met in *Bakke* and were in *Weber,* thus giving different, though not inconsistent, outcomes. *Weber* is the basis for opening scenarios 1 and 3.

1
Scenario

After reading *Weber,* you now realize that in opening scenario 1, it is permissible for an employer to have a voluntary affirmative action plan, but certain factors must be present in order to justify the plan to a court. In opening scenario 1, we do not have all the relevant facts to determine if the employer can take the affirmative action measures the employer wishes. For instance, we do not know why there are such small numbers of minorities and women in upper-level management and skilled labor jobs. We do not know if it is because there is a history of discrimination and exclusion, or that there simply are not sufficient numbers of women and minorities available in the workforce.

3
Scenario

In opening scenario 3, we know from *Weber* that an employer can have a one-for-one affirmative action promotion plan as part of a judicial remedy for past discrimination, and if the *Weber* requirements are met, the employer is protected from liability for discrimination against employees alleging reverse discrimination, that is, that they are adversely impacted by implementation of the plan.

Seven years later, in the case of *Wygant* v. *Jackson Board of Education,*[4] and consistent with language in *Bakke* and *Weber,* the Supreme Court again upheld the concept of affirmative action, this time for protection against layoffs for public employees, though it held that the requirements of demonstrating a compelling state interest and narrowly tailoring the plan to meet the objective had not been met in this case. This answered the question of whether the Court's decision in *Bakke,* involving the admissions policy for a public university, also applied to an affirmative action plan in a public workplace. It did. It also answered the question left after *Weber* as to whether the acceptance of voluntary affirmative action in private employment also applied to public employment. It did.

Johnson v. *Transportation Agency, Santa Clara County, California,*[5] a 1987 Supreme Court decision discussed later, relied heavily on *Weber* to determine that, under circumstances similar to those in *Weber,* but involving a public employer, rather than private, and gender, rather than race, the employer could appropriately take gender into account under its voluntary affirmative action plan as one factor of a promotion decision. The Court said the plan, voluntarily adopted to redress a "conspicuous imbalance in traditionally segregated job categories," represented a "moderate, flexible, case-by-case approach to effecting a gradual improvement in the representation of minorities and women." Consistent with *Weber,* the plan was acceptable, because:

1. It did not unnecessarily trammel male employees' rights or create an absolute bar to their advancement.

2. It set aside no positions for women (as did *Bakke*) and expressly stated that its goals should not be construed as quotas to be met.

[4] 476 U.S. 267 (1986).
[5] 480 U.S. 616 (1987).

3. It unsettled no legitimate, firmly rooted expectation of employees.

4. It was only temporary in that it was for purposes of attaining, not maintaining, a balanced workforce.

5. There was minimal intrusion into the legitimate, settled expectations of other employees.

REVERSE DISCRIMINATION

reverse discrimination
Lawsuit or claim brought by majority member who feels adversely affected by the use of an affirmative action plan benefitting a minority on female.

So-called **reverse discrimination** has often been considered the flip side of affirmative action. When an employer is taking race or gender into account under an affirmative action plan in order to achieve an affirmative action placement goal, someone not in the excluded group alleges she or he is harmed by the employer's consideration of race or gender, or both, in hiring or promotion decisions.

For example, an employer finds an underrepresentation of women in managerial positions in the workplace and develops an affirmative action plan for their inclusion. As part of that plan, one qualified female employee is to be chosen for a managerial training program for each male chosen. The employer chooses one male, then one female. The male employee who feels he would have been chosen next if there were no affirmative action plan requiring a woman to be chosen sues the employer, alleging reverse discrimination. That is, that but for his gender, he would have been chosen for the position the female received.

The case below is the U.S. Supreme Court's recent affirmative action decision regarding the affirmative action plan used in the University of Michigan's law school admissions program. It is a bit longer than your other cases, but this is intentional. We thought you would want to see the language and reasoning of the Court in order to be able to better analyze the decision for yourselves. In the case, a white student sues for reverse discrimination, alleging the university's affirmative action plan was the reason the student was not admitted.

Grutter v. Bollinger *539 U.S. 306 (2003)*

A white student who was not admitted to the University of Michigan Law School sued the university, alleging, essentially, reverse discrimination. Twenty-five years after *Bakke,* the Court once again concluded that a university having a diverse student body is a compelling governmental interest that sustains the use of an affirmative action plan, and affirmative action plans, if implemented correctly, are permissible. The plan was also upheld because it did not have a certain number of students that must be admitted and race was only one of many factors the school considered in creating a diverse class. Though the case involves university admissions, it again reaffirms the Court's position on affirmative action.

O'Connor, J.

This case requires us to decide whether the use of race as a factor in student admissions by the University of Michigan Law School (Law School) is unlawful.

The Law School ranks among the Nation's top law schools. It receives more than 3,500 applications each year for a class of around 350 students. Seeking to "admit a group of students who individually and collectively are among the most capable," the Law School looks for individuals with "substantial promise for success in law school" and "a strong likelihood of succeeding in the practice of law and contributing in diverse ways to the well-being of others." The Law School seeks "a mix of students with varying backgrounds and experiences who will respect and learn from each other."

The hallmark of [the university's admissions policy adopted after *Bakke*] is its focus on academic ability coupled with a flexible assessment of applicants' talents, experiences, and potential "to contribute to the learning of those around them." The policy requires admissions officials to evaluate each applicant based on all the information available in the file, including a personal statement, letters of recommendation, and an essay describing the ways in which the applicant will contribute to the life and diversity of the Law School. In reviewing an applicant's file, admissions officials must consider the applicant's undergraduate grade point average (GPA) and Law School Admissions Test (LSAT) score because they are important (if imperfect) predictors of academic success in law school. The policy stresses that "no applicant should be admitted unless we expect that applicant to do well enough to graduate with no serious academic problems."

The policy makes clear, however, that even the highest possible score does not guarantee admission to the Law School. Nor does a low score automatically disqualify an applicant. Rather, the policy requires admissions officials to look beyond grades and test scores to other criteria that are important to the Law School's educational objectives. So-called "'soft' variables" such as "the enthusiasm of recommenders, the quality of the undergraduate institution, the quality of the applicant's essay, and the areas and difficulty of undergraduate course selection" are all brought to bear in assessing an "applicant's likely contributions to the intellectual and social life of the institution."

The policy does not restrict the types of diversity contributions eligible for "substantial weight" in the admissions process, but instead recognizes "many possible bases for diversity admissions." The policy does, however, reaffirm the Law School's longstanding commitment to "one particular type of diversity," that is, "racial and ethnic diversity with special reference to the inclusion of students from groups which have been historically discriminated against, like African-Americans, Hispanics and Native Americans, who

without this commitment might not be represented in our student body in meaningful numbers." By enrolling a "'critical mass' of [underrepresented] minority students," the Law School seeks to "ensure their ability to make unique contributions to the character of the Law School."

Petitioner Barbara Grutter is a white Michigan resident who applied to the Law School in 1996 with a 3.8 grade point average and 161 LSAT score. The Law School initially placed petitioner on a waiting list, but subsequently rejected her application. In December 1997, Grutter filed suit against the Law School. Grutter alleged that the Law School discriminated against her on the basis of race in violation of the Fourteenth Amendment; Title VI of the Civil Rights Act of 1964; and 42 USC § 1981.

Grutter further alleged that her application was rejected because the Law School uses race as a "predominant" factor, giving applicants who belong to certain minority groups "a significantly greater chance of admission than students with similar credentials from disfavored racial groups." Grutter also alleged that the Law School "had no compelling interest to justify their use of race in the admissions process."

We last addressed the use of race in public higher education over 25 years ago. In the landmark *Bakke* case, we reviewed a racial set-aside program that reserved 16 out 100 seats in a medical school class for members of certain minority groups. The only holding for the Court in *Bakke* was that a "State has a substantial interest that legitimately may be served by a properly devised admissions program involving the competitive consideration of race and ethnic origin."

Justice Powell approved the university's use of race to further only one interest: "the attainment of a diverse student body." With the important proviso that "constitutional limitations protecting individual rights may not be disregarded," Justice Powell grounded his analysis in the academic freedom that "long has been viewed as a special concern of the First Amendment." Today we endorse Justice Powell's view that student body diversity is a compelling state interest that can justify the use of race in university admissions.

The Equal Protection Clause provides that no State shall "deny to any person within its jurisdiction the equal protection of the laws." All racial classifications imposed by government "must be analyzed by a reviewing court under strict scrutiny." This means that such classifications are constitutional only if they are narrowly tailored to further compelling governmental interests. We apply strict scrutiny to all racial classifications to "'smoke out' illegitimate uses of race by assuring that [government] is pursuing a goal important enough to warrant use of a highly suspect tool."

Context matters when reviewing race-based governmental action under the Equal Protection Clause. Strict scrutiny must take "'relevant differences' into account." Not every decision influenced by race is equally objectionable and strict scrutiny is designed to provide a framework for carefully examining the importance and the sincerity of the reasons advanced by the governmental decisionmaker for the use of race in that particular context.

The Law School asserts only one justification for their use of race in the admissions process: obtaining "the educational benefits that flow from a diverse student body." In other words, the Law School asks us to recognize, in the context of higher education, a compelling state interest in student body diversity. Today, we hold that the Law School has a compelling interest in attaining a diverse student body.

The Law School's educational judgment that such diversity is essential to its educational mission is one to which we defer. The Law School's assessment that diversity will, in fact, yield educational benefits is substantiated by the Law School. Our holding today is in keeping with our tradition of giving a degree of deference to a university's academic decisions, within constitutionally prescribed limits. We have long recognized that, given the important purpose of public education and the expansive freedoms of speech and thought associated with the university environment, universities occupy a special niche in our constitutional tradition.

As part of its goal of "assembling a class that is both exceptionally academically qualified and broadly diverse," the Law School seeks to "enroll a 'critical mass' of minority students." The Law School's interest is not simply "to assure within its student body some specified percentage of a particular group merely because of its race or ethnic origin." That would amount to outright racial balancing, which is patently unconstitutional. Rather, the Law School's concept of critical mass is defined by reference to the educational benefits that diversity is designed to produce.

These benefits are substantial. The Law School's admissions policy promotes "cross-racial understanding," helps to break down racial stereotypes, and "enables [students] to better understand persons of different races." These benefits are "important and laudable," because "classroom discussion is livelier, more spirited, and simply more enlightening and interesting" when the students have "the greatest possible variety of backgrounds." Numerous studies show that student body diversity promotes learning outcomes, and "better prepares students for an increasingly diverse workforce and society, and better prepares them as professionals."

These benefits are not theoretical but real, as major American businesses have made clear that the skills needed in today's increasingly global marketplace can only be developed through exposure to widely diverse people, cultures, ideas, and viewpoints. This Court has long recognized that "education . . . is the very foundation of good citizenship."

The Law School does not premise its need for critical mass on "any belief that minority students always (or even consistently) express some characteristic minority viewpoint on any issue." To the contrary, diminishing the force of such stereotypes is both a crucial part of the Law School's mission, and one that it cannot accomplish with only token numbers of minority students. Just as growing up in a particular region or having particular professional experiences is likely to affect an individual's views, so too is one's own, unique experience of being a racial minority in a society, like our own, in which race unfortunately still matters. The Law School has determined, based on its experience and expertise, that a "critical mass" of underrepresented minorities is necessary to further its compelling interest in securing the educational benefits of a diverse student body.

We find that the Law School's admissions program bears the hallmarks of a narrowly tailored plan. Truly individualized consideration demands that race be used in a flexible, nonmechanical way. Universities cannot establish quotas for members of certain racial groups or put members of those groups on separate admissions tracks. We are satisfied that the Law School's admissions program does not operate as a quota. Properly understood, a "quota" is a program in which a certain fixed number or proportion of opportunities are "reserved exclusively for certain minority groups" and "insulate the individual from comparison with all other candidates for the available seats."

In contrast, "a permissible goal . . . requires only a good-faith effort . . . to come within a range demarcated by the goal itself," and permits consideration of race as a "plus" factor in any given case while still ensuring that each candidate "competes with all other qualified applicants." The Law School's goal of attaining a critical mass of underrepresented minority students does not transform its program into a quota. "Some attention to numbers," without more, does not transform a flexible admissions system into a rigid quota.

When using race as a "plus" factor in university admissions, a university's admissions program must remain flexible enough to ensure that each applicant is evaluated as an individual and not in a way that makes an applicant's race or ethnicity the defining feature of his or her application. The importance of this individualized consideration in the context of a race-conscious admissions program is paramount.

Here, the Law School engages in a highly individualized, holistic review of each applicant's file, giving serious consideration to all the ways an applicant might contribute to a diverse educational environment. The Law School affords this individualized consideration to applicants of all races. There is no policy, either *de jure* or *de facto,* of automatic acceptance or rejection based on any single "soft" variable. Unlike the program at issue in *Gratz* v. *Bollinger, ante,* the Law School awards no mechanical, predetermined diversity "bonuses" based on race or ethnicity (distinguishing a race-conscious admissions program that automatically awards 20 points based on race from the Harvard plan, which considered race but "did not contemplate that any single characteristic automatically ensured a specific and identifiable contribution to a university's diversity"). The Law School's admissions policy "is flexible enough to consider all pertinent elements of diversity in light of the particular qualifications of each applicant, and to place them on the same footing for consideration, although not necessarily according them the same weight."

With respect to the use of race itself, all underrepresented minority students admitted by the Law School have been deemed qualified. By virtue of our Nation's struggle with racial inequality, such students are both likely to have experiences of particular importance to the Law School's mission, and less likely to be admitted in meaningful numbers on criteria that ignore those experiences.

The Law School does not, however, limit in any way the broad range of qualities and experiences that may be considered valuable contributions to student body diversity. To the contrary, the 1992 policy makes clear "there are many possible bases for diversity admissions," and provides examples of admittees who have lived or traveled widely abroad, are fluent in several languages, have overcome personal adversity and family hardship, have exceptional records of extensive community service, and have had successful careers in other fields. The Law School seriously considers each "applicant's promise of making a notable contribution to the class by way of a particular strength, attainment, or characteristic—e.g., an unusual intellectual achievement, employment experience, nonacademic performance, or personal background." All applicants have the opportunity to highlight their own potential diversity contributions through the submission of a personal statement, letters of recommendation, and an essay describing the ways in which the applicant will contribute to the life and diversity of the Law School.

The Law School frequently accepts nonminority applicants with grades and test scores lower than underrepresented minority applicants (and other nonminority applicants) who are rejected. This shows that the Law School seriously weighs many other diversity factors besides race that can make a real and dispositive difference for nonminority applicants as well. By this flexible approach, the Law School sufficiently takes into account, in practice as well as in theory, a wide variety of characteristics besides race and ethnicity that contribute to a diverse student body. We agree that, in the context of its individualized inquiry into the possible diversity contributions of all applicants, the Law School's race-conscious admissions program does not unduly harm nonminority applicants.

We are mindful, however, that "[a] core purpose of the Fourteenth Amendment was to do away with all governmentally imposed discrimination based on race." Accordingly, race-conscious admissions policies must be limited in time. This requirement reflects that racial classifications, however compelling their goals, are potentially so dangerous that they may be employed no more broadly than the interest demands. The requirement that all race-conscious admissions programs have a termination point "assures all citizens that the deviation from the norm of equal treatment of all racial and ethnic groups is a temporary matter, a measure taken in the service of the goal of equality itself."

We take the Law School at its word that it would "like nothing better than to find a race-neutral admissions formula" and will terminate its race-conscious admissions program as soon as practicable. It has been 25 years since Justice Powell first approved the use of race to further an interest in student body diversity in the context of public higher education. Since that time, the number of minority applicants with high grades and test scores has indeed increased. We expect that 25 years from now, the use of racial preferences will no longer be necessary to further the interest approved today.

The Equal Protection Clause does not prohibit the Law School's narrowly tailored use of race in admissions decisions to further a compelling interest in obtaining the educational benefits that flow from a diverse student body. The judgment of the Court of Appeals for the Sixth Circuit, accordingly, is AFFIRMED.

Case Questions

1. Do you agree with the Court's decision? Explain.

2. Do you understand why the Court reached the conclusion it did? Explain.

3. Analyze the different positions of the government (through the Supreme Court and the University of Michigan) versus that of a student applying to the school (both minority and nonminority). Did this exercise help you see the different viewpoints more clearly? It is important to be able to do that as a manager or supervisor with responsibilities in this area.

Despite what you may have heard, reverse discrimination accounts for only about 3 percent of the charges filed with EEOC, and most of those claims result in no-cause findings.

As you learned in our discussion of the requirements for an employer to have an affirmative action plan, once the plan is deemed necessary because there is an underrepresentation that cannot be accounted for in virtually any way other than exclusion of certain groups, even unwittingly, then consideration of race or gender becomes a necessary part of the remedy. The law builds in protections for employees who feel they may be adversely affected by ensuring that the plan is only given protection if it complies with the legal requirements.

One of the arguments frequently made in reverse discrimination cases is that affirmative action requires the "sons to pay for the sins of the fathers" and that "slavery is over—why can't we just forget it and move on?" Keep in mind that affirmative action is not about something that happened nearly 150 years ago. It is about underrepresentation in the workplace *today*. Also keep in mind that it is not punishment in any way, but rather a *remedy* for discrimination, or its vestiges, *which has been found to exist*. As for the "sins of the fathers," keep in mind that to the extent that blacks and women were, for the most part, *legally* excluded from the workplace from the beginning of this country's existence until passage of the Civil Rights Act in 1964, and their intentional inclusion only began to become a significant issue in the late 1970s to early 1980s, this gave those groups who were in the workplace for all those years before a huge head start on experience, training, presence, trustworthiness, seniority, perception of appropriateness for the job, and so on.

These factors come into play each time an applicant or employee applies for a job, promotion, training, or other benefit. Without the applicant's intentionally doing anything that may ask for more favorable or less favorable consideration (depending on the group to which the applicant belongs), because of more than 345 years of ingrained history, as shown by study after study, it happens. While it may not be intentional, or even conscious, it has a definite harmful impact on groups traditionally excluded from the workplace—an impact that research has proved to be present time and again. For instance, despite the anecdotal evidence of seemingly omnipresent reverse discrimination situations we may hear about from our friends or colleagues, the U.S. Department of Labor's 1995 Glass Ceiling Report found that though antidiscrimination laws have made a significant impact in bringing women and minorities into the workplace in entry-level positions, there are still significant workplace disparities. Given that, it should come as no surprise that, according to the Glass Ceiling Commission Report, white men are only 43 percent of the Fortune 2000 workforce but hold 95 percent of the senior management jobs. Women are only 8.6 percent of all engineers, less than 1 percent of carpenters, 23 percent of lawyers, 16 percent of police, and 3.7 percent of firefighters. White men are 33 percent of the U.S. population but 65 percent of physicians, 71 percent of lawyers, 80 percent of tenured professors, and 94 percent of school superintendents. This was later borne out again in the Harvard study mentioned earlier.

While we would all love to live in a color-blind society where merit is the only factor considered in the workplace, the truth is, research shows that we aren't there yet. Affirmative action steps in as a measure to help remedy this situation. (For pro and con views, see Exhibit 4.7.) Nevertheless, as you can see from the *Kane* case below, reverse discrimination remains an important tool in effectuating rights under Title VII, as well as further defining its parameters.

Kane v. Freeman *1997 U.S. Dist. LEXIS 4063 (USDC, Mid. Dist. FL, Tampa Div. 1997)*

In 1996, Tampa police officers sued the police department to prohibit the continued use of the affirmative action plan which had been in place since 1976 and was to expire in 1995. The court held that though there had initially been a basis for instituting the plan, since there was no longer an underrepresentation of black police officers and blatant discrimination that created the need for the plan, it was no longer justified and must be stopped.

Kovachevich, J.

The City of Tampa's Police Department (TPD) has granted promotions, assignments and transfers pursuant to an Affirmative Action Plan since 1976. The TPD considers race as one factor in determining the propriety of individual promotions and assignments, and the determination of workforce promotional and assignment goals. The 1990 TPD Plan continues to be effective in 1996, notwithstanding its internal language indicating the Plan was to terminate in 1995.

In this case, there is a basis in the evidence for the Court to find that racial discrimination existed at the Tampa Police Department. Chief Bennie Holder testified that until the late 1970s it was not uncommon to hear derogatory speech toward black and female officers. Chief Holder further testified:

. . . It's been necessary at times to explain to people why we have affirmative action. People don't understand. Some people, because they didn't experience it, or it predates them, they don't know about some of the discriminatory practices that existed in the past. . . . They didn't know that black officers made less money than white officers; and that there was an understanding that they didn't arrest white people, that if they needed to arrest a white person, they had to summon a white officer; that they weren't allowed to drive police vehicles; that they didn't have roll call with black (sic) police officers, they had theirs in the hallway.

Chief Holder also testified that to his knowledge none of the past discriminatory practices described above have existed at the Tampa Police Department for the last five years, and that he did not know the exact date these practices ended. The Court is certain that at one time an affirmative action plan was warranted, and must now determine whether present circumstances warrant the continuation or modification of the plan.

In order to satisfy the "compelling governmental interest" prong of the strict scrutiny test, TPD must show that racial preference guides the affirmative action plan and that some governmental interest allows this discrimination. One way TPD may satisfy the first prong is to demonstrate "gross statistical disparities" between the proportion of minorities hired by the public employer and the proportion of minorities willing and able to do the work.

After reviewing TPD's statistical analyses, the Court concludes that no statistical evidence exists of present discrimination against blacks at the Tampa Police Department sufficient to support a "compelling governmental interest." The conclusions of two statistical analyses performed by the police officers demonstrate this point. The first statistical analysis performed by the police officers was the "rank below analysis of percentages." This analysis represents the overall percentages of blacks in each rank, compared to the percentages of blacks in each rank below (the next rank down). The studies found that black candidates for the rank of Lieutenant were promoted at rates that actually exceed the percentage of blacks in the rank of Sergeant, the eligibility rank below. This Court finds no statistical disparity

The second statistical analysis performed by the police officers was the "Statistical Workforce Analysis." This test demonstrates the racial composition of supervisory sworn personnel compared with the relevant labor market in the relevant geographic area. When performed by the police officers, the test exhibited no statistically significant underrepresentation in each geographic area considered among the Department's supervisory personnel. In fact, the test revealed that black employees are significantly overrepresented among TPD's non-supervisory employees.

The desire to eliminate vestiges of past discrimination may support the "compelling governmental interest" requirement. However, as to the elimination of the vestiges of past discrimination, there is no duty to remedy an imbalance that is not caused by past discrimination so long as the current employment and promotional policies and practices are neutral with respect to race, gender, and ethnicity.

Chief Holder denied any specific knowledge that discrimination toward blacks in the Tampa Police Department continues to the present day. However, he did state "I'm not going to be so naive and say it's not occurring, but it certainly does not occur in my presence. And I would say, if it is going on, it's much more covert. It's just not prevalent because it's just not condoned." Anecdotal evidence may be used to document discrimination, especially if buttressed by relevant statistical evidence, but the Court looked for it in the supporting documents, and did not find it.

Defendants have not brought forth evidence of a compelling state interest sufficient to justify the continuation of the present Affirmative Action Plan. The Court concludes that the evidence presented of the necessity for the subject relief is not sufficient to justify continuation. At the very least, the parties must open discussions as to whether some modified plan may be necessary.

One must attempt to eliminate all vestiges of past discrimination through nondiscriminatory measures before one resorts to discriminatory measures. The TPD has not revealed any evidence that it used, or even experimented with, any viable or meaningful plans to promote black candidates without employing discriminatory measures. The door is therefore now open for the application of alternative means. Limiting the duration of a race-conscious remedy which clearly impacts adversely upon the suing police officers is a keystone of a narrowly tailored plan. The TPD's present plan is perpetual, and establishes "moving targets."

The police officers argue that TPD has not implemented measures to evaluate its affirmative action program to determine whether the Plan at the very least needs revamping. The Court agrees with the officers' contention that TPD fail to show any evidence that they reevaluate the Plan periodically. The methods used by the City of Tampa are critically in need of review.

The TPD's "availability percentage" is rigid. The most recent racial classifying plan developed before 1990 contained availability percentage data for each minority category. However, the TPD still uses percentages calculated before 1990 in 1996, even after the new census data was available. The police officers argue that TPD made no attempt to reassess or adopt available percentages to current data. According to the officers, TPD's calculation of the availability percentage for promotions has flaws. The Court agrees. TPD's calculation uses percentage data obtained from outdated pre-1990 census data when 1990 census data is available.

The Court finds that no compelling interest has been established as to the present Affirmative Action Plan of the Tampa Police Department, and the means employed by the Plan are not narrowly tailored. The Court enjoins the use of the present Affirmative Action Plan for promotions, assignments and transfers within the Tampa Police Department. There is "no universal answer to the problem of remedying racial discrimination." The choice of remedies to redress racial discrimination is a balancing process left, within appropriate constitutional or statutory limits, to the sound discretion of the trial court. Motion for partial summary judgment GRANTED.

Case Questions

1. Why do you think the police department was still using the plan even though the stated expiration date had passed?

2. What do you think the police officers who sued were feeling about the plan?

3. Assuming the suing police officers had their feelings before the expiration date of the plan, how would you have addressed them?

Given what you now know about affirmative action, which side makes most sense to you?

Con—Clarence Pendleton, chair of the U.S. Commission on Civil Rights.

Human resource management departments are "the major force companies have for getting rid of preference (hiring) plans and for not letting the 'new racism' take hold," Clarence Pendleton told his packed luncheon-time audience at a recent monthly meeting of the Metropolitan New York City American Society of Personnel Administrators.

"New racism," Pendleton explained, is a lot like old racism. New racists typically are vociferous supporters of civil rights, but want different treatment for minorities, such as goals, timetables and quotas. "New racists think of blacks as a commodity," he commented, "and, therefore, they set numbers as goals."

Preferential treatment, which Pendleton characterized as "neo-slavery," leads automatically to different results for classes of people. With no equality of results, he said.

Pendleton, who is often and loudly criticized for his conservative Republican beliefs, made no apologies for his work with the Reagan Administration. He defended the civil rights record of the Administration, claiming that "we are not turning our backs on civil rights. Discriminatory affirmative action programs are dead, but those who have been discriminated against should be made whole."

He suggested that a best-selling book could be a compendium of the Civil Rights Act of 1964. "Read it," he challenged his audience, "and you will find that nowhere does the Act call for preferential treatment. The faster we get preferential treatment out of politics, the faster we are going to get to a color-blind society."

Too many black leaders "are peddling pain with federal preference programs, but they don't demand education," Pendleton charged.

And that's where HR professionals come into Pendleton's plan. He challenged the audience to "develop a profile on what it takes to move into corporate America without preferences. Let us know what training and support is necessary to get minorities into the economic system. Tell us—'Here's what it takes to get prepared.' Pass that information on to educators."

He asked that professionals support schools and fight for a reduced minimum wage for teens. "Affirmative action without jobs isn't doing a thing for the 59 percent of black youth who are unemployed and are not qualified for jobs which exist."

"It's time to remove all the chains," he said. "And you in human resources play a major role in the development of public policy. We need a majestic national river of employees, and not these ethnic creeks."

Pro—Richard Womack, director, Office of Civil Rights for the AFL-CIO.

It is all well and good to promote the concept of equality in hiring and promotion, but centuries of discrimination against minorities and women have put them at a disadvantage in the workplace that must first be corrected through aggressive action.

Addressing a June 5 plenary session of the 15th annual American Association of Affirmative Action conference, Womack told several hundred conferees that the challenge facing equal employment and affirmative action officers today is to decide how to proceed "until we reach the day when we can say we have a color-blind society."

Womack likened the state of today's workforce to a football game where the dominant team, which has mounted a huge lead by cheating and putting 15 players on the field, decides to stop cheating and pare its team down to 11 players with just three minutes left to play. "For those three minutes the two teams may be equal, but the cheating that preceded the equality will doom the other team to certain failure," Womack said.

Exhibit 4.7 (continued)

White males have had the advantage of preference in the workplace for years. "Now it's time to do the same thing for women and minorities." Noting that his remarks may be viewed by some as "harsh," Womack said that protected groups must be given preference in order to put all workers on the same level playing field. "After whites used race as a basis for slavery and a standard for the exclusion to education and advancement, why now should we be color-blind? There is too much damage to undo."

Womack urged the EEO officers to provide opportunity to minorities and women in the same manner that white males have in the past. "White males have historically taken care of other whites," Womack said.

Affirmative action is an "imperfect tool" to be used to correct past discrimination and suffers from a perception problem, Womack said. "You mention affirmative action to whites and they conjure up images of incompetent blacks who have been given jobs that should have gone to qualified whites," Womack told the conference. Blacks, on the other hand, view affirmative action as "a paltry effort of reduced bias—a dent in whites favoring whites," he said.

The concept and use of goals and timetables also face perception problems, Womack said. The federal government and corporations alike set goals and timetables for everything from collection of taxes to the implementation of new products or procedures, he noted. "So why are goals and timetables so horrible in the employment context?" Womack asked.

Source: Con—reprinted with the permission of *HR Magazine*, published by the Society for Human Resource Management, Alexandria, VA; *pro*—reprinted with permission from *Daily Labor Report*, No. 107, pp. A-10–A-11 (June 6, 1989). Copyright 1989 by the Bureau of National Affairs, Inc. (800/372-1033), http://www.bna.com.

The *Johnson* case set forth the requirements for a valid affirmative action plan that will pass judicial muster in a reverse discrimination challenge.

Johnson v. Transportation Agency, Santa Clara County, California *480 U.S. 616 (1987)*

A female was promoted over a male pursuant to an affirmative action plan voluntarily adopted by the employer to address a traditionally segregated job classification in which women had been significantly underrepresented. A male employee who also applied for the job sued, alleging it was illegal discrimination under Title VII for the employer to consider gender in the promotion process. The U.S. Supreme Court upheld the promotion under the voluntary affirmative action plan. It held that since it was permissible for a public employer to adopt such a voluntary plan, the plan was reasonable, and since the criteria for the plan had been met, gender could be considered as one factor in the promotion.

Brennan, J.

In December 1978, the Santa Clara County Transit District Board of Supervisors adopted an Affirmative Action Plan (Plan) for the County Transportation Agency. The Plan implemented a County Affirmative Action Plan, which had been adopted because "mere prohibition of discriminatory practices is not enough to remedy the effects of past practices and to permit attainment of an equitable representation of minorities, women and handicapped persons." Relevant to this case, the Agency Plan provides that, in making promotions to positions within a traditionally segregated job classification in which women have been significantly underrepresented, the Agency is authorized to consider as one factor the sex of a qualified applicant.

In reviewing the composition of its workforce, the Agency noted in its Plan that women were represented in numbers far less than their proportion of the County labor force in both the Agency as a whole and in five of seven job categories. Specifically, while women constituted 36.4 percent of the area labor market, they composed only 22.4 percent of Agency employees. Furthermore, women working at the Agency were concentrated largely in EEOC job categories traditionally held by women: women made up 76 percent of Office and Clerical Workers, but only 7.1 percent of Agency Officials and Administrators, 8.6 percent of Professionals, 9.7 percent of Technicians, and 22 percent of Service and Maintenance Workers. As for the job classification relevant to this case, none of the 238 Skilled Craft Worker positions was held by a woman. The Plan noted that this underrepresentation of women in part reflected the fact that women had not traditionally been employed in these positions, and that they had not been strongly motivated to seek training or employment in them "because of the limited opportunities that have existed in the past for them to work in such classifications." The Plan also observed that, while the proportion of ethnic minorities in the Agency as a whole exceeded the proportion of such minorities in the County workforce, a smaller percentage of minority employees held management, professional, and technical positions.

The Agency stated that its Plan was intended to achieve "a statistically measurable yearly improvement in hiring, training and promotion of minorities and women throughout the Agency in all major job classifications where they are underrepresented." As a benchmark by which to evaluate progress, the Agency stated that its long-term goal was to attain a workforce whose composition reflected the proportion of minorities and women in the area labor force. Thus, for the Skilled Craft category in which the road dispatcher position at issue here was classified, the Agency's aspiration was that eventually about 36 percent of the jobs would be occupied by women.

The Agency's Plan thus set aside no specific number of positions for minorities or women, but authorized the consideration of ethnicity or sex as a factor when evaluating qualified candidates for jobs in which members of such groups were poorly represented. One such job was the road dispatcher position that is the subject of the dispute in this case.

The Agency announced a vacancy for the promotional position of road dispatcher in the Agency's Roads Division. Twelve County employees applied for the promotion, including Joyce and Johnson. Nine of the applicants, including Joyce and Johnson, were deemed qualified for the job, and were interviewed by a two-person board. Seven of the applicants scored above 70 on this interview, which meant that they were certified as eligible for selection by the appointing authority. The scores awarded ranged from 70 to 80. Johnson was tied for second with a score of 75, while Joyce ranked next with a score of 73. A second interview was conducted by three Agency supervisors, who ultimately recommended that Johnson be promoted.

James Graebner, Director of the Agency, concluded that the promotion should be given to Joyce. As he testified: "I tried to look at the whole picture, the combination of her qualifications and Mr. Johnson's qualifications, their test scores, their expertise, their background, affirmative action matters, things like that . . . I believe it was a combination of all those."

The certification form naming Joyce as the person promoted to the dispatcher position stated that both she and Johnson were rated as well qualified for the job. The evaluation of Joyce read: "Well qualified by virtue of 18 years of past clerical experience including 3½ years at West Yard plus almost 5 years as a [road maintenance worker]." The evaluation of Johnson was as follows: "Well qualified applicant; two years of [road maintenance worker] experience plus 11 years of Road Yard Clerk. Has had previous outside Dispatch experience but was 13 years ago." Graebner testified that he did not regard as significant the fact that Johnson scored 75 and Joyce 73 when interviewed by the two-person board.

Johnson filed a complaint with the EEOC alleging that he had been denied promotion on the basis of sex in violation of Title VII.

In reviewing the employment decision at issue in this case, we must first examine whether consideration of the sex of applicants for Skilled Craft jobs was justified by the existence of a "manifest imbalance" that reflected underrepresentation of women in "traditionally segregated job categories." In determining whether an imbalance exists that would justify taking sex or race into account, a comparison of the percentage of minorities or women in the employer's work force with the percentage in the area labor market or general population is appropriate in analyzing jobs that require no special expertise or training programs designed to provide expertise. Where a job requires special training, however, the comparison should be with those in the labor force who possess the relevant qualifications. The requirement that the "manifest imbalance" relate to a "traditionally segregated job category" provides assurance both that sex or race will be taken into account in a manner consistent with Title VII's purpose of eliminating the effects of employment discrimination, and that the interests of those employees not benefiting from the plan will not be unduly infringed.

It is clear that the decision to hire Joyce was made pursuant to an Agency plan that directed that sex or race be taken into account for the purpose of remedying underrepresentation. The Agency Plan acknowledged the "limited opportunities that have existed in the past," for women to find employment in certain job classifications "where women have not been traditionally employed in significant numbers." As a result, observed the Plan, women were concentrated in traditionally female jobs in the Agency, and represented a lower percentage in other job classifications than would be expected if such traditional segregation had not occurred. Specifically, 9 of the 10 Para-Professionals and 110 of the 145 Office and Clerical Workers were women. By contrast, women were only 2 of the 28 Officials and Administrators, 5 of the 58 Professionals, 12 of the 124 Technicians, none of the Skilled Craft Workers, and 1—who was Joyce—of the 110 Road Maintenance Workers. The Plan sought to remedy these imbalances through "hiring, training and promotion of . . . women throughout the Agency in all major job classifications where they are underrepresented."

The Agency adopted as a benchmark for measuring progress in eliminating underrepresentation the long-term goal of a workforce that mirrored in its major job classifications the percentage of women in the area labor market. Even as it did so, however, the Agency acknowledged that such a figure could not by itself necessarily justify taking into account the sex of applicants for positions in all job categories. For positions requiring specialized training and experience, the Plan observed that the number of minorities and women "who possess the qualifications required for entry into such job classifications is limited." The Plan therefore directed that annual short-term goals

be formulated that would provide a more realistic indication of the degree to which sex should be taken into account in filling particular positions. The Plan stressed that such goals "should not be construed as 'quotas' that must be met," but as reasonable aspirations in correcting the imbalance in the Agency's workforce. These goals were to take into account factors such as "turnover, layoffs, lateral transfers, new job openings, retirements and availability of minorities, women and handicapped persons in the area workforce who possess the desired qualifications or potential for placement." The Plan specifically directed that, in establishing such goals, the Agency work with the County Planning Department and other sources in attempting to compile data on the percentage of minorities and women in the local labor force that were actually working in the job classifications constituting the Agency workforce. From the outset, therefore, the Plan sought annually to develop even more refined measures of the underrepresentation in each job category that required attention.

As the Agency Plan recognized, women were most egregiously underrepresented in the Skilled Craft job category, since none of the 238 positions was occupied by a woman. In mid-1980, when Joyce was selected for the road dispatcher position, the Agency was still in the process of refining its short-term goals for Skilled Craft Workers in accordance with the directive of the Plan. This process did not reach fruition until 1982, when the Agency established a short-term goal for that year of 3 women for the 55 expected openings in that job category—a modest goal of about 6 percent for that category.

The Agency's Plan emphasized that the long-term goals were not to be taken as guides for actual hiring decisions, but that supervisors were to consider a host of practical factors in seeking to meet affirmative action objectives, including the fact that in some job categories women were not qualified in numbers comparable to their representation in the labor force.

By contrast, had the Plan simply calculated imbalances in all categories according to the proportion of women in the area labor pool, and then directed that hiring be governed solely by those figures, its validity fairly could be called into question. This is because analysis of a more specialized labor pool normally is necessary in determining underrepresentation in some positions. If a plan failed to take distinctions in qualifications into account in providing guidance for actual employment decisions, it would dictate mere blind hiring by the numbers, for it would hold supervisors to "achievement of a particular percentage of minority employment or membership . . . regardless of circumstances such as economic conditions or the number of available qualified minority applicants. . . ."

The Agency's Plan emphatically did not authorize such blind hiring. It expressly directed that numerous factors be taken into account in making hiring decisions, including specifically the qualifications of female applicants for particular jobs. The Agency's management had been clearly instructed that they were not to hire solely by reference to statistics. The fact that only the long-term goal had been established for this category posed no danger that personnel decisions would be made by reflexive adherence to a numerical standard.

Furthermore, in considering the candidates for the road dispatcher position in 1980, the Agency hardly needed to rely on a refined short-term goal to realize that it had a significant problem of underrepresentation that required attention. Given the obvious imbalance in the Skilled Craft category, and given the Agency's commitment to eliminating such imbalances, it was plainly not unreasonable for the Agency to determine that it was appropriate to consider as one factor the sex of Ms. Joyce in making its decision. The promotion of Joyce thus satisfies the first requirement since it was undertaken to further an affirmative action plan designed to eliminate Agency workforce imbalances in traditionally segregated job categories.

We next consider whether the Agency Plan unnecessarily trammeled the rights of male employees or created an absolute bar to their advancement. The Plan sets aside no positions for women. The Plan expressly states that "[t]he 'goals' established for each Division should not be construed as 'quotas' that must be met." Rather, the Plan merely authorizes that consideration be given to affirmative action concerns when evaluating qualified applicants. As the Agency Director testified, the sex of Joyce was but one of numerous factors he took into account in arriving at his decision. The Plan thus resembles the "Harvard Plan" approvingly noted in *Regents of University of California* v. *Bakke,* which considers race along with other criteria in determining admission to the college. As the Court observed: "In such an admissions program, race or ethnic background may be deemed a 'plus' in a particular applicant's file, yet it does not insulate the individual from comparison with all other candidates for the available seats." Similarly, the Agency Plan requires women to compete with all other qualified applicants.

No persons are automatically excluded from consideration; all are able to have their qualifications weighed against those of other applicants.

In addition, Johnson had no absolute entitlement to the road dispatcher position. Seven of the applicants were classified as qualified and eligible, and the Agency Director was authorized to promote any of the seven. Thus, denial of the promotion unsettled no legitimate, firmly rooted expectation on the part of Johnson. Furthermore, while Johnson was denied a promotion, he retained his employment with the Agency, at the same salary and with the same seniority, and remained eligible for other promotions.

Finally, the Agency's Plan was intended to attain a balanced workforce not to maintain one. The Plan contains 10 references to the Agency's desire to "attain" such a balance, but no reference whatsoever to a goal of maintaining it. The Director testified that, while the "broader goal" of affirmative action, defined as "the desire to hire, to promote, to give opportunity and training on an equitable, non-discriminatory basis," is something that is "a permanent part" of "the Agency's operating philosophy," that broader goal "is divorced, if you will, from specific numbers or percentages." The Agency acknowledged the difficulties that it would confront in remedying the imbalance in its workforce, and it anticipated only gradual increases in the representation of minorities and women. It is thus unsurprising that the Plan contains no explicit end date, for the Agency's flexible, case-by-case approach was not expected to yield success in a brief period of time.

Express assurance that a program is only temporary may be necessary if the program actually sets aside positions according to specific numbers. This is necessary both to minimize the effect of the program on other employees, and to ensure that the plan's goals "[are] not being used simply to achieve and maintain . . . balance, but rather as a benchmark against which" the employer may measure its progress in eliminating the underrepresentation of minorities and women. In this case, however, substantial evidence shows that the Agency has sought to take a moderate, gradual approach to eliminating the imbalance in its workforce, one which establishes realistic guidance for employment decisions, and which visits minimal intrusion on the legitimate expectations of other employees. Given this fact, as well as the Agency's express commitment to "attain" a balanced workforce, there is ample assurance that the Agency does not seek to use its Plan to maintain a permanent racial and sexual balance.

In evaluating the compliance of an affirmative action plan with Title VII's prohibition on discrimination, we must be mindful of "this Court's and Congress's consistent emphasis on 'the value of voluntary efforts to further the objectives of the law.'" The Agency in the case before us has undertaken such a voluntary effort, and has done so in full recognition of both the difficulties and the potential for intrusion on males and nonminorities. The Agency has identified a conspicuous imbalance in job categories traditionally segregated by race and sex. It has made clear from the outset, however, that employment decisions may not be justified solely by reference to this imbalance, but must rest on a multitude of practical, realistic factors. It has therefore committed itself to annual adjustment of goals so as to provide a reasonable guide for actual hiring and promotion decisions. The Agency earmarks no positions for anyone; sex is but one of several factors that may be taken into account in evaluating qualified applicants for a position. As both the Plan's language and its manner of operation attest, the Agency has no intention of establishing a workforce whose permanent composition is dictated by rigid numerical standards.

We therefore hold that the Agency appropriately took into account as one factor the sex of Diane Joyce in determining that she should be promoted to the road dispatcher position. The decision to do so was made pursuant to an affirmative action plan that represents a moderate, flexible, case-by-case approach to effecting a gradual improvement in the representation of minorities and women in the Agency's workforce. Such a plan is fully consistent with Title VII, for it embodies the contribution that voluntary employer action can make in eliminating the vestiges of discrimination in the workplace. Accordingly, the judgment of the Court of Appeals is AFFIRMED.

Case Questions

1. What do you think of the Court's decision in this case? Does it make sense to you? Why or why not?
2. If you disagree with the Court's decision, what would you have done, as the employer, instead?
3. Are the Court's considerations for how to institute an acceptable affirmative action program consistent with how you thought affirmative action worked? Explain.

VALUING DIVERSITY/MULTICULTURALISM

Once affirmative action plans accomplished (at least to a limited degree) their purpose of bringing heretofore excluded employees into the workplace, employers discovered that this, in and of itself, was not enough to provide equal opportunity conditions of employment for all. Employees coming into workplaces not used to their presence found the workplace often hostile in subtle, but very real ways.

While the hostilities may have been subtle, the impact on their work lives was not. Employees found they did not move up as quickly as other, more traditional, employees. Many were not included in workplace activities, were reprimanded more often, did not receive the same opportunities, and thus had higher turnover rates. Even subtle differences in their treatment meant the difference between progressing in the workplace and remaining stagnant.

valuing diversity
Learning to accept and appreciate those who are different from the majority and value their contributions to the workplace.

Faced with workplaces filled with new kinds of people, employers sought answers. The search became even more immediate after the release of the Hudson Institute's "Workforce 2000" study for the U.S. Department of Labor in 1987. According to the study, the United States was about to face its largest wave of immigration since World War II, and, unlike the last big wave that was 90 percent European, this one would be about 90 percent Asian and Latin American.

The idea of **valuing diversity** began to take root. Valuing diversity is being sensitive to and appreciative of differences among groups that may be different from the "mainstream" and using those differences, yet basic human similarities, as a positive force to increase productivity and efficiency. For the past several years, employers all

Exhibit 4.8   Cultural Differences

Did you ever think about how much culture affects us, and how we differ culturally? Not only does it impact big things like our holidays, clothing, and so on, but it shapes much smaller things.

A recent list of tips to travelers abroad issued by the Chinese government warned: "Don't squat when waiting for a bus or a person. Don't spit in public. Don't point at people with your fingers. Don't make noise. Don't laugh loudly. Don't yell or call to people from a distance. Don't pick your teeth, pick your nose, blow your nose, pick at your ears, rub your eyes, or rub dirt off your skin. Don't scratch, take off your shoes, burp, stretch or hum."

---

over the country have sponsored workplace programs to sensitize employees to differences among people in the workplace. Being made aware of these differences in various racial, ethnic, religious, and other groups has helped employees learn to better deal with them. Chances are, at some point in your career, you will be exposed to the concept of valuing diversity. It will greatly increase your value to the employer to do so. (See Exhibits 4.8, 4.9, and 4.10.)

Exhibit 4.9   Valuing Diversity

Make a circle with your thumb and forefinger. What does it mean? In America we know it primarily as meaning "okay." But how many of us know that it may also mean the equivalent of "flipping someone the bird," "give me coin change," "I wish to make love with you," or "I wish you dead, as my mortal enemy"? The objective act has not changed, yet the meaning has. The interpretation the act is given depends on the cultural conditioning of the receiver. Welcome to multiculturalism. Knowing what is meant becomes a necessity in processing the act, otherwise the act has little meaning. Culture is what provides that information and, thus, meaning for virtually everything we do, say, wear, eat, value, and where and in what we live, sit, and sleep. Imagine how many other acts we engage in every day which can be misinterpreted based upon differences in cultural conditioning. Yet our cultural conditioning is rarely given much thought. Even less is given to the culture of others. That will not be true much longer.

In the fall 1992 issue of the magazine of the American Assembly of Collegiate Schools of Business, the accrediting body of schools of business, the cover story and lead article was "Teaching Diversity: Business Schools Search for Model Approaches." In the article, it stated that "without integrating a comprehensive diversity message into the entire curriculum, the most relevant management education cannot occur." *Multiculturalism* is learning to understand, appreciate, and value (*not* just "tolerate") the unique aspects of cultures different from one's own. The end product is learning to value others who may be different, for what they contribute, rather than rejecting them simply because they are different.

The concept of "culture" encompasses not only ethnicity, but also gender, age, disability, affinity orientation, and other factors which may significantly affect and in many ways, define, one's life. Multiculturalism is learning that "different from" does

Exhibit 4.9   (continued)

not mean "less than." It is getting in touch with one's cultural conditioning and working toward inclusion, rather than conformity.

Learning to value diversity opens people up to more. A major workplace concern is maximizing production and minimizing liability. Multiculturalism and valuing diversity contribute to this. To the extent that each person, regardless of cultural differences, is valued as a contributor in the workplace, he or she is less likely to sue the employer for transgressions (or perceived transgressions) stemming from not being valued. To the extent they are valued for who they are and what they can contribute in society, they are much less likely to end up engaging in acts such as the Los Angeles riots causing death and destruction in the spring of 1992 after the Rodney King verdict.

The U.S. Department of Labor's Workforce 2000 study conducted by the Hudson Institute and released in 1987 held a few surprises that galvanized America into addressing the issue of multiculturalism. According to the widely cited study, by the year 2000 we will experience the greatest influx of immigrants since World War II. At the same time, the percentage of women entering the workforce is increasing. The net result, according to the study, is that 85% of the net growth in the workforce will be comprised of women and non-Europeans. For the first time, white males will be a minority in the workforce. This need not be viewed as a threatening circumstance, but rather an opportunity for innovation and progress.

These factors, alone, reveal that the workplace (and by implication, schools, universities, recreational facilities and everything else) will be very different from before. It will no longer do to have a white, European, male, standard of operation. Others will be pouring into the workplace and will come with talent, energy, ideas, tenacity, imagination and other contributions the U.S. has always held dear as the basis for the "American Dream." They will come expecting to be able to use those qualities to pursue that dream. They will come feeling that they have much to offer and are valuable for all their uniqueness and the differences they may have from "the norm." And what will happen? There is no choice but to be prepared. It is a simple fact that the workplace cannot continue to operate in the same way and remain productive.

Studies have shown that when the same problem is given to homogeneous groups and heterogeneous groups to solve, the heterogeneous groups come up with more effective solutions. When people feel valued for who they are and what they can contribute, rather than feeling pressed into conformity as if who they are is not good enough, they are more productive. Energy, and creativity can be spent on the task at hand, rather than on worrying about how well they fit into someone's idea of who they should be. A significant number of the problems we face as a society and on which is spent millions in precious tax dollars comes from rejecting multiculturalism and not valuing diversity. If people were judged for who they are and what they contribute, there would not be a need for a civil rights act, affirmative action plans, riot gear, human rights commissions, etc.

There are, of course, naysayers on the topic of multiculturalism such as those who think it is just an attempt at being "politically correct." It has been said that the term "politically correct" is an attempt to devalue, trivialize, demean, and diffuse the substantive value of the issues spoken of; that once something is deemed to be an issue of "political correctness," then there is no need to worry about the real import or impact of it, because it is only a passing fad which need not be taken seriously, as it will die its own natural death soon enough.

(continued)

Exhibit 4.9 (continued)

Multiculturalism is here to stay. People have evolved to the point where it will not go away. Self-worth and valuing oneself is a lesson that it takes many a long time to learn. Once learned, it is hard to give up. And, of course, why should it be given up? Again, "different from" does not mean "less than." Learning to value others as unique human beings whose cultures is an integral part of who they are, rather than something to be shed at the work or school door, and learning to value the differences rather than to try to assimilate them, will benefit everyone.

Source: Reprinted with permission from the University of Georgia's *Columns.*

Exhibit 4.10   Promoting Diversity to Avoid Liability

As managers, part of your duties will be to try to limit the legal liability of your employer. There will be many reasons for this, and one of them will be avoiding discrimination claims. Below are some tips for helping to do so.

A Checklist for Eliminating Barriers to Diversity

✓ Think about and recognize your own cultural biases. Are you making assumptions about people who are different from you? Are you denying or ignoring differences that exist?

✓ Learn more about different cultures within your own organization—make friends with someone from a different cultural background. Recognize that we tend to promote and surround ourselves with people who are like us.

✓ Enhance communication by focusing on the whole person and the content of the message. Some people become distracted or biased by others' gestures, appearance, accent and so on.

✓ Understand that diversity is a bottom-line business issue. To stay competitive, companies need to be reflective of the changing demographics and cultures of the marketplace.

Nine Steps to Fostering Diversity

1. Aggressively recruit qualified, diverse candidates.
2. Speak out about inappropriate behavior.
3. Include employees and volunteers in decision making.
4. Introduce diversity education within the workplace.
5. Mentor a diverse student or colleague.
6. Share diversity development strategies with colleagues.
7. Incorporate diversity into all aspects of the workplace.
8. Review policies and practices for hindrance of diversity.
9. Broaden your definition of diversity to be inclusive of white males.

Source: Rachel Patrick, American Bar Association. Reprinted with permission from the *Wisconsin Bar Journal,* April 1994, p. 11.

Management Tips

Affirmative action can be a bit tricky. Keeping in mind these tips can help avoid liability for instituting and implementing a plan.

- Ensure that the hiring, promotion, training, and other such processes are open, fair, and available to all employees on an equal basis.
- If an affirmative action plan is to be adopted voluntarily, work with the union (if there is one) and other employee groups to try to ensure fairness and get early approval from the constituencies affected to ward off potential litigation.
- Make sure voluntary affirmative action plans meet the judicial requirements of

  —Being used to redress a conspicuous imbalance in traditionally segregated job categories.

  —Being moderate, flexible, and gradual in its approach.

  —Being temporary in order to attain, not maintain, a balanced workforce.

  —Not unnecessarily trammeling employees' rights or creating an absolute bar to their advancement.

  —Unsettling no legitimate, firmly rooted expectations of employees.

  —Presenting only a minimal intrusion into the legitimate, settled expectations of other employees.

- Provide training about the plan so that all employees understand its purpose and intent. Try to allay fears from the outset to ward off potential litigation. The more employees know and understand what is being done, the less likely they are to misunderstand and react adversely. Even so, keep in mind that some employees will still dislike the plan. Reiterating top-level management's commitment to equal employment opportunity will stress the seriousness of management's commitment.
- Implement periodic diversity and related training. This not only provides a forum for employees to express their views about diversity issues, but it also provides information on learning how to deal with their co-workers as diversity issues arise.

Summary

- Affirmative action is intentional inclusion of women, minorities, and others traditionally excluded in the workplace after demonstrated underrepresentation of these historically disadvantaged groups.

- Affirmative action plans may arise voluntarily, as a remedy in a discrimination lawsuit, or as part of an employer's responsibilities as a contractor or subcontractor with the government.

- Employers should conduct voluntary periodic equal employment opportunity audits to monitor their workforce for gender, minority, and other inclusion. If there is underrepresentation, the employer should develop a reasonable, nonintrusive, flexible plan within appropriate guidelines.

- Such plans should not displace nonminority employees or permit people to hold positions for which they are not qualified, simply to meet affirmative action goals. This view should not be encouraged or tolerated.

- A well-reasoned, flexible plan with endorsement at the highest levels of the workplace, applied consistently and diligently, will greatly aid in diminishing negativity surrounding affirmative action and in protecting the employer from adverse legal action.

Chapter-End Questions

1. What is the monetary floor an employer/federal government contractor must meet to have Executive Order 11246 imposed?

2. Anne is employed by Bradley Contracting Company. Bradley has a $1.3 million contract to build a small group of outbuildings in a national park. Anne alleges that Bradley Contracting has discriminated against her, in that she has not been promoted to skilled craft positions with Bradley because it thinks that it is inappropriate for women to be in skilled craft positions and that most of the male skilled craftworkers are very much against having women in such positions. Knowing that Bradley Contracting has a contract with the federal government, Anne brings suit against Bradley under Executive Order 11246 for gender discrimination. Will she be successful? Why or why not?

3. Can employers lawfully consider race or gender when making hiring or promotion decisions? Explain.

4. If so, may it only be used to remedy identified past discrimination? Discuss.

5. Must such discrimination have been committed by the employer or can the discrimination have been committed by society in general? Explain.

6. May preferential treatment be used to benefit those who did not actually experience discrimination? Discuss.

7. Can race or gender be the only factor in an employment decision? Explain.

8. If race or gender can be the only factor in an employment decision, how long can it be a factor?

9. What is the difference between an affirmative action goal and a quota? Is there a difference? Explain.

10. What is the proper comparison to determine if there is an underrepresentation of women or minorities in the workplace?

Chapter Five

Race Discrimination

Opening Scenarios

SCENARIO 1

Scenario 1

An employer has a "no-beard" policy, which applies across the board to all employees. A black employee tells the employer he cannot shave without getting severe facial bumps from ingrown hairs. The employer replies that the policy is without exception and the employee must comply. The employee refuses and is later terminated. The employee brings suit under Title VII on the basis of race discrimination. Does he win? Why? Why not?

SCENARIO 2

Scenario 2

Two truck driver employees are found to have stolen goods from the cargo they were carrying. The black employee is retained and reprimanded. The white employee is terminated. The white employee sues the employer for race discrimination under Title VII. Who wins and why?

SCENARIO 3

Scenario 3

A black female employee is terminated during a downsizing at her place of employment. The decision was made to terminate the two worst employees, and she was one of them. The employer had not told the employee of her poor performance nor given her any negative feedback during evaluations to enable her to assess her performance and govern herself accordingly. In fact, there were specific orders not to give her any negative feedback. The employee sues for racial discrimination, alleging it was a violation of Title VII for the employer not to give her appropriate negative feedback during evaluations to prevent her from being put in the position of being terminated. Does the employee win? Why? Why not?

STATUTORY BASIS

It shall be an unlawful employment practice for an employer—

(1) to fail or refuse to hire or to discharge any individual, or otherwise to discriminate against any individual with respect to his compensation, terms, conditions, or privileges of employment, because of such individual's race, color . . . or

(2) to limit, segregate, or classify his employees or applicants for employment in any way which would deprive or tend to deprive any individual of employment opportunities or otherwise adversely affect his status as an employee, because of such individual's race, color . . . Title VII of the Civil Rights Act of 1964, as amended, 42 U.S.C. 2000e-2(a).

SURPRISED?

Race is the first of the prohibited categories in Title VII, the main reason for passage of the law, and it remains, even today, a factor in the lives of many employees. Would it surprise you to discover that

- Research shows employers would rather hire a white man who had served time in prison than a black man who had not?

- When researchers sent out identical resumes for jobs listed in the newspaper, with the only difference being the names of the applicants, those with "ethnic" names like Jamal or Lakiesha received 50 percent fewer callbacks for jobs than the identical résumés with traditionally white names like Megan or Brad?

- In addition to visual profiling, researchers have found linguistic profiling—blacks who leave messages in response to ads often never receive return calls, while whites almost always do?

- A black man with a college degree makes 30 percent less than a similarly situated white man?

- An employee shooting rampage at a major U.S. defense contractor's Mississippi plant in July 2004 "wasn't all that unexpected" because the white employee had repeatedly threatened to kill black co-workers? Six were murdered and eight injured. All but one of the murdered workers were black.

- A white judge in Louisiana wore blackface makeup, handcuffs, and a jail jumpsuit at a Halloween party as a "joke"? His brother-in-law, the host, was dressed as Buckwheat.

- In the November 2004, elections in Alabama, voters voted to keep the Alabama constitution's language that says "separate schools shall be provided for white and colored children, and no child of either race shall be permitted to attend a school of the other race"?

- That a black Reuters employee received an e-mail from his white supervisor, David Flynn, who routinely called the employee "my n-----," which depicted an electronically altered photo of the employee with a noose around his neck, braids in his hair, and a large penis?

- At Charapp Ford South, a car dealership near Pittsburgh, two black employees who complained about constant racial harassment in the workplace allegedly found a document that suggested "ten ways to kill" blacks in their work areas? They also say a manager told those who complained that "people [around here] wanted to see blacks washing cars, not selling them."

- A temp agency used code words to supply Jamestown Container Co. and Whiting Door Mfg. Co. with white male employees they requested, denying placements to minorities and women?

- A congressionally commissioned study by the Institute of Medicine found that "bias, prejudice, and stereotyping on the part of health care providers" contributes to blacks being less likely than whites to receive appropriate heart medication, coronary artery bypass surgery, and kidney transplants, as well as being more likely to receive a lower quality of basic clinical services such as intensive care?

If any of this surprises you, you are certainly not alone. A 2004 Gallup poll found that 76 percent of whites, *including 9 out of 10 under 30,* thought blacks were now being treated fairly or somewhat fairly, compared to only 38 percent of blacks who thought so. Yet there are so many more things that could be added to this list!

You can see what a problem this would present in the workplace. While much of the discrimination now occurring in the workplace is not as overt as it was before Title VII. (See Exhibit 5.1.) As you can see, it is still very much a factor in employment. (See Exhibits 5.2 and 5.3.) And, as you can also see from some of the items, it does not occur in a vacuum. It is part of a much larger picture of race discrimination outside of the workplace.

Working to get future managers and supervisors to see this larger picture is a big part of what this chapter is about. The more you can see the bigger picture, the less likely you are to be a part of unnecessary claims of workplace race discrimination. That is why we can't simply tell you the law and leave it at that. The law has been in place

Exhibit 5.1   Classified Ads, 1961

The exhibit below, adapted from an actual newspaper classified ad section from 1961, is typical of want ads found in newspapers before Title VII was passed in 1964. For publication purposes names and phone numbers have been omitted. It is now illegal to advertise for males, females, or racial groups.

Male Help Wanted

SOUTH ATLANTA

PERMANENT position for 2 young men 18-35, must be ambitious, high school graduate, and neat appearing. $85 week guaranteed, plus bonus. Opportunity to earn in excess of $100 per week. Must have desire to advance with company. For interview call…

ATTN YOUNG MEN

18-25, SINGLE, free to travel, New York and Florida, returns for clearing house for publishers. New car, transportation furnished. Expense account to start. Salary plus commission. We train you. Apply…

10 BOYS

14 OR OVER. Must be neat in appearance to work this summer. Salary 75 cent per hour. Will be supervised by trained student counselor. Apply…

MAN experienced in selling and familiar with the laundry and dry cleaning business needed to sell top brands of supplies to laundries and dry cleaning plants. This is an excellent opportunity for a man who is willing to work for proper rewards. Salary and comm. Reply to…

EXPERIENCED dairy man to work in modern dairy in Florida. Must be married, sober, and reliable. Salary $60 per week for 6 days with uniform, lights and water—furnished. Excellent house. Write…

SALESMEN

THIS corporation provides its salesmen with a substantial weekly drawing account. New men are thoroughly trained in the field with emphasis directed toward high-executive income bracket. Men experienced in securities, encyclopedias, and other intangibles who can stand rigid investigation, are dependable, and own late-model car. Reply to…

Situations Wanted, Female   24

SECRETARY—RECEPTIONIST (experienced). Ex-Spanish teacher desires diversified permanent position. Responsible, personable, like people, unencumbered. Can travel.

EXPERIENCED executive secretary with college degree, top skills, currently employed—seeks better position with opportunity for advancement and good salary.

SECRETARY desires typing at home, evenings, and weekends.

COLORED EMPLOYMENT

Help Wanted Male, Colored   26

CURB BOYS

DAY or night shift. No experience necessary. Good tips. Apply in person only.

HOUSEMAN, chauffeur. Must be experienced. Recent references, driver's license, health card required. Must be sober, reliable. Write…

RESTAURANT COOK

FOR frying and dinner cooking. Age 22-35. Must be sober, dependable and well-experienced. Salary $250-$275 for good man. Apply…

SOBER, experienced service station porter. No Sundays. Top pay.

PART-TIME lawn and yard maintenance man.

EXP service station porter, 6-day wk. Good sal.

KITCHEN porters, also ware washers. Apply…

Situations Wanted, Male, Col.   28

YOUNG man wants job. Short order and plain cooking, experienced.

Help Wanted, Female, Col.   29

MAID, free to travel with family, $35 to $50 week. Free room and board.

LAUNDRY MARKER—Experienced. 40 hours—pay hourly basis.

SHIRT girl. Experienced.

SHIRT girl, Experienced. Good pay. Good hours. Apply in person.

WAITRESS, experienced, for lunch counter. Over 40. Call…

Situation Wanted, Female, Col.   31

COOK-MAID (experienced)—desires Monday, Wednesday, Friday. References and health card.

MAID wants 5 days week. References.

GIRL WANTS 5 DAYS

MAID wants 5 days work. Will live-in.

MID-TEEN girl desires maid or office work.

for 40 years now and race discrimination claims are still very much a part of Title VII. They have risen every decade since the law was passed. What we are seeing as the Title VII system is still being fine-tuned is that supervisors and managers often do not recognize race discrimination or its effects when they occur (the obvious situations above, notwithstanding). We don't want that to happen to you. We want to provide you

Exhibit 5.2

Equal?

According to U.S. Census and other data:

- More blacks attend college, and work, than ever before.
- Of those, black men earn nearly one-third less than white men.
- The average black male with a master's degree earns 20 percent less than a white man with a master's degree.
- Blacks with master's degrees have a higher unemployment rate than whites with bachelor's degrees.
- Black unemployment was twice that of whites in the early 1960s before Title VII. It was still that in 2002 (4.7 percent versus 10.8 percent).
- The median income for whites is $47,800; for blacks, $29,600.
- The net worth of blacks is $6,000; for whites, $88,000+.
- A black male with a high school diploma earns 25 percent less than a white male with a high school diploma.
- Nearly half of white Bostonians surveyed said that blacks and Hispanics are less intelligent than whites and that blacks are harder to get along with than other ethnic groups.
- A five-year, seven-volume study by the Russell Sage Foundation found that "racial stereotypes and attitudes heavily influenced the labor market, with blacks landing at the very bottom."

with a good basic background in the area of race discrimination so you can have the tools you need to be able to keep liability from attaching for unnecessary workplace discrimination.

This is a chapter about blacks and whites (national origin and ethnicity is a separate category under Title VII and will be discussed in a subsequent chapter), and there is no way to effectively give you the information you need without speaking frankly. That can be uncomfortable for some since race is not a topic often discussed openly. Don't be offended; nothing we say is meant to be offensive and is only said in the context of using our experience and research to teach students and employers how to avoid unnecessary litigation.

We have heard from thousands of white students, managers, supervisors, and business owners that "the law seems to only deal with discrimination against blacks, but what about whites? Why can't we just forget race and move on?" Title VII applies equally to *everyone*. However, given our unique racial history, there are likely to be more claims by blacks because they are, quite simply, the ones more likely to be the objects of discrimination given our country's racial history. That makes sense since this is, in large part, why the law was put in place (which will be detailed more below).

It is also important to keep in mind the difference between racism, which is what the Civil Rights Act was created to curtail, and prejudice, which it was not. Prejudice is liking one group better than another, usually for no logical reason (that is, you *prejudge* them) and is personal. Everyone has a right to feel however they want about whoever they want. This is America and freedom to choose is a freedom we enjoy and hold dear.

Exhibit 5.3   Reality of Intentional Job Discrimination

In 2002, Alfred W. Blumrosen and Ruth G. Blumrosen, noted well-respected lawyers, law professors, and civil rights researchers, released an unprecedented, comprehensive, groundbreaking study of workplace discrimination called *The Reality of Intentional Job Discrimination in Metropolitan America—1999.* The objective of the Ford Foundation–funded study was "to advance the public 'sense of reality' concerning the present extent of intentional job discrimination." The study examined 160,297 EEO-1 reports (discussed in the last chapter) supplied to the federal government by private employers with 100 or more employees and federal contractors with 50 or more employees, for the period 1975–1999. It identified intentional employment discrimination by applying legal standards to statistics of the race, gender, and ethnic composition of large and medium-sized employers in the private sector. The report contained statistical information on 40 individual states, as well as the nation as whole.

The report concluded that "A substantial part of the public has erroneously assumed that intentional job discrimination is either a thing of the past, or the acts of individual 'bad apples' in an otherwise decent work environment . . . Meanwhile, thousands of employers have continued systematic restriction of qualified minority and female workers, and these workers have lost opportunities to develop and exercise the skills and abilities that would warrant higher wages." The report found that blacks "still bear the severest brunt of this discrimination . . . Thirty-five thousand business establishments discriminated against 586,000 blacks. Ninety percent of these black workers were affected by establishments that were so far below the average utilization that there was only a 1 in 100 chance that this happened by accident and half by 'hard core' employers who had been discriminating for at least nine years."

Source: *The Reality of Intentional Job Discrimination in Metropolitan America—1999,* Alfred W. Blumrosen and Ruth G. Blumrosen, 2002, http://www.eeo1.com/1999_NR/Title.pdf.

Though acting on it may be illegal if the act violates the law, prejudice, itself, is not illegal. Nothing we say here is said in an attempt to change personal preferences. You are entitled to your preferences or prejudices, *whatever* they are. Rather, our objective is to teach you what the law requires when dealing with these issues in the workplace so liability does not apply.

While prejudice is personal, racism, on the other hand, *institutionalizes* prejudice and makes it an integral part of the everyday social, political, legal, educational, religious, and other structure of a society, such that it adversely affects all aspects of the lives of the targeted group. Since our country had laws in effect separating blacks from whites since virtually the beginning of the country's history until 1964, that institutionalization is very deep, ingrained, and far-reaching. You see the manifestation of it in some of the items given above.

Blacks have never had any significant control over the overall institutions of this country, thus they have never been able to effectively be racist, though, like everyone else, they may have feelings of prejudice. However, because of our country's racial history and its present-day vestiges, those same feelings in someone white have the potential for being a part of a much larger, long-standing, institutionalized structure of racial inequality and thus are more likely to be harmful to more people. We may want to forget the past and move on, but enough of the vestiges remain and underlie so much of the litigation and discriminatory workplace actions that we ignore it at our peril in the workplace.

For instance, research shows that managers are more likely to evaluate those of their race higher than those not of their race and more likely to recommend them for promotions, raises, and the like. This is true for both blacks and whites. However, since research also shows that there are so many fewer blacks in managerial positions, this is not likely to have the same numerical impact on blacks as it does whites. While any employment discrimination based on race is illegal under Title VII and both employees evaluated unfairly would have a cause of action for race discrimination, it is likely, given our history and its vestiges, that most of the claims will come from blacks because most of the managers are white.

This does not make the white employee's claim any less important; it is simply that given our history, there are less likely to be as many such claims. It also does not mean that all acts of discrimination are racially motivated when they involve people of different races. Nor does it mean that whites are inherently racist, even though we have lived in a racialized society for most of the country's history, or that they willingly participate in institutionalized racism, or will act against the interests of blacks. However, it does mean that we have a serious enough issue that, if not addressed, will continue to cost employers millions in unnecessary litigation.

One of the common issues managers and supervisors face when evaluating complaints of race discrimination is the difference in terminology. Our experience has been that blacks and whites often mean different things when they use the same terms. For instance, a simple term like *racist* commonly has different meanings, depending on the racial background of the user. Blacks tend to think of it in terms of the present-day manifestation of a long history of institutionalized acts of subjugation. Whites tend to mean spirited, patently discriminatory behavior toward one group or another on an ad-hoc basis, rather than in the larger historical context. Our experience in talking to thousands of people over the years is that whites tend not to think in terms of the larger historical context and instead deal with these issues as isolated, temporal occurrences. In fact, they may even view blacks' historically based perspective as paranoia, being overly sensitive, or "playing the race card." It all depends on your perspective and personal narrative.

As future managers and supervisors, it is of the utmost importance that you be aware of this difference in perceptions. Without it, you may miss attaching significance to something that later results in liability for your employer. The *Vaughn* v. *Edel* case in the chapter is a great example of this. This difference in personal narratives that impacts how we view the same facts is one reason why blacks and whites may view the same facts quite differently. (The O.J. Simpson verdict comes to mind.) Blacks look at what may appear to others to be a harmless act (for instance, calling a black man "boy") and see it as part of continuing a system in which the term was once used to keep them subjugated. Whites who have no such history with the word, may think of it as just a word. They may not even be aware that by law in some places and social custom in others, black men were quite intentionally *never* referred to as a "man," but always as a "boy," as an important means of social control and subjugation.

A white person using the term may not have had the least inkling of it being offensive and never would have used it if they had known because they had no intent to express anything negative. The reason the white person does not see it as offensive is because they don't have the same context for the word. The word simply doesn't have the same history and baggage for them since it was not used as a weapon of social oppression against them.

Both views make perfect sense, given each person's context. But we often don't realize our contexts and histories *are* different and that we are products of them. These are our personal narratives we use to operate in the world and each reflects our own experience, acculturation, family, and values. Neither is right or wrong; they simply are. We are fine as long as our narratives are generally similar, but at times, though we may assume they are, they are not. Since we act on the basis of our narratives, trouble can arise when there is conflict. This is particularly true when put into the workplace context.

Southwest Airlines discovered this recently when it was sued because of a nursery rhyme used by one of its flight attendants. Yep, you read it right, a *lawsuit* over a *nursery rhyme*. In an effort to get passengers seated on a crowded flight, the flight attendant said over the plane's intercom, "Eenie, meenie, minie, moe; hurry up, we gotta go!" Two black women, sisters, in the aisle looking for seats, were absolutely shocked. They wrote to the airline about it, but to no avail. Feeling they had not been taken seriously, they sued, alleging humiliation, embarrassment, depression, and other physical effects.

Chances are, you're speechless and can't believe the sisters did this. The old "race card" again. Ready for the "why"? It was not until the flight attendant showed the lawsuit letter to her mother that she found out what all the fuss was about. For generations the rhyme was often used by whites and usually ended, "catch a n----- by the toe." The flight attendant's personal narrative had only known the nursery rhyme as an innocent nursery rhyme. She had no idea of any racial implications, and, of course, meant nothing racial when she said it. She thought she was being lightheartedly humorous under a rather stressful situation. However, in the sisters' personal narrative, the nursery rhyme was a widespread, long-time manifestation of racial oppression and derision. Hearing such a thing over the airplane's intercom was extremely embarrassing and humiliating based on their personal narratives. It only added insult to injury when they did not receive satisfaction from Southwest and felt compelled to sue in order to be heard. The all-white jurors' verdict was for the airline. Now you can figure out why.

Each party's actions reflects his or her own reality, including, most likely, the jurors, the Southwest Airlines personnel who did not respond to the sisters' satisfaction, and, of course, the flight attendant. The flight attendant had no idea what she was saying, the sisters couldn't imagine she did not know how utterly offensive the rhyme was since they had heard it all their lives, and in the end a costly lawsuit and negative publicity resulted. If we are not aware, in some general way, of the racial narratives of our employees, unnecessary lawsuits and embarrassing and expensive litigation will continue to occur.

That is, in part, also why the no-beard policy in the opening scenario would likely catch a nonblack manager or supervisor off guard. Having no history of pseudofolliculitis barbae (PFB), any possible medical exceptions would not likely be something they took into consideration when creating the policy. As it turns out, the policy has a huge, though totally unintentional, disparate impact on black employees. Under the policy, they would be kept out of the workplace in much higher numbers than whites based on a criteria having nothing to do with their ability to do the job. See how much our personal narratives affect our lives and perceptions and how important it is for a manager to have some awareness of this? Do you understand why we can't just tell you the law and let it go at that? If we do, these issues will continue to arise in the workplace, causing lawsuits and damages that could be avoided. If someone told the flight attendant not to discriminate, she would still have said the rhyme, having no idea she was doing so. The same with the no-beard policy; no doubt the manager had no idea he was discriminating. We tend to think of discrimination as an intentional act of ill-will. The law deals with acts, not intent—at least not the way most people picture intent.

As we will see, this does *not* mean that a manager or supervisor must know how each and every employee is going to interpret (or misinterpret) something they say, or that they should tiptoe around like they are on eggshells, trying not to "offend" anyone. Not at all. Rather, it means being open to learning from others who may be unfamiliar to us and listening to the cues they give about serious matters. For instance, you will see that in many cases, and these two are no exception, even if the employer did not know about the particular narratives, litigation could likely have been easily avoided.

We have the dichotomous situation that the farther away we get from the history that caused the need for Title VII, and the more those who knew of and participated in the history pass from the scene, the less those remaining know about that history. We often hear it said that there will be no more discrimination when the older people who were the cause of needing the law in the first place all die off and leave things to the younger generation. Great thought. While it is laudable that those coming into the workplace at this point in time do not act the same as those who created the need for Title VII, racial prejudice has been systemic and enough vestiges remain that there is still a need to address the issues. Ignoring them, being ignorant of them, or thinking they have disappeared will only perpetuate them and continue to create liability for the employer. The flight attendant is an example of what can happen if history is unknown. It wasn't just the nursery rhyme being recited in the airplane that resulted in litigation. It was also the subsequent refusal of the airline to hear and understand the sisters' concern. This could have been avoided simply by listening to them.

Things have certainly changed dramatically in the past 40 years. But keep the previously mentioned poll in mind. It is only the last in many such polls with similar results and it demonstrates that the disappearance of race discrimination may not necessarily be realistic in the near future. In fact, researchers refer to the idea that whites think everything is fair for everyone nowadays, so nothing need be done to ensure equal opportunity anymore, as the "new racism." Because our unique racial history was systemic, those who remain are left with enough of the vestiges to account for much of the racial differences we see reflected in the statistics above. If they do not realize that vestiges remain, they are likely to run afoul of the law. They do not need to engage in deliberate, intentional racial discrimination in order to violate the law and the law does not require that in order to find liability. That is why providing information here to address these matters is so important for making workplace decisions that avoid liability.

So, as much as we would like to think so, racial discrimination and harassment in the workplace, both overt and subtle, are still alive and well 40 years after passage of the Civil Rights Act that was created to eradicate it. Given the wide gap shown in the

Gallup poll, you can also see why it is important for you, as future managers and supervisors, to be aware of issues that can arise in this area. Nine of 10 whites under the age of 30—most of you reading this text—believed that blacks are already being treated fairly. With this mind-set, they would be less likely to respond appropriately to claims of racial discrimination or harassment from black employees and thus increase the likelihood of liability under Title VII.

Despite all this, much progress has been made in the area of race discrimination in the workplace since Title VII was enacted. An extremely comprehensive, four-year, 1,400-page study of intentional workplace discrimination between 1975 and 1999 was released by Alfred and Ruth Blumrosen in 2002. The report found that workplace discrimination against blacks is still the worst of all groups, and "the seriousness of intentional job discrimination against Black workers by major and significant industries is evident; and the 'playing field' is far from level. However, minorities increased their participation in the labor force by 4.6 million workers beyond the increase resulting from economic growth and increased their share of 'better jobs' as officials, managers, professionals, technical, and sales workers." The study showed that 15 percent of blacks experience intentional workplace discrimination.

And there are, in fact, companies that are doing just fine and understand the impact of race in the workplace and work to make sure they do not violate the law. *The Wall Street Journal* reported that after a study of 31,000 of their U.S. jobs showed discrepancies, Eastman Kodak Co. agreed to pay about $13 million in retroactive and current pay raises to 2,000 female and minority employees in New York and Colorado. The pay raise was not in response to a threatened lawsuit, as is generally the case. Employees had complained about it to supervisors the year before, so Kodak conducted the study and determined it would make the correction.

One of the best ways to address this situation is to give you some of the history. We have found in our own classrooms that most of our students fit quite neatly into that "9 out of 10" category. They come into the course thinking everything is fine between blacks and whites and see little reason to still have Title VII in force. Until, that is, we show them video clips of documentaries on historical events like slavery, the Jim Crow era, and school desegregation riots leading up to its passage and discuss it and the information in this introduction. Then they get it. ***Really*** get it. They are absolutely astonished at how clueless (their term, not ours) they were about it all and how little they really knew about this history, yet how important it is to know in order to understand the law, where we are today, and how it impacts their actions in the workplace. It would fill volumes to do it any real justice, but we will give you the most significant highlights leading up to passage of Title VII primarily to address racial discrimination in the workplace, so that you can see what contributes to some of the personal narrative of many employees.

Background

History and its present-day effects account for much of the race discrimination we see manifested today. And make no mistake about it, our history regarding race has been a long, complex, and tortured one. Six months after the death of the erstwhile staunch segregationist, South Carolina Senator Strom Thurmond, in June 2003, it was a national media event when a black woman announced she was his daughter and had been privately, but not publicly, acknowledged by him all her life. She had been the result of a union between Thurmond, then a 22-year-old lawyer living with his parents, and her mother, a 16-year-old maid in the household. Despite the fact that the hallmark of Thurmond's career had been supporting racial segregation, including running for president on a segregationist "Dixiecrat" ticket, he had a daughter by a black woman and was one of the first Southern legislators to hire a black aide in the early 1970s.

Africans arrived in this country in 1619, before the *Mayflower*. Their initial experience was as free people who were contracted as indentured servants. After the first 40 years or so, this changed, and slavery came into existence. While some blacks were free, slavery as an integral part of American life lasted for well over 200 years, until after the Civil War ended in 1865. With a slight pause (11 years) for Reconstruction after the Civil War, the next 99 years saw Black Codes and Jim Crow laws legalize and codify racial discrimination. It is well documented that Africans were brought from Africa specifically to be enslaved or otherwise work for whites and that they had no other place in American life. In many places there were many more slaves than whites (e.g., South Carolina had an 80 percent slave population), so absolute control was necessary in order to prevent slave uprisings which were a *major* concern for whites. Without having sufficient manpower to exercise this control physically, it had to be done psychologically as well. Since there were not enough resources available to be able to watch each black every minute of the day, it was important to devise a system that gave blacks the message, in their every waking moment, that they were to be subjugated to the will of whites. This meant imposing a system so severe that it assured whites that blacks would not forget the place designed for them. The legal system that governed the lives of blacks was codified into laws known as "Slave Codes." Each of the rules and regulations imposed in the Slave Codes, and later, after Reconstruction, in the Black Codes, was designed to do this.

To give you an indication of the extent to which such measures went, a February 21, 2002, *USA Today* news article excerpted a quote from an 1822 South Carolina grand jury in response to complaints about slaves wearing clothes made from ordinary cloth. The grand jury said: "Negroes should be permitted to dress only in coarse stuffs [called "Negro cloth" and manufactured by WestPoint Stevens, today the United States' largest producer of bed and bath textiles]. . . . Every distinction should be created between whites and the Negroes, calculated to make the latter feel the superiority of the former."

When Reconstruction ended, about 11 years after the Civil War was over, the Slave Codes were renamed "Black Codes" and used virtually as if slavery had never ended. This system of laws governing black and white relations was based both on law and social custom and was as ironclad as any legal law ever was. The system, adopted by either law or social custom all over the country, remained in place until the Civil Rights Act of 1964, and in some places well into the 1970s, constantly reasserting the institutionalized role of race in the United States.

But what do we really mean by "a system" and "the institutionalized role of race"? And why can't we just all forget it and move on? Well, let's take a look and see if we can gain some insight. Doing so is helpful in trying to figure out why race is still such a persistent and pervasive issue in the workplace today.

After Reconstruction, as during slavery, every facet of the life of blacks was regulated. Recall from the affirmative action chapter that state and local laws or ironclad customs made it virtually impossible for blacks to vote and made it illegal for blacks to marry whites, have sex with them, go to school with them; to go, on an equal basis with whites, to the same parks, recreational facilities, universities, professional schools, movies, churches, theaters, hospitals, restrooms, libraries, restaurants, transportation facilities, department stores, beaches; to be serviced by the same barbers and beauticians, doctors and lawyers (or, if they were allowed to be, they waited in a separate waiting room and were seen last); to drink from the same water fountains; or, in some places, to drive a car, stay in a town past sundown, go to town on certain days, be out past curfew, or drive taxi customers of a different race. If space was provided for blacks at all in public accommodations, it was separate from that occupied by whites. For instance, blacks were routinely seated in the balconies of movie theaters, or made to attend on different days than whites (some fairs had "Negro days" for blacks to attend, and some towns had "Negro days" for blacks to shop). They were not seated at all in restaurants but were generally sent around to the back, where they ordered their food on a take-out basis long before the advent of drive-throughs. Staying in hotels was generally out of the question.

Blacks could not try on clothes or shoes in clothing or shoe stores; for shoes, blacks had to come in with a tracing of the customer's foot on paper and have it matched to the shoes they wanted to buy, which they then purchased and took away from the store. Although paying full bus fare, in the South blacks could not board the front of the bus. Rather, they were required to pay their fare in the front, get off the bus, and reenter through the back to sit. If whites wanted or needed seats, blacks had to give up their seats even though they had paid the full fare.

Blacks could not testify against whites in court, look whites in the eye, stay on the sidewalk when whites passed by, be called "Mr.," "Mrs.," or "Miss," or contradict anything a white person said. It was not until the Voting Rights Act of 1965 that blacks received full voting rights in the United States. Breach of the law or social policy by blacks resulted in swift retribution, up to and including death—generally by lynching for males—an event that was often attended by whole families of whites, including children, and treated as a festive family outing, complete with picnic baskets.

Segregated public schools were outlawed by the U.S. Supreme Court in *Brown* v. *Board of Education* in 1954, but blacks were not admitted into many schools until much later. For instance, they were not admitted to the University of Georgia until 1961, and not before campus rioting occurred protesting integration. Counties in some states shut down their entire public school system rather than admit blacks. In 1957 the "Little Rock 9" integrated Central High School in Little Rock, Arkansas, but not before President Dwight Eisenhower sent in 10,000 federalized National Guardsmen and 1,000 paratroopers to handle the angry mob of 1,000 whites and guard the nine students. At the University of Mississippi in 1962, two people were killed and more than 150 federal marshals were injured when the first black student enrolled.

Sounds like something out of a bad dream, doesn't it? It was real. And it was not that long ago. If you were not alive during that time, then most certainly your parents or grandparents were. Remember that the system officially ended only in 1964, and in many places it, or its effects, lingered on long after. For instance, in Atlanta, retiring black police officers are suffering because of the police department's racial policy that lingered until the 1970s, which prevented black officers from contributing to a whites-only pension fund. This is now resulting in hundreds of dollars a month less in pension payouts to retiring black officers. Along with the difference in pensions, black officers were not permitted to partner with white officers, were made to dress in separate dressing rooms in separate buildings, and were not permitted to arrest white suspects. Among other examples,

- Between 2000 and 2004, 16 major insurance cases were settled, covering about 14.8 million policies sold by 90 insurance companies between 1900 and the 1980s to blacks who were charged more, as was the custom of the day, simply because they were black. The settlements amounted to more than $556 million. During the high-water mark for burial insurance, as it was known, American insurance companies held policies worth more than $40 billion. According to the Federal Trade Commission, some companies, like Metropolitan Life, built their businesses largely on such policies, which not only charged blacks higher premiums, but were targeted to poor blacks and often paid out less than the premiums paid in.

- In June 2005, reputed KKK member Edgar Ray Killen was convicted for the 1964 murder case involving the three civil rights workers who were helping blacks register to vote. Michael Schwerner, James Chaney, and Andrew Goodman were abducted, killed, and buried in an earthen dam in Mississippi. The murder was the basis of the popular movie, *Mississippi Burning.*

- In 2004, the U.S. Justice Department announced they were reopening the 50-year-old Emmett Till murder investigation to determine whether others were involved in the murder of 14-year-old Till. While visiting family in Mississippi in 1955, Till, from Chicago, allegedly whistled at a white woman and was later taken from his bed at 2:30 A.M., beaten, his eyes gouged out, and shot in the head. He was found in the Tallahatchie River, tied with barbed wire to a heavy metal fan. The two men tried for the crime were acquitted by an all-white jury within an hour (a juror later said they drank a Coke before returning the verdict, to make things look legitimate), and a few months later sold the detailed story of their murder of Till to *Look* magazine. Thousands of people attended the open-casket funeral of Till, and a few months later the trial verdict fueled the Montgomery, Alabama, bus boycott begun by Rosa Parks and led by Dr. Martin Luther King, Jr. which was the opening shot of the Civil Rights Movement.

- In 2002, a federal judge in Mississippi approved a desegregation plan for Mississippi's universities based on a case brought 28 years earlier in 1975.

Notice that this is not dull, dry history from eons ago. This is now. We are living the history as we speak. The last Civil War widow just died in May 2004!

It was not until passage of the Civil Rights Act of 1964 that this country was first forced to deal with blacks as equals. For virtually their entire history in this country, blacks were dealt with in one way, with societal laws and mores totally built around that approach. Then came the Civil Rights Act of 1964, attempting to change this 300+-year history overnight. We have been struggling with the issue ever since.

When race has been as ingrained in a culture as it has been in the United States, it is predictable that it is taking a rather long while to rid the workplace of the vestiges of race discrimination. The effects of racially based considerations and decisions linger long after the actual intent to discriminate may have dissipated.

Department of Labor Glass Ceiling Studies in 1991 and 1995 of barriers to full management participation in the workplace by women and minorities found that minorities had made strides in entering the workplace, but a "glass ceiling" exists, beyond which minorities rarely progress. The study found that minorities plateau at a lower corporate level than women, who plateau at a lower level than white males.

According to the studies, monitoring for equal access and opportunity was almost never considered a corporate responsibility or a part of the planning and developmental programs and policies of the employer, nor as part of participation with regard to senior management levels. Neither employee appraisals nor total compensation systems were usually monitored. Most companies had inadequate records regarding equal employment opportunity and affirmative action responsibilities in recruitment, employment, and developmental activities for management-level positions.

Such factors militate against serious consideration of full participation by all sectors of the work population and prevent the employer from being presented in the best light should lawsuits arise. If an employer analyzed and monitored workplace information based on the Glass Ceiling considerations, much race discrimination could be discovered and addressed before it progressed to the litigation stage.

The cases in this chapter are specifically chosen to help you learn to recognize race discrimination claims when you see them coming and before they turn into litigation. Pay particular attention to the facts in the cases and the questions after them. After thoroughly reading and thinking about the cases, you should feel much more comfortable about being a manager or supervisor who is able to spot trouble in this area and do what needs to be done to avoid it.

GENERAL CONSIDERATIONS

Title VII was enacted primarily in response to discrimination against blacks in this country, but the act applies equally to *all*. Though, as we saw in Chapter 5 on affirmative action, there are times when it *appears* the law does not equally protect rights of nonminorities, this is done only in a remedial context with strict safeguards in place. The *McDonald* case demonstrates that racial discrimination may occur against blacks *or* whites and is equally prohibited under Title VII. Note that the *McDonald* decision is written by Justice Thurgood Marshall, who strenuously fought on the U.S. Supreme Court, and even before, to end racial discrimination. (See Exhibit 5.4.) The *McDonald* case is the basis for opening scenario 2.

Scenario

Thurgood Marshall was born in Baltimore, Maryland, the son of a steward and a school teacher. He graduated from Lincoln University and from Howard University Law School in 1933. While at Howard, Marshall attracted the attention of Dean Charles Houston, a noted black lawyer and chief legal planner for the NAACP. When he met Marshall, Houston was about to begin a campaign challenging the constitutionality of racial segregation laws in the United States. After law school Marshall practiced law for a brief period, joined the NAACP as a staff attorney, then took over as chief counsel after Houston in 1938.

When Marshall assumed leadership of the NAACP legal program, racial segregation pervaded every aspect of life in the United States—its legality was hardly questioned, and blacks were not considered full partners in the American republic. The 13th, 14th, and 15th Amendments and the laws enacted to give meaning to their promise of black equality had been emptied of content by decisions of the U.S. Supreme Court. The most influential decision, *Plessy* v. *Ferguson,* 1896, was understood to give broad approval to providing separate public facilities and services for blacks. The political power of the Southern states was such that neither congress nor the president would support legislation to outlaw lynching, much less to end racial segregation. Marshall and his colleagues determined, therefore, to concentrate their efforts on the courts. Their early cases aimed at documenting the inequalities—for example, in per pupil spending and teacher pay—that made the segregated public facilities and education offered to blacks by the Southern and border states not equivalent to those provided to whites. It was thought that such litigation might lead to significant short-term improvement in the facilities with which blacks were provided. However, the NAACP's ultimate goal and grand design was to persuade the Supreme Court that racial segregation as such was unconstitutional, that regardless of the facilities offered to blacks it inevitably relegated them to a position of inferiority and second-class citizenship.

After World War II the pace of litigation quickened, and the Supreme Court struck down particular instances of racial discrimination in interstate travel, primary elections, housing, and criminal justice. Eventually litigation efforts were concentrated on education. By 1954 when Marshall argued *Brown* v. *Board of Education,* dealing with public school segregation, extensive documentation had been accumulated demonstrating that, as the Court ultimately found, "separate educational facilities are inherently unequal." Soon after, civil rights lawyers won a series of cases that made clear that *Brown* had undermined any constitutional basis for the government to make invidious distinctions in the allocation of goods, services, or benefits on the basis of race.

During his years with the NAACP, Marshall earned a reputation as a tough, shrewd legal tactician with a deceptively easygoing personal style. Southern senators attempted to block his appointment to the U.S. Court of Appeals in 1961, but the nomination was confirmed in 1962. In 1965, President Lyndon B. Johnson named Marshall solicitor-general, and in 1967 Johnson appointed him an associate justice of the Supreme Court.

On the Supreme Court, Marshall usually supported positions taken by civil libertarians, equal rights advocates, and those who construe the procedural guarantees of the Bill of Rights to protect criminal defendants. In the 1970s when many ground-breaking liberal decisions of the later 1950s and the 1960s were restricted by a new conservative majority of justices appointed by President Richard M. Nixon, Marshall became one of the Court's more vocal dissenters, especially in cases such as the *Bakke* decision outlawing reverse racial quotas, where he believed the Court had retreated from a commitment to eliminate racism in public life.

Source: Adapted from "Thurgood Marshall" by Michael Meltsner, *Collier's Encyclopedia,* vol. 15. Copyright © 1983 by Macmillan Educational Company. Reprinted by permission of the publisher.

McDonald v. Santa Fe Trail Transportation *427 U.S. 273 (1976)*

Two white employees and one black employee misappropriated cargo from one of the employer's shipments. The two white employees were discharged and the black employee was not. The white employees sued the employer for race discrimination. The Court held that Title VII is not limited to discrimination against members of any particular race and applies equally to whites and blacks.

Marshall, J.

Santa Fe Transportation employees, McDonald, Laird and Jackson were separately and together accused by their employer of misappropriation of 60-gallon cans of antifreeze which were part of a shipment they were carrying for one of Santa Fe's customers. Six days later, McDonald and Laird, white, were fired by the employer. Jackson, black, was not. We hold that this unequal discipline based on race violates Title VII even though the employees bringing suit are white.

Title VII of the Civil Rights Act of 1964 prohibits the discharge of "any individual" because of "such individual's race." Its terms are not limited to discrimination against any particular race. Thus, although we were not there confronted with racial discrimination against whites, we described the Act in *Griggs* v. *Duke Power Co.* as prohibiting "[d]iscriminatory preference for any [racial] group, minority or majority."

This conclusion is in accord with uncontradicted legislative history to the effect that Title VII was intended to "cover white men and white women and all Americans," 110 Cong. Rec. 2578 (1964), and create an "obligation not to discriminate against whites," *id.,* at 7218.

Santa Fe, while conceding that "across-the-board discrimination in favor of minorities could never be condoned consistent with Title VII," contends never-

theless that "such discrimination in isolated cases which cannot reasonably be said to burden whites as a class unduly," such as is alleged here, "may be acceptable." We cannot agree. There is no exception in the terms of the Act for isolated cases; on the contrary, "Title VII tolerates no racial discrimination, subtle or otherwise." Santa Fe disclaims that the actions challenged here were any part of an affirmative action program, and we emphasize that we do not consider here the permissibility of such a program, whether judicially required or otherwise prompted.

While Santa Fe may decide that participation in a theft of cargo may render an employee unqualified for employment, this criterion must be applied alike to members of all races, and Title VII is violated if, as employees allege, it is not. Thus, we conclude that the district court erred in dismissing the employees' Title VII claims and we REVERSE and REMAND.

Case Questions

1. Does it seem consistent with Title VII for the Court to hold as it did? Why or why not?
2. Do you agree with the employer's "isolated case" argument? Explain.
3. How does this holding square with what you know of affirmative action and race discrimination?

RECOGNIZING RACE DISCRIMINATION

One of the most difficult things for a manager to do in this area is often simply being able to recognize race discrimination when it presents itself. The latest EEOC statistics for FY 2004 indicated that race remains the most frequent type of claim filed with the agency. Of the 79,432 charges filed, 34.9 percent of them were based on race. Many of these claims involve systemic race discrimination affecting hundreds of employees. That is, the glass ceiling is still at work, denying full workplace participation to blacks. Just within the past couple of years, EEOC has settled class action suits with Abercrombie & Fitch ($50 million), Consolidated Freightways ($2.75 million), Milgard Windows ($3.37 million), Home Depot ($5.5 million), Carl Buddig ($2.5 million), and Supercuts

($3.5 million). All of these cases involve widespread workplace discrimination in hiring, promotions, training, and other aspects of work life. Cases of systemic glass ceiling–type discrimination that go to trial are becoming increasingly rare. Even if, as was the case with Abercrombie and Fitch, the employer settles with EEOC for a whopping $50 million, they may still be better off than taking the case to trial where higher compensatory damages, and punitive damages on top of this, are possible.

Often employers are held liable for race discrimination because they treated employees of a particular race differently without even realizing they were building a case of race discrimination for which they could ultimately be liable. As the case below demonstrates, intent may be established by direct evidence of discrimination by the employer even when an employer may discriminate for what it considers to be justifiable reasons.

As you read the case below, think about whether you would have handled things differently to avoid the result the court reached here. *Vaughn* is the basis for opening scenario 3.

Vaughn v. Edel   *918 F.2d 517 (5th Cir. 1990)*

During a retrenchment, a black female was terminated for poor performance. She alleged race discrimination in that her employer intentionally determined not to give her necessary feedback about her performance which would have helped her perform better and perhaps avoid dismissal. The court upheld the employee's claim.

Wiener, J.

Emma Vaughn, a black female attorney, became an associate contract analyst in Texaco's Land Department in August of 1979. Her supervisors were Robert Edel and Alvin Earl Hatton, assistant chief contract analyst. In Vaughn's early years with Texaco, she received promotions and was the highest ranked contract analyst in the department.

The events leading to this dispute began on April 16, 1985, the day after Vaughn returned from a second maternity leave. On that day, Edel complained to Vaughn about the low volume of her prior work and the excessive number of people who visited her office. Vaughn later spoke with Roger Keller, the head of the Land Department, about Edel's criticism of her.

In a memorandum concerning this discussion, Keller wrote that he had told Vaughn that he had been told that Vaughn's productivity "was very low"; that he "had become aware for some time of the excessive visiting by predominantly blacks in her office behind closed doors"; and that "the visiting had a direct bearing on her productivity." Keller then told Vaughn, as he noted in his memo, that "she was allowing herself to become a black matriarch within Texaco" and "that this

role was preventing her from doing her primary work for the company and that it must stop."

Keller's remarks offended Vaughn, so she sought the advice of a friend who was an attorney in Texaco's Legal Department. Keller learned of this meeting and of Vaughn's belief that he was prejudiced. To avoid charges of race discrimination, Keller told Vaughn's supervisor, Edel, "not [to] have any confrontations with Ms. Vaughn about her work." Keller later added that "if he [Edel] was dissatisfied, let it ride. If it got serious, then see [Keller]."

Between April 1985 and April 1987 when Vaughn was fired, neither Edel nor Hatton expressed criticism of Vaughn's work to her. During this period all annual written evaluations of Vaughn's work performance (which, incidentally, Vaughn never saw) were "satisfactory." Vaughn also received a merit salary increase, though it was the minimum, for 1986. Keller testified that for several years he had intentionally overstated on Vaughn's annual evaluations his satisfaction with her performance because he did not have the time to spend going through procedures which would result from a lower rating and which could lead to termination.

In 1985–86 Texaco undertook a study to identify activities it could eliminate to save costs. To meet the cost-reduction goal set by the study, the Land Department fired its two "poorest performers," one of whom was Vaughn, as the "lowest ranked" contract analyst. The other employee fired was a white male.

In passing Title VII, Congress announced that "sex, race, religion, and national origin are not relevant to the selection, evaluation, or compensation of employees."

When direct credible evidence of employer discrimination exists, employer can counter direct evidence, such as a statement or written document showing discriminatory motive on its face, "only by showing by a preponderance of the evidence that they would have acted as they did without regard to the [employee's] race."

Vaughn presented direct evidence of discrimination. Keller testified that to avoid provoking a discrimination suit he had told Vaughn's supervisor not to confront her about her work. His "black matriarch" memorandum details the events that led Keller to initiate this policy. Keller also testified to deliberately overstating Vaughn's evaluations in order not to start the process that might eventually lead to her termination. This direct evidence clearly shows that Keller acted as he did solely because Vaughn is black.

Although Vaughn's race may not have directly motivated the 1987 decision to fire her, race did play a part in Vaughn's employment relationship with Texaco from 1985–1987. Texaco's treatment of Vaughn was not color-blind during that period. In neither criticizing Vaughn when her work was unsatisfactory nor counselling her how to improve, Texaco treated Vaughn differently than it did its other contract analysts because she was black. As a result, Texaco did not afford Vaughn the same opportunity to improve her performance and perhaps her relative ranking, as it did its white employees. One of those employees was placed on an improvement program. Others received informal counselling. The evidence indicates that Vaughn had the ability to improve. As Texaco acknowledges, she was once its highest ranked contract analyst.

Had her dissatisfied supervisors simply counselled Vaughn informally, such counselling would inevitably have indicated to Vaughn that her work was deficient. Had Keller given Vaughn the evaluation that he believed she deserved, Texaco's regulations would have required his placing her on a ninety-day work improvement program, just as at least one other employee—a white male—had been placed. A Texaco employee who has not improved by the end of that period is fired.

When an employer excludes black employees from its efforts to improve efficiency, it subverts the "broad overriding interest" of Title VII—"efficient and trusty workmanship assured through fair and racially neutral employment and personnel decisions." Texaco has never stated any reason, other than that Vaughn was black, for treating her as it did. Had Texaco treated Vaughn in a color-blind manner from 1985–1987, Vaughn may have been fired by April 1987 for unsatisfactory work; on the other hand, she might have sufficiently improved her performance so as not to be one of the two lowest ranked employees, thereby avoiding termination in April 1987.

Because Texaco's behavior was race-motivated, Texaco has violated Title VII. Texaco limited or classified Vaughn in a way which would either "tend to deprive [her] of employment opportunities or otherwise adversely affect [her] status as an employee" in violation of the law.

Case Questions

1. Do you agree with the court's decision? Why or why not?

2. How would you have handled this matter if you were the manager?

3. What do you think of Keller's remarks about Vaughn becoming the "black matriarch" of Texaco, "meeting behind closed doors," and "excessive meetings with predominantly blacks"? What does it signify to you? What attitudes might it reflect that may be inappropriate in the workplace? What concern, if any, might be appropriate?

An employer who has not considered the issue of race may well develop and implement policies that have a racially discriminatory impact, without ever intending to do so. The "no-beard" case below is a good example of this. It is also a good example of why disparate impact cases must be recognized, if Congress' legislative intent of ridding the workplace of employment discrimination is to be at all successful.

Scenario 1

Bradley is the basis for opening scenario 1. *Bradley* also clearly demonstrates why the more an employer knows about diverse groups, the better. Here, it could have saved the employer from liability.

Bradley v. Pizzaco of Nebraska, Inc., d/b/a Domino's Pizza
7 F.3d 795 (8th Cir. 1993)

Employee brought a race discrimination case against his employer after being discharged for failure to comply with the employer's policy requiring employees to be clean-shaven. The court held that the policy had a disparate impact on blacks and violated Title VII.

Bowman, J.

This action arose out of a Title VII employment discrimination claim brought by Langston Bradley, a former Domino's delivery man. Bradley alleged that Domino's discriminated against him on the basis of race when it fired him for failure to appear clean-shaven in compliance with the company's no-beard policy. The no-beard policy is established nationwide by Pizzaco's franchiser, Domino's Pizza, Inc. Bradley alleged that he suffered from pseudofolliculitis barbae ("PFB"), a skin condition affecting approximately fifty percent of African American males, half of which number cannot shave at all. Bradley claimed that the no-beard policy deprived him and other African American males suffering from PFB of equal employment opportunities in violation of Title VII of the Civil Rights Act of 1964.

Domino's offered the testimony of Paul D. Black, Domino's vice president for operations. Black said it was "common sense" that "the better our people look, the better our sales will be." Black also cited a public opinion survey indicating that up to 20 percent of customers would "have a negative reaction" to a delivery person wearing a beard. Further, Black speculated that Domino's would encounter difficulty enforcing any exceptions to their dress and grooming code. Black did not offer evidence of any particular exception that was tried without success; rather, he merely stated that monitoring the hair length and moustaches of employees at five thousand Domino's locations is difficult.

Black's testimony was largely speculative and conclusory. Such testimony, without more, does not prove the business necessity of maintaining the strict no-beard policy.

In addition to Black's testimony, Domino's offered the results of a public opinion survey it commissioned. The survey purported to measure public reaction to beards on pizza shop employees. The survey showed that up to 20 percent of those surveyed would react negatively to a delivery man wearing a beard. Even if the survey results indicated a significant customer apprehension regarding beards, which they do not, the results would not constitute evidence of a sufficient business justification defense for Domino's strict no-beard policy. Although this Circuit has not directly addressed customer preference as a business justification for policies having a disparate impact on a protected class, cases from other circuits have not looked favorably on this kind of evidence. Customer preference may only be taken into account when it goes to a matter affecting the company's ability to perform the primary necessary function or service it offers, rather than a tangential aspect of that service or function. The existence of a beard on the face of a delivery man does not affect in any manner Domino's ability to make or deliver pizzas to their customers. Customer preference, which is at best weakly shown by Domino's survey, is clearly not a colorable business justification defense in this case. Significantly, the survey makes no showing that customers would order less pizza in the absence of a strictly enforced no-beard rule.

Domino's is free to establish any grooming and dress standards it wishes; we hold only that reasonable accommodation must be made for members of the protected class who suffer from PFB. We note the burden of a narrow medical exception for African American males who cannot shave because of PFB appears minimal. The employer, of course, should not be precluded from requiring that any beards permitted under this narrow medical exception be neatly trimmed, clean, and not in excess of a specified length. REVERSED and REMANDED.

Case Questions

1. If you had been the manager, would you have been surprised at this case outcome? Explain.

2. Why do you think Pizzaco had a no-beard policy? What purpose did it serve? Was there another way to get what Pizzaco may have wanted by instituting the policy?

3. Did stereotypes play a role in this policy? What role should stereotypes play in developing workplace policies?

See how important it can be to simply be able to recognize race discrimination when you see it? If you, as a manager, never had to deal with PFB (as 95 percent of the white male population and certainly all of the white female and other ethnicities need not do), you would be blissfully unaware of the impact of your policy on 70 or so percent of the black male population. Simply taking the time to treat the employee's concern as legitimate (rather than merely dismissing it because it was not something with which the manager was familiar) and trying to seek alternatives would have made all the difference.

If the employer in *Bradley* had simply asked the employee to provide documentation for his condition from a reputable and reliable source, such as a dermatologist or barber, the outcome may have been different. The employer would have had a basis for providing an exception to the rule in these particular circumstances, while still maintaining the general rule for other employees. While not satisfied that everyone does not have to obey the policy, the employer at least feels satisfied that sufficient justification was provided to excuse this employee. Other employees seeing the employee treated differently would feel reasonably comfortable knowing that the difference in treatment is based on justifiable medical reasons. If the employer had been flexible, rather than dismissing the employee's assertions out of hand simply because it was not familiar to him, he undoubtedly could have avoided the result in this case. As a manager, make sure you try to consider all angles before making a decision. It is especially important to consider the realities of those who belong to groups with whom you may not be familiar. Don't be afraid to seek help or information from those in a better position to know. (For more examples of discrimination, see Exhibit 5.5.)

Below is another unusual manifestation of racial discrimination that might well slip by a manager, just as it did in this case. In the case below, the action was not brought by the blacks discriminated against by the employer but, rather, by the white manager who was trying *not* to discriminate when her company wanted her to do so.

Chandler v. Fast Lane, Inc. *868 F. Supp. 1138 (E.D. Ark., W. Div. 1994)*

A white employee brought suit against her employer for constructive dismissal under Title VII and other statutes, alleging that she was forced to leave her job when the employer would not allow her to hire and promote blacks. The employer argued that since its policies discriminated only against blacks, the white employee had no right to sue under Title VII. The court disagreed and permitted the case to be brought.

Eisele, J.

In the complaint filed with the Court, Chandler (who is white) alleges that she was the victim of a discriminatory employment practice at the hands of her employers. Chandler, a former manager of employers' restaurant, claims that her employer thwarted her efforts to employ and promote African-American employees, and that as a result the conditions of her employment became so intolerable that she was forced to resign. The employer argues that because they are alleged to have adopted discriminatory hiring and promotional practices targeted only at African-Americans, a white person has no standing to assert a Title VII claim premised upon these policies.

It is true that only individuals whom employers are claimed to have failed or refused to hire or promote were African-Americans. However, by focusing on the "fail or refuse to hire" provision of 2000e-2(a)(1), employers' argument misperceives the unlawful employment practice alleged by Chandler. Chandler does not claim that she was a target of employers' allegedly anti–African-American employment practices. Rather, Chandler argues that employers' insistence that she enforce these practices violated her fundamental right to associate with African-Americans, and as a consequence employer committed a separate violation by engaging in an unlawful employment practice that "otherwise discriminate[d] against an individual," namely Chandler.

Although the Court recognizes that Chandler's Title VII claim is somewhat novel, it is of the opinion that such a claim, if proven, would state a cause of action under Title VII. A white person's right to associate with African-Americans is protected by Sec. 1981. Therefore, the Court concludes that an employer's implementation of an employment practice that impinges upon this right is actionable under Title VII.

Additionally, Chandler's allegations are sufficient to establish a Title VII claim under a separate provision of the statute. The relevant provision of Title VII is found in §42 U.S.C.A. §2000e-3(a), which provides in pertinent part:

> It shall be an unlawful employment practice for an employer to discriminate against any of his employees . . . because [s]he has opposed any practice made an unlawful employment practice by [Title VII].

In order to establish a prima facie case under the "opposition" clause of §2000e-3(a), an employee must show: (1) that she was engaged in an opposition activity protected under Title VII; (2) that she was a victim of adverse employment action; and (3) that a causal nexus exists between these two events. The Court has no doubt that an employee who exercises her authority to promote and employ African-Americans engages in protected "opposition" to her employer's unlawful employment practice which seeks to deprive African-Americans of such benefits. Thus, Chandler's allegations are clearly sufficient to meet the first requirement of a §2000e-3(a) claim. The Court further concludes that employers' insistence that Chandler enforce such an employment practice, if proven, would certainly cause an "adverse employment action" to be visited upon her. Title VII forbids an employer from requiring its employees "to work in a discriminatorily hostile or abusive environment," and included within this prohibition is the right of white employees to a work environment free from discrimination against African-Americans, or any other class of persons. Indeed, subjecting an employee to such a hostile working environment may result in an actionable constructive discharge, a result that is especially likely under facts similar to those presently alleged. Under Title VII, a constructive discharge occurs whenever it is reasonably foreseeable that an employee will resign as a result of her employer's unlawful employment practice, and it is plainly foreseeable that an employee might choose to resign rather than to acquiesce in or enforce her employer's discriminatory and illegal employment practice.

The Court is therefore satisfied that employers' efforts to hinder Chandler from hiring and promoting African-Americans, and their insistence that she discriminate against such persons, if proven, would result in an actionable Title VII claim. Indeed, "[u]nder the terms of §2000e-3(a), requiring an employee to discriminate is itself an unlawful employment practice." Accordingly, it is therefore ordered that employers' motion to dismiss is DENIED.

Case Questions

1. What do you think of the employer's argument that since its policies discriminated against blacks, the white employee should not be able to bring a suit for discrimination? Explain.

2. Do you understand the court's reasoning that the white employee was being discriminated against by not being able to hire and promote black employees? Explain.

3. What reason can you think of as to why the employer had the policy of not hiring or promoting blacks? Do you think it makes good economic sense? (Consider all facets of economics, including the possibility of litigation over the policies.)

Exhibit 5.5   Names and "Hello" Can Keep You Out

Two recent studies have shown just how pervasive, yet subtle, race discrimination can be for employees and job applicants.

In the first, researchers from the University of Chicago and MIT conducted a study in which they sent out nearly 5,000 fictional résumés in response to 1,300 newspaper ads for jobs in Chicago and Boston. To each ad they sent two sets of two résumés: one identical set had a résumé with a "traditionally black" name and one with a "traditionally white" name; the other set of résumés had more experience, and again, one had a "traditionally black" name and the other a "traditionally white" name. "Traditionally black" names included Rasheed, Kareem, Leroy, Tyrone, Ebony, Kenya, LaTonya, Tanisha, Keisha, Hakim, Aisha, and Tamika. "Traditionally white" names included Greg, Jill, Allison, Emily, Laurie, Sarah, Brendan, Brad, Meredith, Kristen, Matthew, and Brett.

Applicants with "traditionally white" names received 50 percent more callbacks than those with "traditionally black" names. The researchers found that increasing credentials resulted in a better chance of whites being called back more often, but not blacks. Applicants with "traditionally white" names were called back at a rate comparable to having eight additional years of experience. The result was the same across occupations, industries, and employer size. Federal contractors or others who indicated they were equal employment opportunity employers were just as likely to discriminate as other employers, according to the researchers. Having more upscale addresses helped whites, but not blacks. The researchers concluded that "Differential treatment by race still appears to still be prominent in the U.S. labor market."

In the second study, Dr. John Baugh, a professor of education and linguistics at Stanford University, presented over 300 university students recordings of voices saying a single word. The students were asked to identify the ethnicity of the speaker. Over 80 percent were able to do so correctly, based solely on hearing the single word, "hello."

Baugh, black, became interested in linguistic profiling when he placed several calls in response to newspaper ads for housing, but when he showed up at the property, he was always given reasons why it could not be rented to him. He suspected that the phenomenon was because he used his professional voice on the phone and the landlords thought he was white, but he showed up and was black. He set out to investigate his suspicions. Dr. Baugh is particularly adept at voices, having grown up in Philadelphia and Los Angeles with many different dialects. He placed over 100 calls inquiring about a rental property, some using his professional voice, and others his "ethnic dialects." He used the exact same sentence each time he called, and only varied his voice and intonation. Dr. Baugh found that when using his "white" voice, he received 50 percent more calls back.

After James Johnson suspected that the same thing happened to him while looking for an apartment in San Francisco, he reported it to the local fair housing agency, the Eden Council for Hope and Opportunity. Eden used five callers to inquire about housing, leaving messages. Three of the callers "sounded white" and two "sounded black." The "white" callers' calls were returned within hours. The "black" callers' calls were not returned. The counselor who ran the investigation said it was "pretty blatant." Shanna Smith, executive director of the National Fair Housing Alliance, says it is a familiar practice for housing, banking, and other industries, such as insurance.

Sources: Marianne Bertrand and Sendhil Mullainathan, 2004, "Are Emily and Greg More Employable than Lakisha and Jamal? A Field Experiment on Labor Market Discrimination," http://post.economics.harvard.edu/faculty/mullainathan/papers/emilygreg.pdf; Patrice D. Johnson, "Linguistic Profiling," The *Black Commentator* 1 (April 5, 2002), http://www.blackcommentator.com/linguistic_profiling_pr.html; Steve Osunsami, "Voice Recognition," ABC News.com, 12/6/01, http://more.abcnews.go.com/sections/wnt/worldnewstonight/linguistic_profiling011206.html; "The Color of Voice: How Inferring Race Can Become Discrimination," ABC News.com, 2/6/2002, http://abcnews.go.com/sections/ Downtown/2020/downtown_linguisticsprofiling_020205.html.

RACIAL HARASSMENT

In addition to an employer being liable for race discrimination under Title VII, the employer may also be liable for workplace racial harassment. To hold an employer liable for racial harassment, the employee must show that the harassment was (1) unwelcome; (2) based on race; (3) so severe or pervasive that it altered the conditions of employment and created an abusive environment; and that (4) there is a basis for imposing liability on the employer. The employer is responsible for such activity if the employer himself or herself is the one who perpetrates the harassment, or if it is permitted in the workplace by the employer or supervisory employees. Actions for racial harassment, like those of race discrimination under Title VII, may be brought under the same alternative statutes as race discrimination, as appropriate—that is, the post–Civil War statutes, state human rights or fair employment practice laws, or constitutional provisions.

As shown by the case below, racial harassment has as its basis the employer imposing on the harassed employee different terms or conditions of employment based on race. The employee is required to work in an atmosphere in which severe and pervasive harassing activity is directed at the employee because of the employee's race or color. As we shall see later with sexual harassment, the employer's best approach to racial harassment is to maintain a workplace in which such activity is not permitted or condoned in any way, to take all racial harassment complaints seriously, and to take immediate corrective action, if necessary, after investigation. As the case below demonstrates, an employer must do this to avoid liability. The case also demonstrates how important it is for a manager to keep up with changes that result in new and different ways to harass. Here, the harassment was done by e-mail.

Daniels v. WorldCom Corp. *1998 U.S. Dist. LEXIS 2335 (N.D. Tex. 1998)*

Employees sued the employer under Title VII and state civil causes of action when jokes with racial undertones were sent to them and other employees on their workplace computers. While the court dismissed the actions based on legal problems with the case, the case is instructive for demonstrating how racial harassment can arise in the workplace, and even changes with technology.

Solis, J.

Angela Daniels and Dimple Ballou allege that they were racially discriminated against while working at WorldCom, Inc. Specifically, they assert that four electronic mail [e-mail] jokes sent by a non-managerial employee of WorldCom were racially harassing. Further, the employees assert that WorldCom was negligent for allowing the e-mail system to be used to send the jokes and that WorldCom retaliated against them for reporting the jokes.

On January 21, 1997, Cathy Madzik, a non-managerial employee at WorldCom, sent a joke to Daniels and two other co-workers across the com-

pany's e-mail system. After receiving this and construing the joke as having racial undertones, Daniels sent a message to Madzik objecting to the joke's contents. Three days later, Madzik sent three more jokes to Daniels and others. Daniels was offended by what she perceived as racial undertones in one of the jokes.

At some point shortly after receiving these jokes, Daniels complained to the manager of the Information Systems Department, Dianne Summers. Daniels also took her concerns to Tom Adams, the Human Resources Manager at WorldCom's Dallas facility. After learning of Daniels' concerns and discussing the situation with the Human Resources Department, Summers issued a "strong verbal warning" to Madzik and placed a written reprimand in her personnel file. On or about January 27, 1997, Summers held a staff meeting which Daniels and Ballou attended. At the close of this meeting, Summers dismissed Madzik and warned the remaining individuals not to use the e-mail system for non-business purposes. On January 29, 1997, Adams held a meeting during which Daniels and Ballou were also allowed to voice their displeasure about the jokes. Adams also addressed the appropriate use of the company e-mail system. In addition to the two meetings discussed above, Summers requested several workers at WorldCom, including Daniels and Ballou, to review the company's Electronic Mail Policy. Daniels and Ballou filed suit on February 27, 1997.

Daniels and Ballou assert that WorldCom was negligent in allowing employees to use the e-mail system to send racially discriminatory jokes. To the extent that they claim an allegation of common-law negligence, this claim fails as a matter of law because WorldCom acted reasonably. Within ten days of the employees' complaints regarding the e-mail jokes, supervisors at WorldCom organized two meetings to discuss the

proper use of the company's e-mail system. Further, Summers verbally reprimanded Madzik and issued a written warning regarding improper use of e-mail. Finally, WorldCom had an established policy regarding the use of e-mail and Summers attached a copy of this policy on February 4, 1997, for the employees in her department to review. Based on all of this evidence, WorldCom acted reasonably and employees' common-law claim of negligence fails as a matter of law. Employer's motion to dismiss is GRANTED.

Case Questions

1. Does it surprise you that there would be liability on the part of the employer for harassing e-mails sent from a workplace computer? Explain.

2. Do you agree with the court that the employer quickly and appropriately addressed the problem here so that liability should not attach?

3. If you were the manager to whom the employees came reporting the e-mail jokes, what would you have done?

Keep in mind that an employer's prompt response to harassment is important. In a recent case in which the EEOC sued the employer for workplace racial harassment, the employer ended up paying a $1.8 million settlement despite the fact that in responding to the racial harassment it had called the police, photographed the "racist graffiti," offered rewards, placed undercover employees in the plant, hired handwriting analysts, sent employees to diversity training, increased plant security, and sought the help of the FBI. The graffiti continued to appear, yet declined to a large extent "after the company started taking the remedial steps and the litigation was in full swing." The EEOC said that the company could have stopped the harassment earlier if it had wanted to. The company was also required to take preventive measures including adopting a policy against racial harassment and instituting camera monitoring of its facilities, training for managers and employees, and periodic reporting to the EEOC on racial harassment complaints.[1]

[1] *EEOC* v. *Scientific Colors, Inc., d/b/a Apollo Colors,* N.D. Ill., No. 99 C 1959 (2002).

Henderson v. Irving Materials Inc. *329 F. Supp. 2d 1002 (S.D. Ind., Indianapolis Div., 2004)*

A black employee was subjected to a number of incidents at work, including racial epithets, threats, greasing of his truck, dead mice placed in his truck and the buttons cut off his uniform, by two of his white co-workers. Several of the incidents were witnessed by their supervisor. The court found that though some of the events, in isolation, may not qualify as harassment, when taken in the total context of the employee's experience as the first black hired to work there and in the greater context of race in our country, they constituted racial harassment.

Hamilton, J.

To survive summary judgment on his hostile work environment claim against SouthSide, Henderson must come forward with evidence that would allow a reasonable jury to find that: (a) he was subject to unwelcome harassment; (b) the harassment was based on his race; (c) the harassment was sufficiently severe or pervasive so as to alter the conditions of his employment and to create a hostile or abusive working environment; and (d) there is a basis for employer liability.

Many of the incidents alleged in this case, when taken alone, would not be sufficient by themselves to reach the "severe or pervasive" standard required to support a hostile work environment claim. However, the court must consider the totality of the relevant circumstances. The court may not consider each incident in isolation. Instead, the court must consider each as part of a larger quilt of racial hostility that could convince a reasonable jury that the conditions of Henderson's employment were materially altered by a racially hostile work environment.

A. TARGET OF UNWELCOME HARASSMENT

The undisputed facts easily support a finding that Henderson was the target of unwelcome harassment, thus satisfying the first required element of his claim.

B. "BASED ON" RACE

There also is no dispute that plaintiff's evidence of Moistner's racial jokes and comments, Moistner's claims to be a member of the Ku Klux Klan and to know the Klan's grand dragon, and Moistner's calling Henderson a "nigger" at the small claims court were racial incidents and stemmed directly from racial hostility. As for the remainder of the incidents alleged by plaintiff, the racial connection might appear more attenuated if the incidents were considered in isolation. However, the court may not view those incidents in isolation. Viewing the other acts of harassment by Moistner and Santerre, tolerated by plant manager Taylor, in combination with the incidents involving the more

blatant racial hostility, a reasonable jury could find that all were part of a racially hostile environment.

Defendants argue that some incidents were not based on race because there was not an explicit racial dimension. Defendants' argument is easily refuted with respect to one incident in particular, the evidence that Moistner threatened to drag Henderson behind his pick-up truck. The court must keep in mind the Seventh Circuit's and Supreme Court's instructions to give careful consideration to "the social context in which particular behavior occurs and is experienced by its target," and to keep in mind that "the real social impact of workplace behavior often depends on a constellation of surrounding circumstances, expectations, and relationships."

Defendants' contention that a threat to drag Henderson behind a pick-up truck was devoid of a racial element is blind to history. In a murder that gained worldwide attention in 1998, James Byrd, a black man, was chained to the back of a pick-up truck by three white men who drove through the streets of Jasper, Texas, dragging Byrd to his death. The murder of Mr. Byrd triggered images of similar past acts of lynching, a tactic used by whites to terrorize and kill members of the black community.

The threat by Moistner, a self-proclaimed member of the Ku Klux Klan, that he "would like" to drag Henderson, a black man, down the street on the back of Moistner's pick-up truck has racial connotations that date back to the days when lynching black people in this manner was commonplace. See Brent Staples "Coming to Grips with the Unthinkable in Tulsa," *New York Times,* Mar. 16, 2003, sec. 4, p. 12, col. 1 (discussing race riot in Tulsa, Oklahoma, where black people were "shot, burned, lynched or tied to cars and dragged to death"). A jury could easily find that Moistner's threat carried as much racist freight as the most vile racial epithets (which Moistner himself also aimed at Henderson), combined with a threat of murder.

A reasonable jury could also draw the reasonable inference that, in light of the explicit racist character of several incidents, the superficially neutral acts of harassment were also all based on race. These forms of harassment include the buttons cut from Henderson's work shirt, the grease slathered inside his truck, the dead mice placed in his truck, the "no one wants you here" comment by Santerre, and Santerre's attempts to hit or frighten Henderson with his truck. The alleged wrongful conduct need not have been explicitly racial in order to create a hostile environment. The complained of conduct must have a racial character *or purpose* to support a Title VII claim. Plaintiff has set forth sufficient evidence to convince a reasonable jury that the conduct that defendants characterize as not based on race did indeed have a racial purpose and/or character.

C. "SEVERE OR PERVASIVE"

The next issue is whether the conduct was sufficiently severe or pervasive to support a claim under Title VII. "For workplace conduct to constitute a hostile work environment actionable under Title VII, the harassment must be sufficiently severe or pervasive to alter the conditions of the plaintiff's employment and create an abusive environment." To be considered severe or pervasive, the conduct must have been objectively hostile or abusive and must have been subjectively perceived as such. Isolated and innocuous incidents will not support a hostile environment claim.

The jury could easily find that Henderson subjectively perceived his work environment to be hostile and abusive. He complained to plant manager Taylor on several occasions. He submitted a detailed letter of complaint to general manager Goins and met with Goins to discuss the incidents that he believed made his work environment intolerable. Henderson also directly told Moistner that he did not appreciate Moistner's racist jokes and comments.

To ascertain whether an environment is objectively hostile or abusive, the court must consider all the circumstances, including the frequency of the discriminatory conduct; the severity of the conduct; whether the conduct is physically threatening or humiliating, or a mere offensive utterance; and whether that conduct unreasonably interferes with an employee's work performance. In other words, a court must consider the totality of the circumstances, rather than merely considering incidents separately and independently of one another.

Applying this standard, plaintiff Henderson's claims are sufficient to survive summary judgment on a hostile work environment claim. Defendants, by characterizing the evidence as "rather tepid events," "tired reasoning," "industrial plant banter," and "teasing," ask the court to close its eyes to the totality of the evidence and to "the social context in which particular behavior occurs and is experienced by its target," and to the "real social impact of workplace behavior."

Defendants also contend that the incidents alleged by plaintiff cannot satisfy the pervasive arm of the "severe or pervasive" test because no specific incident occurred more than once. The argument is specious. The plaintiff need not show that the alleged conduct was both severe *and* pervasive; either is sufficient. Further, the incidents alleged in this case were not isolated incidents. Every incident must be considered in combination with the other incidents. There also is no principle of law requiring the harassers to repeat any particular form of harassment. If we are counting, as defendants suggest, there were a total of at least nine incidents in September and October 2001 alone. A reasonable jury considering the totality of the circumstances in this case could find that the hostile work environment was sufficiently severe and pervasive and that plaintiff worked in a racially abusive environment so severe as to alter the terms and conditions of his employment. Further, although Henderson did not lose his job, proof of termination is not dispositive on the question of severe or pervasive.

In sum, all of the alleged incidents must be considered as a whole when analyzing Henderson's hostile work environment claim. Considering the totality of the circumstances, and giving Henderson the benefit of all reasonable inferences from the evidence, the incidents alleged are sufficient to allow a reasonable jury to find that plaintiff Henderson's work environment was severe, pervasive, and abusive, and was therefore actionable under Title VII.

D. EMPLOYER LIABILITY

Once a Title VII plaintiff establishes that his work environment was both subjectively and objectively hostile, he must also establish a basis for employer liability. To establish employer liability where the harasser is a co-worker, plaintiff must show that the employer was negligent in either discovering or remedying the harassment. In hostile work environment cases, the employer can avoid liability for its employees' harassment if it takes prompt and appropriate corrective action reasonably likely to prevent the harassment from recurring. Generally, the law does not charge an employer with knowledge of the harassment unless the employee makes a concerted effort to inform the employer that a problem exists. If the harassment was sufficiently obvious, however, an employer can be charged with constructive notice.

Plaintiff's evidence could convince a reasonable jury that Henderson's supervisor, plant manager Willie

Taylor, was present and witnessed many of Moistner's racist jokes and comments, as well as his KKK membership renewal comment. There is no evidence that there was any company policy directing employees to report complaints to anyone other than Taylor, a supervisor with an actual presence at the plant. A jury could easily find on this record that plant manager Taylor was fully aware of the racist campaign against Henderson. The evidence is enough to support a finding that SouthSide management had actual notice of the incidents of which Henderson now complains, and that they did nothing about it for months.

Alternatively, defendants argue that the company took adequate corrective action. When Henderson reported to plant manager Taylor that Santerre had tried to hit him with his truck, Taylor spoke with Santerre, who denied the incident. That was the extent of the company's involvement with that incident. A reasonable jury could find that the company's response was insufficient. A reasonable jury could find, for instance, that more intervention and ultimately more supervision were necessary to control such physically dangerous conduct.

After Henderson found the dead mice, the company posted a statement that cautioned drivers to keep their trucks clean to keep mice away. A reasonable jury could find that the company's indirect poster about *hygiene* was insufficient to address the *deliberate* harassing behavior or to remedy the wrongs that Henderson suffered. The poster, moreover, addressed only one problem (and did so as if it had been the result of an oversight by Henderson rather than a deliberate act of others). It failed to address the dead mice as part of a larger campaign of harassment, except to suggest that employees not expose others to rodents. There is no evidence that the company had done anything prior to posting its statement to remedy the other problems alleged by plaintiff.

In addition, Henderson reported the dead mice incident to SouthSide's general manager Goins at the same time that he reported so many of the other alleged harassing incidents that he had endured. The company's response was to reprimand the offenders—only to rescind the reprimands two days later. At the summary judgment stage, the court must assume that Henderson's account of the harassment directed against him is true. Based on that evidence, a reasonable jury could conclude that two days was not adequate time to launch and complete a reasonable investigation into the complaints by plaintiff.

On the issue of remedy, moreover, plaintiff's evidence would as noted above allow a reasonable jury to find that plant manager Willie Taylor was fully aware of the campaign of racial harassment against Henderson, and that he failed—for months—to take any meaningful steps to remedy the harassment. Taylor was the plant manager. He was the senior manager on site at the Harding Street facility. His failure to try to remedy the problems can be attributed to SouthSide, quite apart from the arguably feeble efforts made in response to Henderson's complaint to Goins. There is sufficient evidence to convince a reasonable jury that the defendant company was negligent in remedying the harassment.

CONCLUSION

For the foregoing reasons, Defendants' motion is denied as to plaintiff's Title VII hostile environment claim against SouthSide. GRANTED IN PART AND DENIED IN PART.

Case Questions

1. How could the employer have avoided liability here?
2. Why do you think Taylor did as little as he did about the harassers?
3. Does it make sense to you that the black employee was transferred? Explain.

A WORD ABOUT COLOR

Color is one of the five categories included in Title VII as a prohibited basis for discrimination. Despite the findings reflected in Exhibit 5.6, few cases have been brought using color as a basis for discrimination. However, it should be noted that color may be a basis for discrimination in employment. Most recently, the EEOC filed suit against the Kansas-based chain Applebee's Neighborhood Grill and Bar in Jonesboro, Georgia, for failure to act on a complaint of mistreatment based on color and then firing the dark-skinned employee for complaining to his light-skinned boss.

Exhibit 5.6   Light and Dark

Jet magazine reported that the National Survey of Black Americans across the country, published in a recent issue of the *American Journal of Sociology*, found that "the fairer one's pigmentation (skin color), the higher his or her occupational standing." Researchers found that a light-complexion black, on average, had a 50 percent higher income than darker blacks, regardless of educational, occupational, or family background.

Employers should be aware of this and guard against it, as with the other categories. In both cases, it was a black supervisor who was alleged to have discriminated against a black employee. Employers should not miss the possibility of this problem by thinking there can be no discrimination since two people of the same race are involved.

If you think color doesn't matter, think about whether it was a mere coincidence that the first-ever black Miss America, Vanessa Williams, was light-skinned with green eyes and long hair. Was America ready for Miss America to be dark brown with short, kinky natural hair? No. It didn't appeal to the nation's cultural sensibilities of beauty. That is why blacks and other ethnic groups still hold their own beauty pageants. Despite the historically based titles of the events reflecting a time in which blacks were not welcome or permitted in such functions (e.g., "Miss Black America" pageant), it is not for purposes of segregation. Rather, it is to have a pageant that uses the standards of beauty that arise from, and are appreciated by the group itself, rather than the one imposed by the larger society which may not match the group's own standards.

The recent flap over the third U.S. president, Thomas Jefferson, allegedly having a 38-year-long relationship with his slave Sally Hemmings also reflected this color issue. When several of the Hemmings descendants who claimed to be the descendants of the relationship between Jefferson and Hemmings appeared in public and looked "whiter" than many whites, there was initially widespread public disbelief. If color did not matter, this simply would not have occurred.

Whether or not you agree with the idea of beauty pageants or separate ones, or even that color matters, the point is that skin color exists and has value (negative or positive) in our society that may be reflected in the workplace. Make sure you are aware that Title VII covers color, and be mindful of the subtle, though not necessarily conscious role it may play in how we deal with others.

As the case below demonstrates, liability is still possible, although for other reasons it was not imposed here.

Walker v. Secretary of the Treasury, Internal Revenue Service
742 F. Supp. 670 (N.D. Ga., Atlanta Div. 1990).

A light-skinned black employee sued her employer alleging discrimination by her supervisor based on color. The employee alleged that the supervisor, a brown-skinned black, said and did derogatory things to her because the supervisor resented the employee's lighter skin color. The court recognized that color could be a basis for discrimination under Title VII, but held that the employee failed to demonstrate that the employer had discriminated since there were legitimate nondiscriminatory reasons for the dismissal.

May, J.

Employee, a lighter-skinned black female, filed a complaint alleging, among other things, that she had been terminated by her darker-skinned black female supervisor because of employee's lighter colored skin, in violation of Title VII of the Civil Rights Act of 1964.

The employer maintains that employee's termination was based upon her poor performance, poor attitude and misconduct. Employee argues that these reasons were a mere pretext and that she was actually terminated because of her supervisor's color-based prejudice. We hold that employee failed to meet her burden by proving by a preponderance of the evidence that her termination was the result of a violation of Title VII rather than the stated reasons of poor performance and attitude.

The only significant evidence that employee offered that, if true, would tend to prove that her supervisor did indeed have feelings of prejudice toward her are some derogatory personal comments that her supervisor allegedly made to her, such as: "you need some sun"; "you think you're bad, you ain't about nothing, you think you're somebody, I can do what I want to do to you"; "why don't you go back to where you belong?"; and "why did you come down here?" However, this court holds that employee has failed to prove by a preponderance of the evidence that the comments were in fact made.

But even if the comments were made, employee failed to prove that they were uttered for any reason other than the personal animosity that the two individuals might have had for each other. It appears undisputed that there was a personality conflict between the employee and her supervisor, and that her supervisor was not wholly innocent in the propagation of the conflict. However, a personality conflict alone does not establish invidious discrimination. There is ample evidence in the record to support the supervisor's contention that the reason for the personality conflict, and likewise the subsequent termination of employment, was employee's performance on the job.

Employee has failed to prove by a preponderance of the evidence that she was terminated because of invidious discrimination on the basis of color on the part of her supervisor. Conversely, the employer has offered legitimate reasons for employee's termination which the court finds nonpretextual. JUDGMENT for DEFENDANT.

Case Questions

1. Do you think the court was correct in interpreting Title VII to permit a color discrimination case to be brought by a black employee against a black supervisor? Why or why not?

2. If you were the manager here, what would you have done to deal with employee and her supervisor?

3. Since the statements were insufficient to show discrimination, what else do you think the employee could have used to satisfy the court? Do you think the case would have been decided differently if the supervisor was a different race than the employee? Explain.

THE RECONSTRUCTION CIVIL RIGHTS ACTS

In this chapter we have been discussing race discrimination under Title VII of the Civil Rights Act of 1964. However, the Civil Rights Act of 1964 was not the first piece of legislation aimed at prohibiting racial discrimination. Since these other laws are still used today, a chapter on race discrimination in employment would not be complete without including some mention of them. It is important to know the full range of potential liability an employer has for discrimination lawsuits by employees.

There are three main pre-Title VII laws. Collectively, they are known as the post–Civil War statutes, or the Reconstruction Civil Rights Acts. They were passed by Congress after the Civil War ended in 1865 in an effort to provide a means of enforcing the new status of the ex-slaves as free citizens. In 1865, passage of the 13th Amendment to the Constitution abolishing slavery had merely set them free. Nothing on the books at that point said what that picture had to look like. In fact, largely in response to the 13th Amendment, states enacted "Black Codes"—mostly revisions of their pre–Civil War "Slave Codes," that codified discrimination on the basis of race and limited the rights of the newly free slaves.

Beginning in 1866, Congress began enacting the post–Civil War statutes, understanding that without legislation providing rights for the new status of blacks, little would change from before the Civil War. It passed section 1981, making all blacks born in the United States citizens and ensuring them the right to make and enforce contracts the same "as enjoyed by white citizens." In 1868, Congress passed the 14th Amendment to make its laws applicable to the states, dictating that no state "shall make or enforce any law which shall abridge the privileges or immunities of the citizens of the United States . . . [or] deprive any person of life, liberty, or property without due process of law, [or] deny to any person within its jurisdiction the equal protection of the laws."

The three post–Civil War statutes are now codified as 42 U.S.C. sections 1981, 1983, and 1985. They prohibit discrimination on the basis of race in making and enforcing contracts; prohibit the denial of civil rights on the basis of race by someone acting as if they are acting on behalf of the government (called **"under color of state law"**); and prohibit concerted activity to deny someone their rights based on race.

under color of state law
Government employee is illegally discriminating against another during performance of his or her duties.

Sections 1981 and 1983 are the laws most frequently used in the employment setting if a claim is not brought using Title VII. Since Title VII is part of a statutory scheme to prohibit race and other discrimination, it is more comprehensive and is the preferred method of enforcing employment discrimination claims. A complete administrative structure has been set up to deal with such claims. The post–Civil War statutes do not offer such a structure. Employees bringing claims under Title VII go to EEOC to file their claim and do not have to pay. Employees bringing claims under the post–Civil War statutes must go to an attorney and must pay the attorney. On the other hand, the statute of limitations for the post–Civil War statutes is longer than under Title VII. While Title VII's basic statute of limitations is 180 days from the precipitating event, the U.S. Supreme Court ruled in 2004 that the statute of limitations on race cases under Section 1981 is four years.[2]

When you put the post–Civil War statutes' limitations together with the historical context in which blacks operated after the Civil War until passage of the Civil Rights Act in 1964, 99 years later, it makes sense that these laws were not used as much as Title VII. From the end of the Civil War until passage of the Civil Rights Act of 1964, Jim Crow laws and customs segregated blacks and denied them basic rights. This was often enforced through violence. Few blacks had the money to sue. Between not having the legal right to have a job based on their race, not being able to afford to bring lawsuits, and taking their lives into their hands if they tried to enforce any rights they did have under these law, the post–Civil War statutes provided little relief to blacks facing employment discrimination.

Still, they remain a viable source of employer liability and, as such, you should have some exposure to them. Note also that the laws were created to address the issue of the newly freed slaves, but the language now applies to anyone, so gender and national origin cases are also brought under the statutes. By and large, most of the cases are

---

[2] *Jones v. R.R. Donnelley & Sons, Co.,* 541 U.S.369 (2004).

brought under these statutes as opposed to Title VII either because the claimant missed the Title VII statute of limitations deadline, or because the claim involves a government employer.

42 U.S.C. Section 1981

Section 1981. Equal Rights under the Law
All persons within the jurisdiction of the United States shall have the same right in every State and Territory to make and enforce contracts . . . as is enjoyed by white citizens.

This provision of the post–Civil War statutes has been used to a limited extent in the past as a basis for employees suing employers for racial discrimination in employment. In 1975, the U.S. Supreme Court held that section 1981 prohibits purely private discrimination in contracts, including employment contracts. In *Patterson* the limitations of section 1981 become evident. *Patterson* was nullified by the Civil Rights Act of 1991. As you read the case for historical and analytical purposes, see if you can determine why Congress would want to overrule the Supreme Court's decision by the 1991 legislation. *Patterson* was specifically chosen for inclusion here to demonstrate how seemingly small, insignificant matters can accumulate and provide a solid picture of discriminatory treatment leading to liability.

Patterson v. McLean Credit Union *491 U.S. 164 (1989)*

A black female alleged racial discrimination in violation of section 1981 in that she was treated differently from white employees and not promoted, on the basis of race. The Court held that section 1981 was not available to address this problem since the case did not involve the making of a contract, but rather its performance.

Kennedy, J.

Patterson, a black female, worked for the McLean Credit Union (MCU) as a teller and file coordinator for 10 years. She alleges that when she first interviewed for her job, the supervisor, who later became the president of MCU, told her that she would be working with all white women and that they probably would not like working with her because she was black. According to Patterson, in the subsequent years, it was her supervisor who proved to have the problem with her working at the credit union.

Patterson alleges that she was subjected to a pattern of discrimination at MCU which included her supervisor repeatedly staring at her for minutes at a time while she performed her work and not doing so to white employees; not promoting her or giving her the usually perfunctory raises which other employees routinely received; not arranging to have her work reassigned to others when she went on vacation, as was routinely done with other employees, but rather, allowing Patterson's work to accumulate during her absence; assigning her menial, nonclerical tasks such as sweeping and dusting, while such tasks were not assigned to other similarly situated employees; being openly critical of Patterson's work in staff meetings, and that of one other black employee, while white employees were told of their shortcomings privately; telling Patterson that it was known that "blacks are known to work slower than whites, by nature" or, saying in one instance, "some animals [are] faster than other animals"; repeatedly suggesting that a white would be able to perform Patterson's job better than she could; unequal work assignments between Patterson and other similarly situated white employees, with Patterson receiving more work than others; having her work scrutinized more closely and criticized more severely than white employees; despite her desire to "move up and advance," being offered no training for higher jobs during her 10 years at the credit union, while white employees were offered training, including those at the same level, but with less seniority (such employees were later promoted); not being informed of job openings, nor interviewed for them, while less senior whites were informed of the positions and hired; and when another manager recommended to Patterson's supervisor a different black to fill a position as a data processor, the supervisor said that he did not "need any more problems around here," and would "search for additional people who are not black."

When Patterson complained about her workload, she was given no help, and in fact was given more work and told she always had the option of quitting. Patterson was laid off after 10 years with MCU. She brought suit under 42 U.S.C. section 1981, alleging harassment, failure to promote and discharge because of her race.

None of the racially harassing conduct which McLean engaged in involved the section 1981 prohibition against refusing to make a contract with Patterson or impairing Patterson's ability to enforce her existing contract rights with McLean. It is clear that Patterson is attacking conditions of employment which came into existence after she formed the contract to work for McLean. Since section 1981 only prohibits the interference with the making or enforcement of contracts because of race, performance of the contract is not actionable under section 1981.

Section 1981's language is specifically limited to making and enforcing contracts. To permit race discrimination cases involving post-formation actions would also undermine the detailed and well-crafted procedures for conciliation and resolution of Title VII claims. While section 1981 has no administrative procedure for review or conciliation of claims, Title VII has an elaborate system which is designed to investigate claims and work toward resolution of them by conciliation rather than litigation. This includes Title VII's limiting recovery to backpay, while section 1981 permits plenary compensatory and punitive damages in appropriate cases. Neither party would be likely to conciliate if there is the possibility of the employee recovering the greater damages permitted by section 1981. There is some overlap between Title VII and section 1981, and when conduct is covered by both, the detailed procedures of Title VII are rendered a dead letter, as the plaintiff is free to pursue a claim by bringing suit under section 1981 without resort to those statutory prerequisites.

Regarding Patterson's failure to promote claim, this is somewhat different. Whether a racially discriminatory failure to promote claim is cognizable under section 1981 depends upon whether the nature of the change in positions is such that it involved the opportunity to enter into a new contract with the employer. If so, then the employer's refusal to enter the new contract is actionable under section 1981. AFFIRMED in part, VACATED in part, and REMANDED.

Case Questions

1. Do you think justice was served in this case? Explain. Why do you think Patterson waited so long to sue?
2. If you had been the manager when Patterson was initially interviewed, would you have made the statement about whites not accepting her? Why or why not?
3. When looking at the list of actions Patterson alleged McLean engaged in, do any seem appropriate? Why do you think it was done or permitted?

The Civil Rights Act of 1991 contained provisions specifically addressed to *Patterson.* The act overturned *Patterson's* holding that section 1981 does not permit actions for racial discrimination during the performance of the contract, but only in making or enforcing the contract. Note that the limitation on damages the Court spoke of as part of Title VII's administrative scheme no longer applies. The Civil Rights Act of 1991 now permits recovery of compensatory and punitive damages. How do you think this squares with the Court's statement, "Neither party would be likely to conciliate if there is the possibility of the employee recovering the greater damages permitted by section 1981"?

42 U.S.C. Section 1983

Section 1983. Civil Action for Deprivation of Rights

Every person who, under color of any statute, ordinance, regulation, custom, or usage, of any State or Territory, subjects, or causes to be subjected, any citizen of the United States or other person within the jurisdiction thereof to the deprivation of any rights, privileges, or immunities secured by the Constitution and laws, shall be liable to the party injured in an action at law, suit in equity, or other proper proceeding for redress.

The Civil Rights Act of 1871, codified as 42 U.S.C. section 1983, protects citizens from deprivation of their legal and constitutional rights, privileges, and immunities, under color of state law. That is, someone acting on behalf of the state cannot deprive people of their rights. Examples would be (1) the New Jersey state troopers who were convicted in 2002 when racial profiling admittedly caused them to shoot 11 bullets into a car with four unarmed black and Latino students, wounding three, and (2) the police officers who were videotaped beating Rodney King during his arrest in Los Angeles in 1991. While performing their duties as government employees, they were alleged to have deprived King of his rights by using excessive force and thus depriving him of his rights as if it were a legitimate part of their duties.

In the employment area, section 1983 cases arise when, for instance, a city fire department or municipal police department discriminates against an employee on the basis of race, gender, or one of the other bases protected under federal or state law.

Neither the 14th Amendment nor section 1983 may be used for discrimination by private employers. They both redress actions by government personnel. The government may not be sued without its permission because of the 11th Amendment to the Constitution, so the action is brought against the government official in his or her individual and official capacity.

Jett v. Dallas Independent School District *491 U.S. 701 (1989)*

Plaintiff, a white high school coach and teacher, brought suit under Section 1983 against his employing school district and a black principal, alleging they were responsible for a racially discriminatory diminution in his employment status. A jury held for the coach and awarded compensatory and punitive damages. The U.S. Supreme Court upheld the verdict in part.

O'Connor, J.

Norman Jett, a white male, was employed by Dallas Independent School District (DISD) as a teacher, athletic director, and head football coach at South Oak Cliff High School (South Oak) until his reassignment to another DISD school in 1983. Jett was hired by the DISD in 1957, was assigned to assistant coaching duties at South Oak in 1962, and was promoted to athletic director and head football coach of South Oak in 1970. During Jett's lengthy tenure at South Oak, the racial composition of the school changed from predominantly white to predominantly black. In 1975, the DISD assigned Dr. Fredrick Todd, a black, as principal of South Oak. Jett and Todd clashed repeatedly over school policies, and in particular over Jett's handling of the school's football program. These conflicts came to a head following a November 19, 1982, football

game between South Oak and the predominately white Plano High School. Todd objected to Jett's comparison of the South Oak team with professional teams before the match, and to the fact that Jett entered the officials' locker room after South Oak lost the game and told two black officials that he would never allow black officials to work another South Oak game. Todd also objected to Jett's statements, reported in a local newspaper, to the effect that the majority of South Oak players could not meet proposed National Collegiate Athletic Association academic requirements for collegiate athletes.

On March 15, 1983, Todd informed Jett that he intended to recommend that Jett be relieved of his duties as athletic director and head football coach at South Oak. On March 17, 1983, Todd sent a letter to John Kincaide, the director of athletics for DISD, recommending that Jett be removed based on poor leadership and planning skills and Jett's comportment before and after the PIano game. Jett subsequently met with John Santillo, director of personnel for DISD, who suggested that Jett should transfer schools because any remaining professional relationship with Principal Todd had been shattered. Jett then met with Linus Wright, the superintendent of the DISD. At this meeting, Jett informed Superintendent Wright that he believed that Todd's criticisms of his performance as head coach were unfounded and that in fact Todd was motivated by racial animus and wished to replace Jett with a black head coach. Superintendent Wright suggested that the difficulties between Todd and Jett might preclude Jett from remaining in his coaching position at South Oak, but assured Jett that another position in the DISD would be secured for him.

On March 25, 1983, Superintendent Wright met with Kincaide, Santillo, Todd, and two other DISD officials to determine whether Jett should remain at South Oak. After the meeting, Superintendent Wright officially affirmed Todd's recommendation to remove Jett from his duties as coach and athletic director at South Oak. Wright indicated that he felt compelled to follow the recommendation of the school principal. Soon after this meeting, Jett was informed by Santillo that effective August 4, 1983, he was reassigned as a teacher at the DISD Business Magnet School, a position that did not include any coaching duties. Jett's attendance and performance at the Business Magnet School were poor, and on May 5, 1983, Santillo wrote Jett indicating that he was being placed on "unassigned personnel budget" and being reassigned to a temporary position in the DISD security department. Upon receiving Santillo's letter, Jett filed this lawsuit in the District Court for the Northern District of Texas. The DISD subsequently offered Jett a position as a teacher and freshman football and track coach at Jefferson High School. Jett did not accept this assignment, and on August 19, 1983, he sent his formal letter of resignation to the DISD.

Jett brought this action against the DISD and Principal Todd in his personal and official capacities, under 42 U.S.C. §§ 1981 and 1983, alleging due process, First Amendment, and equal protection violations. Jett's due process claim alleged that he had a constitutionally protected property interest in his coaching position at South Oak, of which he was deprived without due process of law. Jett's First Amendment claim was based on the allegation that his removal and subsequent transfer were actions taken in retaliation for his statements to the press regarding the sports program at

South Oak. His equal protection and §1981 causes of action were based on the allegation that his removal from the athletic director and head coaching positions at South Oak was motivated by the fact that he was white, and that Principal Todd, and through him the DISD, were responsible for the racially discriminatory diminution in his employment status. Jett also claimed that his resignation was in fact the product of racial harassment and retaliation for the exercise of his First Amendment rights and thus amounted to a constructive discharge. These claims were tried to a jury, which found for Jett on all counts. The jury awarded Jett $650,000 against the DISD, $150,000 against Principal Todd and the DISD jointly and severally, and $50,000 in punitive damages against Todd in his personal capacity.

On motion for judgment notwithstanding the verdict [judgment n.o.v.], the District Court set aside the punitive damages award against Principal Todd as unsupported by the evidence, found the damages award against the DISD excessive and ordered a remittitur of $200,000, but otherwise denied the defendants' motions for judgment n.o.v. and a new trial and upheld the jury's verdict in all respects. Principal Todd has reached a settlement with Jett and is no longer a party to this action.

On appeal, the Court of Appeals for the Fifth Circuit reversed in part and remanded. Initially, the court found that Jett had no constitutionally protected property interest "in the intangible, noneconomic benefits of his assignment as coach." Since Jett had received both his teacher's and coach's salary after his reassignment, the change in duties did not deprive him of any state law entitlement protected by the Due Process Clause. The Court of Appeals also set aside the jury's finding that Jett was constructively discharged from his teaching position within the DISD. The court found the evidence insufficient to sustain the claim that Jett's loss of coaching duties and subsequent offer of reassignment to a lesser coaching position were so humiliating or unpleasant that a reasonable employee would have felt compelled to resign. While finding the question "very close," the Court of Appeals concluded that there was sufficient evidence from which a reasonable jury could conclude that Principal Todd's recommendation that Jett be transferred from his coaching duties at South Oak was motivated by impermissible racial animus. The court noted that Todd had replaced Jett with a black coach, that there had been racial overtones in the tension between Todd and Jett before the Plano game, and that Todd's explanation of his unsatisfactory rating of Jett was questionable and was not supported by the testimony of other DISD officials who spoke of Jett's performance in laudatory terms. The court also affirmed the jury's finding that Todd's recommendation that Jett be relieved of his coaching duties was motivated in substantial part by Jett's protected statements to the press concerning the academic standing of athletes at South Oak. These remarks addressed matters of public concern, and Todd admitted that they were

a substantial consideration in his decision to recommend that Jett be relieved of his coaching duties. AFFIRMED in part and REMANDED.

Case Questions

1. Does the decision make sense to you? Explain.
2. What difference do you think it made to the coach's job that the school district's racial composition changed?
3. If you were the principal, what would you have done differently?

42 U.S.C. Section 1985

Section 1985. Conspiracy to Interfere with Civil Rights—Preventing Officer from Performing Duties

Depriving persons of rights or privileges

(3) If two or more persons in any State or Territory conspire or go in disguise on the highway or on the premises of another, for the purpose of depriving, either directly or indirectly, any person or class of persons of the equal protection of the laws, or of equal privileges and immunities under the laws; in any case of conspiracy set forth in this section, if one or more persons engaged therein do, or cause to be done, any act in furtherance of the object of such conspiracy, whereby another is injured in his person or property, or deprived of having and exercising any rights or privileges of a citizen of the United States, the party so injured or deprived may have an action for the recovery of damages, occasioned by such injury or deprivation, against any one or more of the conspirators.

42 U.S.C. section 1985, known as the "Ku Klux Klan Act," addresses conspiracies to interfere with or deprive the civil rights of others. For instance, it was used to convict the murderers of the three student civil rights activists in Mississippi in 1964 who were killed for trying to help blacks register to vote referred to earlier (the *Mississippi Burning* case). It is not used as much as the other post–Civil War statutes for employment because of the types of facts needed are so specific and, for the most part, we've moved away from such acts in the workplace. Title VII is used more than all of them.

Employees can also sue under the state or federal constitution for a denial of equal protection if they work for the government or under state tort laws for defamation, intentional infliction of emotional distress, assault, or any other tort the facts support.

An employer who must remedy racial discrimination may not avoid doing so because of the possibility of a reverse discrimination suit by employees alleging they were adversely affected. If an employer institutes a judicially imposed or voluntary affirmative action plan, which can withstand judicial scrutiny for the reasons set forth in the affirmative action chapter, the employer will not be liable to employees for reverse discrimination.

Management Tips

Race discrimination can seem elusive. Many of us tend to think it no longer exists, or that others feel as neutral as we do about race. That is not necessarily so. Because a manager can be unaware of the presence of race discrimination, he or she can miss it until litigation arises. Think back to the *Patterson case*. Remember that many of the things Patterson alleged as part of a discriminatory pattern of treatment toward her would have been insignificant in and of themselves. However, taken together, the list becomes quite significant. Be aware of what goes on in the workplace and "don't miss the forest for the trees." The following tips may prove useful:

- Believe that race discrimination occurs and be willing to acknowledge it when it is alleged.
- Make sure that there is a top-down message that the workplace will not tolerate race discrimination in any form.
- Don't shy away from discussing race when the issue arises.
- Provide a positive, nonthreatening, constructive forum for the discussion of racial issues. Don't let the only time a discussion of race arises be in the midst of an allegation of racial discrimination.
- Be aware of cultural differences which may be based, at least in part, on race, when doing things as simple as deciding how to celebrate special events in the workplace. Be inclusive regarding what music will be played, what food will be served, what recreation will be offered, what clothes will be worn, and other factors. These all form a part of the atmosphere in which an employee must work and experience workplace leisure. If people do not see themselves reflected in the workplace culture, they will not feel a part of it and will feel isolated. If they feel isolated, they are more likely to experience other factors leading to discrimination and ultimately to litigation. If this seems like a small matter to you, imagine yourself showing up at a gathering at work, and the music, decorations, food, and clothing were all Japanese. There's sushi to eat, saki to drink, and everyone is speaking Japanese. You'd probably feel a bit out of your element and would quickly realize how those seemingly simple things make a big impact. Now imagine that happening at *every* workplace party!

- When an employee reports discrimination based on race, don't let the first move be to tell the employee he or she must be mistaken. Investigate it as any other matter would be investigated.
- Be willing to treat the matter as a misunderstanding if it is clear that is what has taken place. There is no use in making a federal case (literally) out of a matter that could be handled much more simply. Do not, however, underplay the significance of what occurred.
- Offer support groups if there is an expressed need.
- Offer training in racial awareness and sensitivity. Courts have offered language indicating they will look more favorably on employers who do so.
- Constantly monitor workplace hiring, termination, training, promotion, raises, and discipline to ensure that they are fair and even-handed. If there are differences in treatment among races, be sure they are legally justifiable and explainable.

Summary

- Title VII prohibits discrimination on the basis of race.
- The employer must ensure that every employee has an equal opportunity for employment and advancement in the workplace, regardless of race.

- Employers must be vigilant to guard against the more stubborn, subtle manifestations of race discrimination.
- Racial discrimination may be by way of disparate treatment or disparate impact.
- Disparate treatment may be shown by direct or indirect evidence of discrimination.
- Disparate impact may be more difficult to discern, so employers need to closely scrutinize workplace policies and procedures to prevent unintended disparate impact leading to liability.
- Race cannot be used as a bona fide occupational qualification.

Chapter-End Questions

1. A black firefighter alleges that each time he is transferred from one fire station to another, he must take his bed with him, on orders of the fire chief. The chief defends on the basis that it is a legitimate decision, because white firefighters would not want to sleep in the same bed in which a black firefighter slept. Is this illegal under Title VII? Explain. [Georgia newspaper article]

2. A white college receptionist is fired when it is found that she told a black college applicant that the applications for admissions are distinguished by race by the notation of a small *RH* in the corner of black applicants' applications. "RH," she says, is her supervisor's term for "raisin heads," which he calls blacks. Is the employee entitled to reinstatement? [*Jet* magazine article]

3. It is discovered that, at a health club, the owner has been putting a notation on the application of black membership applicants that reads "DNWAM," which means "do not want as member." In addition, the black membership applicants are charged higher rates for the club fee and are much less likely to be financed as other nonblack applicants. Can the black applicants bring a successful action under Title VII?

4. A black female employee is told that she cannot come to work with her hair in decorative braids traditionally worn in Africa, and if she continues to do so, she will be terminated. Does the employee have a claim under Title VII?

5. Bennie's Restaurant chain routinely hires blacks, but it only assigns them to the lower-paying jobs as kitchen help, rather than as higher-paid servers, salad bar helpers, or managers. Bennie's says it does not discriminate because it has many black employees. If suit is brought by the black employees, who will likely win? [Based on Denny's restaurants]

6. A prominent black professor takes an unpaid leave of absence to protest the fact that his extremely prominent university has failed to ever hire any black females in tenure-track (regular, permanent) positions on the faculty. When he does not return after two years, he is terminated. He sues the university, alleging constructive discharge, in that the situation created by the school's policies made it an unlivable situation for him. Is this an effective argument? Explain. [Based on Harvard Law School situation]

7. Ken recruits applicants for several prominent companies. Often when the companies call for Ken's services, they strongly hint that they do not wish to hire blacks, so Ken never places blacks with those companies. Is Ken liable for illegal discrimination?

8. Brie owns a six-person beauty salon. One day a black customer comes in and wants a wash and set. Brie has a cold and does not wish to give it to the customer, so she tells her that

Jerre will take care of her. Jerre starts protesting, in front of the other customers, that she is not going to do the customer's hair, because "she doesn't do black hair" and "she [Jerre] is from New Hampshire." The customer, totally humiliated and crying, leaves the premises. Is Brie liable under Title VII?

9. Jill, the owner of a construction business, says her construction crew will not work if she hires black crew members, so Jill does not do so. Is this a defense to a Title VII action?

10. Sam has worked at Allied for several years with no problems. Avril is transferred into Sam's unit. Sam immediately begins having a strong allergic reaction to the perfume Avril wears each day. After having to take days off work because of his allergies, Sam asks Avril if she can tone down her perfume. Avril does so for a few days, then resumes her usual amount. Sam does not complain any further but is thinking of quitting because his allergies are so bad. He doesn't want to go any further with Avril about it because Sam is white and Avril is black and Sam thinks it might lead to race discrimination liability for his employer. Is Sam correct? [Student's parents dilemma.]

Chapter **Six**

Gender Discrimination

Chapter Outline

Opening Scenarios

SCENARIO 1

1 Scenario
A discount department store has a policy requiring that all male clerks be attired in coats and ties and all female clerks wear over their clothing a smock provided by the store, with the store's logo on the front. A female clerk complains to her supervisor that making her wear a smock is illegal gender discrimination. Is it? Why or why not?

SCENARIO 2

2 Scenario
A male applies for a position as a server for a restaurant in his hometown. The restaurant is part of a well-known regional chain named for an animal whose name is a colloquial term for a popular part of the female anatomy. Despite several years of experience as a server for comparable establishments the male is turned down for the position, which remains vacant. The applicant is instead offered a position as a kitchen helper. The applicant notices that all servers are female and most are blonde. All servers are required to wear very tight and very short shorts, with T-shirts with the restaurant logo on the front, tied in a knot below their, usually ample, breasts. All kitchen help and cooks are male. The applicant feels he has been unlawfully discriminated against because he is a male. Do you agree? Why or why not?

SCENARIO 3

3 Scenario
An applicant for a position of secretary informs the employer that she is pregnant. The employer accepts her application but never seriously considers her for the position because she is pregnant. Is this employment discrimination?

STATUTORY BASIS

It shall be an unlawful employment practice for an employer—

(1) to fail or refuse to hire or to discharge any individual, or otherwise to discriminate against any individual with respect to his compensation, terms, conditions, or privileges of employment, because of such individual's . . . sex [gender]. . . . Title VII of the Civil Rights Act of 1964, as amended. 42 U.S.C. 2000e-2 (a).

(1) No employer . . . shall discriminate between employees on the basis of sex by paying wages to employees . . . at a rate less than the rate at which he pays wages to employees of the opposite sex . . . for equal work on jobs the performance of which requires equal skill, effort, and responsibility, and which are performed under similar working conditions, except where such payment is made pursuant to (i) a seniority system; (ii) a merit system; (iii) a system which measures earnings by quantity or quality of production; or (iv) a differential based on any other factor other than sex. . . . Equal Pay Act, 29 U.S.C.A. §206(d).

(k) The term "because of sex" or "on the basis of sex" includes, but is not limited to, because of or on the basis of pregnancy, childbirth, or related medical conditions; and women affected by pregnancy, childbirth, or related medical conditions shall be treated the same for all employment-related purposes, including receipt of benefits under fringe benefit programs, as other persons not so affected but similar in their ability or inability to work. . . . Pregnancy Discrimination Act, 42 U.S.C. §2000e.

Note: Reread the Preface regarding the use of gender terminology before reading this chapter.

Exhibit 6.1   Gender-Neutral Language?

Attorney Harry McCall, arguing before the U.S. Supreme Court, stated, "I would like to remind you gentlemen" of a legal point. Associate Supreme Court Justice Sandra Day O'Connor asked, "Would you like to remind me, too?" McCall later referred to the Court as "Justice O'Connor and gentlemen." Associate Justice Byron White told McCall, "Just 'Justices' would be fine."

Source: *Newsweek,* Nov. 25, 1991, p. 17.

DOES IT REALLY EXIST?

What does a group of 25 attorney-mediators have to do with a 2005 swimsuit calendar? Good question. The Miami-based Florida Mediation Group has probably been asking itself that same question ever since it received a good deal of flack for having its name emblazoned across one of several themed calendars given away as gifts to clients.

It can be hard to recognize gender discrimination when it plays itself out in the workplace. A woman is required by her employer to wear 2-inch heels to work. Doing so causes her to develop bunions on her feet, which can only be removed by surgery. After surgery she is ordered by her doctor to wear flat shoes for two months. Her employer refuses to permit her to do so. Left with no alternative, she quits. The employer imposes no such requirement or its attendant problems on male employees. When you realize that the employer's 2-inch-heels policy cost the woman her job and had she been male, this would not have happened, it becomes more obvious that the policy is discriminatory. Remember the wires of the bird cage. Those wires are probably what the members of the executive board of the Miami-Dade chapter of the Florida Association of Women Lawyers were thinking of when they registered their objection to the calendar. "We believe this type of advertising, whether picturing men or women, does not promote dignity in the law and is inappropriate when circulated by an organization that serves the legal community."

It is not difficult to discriminate on the basis of gender if an employer is not sensitive to the issues involved. (See Exhibit 6.1.) Once again, as with race discrimination, vigilance pays off. This chapter will address gender discrimination in general, including pregnancy discrimination, fetal protection policies, and the Family and Medical Leave Act. Sexual harassment, another type of gender discrimination, will be considered in the next chapter. Gender discrimination covers both males and females, but because of the unique nature of the history of gender in this country, it is females who feel the effects of gender discrimination in the workplace more so than men, and the vast majority of EEOC gender claims are filed by women.

Women are the single largest group of beneficiaries under affirmative action. They seem to be gaining in all facets of life. Who, you think to yourself, would be dumb enough to discriminate against women these days? It can be hard to believe that gender discrimination still exists when you go to school and work with so many people of both genders; you don't feel like *you* view gender as an issue, and it just seems like everything is okay. However, an EEOC report on the commission's litigation over the years 1997–2000 showed that gender suits accounted for the highest percentage of cases brought under Title VII. Just this semester one of our female students in the master's program was actually told by an employer that if she were a man with her qualifications, he would pay her 50 percent more!

Even professionals can be caught off guard. In February 1999, the media reported that a gender discrimination charge that started with eight female stockbrokers at Merrill Lynch alleging various forms of gender inequality, particularly economic discrimination, had ballooned to 900 women and was still growing. "It's been a flood. I've been stunned. We were expecting 200–300 claims, but the calls are still coming in," said one of the lawyers representing the women.

In April 2004, arbitrators found that it was standard operating procedure at Merrill Lynch to discriminate against women. It was the first time a Wall Street firm had been found to have engaged in systematic gender discrimination. Merrill Lynch has spent more than $100 million settling close to 95 percent of the 900 or so claims. In subsequent press releases, the firm said this is not an accurate picture of the firm today.

Even the September 11, 2001, disaster was not without its gender implications. The observation has been made that rescue efforts were overwhelmingly male. A commentator for the *National Law Journal* noted that "some 20 years after Brenda Berkman sued the New York Fire Department for sex discrimination, only 36 of the department's 11,000 firefighters are women. Of the nation's construction workers, including those involved in Ground Zero rebuilding efforts, only about 3 percent are women." The piece went on to disclose that studies demonstrate that the statistics are not simply a lack of interest on the part of women.

Gender equality is an ever-evolving area, and does not occur in a vacuum. The issues in the workplace are only one part of a much larger environment of different, often unequal, treatment of people based on gender. For instance, imagine if the swimsuit calendar had bikini-clad males instead of females! Manifestations can be as diverse as the group of Massachusetts teens suing the Selective Service System arguing it is an unconstitutional violation of the 5th and 14th Amendments' Equal Protection Clause for females not to be subject to the draft just as men are, asserting that "If people want women's rights, they should want it wholeheartedly, including for women to have to fight in wars," to the protest over General Nutrition Center (GNC) dropping women from its GNC Show of Strength bodybuilding competition and replacing it with the International Federation of Body Builders (IFBB) Pro Figure competition; from New Jersey bars no longer being able to offer "Ladies' Night" discounts as a marketing tool to attract women because such promotions discriminate against men, to the flap over heiress and philanthropist Teresa Heinz Kerry, wife of 2004 Democratic presidential nominee Senator John Kerry saying, when asked if she would be a different first lady than Laura Bush (who had been a teacher and librarian from 1968–1977) "I don't know that she's ever had a real job." She later issued an apology.

New types of gender claims are constantly evolving. In the past few years, at least 21 states have passed "contraceptive equity" laws requiring that any health plan that provides coverage for prescription drugs must also provide coverage for FDA-approved contraceptive drugs. Many employers' plans routinely covered the cost of Viagra for male employees but not the cost of contraceptives for female employees. The need for lactation facilities for nursing mothers has become a growing area of concern in the workplace. Increasing male employee interest in balancing work and family has also found its place into the workplace. The first gender-based Family and Medical Leave Act (FMLA) claim involved a new father who won $40,000 after being denied appropriate FMLA leave to take care of his premature baby and seriously ill wife. Within the past few years, in addition to the female coaches who have sued for gender discrimination, several male coaches have alleged gender discrimination, for instance, the coach at the University of Pennsylvania won his claim of being passed over for crew coach in favor of a female.

As women have increasingly entered the workforce over the past 40 years since passage of Title VII, the focus of claims of gender discrimination have more recently shifted away from hiring discrimination toward on the job issues such as equal pay, promotions, harassment, and pregnancy leave. Eric S. Dreiband, EEOC general counsel, recently said this reflects "new issues erupting in a diverse workforce. As blatant discrimination decreased, other areas like harassment increase."

Viewed in this context, it then comes as no surprise that just in recent months, Wachovia Bank reached a settlement with the Office of Federal Contract Compliance Programs (OFCCP) to pay $5.5 million for compensation discrimination against women (September 2004). In July 2004, the Wall Street investment firm of Morgan Stanley paid $54 million to settle a landmark gender discrimination lawsuit involving claims of nearly 350 women who said they were denied equal pay and promotions in the company's institutional equities division. In August 2004, Home Depot agreed to pay $5.5 million to resolve a class action suit alleging, among other things, gender discrimination in its Colorado stores. In June 2004, the Palm Steak House agreed to a $500,000 settlement for failing to hire women to wait tables at its 29 restaurants because males, who could make up to $80,000 per year, including tips, were viewed as more prestigious.

Washington is the only state in the country that can boast that it has a female governor, both of its U.S. senators are female, four of its nine state supreme court justices are female, and 42 of its 147 state legislators are female, yet Seattle-based aeronautical giant, Boeing, agreed to pay $72.5 million for gender-based compensation discrimination against its female employees. A University of California lab agreed to pay $9.7 million to 3,200 women to whom it had paid less wages and whom it had promoted less often than male employees. The EEOC asked the law firm of Boies, Schiller and Flexner to codify its two-tiered track and compensation system and render objective its "highly subjective" and secretive policy, saying it discriminated against female associates, relegating them to a lower-paid, nonpartnered track. Costco Wholesale Corp., with a workforce of 78,000, was sued by about 650 women in a class action suit who allege the company did not announce openings for higher-paying managerial jobs, relying instead on a "tap the shoulder" policy of choosing managers. That is, top-level male managers would pick other males for high level positions. Fewer than one in six of Costco's managers are women, while nearly 50 percent of its workforce is female.

Then, of course, there is Wal-Mart, whose size alone puts it nearly in a class by itself. With sales of $284 billion for fiscal year 2004, it is the world's largest retailer. More than 70 percent of its hourly sales employees are women. In *Dukes* v. *Wal-Mart Stores,* potentially about 1.6 million present and former female employees (roughly the population of San Francisco) was certified in June 2004 for a class action suit against

Wal-Mart for gender bias. The employees allege that Wal-Mart systematically mistreats women in a variety of ways, including paying them less even though they may have more experience or outrank men, prohibiting women from advancing by denying them training, prohibiting them from working in departments traditionally staffed by men (positions that usually pay more), and not posting all management position openings. Damages could run into the billions if Wal-Mart, which denies any wrongdoing, is found liable for gender discrimination. A study done at the request of the employees' attorney found that of Wal-Mart's top 20 competitors, 56 percent of the managers are women, compared with about one-third of that for Wal-Mart. About 14 percent of the top managers at its 3,000 stores are female. In response to the media surrounding the lawsuit, in late 2004, Wal-Mart took out more than 100 full-page newspaper ads across the country, outlining its wages and benefits and the good the company brings to its communities.

Let's take a look at some of the statistics that might underlie these cases to see if they support the overall picture. Nearly half the workforce is female. At the same time women are nearing the halfway mark in the workforce, they represent two-thirds of all poor adults. Nearly 80 percent of female employees work in traditional "female" jobs—as secretaries, administrative support workers, and salesclerks. Statistics show that 16 percent of the females in the workforce are employed as professionals but 10 percent of them are actually nurses or K-12 teachers—traditionally "pink-collar" female strongholds. For instance, 90 percent of nurses are women, as are 80 percent of teachers. Paradoxically, a March 2004 EEOC report, *Glass Ceilings: The Status of Women as Officials and Managers in the Private Sector,* found that women have the lowest odds of being managers in nursing care facilities. Even though Title VII has been in effect for 40 years, only 15 percent of women work in jobs typically held by men (engineers, stockbrokers, judges), while fewer than 8 percent of men hold female-dominated jobs such as nurses, teachers, or sales clerks. According to the EEOC report, women now represent about 36 percent of all officials and managers in private sector employment, a 7 percent increase over the 12-year period examined. On the other hand, women were 58 percent of the 13 million U.S. undergraduates in 2002 and earned more doctorates than men, yet it is generally recognized that campuses are still predominantly male when it comes to professors, department heads, and other high-level administrators. In a historic move in October 2004, Susan Hockfield was tapped to be the new president of the prestigious Massachusetts Institute of Technology. Shortly thereafter, in January 2005, the president of Harvard University, Lawrence Summers, created quite a stir when he suggested at an academic conference that women represent such a small percentage of math and science faculties because they lack innate ability in math and science. He subsequently apologized, saying, in part, "The human potential to excel in science is not somehow the province of one gender or another."

In 2004, a study by Stephen J. Rose, an economist at the consulting firm of Macro International, Inc., and Heidi I. Hartmann, president of the Institute for Women's Policy Research, found that while the Bureau of Labor Statistics (BLS) reports that women earn about 77 percent of men's pay, over the course of their careers, it is actually more like 44 percent. The researchers say the BLS statistics consider only full-time, year-round employees—a category only about 25 percent of women fit into over the course of their work life—and do not account for the roughly 75 percent of those who work only part time at some point and dip in and out of the labor force to care for children or elderly parents. When the more accurate reality is used for calculation, the figure becomes 44 percent.

In November 2004, the BLS announced that it would no longer collect data on women in employment in its monthly Current Employment Statistics survey, despite its report released on June 2, 2004, indicating that women earn less than men with the same education, at all levels. According to the report, male dropouts earned an average of $36,000 per year during the years between 1983 and 1998, while women with a bachelors' degree earned an average of $35,000 per year. Women with graduate degrees earned an average of $42,000, while men with such degrees earned nearly $77,000 per year. A 2003 report by the U.S. Census Bureau found that the average male working full-time, year-round earned $54,803, while for females the average was $37,123, or 32 percent less. The gender-based wage gap is present in every profession. For instance, female doctors on average earn 58 percent less than male doctors.

The 1991 Civil Rights Act called for the establishment of a Glass Ceiling Commission to investigate the barriers to female and minority advancement in the workplace and suggest ways to combat the situation. In 1995, the U.S. Department of Labor released a study by the bipartisan commission. Findings were based on information obtained from independent studies, existing research, public hearings, and focus groups. The commission reported that while women have gained entry into the workforce in substantial numbers, once there they face all but invisible barriers to promotion into top ranks. "Glass ceilings" prevent them from moving up higher in the workplace. "Glass walls" prevent them from moving laterally into areas that lead to higher advancement. Research indicates that many professional women hold jobs in such areas as public relations, human resources management, and law—areas that are not prone to provide the experience management seeks when it determines promotions to higher level positions. This was further supported by the study by Professor Blumrosen, mentioned in the previous chapter.

Segregation by both race and gender among executives and management ranks is widespread. A survey of top managers in Fortune 1000 industrial and Fortune 500 service firms found that 97 percent are white males. As part of their findings, a survey by Korn/Ferry International found 3 to 5 percent of top managers are women. Of those, 95 percent are white, non-Hispanic. Further, women and minorities are trapped in low-wage, low-prestige, and dead-end jobs, the commission said. It is therefore not difficult to see why, in a *New York Times* poll of women about "the most important problem facing women today," job discrimination won overwhelmingly.

Our country, like many others, has a history in which women's contributions to the workplace have historically been precluded, denied, or undervalued. Prior to the 1964 Civil Rights Act, it was common for states to have laws that limited or prohibited women from working at certain jobs under the theory that such laws were for the protection of women. Unfortunately, those jobs also tended to have higher wages. The effect was to prevent women from entering into, progressing within, or receiving higher wages in the workplace. In *Muller* v. *Oregon*,[1] which upheld protective legislation for women and justified them being in a class of their own for employment purposes, the U.S. Supreme Court stated that a woman must "rest upon and look to her brother for

---

[1] 208 US 412 (1908).

Exhibit 6.2   Sexist Thinking

An *Esquire* magazine poll asked men: "If you received $1.00 for every sexist thought you had in the past year, how much richer would you be today?" The median answer was $139.50.

Source: *Parade Magazine,* December 1991, p. 5.

[We have never had a male student who didn't think the figure should be higher.]

protection . . . to protect her from the greed as well as the passions of man." This is precisely the view our laws took until the Civil Rights Act of 1964.

After women came into the workplace in unprecedented numbers out of necessity during World War II and performed traditional male jobs admirably, it became more difficult to maintain the validity of such arguments. This type of protective legislation was specifically outlawed by Title VII, and the glass ceiling and walls notwithstanding, women have made tremendous strides in the workplace over the past 40 years. In evaluating those strides, keep in mind that women were virtually starting from scratch since there was little or nothing to prevent workplace discrimination, so gaining entry into the workplace and the statistics reflected by that should, of course, be high.

Despite the fact that many of the strides made by women were made with the help of male judges, employers, legislators, and others, much of the cause of the figures is attitudinal. (See Exhibit 6.2.) Workplace policies generally reflect attitudes of management. In a national poll of chief executives at Fortune 1000 companies, more than 80 percent acknowledged that discrimination impedes female employees' progress, yet less than 1 percent regarded *remedying* gender discrimination as a goal that their personnel departments should pursue. In fact, when the companies' human resources officers were asked to rate their departments' priorities, women's advancement ranked dead last.

Interestingly enough, despite the fact that it was not only perfectly legal but also generally accepted that women were either excluded from the workplace or kept from its higher paying jobs, and despite the fact that the biggest gains under protective employment legislation in the last 40 years have been made by women, the truth is, gender was not originally a part of Title VII. Gender was inserted into the civil rights bill at the last moment by Judge Howard Smith, a southern legislator and civil rights foe who was confident that, if gender discrimination was included in the bill, then the bill legislating racial equality would surely be defeated. He was wrong. However, because of the ploy, there was little legislative debate on the gender category, so there is little to guide the courts in interpreting what Congress intended by prohibiting gender discrimination. To date, it has been determined that gender discrimination also includes discrimination due to pregnancy and sexual harassment, but not because of affinity orientation or being transsexual.

The goal of a manager, supervisor, human resources employee, or business owner is to have workplace policies that maximize the potential for *every* employee to contribute to the productivity and growth of the workplace, while minimizing or eliminating irrelevant, inefficient, and nonproductive policies that prevent them from doing so. The underlying consideration to keep in mind when developing, enforcing, or

Exhibit 6.3   Career Stereotyping

Dear Abby: As I begin my second year of medical school, I need some advice on how to respond to those ignorant people who assume that, since I am female, I am studying to be a nurse. Men and women alike are guilty of this.

Please don't get me wrong, I have just as much respect for nurses—they work as hard as some physicians, but women are seldom given the credit they deserve. I once heard this statement: "Oh, so you're in medical school? My sister is a nurse, too!"

I cannot tell you how angry this makes me. Many of my female classmates also feel this way. Do you have a response that expresses our feelings without offending the speaker?—Ms. Future Doctor in L.A.

Dear Future Doctor: Anyone who is confused about the role of a student in medical school should be told that future physicians are trained in medical schools, and future nurses are trained in nursing schools.

Dear Abby: After reading the letter from "Ms. Future Doctor," I felt the need to write and give another view on career sexual stereotypes.

I am 27, a registered nurse for four years, and I am a MALE. I am frequently asked, "When will you become a doctor?" Or, "You're doing this just to put yourself through medical school, right?" Also, "What's the matter, couldn't you get into medical school?"

When I first started my schooling to become a nurse, I considered medical school, but the further I got into nursing, the more I enjoyed being a nurse. I enjoy comforting a patient in pain, teaching my patients about their diseases, and holding the hand of someone who is frightened and hurting. These feelings are experienced by every nurse, and being male did not exclude me from doing them. (Most doctors are too busy.) I still work hard being a competent and compassionate nurse.

More males are choosing nursing as a career, and we need to shed our preconceived notions about who nurses are and what they look like.—Mr. Nurse in Tampa

Source: Taken from "Dear Abby" columns by Abigail Van Buren. Dist. by Universal Press Syndicate. Reprinted with permission. All rights reserved.

analyzing policies is that, no matter what we may have been taught about gender by cultural or societal mores, gender, alone, is considered by the law as irrelevant to one's ability to perform a job. By law, it is the person's *ability* to perform, *not* his or her *gender,* that must be the basis of workplace decisions. (See Exhibits 6.3 and 6.4.) As we shall see, there may be very limited exceptions to this rule if a bona fide occupational qualification (BFOQ) exists. It is not only the law, but it is in the best interest of any employer who is serious about maximizing production, efficiency, and profits, as well as minimizing legal liability for workplace discrimination, to recognize that gender discrimination, whether subtle or overt, is just plain bad business. After all, workplace turnover, morale, and defending against lawsuits cost the employer money, time, and energy better spent elsewhere. (See Exhibit 6.5.)

The aim of this chapter is to provide information about obvious gender discrimination and what factors must be considered in making determinations about the policies in "gray areas." This chapter provides the tools to use when developing, applying, or analyzing policies that may result in gender discrimination claims.

Exhibit 6.4   Gender Myths

Due to the particular historical development of gender in our country, there are many myths about gender that affect how those of a given gender are perceived. These myths impact how we view employees of a given gender in the workplace. See if any are familiar.

- Women are better suited to repetitive, fine motor skill tasks.
- Women are too unstable to handle jobs with a great deal of responsibility or high pressure.
- Men make better employees because they are more aggressive.
- Men do not do well at jobs requiring nurturing skills, such as day care, nursing, elder care, and the like.
- When women marry they will get pregnant and leave their jobs.
- When women are criticized at work, they will become angry or cry.
- A married woman's income is only extra family income.
- It is inappropriate for a male employee to take leave to deal with the arrival of a new child.

GENDER DISCRIMINATION IN GENERAL

Title VII and state fair-employment practice laws regarding gender cover the full scope of the employment relationship. Unless it is a BFOQ, gender may not be the basis of any decision related to employment. This includes the following, taken from actual cases and experiences:

- *Advertising* for available positions and specifying a particular gender as being preferred (see Exhibit 6.6).
- Asking questions on an *application* that are only asked of one gender. For example, for background-check purposes asking the applicant's maiden name, rather than simply asking all applicants if there is another name they may have used.
- Asking questions in an *interview* that are only asked of one gender. For example, asking female interviewees if they have proper day care arrangements for their children and not asking male interviewees who also have children. Or asking female applicants about reproductive plans and not asking males. (Yes, people actually do such things.)
- *Requiring one gender to work different hours or job positions* for reasons not related to their ability or availability for the job. For example, not permitting women to work at night or not giving a promotion to a woman because it involves travel.
- *Disciplining* one gender for an act for which the other gender is not disciplined. For example, chastising a female employee who is late for work because of reasons related to her children while not similarly chastising a male employee who is late because of a sick dog, or chastising a female employee for cursing but not a male.

Exhibit 6.5   Discrimination: Bad for Business and Employees

JURY TELLS NBA TO PAY FEMALE REFEREE $7.85 MILLION

Read what happened when a female rose to number two on the list of those in line to officiate in the NBA, only to be repeatedly passed over:

Sandra Ortiz-Del Valle sued the National Basketball Association (NBA) for gender discrimination for passing her over as a referee, and handed the NBA its first discrimination case loss when the federal jury awarded Ortiz-Del Valle $7.85 million, $7 million of which was punitive damages (the award was later reduced by a judge to $350,000). Ortiz-Del Valle had dreamed of being an NBA referee for years, but kept getting passed over. Despite documents praising Ortiz-Del Valle as being "very knowledgeable about the rules" and having "excellent basketball officiating skills," and although the evaluator said, "I would not hesitate to recommend that at sometime in the near future she be considered to enter our training program," the NBA kept giving her varying reasons for denying her the position. The NBA denied any discrimination and said she was not hired because she failed to upgrade the level of competition in her officiating schedule despite being asked to, and said she was out of shape. Ortiz-Del Valle claimed she had all the qualifications to be an NBA referee, including officiating in top men's amateur and professional basketball leagues for 17 years. She was the first woman in history to officiate a men's professional basketball game. Ortiz-Del Valle said she finally sued after continuously doing everything the league asked of her, and not being promoted, then seeing men she trained hired by the league. "It was like they kept moving the basket," she said.

Source: *Ortiz-Del Valle* v. *NBA,* 42 F. Supp. 2d 334 (S.D.N.Y. 1999).

- Providing or not providing *training* for one gender, while doing so for another. For example, requiring all female employees to be trained on word processing equipment, no matter what position they hold in the company, while not requiring that males undergo the same training. Or, alternatively, providing training opportunities for career advancement to male employees and not to female employees who equally qualify for the training.

- Establishing *seniority systems* specifically designed to give greater seniority to one gender over another. For example, instituting a new seniority system that bases seniority on how long an employee has been working for the employer, rather than how long the employee has been working in a particular department with the intent that, if the employer ever needs to lay off employees for economic reasons, more males will be able to retain their positions because females have been in the workplace a shorter time and thus have less seniority.

- *Paying* employees different wages based on gender, though the job one employee performs is the same or substantially the same as another. This may also violate the Equal Pay Act, which prohibits discrimination in compensation on the basis of gender for jobs involving equal skill, effort, or responsibility.

- Providing different *benefits* for one gender than for another. For example, providing spouses of male employees with coverage for short-term disabilities, including pregnancy, while not providing female employees with similar coverage for short-term disabilities for their spouses.

Exhibit 6.6   Pre-Title VII Newspaper Want Ads for Females

This classified ad excerpt, taken from an actual newspaper, is typical of those found in newspapers in the United States before Title VII was passed in 1964. For publication purposes, all names and phone numbers have been omitted. Title VII made it illegal to advertise for jobs based on gender.

FEMALE EMPLOYMENT

Female Help Wanted   23

ATTRACTIVE, NEAT APPEARING, RELIABLE YOUNG LADIES
FOR permanent employment as food waitresses. Interesting work in beautiful surroundings. Good salary plus tips. UNIFORMS FURNISHED. Vacation with pay. Age 21-35 years. For interview appointment phone…

SETTLED white woman who needs home to live in.

LADY to run used furniture store on…

GIRL FRIDAY
If you are a qualified executive secretary, dependable, and would like a solid connection with a growing corporation, write me your qualifications in confidence…

A REFRESHING CHANGE
FROM your household chores! Use those old talents of yours and become a part-time secretary. You can earn that extra money you have been needing by working when you want. XXX has temporary positions open in all locations in town and you can choose what and where you want. TOP HOURLY RATES…NO FEE

Opening Soon…WAITRESSES…NO EXPERIENCE NECESSARY
Will train neat, trim, and alert applicants to be coffee house and cocktail waitresses. Apply at once.

CLERK FOR HOTEL
CLERK for medium-size, unusually nice motor hotel. 6-day wk. Hours 3-11. Experience not necessary. Must be mature, neat, and refined. Call…

• Subjecting one gender to different *terms or conditions of employment.* For example, requiring female associates in an accounting firm to dress, talk, or act "feminine," when no comparable requirement is imposed on males aspiring to partnership.

• *Terminating* the employment of an employee of one gender for reasons that would not serve as the basis for termination for an employee of the other gender. For example, terminating a female employee for fighting on the job, when males engaged in similar activity are retained and only disciplined.

Clearly the antidiscrimination provisions are comprehensive. The law is broad enough to cover virtually every decision or policy that could possibly be made in the workplace. The scope of antidiscrimination laws is intentionally undefined, so that decisions can be made on a case-by-case basis. Some of the examples above are not illegal per se. Rather, they elicit gender or gender-related information that can form the basis of illegal gender-based employment decisions—or at least make it appear as if that is the case.

The law takes a case-by-case approach to gender discrimination, so it is imperative to know what factors will be considered in analyzing whether gender discrimination has occurred. To the extent that these factors are considered when developing

Exhibit 6.7   Appearance-Based Discrimination

We often discriminate against others without even realizing it. Since only those things prohibited by law are considered illegal, not all discrimination is actionable. Look at the items below:

- Very attractive men and women earn at least 5 percent more per hour than people with average looks.
- Plain women earn an average of 5 percent less than women with average looks.
- Plain men earn 10 percent less than average men.
- Most employers pay overweight women 20 percent less per hour than women of average weight.
- Overweight males earn 26 percent more than underweight co-workers.
- Of men with virtually identical résumés, the taller man will be hired 72 percent of the time.
- Men who are 6 feet 2 inches or taller receive starting salaries 12 percent greater than men under 6 feet.
- Married men earn, on average, 11 percent more per hour than men who have never married.
- White women 65 pounds overweight earn 7 percent less than those of median weight; there is little effect of weight on the earnings of Hispanic women, none on black women, and virtually none on the wages of men.
- Better-looking men get more job offers, higher starting salaries, and better raises; good-looking women get better raises but not usually better jobs or starting salaries.
- Plain women tend to attract the lowest quality husbands (as measured by educational achievement or earnings potential); beautiful women do no better in marriage than average women; looks don't seem to affect men's marriage prospects.

Sources: Taken from *The Paranoid's Pocket Guide,* by Cameron Tuttle, Chronicle Books, 1997. Reprinted with permission; Professors Jeff Biddle and Daniel Hamermesh, "Beauty and the Labor Market," *American Economic Review* 83, no. 1174 (December 1994); John Cawley, *Body Weight and Women's Labor Market Outcomes* 2, no. 1, Joint Center for Poverty Research, 2000.

or implementing policies, it is less likely that illegal considerations or criteria will be used in making workplace decisions and policies. (See Exhibits 6.7 and 6.8.)

RECOGNIZING GENDER DISCRIMINATION

When analyzing employment policies or practices for gender discrimination, first check to see if it is obviously so. See if the policy excludes members of a particular gender from the workplace or some workplace benefit. An example is a policy that recently appeared in a newspaper story on local restaurants. One owner said that he did not hire males as servers because he thought females were more pleasant and better at serving customers. As the following case demonstrates, employers such as the restaurant owner, unaware of how their policies may have negative legal repercussions, may engage in obvious gender discrimination.

Exhibit 6.8 — On the Lighter Side

Women are often accused of being humorless when it comes to gender issues. While the issue of gender discrimination is far from funny, it doesn't mean we can't laugh at ourselves. To wit, the following e-mail:

IS YOUR COMPUTER A HE OR A SHE?

A college professor who was previously a sailor was very aware that ships are addressed as "she" and "her." He often wondered [by] what gender computers should be addressed.

To answer that question, he set up two groups of computer experts. The first was composed of women, and the second of men. Each group was asked to recommend whether computers should be referred to in the feminine gender, or the masculine gender. They were asked to give four reasons for their recommendations.

The group of women reported that the computers should be referred to in the masculine gender because:

1. In order to get their attention, you have to turn them on.
2. They have a lot of data, but they are still clueless.
3. They are supposed to help you solve problems, but half the time they are the problem.
4. As soon as you commit to one, you realize that if you had waited a little longer, you could have had a better model.

The men, on the other hand, concluded that computers should be referred to in the feminine gender because:

1. No one but the Creator understands their internal logic.
2. The native language they use to communicate with other computers is incomprehensible to everyone else.
3. Even your smallest mistakes are stored in long-term memory for later retrieval.
4. As soon as you make a commitment to one, you find yourself spending half your paycheck on accessories for it.

Source: Thanks to Andy Walters, Hobart and William Smith Colleges. Used with permission.

Milligan-Jensen v. Michigan Technological Univ. *767 F. Supp. 1403 (W.D. Mich., N. Div. 1991)*

A female public safety officer (PSO) at Michigan Technological University brings suit for gender discrimination after being treated differently because of her gender. The court found the employer liable.

Hillman, J.

In this case there was a substantial amount of direct evidence that defendant took plaintiff employee's gender into account in her employment and termination. Employer initially welcomed Milligan-Jensen's application, telling her that the department would be receptive to her application because "their woman" had just quit and "they had to hire a female." Two months later, after Milligan-Jensen updated her application, the employer wrote, "We are interested in interviewing female applicants for the position of PSO."

Milligan-Jensen came to work as a PSO. The employer assigned her a badge number that every female before her had previously had. Initially she was assigned another badge number, but her supervisor, Louis Fredianelli, changed it to the "female" number because he said, whenever he called for her, he got the other person assigned that number because he was used to using the number for the female officer. Fredianelli, who made the decision to terminate the employee, criticized her uniform and dress even though he admitted that she was helpless to change the mandatory clothes, which are designed for men to wear. Further, Fredianelli treated the employee differently from a male co-worker when each of them committed the same infraction of the rules of not wearing a hat.

Milligan-Jensen's evaluations were mostly marginal, even though a comparable employee received better ratings. When another officer announced his retirement and Milligan-Jensen asked Fredianelli for his shift, she was asked by Fredianelli, who became angry, what was wrong with the job that she had. He declared, "You've got the lady's job. Don't you like it?" On the same day Fredianelli wrote two notes which he placed in employee's file. One said that she asked why she has the dayshift job and he told her it was the "female's job." Two weeks after Fredianelli's "lady's job" remark, employee was terminated. When she asked why, she was told it was because she did not complete her progress reports to satisfaction and spent too much time in the office.

Direct evidence of discrimination usually entails a general comment about a minority group in society. The courts infer from such a remark that the defendant had discriminatory animus toward the particular plaintiff in the particular job. Here, no inference is necessary: Fredianelli's "lady's job" remark was directed specifically at plaintiff and directly related to her job. The court can only surmise that someone infected by discriminatory animus would be "mad and upset" by such a question. After making the discriminatory remark, Fredianelli documented it. The remark is direct evidence of Fredianelli's discriminatory state of mind toward plaintiff. The uniform criticism, disparate treatment, and badge episode are also direct evidence that Fredianelli's state of mind was affected by employee's gender.

Because Milligan-Jensen made a showing of intentional discrimination, the burden shifts to the employer to convince the court by a preponderance of the evidence that the decision would have been the same absent consideration of the unlawful factor. This is difficult because more than one motive nearly always occupies a decision-maker's mind. As a result, when the court finds that a substantial motivating factor of a decision was unlawful, the burden is then placed squarely on the decisionmaker's shoulders to prove that the identical decision would have been made absent the unlawful motive.

Here, a number of factors suggest that Fredianelli's discrimination terminally infected employee's employment as a PSO. From the testimony, it appears that Fredianelli decided that plaintiff was going to be terminated as early as a month before it occurred. At that time, there were already indications of Fredianelli's discriminatory state of mind toward employee. Thus, the increase in critical notes to her file and heightened watch over her job performance indicate that Fredianelli was simply building a file so that he would have justification to terminate her. Further, on the day he made the "lady's job" comment, he put in employee's file a note about her spending too much time in the office. Two weeks later in her termination meeting, he told her she was being fired for this reason.

Thus, Fredianelli's decision to dismiss employee was infected by his desire to retaliate for her complaint about his acts of discrimination. It is clear that Fredianelli was motivated by discriminatory animus and in the end, by a desire to retaliate against employee.

The next question is whether the employer proved by a preponderance of the evidence that the employment decisions concerning employee would have been identical absent the unlawful motivation. This court cannot separate the good from the bad, the times when Fredianelli's mind was infected by discrimination and the times when he treated employee as he would have treated any other employee. Employer bore the burden of persuading the court that gender discrimination did not infect the decision to dismiss employee. Employer failed to carry its burden. Therefore, based on all of the above, the court concludes that employer did in fact discriminate against employee on the basis of gender in violation of Title VII. JUDGMENT for PLAINTIFF.

Case Questions

1. Would you have said some of the things that Fredianelli said to Milligan-Jensen? Which things and why or why not?

2. Do you think the police department intended to discriminate? Explain.

3. How would you have avoided this situation?

Exhibit 6.9   Illegal or Unfair?

Several courts have wrestled with the issue of what constitutes gender discrimination under Title VII. One issue that has arisen several times is whether it is illegal gender discrimination under Title VII if a female who is having a relationship with a supervisor receives a job or promotion over a qualified male who applies for the position. In *Womack v. Runyon,* 77 FEP Cases 769 (11th Cir. 1998), Paul Womack, having excellent credentials, experience, and training, applied for a carrier supervisor position in Waycross, Georgia. He was unanimously selected as the best qualified candidate by a review board, but O. M. Lee, the newly appointed postmaster of Waycross, instead appointed Lee's paramour, Jeanine Bennett. In rejecting Womack's Title VII claim of gender discrimination, the court held that Title VII did not cover claims of favoritism, saying that such decisions may not be fair, but they are not illegal under Title VII. According to a 1990 EEOC policy guidance, "Title VII does not prohibit . . . preferential treatment based upon consensual romantic relationships. An isolated instance of favoritism toward a paramour . . . may be unfair, but it does not [amount to] discrimination against women or men in violation of Title VII, since both [genders] are disadvantaged for reasons other than their genders."

Not all cases may be as easy to recognize as gender discrimination when making workplace decisions or policies. (See Exhibit 6.9.) It is easier to realize there is gender discrimination when the policy says "no women hired as guards" than when, as with the *Dothard* case below, there is a policy, neutral on its face, saying all applicants must meet a certain height and weight requirement to be guards, yet due to their genetic differences statistically, most women do not generally meet the requirement. In the *Dothard* case, for the first time, the U.S. Supreme Court was faced with whether Title VII's gender discrimination provision applied to the seemingly neutral criteria of height and weight restrictions, which had long been an accepted basis for screening applicants for certain types of jobs such as prison guards, police officers, and firefighters. The Court decided that Title VII did, in fact, apply to such facially neutral policies when they screened out women (later cases extended this standard to shorter and slighter ethnicities as well) at an unacceptable rate and were not shown to be directly correlated to ability to do the job.

Dothard v. Rawlinson *433 U.S. 321 (1977)*

After her application for employment as an Alabama prison guard was rejected because the applicant, Rawlinson, failed to meet the minimum 120-pound weight, 5-foot-2-inch height requirement of an Alabama statute, Rawlinson sued. She challenged the statutory height and weight requirements and a regulation establishing gender criteria for assigning prison guards to "contact" positions (those requiring close physical proximity to inmates) as violative of Title VII of the Civil Rights Act of 1964. The Supreme Court found gender discrimination.

Stewart, J.

At the time she applied for a position as a correctional counselor trainee, Rawlinson was a 22-year-old college graduate whose major course of study had been correctional psychology. She was refused employment because she failed to meet the minimum 120-pound weight requirement established by an Alabama statute. The statute stated that the applicant shall not be less than five feet two inches nor more than six feet ten inches in height, shall weigh not less than 120 pounds nor more than 300 pounds. Variances could be granted upon a showing of good cause, but none had ever been applied for by the Board and the Board did not apprise applicants of the waiver possibility. While this suit was pending the Board adopted Administrative Regulation 204 establishing gender criteria for assigning correctional counselors to maximum-security institutions for "contact positions." Rawlinson amended her complaint by adding a challenge to Regulation 204 as violative of Title VII of the Civil Rights Act of 1964 and the Fourteenth Amendment.

Like most correctional facilities in the U.S., Alabama's prisons are segregated on the basis of gender. Inmate living quarters are for the most part large dormitories, with communal showers and toilets that are open to the dorms and hallways. Two of the facilities carry on extensive farming operations, making necessary a large number of strip searches for contraband when prisoners re-enter the prison buildings. A prison guard's primary duty within these institutions is to maintain security and control the inmates by continually supervising and observing their activities.

At the time this litigation was in the district court, women applicants could under Regulation 204 compete equally with men for only about 25% of the correctional counselor jobs available in the Alabama prison system because of the gender and "contact" restrictions. In considering the effect of the minimum height and weight standards on this disparity in rate of hiring between genders, the district court found that when the height and weight restrictions are combined, Alabama's statutory standards would exclude 41.13% of the female population while excluding less than 1% of the male population.

In enacting Title VII, Congress required "the removal of artificial, arbitrary, and unnecessary barriers to employment when the barriers operate invidiously to discriminate on the basis of racial or other impermissible classification." *Griggs* v. *Duke Power Co.* The District Court found the minimum

height and weight requirements constitute the sort of arbitrary barrier to equal employment opportunity that Title VII forbids. Alabama asserts that the district court erred both in finding the standards discriminate against women, and in its refusal to find that, even if they do, these standards are justified as "job related."

This claim does not involve an assertion of purposeful discriminatory motive. It is asserted, rather, that these facially neutral qualification standards work in fact disproportionately to exclude women from eligibility for employment by the Alabama Board of Corrections.

We turn to Alabama's argument that they have rebutted the prima facie case of discrimination by showing that the height and weight requirements are job related. These requirements, they say, have a relationship to strength, a sufficient but unspecified amount of which is essential to effective job performance as a correctional counselor. In the district court, however, they failed to offer evidence of any kind in specific justification of the statutory standards.

If the job-related quality that the Board identifies is bona fide, their purpose could be achieved by adopting and validating a test for applicants that measures strength directly. But nothing in the present record even approaches such a measurement.

The district court was not in error in holding that Title VII of the Civil Rights Act of 1964 prohibits application of the statutory height and weight requirements to Rawlinson and the class she represents. AFFIRMED in part, REVERSED in part, and REMANDED.

Case Questions

1. What purpose did the height and weight requirement serve? Do you think it was made to intentionally discriminate against women?

2. How could management have avoided this outcome?

3. In your view, should women's access to male prisoners be limited as described here? Why or why not?

"GENDER-PLUS" DISCRIMINATION

There are some situations in which the employer may permit the hiring of women but not if there are other factors present—for example, no hiring of women who are pregnant, married, over a certain age, have children under a certain age, or are unmarried

A federal judge in New York dismissed a gender discrimination and disability suit brought by Alicia Martinez, a cable television producer, alleging that after returning from maternity leave, her employer, MSNBC cable, failed to provide her with a "safe, secure, sanitary and private" place to pump breast milk during work breaks and harassed her for complaining. *Martinez* v. *NBC, Inc. and MSNBC,* 49 F. Supp. 2d 305 (S.D. N.Y. 1999).

Regarding the ADA claim, Judge Kaplan said it was "preposterous to contend a woman's body is functioning abnormally because she is lactating." As to the Title VII claim, the court said this was not "sex plus" discrimination because "to allow a claim based on sex-plus discrimination here would elevate breast milk pumping—alone—to a protected status," and that could only be done by Congress. It was not plain gender discrimination under Title VII because "the drawing of distinctions among persons of one gender on the basis of criteria that are immaterial to the other, while in given cases perhaps deplorable, is not the sort of behavior covered by Title VII."

Note that a similar argument was struck down by Congress in enacting the Pregnancy Discrimination Act, where the court determined it was not illegal gender discrimination to treat pregnant employees differently, since only females could become pregnant. Keep an eye on what happens with breast-feeding in the workplace. Some states (e.g., California) have already enacted laws providing protection for nursing mothers and others are considering legislation. Even in the absence of legislation, many employers are taking this issue quite seriously and creating policies to address lactation. A popular route recently is for the employer to draw up a lactation agreement setting forth the parameters of the workplace lactation provisions, and the responsibilities of both the employer and the employee, and have the employee understand and sign it.

"gender-plus" discrimination
Employment discrimination based on gender and some other factor such as marital status or children.

with children. This is **"gender-plus" discrimination**. Of course, the problem is that such policies are not neutral at all, because males are not subject to the same limitations. (See Exhibit 6.10.)

The *Phillips* case below was the first Title VII case to reach the U.S. Supreme Court and is still widely cited. It is a per curiam or summary decision, rather than a full court opinion, but it provides insight into the considerations the Court will use in deciding gender-plus discrimination cases.

Phillips v. Martin Marietta Corp. *400 U.S. 542 (1971)*

A female applicant was denied employment because of the employer's policy against hiring women with preschool-age children. There was no policy against hiring men with such children. The Supreme Court held the employer's policy violated Title VII.

Per Curiam

Martin Marietta informed Ida Phillips that it was not accepting job applications from women with pre-school-age children. As of the time of this action, Martin Marietta employed men with pre-school-age children. At the time Phillips applied, 70–75% of the applicants for the position she sought were women; 75–80% of those hired for the position, assembly trainee, were women, hence no question of bias against women as such was presented.

Section 703(a) of the Civil Rights Act of 1964 requires that persons of like qualifications be given employment opportunities irrespective of their gender. The Court of Appeals therefore erred in reading this section as permitting one hiring policy for women and another for men—each having pre-school-age children. The existence of such conflicting family obligations, if demonstrably more relevant to job performance for a woman than a man, could arguably be a basis for distinction under 703(3) [BFOQ] of the Act. But that is a matter of evidence tending to show that the condition in question is a BFOQ reasonably necessary to the normal operation of that particular business or enterprise. The record before us, however, is not adequate for resolution of these important issues. VACATED and REMANDED.

Mr. Justice Marshall, concurring.

While I agree that this case must be remanded for a full development of the facts, I cannot agree with the Court's indication that a BFOQ reasonably necessary to the normal operation of Martin Marietta's business could be established by a showing that some women, even the vast majority, with pre-school-age children have family responsibilities that interfere with job performance and that men do not usually have such responsibilities. Certainly, an employer can require that all of his employees, both men and women, meet minimum performance standards, and he can try to insure compliance by requiring parents, both mothers and fathers, to provide for the care of their children so that job performance is not interfered with.

The Court has fallen into the trap of assuming that the Act permits ancient canards about the proper role of women to be the basis for discrimination. Congress, however, sought just the opposite result.

Even characterizations of the proper domestic roles of the genders were not to serve as predicates for restricting employment opportunity. The exception for a BFOQ was not intended to swallow that rule.

Case Questions

1. Why do you think the employer instituted the rule discussed here? Does it actually address the employer's concern?

2. Can you think of a better way for management to handle its concerns about preschool parents?

3. Does Justice Marshall's position make sense to you? Why or why not?

The Court evidently took Justice Marshall's dissent seriously, because in the years after *Martin Marietta* it has not permitted BFOQs to be used in the way he warned against. Keep in mind that, while BFOQs are permitted as a lawful means of discriminating based on gender, they are very narrowly construed. The employer is under a heavy duty to show that the gender requirement is reasonably necessary for the employer's particular business.

GENDER ISSUES

gender stereotypes
The assumption that most or all members of a particular gender must act a certain way.

As we have seen, many issues are included under the umbrella of illegal gender discrimination. Following are some that are more prevalent. Keep in mind that many things we take for granted and dismiss as "that's just the way things are" *may* be illegal in the workplace. It is extremely important to keep this in mind as managers make workplace decisions and to guard against letting such thoughts be the basis of illegal Title VII decisions.

Gender Stereotyping

Much discrimination on the basis of gender is in some way based on **gender stereotypes**. That is, workplace decisions are based on ideas of how a particular

Exhibit 6.11

Stereotyped Humor

"Hey, didja hear the one about the blond bimbo?" Well, you won't hear it here. Whether or not jokes playing on stereotypes of women make you laugh, they might affect your judgments of women. About 100 male and female college students who heard sex-stereotyped jokes before watching female lecturers later rated the women in a more stereotyped fashion than did students who heard nonsexist jokes. "This study suggests we should be on guard about [stereotyped humor]," says co-author Christine Weston, Boston University.

Source: *USA Today,* Aug. 24, 1993, p. D-1.

---

gender should act or dress, or what roles they should perform. An employer may terminate a female employee who is too "abrasive," or not hire a female for a job as a welder because it is "men's work." Stereotypes generally have little or nothing to do with an individual employee's qualifications or ability to perform. Workplace decisions based on stereotypes are prohibited by Title VII. (See Exhibits 6.5 and 6.11.)

As we will see in *Hopkins,* stereotyping frequently leads to actions that form the basis of unnecessary liability for the employer. It is senseless for employers to allow managers and supervisors who hold such views to cause liability that costs the entire company unnecessary loss of revenue.

Price Waterhouse v. Hopkins *490 U.S. 228 (1989)*

Ann Hopkins, a female associate who was refused admission as a partner in an accounting firm, brought a gender discrimination action against the firm. The U.S. Supreme Court held that the evidence was sufficient to show that illegal gender stereotyping played a part in evaluating Hopkins' candidacy.

Brennan, J.

In a jointly prepared statement supporting her candidacy, the partners in Hopkins' office showcased her successful 2-year effort to secure a $25 million contract with the Department of State, labeling it "an outstanding performance" and one that Hopkins carried out "virtually at the partner level." None of the other partnership candidates had a comparable record in terms of successfully securing major contracts for the partnership.

The partners in Hopkins' office praised her character and her accomplishments, describing her as "an outstanding professional" who had a "deft touch," a "strong character, independence, and integrity." Clients appeared to have agreed with these assessments. Hopkins "had no difficulty dealing with clients and her clients appeared to be very pleased with her work" and she "was generally viewed as a highly competent project leader who worked long hours, pushed vigorously to meet deadlines, and demanded much from the multidisciplinary staffs with which she worked."

Virtually all of the partners' negative comments about Hopkins—even those of partners supporting her—had to do with her "interpersonal skills." Both supporters and opponents of her candidacy indicate she was sometimes "overly aggressive, unduly harsh, difficult to work with, and impatient with staff."

There were clear signs, though, that some of the partners reacted negatively to Hopkins' personality because she was a woman. One partner described her as "macho"; another suggested that she "overcompensated for being a woman"; a third advised her to take "a course at charm school." Several partners criticized her use of profanity; in response, one partner suggested that those partners objected to her swearing only "because it['s] a lady using foul language." Another supporter explained that Hopkins "ha[d] matured from a tough-talking somewhat masculine hard-nosed manager to an authoritative, formidable, but much more appealing lady partner candidate." But it was the man who bore responsibility for explaining to Hopkins the reasons for the Policy Board's decision to place her candidacy on hold who delivered the coup de grace; in order to improve her chances for partnership, Thomas Beyer advised, Hopkins should "walk more femininely, talk more femininely, dress more femininely, wear make-up, have her hair styled, and wear jewelry."

Dr. Susan Fiske, a social psychologist and Associate Professor of Psychology at Carnegie-Mellon University, testified at trial that the partnership selection process at Price Waterhouse was likely influenced by gender stereotyping. Her testimony focused not only on the overtly gender-based comments of partners but also on gender-neutral remarks, made by partners who knew Hopkins only slightly, that were intensely critical of her. One partner, for example, baldly stated that Hopkins was "universally disliked" by staff and another described her as "consistently annoying and irritating"; yet these were people who had had very little contact with Hopkins. According to Fiske, Hopkins's uniqueness (as the only woman in the pool of candidates) and the subjectivity of the evaluations made it likely that sharply critical remarks such as these were the product of gender stereotyping.

An employer who acts on the basis of a belief that a woman cannot be aggressive or that she must not be has acted on the basis of gender. Although the parties do not overtly dispute this last proposition, the placement by Price Waterhouse of "sex stereotyping" in quotation marks throughout its brief seems to us an insinuation either that such stereotyping was not present in this case or that it lacks legal relevance. We reject both possibilities. A number of the partners' comments showed gender stereotyping at work. As for the legal relevance of gender stereotyping, we are beyond the day when an employer could evaluate employees by assuming or insisting that they matched the stereotype associated with their group, for "[i]n forbidding employers to discriminate against individuals because of their gender, Congress intended to strike at the entire spectrum of disparate treatment of men and women resulting from sex stereotypes." An employer who objects to aggressiveness in women but whose positions require this trait places women in the intolerable and impermissible Catch-22: out of a job if they behave aggressively and out of a job if they don't. Title VII lifts women out of this bind.

Remarks at work that are based on gender stereotypes do not inevitably prove that gender played a part in a particular employment decision. The plaintiff must show that the employer actually relied on her gender in making its decision. In making this showing, stereotyped remarks can certainly be evidence that gender played a part. REVERSED and REMANDED.

Case Questions

1. What were Price Waterhouse's fatal flaws?
2. Does Hopkins' treatment here make good business sense? Explain.
3. How would you avoid the problems in this case?

Grooming Codes

The issue of gender stereotypes may be closely linked to that of grooming codes since the issue often arises in a gender context (e.g., men being prohibited from wearing earrings at work or women being prohibited from wearing pants). Courts recognize that employers need to be able to control this aspect of the workplace, and a good deal of flexibility is permitted. As *Blockbuster* demonstrates, Title VII does not prohibit an employer from using gender as a basis for reasonable grooming codes.

Note, however, that we here address grooming codes only in the context of gender discrimination. The more recent workplace issues of, for example, applicants or employees with numerous body piercings, tattoos, and the like is generally not a gender issue but, rather, one of pure dress code–based appropriate business attire. Again, employers are given a good deal of leeway in setting workplace dress codes. The codes

Exhibit 6.12

Stereotypes

Do any of the stereotypes below, taken from actual cases, sound familiar? Note that they do not address only gender.

- "Older employees have problems adapting to changes and to new policies."
- One had to be wary around "articulate black men."
- Would not consider "some woman" for the position, questioned plaintiff about future pregnancy plans, and asked whether her husband would object to her "running around the country with men."
- Female employee who spent time talking to other black employees was becoming "the black matriarch" within the company.
- A lesser job position was sufficient for women and no woman would be named to the higher position.
- If it were his company, he would not hire any black people.
- He was "not going to hire a black leasing agent."

---

can be pretty much whatever the employer wants, unless a policy violates law, such as being illegally discriminatory on the basis of gender. In making this determination, employers can use reasonable standards of what is generally thought to be male- or female-appropriate attire in a business setting. That is why it is permissible under Title VII for an employer to prohibit males from wearing earrings, for instance, even though females are permitted to wear them.

Harper v. Blockbuster Entertainment Corporation *139 F. 3d 1385 (11th Cir. 1998)*

Male employees sued employer under Title VII and Florida Civil Rights Act, alleging that employer's grooming policy, which prohibited men, but not women, from wearing long hair, discriminated against them on the basis of gender. The court held that the grooming policy did not violate Title VII or Florida law.

Carnes, J.

The plaintiffs in this case are four males formerly employed by Blockbuster Entertainment Corp. ("Blockbuster"). They brought this suit against Blockbuster under Title VII and the Florida Civil Rights Act alleging that Blockbuster's grooming policy discriminated against them on the basis of their gender and that they were wrongfully terminated in retaliation for protesting that policy. After the district court granted Blockbuster's motion to dismiss the employees' complaint, the employees appealed. For the reasons discussed below, we affirm the district court's order dismissing employees' complaint.

In May of 1994, Blockbuster implemented a new grooming policy that prohibited men, but not women, from wearing long hair. The employees, all men with long hair, refused to comply with the policy. They protested the policy as discriminatory and communicated their protest to supervisory officials of Blockbuster. Two of the employees were the subject of media stories concerning their protest of the policy. All of the employees were subsequently terminated by Blockbuster because they had refused to cut their hair and because they had protested the grooming policy.

The employees timely filed a charge with the EEOC. After the EEOC issued right to sue letters, the employees filed a complaint alleging gender discrimination under Title VII. Blockbuster moved to dismiss the complaint. The district court granted the motion, and this appeal followed. We affirm the dismissal.

The employees allege that Blockbuster's grooming policy discriminates on the basis of gender in violation of Title VII. In *Willingham* v. *Macon Telegraph Pub. Co.,* our predecessor court held that differing hair length standards for men and women do not violate Title VII, a holding which squarely forecloses the employees' discrimination claim. [In *Willingham,* the court stated]:

> Willingham argues that the Telegraph discriminates among employees based upon their gender in that female employees may wear their hair any length they choose, while males must limit theirs to a length deemed acceptable by the Telegraph. He therefore asserts that he was denied employment because of his gender because were he a girl with identical length hair and comparable job qualifications, he (she) would have been employed.

We conclude that the undisputed discrimination practiced by the Macon Telegraph is not based upon gender, but rather upon grooming standards, and thus not a violation of Title VII. We perceive the intent of Congress to have been the guarantee of equal job opportunity for males and females. Providing such opportunity is where the emphasis rightly lies. This is to say that Title VII should lie to reach any device or policy of any employer which serves to deny acquisition and retention of a job or promotion in a job to an individual *because* the individual is either male or female. Equal employment *opportunity* may be secured only when employers are barred from discriminating against employees on the basis of immutable characteristics, such as race and national origin. Similarly, an employer cannot have one hiring policy for men and another for women if the distinction is based on some fundamental right. But a hiring policy that distinguishes on some other ground, such as grooming codes or length of hair, is related more closely to the employer's choice of how to run his business than to equality of employment opportunity. We perceive that a line of distinction must be drawn between distinctions grounded on such fundamental rights as the right to have children as in *Phillips* v. *Martin Marietta* and those interfering with the manner in which an employer exercises his judgment as to the way to operate a business. Hair length is not immutable and in the situation of an employer vis-à-vis employee, enjoys no constitutional protection. If the employee objects to the grooming code he has the right to reject it by looking elsewhere for employment or alternatively he may choose to subordinate his preference by accepting the code along with the job.

We adopt the view, therefore, that distinctions in employment practices between men and women on the basis of something other than immutable or protected characteristics do not inhibit employment *opportunity* in violation of 703(a) of Title VII. Congress sought only to give all persons equal access to the job market, not to limit an employer's right to exercise his informed judgment as to how best to run his shop. AFFIRMED.

Case Questions

1. Do you agree with the court? Why or why not?
2. In your view, how can the court reach its decision simply by saying Title VII deals only with immutable characteristics? Were the discriminatory factors in *Hopkins* immutable (wear more jewelry, have hair styled, dress more femininely, etc.)? What is the distinction?
3. If you were an employer, what policy would you adopt? Why?

Courts have also upheld grooming codes that required, among other things, male supermarket clerks to wear ties, female employees to not wear pants, a female attorney to "tone down" her "flashy" attire, and male and female flight attendants to keep their weight down. Not permitted were a weight restriction policy applied only to the exclusively female category of flight attendants, but not the category of male directors of passenger service, when both were in-flight employees. Also not permitted was requiring male employees to wear "normal business attire" and women to wear uniforms, though both performed the same duties. The court found "there is a natural tendency to assume that the uniformed women have a lesser professional status than their male colleagues attired in normal business clothes."

Scenario

This is the basis for opening scenario 1, and the reason the female clerk made to wear the smock would have a viable claim for gender discrimination. The wearing of the smock (picture the loose-fitting coverall-type button-down overdress that hairdressers often wear) may seem like a small thing to you, and you might say to yourself, "What's the big deal? Why would anybody complain about such a little thing?" Think back to the wires of the cage. It is not the smock itself that presents the problem. Rather, as the court said above, it is how that smock positions the employee to be perceived in the workplace. That perception is a large part of what happens in that employee's worklife, affecting whether that employee receives promotions, training, raises, and so on. When you think of business attire (keep in mind that the males with the same jobs were required to wear the "normal business attire" of coats and ties), a smock does not generally come to mind. If both genders were performing the same job, a female wearing a smock would not qualify as comparable to a male wearing a coat and tie. If you think she would, just turn the facts around and require the males to wear the smock and the females to wear "normal business attire." Not the same picture, is it? And when you think of who should get a promotion, the employee in the smock probably doesn't come to mind. Like the wires, each requirement, in and of itself, may not make a big difference, but taken together, the policies create a picture that is likely to keep the female employee on the low end of the workplace ladder and be more likely to lead to unnecessary litigation.

As a managerial exercise for yourself, try to think of why the employer would have required the smock. Why not require it for all employees if they really are all the same? What is the difference between males wearing them and females wearing them? Once you come up with a reason, ask yourself if it makes sense. Chances are, it doesn't. For instance, if the smock was required to keep the employees' clothes clean, then why not protect the clothing of males also?

Being able to see and really understand the smock case goes a long way toward being able to truly grasp the big picture of how gender discrimination works and how you can think about avoiding liability for it in the workplace when faced with your own situations as a manager.

A gender-based grooming policy which subjects one gender to different conditions of employment would also not be allowed, for instance, where the scant uniform the female lobby attendant was required to wear made her the object of lewd comments and sexual propositions from male entrants, or where a manager required female employees to wear skirts when the "head honcho" visited, because he "liked to look at legs." It is not a defense for an employer to argue that the employee knew about the grooming code when he or she came into the workplace. If the code is illegal, it is illegal, period. Agreeing to it makes it no less so, particularly given the unequal bargaining positions of the employer and employee.

An interesting case arose recently when Harrah's Casino in Reno, Nevada, instituted a new dress code that required female employees to wear makeup. The "Personal Best" program "specified the makeup as foundation or powder, blush, lipstick and mascara, applied precisely the same way every day to match a photograph held by the supervisor." The only requirement for men was that they not wear makeup of any kind and keep their hair and nails trimmed. Darlene Jespersen, a bartender who had been employed by the casino for

21 years and had an excellent work history, was "highly offended she had to doll herself up to look like a hooker." She was terminated for failing to comply with the policy. Jespersen argued that the cosmetics cost hundreds of dollars per year and took a good deal of time to apply and therefore created an unequal burden on female employees. In December 2004, the Ninth Circuit Court of Appeals upheld the policy, saying "there is no evidence in the record in support of [Jespersen's] contention that cosmetics can cost hundreds of dollars per year and that applying them requires a significant investment of time."

Can you reconcile the court's position with that of the U.S. Supreme Court in the *Hopkins* decision, which held that gender stereotyping violated Title VII? Remember that the Court found gender discrimination when, among other things, Hopkins was told she must "walk more femininely, talk more femininely, dress more femininely, wear make-up, have her hair styled and wear jewelry." The Ninth Circuit said its decision did not run afoul of *Hopkins* because *Hopkins* did not address the specific question of whether an employer can impose sex-differentiated appearance and grooming standards on its male and female employees (presumably because the more direct issue before the Court was Hopkins' assertive/aggressive behavior, which her employers used as a large part of their rejection of her as a partner). The full Ninth Circuit reheard the case again *en banc* (that is, with the entire court sitting rather than the usual 3-judge panel) on June 22, 2005, what do you think the court decided?

Customer or Employee Preferences

Frequently an employer uses gender as a basis for assigning work because of the preference of customers, clients, or other employees. Often the work to which one gender is not privy presents a loss of valuable revenue or a professionally beneficial opportunity for that employee. Such considerations may be formidable in client-driven businesses, such as law, brokerages, accounting, sales, and other professions. If a customer does not wish to have a female audit his or her books, can her accounting firm legally refuse to let her service the client? Is an employer in violation of Title VII if the employer does not permit an employee of a certain gender to deal with a customer because the customer does not wish to deal with someone of that gender and the employee is thereby denied valuable work experience or earning potential? What if male employees on a construction site don't want a female to work with them?

The answer is yes, the employer is in violation of Title VII and can be held liable to the employee for gender discrimination. Customer preference is *not* a legitimate and protected reason to treat otherwise-qualified employees differently based on gender.

Hooters is an Atlanta-based restaurant chain known for its buffalo wings and scantily clad (very short shorts and T-shirts tied around the middle, revealing a bare midriff), generally well-endowed, female servers. It came to light that Hooters refuses to hire males as servers. The conventional wisdom is that despite Hooters' claims that it is a family restaurant and "Hooters" refers to its owl logo, "Hooters" is a not-so-subtle reference to female breasts, and the servers are as, or more, important than the food it serves. This is further supported by the servers' outfits, the fact that Hooters is known for its "Hooters' Girls," complete with pin-up calendars and a 10-page *Playboy* magazine spread, and its "more than a mouthful" logo, which few believe refers to chicken wings or owls.

Hooters alleges that customers want only female servers. In 1996, Hooters launched a "no to male servers" billboard campaign featuring husky male servers clad in the

Hooters' attire. Today, Hooters' serving staff is still female, despite the lawsuits brought by EEOC and class action suits by males in Chicago and Maryland. Hooters has chosen to settle cases rather than litigate them, which, of course, it has the right to do as long as it is willing to foot the bill.

Scenario 2

The Hooters situation is the basis for opening scenario 2. Not a semester goes by that one of our students doesn't ask how Hooters can "get away with" hiring only female servers. The short answer is, it can't. At least not legally, in its present incarnation. Hooters has the right to use gender as a BFOQ to protect its females-only server policy if it can show that the gender of its servers is a bona fide occupational qualification reasonably necessary to the particular job done by the servers. For instance, the BFOQ would be defensible if Hooters declared itself to be in the business of entertainment by use of its servers—rather like Playboy Club bunnies. It has chosen, instead, to classify itself as a family restaurant. This means either gender can serve its food and its female-only server policy violates Title VII's prohibition against gender discrimination. The way Hooters "gets away" with hiring only female servers is to settle lawsuits brought by males challenging its exclusionary policy. Obviously, (1) Hooters does not want to classify itself as entertainment and allow the BFOQ defense, and (2) Hooters has concluded that it is worth more to them to keep its female-only server policy and settle claims by males than to change its policy. Again, that approach is something it has every right to take as long as it is willing to foot the bill for that choice.

This issue of customer preference may cause special problems now that the Civil Rights Act of 1991 applies Title VII to U.S. citizens employed by American-owned or controlled companies doing business outside the United States. An employer in a country whose mores may not permit women to deal professionally with men must still comply with Title VII unless doing so would cause the company to actually violate the law of the country in which the business is located.

Logistical Considerations

In some workplaces, males and females working together can present logistical challenges. For instance, female sports reporters going into male athletes' locker rooms, a female firefighter sleeping at a fire station, or lack of bathrooms at a construction site. This issue arose in the context of construction workers in the case below. Note how the employer can take little for granted in making workplace decisions, as even the seemingly smallest decisions can be the basis of a time-consuming and expensive lawsuit.

Lynch v. Freeman *817 F.2d 380 (6th Cir. 1987)*

A female carpenter's apprentice sued her employer for gender discrimination, alleging the failure to furnish adequate sanitary toilet facilities at her worksite. The court found the unsanitary facilities violated Title VII.

Lively, J.

The portable toilets were dirty, often had no toilet paper or paper that was soiled, and were not equipped with running water or sanitary napkins. In addition, those designated for women had no locks or bolts on the doors and one of them had a hole punched in the side.

To avoid using the toilets, Lynch began holding her urine until she left work. Within three days after starting work she experienced pain and was advised that the practice she had adopted, as well as using contaminated toilet paper, frequently caused bladder infections.

The powerhouse, which had large, clean, fully equipped restrooms, was off limits to construction workers. Lynch testified that some of the men she worked with used them regularly and were not disciplined. In late December 1979 or early January 1980, knowing the restrooms were off limits, Lynch began using the powerhouse restrooms occasionally, after her doctor diagnosed her condition as cystitis, a type of urinary infection. When the infection returned in February, Lynch began using a restroom in the powerhouse regularly and she had no further urinary tract infections. Lynch was eventually fired for insubordination in using the powerhouse toilet.

The lower court found that the toilets were poorly maintained. The cleaning was accomplished by pumping out the sewage. This process often left the toilets messy, with human feces on the floors, walls, and seats. The contractors were to scrub down the toilets afterwards, but it appears they often failed to do so. Paper covers were not provided, and the toilet paper, if any, was sometimes wet and/or soiled with urine. No running water for washing one's hands was available near the toilets, although a chemical hand cleaner could be checked out from the "gang-boxes."

The lower court found it credible that most women were inhibited from using the toilets. Further, the inhibitions described were not personal peculiarities, but that Lynch and others reasonably believed that the toilets could endanger their health. Lynch introduced credible medical expert testimony to demonstrate that women are more vulnerable to urinary tract infections than are men.

On the basis of that evidence, the court concluded that all increased danger of urinary tract infections may be linked to the practice of females holding their urine and to the use of toilets under the circumstances where the female's bacteria-contaminated hands came into contact with her external genitalia or where a female's perineal area comes into direct contact with bacteria-contaminated surfaces.

Few concerns are more pressing to anyone than those related to personal health. A prima facie case of disparate impact is established when a plaintiff shows that the facially neutral practice has a significantly discriminatory impact. Any employment practice that adversely affects the health of female employees while leaving male employees unaffected has a significantly discriminatory impact. The burden then shifts to the employer to justify the practice which resulted in this discriminatory impact by showing business necessity; that is, that the practice of furnishing unsanitary toilet facilities at the work site substantially promotes the proficient operation of business.

Title VII is remedial legislation, which must be construed liberally to achieve its purpose of eliminating discrimination from the workplace. Although Lynch was discharged for violating a rule, she did so in order to avoid the continued risk to her health which would have resulted from obeying the rule. The employer created an unacceptable situation in which Lynch and other female construction workers were required to choose between submitting to a discriminatory health hazard or risking termination for disobeying a company rule. Anatomical differences between men and women are "immutable characteristics," just as race, color, and national origin are immutable characteristics. When it is shown that employment practices place a heavier burden on minority employees than on members of the majority, and this burden relates to characteristics which identify them as members of the protected group, the requirements of a Title VII disparate impact case are satisfied. REVERSED and REMANDED.

Case Questions

1. Are you surprised by this outcome? Why or why not?

2. Does the outcome make sense to you? Explain.

3. What would you have done if you were the employer in this situation?

Employers may not forgo hiring those of a certain gender because of logistical issues unless it involves an unreasonable financial burden—usually a matter difficult for an employer to prove. These challenges must be resolved in a way that does not discriminate against the employee based on gender. Generally it is not exceedingly difficult, although it may take thinking about the workplace in a different way. In one situation the employer said he could not hire females because there was only one restroom on the premises. However, if there is no state sanitation or building code prohibiting it, there is no requirement that males and females use separate restrooms as long as privacy is maintained.

Equal Pay and Comparable Worth

> (1) No employer . . . shall discriminate between employees on the basis of sex by paying wages to employees . . . at a rate less than the rate at which he pays wages to employees of the opposite sex . . . for equal work on jobs the performance of which requires equal skill, effort, and responsibility, and which are performed under similar working conditions, except where such payment is made pursuant to (i) a seniority system; (ii) a merit system; (iii) a system which measures earnings by quantity or quality of production; or (iv) a differential based on any other factor other than sex. . . . Equal Pay Act, 29 U.S.C.A §206(d).

Despite the statute quoted above, according to wage data, women earn on average 77 cents for every dollar earned by men. This is up from 60 cents in 1979. Younger women make 80 cents for every dollar a man makes in the same age group. At the rate the gender wage gap is closing, research shows that women's salaries will not be equal until the year 2050. A 2003 General Accounting Office report found that the gender wage gap is not because of less education or experience or because women get on a "mommy track" or choose low-paying professions. Instead, they concluded that discrimination is the biggest factor in the wage gap between genders. While Title VII prohibits discrimination in employment including in the area of compensation, even before Title VII there was legislation protecting employees against discrimination in compensation solely on the basis of gender. The year before Title VII was passed, the Equal Pay Act (EPA), actually part of the Fair Labor Standards Act (FLSA) governing wages and hours in the workplace, became law.

Under the act, employers subject to the minimum wage provisions of the FLSA may not use gender as a basis for paying lower wages to an employee for equal work "on jobs the performance of which requires equal skill, effort, and responsibility, and which are performed under similar working conditions." There are exceptions. Differences in wages are permitted if based on seniority or merit systems, on systems that measure earnings by quantity or quality of production, or on a differential based on "any other factor other than [gender]."

To comply with the Equal Pay Act, the employer may not reduce the wage rate of the higher-paid employees. According to Bureau of Labor Statistics figures, the pay gap that was supposed to be closed by the legislation actually widened at least nine times from one year to the next since passage of the EPA.

The EPA overlaps with Title VII's general prohibition against discrimination in employment on the basis of gender. Title VII's Bennett Amendment was passed so that the exceptions permitted by the EPA would also be recognized by Title VII. The EPA also has a longer statute of limitations (two years from the time of the alleged violation, which may be raised to three years for willful violations, rather than 180 days under Title VII). Perhaps due to the fact that Title VII was passed very soon after the EPA, and more generally proscribed discrimination in employment, there has been less activity under the EPA than under Title VII. However, the prohibitions on pay discrimination should be considered no less important. (See Exhibit 6.13.)

A national study undertaken by the AFL-CIO and the Institute for Women's Policy Research reveals very interesting insights into the issue of pay equality among American workers. Almost two-thirds of *all* working women responded to the survey. When looking at the findings and thinking about the issue of wage equality, keep in mind that the women responding provided half or more of their families' incomes.

- Ninety-four percent of working women described equal pay as "very important"; two of every five cited pay as the biggest problem women face at work.

- Working families lose $200 billion of income annually to the wage gap—an average yearly loss of more than $4,000 for each working woman's family because of unequal pay, even after accounting for differences in education, age, location, and the number of hours worked.

- If married women were paid the same as comparable men, their family income would rise by nearly 6 percent, and their families' poverty rates would fall from 2.1 percent to 0.8 percent.

- If single working mothers earned as much as comparable men, their family incomes would increase by nearly 17 percent, and their poverty rates would be cut in half, from 25.3 percent to 12.6 percent.

- If single women earned as much as comparable men, their incomes would rise by 13.4 percent and their poverty rates would be reduced from 6.3 percent to 1 percent.

- Working families in Ohio, Michigan, Vermont, Indiana, Illinois, Montana, Wisconsin, and Alabama pay the heaviest price for unequal pay to working women, losing an average of roughly $5,000 in family income each year.

- Family income losses due to unequal pay for women range from $326 million in Alaska to $21.8 billion in California.

- Women who work full-time are paid the least, compared with men, in Indiana, Louisiana, Michigan, Montana, North Dakota, Wisconsin, and Wyoming, where women earn less than 70 percent of men's weekly earnings.

- Women of color fare especially poorly in Louisiana, Montana, Nebraska, Oregon, Rhode Island, Utah, Wisconsin, and Wyoming, earning less than 60 percent of what men earn.

- Even where women fare best compared with men—in Arizona, California, Florida, Hawaii, Massachusetts, New York, and Rhode Island—women earn little more than 80 percent as much as men.

- Women earn the most in comparison to men—97 percent—in Washington, DC, but the primary reason women appear to fare so well is the very low wages of minority men.

- For women of color, the gender pay gap is smallest in Washington, DC, Hawaii, Florida, New York, and Tennessee, where they earn more than 70 percent of what men overall in those states earn.

- The 25.6 million women who work in predominantly female jobs lose an average of $3,446 each per year; the 4 million men who work in predominantly female occupations lose an average of $6,259 each per year.

Sources: 1999 AFL-CIO and the Institute for Women's Policy Research (IWPR).

Pollis v. the New School for Social Research   *132 F.3d 115 (2nd Cir. 1997)*

A professor sued her college for, among other things, willful violation of the Equal Pay Act. The jury held in her favor, and the college appealed. The Court of Appeals held that the fact that the professor had complained about discrepancies between her salary and salaries of male professors on many occasions and the college did not rectify the situation was sufficient to show reckless or willful violation of the Equal Pay Act by the college.

Leval, J.

The New School for Social Research ("New School") appeals the judgment of the District Court entered pursuant to jury verdict, awarding damages to Dr. Adamantia Pollis, a retired professor of political science. Among other things, the New School contests the sufficiency of evidence in support of the jury's finding of willfulness, with respect to its violation of the Equal Pay Act, in paying Pollis less than comparable male faculty members. We affirm the jury's finding that the New School's violation of the Equal Pay Act was willful or reckless.

Pollis was hired as a professor of political science at the Graduate Faculty of the New School in 1964. She was granted tenure in 1966, and promoted to full professor in 1976. During her employment at the New School, she twice served as chair of the political science department. Her primary areas of specialty were human rights and Greek politics. According to evidence Pollis submitted at trial, during a 19-year period, her salary was lower than the salaries of five male teachers who were comparable to her.

The Equal Pay Act is violated if an employer whose employees are subject to the Fair Labor Standards Act pays wages to an employee "at a rate less than the rate at which he pays wages to employees of the opposite sex . . . for equal work on jobs the performance of which requires equal skill, effort, and responsibility, and which are performed under similar working conditions. . . ." 29 U.S.C. § 206(d). A violation occurs when an employer pays lower wages to an employee of one gender than to substantially equivalent employees of the opposite gender in similar circumstances. A plaintiff need not prove that the pay disparity was motivated by an intention to discriminate on the basis of gender. The New School contends that there is insufficient evidence to support

the jury's finding that the New School willfully violated the Equal Pay Act.

A defendant's violation of the Equal Pay Act is willful or reckless if "the employer either knew or showed reckless disregard for the matter of whether its conduct was prohibited by the statute." A plaintiff need not show that an employer acted with intent to discriminate or in bad faith. Pollis testified that on multiple occasions over several years, she complained to New School decision-makers about discrepancies between her salary and the salaries of male professors. Responses she received indicated an awareness on the part of the administration that her salary level was below that of comparable male teachers. Nonetheless, the school continued to pay Pollis less than comparable male teachers.

This evidence—that the New School knew that Pollis was paid less than comparable males, but did not rectify the situation—is sufficient to support the jury's finding of reckless or willful violation of the Equal Pay Act. Therefore, compensatory damages for the Equal Pay Act violation should have been calculated by reference to the three-year limitations period for willful violations, and the resulting compensatory award should be doubled pursuant to the Fair Labor Standards Act's liquidated damages provision. AFFIRMED IN PART, VACATED IN PART, and REMANDED.

Case Questions

1. What do you think accounted for the difference in Pollis' salary?

2. If you were the department chair responsible for such things, how would you have avoided this situation?

3. Why do you think the school did not rectify the situation even after the salary differences became clear?

**comparable
worth**
A Title VII
action for pay
discrimination
based on gen-
der, in which
jobs held mostly
by women are
compared with
comparable jobs
held mostly by
men in regard to
pay to deter-
mine if there is
gender discrimi-
nation.

Under the EPA it is the content of the job, not the job title or description, that controls the comparison of whether the jobs are substantially the same. For instance, if a hospital's male "orderlies" and female "aides" perform substantially the same job, they should receive the same pay, despite the difference in job titles.

In *County of Washington* v. *Gunther*[2] the Court held that Title VII's Bennett Amendment only incorporated the four EPA exceptions into Title VII, not the "substantially equal" requirement; therefore, the jobs compared in a Title VII unequal pay action need not be substantially equal. Thus, under Title VII, employees have attempted to bring **comparable worth** cases in which higher-paid predominantly male jobs with similar value to the employer are compared in order to challenge lower wage rates for jobs held mostly by women ("pink-collar jobs"). Federal courts have, however, generally rejected Title VII claims based on comparable worth. Take a look at the historic *AFSCME* case, below, to see some of the considerations involved. *AFSCME* was the first significant statewide case to challenge gender-based pay differences on the basis of the comparable worth theory.

[2] 452 U.S. 161 (1981).

American Federation of State, County, and Municipal Employees, AFL-CIO (AFSCME) v. State of Washington
770 F.2d 1401 (9th Cir. 1985)

The state of Washington conducted studies of prevailing market rates for jobs and wages in order to determine the wages for various state jobs. Under market rates, female-dominated jobs were paid lower wages than male-dominated jobs. The state then compared jobs for comparable worth and after finding that female-dominated job salaries were generally about 20 percent less than wages in male-dominated jobs, legislated that it would begin basing its wages on comparable worth rather than the market rate, over a 10-year period. State employees wanted the scheme to go into effect immediately, and a class of state employees in job categories at least 70 percent female brought a Title VII suit against the state alleging it was a violation of Title VII for the state to know of the wage differences and not remedy the situation immediately. The lower court held for the employees and the state appealed. The court of appeals held that the state's decision to base compensation on the competitive market rather than on a theory of comparable worth did not establish its liability under the disparate impact analysis of Title VII, and the state's participation in a market system did not allow an inference of discriminatory motive in order to establish its liability under a disparate treatment theory, since the state did not create the market disparity and was not shown to have been motivated by illegal gender-based considerations in setting its salaries. Therefore, the employees did not prove liability under Title VII, and the lower court decision was reversed. Note that since the jobs being compared were not the "same or substantially the same," as required by the Equal Pay Act, the employees were constrained to bring suit under Title VII.

Kennedy, J.

It is evident from the legislative history of the Equal Pay Act that Congress, after explicit consideration, rejected proposals that would have prohibited lower wages for comparable work, as contrasted with equal work. In the instant case, the district court found a violation of Title VII, premised upon both the disparate impact and the disparate treatment theories of discrimination.

AFSCME's disparate impact argument is based on the contention that the State of Washington's practice of taking prevailing market rates into account in setting wages has an adverse impact on women, who, historically, have received lower wages than men in the labor market. Disparate impact analysis is confined to cases that challenge a specific, clearly delineated employment practice applied at a single point in the job selection process.

The instant case does not involve an employment practice that yields to disparate impact analysis. The decision to base compensation on the competitive market, rather than on a theory of comparable worth, involves the assessment of a number of complex factors not easily ascertainable, an assessment too multifaceted to be appropriate for disparate impact analysis. Unlike a specific, clearly delineated employment policy contemplated by precedent such as those requiring a height and weight requirement or a certain score on an exam, the compensation system in question resulted from surveys, agency hearings, administrative recommendations, budget proposals, executive actions, and legislative enactments. A compensation system that is responsive to supply and demand and other market forces is not the type of single practice that suffices to support a claim under disparate impact theory. Such cases are controlled by disparate treatment analysis. Under these principles and precedents, we must reverse the district court's determination of liability under the disparate impact theory of discrimination.

Under the disparate treatment theory, our review of the record indicates failure by AFSCME to establish the requisite element of intent by either circumstantial or direct evidence.

AFSCME contends discriminatory motive may be inferred from the Willis study, which finds the State's practice of setting salaries in reliance on market rates creates a sex-based wage disparity for jobs deemed of comparable worth. AFSCME argues from the study that the market reflects a historical pattern of lower wages to employees in positions staffed predominantly by women, and it contends the State of Washington perpetuates that disparity, in violation of Title VII, by using market rates in the compensation system. The inference of discriminatory motive which AFSCME seeks to draw from the State's participation in the market system fails, as the State did not create the market

disparity and has not been shown to have been motivated by impermissible sex-based considerations in setting salaries.

The requirement of intent is linked at least in part to culpability. That concept would be undermined if we were to hold that payment of wages according to prevailing rates in the public and private sectors is an act that, in itself, supports the inference of a purpose to discriminate. Neither law nor logic deems the free market system a suspect enterprise. Economic reality is that the value of a particular job to an employer is but one factor influencing the rate of compensation for that job. Other considerations may include the availability of workers willing to do the job and the effectiveness of collective bargaining in a particular industry. Employers may be constrained by market forces to set salaries under prevailing wage rates for different job classifications. We find nothing in the language of Title VII or its legislative history to indicate Congress intended to abrogate fundamental economic principles such as the laws of supply and demand or to prevent employers from competing in the labor market. While the Washington legislature may have the discretion to enact a comparable worth plan if it chooses to do so, Title VII does not obligate it to eliminate an economic inequality that it did not create. Title VII was enacted to ensure equal opportunity in employment to covered individuals, and the State of Washington is not charged here with barring access to particular job classifications on the basis of sex.

We have recognized that in certain cases an inference of intent may be drawn from statistical evidence. We have admonished, however, that statistics must be relied on with caution. Though the comparability of wage rates in dissimilar jobs may be relevant to a determination of discriminatory animus, job evaluation studies and comparable worth statistics alone are insufficient to establish the requisite inference of discriminatory motive critical to the disparate treatment theory. The weight to be accorded such statistics is determined by the existence of independent corroborative evidence of discrimination. We conclude the independent evidence of discrimination presented by AFSCME is insufficient to support an inference of the requisite discriminatory motive under the disparate treatment theory.

AFSCME offered proof of isolated incidents of sex segregation as evidence of a history of sex-based wage discrimination. The evidence consists of "help wanted" advertisements restricting various jobs to members of a particular sex. These advertisements were often placed in separate "help wanted—male" and "help wanted—female" columns in state newspapers between 1960 and 1973, though most were discontinued when Title VII became applicable to the states in 1972. At trial, AFSCME called expert witnesses to testify that a causal relationship exists between sex segregation practices and sex-based wage discrimination, and that the effects of sex segregation practices may persist even after the practices are discontinued. However, none of the individually named plaintiffs in the action ever testified regarding specific incidents of discrimination. The isolated incidents alleged by AFSCME are insufficient to corroborate the results of the Willis study and do not justify an inference of discriminatory motive by the State in the setting of salaries for its system as a whole. Given the scope of the alleged intentional act, and given the attempt to show the core principle of the State's market-based compensation system was adopted or maintained with a discriminatory purpose, more is required to support the finding of liability than these isolated acts, which had only an indirect relation to the compensation principle itself.

We also reject AFSCME's contention that, having commissioned the Willis study, the State of Washington was committed to implement a new system of compensation based on comparable worth as defined by the study. Whether comparable worth is a feasible approach to employee compensation is a matter of debate. Assuming, however, that like other job evaluation studies it may be useful as a diagnostic tool, we reject a rule that would penalize rather than commend employers for their effort and innovation in undertaking such a study. The results of comparable worth studies will vary depending on the number and types of factors measured and the maximum number of points allotted to each factor. A study that indicates a particular wage structure might be more equitable should not categorically bind the employer who commissioned it. The employer should also be able to take into account market conditions, bargaining demands, and the possibility that another study will yield different results.

We hold there was a failure to establish a violation of Title VII under the disparate treatment theory of discrimination, and reverse the district court on this aspect of the case as well. The State of Washington's initial reliance on a free market system in which employees in male-dominated jobs are compensated at a higher rate than employees in dissimilar female-dominated jobs is not in and of itself a violation of Title VII, notwithstanding that the Willis study deemed the positions of comparable worth. Absent a showing of discriminatory motive, which has not been made here, the law does not permit the federal courts to interfere in the market-based system for the compensation of Washington's employees. REVERSED.

Case Questions

1. Do you think that using comparable worth is an effective way to determine salaries?
2. Why do you think male-dominated jobs tend to pay less than female-dominated jobs, even if both have virtually the same value to the employer?
3. What would you do to avoid this situation?

Prompted by the flap over pay disparities in women's soccer in January 2000, there was a flurry of activity surrounding the issue of gender-based wage differences. Twenty members of the U.S. Women's Soccer Team refused to play in an Australian tournament and demanded pay equal to that of the U.S. Men's Soccer Team. The women were scheduled to be paid $3,150 per month for the most experienced player and about $250 per game. Men were to receive $5,000 per month and an additional $2,000 for the 18 players going to Australia. In the wake of the incident, at least two pieces of legislation were introduced into Congress (the Fair Pay Act and the stronger Fair Paycheck Act) to amend the Fair Labor Standards Act to address the issue of gender-based wage disparities. In February 2000, President Clinton, accompanied by women's soccer player Michelle Akers, announced that he was seeking an Equal Pay Initiative of $27 million to close the gap between men's and women's pay, of which

$10 million would be allocated to the EEOC to deal with the issue of gender-based wage violations. However, nothing much came of the flurry of activity and the laws were not enacted by Congress.

Under existing law, employers should be aware of any pay differentials between specific males and females, as well as between jobs that are held primarily by males and those held primarily by females. Employers should perform periodic audits to ensure that they are not operating under gender-based pay differentials, which may lead to preventable wage discrimination litigation against the employer.

GENDER AS A BFOQ

Title VII permits gender to be used as a bona fide occupational qualification (BFOQ) under certain limited circumstances. Under the EEOC guidelines, a BFOQ may be used when there is a legitimate need for authenticity such as for the part of a female in a theater or film production. More often than not, when employers have attempted to use BFOQ as a defense to gender discrimination, courts have found the defense inapplicable. As the case below demonstrates, it is not always females who are kept out of the workplace because of gender.

EEOC v. Audrey Sedita, d/b/a Women's Workout World
755 F. Supp. 808 (N. Dist. Ill. E.D. 1991)

The employer, Women's Workout World (WWW), refused to hire males as managers, assistant managers, or instructors in the employer's exercise studio. Employer argued that being a female was reasonably necessary for the particular business. The court did not agree.

Williams, J.

The employer asserts that the jobs at issue require a substantial amount of physical contact with members' bodies and that they are exposed to nudity in the club locker room, shower, and bathroom, during orientation sessions when they show club facilities to new members. They argue that it would be impossible for WWW to reassign job duties in order to avoid intruding on members' privacy interests, since the conduct which infringes on privacy interests amounts to the essence of the jobs in question.

EEOC argues that the essence of the jobs in question does not require employees to intimately touch health club members, or force employees to be exposed to nudity of members. They suggested WWW could hire male

employees by changing the duties of the jobs in question, such as hiring females to assist clients who objected to being touched by males, posting a schedule to inform clients of when male employees would be on duty, or letting clients take themselves through the locker rooms.

The BFOQ exception is meant to be an extremely narrow exception to the general prohibition of discrimination on the basis of gender. Hence, a defendant asserting a BFOQ defense has a heavy burden in terms of justifying his employment practice. An employer asserting a privacy-based BFOQ defense must satisfy a three-part test. First, the employer must assert a factual basis for believing that hiring any members of one gender would undermine the business operation. Second, the employer must prove that the customer's privacy interest is entitled to protection under the law, and third, that no reasonable alternatives exist to protect those interests other than the gender-based hiring policy.

WWW contends a factual basis for their hiring policy exists because their clients have consciously chosen to join an all-female health club. They present the owner's testimony that members have, in the past, been disturbed by the presence of males in the club.

We find that WWW failed to prove either that a factual basis exists for their discriminatory hiring policies, or that no reasonable alternatives exist to protect their customers' privacy interests other than sex-based hiring.

A defendant in a privacy rights case may satisfy its burden of proving a factual basis for sex-based hiring policies by showing that the clients or guests of a business would not consent to service of the opposite gender and would stop patronizing the business if members of the opposite gender were allowed to perform the service. This, WWW has failed to do. Also, WWW has previously hired males as "class givers," suggesting that there is no basis in the law for their present refusal to hire men. The EEOC's evidence of feasibility exists in the nation's other health clubs, which hire both genders, and allow members to be served both by assistants of their own gender and by members of the opposite gender.

The purpose of WWW's business operation is to provide individualized fitness and exercise instruction to the club's women members. Hence, WWW must prove that they cannot achieve their business purpose without engaging in single-gender hiring. In response to EEOC's alternatives, WWW produced nothing more than the owner's assertions that the alternatives were not feasible because of the views of her clientele, and the difficulties of accommodating men in the health club. This is not strong enough to prove that no alternatives were feasible. WWW needed to provide evidence to prove their argument such as data on costs, studies on the feasibility of changing their present operation, or projections on the impact of such changes in terms of lost profits.

The motion for PARTIAL SUMMARY JUDGMENT for EEOC is GRANTED.

Case Questions

1. Do you agree with the court's decision? Why or why not? Do you think the outcome would have been the same if the genders were reversed and females were prevented from working at the club?

2. If you were the employer in this case, what would you do?

3. Do you think Title VII was made to address this type of situation, that is, where a private commercial enterprise wishes to have a particular clientele served a particular way? Explain.

PREGNANCY DISCRIMINATION

> *It didn't bother me at all that she was pregnant. But whether or not she was going to be able to spend the time to actually perform the job and to be a mom and do all that, yeah, we factored it in, sure. We were concerned.*

This statement by Robert DiFazio, head of Smith-Barney's equities division regarding why someone other than the pregnant applicant was promoted to head the over-the-counter sales desk, is typical of many employers' views about pregnant employees. The employee here filed a claim and the arbitration panel said "it is hard to imagine sentiments more universally regarded as symbolic of illegal gender bias" and ruled the remarks constituted evidence of gender discrimination. A study in the *Journal of Personality and Social Psychology* found that while "business women" were rated similar in competence to "business men" or "millionaires," women who became mothers were rated as similar in competence to the "elderly," "blind," "retarded," or "disabled."

The EEOC recently reported that there has been at least a 182 percent increase in the filing of pregnancy discrimination charges over the past 10 years. While the EEOC says the most common scenario in pregnancy discrimination claims is termination of the pregnant employee (like the car dealer who fired the employee for fear she'd have morning sickness and throw up in the vehicles), employers take all kinds of measures. Wal-Mart rejected pregnant job applicants, thousands of female Verizon Wireless employees lost benefits during maternity leave, Delta Airlines fired one pregnant ramp attendant and forced another to take unpaid leave, a producer on Spelling Entertainment's *Melrose Place* fired pregnant actress Hunter Tylo on the grounds that she was "unable to play the role of a seductress," a Dallas attorney at the law firm of Jenkins & Gilchrist claimed she was constructively discharged due to her pregnancy, and a New York City police commander claims she was passed over because of her pregnancies, as does the first woman promoted within the Annapolis Fire Department and the education reporter for television station WLOX in Biloxi.

The Supreme Court determined in *General Electric Co.* v. *Gilbert*[3] that discrimination on the basis of pregnancy was not gender discrimination under Title VII. Two years later Congress passed the Pregnancy Discrimination Act (PDA) amending Title VII's definitions to include discrimination on the basis of pregnancy. Despite the fact that women comprise nearly 50 percent of the workforce, and statistics show that about 75 percent of those of childbearing age will have children sometime during their work life, pregnancy discrimination is still a serious workplace concern.

Many employers have maternity leave policies to address this more-than-likely event, but others, particularly smaller employers, do not. Based on traditional notions about the inappropriateness of women in the workplace in general, or pregnant women in particular, some employers are actually hostile to pregnant employees and run the very real risk of being sued for pregnancy discrimination.

The PDA prohibits an employer from using pregnancy, childbirth, or related medical conditions as the basis for treating an employee differently than any other employee with a short-term disability if that employee can perform the job. This is why in opening scenario 3, it is illegal for the employer to evaluate the pregnant employee differently than it would any other. Employers illegally treat employees differently in many ways. For instance, the employer:

Scenario

- Refuses to hire pregnant applicants.
- Terminates an employee on discovering the employee's pregnancy.
- Does not provide benefits to pregnant employees on an equal basis with short-term disabilities of other employees.
- Refuses to allow a pregnant employee to continue to work even though the employee wishes to do so and is physically able to do so.
- Does not provide the employee with lighter duty if needed, when such accommodations are made for employees with other short-term disabilities.

[3] 429 U.S. 125 (1976).

- Eliminates the pregnant employee by moving her to a new job title with the same pay, then eliminates the position in a job restructuring or a reduction in force.
- Evaluates the employee as not having performed as well or as much as other employees when the basis for the evaluation is the employer's own refusal or hesitation to assign equal work to the employee because the employee is pregnant and the employer feels the need to "lighten" the employee's load, though the employee has not requested it.
- Does not permit the pregnant employee to be a part of the normal circle of office culture so she becomes less aware of matters of importance to the office or current projects, resulting in more likelihood that the employee will not be able effectively to compete with those still within the circle.

Zaken v. Boerer *964 F.2d 1319 (2nd Cir. 1992)*

Employee's performance was above average until employer found out employee was pregnant, at which time she was terminated. Court held for employee.

Cardamone, J.

Defendant, Bonnie Boerer, was the chief executive officer of Bonnie Boerer & Company and the owner of 98 percent of its stock. Boerer had owned the now-defunct company since 1983. Boerer designed clothing which was then manufactured by her Hong Kong corporation and sold through her New York City showroom where plaintiff, Zaken was employed. Boerer controlled almost every aspect of her business and had ultimate decision-making power with respect to all corporate activities including personnel decisions. Boerer made the final decision to terminate Zaken.

Zaken was hired in September 1988 as a sales manager of the company's large size clothing division in their New York office. When Zaken was hired, she was brought on at a salary of $46,000 per year and promised a bonus at the end of the year (1988). At the time she was hired, Zaken did not realize that she was replacing Robin Weinberg, who had been discharged during her fifth month of pregnancy.

Shortly after beginning employment in September, Zaken learned that she was pregnant and told this to her supervisor in October. Zaken planned to work as long as possible before the baby was born, then return as soon as possible after delivery. When Zaken told her supervisor she was pregnant, he told her that she should not tell Boerer or anyone else at the company she was pregnant, and suggested it would be best if he broke the news to Boerer at a later time.

At the end of December 1988, Boerer returned to her New York office from the Orient where she had been overseeing her product line since Zaken was hired in September. It was then that Boerer learned of Zaken's pregnancy.

Zaken was not given her bonus at the end of 1988. When Zaken asked why, she was told by her supervisor that Boerer had decided Zaken was "not qualified" for her sales position. Zaken testified that she told her supervisor then that she believed Boerer was discriminating against her because of her pregnancy.

A month later, on January 23, 1989, Zaken's supervisor told Zaken that Boerer had decided to terminate Zaken, who was now five months pregnant. When Zaken asked why she was being fired, her supervisor told her that Boerer had decided Zaken was "not qualified" as a sales manager. The supervisor testified that he also told Zaken that he had fought to convince Boerer not to fire Zaken. In Zaken's subsequent recommendation letter, the supervisor stated that Zaken's "administrative skills, attention to detail, work ethics and ability to communicate were outstanding."

Zaken brought suit alleging that she was denied a bonus and her employment was terminated because she was pregnant, in violation of Title VII of the Civil Rights Act of 1964, as amended, and New York's Human Rights Law. At the trial, Zaken's predecessor, Weinberg, testified that she had also been discharged by Boerer when she was five months pregnant after working for Boerer for a little over a year.

She testified that at the time she was terminated, she had a very good sales record and before becoming pregnant, had received very positive comments from Boerer. Weinberg had received a bonus after working for Boerer for only five months, and a raise after eight months. After Boerer discovered she was pregnant, Weinberg testified, Boerer became cold and hostile and terminated Weinberg a few months later. Weinberg also testified that, at the time of her hiring interview, Boerer asked whether Weinberg planned to have children and told Weinberg she hoped Weinberg would not become pregnant while Weinberg was employed by Boerer's company.

Boerer insisted in her testimony that she fired Zaken because Zaken was not qualified to fill the sales manager position and Weinberg because of excessive absenteeism, low productivity and dishonesty. Boerer also testified that she employed about 30 people in her New York showroom, of whom 24 were women and 5 had become pregnant during their employment without losing their jobs.

Plaintiff need not show pregnancy was the primary reason for defendant's decision to discharge plaintiff and deny her a bonus, but only that it was a factor relied upon by defendant. Moreover, the trial court's statement could have been interpreted to require that pregnancy had to be the factor that "prompted" the defendant to deny plaintiff a bonus and terminate her employment, rather than simply a factor that made a difference in these decisions.

The jury should have been instructed that if it found Zaken had demonstrated by a preponderance of the evidence that her pregnancy played a part in Boerer's decision, then it should find for Zaken unless Boerer demonstrated by a preponderance of the evidence that the same decision would have been made even if pregnancy would not have been one of the factors contributing to it. REVERSED and REMANDED.

Case Questions

1. Point out some of the things that you think Boerer and the supervisor should not have done in this case. How would you have handled it differently?

2. Can you think of reasons why Boerer may have terminated pregnant employees, if she did as Zaken alleged?

3. Do you think that the type of business had an impact here—that is, the fashion industry, rather than some other workplace? Should it?

If the employee is temporarily unable to perform the duties of the job because of pregnancy, then the law requires that the inability to perform to be the issue, not the fact that the employee is pregnant. The employee should therefore be treated just as any other employee who is temporarily unable to perform job requirements. Whatever arrangements the employer generally makes in such circumstances must be extended to the pregnant employee. Note, however, that the EEOC has ruled that an employer's adherence to a facially neutral sick leave policy and its consequent refusal to provide pregnant employees with a reasonable leave of absence, in the absence of a showing of business necessity, discriminates on the basis of gender because of its disproportionate impact on women.[4] Pregnancy can, of course, be used as a BFOQ.

As a manager, you should be aware of the ingrained ideas people hold about pregnancy and work and be sure to ward off any trouble. According to a recent Jury Verdict Research study, if job applicants or employees with pregnancy discrimination claims go to jury trial, they win 54 percent of the time. On the other hand, while the study shows that pregnancy discrimination claimants are more likely than other kinds of discrimination claimants to recover from a jury, the amount they recover is substantially less. The median jury award in a pregnancy discrimination case was $56,360, while for others it was $146,468. But since the discrimination is avoidable, even a verdict of $56,360 is unnecessary.

[4] EEOC Dec. No. 74-112, 19 FEP Cases 1817 (4/15/74); EEOC Guidelines, 29 CFR section 1604.10(c).

PARENTAL LEAVE POLICIES: THE FAMILY AND MEDICAL LEAVE ACT

Leave Requirement

(a) (1) Entitlement to leave.—an eligible employee shall be entitled to a total of 12 workweeks of leave during any 12-month period for one or more of the following:

(A) Because of the birth of a son or daughter of the employee and in order to care for such son or daughter.

(B) Because of the placement of a son or daughter with the employee for adoption or foster care.

(C) In order to care for the spouse, or a son, daughter, or parent, of the employee, if such spouse, son, daughter, or parent has a serious health condition.

(D) Because of a serious health condition that makes the employee unable to perform the functions of the position of such employee. The Family and Medical Leave Act of 1993, 29 U.S.C. §2601 et seq.

Closely related to the issue of pregnancy discrimination is protection of employees who take time off work to have a baby or to adopt a child. This had been a real problem before the FMLA was enacted in 1993 because employees taking time off to care for a new child had no job security.

The FMLA is included in the gender chapter because it was enacted primarily in response to women's concerns about keeping their job or not being demoted or losing benefits after the birth or arrival of a child. Since its passage, the law has evolved into a much broader piece of legislation. With baby boomers playing such a large part in the national conscience and policies, it was inevitable that since the law also covers taking time off to care for parents, this would also become a fertile area under the law. However, it is the gender matters with which we are concerned in this chapter.

On February 5, 1993, President Clinton signed into law the first piece of legislation of his administration: The Family and Medical Leave Act (FMLA). The act guarantees employees who have been on the job at least a year up to 12 weeks of unpaid leave per year for a birth, an adoption, or care of sick children, spouses, or parents (or their own serious illness) and the same or an equivalent job upon their return. The act applies to employers with 50 or more employees within a 75-mile radius. Employees must have worked for their employer for at least one year and for at least 1,250 hours during the 12 months preceding the time off. They must give the employer at least 30 days' notice when practical (such as for a birth).

Employers may require employees to first use vacation or other leave before applying for the unpaid leave, but employees must be compensated for the vacation days as they normally would. Where both members of the couple work for the same employer, the employer can restrict the couple to a total of 12 weeks leave per year. Employers must continue to provide employees with health insurance during their leave and may exclude the highest-paid 10 percent of their employees from FMLA coverage.

Employers can also require medical confirmation of an illness, which the U.S. Department of Labor, which has issued regulations on the act, defines as requiring at least one night in the hospital. Complaints may be filed with the Wage and Hour Division of the Labor Department, or the employee can file a lawsuit if he or she feels the employer violated the act. (See Exhibit 6.14.)

Exhibit 6.14 FMLA: Societal Impediments and Working Fathers

God decided only women can give birth and therefore could be the only primary care giver . . . Unless your wife is in a coma or dead you can't be a primary care giver . . . Until you have breast-fed a baby, there is no way you can be a primary care giver.

While the FMLA applies to both mothers and fathers, there are still societal impediments to fathers taking advantage of their rights under the law as reflected in the above-quoted statements made by a human resources department to the male employee described below. Many don't do so because they feel they will be perceived as not being committed to their jobs if they take off for the birth or adoption of a child. If you think the teasing and jokes don't matter, read on.

WORKING DADS FEAR "SLACKER" LABEL

There were snide comments and many, many jokes. And when Maryland state trooper Kevin Knussman won his four-year legal fight this week against the bosses who denied him parental leave, only a couple of colleagues called to congratulate him.

Knussman's victory highlights the rights of working fathers to take time off with their babies. But his isolation shows how balancing a job and family remains a silent struggle for many men.

"Much of the progress (for working fathers) is still going on underground," says James Levine, a leading researcher on fatherhood and co-author of the book "Working Fathers."

Fearing—often with reason—that they'll be labeled slackers, fathers cobble together sick days and vacation time to create leave time after a baby is born. When they want to go to a school play, they dash for the door, under cover of attending a "late meeting." Progress has been made, albeit slowly, in accepting men's growing desire to be involved parents.

Asked 15 years ago how much unpaid parental leave time was reasonable for men to take, 63 percent of business leaders at large companies said "none." Even 40 percent of executives at companies with a parental leave policy at the time nixed the idea of actually using it, according to Catalyst, a non-profit group that studies women in business.

Today, half a million men take some sort of parental leave each year to care for a new child, under the auspices of the 1993 federal Family and Medical Leave Act. That compares with 1.4 million women. A total of 20 million people have taken leave under the federal law.

Knussman, a helicopter paramedic, sued the state police after he was denied 12 weeks leave following the birth of his daughter in 1994. He was given 10 days off, but sought more time because his wife experienced childbirth complications.

A jury awarded him $375,000* in damages for mental anguish, in the first sex discrimination case under the Family Leave Act. Attorneys for the state police said they may appeal.

"There's still a presumption that women are going to be the primary caretaker," said Sara Mandelbaum, an ACLU lawyer who represented Knussman. "Those studies are hard to change, especially a male-dominated organization like the state police."

Money also plays a role. A few companies, including Merrill Lynch and the software maker Lotus Development Corp., offer paid leaves for men. But most don't, and since men are major breadwinners, it's hard for them to take unpaid time off.

Exhibit 6.14 (continued)

For now, many men choose to do what they can, when they can. Still, Knussman is glad he took a stand. After he filed his suit, the state police gave him a full 12 weeks off following the birth of his second child.

"Biting the hand that feeds you is never easy," he said by telephone as his daughters giggled in the background. But taking three months off was "just a great, great time. I will never, ever regret that."

*This figure was later reduced by a Court of Appeals to $40,000 for reasons related to civil procedure issues.

Source: Courtesy of the Associated Press.

In 1997, Congress declined to grant President Clinton's request to extend the FMLA to permit employees to take up to 24 hours of unpaid leave each year to fulfill certain family obligations such as attending parent-teacher conferences, taking a child to the doctor, finding child care, or caring for elderly relatives.

The FMLA affects about 5 percent of U.S. employers and about 40 percent of U.S. employees. The number of employees who will be able to take 12 weeks without pay is significantly fewer than those who are covered by the law. However, since its passage, over 35 million employees have used the FMLA. Research shows that almost one-third of all workers who needed leave but did not take it cited worry about losing their jobs as a reason for not taking leave. Eighty-eight percent of those who needed leave but did not take it said they would have done so if they could have received more (or at least some) pay during their leave. Societal impediments can also be a factor (see Exhibit 6.14).

The FMLA has been the subject of a great deal of uncertainty ever since its passage. The law, particularly the Department of Labor's regulations, has been a constant source of confusion for employers. There have been questions as to how serious an illness must be for the employee to qualify for the leave, assessment of eligibility requirements for the leave, what to do about intermittent leave, reinstatement after taking leave, and notification and certification requirements for leave, just to name a few issues. These questions have resulted in a steadily increasing number of FMLA claims, causing it to develop into one of the most active areas of employment law. An informal survey of 237 human resources professionals conducted by business publisher HR Next found the majority calling the FMLA the "most bothersome U.S. regulation to administer."

In 2002, the U.S. Supreme Court decided its first FMLA case, nearly 10 years after the law was enacted. In *Ragsdale* v. *Wolverine Worldwide, Inc.,*[5] the Court determined that it is not always fatal for an employer not to notify an employee that the employee is using FMLA leave. In the case, an employee who took seven months of unpaid sick leave after being diagnosed with cancer was terminated after asking for additional leave or part-time work. The employee claimed the employer never told her that the leave she took included FMLA leave, so she thought she was still entitled to the 12

[5] 535 U.S. 81 (2002).

weeks provided by the FMLA. Even though the Department of Labor agreed with this position, the Supreme Court disagreed. The Court reasoned that the employer's failure to notify the employee that she was using FMLA leave did not interfere with the exercise of her FMLA rights since she could not show that she was harmed by the lack of notice or would have acted differently had she been notified. Since the employer had given her much more than the 12 weeks required by law, giving her 12 more weeks seemed to the Court an inappropriate penalty.

Despite the Court's ruling, know that the regulatory notification requirements are an important part of the FMLA, and it is preferable to let the employee know when FMLA leave is being charged. Given the growing number of FMLA claims in recent years, compliance with the regulations is imperative if an employer wants to avoid liability.

The case below goes a long way toward demonstrating why employers have such a problem with this law. Think about how you would have handled the situation.

Spangler v. Federal Home Loan Bank of Des Moines 278 F.3d 847 (8th Cir. 2002)

The employee called in to her employer and left a message that she would not be in because of "depression again." The issue became whether this statement was sufficient to put the employer on notice that the employee was invoking the FMLA and taking FMLA leave. The district court held for the employer, but the court of appeals reversed, determining that given the employer's background and history with the employee, the employee's statement was sufficient.

Riley, J.

Theresa Spangler began working for the Bank in the Demand Services Department in 1982. Spangler suffers from dysthymia, a form of depression, along with phobia and bouts of more intense depression. Her former therapist first diagnosed Spangler with this mental illness in 1993. At that time, Spangler took a six-week leave of absence from the Bank and went through treatment. Spangler's current psychiatrist also diagnosed Spangler with dysthymia in 1997. At that time, she took another leave of absence to undergo treatment. After her 1997 diagnosis, Spangler informed her supervisor that she took this leave to obtain treatment for her depression. Spangler also recalls later telling a variety of other supervisors and Bank personnel about her depression.

The Bank's attendance policy allowed supervisors to excuse occasional absences due to illness or injury depending on the circumstances and on the employee's past attendance. The Bank dealt with exces-

sive absenteeism through counseling, warning, and, on occasion, termination if necessary. Employees were to arrange time off for personal business and medical appointments in advance. The Bank's FMLA policy required employees to request leave 30 days in advance or, if the leave was not predictable, the employee needed to provide as much notice as was practicable. The Bank posted this information about the FMLA in the employee break room and printed it on the back of employee time cards.

Bank records show a persistent pattern of absenteeism and tardiness throughout Spangler's employment with the Bank. Spangler was absent for family or medical reasons for 32 days in 1993, 17.6 days in 1994, 12.4 days in 1995, and 29.3 days in 1996.

One morning in September of 1997, Spangler left a voice mail message on a supervisor's machine in the morning stating she would not be at work that day, thus forcing the supervisor to do Spangler's work instead of attending a scheduled training session.

Throughout 1997 and 1998, Spangler's many unscheduled absences and her persistent tardiness were routinely noted by the Bank. Spangler used five days of unscheduled vacation for personal reasons from September 15 through 19, 1997. Each morning when she was absent, Spangler notified her supervisor by leaving a voice mail message. In September, Spangler was warned that she needed to be on time to work and to talk to someone instead of leaving voice mail messages when she was unable to make it to work. Her 1997 performance appraisal noted that her 21 absences that year were excessive and that absenteeism was a problem for Spangler.

Due to more absences, Spangler was again put on probation in January and again August 31, 1998. On September 15 she missed work because of transportation problems. The following day, a Bank employee noted in a memorandum to Spangler's manager that Spangler phoned and stated she would not be in that day because it was "depression again."

On September 17, when Spangler had not yet arrived at work in the middle of the morning, and had not yet called with any explanation, Spangler's manager terminated her employment.

Discussion

An employee is to provide his or her employer with 30 days notice or as much notice as is practicable of the intention to use FMLA leave, when the necessity for leave "is foreseeable." 29 U.S.C. §2612(e)(2). Less than 30 days notice is permissible for reasons "such as because of a lack of knowledge of approximately when leave will be required to begin, a change in circumstances, or a medical emergency." 29 C.F.R. §825.302(a). Notice is required "as soon as practicable," meaning "as soon as both possible and practical, taking into account all of the facts and circumstances in the individual case." 29 C.F.R. §825.302(b). "This ordinarily . . . mean[s] at least verbal notification to the employer within one or two business days of when the need for leave becomes known to the employee." If the need for FMLA leave is not foreseeable, the employee "should give notice to the employer of the need for FMLA leave as soon as practicable under the facts and circumstances of the particular case." 29 C.F.R. §825.303(a).

Although "[a]n employer may also require an employee to comply with the employer's usual and customary notice and procedural requirements for requesting leave," "failure to follow such internal employer procedures will not permit an employer to disallow or delay an employee's taking FMLA leave if the employee gives timely verbal or other notice." 29 C.F.R. §825.302(d). The acceptable ways for an employee to provide notice include, "in person, by telephone, telegraph, facsimile, . . . or other electronic means." 29 C.F.R. §825.303(b).

Employee argues that by alerting the Bank of her need for time off due to "depression again" the day before her dismissal, she put the Bank on notice that she would need time off that would qualify under the FMLA. Spangler presented a great deal of evidence of the Bank's awareness of her mental condition. She informed several supervisors of her illness throughout the time she was employed with the Bank. Furthermore, it is undisputed that in her final request for time off work, she stated it was because of "depression again." We have held that "[a]n employee need not invoke the FMLA by name in order to put an employer on notice that the Act may have relevance to the employee's absence from work." "Under the FMLA, the employer's duties are triggered when the employee provides enough information to put the employer on notice that the employee may be in need of FMLA leave."

We view Spangler's uncontroverted statement that it was "depression again" as a potentially valid request for FMLA leave. The Bank here knew Spangler suffered from depression, knew she needed leave in the past for depression and knew from Spangler specifically on September 16, 1998, she was suffering from "depression again."

When an employee provides the employer with notice that she may be in need of FMLA leave before the fact of the absence, it then becomes the employer's duty to determine whether or not the employee actually requires FMLA leave if there is some doubt as to whether or not the request would qualify. Once the employer is notified, it has a duty either to provide FMLA time or follow the procedures set forth in the statute and regulations to verify the validity of the employee's request for time off "by a certification issued by the health care provider." 29 U.S.C. §2613(a). "The responsibility to request FMLA certification is the employer's."

We have noted that an employee "cannot claim protection from the FMLA for disciplinary action . . . as a result of absences that are not attributable to his serious health conditions." The Bank is free to present evidence before the jury of its legitimate disciplinary reasons for dismissing Spangler, reasons not attributable to any FMLA request.

Finally, we emphasize the FMLA does not provide an employee suffering from depression with a right to "unscheduled and unpredictable, but cumulatively substantial, absences" or a right to "take unscheduled leave at a moment's notice for the rest of her career." On the contrary, such a situation "implies that she is not qualified for a position where reliable attendance is a bona fide requirement. . . ." REVERSED.

Case Questions

1. Put yourself in the position of a manager. What would you do to cope with Spangler?
2. Do you understand the court's decision about Spangler's last phone message? Explain. Do you agree? Why or why not?
3. Do you understand why employers have so much trouble with the FMLA regulations and find them so bothersome? Explain.

FETAL PROTECTION POLICIES

fetal protection policies
Policies an employer institutes to protect the fetus or the reproductive capacity of employees.

The issue of **fetal protection policies** will be given attention here because of the unique gender employment problems involved. Fetal protection policies are policies adopted by an employer that limit or prohibit employees from performing certain jobs or working in certain areas of the workplace because of the potential harm presented to pregnant employees, their fetuses, or the reproductive system or capacity of employees.

The problem with these policies is that, as in *Johnson,* below, many times, even though there is a danger presented to male employees, the policies only exclude females (and do so very broadly), and the jobs from which the females are excluded pay more or have more promotion potential.

UAW v. Johnson Controls, Inc. *499 U.S. 187 (1991)*

A group of employees challenged the employer's policy barring all women except those whose infertility was medically documented from jobs involving actual or potential lead exposure exceeding Occupational Safety and Health Administration (OSHA) standards. The Court found the policy to be illegal gender discrimination.

Blackmun, J.

In this case we are concerned with an employer's gender-based fetal protection policy. May an employer exclude a fertile female employee from certain jobs because of its concern for the health of the fetus the woman might conceive? Our answer is no.

Employees involved in the suit include Elsie Nelson, a 50-year-old divorcee, who suffered a loss in compensation when she was transferred out of a job where she was exposed to lead, Mary Craig who chose to be sterilized in order to avoid losing her job, and Donald Penny, who was denied a request for leave of absence for the purpose of lowering his lead level because he intended to become a father.

The bias in Johnson Control's policy is obvious. Fertile men, but not fertile women, are given the choice as to whether they wish to risk their reproductive health for a particular job. Johnson Control's fetal protection policy explicitly discriminates against women on the basis of their gender. The policy excludes women with childbearing capacity from lead-exposed jobs and so creates a facial classification based on gender.

The policy classifies on the basis of gender and childbearing capacity, rather than fertility alone. The employer does not seek to protect the unconceived children of all its employees. Despite evidence in the record about the debilitating effect of lead exposure on the male reproductive system, Johnson Controls is concerned only with the harms that may befall the unborn offspring of its female employees. Johnson Controls' policy is facially discriminatory because it requires only a female employee to produce proof that she is not capable of reproducing.

Our conclusion is bolstered by the Pregnancy Discrimination Act of 1978 in which Congress explicitly provided that, for purposes of Title VII, discrimination "on the basis of sex" included discrimination "because of or on the basis of pregnancy, childbirth, or related medical conditions." The PDA has now made clear that, for all Title VII purposes, discrimination based on a woman's pregnancy is, on its face, discrimination because of her gender. Johnson Controls has chosen to treat all its female employees as potentially pregnant; that choice evinces discrimination on the basis of gender.

An employer may discriminate on the basis of gender in those certain instances where religion, gender or national origin is a BFOQ reasonably necessary to the normal operation of that particular business or enterprise. We conclude that the language of both the BFOQ provision and the PDA, which amended it, as well as the legislative history and case law, prohibit employers from discriminating against a woman because of her capacity to become pregnant unless her reproductive potential prevents her from performing the duties of her job. We have said before, an employer must direct its concerns about a woman's ability to perform her job safely and efficiently to those aspects of the woman's job-related activities that fall within the "essence" of the particular business.

Johnson Controls cannot establish a BFOQ. Fertile women, as far as appears on the record, participate in the manufacture of batteries as efficiently as anyone else. Johnson Controls' professed moral and ethical concerns about the welfare of the next generation do not suffice to establish a BFOQ of female sterility. Nor can concerns about the welfare of the next generation be considered a part of the "essence" of Johnson Controls' business. It is word play to say that the job at Johnson Controls is to make batteries without risk to fetuses in the same way the job at an airline is to fly planes without crashing. Decisions about the welfare of future children must be left to the parents who conceive, bear, support and raise them rather than to the employers who hire those parents.

A word about tort liability and the increased cost of fertile women in the workplace is perhaps necessary. It is correct to say that Title VII does not prevent an employer from having a conscience. The statute, however, does prevent gender-specific fetal protection policies. These two aspects of Title VII do not conflict. More than 40 states currently recognize a right to recover for a prenatal injury based either on negligence or on wrongful death. According to Johnson Controls, however, the company complies with the lead standard developed by OSHA and warns its female employees about the damaging effects of lead. It is worth noting that OSHA gave the problem of lead lengthy consideration and concluded that "there is no basis whatsoever for the claim that women of childbearing age should be excluded from the workplace in order to protect the fetus or the course of the pregnancy." 43 Fed. Reg. 52952, 22996 (1978). Instead, OSHA established a series of mandatory protections, which, taken together, "should effectively minimize any risk to the fetus and newborn child." Without negligence, it would be difficult for a court to find liability on the part of the employer. If, under general tort principles, Title VII bans gender-specific fetal protection policies, the employer fully informs the woman of the risk, and the employer has not acted negligently, the basis for holding an employer liable seems remote at best.

Our holding today that Title VII, as so amended, forbids gender-specific fetal protection policies is neither remarkable nor unprecedented. Concern for a woman's existing or potential offspring historically has been the excuse for denying women equal employment opportunities. Congress and the PDA prohibited discrimination on the basis of a woman's ability to become pregnant. We do no more than hold that the PDA means what it says.

It is no more appropriate for the courts than it is for individual employers to decide whether a woman's reproductive role is more important to herself and her family than her economic role. Congress has left this choice to the woman as hers to make. REVERSED and REMANDED.

Case Questions

1. Do you agree with the Court that the welfare of the child should be left to the parents, not the employer?
2. What do you find most troublesome about the decision, if anything? Explain.
3. As an employer, what would you do in this situation?

Management Tips

As you have seen from the chapter, gender discrimination can manifest itself in many forms, some of which may take the employer by surprise. Following these tips can help keep the surprises to a minimum.

- Let employees know from the beginning that gender bias will not be tolerated in any way. Give them examples of unacceptable behavior.
- Back up the strong gender message with appropriate enforcement.
- Take employee claims of gender discrimination or bias seriously.
- Promptly and thoroughly investigate all complaints, keeping privacy issues in mind.
- Don't go overboard in responding to offenses substantiated by investigation. Make sure the "punishment fits the crime."

- Conduct periodic training to keep communication lines open and to act as an ongoing reminder of the employer's antibias policy.
- Conduct periodic audits to make sure gender is not adversely affecting hiring, promotion, and raises.
- Review workplace policies to make sure there are no hidden policies or practices that could more adversely impact one gender than another.
- In dealing with gender issues, keep in mind that none of the actions need make the workplace stilted and formal. Employees can respect each other without discriminating against each other.

Summary

- Discrimination on the basis of gender is illegal and not in keeping with good business practices of efficiency, maximizing resources, and avoiding unnecessary liability.
- Gender discrimination has many manifestations, including discrimination in hiring, firing, compensation, training, fetal protection policies, client preferences, dress codes, and child care leave.
- In determining whether employment policies are gender biased, look at the obvious, but also look at the subtle bias that may arise from seemingly neutral policies adversely impacting a given gender, such as height and weight requirements. Both types of discrimination are illegal.
- Where employees must be treated differently, ensure that the basis for differentiation is grounded in factors not gender-based but, instead, address the actual limitation of the employee or applicant's qualifications.
- Under the PDA, employers must treat a pregnant employee who is able to perform the job just as they treat any other employee with a short-term disability.
- Because of health and other considerations, an employer may use pregnancy as a BFOQ and may have policies excluding or limiting pregnant employees if there is a reasonable business justification for such policies.
- If there are legitimate bases for treating pregnant employees differently, an employer has ample flexibility to make necessary decisions.
- Outmoded ideas regarding pregnant employees may not be the basis of denying them equal employment opportunities.
- Covered employers must provide covered employees with leave under the FMLA.
- Fetal protection policies may not operate to discriminate against employees and fail to extend to them equal employment opportunities.

Chapter-End Questions

1. A female restaurant employee is on the phone in the kitchen talking to her mother. The chef of the restaurant comes up to the employee, throws off his chef's hat, grabs both the employee's arms and begins shaking her violently and screaming at her. She reports this to the police. She is later terminated and sues for gender discrimination. Will she win? Why or why not? [*Labonia* v. *Doran Assoc., LLC,* 2004 U.S. Dist. LEXIS 17025 (D. Conn. 2004).]

2. Employee says she was forced to quit her job because of her status as a mother of young children. She claimed that her female supervisor created a hostile work environment that violated Title VII. She was replaced by another mother. Does she win? [*Fuller* v. *GTE Corp./Contel Cellular, Inc.,* 926 F. Supp. 653 (M.D. Tenn. 1996).]

3. Employer had only one promotion to give, but he was torn between giving it to the single female and the male who had a family and, the employer thought, most needed and could best use the money. He finally decided to give the promotion to the male and told the female he gave it to the male because the male was a family man and needed the money. If the female employee sues, will she win? [*Taylor* v. *Runyon,* 175 F.3d 861 (11th Cir. 1999).]

4. An accounts receivable supervisor was laid off by her employer after taking an extended disability leave for pregnancy. She claimed that the employer discriminated against her on the basis of gender and ability to bear children, stating that two male employees were retained and her replacement was a childless, 40-year-old unmarried female. She files suit, alleging gender discrimination. The employer said it was a legitimate layoff. What should the court consider in determining whether the employer's argument is true? [*Leahey* v. *Singer Sewing Co.,* 694 A.2d 609 (N.J. Super. 1996).]

5. Employee becomes pregnant while she is having an affair with a married co-worker. Employer said that employee violated its norms of conduct by committing the crime of adultery, and both employee and the father of the child are dismissed. Is employee's dismissal a violation of the PDA? [*Cumpiano* v. *Banco Santander Puerto Rico,* 902 F.2d 148 (1st Cir. 1990).]

6. A cable company closed its door-to-door sales department and released all employees of that department after settling a discrimination complaint by one of the department's employees. The employee's mother, sister, and two close friends had also been employed in the department. Eighteen months later, the company resumed its door-to-door sales, but refused to rehire three of the former employees connected with the employee who had previously sued. The former employees sue, alleging gender discrimination. Will they be successful in their suit? Explain. [*Craig* v. *Suburban Cablevision, Inc.,* 660 A.2d 505 (N.J. 1995).]

7. A power company began employing women as meter readers, and the job classification went from all-male to all-female within a few years. The labor union that represented bargaining unit employees negotiated a new collective bargaining agreement that froze wages in the meter reader classification and lowered the wage for new hires. There was evidence that the company president made comments concerning the desirability of housewives to read meters and that he admitted the contract was unfavorable to women. A number of women in the meter reader category filed a state court lawsuit against the employer and union for gender discrimination on the basis of state law and wage discrimination under federal law. The employer argued that the federal labor law preempted the state law gender discrimination complaint, therefore the gender complaint should be dismissed. Is the state law preempted? [*Donajkowski* v. *Alpena Power Co.,* 556 N.W.2d 876 (Mich. App. 1996).]

8. On employee's first day on the job, employer withdraws an offer of employment as a medical claims examiner after learning that employee is four months pregnant. Is this a

violation of the PDA? Does it matter if the point at which employee would be taking leave would likely have been the beginning of her paying small claims without close supervision? [*Ahmad* v. *Loyal American Life Ins. Co.,* 767 F. Supp. 1114 (S.D. Ala. S. Div. 1991).]

9. Employer decides to shut down one of its three plants because the employees at that plant are almost exclusively women. The males who worked at the plant and lost their jobs as a result of the closing wish to sue for gender discrimination under Title VII. If they do, will they be successful? [*Allen* v. *American Home Foods, Inc.,* 644 F. Supp. 1553 (N.D. Ind. 1986).]

10. Employer terminates female employee because employer's daughter-in-law feels the female employee is having an affair with her husband, the employer's son, who is also employed by employer. Female employee sues for gender discrimination. Does she win?

Chapter **Seven**

Sexual Harassment

Opening Scenarios

SCENARIO 1

Scenario

A female employee tells her supervisor that she is disturbed by the workplace display of nude pictures, calendars, and cartoons. He replies that, if she is bothered, she should not look. The employee suspects this is a form of sexual harassment. Do you agree? Why or why not?

SCENARIO 2

Scenario

A male and female employee have engaged in a two-year consensual personal relationship, which ends. The male continues to attempt to get the female to go out with him on dates. When she does not, she is eventually fired by the male, who is her supervisor. She sues, alleging sexual harassment. Who wins and why?

SCENARIO 3

Scenario

An employee routinely compliments colleagues about their appearance, hair, and body. Is this sexual harassment? Why or why not?

STATUTORY BASIS

It shall be unlawful employment practice for an employer—
   (1) to fail or refuse to hire or to discharge any individual, or otherwise to discriminate against any individual with respect to his compensation, terms, conditions, or privileges of employment, because of such individual's . . . sex [gender]. . . . Title VII of the Civil Rights Act of 1964, as amended. 42 U.S.C. 2000e2(a).

Unwelcome sexual advances, requests for sexual favors, and other verbal or physical conduct of a sexual nature constitute sexual harassment when (1) submission to such conduct is made either explicitly or implicitly a term or condition of an individual's employment, (2) submission to or rejection of such conduct by an individual is used as the basis for employment decisions affecting such individual, or (3) such conduct has the purpose or effect of unreasonably interfering with an individual's work performance or creating an intimidating, hostile, or offensive working environment. 29 C.F.R. Section 1604.11 (a) (EEOC Sexual Harassment Guidelines).

SINCE EDEN . . . AND COUNTING

Introduction

As we approach the 40th anniversary of the landmark Civil Rights Act in July, sexual harassment and retaliation in the workplace are still far too common occurrences

6/17/2004 EEOC Miami District Director Federico Costales

Mr. Costales is absolutely right.

For that reason, we think that of all the chapters you will read in this book, this is probably the single most perplexing one. Why in the world would someone engage in such an unnecessary act that can have such wide-ranging negative consequences for the employer? Why would an employer permit it? You will probably find yourself asking this over and over as you read this chapter. Not that any discrimination ever is, but how could this ever be worth it to an employer when it is so *purely* personal?

No matter what the workplace, whether employees are driving taxis or making them, practicing law or executing it, serving customers or hosting television shows, the fact that it is a workplace means we presume a certain standard for our interaction with coworkers. It may be loosely defined, but we know it is there. Just picture what you think your workplace will be like when you graduate. You worked long and hard to get that diploma, you step out into the workplace feeling a degree of trepidation and uncertainty, but knowing that if given a chance, you'll be able to work hard and make your dreams come true. You will take a job where you will have dignity and respect and be allowed to contribute your time and energies to the productivity of your employer. You may expect there to be some unpleasant personalities and even jerks in your workplace, but you still expect a certain level of decorum.

With this picture in mind, we guarantee that the following situations do not comport with your idea of an appropriate standard of workplace interaction, or a workplace you would like to step into. Keep in mind that these incidents are only from the past couple of years.

- In April 2003, Lutheran Medical Center in Brooklyn, New York, agreed to pay nearly $5.5 million to settle a sexual harassment case in which a hospital doctor allegedly subjected more than 50 female employees to invasive touching and intrusive questions about their sex life during mandatory physical exams. He threatened to delay or deny their employment if they did not cooperate.

- In February 2004, the city of Richmond, Virginia, agreed to pay $100,000 to settle a suit by a female employee claiming police administrators ignored sexual harassment complaints against a high-ranking official and for months after she formally complained, allowing him to continue to supervise her. She claims he repeatedly made sexually explicit comments to her and asked her out, used derogatory language to describe female employees, and engaged in unwelcome, offensive, or other unwanted conversations of a sexual or personal nature.

- In June 2004, Airguide Corporation and Pioneer Metals, Inc., entered into a consent decree with EEOC, agreeing to pay $1 million for sexual harassment and retaliation to three former female employees allegedly subjected to sexually explicit slurs and comments by their supervisors. Though they complained repeatedly, the harassment persisted.

- In December 2004, Burger King entered into a consent decree with EEOC to pay $400,000 to settle a claim for sexual harassment of seven female employees, *six of whom were high school students,* after the manager subjected them to repeated groping, vulgar sexual comments, and demands for sex. Nothing was done when this was reported to assistant managers at the restaurant or to the district manager.

- In January 2005, a New Hampshire judge resigned from the bench after groping five female victim advocates of his court at a conference on sexual assault and domestic violence. Late night partying at the conference also led to the Attorney General's resignation after an investigation into his inappropriate touching of a woman while dancing.

- In February 2005, a judge, married and the father of three grown children, resigned from the bench after allegations that he habitually masturbated with a penis pump under his robe at trials—a claim bolstered by semen samples on his robe, chair, and carpet samples collected from behind the bench, as well as witnesses such as the court reporter, lawyers who heard the "whooshing" sound made by the pump, and police officers who took photos of the pump under the desk during a break in a murder trial after seeing a piece of plastic tubing disappear under the judge's robe. It is expected that a number of defendants will appeal, alleging the judge was not paying sufficient attention while presiding over their trials since, it was reported, "During one trial, the judge seemed so distracted that some jurors thought he was playing a handheld video game or tying fishing lures behind the bench."

We could go on, but we will stop here. You get the message. From *The Price Is Right* game show host, Bob Barker, to governor and actor Arnold Schwarzenegger (who, after being dogged by allegations of sexual misconduct with up to 16 women during his campaign for governor of California, underwent a voluntary course in preventing sexual harassment after his election); from the founder of Habitat for Humanity, to the conservative talk show host Bill O'Reilly, no one seems to be immune from engaging in sexual harassment. (See Exhibit 7.12.) Sexual harassment suits are still far more frequent an occurrence than we would like them to be, if for no other reason than they cost the employer totally unnecessary time, effort, energy, bad press, and money. Who needs it?

In 1991, the first sexual harassment class action was approved in *Jenson* v. *Eveleth Taconite, Inc.*[1] Leading up to the class action certification proceedings there was much speculation in the legal community as to whether such a thing could be done, or even if it really needed to be done. How frequently could there possibly be a case with so many charges that a class action suit was needed? Unfortunately, in the years since, many such cases have been brought, involving both men and women. Few are brought to trial. The risk to the employer is too great. Sexual harassment class action trials have been called "a white buffalo" by one lawyer because so few are seen. Many cases are filed, but they are settled rather than litigated as a means of avoiding bad publicity and the possibility of even greater damages if the matter goes to trial. Keep in mind that at trial the jury would hear employee after employee get up and tell similar stories, often from offices all over the country. To think that there would be enough employees experiencing sexual harassment at a workplace to even be certified as a class action (no small feat!) ought to give you cause for concern as a future manager, supervisor or business owner. Again, *who needs it?* In addition to the class action suits set forth above, consider these:

- In September 2004, CB Richard Ellis, a $1.6 billion, publicly traded commercial real estate brokerage firm with 17,000 employees in 300 offices around the world, was sued by female employees whose affidavits allege management condoned and perpetuated discrimination and sexual harassment against women through such things as its decades-old, much-touted, annual "Fight Night" event in Atlanta. This was characterized as a "rowdy, black-tie Vegas-style boys night out of cigar smoke, boxing, and women on display." Female employees were chosen to wear evening clothes and serve them and their clients drinks and cigars. At work, female employees across the country allege they were subjected to groping, degrading comments, and vulgar discussions about sex and women's body parts. Male employees also

---

[1] 139 F.R.D. 657 (D. Minn. 1991).

exposed themselves to female employees. The plaintiffs alleged daily circulation of offensive, lewd, and pornographic e-mails; granting or withholding permission to interface with customers based on a female employee's looks; viewing of pornographic Web sites and videos in the office; and the display of offensive, lewd, and pornographic pictures and calendars in the office.

- In April 2003, Dial Corporation, maker of Dial soap, entered into a consent decree with EEOC to settle a class action by 91 women who alleged that the Dial Corporation's soap factory in Montgomery, Illinois, had a sexually abusive environment for years and management either participated in the activities or did nothing when it was reported. Harassing activity included everything from grabbing female employees and fondling their breasts, to sexual comments and propositions, to placing a sanitary napkin doused with ketchup and beside a female employee's tool box, a life-sized penis carved from pink soap.

- In June 2003, 32 female employees at the U.S. Mint Denver plant, nearly one-third of the females filed suit alleging they were subjected to sexist comments, treated more favorably if they had sex with some managers, disciplined more harshly than men, discouraged from complaining about the treatment, and ignored after they met with Mint officials. Until they met with higher authorities at the U.S. Treasury Department, the harassment continued. The harassment occurred even though the Mint director was female.

- In October 2002, the EEOC sued Kraft on behalf of a class of male employees who were subjected to "egregious" same-sex harassment and retaliation by their male supervisor in Birmingham, Alabama. The employees were the subject of sexual comments, propositioned for sex, touched, grabbed, and sexually assaulted by a Nabisco male supervisor.

- In October 2004, the EEOC filed for class action certification in an action against Federal Express Corp. for same-gender sexual harassment in Kankakee, Illinois. One of the employees alleged that he repeatedly complained to management about the harassment by another male employee, but he was told to "act like a man" and "nothing can be done."

Sounds awful, doesn't it? If it sounds like we're preaching, we are. Nothing is more frustrating than seeing millions of hard earned dollars go out of business' coffers for such unnecessary, avoidable, and totally useless actions. Impeachment of a president, resignation of multi-starred generals and other high-level military personnel, resignation of company and university presidents and long-term legislators, and embarrassing televised hearings of a U.S. Supreme Court nominee have all been a part of our national consciousness and abrupt introduction to, and education in, the area of sexual harassment. It is frustrating to see the same thing over and over again, yet liability is so avoidable if employers will only take a few steps we will discuss.

But before we do that, let's get a bit of context first.

It seems like such a short time ago that most of us were blissfully unaware that the legal cause of action of sexual harassment even existed. Though it had been around for more than 10 years, most people knew very little about it. Until, that is, it was thrust into the limelight when then-University of Oklahoma law professor Anita Hill took her seat at a table before the Senate Judiciary Committee in the confirmation hearings for associate justice of the U.S. Supreme Court, Clarence Thomas. Hill had worked for Thomas when he was head of the EEOC about 10 years before. When Thomas came up for confirmation, friends of Hill reported to the Judiciary Committee that she had at one time revealed to them details of unprofessional exchanges with Thomas that could have amounted to sexual harassment. The committee contacted Hill and made clear that she would either testify about the matter and set the record straight herself or leave them to their own devices of discovery. Hill very reluctantly chose to testify, and the country hasn't been the same since.

Hill's testimony over the next several days, and Thomas' barely concealed anger about it, were painful for the millions of Americans who sat glued to their television sets during those unbelievable autumn days in 1991. People who had never even heard the term *sexual harassment* now had implacable opinions about it. From barber shops to executive suites, and everywhere in between, *everyone* discussed the pros and cons of not only Hill's and Thomas' truthfulness, but also the concept of sexual harassment itself. Men who had thought nothing of what they considered harmless sexually suggestive jokes, comments, and gestures suddenly felt themselves looked upon as virtual lechers. Women who had found themselves on the uncomfortable receiving end of such unwanted attentions now discovered that those attentions might be not just uncomfortable situations for them but also actually illegal acts that violate Title VII. Eight months after the Hill–Thomas hearings, sexual harassment complaints filed with the EEOC increased by more than 50 percent. Ninety percent of the charges were from women. In the elections of 1992, called the "Year of the Woman," unprecedented numbers of female politicians rode the backlash wave of women who wanted to change "politics as usual" after witnessing what they perceived as the Senate's poor treatment of Hill during the hearings and Thomas' confirmation despite Hill's revelations. Thomas was head of the very agency charged with enforcing sexual harassment claims at the time he engaged in the alleged activity.

Much happened in the wake of this fiasco. (See Exhibit 7.13, page 354.) Almost overnight, the country's offices and workplaces went from friendly to foul. Sexual harassment captivated the national consciousness much the way President Clinton's Monica Lewinsky affair did in 1998, or Terry Schiavo's husband's fight to allow his brain-dead wife to die peacefully in 2005, only there was an immediate, acerbic, often acrimonious air to it. Lines were drawn in offices, bars, universities, churches, and homes all across the country, and people took their places on one side or the other and held their ground.

Whew! Scary, huh? Why do we bother to tell you all this instead of launching right into a narrative on sexual harassment? Because it is important for you to understand the context of this issue. Sexual harassment law is not something that has been around forever that we've grown accustomed to and learned to live with over hundreds of years or even in the 40+ years since Title VII was born. Even though it may seem like old hat today, it's still pretty new in the legal sense. It is still evolving. The U.S. Supreme Court didn't hear its first sexual harassment case until 1986, and the next one didn't come until seven years later. And of course, as we saw earlier, there are still many who don't yet "get it."

We also told you the background of sexual harassment because there's a lot of baggage that comes with the issue. Often, managers, supervisors, and employees don't recognize sexual harassment when it occurs. Our society preaches sexual permissiveness on the one hand, through music, movies, television, advertising, and so

Sometimes, trying to stamp out sexual harassment in the workplace can seem like an unwinnable battle, given the greater context in which we live. The excerpt below gives a compelling view of that context. But, as we discussed in the introduction to sexual harassment, the concept of sexual harassment does carry baggage, and not everyone agrees that something should be done about stamping it out.

Sex is everywhere you look in America. No escaping it. Newsstands spill over with glossy photos of bikini-popping babes. Radio jocks like Don Imus and Howard Stern dole out sexually tinged humor to go with your morning coffee. There are sexual fantasy telephone lines advertised on matchbook covers. Pay TV channels show male and female stripteasers and porn films day and night. Condoms are handed out like bubble gum, even to kids, sometimes courtesy of the Board of Education. Porn CD-ROMs like *Virtual Valerie* are big sellers.

Sex screams at us from the sides of buses with their underwear ads, and from TV sets carrying afternoon soap operas. But let anyone complain, and the affected interests, backed by the civil libertarians, scream censorship.

Except. Except in the workplace. Don't pin a *Penthouse* centerfold onto your office wall. Don't repeat to a co-worker an off-color joke about the guy in the White House. And for heaven's sake, don't leave *Virtual Valerie* on your office desk.

Do any of these things and the federal government suddenly forgets about the First Amendment. It could easily slap your employer with a six-figure lawsuit because you've created a "hostile environment" in the workplace.

"Outside of work, we face an incredibly permissive society," notes Louis DiLorenzo, a senior partner at Bond, Schoeneck & King, in Syracuse, NY, which represents companies in sexual harassment cases. "Yet we're told, at work, make sure no one talks about race or sex."

Of all the crusades Washington has ever embarked upon, the current commitment to stamp out sex in the workplace surely ranks among the daffiest.

Source: Reprinted by permission of *Forbes* Magazine © 2000, *Forbes* 1996.

---

forth, but when it comes to the workplace, the rules are different and some people don't make the transition very well. Remember the brouhaha on Donald Trump's popular television show, *The Apprentice,* in January 2004 when Trump admonished the women, who beat the men in trying to boost alcohol sales at the Times Square Planet Hollywood, for relying too heavily on their sexuality? Of course, it doesn't help matters to have *The Washington Post* run a story on clothing designers a couple of months later making "a strong case for sex in the office" by featuring sexier business attire for women. "Donatella Versace set the standard for the corporate siren by pairing businesslike jackets and sweater sets with skirts that could be mistaken for sausage casings." It is understandable why employees and employers alike could be confused. (See Exhibit 7.1.)

But despite all this, does sexual harassment really exist? Is it really widespread? Should we really be concerned? Is it that big a deal? Well, let's see.

In one of the first and still one of the most comprehensive studies ever conducted on the issue, the U.S. Merit Systems Protection Board in 1980 found that over 40 percent of federal employees had reported incidents of sexual harassment; seven years later the results were nearly the same (42 percent). A survey by *Working Woman* magazine of 160 of the Fortune 500 companies showed that nearly 40 percent of the companies had received at least one sexual harassment complaint in the previous 12 months. A *New York Times* poll found that 4 of every 10 women reported having experienced sexual harassment. The *National Law Journal* reported that 60 percent of female attorneys nationally said they had experienced some form of sexual harassment. A *Parade Magazine* poll discovered that 70 percent of the women polled who served in the military said they had been sexually harassed (see Exhibit 7.3), as had 50 percent of the women who worked in congressional offices on Capitol Hill. Despite the numbers, only about 5 percent of the incidents of sexual harassment are reported. Those who experience sexual harassment "pay all the intangible emotional costs inflicted by anger, humiliation, frustration, withdrawal, [and] dysfunction in family life."[2]

In *Robinson* v. *Jacksonville Shipyards, Inc.,*[3] the court found, based on expert testimony, that:

> [v]ictims of sexual harassment suffer stress effects from the harassment. Stress as a result of sexual harassment is recognized as a specific, diagnosable problem by the American Psychiatric Association. Among the stress effects suffered is "work performance stress," which includes distraction from tasks, dread of work, and an inability to work. Another form is "emotional stress," which covers a range of responses, including anger, fear of physical safety, anxiety, depression, guilt, humiliation, and embarrassment. Physical stress also results from sexual harassment; it may manifest itself by sleeping problems, headaches, weight changes, and other physical ailments. A study by the Working Women's Institute found that 96 percent of sexual harassment victims experienced emotional stress, 45 percent suffered work performance stress, and 35 percent were inflicted with physical stress problems.
>
> Sexual harassment has a cumulative, eroding effect on the victim's well-being. When women feel a need to maintain vigilance against the next incidence of harassment, the stress is increased tremendously. When women feel that their individual complaints will not change the work environment materially, the ensuing sense of despair further compounds the stress.

Regarding tangible costs, according to the classic 1987 MSPB update study, sexual harassment cost the federal government $267 million from May 1985 to May 1987 for losses in productivity, sick leave costs, and employee replacement costs. The *Working Woman* magazine survey found the actual cost of sexual harassment in the responding companies to be $6.7 million in low productivity, absenteeism, and employee turnover. In addition, along with the nontangible price they pay, MSPB found that employees who are sexually harassed pay medical expenses, litigation expenses, job search expenses, and the loss of valuable sick leave and annual leave.

---

[2] *Ellison* v. *Brady,* 924 F.2d 872, 881, n. 15 (9th Cir. 1991), quoting from the MSPB update study, "United States Merit Systems Protection Board, Sexual Harassment in the Federal Government: An Update" at 42 (1988).

[3] 760 F. Supp. 1486, 1506–07 (M.D. Fla., 1991).

Exhibit 7.2   Employer Confusion over Harassment Issues

Dear Ann Landers: I am married. I am also the boss. I have several competent women employees who come on to me in subtle ways. They wear see-through blouses in the office, which I consider in poor taste. I do not wear see-through pants to work. Their thigh-high short skirts may be fashionable but when they sit down I am afraid to look for fear of what might be showing.

If I were to bring up this subject, they might charge me with "sexual harassment," so once they are hired and their work skills are up to par, there is very little I can do. The law is now on their side.

I often wonder if these women are trying to trap me into making passes at them. When I once mentioned "appropriate clothing" in the office, they pointed out that they dress like everyone else in the building—which is true.

I am proud to say that in the 28 years I've been married, cheating never once crossed my mind. Why, then, do these women come on to me? I don't flirt and am very businesslike. Of course, I could not ask my secretary to type this letter, so please excuse the mistakes.—Business Man, USA.

Source: Permission to reprint granted by Ann Landers/Creators Syndicate.

Whether it occurs through joking, e-mails, touching, staring, unwanted requests for dates, denials of job opportunities, or some other means, sexual harassment is not just kidding or a joke or workplace fraternization. It is illegal as a form of gender discrimination that violates Title VII of the 1964 Civil Rights Act. But it is not only illegal: Given the toll it takes on the workplace, it is simply not good business. Since it is purely personal on the part of the harasser, it makes little sense for an employer not to take simple steps to prevent this totally unnecessary liability. It has become even less justifiable in the face of the 1991 Civil Rights Act permitting jury trials and compensatory and punitive damages.

The Civil Rights Act was passed in 1964, but it was the mid- to late 1970s before courts began to seriously recognize sexual harassment as a form of gender discrimination under Title VII. In 1980, soon after the first few significant sexual harassment cases were decided, the EEOC issued guidelines on sexual harassment. The guidelines, quoted in the opening of this chapter, are not law in the sense of Title VII but carry a great deal of weight when it comes to how courts will view and analyze the issue.

Where Do Sexual Harassment Considerations Leave the Employer?

The letter to Ann Landers in Exhibit 7.2 evidences a common frustration with and ignorance of sexual harassment issues. The intent of the law is *not* that the workplace either become totally devoid of sexuality on the one hand or be given completely over to employees who would misuse the law on the other. Consensual relationships are not forbidden, and employees may date consistent with appropriate company policy. It is only when the activity directed toward an employee is *unwelcome* and imposes terms or conditions different for one gender than another that it becomes a problem. For instance, a female employee might be required as a condition of employment to date her supervisor, while the male employees have no such condition imposed. (See Exhibit 7.2.) Most workplaces have now adopted antisexual harassment policies (see Exhibit 7.14) to govern this workplace issue.

SEXUAL HARASSMENT IN GENERAL

quid pro quo sexual harassment
Sexual harassment in which the harasser requests sexual activity from the harassee in exchange for workplace benefits.

hostile environment sexual harassment
Sexual harassment in which the harasser creates an abusive, offensive, or intimidating environment for the harassee.

There are two theories on which an action for sexual harassment may be brought: **quid pro quo sexual harassment** and **hostile environment sexual harassment**. The first generally requires the employer to require some type of sexual activity from the harassee as a condition of employment. The second addresses an offensive work environment to which one gender is subjected but not the other. (See Exhibit 7.8.) While there are two different types of sexual harassment and each has its own requirements, the U.S. Supreme Court has said that the distinction need not be rigid. In *Burlington Industries, Inc.* v. *Ellerth,*[4] the supervisor made threats to the harassee, but did not carry them out. The harassee brought suit on the theory of quid pro quo sexual harassment, but rather than deny relief because there had been no loss of a tangible job benefit which would impose liability on the employer, the Court said that the terms *quid pro quo* and *hostile environment* are not controlling for purposes of determining employer liability for harassment by a supervisor. Rather, they are helpful in making rough demarcations between Title VII cases in which sexual harassment threats are carried out and where they are not or are absent altogether.

In order to see the context within which sexual harassment operates and many of the ideas that underlie courts' consideration of the issue, take a look at both the majority decision in the following case as well as the dissent. Read the case with the idea in mind that you are looking at the competing interests at issue as society continues to struggle with this sometimes difficult issue. Note that the dissent in *Rabidue* has pretty much become the majority view in the way courts now approach the issue of sexual harassment, but the case is instructive in forcing you to think about the "subtext" of sexual harassment claims and why there is often so much acrimony around the issue. *Rabidue* can also be used to discuss a classic hostile environment sexual harassment case.

[4] 524 U.S. 742 (1998).

Rabidue v. Osceola Refining Co. *805 F.2d 611 (6th Cir. 1986)*

An employee asserted gender discrimination and sexual harassment in violation of Title VII due to "vulgarity" and nude posters in the workplace. The court rejected her claim. However, the case is probably cited more for the dissent than the majority opinion. The dissenting view is now the one that generally prevails in sexual harassment cases. The majority opinion helps you see the evolution of sexual harassment claims from the more provincial view, to the more enlightened position now taken by the courts.

Krupansky, J.

Rabidue was a credit manager and office manager. Her charge of sexual harassment arose primarily as a result of her unfortunate acrimonious working relationship with Douglas Henry, a supervisor of the company's key punch and computer sections. Henry exercised no supervisory authority over Rabidue nor

Rabidue over him. Henry was an extremely vulgar and crude individual who customarily made obscene comments about women generally, and, on occasion, directed such obscenities to Rabidue. Management was aware of Henry's vulgarity, but it had been unsuccessful in curbing his offensive personality traits. Rabidue, and other female employees, were annoyed by Henry's vulgarity. In addition to Henry's obscenities, other male employees from time to time displayed pictures of nude or scantily clad women in their offices and/or work areas, to which Rabidue and other women employees were exposed. Rabidue was discharged from her employment at the company as a result of her many job-related problems, including her irascible and opinionated personality and her inability to work harmoniously with co-workers and customers.

Rabidue to have prevailed in her cause of action against Osceola on this record must have proved that she had been subjected to unwelcome verbal conduct and poster displays of a sexual nature which had unreasonably interfered with her work performance and created an intimidating, hostile, or offensive working environment that affected seriously her psychological well-being.

The record disclosed that Henry's obscenities, although annoying, were not so startling as to have affected seriously the psyches of the plaintiff or other female employees. The evidence did not demonstrate that Henry's vulgarity substantially affected the totality of the workplace. The sexually oriented poster displays had a negligible effect on Rabidue's work environment when considered in the context of a society that condones and publicly features and commercially exploits open displays of written and pictorial erotica at the newsstands, on prime-time television, at the cinema, and in other public places. In sum, Henry's vulgar language and the sexually oriented posters did not result in a working environment that could be considered intimidating, hostile, or offensive under the guidelines. AFFIRMED.

Keith, Circuit Judge, concurring in part, dissenting in part.

I dissent, for several reasons, as I believe the majority erroneously resolves Rabidue's substantive claims.

First, after review of the entire record I am firmly convinced that although supporting evidence exists, the court is mistaken in affirming the findings that Osceola's treatment of Rabidue evinced no anti-female animus and that gender-based discrimination played no role in her discharge. The overall circumstances of Rabidue's workplace evince an anti-female environment. For seven years plaintiff worked at Osceola as the sole woman in a salaried management position. In common work areas Rabidue and other female employees were exposed daily to displays of nude or partially clad women belonging to a number of male employees at Osceola. One poster, which remained on the wall for eight years, showed a prone woman who had a golf ball on her breasts with a man standing over her, golf club in hand, yelling "Fore." And one desk plaque declared "Even male chauvinist pigs need love." Plaintiff testified the posters offended her and her female co-workers.

In addition, Henry regularly spewed anti-female obscenity. He routinely referred to women as "whore," "cunt," "pussy," and "tits." Of plaintiff, Henry specifically remarked "All that bitch needs is a good lay" and called her "fat ass." Plaintiff arranged at least one meeting of female employees to discuss Henry and repeatedly filed written complaints on behalf of herself and other female employees who feared losing their jobs if they complained directly. Osceola Vice President Charles Meutzel stated he knew that employees were "greatly disturbed" by Henry's language. However, because Osceola needed Henry's computer expertise, Meutzel did not reprimand or fire Henry. In response to subsequent complaints about Henry, a later supervisor testified that he gave Henry "a little fatherly advice" about Henry's prospects if he learned to become "an executive type person."

In addition to tolerating this anti-female behavior, Osceola excluded Rabidue, the sole female in management, from activities she needed to perform her duties and progress in her career. Unlike male salaried employees, she did not receive free lunches, free gasoline, a telephone credit card or entertainment privileges. Nor was she invited to the weekly golf matches. Without addressing Osceola's disparate treatment of Rabidue, the district court dismissed these perks and business activities as fringe benefits. After Rabidue became credit manager, Osceola prevented her from visiting or taking customers to lunch as all previous male credit managers had done. Upon requesting such privileges, Rabidue's supervisor replied that it would be improper for a woman to take a male customer to lunch and that she might have car trouble on the road. On another occasion, he asked her "how would it look for me, a married man, to take you, a divorced woman, to the West Branch Country Club in such a small town?" Osceola saw no problem in male managers entertaining female clients regardless of marital status. Rabidue's later supervisor stated to another female worker, "[Rabidue] is doing a good job as credit manager, but we really need a man on that job," adding "She can't take customers out to lunch."

Rabidue was consistently accorded secondary status. At a meeting to instruct clerical employees of their duties after a corporate takeover, Rabidue was seated with female hourly employees. The male salaried employees, apparently pre-informed of the post-takeover procedures, stood at the front of the room. There are many other instances in the record of how Rabidue was treated differently in negative ways because of her gender. I conclude that the misogynous language and decorative displays tolerated at the workplace, the primitive views of working women expressed by Osceola supervisors and Osceola's treatment for their only female salaried employee clearly evinces anti-female animus.

Nor do I agree with the majority's holding that a court considering hostile environment claims should adopt the perspective of the reasonable person's reaction to a similar environment. In my view, the reasonable person perspective fails to account for the wide divergence between most women's views of appropriate sexual conduct and those of men. I would have courts adopt the perspective of the reasonable victim which simultaneously allows courts to consider salient sociological differences as well as shield employers from the neurotic complaint.

The majority also mandates that we consider the "prevailing work environment," the obscenity that pervaded the environment before and after Rabidue came there and her reasonable expectations upon "voluntarily" entering the environment. The majority suggests through these factors that a woman assumes the risk of working in an abusive anti-female environment. Moreover, the majority contends that such work environments somehow have an innate right to perpetuation and are not to be addressed under Title VII. In my view, Title VII's precise purpose is to prevent such behavior and attitudes from poisoning the work environment of classes protected under the Act. As I believe no woman should be subjected to an environment where her sexual dignity and reasonable sensibilities are visually, verbally, or physically assailed as a matter of prevailing male prerogative, I dissent.

Nor can I agree with the majority's notion that the effect of pin-up posters and misogynous language in the workplace can have only a minimal effect on female employees and should not be deemed hostile or offensive "when considered in the context of a society that condones and publicly features and commercially exploits open displays of erotica." "Society" in this scenario must primarily refer to the unenlightened; I hardly believe reasonable women condone the pervasive degradation and exploitation of female sexuality perpetuated in American culture. In fact, pervasive societal approval thereof and of other stereotypes stifles female potential and instills the debased sense of self worth which accompanies stigmatization. The presence of pin-ups and misogynous language in the workplace can only evoke and confirm the debilitating norms by which women are primarily and contemptuously valued as objects of male sexual fantasy. That some men would condone and wish to perpetuate such behavior is not surprising. However, the relevant inquiry at hand is what the reasonable woman would find offensive, not society, which at one point also condoned slavery. I conclude that sexual posters and anti-female language can seriously affect the psychological well-being of the reasonable woman and interfere with her ability to perform her job.

In conclusion, I dissent because the record shows that Osceola's treatment of Rabidue evinces anti-female animus and that Rabidue's gender played a role in her dismissal. I also believe the hostile environment standard set forth in the majority opinion shields and condones behavior Title VII would have the courts redress.

Case Questions

1. Is the majority decision or the dissent closer to your view of sexual harassment? Explain.

2. Why do you think the majority decision did not cite the factors brought out in the dissent and conclude that they presented a hostile environment?

3. If you were management and needed Henry's expertise, what would you have done about his actions?

Exhibit 7.3   Supporting Our Troops?

If your community is like ours, you have seen ribbon car stickers appearing all over in support of our troops in Iraq. Ironically, women in the military face the possibility of attack from not only their military foes, but also their own comrades. Sexual trauma in the military has reportedly reached epidemic proportions. A Department of Defense study shows twice the number of cases as in the civilian population. In January 2005, in response to a rash of sexual assaults among troops in Iraq, at the Air Force Academy (which resulted in the Pentagon announcing that top Air Force Academy officials would be replaced in an effort to change the school's culture) and elsewhere in the military, the Pentagon announced it will begin allowing sexual assault victims confidentiality immediately after their attack in an effort to have more victims report their attacks.

There were courts that followed the majority in *Rabidue,* and those that preferred the dissent. Those preferring the dissent were more prevalent, and ultimately prevailed when the U.S. Supreme Court decided *Harris* v. *Forklift Systems, Inc.*[5] *Harris* was also a Sixth Circuit decision with facts similar to *Rabidue*'s. That is why the employee would be correct in opening scenario 1. (See Exhibit 7.3 for the military's change in this area.)

1
Scenario

In *Harris,* a female managerial employee was subject to several embarrassing and demeaning actions by Charles Hardy, president of Forklift, who admitted to the acts but considered it "joking." Women were requested to retrieve coins from his front pants pockets; he threw objects on the ground in front of Harris and other females and asked them to pick them up; he made sexual innuendoes about Harris and other women's clothing; in front of others, he suggested that he and Harris negotiate her raise at the Holiday Inn; he told her on several occasions "You're a woman, what do you know?" "We need a man as the rental manager," and that she was a "dumb ass woman." After Harris requested that Hardy curtail his activities because she was offended, he promised to stop, but then he resumed. Harris quit after Hardy asked her again, in front of others while she was arranging a deal with a customer, "What did you do, promise the guy . . . some [sex] Saturday night?" The U.S. Supreme Court rejected the notion that such activity in the workplace does not violate Title VII.

Most sexual harassment takes place between males and females, with the male as the harasser and the female as the harassee. But the gender of the harasser need not be male. Males can be sexually harassed, just as females can be sexually harassed. (See Exhibit 7.4.) Unfortunately, because society views males and sex so differently from females and sex, many males do not bring cases for fear of ridicule. Males who are being sexually harassed and wish to put a stop to it often find themselves the object of workplace jokes, teasing, and questioned sexuality, so they forgo filing claims. Even so, statistics show that claim by men are increasing. In *Showalter,* below, males alleged sexual harassment when they were forced to have sex with their supervisor's secretary in order to keep their jobs.

[5] 510 U.S. 17 (1993).

Exhibit 7.4   Trading Places

SEXUALLY HARASSED AT WORK, A CALIFORNIA MAN IS AWARDED $1 MILLION

When Sabino Gutierrez asked his boss, Maria Martinez, for a few days off back in 1986 to visit his native Mexico, she promptly approved the vacation. As a token of his appreciation, he brought her back a gift of two embroidered pillowcases. When Martinez, who was personnel manager at Cal-Spas, a hot-tub manufacturing company in Pomona, Calif., dropped by Gutierrez's office to thank him personally for the gift, she closed the door and embraced him. He thought she was going to give him a peck on the cheek. "But the kiss," says Gutierrez, "was coming straight to the mouth." He says his supervisor told him, "I want to give you my thanks this way."

That, according to Gutierrez, 33, was the beginning of a six-year campaign of sexual harassment during which he was subjected to the advances of Martinez, 39, almost daily. He says the torment included unwanted caresses, kissing, fondling of genitals and demands for sex. In her defense, Martinez, who is married and the mother of two children, contends that it was Gutierrez who was coming on to her, as well as to other women at the company. "He walked around here like a peacock," she says. "Nobody stood in this man's way." However, a Los Angeles jury found that Martinez had indeed sexually harassed Gutierrez and awarded him more than $1 million in damages. The decision is the largest award ever handed down in the United States for a male victim of sexual harassment.

Nonetheless, the facts of the case are far from cut-and-dried. Gutierrez, then a division manager at Cal-Spas, admits that after Martinez's initial advances, he had sex with her—once—in the summer of 1988. "It got to the point where I had to do it to keep her happy," he says. After that, he says, he managed to fend her off despite her continuing overtures. Still, says Gutierrez, he was afraid to reject Martinez outright for fear of losing his job.

The real crisis came in May 1990, Gutierrez says, when he fell in love and became engaged in the span of a few weeks. When Martinez heard, says Gutierrez, she offered her congratulations—then stormed out of his office and slammed the door. The next day, he testified, she vowed to get revenge. During the next several months, she humiliated him by tearing down his office and paring away his duties.

The low point came when she stripped him of all his managerial responsibilities. "She was treating me like a sweeper," he says. "It's terrible even to remember this." According to Martinez, though, the only source of stress for Gutierrez was his own incompetence on the job, which she attributed to his being promoted beyond his capabilities. As for the allegations of harassment, Martinez, who like Gutierrez emigrated from Mexico, scoffs at the notion. "Look at me," she says, incredulous, "I'm a well-educated woman. I've been married for 15 years. I have two children. I grew up with very high morals in my family."

At the trial, Gutierrez's lawyer produced a few witnesses who could corroborate his accounts of harassment. But in the end, a key factor for the 10-woman, two-man jury was the demeanor of the accused and her accuser. While Gutierrez, who has a 22-month-old son, Geovanni, with wife Angelica and now works at another spa company in Ontario, Calif., came across as genuine and sympathetic, Martinez appeared calculating and defensive. "I found him to be very credible right from the beginning," says jury forewoman Clara Riles. By contrast, "it was like [Martinez] had an agenda and she was following that agenda."

Exhibit 7.4 (continued)

The long-term implications of the decision are hard to gauge. If nothing else, the case put some women's rights advocates in the unusual position of arguing against a woman. Yet, in their eyes, the verdict was a solid victory for their cause, since they believe it will strengthen harassment protection for everyone. "The message is that this country is not about justice for some, but about justice for all," says noted feminist lawyer Gloria Allred, whose firm represented Gutierrez. "And that includes men."

Source: Bill Hewitt and Nancy Matsumoto/*People Weekly* © 1993 Time Inc. Reprinted with permission.

Showalter v. Allison Reed Group, Inc. *767 F. Supp. 1205* (D.C. R.I. 1991)

Two male employees allege sexual harassment in violation of Title VII of the Civil Rights Act of 1964 because their manager forced them to engage in sexual activities with his secretary by threatening them with the loss of their jobs if they did not comply. The court found sexual harassment even though the harassees were male.

Lagueux, J.

Employees allege that a series of several sexual incidents occurred on the Techni-Craft premises beginning the summer of 1988 and lasting until June or July of 1989. Defendants Smith and Marsella deny that most of it ever occurred, as does the Allison Reed Group.

Smith, the general manager, was having a sexual liaison with his secretary, Marsella. Employee Showalter alleges that in the Spring of 1988, Smith began talking incessantly and obsessively about Marsella to Showalter. The talks were of a sexual nature and usually described to Showalter Smith's sexual relationship with Marsella, including showing Showalter nude photos, pornographic drawings, and X-rated letters, all involving Marsella. By the end of the summer, Smith began telling Showalter that Marsella was interested in Showalter and prodding Showalter to join his sexual liaison with Marsella. Showalter declined on the ground that he was married, but Smith immediately told Showalter that he and Marsella were also married, but what their spouses didn't know wouldn't hurt them. Angrily, Smith told Showalter that Marsella controlled the hiring and firing decisions at Techni-Craft, and that if he valued his job he would follow Smith's demands. Smith continued to press Showalter to engage in a ménage-à-trois, and reminded Showalter of Smith's extensive connections in the jew-

elry business in Rhode Island, implying that Showalter would be shut out of the jewelry business if he did not comply with Smith's request. Smith also told Showalter that he had to please Marsella in order for everything between Smith and Marsella "to be okay." At one point, Smith also threatened Showalter with the loss of his medical benefits if he failed to participate in the sexual activity. Smith knew that this was especially important to Showalter because Showalter's son had a heart defect and had undergone three open heart surgeries.

Showalter first acceded to Smith's demands in September 1988 when Smith orchestrated an after hours strip-tease performance by Marsella on company premises. Before the actual event Smith gave Showalter explicit instructions outlining the various sexual activity Smith expected Showalter to engage in with Marsella and him. This occurred at least twice and each time Showalter was unable to maintain an erection to do what was demanded of him, and was berated by Smith and Marsella. Showalter was also forced to observe and engage in other sexual activity at Techni-Craft from September 1988 to June 1989, including during work hours and after work hours. Smith tried to get Showalter to bring his wife into the activity in the Spring of 1989, but Showalter resisted. [Employee] Phetosomphone [Fet'-ō-som'-fō-nee] was also forced by Smith to engage in sexual activity at Techni-Craft

321

and observe it between Smith and Marsella. He feared he would lose his job if he did not accede.

Here, Showalter and Phetosomphone were clearly the victims of both hostile environment sexual harassment and quid pro quo sexual harassment. For the quid pro quo sexual harassment, the employees were clearly required to trade the requested sexual activity for the privilege of keeping their jobs. The hostile environment sexual harassment occurred and drastically altered the conditions of plaintiffs' employment and created a hostile and abusive work environment. The frequency and nature of the unwelcome sexual activity certainly was severe and pervasive. Sexual advances were made to plaintiffs for months and the harassment completely infected the work environment. JUDGMENT for PLAINTIFFS on this issue.

Case Questions

1. What can an employer do to protect against liability for sexual harassment in situations such as this, where the person responsible for the workplace is the perpetrator?

2. This is a 1991 case. Do you think males who complain of sexual harassment are still less likely to be believed today? Explain. Do you think they are less likely to sue? Explain.

3. Should it make any difference that the request for sex with Showalter did not come directly from Marsella, the person who wanted to engage in the activity with him, but rather came from Smith? Explain.

As a final preliminary matter, Title VII does not protect employees from discrimination on the basis of affinity orientation, but the U.S. Supreme Court held, after many lower court cases to the contrary, that even though both the harasser and the harassee are the same gender, a harassee can bring a sexual harassment claim and be protected by Title VII. Of course, the reason for the harassment cannot be because the harassee is gay or lesbian, since that is not covered by Title VII, but there is no longer a presumption that if both parties are the same gender the claim is not covered by Title VII, as many cases had held.

QUID PRO QUO SEXUAL HARASSMENT

In quid pro quo sexual harassment, the employee is required to engage in sexual activity in exchange for workplace entitlements or benefits such as promotions, raises, or continued employment. This is the more obvious type of sexual harassment and is not generally difficult to recognize. (See Exhibit 7.5.) Actually, we say it is not difficult to recognize, but notice the difference of opinion between the district court and the lower court in the *Bryson* case, below or the *Rabidue* case discussed previously.

Bryson v. Chicago State University *96 F.3d 912 (1996)*

A Chicago State University tenured professor alleged that she lost her job title and was banished from university committee work because of rejecting requests for sexual activity from her supervisor. The court looked at the causation between the loss of her job benefits and the activity by the supervisor and determined that the rejection caused the loss, thus resulting in quid pro quo sexual harassment.

Wood, J.

Emily Bryson is a tenured full professor at Chicago State University. She claimed, in a lawsuit brought

under Title VII, that she had been the victim of quid pro quo sexual harassment inflicted by then-Provost Chernoh Sesay. The district court granted summary judgment to Chicago State University, Sesay, and the

Demonstrating that no one seems to be exempt from claims of sexual harassment, in what is probably the most famous sexual harassment case in history, Paula Jones, a former Arkansas state employee, filed suit against a state trooper and a sitting president of the United States. Jones claimed that she was the victim of a sexual advance from President Bill Clinton while he was serving as governor of Arkansas prior to his presidency. The decision of whether the sexual harassment case could be brought against a sitting president went all the way to the U.S. Supreme Court, and the Court saw no impediment to Jones' bringing the suit. In the end, the Eighth Circuit Court of Appeals affirmed the district court's dismissal of Jones's case. [990 F. Supp. 657 (E.D. Ark. W. Div. 1998)] The Court held that the facts alleged by Jones, even if taken to be true, were insufficient to establish a basis for either quid pro quo or hostile work environment sexual harassment. In the court's view, the president's dropping his trousers, fondling his penis, and asking Jones to kiss it, and then backing off when she said no, while boorish, was not sufficiently severe or pervasive to constitute a violation of the statute.

---

other defendants named in the suit, on the ground that Bryson failed adequately to demonstrate that she had lost any tangible employment benefit as a result of her rejections of Sesay. Because we conclude that the record reveals genuine issues of fact on this point, we reverse and remand for further proceedings.

Chernoh Sesay was appointed Provost and Vice-President of Academic Affairs at Chicago State in July 1990. The Provost has full control and responsibility over faculty affairs at the university; he reports directly to the President. Sesay knew Bryson and supported her in her successful bid for an Administrative Fellowship. In January 1991 (after her selection but before she began her Fellowship), he began to make sexually suggestive and derogatory comments to her and to attempt to engage in improper physical contact with her. For example, in December 1990 at the President's Christmas party, Sesay approached Bryson, caressed her shoulders, pushed his body against hers, and whispered "when are you going to come over and start cooking for me?" Bryson jerked away and retorted, "I don't cook for anybody." In February 1991, while both Sesay and Bryson were visiting Governor's State (another campus in the system), Sesay asked Bryson to get into his car and go back to his hotel with him, so that they could "relax." Bryson refused. On numerous other occasions, he also suggested that they "relax" together, but she consistently rejected him. Several times in his office, he tried to kiss her. Once he asked her into his office to discuss a library-related matter, but when she stood up to leave, he ran his hand up her dress and fondled her behind.

Sesay's inappropriate behavior continued during Bryson's fellowship at Eastern Illinois University. At a President's function in October 1991, he approached Bryson and asked, "Why aren't you going to let me up into your room? Let's go relax. I have something big to show you." Her rejections continued, however, and when in May 1992 he again asked her to come to his room to "relax" and she again refused, he warned her, "You had better do what I say or you're going to be sorry."

In June 1992, Bryson met with Chicago State President Dolores E. Cross to discuss her return. She said that she intended to return to her old position of Special Assistant to the Dean. Cross then called Sesay into the meeting. Sesay told her that the administrative title of "Special Assistant to the Dean" had never existed and that she had never performed those duties. Bryson interpreted this to mean that if she did not give in to his advances, she would have to work her way back up again. Sesay also told Bryson that all her tasks of special assistance to the dean had been reassigned to other people, and that she would be returned to bibliographic instruction work, her entry level position in 1980. Guy Craft, the Dean of LLR, told Bryson the next day that he had been instructed by his supervisors to "put [her] back as bibliographic instruction librarian."

Upon her return to Chicago State, although her work assignment "units" reflected the same number devoted to special assistance tasks as before, both her job description and her actual duties were diminished. By January 1993, all her special assistance responsibilities were deleted from her assignment. She filed a grievance with her union, which had the effect of permitting her to continue performing the disputed administrative tasks pending the outcome of the proceeding. In the end, she retained her duties as Special Assistant to the Dean, but she lost her in-house title. She also found herself frozen out of the university's administrative committees, even though appointments were made on an annual basis to most of them. She was denied reappointment to the Budget Committee, the Assessment Committee, and the Retention Committee, in spite of her expressed desire to continue serving. Her written request to serve on several other committees also fell on deaf ears.

In Bryson's view, Sesay had made good on his threats. She filed a charge with the EEOC alleging that she was the victim of sexual harassment by Sesay. She argued that she was denied the employment benefits of membership on various administrative committees and the title of Special Assistant to the Dean as a direct result of her rebuffing Sesay's unwanted sexual advances. She received her right to sue letter and filed a complaint with the district court alleging both quid pro quo and hostile work environment sexual harassment.

In order to prove such a claim, many courts of appeals use a five-part test, asking whether the plaintiff has shown (1) that she or he is a member of a protected group, (2) the sexual advances were unwelcome, (3) the harassment was sexually motivated, (4) the employee's reaction to the supervisor's advances affected a tangible aspect of her employment, and (5) respondeat superior has been established. Element (1) is plain enough, and a common part of many kinds of discrimination claims. Element (2) focuses on the unwelcome nature of the sexual advances from the point of view of the recipient, while element (3) asks whether the harasser was looking for sexual favors or something else. Element (4) asks what the "quo" part of the quid pro quo was: what tangible aspect of employment was affected? Finally, element (5) recognizes that there is a need to link the employer to the actions of the harasser. We have no occasion here to decide whether these five elements perfectly capture today's law of quid pro quo harassment, or if it would be better to consolidate some or add others. For present purposes, they provide a useful framework for our discussion, which turns on only one element that we agree is critical.

That element is number 4: what was the "tangible employment benefit" that was denied to Bryson, and was the denial a result of her refusal to submit to Sesay's demands? The question whether an employee has suffered a materially adverse employment action will normally depend on the facts of each situation.

Bryson relies on the loss of two types of tangible employment benefits to meet this flexible test: first, she claims that her loss of the title Special Assistant to the Dean was a tangible adverse action, and second, she claims that her banishment from university committee work was such an action.

Chicago State responds that the title had no independent meaning, and that committee work was nothing she could expect to do in any event. It stresses that she succeeded in retaining her tasks. The district court found that committee work was not essential to a tenured academic, and it expressed skepticism that anyone would really want to serve on committees in any event. It was similarly unimpressed with the loss of the title, which it found had only speculative value. The case would have been different, the court suggested, if Bryson had applied for tangible promotions such as a deanship and been unsuccessful.

With respect, we believe that the district court failed to recognize that Bryson raised disputed issues of fact on the issue of loss of tangible employment benefit. Bryson came forward with evidence that her title conferred prestige and was important to further professional advancement. She came forward with similar evidence regarding her committee work. The title, for example, would communicate to others both within the State Colleges and Universities system and outside it what kind of responsibilities had been entrusted to her. Committee work, especially on important committees like Budget and Retention, is often a prelude to an administrative career.

Bryson herself, it is undisputed, had been on a promising job track for such a career, since she won the coveted position of Board Administrative Fellow for 1991–92. A sudden loss of all committee responsibilities and the stripping of a title one formerly held (when similar titles continued to be used throughout the university), if proven at trial, would be a loss of tangible employment benefits just as serious as moving an office to an undesirable location, relocating someone's personal files, or isolating the employee from others—all actions courts have held to qualify under Title VII in other cases.

Universities have few "carrots" to dangle in front of tenured faculty members who reach full professorhood. The subtle indicia of job status and reward thus may, in a particular institution, take on an importance that may be far greater in context than would appear on the outside—indicia like honorary or in-house titles (that may have no budgetary effect, unlike their administrative counterparts) and committee assignments. The trier of fact must resolve the factual dispute over the reward structure that prevailed at Chicago State and how it related to the particular actions taken in Bryson's case. As the district court implicitly recognized, committee assignments and titles may play a part in preparing for an administrative academic career.

The court erred in assuming that nothing adverse had happened to Bryson because she had not yet applied for a deanship. Depriving someone of the building blocks for such a promotion, if that is what a trier of fact thinks Chicago State did, is just as serious as depriving her of the job itself.

Chicago State also claims that Bryson did not offer sufficient evidence of causation. Here again, the record shows genuine issues of fact. Bryson pointed both to direct evidence of causation and circumstantial evidence. The direct evidence was Sesay's remark to her in May 1992 that she "had better do what I say or [she'll] be sorry."

The circumstantial evidence began building immediately thereafter. In the June 1992 meeting, Sesay made a statement that a trier of fact could interpret as a veiled threat, when he told her the administrative title of "Special Assistant to the Dean" had never existed and that she had never performed those duties. The title had obviously existed, whether it was an "in-house" title or something more formal, and she had just as plainly performed the duties. The contrast between her position at Chicago State prior to her fellowship and her position upon her return might also strike a trier of fact as telling. As Provost, Sesay was in a position to effect all these changes. This was all Bryson needed to defeat Chicago State's motion for summary judgment on the quid pro quo harassment charge. REVERSED.

Case Questions

1. If you were the university president, what would you have done about this situation?

2. Do you agree with the lower court that there was not sufficient evidence of a connection between what the provost did and what happened to Bryson's job, or with the Court of Appeals, which said there was sufficient evidence of the connection? Explain.

3. How could this situation have been avoided or liability lessened?

An employer can limit a supervisor's ability to abuse power by choosing supervisory employees carefully and having in place a system with adequate monitors and checks. It greatly decreases morale, and thus lowers workplace productivity, for other employees to witness quid pro quo harassment by the supervisor. In fact, it has even been held that the other employees witnessing such activity may bring a cause of action of their own.

HOSTILE ENVIRONMENT SEXUAL HARASSMENT

The more difficult sexual harassment issues have been in the area of hostile environment because there remains confusion about what activity constitutes the offense. Part of the difficulty lies in the fact that many of the causes that may serve as a basis for liability have until recently gone unchallenged. However, a closer look at what courts have held to constitute a hostile environment lends more predictability.

To sustain a finding of hostile environment sexual harassment, it is generally required that:

• The harassment be unwelcome by the harassee.

• The harassment be based on gender.

- The harassment be sufficiently severe or pervasive to create an abusive working environment.
- The harassment affect a term, condition, or privilege of employment.
- The employer had actual or constructive knowledge of the sexually hostile working environment and took no prompt or adequate remedial action.

Scenario

In light of these requirements, it becomes clear why simply giving polite compliments as in opening scenario 3, is not, in and of itself, sexual harassment. Sexual harassment involves much more.

The case below was the first sexual harassment case to reach the U.S. Supreme Court. See if you can now distinguish between quid pro quo and hostile environment sexual harassment.

Meritor Savings Bank, FSB v. Vinson   *477 U.S. 57 (1986)*

An employee alleged sexual harassment even though she lost no tangible job benefits. The Court determined that quid pro quo was not the only type of sexual harassment. For the first time, the U.S. Supreme Court determined that this kind of situation constituted hostile environment sexual harassment.

Rehnquist, J.

Mechelle Vinson worked at Meritor Savings Bank, initially as a teller-trainee, but was later promoted to teller, head teller, and assistant branch manager, admittedly based upon merit. Sidney Taylor was the bank branch manager and the person who hired Vinson. Vinson alleged that in the beginning Taylor was "fatherly" toward her and made no sexual advances, but eventually he asked her to go out to dinner. During the course of the meal Taylor suggested that he and Vinson go to a motel to have sexual relations. At first she refused, but out of what she described as fear of losing her job, she eventually agreed. Taylor thereafter made repeated demands upon Vinson for sexual activity, usually at the branch, both during and after business hours. She estimated that over the next several years she had intercourse with him some 40 or 50 times. In addition, she testified that Taylor fondled her in front of other employees, followed her into the women's restroom when she went there alone, exposed himself to her, and even forcibly raped her on several occasions. These activities ceased in 1977 when Vinson started going with a steady boyfriend.

Courts have applied Title VII protection to racial harassment and nothing in Title VII suggests that a hostile environment based on discriminatory *sexual* harassment should not be likewise prohibited. The Guidelines thus appropriately drew from, and were fully consistent with, the existing case law.

Of course, not all workplace conduct that may be described as "harassment" affects a "term, condition, or privilege" of employment within the meaning of Title VII. For instance, mere utterance of an ethnic or racial epithet which engenders offensive feelings in an employee would not affect the condition of employment to a sufficiently significant degree to create an abusive working environment. For sexual harassment to be actionable, it must be sufficiently severe or pervasive to alter the conditions of the victim's employment and create an abusive working environment. Vinson's allegations in this case—which include not only pervasive harassment, but also criminal conduct of the most serious nature—are plainly sufficient to state a claim for hostile environment sexual harassment.

The District Court's conclusion that no actionable harassment occurred might have rested on its earlier finding that if Vinson and Taylor had engaged in intimate or sexual relations, that relationship was a voluntary one. But the fact that sex-related conduct was "voluntary" in the sense that the complainant was not forced to participate against her will, is not a defense to a sexual harassment suit brought under Title VII. The gravamen of any sexual harassment claim is the alleged sexual advances were "unwelcome." While the question whether particular conduct was indeed unwelcome presents difficult problems of proof and turns largely on credibility determinations committed to the trier of fact, the District Court in this case erroneously focused on the "voluntariness" of Vinson's participation in the claimed sexual episodes. The correct inquiry is whether Vinson, by her conduct, indicated that the alleged sexual advances were unwelcome, not whether her participation in sexual intercourse was voluntary.

The district court admitted into evidence testimony about Vinson's "dress and personal fantasies." The court of appeals stated that testimony had no place in the litigation, on the basis that Vinson's voluntariness in submitting to Taylor's advances was immaterial to her sexual harassment claim. While "voluntariness" in the sense of consent is not a defense to such a claim, it does not follow that a complainant's sexually provoca-

tive speech or dress is irrelevant as a matter of law in determining whether she found particular sexual advances welcome. To the contrary, such evidence is obviously relevant. The EEOC Guidelines emphasize that the trier of fact must determine the existence of sexual harassment in light of "the record as a whole" and the "totality of circumstances," such as the nature of the sexual advances and the context in which the alleged incidents occurred.

In sum we hold that a claim of "hostile environment" sexual harassment gender discrimination is actionable under Title VII. AFFIRMED.

Case Questions

1. As a manager, what would you have done if Vinson had come to you with her story?

2. Under the circumstances, should it matter that Vinson "voluntarily" had sex with Taylor? That she received her regular promotions? Explain.

3. As a manager, how would you determine who to believe?

In *Meritor* it is clear that the supervisor's actions changed the terms and conditions of Vinson's employment. There is a big difference between the ongoing, pervasive actions of Vinson's supervisor and merely giving someone an occasional nonsexual compliment. Be sure that you understand that in a hostile environment action, the action must be more than someone committing a boorish, stupid, inappropriate act. The act must come up to the standards the courts and the EEOC have set forth for the cause of action. Contrary to what you may have been led to believe by the press or other information you've received, not every act, even if it is unwanted or offensive, will do so; thus, not every act, though considered offensive by the employee, constitutes sexual harassment as set forth by law. (see Exhibit 7.5.) Note too, that in *Bryson,* it was clear that Bryson's job suffered because of her failure to accede to her supervisor's requests for sexual activity (quid pro quo), while in *Meritor,* the employee lost no tangible job benefits such as raises or promotions.

Unwelcome Activity

The basis of hostile environment sexual harassment actions is unwanted activity by the harasser. (See Exhibit 7.6.) If the activity is wanted or welcome by the harassee, there is no sexual harassment. Even if the activity started out being consensual, if one employee calls a halt to it and the other continues, it can become sexual harassment at the time the activity is no longer consensual, as in opening scenario 2.

In making the determination of whether the harasser's activity was welcome, the actions used as a basis for the determination can be direct or indirect. In *McLean* v.

QUID PRO QUO SEXUAL HARASSMENT

- Workplace benefit promised, given to, or withheld from harassee by harasser
- In exchange for sexual activity by harassee
- Generally accompanied by a paper trail (e.g., promotion, raise, or termination paperwork).

HOSTILE ENVIRONMENT SEXUAL HARASSMENT

Activity by harasser, toward harasee that

- Is unwanted by the harassee.
- Is based on harassee's gender.
- Creates for harassee a hostile or abusive work environment.
- Unreasonably interferes with harassee's ability to do his or her job.
- Is sufficiently severe and/or pervasive.
- Affects a term or condition of harassee's employment.

Satellite Technology Services, Inc. the court had no trouble in determining that harassee welcomed the activity of harasser, if, in fact, it took place at all. It also demonstrates that there is more to winning a sexual harassment case than alleging simply that sexual harassment occurred.

McLean v. Satellite Technology Services, Inc. *673 F. Supp. 1458 (E.D. Mo. 1987)*

An assistant salesperson contends she was wrongfully terminated after she spurned romantic advances by her supervisor. The court found no sexual harassment because it held that the supervisor's actions, if they occurred, were not unwelcome.

Gunn, J.

McLean alleges she was at a business seminar meeting in Florida with Manning, who was making a presentation. McLean was to observe so she would ultimately be able to conduct a seminar. After one day's work, McLean, Manning, and another Satellite employee had dinner and went to the hotel's hot tub. Manning suggested to McLean that she should review his presentation, so he went to her hotel room. McLean claims that while they were in the room, with her dressed in a swimsuit and towel, and Manning in shorts and a shirt,

they sat on the couch together and while Manning talked about his presentation, he put his arm around her back, touched her leg, and made an effort to kiss her once. McLean testified the effort was easily rebuffed and Manning then left the room. Manning denies making any advances to McLean. Following the trip McLean alleges Manning was cool to her. She attributes this and her subsequent dismissal to her rebuff of his advances.

The court finds that there was a multitude of legitimate business reasons for terminating McLean and that her discharge was not based upon sexual harassment.

It is undisputed that McLean was anything but demure, that she possessed a lusty libido and was no paragon of virtue. From the beginning of her short term of employment with Satellite in November of 1985, to its end in February 1986, she displayed a remarkable lust for those of the opposite sex. She displayed her body through semi-nude photos or by lifting her skirt to show her supervisor an absence of undergarments. Also, during work hours, she made offers of sexual gratification or highly salacious comments to employees, customers and competitors alike, though warned by Manning not to do so. There was uncontroverted evidence of acceptance of her offers.

Though specifically ordered by her supervisor, Manning, to refrain from an obviously flirtatious telephone relationship with an employee of a customer, McLean flouted the order and carried on the dalliance. It was McLean's activities at a trade show in Las Vegas, Nevada, on February 22–23, 1986 that finally led to McLean's discharge. At the trade show, McLean missed meetings she was expected to attend, was not at her job station a large percentage of the time and continued her libidinous behavior, acknowledging she was "intimate" with an employee of a customer at least two or three times, entertaining him in her hotel room during the period of the trade show. This was despite orders from her supervisor to abstain from promiscuity with customers or dealers.

On her return from Las Vegas, McLean was summarily discharged from her employment by the president of Satellite. His basis was McLean's performance at the Las Vegas trade show as related by Satellite's chief operating officer who was there and observed McLean's actions. Specifically, she was dismissed for missing work and meetings in Las Vegas.

The court specifically finds that there was no sexual harassment of McLean by her supervisor. From McLean's character, it is apparent that she would have welcomed rather than rejected Manning's advance, if he did indeed do so. But the court finds that Manning made no sexual advance. McLean was not subjected to any unwelcome sexual harassment. Indeed, it is McLean who bears the responsibility for whatever sexually suggestive conduct is involved in this case. Satellite has stated nonpretextual, legitimate and absolutely nondiscriminatory reasons for its discharge of McLean. She was insubordinate, and displayed total disrespect for her supervisor, which would serve as a legitimate basis for termination. It is also abundantly clear that McLean was terminated because of her poor work performance, attitudes, and habits, e.g., excessively long lunch hours, personal phone calls, entertaining nonbusiness visitors during working hours, and being inattentive to her work, particularly at the Las Vegas trade show. As such, her termination was proper. JUDGMENT FOR DEFENDANT, COSTS TO BE PAID BY PLAINTIFF.

Case Questions

1. Do you agree with the court's assessment of the evidence? Why or why not?

2. If you were McLean's supervisor and she exhibited the behavior alleged, what could you have done?

3. Do you think the court would have held the same way if McLean had been a male? Explain. Do you think a male employee would have been ordered by his supervisor to "abstain from promiscuity with customers"? Would it be gender discrimination to give such orders to employees of one gender and not the other? Explain.

There may also be a finding that the harassee did not welcome the activity by the harasser. Evidence can be direct, such as the harassee telling the harasser to discontinue the offending activity, or indirect, such as the harassee using body language, eye signals, and the like to show disapproval of the harasser's actions. Employees should be told to make it clear to a harasser that the activity is unwelcome; otherwise, the signals may become confused and the harasser may think his or her actions are wanted by the harassee. In Exhibit 7.7 you can see how some employers are trying to address the issue in novel ways.

Exhibit 7.7   Wanna Fool Around? Sign on the Dotted Line, Please . . .

In the face of increasingly expensive and embarrassing sexual harassment litigation, there have been all sorts of attempts to lessen employer liability. See how you like this workplace idea. You may recall hearing about a similar plan imposed on the students by the administration at a large midwestern university a few years ago to prevent date rape.

"LOVE CONTRACTS" HELP FEND OFF HARASSMENT SUITS

No matter how many training sessions or awareness workshops they conduct, companies still find themselves facing sexual harassment claims. Alarmingly, claims keep going higher up the chain of command, increasingly hitting CEOs. And when such a suit reaches a top executive, it's not just a department in trouble, but the entire company itself.

The latest trend in fending off sexual harassment suits is a "love contract." Teresa Butler, managing partner in the Atlanta office of employment law firm Littler Mendelson, explains.

Can you talk about the "love contract" and how it works?

It's really only intended for higher-level executives. This isn't something we advise employers to put in their handbooks, and we don't recommend that all supervisors issue them to subordinates. We talk about this for CEOs and officers, top-level executives, and maybe directors; that's a judgment call for the company. It's basically for people who have broad power in the workplace—not the average first-level supervisor.

What's included in the contract?

The love contract does three things. First it restates the voluntary nature of the relationship. The CEO, or whoever is in this situation, issues the agreement to a subordinate employee, basically explaining to the individual, "I want to have this relationship with you. My understanding is you want to have this relationship with me. But I'm concerned that over time you might believe that the continuation of this relationship— even though you don't want it anymore—might be necessary for you to be successful here. As you know, we have a harassment policy, and I want you to understand that I'm aware of that policy and would never allow [the end of the relationship] to influence my decision making with regard to your employment." So the agreement is actually a formal contract. It restates the voluntary nature of the relationship.

What else should a love contract do?

Secondly, it affirms that the parties will use the company's sexual harassment policies if a problem arises, and it confirms the existence of those policies and [procedures]. It also states that if the policies aren't used, it's fair to assume there isn't a problem. And thirdly, the parties agree if work-related disputes arise, they'll resolve their differences using alternative dispute resolution (ADR) rather than resorting to the courts. Some might want to use that third piece and some might not, but we recommend ADR from a legal standpoint.

How are these contracts useful?

Often these relationships go bad at some point; one party wants to end it and the other doesn't. And then there's retaliatory conduct by the other, sometimes by the subordinate in the form of a sexual harassment complaint. So this contract is a method for the top-level executives to just say out loud what is actually the case. It's assurance for the company and the individuals that everybody understands what the rules are.

Exhibit 7.7   (continued)

How legally defensible is a love contract?

The first response we typically hear, especially from lawyers, is: How could this possibly be enforceable? The idea is this person can always come back and say this was coerced, that he or she was forced to sign this agreement. That's a risk you take with any contractual relationship because an employee is always in a subordinate role to the employer. If you take that to its logical end, you might as well say you could never have an enforceable contract with an employee.

So can they raise that issue?

Of course they can. But are you better off with the contract than without it? Yes. I think it's a pretty tough argument for an individual who signs this agreement to say that he or she was coerced into having this consensual relationship that you'll be able to [prove] the person had. There's usually evidence in these cases of a consensual relationship: You've got birthday cards, receipts for dinner, letters and other types of communications that the subordinate employee has clearly engaged in on a voluntary basis.

"LOVE CONTRACT" SAMPLE LETTER

Dear [Name of Object of Affection]:

As we discussed, I know that this may seem silly or unnecessary to you, but I really want you to give serious consideration to the matter as it is very important to me. [Add other materials as appropriate]

I very much value our relationship and I certainly view it as voluntary, consensual and welcome, and I have always felt that you feel the same. However, I know that sometimes an individual may feel compelled to engage in or continue in a relationship against their will out of concern that it may affect the job or working relationships.

It is very important to me that our relationship be on an equal footing and that you be fully comfortable that our relationship is at all times fully voluntary and welcome. I want to assure you that under no circumstances will I allow our relationship or, should it happen, the end of our relationship, to impact on your job or our working relationship. Though I know you have received a copy of [our company's name] sexual harassment policy, I am enclosing a copy [Add specific reference to policy as appropriate] so that you can read and review it again. Once you have done so, I would greatly appreciate your signing this letter below, if you are in agreement with me.

[Add personal closing]

Very truly yours,

[Name]

I have read this letter and the accompanying sexual harassment policy, and I understand and agree with what is stated in both this letter and the sexual harassment policy. My relationship with [name] has been (and is) voluntary, consensual and welcome. I also understand that I am free to end this relationship any time, and in doing so, it will not adversely impact on my job.

[Signature of Object of Affection]

Sources: Teresa Butler, Littler Mendelson, Atlanta, 888-LITTLER; Gillian Flynn, *Workforce Magazine*, March, 1999, pp. 106–108. Used with permission.

In another type of welcomeness issue, the Hooters restaurant chain was involved in several cases that, among other things, brought up the question of unwelcomeness parameters. As discussed in the previous chapter, Hooters is an Atlanta-based chain of over 235 restaurants in 46 states and 14 countries. It is noted for its buffalo chicken wings and scantily clad female servers. At least seven lawsuits have been filed by female servers who were allegedly illegally fired or forced to quit because of sexual harassment.

The suits allege that the environment created by management for female servers was hostile, starting with the name "Hooters," which is a slang term for women's breasts. Servers (a position for which Hooters only hires females), who are required to wear uniforms of revealing shorts and T-shirts, alleged that they were required to endure an atmosphere of sexually offensive remarks, touching, and other conduct by both management and customers. For example, the sign on entering Hooters reads "Men: no shirt, no shoes: no service. Women: no shirt: free food."

An important issue in the lawsuits has been whether, as the company argued, the women assumed the risk of the activities directed at them by agreeing to work for the company—that is, whether the conduct was welcomed by the fact that the servers worked for a company whose concept encouraged such behavior. What do you think? Should it matter, if as it turns out, the requirement is illegal under Title VII? Check out the Hooters website and see if you agree, as Hooters argued, that it is merely a neighborhood restaurant (previously it had argued it was a family restaurant), complete with a children's menu. There is at least some truth to this. One of our students said his Little League baseball coach took the all-male team to Hooters to celebrate the student's birthday and they *loved* it. It was the student's 12th birthday and the coach was his dad!

Severe and Pervasive Requirement

severe and pervasive activity
Harassing activity that is more than an occasional act or is so serious that it is the basis for liability.

One of the most troublesome problems with hostile environment is determining whether the harassing activity is **severe and pervasive** enough to amount to an unreasonable interference with an employee's ability to perform. (See Exhibit 7.8.) Built into the elements of hostile environment sexual harassment is a requirement that the offending activity be sufficiently severe and pervasive. That is, the activity is not an isolated occurrence that is not serious enough to warrant undue concern. The more frequent or serious the occurrences, the more likely it is that the severe and pervasive requirement will be met. If it is egregious enough, one time may meet the severity requirement, for example, in the case of rape.

Regarding the "unreasonable interference" requirement, in *Harris* v. *Forklift Sys.* mentioned earlier, the U.S. Supreme Court decided that sexual harassment claims do not require findings of severe psychological harm to be actionable. The Court said that "so long as the environment would reasonably be perceived, and is perceived, as hostile or abusive, there is no need for it also to be psychologically injurious."

In *Ross* v. *Double Diamond, Inc.,* events over a two-day period were determined to meet the requirement for one employee but not for her sister. See if you agree with the different conclusions or can understand the difference in the court's decision about one sister versus the other.

Exhibit 7.8   Wanted?

One of the requirements of sexual harassment is that the activity be unwelcome. Look at *these* cases!

A jury awarded over $4 million to a hospital administrator who sued for retaliation under Title VII for being forced to resign when she attempted to prevent sexual harassment in the hospital's operating room. There were complaints of the nurse bugging, kissing, embracing, and rubbing doctors and other staff. The administrator verbally warned the nurse that this was inappropriate behavior. The nurse complained to doctors and staff about unfair treatment and quit. Several doctors complained about the administrator and a prominent doctor threatened to leave the hospital unless the administrator was terminated and the nurse reinstated. The administrator, given the choice to resign or be terminated for "breach of confidentiality," left, and six days later the nurse returned.

EEOC v. *Bon Secours DePaul Med. Ctr.,* Civil Action No. 2:02cv728 (E. D. Va, 2002).

In July 2005, the California Supreme Court held that an employee can sue a supervisor engaging in consensual sexual conduct with other employees when it has the effect of creating a "widespread atmosphere of sexual favoritism in the workplace." This decision forces employers to closely monitor employee relationships.

Miller v. *Department of Corrections,* 2005 LEXIS 7606 (July 18, 2005).

Ross v. Double Diamond, Inc. *672 F. Supp. 261*
(N.D. Tex. 1987)

Two discharged employees, sisters, brought this action against their former employer, alleging that he violated Title VII by creating a sexually harassing work environment and then constructively discharging them because they reported it and also because of their gender. The court found a hostile environment for acts occurring during a two-day period for one sister, Beverly Ross, but not the other, Sheila Stroudenmire.

Mahon, J.

Within the first hour that twenty-year-old Ross was on her new job at Double Diamond, her supervisor, Larry Womack, asked her if she "fooled around," to which she answered no. A short time later, Womack asked Ross to bring him a cup of coffee. When she entered his office with the coffee, he told her he wanted to take her picture. She protested, he insisted, and Ross agreed for fear of Womack's reaction if she continued to refuse. Womack then told Ross to pull up her dress for the picture. Still afraid of his reaction to her refusal, she pulled her dress up two inches above her knee and Womack took the picture. A short time later Ross asked for the picture and Womack refused to give it to her.

Later that day Womack called Ross on the phone and asked her to pant heavily for him. Ross immediately hung up. Still later the same day, Ross entered Womack's office during a meeting to give a message to one of the attendees. A salesman, Larry West, placed a Polaroid camera on the floor directly under Ross and took a picture up Ross's dress. The salesmen at the meeting laughed. Ross attempted to take the camera, but Womack prevented it. Ross asked for the picture and Womack refused, told her the picture did not develop and that she could not look for it in the trash can. Womack later called Ross on the phone and again

333

asked her to pant heavily into the phone. Ross immediately hung up.

The next day, when Ross came into Womack's office to bring him coffee, he told her to come over to him by the desk. She did so and Womack pulled her onto his lap. A salesman came into the office. The salesman testified that Ross was on Womack's lap and Womack had his arms around Ross's waist and Ross was feverishly trying to pull away. After the salesman came in, Womack, who the salesman said looked "perverted," released his hold on Ross.

During this same day, Ross's sister, Stroudenmire, came to work for her first day of work as a sales trainee. She heard some employees laughing while looking at a picture in Womack's office. She told Ross and they went into the office to obtain the picture. Two salesmen were laughing at a picture, but slipped it into Womack's desk drawer when the two came in. Stroudenmire removed the picture from the drawer. It was the one taken up Ross's dress. Ross left the office in tears and went to the ladies' room. Later that day Womack called Ross into his office and told her to "bend over" and clean something off the wall. She refused to do so and started to leave. Womack proceeded to close the door to prevent her from leaving and trapped Ross against the door. Ross escaped by crawling out from under Womack's arm. Womack later entered a room in which Stroudenmire was studying and told her that he bet she liked to wear black boots and carry a whip in the bedroom. Womack also segregated Stroudenmire from the other sales trainees who were studying together, refused to allow her to take materials home to study with, and threatened in a loud voice to have Stroudenmire's husband fired and to make Stroudenmire and her husband lose their home because Stroudenmire reported Womack's activities to his supervisor. Stroudenmire and Ross called the sheriff and told him of the threats and asked him to come to Double Diamond. When he came and inquired as to what was going on, Womack said they were just having fun. Ross and Stroudenmire soon after left their jobs after being told they could not take the rest of the afternoon off or if they did so, they could not return.

To determine severity or pervasiveness the court should consider several things. First, the nature of the unwelcome sexual acts or words. Generally unwelcome physical touching is more offensive than unwelcome verbal abuse. However, this is only a generalization and in specific situations, the type of language used may be more offensive than the type of physical touching. Second, a court should consider the frequency of the offensive encounters. It is less likely that a hostile work environment exists when, for instance, the offensive encounters occur once every year than if the encounters occur once every week. Third, the court would consider the total number of days over which all the offensive meetings occur. Lastly, the court should consider the context in which the sexually harassing conduct occurred. The court emphasizes that none of these factors should be given more weight than others. In addition, the nonexistence of one of these factors does not, in and of itself, prevent a Title VII claim. The trier of fact must consider the totality of the circumstances.

Because of its importance in this case, the court chooses to elaborate on the reasons why a short duration of sexual harassment does not prohibit a Title VII claim. The courts are looking for a pattern of sexual harassment inflicted upon an employee because of her gender because this type of activity is a pattern of behavior that inflicts disparate treatment upon a member of one gender with respect to terms, conditions, or privileges of employment. Sexual harassment need not exist over a long period for it to be considered a pattern. If the sexual harassment is frequent and/or intensely offensive, a pattern can be established over a short period of time.

The court finds that the acts and communications perpetrated against Ross at Double Diamond are sufficiently severe or pervasive to alter the conditions of Ross's employment and create an abusive work environment.

This is not so with Stroudenmire. Title VII is not a shield which protects people from all sexual discrimination. The type of conduct listed above does not rise to the level of harassment which is actionable. It is not sufficiently severe and pervasive to alter the conditions of employment or create an abusive work environment. JUDGMENT for ROSS.

Case Questions

1. Do you agree with the court's decision about Stroudenmire? Ross? Explain.

2. As the manager, what would you have done about Womack?

3. Do you agree that there was sufficient severity and pervasiveness in the two-day period here? Specifically what makes you reach your conclusion?

Exhibit 7.9   Is "Discomfort" Enough?

Students often think that merely feeling uncomfortable about something going on in the workplace is sufficient to sustain a claim under Title VII for hostile environment sexual harassment. As you can see from this situation, this is far from the case—or is it?

Canon, Inc.'s male sales representative had, as part of his territory, a store owned by a woman, his client. At a Christmas party, the female store owner/client was inappropriately touched, hugged, and kissed on the face and forehead by the sales rep's immediate supervisor. The client decided she did not want to complain about it. The sales rep complained to the company anyway. When the supervisor to whom the complaint was made called the client to discuss it as part of its investigation of the claim, the client again said she did not want to pursue the matter. When the sales rep was told this, he called the client and left a voice mail message expressing his anger at her refusal to corroborate his claims against his supervisor. In a "loud, rapid" voice, he used abusive language, and told her he was "pissed off," he accused her of lying to Canon, and said that he was going to "lose his f_ing job" and she needed to back up his claim of the harassment against her. Because of the message, the client was so afraid of the sales rep that she would no longer allow him in her store. When the company found out about the voice mail message, the sales rep was fired. Canon, Inc., told him his conduct toward the client was unprofessional and unacceptable and would not be tolerated under any circumstances. The employee filed suit for retaliation under Title VII, claiming that the company terminated his employment because he complained about the sexual harassment of his client. Canon said the termination was for sufficient cause based on his actions toward the client.

As part of his claim, the employee alleged that the sexual harassment action against the client presented a hostile environment for him because he was "made uncomfortable" by his boss's alleged advances toward his client.

The court did not agree. The court said "feelings of 'discomfort' cannot support a hostile environment claim. Instead, such a claim is stated only where plaintiff alleges that the conditions of his workplace were so permeated with discriminatory intimidation, ridicule, and insult that is sufficiently severe or pervasive as to alter the conditions of the victim's employment and create an abusive working environment." [*Kunzler* v. *Canon, USA, Inc.,* 257 F. Supp. 3d 574 (E.D.N.Y. 2003).]

On the other hand, in August 2003, the Minneapolis Public Library entered into a settlement agreement with its employees for $435,000 after the employees accused the library administration of subjecting them to a hostile environment by leaving them exposed to patrons' displays of explicit Web sites.

Do the two square for you?

---

reasonable person standard Viewing the harassing activity from the perspective of a reasonable person in society at large (generally tends to be the male view).

Whether an environment is hostile or abusive can be determined only by looking at all the circumstances. These may include the frequency of the discriminatory conduct, its severity, whether it is physically threatening or humiliating or a mere offensive utterance, and whether it unreasonably interferes with an employee's work performance. According to the court, no single factor is determinative. (See Exhibit 7.9.)

Perspective Used to Determine Severity

Until recently the determination of whether the harasser's activity was sufficiently severe and pervasive was generally based on a **reasonable person standard**, which is supposed to be a gender-neutral determination. That is, the activity would be judged as

reasonable victim standard
Viewing the harassing activity from the perspective of a reasonable person experiencing the harassing activity including gender-specific sociological, cultural, and other factors.

offensive (or not) based on whether the activity would offend a reasonable person under the circumstances. Since this "neutral" standard generally turned out to be instead a male standard, the EEOC issued a policy statement in which it required that the victim's perspective must also be considered, so as not to perpetuate stereotypical notions of what behavior is acceptable to those of a given gender. Sound familiar? It is the concept argued by Judge Keith in the *Rabidue* dissent, earlier in the chapter. This notion, labeled the "reasonable woman" or **"reasonable victim" standard**, has been used increasingly by courts and should be given serious consideration when evaluating harassing activity. If the victim is a male, it would, of course, be a reasonable man standard.

In *Ellison* v. *Brady* below, the Court adopted a reasonable woman standard for analyzing whether the harasser's behavior was severe and pervasive enough to create a hostile work environment, and it explains why viewing severity and pervasiveness from this perspective may render different results. The U.S. Supreme Court has not addressed the reasonable victim versus reasonable person dichotomy as a direct issue, but in *Oncale* it said "the objective severity of harassment should be judged from the perspective of a reasonable person *in the plaintiff's position*," which sounds like the reasonable victim standard.

Ellison v. Brady *924 F.2d 872 (9th Cir. 1991)*

An employee brought a sexual harassment suit because, among other things, her co-worker, whom she barely knew, kept sending her personal letters. The court found that while some may think it only a small matter, viewed from the employee's perspective as a female in a society in which females are often the victims of violence, the action was offensive and a violation of Title VII.

Beezer, J.

The case presents the important issue of what test should be applied to determine whether conduct is sufficiently severe or pervasive to alter the conditions of employment and create a hostile working environment.

Ellison worked as a revenue agent for the IRS in San Mateo, California. During her initial training in 1984 she met Sterling Gray, another trainee also assigned to that office. The two never became friends and did not work closely together. Gray's desk was twenty feet from Ellison's, two rows behind and one row over.

In June of 1986 when no one else was in the office, Gray asked Ellison to go to lunch. She accepted. They went past Gray's house to pick up his son's forgotten lunch and Gray gave Ellison a tour of his house. Ellison alleges that after that June lunch, Gray began to pester her with unnecessary questions and hang around her desk.

On October 9, when Gray asked Ellison out for a drink after work, she declined, but suggested lunch the following week. Ellison did not want to have lunch alone with him and she tried to stay away from the office during lunch time. The next week Gray asked her out to lunch and she did not go.

On October 22, 1986 Gray handed Ellison a note written on a telephone message slip which read: "I cried over you last night and I'm totally drained today. I have never been in such constant termoil (sic). Thank you for talking with me. I could not stand to feel your hatred for another day." Ellison was shocked at the note, became frightened and left the room. Gray followed Ellison into the hallway and demanded that she talk to him. Ellison left the building. While Gray reported this to her supervisor and asked to try to handle it herself, she asked a male co-worker to talk to Gray and tell him she was not interested in him and to leave her alone. The next day, Gray called in sick. Ellison did not work the following day, Friday, and on Monday started a four-week training session in Missouri.

While Ellison was at the training session, Gray mailed her a card and a three-page, typed, single spaced letter.

Ellison described the letter as "twenty times, a hundred times weirder" than the prior note. In part, Gray wrote:

> I know that you are worth knowing with or without sex. . . . Leaving aside the hassles and disasters of recent weeks. I have enjoyed you so much over these past few months. Watching you. Experiencing you from O so far away. Admiring your style and elan. . . . Don't you think it odd that two people who have never even talked together, alone, are striking off such intense sparks . . . I will [write] another letter in the near future.

Ellison stated that she thought Gray was "crazy. I thought he was nuts. I didn't know what he would do next. I was frightened." Ellison immediately called her supervisor and reported this and told her she was frightened and wanted one of them transferred. Gray was told many times over the next few weeks not to contact Ellison in any way. On November 24 Gray transferred to the San Francisco office. Ellison returned from Missouri in late November. After three weeks in San Francisco, Gray filed a grievance to return to San Mateo and as part of the settlement in Gray's favor, he agreed to be transferred back provided he spend four more months (a total of six months) in San Francisco and promise not to bother Ellison. When Ellison learned of Gray's request to return in a letter from her supervisor indicating Gray would return after a six-month separation, she said she was "frantic" and filed a formal sexual harassment complaint with IRS. The letter to Ellison also said that they could revisit the issue if there was further need.

Gray sought joint counseling. He wrote another letter to Ellison seeking to maintain the idea that he and Ellison had a relationship.

We do not agree with the standard set forth in *Rabidue*. We believe that Gray's conduct was sufficiently severe and pervasive to alter the conditions of Ellison's employment and create an abusive working environment. We believe that, in evaluating the severity and pervasiveness of sexual harassment, we should focus on the perspective of the victim. If we examined whether a reasonable person would engage in allegedly harassing conduct, we would run the risk of reinforcing the prevailing level of discrimination. Harassers could continue to harass merely because a particular discriminatory practice was common, and victims of harassment would have no remedy.

We therefore prefer to analyze harassment from the victim's perspective. A complete understanding of the victim's view requires, among other things, an analysis of the different perspectives of men and women. Conduct that many men consider unobjectionable may offend many women. See, e.g., *Lipsett* v. *University of Puerto Rico,* 864 F.2d 881, 898 (1st Cir. 1988) ("A male supervisor might believe, for example, that it is legitimate for him to tell a female subordinate that she has a 'great figure' or 'nice legs.' The female subordinate, however, may find such comments offensive"); Yates, 819 F.2d at 637, n.2 ("men and women are vulnerable in different ways and offended by different behavior"). See also, Ehrenreich, Pluralist Myths and Powerless Men: The Ideology of Reasonableness in Sexual Harassment Law, 99 Yale L. J. 1177, 1207–1208 (1990) (men tend to view some forms of sexual harassment as "harmless social interactions to which only overly-sensitive women would object"); Abrams, Gender Discrimination and the Transformation of Workplace Norms, 42 Vand. L. Rev. 1183, 1203 (1989) (the characteristically male view depicts sexual harassment as comparatively harmless amusement).

We realize that there is a broad range of viewpoints among women as a group, but we realize that many women share common concerns which men do not necessarily share. For example, because women are disproportionately victims of rape and sexual assault, women have stronger incentives to be concerned with sexual behavior. Women who are victims of mild forms of sexual harassment may understandably worry whether a harasser's conduct is merely a prelude to violent sexual assault. Men, who are rarely victims of sexual assault, may view sexual conduct in a vacuum without a full appreciation of the social setting or the underlying threat of violence that a woman may perceive.

In order to shield employers from having to accommodate the idiosyncratic concerns of the rare hypersensitive employee, we hold that a female plaintiff states a prima facie case of hostile environment sexual harassment when she alleges conduct that a reasonable woman would consider sufficiently severe or pervasive to alter the conditions of employment and create an abusive working environment. Of course, where male employees allege that co-workers engage in conduct which creates a hostile environment, the appropriate victim's perspective would be that of a reasonable man.

We adopt the perspective of a reasonable woman primarily because we believe that a gender-blind reasonable person standard tends to be male-biased and tends to systematically ignore the experiences of women. The reasonable woman standard does not establish a higher level of protection for women than men. Instead, a gender-conscious examination of sexual harassment enables women to participate in the workplace on an equal footing with men. By acknowledging and not trivializing the effects of sexual harassment on reasonable women, courts can work towards ensuring that neither men nor women will have to "run a gauntlet of sexual abuse in return for the privilege of being allowed to work and make a living."

We note that the reasonable woman victim standard we adopt today classifies conduct as unlawful sexual harassment even when harassers do not realize that their conduct creates a hostile working environment. Well-intentioned compliments by co-workers or supervisors can form the basis of a sexual harassment cause of action if a reasonable victim of the same gender as plaintiff would consider the comments sufficiently severe or pervasive to alter a condition of employment and create an abusive working environment. That is because Title VII is not a fault-based tort scheme. Title VII is aimed at the consequences or effects of an employment practice and not the motivation of co-workers or employers.

The facts of this case illustrate the importance of considering the victim's perspective. Analyzing the facts from the alleged harasser's viewpoint, Gray could be portrayed as a modern-day Cyrano de Bergerac wishing no more than to woo Ellison with his words. There is no evidence that Gray harbored ill-will toward Ellison. He even offered in his "love letter" to leave her alone if she wished [though he said he would not be able to forget her]. Examined in this light, it is not difficult to see why the district court characterized Gray's conduct as isolated and trivial.

Ellison, however, did not consider the acts to be trivial. Gray's first note shocked and frightened her. After receiving the three-page letter, she became really upset and frightened again. She immediately requested that she or Gray be transferred. Her supervisor's prompt response suggests that she too did not consider the conduct trivial. When Ellison learned that Gray arranged to return to San Mateo, she immediately asked to transfer and she immediately filed an official complaint.

We cannot say as a matter of law that Ellison's reaction was idiosyncratic or hyper-sensitive. We believe that a reasonable woman could have had a similar reaction. After receiving the first bizarre note from Gray, a person she barely knew, Ellison asked a co-worker to tell Gray to leave her alone. Despite her request, Gray sent her a long, passionate, disturbing letter. He told her he had been "watching" and "experiencing" her, he made repeated references to sex; and he said he would write again. Ellison had no way of knowing what Gray would do next. A reasonable woman could consider Gray's conduct, as alleged by Ellison, sufficiently severe and pervasive to alter a condition of employment and create an abusive working environment.

Sexual harassment is a major problem in the workplace. Adopting the victim's perspective ensures that courts will not "sustain ingrained notions of reasonable behavior fashioned by the offenders." Congress did not enact Title VII to codify prevailing sexist prejudices. To the contrary, "Congress designed Title VII to prevent the perpetuation of stereotypes and a sense of degradation which serve to close or discourage employment opportunities for women." We hope that over time both men and women will learn what conduct offends reasonable members of the other gender. When employers and employees internalize the standard of workplace conduct we establish today, the current gap in perception between the genders will be bridged. REVERSED and REMANDED.

Case Questions

1. Do you agree with the court's use of the "reasonable victim" standard? Explain.

2. Do you think the standard creates problems for management? If so, what are they? If not, why not?

3. Do you think Ellison was being "overly sensitive?" What would you have done if you had been the supervisor to whom she reported the incidents?

"Sexual" Requirement Explained

While the harassment of the employee must be based on gender, it need not involve sex, requests for sexual activity, sexual comments, or other such activity. Even today, a female entering a workplace with few or no other females is often verbally harassed about "doing men's work," "taking away the job a man should have," or simply inappropriately working at a traditionally male job. This, despite the lack of sexual overtones, could well constitute sexual harassment. In the case below, the sexual activity was only a small part of what the females who came into the traditionally male job were subjected to in being harassed. Notice how little of what they went through conforms to what we usually think of as sexually based hostile environment. This "nonsex" requirement is also one of the reasons it is better to use the term "gender" in sexual harassment discussions so that sex in the traditional sense, and gender, meaning whether one is male or female, are clearly differentiated and the discussion is less confusing.

Andrews v. City of Philadelphia *895 F.2d 1469 (3d Cir. 1990)*

Two female police officers, Andrews and Conn, filed a Title VII action against their employer and supervisors for sexual harassment. The court found sufficient basis for hostile environment sexual harassment even though sex, per se, was not the basis of the activity directed toward them though gender clearly was.

Rosenn, J.

While employees were assigned to the Auto Investigation Division (AID) of the Philadelphia police department, males dominated the division and according to Andrews, the AID squadroom was charged with sexism. Women were regularly referred to in an offensive and obscene manner and they personally were addressed by obscenities. There was evidence that the language was commonplace in police headquarters, but also testimony that one of the plaintiffs, a twelve-year police veteran, "had never been called some of the names that [she] was called in AID." There was also evidence of pornographic pictures of women displayed in the locker room on the inside of a locker which most often was kept open. Plaintiffs contend that the language and pictures embarrassed, humiliated, and harassed them.

Both employees further claimed that their files often disappeared from their desks, or were ripped or sabotaged. When Conn reported the sabotage, she was told by her supervisor, "You know, you're no spring chicken. You have to expect this working with the guys." Male officers who were to assist them in their work often hindered them or refused to help, although the men would help each other. The women experienced vandalism of their personal property, with Andrews having her car thrice vandalized while parked on the AID lot, with tires slashed, car scratched and windshield wipers removed; soda was poured into her typewriter; someone tore the cover off Andrews' book needed to keep track of investigations. Someone spit on Conn's coat, cut the band off her hat, and scratched her car. A roll of film Conn was using in an investigation disappeared before it was dispatched for developing.

Both employees also received obscene phone calls at their unlisted home phone numbers which AID had access to. One of the time periods for the calls was after the lawsuit was filed. One caller told the daughter of Andrews that her mother was sleeping with Conn, and that "those bitches ain't getting no money because they think they trying to get money but they not going to get none." During one of the conversations Andrews heard someone say "Yoh, sarge" in the background. Conn testified that the calls made her very scared and nervous and unable to function emotionally. She was also harassed by co-workers placing sexual devices and pornographic magazines in her desk drawer and gathering around and laughing at her reaction. When she reported this to her superior, he remained unresponsive. Another time a caustic substance was placed inside Andrews' shirt in her locker in the women's locker room. Andrews' back was severely burned by what was later determined to be a lime substance. Lime was found in other clothing in the locker and on the handle. Andrews also says that lewd pictures were posted on the walls and that she was embarrassed by pornographic pictures placed in her personal desk drawer.

Some of Conn and Andrews' complaints were investigated, others were not, but nothing significant came of any investigations. In both cases there was some sexually-based activity directed toward the women, such as suggestive remarks or tones used in connection with them.

We believe that the trial court too narrowly construed what type of conduct can constitute sexual harassment. Great emphasis was put on the lack of sexual advances, innuendo, or contact. In the lower court's opinion, evidence was extremely minimal and would not, standing alone, support a finding of a sexually hostile work environment, noting the lack of evidence of direct sexual harassment. To the extent that the court ruled that overt sexual harassment is necessary to establish a sexually hostile environment, we are constrained to disagree.

To make out a case under Title VII it is only necessary to show that gender is a substantial factor in the discrimination, and that if the plaintiff had been a man she would not have been treated in the same manner. To constitute impermissible discrimination, the offensive conduct is not necessarily required to include sexual overtones in every instance or that each incident be sufficiently severe to detrimentally affect a female employee. Intimidation and hostility toward women because they are women can obviously result from conduct other than explicitly sexual advances. *Meritor* appears to support this proposition as well, "Title VII affords employees the right to work in an environment free from discriminatory intimidation, ridicule and insult." The Supreme Court in no way limited this concept to intimidation or ridicule of an explicitly sexual nature.

More specifically, we hold that the pervasive use of derogatory and insulting terms relating to women generally and addressed to female employees personally may serve as evidence of a hostile environment. Similarly, so may the posting of pornographic pictures in common areas and in the plaintiff's personal work spaces.

Although the employer's attorney argues vigorously that a police station need not be run like a day care center, it should not, however, have the ambience of a nineteenth century military barracks. We realize that it is unrealistic to hold an employer accountable for every isolated incident of sexism; however, we do not consider it an unfair burden of an employer of both genders to take measures to prevent an atmosphere of sexism to pervade the workplace.

On remand, the trial judge should look at all incidents to see if they produce a work environment hostile and offensive to women of reasonable sensibilities. The evidence in this case includes not only name calling, pornography, displaying sexual objects in desks, but also the recurrent disappearance of plaintiffs' case files and work products, anonymous phone calls, and destruction of other property. The court should view this evidence in its totality, as described above, and then reach a determination. VACATED and REMANDED.

Case Questions

1. Why do you think the employer did nothing much to remedy this situation?
2. Do you think sexual overtones should have been required here?
3. What would you have done if you were the manager?

A common element of hostile environment sexual harassment cases that may lack an actual sexuality factor is *anti-female animus* exhibited by the harasser toward those of the harassee's gender. (See Exhibit 7.10.) This is manifested through, for instance, the use of derogatory terms when referring to women. Recall that the *Rabidue* dissent said it was exhibited, among other things, by workplace references to women or female employees as "bitches," "cunts," "pussy," or "whores." Courts have also found anti-female animus in derogatory statements to or about women in the context of their jobs, such as "women have shit for brains," "should be barefoot and pregnant," "should not be surgeons because it takes them too long to bathe and put on makeup," "could never stand up to union representatives," "are unstable when they are 'in heat' [having their menstrual cycle, said to a female doctor]," or "all she needs is a good lay." Often anti-female animus is accompanied by sexually based activity, but need not be to be considered hostile environment sexual harassment. A harassee's complaint should not be dismissed simply because it does not involve sexually related activity. (See Exhibit 7.11.)

One of the more intriguing developments in the area of hostile environment sexual harassment has been such harassment by electronic means. Claims involving sexual harassment through workplace e-mail, bulletin boards, and chat rooms have increased

Exhibit 7.10   Foul Play?

Knowing what you do about hostile environment and anti-female animus, take a look at this situation from recent news headlines. See whether you think it indicates an anti-female animus. It is in the context of a college football team, but it could just as likely have been in a pro setting or other traditionally male workplace.

You may recall that the University of Colorado football team was plagued by several allegations of misconduct. Civil lawsuits filed by three women against the school alleged they were raped by players or recruits in December 2001. Police released a report alleging that when a woman brought rape allegations against a player, she later dropped the charges because Coach Gary Barnett told her he "would back his player 100 percent if rape charges were pursued." An independent committee investigated allegations involving the football program, including rapes, recruiting parties featuring alcohol and sex, use of escort service, and hiring strippers.

In February 2004, team kicker Katie Hnida filed a police report saying she had been raped four years before by another football player. Upon being asked about the allegations, Coach Barnett told the reporter "Katie was not very good. She was awful," and couldn't "kick the ball through the uprights." "Katie was not only a girl, she was terrible, OK? There's no other way to say it." University President Elizabeth Hoffman (who resigned in 2005) was "utterly distressed" by Barnett's "insensitive" and "inappropriate" response, and put him on a paid suspension.

Did Barnett's comments indicate anti-female animus to you? Was there anything that would make you think that Hnida's performance may not have being judged totally on its own merits, and instead, that gender may have played a part in the assessment? Explain.

dramatically in the past few years. Since this means of communication is here to stay for the foreseeable future, it is best to be aware of the potential for liability. Again, there need not be a sexual element involved, and as the case below demonstrates, the activity need not even take place on the premises of the workplace in order to be considered sexual harassment. It is a good idea to have a well-enforced workplace policy giving guidelines for this kind of activity and to keep up with any changes that may result in new ways for liability to occur.

Blakely v. Continental Airlines, Inc. *164 N.J. 38, 751 A.2d 538 (2001)*

An airline employee brought suit against her employer for sexual harassment because of, among other things, statements posted about her on an electronic bulletin board that the employer maintained offsite for the use of employees. The court had to answer the question of whether the employer could be held liable for sexual harassment committed in this way. The Supreme Court of New Jersey decided that it could.

O'Hern, J.

In this employment discrimination case against Continental Airlines and certain of its employers, one way of framing the issues is whether "If an employer provides an [I]nternet 'forum'—an electronic bulletin board—for

employees' use, does it have a duty to monitor e-mail postings to ensure that employees are not harassing one another?"

The answer to [this question] is easy. The case appears to have proceeded on the thesis that there could be no liability if the harassment by co-employees did

Exhibit 7.11   All in Good Fun? Just Joking . . .

A number of sexual harassment cases arise from situations having nothing to do with "sex" as we ordinarily think of it. It has to do instead with gender—more specifically, anti-female animus, or feelings against women who are in male-dominated or traditionally male jobs such as truck driving. Even when males are in traditionally female jobs, they rarely are subjected to the same kind of actions directed toward them that women in traditionally male fields are. And often, when men in a traditionally female job, are subjected to harassing activity, it is by other males who tease, joke, make derogatory comments and more, rather than by their female colleagues. Case law indicates that male nurses generally do not get hassled by female nurses or male kindergarten teachers by female kindergarten teachers, while female truck drivers, firefighters, or police officers are more likely to be hassled by their male colleagues.

Students, and even managers and supervisors in the workplace, often comment that "it's only joking" and that women who complain seem to be "overly sensitive." "Why can't they just suck it up and stop whining about something so trivial?" What they don't understand is that rarely is the ribbing or joking an isolated event, but rather, it is usually accompanied by other indicators in the workplace that one gender is being treated differently, less well, than another. Rarely will you find women progressing in a workplace when the atmosphere exhibits anti-female animus through jokes, ribbing, and derogatory gender-based comments. It all goes together. The thought is parent to the act. If anti-female animus is manifested through jokes, comments, and ribbing, it is very likely to also be manifested in lack of full participation in the workplace for women through pay, training, discipline and advancement. It's never "just jokes." That is why it is such a serious matter.

Keep in mind that as a manager or supervisor, how you handle these events as they occur can make all the difference in the world for your employer. It may seem like only joking, ribbing, or all in good fun, but as a manager, you ignore it at the peril of your company. Heaped on an employee day after day, it places upon them different terms or conditions of employment than it does other employees of the other gender who do not have to contend with this hostile environment.

After an 11-day trial, Marion Shaub, a female FedEx truck driver, won a $3.2 million verdict against FedEx. She alleged that her brakes were loosened, the brake lines were cut, and the lines were filled with dirt. Luckily, she was always able to maintain control over the vehicle and incur no injuries or property damage. She was also subjected to such "anti-female remarks" by her coworkers as women should be "barefoot and pregnant," she "looked like a porn star," and that "if she were his daughter, he would 'abort her'." [*EEOC* v. *Federal Express Corp.*, 02-CV-1194 (MD Pa. 2004).]

not take place within the workplace setting at a place under the physical control of the employer. Although the electronic bulletin board may not have a physical location within a terminal, hangar or aircraft, it may nonetheless have been so closely related to the workplace environment and beneficial to Continental that a continuation of harassment on the forum should be regarded as part of the workplace. As applied to this hostile environment workplace claim, we find that if the employer had notice that co-employees were engaged on such a work-related forum in a pattern of retaliatory harassment directed at a co-employee, the employer would have a duty to remedy that harassment. We find that the record is inadequate to determine whether the relationship between the bulletin board and the employer establishes a connection with the workplace sufficient to impose such liability on the employer. We remand that aspect of the matter to the Law Division for further proceedings in accordance with this opinion.

Tammy S. Blakey, a pilot for Continental Airlines since 1984, appears from the record to be a highly qualified commercial airline pilot. In December 1989, Blakey became that airline's first female captain to fly an Airbus or A300 aircraft (A300). The A300 is a wide-body twin-engine jet aircraft seating 250 passengers. Plaintiff was one of five qualified A300 pilots in the service of Continental Airlines. Shortly after qualifying to be a captain on the A300, Blakey complained of sexual harassment and a hostile working environment based on conduct and comments directed at her by male co-employees. According to Blakey, in February 1991, she began to file systematic complaints with various representatives of Continental about the conduct of her male co-employees. Specifically, Blakey complained to Continental's management concerning pornographic photographs and vulgar gender-based comments directed at her that appeared in the workplace, specifically in her plane's cockpit and other work areas.

In February 1993, Blakey filed a charge of sexual discrimination and retaliation in violation of Title VII of the Civil Rights Act of 1964 and the Civil Rights Act of 1991 against Continental with the Equal Employment Opportunity Commission in Seattle, Washington, her home state. She simultaneously filed a complaint in the United States District Court in Seattle, Washington, against Continental for its failure to remedy the hostile work environment. At her own request, Blakey transferred to Houston in May 1993. To be relieved of the continuing stress that she had experienced in Newark, Blakey assumed a voluntary unpaid leave of absence beginning in August 1993.

In the midst of that federal litigation, her fellow pilots continued to publish a series of what plaintiff views as harassing gender-based messages, some of which she alleges are false and defamatory. From February to July 1995, a number of Continental's male pilots posted derogatory and insulting remarks about Blakey on the pilots on-line computer bulletin board called the Crew Members Forum ("Forum"). The Forum is accessible to all Continental pilots and crew member personnel through the Internet provider, CompuServe. When Continental employees access CompuServe, one of the menu selections listed in the "Continental Airlines Home Access" program includes an option called "Continental Forum." Like many other large corporations today, Continental's computer technology operations are "outsourced" or contracted-out, in this case to a company called Electronic Data Systems ("EDS"). EDS manages Continental's information systems including the CMS, which contains information on flights, crew member schedules, pay and pilot pairings. Continental requires that pilots and crew "access" the CMS in order to learn their flight schedules and assignments. To access such a system is, in essence, to call in through a computer or telephone.

CompuServe charges pilots and crew members a monthly fee for Internet access. Perhaps to enhance the appeal of its product, CompuServe provides the Crew Members Forum for pilots and crew members to exchange messages. In the parlance of the Internet, this is described as a virtual community. Community is about communication and interaction among people of shared interests, objectives or purposes. When community members such as employees communicate with each other, they build relationships. The Crew Members Forum essentially serves as an Intranet system.

Access to the Crew Members Forum is available only through CompuServe. The Forum is like a bulletin board where employees can post messages or "threads" for each other. At the time of trial, the Law Division stated that "only 250 employees nationwide had access to the Forum at the time that defendants published their statements." Although it was said that Continental management was not permitted to post messages or reply to any messages on the Forum, its chief pilots and assistant chief pilots had access to the Forum if they signed up with CompuServe to utilize the CMS. Relying on deposition testimony of the Director of Crew Systems and Planning, plaintiff asserts that chief pilots are considered management within Continental. Although Continental may have no duty to monitor the Forum, it is possible that a jury could find that Continental had knowledge, either direct or vicarious through managerial employees, of the content of certain messages posted on the Forum.

To put the issue in perspective, we need to shrink the context a bit. There was a television series a few years ago called "Wings." (NBC television broadcast, April 1990 through May 1997.) The program concerned a small, regional airline, its pilots, ground crew, and maintenance people. If there were at that small airport a lounge used exclusively by the pilots and crew of that airline and a bulletin board in that lounge contained the same or similar comments and asides by the pilots and crew, there would be little doubt that if management had notice of messages that met the required substantive criteria of being "sufficiently severe or pervasive to alter the conditions of employment and to create an intimidating, hostile, or offensive working environment," a cause of action for hostile work environment sexual harassment could be asserted. And if there had been a nearby place frequented by senior management, pilots and crew where one of the crew was regularly subjected to sexually offensive insults and if that harassing conduct was a continuation of a pattern of harassment in the workplace, an employer that had notice of the pattern of severe and pervasive harassment in and out of the workplace would not be entirely free to disregard the conduct.

The question in this more complex case is whether the Crew Members Forum is the equivalent of a bulletin board in the pilots' lounge or a work-related place in which pilots and crew members continue a pattern of harassment. The trial court correctly perceived the role of the Forum when it asked:

So what's the difference? What's the critical difference now we've taken it off this wood and whatever it is, cork material, that a bulletin board is made out of, and now we've electronically put it on the Internet. Now, what are the critical differences that now take it out of something that Continental could be responsible for as a workplace, or work-related item?

This Court has recognized that harassment by a supervisor that takes place outside of the workplace can be actionable. The Court "note[d] that whether specific acts of harassment or discrimination took place outside of the workplace, such as harassing telephone calls . . . , is of no consequence because such conduct nevertheless would have arisen out of the employment relationship between [the plaintiff and the defendant corporation]."

Thus, standing alone, the fact that the electronic bulletin board may be located outside of the workplace (although not as closely affiliated with the workplace as was the cockpit in which similar harassing conduct occurred), does not mean that an employer may have no duty to correct off-site harassment by co-employees. Conduct that takes place outside of the workplace has a tendency to permeate the workplace. A worker need not actually hear the harassing words outside the workplace so long as the harassment contributes to the hostile work environment. In a case involving harassment that occurred in a tavern outside of the workplace, the New Hampshire federal court refused to dismiss any evidence of harassment related to activities at the tavern on the basis that the conduct was irrelevant. (There had been harassment taking place in the workplace.) The court observed that "[a]n employer's liability for a hostile environment caused by lower-level supervisory employees or plaintiff's co-worker exists, 'if an official representing the institution knew, or in the exercise of reasonable care, should have known, of the harassment's occurrence, unless that official can show that he or she took appropriate steps to halt it.'"

On remand, the trial court should first determine whether Continental derived a substantial workplace benefit from the overall relationship among CompuServe, the Forum, and Continental. The record does not disclose that Continental sought the Forum's inclusion on CompuServe's menu. Still, it appears to us that a business enterprise would derive the same benefits from having its employees connected as would a law firm or the judiciary itself. We have become familiar with the process through which the judiciary's employees and its several jurisdictions may be connected by the Internet. That process is well known by now. The problems that developed in our fathers' offices are likely to develop in the offices of the future. Business counselors caution employers that they should have policies that deal with sexual harassment on the message centers of this changing world. That does not mean that employers have a duty to monitor employees' mail. Grave privacy concerns are implicated. It may mean that employers may not disregard the posting of offensive messages on company or state agency e-mail systems when the employer is made aware of those messages. The Law Division should initially determine whether a triable issue of fact is presented concerning whether the Crew Members Forum should be considered sufficiently integrated with the workplace to require such a response by an employer.

For example, the record does not contain the contract between CompuServe and Continental. In addition, at the time of these proceedings, use of the Internet was in the beginning stages. The number of current users would be relevant to the benefit that Continental might derive from the service. It appears to us

Exhibit 7.12   Even a Professor . . .

Inbal Hayut, a female student of political science professor Alex Young at the University of New York at New Paltz, sued Professor Young for nicknaming her "Monica" and subjecting her to harassment about it over the course of the semester. Hayut apparently resembled Monica Lewinsky, the White House intern who had an affair with then-President Bill Clinton and was much in the news at the time. Professor Young opened virtually every class session by asking Hayut in front of the entire class, "How was your weekend with Bill?" Hayut alleged that twice in class Professor Young told her "Be quiet, Monica. I'll give you a cigar later." She asked Professor Young to stop referring to her as "Monica," but was ignored. Classmates mockingly addressed Hayut as "Monica" outside class.

Hayut said the comments affected her deeply, humiliated her in front of her classmates, and made it difficult for her to sleep or concentrate at school or work. She barely passed her courses that semester, received failing grades the next term, withdrew from the school, and had to complete a year of remedial work before she could transfer to another school.

Hayut sued the university, the professor, and several school administrators for, among other things, violating the Title IX Educational Amendments of 1972 which prohibits gender discrimination in any education program or activity receiving federal financial assistance. Professor Young, who had been teaching for 30 years, admitted making the statements, but said they were a joke. He retired a month after school administrators met to decide what to do about the situation.

In the lawsuit the school claimed the actions by Professor Young did not amount to sexual harassment. The court ruled that Professor Young, as "a teacher at a state university, was a state actor vested with considerable authority over his students." His comments were severe and pervasive enough to transcend the bounds of propriety and decency and became actionable harassment and Hayut's academic performance suffered as a result. [*Hayut* v. *SUNY at New Paltz, et al.*, 352 3d 733 (2d Cir. 2003).]

likely that Continental crew members who subscribed to CompuServe did so because of access to the CMS. In essence, Continental "outsourced" what another organization might call its own network. When a crew member accesses the CMS through CompuServe, the menu of options listed under the "Continental Airlines Home Access" includes both the "Crew Services/Forum" and "Continental Forum." The ability of Continental employees to access the information provided on the CMS benefits Continental by improving its efficiency and operations. The ability of the Continental employees to communicate with each other on the Forum would likewise appear to be a benefit.

CompuServe's role may thus be analogized to that of a company that builds an old-fashioned bulletin board. If the maker of an old-fashioned bulletin board provided a better bulletin board by setting aside space on it for employees to post messages, we would have little doubt that messages on the company bulletin board would be part of the workplace setting. Here, the Crew Members Forum is an added feature to the company bulletin board.

To repeat, employers do not have a duty to monitor private communications of their employees; employers do have a duty to take effective measures to stop co-employee harassment when the employer knows or has reason to know that such harassment is part of a pattern of harassment that is taking place in the workplace and in settings that are related to the workplace. Besides, it may well be in an employer's economic best interests to adopt a proactive stance when it comes to dealing with co-employee harassment. The best defense may be a good offense against sexual harassment. "[W]e have afforded a form of a safe haven for employers who promulgate and support an active, anti-harassment policy." Effective remedial steps reflecting a lack of tolerance for harassment will be "relevant to an employer's affirmative defense that its actions absolve it from all liability. Surely an anti-harassment policy directed at any form of co-employee harassment would bolster that defense. REVERSED and REMANDED.

Case Questions

1. Does the court's decision surprise you? Discuss. Does it make sense to you? Explain.

2. What would you have done if you were a manager and had seen the postings about Blakely on the bulletin board?

3. What provisions would you include in a workplace policy you developed for electronic harassment?

EMPLOYER LIABILITY FOR SEXUAL HARASSMENT

The U.S. Supreme Court (and therefore employers and employees) has been wrestling with the issue of employer liability for sexual harassment since it decided the first case on the subject in 1986 *(Meritor,* discussed earlier in the chapter). In its 1998 *Ellerth* case, also discussed in this chapter, the Court said that it was hearing the case in order to assist in defining the relevant standards of employer liability since "Congress has left it to the courts to determine controlling agency law principles in a new and difficult area of federal law." Without trying to drag you into the legal mire that has surrounded the issue, we will give you some general rules with which to operate and leave the intricacies for the courts to continue to unravel.

Supervisor toward Employee (tangible employment action)

This is generally going to be quid pro quo sexual harassment (for instance, the employee's supervisor denies the employee an expected raise or promotion because she refuses to have sex with him), but the courts have said that the categories are not cast in stone. An employer is strictly liable for the tangible acts of its supervisors regardless of whether the specific acts complained of were authorized or even forbidden by the employer and regardless of whether the employer knew or should have known of their occurrence. Since the supervisor is, in effect, the employer, the supervisor's acts are considered those of the employer.

The employer has control of the situation by carefully choosing supervisory employees. Also, in a tangible job action there is usually a paper trail involved, so it also gives the employer a measure of control by keeping tabs on what is going on in the workplace and monitoring for actions that may violate the law. For instance, if an employee is precipitously terminated or demoted, not given a raise if it is expected, or given a raise if none is expected, there will be a paper trail and the law holds the employer responsible for taking steps to keep track of what is going on in the employer's workplace. The law says the employer cannot engage in sexual harassment, so doing so through a supervisor is tantamount to the employer doing it and the employer is strictly liable for the harassment.

Supervisor toward Employee (no tangible employment action)

If there is no tangible employment act by a supervisor, and instead there is activity by a supervisor causing a severe and/or pervasive hostile environment resulting in harm to the harassed employee (for instance, the supervisor may constantly ask the employee out on dates and make sexual comments, but still give the employee her usual raises and promotions), the employer is not strictly liable. This is also true of a constructive discharge. Recall that in constructive discharge, the workplace becomes so unbearable, objectively speaking, that the employee has no real option except to leave. In these situations, the harassed employee can bring a claim, but there is no virtually automatic liability like there is for strict liability offenses. Here, the employer has an affirmative defense available. The employer can use the *Ellerth/Faragher* defense to show that the employer had a reasonable antidiscrimination policy to prevent and address sexual harassment and the harassed employee unreasonably failed to use it. This defense is not permitted in a case where there is a tangible unfavorable job action by a supervisor.

Coworker Harassment or Third Party Harassment of Employee   When the harassment is by one employee toward another on the same level (rather than by a supervisory employee to a subordinate) or the harassment is by someone who is not employed by the employer, such as a client or someone who comes in to service the machinery at the employer's business, the employer is liable if the employer knew or should have known of the acts of the harasser and took no immediate corrective action. For instance, if the computer repairer comes in to the workplace to service computers and regularly feels the employee's legs while working with wires under the desk or makes suggestive sexual comments, the employer would be liable even though the repairer does not work for the employer. The employee would usually have to make the employer aware of the situation and the employer would have to take no steps to remedy the situation before liability would attach. If the employer saw what was happening and saw that the employee was clearly unhappy with the situation, the employer would be put on notice that something should be done and liability could attach. The same is true with coworkers. That is why it is so important for managers and supervisors to be aware of what is going on around them in the workplace and deal with it effectively. The law will hold the employer responsible through the acts of the supervisory employees who were aware and took no action to rectify the situation.

In the following important U.S. Supreme Court case, the Court discussed employer liability for sexual harassment. The Court provided employers not only with a defense they could use when sued by an employee who had not acted reasonably in seeking to avoid harm (the *Ellerth/Faragher* affirmative defense) but also with ammunition for an employee who could allege that the employer did not use reasonable measures to prevent sexual harassment.

Faragher v. City of Boca Raton   *524 U.S. 775 (1998)*

A former city lifeguard sued the city under Title VII for sexual harassment based on the conduct of her supervisors. The Supreme Court held that an employer is subject to vicarious liability under Title VII for actionable discrimination caused by a supervisor, but the employer may raise an affirmative defense that looks to the reasonableness of the employer's conduct in seeking to prevent and correct harassing conduct and to the reasonableness of employee's conduct in seeking to avoid harm. The Court held that the employer was vicariously liable here because it failed to exercise reasonable care to prevent harassing behavior.

Souter, J.

This case calls for identification of the circumstances under which an employer may be held liable under Title VII of the Civil Rights Act for the acts of a supervisory employee whose sexual harassment of subordinates has created a hostile work environment amounting to employment discrimination. We hold that an employer is vicariously liable for actionable discrimination caused by a supervisor, but subject to an affirmative defense looking to the reasonableness of the employer's conduct as well as that of a plaintiff victim.

Between 1985 and 1990, while attending college, petitioner Beth Ann Faragher worked part time and during the summers as an ocean lifeguard for the Marine Safety Section of the Parks and Recreation Department of respondent, the City of Boca Raton, Florida (City). During this period, Faragher's immediate supervisors were Bill Terry, David Silverman, and Robert Gordon. In June 1990, Faragher resigned. In 1992, Faragher brought an action against Terry, Silverman, and the City, asserting claims under Title VII, and Florida law. The complaint alleged that Terry and Silverman were agents of the City, and that their conduct created a "sexually hostile atmosphere" that amounted to discrimination in the "terms, conditions, and privileges" of her employment at the beach by repeatedly subjecting Faragher and other female lifeguards to "uninvited and offensive touching," by making lewd remarks, and by speaking of women in offensive terms.

Throughout Faragher's employment with the City, Terry served as Chief of the Marine Safety Division, with authority to hire new lifeguards (subject to the approval of higher management), to supervise all aspects of the lifeguards' work assignments, to engage in counseling, to deliver oral reprimands, and to make a record of any such discipline. Silverman and Gordon were captains and responsible for making the lifeguards' daily assignments, and for supervising their work and fitness training. The lifeguards and supervisors were stationed at the city beach. The lifeguards had no significant contact with higher city officials like the Recreation Superintendent.

In February 1986, the City adopted a sexual harassment policy, which it stated in a memorandum from the City Manager addressed to all employees. In May 1990, the City revised the policy and reissued a statement of it. Although the City may actually have circulated the memos and statements to some employees, it completely failed to disseminate its policy among employees of the Marine Safety Section, with the result that Terry, Silverman, Gordon, and many lifeguards were unaware of it.

Faragher did not complain to higher management about Terry or Silverman. In April 1990, however, two months before Faragher's resignation, Nancy Ewanchew, a former lifeguard, wrote to Richard Bender, the City's Personnel Director, complaining that Terry and Silverman had harassed her and other female lifeguards. Following investigation of this complaint, the City found that Terry and Silverman had behaved improperly, reprimanded them, and required them to choose between a suspension without pay or the forfeiture of annual leave.

Since our decision in *Meritor,* Courts of Appeals have struggled to derive manageable standards to govern employer liability for hostile environment harassment perpetrated by supervisory employees. While indicating the substantive contours of the hostile environments forbidden by Title VII, our cases have established few definite rules for determining when an employer will be liable for a discriminatory environment that is otherwise actionably abusive.

A "master is subject to liability for the torts of his servants committed while acting in the scope of their employment." Restatement §219(1). This doctrine has traditionally defined the "scope of employment" as including conduct "of the kind [a servant] is employed to perform," occurring "substantially within the authorized time and space limits," and "actuated, at least in part, by a purpose to serve the master," but as excluding an intentional use of force "unexpectable by the master."

A justification for holding the offensive behavior within the scope of Terry's and Silverman's employment was well put in Judge Barkett's dissent: "[A] pervasively hostile work environment of sexual harassment is never (one would hope) authorized, but the supervisor is clearly charged with maintaining a productive, safe work environment. The supervisor directs and controls the conduct of the employees, and the manner of doing so may inure to the employer's benefit or detriment, including subjecting the employer to Title VII liability."

It is by now well recognized that hostile environment sexual harassment by supervisors (and, for that matter, co-employees) is a persistent problem in the workplace. An employer can, in a general sense, reasonably anticipate the possibility of such conduct occurring in its workplace, and one might justify the assignment of the burden of the untoward behavior to the employer as one of the costs of doing business, to be charged to the enterprise rather than the victim. As noted, developments like this occur from time to time in the law of agency.

We agree with Faragher that in implementing Title VII it makes sense to hold an employer vicariously liable for some tortious conduct of a supervisor made possible by abuse of his supervisory authority. The agency relationship affords contact with an employee subjected to a supervisor's sexual harassment, and the victim may well be reluctant to accept the risks of blowing the whistle on a superior. When a person with supervisory authority discriminates in the terms and conditions of subordinates' employment, his actions necessarily draw upon his superior position over the people who report to him, or those under them, whereas an employee generally cannot check a supervisor's abusive conduct the same way that she might deal with abuse from a co-worker. When a fellow employee harasses, the victim can walk away or tell the offender where to go, but it may be difficult to offer such responses to a supervisor, whose "power to supervise—[which may be] to hire and fire, and to set work schedules and pay rates—does not disappear . . . when he chooses to harass through insults and offensive gestures rather than directly with threats of firing or promises of promotion." Recognition of employer liability when discriminatory misuse of supervisory authority alters the terms and conditions of a victim's employment is underscored by the fact that the employer has a greater opportunity to guard against misconduct by supervisors than by common workers; employers have greater opportunity and incentive to screen them, train them, and monitor their performance.

In order to accommodate the principle of vicarious liability for harm caused by misuse of supervisory authority, as well as Title VII's equally basic policies of encouraging forethought by employers and saving action by objecting employees, we adopt the following holding in this case and in *Burlington Industries, Inc.* v. *Ellerth,* also decided today. An employer is subject to vicarious liability to a victimized employee for an actionable hostile environment created by a supervisor with immediate (or successively higher) authority over the employee.

When no tangible employment action is taken, a defending employer may raise an affirmative defense to liability or damages, subject to proof by a preponderance of the evidence. The defense comprises two necessary elements: (a) that the employer exercised reasonable care to prevent and correct promptly any sexually harassing behavior, and (b) that the plaintiff employee unreasonably failed to take advantage of any preventive or corrective opportunities provided by the employer or to avoid harm otherwise.

While proof that an employer had promulgated an antiharassment policy with complaint procedure is not necessary in every instance as a matter of law, the need for a stated policy suitable to the employment circumstances may appropriately be addressed in any case when litigating the first element of the defense. And while proof that an employee failed to fulfill the corresponding obligation of reasonable care to avoid harm is not limited to showing an unreasonable failure to use any complaint procedure provided by the employer, a demonstration of such failure will normally suffice to satisfy the employer's burden under the second element of the defense. No affirmative defense is available, however, when the supervisor's harassment culminates in a tangible employment action, such as discharge, demotion, or undesirable reassignment.

Applying these rules here, it is undisputed that these supervisors "were granted virtually unchecked authority" over their subordinates, "directly controll[ing] and supervis[ing] all aspects of [Faragher's] day-to-day activities." It is also clear that Faragher and her colleagues were "completely isolated from the City's higher management."

While the City would have an opportunity to raise an affirmative defense if there were any serious prospect of its presenting one, it appears from the record that any such avenue is closed. The City entirely failed to disseminate its policy against sexual harassment among the beach employees and its officials made no attempt to keep track of the conduct of supervisors like Terry and Silverman. The City's policy did not include any assurance that the harassing supervisors could be bypassed in registering complaints. Under such circumstances, we hold as a matter of law that the City could not be found to have exercised reasonable care to prevent the supervisors' harassing conduct. Unlike the employer of a small workforce, who might expect that sufficient care to prevent tortious behavior could be exercised informally, those responsible for city operations could not reasonably have thought that precautions against hostile environments in any one of many departments in far-flung locations could be effective without communicating some formal policy against harassment, with a sensible complaint procedure. REVERSED and REMANDED.

Case Questions

1. How could the city have avoided this outcome? Explain.

2. Do you think that it would have made sense for the city to consider the particulars of the circumstances here, such as that these were lifeguards, in a remote location, who by the nature of the job would be dressed in fairly little clothing, and who, because of the environment (the beach and recre-

ational facilities) might need a different approach to sexual harassment than, say, office employees? Explain.

3. What do you think of the Court's affirmative defense given to employers and employees? What are the pros and cons?

In the *Suders* case below, the court addressed what to do if a supervisor's actions result in a constructive discharge for an employee and whether such a discharge is loss of a tangible job benefit, resulting in strict liability for the employer.

Pennsylvania State Police v. Suders *542 U.S. 129 (2004)*

In the U.S. Supreme Court's latest sexual harassment case, it further defined employer liability for supervisory employees. The *Suders* case, seen earlier, here addresses liability in constructive discharge cases. The plaintiff was subjected to fairly intense sexual harassment by her supervisors over the course of her employment. She eventually left, but without first going through the employer's sexual harassment complaint procedures. The U.S. Supreme Court heard the case in order to determine if constructive discharge is a tangible job benefit that made the employer strictly liable for the acts of its supervisor. It decided that it was not. Take a look at the facts and see if you think constructive discharge was warranted.

Ginsburg, J.

Plaintiff-respondent Nancy Drew Suders alleged sexually harassing conduct by her supervisors, officers of the Pennsylvania State Police (PSP), of such severity she was forced to resign. The question presented concerns the proof burdens parties bear when a sexual harassment/constructive discharge claim of that character is asserted under Title VII of the Civil Rights Act of 1964.

Suders' supervisors were Sergeant Eric D. Easton, Station Commander at the McConnellsburg barracks, Patrol Corporal William D. Baker, and Corporal Eric B. Prendergast. Those three supervisors subjected Suders to a continuous barrage of sexual harassment that ceased only when she resigned from the force.

Easton "would bring up [the subject of] people having sex with animals" each time Suders entered his office. He told Prendergast, in front of Suders, that young girls should be given instruction in how to gratify men with oral sex. Easton also would sit down near Suders, wearing spandex shorts, and spread his legs apart. Apparently imitating a move popularized by television wrestling, Baker repeatedly made an obscene gesture in Suders' presence by grabbing his genitals and shouting out a vulgar comment inviting oral sex. Baker made this gesture

as many as five to ten times per night throughout Suders' employment at the barracks. Suders once told Baker she "d[id]n't think [he] should be doing this"; Baker responded by jumping on a chair and again performing the gesture, with the accompanying vulgarity. Further, Baker would "rub his rear end in front of her and remark 'I have a nice ass, don't I?'" Prendergast told Suders "the village idiot could do her job"; wearing black gloves, he would pound on furniture to intimidate her.

In June 1998, Prendergast accused Suders of taking a missing accident file home with her. After that incident, Suders approached the PSP's Equal Employment Opportunity Officer, Virginia Smith-Elliott, and told her she "might need some help." Smith-Elliott gave Suders her telephone number, but neither woman followed up on the conversation. On August 18, 1998, Suders contacted Smith-Elliott again, this time stating that she was being harassed and was afraid. Smith-Elliott told Suders to file a complaint, but did not tell her how to obtain the necessary form. Smith-Elliott's response and the manner in which it was conveyed appeared to Suders insensitive and unhelpful.

Two days later, Suders' supervisors arrested her for theft, and Suders resigned from the force. The theft arrest occurred in the following circumstances. Suders had several times taken a computer-skills exam to satisfy a PSP job requirement. Each time, Suders' supervisors told her that she had failed. Suders one day came upon her exams in a set of drawers in the women's locker room. She concluded that her supervisors had never forwarded the tests for grading and that their reports of her failures were false. Regarding the tests as her property, Suders removed them from the locker room. Upon finding that the exams had been removed, Suders' supervisors devised a plan to arrest her for theft. The officers dusted the drawer in which the exams had been stored with a theft-detection powder that turns hands blue when touched. As anticipated by Easton, Baker, and Prendergast, Suders attempted to return the tests to the drawer, whereupon her hands turned telltale blue. The supervisors then apprehended and handcuffed her, photographed her blue hands, and commenced to question her. Suders had previously prepared a written resignation, which she tendered soon after the supervisors detained her. Nevertheless, the supervisors initially refused to release her. Instead, they brought her to an interrogation room, gave her [Miranda] warnings, and continued to question her. Suders reiterated that she wanted to resign, and Easton then let her leave. The PSP never brought theft charges against her.

In September 2000, Suders sued the PSP. This Court granted certiorari to resolve the disagreement among the Circuits on the question whether a constructive discharge brought about by supervisor harassment ranks as a tangible employment action and therefore precludes assertion of the affirmative defense articulated in *Ellerth* and *Faragher.* This case concerns an employer's liability for one subset of Title VII constructive discharge claims: constructive discharge resulting from sexual harassment, or "hostile work environment," attributable to a supervisor.

The constructive discharge here at issue stems from, and can be regarded as an aggravated case of sexual harassment or hostile work environment. For an atmosphere of sexual harassment or hostility to be actionable, the offending behavior "must be sufficiently severe or pervasive to alter the conditions of the victim's employment and create an abusive working environment." A hostile-environment constructive discharge claim entails something more: A plaintiff who advances such a compound claim must show working conditions so intolerable that a reasonable person would have felt compelled to resign. Essentially, Suders presents a "worse case" harassment scenario, harassment ratcheted up to the breaking point. Harassment so intolerable as to cause a resignation may be effected through co-worker conduct, unofficial supervisory conduct, or official company acts.

Unlike an actual termination, which is *always* effected through an official act of the company, a constructive discharge need not be. A constructive discharge involves both an employee's decision to leave and precipitating conduct: The former involves no official action; the latter, like a harassment claim without any constructive discharge assertion, may or may not involve official action.

To be sure, a constructive discharge is functionally the same as an actual termination in damages-enhancing respects. Both end the employer–employee relationship, and both inflict direct economic harm. But when an official act does not underlie the constructive discharge, the *Ellerth* and *Faragher* analysis, we here hold, calls for extension of the affirmative defense to the employer. Official directions and declarations are the acts most likely to be brought home to the employer, the measures over which the employer can exercise greatest control. Absent "an official act of the enterprise," as the last straw, the employer ordinarily would have no particular reason to suspect that a resignation is not the typical kind daily occurring in the work force. An official act reflected in company records—a demotion or a reduction in compensation, for example—shows beyond question that the supervisor has used his managerial or controlling position to the employee's disadvantage. Absent such an official act, the extent to which the supervisor's misconduct has been aided by the agency relation is less certain. That uncertainty, our precedent establishes, justifies affording the employer the chance to establish, through the *Ellerth/Faragher* affirmative defense, that it should not be held vicariously liable.

The plaintiff who alleges no tangible employment action has the duty to mitigate harm, but the defendant bears the burden to allege and prove that the plaintiff failed in that regard. The plaintiff might elect to allege facts relevant to mitigation in her pleading or to present those facts in her case in chief, but she would do so in anticipation of the employer's affirmative defense, not as a legal requirement. VACATE AND REMAND.

Case Questions

1. What would you have done about the situation if you were Suders?

2. How do you think this situation could have been avoided?

3. Do you understand the distinction between allowing employers to use the *Ellerth/Faragher* affirmative defense in cases involving tangible job actions versus constructive dismissal or hostile environment cases?

1

Scenario

In the following case, the Court provides important information as to how sexual harassment cases should be handled. It is the basis for Opening Scenario 1.

Robinson v. Jacksonville Shipyards, Inc. *760 F. Supp. 1486 (M.D. Fla. Jacksonville Div. 1991)*

An employee brought this action against her employer because of the prevalence of nude photos, posters, reading material, plaques and other nude representations in the workplace. She alleged that this, and the harassing activity toward her constituted hostile environment sexual harassment in violation of Title VII of the Civil Rights Act of 1964. After an exhaustive 59-page, extremely detailed opinion, the court held for the employee and discussed the employer's handling of its sexual harassment complaints.

Melton, J.

The shipyard had very few female skilled employees, so males greatly outnumbered females in the workplace. The employees bringing the complaint were skilled female craftworkers who had been subjected to a full range of harassing activity in the workplace including repeated requests for sexual activity, lewd comments, propositions, jokes, nude photos, posters, magazines and sexual teasing, all of the most egregious kind.

In addressing the employer's response to the harassing activity in the workplace, the court finds that the policies and procedures at JSI for responding to complaints of harassment are inadequate. The company has done an inadequate job of communicating with employees and supervisors regarding the nature and scope of sexually harassing behavior. This failure is compounded by a pattern of unsympathetic response to complaints by employees who perceive that they are victims of harassment. This pattern includes an unwillingness to believe the accusations, an unwillingness to take prompt and stern remedial action against admitted harassers, and an express condonation of behavior that is and encourages sexually harassing conduct (such as the posting of nude and partially nude women). In some instances, the process of registering a complaint about sexual harassment became a second episode of sexual harassment.

JSI cannot stand on an "ostrich defense" that it lacked knowledge of many of the complaints, because its handling of sexual harassment complaints deterred reporting and it did not conduct adequate investigation of the complaints it did receive. JSI received reports at the supervisory level and at the line level concerning incidents of sexual harassment. Additionally, many supervisory personnel admitted that they knew of the sexually

oriented pictures throughout the workplace. JSI concedes it had reports of this and those reports should have alerted them to the need to conduct a more thorough investigation of conditions in the shipyards. Such a duty arises when reports show that the workplace may be charged with a sexually hostile atmosphere.

JSI instead ignored the warning signs of a hostile environment. The evidence reveals a supervisory attitude that sexual harassment is an incident-by-incident matter; records were not maintained that would have permitted an analysis of sexual harassment complaints to determine the level of sexual hostility in the workplace. Under these circumstances, the court concludes that JSI received adequate actual knowledge of the state of the work environment, but, like an ostrich, the company elected to bury its head in the sand rather than learn more about the conditions to which female employees, Robinson in particular, were subjected.

The court additionally imposes constructive knowledge on JSI for the sexually hostile state of its work environment. Constructive knowledge is measured by a practical threshold. An employer escapes liability for isolated and infrequent slurs and misogynist behaviors because even a reasonably prudent employer cannot exercise sufficient control over the workplace to put an end to such conduct; conversely, an employer incurs liability when harassing behavior happens frequently enough that the employer can take steps to halt it. The sexually harassing behaviors described here are too pervasive to have escaped the notice of a reasonably alert management. Moreover, the extent to which co-workers and supervisory personnel actually knew of the existence of sexually harassing behaviors is a good barometer of the company's constructive knowledge. The testimony establishes that Robinson's plight was widely known.

To the extent that JSI contends that the physical size of its work environment diminished its ability to monitor incidents of sexual harassment, the company must realize that its expansive size may increase its burden in providing a workplace free of discrimination, but that expanse does not decrease the responsibility in its task. JUDGMENT for PLAINTIFF on the Title VII issue.

Case Questions

1. How would you have handled this workplace if you had been manager?
2. Do you think the court imposed too heavy a burden on the employer for monitoring the workplace?
3. Should the "ostrich defense" be permitted?

The question often arises as to whether an employer can be held liable for sexual harassment committed by someone who is not an employee, such as a customer or client. As you saw in the initial information setting for employee liability, the answer is yes. Liability for hostile environment sexual harassment by nonemployees is judged by the same standard as for coworkers. That is, the employer will be liable when the employer knows or should have known of the harassment through its employees and failed to take appropriate corrective action. It may seem unfair to hold an employer responsible for the actions of someone like a computer repairer who routinely comes to service the company's machines. However, on close inspection it makes sense. Once made aware of the situation by the harassee, the employer can speak to the repairer and request that the harassing behavior be curtailed, speak to the repairer's supervisor, request that a different repairer service the computers, or even cancel the contract altogether, as appropriate. The employer is also responsible for an outsider's harassment if the employer set up a situation encouraging harassing activity, such as requiring employees to dress in revealing uniforms.

Remember that it is a defense to liability if an employer can show that the harassee unreasonably failed to avail himself or herself of a mechanism the employer had in place for preventing or correcting sexual harassment. Likewise, it is helpful to a harassee if he or she can show that the employer had unreasonable means of preventing or correcting sexual harassment (for instance, the only one to whom claims are reported is the harasser). This makes it more important than ever for an employer to have an antisexual harassment policy as well as effective training, monitoring, and reporting of sexual harassment. The EEOC has determined that since harassment of any kind is the only type of discrimination carried out by a supervisor for which an employer can avoid liability, that limitation is to be narrowly construed.

OTHER IMPORTANT CONSIDERATIONS

There are several other important miscellaneous matters you should be aware of that are often at issue in sexual harassment claims.

Determining the Truth of Allegations

The number-one problem managers have with responding to sexual harassment complaints (other than their discomfort in dealing with such matters) is determining the truth of sexual harassment allegations. Appropriate investigation should provide the employer a basis on which to decide and to appropriately respond. Both parties, as well as any witnesses, should be questioned. The investigator's objective is to find out the "who," "what," "when," "where," and "how" of the allegations as quickly and as

26 MAINE REVISED STATUTES SECTIONS 806, 807

In an effort to ensure a workplace free of sexual harassment, Maine was the first state to pass a sexual harassment law. Connecticut passed such a law in May 1992 and was followed by other states, including Rhode Island, Massachusetts, and Vermont. While the EEOC guidelines are voluntary on the part of employers, Maine's law, which took effect in 1991, imposes affirmative duties on all employers, whether or not they have been found to have violated Maine's human rights law. The law, which in large part tracks the EEOC guidelines, requires employers to provide employees with information regarding sexual harassment, including:

- A statement that it is illegal.
- Defining sexual harassment under the state law.
- Descriptions of sexual harassment using examples.
- Descriptions of the internal complaint process available to employees.
- The availability of legal recourse and complaint process through the state's Human Rights Commission.
- Directions on how to contact the Commission.
- The availability of protection against retaliation for invoking rights under the discrimination law.

The employer must provide this information in three ways:

- Posting a poster (which cannot exceed a 6th grade literacy level and may be purchased from Maine's Human Rights Commission) in a prominent and accessible location in the workplace.
- Providing employees each year with an individual written notice about sexual harassment delivered in a manner to ensure its receipt, such as with employees' pay.
- If the employer has 15 or more employees, the employer must conduct an education and training program for all new employees within one year of the employee starting work. Additional training is required for supervisory and managerial employees within a year of commencing work to ensure that those employees take immediate and appropriate corrective action addressing sexual harassment complaints.

In an interesting note, in March 2001, after several sexual harassment complaints against the U.S. Postal Service (USPS) in Maine, Senator Olympia Snow (R-Maine) requested that the federal office of the Inspector General (IG) conduct an investigation. In March 2002, the IG's office reported, among other things, that while there were strong sexual harassment policies in place, they were not well enforced. Supervisors who knew of sexual harassment complaints had routinely been given promotions, and one employee even committed suicide, leaving a note blaming sexual harassment for her despair. Based on the findings in Maine, the USPS ordered a nationwide investigation of its facilities. The lesson here is vigilance. Even though Maine was the first state to enact sexual harassment regulations into law, including requirements for training, the legislation is useless without vigorous enforcement.

Source: CBC Employment Alert, August 15, 1991, pp. 2–3, © 1994 by Clark Boardman Callahan, a division of Thomson Legal Publishing, Inc.

Exhibit 7.14　　　Example of an Antisexual Harassment Policy

Often the employer doesn't really know what is appropriate to include in an antisexual harassment policy. In the *Jacksonville Shipyards* case, as part of the court's order, it required the employer to adopt an antisexual harassment policy, which it included in an appendix. In order for you to see what one actually looks like and make the theoratical more practical for you, it is reproduced below, with changes as appropriate to generalize the policy (rather than have it be specific to JSI).

XYZ COMPANY ANTISEXUAL HARASSMENT POLICY

Statement of Policy. Title VII of the Civil Rights Act of 1964 prohibits employment discrimination on the basis of race, color, gender, religion, or national origin. *Sexual harassment is included among the prohibitions.*

Sexual harassment, according to the federal Equal Employment Opportunity Commission (EEOC), consists of unwelcome sexual advances, requests for sexual favors, or other verbal or physical acts of a sexual or sex-based nature where (1) submission to such conduct is made either explicitly or implicitly a term or condition of an individual's employment; (2) an employment decision is based on an individual's acceptance or rejection of such conduct; or (3) such conduct interferes with an individual's work performance or creates an intimidating, hostile, or offensive working environment.

It is also unlawful to retaliate or take reprisal in any way against anyone who has articulated any concern about sexual harassment or discrimination, whether that concern relates to harassment of or discrimination against the individual raising the concern or against another individual.

Examples of conduct that would be considered sexual harassment or related retaliation are set forth in the Statement of Prohibited Conduct, which follows. These examples are provided to illustrate the kind of conduct proscribed by this policy; the list is not exhaustive.

XYZ Company and its agents are under a duty to investigate and eradicate any form of sexual harassment, gender discrimination, or retaliation. To further that end, XYZ Company has issued a procedure for making complaints about conduct in violation of this policy and a schedule for violation of this policy.

Sexual harassment is unlawful, and such prohibited conduct exposes not only XYZ Company but individuals involved in such conduct to significant liability under the law. Employees at all times should treat other employees respectfully and with dignity in a manner so as not to offend the sensibilities of a coworker. Accordingly, XYZ's management is committed to vigorously enforcing its Antisexual Harassment Policy at all levels within the company.

Statement of Prohibited Conduct. The management of XYZ Company considers the following conduct to represent some of the types of acts which violate XYZ's Antisexual Harassment Policy:

A. *Physical assaults of a sexual nature, such as:*
   (1) rape, sexual battery, molestation, or attempts to commit these assaults; and
   (2) intentional physical conduct, which is sexual in nature, such as touching, pinching, patting, grabbing, brushing against another employee's body, or poking another employee's body.

B. *Unwanted sexual advances, propositions, or other sexual comments, such as:*
   (1) sexually oriented gestures, noises, remarks, jokes, or comments about a person's sexuality or sexual experience directed at or made in the presence of any

(continued)

Exhibit 7.14 (continued)

employee who indicates or has indicated in any way that such conduct in his or her presence is unwelcome;

(2) preferential treatment or promise of preferential treatment to an employee for submitting to sexual conduct, including soliciting or attempting to solicit any employee to engage in sexual activity for compensation or reward; and

(3) subjecting, or threats of subjecting, an employee to unwelcome sexual attention or conduct or intentionally making performance of the employee's job more difficult because of that employee's gender.

C. *Sexual or discriminatory displays or publications anywhere in XYZ's workplace by XYZ's employees, such as:*

(1) displaying pictures, posters, calendars, graffiti, objects, promotional materials, reading materials, or other materials that are sexually suggestive, sexually demeaning, or pornographic, or bringing into the XYZ work environment or possessing any such material to read, display, or view at work.

A picture will be presumed to be sexually suggestive if it depicts a person of either gender who is not fully clothed or in clothes that are not suited to or ordinarily accepted for the accomplishment of routine work in and around the workplace and who is posed for the obvious purpose of displaying or drawing attention to private portions of his or her body;

(2) reading or otherwise publicizing in the work environment materials that are in any way sexually revealing, sexually suggestive, sexually demeaning, or pornographic; and

(3) displaying signs or other materials purporting to segregate an employee by gender in any area of the workplace (other than restrooms and similar semiprivate lockers/changing rooms).

D. *Retaliation for sexual harassment complaints, such as:*

(1) disciplining, changing work assignments of, providing inaccurate work information to, or refusing to cooperate or discuss work-related matters with any employee because that employee has complained about or resisted harassment, discrimination, or retaliation; and

(2) intentionally pressuring, falsely denying, lying about, or otherwise covering up or attempting to cover up conduct such as that described in any item above.

E. *Other acts:*

(1) The above is not to be construed as an all-inclusive list of prohibited acts under this policy.

(2) Sexual harassment is unlawful and hurts other employees. Any of the prohibited conduct described here is sexual harassment of anyone at whom it is directed or who is otherwise subjected to it. Each incident of harassment, moreover, contributes to a general atmosphere in which all persons who share the victim's gender suffer the consequences. Sexually oriented acts or gender-based conduct have no legitimate business purpose; accordingly, the employee who engages in such conduct should be and will be made to bear the full responsibility for such unlawful conduct.

Schedule of Penalties for Misconduct. The following schedule of penalties applies to all violations of this policy, as explained in more detail in the Statement of Prohibited Conduct.

Exhibit 7.14 (continued)

Where progressive discipline is provided for, each instance of conduct violating the policy moves the offending employee through the steps of disciplinary action. In other words, it is not necessary for an employee to repeat the same precise conduct in order to move up the scale of discipline.

A written record of each action taken pursuant to the policy will be placed in the offending employee's personnel file. The record will reflect the conduct, or alleged conduct, and the warning given, or other discipline imposed.

A. *Assault:*
Any employee's first proven offense of assault or threat of assault, including assault of a sexual nature, will result in dismissal.

B. *Other acts of harassment by coworkers:*
An employee's commission of acts of sexual harassment, other than assault, will result in nondisciplinary oral counseling upon alleged first offense; written warning, suspension, or discharge upon the first proven offense, depending upon the nature and severity of the misconduct; and suspension or discharge upon the second proven offense, depending upon the nature and severity of the misconduct.

C. *Retaliation:*
Alleged retaliation against a sexual harassment complainant will result in nondisciplinary oral counseling. Any form of proven retaliation will result in suspension or discharge upon the first proven offense, depending upon the nature and severity of the retaliatory acts, and discharge upon the second proven offense.

D. *Supervisors:*
A supervisor's commission of acts of sexual harassment (other than assault) with respect to any employee under that person's supervision will result in nondisciplinary oral counseling upon alleged first offense, final warning or dismissal for the first offense, depending upon the nature and severity of the misconduct, and discharge for any subsequent offense.

Procedures for Making, Investigating, and Resolving Sexual Harassment and Retaliation Complaints

A. *Complaints:*
XYZ Company will provide its employees with convenient, confidential, and reliable mechanisms for reporting incidents of sexual harassment and retaliation. Accordingly, XYZ designates at least two employees in supervisory or managerial positions to serve as investigative officers for sexual harassment issues. The names, responsibilities, work locations, and phone numbers of each officer will be routinely and continuously posted so that an employee seeking such name can enjoy anonymity and remain inconspicuous to all of the employees in the office in which he or she works.

The investigative officers may appoint "designees" to assist them in handling sexual harassment complaints. Persons appointed as designees shall not conduct investigations until they have received training equivalent to that received by the investigative officers. The purpose of having several persons to whom complaints may be made is to avoid a situation where an employee is faced with complaining to the person, or a close associate of the person, who would be the subject of the complaint.

Complaints of acts of sexual harassment or retaliation that are in violation of the sexual harassment policy will be accepted in writing or orally, and anonymous

(continued)

Exhibit 7.14   (continued)

complaints will be taken seriously and investigated. Anyone who has observed sexual harassment or retaliation should report it to a designated investigative officer. A complaint need not be limited to someone who was the target of harassment or retaliation. Only those who have an immediate need to know, including the investigative officers and/or his/her designee, the alleged target of harassment or retaliation, the alleged harasser(s) or retaliator(s), and any witnesses will or may find out the identity of the complainant. All parties contacted in the course of an investigation will be advised that all parties involved in a charge are entitled to respect and that any retaliation or reprisal against an individual who is an alleged target of harassment or retaliation, who has made a complaint, or who has provided evidence in connection with a complaint is a separate actionable offense as provided in the schedule of penalties. This complaint process will be administered consistent with federal labor law when bargaining unit members are affected.

B. *Investigations:*

Each investigative officer will receive thorough training about sexual harassment and the procedures herein and will have the responsibility for investigating complaints or having an appropriately trained and designated XYZ investigator do so.

All complaints will be investigated expeditiously by a trained XYZ investigative officer or his/her designee. The investigative officer will produce a written report, which, together with the investigation file, will be shown to the complainant upon request within a reasonable time. The investigative officer is empowered to recommend remedial measures based upon the results of the investigation, and XYZ management will promptly consider and act upon such recommendation. When a complaint is made, the investigative officer will have the duty of immediately bringing all sexual harassment and retaliation complaints to the confidential attention of the office of the president of XYZ, and XYZ's EEO officer. The investigative and EEO officers will each maintain a file on the original charge and follow up investigation. Such files will be available to investigators, to federal, state, and local agencies charged with equal employment or affirmative action enforcement, to other complainants who have filed a formal charge of discrimination against XYZ, or any agent thereof, whether that formal charge is filed at a federal, state, or local law level. The names of complainants, however, will be kept under separate file.

C. *Cooperation:*

An effective antisexual harassment policy requires the support and example of company personnel in positions of authority. XYZ agents or employees who engage in sexual harassment or retaliation or who fail to cooperate with company-sponsored investigations of sexual harassment or retaliation may be severely sanctioned by suspension or dismissal. By the same token, officials who refuse to implement remedial measures, obstruct the remedial efforts of other XYZ employees, and/or retaliate against sexual harassment complainants or witnesses may be immediately sanctioned by suspension or dismissal.

Procedures and Rules for Education and Training. Education and training for employees at each level of the workforce are critical to the success of XYZ's policy against sexual harassment. The following documents address such issues: the letter to be sent to all employees from XYZ's chief executive officer/president; the Antisexual Harassment Policy; Statement of Prohibited Conduct; the Schedule of Penalties for Misconduct; and Procedures for Making, Investigating, and Resolving Sexual Harassment Complaints.

Exhibit 7.14 (continued)

These documents will be conspicuously posted throughout the workplace at each division of XYZ, on each company bulletin board, in all central gathering areas, and in every locker room. The statements must be clearly legible and displayed continuously. The antisexual harassment policy under a cover letter from XYZ's president will be sent to all employees. The letter will indicate that copies are available at no cost and how they can be obtained.

XYZ's antisexual harassment policy statement will also be included in the Safety Instructions and General Company Rules, which is issued in booklet form to each XYZ employee. Educational posters using concise messages conveying XYZ's opposition to workplace sexual harassment will reinforce the company's policy statement; these posters should be simple, eye-catching, and graffiti resistant.

Education and training include the following components:

1. *For all XYZ employees:* As part of the general orientation, each recently hired employee will be given a copy of the letter from XYZ's chief executive officer/president and requested to read and sign a receipt for the company's policy statement on sexual harassment so that they are on notice of the standards of behavior expected. In addition, supervisory employees who have attended a management training seminar on sexual harassment will explain orally at least once every six months at general meetings attended by all employees the kind of acts that constitute sexual harassment, the company's serious commitment to eliminating sexual harassment in the workplace, the penalties for engaging in harassment, and the procedures for reporting incidents of sexual harassment.

2. *For all female employees:* All women employed at XYZ will participate on company time in annual seminars that teach strategies for resisting and preventing sexual harassment. At least a half-day in length, these seminars will be conducted by one or more experienced sexual harassment educators, including one instructor with work experience in the trades for skilled employees in traditionally male-dominated jobs.

3. *For all employees with supervisory authority of any kind over other employees:* All supervisory personnel will participate in an annual, half-day-long training session on gender discrimination. At least one-third of each session (of no less than one and one-half hours) will be devoted to education about workplace sexual harassment, including training (with demonstrative evidence) as to exactly what types of remarks, behavior, and pictures will not be tolerated in the XYZ workplace. The president of XYZ will attend the training sessions in one central location with all company supervisory employees. The president will introduce the seminar with remarks stressing the potential liability of XYZ and individual supervisors for sexual harassment. Each participant will be informed that they are responsible for knowing the contents of XYZ's antisexual harassment policy and for giving similar presentations at meetings of employees.

4. *For all investigative officers:* The investigative officers and their designees, if any, will attend annual full-day training seminars conducted by experienced sexual harassment educators and/or investigators to educate them about the problems of sexual harassment in the workplace and the techniques for investigating and stopping it.

discreetly as possible. Employees should be involved only on a "need to know" basis. When all appropriate evidence is gathered, much like the members of a jury, the employer must determine the facts. The employer bases the determination on who seems most credible, whose version of the alleged incidents is more likely to be closer to the truth, what interests the parties have in telling their version of the events, and any credible corroboration presented. The common problem of the employer's discomfort with making judgments should not, as it so often does, prevent moving quickly and appropriately on complaints.

The EEOC's June 1999 Policy Guidance on Harassment provides insight into how credibility determinations are to be made. According to the EEOC, while none of the following is necessarily determinative, factors to consider in deciding credibility include:

- *Inherent plausibility.* Is the testimony believable on its face? Does it make sense?
- *Demeanor.* Did the person seem to be telling the truth or lying?
- *Motive to falsify.* Did the person have a reason to lie?
- *Corroboration.* Is there *witness testimony* (such as testimony of eyewitnesses, people who saw the person soon after the alleged incidents or people who discussed the incidents with him or her at or around the time that they occurred) or *physical evidence* (such as written documentation) that corroborates the party's testimony?
- *Past record.* Did the alleged harasser have a history of similar behavior in the past?

We wish there was more we could tell you, but the truth is, there isn't much more that can be said. It can be uncomfortable, but investigating and making a decision must be done, and there are no special tools to do it, much like a jury has no special tools when deciding a murder case. They just come in, listen carefully to the evidence, observe carefully, and make a determination using their best judgment based on what they have taken in. There is no magic, no easy way to do it. Responding quickly, taking the matter seriously, using your best judgment to evaluate what you find, and going where the information leads you are the best tools you can use in determining the truth of the matter.

Retaliation and Employee Privacy

Often harassees report sexual harassment and, out of fear of retaliation, want the employer to provide relief without informing the alleged harasser of the complaint or of the complainant's identity. Harassees should be informed that the alleged harasser must be told of the complaint for the employer to effectively address it, but that retaliation will not be tolerated, as the law has separate retaliation provisions. Even alleged harassers are not required to play hide-and-seek with claims and claimants. As uncomfortable as the claimant may be in coming forward, the alleged harasser must be notified.

According to the EEOC, there has been a dramatic increase in the number of retaliation claims in recent years. EEOC has been clear in reiterating that it takes such cases very seriously. Courts and juries have been clear in sending the message that they do not like retaliation by employers for employees pursuing their legal rights under the law. Punitive damages are likely to be granted in such cases since retaliation, in a manner of speaking, adds insult to injury and is much more deliberate. Think back to Exhibit 7.8 about the nursing supervisor who was terminated in retaliation for giving a verbal warning to the nurse who was feeling people up in the operating room. The claimant received $4 million in her jury verdict, $3 million of which was punitive damages—all totally unnecessary as well as avoidable. Do you think a company really has an extra $4 million in its coffers to pay out to someone for a retaliation claim? We don't think so. If they have that kind of money to throw away, they can throw it in our direction! ☺

Corrective Action

The guidelines state that the employer must take "immediate and appropriate corrective action" to remedy sexual harassment. The most appropriate thing to do under the specific circumstance depends on the facts. Consideration should be given to such factors as the employment position of the employees, the activity involved, the duration of the actions, the seriousness of the actions, the employer's antisexual harassment policy and other methods used to deter sexual harassment, the alleged harasser's prior history of sexual harassment, and so on. While the remedy must be calculated to stop the harassment and must not have the effect of punishing the harassee, neither should it be out of proportion to the act. Make sure "the punishment fits the crime." Every act of sexual harassment need not result in automatic termination, the "capital punishment" of the workplace.

With all this in mind, the good news is that there is now a more formalized purpose to all this. For years, courts admonished employers to take claims seriously and respond accordingly, but this had no consistent, formalized result for the employer. Employers could do the best they could and still get into trouble with the law. That is no longer so for certain cases. Through two cases, one of which, *Faragher,* you have already been introduced to in this chapter, the U.S. Supreme Court created the *Ellerth/Faragher* affirmative defense we spoke of earlier, which employers could use to protect themselves from liability when they have tried to consistently obey the law. In *Ellerth,* below, the Court outlines that defense and provides employers with a good deal of control over avoiding and/or limiting liability for violations of Title VII when there is no loss of tangible job benefits because of a harasser's action. Keep in mind that the defense can only be used where there was no tangible employment action by a supervisor. We include the case here so that you can see the second case that accounts for the employer's defense, and also to give it to you in the context of employer's corrective action rather than in the context of employer liability.

Burlington Industries, Inc. v. Ellerth *524 U.S. 742 (1998)*

Employee claimed she was constructively discharged because of unwanted, persistent sexual advances by her supervisor. While she lost no tangible job benefit because of his actions toward her, and even had a promotion during her employment, the Court held she could still bring a cause of action based on hostile environment sexual harassment. Though employer had an antisexual harassment policy, employee did not report the harassment until a few weeks after she left. The Court said that employee could still bring the sexual harassment action, but in cases such as this where there is no loss of tangible job benefits, the employer could use as an affirmative defense the existence of procedures for reporting and handling sexual harassment complaints, and an employee's failure to use them.

Kennedy, J.

The employee is Kimberly Ellerth. From March 1993 until May 1994, Ellerth worked as a salesperson in one of Burlington's divisions in Chicago, Illinois. During her employment, she alleges, she was subjected to constant sexual harassment by her supervisor, one Ted Slowik.

Against a background of repeated boorish and offensive remarks and gestures which Slowik allegedly made, Ellerth places particular emphasis on three alleged incidents where Slowik's comments could be construed as threats to deny her tangible job benefits. In the summer of 1993, while on a business trip, Slowik invited Ellerth to the hotel lounge, an invitation Ellerth felt compelled to accept because Slowik was her boss. When Ellerth gave no encouragement to remarks Slowik made about her breasts, he told her to "loosen up" and warned, "you know, Kim, I could make your life very hard or very easy at Burlington."

In March 1994, when Ellerth was being considered for a promotion, Slowik expressed reservations during the promotion interview because she was not "loose enough." The comment was followed by his reaching over and rubbing her knee. Ellerth did receive the promotion; but when Slowik called to announce it, he told Ellerth, "you're gonna be out there with men who work in factories, and they certainly like women with pretty butts/legs."

In May 1994, Ellerth called Slowik, asking permission to insert a customer's logo into a fabric sample. Slowik responded, "I don't have time for you right now, Kim—unless you want to tell me what you're wearing." Ellerth told Slowik she had to go and ended the call. A day or two later, Ellerth called Slowik to ask permission again. This time he denied her request, but added something along the lines of, "are you wearing shorter skirts yet, Kim, because it would make your job a whole heck of a lot easier."

A short time later, Ellerth's immediate supervisor cautioned her about returning telephone calls to customers in a prompt fashion. In response, Ellerth quit. She faxed a letter giving reasons unrelated to the alleged sexual harassment we have described. About three weeks later, however, she sent a letter explaining she quit because of Slowik's behavior.

During her tenure at Burlington, Ellerth did not inform anyone in authority about Slowik's conduct, despite knowing Burlington had a policy against sexual harassment. In fact, she chose not to inform her immediate supervisor (not Slowik) because "it would be his duty as my supervisor to report any incidents of sexual harassment." On one occasion, she told Slowik a comment he made was inappropriate.

We must decide, then, whether an employer has vicarious liability when a supervisor creates a hostile work environment by making explicit threats to alter a subordinate's terms or conditions of employment, based on sex, but does not fulfill the threat.

Tangible employment actions are the means by which the supervisor brings the official power of the enterprise to bear on subordinates. A tangible employment decision requires an official act of the enterprise, a company act. The decision in most cases is documented in official company records, and may be subject to review by higher level supervisors. The supervisor often must obtain the imprimatur of the enterprise and use its internal processes. For these reasons, a tangible employment action taken by the supervisor becomes for Title VII purposes the act of the employer. Whatever the exact contours of the aided in the agency relation standard, its requirements will always be met when a supervisor takes a tangible employment action against a subordinate. In that instance, it would be implausible to interpret agency principles to allow an employer to escape liability.

An employer is subject to vicarious liability to a victimized employee for an actionable hostile environment created by a supervisor with immediate (or successively higher) authority over the employee. When no tangible employment action is taken, a defending employer may raise an affirmative defense to liability or damages, subject to proof by a preponderance of the evidence. The defense comprises two necessary elements: (a) that the employer exercised reasonable care to prevent and correct promptly any sexually harassing behavior, and (b) that the plaintiff employee unreasonably failed to take advantage of any preventive or corrective opportunities provided by the employer or to avoid harm otherwise.

While proof that an employer had promulgated an anti-harassment policy with complaint procedure is not necessary in every instance as a matter of law, the need for a stated policy suitable to the employment circumstances may appropriately be addressed in any case when litigating the first element of the defense. And while proof that an employee failed to fulfill the corresponding obligation of reasonable care to avoid harm is not limited to showing any unreasonable failure to use any complaint procedure provided by the employer, a demonstration of such failure will normally suffice to satisfy the employer's burden under the second element of the defense. No affirmative defense is available, however, when the supervisor's harassment culminates in a tangible employment action, such as discharge, demotion, or undesirable reassignment.

Although Ellerth has not alleged she suffered a tangible employment action at the hands of Slowik, which would deprive Burlington of the availability of the affirmative defense, this is not dispositive. In light of our decision, Burlington is still subject to vicarious liability for Slowik's activity, but Burlington should have an opportunity to assert and prove the affirmative defense to liability. AFFIRMED.

Case Questions

1. What do you think of the Court not allowing the affirmative defense if there was a tangible employment action such as a discharge, demotion, or undesirable reassignment?

2. Does it make sense to you to allow an employee to bring a sexual harassment cause of action if the employee suffered no adverse tangible employment action?

3. Do you understand why the Court would allow this affirmative defense in cases where there is no loss of tangible job benefit, but not in cases where there is such a loss?

Damages and Jury Trials

Under the Civil Rights Act of 1991, an employee suing for sexual harassment can now ask for up to $300,000 in compensatory and punitive damages (and unlimited medical damages) and request a jury trial. Both these factors greatly increase the employer's potential liability for sexual harassment and make avoiding liability for this unnecessary activity even more imperative.

As you can imagine, after the 1991 amendments allowed damages and jury trials, Title VII claims increased dramatically. It finally made economic sense to go through the time-consuming, arduous process of suing, for both claimants and their attorneys. Of course, this was not a welcome event for employers. In response to our country's exploding litigation dockets, the use of alternative dispute resolution, or ADR, went from a backwater alternative to litigation to one of the most-used methods. As we discussed in the chapter on Title VII, EEOC has now institutionalized the used of ADR in its proceedings in several ways and has gotten employers to do the same, using their own extensive, in-house ADR resources. Among other things, EEOC conducts mediation on appropriate claims filed with them, and in 2003, it began pilot or start-up programs for handling its own internal complaints, a program to have Fair Employment Practice Agencies mediate private sector claims, and a program in which national employers handle claims of their employees informally before handing it over to EEOC (if it necessary to do so). Many attorneys and court systems now also offer ADR as a part of their services.

ADR is a much less acrimonious, expensive, time-consuming alternative that also has the bonus of not being on the public record, for the most part, or precedent setting, in the formal sense. If you are an employer or employee, it would probably be in your best interest to try this route before going to court. You have little to lose and a host of benefits to gain.

Tort and Criminal Liability

In addition to bringing an action under Title VII, harassees may also bring civil actions in state court—or if permitted, federal court—based on state laws that may also be violated by the actions of the alleged harasser. Recall that in *Meritor*, the first sexual harassment case to come before the U.S. Supreme Court, the bank manager was alleged to have fondled plaintiff in public, followed her to and entered the ladies' restroom with her, and engaged in unwelcome sexual intercourse, including while in the bank's vault.

Management Tips

Sexual harassment doesn't have to be the employer's worst nightmare. Don't ever expect to have absolute control over every employee in the workplace, but following the tips below can substantially decrease the chances of a recalcitrant employee causing liability.

Zero tolerance, both in word and deed, should be the rule for sexual harassment. The EEOC and courts take the position that the best thing an employer can do to effectively keep sexual harassment complaints to a minimum—and to minimize liability for sexual harassment complaints that do occur—is to take a preventive approach. This may include the following:

- Adopt an antisexual harassment policy discouraging such activity. This should be separate from the general antidiscrimination policy, and every employee should be aware of it.

- Make sure, from the top down, that all employees understand that sexual harassment in the workplace simply will not be tolerated. *Period.*

- Create and disseminate information about an effective reporting mechanism for harassees.

- After adopting the policy, don't let it sit in a drawer somewhere. Use it.

- Provide employees with training or information apprising them of what sexual harassment is and of what specific activities are appropriate and inappropriate in the workplace. This will go a very long way toward decreasing potential liability for the employer.

- Ensure that reported incidents of sexual harassment are taken seriously by supervisors and others involved in reporting. Do not tell the employee to "get over it," or that it is to be expected.

- Ensure that the training employees receive is effective and answers their questions and concerns.

- Keep in mind that creating an atmosphere in which sexual harassment is not tolerated is a big part of what the EEOC and courts want employers to do. Operationalize this on a real-life basis. That is, when employees engage in activity that helps to create an atmosphere that accepts harassing activity, challenge it. Don't tolerate the jokes, sneers, leers, teasing, gestures, and so forth.

- Promptly investigate all sexual harassment claims and only circulate information on a need-to-know basis.

- If investigation warrants discipline for the harasser, ensure that immediate appropriate corrective action is taken against harasser. Make sure the corrective action is commensurate with the policy violation. Termination is not the response to every sexual harassment claim.

- Work to keep the workplace friendly and open. Having a workplace free of sexual harassment does not mean employees can't still work in a pleasant atmosphere.

These acts, while constituting sexual harassment under Title VII, also could form the basis for the tort actions of

Assault: Intentionally putting the victim in fear or apprehension, or both, of immediate unpermitted bodily touching.

Battery: Intentional unpermitted bodily touching.

Intentional infliction of emotional distress: An intentional outrageous act that goes outside the bounds of common decency, for which the law will provide a remedy.

False imprisonment: Intentionally preventing the harassee's exit from a confined space.

Intentional interference with contractual relations: Intentionally causing the harassee to be unable to perform her employment contract as agreed upon.

These cases are generally heard by juries, and there is the possibility of unlimited compensatory and punitive damages. In addition, the harasser's action could also form the basis of criminal prosecution for, at a minimum, criminal assault, battery, and rape. Of course, the criminal cases would be against the harasser, rather than the employer, and would result in punishment for the harasser, rather than money damages to the harassee (unless the state has a victim assistance or restitution program).

Summary

- Consensual activity is not a violation of Title VII.
- Unwelcome sexual advances that cause one gender to work under conditions or terms of employment different from those of the other gender constitute sexual harassment for which the employer may be liable.
- Employers will be responsible only if the sexual harassment is severe and pervasive.
- Activity does not have to be sexual in nature to constitute sexual harassment.
- Employers should treat all sexual harassment complaints seriously and act on them quickly.
- Prevention is imperative to avoid sexual harassment claims and lessen liability. The employer must make it clear that sexual harassment will not be tolerated. This should be clearly stated and followed up and monitored by appropriate mechanisms.
- Employers need a strong antisexual harassment policy that is vigorously enforced.

Chapter-End Questions

1. Dave comes into the office and says to Sue, "Good morning! You look great today! Ooops, I'd better not say that. That's sexual harassment." Is Dave correct? Explain.

2. Employee, a 33-year-old unmarried male, is frequently teased by the other males in his plant about being unmarried and still living at home with his mother. Is this sexual harassment? [*Goluszek* v. *Smith,* 697 F. Supp. 1452 (N.D. Ill. 1988).]

3. Employee sues employer for sexual harassment, because her supervisor once touched her on her back and made an "untoward" statement to her. Will she win? Explain. [*Strickland* v. *Sears Roebuck and Co.,* 693 F. Supp. 403 (E.D. Va. 1988).]

4. Two employees, Marge and Ben, are having a relationship that later turns sour. When Marge does not get the promotion she goes up for, she sues the employer for sexual harassment, alleging it was committed by her ex-boyfriend Ben, who has, since their breakup, left Marge

alone. Will Marge win her suit? [*Koster* v. *Chase Manhattan Bank,* 687 F. Supp. 848 (S.D. N.Y. 1988).]

5. Dennis comes up to his supervisor, Mae, at a Christmas party and tells Mae he wants to sue for sexual harassment. Mae asks what happened. Dennis says that Linda came over to him and tweaked his cheek and called him sweetie. Dennis pursues the case. Does he win? Why or why not?

6. Is it possible for a subordinate to sexually harass a supervisor? Explain.

7. A female employee has an operation on her breast and, when she returns to work, a male employee "jokingly" asks to see the scar. Actionable sexual harassment? [*Keziah* v. *W. M. Brown Son, Inc.,* 683 F. Supp. 542 (W.D.N.C. 1988).]

8. Joan, a female manager, asks Margaret, one of her subordinates, out on a date. When Margaret refuses, Joan becomes mean to her at work and rates Margaret's work poorly on her next evaluation. Margaret wants to bring a sexual harassment claim, but feels she cannot do so since her boss is female. Is Margaret correct?

9. At the door of church each Sunday as his church members are leaving, Reverend Bill kisses the females on the cheek and calls them names like "honey" and "sweetheart." Is this sexual harassment? Explain.

10. Trudy comes to Pat, her supervisor, and tells her that Jack has been sexually harassing her by making suggestive remarks, comments, and jokes, constantly asking her for dates, and by using every available opportunity to touch her. Pat has been friends with Jack for a long time and can't imagine Jack would do such a thing. Pat is hesitant to move on Trudy's complaint. What should Pat do?

Chapter **Eight**

Affinity Orientation Discrimination

Opening Scenarios

STATUTORY BASIS

It shall be an unlawful employment practice for an employer—

(1) to fail or refuse to hire or to discharge any individual, or otherwise to
discriminate against any individual with respect to his compensation, terms, conditions,
or privileges of employment, because of such individual's . . . sex. Title VII of the Civil
Rights Act of 1964, as amended. 42 U.S.C. 2000e-2(a).

**affinity
orientation**
Whom one is
attracted to for
personal and
intimate rela-
tionships.

The above does *not* prohibit discrimination on the basis of **affinity orientation**.

Nor shall any State deprive any person of life, liberty, or property, without due process
of law; nor deny to any person within its jurisdiction the equal protection of the laws.
Amendment XIV of the U.S. Constitution.

OUT OF THE CLOSET

"Look," the angry gentleman in the audience said gruffly as the diversity consultant
walked into the room and up to the stage in preparation for conducting a training session. "Does this diversity training mean that I have to deal with homosexuals? Because
if it does, I'm not doing it, because homosexuality is against my religion and I just
don't think it's right!" This employee's attitude is not unique, nor are the social trends
that are provoking such reactions:

- SpongeBob SquarePants' creator, Stephen Hillenburg, defends against charges that
  SpongeBob and his starfish friend Patrick, are gay.

- Newly appointed Secretary of Education, Margaret Spellings, makes one of her first
  official duties firing off a letter of reprimand to the Public Broadcasting Station
  (PBS) for its plans to air an episode of *Postcards from Buster*, with a cartoon bunny
  who travels around the world visiting different places to teach children about culture,

geography, and diversity, because Buster stops in Vermont and visits a family that has two moms.

- A farmer acknowledges spreading three tons of manure along the route of a gay rights parade, saying he was exercising his constitutional right to free speech.
- Republican California governor Arnold Schwarzenegger causes an uproar when he calls Democratic legislators who oppose his budget "girlie men."
- Hofstra Law School creates three $25,000 scholarships for the Equality of Lesbian, Gay, Bisexual and Transgender People in response to the university's decision to allow the military to recruit on campus, despite objections from faculty and students that the military's "don't ask, don't tell" policy is discriminatory.
- Kelli O'Donnell, life partner of celebrity Rosie O'Donnell, launches R Family Vacations, the first travel company dedicated to the gay family market.
- An immigration judge refuses to grant asylum to a gay Mexican seeking asylum due to his treatment in his country because he is gay, saying he "does not see anything in his appearance, his dress, his manner, his demeanor his gestures or his voice or anything of that nature that remotely approaches some of the stereotypical things that society assesses to gays, whether those are legitimate or not."
- A seven-year-old is scolded and forced to write repeatedly "I will never use the word 'gay' in school again" after he told a classmate about his lesbian mom in response to a question during recess by a classmate about the boy's parents.
- A gay inmate is not able to send letters to his life partner of 18 years because letters can only go to family or spouses.
- Athletes who undergo gender change operations will be eligible to compete in the Olympics for the first time under new rules finalized by the International Olympic Committee.
- An Atlanta golf club retains a prominent attorney after the city commission finds the club discriminates by not extending marital benefits to partners of gay members.
- The federal government awards more than $500,000 from the federal fund created to compensate victims of the 9/11 attacks to the 18-year lesbian partner of a woman killed in the attack on the Pentagon.
- The Episcopal Church ordains its first gay bishop.
- As part of "dirty" recruiting tactics, parents of highly sought-after female high school basketball players are told that female coaches of competing teams are lesbian in what is called the "fear of a gay boogeyman who will make their daughters choose a lesbian sexual orientation" (partly in response, the NCAA is studying whether homophobia is a reason that the number of female head basketball coaches dropped from 79 percent in 1977 to 63 percent in 2002).
- A high school student sues her school because the teacher who found out the student is a lesbian kicked her out of gym class and made her sit in the principal's office during gym for a week and a half.
- Two days after unanimously requesting that the county attorney find a way to enact an ordinance banning gays and lesbians from living in the county (saying "We need

to keep them out of here"), the Rhea County, Tennessee, commissioners withdraw the request because of the outcry outside the county.

And this is just in the past few years!

As you can see, same-gender affinity orientation[1] pushes a lot of buttons in society in general, and the workplace is just a microcosm of society. Though a bit gruff, the employee's assertion that homosexuality was against his religion, mentioned above, was a manifestation of that. This employee spoke for many others when he made his statement. The good thing is that he got it out onto the table where it could be discussed, put into perspective, and fitted into what his employer wanted this program to accomplish: less exposure to liability for violations of the law on this and other bases of discrimination. Since we understand that this sentiment is a fairly common one, let's take a bit of time up front to discuss it and give you some things to keep in mind as you go through the chapter and think about the subject matter.

From the battle with the Boy Scouts of America and whether a California Eagle Scout can be excluded from the largest youth organization in the United States, to celebrity and adoptive mother Rosie O'Donnell announcing that she is a lesbian and taking up the issue of Florida law not permitting adoptions by gays and lesbians, to whether a transgender employee can lawfully sue for the use of certain toilet facilities, the issue of affinity orientation is being debated and discussed all across the country, and even around the world, in every conceivable context. From whether gays and lesbians can marry and have children or can visit a partner in a hospital when only "family" members are permitted, to whether they can be terminated from a job because of being gay or lesbian or whether their partners can receive job benefits as spouses do, the issue has vast implications for people's everyday lives. And, of course, anything that is of any great social importance generally ends up finding its way into the workplace. The issue of affinity orientation is no different. The increasing presence of the issue in the workplace and the legal implications arising therefrom make it essential that we include coverage here.

Discrimination on the basis of affinity orientation is not included in Title VII, but the fact that hundreds of local ordinances, 15 state laws, and thousands of workplaces include it as part of prohibited bases for employment discrimination also dictate we include coverage here. As exhibited by the gentleman in the opening paragraph (one of your authors was actually the consultant involved), affinity orientation discrimination is also one of the types of discrimination that may call into question ideas we hold dear and wish to protect, so we may think of this type of discrimination differently—as more justifiable—than we do others. In order to prevent those thoughts from turning into actions that lead to litigation and liability for the employer, we must learn to view the costly and avoidable matter in its proper *workplace* perspective.

As you read the chapter, keep this thought in the front of your mind: The intent of this chapter is not to get you to "accept" homosexuality. This chapter is not about going against your religious dictates, moral values, or conscience. As with our other chapter topics, you are free to believe whatever you wish. Rather, this chapter is about what the law requires in this area and what will lessen or prevent costly liability from attaching

---

[1] Also included in this general discussion are persons of bi-gender affinity orientation and transgenders. Since their workplace issues generally stem from exercise of their same-gender component, they are not specifically delineated here separately except as necessary.

for violations of the law. This is especially important as things in this area are changing so rapidly to include new rights.

Before choosing to engage in activity that may cause the employer liability for discrimination and result in your termination, keep in mind that this is the *employer's* workplace, not yours. Employees don't have the right to engage in activities that will cause unnecessary liability for their employer. Since this is the employer's workplace, the employer gets to call the shots. If the employer has hired someone you don't like, for whatever reason, you have to decide what it's worth to you. Do you create trouble for the employer and run the risk of getting fired, or do you conduct yourself in a professional manner and keep your personal issues to yourself and collect a check? If you feel like you can't do the latter, then you are free to seek employment elsewhere. But if you choose to stay, you have no right to impose your personal beliefs on the workplace in a way that increases the employer's liability.

If you think your religious beliefs don't permit same-gender affinity orientation, then don't take your gay or lesbian coworker to lunch. Don't take him or her home for dinner. But refusing to work with him or her as required or otherwise treating the coworker in ways that discriminate and expose the *employer* to liability is simply not an option. It might help to think about whether you discriminate against other employees who do things that are against your religion. If you also refuse to deal with coworkers who are alcoholics, fornicators, adulterers, or engage in other activity against your religious beliefs, at least the religious justification is consistent. For most, it rarely is. Working with someone who is gay or lesbian does not mean you "accept homosexuality" any more than working with adulterers means you "accept adultery." Many people put affinity orientation into another category that permits them to treat it differently. That may be fine for your personal life, but work is work, and your personal life is your personal life, and the considerations for one are not always the same as the considerations for the other. When it's a matter of business and someone else's pocket that will suffer, you have to rein in your personal feelings. Again, if all else fails, and you just can't bring yourself to think of this differently for work purposes, you ought to find another job where you'd be more comfortable. If this sounds like we have an agenda, then you heard us correctly. Our agenda is to protect the employer from unnecessary and costly liability.

With that out of the way, let's explore this area and see what's here.

Despite the stereotypes of gay males as florists, designers, or interior decorators, a survey by the Chicago marketing research firm, Overlooked Opinions, found that more gay males work in science and engineering than in social services, 40 percent more are employed in finance and insurance than in entertainment and the arts, and 10 times as many work in computers as in fashion. (See Exhibit 8.1) Once, gays and lesbians in the workplace were virtually invisible, but diverse circumstances have begun to change that in dramatic ways.

You have the blessing (or curse, depending on your view) of actually living history as it relates to this issue. There have been dramatic changes in just the past 12 years or so. From never speaking the world *gay* on TV, to having award-winning TV shows like *Will and Grace, Queer Eye for the Straight Guy,* or *The L Word* be top performers, the landscape has changed. You may wonder how it happened.

Recent historical issues such as the impact of AIDS in the workplace, the military's "don't ask, don't tell" policy, the 1992 presidential election in which President Bill

Exhibit 8.1   Heterosexual Myths

QUESTIONNAIRE

The questions below provide a somewhat humorous yet insightful look at some of the more frequent assumptions surrounding gays and lesbians, which affect how they may be perceived in the workplace and society at large. The approach of reversing the questions subtly challenges commonly held heterosexually based notions.

1. What do you think caused your heterosexuality?
2. When and how did you first decide you were heterosexual?
3. Is it possible your heterosexuality is just a phase you may grow out of?
4. Is it possible your heterosexuality stems from a neurotic fear of others of the same gender?
5. Heterosexuals have histories of failures in gay relationships. Do you think you may have turned to heterosexuality out of fear of rejection?
6. If you've never slept with a person of the same gender, how do you know you wouldn't prefer that?
7. To whom have you disclosed your heterosexual tendencies? How do they react?
8. Your heterosexuality doesn't offend me as long as you don't try to force it on me. Why do you people feel compelled to seduce others into your sexual orientation?
9. Why do you insist on being so obvious and making a public spectacle of your heterosexuality by holding hands or kissing in public? Can't you just be what you are and keep it quiet?
10. How would the human race survive if everyone were heterosexual like you, considering the menace of overpopulation?
11. Why do heterosexuals place so much emphasis on sex?
12. How can you be heterosexual if you've never had sex?

Source: Adapted from Martin Rochlin, Ph.D., by Dr. Miranda Pollard, University of Georgia.

Clinton voiced support for gays (he later supported the Employment Nondiscrimination Act [ENDA] prohibiting workplace discrimination against gays and lesbians, which has not yet passed, and appointed over 150 gays and lesbians in his administration, including an ambassador and cabinet-level positions—see Exhibit 8.2) and Colorado's attempted constitutional ban on protection for gays and lesbians (which the U.S. Supreme Court struck down) put the issue of gays and lesbians on the national agenda for the first time. On April 25, 1993, the Cable News Network (CNN) broadcast day-long national television coverage of the convergence of nearly a million people, gay and straight, on Washington, D.C., for the March on Washington for Lesbian, Gay, and Bi Equal Rights and Liberation. It was clear that it was one of the largest marches ever held, and that gays and lesbians could no longer be ignored. Since that time, states have seen a good deal of legislation about gays and lesbians, and courts have seen cases on issues ranging from parental rights to military discharges, from domestic partner benefits to gay marriage, and from hate crimes to workplace discrimination.

Earning a living is a necessity for most people, so the issue of gays and lesbians is increasingly surfacing in the workplace and has become one an employer must deal with. There is an increasing realization that gays and lesbians are everywhere and

Exhibit 8.2   Lesbian Confirmed for No. 2 HUD Post

On May 24, 1993, President Clinton's nominee for assistant secretary of Housing and Urban Development, Roberta Achtenberg, was confirmed by the Senate 58–31 after a three-day debate. Ms. Achtenberg was a member of the San Francisco Board of Supervisors who had won numerous awards for her community service, and the Senate's vote made her the first open lesbian appointed to such a high government position.

During the Senate debate, Senator Jesse Helms (R-N.C.) brought up that Ms. Achtenberg was seen with her partner, municipal court judge Mary Morgan, kissing and hugging while leading a 1992 gay pride parade. The Christian Action Network sent a copy of the videotape to every member of the Senate, and senators received thousands of calls from opponents after being urged to call from TV shows like Reverend Pat Robertson's *700 Club*.

During the Senate debate, Senator Dianne Feinstein (D-Calif.), former mayor of San Francisco, said "Today we have a chance to turn our back to prejudice. Today we can vote down the politics of hate and take a small step to make sure our government is representative of all the people it seeks to serve."

Note: Achtenberg resigned in 1995 to run for elected office in San Francisco.

---

should be judged for who they are as people, not for the singular measure of the private matter of sex. With the rules changing almost daily, and more state and local legislation both for and against civil rights for gays, it has become imperative for employers to know what their potential legal liability is in this area.

A fairly recent development has been the emergence of nondiscrimination policies and gay and lesbian employee support groups within the workplace. There are well over 2,000, including groups in over 300 Fortune 500 companies, many colleges and universities, nonprofits, unions, and state and local governments. Now listed among such employers are Apple Computer, Digital Equipment, AT&T, Coca-Cola, IBM, Kodak, Du Pont, Hewlett-Packard, Lucent Technologies, Sun Microsystems, Pacific Gas and Electric Company, Walt Disney Co., J. P. Morgan, Chase & Co., Goldman Sachs, Merrill Lynch, and United Parcel Service, to name a few. The groups tackle such issues as workplace hostility, extending employee benefits to domestic partners, making sure that partners are welcome at company social functions, and generally making the workplace less threatening to the worklife and workplace progress of gays and lesbians.

Some companies sponsor their gay and lesbian employees at events like Gay Pride, a nationwide celebration each June, culminating in a parade comprised of many types of contingents, including businesses. Companies provide employees with such things as novelty items to be passed out to attendees or T-shirts with slogans, such as "ABC Company Supports Its Gay and Lesbian Employees." (See Exhibit 8.3.) A recent poll showed that this type of workplace support is important to 71 percent of the gays and lesbians polled.

Gay Pride Month is not just a fun time. And despite what your local news coverage may choose to show, it not only has parade participants with their behinds hanging out of leather clothing or "freaky" looking characters. It is actually the commemoration of the historic events of June 1969. Being gay or lesbian is often a life-threatening proposition, but it was even more so then. As a result, most gays and lesbians led an extremely closeted existence and often congregated in gay bars in order to be sure of the safety of their surroundings. Since gays and lesbians were considered social outcasts

Exhibit 8.3   AT&T's Gay Employee Resource Group

This is part of a full-color brochure handed out at the 1993 March on Washington for Gay, Lesbian, and Bisexual Equal Rights and Liberation. The 1987 march referred to is the first national gay and lesbian march that had been held in Washington, D.C. six years before.

IT'S
GREAT
TO BE GAY
AT
AT&T

PROVIDED

BY THE

LESBIAN,

BISEXUAL &

GAY UNITED

EMPLOYEES

AT AT&T

LEAGUE

HISTORY OF LEAGUE

In 1987 a handful of AT&T employees returned home from the March on Washington inspired, energized and convinced that they could change their part of the world . . . that they could make AT&T a place that welcomed ALL its employees!

Meeting in restaurants and private homes, they formed an informal support group called LEAGUE. In 1988, these brave people brought LEAGUE to the corporation where it was recognized as the two-way communication vehicle between the decision-makers and the AT&T gay community. Soon, word about LEAGUE came out on informal gay bulletin boards across the country . . . chapters sprang up in Denver, then New Jersey, then Ohio and Illinois! In 1992, LEAGUE National was created and bound the loosely associated chapters together to form a common voice, with a common vision: To share the AT&T values, we commit ourselves to advancing changes that will help people respect and value lesbian, bisexual and gay employees and further AT&T's quest for excellence and customer satisfaction. Today there are over 20 LEAGUE chapters across the country that provide its members:

- Advocacy and access to all levels of management
- Professional development courses and conferences
- Workplace community support via electronic mail and regular meetings
- The "Safe Place" ™ program
- Help with community service projects
- Social and networking opportunities
- Resources for solving workplace issues
- Opportunities to educate the AT&T community via homophobia workshops and speaking engagements.

LEAGUE has become a proud and visible leader in the global business community, offering an example for other gay employee resource groups to follow.

Exhibit 8.3   (continued)

I LOVE WORKING FOR AT&T BECAUSE...

...I have something special here: a non-discrimination policy, the respect of my management, the support of fellow lesbian, bisexual, gay and straight co-workers, the empowerment to help make AT&T a better place for everyone and the freedom to bring my partner to Family Day at my office.

Rich Mielke, Network Systems, LEAGUE, N. Illinois

...I can aspire toward my professional goals without compromising my personal values or pretending to be someone I'm not. It's inspiring to see gay role models and rewarding to be one in a corporation that takes valuing the diversity of its workforce as seriously as its other business imperatives.

Linda Escalante, Mgr.-Int'l Sales Support, LEAGUE, N. Jersey

...I can finally be open about who I am. I feel very supported by AT&T knowing that if anyone gives me a hard time because of my sexual orientation, more education will take place. I am a much more powerful manager now that I am open about who I am. My personal and professional relationships are moving to deeper levels as I share more of myself with others.

Don Shuart, Programmer/Analyst, LEAGUE, Atlanta

...I believe that our management is honestly committed to understanding our issues and to promoting a healthy, diverse work place and that this will give us a competitive advantage in the decades to come.

Bill Thacker, Quality Engineer, LEAGUE, Columbus

...while recognizing that this is not a perfect place to work, AT&T is committed to making it an attractive, supportive place for all employees. I feel safe being out at work because people around me make it a supportive, caring place.

Terry Teeter, QA Specialist, LEAGUE, Central Florida

...it has taught me the true value of a supportive community on the job. When my life partner became ill with AIDS seven years ago, I "came out" to my boss and my co-workers in order to help them understand why I might suddenly be absent to deal with a health crisis at home. My boss cried and offered me her complete support. When my partner died a year later, about half of the workers in our office—secretaries, paralegals and attorneys—came to his memorial service. I knew then that I was "at home" and "with family" here at AT&T and have felt even closer to my colleagues in the years since.

Glenn Stover, Senior Attorney, LEAGUE, At-Large

...since my involvement with LEAGUE-Atlanta, I've gained a deeper self-respect and found that the people I work with respect me more as a person. I used to live my life in fear of what a few people may have thought of me rather than accepting the positive support that I now know was out there all along. After 25 years with the company, I now know that AT&T really is its people.

Jane Darby, Quality Specialist, LEAGUE, Atlanta

Source: Reprinted with permission of AT&T.

of the highest order, they did not want to risk their own lives, or embarrass their families and friends by being honest about who they were. Fearing discovery made them a very vulnerable group who rarely fought against their circumstances. Gay bars, often the only place gays and lesbians could go and feel accepted for who they were, were routinely raided by police officers and the patrons hauled off to jail for one minor infraction or another. Fearing publicity, most patrons went quietly.

In June 1969, this changed. When plainclothes police raided the Stonewall Inn in New York's Greenwich Village, there was uncharacteristic resistance by the bar patrons and people on the street that resulted in a weekend of riots. The next year in New York, the first legislative hearings on gay issues were held, as was the first parade to commemorate the events at Stonewall. The resistance at Stonewall in 1969 is considered the beginning of the modern gay rights movement. Over the years the commemoration has grown and spread as more people, gay and straight, determine that being gay should not equal being vulnerable to discrimination or death. Each June there are now Gay Pride Month celebrations across the country and around the world. While in office, President Clinton issued proclamations declaring June Gay Pride Month, as do many state governors. President Bush broke with this tradition, saying he considers affinity orientation a personal matter.

The Clinton administration's first U.S. Department of Transportation secretary, Federico Peña, held a lunch hour gay pride day ceremony for department employees, stating, "We need to draw on the talents of everyone. It's not about special privileges. It's about equal treatment." In June 2002, among others, the U.S. Environmental Protection Agency's director of the Office of Administration and Resource Management, William E. Laxton, issued a memo setting forth support for, and listing, Gay Pride Month activities and encouraging managers and supervisors to do likewise. AT&T handed out slick, three-color brochures during the 1993 march on Washington (see Exhibit 8.3) providing information for gay and lesbian AT&T employees about AT&T and its policies and attitudes regarding them. Each year there is a National Conference on Gay Issues in the Workplace held for human resources professionals needing guidance in this area. Each October 11 is National Coming Out Day, the purpose of which is to bring attention to the importance of gays' and lesbians' being open about who they are in an effort to help dispel the myths and stereotypes society holds, which have resulted from their historic silence and invisibility. The question often arises as to why a gay person has to let people know. "I don't go around telling people I'm straight, so why do they have to say they are gay?" The reason is that there is an overriding presumption that people are heterosexual, and if the gay person does not say otherwise, he or she ends up feeding into it and living a lie.

The issue of gays in the workplace can surface in some surprising ways, making it all the more compelling for an employer to be aware of the possibilities and take them into consideration when making policy in this area. Apple computer company was thinking of moving its operations to Williamson County, Texas. The city council refused to vote Apple concessions as an incentive to move there after it discovered that Apple had domestic partnership benefits for its employees. Apple refused to take away these benefits, and the city council finally voted to give Apple the concessions. The Walt Disney Company took a real beating from conservatives when it extended benefits to domestic partners of its employees. The company chose to continue the benefits. Anheuser-Busch took flak for its ads featuring two men holding hands, but the ads continued. In May 2005, two weeks after dropping the protection for gays and lesbians from its legislative agenda due to threats of boycotts from religious groups, Microsoft's CEO, Steve Ballmer, said "After looking at the question from all sides, I've concluded that diversity in the workplace is such an important issue for our business that it should be in our legislative agenda."

Based on the potential for increased productivity and the possibility of litigation or other business problems, some employers conclude that the safer practice is to base workplace decisions solely on an employee's ability to effectively perform the job, rather than on his or her affinity orientation. If the employee's *conduct* interferes with the workplace, it may be the basis for a disciplinary action, but this is not the same as the employee's affinity *orientation*. The focus should not be on the employee's *status* as gay or lesbian but, rather, on the employee's workplace *performance*.

The above notwithstanding, affinity orientation is *not* a protected category under Title VII of the Civil Rights Act. It has been judicially and administratively determined that gender discrimination under Title VII does not include discrimination on the basis of same-gender affinity orientation, **gender/sexual reassignment surgery (transsexuals)** or

gender/sexual reassignment surgery
The surgery required to change a person's gender. Gender dysphoria is the condition of the physical gender not matching the emotional/psychological gender of the candidate for the operation. A prerequisite for surgery.

transsexual
Someone who undergoes a change from one gender to another.

- There are state employment antidiscrimination laws in Washington, D.C., California, Connecticut, Hawaii, Maryland, Massachusetts, Minnesota, Nevada, New York, Illinois, New Mexico, New Jersey, New Hampshire, Rhode Island, Vermont, and Wisconsin.
- An executive order prohibits discrimination in the federal civilian workforce and mandates that security clearances no longer be denied based on affinity orientation.
- At least 532 cities or counties prohibit discrimination in public and/or private employment. Jurisdictions include:

Fayetteville, AR	Lawrence, KS	Portland, OR
Phoenix, AZ	Louisville, KY	Philadelphia, PA
Boulder, CO	New Orleans, LA	Charleston, SC
Wilmington, DE	Detroit, MI	Minnehaha County, SD
Broward County, FL	St. Louis, MO	Austin, TX
Atlanta, GA	Durham, NC	Salt Lake County, UT
Ames, IA	Albuquerque, NM	Alexandria, VA
Chicago, IL	New York, NY	Seattle, WA
Bloomington, IN	Toledo, OH	Morgantown, WV

Source: Human Rights Campaign, www.hrc.org.

---

bi-gender affinity orientation
Someone attracted to both genders.

bi-gender affinity orientation (bisexuality). Those who are terminated or not hired solely on the basis of affinity orientation have no claim for relief under this law. This was reaffirmed once again when Congress failed to pass the Employment Nondiscrimination Act (ENDA) in 2001. It is again before Congress. The Senate's Health, Education, Labor, and Pensions Committee considered the bill and recommended that the entire Senate consider it for passage. It has not yet been acted upon. ENDA would basically extend Title VII's reach to include discrimination on the basis of affinity orientation, without, of course, the affirmative action aspect. Corporations endorsing ENDA include NYNEX Corp., Polaroid, Bethlehem Steel Corp., Harley-Davidson, Merrill Lynch, Quaker Oats, and, of course, Microsoft, to name a few.

A U.S. Government Accounting Office report on states with antidiscrimination laws protecting gays and lesbians found that the laws had not generated a significant amount of litigation. Separate nationwide polls by Gallup and Harris found widespread public support (85 percent and 61 percent, respectively) for protective legislation. Interestingly, the Harris poll showed that 42 percent of those surveyed already thought such a law existed.

Having no federal legislation protecting gays and lesbians from workplace discrimination does not mean that employers are totally free to discriminate against them. To date, legislation has been passed protecting gays and lesbians from workplace discrimination in over 530 municipalities and 15 states (Wisconsin, California, Nevada, Massachusetts, Hawaii, Connecticut, New Mexico, Illinois, New York, New Jersey, Minnesota, Vermont, Rhode Island, Maryland, and New Hampshire) and the District of Columbia. Between state laws and local ordinances or executive orders, every single state in the union now has *some* form of job antidiscrimination protection for gays and lesbians. (See Exhibit 8.4.) In

gender identity statutes
Laws providing protection for transsexuals.

addition, 73 local jurisdictions, five states, and Washington, D.C., provide workplace protection for transsexuals, called **gender identity statutes**. There are such statutes in California, Illinois, New Mexico, Minnesota, Rhode Island, and Washington, D.C. A study of states with job discrimination laws for gays and lesbians found little, if any, increase in the number of affinity orientation job discrimination lawsuits filed.

In addition to rights that may be provided by state and local legislation, gay and lesbian public employees adversely affected by an employment decision based on affinity orientation may, under appropriate circumstances, use state constitutions or the 1st, 5th, or 14th Amendments of the U.S. Constitution as a basis for suit, as well as the constitutional right to privacy. This applies to federal, state, and local employees. These lawsuits have traditionally been decided in the employer's favor, but recent decisions have impacted this trend and increasingly recognize the rights of gays and lesbians. This means employers should take note.

Gay and lesbian employees may also bring tort actions, such as intentional infliction of emotional distress, intentional interference with contractual relations, invasion of privacy, or defamation. The outcome depends on the particular circumstances, but employers should be mindful of the possibility of civil suits with unlimited damages.

Employers should also be aware of the possibility of several closely related matters that may arise in affinity orientation cases and cause liability based on the protected category of gender—for instance, gender stereotyping as discussed in the gender chapter. Judging employees based on an idea of how they measure up to qualities a given gender should or should not possess (i.e., females who are "too aggressive" or "too macho" or males who are "too effeminate"), rather than on legitimate job requirements, may result in liability for gender discrimination, rather than affinity orientation, and should be avoided (see *Williamson,* later in this chapter). Similarly, if an employer knowingly hires lesbians but not gay men, this could be the basis for gender discrimination. In such a case, under Title VII, affinity orientation is clearly not an issue for the employer, since the employer knowingly hired lesbians.

So, unlike the rest of the categories we have discussed, affinity orientation is not nearly as settled as other types of employment discrimination. The patchwork quilt of constitutional guarantees, state and local laws and ordinances, and employer policies, as well as the public relations and political aspects of the issue, make it one in which careful thought to policy is critical. We are in the rare position of seeing an entirely new area of law unfold. As exciting as this is from a legal standpoint, it can have traps for the unwary employer. Sticking with only relevant qualifications and watching trends in case law and legislation at all levels will greatly aid in making policy decisions much less likely to result in liability.

Seeing how the court handles this issue in the case below is instructive in trying to shape policies consistent with its pronouncements.

Weaver v. Nebo School District *29 F. Supp. 2d 1279*
(D. Utah, CD 1998)

A schoolteacher was reprimanded when she said "yes" when asked by a student if she was gay. Her coaching job was taken away and a notation put in her personnel file. The court held that treating her this way based on affinity orientation was an unconstitutional denial of equal protection.

Jenkins, J.

For the past nineteen years, plaintiff Wendy Weaver has been a teacher at Spanish Fork High School in the Nebo School District. Ms. Weaver, a tenured faculty member since 1982, teaches psychology and physical education. Her reputation as an educator at Spanish Fork is unblemished: she has always been considered an effective and capable teacher, her evaluations range from good to excellent, and she has never been the subject of any disciplinary action. In addition to her teaching responsibilities, Ms. Weaver has served as the girl's volleyball coach since 1979. She has been effective in this endeavor, leading the team to four state championships.

Unlike her teaching position, however, Ms. Weaver's position as coach was not tenured. Instead, as is the case with all coaching positions at Spanish Fork High School, Ms. Weaver was hired as volleyball coach on a year-to-year basis. For each year she was hired as coach, Ms. Weaver received a stipend, which in her most recent year of coaching was $1,500. The practice of hiring coaches, however, is somewhat informal. It is the policy of the School District that Principal Wadley has final decision-making authority in selecting a coach. Generally, Principal Wadley finds out who has an interest, selects a coach from the interested candidates, and notifies the coach that he or she has the position. No written contract is prepared. In practice, the coach from the previous year is routinely offered the position for the following year, or, as Principal Wadley stated, "you assign them once and they stay assigned until you assign someone else."

In the late spring and early summer of 1997, Ms. Weaver began preparing for the upcoming school volleyball season—as she did in the past—by organizing two summer volleyball camps for prospective team players. As usual, these camps were to be held at Spanish Fork High School in June and July of 1997. Ms. Weaver telephoned prospective volleyball team members to inform them of the camp schedules. One of the calls went to a senior team member. During the conversation, the team member asked Ms. Weaver. "Are you gay?" Ms. Weaver truthfully responded, "Yes." The team member then told Ms. Weaver that she would not play on the volleyball team in the fall. On July 14, 1997, the team member and her parents met with defendants Almon Mosher, Director of Human Resources for the Nebo School District, and Larry Kimball, Director of Secondary Education for the Nebo School District, and told them that Ms. Weaver told them that she is gay and that the team member decided she would not play volleyball.

In April of 1997, Gary Weaver, Ms. Weaver's ex-husband and a school psychologist for the Nebo School District, spoke with Principal Wadley about Ms. Weaver's sexual orientation. In May of 1997, Nedra Call, the Curriculum Coordinator for the School District, received two calls concerning Ms. Weaver's "lifestyle and her actions." She related the substance of these calls to defendant Mosher. Defendant Dennis Poulsen, Superintendent of the Nebo School District, also received calls about Ms. Weaver. In addition, several adults affiliated or formerly affiliated with the school contacted Principal Wadley with comments or questions about Ms. Weaver's sexual orientation. Principal Wadley held a meeting with his two assistant principals to discuss Ms. Weaver's sexual orientation. On May 22, 1997, before the phone conversation with Ms. Weaver, the team member and her mother telephoned Principal Wadley to let him know that the team member would not be playing volleyball because she was uncomfortable playing on the team knowing that Ms. Weaver is gay. On May 22nd, Principal Wadley discussed Ms. Weaver's sexual orientation with defendant Larry Kimball. Even the School Advisory Council wanted to discuss Ms. Weaver's sexual orientation.

In response to these reports, and after meeting again with the team member's family on July 14, 1997, defendants Mosher and Kimball discussed taking some action against Ms. Weaver because they felt Ms. Weaver's comments about her sexual orientation were in "violation of district policy." Several days later, on July 21, 1997, Ms. Weaver met with Principal Wadley, who informed her that she would not be assigned to coach volleyball for the 1997–98 school year. This discussion was memorialized in a letter to Ms. Weaver dated the same day but sent subsequently. The following day, Ms. Weaver was called to a meeting at the School District office and presented a letter, printed on the School District letterhead. The letter was drafted by defendant Mosher, signed by him and Larry Kimball, was reviewed by defendant Dennis Poulsen, delivered to Ms. Weaver, and placed in her personnel file. On August 8, 1997, a similar letter was issued to Gary Weaver. This letter was delivered to Mr. Weaver and placed in his personnel file.

Despite mounting evidence that gay males and lesbians suffer from employment discrimination and, as recent events in Wyoming [the brutal murder of gay college student Matthew Shepard] remind us, other more life-threatening expressions of bias, courts, including the Supreme Court, have not yet recognized a person's sexual orientation as a status that deserves heightened protection. The deep-seated prejudice on the part of some persons against the gay and lesbian community can be summed up in a single quote from ardent anti-gay activist and former entertainer Anita Bryant: "I'd rather my child be dead than be a homosexual." See Millie Ball, "I'd Rather My Child Be Dead Than Homo," The *Times-Picayune,* June 19, 1977, at 3 (quoting Ms. Bryant). To date, Congress has expressly prohibited employment discrimination on the basis of race, religion, national origin, gender, age, and disability, but not sexual orientation. As of this year, eleven states and the District of Columbia offer statutory protection against discrimination on the basis of sexual orientation; thirty-nine states, including Utah, do not.

Nevertheless, the Fourteenth Amendment of the United States Constitution entitles all persons to equal protection under the law. It appears that the plain language of the Fourteenth Amendment's Equal Protection Clause prohibits a state government or agency from engaging in intentional discrimination—even on the basis of sexual orientation—absent some rational basis for so doing.

The Supreme Court has recognized that an "irrational prejudice" cannot provide the rational basis to support a state action against an equal protection challenge. "A bare desire to harm a politically unpopular group" is not a legitimate state interest. Indeed, mere negative attitudes, or fear, unsubstantiated by factors which are properly cognizable in [the circumstances], are not permissible bases for differential treatment by the government.

Supreme Court precedent has recognized that when state action reflects an animus directed at a defined minority, it cannot be supported under the Equal Protection Clause. More recently, in *Romer* v. *Evans,* 517 U.S. 620 (1996), the Court was called upon to examine whether an amendment to Colorado's state constitution, prohibiting any legislation or judicial action designed to protect the status of a person based on sexual orientation violated the Fourteenth Amendment. It had no trouble finding that it did. In *Romer,* the Court noted that under the ordinary deferential equal protection standard—that is, rational basis—the Court would "insist on knowing the relation between the classification adopted and the object to be obtained." It is this search for a "link" between classification and objective,

noted the Court, that "gives substance to the Equal Protection Clause." In *Romer,* such a "link" was noticeably absent. Noting that the "inevitable inference" that arises from a law of this sort is that it is "born of animosity toward the class of persons affected," the Court described the amendment as "a status-based enactment divorced from any factual context from which we could discern a relationship to legitimate state interests."

The question then is whether bias concerning Ms. Weaver's sexual orientation furnishes a rational basis for the defendants' decision not to assign her as volleyball coach. The "negative reaction" some members of the community may have to homosexuals is not a proper basis for discriminating against them. So reasoned the Supreme Court in the context of race. See, e.g., *Brown* v. *Board of Education,* 347 U.S. 483 (1954) (declaring that racial school segregation is unconstitutional despite the widespread acceptance of the practice in the community and in the country). If the community's perception is based on nothing more than unsupported assumptions, outdated stereotypes, and animosity, it is necessarily irrational and under *Romer* and other Supreme Court precedent, it provides no legitimate support for the School District's decisions.

The record now before the court contains no job-related justification for not assigning Ms. Weaver as volleyball coach. Nor have the defendants demonstrated how Ms. Weaver's sexual orientation bears any rational relationship to her competency as teacher or coach, or her job performance as coach—a position she has held for many years with distinction. As mentioned earlier, it is undisputed that she was an excellent coach and apparently, up until the time her sexual orientation was revealed, the likely candidate for the position. Principal Wadley's decision not to assign Ms. Weaver (a decision reached after consulting with the other defendants) was based solely on her sexual orientation. Absent some rational relationship to job performance, a decision not to assign Ms. Weaver as coach because of her sexual orientation runs afoul of the Fourteenth Amendment's equal protection guarantee.

Although the Constitution cannot control prejudices, neither this court nor any other court should, directly or indirectly, legitimize them. The private antipathy of some members of a community cannot validate state discrimination. Because a community's animus towards homosexuals can never serve as a legitimate basis for state action, the defendants' actions based on that animus violate the Equal Protection Clause. Because this perceived negative reaction arose solely from Ms. Weaver's sexual orientation, and not from her abilities as coach, it does not furnish a rational job-related basis for the defendants' decision. Therefore, Ms. Weaver's motion for summary judgment is granted as to this claim.

In Ms. Weaver's second equal protection claim, she asserts that the defendants violated her rights to equal protection by imposing a viewpoint and content-based restriction on her speech. She argues that she was prohibited from discussing her sexual orientation only because she would have discussed her homosexuality, and points out that other teachers were free to discuss their heterosexual orientations.

Ms. Weaver was threatened with disciplinary action for discussing her intimate associations and sexual orientation. At the same time, no other teacher in the School District was prohibited from discussing these topics. Indeed, as the School District conceded at the hearing, no similar restriction was placed on heterosexual teachers at all. Clearly then, the School District wanted to silence Ms. Weaver's speech because of its expected pro-homosexual viewpoint. Such viewpoint-based restriction is constitutionally impermissible.

Simple as it may sound, as a matter of fairness and evenhandedness, homosexuals should not be sanctioned or restricted for speech that heterosexuals are not likewise sanctioned or restricted for. Because the School District has not restricted other teachers in speaking out on their sexual orientation, the School District has not only violated the First Amendment, but also the Fourteenth Amendment's Equal Protection Clause. In such an instance, when an equal protection claim is based on a person's exercise of a fundamental constitutional right, the proper standard of review is strict scrutiny—that is, is the restriction supported by a compelling state interest. Because the Court has concluded that the School District's actions cannot be supported on any rational basis, the District's actions obviously fail the strict scrutiny test. Ms. Weaver is granted summary judgment on this claim as well.

For the foregoing reasons, it is ordered that plaintiff's motion for summary judgment is GRANTED and defendants' motion is DENIED; that the School District shall remove the letters from plaintiff's personnel file; the School District is directed to offer the plaintiff the Spanish Fork High School girl's volleyball coaching position for the 1999–2000 school year; and the School District pay damages to the plaintiff in the sum of $1,500.

Case Questions

1. What would you have done if you had been the school administrator receiving calls in this situation?
2. Do you think the school was correct in ignoring the teacher's record?
3. Does it make a difference that this matter did not arise at the teacher's instigation, but in response to a question from a student? Explain.

Romer, mentioned in the *Weaver* decision, was one of the first major U.S. Supreme Court cases that challenged states' rights to pass laws restricting rights of gays and lesbians. As such, it sent an important message to states regarding their ability to exclude certain groups from constitutional protections. To some extent, this paved the way of much of what was to come, as you can see from the *Weaver* case. Note, too, that as the court mentioned, Title VII did not protect Weaver on the basis of affinity orientation, and the state did not have a law protecting her, but because she was a public school teacher, and thus a government employee, she had a cause of action for an unconstitutional denial of equal protection under the law.

AFFINITY ORIENTATION AS A BASIS FOR ADVERSE EMPLOYMENT DECISIONS

As you will see from the cases below, not all affinity orientation issues arise in the same contexts. The employee may be the basis of employer concern because the employee, among other things:

- Is gay or lesbian (i.e., status or orientation).
- Has primary relationships with those of the same gender (i.e., activity rather than status).

- Exhibits inappropriate workplace behavior, such as detailed discussions of intimate sexual behavior or improperly propositioning others in the workplace (this is certainly not *presumed* of gays and lesbians, and as you saw from the sexual harassment chapter, this is not solely a gay or lesbian phenomenon).
- Wears clothing, jewelry, or makeup in violation of workplace grooming codes.
- Undergoes gender reassignment surgery.
- Is in the presurgery adjustment stages of such gender reassignment surgery.

Note that some of the activity presents a problem no matter who the employee is. An employer should not tolerate from any employee inappropriate workplace behavior, such as improperly propositioning other employees. A distinction should also be made between *status* or *orientation* as a gay or lesbian, on the one hand, and, on the other, *activity* that may be inappropriate. Basing decisions and policies on actions is more defensible than basing them on status. But even then the action should not be singled out solely based on the actor's orientation. Each of the above contexts of gay or lesbian issues presents its own unique issues.

Scenario

In the following case, the court set forth the reasoning for not extending Title VII protection to discrimination on the basis of affinity orientation. Notice that it is directed toward status, more so than any particular activity in which the employee may have engaged. It is this basic approach that underlies why the employee would not be protected in opening scenario 1. As you will see later, this court in the *Nichols* case reversed itself to some extent, but *DeSantis* is an important historical case.

DeSantis v. Pacific Telephone & Telegraph Co., Inc.
Strailey v. Happy Times Nursery School, Inc.
Lundin and Buckley v. Pacific Tel. & Tel. Co., Inc.
608 F.2d 327 (9th Cir. 1979)

Gays and lesbians brought these actions claiming their employers and former employers discriminated against them in employment decisions because they were gay and lesbian. The Court of Appeals dismissed the cases, holding that Title VII does not include protection for gays and lesbians, within its prohibition of discrimination on the basis of gender.

Choy, J.

Employee Strailey, a male, was fired by the Happy Times Nursery School after two years as a teacher. He alleged he was fired because he wore a small gold earloop to school before the beginning of the school year.

DeSantis, Boyle and Simard, all males, claimed that Pacific Telephone & Telegraph (PT&T) impermissibly discriminated against them because they were gay. DeSantis alleged he was not hired when a PT&T supervisor concluded he was gay. Boyle was continually harassed by his coworkers and had to quit to preserve his health

after only three months because his supervisor did nothing to alleviate this condition. Finally, Simard was forced to quit under similar conditions after almost four years of employment with PT&T, but he was harassed by his supervisors as well. In addition, his personnel file has been marked as not eligible for rehire, and his applications for employment were rejected by PT&T in 1974 and 1976. All three alleged that PT&T officials have publicly stated that they would not hire gays and lesbians. EEOC rejected all claims for lack of jurisdiction.

Employees argue first that the district courts erred in holding that Title VII does not prohibit discrimination on the basis of affinity orientation. They claim that in prohibiting certain employment discrimination on the basis of "gender," Congress meant to include discrimination on the basis of affinity orientation. They add that in trial they could establish that discrimination against such employees disproportionately affects men and that this disproportionate impact and correlation between discrimination on the basis of affinity orientation and discrimination on the basis of gender requires that affinity orientation be considered a subcategory of the gender category of Title VII.

Congress has not shown any intent other than to restrict the term gender to its traditional meaning. Therefore, this court will not expand Title VII's application in the absence of Congressional mandate. The manifest purpose of Title VII's prohibition against gender discrimination in employment is to insure that men and women are treated equally, absent a bona fide relationship between the qualifications for the job and the person's gender. Based on similar readings of the legislative history and the principle that "words used in statutes are to be given their ordinary meaning," the EEOC has concluded "that when Congress used the word 'sex' in Title VII, it was referring to a person's 'gender' and not to 'sexual practices.'" EEOC Dec. No. 76-75 (1976) Employment Practice Guide (CCH) section 6495 at 4266. We conclude that the prohibition against gender discrimination does not include same gender affinity orientation.

Employees further argue that recent decisions dealing with disproportionate impact require that discrimination against gays and lesbians fall within the purview of Title VII. They contend that recent decisions like *Griggs* v. *Duke Power Co.,* establish that any employment criterion that affects one gender more than the other violates Title VII. They quote from *Griggs* at 431, that "what is required by Congress is the removal of artificial, arbitrary and unnecessary barriers to employment when the barriers operate invidiously to discriminate on the basis of racial or other impermissible classifications." They claim that they can prove that discrimination against gays and lesbians disproportionately affects males both because of the greater likelihood of an employer discovering males with such orientation compared to females similarly situated.

Assuming that the employees can otherwise satisfy the requirements of *Griggs,* we do not believe that *Griggs* can be applied to extend Title VII protection to those in employees' position. In finding that the disproportionate impact of educational tests on blacks violated Title VII when they were not job related, the Supreme Court in *Griggs* sought to effectuate a major congressional purpose in enacting Title VII: protection of blacks from employment discrimination. Our objective is to ascertain the congressional intent and give effect to the legislative will. Congress did not intend to protect affinity orientation and has repeatedly refused to extend such protection. Employees now ask us to employ the disproportionate impact decisions as an artifice to "bootstrap" Title VII protection for this group under the guise of protecting men generally.

This we are not free to do. Adoption of this bootstrap device would frustrate congressional objectives, not effectuate congressional goals as in *Griggs*. It would achieve by judicial "construction" what Congress did not do and has consistently refused to do on many occasions. We conclude that the *Griggs* disproportionate impact theory may not be applied to extend Title VII protection to affinity orientation.

Employees next contend that recent decisions have held that an employer generally may not use different employment criteria for men and women. They claim that if a male employee prefers males, he will be treated differently from a female who prefers males. They conclude that the employer thus uses different employment criteria for men and women and violates *Phillips* v. *Martin-Marietta Corp.,* 400 U.S. 542 (1971). We must again reject employees' efforts to "bootstrap" Title VII protection for their group. While we do not express approval of an employment policy that differentiates according to affinity orientation, we note that, whether dealing with men or women, the employer is using the same criterion: it will not hire or promote a person who prefers sexual partners of the same gender. Thus the policy does not involve different decisional criteria for the genders.

Employees argue that EEOC has held that discrimination against an employee because of the race of the employee's friends may constitute discrimination based on race in violation of Title VII. They contend that analogously discrimination because of gender of the employee's sexual partner should constitute discrimination based on gender. They have not, however, alleged that the employers have policies of discriminating against employees because of the gender of their friends. That is, they do not claim that the employers will terminate anyone with male (or female) friends. They claim instead that the employees discriminate against employees who have a certain type of relationship—i.e., a same-gender affinity orientation—with certain friends. As noted earlier, that relationship is not protected by Title VII. Thus, assuming it would violate Title VII for an employer to discriminate against employees because of the gender of their friends, the employees' claims do not fall within the purported rule. AFFIRMED.

Case Questions

1. The court said that the employer was discriminating against the parties because of their choice of sexual partners. Notwithstanding the way the issue has historically been treated, does this seem to be a valid basis for judging an applicant for employment? Explain.

2. Do you agree with the parallels that the parties attempted to draw between race discrimination and discrimination on the basis of affinity orientation? Discuss.

3. What do you think of the employees' argument that the Title VII should be interpreted to include affinity orientation since it can be shown that affinity orientation discrimination has a disproportionate impact on men and is, essentially, a type of gender discrimination? Explain.

Realizing the effect of *DeSantis,* which has been widely used as precedent in other jurisdictions, employees have often tried to get around the Title VII limitation on affinity orientation by attempting to allege some other recognized basis for discrimination under Title VII. As you will see in the following case, it may not work. When the employer terminates the employee for a combination of reasons, some protected and some not, liability may ensue. For instance, if an employer terminates a black female after the employer finds that she is a lesbian, the employee is not able to use her status as a lesbian as the basis for a claim under Title VII. However, the employee could allege discrimination based on her gender or race as a basis for suit but would have to prove this was actually the basis for termination. On the other hand, look at Exhibit 8.5 to see how much the workplace is changing.

Allegations and actual proof to the satisfaction of EEOC or the court are two very different things. The employee may not be able to prove a case of race or gender discrimination because the evidence simply is not present. To be fully protected in the decision to terminate, an employer must be certain there are no facts that will support the other categories the employee may allege as a basis for suit. The following case illustrates the use of both protected and unprotected status as a basis for a discrimination suit and how the courts analyze such a case.

Williamson v. A. G. Edwards & Sons, Inc. *876 F.2d 69* *(8th Cir. 1989)*

A gay black male who wore makeup to work brought suit alleging his dismissal was illegally based on race in violation of Title VII of the Civil Rights Act of 1964. The court disagreed and held for the employer.

Per Curiam

Employee Williamson worked for the employer from November 1979 until May 1985 when he was discharged for his disruptive and inappropriate conduct at work. Williamson alleged that his supervisor, Bruce Morgan, falsely accused him of disrupting the workflow by continuing to discuss the details of his gay lifestyle in the workplace and harassing another employee, and that similarly situated white employees who behaved as he did were not disciplined. The lower court found that the employee's complaint and deposition clearly indicated that Williamson believed he had been treated differently because of his affinity orientation and not his race. On appeal Williamson argues that the lower court erred in failing to consider his allegations that similarly situated white employees working in the same department as Williamson, were not harassed or terminated as he had been.

Title VII does not prevent discrimination on the basis of affinity orientation. *DeSantis* v. *Pacific Tel. & Tel. Co.,* 608 F.2d 327 (9th Cir. 1979). Although employee stated that he believed he was treated differently because he was black, he failed to allege facts sufficient to establish that other similarly situated white employees were treated differently. He did not claim that the other white employees who also allegedly were gay behaved as he did in openly discussing their lives while at work, but only compared his behavior in that regard to the behavior of other heterosexuals. Although he alleged he was reprimanded for wearing makeup at work while two other white males, allegedly gay, were only reprimanded for wearing jewelry, there is no indication in the record that the other two men wore any makeup. Accordingly, we AFFIRM.

Case Questions

1. How would you have handled this issue if you had been the manager?

2. Do you accept the argument that, if things were as the employee alleged, it was racial discrimination?

3. What do you think of the court saying the employee openly discussed details of his gay lifestyle at work? Does this appear to unfairly presume that gays discuss only sex? Explain. What if this simply meant he discussed, as did other employees, who he went out with over the weekend?

Exhibit 8.5   New Push to Recruit Gay Students

In February 2000, in a *Wall Street Journal* article, Rachel Emma Silverman reported that Wall Street financial firms were, for the first time, targeting their recruitment toward gay and lesbian business students. Firms such as Goldman Sachs Group, Inc., J. P. Morgan & Co., and American Express Co. have gone to great lengths to woo gay students. According to the employers, the tightening labor market as well as the increasingly vocal employees of the firms caused them to use this as a tool to be or remain competitive in their recruiting efforts. The recruitment efforts include wining and dining the students at posh restaurants, co-hosting dinners for gay students, having gay and lesbian support groups in the workplace, having gay recruiting events with well-known speakers, and having discussion groups about being gay in the workplace.

Other firms, in an effort to thwart the criticism from students that the students want to be chosen for their qualifications, not their affinity orientation, declined to target gays and lesbians in recruiting. Students were clear, however, that it was important for them to feel comfortable in their workplace, including feeling comfortable about their affinity orientation. Since this time, there have also been gay and lesbian job fairs and college fairs, among other things, organized to ensure that gays and lesbians would be able to seek opportunities in settings in which they would be comfortable, given the usual hostile environment they can encounter.

It was previously stated that employers should not base workplace decisions on stereotyped ideas of gender any more than necessary. *Williamson* indicates when it may be necessary (i.e., when a male is wearing makeup). As mentioned in the section on dress codes in the gender chapter, employers have the flexibility to impose reasonable rules about workplace appearance. The Washington State Supreme Court ruled that Boeing Company had sufficient basis for terminating a male engineer who was undergoing gender reassignment surgery. Boeing attempted to accommodate the employee by permitting him to wear "unisex" clothing; but the employee was terminated when he added pink pearls to such an outfit and insisted on using the women's bathroom.

For years male employees also tried to argue that their effeminacy should not be a basis on which employers can refuse to hire them or to terminate them from their jobs. Until recently, this argument rarely succeeded and courts routinely sided with the employer, usually using *DeSantis* for precedent. The court in *DeSantis* had stated:

> Employee Strailey contends he was terminated by the Happy Times Nursery School because the school felt that it was inappropriate for a male teacher to wear an earring to school. He claims that the school's reliance on a stereotype—that a male should have a virile, rather than an effeminate, appearance—violates Title VII. This does not fall within Title VII. We hold that discrimination because of effeminacy, like discrimination because of [affinity orientation], does not fall within the purview of Title VII.

However, in the *Nichols* case in the next section, the *DeSantis* court reversed itself as it related to this issue and determined that under certain circumstances, Title VII does, in fact, permit employees claiming discrimination based on failing to fit a certain gender-based stereotype (usually effeminate men) to bring a cause of action based on gender stereotyping as a type of gender discrimination. In doing so, the court interpreted the U.S. Supreme Court's *Price Waterhouse* v. *Hopkins* case discussed in the gender chapter, as being inconsistent with its *DeSantis* holding. The court said:

> *Price Waterhouse* sets a rule that bars discrimination on the basis of sex stereotypes. That rule squarely applies to preclude the harassment here. We do not imply that all gender-based distinctions are actionable under Title VII. For example, our decision does not imply that there is any violation of Title VII occasioned by reasonable regulations that require male and female employees to conform to different dress and grooming standards.
>
> The only potential difficulty arises out of a now faint shadow cast by our decision in *DeSantis* holding that discrimination based on a stereotype that a man "should have a virile rather than an effeminate appearance" does not fall within Title VII's purview. This holding, however, predates and conflicts with the Supreme Court's decision in *Price Waterhouse*. And, in this direct conflict, *DeSantis* must lose. To the extent it conflicts with *Price Waterhouse,* as we hold it does, *DeSantis* is no longer good law.

SAME-GENDER SEXUAL HARASSMENT

Since Title VII does not include a prohibition against discrimination on the basis of affinity orientation, an important question had been whether an employee sexually harassed by someone of the same gender could bring an action under Title VII. Some courts said no because they considered any sexual harassment between employees of the same gender to be based on same-gender affinity orientation (regardless of the nature of the harassment) and since Title VII excluded affinity orientation coverage, a harassee had no cause of action.

Other courts looked at the nature of the harassment and allowed a cause of action if it was not based on affinity orientation (rather than presuming that because it was between employees of the same gender it *must* be). And there were many other variations on the theme. In the *Oncale* case below, the U.S. Supreme Court finally made sense of it all.

Oncale v. Sundowner Offshore Services, Inc. *523 U.S. 75 (1998)*

Employee sued for sexual harassment under Title VII after being harassed by his coworkers. For the first time, the U.S. Supreme Court dealt with the question of whether there can be a sexual harassment claim under Title VII if the harassers and the harassee are the same gender. The Court determined that Title VII's exclusion of discrimination on the basis of affinity orientation did not prevent a cause of action for sexual harassment under Title VII even when the harasser and harassee are both the same gender.

Scalia, J.

This case presents the question whether workplace harassment can violate Title VII's prohibition against "discriminat[ion] . . . because of . . . sex," when the harasser and the harassed employee are of the same sex.

Oncale was working for Sundowner Offshore Services on a Chevron U.S.A., Inc., oil platform in the Gulf of Mexico. He was employed as a roustabout on an eight-man crew which included John Lyons, Danny Pippen, and Brandon Johnson. Lyons, the crane operator, and Pippen, the driller, had supervisory authority. On several occasions, Oncale was forcibly subjected to sex-related, humiliating actions against him by Lyons, Pippen, and Johnson in the presence of the rest of the crew. Pippen and Lyons also physically assaulted Oncale in a sexual manner, and Lyons threatened him with rape. Oncale's complaints to supervisory personnel produced no remedial action; in fact, the company's Safety Compliance Clerk, Valent Hohen, told Oncale that Lyons and Pippin "picked [on] him all the time too," and called him a name suggesting homosexuality. Oncale eventually quit—asking that his pink slip reflect that he "voluntarily left due to sexual harassment and verbal abuse." When asked at his deposition why he left Sundowner, Oncale stated "I felt that if I didn't leave my job, that I would be raped or forced to have sex." The district court held that "Mr. Oncale, a male, has no cause of action under Title VII for harassment by male co-workers." The Fifth Circuit affirmed.

Title VII of the Civil Rights Act of 1964 not only covers "terms" and "conditions" in the narrow contractual sense, but "evinces a congressional intent to strike at the entire spectrum of disparate treatment of men and women in employment." "When the workplace is permeated with discriminatory intimidation, ridicule, and insult that is sufficiently severe or pervasive to alter the conditions of the victim's employment and create an abusive working environment, Title VII is violated."

Title VII's prohibition of discrimination "because of . . . gender" protects men as well as women, and in the related context of racial discrimination in the workplace we have rejected any conclusive presumption that an employer will not discriminate against members of his own race. "Because of the many facets of human motivation, it would be unwise to presume as a matter of law that human beings of one definable group will not discriminate against other members of that group." We hold today that nothing in Title VII necessarily bars a claim of discrimination "because of . . . gender" merely because the plaintiff and the defendant are of the same sex.

Courts have had little trouble with that principle in cases where an employee claims to have been passed over for a job or promotion. But when the issue arises in the context of a "hostile environment" sexual harassment claim, the state and federal courts have taken a bewildering variety of stances. Some, like the Fifth Circuit in this case, have held that same-gender sexual harassment claims are never cognizable under Title VII. Other decisions say that such claims are actionable only if the plaintiff can prove that the harasser is homosexual (and thus presumably motivated by sexual desire). Still others suggest that workplace harassment that is sexual in content is always actionable, regardless of the harasser's gender, sexual orientation, or motivations.

We see no justification in the statutory language or our precedents for a categorical rule excluding same-sex harassment claims from the coverage of Title VII. As some courts have observed, male-on-male sexual harassment in the workplace was assuredly not the principal evil Congress was concerned with when it enacted Title VII. But statutory prohibitions often go beyond the principal evil to cover reasonably comparable evils, and it is ultimately the provisions of our laws rather than the principal concerns of our legislators by which we are governed. Title VII prohibits "discriminat[ion] . . . because of . . . gender" in the "terms" or "conditions" of employment. Our holding that this includes sexual harassment must extend to sexual harassment of any kind that meets the statutory requirements.

Respondents contend that recognizing liability for same-gender harassment will transform Title VII into a general civility code for the American workplace. But that risk is no greater for same-gender than for opposite-gender harassment, and is adequately met by careful attention to the requirements of the statute. Title VII does not prohibit all verbal or physical harassment in the workplace; it is directed only at "discriminat[ion] . . . because of . . . gender." We have never held that workplace harassment, even harassment between men and women, is automatically discrimination because of sex merely because the words used have sexual content or connotations. "The critical issue, Title VII's text indicates, is whether members of one gender are exposed to disadvantageous terms or conditions of employment to which members of the other gender are not exposed."

Courts and juries have found the inference of discrimination easy to draw in most male–female sexual harassment situations, because the challenged conduct typically involves explicit or implicit proposals of sexual activity; it is reasonable to assume those proposals would not have been made to someone of the same gender. The same chain of inference would be available to a plaintiff alleging same-gender harassment, if there were credible evidence that the harasser was homosexual. But harassing conduct need not be motivated by sexual desire to support an inference of discrimination on the basis of gender. A trier of fact might reasonably find such discrimination, for example, if a female victim is harassed in such gender-specific and derogatory terms by another woman as to make it clear that the harasser is motivated by general hostility to the presence of women in the workplace.

A same-gender harassment plaintiff may also, of course, offer direct comparative evidence about how the alleged harasser treated members of both sexes in a mixed-gender workplace. Whatever evidentiary route the plaintiff chooses to follow, he or she must always prove that the conduct at issue was not merely tinged with offensive sexual connotations, but actually constituted "discriminat[ion] . . . because of . . . gender."

And there is another requirement that prevents Title VII from expanding into a general civility code: The statute does not reach genuine but innocuous differences in the ways men and women routinely interact with members of the same gender and of the opposite gender. The prohibition of harassment on the basis of gender requires neither asexuality nor androgyny in the workplace; it forbids only behavior so objectively offensive as to alter the "conditions" of the victim's employment. "Conduct that is not severe or pervasive enough to create an objectively hostile or abusive work environment—an environment that a reasonable person would find hostile or abusive— is beyond Title VII's purview." We have always regarded that requirement as crucial, and as sufficient to ensure that courts and juries do not mistake ordinary socializing in the workplace—such as male-on-male horseplay or intersexual flirtation—for discriminatory "conditions of employment."

We have emphasized, moreover, that the objective severity of harassment should be judged from the perspective of a reasonable person in the plaintiff's position, considering "all the circumstances." In same-gender (as in all) harassment cases, that inquiry requires careful consideration of the social context in which particular behavior occurs and is experienced by its target. A professional football player's working environment is not severely or pervasively abusive, for example, if the coach smacks him on the buttocks as he heads onto the field— even if the same behavior would reasonably be experienced as abusive by the coach's secretary (male or female) back at the office. The real social impact of workplace behavior often depends on a constellation of surrounding circumstances, expectations, and relationships which are not fully captured by a simple recitation of the words used or the physical acts performed. Common sense, and an appropriate sensitivity to social context, will enable courts and juries to distinguish between simple teasing or roughhousing among members of the same gender, and conduct which a reasonable person in the plaintiff's position would find severely hostile or abusive. In light of our holding, the case is REVERSED and REMANDED.

Case Questions

1. Do you understand why the Court allowed Oncale to prevail here, despite the fact that the sexual harassment was between males? Explain.

2. What about the idea of men "roughhousing" and otherwise interacting with each other in ways that may cause claims to arise? As the employer, what would you do to lessen liability exposure?

3. As an employer, how would you be able to distinguish between activity that is directed at an employee because he or she is gay or lesbian, which is not protected by Title VII, and activity that is not based on affinity orientation, which is protected by Title VII? Explain.

Oncale was a *huge* case. Not only had courts across the country been absolutely splintered in their approaches to the same facts, but legal scholars, employers, as well as the public debated the issue at length. The U.S. Supreme Court finally came down on the side of the intent of Title VII in striking at the full spectrum of gender-based employment discrimination. It made sense that if the issue involved was workplace harassment and discrimination, then the gender or affinity orientation of either party should not matter. That inquiry is not made in other harassment cases, and it made little sense to make it in this instance. As the Court determined, the important inquiry is whether "the workplace is permeated with discriminatory intimidation, ridicule, and insult that is sufficiently severe or pervasive to alter the conditions of the victim's employment and create an abusive working environment." If so, then Title VII is violated. Clearly that happened in *Oncale*. There have been several similar cases since the *Oncale* decision, including the two class action suits in the introductory material.

Under the *Oncale* decision, the Court preserved Title VII's exclusion of discrimination on the basis of affinity orientation by holding that the sexual harassment of an employee by someone of the same gender is prohibited unless it can be shown that it was actually based on affinity orientation. That is, if a female employee can show that a female harassed her by calling her negative names, undermining her work productivity, spreading lies about her, negatively commenting on her personality, actions, friends, speech, or clothing, as it relates to gender, and so on, then she can bring a claim under Title VII. If, however, the harassee is a lesbian and the harassment is in the form of something such as constantly calling her a lesbian, "dyke," or other terms related to her orientation, directing teasing, joking, and comments on homosexuality toward her, or persistently asking for dates or making sexual comments, then the harassee would not have a cause of action under Title VII. The first situation is plain old sexual harassment even though the parties are both the same gender, and it is covered by Title VII. The second is harassment based on affinity orientation and it is not covered. What the Supreme Court did is to not presume that every harassment between employees of the same gender is based on same-gender affinity orientation. See if you can make the distinction in the case below.

Nichols v. Azteca Restaurant Enterprises, Inc.   *256 F.3d 864* *(9th Cir. 2001)*

Employee brought suit under Title VII for gender harassment directed toward him at work which employer did little to stop. The court agreed with the employee that this constituted a violation of Title VII even though the employee was gay.

Gould, J.

Throughout his tenure at Azteca, Sanchez was subjected to a relentless campaign of insults, name-calling, and vulgarities. Male co-workers and a supervisor repeatedly referred to Sanchez in Spanish and English as "she" and "her." Male co-workers mocked Sanchez for walking and carrying his serving tray "like a woman," and taunted him in Spanish and English as, among other things, a "faggot" and a "f**king female whore." The remarks were not stray or isolated. Rather, the abuse occurred at least once a week and often several times a day.

This conduct violated company policy. Since 1989, Azteca has expressly prohibited sexual harassment and retaliation and has directed its employees to bring complaints regarding such conduct directly to the attention of the corporate office. Upon receipt of a complaint, Azteca's policy is to conduct a thorough investigation, the results of which are reviewed by the company's EEO Board, which is then responsible for implementing an appropriate remedy.

In addition to this policy, Azteca has a bilingual (English and Spanish) training program about sexual harassment. This training, which all employees attend when hired, and annually thereafter, defines sexual harassment and instructs employees how to report complaints.

Under Title VII, it is unlawful for an employer "to discriminate against any individual with respect to his compensation, terms, conditions, or privileges of employment, because of . . . sex. It is by now clear that sexual harassment in the form of a hostile work environment constitutes sex discrimination.

To prevail on his hostile environment claim, Sanchez was required to establish a "pattern of ongoing and persistent harassment severe enough to alter the conditions of employment." To satisfy this requirement, Sanchez needed to prove that his workplace was "both objectively and subjectively offensive, one that a reasonable person would find hostile or abusive, and one that the victim in fact did perceive to be so." In addition, Sanchez was required to prove that any harassment took place "because of sex." The district court ruled against Sanchez on each of these elements, concluding that: (1) Sanchez's workplace was not objectively hostile; (2) Sanchez did not perceive his workplace to be hostile; and (3) the alleged conduct did not occur because of sex. We disagree with each of these conclusions and, where applicable, the clearly erroneous findings upon which they are based.

Having reviewed the record, we hold that a reasonable man would have found the sustained campaign of taunts, directed at Sanchez and designed to humiliate and anger him, sufficiently severe and pervasive to alter the terms and conditions of his employment. Indeed, even Azteca does not contend otherwise on appeal.

Assuming that a reasonable person would find a workplace hostile, if the victim "does not subjectively perceive the environment to be abusive, the conduct has not actually altered the conditions of the victim's employment, and there is no Title VII violation." We must determine whether Sanchez, by his conduct, indicated that the alleged harassment was "unwelcome."

The district court concluded that the frequent verbal abuse was not unwelcome. Although the court made no factual finding directly on point, its determination may have been influenced by its findings that: (1) Sanchez made no complaint of sexual harassment to Serna, or anyone else from the corporate office; (2) Sanchez never sought mental health treatment; and (3) Sanchez engaged in horseplay with his male co-workers. We see the evidence another way.

The first of these findings by the district court, which forms the crux of Azteca's appeal, is clearly erroneous. It is undisputed that in May 1995 Sanchez told Serna, in considerable detail, about the fact and nature of the verbal abuse. Sanchez also complained to the Southcenter general manager and an assistant manager, though in less detail. That Sanchez complained about the frequent, degrading verbal abuse supports our conclusion that the conduct was unwelcome, as does Sanchez's unrebutted testimony to that effect. We hold that Sanchez perceived his workplace to be hostile.

Nor do the other potentially relevant findings noted above—that Sanchez never sought mental health treatment, and that he engaged in horseplay with some of his harassers—warrant a different result. As to the first, the scope of Title VII is not limited to conduct that affects a victim's psychological well-being. As to the second, the fact that not all of Sanchez's interactions with his harassers were hostile does not mean that none of them was. As any sensible person would, Sanchez drew a distinction between conduct he perceived to be objectionable, and conduct that was not. He viewed horseplay as "male bonding" and excluded it from his hostile environment claim; he viewed relentless verbal affronts as sexual harassment, and sought legal recourse for that conduct. And, in complaining to Serna about the verbal abuse, he demonstrated a subjective belief that he was being harassed.

Sexual harassment is actionable under Title VII to the extent it occurs "because of" the employee's gender. Sanchez asserts that the verbal abuse at issue was based upon the perception that he is effeminate and, therefore, occurred because of gender. In short, Sanchez contends that he was harassed because he failed to conform to a male stereotype.

At its essence, the systematic abuse directed at Sanchez reflected a belief that Sanchez did not act as a man should act. Sanchez was attacked for walking and carrying his tray "like a woman"—i.e., for having feminine mannerisms. Sanchez was derided for not having sexual intercourse with a waitress who was his friend. Sanchez's male co-workers and one of his supervisors repeatedly reminded Sanchez that he did not conform to their gender-based stereotypes, referring to him as "she" and "her." And, the most vulgar name-calling directed at Sanchez was cast in female terms. We conclude that this verbal abuse was closely linked to gender.

We hold that the verbal abuse at issue occurred because of gender. Because we hold that Sanchez has established each element of his hostile environment claim, we further hold that the conduct of Sanchez's co-workers and supervisor constituted actionable harassment under Title VII AFFIRMED IN PART, REVERSED IN PART, and REMANDED.

Case Questions

1. Title VII does not prohibit discrimination on the basis of affinity orientation. How would you characterize this case? Do you see the discrimination as being based on affinity orientation and thus not protected by Title VII, or as based on gender, and thus protected by Title VII?

2. Why do you think the managers did not address the employee's complaints?

3. What would you have done differently here if you had been Sanchez's manager?

TRANSSEXUAL DISCRIMINATION

Scenario

Think the issue of transsexuals is far-fetched? In one of the cases below, Boeing was faced with the requests for accommodating transgender employees so frequently (at least nine times) that it finally developed a carefully crafted policy. Transsexual discrimination is one of the fastest-growing issues related to affinity orientation. As a result, it is presenting itself more and more frequently as a workplace issue. Several of the state and local laws include transsexuals within their protection for gays and lesbians. As you can imagine, the issue presents rather interesting, confusing, and complicated workplace challenges that must be addressed.

The argument has been made by transsexuals who have had gender reassignment surgery that they should be afforded the protection of Title VII, because they have changed their gender status from male to female or vice versa and now are being discriminated against in employment because they are of a particular gender. Courts have not upheld this position. As stated in the case below, the basis for opening scenario 2, it is not the status of the employee as a member of the gender to which he or she has been reassigned that has created the problem. That is, a male who is terminated on becoming a female is not discriminated against because he is a female as contemplated by Title VII. Rather, he is discriminated against because he changed from male to female. These are considered two very different arguments, with the former being provided Title VII protection, but not the latter.

Ulane v. Eastern Airlines, Inc. *742 F.2d 1081 (7th Cir. 1984)*

A male airline pilot underwent a gender change operation and became a female. After being terminated by the airline, he brought suit. The court upheld the termination, concluding that the matter was not protected by Title VII.

Wood, J.

Employee, Ulane, became a licensed pilot in 1964 serving in the U.S. Army from that time until 1968 with a record of combat missions in Viet Nam for which he received the Air Medal with eight clusters. Upon discharge in 1968, Ulane began flying for Eastern. With Eastern he progressed from Second to First Officer, and also served as a flight instructor, logging over 8,000 flight hours.

Ulane was diagnosed a transsexual in 1979. Transsexualism is a condition that exists when a physiologically normal person experiences discomfort or discontent about nature's choice of his or her gender and prefers to be the other gender. This discomfort is generally accompanied by a desire to utilize hormonal, surgical, and civil procedures to allow the individual to live in his or her preferred gender role. The diagnosis is appropriate only if the discomfort has been continuous for at least two years, and is not due to a mental disorder such as schizophrenia. This is to be distinguished from homosexuals who are sexually attracted to persons of the same gender and transvestites, who are generally male heterosexuals who cross-dress, i.e., dress as females, for sexual arousal rather than social comfort. Both homosexuals and transvestites are content with the gender into which they were born.

Ulane explains that although embodied as a male, from early childhood she felt like a female. She first sought psychiatric and medical assistance in 1968 while in the military. Later she began taking female hormones as part of her treatment, and eventually developed breasts from the hormones. In 1980 she underwent "gender reassignment surgery" and afterwards was issued a revised birth certificate indicating she was female and the FAA certified her for flight status as a female. Eastern was not aware of Ulane's transsexuality, her hormone treatments, or her psychiatric counseling until she attempted to return to work after her reassignment surgery. Eastern knew Ulane only as one of its male pilots.

The district court found Eastern discharged Ulane because she was a transsexual, and that Title VII does not prohibit discrimination on this basis. While we do not condone discrimination in any form, we are constrained to hold that Title VII does not protect transsexuals. AFFIRMED.

Case Questions

1. As the manager to whom Ulane reported after surgery, how would you have handled this?

2. Why do you think Eastern terminated Ulane?

3. What should be the significance of Ulane's prior flight history and experience? In your view, how should it be analyzed with the other relevant factors here?

Employees have also argued that being a transsexual is a disability which must be accommodated. The "pink pearls" case below rejected that view in Washington state. It also provides great insight into how an employer can approach these issues to best provide protection against liability for discrimination.

Jane Doe v. Boeing Company *121 Wash. 2d 8 (1993)*

A biological male employee who was planning to have gender reassignment surgery sued his employer, Boeing, for employment discrimination, alleging an unaccommodated disability. He was discharged by Boeing for wearing "excessively" feminine attire (pink pearls) in violation of company directives. The Washington Supreme Court found that Boeing had done enough to reasonably accommodate the employee, even though it had no duty to do so under Washington's law against discrimination.

Guy, J.

Jane Doe was hired as a Boeing engineer in 1978. At the time of hire, Doe was a biological male and presented herself as such on her application for employment. In 1984, after years of struggling with her sexual identity, Doe concluded that she was a transsexual. Transsexualism is also known in the psychiatric and medical communities as gender dysphoria.

Doe's treating physician confirmed Doe's self-assessment and diagnosed Doe as gender dysphoric. In April 1984, Doe began hormone treatments, as prescribed by Dr. Smith, as well as electrolysis treatments. In December 1984, Doe legally changed her masculine name to a feminine name.

In March 1985, Doe informed her supervisors, management and co-workers at Boeing of her transsexualism and of her intent to have gender reassignment surgery.

Doe informed Boeing of her belief that in order to qualify for gender reassignment surgery, she would have to live full time, for 1 year, in the social role of a female. Doe based her belief on discussions with her treating psychologist and her physician about a treatment protocol for transsexuals known as the Harry Benjamin International Gender Dysphoria Standards (Benjamin Standards). Benjamin Standard 9 states: "Genital sex reassignment shall be preceded by a period of at least 12 months during which time the patient lived full-time in the social role of the genetically other sex."

Upon being notified of Doe's intentions, Boeing informed Doe that while Doe was an anatomical male, she could not use the women's rest rooms or dress in "feminine" attire. Boeing informed Doe that she could dress as a woman at work and use the women's rest rooms upon completion of her gender reassignment surgery.

While Doe was an anatomical male, Boeing permitted Doe to wear either male clothing or unisex clothing. Unisex clothing included blouses, sweaters, slacks, flat shoes, nylon stockings, earrings, lipstick, foundation, and clear nail polish. Doe was instructed not to wear obviously feminine clothing such as dresses, skirts, or frilly blouses. Boeing applied its unwritten dress policy to all employees, which included eight other transsexuals who had expressed a desire to have gender reassignment surgery while working for Boeing. Both Doe's psychologist and treating physician testified that what Doe was allowed to wear at Boeing was sufficiently feminine for Doe to qualify for gender reassignment surgery.

Between June and late September 1985, Boeing management received approximately a dozen anonymous complaints regarding Doe's attire and use of the women's rest rooms. On October 25, 1985, following the receipt of a complaint about Doe using the women's rest room, Boeing issued Doe a written disciplinary warning. The warning reiterated Boeing's position on acceptable attire and rest room use and stated that Doe's failure to comply with Boeing's directives by November 1, 1985, would result in further corrective action, including termination. During this "grace" period, Doe's compliance with Boeing's "acceptable attire" directive was to be monitored each day by Doe's direct supervisor. Doe was told that her attire would be deemed unacceptable when, in the supervisor's opinion, her dress would be likely to cause a complaint were Doe to use a men's rest room at a Boeing facility. No single article of clothing would be dispositive. Doe's overall appearance was to be assessed.

Doe's transsexualism did not interfere with her ability to perform her job duties as a software engineer at Boeing. There was no measurable decline in either her work group's performance or in Doe's own job performance. There was no testimony to indicate that Boeing's dress restrictions hindered Doe's professional development.

On November 4, 1985, the first day Doe worked after the grace period, Doe wore attire that her supervisor considered acceptable. Doe responded that she was disappointed that her attire was acceptable, and that she would "push it" the next day. By "push it," Doe testified that she meant she would wear more extreme feminine attire. The next day, Doe came to work wearing similar attire, but she included as part of her outfit a strand of pink pearls which she refused to remove. This outfit was similar to one she had been told during the grace period was unacceptable in that the addition of the pink pearls changed Doe's look from unisex to "excessively" feminine. Doe was subsequently terminated from her position at Boeing as a result of her willful violation of Boeing's directives. Doe filed a handicap discrimination action against Boeing pursuant to Washington's Law Against Discrimination (hereafter Act) RCW49.60. The trial court held that Doe was "temporarily handicapped" under its construction of the law. The Court of Appeals reversed, finding Boeing failed to accommodate Doe. We reverse the Court of Appeals.

This case presents two issues for review. First, is Jane Doe's gender dysphoria a "handicap" under RCW 49.60.180? We hold that Doe's gender dysphoria is not a handicap under the Act. The definition of "handicap" for enforcement purposes in unfair practice cases under RCW 49.60.180, as defined in WAC 162-22-040, requires factual findings of both (1) the presence of an abnormal condition, and (2) employer discrimination against the plaintiff because of that condition. While gender dysphoria is an abnormal condition, we hold that Doe was not "handicapped" by her gender dysphoria because Boeing did not discharge her because of that condition.

Second, did Boeing have to provide Doe's preferred accommodation under RCW 49.60.180? We hold that the scope of an employer's duty to reasonably accommodate an employee's abnormal condition is limited to those steps necessary to enable the employee to perform his or her job. We hold that Boeing's actions met this standard and did not discriminate against Doe by reason of her abnormal condition.

It is uncontested that gender dysphoria is an abnormal, medically cognizable condition with a prescribed course of treatment. Assuming the presence of an abnormal condition, the next inquiry is whether the employer discriminated against the employee because of that condition. Boeing did not discriminate against Doe because of her condition. Boeing discharged Doe because she violated Boeing's directives on acceptable attire, not because she was gender dysphoric. Doe was treated in a respectful way by both her peers and supervisors at Boeing. Doe's supervisor consistently rated her work as satisfactory on her performance evaluations. While complaints were filed with Boeing management about Doe's use of the women's rest room, the record is void of any evidence that Doe suffered harassment because of her use of the rest room or because of her attire.

Inasmuch as Boeing did not discharge Doe based on her abnormal condition but on her refusal to conform with directives on acceptable attire, we must turn our attention to whether Boeing discriminated against Doe by failing to reasonably accommodate her condition of gender dysphoria.

We recognize that employers have an affirmative obligation to reasonably accommodate the sensory, mental, or physical limitations of such employees unless the employer can demonstrate that the accommodation would impose an undue hardship on the conduct of the employer's business. The issue before us is whether Boeing had a duty to accommodate Doe's preferred manner of dress prior to her gender reassignment surgery. We hold that the scope of an employer's duty to accommodate an employee's condition is limited to those steps reasonably necessary to enable the employee to perform his or her job.

Doe contends that Boeing's dress code failed to accommodate her condition and, thus was discriminatory. We disagree. The record substantially supports the trial court's findings that Boeing reasonably accommodated Doe in the matter of dress by allowing her to wear unisex clothing at work. Despite this accommodation, Doe determined unilaterally, and without medical confirmation, that she needed to dress as a woman at her place of employment in order to qualify for gender reassignment surgery. We find substantial support for the trial court's finding that Doe had no medical need to dress as a woman at work in order to qualify for her surgery.

[P]laintiff's experts declined to state that any particular degree of feminine dress was required in order for plaintiff to fulfill any presurgical requirements. In fact, the evidence was uncontradicted that the unisex dress permitted by Boeing . . . would not have precluded plaintiff from meeting the Benjamin Standards presurgical requirement of living in the social role of a woman. The trial court's findings are well supported by the testimony of Doe's own treating physician and psychologist, as well as other medical evidence.

Doe argues, however, that the trial court's findings on this point are irrelevant since Boeing did not have the benefit of such medical testimony prior to enforcing its dress policy. We disagree. The trial court found that Boeing's policy on accommodation of transsexuals was developed with input from Boeing's legal, medical, personnel and labor relations departments. The Boeing medical department consulted with outside experts in the field and reviewed the literature on transsexualism. The trial court also held that Boeing has a legitimate business purpose in defining what is acceptable attire and in balancing the needs of its work force as a whole with those of Doe. The record supports the trial court's findings of fact and conclusions of law that Boeing developed and reasonably enforced a dress policy which balanced its legitimate business needs with those of its employees.

Doe further argues that, as a gender dysphoric, her perceived needs should have been accommodated. We disagree. The Act does not require an employer to offer the employee the precise accommodation he or she requests. Her perceived need to dress more completely as a woman did not impact her job performance. Doe's condition had no measurable effect on either Doe's job performance or her work group's performance. That is not to say that Doe did not have emotional turmoil over the changes that were taking place in her life, but that turmoil did not prevent her from performing her work satisfactorily. Based on the record, there was no need for any further action by Boeing to facilitate Doe in the performance of job-related tasks.

Doe also argues that Boeing failed to accommodate her unique condition because its dress policy was uniformly applied.

In determining what is a reasonable accommodation, the evaluation must begin with the job specifications and how those tasks are impacted by the abnormal condition. In the case of trauma or physical deterioration, the answers are generally apparent and the issue becomes one of whether the accommodation is reasonable, not what is the accommodation. In Doe's case, the analysis is not so simple. Doe's job performance was unchanged by reason of her condition. Based on the record, there was no accommodation that Boeing could have provided that would have aided Doe in the performance of her work.

How she dressed or appeared had no impact on the physical or mental requirements of her employment responsibilities.

Doe's gender dysphoria did not impede her ability to perform her engineering duties. Therefore, Boeing had no duty to provide any further accommodation to Doe beyond what it provided for all employees. REVERSED.

Case Questions

1. What do you think the real problem was here? If you say that it was Jane trying to push too hard, explore what that really means. How responsible should the employer be for the discomfort of other employees? What about when the discomfort arises from long-

held beliefs based on misinformation, which society may have taken for granted until now? Would it be different if the issue was race instead of affinity orientation (i.e., employees did not want to deal with employees of other races in the workplace and were uncomfortable doing so)? Explain.

2. Are you surprised that Boeing had eight other employees to deal with on this issue? Explain. Are you surprised that an employer dealt with this issue with the depth that Boeing did? Why do you think it did so?

3. Doe evidently kept going to the female toilet, but it was the pink pearls that got her fired. Any thoughts as to why? Explain.

EMPLOYMENT BENEFITS

In the past few years, one of the most active issues regarding affinity orientation and the workplace has been that of employment benefits. Benefits that other employees take for granted are major hurdles for gays and lesbians. For instance, bereavement leave routinely granted for the death of a loved one is often not provided to gays and lesbians when their life partners die. Sick leave routinely granted to take care of a family member is often not given when the family is the gay or lesbian employee's life partner. (See Exhibits 8.6 and 8.7.)

In recent years, cities like Atlanta, Georgia; Ithaca, New York; Madison, Wisconsin; and West Hollywood, California, provided for the registration of unmarried couples (gay or straight) as domestic partners. Domestic partners generally must be able to prove that for a specified length of time they have lived together and given mutual aid and support. Upon proof of the jurisdiction's requirements, domestic partners may qualify for certain benefits. For instance, Delta Airlines expanded its definition of "family" to whom frequent flyer miles can be transferred to include registered gay partners. In June 1994, Vermont became the first state to offer health benefits to domestic partners of state workers. Other jurisdictions followed. More than 5,000 private companies and city governments now permit their employees to include domestic partners in their health insurance coverage. Included among them are Goldman Sachs and J. P. Morgan, both major Wall Street investment firms generally considered rather staid and conservative.

As the labor market continues to tighten, such benefits are used as a marketing tool to attract and retain gay and lesbian employees. (See Exhibit 8.5.) In 2002, the state of Connecticut passed legislation extending many rights to same-gender partners, such as allowing them to name someone to make their medical decisions, allowing private visits in nursing homes, and requiring employers to allow emergency calls from a legally designated person.

What might seem like purely social issues have workplace implications that are quite far-reaching. For instance, a San Francisco UPS employee sued after the employer denied his request for an out-of-state transfer so he could follow his male life

- *Nondiscrimination policies.* Corporate antidiscrimination policies are a primary concern for lesbians and gays who don't have state or local civil rights ordinances protecting them. A basic statement that employees are given the same opportunity to enter, advance, and succeed in an organization sets the tone for how that organization relates to lesbians and gays.
- *Bereavement leave for domestic partners.* Many corporations have policies granting employees paid leave to attend the funerals of spouses and immediate members of the family. These policies don't help unmarried domestic partners of gays or straights. This was a particularly important issue, given the devastating impact of the AIDS crisis.
- *Vacation leave transfer.* Another issue is the enormous financial burden placed on employees with AIDS. Other employees often want to help these employees by donating their earned vacation time. Gay and lesbian groups are lobbying companies to consider allowing employees to offer support in this way.
- *Benefits for domestic partners.* Earning health care benefits for their partners is an important goal for lesbian and gay employees. They're asking corporations to respect alternative families and recognize their benefit needs, and they argue that the family partner of an unmarried employee is just as likely to need health insurance as is the spouse of a married employee. Gays and lesbians also are asking for parental leave benefits when appropriate.

Source: G. K. Kronenberger, "Out of the Closet," *Workforce Magazine,* June 1991, p. 40.

partner's move to Chicago. The recent and ongoing gay marriage debate has huge implications for employers. In response to mounting concerns that gay marriage could result in mandatory domestic partner benefits or mandatory family leave for domestic partners, regardless of what states or Congress choose to do, employers have already begun to address the issue of gay families in significant ways. Nearly half of the Fortune 500 companies offer domestic partner benefits. Many companies go beyond. Of companies that provide such benefits, 90 percent cover a domestic partner's dependents or children, 60 percent extend adoption assistance to domestic partners, and 72 percent also allow employees to take extended family leave to care for a domestic partner or their dependents. According to the U.S. Census, the National Adoption Information Clearinghouse, and the Urban Institute, the number of children who have a gay or lesbian parent could be anywhere from 6 to 14 million. The most conservative estimates, based on underreported census data, puts the number of children growing up in single-gender parent households at over 1 million.

This means that workplace leave policies, adoption policies, and flexible schedule issues will become more pronounced as gay families continue to seek workplace rights provided to others. According to the Urban Institute, in 1990, 1 in 20 male single-gender couples had children under 18. By the year 2000, that number was 1 in 5. For women, 1 in 5 rose to 1 in 3 by 2000. Data indicate that gay dads are as likely to have one stay-at-home partner as heterosexual couples with children. Gay and lesbian parents are quitting their jobs and moving to part-time work in order to deal with their

USA TODAY EDITORIAL: OUR VIEW

Shouldn't you be able to decide who should care for you in crisis or [should] benefit if you die?

Unmarried couples should keep an eye on California. A bill awaiting the governor's signature would bring some needed changes to Californians' lives. The concept could, and should, spread to other states.

There's nothing earthshaking about the bill. In fact, it's surprising no state yet offers three basic protections to unmarrieds:

- The right to have your partner visit if you're hospitalized.
- The right to have your partner act as guardian if you're incapacitated.
- And the right to leave your money and property to whom you wish in your will, avoiding nasty court battles with relatives.

Spouses, of course, already have these rights. But there are plenty of couples—nearly half a million in California alone—who aren't married, 93 percent of them heterosexual. Many will marry later; some never will, for a variety of reasons. And for gay couples, marriage is out of the question.

Domestic partner programs have expanded rapidly in the past decade. Two states and several cities grant full health benefits to employees' partners.

Others offer domestic partner registration, which offers varying degrees of legal protection. Ordinances in Minneapolis, Minn., and West Hollywood, Calif., for example, allow hospital visitation. In other places, registration provides psychological benefits but not legal ones.

How important is legal recognition of a partnership? Anyone who pooh-poohs it could use a lesson from Karen Thompson and Sharon Kowalski. The two women, teachers in Minnesota, began living together in 1979. In 1983, Kowalski was injured in an accident caused by a drunken driver. She was brain damaged and comatose for five months.

Thompson battled Kowalski's parents over guardianship, and when the parents won in 1985, they banned Thompson from even visiting their daughter. The case went to the Minnesota Court of Appeals, and Thompson, who had built a wheelchair-accessible home for Kowalski, finally gained custody in 1991.

When it comes to the law, spouses and blood relatives come first regardless of the wishes of the victim. That's why legislation such as the one in California [is] so important.

[It allows] people to say, in effect, "Hey, world. This is my life partner. This is the person I want when I'm sick or need to be taken care of, and it's the person I want taken care of if I die first."

The California proposal is such a little step in the legal scheme of things, but it's an important one.

Growth of Benefits

More than 2,800 firms and organizations offer some type of domestic partner benefits. Two states, Vermont and New York, have granted health and dental benefits to domestic partners of state employees. Some cities with similar provisions:

Health benefits; Ann Arbor and East Lansing, Mich.; Berkeley, Calif.; Cambridge, Mass.; Seattle, Wash.; New York, N.Y.

Registration and/or sick and bereavement leave: Atlanta, Ga.; Madison, Wis.; Takoma Park, Md.; Los Angeles, Calif.; West Palm Beach, Fla.

(continued)

Exhibit 8.7   (continued)

OPPOSING VIEW

This law isn't necessary. Stop this campaign to legitimize cohabitation.

Hold on to your checkbook, because the liberal/left is pushing another nearsighted social experiment called "domestic partners," which will cost taxpayers and redefine the institution of marriage.

The goal of the homosexual special interest lobby is to change the public policy of this nation by expanding the definition of marriage and family to include two homosexuals or heterosexuals living together. This new quasi-marital union impacts the way our judges make their rulings on issues that relate to marriage and family, and it devalues the concept of marriage.

So far, courts have denied marital status to cohabiting homosexuals. But this could change. If government expands the definition of marriage, the courts will then be compelled to force businesses to pay benefits for the domestic partners of employees just like benefits for employees' spouses. And governments could be forced to use scarce tax dollars for benefits for domestic partners of government employees. Most states allow consenting adults to live together, but that doesn't mean taxpayers should have to subsidize this arrangement.

Also, domestic partnerships weaken the institution of marriage and encourage relationships without the responsibility of marriage. Some may argue this new legislation promotes monogamous relationships, but these laws typically allow for a new "partner" every six months and erode the cultural support for the permanency of marriage.

Homosexual activists are good at marketing. They have tried to mainstream themselves by garnering some senior citizens' support. But domestic partners is an unnecessary shotgun approach to remedy some senior-citizen concerns.

Moreover, medical facilities already allow visitation in intensive care units and hospital rooms by friends or relatives. Existing law allows a testator to will property to anyone—friend or stranger. Existing law allows any "interested person" to file petitions or receive notice regarding conservatorship or guardianship.

The man/woman marriage relationship is best for society.

Note: The law was, in fact, enacted.

Source: "Our View"—Copyright 1994, *USA Today,* reprinted with permission; "Opposing View"—courtesy of the Rev. Louis P. Sheldon, chairman of Traditional Values Coalition, Anaheim, Calif.

---

children, and many employers are responding by offering work–life programs and benefits to gay parents.

Since research shows that gay couples with children are more likely to settle where there are more families with children, rather than in areas considered more "gay-friendly," this is not an issue for only a limited area of the country. Would it surprise you to know that the Urban Institute's research shows that the state where gay couples are most likely to raise children is—are you ready for this?—*Mississippi?!*

While there are employers who treat gay and lesbian employees much like any other employees when it comes to these issues, others do not. Lately, gay and lesbian employees have been fighting back. In the case below, lesbians sued their employer to have the right to include their long-term life partners on their insurance policies. They won.

Tanner v. Oregon Health Sciences University *971 P.2d 435 (Ore. 1998)*

Three lesbian university employees sued when the university denied insurance benefits to their domestic partners. The Oregon Court of Appeals held that the university's denial of insurance benefits to the employees' domestic partners violated the Oregon constitution's privileges and immunities clause.

Landau, J.

At issue in this case is the lawfulness of Oregon Health Science University's (OHSU) denial of health and life insurance benefits to the unmarried domestic partners of its homosexual employees. Plaintiffs, who are three lesbian employees of OHSU and their domestic partners, initiated this action for judicial review of State Employees' Benefits Board (SEBB) orders affirming the lawfulness of the denial and for declaratory and injunctive relief. Plaintiffs contend that OHSU's actions violate Article I, section 20, of the Oregon Constitution, which prohibits granting privileges or immunities not equally belonging to all citizens.

Article I, section 20, of the Oregon Constitution provides:

> "No law shall be passed granting to any citizen or class of citizens privileges or immunities, which, upon the same terms, shall not equally belong to all citizens."

Article I, section 20 generally is understood to express two separate prohibitions. The clause "forbids inequality of privileges or immunities not available upon the same terms, first, to any citizen, and second, to any class of citizens." In this case, employees contend that they are members of a class of citizens—homosexual couples—to whom certain privileges—insurance benefits—are not made available.

There is no question but that employees are members of a true class. That class—unmarried homosexual couples—is not defined by any statute nor by the practices that are the subject of employees' challenges. Moreover, the class clearly is defined in terms of ad hominem, personal, and social characteristics. The question then is whether employees are members of a suspect class. Here, too, we have no difficulty concluding that employees are members of a suspect class. Sexual orientation, like gender, race, alienage, and religious affiliation is widely regarded as defining a distinct, socially recognized group of citizens, and certainly it is beyond dispute that homosexuals in our society have been and continue to be the subject of adverse social and political stereotyping and prejudice.

Because employees are members of a suspect class to which certain privileges and immunities are not made available, we must determine whether the fact that the privileges and immunities are not available to that class may be justified by genuine differences between the class and those to whom the privileges and immunities are made available. Stated perhaps more plainly, we must determine whether the fact that the domestic partners of homosexual OHSU employees cannot obtain insurance benefits can be justified by their homosexuality. The parties have suggested no such justification, and we can envision none.

OHSU's defense is that it determined eligibility for insurance benefits on the basis of marital status, not sexual orientation. According to OHSU, the fact that such a facially neutral classification has the unintended side effect of discriminating against homosexual couples who cannot marry is not actionable under Article I, section 20. We are not persuaded by the asserted defense. Article I, section 20, does not prohibit only intentional discrimination. OHSU has taken action with no apparent intention to treat disparately members of any true class of citizens. Nevertheless, its actions have the undeniable effect of doing just that. OHSU's intentions in this case are not relevant. What is relevant is the extent to which privileges or immunities are not made available to all citizens on equal terms.

OHSU insists that in this case privileges and immunities are available to all on equal terms: All married employees—heterosexuals and homosexuals alike—are permitted to acquire insurance benefits for their spouses. That reasoning misses the point, however. Homosexual couples may not marry. Accordingly, the benefits are not made available on equal terms. They are made available on terms that, for gay and lesbian couples, are a legal impossibility.

We conclude that OHSU's denial of insurance benefits to the unmarried domestic partners of its homosexual employees violated the Oregon Constitution and that the trial court correctly entered judgment in favor of plaintiffs on that ground. AFFIRMED.

Case Questions

1. While this case was pending, the employer decided to revise its policies to extend insurance coverage to gays and lesbians. Why do you think it did so?

2. List what you consider to be the five best reasons for not extending benefits to gay and lesbian employees. Explain. Now give the arguments for why these reasons may not be good ones. Which do you prefer? Why?

3. Do you understand why the court would hold that the Oregon Constitution's privileges and immunities clause requires that the employer not extend benefits to one group that it will not extend to another unless it can show there is a valid reason for the differentiation? Can you think of a valid reason here?

MANAGEMENT CONSIDERATIONS

Since affinity orientation is not a protected category under Title VII, employers have more flexibility in making workplace policies and decisions on this issue. The approach the employer takes will depend in large part on the employer's own views and preferences. Those employers who prefer the benefits of a diverse workplace—and who wish to maximize the potential the employee has for growth and contribution within the workplace and who wish to avoid legal wrangling—will likely choose to deal with the affinity orientation issue in a less restrictive manner.

Such employers will likely not have policies that have a hard-and-fast rule of "no gays or lesbians allowed." Rather, they will judge all employees on the basis of work-related criteria.

If some action of the lesbian or gay employee presents an issue, it should be dealt with as a legitimate workplace issue, rather than one that arose solely because of the employee's affinity orientation. The fact that the employee happens to be gay or lesbian should not be treated as the "why," any more than it would be if the employee were not gay or lesbian. It is irrelevant to the activity. The focus is on the conduct itself, not on the affinity orientation of the employee. It greatly reduces the potential for liability to deal with all employees this way.

Employers who decide to have a policy that treats gays and lesbians as full contributors to the workplace should ensure that the message goes out from the very top. It is more likely to be accepted, appreciated, and understood and therefore will be more likely to accomplish its purpose. Other employees will be more likely to comport themselves consistently with the policy if it comes from the top of the hierarchy. It should be made clear that not only will the employer not discriminate on the basis of affinity orientation, but that it will not be tolerated from other employees, particularly in the form of harassment of gays and lesbians.

The employer who does not prefer this approach may have more latitude under the law (depending on the jurisdiction in which the employer is located) not to take this view, than they would, say, about having women in the workplace, or having Jews, or blacks, or Hispanics. Some employers may even wish to take an adverse workplace decision involving a gay or lesbian employee to court to maintain maximum control over areas not as heavily regulated as the other protected categories. That is the employer's personal choice, but at least the employer now knows both sides of the issue. (See Exhibit 8.7.)

Management Tips

Policies and decisions in the affinity orientation area are rapidly evolving. The patchwork of state, federal, local, public, and private laws and policies we have discussed present the employer with the challenge of trying to do what is required for each jurisdiction, when, in fact, the requirements may be quite different. However, conclusions can be drawn about creating policy in the midst of such seeming chaos. In order to provide the maximum protection from liability for affinity orientation–related issues, an employer can do several things:

- Hire using only relevant, work-related criteria.
- Keep inquiries about applicants' personal lives at a minimum, and make sure the information is relevant.
- Have a policy ensuring all employees respect in the workplace, and ensure that all employees are aware of the policy and what it means.
- No matter what the employer's policy about gays in the workplace, the respect policy should protect everyone from things like unsolicited negative statements about immutable

and other characteristics such as race, religion, gender, and affinity orientation.

- Take prompt action whenever there are complaints of violations of the policy or it sends the message that the policy is meaningless.
- Deciding what position to take on affinity orientation–related issues for policy purposes can be done proactively before the issue arises, or defensively to meet the issue when it comes about; the latter has the benefit of specificity, the former the advantage of deliberate, strategic thinking.
- Be aware of the potential impact on gays and lesbians of workplace policies regarding issues like bereavement leave, benefits, bringing significant others to office functions, accepting personal calls during work hours, display of personal items at work (photos, cards, political buttons, and so forth).
- If the employer decides to institute policies inclusive of gays and lesbians, ensure that they are fair and evenly handled.

Some employers take a middle-ground position. That is, they do not have a specific policy of either support or prohibition, but they deal with issues as they arise on a case-by-case basis. Again, because the law is not as restrictive for this category of employees as it is for others and does not extend the same Title VII protections, the employer potentially (again, depending on the state the employer is in) has more leeway to choose the management approach that best suits his or her needs or desires.

The caution to be heeded is that simply because Title VII or the majority of state fair-employment practice laws do not prohibit discrimination on the basis of affinity orientation does not mean that it is not prohibited by relevant state or local laws relating to closely connected issues, such as privacy, right to free speech, interference with contractual relations, and so on. And the laws are changing every day. Employers concerned about workplace decisions should, at the very least, check such laws or case law in their jurisdiction before making final decisions. Remember that every single state either has a state or local law protecting gays and lesbians.

Even if the law is on the employer's side, the employer may wish to consider other possible repercussions of restrictive employment policies in this area. An example of this is the Cracker Barrel restaurant chain headquartered in Tennessee. Cracker Barrel operates a number of restaurants around the country. With no apparent motivating event, in 1991 the company announced that it would no longer employ people "whose sexual preferences fail to demonstrate normal heterosexual values which have been the foundation of families in our society." Pursuant to this policy, Cracker Barrel summarily dismissed its gay and lesbian employees.

After doing so, it was the subject of vigorous opposition, mainly by the gay and lesbian community. Many of Cracker Barrel's restaurants were picketed and denounced by vocal protesters. Gays and lesbians bought stock in order to have a say in its policies. Cracker Barrel later revoked the policy as overreactive. Even though the law permitted Cracker Barrel's actions, some employers may wish to avoid the controversy exhibited here, particularly if there is no pressing need to address the issue. In a complete about-face, in 2002, Cracker Barrel's board of directors voted to include gays and lesbians in its antidiscrimination policy.

Despite all the information in this chapter, it is still up to the employer how the issue of gays and lesbians in the workplace is to be handled. A word of caution should be given, however. If the employer decides to create a workplace inclusive of gays and lesbians, he or she should be aware of the religious conflicts employees have alleged based on diversity policies. As the case below demonstrates, the employer should not trample over the rights of other employees in order to address the issue of diversity and avoiding liability.

Buonanno v. AT&T Broadband, LLC *313 F. Supp. 2d 1069 (D. CO 2004)*

Employee was terminated for refusing to sign a workplace document containing language that he would "value" diversity, under the employer's diversity policy. His refusal was based on his religion rejecting homosexuality. The employee sued the employer for terminating him without trying to reasonably accommodate the employee's religious belief or practice. The court sided with the employee.

Krieger , J.

Buonanno is a Christian who believes that the Bible is divinely inspired. He attempts to live his life in accordance with its literal language. Because the Bible requires that he treat others as he would like to be treated, Buonanno values and respects all other AT&T employees as individuals. He never has nor would he discriminate against another employee due to differences in belief, behavior, background, or other attribute. However, his religious beliefs prohibit him from approving, endorsing, or esteeming behavior or values that are repudiated by Scripture.

In January 2001, AT&T promoted a new "Employee Handbook" that addressed "How We Work: Employee Guidelines" and "Doing What's Right: Business Integrity

& Ethics Policies." AT&T maintains a "Certification Policy," which provides that "each AT&T Broadband employee must sign and return the Acknowledgment of Receipt and Certificate of Understanding form indicating that you have received a copy of the handbook and the AT&T Code of Conduct and that you will abide by our employment policies and practices." The parties agree that one of the "employment policies and practices" to which Buonanno was required to adhere is AT&T's "Diversity Policy." The Handbook, however, does not contain a single policy clearly denoted as such; instead, it contains numerous references in various locations to AT&T's philosophy and goals with regard to diversity in the workplace. The parties' references to a "Diversity Policy" appear to be primarily referring to a section of the Handbook entitled "A Summary of Our Business

Philosophy," a subsection of which is entitled "Diversity." It reads as follows:

> The company places tremendous value on the fresh, innovative ideas and variety of perspectives that come from a diverse workplace. Diversity is necessary for a competitive business advantage—and the company is competing for customers in an increasingly diverse marketplace. To make diversity work to our advantage, it's our goal to build an environment that:
>
> * Respects and values individual differences.
> * Reflects the communities we serve.
> * Promotes employee involvement in decision making.
> * Encourages innovation and differing perspectives in problem solving.
> * Allows our diverse employee population to contribute richly to our growth.
>
> We want to create a team that is diverse, committed and the most talented in America. To that end, AT&T Broadband has a "zero tolerance" policy toward any type of discrimination, harassment, or retaliation in our company. Each person at AT&T Broadband is charged with the responsibility to fully recognize, respect and value the differences among all of us. This is demonstrated in the way we communicate and interact with our customers, suppliers and each other every day.

There was no uniform understanding at AT&T as to what comprised the company's "Diversity Policy," or, more importantly, what an employee was required to do or not do to comply with it. Buonanno questioned the meaning of the third sentence in the second paragraph of the Diversity Philosophy, which reads "Each person at AT&T Broadband is charged with the responsibility to fully recognize, respect and value the differences among all of us." (The Court will hereinafter refer to this phrase as "the challenged language.") He believed that some behavior and beliefs were deemed sinful by Scripture, and thus, that he could not "value"—that is hold in esteem or ascribe worth to—such behavior or beliefs without compromising his own religious beliefs. Buonanno was fully prepared to comply with the principles underlying the Diversity Philosophy; he recognized that individuals have differing beliefs and behaviors and he would not discriminate against or harass any person based on that person's differing beliefs or behaviors. However, he could not comply with the challenged language insofar as it apparently required him to "value" the particular belief or behavior that was repudiated by Scripture. Accordingly, if the chal-

lenged language literally required him to do so, he could not sign the Certificate of Understanding, agreeing to "abide by" such language.

No AT&T representative explored or explained the intended meaning (or any of the various interpretations) of the challenged language to Buonanno. No AT&T employee inquired as to the particulars of Buonanno's concerns, sought to devise ways to accommodate Buonanno's religious beliefs, or reassured him that the challenged language did not require him to surrender his religious beliefs. At all relevant times, Buonanno was presented with a choice between accepting the language of the Handbook without any additional clarification and signing the Certificate, or losing his employment.

AT&T's Diversity Philosophy reflects a legitimate and laudable business goal. The Court accepts AT&T's contention that allowing employees to strike piecemeal portions of the Handbook or Certification could pose an undue hardship on its business, making uniform application of company policies much more difficult. Nevertheless, had AT&T gathered more information about Buonanno's concerns before terminating his employment, it may have discovered that the perceived conflict between his beliefs and AT&T's policy was not an actual conflict at all, or that if a true conflict existed, it was possible to relieve that conflict with a reasonable accommodation.

Had [Human Resources Manager] Batliner sought more details about Buonanno's concerns, rather than steadfastly insisting that he had to agree with the ambiguous "Diversity Policy" to retain his job, she would have discovered that, but for the challenged language, Buonanno agreed with the entirety of the Handbook, including the Diversity Philosophy, the non-discrimination policy, and all other aspects of AT&T's policies and practices. His only objection was to a literal interpretation of the challenged language that required him to "value" particular behavior and beliefs of co-workers. Had Batliner followed [vice president of Human Resources for Colorado operations] Davis' instructions and engaged in a conversation through which she gathered information about Buonanno's concerns, based on her interpretation of the challenged language, she would have discovered no actual conflict between the challenged language and Buonanno's religion. If Batliner had, as directed, reported these findings back to Davis, based on Davis' interpretation of the challenged language, Buonanno's religious beliefs would not have been in conflict with the challenged language. Had Batliner reported this information to [Senior vice president for

Human Resources] Brunick, he would have observed that, like the Jewish employee who must recognize—but not adopt—the differing beliefs of his Muslim co-worker, the challenged language did not require Buonanno to actually "value" the particular conduct of his co-workers that he considered sinful. Had [Director of Employee Relations] Wilson been consulted, Buonanno's promise to recognize that there were differences between what he believed and did and what his co-workers believed and did and to treat everyone with respect regardless of their beliefs and behavior would have been sufficient to accomplish the goals of the challenged language. Had Batliner, Davis, Brunick, or Wilson ever explained that they understood the challenged language to have a figurative, rather than literal, meaning and listened to his concerns, the issue could have been resolved without any need for accommodation. Accordingly, AT&T has failed to show that it could not have accommodated Buonanno's beliefs without undue hardship.

Even assuming that—despite the testimony of Batliner, Davis, and, at times, Brunick and Wilson—AT&T intended that the challenged language be applied literally and that all employees were affirmatively required to ascribe value in the various beliefs and behaviors of their co-workers, AT&T could nevertheless have accommodated Buonanno without suffering undue hardship. Although AT&T's Diversity Philosophy confers a business advantage, AT&T did not show that the literal application of the challenged language was necessary to obtain such advantage. For example, Wilson explained the advantages conferred by the "Diversity Policy" by relating an anecdote in which homosexual employees at American Express, sensing a need for estate-planning services in the gay community, proposed the creation of a successful new targeted product. In such example, no employee at American Express was required to ascribe any "value" to the practice of homosexuality in order to capitalize on the opportunity. Rather, American Express officials simply recognized that homosexual employees had a unique perspective on ways to market the company's product. Thus, as Wilson admitted, a minor revision of the challenged language, requiring all employees company-wide to "fully recognize, respect and value that there are differences among all of us" would have "accomplished [AT&T's] goals" as set forth in the Diversity Philosophy, without imposing any apparent hardship on AT&T. Whether such a change is characterized as clarifying AT&T's interpretation of the existing Handbook language or a reasonable accommodation for Buonanno is irrelevant.

AT&T violated Title VII by failing to engage in the required dialogue with Buonanno upon notice of his concerns and by failing to clarify the challenged language to reasonably accommodate Buonanno's religious beliefs. Accordingly, Buonanno is entitled to damages.

Case Questions

1. If you were Buonanno's manager, how would you have handled this situation?

2. Think about the issue of an employee deciding not to accept a coworker because of religious reasons. If you were the manager, how would you balance the two (workplace requirements versus religion)? What if, as in the chapter on religion, the employee's religion teaches them to hate blacks and Jews? Is it the same? Explain.

3. What considerations should an employer be concerned with when coming up with approaches to promote workplace cohesion and avoidance of discrimination claims?

Summary
- Affinity orientation is not protected by Title VII.
- Washington, D.C., 15 states, and hundreds of municipalities have passed protective legislation. Constitutional protection may also apply to public employees.
- Employers in most jurisdictions have more leeway in this area to make employment decisions without regard to the same legal strictures applicable to other categories of employees included within Title VII.
- The safer approach is to base employment decisions on the person's qualifications and fitness for the job, rather than on questionably relevant characteristics about his or her personal life.

Chapter-End Questions

1. Applicant applies for a position with Ace Corporation. During the interview, Ace suspects that applicant is gay. When asked why the suspicion, Ace says that the male applicant acted effeminately. Ace decides not to hire the applicant, who is otherwise qualified. Does the applicant have a cause of action against Ace? [*Jantz* v. *Muci,* 759 F. Supp. 1543 (D. Kan, 1991).]

2. When the FBI learns that Mary, its FBI agent, is a lesbian, Mary is fired. Mary goes to an attorney to find out about the possibility of suing to get her job back. What does the attorney likely tell her?

3. As a manager, an employee comes to you and tells you that he has a hunch that one of the other employees is probably gay. What do you do?

4. Charlie, the manager, does not like it that Chester wears an earring and orders Chester to get rid of it or run the risk of termination. Chester refuses. Can Charlie terminate Chester?

5. Employee sues employer, saying that he is being sexually harassed by gay males, who only harass young male employees. Does he have a cause of action? [*Wrightson* v. *Pizza Hut of America, Inc.,* 99 F.3d 138 (4th Cir. 1996).]

6. Maureen brings her same-gender partner of 14 years to a company picnic. One of the other employees treats Maureen poorly after realizing she is a lesbian. Does Maureen have any recourse?

7. A male firefighter is diagnosed with gender dysphoria seven years after coming onto the force and having no negative incidents with coworkers. As he begins to exhibit a more feminine demeanor, he begins to have administrative troubles, which he attributes to his failing to conform to gender stereotypes. Does he have a cause of action under Title VII? [*Smith* v. *City of Salem, Ohio,* 378 F.3d 566 (6th Cir. 2004).]

8. A female assistant at a hair salon is terminated. She brings suit under Title VII, alleging that it is because she is a lesbian whose overall appearance is more male than female. The employer counters that the termination was due to poor performance, there was no dress code, and the employee was allowed to wear her hair in a Mohawk cut as long as it was styled by someone at the salon. Is the employee likely to win? [*Dawson* v. *Bumble & Bumble,* 398 F.3d 211 (2d Cir. 2005).]

9. Employee was designated male at birth and on her driver's license, but considered herself a woman. When she used both the male and female bathroom at work, her employer asked her to supply a letter from her doctor indicating her gender. Her attorney wrote saying that she was not entirely male or female, and was, instead, intersexed. Employer tells employee she can only use the men's restroom. If the employee had not notified the employer that she was intersexed, and possibly within Title VII, would employer be held liable for discrimination? [*Johnson* v. *Fresh Mark, Inc.,* 337 F. Supp. 2d 996 (N.D. Ohio 2003).]

10. Employee is harassed by a male coworker, who makes repeated statements to him in the men's locker room such as "your hands are so soft—what are you doing after work?" and "why don't you come strip for me?" Employee complains to management. Does management have to respond? [*Jones* v. *Pacific Rail Services,* 85 Fair Empl. Prac. Cas. (BNA) 90 (N.D. Ill. 2001).]

Chapter **Nine**

Religious Discrimination

Chapter Outline

Opening Scenarios

SCENARIO 1

1 Scenario

In his preemployment interview, Mosley stated that he would not work on Saturdays because that is the day of his Sabbath. As a result, he is not hired. Is this religious discrimination?

SCENARIO 2

2 Scenario

Three months after coming to work for Steel Bank, Jon joins a religious group whose Sabbath is on Tuesdays. Members of the religion are not to work on the Sabbath. Jon refuses to work on Tuesdays. He is terminated. Jon sues the employer, alleging religious discrimination. The employer defends by saying that (1) Jon was not of this religion when he was hired, (2) Tuesday is not a valid Sabbath day, and (3) any religious group that celebrates a Sabbath on Tuesday is not a valid religion and the employer does not have to honor it. Are any of the employer's defenses valid?

SCENARIO 3

3 Scenario

Mohammed, a member of the Sikh religion, wears a turban as part of his religious mandate. His supervisor tells him the turban makes his coworkers "uncomfortable." Must he stop wearing it?

STATUTORY BASIS

It shall be an unlawful employment practice for an employer—

(1) to fail or refuse to hire or to discharge any individual, or otherwise to discriminate against any individual with respect to his compensation, terms, conditions, or privileges of employment, because of such individual's . . . religion . . . or

(2) to limit, segregate, or classify his employees or applicants for employment in any way which would deprive or tend to deprive any individual of employment opportunities or otherwise adversely affect his status as an employee, because of such individual's religion . . . Title VII of the Civil Rights Act of 1964, as amended; 42 U.S.C. 20002-2(a).

Congress shall make no law respecting an establishment of religion, or prohibiting the free exercise thereof . . . First Amendment to the U.S. Constitution.

THIS IS NOT YOUR FOREFATHER'S RELIGIOUS DISCRIMINATION

- An employee sues to have the court impose an injunction allowing her to say "have a blessed day" in written communications to clients and customers.
- An employee sues after being terminated for eating a bacon, lettuce, and tomato sandwich (BLT) at work, in violation of the "no pork or pork products" rule put in place in deference to Muslim employees and clients.
- A Muslim trucker is fired for refusing to pick up a load of beer from a brewer because Muslims are forbidden from handling alcohol.
- Muslim taxi drivers refuse to pick up passengers who carry alcohol purchased at airport duty-free shops.
- A Jewish employee alleges his coworkers call him "Jew Boy" and other slurs and would not stop witnessing to him at work about their Christian faith.

- An Indiana state police officer is terminated for refusing a casino detail, saying gambling or being around it is against his religion.
- The New York Police Department is found guilty of religious discrimination for banning the wearing of a turban on the job by a Sikh.
- Alabama supreme court chief justice Roy S. Moore is removed from office for refusing a court's order to remove a 5,280-pound granite carving of the Ten Commandments from the courthouse rotunda.
- A television producer is fired for complaining about the company including biblical scriptures inside paycheck envelopes and promoting office Bible study.
- A son sues his father, who is also his boss, alleging religious discrimination in that his father terminated him because the son was involved in an extramarital affair in violation of the father's religious beliefs.
- An AT&T employee is terminated for refusing to sign a "Certificate of Understanding" requiring him to adhere to the company's diversity policy, which conflicted with the employee's religious beliefs about homosexuality.
- At Hewlett-Packard, in the same situation, an employee is terminated for refusing to remove biblical scriptures he placed on an overhead bin in his workplace cubicle, hoping his gay and lesbian coworkers would see them, be hurt, repent, and be saved.
- In Minnesota, employees who bring their Bibles to the diversity session on working with gays and lesbians sue their employers, saying punishing them for this was a violation of their constitutional rights.
- A UPS employee sues for religious discrimination after he is fired for refusing to cover his dreadlocks, which he says are a part of his religion, with a cap.
- An employee belonging to the World Church of the Creator that teaches that "all people of color are savages who should go back to Africa and the Holocaust never happened and if it did, Nazi Germany would have done the world a tremendous favor" sues his employer after being terminated for giving a newspaper interview espousing these views.

Wow! Can you believe it?! Incredible! And those were just examples of religious issues in the *workplace!* That doesn't even include issues outside the workplace like the recent Supreme Court case challenging the pledge of allegiance phrase, "One nation under God," the Supreme Court's recent decision on the exhibition of Ten Commandment monuments on federal or state premises; the Pennsylvania Amish winning a suit allowing them to use, for safety purposes, retroreflective tape to outline their buggies rather than the bright orange triangles, whose color and shape deeply offend their religious sensibilities; the University of Georgia Jewish cheerleader (actually one of our students!) who alleged that the Christian cheerleading coach did not appoint her to the prestigious football cheering squad because she did not participate in pre-game prayers or attend Bible studies held in the coach's home; the female Muslim University of South Florida basketball player who voluntarily resigned from the team after the coach refused to allow her to wear a uniform with long pants, long sleeves, and a head scarf in conformity with her religious dictates; or the Muslim sixth-grader who caused a stir in Oklahoma when she refused to remove her *hijab,* the head covering required by her religion, which the school said violated its dress code.

There are many more we could add, but one thing is for sure: religious discrimination is no longer the backwater issue of Title VII. Religious discrimination has certainly come a long way from what was likely envisioned by our forefathers when they wrote its protection into our constitution.

Religion has unique significance in our country's creation and development. In the 16th century, when the Catholic Church did not allow King Henry VIII to divorce his wife, Catherine of Aragon, and to marry Anne Boleyn, Henry broke with Rome. This led to the establishment of a separate national church in England under the supreme headship of the king. Henry VIII was allowed to divorce Catherine (he eventually took six wives) and marry Anne, whom he ordered beheaded in 1536.

The aftermath of Henry's maneuvers was that the church became inextricably woven with the government, and religious freedom was virtually nonexistent. The right to practice religion freely and not be required to blindly accept the government's state-imposed religious beliefs was a large part of what made America break away from Great Britain and its Church of England more than a century later.

Of course, this is only a simplified version of a very long and complex developmental process for our relationship as a country with religion. But the end product was that, rejecting the tyranny of this state-imposed religion, religious freedom was included in the U.S. Constitution, and freedom of religion has since always been highly valued and closely held, and it has enjoyed a protected position in American law. Title VII embodies this in the employment arena by prohibiting discrimination in employment based on religion—either its beliefs or practices (see Exhibits 9.1 and 9.2). While litigation on the basis of religious discrimination does not occur as frequently as some of the other categories, or may not have as high a profile, it is just as important a concern for employers. The percentage of claims may seem small, but the more important factor is that there has been a steady increase in claims since 1993. In its 2002 comprehensive litigation report covering the five-year period of fiscal years 1997 through 2001, the EEOC stated that of the total suits filed, cases alleging religious discrimination comprised 4.3 percent. This is in stark contrast to the 30.1 percent for gender cases or the 22.2 percent for retaliation cases, or even the 13.5 percent for race discrimination cases. However, religious discrimination is no less important. It is clear that this issue has taken on an even more pressing note since the tragic events of September 11, 2001. According to the EEOC, federal, state, and local fair employment practice agencies have documented a significant increase in the number of charges of workplace harassment and discrimination claims based on national origin (with those perceived to be of Arab and South Asian descent being the target) and religion (Muslims, Sikhs). Employment discrimination claims increased by 4.5 percent from 2001 to 2002, with much of that increase coming from ethnicity and religion after 9/11.

Actually, the increase in litigation involving religious issues began to pick up when issues of workplace activities and harassment issues surrounding religious practices became more active in the late 1980s and early 1990s with the rising popularity of Fundamentalist Christianity. Many of the Fundamentalists, commonly referred to as "born-again Christians," ran into trouble when, as an article of faith, they attempted to share their religion with others in the workplace, sometimes whether the coworker wished to have it so or not. On the other hand, Fundamentalists experienced trouble

Exhibit 9.1

World Religions

Group	Adherents	Percent of World Pop.
Major World Religions		
Christianity	2 billion	33.0%
Islam	1.3 billion	22.0
Hinduism	900 million	15.0
Buddhism	360 million	6.9
Judaism	14 million	0.4
Other Broad Religious Groupings		
Chinese folk religions	225 million	4.0%
African traditional and diasporic religions	95 million	3.0
Regional and Smaller Religious Groups		
Sikhism	23 million	0.34%
Spiritism	14 million	0.14
Bahaism	6 million	0.09
Jainism	4 million	0.07
Shintoism	4 million	0.07
Parsiism (Zoroastrianism)	150,000	0.01
Unaffiliated		
Secular/Nonreligious/ Agnostic/Atheist	850 million	16.9%

Source: www.adherents.com, Sept. 6, 2002.

when they were mocked, teased, or otherwise singled out for their religious beliefs at work.

These religious discrimination issues have now extended into issues surrounding the practices and dictates—and harassment—involving those of primarily Middle Eastern religions. Can a Sikh be required to remove his religiously dictated turban at work? Can a Muslim woman be terminated for wearing a religiously dictated head covering? Must a Muslim employee be allowed to attend midday Friday religious service or have a place provided for religion-required prayer five times a day? All of these issues and those mentioned at the beginning of the chapter have been a part of the post–September 11, 2001, landscape and must be addressed consistent with Title VII and other legal dictates.

duty to reasonably accommodate
The employer's Title VII duty to try to find a way to avoid conflict between workplace policies and an employee's religious practices or beliefs.

Federal and state constitutional guarantees of due process, equal protection, and freedom of religion also provide protection for federal, state, and local government employees. If the employer is a governmental entity, the employer must avoid workplace policies that have the effect of tending to establish or to interfere with the practice of the employee's religion. In determining whether the employer has discriminated on the basis of religion, the court must sometimes first address whether even deciding the issue entangles the government excessively in the practice of religion. Title VII is the only legislation specifically prohibiting religious discrimination in employment, and consideration is given to constitutional issues where necessary.

Exhibit 9.2

Major Religions and Denominations in the United States, 2001

Top Organized Religions

Christianity	76.5%
Judaism	1.3
Islam	0.5
Buddhism	0.5
Hinduism	0.4
Unitarian Universalist	0.3
Wiccan/Pagan/Druid	U.1

Largest Denominational Families

Catholic	24.5%
Baptist	16.3
Methodist	6.8
Lutheran	4.6
Pentecostal	2.1
Presbyterian	2.7
Mormon	1.3
Nondenominational Christians	1.2
Church of Christ	1.2
Episcopal/Anglican	1.7
Assemblies of God	0.5
Congregational/United Church of Christ	0.7
Seventh Day Adventist	0.3

Source: www.adherents.com/rel_usa.htm/families.

undue hardship
A burden imposed on an employer, by accommodating an employee's religious conflict, that would be too onerous for the employer to bear.

Unlike the other categories included in Title VII, there is not an absolute prohibition against discrimination on the basis of religion. Rather, for the first time under Title VII, we see that a category has built into it a **duty to reasonably accommodate** the employee's religious conflict unless to do so would cause the employer **undue hardship**. There is no such reasonable accommodation requirement for race, gender, color, or national origin, but there is under the Americans with Disabilities Act (ADA) as we shall see in that chapter. However, the nature of the accommodation in the ADA is quite different.

To a great extent, religious organizations are exempt from the prohibitions in Title VII. As a general rule, they can discriminate so that, for instance, a Catholic church may legitimately refuse to hire a Baptist minister as its priest. That is, religion is recognized as a basis for a BFOQ reasonably necessary to the normal operation of that particular business or enterprise under section 703(e)(1) of Title VII. If the church has nonsectarian activities, such as running a day care center, bookstore, or athletic club, it may enjoy the same broad type of freedom to discriminate on the basis of religion, since these activities may have religion or propagation of the religion as an integral part of their activity. Employers should be cautioned that the specific facts play an important role in making this determination.

Corporation of the Presiding Bishop of the Church of Jesus Christ of Latter-day Saints v. Amos *483 U.S. 327 (1987)*

Employee terminated from his job as a janitor in a church-owned gym brought suit for religious discrimination under Title VII. The U.S. Supreme Court held that applying the religious exemption to Title VII's prohibition against religious discrimination in employment to secular nonprofit activities of religious organization did not violate the U.S. Constitution's Establishment Clause. That is, it is not a violation of Title VII for a religious employer to discriminate against employees on the basis of religion, even if the employees are not performing strictly religious functions.

White, J.

Section 702 of the Civil Rights Act of 1964 exempts religious organizations from Title VII's prohibition against discrimination in employment on the basis of religion. The question presented is whether applying the exemption to the secular nonprofit activities of religious organizations violates the Establishment Clause of the First Amendment. The District Court held that it does. We reverse.

The Deseret Gymnasium (Gymnasium) in Salt Lake City, Utah, is a nonprofit facility, open to the public, run by religious entities associated with The Church of Jesus Christ of Latter-day Saints (Church), an unincorporated religious association sometimes called the Mormon or LDS Church.

Employee Mayson worked at the Gymnasium for some 16 years as an assistant building engineer and then as building engineer. He was discharged in 1981 because he failed to qualify for a temple recommend, that is, a certificate that he is a member of the Church and eligible to attend its temples. Temple recommends are issued only to individuals who observe the Church's standards in such matters as regular church attendance, tithing, and abstinence from coffee, tea, alcohol, and tobacco.

Mayson brought an action against the Church alleging, among other things, discrimination on the basis of religion in violation of §703 of the Civil Rights Act of 1964. The Church moved to dismiss this claim on the ground that §702 shields them from liability. The employees contended that if construed to allow religious employers to discriminate on religious grounds in hiring for nonreligious jobs, the exemption of §702 violates the Establishment Clause.

It is a significant burden on a religious organization to require it, on pain of substantial liability, to predict which of its activities a secular court will consider religious. The line is hardly a bright one, and an organization might understandably be concerned that a judge would not understand its religious tenets and sense of mission. Fear of potential liability might affect the way an organization carried out what it understood to be its religious mission.

Congress's purpose was to minimize governmental "interfer[ence] with the decision-making process in religions." We agree that this purpose does not violate the Establishment Clause.

The religious groups have been better able to advance their purposes on account of many laws that have passed constitutional muster. A law is not unconstitutional simply because it allows churches to advance religion, which is their very purpose. For a law to have forbidden "effects," it must be fair to say that the government itself has advanced religion through its own activities and influence.

The case before us involves a nonprofit activity instituted over 75 years ago in the hope that "all who assemble here, and who come for the benefit of their health, and for physical blessings, [may] feel that they are in a house dedicated to the Lord." Dedicatory Prayer for the Gymnasium. Mayson was not legally obligated to take the steps necessary to qualify for a temple recommend, and his discharge was not required by statute. We find no merit in his contention that §702 "impermissibly delegates governmental power to religious employees and conveys a message of governmental endorsement of religious discrimination."

§702 is rationally related to the legitimate purpose of alleviating significant governmental interference with the ability of religious organizations to define and carry out their religious missions.

It cannot be seriously contended that §702 impermissibly entangles church and state; the statute effectuates a more complete separation of the two and avoids intrusive inquiry into religious belief. The statute easily passes muster. REVERSED and REMANDED.

Case Questions

1. Are you surprised at the outcome of this case? Why?

2. As a church employer in your religion, what reason would you give for requiring that the building engineer be of the same religion?

3. Are you able to draw a bright line between excessive interference with church business and the government wanting to ensure employment protection for all? Explain.

Section 703(e)(2) of Title VII states that it is not an unlawful employment practice for a school, college, university, or other educational institution to hire or employ employees of a particular religion if the institution is in whole or in substantial part owned, supported, controlled, or managed by a particular religion or by a religious corporation, association, or society or if its curriculum is directed toward the propagation of a particular religion.

Not very long ago it was fairly routine for employers to be nearly as adamant about not hiring those of certain religious faiths, such as Jews, as it was about not hiring people of a certain race, ethnic background, or gender. Universities routinely imposed quotas on the number of Jewish students they would accept. The issue has usually been more covertly handled, but it existed extensively, nonetheless. Title VII was enacted to remedy such practices in the workplace.

The more frequent basis for lawsuits today is that an employee is not hired or is terminated because of some religious practice that comes into conflict with the employer's workplace policies. The employee may wish not to work on a particular day because it is the employee's Sabbath. Or the employee may wish to dress a certain way for religious reasons, or to take certain days off for religious holidays or observances. When it conflicts with the employer's policies and the employee refuses to accede, the employee is terminated and Title VII comes into play.

Frequently the employer discovers religious information through questions on an employment application or during a preemployment interview, either of which relates to notifying a religious figure or taking employee to a particular hospital in the event of on-the-job injury. To eliminate the appearance of illegal consideration of religion in hiring, employers should, instead, ask such questions after hire.

In this chapter, we will learn what is meant by religious discrimination, what the duty to accommodate involves, and how far an employer can go in handling management considerations when religious conflict is at issue.

In the case below, we see one of the growing post-9/11 areas of religious conflict: employers accommodating religious conflicts of those practicing the Muslim faith.

Tyson v. Clarian Health Partners, Inc. *2004 U.S. Dist. LEXIS 13973 (S.D. Ind. 2004)*

Employee, a Muslim, was terminated, in part, for using an empty patient room bathroom to perform her religiously required preprayer ablutions of washing her hands, feet, and forehead, while at work. She also alleged the employer failed to reasonably accommodate her praying up to three times per day at work as required by her religion. The court held that the employer failed to reasonably accommodate the employee's religious conflict as to the ablutions, but not the prayer.

Hamilton, J.

Employee Fatou Tyson, a Muslim woman, worked as a Patient Service Assistant at Methodist Hospital, which is operated by defendant Clarian Health Partners. Clarian fired Tyson while she was still a probationary employee in her first six months of employment. Tyson has sued Clarian under Title VII of the Civil Rights Act of 1964, claiming [among other things] that it failed to reasonably accommodate her religion.

Tyson is a Muslim. Her religion calls for her to pray five times a day. The times at which she was required to pray varied somewhat over the course of her employment, but generally three of her daily prayer sessions coincided with her work shift at the hospital. Before she prayed, Tyson engaged in a religious cleaning ritual known as ablution. Typically, ablution takes two to three minutes and involves cleaning the feet, hands, and forehead.

Title VII defines "religion" to include:

> all aspects of religious observance and practice, as well as belief, unless an employer demonstrates that he is unable to reasonably accommodate to an employee's or prospective employee's religious observance or practice without undue hardship on the conduct of the employer's business.

This definition imposes on employers a duty to provide a reasonable accommodation for an employee's religious beliefs and observances unless the employer can show it is unable to do so without undue hardship.

To establish a *prima facie* case of religious discrimination by failure to accommodate, a plaintiff must show that: (1) she follows a bona fide religious practice that conflicts with an employment requirement; (2) she brought the practice to the employer's attention; and (3) the religious practice was the basis for an adverse employment action. The employer may respond to the *prima facie* case by proving either that it offered a reasonable accommodation that the employee did not accept, or that it was unable to provide a reasonable accommodation without undue hardship. The employer bears the burden of proof on these issues. An employee is not required to propose a specific accommodation.

Two of Tyson's religious practices are at issue: the requirement that she pray several times a day and the requirement that she perform ablution before prayer. As to the prayer issue, the parties agree on the essential facts, which show that Clarian accommodated Tyson's religious practice of prayer. Approximately a week into her employment with Clarian, Tyson told [her supervisor] Rios that she was a Muslim and would need to pray as many as three times during her work shift. Rios said that was "okay," and he showed her the hospital's two non-denominational chapels where she could pray.

Previously, Tyson had learned that other Muslims who worked at Methodist used the basement of the hospital for prayer. Tyson indicated to Rios that she would prefer to pray in the basement. He replied that this was "fine" and that she should just inform him when she went to pray. Although Tyson eventually moved her place of prayer from the basement to a room on Floor 3S, she was able to continue praying throughout the course of her employment with Clarian.

Tyson testified that she was forced to change the location where she prayed because Rios complained about her coming back late from the basement. She seems to suggest that this fact alone establishes Clarian's failure to accommodate her religious practices. There are several flaws in this theory. First, even if Rios complained about Tyson returning late from her prayers in the basement, there is no indication that she was ever disciplined on this ground or that this complaint was the basis for an adverse employment action. None of the reasons given for Tyson's termination are even tangentially related to complaints concerning lateness.

Second, regardless of where Tyson ultimately chose to pray, the undisputed evidence shows that Clarian offered and Tyson accepted a reasonable accommodation that enabled her to pursue her practice of prayer throughout the course of her employment. A reasonable accommodation of an employee's religion is one that "eliminates the conflict between employment requirements and religious practices." "Title VII requires only 'reasonable accommodation,' not satisfaction of an employee's every desire." Clarian provided Tyson with several spaces in the hospital where she could pray and allowed her to do so during work hours while she was on duty. According to the evidence, the only limit Clarian placed on Tyson's religious practice was the requirement that she notify Rios when she went to pray. As a matter of law, Clarian provided reasonable accommodation for prayer.

The same cannot be said, however, concerning Tyson's practice of ablution. At issue is the third element of the *prima facie* test—whether Tyson has come forward with sufficient evidence to suggest that her practice of ablution was the basis for an adverse personnel action.

According to Clarian, Tyson was fired because she accumulated three relatively serious disciplinary violations within the probationary period of her employment. However, one of the violations was the disputed shower incident where Tyson has alleged that she was performing ablution in the shower of an empty patient room. Tyson contends that, to the extent Clarian based its decision to terminate her on this incident, she was in effect discharged for engaging in a religious practice, specifically ablution.

Clarian's position is that regardless of Tyson's activities in the shower, it was a serious breach of hospital policy for her to be using a patient room shower without permission for *any* reason. Viewing the facts in the light most favorable to Tyson, her religious practice of ablution was at least a factor, and more likely the decisive factor, in Clarian's decision to fire her. Tyson has met her burden of establishing a *prima facie* case that Clarian failed to accommodate her religious practices.

Clarian seems to view the Islamic practices of prayer and ablution as one religious practice that it reasonably accommodated by offering to let Tyson pray in the hospital's non-denominational chapels and basement. It is true that Tyson performed ablution in the basement and public restrooms of the hospital, but the record also contains evidence indicating that these venues were ill-suited for her needs. She testified that the sinks in public restrooms were too high for her to be able to wash her feet. The record is sparse regarding the precise practical requirements of ablution. The court does not find as a matter of law that Clarian provided Tyson with a reasonable accommodation for her religious practice of ablution. In this respect, summary judgment on Tyson's accommodation claim is DENIED.

Case Questions

1. Does this situation surprise you? Think about it. How much of your reaction is based on rejection of the situation itself, and how much is based on your discomfort with customs different from what you may be used to?

2. We had a student who confronted this situation during a summer internship when she walked into the bathroom and a Muslim employee was standing on the bathroom counter performing ablutions. What should be done about the discomfort of those not of the same religion?

3. As the employer, explore how you feel about having to accommodate religious practice differences. If your feelings run toward resentment, keep this in mind as you run into religious conflicts at work that must be accommodated.

WHAT IS RELIGION?

Title VII originally provided no guidance as to what it meant by the word *religion*. In the 1972 amendments to Title VII, Congress addressed the issue. In section 701 providing definitions for terms within Title VII, section (j) states: "The term 'religion' includes all aspects of religious observance and practice, as well as belief, unless an employer demonstrates that he is unable to reasonably accommodate an employee's or prospective employee's religious observance or practice without undue hardship on the conduct of the employer's business."

The question frequently arises: "What if I never heard of the employee's religion. Must I still accommodate it?" The answer is based on two considerations: Whether the belief is closely held and whether it takes the place of religion in the employee's life. The latter requirement means that even atheism has been considered a "religion" for Title VII purposes.

The religious belief need not be a belief in a religious deity as we generally know it. However, courts have determined that groups like the Ku Klux Klan are political, not religious organizations, even though their members have closely held beliefs. The employer need not previously know of, or have heard of, or approve of the employee's religion in order to be required to accommodate it for Title VII purposes. Also, the employer cannot question the sincerity of the belief merely because it appears to the employer unorthodox.

In the case below, the Supreme Court held that the employee need not be a member of an organized religion at all. The case involves the Free Exercise Clause of the First Amendment to the U.S. Constitution, made applicable to the states by the 14th Amendment, but the considerations are similar to those of Title VII.

Frazee v. Illinois Dep't. of Employment Security
489 U.S. 829 (1989)

Unemployment compensation was denied to an applicant who refused a temporary retail position because he would not work on Sundays for religious reasons. The Court held that the fact that the applicant did not belong to a particular religious organization did not mean he could not claim his religious freedom had been abridged.

White, J.

Frazee refused a temporary retail position offered him by Kelly Services because the job would have required him to work on Sunday. Frazee told Kelly that, as a Christian, he could not work on "the Lord's day." Frazee applied to the Illinois Department of Employment Security for unemployment benefits claiming there was good cause for his refusal to work on Sunday. His application was denied. Frazee appealed the denial of benefits to the Department's Board of Review, which also denied his claim. The Board of Review stated: "When a refusal of work is based on religious convictions, the refusal must be based upon some tenets or dogma accepted by the individual of some church, sect, or denomination, and such a refusal based solely on an individual's personal belief is personal and noncompelling and does not render the work unsuitable."

To the Illinois court, Frazee's position that he was "a Christian" and as such felt it wrong to work on Sunday was not enough. For a Free Exercise Clause claim to succeed, said the Illinois Appellate Court, "the injunction against Sunday labor must be found in a tenet or dogma of an established religious sect. Frazee does not profess to be a member of any such sect."

The courts below did not question his sincerity, and the State concedes it. Furthermore, the Board of Review characterized Frazee's views as "religious convictions," and the Illinois Appellate Court referred to his refusal to work on Sunday as based on a "personal professed religious belief."

Frazee asserted that he was a Christian, but did not claim to be a member of a particular Christian sect. It is also true that there are assorted Christian denominations that do not profess to be compelled by their religion to refuse Sunday work, but this does not diminish Frazee's protection flowing from the Free Exercise Clause. Undoubtedly, membership in an organized religious denomination, especially one with a specific tenet forbidding members to work on Sunday, would simplify the problem of identifying sincerely held religious beliefs, but we reject the notion that, to claim the protection of the Free Exercise Clause, one must be responding to the commands of a particular religious organization. Here, Frazee's refusal was based on a sincerely held religious belief. Under our cases, he was entitled to invoke First Amendment protection. REVERSED and REMANDED.

Case Questions

1. As the employer here, how could you stay within the law and still have a policy in the best interest of your company?

2. If you were Kelly Services, what would you have done to avoid a conflict with Frazee?

3. As an employer, would you be concerned about how you could tell when an employee had a right to be protected under the law and when an employee was simply trying to get out of work? What would you do about it?

Perhaps the single most-asked question in this area is: "Must I accommodate the employee's religious conflict if it did not exist when the employee was hired?" The answer is yes. The duty attaches to the conflict itself, not to when the conflict arises. The duty to accommodate, however, is only to the extent that it does not cause the employer undue hardship. What constitutes undue hardship will be discussed shortly.

The duty to accommodate only applies to religious *practices,* not religious *beliefs.* An employer is only required to accommodate a religious practice to the extent that it does not present an undue hardship on the employer, but religious beliefs do not have that limitation. That is, no matter how unorthodox, or even outrageous, an employee's religion may seem to the employer, the employer cannot take an adverse employment action against the employee simply because the employee holds that religious belief. In the case below, the employer was called upon to deal with one of the more unorthodox religions.

Peterson v. Wilmur Communications, Inc. *205 F. Supp. 2d 1014* *(E.D. Wisc. 2002)*

Employee, a member of a religious group that believed in white supremacy, was demoted when a newspaper article was published giving his religious views. The court held that though the employee's belief was similar to groups such as the KKK, which were political groups not given protection under Title VII, this was a religion that required Title VII protection and employee could not be demoted simply for having this religious belief.

Adelman, J.

Plaintiff/employee, Christopher Lee Peterson, is a follower of the World Church of the Creator, an organization that preaches a system of beliefs called Creativity, the central tenet of which is white supremacy. Creativity teaches that all people of color are "savage" and intent on "mongrelizing the White Race," that African-Americans are subhuman and should be "shipped back to Africa"; that Jews control the nation and have instigated all wars in this century and should be driven from power, and that the Holocaust never occurred, but if it had occurred, Nazi Germany "would have done the world a tremendous favor."

Creativity considers itself to be a religion, but it does not espouse a belief in a God, afterlife, or any sort of supreme being. "Frequently Asked Questions about CREATIVITY," a publication available on the World Church of the Creator's website, characterizes such beliefs as unsubstantiated "nonsense about angels and devils and gods and . . . silly spook craft" and rejects them in favor of "the Eternal Laws of Nature, about which [Creators say] the White Man does have an impressive

fund of knowledge." The White Man's Bible, one of Creativity's two central texts, offers a vision of a white supremacist utopian world of "beautiful, healthy [white] people," free of disease, pollution, fear and hunger. This world can only be established through the degradation of all non-whites. Thus, Creativity teaches that Creators should live their lives according to the principle that what is good for white people is the ultimate good and what is bad for white people is the ultimate sin. According to The White Man's Bible, the "survival" of white people must be ensured "at all costs." Employee holds these beliefs and, in June 1998, became a "reverend" in the World Church of the Creator.

In 2000, employee was employed by employer Wilmur Communications, Inc. as a Day Room Manager, a position which entailed supervising eight other employees, three of whom were not white. On Sunday, March 19, 2000, an article appeared in the *Milwaukee Journal Sentinel* discussing the World Church of the Creator, interviewing employee, and describing his involvement in the church and beliefs. The article included a photograph of him holding a tee-shirt bearing a picture of Benjamin Smith, who, carrying a copy of

The White Man's Bible, had targeted African-American, Jewish and Asian people in a two-day shooting spree in Indiana and Illinois before shooting himself in the summer of 1999. The caption under the photograph read "Rev. C. Lee Peterson of Milwaukee holds a T-shirt commemorating Benjamin Smith, who killed two people and wounded nine others before shooting himself in a two-day spree last summer."

When employee arrived at work the next day, his supervisor and the president of the company, Dan Murphy, suspended him without pay. Two days later, employee received a letter from Murphy demoting him to the position of "telephone solicitor," a position with lower pay and no supervisory duties. During his six years of employment at Wilmur Communications, employee had been disciplined once for a data entry error but had never been disciplined for anything else.

Title VII makes it unlawful for an employer to "discriminate against any individual with respect to his compensation, terms, conditions, or privileges of employment, because of such individual's . . . religion." The statute defines "religion" to include "all aspects of religious observance and practice, as well as belief." § 2000e(j).

A test has emerged to determine whether beliefs are a religion for purposes of Title VII. Rather than define religion according to its content, the test requires the court should find beliefs to be a religion if they "occupy the same place in the life of the [individual] as an orthodox belief in God holds in the life of one clearly qualified." To satisfy this test, the employee must show that the belief at issue is "'sincerely held' and 'religious' in his [or her] own scheme of things." In evaluating whether a belief meets this test, courts must give "great weight" to the employee's own characterization of his or her beliefs as religious.

To be a religion under this test, a belief system need not have a concept of a God, supreme being, or afterlife. Courts also should not attempt to assess a belief's "truth" or "validity." So long as the belief is sincerely held and is religious in the employee's scheme of things, the belief is religious regardless of whether it is "acceptable, logical, consistent, or comprehensible to others." Once an employee establishes that his or her beliefs are a religion, the employee must offer evidence that his or her religion "played a motivating role" in the adverse employment action at issue. An employee can meet this burden by presenting direct evidence of the employer's discriminatory intent, the method that employee has chosen here, or by the indirect method.

The parties hotly dispute whether Creativity is a religion under Title VII. Thus, as an initial matter, I must determine whether employee's beliefs are "sincerely held" and "religious in his own scheme of things."

Here, the first prong is undisputed. Employee states that he has "a sincere belief" in the teachings of Creativity and employer offers no contrary evidence. Thus, employee meets the first prong of the test.

The second prong is also undisputed. Employee considers his beliefs religious and considers Creativity to be his religion. I must give "great weight" to that belief. In addition, Creativity plays a central role in employee's life. Employee has been a minister in the World Church of the Creator for more than three years.

Employee states that he "work[s] at putting [the teachings of Creativity] into practice every day." Thus, all the evidence conclusively reveals that the teachings of Creativity are "religious" in employee's "own scheme of things." These beliefs occupy for employee a place in his life parallel to that held by a belief in God for believers in more mainstream theistic religions. Thus, Creativity "functions as" religion for employee. Employee has met his initial burden of showing that his beliefs constitute a "religion" for purposes of Title VII.

Employer argues that the World Church of the Creator cannot be a religion under Title VII because it is similar to other white supremacist organizations that have been found to be political organizations and not religions. To be sure, Creativity shares some of the white supremacist beliefs of the KKK and the National Socialist White People's Party. However, the fact that employee's beliefs can be characterized as political does not mean they are not also religious. Thus, employee could share the beliefs of political organizations yet still establish that his beliefs function as religion for him.

Employer also argues that Creativity's beliefs cannot be religious because they are immoral and unethical, and EEOC regulations define religious beliefs as "moral or ethical beliefs as to what is right and wrong." The EEOC regulation means that "religion" under Title VII includes belief systems which espouse notions of morality and ethics and supply a means of distinguishing right from wrong. Creativity has these characteristics. Creativity teaches that followers should live their lives according to what will best foster the advancement of white people and the denigration of all others. This precept, although simplistic and repugnant to the notions of equality that undergird the very non-discrimination statute at issue, is a means for determining right from wrong. Thus, employer's argument must be rejected. Employee has shown that Creativity functions as religion in his life; thus, Creativity is for him a religion regardless of whether it espouses goodness or ill. Employer's argument is again rejected.

Having established that Creativity is for employee a religion, the employee must offer evidence that his religion played a motivating role in the adverse employment action, in this case his demotion. Employee argues that Murphy's letter of demotion provides direct evidence that he was demoted because of his religion. The letter of demotion from Murphy plainly states that employee was being demoted because of his membership in the World Church of the Creator and his white supremacist beliefs.

Thus, employee's beliefs caused employer to demote him and employer is, therefore, liable.

Employee's motion for summary judgment on the issue of liability must be GRANTED. Employer's motion for summary judgment is DENIED.

Case Questions

1. What would you have done if you were the employer who saw this news article? Why?
2. Does the court's decision surprise you? Explain.
3. If you were the employer, what would you do if the employee mistreated non-white employees in the workplace?

RELIGIOUS CONFLICTS

Workplace conflict between employee religious practices at odds with workplace policies is probably the most frequent type of religious discrimination case. That is, it is not so much that the employer dislikes a particular religion and refuses to hire members of that religion. Rather, it is that the employee may engage in some religious practice that is not perceived to be compatible with the workplace. For instance, the employer may have a no-beard policy, but the employee's religion forbids shaving; the employer may have a policy forbidding the wearing of headgear, but the employee's religion requires the wearing of some sort of head cover; the employer may have a policy forbidding the wearing of long hair on males, but the employee's religion forbids the cutting of male hair except in certain limited circumstances; the employer may have a policy that all employees must work on Saturdays, but the employee's religious Sabbath may be on Saturday and followers may be forbidden to work on the Sabbath.

In fact, sometimes the conflict comes not with the employee's religion, but with that of the employer. In Exhibit 9.3 the atheist employee is upset at having to attend mandatory Fundamentalist Christian workplace church services at the manufacturing plant in which he is employed.

As more and more employees come into the workplace who are not of the "traditional" religions with which an employer may be more familiar, and these employees have an expectation of being accommodated in accordance with the law, employers will need to learn to effectively handle the religious differences which arise. The religious conflicts serving as the basis for discrimination claims have become more and more fascinating over the years. Recent conflicts have included such diverse situations as employees with dreadlocks claiming religious discrimination when told to wear a more conventional hairstyle; a woman suing for religious discrimination because her religion does not allow her to wear men's clothing, but her employer banned the wearing of loose-fitting clothing such as skirts and dresses because they might get caught in the metal-fabricating factory's machinery; a Jehovah's Witness who sued Chi-Chi's

Exhibit 9.3   The Lord at Work

Mandatory Prayer Meetings Pit Christian Boss against Atheist Worker

Jake Townley can't understand it—why this atheist from Arizona complained about these weekly devotional meetings, why anyone would. It's *paid* work time. Nobody's asking him to do anything except show up, just like all Townley Manufacturing employees are required to do. The meetings only last half an hour. They're harmless. They've been a Townley tradition for 25 years.

Until this Louis Pelvas came along.

Pelvas, a machinist in the Townley plant in Arizona, objected to the prayer meetings. He filed a complaint of religious discrimination with the Equal Employment Opportunity Commission raising questions about religion in the workplace. Questions Jake Townley thinks the government has no right asking.

Townley is seated on one of about 50 metal folding chairs in the Townley Manufacturing Company workshop in Candler [Florida]. It is 7 A.M. Tuesday, time for the weekly devotional meeting held at this and five other Townley Manufacturing plants in the United States.

The working men file through the door slow and easy, the way people amble into church on Sundays. The preacher sits, Bible in hand, by the welding station. The meeting begins. A man strums a red electric guitar and sings: "I won't walk without Jesus and I won't talk without Jesus . . ."

After the song, one manager speaks briefly about production schedules. Another manager talks just as quickly about safety regulations. Then the preacher rests his large hands on the lectern.

"Good morning," he says. "Praise the Lord."

He points out "Brother and Sister Townley," the company owners, and speaks of their blessed mission of gospel-sharing and toolmaking. He begins conversationally, as if he were addressing the family at the dinner table, but then picks up steam. "God is the one that breathes in us the breath of life, he made us, he created us, he loves us. . . ." The preacher's words rise from his belly, his voice swells. He cups his arms toward the ceiling. Tears moisten his cheeks.

The workers sit motionless, a sea of wooden faces. Twenty minutes pass. The preacher closes with a prayer. The men bow their heads.

Seconds later, the men are at their stations and Townley looks proud: That wasn't so bad, now was it?

The Townleys think they have a right to keep it that way.

But that may not be possible. The EEOC sued Townley Manufacturing, charging its policy of requiring attendance at devotional meetings violates Title VII of the Civil Rights Act of 1964.

Townley says the case will determine whether owners of private, for-profit companies can operate their businesses according to their religious beliefs.

The EEOC says Title VII requires employers to accommodate an employee's religious beliefs and practices unless it presents undue hardship.

All newly hired employees must read and sign an employee handbook, which states that all employees must attend weekly "non-denominational" services; missing them is grounds for termination. Profanity is also prohibited, and the handbook encourages employees to keep track of "how our politicians stand on various issues and to vote for those candidates who support a realistic and stable government policy toward business."

Exhibit 9.3 (continued)

"We run the business according to Christian principles," Townley says. "Everyone may not agree with it, but we feel the Lord gave us the business and it's inseparable from what we do."

Pelvas says his family never went to church. "I was always brought up to the fact that religion and politics should never enter industry."

If he had known the meetings would start in Eloy [Arizona], he says, "I don't believe I would ever have taken the job."

Townley pressured the manager to comply with company policy, and pretty soon one atheist and a roomful of Hispanic Catholics got weekly doses of Bible readings. Pelvas asked to be allowed to work, instead, but was told to show up, even if he didn't pay attention.

Pelvas acquiesced. He listened to music from an ear plug attached to a radio. Sometimes he read. Company business was never discussed, he says. Nor were the services "nondenominational."

"It was strictly born-again services. There were three different preachers. All three of 'em would start off with what a bad person they was—alcohol, woman chaser—and they must have seen the light because they're all different now. I'm 60-some years old, and I haven't seen the light yet."

"I went along with 'em for quite a while until I got disgusted with the whole thing."

The other employees wouldn't object because they were afraid of being fired, Pelvas said. Besides, they didn't mind "listening to some yo-yo blabber away as long as they're gettin' paid for it—I can't blame 'em for that."

Two men, two views: America means freedom of religion; America means freedom *from* religion.

Note: The EEOC decided in favor of Pelvas, 859 F.2d 610 (9th Cir. 1988).
Source: *St. Petersburg Times,* Apr. 24, 1988, p. 1F.

Mexican Restaurant for religious discrimination after being fired for not adhering to Chi-Chi's policy of all employees singing birthday songs to patrons on their birthday because the policy conflicted with her religion, which does not observe personal birthdays, believing they arise out of pagan celebrations; an employee refusing to answer the telephone with the hotel's required "happy holidays" greeting during the Christmas season, claiming her religious beliefs prohibited her from doing so; and a strict vegetarian bus driver who was fired for refusing to hand out coupons to riders for free hamburgers as part of a promotion between the bus company and a hamburger chain. Wow!

The key is to make sure that the basis for the conflict is a religious one and then to try to work out an accommodation. Once the employer is aware of the conflict, the employer must attempt a good-faith accommodation of the religious conflict and the employee must assist in that attempted accommodation. This is why in opening scenario 3, the Sikh need not stop wearing his religiously mandated turban simply because other employees are "uncomfortable." If none can be worked out and the employer has tried everything available that does not present an undue hardship, then the employer has fulfilled his or her Title VII obligation and there is no liability, even if the employee's religious conflict cannot be accommodated. Of course, because of the diversity of religious conflicts that are possible, there is no single set of rules that can be given to handle all religious conflicts.

Scenario

Goldman v. Weinberger   *475 U.S. 503 (1986)*

A member of the military, an Orthodox Jew and ordained rabbi, brought suit against the Secretary of Defense claiming that application of Air Force regulation to prevent him from wearing his yarmulke infringed upon his First Amendment freedom to exercise his religious belief. The Supreme Court held that the First Amendment did not prohibit a regulation that prevented the wearing of a yarmulke by a member of the military while on duty and in uniform.

Rehnquist, J.

Petitioner S. Simcha Goldman contends that the Free Exercise Clause of the First Amendment to the United States Constitution permits him to wear a yarmulke while in uniform, notwithstanding an Air Force regulation mandating uniform dress for Air Force personnel.

The military need not encourage debate or tolerate protest to the extent that such tolerance is required of the civilian state by the First Amendment; to accomplish its mission the military must foster instinctive obedience, unity, commitment, and esprit de corps. The essence of military service "is the subordination of the desires and interests of the individual to the needs of the service."

These aspects of military life do not, of course, render entirely nugatory in the military context the guarantees of the First Amendment. But "within the military community there is simply not the same [individual] autonomy as there is in the larger civilian community." In the context of the present case, when evaluating whether military needs justify a particular restriction on religiously motivated conduct, courts must give great deference to the professional judgment of military authorities concerning the relative importance of a particular military interest. Not only are courts "ill-equipped to determine the impact upon discipline that any particular intrusion upon military authority might have," but the military authorities have been charged by the Executive and Legislative Branches with carrying out our Nation's military policy. "[J]udicial deference . . . is at its apogee when legislative action under the congressional authority to raise and support armies and make rules and regulations for their governance is challenged."

The considered professional judgment of the Air Force is that the traditional outfitting of personnel in standardized uniforms encourages the subordination of personal preferences and identities in favor of the overall group mission. Uniforms encourage a sense of hierarchical unity by tending to eliminate outward individual distinctions except for those of rank. The Air Force considers them as vital during peacetime as during war because its personnel must be ready to provide an effective defense on a moment's notice; the necessary habits of discipline and unity must be developed in advance of trouble. We have acknowledged that "[t]he inescapable demands of military discipline and obedience to orders cannot be taught on battlefields; the habit of immediate compliance with military procedures and orders must be virtually reflex with no time for debate or reflection."

To this end, the Air Force promulgated AFR 35-10, a 190-page document, which states that "Air Force members will wear the Air Force uniform while performing their military duties, except when authorized to wear civilian clothes on duty." The rest of the document describes in minute detail all of the various items of apparel that must be worn as part of the Air Force uniform. It authorizes a few individualized options with respect to certain pieces of jewelry and hairstyle, but even these are subject to severe limitations. In general, authorized headgear may be worn only out of doors. Indoors, "[h]eadgear [may] not be worn . . . except by armed security police in the performance of their duties." A narrow exception to this rule exists for headgear worn during indoor religious ceremonies. In addition, military commanders may in their discretion permit visible religious headgear and other such apparel in designated living quarters and nonvisible items generally.

Goldman contends that the Free Exercise Clause of the First Amendment requires the Air Force to make an exception to its uniform dress requirements for religious apparel unless the accouterments create a "clear danger" of undermining discipline and esprit de corps. He asserts that in general, visible but "unobtrusive" apparel will not create such a danger and must therefore be accommodated. He argues that the Air Force failed to prove that a specific exception for his practice of wearing an unobtrusive yarmulke would threaten discipline. He contends that the Air Force's assertion to the contrary is mere ipse dixit [a bare assertion], with no support from actual experience or a scientific study in the record, and is contradicted by expert testimony that religious exceptions to the policy are in fact desirable and will increase morale by making the Air Force a more humane place.

But whether or not expert witnesses may feel that religious exceptions to AFR 35-10 are desirable is quite beside the point. The desirability of dress regulations in the military is decided by the appropriate military officials, and they are under no constitutional mandate to abandon their considered professional judgment. Quite obviously, to the extent the regulations do not permit the wearing of religious apparel such as a yarmulke, a practice described by Goldman as silent devotion akin to prayer, military life may be more objectionable for him and probably others. But the First Amendment does not require the military to accommodate such practices in the face of its view that they would detract from the uniformity sought by the dress regulations. The Air Force has drawn the line essentially between religious apparel that is visible and that which is not, and we hold that those portions of the regulations challenged here reasonably and evenhandedly regulate dress in the interest of the military's perceived need for uniformity. The First Amendment therefore does not prohibit them from being applied to Goldman even though their effect is to restrict the wearing of the headgear required by his religious beliefs. The judgment of the Court of Appeals is AFFIRMED.

Case Questions

1. Do you agree with the Court's decision? Explain.
2. What do you think of Goldman's argument that wearing the yarmulke will help morale? Does that seem a valid argument for permitting the apparel exception?
3. Can you think of other types of clothing that people may want to wear as part of their religious practice that may present the same situation as here? Do you understand why it should not be permitted? Explain.

We chose to include this case for several reasons. First, it presents a conflict between religious practice (wearing a yarmulke) and work (being a member of the military). It also allows you to see the U.S. Supreme Court's position on matters military and how they interact with Title VII and other protective legislation. As we are discussing Title VII, students frequently ask how the military can have the rules it has, which seem to be at odds with Title VII. Our answer is that the Court tends to view the military as being in a class all its own for most purposes. The military's need for "good order," cohesion, instant and unquestioning obedience, esprit de corps, morale, and other such interests as the Court discussed in the case usually end up with the Court deferring to the military when there are conflicts, for the reasons set forth in the *Goldman* opinion.

We also wanted you to understand that the right to be free of religious discrimination is not absolute. There are limitations to the right where there may be overriding considerations such as the military cohesion in *Goldman* or the undue hardship in Title VII.

Not every conflict involving religion will necessarily be a religious conflict recognized by the law. In *Lumpkin* below, the legitimate nondiscriminatory basis for termination was not deemed a religious conflict at all, even though it involved religion to an extent.

Lumpkin v. Jordan   *49 Cal. App. 4th 1223 (1996)*

A minister who was a member of the San Francisco Human Rights Commission was terminated after making public statements to the press about homosexuality being an abomination, a position at odds with the work of the Commission. The minister sued the city for religious discrimination under

California's civil rights laws (comparable to Title VII). The court held for the city, deciding that the termination was based not on religion but rather on the minister's position being at odds with the position he held on the Commission.

Champlin, J.

This case concerns the alleged unlawful removal of Reverend Lumpkin from the City's Human Rights Commission (the Commission). Mayor Jordan, then Mayor of the City, appointed Reverend Lumpkin to serve as a member of the Commission. At the time of his appointment, Reverend Lumpkin was a Baptist minister who served as Pastor of the Ebenezer Baptist Church. Mayor Jordan and Reverend Lumpkin had known one another for over 15 years and, at the time of the appointment, Mayor Jordan was aware that Reverend Lumpkin was a Baptist minister.

Later the *San Francisco Chronicle* quoted Reverend Lumpkin as saying: "It's sad that people have AIDS and what have you, but it says right there in the scripture that the homosexual lifestyle is an abomination against God. So I have to preach that homosexuality is a sin." These remarks provoked a public controversy surrounding Reverend Lumpkin's membership on the Commission.

After meeting with Reverend Lumpkin, Mayor Jordan issued a press release announcing that he would not remove Reverend Lumpkin from the Commission. In this statement, Mayor Jordan stated that Reverend Lumpkin "has a solid and unambiguous record as a member of the Human Rights Commission. As a commissioner he has protected and advanced gay and lesbian civil rights."

In reaction to Mayor Jordan's announcement, the San Francisco Board of Supervisors adopted a resolution calling for Reverend Lumpkin's resignation or removal from the Commission. The resolution demanded that Mayor Jordan "restore public confidence in the role and mission of the Commission, especially with regards to the ability of the Commission to consider complaints and lead the community toward equality and respect for all lesbian and gay San Franciscans."

Reverend Lumpkin was interviewed during a live broadcast of a television news show, *Mornings on 2*. After the interviewer identified Reverend Lumpkin as a member of the Commission, he asked him if he believed homosexuality to be an "abomination." Reverend Lumpkin replied, "Sure, I believe, I believe everything the Bible sayeth." The following exchange ensued:

"Interviewer: Leviticus also says that a man who sleeps with a man should be put to death. Do you believe that? Reverend Lumpkin: That's what it sayeth. Interviewer: Do you believe that? Reverend Lumpkin: That's—I said that's what the Book sayeth."

Later that day, after learning of the interview, Mayor Jordan asked Reverend Lumpkin to resign from the Commission. In a press release explaining his decision, Mayor Jordan stated: "While religious beliefs are constitutionally protected and cannot be the grounds to remove anyone from elected or appointed public office, the direct or indirect advocacy of violence is not, cannot and will not be condoned by this administration. . . . On the grounds of religious freedom and an unblemished record as a Human Rights Commissioner, I have supported Reverend Lumpkin for holding fundamentalist beliefs which are not my own. We part company when those beliefs imply that attacks against anyone can be justified by the scripture or on any other grounds."

Mayor Jordan met with Reverend Lumpkin, who refused to resign. After this meeting, Mayor Jordan announced his decision to remove Reverend Lumpkin from the Commission.

After his removal from the Commission, Reverend Lumpkin brought suit against Mayor Jordan, alleging that he had been terminated "solely because of his religious beliefs" in violation of the FEHA. The second cause of action alleged that defendants, acting under color of state law, deprived Reverend Lumpkin of the right to exercise his constitutionally protected religious beliefs as guaranteed by 42 United States Code section 1983.

Reverend Lumpkin's removal from the Commission did not violate his freedom of expression. The court reasoned that he was a policymaker with the Jordan administration and "Reverend Lumpkin's televised remarks regarding homosexuality could reasonably have been interpreted by the Mayor as undermining the very policies of the Commission to promote good will toward all people."

Reverend Lumpkin's removal did not violate his rights under the Free Exercise Clause. The court found that Mayor Jordan's interest in preventing disruption of the goals of his administration outweighed Reverend Lumpkin's right to religious expression. The court's opinion points out that "critical to this analysis is the fact that

Reverend Lumpkin was not removed solely for exercising his constitutional rights. He is, and at all times was, free to hold and to profess his religious beliefs; however, when the expression of those beliefs clashed with the goals of the Jordan Administration and undermined the public confidence in the ability of the Commission to effect its goals, the Mayor was justified in removing him."

Finally, the court's order held that Reverend Lumpkin's removal did not violate the Establishment Clause. The court explained that Reverend Lumpkin's removal could not reasonably be construed as sending a message either endorsing or disapproving of religion and that "his removal was based on secular concerns." The court emphasized that Reverend Lumpkin "was not removed because he believed in the inerrancy of the Bible; rather, he was removed because his religious beliefs were at odds with the goals of the Commission and disrupted Mayor Jordan's administration." AFFIRMED.

Case Questions

1. Do you agree that this case was not about religious discrimination? Explain.

2. Can you think of some other way to have handled this matter? Explain.

3. Do you agree with the minister that he could continue to do his job with no problems, despite the feelings he expressed to the media? Explain.

EMPLOYER'S DUTY TO REASONABLY ACCOMMODATE

Again, unlike the other categories under Title VII, the prohibition against religious discrimination is not "absolute." An employer can discriminate against an employee for religious reasons if to do otherwise causes the employer undue hardship. When the employer discovers a religious conflict between the employer's policy and the employee's religion, the employer's first responsibility is to attempt accommodation. If accommodation is not possible, the employer can implement the policy even though it has the effect of discriminating against the employee on the basis of religion.

The duty to reasonably accommodate is not a static concept. Due to the nature of religious conflicts and the fact that they can arise in all types of contexts and in many different ways, there is not one single action an employer must take to show that she or he has reasonably accommodated conflicting religious considerations. It depends on the circumstances and will vary from situation to situation. For example:

- The employer owns a sandwich shop. The employer's policy entitles employees to eat all the restaurant food they wish during their meal break free of charge. Employee's religion does not allow eating meat. Aside from the meat used for sandwiches, the employer has little else, other than sandwich trimmings like lettuce and tomatoes. The employee alleges it is religious discrimination to provide the benefits of free meals that the employee cannot eat for religious reasons while other employees receive full free meals. The duty to accommodate may be as simple as the employer arranging to have peanut butter and jelly, eggs, or a variety of vegetables or pasta available for the employee.

- The employer requires employees to work six days per week. An employee cannot work on Saturdays due to a religious conflict. The accommodation may be that the employee switches days with an employee who does not wish to work on Sundays—a day that the employee with the religious conflict is available to work.

- Employer grocery store has a policy requiring all counter clerks to be clean-shaven, to present the employer's view of a "clean-cut" image to the public. Employee cannot shave for religious reasons. The accommodation may be that the employer switches the employee to a job the employee can perform, which does not require public contact, such as stocking shelves or handling paperwork.

If it can be shown that the employer reasonably accommodated the employee, then the employer is relieved of liability under Title VII. In the *Wilson* case, the court found the accommodation to be reasonable, but also found that the employee's claim of the problematic activity of 'needing' to wear an antiabortion button with a graphic picture of a fetus on it was not based on religious requirements.

Wilson v. U.S. West Communications *58 F.3d 1337 (8th Cir. 1995)*

Employee was terminated when she refused to remove or cover a button she wore on her clothing depicting a graphic anti-abortion message that caused immediate and emotional reactions from co-workers. She brought suit against the employer claiming religious discrimination in violation of Title VII, claiming her religious "living witness" commitment required further accommodation. The court held that the employer reasonably accommodated the employee.

Gibson, J.

Wilson worked for U.S. West for nearly 20 years before U.S. West transferred her to another location as an information specialist, assisting U.S. West engineers in making and keeping records of the location of telephone cables. This facility had no dress code.

In late July 1990, Wilson, a Roman Catholic, made a religious vow that she would wear an anti-abortion button "until there was an end to abortion or until [she] could no longer fight the fight." The button was two inches in diameter and showed a color photograph of an eighteen to twenty-week old fetus. The button also contained the phrases "Stop Abortion," and "They're Forgetting Someone." Wilson chose this particular button because she wanted to be an instrument of God like the Virgin Mary. She believed that the Virgin Mary would have chosen this particular button. She wore the button at all times, unless she was sleeping or bathing. She believed that if she took off the button she would compromise her vow and lose her soul.

Wilson began wearing the button to work in August 1990. Another information specialist asked Wilson not to wear the button to a class she was teaching. Wilson explained her religious vow and refused to stop wearing the button. The button caused disruptions at work. Employees gathered to talk about the button. U.S. West identified Wilson's wearing of the button as a "time robbing" problem. Wilson acknowledged that the button caused a great deal of disruption. A union representative told Wilson's supervisor, Mary Jo Jensen, that some employees threatened to walk off their jobs because of the button. Wilson's co-workers testified that they found the button offensive and disturbing for "very personal reasons," such as infertility problems, miscarriage, and death of a premature infant, unrelated to any stance on abortion or religion.

In early August 1990, Wilson met with her supervisors, Jensen and Gail Klein, five times. Jensen and Klein are also Roman Catholics against abortion. Jensen and Klein told Wilson of co-workers' complaints about the button and an anti-abortion T-shirt Wilson wore which also depicted a fetus. Jensen and Klein told Wilson that her co-workers were uncomfortable and upset and that some were refusing to do their work. Klein noted a 40 percent decline in the productivity of the information specialists since Wilson began wearing the button.

Wilson told her supervisors that she should not be singled out for wearing the button because the company had no dress code. She explained that she "just wanted to do [her] job," and suggested that co-workers offended by the button should be asked not to look at it. Klein and Jensen offered Wilson three options: (1) wear the button only in her work cubicle, leaving the button in the cubicle when she moved around the office; (2) cover the button while at work; or (3) wear a different button with the same message but without the photograph. Wilson responded that she could neither cover nor remove the button because it would break her promise to

God to wear the button and be a "living witness." She suggested that management tell the other information specialists to "sit at their desks and do the job U.S. West was paying them to do."

On August 22, 1990, Wilson met with Klein, Jensen, and the union's chief steward. During the meeting, Klein again told Wilson that she could either wear the button only in her cubicle or cover the button. Klein explained that, if Wilson continued to wear the button to work, she would be sent home until she could come to work wearing proper attire.

In an August 27, 1990 letter, Klein reiterated Wilson's three options. He added that Wilson could use accrued personal and vacation time instead of reporting to work. Wilson filed suit but later dismissed the action when U.S. West agreed to allow her to return to work and wear the button pending an investigation by the Nebraska Equal Opportunity Commission.

Wilson returned to work on September 18, 1990, and disruptions resumed. Information specialists refused to go to group meetings with Wilson present. The employees complained that the button made them uneasy. Two employees filed grievances based on Wilson's button. Employees accused Jensen of harassment for not resolving the button issue to their satisfaction. Eventually, U.S. West told Wilson not to report to work wearing anything depicting a fetus, including the button or the T-shirt. U.S. West told Wilson again that she could cover or replace the button or wear it only in her cubicle. U.S. West sent Wilson home when she returned to work wearing the button and fired her for missing work unexcused for three consecutive days. Wilson sued U.S. West, claiming that her firing constituted religious discrimination.

The court considered the three offered accommodations and concluded that requiring Wilson to leave the button in her cubicle or to replace the button were not accommodations of Wilson's sincerely held religious beliefs because: (1) removing the button at work violated Wilson's vow to wear the button at all times; and (2) replacing the button prohibited Wilson from wearing the particular button encompassed by her vow. However, the court concluded that requiring Wilson to cover the button while at work was a reasonable accommodation. The court based this determination on its factual finding that Wilson's vow did not require her to be a living witness. The court reasoned that covering the button while at work complied with Wilson's vow but also reduced office turmoil. The court also concluded that, even if Wilson's vow required Catholic

Voice, she said nothing about being a living witness. Klein testified that he never heard Wilson use the word *witness* in explaining her vow, but rather, that he understood Wilson's vow was to "wear the button until abortions were ended." Accordingly, the district court's finding is supported by the evidence and is not clearly erroneous.

We next consider Wilson's argument that the district court erred as a matter of law in concluding that U.S. West offered to reasonably accommodate Wilson's religious views. Wilson argues that her religious beliefs did not require her or any other employee to miss or rearrange work schedules, as typically causes a reasonable accommodation dispute. She argues that it was her co-workers' response to her beliefs that caused the workplace disruption, not her wearing the button. Wilson contends that U.S. West should have focused its attention on her co-workers, not her. Wilson's brief states: "Quite frankly, . . . Klein and Jensen should have simply instructed the troublesome co-workers to ignore the button and get back to work."

The district court, however, succinctly answered Wilson's argument: Klein was unable to persuade the co-workers to ignore the button. Although Wilson's religious beliefs did not create scheduling conflicts or violate dress code or safety rules, Wilson's position would require U.S. West to allow Wilson to impose her beliefs as she chooses. Wilson concedes the button caused substantial disruption at work. To simply instruct Wilson's co-workers that they must accept Wilson's insistence on wearing a particular depiction of a fetus as part of her religious beliefs is antithetical to the concept of reasonable accommodation.

Moreover, U.S. West did not oppose Wilson's religious beliefs, but rather, was concerned with the photograph. The record demonstrates that U.S. West did not object to various other religious articles that Wilson had in her work cubicle or to another employee's anti-abortion button. It was the color photograph of the fetus that offended Wilson's co-workers, many of whom were reminded of circumstances unrelated to abortion. Indeed, many employees who opposed Wilson's button shared Wilson's religion and view on abortion.

Wilson also argues that requiring her to cover the button is not a reasonable accommodation. She argues that the accommodation offered required her to abandon her religious beliefs, and therefore, that the accommodation was no accommodation at all. Having affirmed the finding that Wilson's religious vow did not require her to be a living witness, we summarily reject this argument.

U.S. West's proposal allowed Wilson to comply with her vow to wear the button and respected the desire of co-workers not to look at the button. Hence, the district court did not err in holding that U.S. West reasonably accommodated Wilson's religious beliefs.

Finally, Wilson argues that the district court erred in concluding that her suggested proposals would be an undue hardship for U.S. West.

The Supreme Court held that an employer is not required to select the employee's proposal of reasonable accommodation and that any reasonable accommodation by the employer is sufficient to comply with the statute. "The employer violates the statute unless it 'demonstrates that [it] is unable to reasonably accommodate . . . an employee's . . . religious observance or practice without undue hardship on the conduct of the employer's business.'" When the employer reasonably accommodates the employee's religious beliefs, the statutory inquiry ends. The employer need not show that the employee's proposed accommodations would cause an undue hardship. Undue hardship is at issue "only where the employer claims that it is unable to offer any reasonable accommodation without such hardship."

Because we hold that U.S. West offered Wilson a reasonable accommodation, our inquiry ends, and we need not consider Wilson's argument that her suggested accommodations would not cause undue hardship.

We recognize that this case typifies workplace conflicts which result when employees hold strong views about emotionally charged issues. We reiterate that Title VII does not require an employer to allow an employee to impose his religious views on others. The employer is only required to reasonably accommodate an employee's religious views. AFFIRMED.

Case Questions

1. What do you think of the coworker reaction to Wilson's button? Does it seem reasonable? Explain.

2. What do you think of Wilson's response to her supervisors that those who did not like the button should simply be told not to look at it? Does this seem to be a reasonable response for the employer to make? Explain.

3. If you were the employer here, what would you have done about Wilson?

Scenario   Scenario

If an accommodation cannot be found, as *Williams,* below, demonstrates, the employer's duty is discharged. This case is the basis for opening scenarios 1 and 2. The important factor is to attempt an accommodation rather than simply dismissing the conflict without trying.

Williams v. Southern Union Gas Company *529 F.2d 483* *(10th Cir. 1976)*

Employee was terminated for not working on Saturday. His reason for not doing so was that it was against his religion to work on his sabbath. The court found that accommodating this religious conflict would cause the employer an undue hardship; therefore the termination did not violate Title VII.

McWilliams, J.

When Williams went to work for Southern Union he was informed that it was a company policy that all employees should be available for work seven days a week 24 hours per day inasmuch as it was a public utility and was obligated to provide continuous and uninterrupted natural gas service to the general public. It was also Southern Union's policy, however, to schedule its em-

ployees for only five days of work each week, eight hours per day. Williams in 1962 did not belong to any church and hence was under no prohibition, religious or otherwise, from working any day in the week.

During the fall of 1969 Williams became a member of the Worldwide Church of God. He informed his supervisor of his conversion and advised him that he would no longer be able to work between Friday at sundown and Saturday at sundown. The supervisor,

Al Dean, explained that it would be difficult to promise that Williams would never be called on to work on a Saturday, but that he would do what he could. Coincidentally, or otherwise, at the time of his conversion Williams' regular work week was from Sunday through Thursday, with both Friday and Saturday off. It would appear that for obvious reasons most all employees desired to have Saturday off. At his supervisor's suggestion Williams checked back with his minister and was informed that he could work on Saturdays if there were an emergency, but that since this was a matter between Williams and his God, he (Williams), and not his employer, would have to make the decision as to whether a true emergency existed.

From the date of his conversion in the fall of 1969 until October 3, 1970, Williams was never asked to work on Saturday. During the fall of 1970 Williams was assigned to work on the Dogie Canyon project in northwest New Mexico, a rather isolated location. This was a new pipeline about 25 miles long that was to expand the capacity of the pipeline system which took natural gas from the production area of the San Juan Basin and supplied the Los Alamos–Santa Fe area with natural gas. This project was running somewhat behind schedule and Southern Union, at least, was of the view that the pipeline had to be completed, purged of air, and brought up to pressure by Saturday, October 3, 1970.

On Wednesday, September 30, 1970, Williams went to Dean and told him that the next day, Thursday, was a special religious holiday in his church and that he would have to have the day off. Dean agreed that Williams could take Thursday off, but explained that the pipeline would have to be pressured up by Saturday, and that if the work were not completed by Friday night Williams would have to work Saturday. Williams testified that he made no protest at this time about the possibility of Saturday work, as he thought the project might very possibly be completed by Friday, and any confrontation would thereby be avoided.

Williams took Thursday off. Unfortunately for Williams, the job was not completed on Friday, and Friday evening Williams called Dean at the latter's home and told Dean that he would not report for work on Saturday morning, as he had been directed. Dean's response was that if Williams didn't show up he would be fired. Dean himself was scheduled to go on vacation starting Saturday. When Williams didn't show up for work on Saturday, Dean delayed the start of his vacation and completed the work himself. There was no one

else with the expertise who could be called. It was in this factual setting that Dean fired Williams.

42 U.S.C. 2000e-2(a) provides that it is an unlawful employment practice for an employer to discriminate against an employee because of his religion. Under a regulation promulgated in 1966 an employer was allowed to establish a "normal work week" which would be generally applicable to all employees even though such would not operate uniformly in its effect upon the religious observances of all employees. In 1967 the following regulation which now appears as 29 C.F.R. 1605.1 (1975) was promulgated:

> Observation of the Sabbath and other religious holidays.
>
> (a) Several complaints filed with the Commission have raised the question whether it is discrimination on account of religion to discharge or refuse to hire employees who regularly observe Friday evening and Saturday, or some other day of the week, as the Sabbath or who observe certain special religious holidays during the year and, as a consequence, do not work on such days.
>
> (b) The Commission believes that the duty not to discriminate on religious grounds, required by section 703(a)(1) of the Civil Rights Act of 1964, includes an obligation on the part of the employer to make reasonable accommodations to the religious needs of employees and prospective employees where such accommodations can be made without undue hardship on the conduct of the employer's business. Such undue hardship, for example, may exist where the employee's needed work cannot be performed by another employee of substantially similar qualifications during the period of absence of the Sabbath observer.
>
> (c) Because of the particularly sensitive nature of discharging or refusing to hire an employee or applicant on account of his religious beliefs, the employer has the burden of proving that an undue hardship renders the required accommodations to the religious needs of the employee unreasonable.

The foregoing regulation was given legislative approval when Congress amended the definition of religion, as that term is read in the Act, to read as follows:

> The term "religion" includes all aspects of religious observance and practice, as well as belief, unless an employer demonstrates that he is unable to reasonably accommodate to an employee's or prospective employee's religious observance or practice without undue hardship on the conduct of the employer's business. 42 U.S.C. 2000e(j).

Under the applicable statute and regulations the question before the trial court was whether Southern Union demonstrated that it was unable to reasonably accommodate to Williams' religious practice without undue hardship in the conduct of its business. The key phrases are "reasonably accommodate" and "undue hardship." The trial court's findings are not clearly erroneous and we affirm.

Most of the civil rights cases concerning those who celebrate the Sabbath on Saturday involve situations where the employer attempts to compel the employee to work on Saturdays as a part of his normal work week. Such is not true in the instant case. On the contrary Williams' normal work week was Sunday through Thursday. Furthermore, Southern Union did not ask Williams to perform work on a Saturday until approximately one year after his conversion. Williams' boss earlier explained that he could not promise Williams that he would never be asked to work on Saturday, and that he might well be asked to work in an emergency situation. The very nature of Southern Union's business required that service be available to the public 24 hours a day, 7 days per week. Someone was going to have to work on Saturdays, even though all employees understandably preferred Saturday off. Indeed, Williams himself recognized that his religion did not preclude him from working on Saturdays in the event of a special emergency. However, Williams insisted that he, rather than his employer, had the exclusive right to determine just what constituted an emergency.

Getting down to the events which immediately preceded Williams' discharge, Southern Union was engaged in certain pipeline construction which it felt had to be completed by Saturday, October 3, 1970. The record is such as to permit the inference that completion of the pipeline by that date was of critical importance. And such fact we deem to be of great significance and distinguishes the instant case from other cases cited to us by counsel, i.e., we are not concerned here with the employer's effort to compel Williams to work on a Saturday as a part of his normal work week; rather this is a situation where the employer was faced with an emergency situation in an isolated work area where there was no reserve of manpower who were qualified to complete the project and could be called in on a moment's notice. Williams, apparently without giving notice, advised his boss on Wednesday that he was taking off Thursday, a regular work day, for a special religious holiday. Whether this absence in anywise contributed to the failure to complete the project by Friday is not disclosed by the record. In any event, the project was not completed by Friday and it was only in this circumstance that Southern Union for the first time asked Williams to work on Saturday. When Williams refused, his boss had to delay his long scheduled vacation in which he was to meet someone from out of town at a remote location for an elk hunt, and he completed the job himself.

The phrases "reasonably accommodate" and "undue hardship" are relative terms and cannot be given any hard and fast meaning. In a sense the case boils down to a determination as to whether Southern Union acted reasonably under all the circumstances. On the one hand it had a duty to at least try to accommodate Williams' religious practices. On the other hand it also had a duty not only to serve the consuming public on a continuous and uninterrupted basis but also to adhere to employment practices that were fair to its other employees. In our view whether Southern Union in the instant case acted in a reasonable manner is a matter upon which reasonable minds might conceivably differ. Such fact, however, does not permit us to substitute our judgment for that of the trial court. It was the trial judge who heard the testimony and saw the various witnesses. He is the one who draws the inferences and finds the facts. He found that to have accommodated William's refusal to work on Saturday, October 3, 1970, would have placed an undue hardship on the Southern Gas and the conduct of its business, and as a result, Southern was justified in discharging Williams because of his refusal to work. In such circumstances we should not disturb his determination of the matter. Judgment AFFIRMED.

Case Questions

1. Do you agree with the court that the employer's duty was discharged in this case?

2. If you had been the employer, what would you have done when Williams came to you after his conversion, and later (if you decided to keep him on) when he requested the Thursday off?

3. As an employer, what questions would you ask yourself before deciding on a policy to handle religious conflicts?

Even where an employee's activity is religiously based, it need not be accommodated if doing so presents real problems for the employer. In the very interesting *Chalmers* case, below, the court refused to find a basis for accommodation, even though the employee claimed she was doing what her religion dictated she do.

Chalmers v. Tulon Company of Richmond *101 F.3d 1012* *(4th Cir. 1996)*

The supervisory employee sued for religious discrimination and a failure to accommodate after being terminated for sending employees letters at home about their personal and religious lives. One employee received the letter while ill at home on leave after delivering a baby out of wedlock, and the other employee's wife opened the letter and became distraught because she thought the references in the letter meant her husband was having an affair. The court held that there was no duty to accommodate the terminated employee's religious practice of sending such letters.

Motz, J.

Chalmers, a supervisor, has been a Baptist all of her life, and in June 1984 became an evangelical Christian. At that time, she accepted Christ as her personal savior and determined to go forth and do work for him. As an evangelical Christian, Chalmers believes she should share the gospel and looks for opportunities to do so.

Chalmers felt that her supervisor, LaMantia, respected her, generally refraining from using profanity around her, while around other employees who did not care, "he would say whatever he wanted to say." She felt that she and LaMantia had a "personal relationship" and that she could talk to him. Chalmers stated that "in the past we have talked about God." Chalmers further testified that "starting off" she and LaMantia had discussed religion about "everytime he came to the service center . . . maybe every three months" but "then, towards the end maybe not as frequently." LaMantia never discouraged these conversations, expressed discomfort with them, or indicated that they were improper. In one of these conversations, LaMantia told Chalmers that three people had approached him about accepting Christ.

Two or three years after this conversation, Chalmers "knew it was time for [LaMantia] to accept God." She believed LaMantia had told customers information about the turnaround time for a job when he knew that information was not true. Chalmers testified that she was "led by the Lord" to write LaMantia and tell him "there were things he needed to get right with God, and that was one thing that . . . he needed to get right with him."

Accordingly, on Labor Day, September 6, 1993, Chalmers mailed the following letter to LaMantia at his home:

> Dear Rich:
>
> The reason I'm writing you is because the Lord wanted me to share somethings [sic] with you. After reading this letter you do not have to give me a call, but talk to God about everything.
>
> One thing the Lord wants you to do is get your life right with him. The Bible says in Romans 10:9vs that if you confess with your mouth the Lord Jesus and believe in your heart that God hath raised him from the dead, thou shalt be saved. vs 10—For with the heart man believeth unto righteousness, and with the mouth confession is made unto salvation. The two verse are [sic] saying for you to get right with God now.
>
> The last thing is, you are doing somethings [sic] in your life that God is not please [sic] with and He wants you to stop. All you have to do is go to God and ask for forgiveness before it's too late.
>
> I wrote this letter at home so if you have a problem with it you can't relate it to work.
>
> I have to answer to God just like you do, so that's why I wrote you this letter. Please take heed before it's too late.
>
> In his name,
> Charita Chalmers

On September 10, 1993 when Chalmers' letter arrived at LaMantia's home, he was out of town on Tulon business and his wife opened and read the letter in his absence. Mrs. LaMantia became distraught, interpreting the references to her husband's improper conduct as indicating that he was committing adultery. In tears, she called Chalmers and asked her if LaMantia was having an affair with someone in the New Hampshire area where LaMantia supervised another Tulon facility. Mrs. LaMantia explained that three years before she and LaMantia had separated because of his infidelity. Chalmers told Mrs. LaMantia that she did not know about any affair because she was in the Richmond area. When Mrs. LaMantia asked her what she had meant by writing that there was something in LaMantia's life that "he needed to get right with God," Chalmers explained about the turnaround time problem. Mrs. LaMantia responded that she would take the letter and rip it up so LaMantia could not read it. Chalmers answered, "Please don't do that, the Lord led me to send this to Rich, so let him read it." The telephone conversation then ended.

Mrs. LaMantia promptly telephoned her husband, interrupting a Tulon business presentation, to accuse him of infidelity. LaMantia, in turn, called the Richmond office and asked to speak with Chalmers; she was in back and by the time she reached the telephone, LaMantia had hung up. Chalmers then telephoned the LaMantias' home and, when she failed to reach anyone, left a message on the answering machine that she was sorry "if the letter offended" LaMantia or his wife and that she "did not mean to offend him or make him upset about the letter."

LaMantia also telephoned Craig A. Faber, Vice President of Administration at Tulon. LaMantia told Faber that the letter had caused him personal anguish and placed a serious strain on his marriage. LaMantia informed Faber that he felt he could no longer work with Chalmers. LaMantia recommended that Tulon management terminate Chalmers' employment.

While investigating LaMantia's complaint, Faber discovered that Chalmers had sent a second letter, on the same day as she sent the letter to LaMantia, to another Tulon employee. That employee, Brenda Combs, worked as a repoint operator in the Richmond office and Chalmers was her direct supervisor. Chalmers knew that Combs was convalescing at her home, suffering from an undiagnosed illness after giving birth out of wedlock. Chalmers sent Combs the following letter:

Brenda,
You probably do not want to hear this at this time, but you need the Lord Jesus in your life right now.
One thing about God, He doesn't like when people commit adultery. You know what you did is

wrong, so now you need to go to God and ask for forgiveness.
Let me explain something about God. He's a God of Love and a God of Wrath. When people sin against Him, He will allow things to happen to them or their family until they open their eyes and except [sic] Him. God can put a sickness on you that no doctor could ever find out what it is. I'm not saying this is what happened to you, all I'm saying is get right with God right now. Romans 10:9;10vs says that is [sic] you confess with your mouth the Lord Jesus and believe in your heart that God has raised him from the dead thou shalt be saved. For with the heart man believeth unto righteousness; and with the mouth confession is made unto salvation. All I'm saying is you need to invite God into your heart and live a life for Him and things in your life will get better.
That's not saying you are not going to have problems but it's saying you have someone to go to.
Please take this letter in love and be obedient to God.
In his name,
Charita Chalmers

Upon receiving the letter Combs wept. Faber discussed the letter with Combs who told him that she had been "crushed by the tone of the letter." Combs believed that Chalmers implied that "an immoral lifestyle" had caused her illness and found Chalmers' letter "cruel." Combs, in a later, unsworn statement, asserted that although the letter "upset her" it did not "offend" her or "damage her working relationship" with Chalmers.

Faber consulted with other members of upper management and concluded that the letters caused a negative impact on working relationships, disrupted the workplace, and inappropriately invaded employee privacy. On behalf of Tulon, Faber then sent Chalmers a memorandum, informing her that she was terminated from her position. The memorandum stated in relevant part:

We have decided to terminate your employment with Tulon Co. effective today, September 21, 1993. Our decision is based on a serious error in judgment you made in sending letters to LaMantia and Combs, which criticized their personal lives and beliefs. The letters offended them, invaded their privacy, and damaged your work relationships, making it too difficult for you to continue to work here.
We expect all of our employees to show good judgment, especially those in supervisory positions,

such as yours. We would hope you can learn from this experience and avoid similar mistakes in the future.

As a result of the preceding events, Chalmers filed suit, alleging that Tulon discriminated against her based on her religion, in violation of Title VII. She contended that her letter writing constituted protected religious activity that Tulon, by law, should have accommodated with a lesser punishment than discharge.

In a religious accommodation case, an employee can establish a claim even though she cannot show that other (unprotected) employees were treated more favorably or cannot rebut an employer's legitimate, nondiscriminatory reason for her discharge. This is because an employer must, to an extent, actively attempt to accommodate an employee's religious expression or conduct even if, absent the religious motivation, the employee's conduct would supply a legitimate ground for discharge.

Tulon's proffered reasons for discharging Chalmers—because her letters, which criticized her fellow employees' personal lives and beliefs, invaded the employees' privacy, offended them and damaged her working relationships—are legitimate and nondiscriminatory.

To establish a prima facie religious accommodation claim, a plaintiff must establish that: "(1) he or she has a bona fide religious belief that conflicts with an employment requirement; (2) he or she informed the employer of this belief; (3) he or she was disciplined for failure to comply with the conflicting employment requirement."

Chalmers has alleged that she holds bona fide religious beliefs that caused her to write the letters. Tulon offers no evidence to the contrary. The parties agree that Tulon fired Chalmers because she wrote the letters. Accordingly, Chalmers has satisfied the first and third elements of the prima facie test. However, in other equally important respects, Chalmers' accommodation claim fails.

Chalmers cannot satisfy the second element of the prima facie test. She has forecast no evidence that she notified Tulon that her religious beliefs required her to send personal, disturbing letters to her co-workers. Therefore she did not allow the company any sort of opportunity to attempt reasonable accommodation of her beliefs.

Chalmers concedes that she did not expressly notify Tulon that her religion required her to write letters like those at issue here to her co-workers, or request that Tulon accommodate her conduct. Nonetheless, for several reasons, she contends that such notice was unnecessary in this case.

Initially, Chalmers asserts that Tulon never explicitly informed her of a company policy against writing religious letters to fellow employees at their homes and so she had "no reason to request an accommodation." However, companies cannot be expected to notify employees explicitly of all types of conduct that might annoy co-workers, damage working relationships, and thereby provide grounds for discharge. Chalmers implicitly acknowledged in the letters themselves that they might distress her co-workers. Moreover, she conceded that, as a supervisor, she had a responsibility to "promote harmony in the workplace."

Although a rule justifying discharge of an employee because she has disturbed co-workers requires careful application in the religious discrimination context (many religious practices might be perceived as "disturbing" to others), Chalmers, particularly as a supervisor, is expected to know that sending personal, distressing letters to co-workers' homes, criticizing them for assertedly ungodly, shameful conduct, would violate employment policy. Accordingly, the failure of the company to expressly forbid supervisors from disturbing other employees in this way provides Chalmers with no basis for failing to notify Tulon that her religious beliefs require her to write such letters.

Alternatively, Chalmers contends that the notoriety of her religious beliefs within the company put it on notice of her need to send these letters. In her view, Chalmers satisfied the notice requirement because Tulon required "only enough information about an employee's religious needs to permit the employer to understand the existence of a conflict between the employee's religious practices and the employer's job requirements."

Knowledge that an employee has strong religious beliefs does not place an employer on notice that she might engage in any religious activity, no matter how unusual. Chalmers concedes that she did not know of any other employee who had ever written distressing or judgmental letters to co-workers before, and that nothing her co-workers had said or done indicated that such letters were acceptable. Accordingly, any knowledge Tulon may have possessed regarding Chalmers' beliefs could not reasonably have put it on notice that she would write and send accusatory letters to co-workers' homes.

Chalmers appears to contend that because Tulon was necessarily aware of the religious nature of the letters after her co-workers received them and before her discharge, Tulon should have attempted to accommodate her by giving her a sanction less than a discharge, such as a warning. This raises a false issue. There is nothing in Title VII that requires employers to give lesser punishments to employees who claim, after they violate company rules (or at the same time), that their religion caused them to transgress the rules.

Part of the reason for the advance notice requirement is to allow the company to avoid or limit any "injury" an employee's religious conduct may cause. Additionally, the refusal even to attempt to accommodate an employee's religious requests, prior to the employee's violation of employment rules and sanction, provides some indication, however slight, of improper motive on the employer's part. The proper issue, therefore, is whether Chalmers made Tulon aware, prior to her letter writing, that her religious beliefs would cause her to send the letters. Since it is clear that she did not, her claims fail.

In sum, Chalmers has not pointed to any evidence that she gave Tulon—either directly or indirectly—advance notice of her need for accommodation. For this reason, Chalmers has failed to establish a prima facie case of discrimination under the religious accommodation theory.

If we had concluded that Chalmers had established a prima facie case, Chalmers' religious accommodation claim would nonetheless fail. This is so because Chalmers' conduct is not the type that an employer can possibly accommodate, even with notice.

Chalmers concedes in the letters themselves that she knew the letters to her co-workers, accusing them of immoral conduct (in the letter to Combs, suggesting that Combs' immoral conduct caused her illness), might cause them distress. Even if Chalmers had notified Tulon expressly that her religious beliefs required her to write such letters, i.e. that she was "led by the Lord" to write them, Tulon was without power under any circumstances to accommodate Chalmers' need.

Typically, religious accommodation suits involve religious conduct, such as observing the Sabbath, wearing religious garb, etc., that result in indirect and minimal burdens, if any, on other employees. An employer can often accommodate such needs without inconveniencing or unduly burdening other employees.

In a case like the one at hand, however, where an employee contends that she has a religious need to impose personally and directly on fellow employees, invading their privacy and criticizing their personal lives, the employer is placed between a rock and a hard place. If Tulon had the power to authorize Chalmers to write such letters, and if Tulon had granted Chalmers' request to write the letters, the company would subject itself to possible suits from Combs and LaMantia claiming that Chalmers' conduct violated their religious freedoms or constituted religious harassment. Chalmers' supervisory position at the Richmond office heightens the possibility that Tulon (through Chalmers) would appear to be imposing religious beliefs on employees.

Thus, even if Chalmers had notified Tulon that her religion required her to send the letters at issue here to her co-workers, Tulon would have been unable to accommodate that conduct.

We do not in any way question the sincerity of Chalmers' religious beliefs or practices. However, it is undisputed that Chalmers failed to notify Tulon that her religious beliefs led her to send personal, disturbing letters to her fellow employees accusing them of immorality. It is also undisputed that the effect of a letter on one of the recipients, LaMantia's wife, whether intended or not, caused a co-worker, LaMantia, great stress and caused him to complain that he could no longer work with Chalmers. Finally, it is undisputed that another employee, Combs, told a company officer that Chalmers' letter upset her (although she later claimed that her working relationship with Chalmers was unaffected). Under these facts, Chalmers cannot establish a religious accommodation claim. Accordingly, the district court's order granting summary judgment to Tulon is AFFIRMED.

Case Questions

1. Is there any way the employer could have avoided this situation? Explain.

2. If the employee had initially told the employer of her plan to write the letters and the employer had told her not to send them, would the outcome be any different if she had done so anyway?

3. What would you have done if your employee's wife called as Ms. LaMantia did?

EMPLOYEE'S DUTY TO COOPERATE IN ACCOMMODATION

The U.S. Supreme Court has held that, in attempting to accommodate the employee, all that is required is that the employer make any reasonable accommodation and this need not necessarily be the most reasonable accommodation. The employee must also be reasonable in considering accommodation alternatives. In *Vargas,* which follows, the employer attempted to accommodate the employee's conflict and the employee refused to compromise. The employer's only alternative may involve demoting the employee. This is not forbidden if all other alternatives present the employer with an undue hardship. The EEOC and the courts will look to the following factors in determining whether the employer has successfully borne the burden of reasonably accommodating the employee's religious conflict:

- Whether the employer made an attempt at accommodation.
- The size of the employer's workforce.
- The type of job in which the conflict is present.
- The employer's checking with other employees to see if anyone was willing to assist in the accommodation.
- The cost of accommodation.
- The administrative aspects of accommodation.

Each factor will be considered and weighed as appropriate for the circumstances. If on balance the employer has considered the factors appropriate for the employer's particular circumstances and accommodation was not possible, there is usually no liability for religious discrimination.

Vargas v. Sears, Roebuck & Company   *1998 U.S. Dist. LEXIS 21148 (E.D. Mich. 1998)*

A Mexican-American who practiced traditional Native American religion, which considers the wearing of long hair on men to be sacred, sued his employer when he was terminated for refusing to cut his hair or to wear it tucked into his shirt as an accommodation. The court held that the employee was required to try to help in making the accommodation, and the employee had not done so. The court therefore granted the employer's motion to dismiss the employee's complaint.

Rosen, J.

Vargas was employed as a salesperson in Ann Arbor, Michigan's Briarwood Mall Sears store from October 1994 until February 1996. He worked on the selling floor in the Sears "Brand Central" home electronics department. When he was hired in the fall of 1994, Vargas was given a copy of the "Sears Associate Handbook," which provides, in pertinent part that all associates were to be neatly dressed in professional, businesslike clothing and for men, beards and contemporary hair styles are acceptable, but should be maintained in a neat, trimmed manner. When Vargas was hired by Sears in the fall of 1994, his hair was collar-length, and therefore, according to Sears, in compliance with store policy.

Vargas' supervisor Kevin Jones confronted Vargas about his hair in late summer 1995 when Vargas had his hair in a short pony tail. Jones did not discipline or direct Vargas to do anything about his hair, but rather, merely advised him that Walter Crockrel, the General Store Manager, did not approve of male salespersons wearing their hair in ponytails. Vargas did not tell Mr. Jones that wearing his hair long or in a ponytail was part of his Native American religion.

Vargas testified in his deposition that he adheres to the practices and customs of Native American religion, that he participates in Native American religious ceremonies, including conducting sweat lodge ceremonies. He further testified that in Native American religious practice, many of the beliefs and practices are "personal," and although long hair is not a requirement of his religion, he believes that the practice of Native American religion is dependent upon "your own spiritual development and the sacrifices you want to make for that." Shortly after Jones had this conversation with Vargas, Jones was replaced by Zerry Rue as Vargas' supervisor.

Zerry Rue addressed Vargas' hair with him in October 1995 upon the direction of Walter Crockrel. On October 25, 1995, Rue gave Vargas a memo stating that his ponytail and hair length were not in compliance with Sears personal appearance policies, and that he had until November 1st to bring himself within compliance with the policies. It was in connection with Rue's memo that Sears was informed that Vargas objected to Sears' hair length policy on religious grounds. On October 30, 1995, Vargas' attorney, Jane Bassett, wrote Crockrel that

> [Vargas] is of Mexican-American descent and he practices traditional Native American religion. Traditionally, growing the hair long has sacred significance in Native American religion. A policy which unequivocally prohibits male employees to have long hair discriminates against men who practice traditional Native American religion.

Upon becoming aware that Vargas' religious beliefs precluded him from cutting his hair, Mr. Crockrel, Mr. Rue and Susan Wisniewski, Sears' Human Resources Director, met with Vargas in the first week of November 1995 in an attempt to accommodate his religious beliefs, and asked him to tuck his hair into the collar of his shirt or jacket. Sears had used this accommodation with another Native American employee, Tony Goulet, who also worked at the Briarwood Mall store.

Vargas flatly refused to even attempt to tuck his hair in. He stated "I felt that it was an inhumane accommodation that was not reasonable. . . . It . . . put me in a position of ridicule and . . . didn't allow a conducive

position for my spirit to be, you know, free. I felt that I was being made to do something that I didn't feel comfortable doing. I felt that this was another form of religious oppression. . . ."

At his deposition, Vargas, whose hair is now nearly waist-length, took the position that tucking his hair into his collar, no less than cutting his hair, would violate his religious convictions. He actually testified that any demand made upon him would violate his religious beliefs. It is undisputed, however, that during the course of his employment Vargas never told his employer that tucking his hair into his collar would violate his religious beliefs.

Despite Vargas' refusal to attempt to comply with Sears' proposed accommodation, Sears did not immediately terminate his employment. Rather, he was urged by his supervisor to go home and reconsider his position. Vargas eventually chose not to comply with Sears' proposed accommodation and thereby terminated his employment. At no time did Vargas offer any alternatives, but instead demanded that he be allowed to work and wear his hair any way he wanted.

In order for an employee to proceed with a claim of religious discrimination, he must first establish a prima facie case by establishing that (1) he holds a sincere religious belief that conflicts with an employment requirement; (2) he has informed the employer about the conflict; and (3) he was discharged or disciplined for failing to comply with the conflicting employment requirement. If an employee establishes a prima facie case, the burden shifts to the employer to show that it offered a reasonable accommodation to the employee or that it could reasonably accommodate the employee without incurring undue hardship.

Although the burden is on the employer to accommodate the employee's religious needs, the employee must make some effort to cooperate with an employer's attempt at accommodation. Where an employee "will not attempt to . . . cooperate with his employer in its conciliatory efforts, he may forgo the right to have his beliefs accommodated by his employer." An employee cannot shirk his duties to try to accommodate himself or to cooperate with his employer in reaching an accommodation by a mere recalcitrant citation of religious precepts. Nor can he thereby shift all responsibility for accommodation to his employer. Where an employee refuses to attempt to accommodate his own beliefs or to cooperate with his employer's attempt to reach a reasonable accommodation, he may render accommodation impossible. Moreover, any reasonable accommodation fulfills the employer's duty. The employee cannot reject the accommodation simply because he desires an alternative accommodation.

In this case, Vargas has not established a prima facie case of failure to accommodate. While Sears does not dispute that Vargas has religious beliefs that prohibit him from cutting his hair, it is clear from the record that Vargas was not terminated for failing to cut his hair. Vargas admitted in his deposition that he was given the option to tuck his hair into his collar to avoid termination of his employment. He, therefore, has not shown that he was discharged for failing to comply with an employment requirement that conflicted with his religious beliefs.

Although Vargas now takes the position that tucking his hair into his collar would also violate his religious beliefs, one of the elements that Vargas must satisfy in order to establish a prima facie case of religious discrimination is to establish that "he informed his employer about his [religious] conflict." There is no evidence whatsoever to establish that Vargas ever told any of his supervisors that his religion precluded him from tucking his hair into his collar. For all of the foregoing reasons, the Court finds that Vargas has failed to make out a prima facie claim of religious discrimination.

Moreover, even if the Court were to find that Vargas had established a prima facie claim, the Court finds that Sears attempted in good faith to reasonably accommodate Vargas' religious beliefs. As set forth above, where an employee refuses to attempt to accommodate his own beliefs or to cooperate with his employer's attempt to reach a reasonable accommodation, accommodation is deemed to be impossible. Vargas does not have the right to insist on his preferred accommodation. Vargas flatly refused to even attempt to comply with the accommodation of tucking his hair into his collar. He did not propose any alternative accommodation to his employer. In fact, Vargas testified that it was not "his job" to offer alternatives or cooperate in any accommodation proposals that were "imposed" on him or caused him any discomfort. Vargas' refusal to cooperate with Sears with respect to attempts to accommodate his religious beliefs precludes Vargas from challenging the sufficiency or "reasonableness" of Sears' offered accommodation.

For all of the foregoing reasons, Sears' Motion for Summary Judgment on Vargas' Title VII religious discrimination claim will be GRANTED.

Case Questions

1. Do you think that Sears' accommodation was sufficient? Explain.
2. Do you think Sears' policies adequately reflected its workforce? Explain.
3. What approach would you take to developing policies such as these?

WHAT CONSTITUTES UNDUE HARDSHIP?

Just as reasonable accommodation varies from situation to situation, so, too, does what constitutes undue hardship. There are no set rules about what constitutes undue hardship since each employer operates under different circumstances. What may be hardship for one employer may not be for another. What constitutes an undue hardship is addressed by the EEOC and courts on an individual basis.

It is clear, however, that the undue hardship may not be a mere inconvenience to the employer. The EEOC has provided guidelines as to what factors it will consider in deciding whether the employer's accommodation would cause undue hardship.[1] Such factors include:

- The nature of the employer's workplace.
- The type of job needing accommodation.
- The cost of the accommodation.
- The willingness of other employees to assist in the accommodation.
- The possibility of transfer of the employee and its effects.

[1] 29 C.F.R. 1605.1.

- What is done by similarly situated employers.
- The number of employees available for accommodation.
- The burden of accommodation on the union (if any).

The factors are similar to those used to determine if the employer has reasonably accommodated. Generally speaking, the EEOC's interpretation of what constitutes undue hardship and reasonable accommodation has been more stringent than the interpretation of undue hardship by the courts. However, since the EEOC's guidelines are not binding, and court decisions are, employers must look to the interpretation by courts in their own jurisdictions. Courts have found, among other things, that it would be an undue hardship if an employer had to violate the seniority provision of a valid collective bargaining agreement, to pay out more than a "de minimis" cost (in terms of money or efficiency) to replace a worker who has religious conflicts, or to force other employees who do not wish to do so to trade places with the employee who has a religious conflict. The U.S. Supreme Court's determination of what constitutes undue hardship was established in the following case, which still stands today. As you can see, it did not offer a very heavy burden on the employer.

Trans World Airlines, Inc. v. Hardison   *432 U.S. 63 (1977)*

Employer was unable to accommodate employee's religious conflict of working on the sabbath, without undue hardship. The Court set forth the guidelines for determining what constitutes undue hardship.

White, J.

The employee, Hardison, was employed by Trans World Airlines (TWA), in a department that operated 24 hours a day throughout the year in connection with an airplane maintenance and overhaul base. Hardison was subject to a seniority system in a collective bargaining agreement between TWA and the International Association of Machinists & Aerospace Workers (union), whereby the most senior employees have first choice for job and shift assignments as they become available, and the most junior employees are required to work when enough employees to work at a particular time or in a particular job to fill TWA's needs cannot be found.

Because Hardison's religious beliefs prohibit him from working on Saturdays, attempts were made to accommodate him, and these were temporarily successful mainly because on his job at the time he had sufficient seniority regularly to observe Saturday as his Sabbath. But when he sought, and was transferred to, another job where he was asked to work Saturdays and where he had low seniority, problems began to arise. TWA

agreed to permit the union to seek a change of work assignments, but the union was not willing to violate the seniority system, and Hardison had insufficient seniority to bid for a shift having Saturdays off. After TWA rejected a proposal that Hardison work only four days a week on the ground that this would impair critical functions in the airline operations, no accommodation could be reached, and Hardison was discharged for refusing to work on Saturdays.

We hold that TWA, which made reasonable efforts to accommodate Hardison's religious needs, did not violate Title VII, and each of the Court of Appeals' suggested alternatives would have been an undue hardship within the meaning of the statute as construed by the EEOC guidelines. The employer's statutory obligation to make reasonable accommodation for the religious observances of its employees, short of incurring an undue hardship, is clear, but the reach of that obligation has never been spelled out by Congress or by EEOC guidelines. With this in mind, we turn to a consideration of whether TWA has met its obligation under Title VII to accommodate the religious observances of its employees.

The Court of Appeals held that TWA had not made reasonable efforts to accommodate Hardison's religious needs. In its view, TWA had rejected three reasonable alternatives, any one of which would have satisfied its obligation without undue hardship. First, within the framework of the seniority system, TWA could have permitted Hardison to work a four-day week, utilizing in his place a supervisor or another worker on duty elsewhere. That this would have caused other shop functions to suffer was insufficient to amount to undue hardship in the opinion of the Court of Appeals. Second, also within the bounds of the collective-bargaining contract the company could have filled Hardison's Saturday shift from other available personnel competent to do the job, of which the court said there were at least 200. That this would have involved premium overtime pay was not deemed an undue hardship. Third, TWA could have arranged a "swap between Hardison and another employee either for another shift or for the Sabbath days." In response to the assertion that this would have involved a breach of the seniority provisions of the contract, the court noted that it had not been settled in the courts whether the required statutory accommodation to religious needs stopped short of transgressing seniority rules, but found it unnecessary to decide the issue because, as the Court of Appeals saw the record, TWA had not sought, and the union had therefore not declined to entertain, a possible variance from the seniority provisions of the collective-bargaining agreement. The company had simply left the entire matter to the union steward who the Court of Appeals said "likewise did nothing."

We disagree with the Court of Appeals in all relevant respects. It is our view that TWA made reasonable efforts to accommodate and that each of the suggested alternatives would have been an undue hardship within the meaning of the statute as construed by the EEOC guidelines.

It might be inferred from the Court of Appeals' opinion and from the brief of the EEOC in this Court that TWA's efforts to accommodate were no more than negligible. The findings of the District Court, supported by the record, are to the contrary. In summarizing its more detailed findings, the District Court observed:

"TWA established as a matter of fact that it did take appropriate action to accommodate as required by Title VII. It held several meetings with plaintiff at which it attempted to find a solution to plaintiff's problems. It did accommodate plaintiff's observance of his special religious holidays. It authorized the union steward to search for someone who would swap shifts, which apparently was normal procedure." It is also true that TWA itself attempted without success to find Hardison another job. The District Court's view was that TWA had done all that could reasonably be expected within the bounds of the seniority system.

We are also convinced, contrary to the Court of Appeals, that TWA itself cannot be faulted for having failed to work out a shift or job swap for Hardison. Both the union and TWA had agreed to the seniority system; the union was unwilling to entertain a variance over the objections of men senior to Hardison; and for TWA to have arranged unilaterally for a swap would have amounted to a breach of the collective-bargaining agreement.

Hardison and the EEOC insist that the statutory obligation to accommodate religious needs takes precedence over both the collective-bargaining contract and the seniority rights of TWA's other employees. We agree that neither a collective-bargaining contract nor a seniority system may be employed to violate the statute, but we do not believe that the duty to accommodate requires TWA to take steps inconsistent with the otherwise valid agreement. Collective bargaining, aimed at effecting workable and enforceable agreements between management and labor, lies at the core of our national labor policy, and seniority provisions are universally included in these contracts. Without a clear and express indication from Congress, we cannot agree with Hardison and the EEOC that an agreed-upon seniority system must give way when necessary to accommodate religious observances.

The Court of Appeals also suggested that TWA could have permitted Hardison to work a four-day week if necessary in order to avoid working on his Sabbath. Recognizing that this might have left TWA short-handed on the one shift each week that Hardison did not work, the court still concluded that TWA would suffer no undue hardship if it were required to replace Hardison either with supervisory personnel or with qualified personnel from other departments. Alternatively, the Court of Appeals suggested that TWA could have replaced Hardison on his Saturday shift with other available employees through the payment of premium wages. Both of these alternatives would involve costs to TWA, either in the form of lost efficiency in other jobs or higher wages.

To require TWA to bear more than a de minimis cost in order to give Hardison Saturdays off is an undue hardship. Like abandonment of the seniority system, to require TWA to bear additional costs when no such costs are incurred to give other employees the days off that they want would involve unequal treatment of employees on the basis of their religion. By suggesting that TWA should incur certain costs in order to give Hardison Saturdays off the Court of Appeals would in effect require TWA to finance an additional Saturday off and then to choose the employee who will enjoy it on the basis of his religious beliefs. While incurring extra costs to secure a replacement for Hardison might remove the necessity of compelling another employee to work involuntarily in Hardison's place, it would not change the fact that the privilege of having Saturdays off would be allocated according to religious beliefs. While the cost may seem small for one employee compared to TWA's resources, TWA may have many employees who need such accommodation.

Case Questions

1. In your opinion, were the alternatives suggested by the court of appeals viable for TWA? Why or why not?

2. Does it seem inconsistent to prohibit religious discrimination yet say that collective bargaining agreements cannot be violated to accommodate religious differences? Explain.

3. If you had been Hardison's manager and he came to you with this conflict, how would you have handled it? Does that change now that you have seen the Court's decision? If so, how?

RELIGION AS A BFOQ

Title VII permits religion to be a bona fide occupational qualification if it is reasonably necessary to the employer's particular normal business operations. It also specifically permits educational institutions to employ those of a particular religion if they are owned in whole or in substantial part by a particular religion. In *Pime*, the court looked at whether a historically Jesuit university could have Jesuit membership as a BFOQ for philosophy professors. Exhibit 9.4 discusses the issue of being male as a BFOQ for being a Catholic priest.

Pime v. Loyola University of Chicago *803 F.2d 351 (7th Cir. 1986)*

The employee, Pime, brought suit against the university under Title VII for religious discrimination in the hiring of tenure track professors in its College of Arts and Sciences, Department of Philosophy. The Department passed a resolution reserving its next three vacancies in tenure track teaching positions for Jesuits, members of the Society of Jesus. The court held the Jesuit requirement to be a BFOQ and not violative of Title VII.

Fairchild, J.

Loyola asserts two affirmative defenses. First, it claimed that it could require its employees to be Jesuits (and thus Catholics) under 42 U.S.C. 2000e-2(e) permitting an educational institution to employ persons of a particular religion if the institution is "in whole or in substantial part, owned, supported, controlled, or managed by a particular religion or by a particular religious corporation, . . . association, or society." It also claimed it could require those employees to be Jesuits according to 42 U.S.C.

2000e-2(e)(1) permitting an employer to employ an individual "on the basis of his religion, gender or national origin in those certain situations where religion, gender or national origin is a bona fide occupational qualification reasonably necessary to the normal operation of that particular business or enterprise." (BFOQ)

After a bench trial, the district court granted judgment in favor of Loyola, finding that being a Jesuit is a BFOQ. Employee challenges the finding of BFOQ. Loyola challenges the trial court's finding that it could not rely on subsection (e)(2).

Exhibit 9.4

Document on Women's Role in Church, Society Rejected

WASHINGTON—Nine years of sharp debate and soul searching over the ordination of women priests ended Wednesday as the United States' Roman Catholic bishops rejected a controversial statement on the role of women in society and the church.

On a 137–110 vote, 53 short of the required two-thirds of eligible voters needed for passage, the prelate sealed a tumultuous chapter in the history of the American church over the ordination of women.

But it did not close the book on the debate over admitting women to the priesthood.

While the letter, which was repeatedly revised, strongly reaffirmed the church's ancient tradition of an all-male priesthood, many advocates of women's ordination said the mere fact that the bishops were debating the issue was a victory.

Some bishops stressed that the vote against the letter was not a vote against banning women priests.

Those bishops, including Cardinal Joseph Bernardin of Chicago, said the missive was rejected because it was either too insensitive in dealing with the subject of women's ordination, or too weak in advancing a rationale for upholding a male priesthood.

Others said the letter had strayed from the bishops' original intent to address pressing social concerns affecting women, such as sexism and domestic violence, and had become too political and divisive.

It marked the first time that a proposed pastoral letter, an authoritative teaching of bishops, had been defeated in the United States.

The letter's defeat came on the eve of the Episcopal Church's plans tonight to consecrate the Rev. Jane Holmes Dixon as the second woman bishop in its history and the third in the 70 million member worldwide Anglican Communion.

Last week, the Church of England—mother church of the Anglican Communion, which broke with Rome in the 16th century—voted to admit women to its priesthood.

Note: On June 29, 2002, seven women were ordained as Catholic priests near Passau, Germany. Less than two weeks later, the Vatican threatened to excommunicate them unless they admitted that the ceremony was invalid and expressed repentance. www.womenpriests.org/called/woc_usa.htm.

Source: L. B. Stammer, *Palm Beach Post,* Nov. 19, 1992, p. 1A. Copyright 1992, *Los Angeles Times.* Reprinted by permission.

The Society of Jesus is a religious order of the Roman Catholic Church. Its members, who are, with few exceptions, priests, are called Jesuits. The order has been characterized by interests and particular energy in the promotion of education, and has established twenty-eight universities in the United States. Jesuits are required to complete a protracted course of training and to make perpetual vows. Once they accept positions as professors they continue to incorporate their religious mission into their professional work.

Loyola University of Chicago has a long Jesuit tradition. Since 1909 its legal entity has been an Illinois not-for-profit corporation. Until 1970, it was governed by a Board of Trustees, all members of which were Jesuits. It has become a large university, consisting of ten schools and colleges, a medical center and a hospital. Presently 93% of the academic administrators are non-Jesuits, as are 94% of the teaching staff.

Every undergraduate must take three Philosophy courses. About 75% of the students come from Catholic backgrounds. There was testimony by the President that, "I'm convinced that of all the things we say about Loyola, the most effective single adjective in attracting students and alumni support and benefactors is its Jesuitness."

In the fall of 1978, there were 31 tenure track positions in the Philosophy Department. Seven had been held by Jesuits, but one had resigned and two more retirements were imminent. On October 12, the department chair reported to a meeting of the department and faculty as follows:

We anticipate 3 full-time faculty openings in the Philosophy Department beginning September 1979. They are the position of Fr. Dehler and those of Fr. Grant and Fr. Loftus after they retire at the end of the current academic year.

There are two different kinds of departmental needs which seem to bear heavily on the decisions as to the kind of persons we should seek to hire for these openings.

1. The first is a need which the Chair voiced two years ago just after Fr. Dehler's resignation. That is, the need for an adequate Jesuit presence in the Department. We are a philosophy Department in a University with a Jesuit tradition. It is mainly by reason of this tradition that philosophy has the importance it does in the education of Loyola undergraduates. Therefore, it behooves us, however strong we may feel about "the autonomy of philosophy," to acknowledge our association with this tradition. One very basic and obvious way of making such acknowledgments is by insisting upon an adequate Jesuit presence in the faculty of the Department. With the retirement of Father Grant and Father Loftus, we shall be left with 4 out of 31 faculty positions occupied by Jesuits. Four out of 31 is not an adequate Jesuit presence in the Department. In the judgment of the Chair, it would be highly desirable to fill all three openings with professionally competent Jesuit philosophers. And it is his recommendation that we do so if we can.

The second kind of departmental need is for faculty, especially qualified to teach courses in the following areas: *a.* Applied ethics, especially medical ethics. There is an increasing student demand for such courses and for additional undergraduate course offerings at the Medical School. *b.* Philosophy of Law. This is one of the most popular of our 300-level course offerings. It needs to be offered annually both at Lake Shore Campus and Water Tower Campus. *c.* Logic. There is an exceedingly heavy student enrollment at both Lake Shore Campus and Water Tower Campus. Additional sections of courses in logic should be offered in each campus.

Consequently, we should seek persons who have special competence and interest in teaching courses in these areas. The Chair's recommendation is that we seek to hire persons who will help teach in these two areas.

These two kinds of needs are different, though not incompatible. The Chair's recommendation as to hiring is the following:

That for each of these 3 positions we seek to hire a professionally competent Jesuit philosopher— preferably a young Jesuit with competence to teach in one or several of the following areas: *a*) applied ethics, especially medical ethics; *b*) philosophy of law; and *c*) logic; and that if we should be unable to hire such, we hire temporary full-time person(s) with special competence to teach in one or several of these areas.

Pime, a Jew, had been employed in 1976 as a part-time lecturer in the department. He taught several courses. He expected to receive his doctorate in June 1979 and had received indications of approval of his work. He knew of the resolution of November 30, and asked the department chair when there would be a full-time tenure track position for him. The chair said he saw nothing in the way of a position for Pime in the next three or four years. Disappointed, Pime left Loyola after the spring semester.

There is no hint of invidious action against Pime on account of his religion. The faculty resolution excluded every non-Jesuit from consideration, whether of the Catholic faith or otherwise. We shall assume, however, that because Pime's faith would prevent his being a Jesuit, he has a claim on discrimination on account of religion.

The BFOQ involved in this case is membership in a religious order of a particular faith. There is evidence of the relationship of the order to Loyola and that Jesuit "presence" is important to the successful operation of the university. It appears to be significant to the educational tradition and character of the institution that students be assured a degree of contact with teachers who have received the training and accepted the obligation which are essential to membership in the Society of Jesus. It requires more to be a Jesuit than just adherence to the Catholic faith, and it seems wholly reasonable to believe that the educational experience at Loyola would be different if Jesuit presence were not maintained. As priests, Jesuits perform rites and sacraments, and counsel members of the university community, including students, faculty and staff. One witness expressed the objective as keeping a presence "so that students would occasionally encounter a Jesuit."

It is true that it has not been shown that Jesuit training is a superior academic qualification, applying objective criteria, to teach the particular courses. It is also true that in looking at claims of BFOQ, courts have considered only the content of the particular jobs at issue. Yet it seems to us here the evidence supports the more general proposition that having a Jesuit presence in the Philosophy faculty is "reasonably necessary to the normal operation" of the enterprise, and that fixing the number at 7 out of 31 is a reasonable determination.

Case Questions

1. Does the decision make sense to you? Explain.

2. Since such a high percentage of Loyola's faculty and administrators are non-Jesuits, does it seem as if an argument could be made that the school has thereby given up its legitimate claim to have being Jesuit be a BFOQ?

3. As an employer, do you think you would have to face dealing with the policy adopted here making other employees or applicants feel unwelcome? If so, what would you do?

RELIGIOUS HARASSMENT

One of the most active areas under religious discrimination lately has been religious harassment. Several factors have come together and caused many employees to decide that expressing their religious views in some way in the workplace is something they are compelled to do, either by their religious dictates or their own interpretations of them.

For instance, employees may feel they must, or wish to, display crosses or other religious artifacts at work, display religious tracts on their desk or pass them out to coworkers, hold Bible or other religious study groups during the workday, preach, teach, testify, or "witness" to their coworkers in order to practice their religion, or engage in other such activities. As mentioned earlier, after the events of September 11, 2001, there was an increase in the number of claims of religious harassment. In one incident cited by the EEOC, a Muslim employee who had experienced no workplace problems before September 11, 2001, reported that afterward none of his coworkers would speak to him and that when they did, they referred to him as "the local terrorist" or "camel jockey."

An article in *The Wall Street Journal* reported that a survey of 743 human resource professionals by the Society for Human Resource Management indicated that the most common religion-related issues among employees are employee proselytizing (20 percent), employees feeling harassed by coworkers' religious expressions (14 percent), employees objecting to job duties (9 percent), and employees harassing coworkers for their religious beliefs (6 percent).

This activity surrounding the issue of religious harassment is due, in part, to matters peripheral to workplace religious discrimination. In 1990, the U.S. Supreme Court rejected Native Americans' argument that they should be permitted the ritual use of peyote (a hallucinogenic drug) in their tribal religious ceremonies as a part of their First Amendment right to freedom of religion. With tremendous support from many quarters, in 1993 Congress passed the Religious Freedom Restoration Act (RFRA) in order to ensure the free exercise of religious practices. RFRA was an attempt to restore the previous status quo under which religious practices must be accommodated unless a compelling governmental interest can be demonstrated and advanced in the least restrictive manner. In 1997, the U.S. Supreme Court overturned RFRA as giving a governmental preference for religion, in violation of the First Amendment to the Constitution.[2]

---

[2] *City of Boerne, Texas v. Flores,* 521 U.S. 507 (1997).

While the matter of religious practices in the workplace was not at issue in these cases or this legislation, the national attention and debate about it, along with a growing religious presence in political issues, extended the religious practices issue to the workplace by extrapolation. When the religious practices were challenged, religious harassment claims rose.

Of course, with all different types of religions in the workplace (see Exhibit 9.2), it is predictable that there would be religious conflicts and that those with religions considered out of the ordinary or with religious practices that coworkers consider extreme would be the subject of religious harassment. In addition, it is often the nonreligious employees who allege they are being harassed by religious employees. (See Exhibit 9.3.) For instance, in a case filed in 1998 by information systems manager Rosamaria Machado-Wilson of DeLand, Florida, the employee alleged that she was fired after less than six months on the job after reporting religious harassment to the human resource office of her employer, BSG Laboratories. According to Machado-Wilson, a simple walk to the coffeepot sometimes meant "weaving past prostrate, praying co-workers and stopping for impromptu ceremonies spoken in tongues." She says she was forced to attend company prayer meetings and be baptized, employees were subjected to inquiries into and comments about their religious beliefs, and those found to be nonbelievers were fired.[3]

Of course, since Title VII prohibits religious discrimination, it also prohibits religious harassment. The EEOC's guidelines on liability for workplace harassment issued in June of 1999 explicitly cover religious harassment. In the wake of the RFRA situation, on August 14, 1997, President Clinton issued guidelines for the religious freedom of federal employees. The purpose of the guidelines is to accommodate religious observance in the workplace as an important national priority by striking a balance between religious observance and the requirements of the workplace. Under the guidelines, employees:

- Should be permitted to engage in private religious expression in personal work areas not regularly open to the public to the same extent that they may engage in nonreligious private expression.
- Should be permitted to engage in religious expression with fellow employees, to the same extent they may engage in comparable nonreligious private expression, subject to reasonable restrictions.
- Are permitted to engage in religious expression directed at fellow employees, and may even attempt to persuade fellow employees of the correctness of their religious views. But employees must refrain from such expression when a fellow employee asks that it stop or otherwise demonstrates that it is unwelcome.

In order to best prevent liability for religious harassment, employers should be sure to protect employees from those religious employees who attempt to proselytize others who do not wish to be approached about religious matters, as well as to protect employees with permissible religious practices who are given a hard time by those who do not.

---

[3] *Rosamaria D. Machado-Wilson* v. *BSG Laboratories, Inc.,* Case No. 98-106601 CIDL (Cir. Ct., 7th Jud. Cir., Volusia County, Fla., 1998).

Making sure that employees are given comparable opportunities to use workplace time and resources for religious practices if given for secular ones is also an important consideration.

The following case sets forth the very interesting issue of what to do when an employer's workplace diversity policy is at odds with an employee's religious beliefs, so much so that the employee who opposes the policy feels harassed.

Peterson v. Hewlett-Packard Co. *358 F.3d 599 (9th Cir. 2004)*

Employee sued employer for religious discrimination and alleged religious harassment after being terminated for repeatedly refusing to remove biblical passages he posted in his workplace cubicle, easily seen by all, in response to employer's workplace diversity posters which included affinity orientation. The court upheld the termination, concluding that the employer was not required to go along with employee's admitted goal of hurting gay and lesbian employees in an effort to get them to "repent and be saved."

Reinhardt, J.

In this religious discrimination action under Title VII of the Civil Rights Act of 1964, Richard Peterson claims that his former employer, the Hewlett-Packard Company, engaged in disparate treatment by terminating him on account of his religious views and that it failed to accommodate his religious beliefs.

The conflict between Peterson and Hewlett-Packard arose when the company began displaying "diversity posters" in its Boise office as one component of its workplace diversity campaign. The first series consisted of five posters, each showing a photograph of a Hewlett-Packard employee above the caption "Black," "Blonde," "Old," "Gay," or "Hispanic." Posters in the second series included photographs of the same five employees and a description of the featured employee's personal interests, as well as the slogan "Diversity is Our Strength."

Peterson describes himself as a "devout Christian," who believes that homosexual activities violate the commandments contained in the Bible and that he has a duty "to expose evil when confronted with sin." In response to the posters that read "Gay," Peterson posted two Biblical scriptures on an overhead bin in his work cubicle. The scriptures were printed in a typeface large enough to be visible to co-workers, customers, and others who passed through an adjacent corridor.

***

Peterson's direct supervisor removed the scriptural passages after consulting her supervisor and determining that they could be offensive to certain employees, and that the posting of the verses violated Hewlett-Packard's policy prohibiting harassment. Throughout the relevant period, Hewlett-Packard's harassment policy stated as follows: "Any comments or conduct relating to a person's race, gender, religion, disability, age, sexual orientation, or ethnic background that fail to respect the dignity and feeling [sic] of the individual are unacceptable."

Over the course of several days after Peterson posted the Biblical materials, he attended a series of meetings with Hewlett-Packard managers, during which he and they tried to explain to each other their respective positions. Peterson explained that he meant the passages to communicate a message condemning "gay behavior." The scriptural passages, he said, were "intended to be hurtful. And the reason [they were] intended to be hurtful is you cannot have correction unless people are faced with truth." Peterson hoped that his gay and lesbian co-workers would read the passages, repent, and be saved.

In these meetings, Peterson also asserted that Hewlett-Packard's workplace diversity campaign was an initiative to "target" heterosexual and fundamentalist Christian employees at Hewlett-Packard, in general, and him in particular. Ultimately, Peterson and the managers were unable to agree on how to resolve the conflict. Peterson proposed that he would remove the offending scriptural passages if Hewlett-Packard removed the "Gay" posters; if, however, Hewlett-Packard would not remove the posters, he would not remove the passages. When the managers rejected both options, Peterson responded: "I don't see any way that I can compromise what I am doing that would satisfy both [Hewlett-Packard] and my own conscience." He further remonstrated: "as long as [Hewlett-Packard] is condoning [homosexuality] I'm going to oppose it. . . ."

Peterson was given time off with pay to reconsider his position. When he returned to work, he again posted the scriptural passages and refused to remove them. After further meetings with Hewlett-Packard managers, Peterson was terminated for insubordination.

Following receipt of a right to sue notice from the EEOC, Peterson filed a complaint alleging religious discrimination in violation of Title VII and the Idaho Human Rights Act. Both parties moved for summary judgment. The district court granted Hewlett-Packard's motion and denied Peterson's. We affirm.

Title VII makes it unlawful for an employer "to discharge any individual . . . because of such individual's . . . religion[.]" "The term 'religion' includes all aspects of religious observance and practice, as well as belief, unless an employer demonstrates that he is unable to reasonably accommodate to an employee's . . . religious observance or practice without undue hardship on the conduct of the employer's business." Our analysis of Peterson's religious discrimination claims under the Idaho Human Rights Act is the same as under Title VII.

A claim for religious discrimination under Title VII can be asserted under several different theories, including disparate treatment and failure to accommodate. In arguing that Hewlett-Packard discriminated against him on account of his religious beliefs, Peterson relies on both these theories.

To survive summary judgment on his disparate treatment claim, Peterson must establish that his job performance was satisfactory and provide evidence, either direct or circumstantial, to support a reasonable inference that his termination was discriminatory. The amount of evidence that Peterson must produce is "very little," so long as it is more than "purely conclusory allegations of alleged discrimination, with no concrete, relevant particulars."

Peterson has the burden of establishing a prima facie case by showing that (1) he is a member of a protected class; (2) he was qualified for his position;

(3) he experienced an adverse employment action; and (4) similarly situated individuals outside his protected class were treated more favorably, or other circumstances surrounding the adverse employment action give rise to an inference of discrimination. It is with respect to the fourth requirement that Peterson's case fails.

Initially, we address Peterson's argument that Hewlett-Packard's workplace diversity campaign was "a crusade to convert fundamentalist Christians to its values," including the promotion of "the homosexual lifestyle." The undisputed evidence shows that Hewlett-Packard carefully developed its campaign during a three-day diversity conference at its Boise facility in 1997 and subsequent planning meetings in which numerous employees participated. The campaign's stated goal—and no evidence suggests that it was pretextual—was to increase tolerance of diversity. Peterson may be correct that the campaign devoted special attention to combating prejudice against homosexuality, but such an emphasis is in no manner unlawful. To the contrary, Hewlett-Packard's efforts to eradicate discrimination against homosexuals in its workplace were entirely consistent with the goals and objectives of our civil rights statutes generally.

In addition to Peterson's allegations about the general purposes of the diversity initiative, he asserts that the campaign that Hewlett-Packard conducted, as well as "the entire disciplinary process" that it initiated in response to his posting of the scriptural passages, constituted "an inquisition serving no other purpose than to ferret out the extremity of Peterson's views on homosexuality." According to Peterson, Hewlett-Packard managers harassed him in order to convince him to change his religious beliefs. However, the evidence that Peterson cites in support of this theory shows that Hewlett-Packard managers acted in precisely the opposite manner. In numerous meetings, Hewlett-Packard managers acknowledged the sincerity of Peterson's beliefs and insisted that he need not change them. They did not object to Peterson's expression of his anti-gay views in a letter to the editor that was published in the *Idaho Statesman*—a letter in which Peterson stated that Hewlett-Packard was "on the rampage to change moral values in Idaho under the guise of diversity," and that the diversity campaign was a "platform to promote the homosexual agenda." Nor did the Hewlett-Packard managers prohibit him from parking his car in the company lot even though he had affixed to it a bumper sticker stating, "Sodomy is Not a Family Value." All that the managers did was explain Hewlett-Packard's diversity program to Peterson and ask him to treat his co-workers with respect. They simply requested that he remove the posters and not violate the company's harassment policy—a policy that was uniformly applied to all employees. No contrary inference may be drawn from anything in the record.

Peterson also maintains that the disciplinary proceedings and his subsequent termination stand in marked contrast to Hewlett-Packard's treatment of three other groups of similarly situated employees. Peterson compares himself, first, to the employees who hung the diversity posters. He argues that these posters were intended "to make people uncomfortable so they would think again about diversity and change their actions to be more positive." He likens these actions to his own intentions to make his "scriptures [] hurtful so that people would repent (change their actions) and experience the joys of being saved." This comparison fails because the employees who hung the diversity posters were simply communicating the views of Hewlett-Packard as they were directed to do by management, whereas Peterson was expressing his own personal views which contradicted those of management. Moreover, unlike Peterson's postings, the company's workplace diversity campaign did not attack any group of employees on account of race, religion, or any other important individual characteristic. To the contrary, Hewlett-Packard's initiative was intended to promote tolerance of the diversity that exists in its workforce. Hewlett-Packard's failure to fire employees for following management's instructions to hang the posters prepared by management provides no evidence of disparate treatment.

Second, Peterson compares himself with other employees who posted religious and secular messages and symbols in their work spaces. Yet Peterson failed to present any evidence that the posters in other Hewlett-Packard employees' cubicles were intended to be "hurtful" to, or critical of, any other employees or otherwise violated the company's harassment policy. In fact, the only posters in other employees' work spaces that Peterson identified were of "Native American dream catchers," "New Age pictures of whales," and a yinyang symbol.

Third, Peterson argues that he was similarly situated to the network group of homosexual employees that

Hewlett-Packard permitted to organize in the workplace and advertise in the company's e-mail and its newsletter. Yet Peterson failed to present any evidence that communications from this network group were, let alone were intended to be, hurtful to any group of employees. Nor does anything in the record indicate that Hewlett-Packard permitted or would have permitted any network group or any individual employee to post messages of either a secular or religious variety that demeaned other employees or violated the company's harassment policy.

In short, we conclude that Peterson's evidence does not meet the threshold for defeating summary judgment in disparate treatment cases. Peterson offered *no* evidence, circumstantial or otherwise, that would support a reasonable inference that his termination was the result of disparate treatment on account of religion. Viewing the record in the light most favorable to Peterson, it is evident that he was discharged, not because of his religious beliefs, but because he violated the company's harassment policy by attempting to generate a hostile and intolerant work environment and because he was insubordinate in that he repeatedly disregarded the company's instructions to remove the demeaning and degrading postings from his cubicle.

Peterson also appeals the district court's rejection of his failure-to-accommodate theory of religious discrimination. An employee who fails to raise a reasonable inference of disparate treatment on account of religion may nonetheless show that his employer violated its affirmative duty under Title VII to reasonably accommodate employees' religious beliefs. To establish religious discrimination on the basis of a failure-to-accommodate theory, Peterson must first set forth a prima facie case that (1) he had a bona fide religious belief, the practice of which conflicts with an employment duty; (2) he informed his employer of the belief and conflict; and (3) the employer discharged, threatened, or otherwise subjected him to an adverse employment action because of his inability to fulfill the job requirement. If Peterson makes out a prima facie failure-to-accommodate case, the burden then shifts to Hewlett-Packard to show that it "initiated good faith efforts to accommodate reasonably the employee's religious practices or that it could not reasonably accommodate the employee without undue hardship."

As we explain below, it is readily apparent that the only accommodations that Peterson was willing to accept would have imposed undue hardship upon Hewlett-Packard. Therefore, we will assume *arguendo* that Peterson could establish a prima facie case that his posting of the anti-gay scriptural passages stemmed from his religious beliefs that homosexual activities "violate the commandments of God contained in the Holy Bible" and that those same religious beliefs imposed upon him "a duty to expose evil when confronted with sin." We make that assumption with considerable reservations, however, because we seriously doubt that the doctrines to which Peterson professes allegiance compel any employee to engage in either expressive or physical activity designed to hurt or harass one's fellow employees.

An employer's duty to negotiate possible accommodations ordinarily requires it to take "some initial step to reasonably accommodate the religious belief of that employee." Peterson contends that the company did not do so in this case even though Hewlett-Packard managers convened at least four meetings with him. In these meetings, they explained the reasons for the company's diversity campaign, allowed Peterson to explain fully his reasons for his postings, and attempted to determine whether it would be possible to resolve the conflict in a manner that would respect the dignity of Peterson's fellow employees. Peterson, however, repeatedly made it clear that only two options for accommodation would be acceptable to him, either that (1) both the "Gay" posters and anti-gay messages remain, or (2) Hewlett-Packard remove the "Gay" posters and he would then remove the anti-gay messages. Given Peterson's refusal to consider other accommodations, we proceed to evaluate whether one or both of the "acceptable" accommodations would have imposed undue hardship upon Hewlett-Packard, or to determine whether Hewlett-Packard carried its burden of showing that no reasonable accommodation was possible.

As we explain further below, Peterson's first proposed accommodation would have compelled Hewlett-Packard to permit an employee to post messages intended to demean and harass his co-workers. His second proposed accommodation would have forced the company to exclude sexual orientation from its workplace diversity program. Either choice would have created undue hardship for Hewlett-Packard because it would have inhibited its efforts to attract and retain a qualified, diverse workforce, which the company reasonably views as vital to its commercial success; thus, neither provides a reasonable accommodation.

With respect to Peterson's first proposal, an employer need not accommodate an employee's religious beliefs if doing so would result in discrimination against his co-workers or deprive them of contractual or other statutory rights. Nor does Title VII require an employer to accommodate an employee's desire to impose his religious beliefs upon his co-workers.

That is not to say that accommodating an employee's religious beliefs creates undue hardship for an employer merely because the employee's co-workers find his conduct irritating or unwelcome. Complete harmony in the workplace is not an objective of Title VII. If relief under Title VII can be denied merely because the majority group of employees, who have not suffered discrimination, will be unhappy about it, there will be little hope of correcting the wrongs to which the Act is directed. While Hewlett-Packard must tolerate some degree of employee discomfort in the process of taking steps required by Title VII to correct the wrongs of discrimination, it need not accept the burdens that would result from allowing actions that demean or degrade, or are designed to demean or degrade, members of its workforce. Thus, we conclude that Peterson's first proposed accommodation would have created undue hardship for his employer.

The only other alternative acceptable to Peterson—taking down all the posters—would also have inflicted undue hardship upon Hewlett-Packard because it would have infringed upon the company's right to promote diversity and encourage tolerance and good will among its workforce. The Supreme Court has acknowledged that "the skills needed in today's increasingly global marketplace can only be developed through exposure to widely diverse people, cultures, ideas, and viewpoints." These values and good business practices are appropriately promoted by Hewlett-Packard's workplace diversity program. To require Hewlett-Packard to exclude homosexuals from its voluntarily adopted program would create undue hardship for the company.

Because only two possible accommodations were acceptable to Peterson and implementing either would have imposed undue hardship upon Hewlett-Packard, we conclude that the company carried its burden of showing that no reasonable accommodation was possible, and we therefore reject Peterson's failure-to-accommodate claim.

Peterson failed to raise a triable issue of fact that his termination from employment at Hewlett-Packard was on account of his religious beliefs. The ruling of the district court is therefore AFFIRMED.

Case Questions

1. Do the employer's actions here seem reasonable to you (both those in response to diversity and in response to the employee's reaction)?

2. Would you have balanced the two sides here the same as the court? Explain.

3. How would you design a diversity program that no employee would have problems with?

Keep in mind here that as an employer, the employer gets to call the shots within the confines of the law. Hopefully, they are consistent with law and promote workplace productivity. Employees who decide, for whatever reason, that they cannot abide the employer's lawful and legal policies always have the choice of either toughing it out or looking for a job which presents no such conflict. While the employer has no right to make employees choose between their religion and work, where a religious conflict does not pose an undue hardship, the employee also has no right to dictate to the employer what workplace policies must be. And, of course, harassment on the basis of religion is illegal under Title VII.

UNION ACTIVITY AND RELIGIOUS DISCRIMINATION

As *Hardison* discussed earlier, at times the religious conflicts that arise between the employee and the employer are caused by collective-bargaining agreement provisions, rather than by policies unilaterally imposed by the employer. It has been determined that, even though Title VII defines the term "religion" with reference to an employer having a duty to reasonably accommodate, unions are also under a duty to reasonably accommodate religious conflicts.

The most frequent conflicts are requirements that employees be union members or pay union dues. Union membership, payment of union dues, or engaging in concerted activity, such as picketing and striking, conflicts with some religious beliefs. Employees have also objected to the payment of union dues as violating their First Amendment right to freedom of religion and Title VII's prohibition against religious discrimination. Unions have claimed that applying the religious proscription of Title VII violates the Establishment Clause of the First Amendment to the U.S. Constitution, ensuring government neutrality in religious matters.

Courts have ruled that union security agreements requiring that employees pay union dues within a certain time after the effective date of their employment or be discharged does not violate an employee's First Amendment rights. However, it violates Title VII for an employer to discharge an employee for refusal to join the union because of his or her religious beliefs.

Employees with religious objections must be reasonably accommodated, including the possibility of the alternative of keeping their job without paying union dues. However, the union could prove undue hardship if many of the employees chose to have their dues instead paid to a nonunion, nonsectarian charitable organization chosen by the union and the employer, since the impact on the union would not be insubstantial.

In *Tooley* v. *Martin-Marietta Corp,*[4] Seventh Day Adventists who were prohibited by their religion from becoming members of, or paying a service fee to, a union offered

[4] 648 F.2d 1239 (9th Cir. 1981).

Management Tips

One of the primary reasons employers get into trouble in this area is because they simply miss realizing the religious conflict when an employee notifies them, or they refuse to adequately address it if they do. Many of the conflicts can be avoided by following a few basic rules:

- Take all employee notices of religious conflicts seriously.
- Once an employee puts the employer on notice of a religious conflict, immediately try to find ways to avoid the conflict.
- Ask the employee with the conflict for suggestions on avoiding the conflict.
- Ask other employees if they can be of assistance, but make it clear that they are not required to do so.
- Keep workplace religious comments and criticisms to a minimum.
- Make sure all employees understand that they are not to discriminate against employees on the basis of religion.
- Once an employee expresses conflict based on religion, do not challenge the employee's religious beliefs, though it is permissible to make sure of the conflict.

- Make sure undue hardship actually exists if it is claimed.
- Revisit issues such as "Christmas" bonuses and "Christmas" parties to see if it is more appropriate to use more inclusive language such as "holiday" to cover employees who do not celebrate the Christian Christmas—further, revisit the issue of whether all employees are being fairly covered by such policies and events.
- Revisit the issue of granting leave for religious events and make sure it does not favor one religion over another, such as giving employees paid leave for Christmas but requiring them to take their own leave for other religious holidays such as Rosh Hashana, Yom Kippur, or Ramadan.
- Make sure food at workplace events is inclusive of all employees, regardless of religion, such as having kosher (or at least nonpork or seafood) items for Jewish employees, having alternatives to alcoholic beverages for those who do not drink for religious reasons, having nonpork items for Muslims, and so on. Asking employees what religious dietary limitations they have or having employees bring a dish to share is an easy way to handle this.

to pay an amount equal to union dues to a mutually acceptable charity. The union refused and argued that to accommodate the employees violated the Establishment Clause ensuring governmental neutrality in matters of religion. The court said that the government could legitimately enforce accommodation of religious beliefs when the accommodation reflects the obligation of neutrality in the face of religious differences and does not constitute sponsorship, financial support, or active involvement of the sovereign in religious activities with which the Establishment Clause is mainly concerned. The Establishment Clause, typically applied to state legislation, such as in *Frazee,* discussed earlier, requires that the accommodation reflect a clearly secular purpose, have a primary effect that neither inhibits nor advances religion, and avoids excessive government entanglement with religion.

Whether the objection under Title VII is directed toward the employer or the union, a government employer still has a duty to reasonably accommodate the employee's religious conflict unless to do so would cause undue hardship or excessive entanglement with religion or violate the Establishment Clause.

Summary

- Employees are protected in the workplace in their right to adhere to and practice their religious beliefs, and the employer cannot discriminate against them on this basis unless to do so would be undue hardship on the employer.

- Employer cannot question the acceptability of employee's religion or when the employee came to believe.

- Employer should be conscious of potential religious conflicts in developing and implementing workplace policies.

- The prohibition on religious discrimination is not absolute, as employer has only the duty to reasonably accommodate the employee's religious conflict unless to do so would cause the employer undue hardship.

- While employer must make a good-faith effort to reasonably accommodate religious conflicts, if such efforts fail, employer will have discharged his or her legal duties under Title VII.

Chapter-End Questions

1. The *Christian Science Monitor* refused to hire Feldstein because he was not a Christian Scientist. The newspaper said they only hired those who were of the Christian Science religion, unless there are none qualified for a position. Is the newspaper's policy legal? Explain. [*Feldstein* v. *EEOC,* 547 F. Supp. 97 (D. Mass. 1982).]

2. Cynthia requested a two-week leave from her employer to go on a religious pilgrimage. The pilgrimage was not a requirement of her religion, but Cynthia felt it was a "calling from God." Will it violate Title VII if Cynthia's employer does not grant her the leave? Explain. [*Tiano* v. *Dillard Department Stores, Inc.,* 1998 WL117864 (9th Cir. 1998).]

3. At the end of all her written communications, employee writes "have a blessed day." One of employer's most important clients requests that employee not do so and employer asks employee to stop. Employee refuses, saying it is a part of her religion. If employee sues the employer for religious discrimination, is she likely to win? [*Anderson* v. *USF Logistics (IMC); Inc.,* 274 F.3d 470 (7th Cir. 2001).]

4. Employee is terminated for refusal to cover or remove his confederate flag symbols as requested by his employer. He sues the employer, claiming discrimination on the basis of his religion as a Christian and his national origin as a "Confederate Southern American." Is he likely to win? [*Storey* v. *Burns International Security Service,* 390 F.3d 760 (3d Cir. 2004).]

5. A Michigan Holiday Inn fired a pregnant employee because the "very Christian" staff members were very upset by her talk of having an abortion. Has the employer violated Title VII? [*Turic* v. *Holland Hospitality, Inc.,* No. 1-93-CV-379 (W.D. Mich. 1994).]

6. A police officer who is assigned to a casino refuses the assignment, claiming his Baptist religion prohibits him from gambling or being around gambling. Is he legitimately able to do so? [*Endres* v. *Indiana State Police,* 349 F.3d 922 (7th Cir. 2003).]

7. Employer has a strict policy of not allowing employees with beards to work in public contact positions. All managerial positions are public contact positions. Employer does not make exceptions to its policies for those with religious objections to shaving, but it reasonably accommodates them by offering them other positions within the company. When employee applies for a driver position and is turned down, he sues employer. Does he win? [*EEOC* v. *UPS,* 94 F.3d 314 (7th Cir. 1996).]

8. Employee, a Muslim, is a management trainee at an airport car rental office. As part of her religious practice, employee wears a *hijab* (headscarf). She is told by her supervisor that the *hijab* does not match the uniforms she is required to wear, so she must stop wearing it or be

transferred to another position with less customer interaction. Employee was later terminated as a part of a company cutback. She sues for religious discrimination. Does she win? Explain. [*Ali* v. *Alamo Rent-A-Car,* 246 F.3d 662 (4th Cir. 2001).]

9. A Pentecostal nurse claims she was constructively discharged after refusing to assist in medical procedures she considered to be abortions because of her religious beliefs. She was initially transferred from labor and delivery to the newborn intensive care unit. Employee found this unacceptable because she says she would once again be forced to refuse tasks that involved allowing infants to die. The hospital invited the employee to meet with human resources and to investigate available positions, but she refused. Employee says the duty to assist in an accommodation never arose because a transfer to any other department is not a viable option since it would require her to give up her eight years of specialized training and education and undertake retraining. Employee is terminated and sues for religious discrimination. Does she win? Explain. [*Shelton* v. *University of Medicine & Dentistry of New Jersey,* U.S. App. LEXIS 19099 (3d Cir. 2000).]

10. A Baptist-run home for troubled youngsters terminates an employee for being a lesbian. Can it do so? [*Pedreira* v. *Kentucky Baptist Home for Children,* 186 F. Supp. 2d 757 (W.D. Ky. 2001).]

Chapter **Ten**

National Origin Discrimination

Opening Scenarios

SCENARIO 1

Scenario

Muhammad, an Arab-American Muslim high school student, had a job after school at a fast-food restaurant. A few coworkers started asking him why his "cousins" bombed the World Trade Center. Muhammad ignored their taunts. Then a manager began to add comments such as, "Hey Muhammed, we're going to have to check you for bombs." Muhammed felt humiliated and angry. Soon after, he was terminated for accidentally throwing away a paper cup that the manager was using. Muhammed suspects that his religious and ethnic background was the reason he was fired.

SCENARIO 2

Kayla, a supervisor, recently hired a new manager, Alex, but has received complaints from customers that they cannot understand him when they speak to him on the telephone. Alex is a Romanian employee visiting from the company's Romanian office and is scheduled to remain with the firm for two years. Kayla is concerned that if she allows Alex to perform duties similar to other managers, the firm will lose customers; however, she is unsure about the firm's liability for decreasing Alex's responsibilities as a result of his foreign accent.

STATUTORY BASIS

The statutory basis for protection against national origin discrimination is presented in Exhibit 10.1. These statutes include Sec. 703(a) of Title VII of the Civil Rights Act of 1964 and the Immigration Reform and Control Act of 1986.

CHEZ/CASA/FALA/WUNDERBAR UNCLE SAM

America has always considered itself to be a melting pot. Under this theory, different ethnic, cultural, and racial groups came together in America, but differences were melted into one homogeneous mass composed of all cultures. Recently, this characterization has been revisited and other, more accurate terms have been proposed. They include such terms as a *salad bowl,* in which all the ingredients come together to make an appetizing, nutritious whole but each ingredient maintains its own identity, or a *stew,* in which the ingredients are blended together but maintain their distinct identity, with the common thread of living in America acting as the stew base that binds the stew's ingredients together.

While the words on the Statue of Liberty—"Give me your tired, your poor, your huddled masses yearning to breathe free"—have always acted as a beacon to those of other countries to find solace on our shores, the reality once they get here, even sometimes after being here for generations, is that they are often discriminated against, rather than consoled. National origin was included in Title VII's list of protected classes to ensure that employers did not base employment decisions on preconceived notions about employees or applications based on their country of origin. Note that Section 1981 of the Civil Rights Act of 1866 may also apply in those circumstances where national origin is a proxy for or equivalent to race. See, for example, *DeSalle* v. *Key Bank,* 47 F.E.P. Cas. 37 (D. Me. 1988).

Exhibit 10.1   Legislation Prohibiting National Origin Discrimination

TITLE VII, CIVIL RIGHTS ACT OF 1964

Sec. 703(a)

It shall be an unlawful employment practice for an employer—

(1) to fail or to refuse to hire or to discharge any individual, or otherwise to discriminate against any individual with respect to his compensation, terms, conditions, or privileges of employment, because of such individual's . . . national origin.

IMMIGRATION REFORM AND CONTROL ACT OF 1986

Sec. 274A(a)

(1) It is unlawful for a person or other entity:

    (A) to hire or to recruit or refer for a fee for employment in the United States an alien knowing the alien is an unauthorized alien with respect to such employment, or

    (B) to hire for employment in the United States an individual without [verification of employment eligibility].

(2) It is unlawful for a person or other entity, after hiring an alien for employment in accordance with paragraph (1), to continue to employ the alien in the United States knowing the alien is (or had become) an unauthorized alien with respect to such employment.

(3) A person or entity that establishes that it has complied in good faith with the [verification of employment eligibility] with respect to hiring, recruiting or referral for employment of an alien in the United States has established an affirmative defense that the person or entity has not violated paragraph (1)(A).

Sec. 274(B)(a)

(1) It is an unfair immigration-related practice for a person or other entity to discriminate against any individual (other than an unauthorized alien) with respect to the hiring, or recruitment or referral for a fee, or the individual for employment or the discharging or the individual from employment—

    (A) because of such individual's national origin, or

    (B) in the case of a protected individual [a citizen or authorized alien], because of such individual's citizenship status.

On its face, national origin discrimination appears to be relatively simple to determine; however, it has surprising complexities. Employers have always been uncertain of the scope of Title VII's coverage in this area and what could be used as a defense to decisions based on national origin. (See Exhibit 10.2.) Notwithstanding its complexity, however, complaints to the EEOC have been on the rise since 1999 with 8,450 complaints received in 2003 based on alleged national origin discrimination, culminating in more than $21 million of collected benefits (this figure does not include monetary benefits collected through private litigation).

1. "Citizenship" and "national origin" are synonymous.
2. A restaurant may hire whomever it wishes to represent the national origin of the restaurant.
3. It is not illegal discrimination for an employer to require that employees speak only English at work.

BACKGROUND

national origin discrimination protection
It is unlawful for an employer to limit, segregate, or classify employees in any way on the basis of national origin that would deprive them of the privileges, benefits, or opportunities of employment.

The **protection** offered by Title VII in connection with national origin is similar to that of gender or race and is used somewhat synonymously with "ethnicity," though they are distinguishable. That is, it is an unlawful employment practice for an employer to limit, segregate, or classify employees in any way that would deprive them of employment opportunities because of national origin. An employer may not group its employees on the basis of national origin, make employment decisions on that basis, or implement policies or programs which, though they appear not to be based on an employee or applicant's country of origin, actually affect those with one national origin differently than those of a different group.

An employee may successfully claim discrimination on the basis of national origin if it is shown that:

1. He or she is a member of a protected class (i.e., articulate the employee's national origin).
2. He or she was qualified for the position for which she applied or in which she was employed.
3. The employer made an employment decision against this employee or applicant.
4. The position was filled by someone who was not a member of the protected class.

Each of the above will be discussed in turn.

Member of the Protected Class

national origin
Individual's or her or his ancestor's place of origin (as opposed to citizenship), or physical, cultural, or linguistic characteristics of an origin group.

In connection with the first requirement, what is meant by "national origin"? While the term is not defined in Title VII, the EEOC guidelines on discrimination define **national origin** discrimination as "including, but not limited to, the denial of equal employment opportunity because of [an applicant or employee's] or his or her ancestor's place of origin; or because an applicant has the physical, cultural, or linguistic characteristics of a national origin group."

Note that the term includes protection against discrimination based only on country of origin, not on country of *citizenship*. Title VII protects employees who are not U.S. citizens from employment discrimination based on the categories of the act, but it does not protect them from discrimination based on their status as aliens, rather than as U.S. citizens. That is, it protects a Somali woman from gender discrimination, but not from discrimination on the basis of the fact that she is a Somali citizen, rather than an American citizen. The issue of citizenship as it relates to national origin is discussed later in this chapter.

Many national origin cases under Title VII involve claims of discrimination by those who were not born in America; however, American-born employees are also protected against discrimination on the basis of their *American* origin. For example, the court has held that the employer's conscious decision to decide whom to dismiss on the basis of the national origin of its employees (in an effort toward "affirmative action") was not acceptable because that method tended to disfavor Americans, in favor of other nationalities.

In addition to national origin encompassing the employee's place of birth, it also includes ethnic characteristics or origins, as well as physical, linguistic, or cultural traits closely associated with a national origin group. For instance, it has been held that Cajuns, Gypsies, and Ukrainians are protected under Title VII. It may also serve as the basis for a national origin discrimination claim if the employee:

- Is identified with or connected to a person of a specific national origin, such as where someone suffers discrimination because he or she is married to a person of a certain ethnic heritage.
- Is a member of an organization that is identified with a national group.
- Is a participant in a school or religious organization that is affiliated with a national origin group.
- Has a surname that is generally associated with a national origin group.
- Is perceived by an employer as a member of a particular national origin group, whether or not the individual is in fact of that origin.

Qualification/BFOQs

The second factor that must be shown for an employee to claim national origin discrimination is that the applicant or employee is *qualified* for the position. That is, the claimant must show that he or she meets the job's requirements.

Contrary to situations involving disability or religion, the employee must show that she or he is qualified for the position without benefit of accommodation. No accommodation of one's national origin is required of employers. For example, while an employer would be required to reasonably accommodate an employee's religious attire, there is no similar responsibility to accommodate an employee's attire of national origin, such as traditional African dress. The employer may rebut this contention of qualification by showing that national origin is a **bona fide occupational qualification (BFOQ)** for the job. That is, the employer may set forth why an employee's being of a specific national origin is necessary for the position applied for, in that it is a legitimate job requirement reasonably necessary for the employer's particular business. However, it is important to note that customer, client, or coworker discomfort or preference may not be relied upon by the employer. On the other hand, national origin was allowed as a BFOQ in a case involving a subsidiary of a Japanese company. The court found that the firm could enact a preference for Japanese nationals based on the unique requirements of international trade.[1] In addition, where the provisions of an international

BFOQ
Bona fide occupational qualification.

---

[1] *Avigliano v. Sumitomo Shoji America, Inc.,* 638 F.2d 552 (2d Cir. 1981).

treaty apply and the BFOQ is citizenship rather than national origin, a foreign-based multinational may be allowed to express a preference for its citizens.[2]

English Fluency and Speaking Native Languages in the Workplace

Employers have also had to address the matter of either requiring employees to be fluent in English or requiring that only English be spoken in the workplace, even when employees are speaking only among themselves. This issue is of increasing relevance. In 2000, 45 million Americans (17.5 percent of the U.S. population) spoke a language other than English in the home, with 10.3 million of these same people speaking little or no English at all. Employers have argued that fluency in English is a BFOQ and, therefore, that they should not be required to hire someone who is not fluent in English because of his or her national origin.

Scenario

Diversity in the workplace brings many benefits, including a greater breadth of skills and life experiences among the workforce. It may also present unique challenges to employers, particularly in the form of poor communication among those who may prefer to speak in their native tongue, which might be not English but Spanish, Hindi, or Tagalog. While such communication problems may cause confusion, severe English-only restrictions may create frustration and resentment among employees for whom English is a second language. To avoid alienating these employees, to ensure realistic and reasonable job qualifications, and to decrease the risk of litigation, employers should not permit managers to arbitrarily impose language restrictions.[3]

To best be protected from possible Title VII liability, the employer must be able to show that English fluency is required for the job, and that the requirement is necessary to maintain supervisory control of the workplace. Perhaps it may be required of an employee who has much communication with clients, or it may be justified as a BFOQ where the employee could not speak or understand English sufficiently to perform required duties.

For example, where a teacher was fluent in English but spoke with such a thick accent that her students had a difficult time understanding her, her discharge was upheld. On the other hand, if the employee is in a job requiring little speaking and the employee can understand English, the requirement may be more difficult to defend—for instance, requiring English fluency for a janitor who talks little, has little reason to speak to carry out the duties of the job, and who understands what is said to him or her.

Scenario

Unlike the teacher above, in scenario 2 Kayla is considering *decreasing* Alex's responsibilities due to his foreign accent, not terminating him. However, like the teacher, it is quite possible in this scenario to show that speaking clear English is a BFOQ, especially if it can be shown that customers have been complaining that they cannot understand him.

Closely related is the employer's policy requiring employees capable of speaking English to speak only English in the workplace. These policies may be based in well-intentioned employer efforts that may include decreasing workplace tension where multiple languages have segregated a workplace, improving employees' English, or

---

[2] *Bennett* v. *Total Minatome Corp.*, 138 F.3d 1053 (5th Cir. 1998).

[3] See "English-Only Rules May Spell Trouble for Employers," Oct. 11, 2001, "special to law.com," www.law.com.

promoting a safe and efficient workplace. Courts have gone both ways on this issue. Some have held the policy to be discriminatory, excessively prohibitive, and a violation of Title VII. Others have held that it is not national origin discrimination if all employees, regardless of ancestry, were prohibited from speaking all but English on the job and that there is no statutory right to speak English at work. It has been held that the right to speak one's native language when the employee is bilingual is not an immutable characteristic that Title VII protects.

In general, though, English only rules have been upheld (see *Garcia* on p. 460). However, challenges to the rules have increased dramatically in recent years and have resulted in large awards and settlements to affected employees. In 2002, the EEOC received 228 complaints regarding English-only rules, while in 1996 there were only 77 complaints.

The EEOC takes the position that English-only rules *applied at all times* or only applied to certain foreign speakers are presumptively discriminatory, although the courts have not always agreed with that approach.[4] When a rule is applied only at certain times, the EEOC recommends that it must be justified by a business purpose in order to avoid discrimination claims. Rules applied during work time *only* are less likely to be considered harassment and more likely to show a business purpose. When an employer is considering an English-only rule, it should take into consideration the legal considerations as well as the fact that such a rule can create an atmosphere of inferiority, isolation, and intimidation that may result in a discriminatory work environment.

According to the EEOC, an employer may justify the business necessity of an English-only rule

- For communications with customers, coworkers, or supervisors who only speak English.
- In emergencies or other situations in which workers must speak a common language to promote safety.
- For cooperative work assignments in which the English-only rule is needed to promote efficiency.
- To enable a supervisor who only speaks English to monitor the performance of an employee whose job duties require communication with coworkers or customers.

In September 2000, a federal magistrate ruled that Dallas-based Premier Operator had illegally discriminated against 13 Hispanic employees in enacting and implementing a "Speak English-Only" rule. Some of the affected employees had been hired for their ability to speak both English and Spanish to customers. The court awarded the plaintiffs more than $700,000, the largest monetary award ever won by the EEOC for such a violation. Earlier in the same month, the EEOC won a $192,000 settlement for eight Hispanic employees in a lawsuit against Illinois-based Watlow Batavia, based on the company's implementation of an English-only policy on its assembly line.[5] *Garcia* v. *Spun Steak Co.,* below, is one of the seminal cases on the subject.

---

[4] See *Garcia,* below. For the contrary opinion supporting the EEOC'S contention, see *EEOC* v. *Premier Operator Services, Inc.,* 75 F. Supp. 550 (N.D. Tex. 1999) and *EEOC* v. *Synchro-Start,* 29 F. Supp. 2d 911 (N.D. Ill. 1999).

[5] Ibid.

Garcia v. Spun Steak Co. *998 F.2d 1480 (9th Cir. 1993)*

Defendant, Spun Steak Co., employs 33 workers, 24 of whom are Spanish-speaking. Two of the Spanish-speakers speak no English. Plaintiffs Garcia and Buitrago are production line workers for the defendant and both are bilingual. After receiving complaints that some workers were using their second language to harass and to insult other workers, defendant enacted an English-only policy in the workplace in order to (1) promote racial harmony; (2) enhance worker safety because some employees who did not understand Spanish claimed that they were distracted by its use; and (3) enhance product quality because the USDA inspector in the plant spoke only English. Plaintiffs received warning notices about speaking Spanish during working hours, and they were not permitted to work next to each other for two months. They filed charges with the EEOC, which found reasonable cause to believe that the defendant had violated Title VII. The District Court awarded summary judgment to the plaintiffs and Spun Steak appealed.

O'Scannlain, J.

The Spanish-speaking employees do not contend that Spun Steak intentionally discriminated against them in enacting the English-only policy. Rather, they contend that the policy had a discriminatory impact on them because it imposes a burdensome term or condition of employment exclusively upon Hispanic workers and denies them a privilege of employment that non-Spanish-speaking workers enjoy.

The employees argue that denying them the ability to speak Spanish on the job denies them the right to cultural expression. It cannot be gainsaid that an individual's primary language can be an important link to his ethnic culture and identity. Title VII, however, does not protect the ability of workers to express their cultural heritage at the workplace. Title VII is concerned only with disparities in the treatment of workers; it does not confer substantive privileges. It is axiomatic that an employee must often sacrifice individual self-expression during working hours. Just as a private employer is not required to allow other types of self-expression, there is nothing in Title VII which requires an employer to allow employees to express their cultural identity.

Next, the Spanish-speaking employees argue that the English-only policy has a disparate impact on them because it deprives them of a privilege given by the employer to native-English speakers: the ability to converse on the job in the language with which they feel most comfortable. It is undisputed that Spun Steak allows its employees to converse on the job. The ability to converse—especially to make small talk—is a privilege of employment, and may in fact be a significant privilege of employment in an assembly-line job. It is inaccurate, however, to describe the privilege as broadly as the Spanish-speaking employees urge us to do.

The employees have attempted to define the privilege as the ability to speak in the language of their choice. A privilege, however, is by definition given at the employer's discretion; an employer has the right to define its contours. Thus, an employer may allow employees to converse on the job, but only during certain times of the day or during the performance of certain tasks. The employer may proscribe certain topics as inappropriate during working hours or may even forbid the use of certain words, such as profanity.

Here, as is its prerogative, the employer has defined the privilege narrowly. When the privilege is defined at its narrowest (as merely the ability to speak on the job), we cannot conclude that those employees fluent in both English and Spanish are adversely impacted by the policy. Because they are able to speak English, bilingual employees can engage in conversation on the job. It is axiomatic that "the language a person who is multilingual elects to speak at a particular time is . . . a matter of choice." The bilingual employee can readily comply with the English-only rule and still enjoy the privilege of speaking on the job. "There is no disparate impact" with respect to a privilege of employment "if the rule is one that the affected employee can readily observe and nonobservance is a matter of individual preference."

This analysis is consistent with our decision in *Jurado* v. *Eleven-Fifty Corporation.* In *Jurado,* a bilingual disc jockey was fired for disobeying a rule forbidding him from using an occasional Spanish word or phrase on the air. We concluded that Jurado's disparate impact claim failed "because Jurado was fluently bilingual and could easily comply with the order" and thus could not have been adversely affected.

The Spanish-speaking employees argue that fully bilingual employees are hampered in the enjoyment of the privilege because for them, switching from one language to another is not fully volitional. Whether a bilingual speaker can control which language is used in a given circumstance is a factual issue that cannot be resolved at the summary judgment stage. However, we fail to see the relevance of the assertion, even assuming that it can be proved. Title VII is not meant to protect against rules that merely inconvenience some employees, even if the inconvenience falls regularly on a protected class. Rather, Title VII protects against only those policies that have a *significant* impact. The fact that an employee may have to catch himself or herself from occasionally slipping into Spanish does not impose a burden significant enough to amount to the denial of equal opportunity. This is not a case in which the employees have alleged that the company is enforcing the policy in such a way as to impose penalties for minor slips of the tongue. The fact that a bilingual employee may, on occasion, unconsciously substitute a Spanish word in the place of an English one does not override our conclusion that the bilingual employee can easily comply with the rule. In short, we conclude that a bilingual employee is not denied a privilege of employment by the English-only policy.

By contract, non-English speakers cannot enjoy the privilege of conversing on the job if conversation is limited to a language they cannot speak. As applied "[t]o a person who speaks only one tongue or to a person who has difficulty using another language than the one spoken in his home," an English-only rule might well have an adverse impact. Indeed, counsel for Spun Steak conceded at oral argument that the policy would have an adverse impact on an employee unable to speak English. There is only one employee at Spun Steak affected by the policy who is unable to speak any English. Even with regard to her, however, summary judgment was improper because a genuine issue of material fact exists as to whether she has been adversely affected by the policy. She stated in her deposition that she was not bothered by the rule because she preferred not to make small talk on the job, but rather preferred to work in peace. Furthermore, there is some evidence suggesting that she is not required to comply with the policy when she chooses to speak. For example, she is allowed to speak Spanish to her supervisor. Remand is necessary to determine whether she has suffered adverse effects from the policy. It is unclear from the record whether there are any other employees who have

such limited proficiency in English that they are effectively denied the privilege of speaking on the job. Whether an employee speaks such little English as to be effectively denied the privilege is a question of fact for which summary judgment is improper.

We do not foreclose the prospect that in some circumstances English-only rules can exacerbate existing tensions, or, when combined with other discriminatory behavior, contribute to an overall environment of discrimination. Likewise, we can envision a case in which such rules are enforced in such a draconian manner that the enforcement itself amounts to harassment. In evaluating such a claim, however, a court must look to the totality of the circumstances in the particular factual context in which the claim arises.

In holding that the enactment of an English-only while working policy does not inexorably lead to an abusive environment for those whose primary language is not English, we reach a conclusion opposite to the EEOC's long standing position. The EEOC Guidelines provide that an employee meets the prima facie case in a disparate impact cause of action merely by proving the existence of the English-only policy. Under the EEOC's scheme, an employer must always provide a business justification for such a rule. The EEOC enacted this scheme in part because of its conclusion that English-only rules may "create an atmosphere of inferiority, isolation and intimidation based on national origin which could result in a discriminatory working environment."

We do not reject the English-only rule Guideline lightly. We recognize that "as an administrative interpretation of the Act by the enforcing agency, these Guidelines . . . constitute a body of experience and informed judgment to which courts and litigants may properly resort for guidance." But we are not bound by the Guidelines. We will not defer to "an administrative construction of a statute where there are 'compelling indications that it is wrong.'"

In sum, we conclude that the bilingual employees have not made out a prima facie case and that Spun Steak has not violated Title VII in adopting an English-only rule as to them. Thus, we reverse the grant of summary judgment in favor of Garcia, Buitrago, and Local 115 to the extent it represents the bilingual employees, and remand with instructions to grant summary judgment in favor of Spun Steak on their claims. A genuine issue of material fact exists as to whether there are one or more employees represented by Local 115 with limited proficiency in English who were adversely impacted by the policy. As to such employee or employees, we reverse the grant of summary judgment in favor of Local 115, and remand for further proceedings. REVERSED and REMANDED.

Case Questions

1. Do you agree with the contention that denying a group the right to speak their native tongue denies them the right to cultural expression?

2. Do employees have a "right" to cultural expression in the workplace?

3. Do you agree with the court that an English-only rule is not abusive per se to those whose primary language is not English? Do you believe that it creates a "class system" of languages in the workplace and therefore inherently places one group's language above another's?

Scenario

An employer, therefore, may properly enforce a limited, reasonable, and business-related, English-only rule against an employee who can readily comply. However, if the practice of requiring only English on the job is mere pretext for discrimination on the basis of national origin (i.e., the employer imposes the rule *in order to* discriminate, or the rule produces an atmosphere of ethnic oppression), such a policy would be illegal. This might be the case where an employer requires English to be spoken in all areas of the workplace, even on breaks or in discussions between employees during free time.

Adverse Employment Action and Dissimilar Treatment

The third and fourth requirements will be addressed together because they often arise together. The third element of the prima facie case for national origin discrimination is that the employee is **adversely affected** by the employer's employment decision. This may include a demotion, termination, or removal of privileges afforded to other employees. The adverse effect may arise either because employees of different national origin are treated differently (disparate treatment) or because the policy, though neutral, adversely impacts those of a given national origin (disparate impact).

The fourth element requires that the employee show that her position was filled by someone who is not a member of her protected class or, under other circumstances, that those who are not members of her protected class are treated differently than she. For example, assume an Asian employee is terminated after the third time he is late for work. There is a rule that employees will be terminated if they are late for work more than twice. However, the employer does not enforce the rule against the other employees, only against Asian employees. This would be a case of disparate treatment, because the employee could show that he was treated differently from other employees who were similarly situated but not members of his protected class.

Alternatively, disparate impact has been found, for example, with physical requirements, such as minimum height and weight. Such requirements may have a disparate impact on certain national origin groups as a result of genetic differences among populations and these requirements disproportionately precluded the groups from qualifying for certain jobs. These requirements violate Title VII and must be justified by business necessity. For instance, a requirement that a firefighter be at least 5 feet 7 inches tall was found to be unlawful where the average height of an Anglo man in the United States is 5 feet 8 inches, where Spanish-surnamed American men average 5 feet $4\frac{1}{2}$ inches, and females average 5 feet 3 inches. On the other hand, if the rule can be shown to be a business necessity, it may be allowed (such as some English fluency requirements, as discussed earlier).

adverse employment action
Any action or omission that takes away a benefit, opportunity, or privilege of employment from an employee.

Once the employee has articulated a prima facie case of discrimination based on national origin, the burden falls to the employer to identify either a BFOQ or a legitimate nondiscriminatory reason (LNDR) for the adverse employment action. In the following case, the employer offers two such LNDRs.

Prudencio v. Runyon, Postmaster General, United States Postal Service *986 F. Supp. 343 (W.D. Vir. 1997)*

A brother and sister of Philippine origin took the U.S. Postal Service (USPS) test, scored high marks, and were never hired during a four-year period, while other non-Philippines with lower scores were hired. They sued for national origin discrimination.

Michael, J.

The plaintiffs, Maritess and Robin Prudencio ("Prudencio"), are brother and sister. Both are of Asian (specifically, Philippine) origin. In 1989, both took a United States Postal Service ("USPS" or "Post Office") qualifying examination in an effort to secure employment with the Post Office. Both of the plaintiffs passed the test; Maritess Prudencio received a score of 98.80 out of a possible score of 100 and Robin Prudencio got a score of 94.00. Upon receipt of such passing scores, the plaintiffs were qualified in all respects to be considered for employment.

After the test, in May 1989, the Post Office apparently placed job applicants' names on an eligibility "register" in Richmond from which names are drawn as and when positions become available at designated branches. Names were to be placed on the register in numerical order by the score each applicant received on the qualifying test. When a position opened up, a computer-generated list of names was to be produced in the order of the scores received on the test.

Between 1989 and November 1993, the Post Office never contacted the plaintiffs concerning their status for potential employment. Although on three separate occasions names were drawn, in which Maritess ranked within the applicants on three occasions and Robin met the scoring on two occasions, the plaintiffs were never on the hiring list. Of the four persons hired from the worksheet's list of names all had lower test scores than the plaintiffs; three of the persons hired were white, one was black, and none was Asian.

***

The applicants have alleged sufficient facts in their complaint to state a claim for discriminatory failure to hire. The Prudencios are members of a protected class because of their national origin (Philippine); they were qualified, by virtue of their high scores on the Post Office tests, for the job in the Charlottesville branch for which the USPS was seeking applicants; they were not hired despite their qualifications; and the positions remained open and the USPS continued to seek or accept applications. The employer filled the positions in question with persons of the applicants' qualifications, but from outside the Title VII protected class (i.e., the white persons hired). Moreover, in the administrative proceedings below, the Post Office admitted that the plaintiffs met all elements of the prima facie test.

The USPS objects . . . that the plaintiffs established a prima facie case of national origin discrimination. The defendant argues . . . [that] the USPS did not know that the Prudencios are of Asian ancestry and, thus, within a Title VII protected class. Of course, while knowledge of a job applicant's race by an employer is a prerequisite for intentional discrimination, the necessary knowledge (or constructive knowledge) is present here. As an initial matter, the Prudencios' father, possessing the same surname, has been employed by the Post Office they applied to in Charlottesville for over fifteen years. Additionally, the USPS acquired actual notice of the Prudencios' national origin when the plaintiffs personally appeared before postal employees to take the employment test in 1989 and again in 1993 to request copies of the "Individual Applicant Ranking Report." Because the burden of establishing a prima facie case of discrimination is not an "onerous" one, and because the USPS had either actual or constructive notice of the plaintiffs' protected national origin status, defendant's motion to dismiss or for summary judgment shall be denied. The Prudencios make out a classic prima facie case of employment discrimination under the *McDonnell Douglas* paradigm.

The defendant-employer must "articulate some legitimate, nondiscriminatory reason for the employee's rejection." Once a plaintiff has established a prima facie case of discrimination, "the employer must respond or lose."

***

Here, the Post Office's attempts to proffer two "legitimate nondiscriminatory reasons" that accounted for the omission of the Prudencios' names from the worksheet issued for the Charlottesville branch's vacancies. One such reason is that an administrative or computer error of some type in the Richmond office removed the Prudencios' names from the active list of applicants when the registry was automated; the Post Office headquarters in Richmond failed to forward the full list of qualified applicants to the branch office in Charlottesville where the ultimate hiring decision was made. Thus, because the Richmond Post Office, for whatever reason, omitted the plaintiffs' names from the registry, the Charlottesville branch was operating on a legitimate, nondiscriminatory basis when it failed to hire the Prudencios.

The plaintiffs argue, and the court agrees, however, that in addition to the above reason's overly syllogistic logic, the USPS cannot and does not know that an innocent error (administrative, computer, or otherwise) accounted for the plaintiffs' exclusion from the Charlottesville job candidates' list. Indeed, as the Post Office itself stated

> The Postal Service merely speculate[s] that the omission of the Plaintiffs' names from the hiring work sheets resulted from administrative or computer error. What actually caused the apparent error is not known.

In this court's view, the USPS's concession that it does not know the reason for the exclusion of the plaintiffs from the employment candidates' list is the logical and legal equivalent of proffering no reason for the omission. Because, as a matter of law, "no reason" cannot serve as a "legitimate, nondiscriminatory reason," the plaintiffs' prima facie showing of national origin discrimination remains unrebutted. Under the *McDonnell Douglas* framework, then, the Prudencios are entitled to judgment as a matter of law. Judgment GRANTED for the Prudencios.

Case Questions

1. Who has to prove a company discriminated against an employee or applicant? Do you agree with this?

2. Do you think this was an "honest mistake" by the Post Office? If so, how can the Post Office prove that it had unintentionally removed the plaintiffs from the list?

3. As an employer, what is the best way for you to protect the company from charges accusing the employer of hiring discrimination?

HARASSMENT ON THE BASIS OF NATIONAL ORIGIN

In addition to traditional claims of discrimination under Title VII, employees are also protected under Title VII against harassment on the basis of national origin. Unfortunately, claims of national origin harassment have been on a sharp increase, rising from 1,383 charges filed with the EEOC in 1993 to practically double that amount (2,719) in 2002. In fact, in 2002, 30 percent of all national origin charges filed with the EEOC included a claim of harassment.

Not all harassment is prohibited under Title VII. Similar to claims of sexual harassment, claims of national origin harassment are only actionable if the harassment was so severe or pervasive that the employee reasonably finds the workplace to be hostile or abusive. Common concerns include ethnic slurs, workplace graffiti, or other offenses based on traits such as an employee's birthplace, culture, accent, or skin color. In considering employer liability, the court will look to whether the conduct was physically threatening or intimidating, its severity, pervasiveness throughout the working environment, whether a reasonable person would find the conduct offensive and/or hostile, and how the employer responded. The EEOC offers the following examples of conduct that do and do not satisfy this review:[6]

Offensive Conduct Based on National Origin that Violates Title VII

Muhammad, an Arab-American, works for XYZ Motors, a large automobile dealership. His coworkers regularly call him names like "camel jockey," "the local terrorist," and "the ayatollah," and intentionally embarrass him in front of customers by claiming that he is incompetent. Muhammad reports this conduct to higher management, but XYZ does not respond. The constant ridicule has made it difficult for Muhammad to do his job. The frequent, severe, and offensive conduct linked to Muhammad's national origin has created a hostile work environment in violation of Title VII.[7]

Offensive Conduct Based on National Origin that Does Not Violate Title VII

Henry, a Romanian emigrant, was hired by XYZ Shipping as a dockworker. On his first day, Henry dropped a carton, prompting Bill, the foreman, to yell at him. The same day, Henry overheard Bill telling a coworker that foreigners were stealing jobs from Americans. Two months later, Bill confronted Henry about an argument with a coworker, called him a "lazy jerk," and mocked his accent. Although Bill's conduct was offensive, it was not sufficiently severe or pervasive for the work environment to be reasonably considered sufficiently hostile or abusive to violate Title VII.

Employers have the responsibility to prevent and correct any national origin harassment that may take place within its working environment. However, that responsibility is limited to occurrences of harassment of which the employer knows or should have known. Consequently, if an employee is consistently subject to abuse but never informs the employer and the supervisors at her or his workplace have no other way of knowing the abuse is taking place, the employer may not be liable. In addition, if the employer is aware of or is made aware of the harassment and takes reasonable steps to prevent and correct it, the employer may likewise be relieved of any liability.

---

[6] http://www.eeoc.gov/policy/docs/national-origin.html.

[7] The EEOC based this example on *Amirmokri* v. *Baltimore Gas & Electric Co.*, 60 F.3d 1126 (4th Cir. 1995) (finding that Iranian emigrant employed as an engineer at a nuclear power plant established a prima facie case of national origin harassment).

Kang v. U. Lim America, Inc. *296 F.3d 810 (9th Cir. 2002)*

Kang is a United States citizen of Korean national origin working for a California corporation called U. Lim America, Inc. All of U. Lim America's employees shared Korean heritage. Tae Jin Yoon was Kang's supervisor. Yoon subjected Kang and other Korean workers to verbal and physical abuse and discriminatorily long work hours. The verbal abuse consisted of Yoon screaming at Kang for up to three hours a day and calling him "stupid," "cripple," 'jerk," "son of a bitch," and "asshole." The physical abuse consisted of striking Kang in the head with a metal ruler on approximately 20 occasions, kicking him in the shins, pulling his ears, throwing metal ashtrays, calculators, water bottles, and files at him, and forcing him to do jumping jacks. Kang began to cut back on the required overtime in order to spend time with his pregnant wife; Yoon fired him. Kang filed suit in California state court against U. Lim America and Yoon for national origin discrimination and harassment in violation of Title VII and the California Fair Employment and Housing Act. The district court granted summary judgment to U. Lim America and Yoon on all Kang's causes of action. Kang appealed.

Browning, C.J.

We reverse summary judgment for the employer on Kang's harassment claim.

To prevail on his harassment claim, Kang must show: (1) that he was subjected to verbal or physical conduct because of his national origin; (2) "that the conduct was unwelcome"; and (3) "that the conduct was sufficiently severe or pervasive to alter the conditions of the plaintiff's employment and create an abusive work environment." Generally, a plaintiff alleging racial or national origin harassment would present facts showing that he was subjected to racial epithets in the workplace. Here, however, Kang alleged that he and other Korean workers were subjected to physical and verbal abuse because their supervisor viewed their national origin as superior. The form is unusual, but such stereotyping is an evil at which the statute is aimed. See *Nichols* v. *Azteca Rest. Enters., Inc.,* 256 F.3d 864, 874–75 (9th Cir. 2001) (holding that a plaintiff proved harassment "because of sex" where he was harassed because he failed to conform to male stereotypes).

Kang presented evidence that Yoon abused him because of Yoon's stereotypical notions that Korean workers were better than the rest and Kang's failure to live up to Yoon's expectations. On numerous occasions, Yoon told Kang that he had to work harder because he was Korean; he contrasted Koreans with Mexicans and Americans who he said were not hard workers; and although U. Lim America employed 50–150 Mexican workers, Yoon did not subject any of them to physical abuse. This evidence created a genuine issue of material fact as to whether Yoon's abuse and imposition of longer working hours was based on Kang's national origin.

Kang also presented evidence that the physical and verbal abuse and long working hours were in fact unwelcome. See *Faragher* v. *City of Boca Raton* (1998) (discussing the requirement that the victim perceive the environment as offensive).

Kang's evidence further showed that the verbal and physical abuse and discriminatory working hours created a work environment that was "objectively offensive . . . one that a reasonable person would find hostile or abusive." *Id.* "The more outrageous the conduct, the less frequent [sic] must it occur to make a workplace hostile." After considering all the circumstances including the frequency and severity of the conduct, the fact that the abuse was frequently "physically threatening or humiliating" and that it unreasonably interfered with Kang's work performance, we conclude that Kang presented evidence sufficient to survive summary judgment that Yoon subjected Kang to an objectively hostile environment.

Case Questions

1. Do you agree that harassment because a worker is viewed as superior is as "evil" as harassment based on a perception that someone is inferior?

2. Does the conduct described seem sufficiently severe and pervasive as to constitute harassment under the *Faragher* definition?

3. Can you make any argument that the definition of sexual harassment and of harassment based on national origin should be different?

GUIDELINES ON DISCRIMINATION BECAUSE OF RELIGION OR NATIONAL ORIGIN

Federal agencies or employers who enter into contracts with a government agency are required by the **Guidelines on Discrimination Because of Religion or National Origin** to ensure that individuals are hired and retained without regard to their religion or national origin. These guidelines impose on the federal contractor an affirmative

Guidelines on Discrimination Because of Religion or National Origin
Federal guidelines that apply only to federal contractors or agencies and that impose on these employers an affirmative duty to prevent discrimination.

obligation to prevent discrimination. The provisions include the following ethnic groups: Eastern, Middle, and Southern European ancestry, including Jews, Catholics, Italians, Greeks, and Slavs. Blacks, Spanish-surnamed Americans, Asians, and Native Americans are specifically excluded from the guidelines' coverage because of their protection elsewhere in Office of Federal Contract Compliance Rules.

The guidelines provide that, subsequent to a review of the employer's policies, the employer should engage in appropriate outreach and positive recruitment activities to remedy existing deficiencies (i.e., affirmative action). Various approaches to this outreach requirement include the following:

1. Internal communication of the obligation to provide equal employment opportunity without regard to religion or national origin.
2. Development of reasonable internal procedures to ensure that the equal employment policy is fully implemented.
3. Periodic informing of all employees of the employer's commitment to equal employment opportunity for all persons, without regard to religion or national origin.
4. Enlistment of the support and assistance of all recruitment sources.
5. Review of employment records to determine the availability of promotable and transferable members of various religious and ethnic groups.
6. Establishment of meaningful contacts with religious and ethnic organizations and leaders for such purposes as advice, education, technical assistance, and referral of potential employees (many organizations send job announcements to these community groups when recruiting for positions).
7. Significant recruitment activities at educational institutions with substantial enrollments of students from various religious and ethnic groups.
8. Use of the religious and ethnic media for institutional and employment advertising.

MIDDLE EASTERN DISCRIMINATION AFTER SEPTEMBER 11, 2001

In the aftermath of September 11, hate crimes against individuals of Middle Eastern descent dramatically increased. Workplace discrimination complaints brought by Muslims and those of Middle Eastern descent also rose sharply. From September 11, 2001, to February 2002, the EEOC received 260 such claims, an increase of 168 percent over the same period a year earlier. The EEOC even created a special classification, "Code Z," to designate complaints tied to September 11.[8]

Scenario 1 exhibits one post–September 11 incident. Further examples include a California employee who was allegedly fired without explanation after being told by her boss not to reveal to anyone that her husband is Palestinian and a New York City nurse who was ordered to take some time off and then was given a lesser

[8] See Eric Lichtblau, "Bias against U.S. Arabs Taking Subtler Forms," *Los Angeles Times,* Feb. 10, 2002, p. A20.

position "for her own safety" after she reported that a coworker threatened to "kill Muslims."[9]

The U.S. Department of Justice (DoJ), through its National Origin Working Group, is working proactively to combat civil rights violations against Arab, Sikh, and South-Asian Americans, as well as those who are perceived to be members of those groups. The initiative is striving to battle against these crimes and discrimination by identifying cases involving bias crimes, conducting outreach and working with other DoJ offices. As of February 2004, the initiative had helped to respond to 546 incidents of bias crime, alone, resulting in federal charges in 13 cases with 18 defendants and a 100 percent conviction rate. In one case, *EEOC* v. *Fairfield Toyota* [No. Cir-S-03-657 (E.D. Calif. 2004)], two auto dealerships agreed to pay seven former workers $550,000. The suit was filed by workers of Afghani national origin and Muslim faith as a result of harassment they suffered on the job. One worker claimed constructive discharge and others suffered retaliation after complaining about the harassment.

Issues of concern and questions that have arisen from these cases have centered on a few key issues. Employers may not treat workers differently because of their religious attire, such as a Muslin *hijab* (head scarf). Employers also need to be sensitive to possible instances of ethnic harassment, especially that which may unfairly relate to security concerns. Finally, employers may not require individuals of one ethnic background to undergo more significant security checks or other preemployment requirements unless all applicants for that position are required to do so.

In the post–September 11 era, employers actually have a unique opportunity to raise awareness of and sensitivity to cultural diversity in the workplace. Elmer Johnson, head of the Aspen Institute, which seeks to improve corporate leadership, has stated that corporate leaders should inspire employees and inculcate a sense of shared values.[10] Perhaps this can be achieved by reaching out to employees of Middle Eastern descent who may be experiencing fear of discrimination. Jaffe Dickerson, a partner of the Littler, Mendelson law firm, had a client's Middle Eastern employee confide that he no longer wants to travel by air or go out to clubs after work out of fear of being victimized by bias.[11] Remaining sensitive to such employees' concerns in job assignments and work-related activities is key to their effective resolution. "Quick fixes," such as compulsory transfer to another position, must be avoided. To further promote a healthy environment at work, employers should also consider the post–September 11 issues in diversity training.

It should be noted that, under certain limited circumstances, employers may reach decisions on the basis of national origin by relying on security requirements, where the security requirements are imposed "in the interest of national security under any security program in effect pursuant to federal statute or executive order."[12]

---

[9] Ibid.

[10] See "CEOs: Human and Humane," *Corporate Counsel,* Oct. 19, 2001.

[11] See "Employment Counsel Tackle Anxieties and Problems after September 11," *National Law Journal,* Oct. 29, 2001.

[12] 42 U.S.C. 2000e-2(g).

CITIZENSHIP AND THE IMMIGRATION REFORM AND CONTROL ACT

As mentioned earlier in this chapter, Title VII's prohibition against discrimination on the basis of national origin does not necessarily prohibit discrimination on the basis of citizenship; this only occurs where citizenship discrimination "has the purpose or effect" of national origin discrimination or where it is pretext for national origin discrimination. In fact, legal aliens (noncitizens residing in the United States) are often restricted from access to certain government or other positions by statute. For instance, in *Foley* v. *Connelie,* 435 U.S. 291 (1978), the Supreme Court held that a rule requiring citizenship was valid in connection with certain nonelected positions held by officers who participate directly in the formulation, execution, or review of broad public policy. This is called the "political function" exception for positions that are intimately related to the process of self-government. In cases where the restricted position satisfies this exception, discrimination against legal aliens is permitted. *Espinoza* (on page 470) is the seminal case in the area of discrimination on the basis of citizenship.

The Immigration Reform and Control Act (IRCA), *in contrast to Title VII,* does prohibit employers in certain circumstances from discriminating against employees on the basis of their citizenship or intended citizenship, and from hiring those not legally authorized for employment in the United States. However, IRCA does allow discrimination in favor of United States citizens as against legal aliens. While aliens are guaranteed various rights pursuant to the Constitution, citizenship confers certain benefits only to those who are citizens and not to those who are legal aliens in the United States. For instance, while rights pursuant to the National Labor Relation Act and Fair Labor Standards Act are provided to citizens and aliens alike, government-provided benefits, such as Medicare and Medicaid, are limited to citizens. Also, the IRCA allows employers to enact a preference for U.S. citizens if the applicants are all equally qualified. Employers may not act on this preference if the foreign national is more qualified for the position than the U.S. citizen.

Employers not subject to Title VII's prohibitions because of their small size may still be sufficiently large to be covered by IRCA's antidiscrimination provisions; those employers with 4 through 14 employees are prohibited from discriminating on the basis of national origin; and employers with 4 or more employees may not discriminate on the basis of citizenship.

Two acceptable BFOQs are statutorily allowed under IRCA:

1. English-language skill requirements that are reasonably necessary to the normal operation of the particular business or enterprise.
2. Citizenship requirements specified by law, regulation, executive order, or government contracts, along with citizenship requirements that the U.S. attorney general determines to be essential for doing business with the government.

The main difference between a proof of discrimination under Title VII and IRCA is that, in proving a case of disparate impact, Title VII does not require proof of discriminatory intent, while IRCA requires that the adverse action be knowingly and intentionally discriminatory. Therefore, innocent or negligent discrimination is a complete defense to a claim of discrimination under IRCA.

For example, consider a hypothetical firm, Talbort Industries, which was interviewing for customer service representatives in their large order processing department. They required all applicants to speak fluent English. Ching Lee applied and was denied employment due to his accent, which some thought was heavy. It turns out that only 3 applicants out of 20 of Asian descent obtained jobs at Talbort. Talbort explained to Lee that not many Chinese applicants apply and those who do have had strong accents. They claim customers have complained of not understanding these individuals. Does Lee have a claim under Title VII? Under IRCA? Without the showing of knowing and intentional discrimination, Talbort Industries could survive the IRCA claim if Lee could not prove they discriminated against him intentionally; however, such knowledge and intention is not required under Title VII and Lee might prevail.

Espinoza v. Farah Manufacturing Co. *414 U.S. 86 (1973)*

Cecilia Espinoza, a lawful Mexican alien, applied for a position at Farah Manufacturing's San Antonio Division. She was denied the position, however, as a result of Farah's policy to hire only U.S. citizens. The issue to be decided by the court is whether Title VII's proscription against discrimination on the basis of national origin protects against discrimination on the basis of citizenship.

Marshall, J.

The term "national origin" on its face refers to the country where a person was born, or, more broadly, the country from which his or her ancestors came.

There are other compelling reasons to believe that Congress did not intend the term "national origin" to embrace citizenship requirements. Since 1914, the Federal Government itself, through Civil Service Commission regulations, has engaged in what amounts to discrimination against aliens by denying them the right to enter competitive examination for federal employment. But it has never been suggested that the citizenship requirement for federal employment constitutes discrimination because of national origin. To interpret the term "national origin" to embrace citizenship requirements would require us to conclude that Congress itself has repeatedly flouted its own declaration of policy. This Court cannot lightly find such a breach of faith. Certainly Title VII prohibits discrimination on the basis of citizenship whenever it has the purpose or effect of discriminating on the basis of national origin. However, there is no indication in the record that Farah's policy against employment of aliens had the purpose or effect of discriminating against persons of Mexican national origin.

Douglas, J., dissenting

It is odd that the Court which holds that a State may not bar an alien from the practice of law or deny employment to aliens can read a federal statute that prohibits discrimination in employment on account of "national origin" so as to permit discrimination against aliens.

Alienage results from one condition only: being born outside the United States. Those born within the country are citizens from birth. It could not be more clear that Farah's policy of excluding aliens is *de facto* a policy of preferring those who were born in this country.

Case Questions

1. Which argument, the majority's or the dissent, do you find more compelling?

2. What implications does this case have for hiring practices in parts of the United States where aliens are prevalent?

3. If Espinoza could show that this policy, while arguably "facially neutral," actually impacts people of

Mexican origin differently than people of American origin, wouldn't Espinoza have a claim for disparate impact?

"Undocumented Workers"

A section of the IRCA was established to correct an unfair double standard that prohibited unauthorized aliens from working in the United States but permitted employers to hire them. Among other things, IRCA makes it unlawful for any person knowingly to hire, recruit, or refer for a fee any alien not authorized to work. Employers are required to verify all newly hired employees by examining documents that identify the individual and show his or her authority to work in the United States using an I-9 form. (See Exhibits 10.3 and 10.4.) Further, employers, recruiters, and those who refer individuals for employment are required to keep records pertaining to IRCA requirements. (For a list of employer responsibilities under IRCA, see Exhibit 10.5.)

IRCA also established civil and criminal penalties for hiring illegal aliens. Employers are selected at random for compliance inspections under the General Administrative Plan (GAP) developed by the Immigration and Naturalization Services (INS), the administrative agency charged with oversight of IRCA. Generally fines are not imposed for paperwork violations alone or for employment of aliens whose illegal status was unknown, unless the employer refused to comply or other egregious factors existed. However, employers who knowingly employed illegal aliens after receiving education regarding IRCA or visits or GAP inspections will receive a Notice of Intent to Fine.[13]

However, in its October 1999 "Enforcement Guidance on Remedies Available to Undocumented Workers," the EEOC emphasized that workers' undocumented status does not justify workplace discrimination. The EEOC also set forth that employers' liability for monetary remedies irrespective of a worker's unauthorized status promotes the goal of deterring unlawful discrimination without undermining the purposes of IRCA. The EEOC's position on available remedies is that unauthorized workers are entitled to the same remedies as any other worker, including back pay and reinstatement. The National Labor Relations Board took a similar position with respect to discrimination based on union activity.

However, in *Hoffman Plastic Compounds Inc.* v. *NLRB,* 122 S. Ct. 1275 (2002), the U.S. Supreme Court held that the NLRB could not award back pay to unauthorized workers who had been unlawfully discriminated against for engaging in union-organizing activities. According to the Court, to do so would contravene federal immigration policy embodied in IRCA. *Hoffman* opens the possibility that back pay will not be available to unauthorized workers who have been illegally discriminated against under

---

[13] See www.ins.gov/graphics/aboutins/history/sanctions.htm.

Exhibit 10.3 INS Employment Form and Document List

U.S. Department of Justice
Immigration and Naturalization Service

OMB No. 1115-0136
Employment Eligibility Verification

Please read instructions carefully before completing this form. The instructions must be available during completion of this form. ANTI-DISCRIMINATION NOTICE: It is illegal to discriminate against work eligible individuals. Employers CANNOT specify which document(s) they will accept from an employee. The refusal to hire an individual because of a future expiration date may also constitute illegal discrimination.

Section 1. Employee Information and Verification. To be completed and signed by employee at the time employment begins.

Print Name: Last	First	Middle Initial	Maiden Name

Address (Street Name and Number)	Apt. #	Date of Birth (month/day/year)

City	State	Zip Code	Social Security #

I am aware that federal law provides for imprisonment and/or fines for false statements or use of false documents in connection with the completion of this form.

I attest, under penalty of perjury, that I am (check one of the following):
☐ A citizen or national of the United States
☐ A Lawful Permanent Resident (Alien # A_____)
☐ An alien authorized to work until ___/___/___
(Alien # or Admission #) _____

Employee's Signature	Date (month/day/year)

Preparer and/or Translator Certification. (To be completed and signed if Section 1 is prepared by a person other than the employee.) I attest, under penalty of perjury, that I have assisted in the completion of this form and that to the best of my knowledge the information is true and correct.

Preparer's/Translator's Signature	Print Name

Address (Street Name and Number, City, State, Zip Code)	Date (month/day/year)

Section 2. Employer Review and Verification. To be completed and signed by employer. Examine one document from List A OR examine one document from List B and one from List C, as listed on the reverse of this form, and record the title, number and expiration date, if any, of the document(s)

List A	OR	List B	AND	List C
Document title: _____		_____		_____
Issuing authority: _____		_____		_____
Document #: _____		_____		_____
Expiration Date (if any): ___/___/___		___/___/___		___/___/___
Document #: _____				
Expiration Date (if any): ___/___/___				

CERTIFICATION - I attest, under penalty of perjury, that I have examined the document(s) presented by the above-named employee, that the above-listed document(s) appear to be genuine and to relate to the employee named, that the employee began employment on *(month/day/year)* ___/___/___ **and that to the best of my knowledge the employee is eligible to work in the United States. (State employment agencies may omit the date the employee began employment.)**

Signature of Employer or Authorized Representative	Print Name	Title

Business or Organization Name	Address (Street Name and Number, City, State, Zip Code)	Date (month/day/year)

Section 3. Updating and Reverification. To be completed and signed by employer.

A. New Name (if applicable)	B. Date of rehire (month/day/year) (if applicable)

C. If employee's previous grant of work authorization has expired, provide the information below for the document that establishes current employment eligibility.

Document Title:_____   Document #: _____   Expiration Date (if any): ___/___/___

I attest, under penalty of perjury, that to the best of my knowledge, this employee is eligible to work in the United States, and if the employee presented document(s), the document(s) I have examined appear to be genuine and to relate to the individual.

Signature of Employer or Authorized Representative	Date (month/day/year)

Form I-9 (Rev. 11-21-91)N Page 2

Exhibit 10.3 (continued)

LISTS OF ACCEPTABLE DOCUMENTS

LIST A		LIST B		LIST C
Documents that Establish Both Identity and Employment Eligibility	**OR**	Documents that Establish Identity	**AND**	Documents that Establish Employment Eligibility

LIST A — Documents that Establish Both Identity and Employment Eligibility

1. U.S. Passport (unexpired or expired)

2. Certificate of U.S. Citizenship (INS Form N-560 or N-561)

3. Certificate of Naturalization (INS Form N-550 or N-570)

4. Unexpired foreign passport, with I-551 stamp or attached INS Form I-94 indicating unexpired employment authorization

5. Permanent Resident Card or Alien Registration Receipt Card with photograph (INS Form I-151 or I-551)

6. Unexpired Temporary Resident Card (INS Form I-688)

7. Unexpired Employment Authorization Card (INS Form I-688A)

8. Unexpired Reentry Permit (INS Form I-327)

9. Unexpired Refugee Travel Document (INS Form I-571)

10. Unexpired Employment Authorization Document issued by the INS which contains a photograph (INS Form I-688B)

OR

LIST B — Documents that Establish Identity

1. Driver's license or ID card issued by a state or outlying possession of the United States provided it contains a photograph or information such as name, date of birth, gender, height, eye color and address

2. ID card issued by federal, state or local government agencies or entities, provided it contains a photograph or information such as name, date of birth, gender, height, eye color and address

3. School ID card with a photograph

4. Voter's registration card

5. U.S. Military card or draft record

6. Military dependent's ID card

7. U.S. Coast Guard Merchant Mariner Card

8. Native American tribal document

9. Driver's license issued by a Canadian government authority

For persons under age 18 who are unable to present a document listed above:

10. School record or report card

11. Clinic, doctor or hospital record

12. Day-care or nursery school record

AND

LIST C — Documents that Establish Employment Eligibility

1. U.S. social security card issued by the Social Security Administration (other than a card stating it is not valid for employment)

2. Certification of Birth Abroad issued by the Department of State (Form FS-545 or Form DS-1350)

3. Original or certified copy of a birth certificate issued by a state, county, municipal authority or outlying possession of the United States bearing an official seal

4. Native American tribal document

5. U.S. Citizen ID Card (INS Form I-197)

6. ID Card for use of Resident Citizen in the United States (INS Form I-179)

7. Unexpired employment authorization document issued by the INS (other than those listed under List A)

Illustrations of many of these documents appear in Part 8 of the Handbook for Employers (M-274)

Exhibit 10.4   Frequently Asked Questions About Employment Eligibility

FREQUENTLY ASKED QUESTIONS ABOUT EMPLOYMENT ELIGIBILITY

Do citizens and nationals of the U.S. need to prove, to their employers, they are eligible to work?

Yes, While citizens and nationals of the U.S. are automatically eligible for employment, they too must present proof of employment eligibility and identity and complete an Employment Eligibility Verification form (Form I-9). Citizens of the U.S. include persons born in Puerto Rico, Guam, the U.S. Virgin Islands, and the Northern Mariana Islands. Nationals of the U.S. include persons born in American Samoa, including Swains Island.

Do I need to complete a Form I-9 for everyone who applies for a job with my company?

No. you need to complete Form I-9 only for people you actually hire. For purposes of the I-9 rules, a person is "hired" when he or she begins to work for you for wages or other compensation.

I understand that I must complete a Form I-9 for anyone I hire to perform labor or services in return for wages or other remuneration. What is "remuneration"?

Remuneration is anything of value given in exchange for labor or services rendered by an employee, including food and lodging.

Can I fire an employee who fails to produce the required document(s) within three (3) business days?

Yes. You can terminate an employee who fails to produce the required document(s), or a receipt for a replacement document(s) (in the case of lost, stolen or destroyed documents), within three (3) business days of the date employment begins. However, you must apply these practices uniformly to all employees. If an employee has presented a receipt for a replacement document(s), he or she must produce the actual document(s) within 90 days of the date employment begins.

What happens if I properly complete a Form I-9 and the BICE discovers that my employee is not actually authorized to work?

You cannot be charged with a verification violation; however, you cannot knowingly continue to employ this individual. You will have a good faith defense against the imposition of employer sanctions penalties for knowingly hiring an unauthorized alien unless the government can prove you had actual knowledge of the unauthorized status of the employee.

What is my responsibility concerning the authenticity of document(s) presented to me?

You must examine the document(s) and, if they reasonably appear on their face to be genuine and to relate to the person presenting them, you must accept them. To do otherwise could be an unfair immigration-related employment practice. If a document does not reasonably appear on its face to be genuine and to relate to the person presenting it, you must not accept it. You may contact your local BICE office for assistance. To get the address and telephone number of the BICE office nearest you, please click the BICE district office directory.

May I accept a photocopy of a document presented by an employee?

No. Employees must present original documents. The only exception is an employee may present a certified copy of a birth certificate.

Source: Publication of the U.S. Citizenship and Immigration Service, http://uscis.gov/graphics/howdoi/eev.htm.

Exhibit 10.5
Employer Responsibilities under IRCA: Dos and Don'ts

Subject	Do	Don't
Completion of Form I-9, Section 1	New employees must complete Section 1 in full before the end of their first day of work if expected to work fewer than three days; otherwise they have until the end of their third day of work. Applies to all workers hired to perform labor or services in return for wages or other remuneration.	Do not require only certain employees to comply before the end of their first day of work.
Completion of Form I-9, Section 2	Employer must examine proper documentation (one from List A or one each from List B and C). Employer must accept the documents if they reasonably appear to be genuine. This must be completed by the end of the new employee's third day of work. Employer must refuse acceptance of documents that do not reasonably appear to be genuine.	Do not accept copies or faxes of documents. (Note: The only exception is for a certified copy of a birth certificate.) Do not require more or different documentation than the minimum necessary to avoid an unfair immigration-related employment practice. Do not require completion of the I-9 in the preoffer stage.
Genuineness of documents and reporting	If a document does not reasonably appear to be genuine, employer may ask for assistance from INS.	[If a document that reasonably appeared to be genuine is in fact not genuine, the employer will not be held responsible by the INS.]
Discovering unauthorized employees	Employer should question the employee and provide another opportunity for review of proper I-9 documentation.	If the employee is not able to provide satisfactory documentation after an opportunity to do so, the employer should not retain the employee. Do not make threats of reporting the employee to the INS in retaliation for discrimination complaints or other protected activity.
Discovering false documentation	If an employee gains employment with false documentation but then later obtains and presents proper work authorization, the employer should correct the relevant information on Form I-9. Personnel policies regarding provision of false information to the employer may apply.	Employers do not have to terminate an employee who presents subsequent work authorization.

(continued)

475

Exhibit 10.5   (continued)

Subject	Do	Don't
"Green cards"	Resident Alien cards, Permanent Resident card, Alien Registration Receipt card, and Form I-551 grant permanent residence in the U.S. Proof of this status may expire. Alien cardholders must obtain new cards. Employers should check that unexpired "green cards" used for Form I-9 appear genuine and establish identity of the cardholder.	Employers should not accept an expired card for purposes of Form I-9. Employers are neither required nor permitted to reverify the employment authorization of aliens who have presented one of these cards to satisfy I-9 requirements.
Social Security cards	For purposes of payroll, employers may accept SSA cards that bear the restriction "Not Valid for Employment" from employees who satisfy I-9 requirements. Often those who initially got such a restricted SSA card proceed to permanent residence or U.S. citizenship.	Employers must not accept restricted SSA cards for purposes of I-9 requirements. Employers must not accept Individual Taxpayer Identification numbers for purposes of I-9 requirements.
Retention of I-9 forms	Generally, retain during an employee's employment and the longer of either three years past the hire date or one year past the termination date.	While not prohibited from doing so, private employers should not store I-9 records in employee personnel files.
Official inspection of I-9 records	Generally, all I-9 forms of current employees must be made available in their original form or on microfilm or microfiche to an authorized official upon request. The official will give employers at least three days advance notice before the inspection.	Employers should not leave preparation for such an inspection to the last minute! Storing I-9 records in employee personnel files makes this task unduly difficult.

Sources: INS, "IRCA and Employer Sanctions," uscis.gov/graphics/aboutins/history/sanctions.htm, last modified Feb. 28, 2003; INS, "About Form I-9, Employment Eligibility Verification," uscis.gov/graphics/howdoi/faqeev.htm, last modified Feb. 9, 2004; INS, "Frequently Asked Questions about Employment Eligibility," uscis.gov/graphics/howdoi/EEV.htm, last modified Feb. 19, 2003.

Title VII, the Americans with Disabilities Act (ADA), and the Age Discrimination in Employment Act (ADEA).[14] The court reviews the pre-Hoffman history and implications in the following case.

[14] See Donna Y. Porter, "Undocumented Workers Have NLRA Rights, but Not Monetary Remedies," *Employment Law Strategies,* June 6, 2002.

Singh v. Jutla & C.D. & R's Oil, Inc., *214 F. Supp.2d 1056 (N.D.C.A. 2002)*

Macan Singh sued his employer, alleging that his employer reported Singh to the Immigration and Naturalization Service (INS) in retaliation for Singh's filing of wage claim, in violation of Fair Labor Standards Act (FLSA). On employer's motion to dismiss, the District Court held that: (1) employee's filing of wage claim was protected activity, and (2) employee's allegations were sufficient to state claim for retaliation.

Breyer, District Judge

BACKGROUND

As alleged, defendant Jutla recruited plaintiff, Macan Singh, to come work for him in the United States. Jutla promised plaintiff a place to live, tuition for education, and that plaintiff would eventually become Jutla's business partner in his corporation, C.D. & R's Oil Inc. Plaintiff, in the United States illegally, worked for Jutla from approximately May 1995 to February 1998 and received no pay.

On January 6, 1999, plaintiff filed a wage claim against defendants with the California Department of Industrial Relations ("Labor Commissioner"), pursuant to section 98 of the California Labor Code. Plaintiff sought unpaid wages and overtime pay for work actually performed. After plaintiff filed the claim, Jutla threatened to report him to the Immigration and Naturalization Services ("INS") unless the claim was dropped. Jutla also tried to force Singh to sign a written waiver of his claims. Plaintiff, however, refused to submit to Jutla. The Labor Commissioner awarded plaintiff $69,633.73. Defendants appealed from the Labor Commission's judgment by filing an action in the Alameda Superior Court. On February 23, 2001, the first day of the trial, the parties settled. In a written agreement signed by both parties on May 3, 2001, Jutla agreed to make scheduled payments to Singh.

The following day, May 4, 2001, the INS arrested and detained plaintiff. Plaintiff has been in INS custody for fourteen months. He alleges that defendant Jutla contacted the INS and provided them with information of plaintiff's status in an act of retaliation.

On March 7, 2002, plaintiff filed a complaint with this Court against defendants for retaliation under the FLSA and the California Labor Code, requesting declaratory, injunctive, and monetary relief.

DISCUSSION

***

II. Pre-*Hoffman* Law

Defendants contend that under *Hoffman Plastic Compounds, Inc.* v. *NLRB,* plaintiff has no cause of action. Before this argument can be addressed, however, it is necessary to briefly discuss the relevant law prior to *Hoffman.*

A. Undocumented Aliens Have a Cause of Action under the National Labor Reform Act ("NLRA")

In *Sure-Tan, Inc.* v. *NLRB,* the Supreme Court held that undocumented aliens could bring an action under the NLRA. Broadly speaking, *Sure-Tan* stands for the proposition that undocumented workers are protected from unfair labor practices under the NLRA, and specifically, that when the evidence establishes that an employer reported the presence of an illegal employee to the INS In retaliation for the employee's protected union activity that the alien has a cause of action under section 8(a)(3) of the NLRA. The *Sure-Tan* court recognized, however, that if there is no specific finding of anti-union animus, reporting an undocumented alien employee would not be an unfair labor practice.

The *Sure-Tan* Court also recognized that undocumented aliens are "employees" within the meaning of section 2(3) of the Act. That provision broadly provides that "[t]he term 'employee' shall include any employee," subject only to certain specifically enumerated exceptions.

The *Sure-Tan* Court reasoned that allowing undocumented workers to bring a cause of action under the NLRB furthered the purposes of the NLRA because "[i]f undocumented alien employees were excluded from participation in union activities and from protections against employer intimidation, there would be created a subclass of workers without a comparable stake in the collective goals of their legally resident co-workers, thereby eroding the unity of all the employees and impeding effective collective bargaining." See *NLRB* v. *Jones & Laughlin Steel Corp.*

The Court held that application of the NLRA to illegal aliens "helps to assure that the wages and employment conditions of lawful residents are not adversely affected by the competition of illegal alien employees who are not subject to the standard terms of employment. If an employer realizes that there will be no advantage under the NLRA in preferring illegal aliens to legal resident workers, any incentive to hire such illegal aliens is correspondingly lessened."

B. FLSA Covers Undocumented Aliens

The underlying rationale in *Sure-Tan,* that the NLRA applies to illegal aliens, was extended in *Patel* v. *Quality Inn South,* where the Eleventh Circuit held that the FLSA applies to illegal aliens. Applying the *Sure-Tan* analysis, the court looked to the reasoning behind the FLSA and what its objectives were in terms of both legal and illegal workers. The *Patel* court also had to consider the Immigration Reform Control Act ("IRCA") which had not yet been passed when the Supreme Court handed down *Sure-Tan.* The IRCA is a comprehensive scheme that made combating the employment of illegal aliens in the United States central to the policy of immigration law. Consistent with *Sure-Tan,* the *Patel* court held that "the FLSA's coverage of undocumented aliens goes hand in hand with the policies behind the IRCA . . . If the FLSA did not cover undocumented aliens, employers would have an incentive to hire them . . . By reducing the incentive to hire such workers the FLSA's coverage of undocumented aliens helps discourage illegal immigration and is thus fully consistent with the objectives of the IRCA. We therefore conclude that undocumented aliens continue to be 'employees' covered by the FLSA."

1. The FLSA's Anti-Retaliation Provision

The FLSA's anti-retaliation provision provides that it shall be unlawful for "any person" to "discharge or in any other manner discriminate against any employee because such employee has filed any complaint or instituted or caused to be instituted any proceeding under or related to this Act . . . "

2. Reporting an Undocumented Worker to the INS with a Retaliatory Motive

In *Contreras* v. *Corinthian Vigor Ins. Brokers, Inc.,* the court denied a motion to dismiss an undocumented worker's FLSA retaliation suit under circumstances virtually identical to the present case. The court concluded that "[t]here is no question that the protections provided by the FLSA apply to undocumented aliens." Though reporting an illegal alien to the INS is generally encouraged conduct because it is consistent with the labor and immigration policies established by the IRCA, the court in *Contreras* concluded that reporting an illegal alien *with* a retaliatory motive was prohibited conduct under §15(a)(3).

C. Pre-Hoffman, *Plaintiff has a Cause of Action*

Under *Sure-Tan* and *Patel,* plaintiff would have a cause of action. According to *Sure-Tan,* an illegal employee has standing to bring a claim under the NLRA for a retaliatory reporting due to a protected union activity. The extension of *Sure-Tan* in *Patel* indicates that an illegal employee would also have standing to bring an anti-retaliation claim under the FLSA for protected FLSA conduct. Under this pre-*Hoffman* line of jurisprudence plaintiff would have a cause of action under section 215(a)(3), as the Northern District found in *Contreras* by applying both *Sure-Tan* and *Patel* specifically to the retaliatory act of reporting an undocumented worker's immigration status to the INS.

III. *Hoffman*

Defendants contend that under *Hoffman* plaintiff's action is barred. Defendants claim that *Hoffman* does not just merely carve out the particular remedy of back pay, but rather, has greater significance in terms of the remedies available to an undocumented worker under the FLSA. The question before this Court is whether *Hoffman* has so altered the legal landscape that the underlying premises of both *Sure-Tan* and *Patel*—that undocumented workers have the right to particular remedies—have changed such that plaintiff no longer has a cause of action.

Hoffman does not compel the conclusion that plaintiff in this case is precluded from seeking a legal remedy. Given the facts in this case, the Court declines to extend *Hoffman* to bar plaintiff's action.

A. Hoffman *Background*

In *Hoffman,* the Supreme Court held that back pay is not an available remedy for undocumented workers who bring claims pursuant to the NLRA. The Court held that to award back pay to an illegal alien for years of work "not performed" ran counter to the policies underlying the IRCA of 1986. *Hoffman* does not, however, hold that an undocumented employee is barred from recovering unpaid wages for work actually performed, nor does it preclude other traditional remedies.[1] In fact, the Court awarded injunctive and declaratory relief.

According to defendants, *Hoffman* should be read broadly, focusing not simply on the narrow issue of whether an undocumented worker is entitled to back pay, but rather, defendants' claim that it should be read to indicate that undocumented workers are not entitled to a wider array of remedies under the national labor laws. Defendants' argument likens all other forms of relief to back pay, thereby extending *Hoffman* so that an undocumented worker is precluded from bringing a claim under the FLSA's anti-retaliation provisions.

The *Hoffman* Court reaffirmed its holding in *Sure-Tan* that undocumented aliens are employees under the NLRA. Though *Hoffman* prevents an undocumented worker from seeking back pay, it does not preclude an undocumented worker from seeking *any* form of relief, as shown through the Court's granting of both injunctive and declaratory relief. While *Hoffman* did not address the remedies of compensatory and punitive damages, which are central here, given the factual circumstances of this case and the interplay with national immigration policy, the Court declines to extend *Hoffman* to bar the remedies that plaintiff seeks.

---

[1] *Hoffman* holds that undocumented employees are entitled to "traditional remedies" under the NLRA: "We have deemed such 'traditional remedies' sufficient to effectuate national labor policy regardless of whether the 'spur and catalyst' of backpay accompanies them (*Sure-Tan*). The remedies awarded in *Hoffman* included a cease-and-desist order and the requirement that the employer "conspicuously post a notice to employees setting forth their rights under the NLRA and detailing its prior unfair practices." Compensatory damages are included in the NLRB's "remedial arsenal." In determining an appropriate remedy under the NLRA, "the Board draws on a fund of knowledge and expertise all its own, and its choice of remedy must therefore be given special respect by reviewing courts" (*Hoffman*).

B. *Defendant in this Case Is a "Knowing Employer"*

Defendant in this case was not just a knowing employer, but allegedly, actively recruited plaintiff to come work in the United States. Defendants continued to employ him for approximately three years, throughout which they were aware of his illegal status.

***

D. *Including Undocumented Workers in the FLSA's Coverage Is Consistent with Immigration policy*

Allowing an undocumented worker to bring an anti-retaliation claim under the FLSA is consistent with the immigration policies underlying the IRCA. Congress enacted the FLSA to eliminate substandard working conditions by requiring employers to pay their employees a statutorily prescribed minimum wage and prohibiting employers from requiring their employees to work more than forty hours per week unless the employees are compensated at one and one half times their regular hourly rate. Congress enacted the IRCA to reduce illegal immigration not only to eliminate the economic incentive for illegal workers to come to this country, but also to eliminate employers' incentive to hire undocumented workers by imposing sanctions on employers who hire such workers. Though the FLSA does not impose sanctions, it also discourages employers from hiring such workers because it eliminates employers' ability to pay them less than minimum wage or otherwise take advantage of their status. As the *Patel* Court noted, "[i]f the FLSA did not cover undocumented aliens, employers would have an incentive to hire them. Employers might find it economically advantageous to hire and underpay undocumented workers and run the risk of sanctions under the IRCA." If employers know they have to pay illegal aliens the same wage as legal workers, they are far less likely to hire an illegal worker and run the risk of subjecting themselves to sanctions under the IRCA. As a result, there are fewer employment opportunities and therefore fewer incentives to enter this country illegally. Admittedly, similar arguments could be used to support the award of back pay, which was rejected In *Hoffman.* Indeed, every remedy extended to undocumented workers under the federal labor laws provides a marginal incentive for those workers to come to the United States. It is just as true, however, that every remedy denied to undocumented workers provides a marginal incentive for employers to hire those workers. The economic incentives are in tension. Given this tension, the courts must attempt to sensibly balance competing considerations. In this case, the balance tips sharply in favor of permitting this cause of action, and the remedies it seeks, to go forward. Prohibiting plaintiff from bringing this claim under the FLSA would provide a perverse economic incentive to employers to seek out and knowingly hire illegal workers, as defendant did here, in direct contravention of immigration laws. Though employers that succumbed to these incentives would run the risk of sanctions under the IRCA, that risk may be worth taking.[2] National labor and immigration policy is most appropriately balanced by permitting this case to go forward.

[2] Indeed, it is the employees who face the most significant and immediate immigration sanctions.

CONCLUSION

Because this Court finds that plaintiff's action under the FLSA is not barred for the aforementioned reasons, defendants' motion to dismiss is DENIED.

Case Questions

1. In your opinion, is there a conundrum created by legal protection of individuals who work in the United States illegally? What is your impression of the dicta and holding in this case?

2. Is it relevant to your above response that Jutla recruited Singh to come work for him in the United States?

3. Do you agree with the Court in *Patel* that protecting undocumented aliens by requiring that employers treat them the same as other workers will discourage illegal immigration?

Unauthorized workers are particularly vulnerable to threats to report them to the INS. In every case in which the employer asserts that the worker is unauthorized and the employer appears to have acquired that information *after* the worker complained of discrimination, the EEOC will determine whether the information was acquired through a retaliatory investigation. If the investigation is retaliatory, the employer will be liable for equitable relief as well as monetary damages without regard to the worker's actual work status. However, a worker's unauthorized status may serve as a legitimate reason for an adverse employment action, although employers who knowingly employ unauthorized workers could not assert this defense in a discrimination claim.[15]

The Fair Labor Standards Act also protects unauthorized workers from abuse. In a dramatic 2001 case, a group of mostly Mexican workers in New Jersey claimed that the operators of a bargain retail chain subjected them to "inhumane" working conditions and failed to pay them fair wages and overtime compensation in working to perform such tasks as building and stocking new stores. Workers generally received $230 for a seven-day workweek of about 12 hours per day, which amounted to $2.74 an hour. These workers were also often forced to work in stores without heat, access to meals, or adequate water, proper ventilation, or adequate bathroom facilities. Bosses also called workers derogatory names.[16] The case was settled when the defendants apologized, agreed to ensure future compliance, and agreed to pay damages to the workers.[17]

[15] See "Workforce Online," *CCH*, November 1999, citing "Policy Guidance: Remedies Available to Undocumented Workers under Federal Employment Discrimination Laws," Oct. 26. 1999, Appendix B of sec. 622, vol. II of *EEOC Compliance Manual*.

[16] See Associated Press, "Mexican Workers Claim U.S. Bargain Store Chain Exploited Them," www.law.com, Jan. 10, 2001.

[17] Internet Bankruptcy Library, *Class Action Reporter III*, no. 67 (4/5/01), http://bankrupt.com/CAR_Public/010405.MBX.

ALTERNATE BASIS FOR NATIONAL ORIGIN OR CITIZENSHIP DISCRIMINATION

While it is probably the most popular basis for the claim of discrimination based on national origin, Title VII is not the only basis for such a claim. In *St. Francis College* v. *Al-Khazraji,* 481 U.S. 604 (1987) [*cert. denied,* 483 U.S. 1011 (1987)], the Supreme Court held that section 42 U.S.C. § 1981 addressed national origin also. In this case, a U.S. citizen who was born in Iraq sued under section 1981, alleging discrimination when he was denied tenure. The Court held that, though originally designed to prohibit racial discrimination, the law also applied to "identifiable classes of persons who are subjected to intentional discrimination solely because of their ancestry or ethnic characteristics." The requirement for section 1981 actions is that employees show they were discriminated against because of what they are (in this case, Iraqi) and not just because of their place of origin or religion. In other words, they must show some nexus between their national origin and the major concern of section 1981, their ethnic characteristics or race.

Since *St. Francis College,* however, several courts have declined to extend section 1981 to more traditional claims of national origin discrimination. In *King* v. *Township of East Lampeter* [17 F. Supp. 2d 394 (E.D. Pa 1998)], for instance, plaintiffs sought section 1981 protection on the basis of their "Amish ethnic culture." The court denied the plaintiffs protection on this basis, distinguishing a New York case that found Orthodox Jews were indeed protected under section 1981. The court in *King* found that Jews are a distinct race for civil rights purposes but did not find the Amish to be a similarly distinct racial group and, without evidence that it has an independent, separate ethnic identity beyond religious observance, they were not protected under section 1981. Interestingly, the court was persuaded by the contention that one could fail to "practice" Judaism but still be a Jew, while "there is no proof of a similar population of 'non-practicing' Amish." Perhaps an argument could be made that the door therefore remains open on this issue.

THE CHANGING WORKFORCE

The 1990s saw a dramatic increase in the number of immigrants to the United States, particularly from Hispanic and Asian countries. Census figures released in 2001 show that the number of Hispanics rose 60 percent since 1990, to 35.3 million people, representing 15.2 percent of the workforce employed by private employers with over 100 employees, creating a virtual tie between Hispanics and African-Americans as the nation's largest minority group.[18] In 1999, immigrant workers numbered 15.7 million, representing 12 percent of U.S. workers.[19]

In 1998, African-Americans made up 11.3 percent of the workforce, Hispanics made up 10.4 percent, and Asians, Pacific Islanders, American Indians, and Alaska

---

[18] See "English-Only Rules May Spell Trouble for Employers," special to law.com, Oct. 11, 2001, www.law.com. See also EEOC, "Job Patterns for Minorities and Women" (2000), p.1.
[19] Ibid.

Management Tips

- While a specific national origin may be a BFOQ, make sure that only individuals of that origin can do the specific job since courts have a high standard for BFOQs in this area.
- An employee may have a claim for national origin discrimination if the worker is simply *perceived* to be of a certain origin, even if the individual is not, in fact, of that origin.
- While English fluency may be required, you are not allowed to discriminate because of an accent (unless the accent makes it impossible to understand the individual). However, be cautious to evaluate the requirement of the job since there may be positions that do not actually require English speaking.
- An employer may not point to customer, client, or coworker preference, comfort, or discomfort as the source of BFOQ.

- If you are a federal contractor, remember that you have additional responsibilities to engage in outreach and positive recruitment activities under the Guidelines on Discrimination Because of Religion or National Origin.
- While you are not prohibited from discriminating on the basis of citizenship under Title VII, you may be prohibited from discriminating on this basis under IRCA. Before instituting a policy, consider the implication of both statutes.
- Recognize the concerns of Middle Eastern employees in the post–September 11 era: Include topic of ethnic diversity in any workplace diversity training. Intervene promptly on incidents of harassment. Remain sensitive and flexible. Refrain from mandatory transfers and other short-term solutions to harassment, intimidation, and discrimination.

Natives made up 4.2 percent. It is projected that in 2008, African-Americans will make up 11.5 percent of the workforce, Hispanics will make up 12.7 percent, and Asians, Pacific Islanders, American Indians, and Alaska Natives will make up 5.2 percent.[20] The number of African-Americans in the workforce by 2008 is expected to increase by 19.5 percent, Asians, Pacific Islanders, American Indians, and Alaska Natives by 40.3 percent, and Hispanics by 36.8 percent.[21]

If the increases are anywhere near the projections, then entry, development, or promotion barriers to full use of the total diversity of the workplace will likely result in loss in the business's effectiveness and productivity. For any business wishing to be on the cutting edge, or simply to effectively use its resources and encourage the best performance from employees, adherence to Title VII's requirements regarding race and national origin should be viewed as a business imperative and not merely as compliance with the law.

The significance to managers of this protection is there must be a complete review of all policies that may have an impact on employees or applicants of diverse national origin. As stated above, this impact may not be obvious.

[20] Howard N. Fullerton, Jr., "Civilian Labor Force 16 Years and Older by 1988, 1998, and Projected 2008," stats.bls.gov/emplt986.htm, Nov. 30, 1999.

[21] Bureau of Labor Statistics, "Civilian Labor Force 16 Years and Older by Sex, Age, Race, and Hispanic Origin, 1988, 1998, and Projected 2008," stats.bls.gov/news.release/ecopro.t05.htm, Feb. 9, 2000.

Employers must be cognizant of the varying needs of employees from different backgrounds. For instance, employers may address the perceived problem of bilingual employees in a number of ways, such as offering English-as-a-second-language classes or tutors for semibilingual employees. Not only would this foster less isolation and exclusion of the employee, but it would also create greater confidence and less intimidation when the employees are speaking English. This type of proactive approach may prevent problems in this area before they emerge.

Summary

- Title VII, the Civil Rights Act of 1964, makes it an unlawful employment practice for employers to limit, segregate, or classify employees in any way that would deprive them of employment opportunities based on their national origin.

- An employee or applicant must show the following to be successful in a claim of discrimination based on national origin discrimination:
  1. The individual is a member of a protected class.
  2. The individual was qualified for the position at issue.
  3. The employer made an employment decision against the individual.
  4. The position was filled by someone not in a protected class.

- "National origin" refers to an individual's ancestor's place of origin or physical, cultural, or linguistic characteristics of an origin group.

- An employer has a defense against a national origin discrimination claim if it can show that the national origin is a bona fide occupational qualification. However, in general, this is very difficult to do. An exception to the difficulty is the requirement of English fluency, if speaking English is a substantial portion of the individual's job.

- No accommodation of a worker's national origin is required, as it would be required in situations involving disability or religion.

- English-only rules applied at all times are presumptively discriminatory, according to the EEOC. If the employer is considering an English-only rule, it is recommended that the employer should:
  1. Consider whether the rule is necessary.
  2. Determine if the rule is a business necessity.
  3. Consider if everybody is fluent in English.
  4. Communicate the rule to employees.
  5. Enforce the rule fairly.

- An alternative basis for national origin or citizenship discrimination is section 42 U.S.C. 1981.

- Guidelines on Discrimination Because of Religion or National Origin are federal guidelines that apply to federal contractors or agencies and impose on those employers an affirmative duty to prevent discrimination.

- The Immigration Reform and Control Act, unlike Title VII, prohibits, in certain circumstances, discrimination on the basis of citizenship. The act does allow for discrimination in favor of U.S. citizens where applicants are equally qualified.

- Two statutorily allowed BFOQs under IRCA are:
  1. English-language skill requirements that are reasonably necessary.
  2. Citizenship requirements specified by law, regulation, executive order, government contracts, or requirements established by the U.S. attorney general.

Chapter-End Questions

1. Which, if any, of the following scenarios would support an employee's claim of discrimination on the basis of national origin?

   a. A Dominican chambermaid in a hotel is denied promotion to front-desk duties primarily because of her inability to clearly articulate and to make herself adequately understood in English. [*Majia* v. *New York Sheraton Hotel,* 459 F. Supp. 375 (S.D.N.Y. 1978).]

   b. Applicant with a speech impediment is unable to pronounce the letter "r." The applicant therefore often has difficulty being understood when speaking and is denied a position.

   c. The owner of a manufacturing facility staffed completely by Mexicans refuses employment to a white American manager because the owner is concerned that the Mexicans will only consent to supervision by and receive direction from another Mexican.

   d. An Indian restaurant seeks to fill a server position. The advertisement requests applications from qualified individuals of Indian descent to add to the authenticity of the restaurant. In the past, the restaurant found that its business declined when it used Caucasian servers because the atmosphere of the restaurant suffered. An Italian applies for the position and is denied employment.

   e. A company advertises for Japanese-trained managers, because the employer has found that they are more likely to remain at the company for an extended time, to be loyal and devoted to the firm, and to react well to direction and criticism. An American applies for the position and is denied employment in favor of an equally qualified Japanese-trained applicant, who happens to also be Japanese.

2. Hector Garcia, a bilingual Mexican-American, is a salesperson for Gloor Lumber and Supply, Inc. Management complimented Hector's work on several occasions and gave him a $250 bonus at the end of his first year. The company had a rule that the employees could not speak Spanish on the job (except during breaks) unless they were dealing with customers who could not speak English. On one occasion, Garcia was asked a question on the job by another Mexican-American employee, and when he replied in Spanish he was discharged. The employer claims Garcia's infraction of the rule was only one of the reasons for his discharge. The employer offered evidence of Garcia's general failure to perform other aspects of his job and claims that the compliments and bonus Garcia received were motivational tools used by the company to encourage him to perform better, not evidence that he was doing a good job. Garcia claims that the English-only rule is discrimination based on national origin. What do you think? [*Garcia* v. *Gloor,* 618 F.2d 264 (5th Cir. 1980).]

3. Calvin Roach, a native-born American of Acadian descent, was fired by Dresser Industrial. Roach claimed that he was fired because of his "Acadian" national origin ("Cajun" descent) and his association with Dresser employees of the same origin. Employer claims that, since there is not and never was such a country as Acadia, employee's claim of national origin discrimination is not covered under Title VII. Do you agree? [*Roach* v. *Dresser Ind. Valve & Instrument Division,* 494 F. Supp. 215 (W.D. La. 1980).]

4. Valentine Jurado, of Mexican-American and Native American descent, was a disc jockey for KIIS radio station. After broadcasting in English for several years, Jurado was asked by the program director to incorporate some "street" Spanish words into the program to attract more Hispanic listeners. A consultant was hired by the radio station to analyze the effects of Jurado's bilingual broadcasting on the listening audience. The consultant concluded that the attempt to increase the Hispanic audience had actually resulted in hurting the overall ratings of the station because it confused many of the listeners, and there was no quantifiable rise in the station's Hispanic audience. Jurado was told to stop speaking Spanish on the air, and he was fired the next day for refusing to comply with this order. Jurado claims that the English-only order disproportionately disadvantaged Hispanics and that he was also fired before

being given a chance to attempt to comply. [*Jurado* v. *Eleven-Fifty Corp.,* 813 F.2d 1406 (9th Cir. 1987).]

5. Ray Wardle was police officer for the Ute Indian tribe in Utah for more than 17 years; he was not a member of this tribe. After 17 years of service, he was discharged because the tribe was hiring a tribal member to fill his position. Wardle filed an action against the tribe, claiming that he was fired based purely on the basis of his national origin. Who will win? [*Wardle* v. *Ute Indian Tribe,* 623 F.2d 670 (10th Cir. 1980).]

6. Hannoon, a Kuwaiti employee who worked as an information systems manager, requested Friday afternoons off to observe weekly Muslim prayer services. His supervisor noted in his personnel file, "first week on job requested Fri. off." In fact, Hannoon was permitted to take the time off and to work at other times to make up for those afternoons. Hannoon was terminated for poor performance and he filed an action claiming national origin and race discrimination. What flaws can you find in his claim? [*Hannoon* v. *Fawn Eng'g Corp.,* 84 EPD ¶41, 370 (8th Cir. 2003).]

7. Samsung Heavy Industries Co. replaced its American national sales manager with a Korean executive. The American sales manager filed suit claiming national origin discrimination though the countries are both party to the Treaty of Friendship, Commerce and Navigation, which would allow this. Is the company nevertheless barred by any other prohibition? Does the American manager have a viable claim? [*Weeks* v. *Samsung Heavy Indus. Co.,* 72 EPD ¶45, 262 (7th Cir. 1998).]

8. In 1979, Xieng, a Cambodian, began working at Peoples National Bank in its management training program for minorities. The program involved a great deal of customer contact. In 1981, Xieng was awarded a certificate of successful completion of the program and received consistently positive performance appraisals. At the bank's suggestion, Xieng received English-language training and his tutor viewed his ability to communicate in English as "dramatically improved." However, in each of his reviews, Xieng's supervisors noted that his communication skills needed future improvement. In 1986, Xieng was passed over for promotion in favor of a white woman with no previous experience in that position. What does the bank need to show to establish that the promotion decision does not violate Title VII? [*Xieng* v. *Peoples National Bank,* 821 P.2d 520 (Wash. 1991).]

9. Rush Presbyterian requires that employees in all job classifications be able to speak and write English. Garcia, a Latino, contends that this rule discriminates against those for whom English is not a first language. The court held that, because there was no evidence that Latinos had been excluded from Rush's workforce in greater numbers than people of other origins, there was no adverse impact on Latinos. Is this true? Couldn't Latinos have been discouraged from even applying and, therefore, those nonapplicants do not appear in the numbers presented in the court? Can you imagine that a rule requiring proficiency in English does not have an adverse effect on minorities? [*Garcia* v. *Rush Presbyterian,* 660 F.2d 1217 (7th Cir. 1981).]

Chapter **Eleven**

Age Discrimination

Opening Scenarios

SCENARIO 1

1 In an effort to reduce costs across the board, Pilchard wishes to hire recent graduates of MBA programs who have little experience. His firm would be paying them above competitive salaries even if it offered them one-half the salaries of its present staff members who are over age 40. Should Pilchard terminate the older employees in favor of the younger, less-expensive workers?

Scenario

SCENARIO 2

2 Beth, an employer, wants to hire someone for a strenuous job that requires a great deal of training, which will take place over the course of several years. The applicant who appears most qualified is 58 years old; however, Beth is concerned that the applicant will not be able to handle the physical demands of the position in the long run. Further, she is concerned that the applicant will only continue working for several more years before she

Scenario

retires. Does Beth hire the applicant, anyway? What advice would you give Beth?

SCENARIO 3

3 Mary had worked as an accountant for Andrew Arthurson, a once prestigious accounting firm, for over 20 years before she was laid off after the firm suffered a great loss of clients due to a scandal. Fifty-year-old Mary applies for a position as an accountant at Knott Hower Phault, an accounting firm with 25 employees in Chicago, Illinois. Thirty-eight-year-old Senior Partner Dan Knott is impressed by Mary's credentials and understands that Mary had no involvement in the Arthurson scandal. Still, he fears that Mary's years of experience make her overqualified for the accountant position at his firm. Dan thinks that a professional at Mary's stage would not care to take direction from him or his partners, who are either Dan's age or younger. What advice would you give Dan?

Scenario

STATUTORY BASIS

The statutory basis is presented in Exhibit 11.1.

OLDIE . . . BUT GOLDIE?

America is a culture in which youth is valued. It must be very strange indeed to those of other cultures, like the Japanese, who revere age and believe that with it comes wisdom and insight unobtainable by the young. In our culture, the general perception is that with youth comes energy, imagination, and innovation. With age comes decreasing interest, lack of innovation and imagination, and a lessening of the quality of the person. Television networks, studios, and talent agencies have been accused of stereotyping "older" television writers as not having the energy and ability to write for the younger demographic group they want to attract.[1]

Older employees suffer from these misperceptions in the workplace, subtle and subconscious though they may be. While statistics show that older workers are more reliable, harder working, more committed, and have less absenteeism than younger workers—all characteristics that employers say they value—the general perception

---

[1] See Erin Carroll, "Television Writers' Age-Bias Case Moves to State Court," *Los Angeles Daily Journal,* Feb. 27, 2002, p. 3.

Sec. 4 (a) It shall be unlawful for an employer—

(1) to fail or refuse to hire or to discharge any individual or otherwise discriminate against any individual with respect to his compensation, terms, conditions, or privilege of employment, because of such individual's age;

(2) to limit, segregate, or classify his employees in any way which would deprive or tend to deprive any individual of employment opportunities or otherwise adversely affect his status as an employee, because of such individual's age; or

(3) to reduce the wage rate of any employee in order to comply with this chapter.

Source: 20 U.S.C. §623.

---

of them as employees is exactly the opposite. This adversely affects employees who may not be treated as well because they are perceived as less-desirable employees. In addition, older workers are now more likely to remain on the job than their counterparts earlier in this century. Fifteen percent of Americans over 65 (about 4.7 million) are working full or part time. While 47 percent of those workers claim that they do so because they need the money, more than 80 percent say that they do it because they like being with other people and want to be productive.[2] The proportions of the workforce in the United States are changing, too. By 2012 the number of workers 55 and over will almost double, resulting in an additional 10.2 million workers over the age of 55. This influx will constitute almost 60 percent of all new workers (17.4 million) for a growth rate almost four times that of the overall workforce, which will increase the percentage of older workers in the workforce from 14.3 percent to 19.1 percent.[3] Of course, this presents a workforce challenge since more than 50 percent of companies do not actively recruit or strive to retain older workers.[4]

The scenarios above are merely generalizations, but they are omnipresent in the workplace. Many employers feel older employees may be more expensive to retain because they have greater experience and seniority. Each year they may receive a raise until their salary becomes a burden on the firm. Management realizes that it could reduce costs by terminating older employees, who have more experience than may be necessary to perform the requirements of the position, and by hiring younger, less experienced employees.

This may seem to be a realistic and legitimate business decision, but, once terminated, older workers are disadvantaged in the search for new employment. They are either viewed as overqualified or employers express concern about their ability to adequately perform. The concerns are usually based on preconceived stereotypical

[2] Arthur Shostak, "Futures Poll on Americans, Work and Education," Drexel University Center for Employment Futures.

[3] M. Toossi, "Labor Force Projections to 2012: The Graying of the U.S. Workforce," *Monthly Labor Review Online* (Bureau of Labor Statistics) 127, no. 2 (Feb. 2004), http://www.bls.gov/opub/mlr/2004/02/art3full.pdf.

[4] J. Collison, "Older Workers Survey," Society for Human Research Management (SHRM/NOWCC/CED), 2003.

1. In a reduction in force caused by economic reasons, employers should always terminate the older workers, since they are usually the highest paid.
2. If most people in a certain age group have a common weakness, it can be generalized that all in that group have the weakness, and age can be used as a job qualification.
3. If an employee is discriminated against because of youth, the employee has a claim under the Age Discrimination in Employment Act.
4. Employees must retire at age 65 in the United States.
5. As workers, older employees

   - Are not hard workers.
   - Will get tired more easily than younger workers.
   - Are less able to perform than younger workers.
   - Don't understand technology.
   - Don't want to travel too much and are generally more stubborn and uninterested in learning.
   - Make too much money since it often based on seniority and not performance.
   - Are just marking time before they can retire.

6. As workers, younger employees

   - Have it easy; they never suffer discrimination.
   - Always win the job when competing against older workers.
   - Have a lower unemployment rate than older workers.
   - Can easily find jobs since older workers are retiring all the time.

notions about the deterioration of the older worker's senses, physical capabilities, response time, and competence. (See Exhibit 11.2.)

In addition, younger workers, as a group, may be better educated and better qualified when entering the workforce. Instead of making a time-consuming individualized determination of the abilities of each applicant, employers generalize about classes of workers and only choose employees from those classes they perceive as more desirable. While some of these generalizations may be grounded in fact, it is the act of generalizing, rather than making individualized conclusions, that constitutes the wrongful discrimination.

In this chapter, we will discuss older employees and the legal rights that the law provides for them through the Age Discrimination in Employment Act.

REGULATION

Age Discrimination in Employment Act

Baseless discrimination against older workers occurs with such consistency that Congress was compelled to enact legislation to protect older workers from discrimination to prevent increased unemployment for those over 40. In 1967, Congress enacted the

**Age Discrimi-
nation in
Employment
Act**
Prohibits dis-
crimination in
employment on
the basis of age;
applies to indi-
viduals who are
at least 40 years
old. Individuals
who are not yet
40 years old are
not protected by
the act and *may*
be discriminated
against on the
basis of their
age.

Age Discrimination in Employment Act (ADEA) for the express purpose of "promot[ing the] employment of older people based on their ability rather than age [and prohibiting] arbitrary age discrimination in employment." The act applies to employment by public and private employers and by unions and employment agencies, as well as by foreign companies with more than 20 workers located in the United States. In 2003, more than 19,000 claims were filed with the EEOC based on the act, resulting in monetary awards of almost $50 million, not including amounts awarded in private litigation.

On its effective date, the act covered employees between the ages of 40 and 65. The upper limit was extended to 70 in 1978 and later removed completely. There is no longer an upper age limit, in recognition that an 80-plus-year-old may be just as qualified for a position as a 30-year-old and should have the opportunity to prove her or his qualifications and to obtain or retain employment based on them. With few exceptions, mandatory retirement has now become a dinosaur. It is also important to recognize that the act will become all the more critical as health care advances allow people to live more vital lives to longer ages. Many people today feel healthy enough to work long beyond the age at which most people used to retire.

Courts and Congress have recognized there is a trade-off for the required employment of qualified older workers. In *Graefenhain* v. *Pabst Brewing Co.,* 827 F.2d 13, n.8 (7th Cir. 1987), overruled on other grounds, 860 F.2d 834 (7th Cir. 1988), the court said:

> Although the ADEA does not hand federal courts a roving commission to review business judgments, the ADEA *does* create a cause of action against business decisions that merge with age discrimination. Congress enacted the ADEA precisely because many employers or younger business executives act as if they believe that there are good business reasons for discriminating against older employees. Retention of senior employees who can be replaced by younger lower-paid people frequently competes with other values, such as profits or conceptions of economic efficiency. The ADEA represents a choice among these values. It stands for the propositions that this is a better country for its willingness to pay the costs for treating older employees fairly.

You may wonder, Why wasn't age merely included as an amendment to Title VII since the laws have several similarities? Both are enforced by the EEOC, as well as through private actions. However, discrimination based on age is substantively different from discrimination based on factors covered by Title VII in three important ways. First, the ADEA is more lenient than Title VII regarding the latitude afforded employers' reasons for adverse employment decisions. The ADEA allows an employer to rebut a prima facie case of age discrimination by identifying any "reasonable factor other than age" that motivated the decision.

Second, an employee is not barred from pursuing a claim simply because the employer treated another older worker better. In other words, a 62-year-old is not barred from a claim when terminated simply because her replacement was 55 (that is, also in the protected class).

Third, the act only protects employees over 40 from discrimination. Unlike Title VII, there is no protection from "reverse" discrimination. In other words, an individual under 40 cannot file a claim under the act based on the claim that she was discriminated against because of her youth—that it was because she was too young. Moreover, in a 2004 decision, the Supreme Court held that the ADEA does not protect workers over

40 who were discriminated against (in this case) in favor of workers over 50 with regard to benefits. As Justice Souter noted, "The law does not mean to stop an employer from favoring an older employee over a younger one . . . The enemy of 40 is 30, not 50."[5] Note, however, that certain state laws or precedents allow for what might be considered a youth's "reverse-discrimination" claim under state age discrimination statutes. One New Jersey man who claimed he was fired from a bank vice president position because of his young age (25) was allowed to proceed in court in that state. It is interesting to note that, in recent years, there has been somewhat of an upward trend in seeking to hire and retain older workers. The American Association of Retired People (AARP) reports that some businesses, particularly in healthcare and retail, are increasingly focusing on hiring and retaining older workers as the nation's 78 million baby boomers age. CNBC adds, "With the prospect of shortfalls in funding for Social Security and the potential for a real labor shortage when the economy expands, employment forecasters say the country can't afford to lose older workers in the years ahead."[6]

Another restriction on the ADEA's protection came from the U.S. Supreme Court's 2000 decision in *Kimel* v. *Florida Board of Regents*.[7] In *Kimel,* state employees alleged that their state employers had discriminated against them on the basis of age in violation of the ADEA. Under the U.S. Constitution's Eleventh Amendment, states cannot be sued by citizens of another state. Federal courts have interpreted the Eleventh Amendment to extend immunity to states not consenting to being sued by their citizens. The U.S. Supreme Court determined that while Congress intended to allow state employees to sue their state employers under the ADEA, this attempt exceeded congressional authority. Therefore, state employees are not able to sue their state employers under the ADEA.

To ensure that appropriate and adequate information exists as to hiring practices in connection with age, the act has specific recordkeeping provisions for employers. Employers are required to maintain the following information for *three years* for each employee and applicant, where applicable:

- Name.
- Address.
- Date of birth.
- Occupation.
- Rate of pay.
- Compensation earned each week.

Employers are required to maintain the following information for *one year* for each employee and for both regular and temporary workers:

- Job applications, résumés, or other employment inquiries in answer to ads or notices, plus records about failure or refusal to hire.

---

[5] *General Dynamics Land Systems, Inc.* v. *Cline,* 124 S. Ct. 1236 (2004).

[6] Bertha Coombs, "Demand Grows for Older Workers: Firms Focus on Hiring and Retaining Baby Boomers," CNBC TV (5/7/04).

[7] 528 U.S. 62 (2000).

- Records on promotion, demotion, transfer, selection for training, layoff, recall, or discharge of any employee.
- Job orders given to agencies or unions for recruiting personnel for job openings.
- Test papers.
- Results of physical exams that are considered in connection with any personnel action.
- Ads or notices relating to job openings, promotions, training programs, or opportunities for overtime.

The ADEA also addresses discrimination in the provision of benefits. Specifically, employers are held to an equal benefit/equal cost rule. Under the rule, employers can comply with the ADEA by either providing equal benefits to workers of all ages or spending an equal amount to purchase the benefits. In recognizing that it may cost more to provide equivalent benefits to older workers, Congress was striving to encourage the hiring of older workers.

Proving Discrimination

The Employee's Prima Facie Case: Disparate Treatment

An employee believes that his employer has made a decision about him on the basis of age. What does he do now? The employee may file an action against the employer under the ADEA and prove age discrimination on the basis of disparate treatment by utilizing the method of proof for Title VII cases originally set forth in *McDonnell Douglas Corp.* v. *Green* and later adapted to age discrimination claims under the ADEA. Under this approach, an employee must establish the following four elements to persuade the court that she or he even has a claim for age discrimination:

1. The employee is in the protected class.
2. She or he was terminated or demoted.
3. The employee was doing her or his job well enough to meet her employer's legitimate expectations.
4. Others not in the protected class were treated more favorably.

Member of the Protected Class   To satisfy the first requirement of the prima facie case, the employee must merely show that she or he is 40 years old or older.

Adverse Employment Action   The second requirement is proof that the employer made an employment decision that adversely affected the employee. This may include a decision not to hire the applicant or to terminate the employee.

Qualified for the Position   With the third requirement, the applicant must prove that he or she was **qualified for the position**. If the applicant is not qualified, then the employer's decision would be justified and the applicant's claim fails. The position requirements, however, must be legitimate requirements, and not merely devised for the purpose of terminating or refusing to hire older workers. Courts have allowed this requirement to be met by the employee simply by showing that the employee was never told that performance was unacceptable. The qualifications requirement is not a difficult one. Courts

qualified for the position
Able to meet the employer's legitimate job requirements.

Exhibit 11.3   EEOC Guidance

The EEOC Interpretive Rules offer the following guidance:

> When help wanted notices or advertisements contain terms and phrases such as "age 25 to 35," "young," "boy," "girl," "college student," "recent college graduate," or others of a similar nature, such a term or phrase discriminates against the employment of older people, and will be considered in violation of the act. Such specifications as "age 40 to 50," "age over 50," or "age over 65" are also considered to be prohibited. Where such specifications as "retired person" or "supplement your pension" are intended and applied so as to discriminate against others within the protected group, they, too, are regarded as prohibited unless one of the exceptions applies.

have even held that the fact that the employee was hired initially indicates that he or she has the basic qualifications.

Dissimilar Treatment   In connection with the fourth requirement for a prima facie case of age discrimination, the employee or applicant must show that he was treated differently than other employees who are not in the protected class. This requires an employer to explain its actions if it terminates (or refuses to hire) an older qualified employee, while simultaneously hiring younger employees. For instance, where an employer terminates a 57-year-old worker and hires, in her place, a 34-year-old employee, and the 57-year-old employee can show that she remains qualified for her position, the employer must defend its decision.

This requirement has presented the most difficulty for courts. What if an 80-year-old is fired and replaced by a 78-year-old? Is this discriminatory action? The basic ADEA case is filed where an employee is replaced by or not hired in favor of an employee who is not a member of the protected class. However, the Supreme Court has held, in *O'Connor* v. *Consolidated Coin Caterers,* 116 S. Ct. 1307 (1996), that a plaintiff can state a claim as long as she or he is replaced by someone younger, even if the replacement is 40 years old or older.

One other provision of the ADEA merits special attention; section 4(e) makes it unlawful to "print or publish or cause to be printed or published, any notice or advertisement . . . indicating any preference, limitation, specification, or discrimination, based on age."

The court in *Hodgson* v. *Approved Personnel Serv., Inc.,* 529 F.2d 760 (4th Cir. 1975) found that, in determining whether an advertisement had a discriminatory effect on older individuals, "the discriminatory effect of an advertisement is determined not by 'trigger words' but rather by its context." That is, the ad is not considered discriminatory because of a word or words but rather because of the intent of the ad to discriminate against older individuals.

The use of certain trigger words like "girl" or "young" may establish an ADEA violation under most circumstances so the context of the statement is important to determine its discriminatory effect. For instance, the use of "recent college graduate" is not discriminatory if a personnel agency merely intended to identify those *services* that it offered to that specific class of individuals. (See Exhibit 11.3.) The EEOC specifically explains as follows:

Exhibit 11.4   Employer's Defenses

The employer may present a legitimate and nondiscriminatory reason for its actions in one of several ways. The act states:

It shall not be unlawful for an employer

(1) to take any action otherwise prohibited where age is a bona fide occupational qualification reasonably necessary to the normal operation of the particular business, or where the differentiation is based on reasonable factors other than age.
(2) to observe the terms of a bona fide seniority system or any bona fide employee benefit plan such as a retirement, pension, or insurance plan.
(3) to discharge or otherwise discipline an individual for good cause.

The ADEA generally makes it unlawful to include age preferences, limitations, or specifications in job notices or advertisements. A job notice or advertisement may specify an age limit only in the rare circumstances where age is shown to be a "bona fide occupational qualification" (BFOQ) reasonably necessary to the normal operation of the business.[8]

Employer's Defenses

Once the employee has presented evidence relating to the employer's actions, the burden of proof shifts to the employer to present a legitimate and nondiscriminatory reason for its actions.

What does "articulate" mean in the *McDonnell Douglas* requirement that the employer "articulate" a legitimate, nondiscriminatory reason for the adverse employment decision? Courts have differed, with some holding that the employer must merely identify a reason why the individual was terminated or not hired and others requiring that the employer present evidence of its nondiscriminatory reason and also persuade the court that the reason actually constitutes the basis for its decision. (See Exhibit 11.4.)

Bona Fide Occupational Qualification   If an employer is sued for age discrimination, the defense of BFOQ is available. In fact, age is one of the most consistently applied BFOQs. The employer's proof of a bona fide occupational qualification under the ADEA is slightly different and less exacting than under Title VII. Title VII requires that the employer demonstrate that the essence of the business requires the exclusion of the members of a protected class and all or substantially all of the members of that class are unable to perform adequately in the position in question. The EEOC follows the requirements of Title VII in connection with the ADEA but adds one further possibility for the employer's proof. The EEOC identifies what the employer must prove in an age discrimination case brought under the ADEA as:

1. The age limit is reasonably necessary to the essence of the employer's business; and either
2. All or substantially all of the individuals over that age are unable to perform the job's requirements adequately; or
3. Some of the individuals over that age possess a disqualifying trait that cannot be ascertained except by reference to age.

[8] http://www.eeoc.gov/types/age.html.

The third element of the proof allows an employer to exclude an older worker from a position that may be unsafe to *some* older workers. This defense would only be accepted by a court where there is no way to individually assess the safety potential of a given applicant or employee.

Scenario

For example, assume there existed a medical disorder that was prevalent among those over 80 and was not discoverable under standard medical investigation. Assume also that this medical condition caused its sufferers to lose consciousness without warning. An employer who refused to place those over 80 in the position of a school bus driver would satisfy the proof of a BFOQ. Note that it is not enough for an employer to simply think there is a condition related to age that supports a BFOQ. The decision must be based on competent expert evidence of a connection between age and the component of the job affected.

mandatory retirement
Deemed illegal by the 1986 amendments to the ADEA, with few exceptions.

When Congress passed the 1986 amendments to the ADEA prohibiting **mandatory retirement** on the basis of age for most workers, it included several temporary exemptions, notably one for tenured faculty in higher education. That exemption expired December 31, 1993. Mandatory retirement has been limited to two circumstances. First, a small number of high-level employees with substantial executive authority can be subjected to compulsory retirement at age 65 or beyond if the individual will receive a company pension of $44,000 or more. This exception is a very narrow one and does not allow for compulsory retirement policies for midlevel managers. Perhaps this exception is narrowly confined to those with decision-making authority based on stereotypes that the majority of powerful executives tend to be over 40, with wealth and opportunity that make a mandatory retirement policy less burdensome. Second, persons in two specific occupations, police officers and firefighters, have been subject to mandatory retirement. However, age is not necessarily a BFOQ in these occupations.

Reasonable Factor Other Than Age   Is there discrimination if an employer who owns a steel manufacturing plant wants all its employees to be super strong, just in case their strength is needed during the business day, even if each particular job may not require that much strength, for instance, an office position? This requirement may seriously impair the ability of an older worker to be hired. The employer's defense that the adverse action was taken as a result of "reasonable factors other than age" appears to allow employers to discriminate against protected persons for reasons that may have an adverse *effect* on older workers, such as dexterity or strength.

In fact, the EEOC regulations require that the factor be *job-related* if the distinction has a disparate impact on employees over 40. Reasonable factors, therefore, may include any requirement that does not have an adverse impact on older workers, as well as those factors that do adversely affect this protected class but are shown to be job-related. For example, if an employee is not performing satisfactorily and is terminated, her failure to meet reasonable performance standards would constitute a reasonable factor other than age.

In addition, if an employee is terminated as a result of his failure to maintain a certain speed on an assembly line, he may claim that this speed requirement adversely affects older workers because they are not able to maintain similar speeds as younger workers. However, if the employer can show that speed of performance in this position is job-related and necessary to the operations of the business, then the termination does not constitute an ADEA violation.

Scenario

In scenario 2, the applicant's age appears to be of some concern; however the real issue is whether the applicant can do the strenuous job. If it can be shown that the applicant can perform all the necessary job functions, he should be hired because he is the most qualified. In the future, if he becomes unable to meet the demands of the job, his termination would be a result of his lack of ability, not his age. Furthermore, regarding the concerns about the applicant leaving after a few years, *any* employee can leave an employer at any time unless there is a contract. This is not only a concern with older individuals.

The case below presents a basic outline of a court's ADEA inquiry.

Parrish v. Immanuel Medical Center   *92 F.3d 727 (8th Cir. 1996)*

A 66-year-old employee resigned after being summarily transferred to a new position and after her supervisor made age-based remarks. She sued for age discrimination and the jury found for the employee. The employer appealed but the judgment is upheld.

Beam, J.

Mary Ruth Parrish was hired as a registrar at Immanuel Medical Center (Immanuel) in 1979 at the age of 57. Although her position became computerized after she was hired, she did not have a problem learning the new technology and received satisfactory evaluations from her superiors, received no negative evaluations, and largely positive comments from her supervisors, save for an admonishment to refrain from criticizing fellow employees in the department.

Although Parrish was slower in admitting patients than many of the other registrars, she was also one of the most accurate workers in the department. When the computer system was upgraded and additional training was required, Mary attended day one of the two-day sessions but missed the second session because she was admitted to the hospital due to depression and anxiety. On at least one occasion, Mary's supervisor was said to have commented that younger registrars were having problems with the new computers.

When she returned to work a month later, Mary was assigned to a new position with new hours. Mary was not given the option of returning to her position as a part-time registrar and was presented the offer to transfer as an all-or-nothing proposition. The following day Mary did not report to work but called her supervisor to ask her to reconsider the transfer. The supervisor refused so Mary, at the age of sixty-six, resigned. Mary sued

Immanuel, alleging that she was constructively discharged because of her age and her disability. Immanuel contended that it legitimately sought to transfer Mary because of her inefficiency and her difficulties with the new computer system. The jury rejected Immanuel's explanation and found that Immanuel had discriminated against Mary due to her age and disability.

* * *

We are satisfied that there is sufficient evidence to support the jury's finding of age discrimination. First of all, Parrish produced ample evidence from which a reasonable jury could conclude that Immanuel's stated reasons for transferring Parrish were pretextual. Immanuel alleges that Parrish was inefficient, slow, and incapable of adjusting to the new computers. Parrish proved, however, that she was an accurate and reliable employee during her ten years at Immanuel. She consistently received above average ratings on her yearly evaluations. Although her rate of production was slower than the average registrar, [a supervisor] did not think the problem significant enough to warrant more than a single comment. Moreover, there was undisputed evidence that Parrish was given only one day of training on the new computer system, and that all of the trainees were helping each other learn the new software on the first day of training. Several witnesses testified that they did not recall Parrish having significant problems learning the new system.

Erickson's comment to Parrish that even "younger registrars" were having difficulty with the computers also supports the jury's verdict. As the Supreme Court has noted, "[i]t is the very essence of age discrimination for an older employee to be fired because the employer believes that productivity and competence decline with old age." The ADEA was enacted to combat stereotypes regarding the ability of older employees to keep pace with changes in the workplace. From comments comparing Parrish's ability to learn computers to the abilities of younger registrars, reasonable minds could infer that the decision to create the new position for Parrish was based on such stereotypes.

Parrish produced ample evidence from which a jury could conclude that Immanuel constructively discharged Parrish not for its proffered reasons but because of her age. Consequently, the district court properly denied Immanuel's motion for judgment as a matter of law with respect to Parrish's age claim. AFFIRMED.

Case Questions

1. Should employers be able to terminate or transfer older workers when they cannot grasp new technology? What can employers do to protect themselves?

2. What do you think is the purpose of the ADEA? What do you think should be its purpose?

3. Do you believe that there is an age after which most people should not be allowed in certain positions? What type of positions? What age would you decide is appropriate for removing these people from the position? How would you decide?

As the next case demonstrates, the employer cannot simply base employment decisions on age-related stereotypes. The employer must base such decisions on credible evidence. Under *Western Airlines, Inc.* v. *Criswell,* an airline attempted to defend its mandatory retirement policy for flight engineers over the age of 60 as a BFOQ. This defense ultimately failed because individual determinations of health could help achieve the airline's goal of safe transportation of passengers in a less restrictive manner.

The policy was apparently based on the Federal Aviation Administration's "Age 60 Rule," prohibiting those who have reached the age of 60 from acting as pilots or co-pilots.[9] Interestingly, while the FAA requires individual pilot medical certifications, and a semiannual exam of pilots, it maintains the Age 60 Rule. A Notice of Proposed Rule Making issued by the FAA in 1982 that would have created a test group of pilots over the age of 60 to determine whether the Age 60 Rule was effective was withdrawn in 1984. Determining a method for selection of the test group became too problematic to justify the possible public safety risks created by such a study.[10]

[9] See 14 CFR 121.383(c).

[10] See www.faa.gov.

Western Air Lines, Inc. v. Criswell   *472 U.S. 400 (1985)*

Western Air Lines requires that its flight engineers, who are members of the cockpit crew but do not operate flight controls unless both the pilot and the co-pilot become incapacitated, retire at age 60. The Federal Aviation Administration prohibits anyone from acting as a pilot or co-pilot after they have reached the age of 60. The respondents in this case include both pilots who were denied reassignment to the position of flight engineers at age 60 and flight engineers who were forced to retire at that age. The airline argued that the age 60 retirement requirement is a BFOQ reasonably necessary to the safe operation of the business. The lower court instructed the jury as follows: The airline could establish age as a BFOQ only if "it was highly impractical for [petitioner] to deal with each [flight engineer] over age 60 on an individualized basis to determine his particular ability to perform his job safely" and that some flight engineers "over 60 possess traits of a physiological, psychological or other nature which preclude safe and efficient job performance that cannot be ascertained by means other than knowing their age." The Supreme Court evaluated whether this instruction was appropriate and determined that it correctly stated the law.

Stevens, J.

As the district court summarized, the evidence at trial established that the flight engineer's "normal duties are less critical to the safety of flight than those of a pilot." The flight engineer, however, does have critical functions in emergency situations and, of course, might cause considerable disruption in the event of his own medical emergency.

The actual capabilities of persons over age 60, and the ability to detect diseases or a precipitous decline in their faculties, were the subject of conflicting medical testimony. Western's expert witness, a former FAA [Federal Aviation Administration] deputy federal air surgeon, was especially concerned about the possibility of a "cardiovascular event," such as a heart attack. He testified that "with advancing age the likelihood of onset of disease increases and that in persons over age 60 it could not be predicted whether and when such diseases would occur."

The plaintiff's experts, on the other hand, testified that physiological deterioration is caused by disease, not aging, and that "it was feasible to determine on the basis of individual medical examinations whether flight deck crew members, including those over age 60, were physically qualified to continue to fly." Moreover, several large commercial airlines have flight engineers over age 60 "flying the line" without any reduction in their safety record.

Throughout the legislative history of the ADEA, one empirical fact is repeatedly emphasized: the process of psychological and physiological degeneration caused by aging varies with each individual. "The basic research in the field of aging has established that there is a wide range of individual physical ability regardless of age." As a result, many older workers perform at levels equal or superior to their younger colleagues.

In 1965, the Secretary of Labor reported to Congress that despite these well-established medical facts, "there is persistent and widespread use of age limits in hiring that in a great many cases can be attributed only to arbitrary discrimination against older workers on the basis of age and regardless of ability." Two years

later, the President recommended that Congress enact legislation to abolish arbitrary age limits on hiring. Such limits, the President declared, have a devastating effect on the dignity of the individual and result in a staggering loss of human resources vital to the national economy.

The legislative history of the 1978 amendments to the ADEA makes quite clear that the policies and substantive provisions of the act apply with especial force in the case of mandatory retirement provisions. The House Committee on Education and Labor reported: "Increasingly, it is being recognized that mandatory retirement based solely upon age is arbitrary and that chronological age alone is a poor indicator of ability to perform a job."

In *Usery* v. *Tamiami Trail Tours, Inc.,* the court of appeals for the Fifth Circuit was called upon to evaluate the merits of a BFOQ defense to a claim of age discrimination. Tamiami Trail Tours had a policy of refusing to hire persons over age 40 as intercity bus drivers. At trial, the bus company introduced testimony supporting its theory that the hiring policy was a BFOQ based upon safety considerations—the need to employ persons who have a low risk of accidents. The court concluded that "the job qualifications which the employer invokes to justify his discrimination must be *reasonably necessary* to the essence of his business—here, the safe transportation of bus passengers from one point to another. The greater the safety factor, measured by the likelihood of harm and the probable severity of that harm in case of an accident, the more stringent may be the job qualifications designed to insure safe driving."

In the absence of persuasive evidence supporting its position, Western nevertheless argues that the jury should have been instructed to defer to "Western's selection of job qualifications for the position of flight engineer that are reasonable in light of safety risks." This proposal is plainly at odds with Congress' decision, in adopting the ADEA, to subject management decisions to a test of objective justification in a court of law. The BFOQ standard adopted in the statute is one of "reasonable necessity," not reasonableness.

In adopting that standard, Congress did not ignore the public interest in safety. That interest is adequately reflected in instructions that track the language of the statute. When an employer establishes that a job qualification has been carefully formulated to respond to documented concerns for public safety, it will not be overly burdensome to persuade a trier of fact that the qualification is "reasonably necessary" to safe operation of the business. The uncertainty implicit in the concept of managing safety risks always makes it "reasonably necessary" to err on the side of caution in a close case. . . . Since the instructions in this case would not have prevented the airline from raising this contention to the jury in closing argument, we are satisfied that the verdict is a consequence of a defect in Western's proof, rather than a defect in the trial court's instructions.

Case Questions

1. What is the difference between the two cases cited in full above? What is the basis for the determination that an employer should or should not be required to test applicants on an individual basis?

2. Should an employer have available as a defense that the cost of the tests would impose a great burden on the employer? Why or why not?

3. What is the distinction the Criswell opinion makes between "reasonable necessity" and "reasonableness"?

1
Scenario

Economic Concerns   Would a company's desire to cut payroll costs constitute a reasonable factor other than age? As stated in the beginning of this chapter, it is likely to be more expensive under certain circumstances to maintain older workers than younger; so cutting the numbers of older workers may reduce costs in some firms.

This issue is unique to ADEA discrimination claims as it is not more costly, for instance, to hire an Asian employee than a Caucasian employee. However, in many cases, it is more expensive to hire or to retain older workers since, among other reasons, they have more experience and thereby command a higher wage. Courts disfavor this justification for the termination of older workers. As stated by the Illinois district court in *Vilcins* v. *City of Chicago,* 1991 WL 74610 (N.D. Ill. 1991), "[n]othing in the ADEA prohibits elimination of a protected employee's position for budgetary reasons. In fact, the case law establishes that economic or budgetary factors may provide valid reasons for discharging a protected employee. A termination allegedly based on economic factors may constitute impermissible discrimination, however, *when the economic reasons proffered serve merely to obscure the fact that age was the true determinant.*" (Emphasis added.)

This brings to mind one of the most interesting case opinions in this area: *Metz* v. *Transit Mix, Inc.,* 828 F.2d 1202 (7th Cir. 1987). In that case, the appellate court noted that salary is often a direct function of seniority. Individual salary increases may occur on a yearly basis with no regard to the financial condition of the employer; consequently, those who have been employed for the longest times, and have accrued the most seniority, are also the highest paid employees. In disallowing the termination of older workers for financial reasons, the court then cited Willie Loman, the salesman who was fired after working for his boss for 34 years (in Arthur Miller's *Death of a Salesman*): "You can't eat the orange and throw the peel away—a man is not a piece of fruit." Courts have emphatically rejected business practices in which the "plain intent and effect was to eliminate older workers who had built up, through years of satisfactory service, higher salaries than their younger counterparts."

The court stated that where salary is tied directly to seniority (and therefore age), seniority then serves as a "proxy" for age, supporting a claim of age discrimination.

The court of appeals noted that one possible solution to the high-pay quandary for the continued employment of older workers is to offer the older worker the option of accepting a pay cut in lieu of termination. The pay cut, of course, must be warranted by business necessity, such as economic difficulties; but at least the older worker would be retained and not replaced by a younger worker who would be willing to accept the lower salary offered. Such an offer to the older worker would be evidence of the intent to reduce costs, as opposed to the intent to relieve the firm of its older workforce. In addition, terminations pursuant to bona fide reductions in force, bankruptcy, or other legitimate business reasons are generally legal, even if the economic considerations that have necessitated the reduction in force require the termination of more older workers than younger employees. In the first case below, the Seventh Circuit revisits the issue of age discrimination in the face of economic duress and, under the facts of this case, finds the employer's arguments persuasive. In the second case below, the employee claimed he was fired to prevent his pension from vesting, rather than for a bona fide reason.

Schuster v. Lucent Technologies, Inc.   *327 F.3d 569 (7th Cir. 2003)*

Schuster, age 56, worked for Lucent Technologies as a vice president of product development; along with two direct reports, he managed the software development process. Schuster was terminated as part of an effort to consolidate the software development process management into one lower-level position, and younger workers took responsibility for his original obligations. Schuster filed a claim for age discrimination by inference that he was over 40, he performed well, he was terminated, and he was treated less favorably that those under 40 who were similarly situated. To counter the employer's economic justifications for the termination, Schuster presented evidence of derogatory comments based on his age and inconsistencies in the proffered reasons for his termination. The court agreed with the employer and affirmed the lower court's dismissal in favor of the employer.

Kanne, Circuit Judge

Paul Schuster brought this suit claiming that his employment with Lucent Technologies, Inc. ("Lucent") was terminated because of his age in violation of the Age Discrimination in Employment Act ("ADEA"). Lucent denied age was the motivation for the discharge, stating that Schuster was terminated as part of an effort to address adverse financial conditions and to eliminate overlapping management positions. Lucent moved for summary judgment, contending that Schuster had not raised an issue of material fact that Lucent's proffered reasons for his discharge were only a pretext for age discrimination. The district court granted summary judgment in favor of Lucent, and Schuster now appeals.

* * *

The ADEA prohibits an employer from "discharg-[ing] any individual . . . because of such individual's age." To establish a claim under the ADEA, a plaintiff-employee must show that "the protected trait (under the ADEA, age) actually motivated the employer's decision"—that is, the employee's protected trait must have "actually played a role in [the employer's decision-making] process and had a determinative influence on the outcome." Such a claim may be proven through direct evidence of the employer's discriminatory motive, or through the indirect, burden-shifting approach articulated by the Supreme Court in *McDonnell Douglas Corp.* v. *Green.* Lacking any direct evidence of age animus on Lucent's part, Schuster here relies on the indirect method.

* * *

For purposes of its summary-judgment motion, Lucent conceded that Schuster could establish a *prima facie* case of discrimination. The company contends, however, that the business reasons it gave for the September 1999 RIF provide a legitimate, nondiscriminatory explanation for Schuster's termination. These reasons all center around the need to make Visual Insights a leaner, financially independent entity, both to reduce Lucent's costs (at this point, Lucent was still funding Visual Insights) and to make Visual Insights a more attractive prospect for outside investors. To meet this financial goal, the senior management proposed, quite sensibly, to eliminate management overlap and reduce the overall workforce size. Research and development was identified as a key area in which streamlining would lead to savings—in its brief, Lucent contends that it did not make fiscal sense to have three of its approximately 35 employees at that time engaged in *managing* the process of developing software, rather than actually *developing* it. This area was thus targeted by the management for savings, and Schuster, as Vice President for Product Development—along with Burkwald as Project Manager and Biernat as Director of Software Development, the two employees who reported to Schuster—was included in the second RIF.

In light of this legitimate, nondiscriminatory reason for the termination, the burden shifts to Schuster to demonstrate that the proffered explanation is merely a pretext for what was actually a discriminatory motivation. Pretext may be proven "directly with evidence that [an] employer was more likely than not motivated by a discriminatory reason, or indirectly by evidence that the employer's explanation is not credible." A plaintiff-employee may proceed indirectly by attempting to show that the employer's "ostensible justification is unworthy of credence" through evidence "tending to prove that the employer's proffered reasons are factually baseless, were not the actual motivation for the discharge in question, or were insufficient to motivate the discharge." That is to say, "[i]f the only reason an employer offers for firing an employee is a lie, the inference that the real reason was a forbidden one, such as age, may rationally be drawn." *Id.* (quotation omitted). Whether a court finds sufficient evidence to create an issue of material fact depends upon the entire record: "When a plaintiff uses the indirect method of proof, no one piece of evidence need support a finding of age discrimination, but rather the court must take the facts as a whole." We also note that "the ultimate burden of persuading the trier of fact that

the defendant intentionally discriminated against the plaintiff remains at all times with the plaintiff."

Even taking the facts alleged by Schuster in a light most favorable to him, we cannot say that he has raised a genuine issue of material fact as to the true reason for his termination. In reviewing the evidence offered by Schuster, we are well aware that "we deal with small gradations, with an employer's subjective comparison of one employee to another, and it is incumbent upon us to remember that what is at issue is not the wisdom of an employer's decision, but the genuineness of the employer's motives."

Based on the evidence presented, the reasons offered by Lucent—that Schuster was terminated as part of its restructuring efforts at a time of financial difficulty—appear based on sufficient facts to justify its decision and constitute the actual motivation for the termination decision it made.

In arguing that Lucent's proffered reasons are pretextual, Schuster first offers affirmative evidence that he says shows that Lucent was more likely than not motivated by discriminatory intent rather than any fiscal concerns. He points to several age-based derogatory comments made by members of the Visual Insights management team which, he argues, reveal their desire to remove or replace older workers. Among the comments cited by Schuster: Shortly after Cogswell began as CEO, he asked Schuster "how long [he] intended to remain employed" and "how long [he] intended to work." At one executive team meeting, Cogswell noted that while young employees are willing to work 100 hours per week. "more mature people aren't willing to do that" (Schuster fails to note that Cogswell went on to say that mature workers "make up for it with skills and experience"). At another meeting, Cogswell remarked that, "younger employees were more energetic and harder working and had a better work ethic." Tatelman, who Lucent admits was involved in the decision to terminate Schuster, was heard telling another employee, "You've got to think like a 25 year old. . . . Well, seriously, all the guys at Microsoft are 25" (this last comment was made approximately one month after Schuster had left Visual Insights).

We have previously stated that age-based derogatory remarks made around the time of and in reference to an employment action are relevant to a finding of discrimination, but we have also noted that less directly related comments, in combination with other evidence, might support an indirect case under the *McDonnell Douglas* approach. The less direct the connection between the comment and the employment action—that is, if the comment was not made in temporal proximity to the employment action, or if the comment was not made in reference to that action—the less evidentiary value the comment will have.

The district court found that these were "stray" workplace remarks that were insufficient to raise an issue of material fact as to the real reason behind Schuster's termination. We agree that the remarks cited by Schuster are too tenuously connected to the termination decision to raise a genuine issue of material fact as to the motivation behind the decision.

Cogswell's inquiry into Schuster's future employment plans was made some two years prior to Schuster's termination; his discussion of "mature people" and the work ethic of younger employees came approximately five months before the termination (and, as Lucent points out in its brief, may not have been derogatory at all). *Cf. Kennedy* v. *Schoenberg, Fisher & Newman, Ltd.,* 140 F.3d 716, 724 (7th Cir. 1998) (finding that a comment made five months prior to employee's termination was not temporally related to the discharge decision). Tatelman's references to 25-year-old employees came about one month after Schuster's termination. Because of the temporal distance between the comments and the termination decision, as well as the lack of any connection to that decision, the district court properly viewed them as "stray" workplace remarks, rather than evidence of the thought process behind Schuster's termination.

In addition, the cited comments may have less to do with age and more to do with business climate. This case arose at a time when the "dot.com" marketplace was intensely competitive. In order to succeed in that environment, Cogswell spoke of the need to "create a team that was faster-moving, was more amenable to a very rapidly changing marketplace . . . and . . . was quicker in decision making." O'Donnell testified that Cogswell's goal was "to migrate the company to a fast-paced, agile dynamic dot.com environment." Taking the Cogswell and Tatelman remarks in this context suggests that they may have been motivated less by age animus than by the realities of the marketplace. The district court noted that these comments "only establish the type of thinking that each person wanted Visual Insights to reflect. Neither comment suggests that either person wanted his subordinates to be a certain age, nor does either comment suggest that . . . an employee who thought in an appropriate manner would nonetheless [be] summarily dismissed because of that employee's

age." While making any distinction between a person's mindset and his or her age may present a close question, such a potential distinction certainly reduces the likelihood that discrimination, rather than competitive desire, was the motivating influence for Schuster's termination.

Schuster next points to the fact that two younger workers—Eick at age 45 and Hammond at age 40—took over his responsibilities after he was terminated, which he argues is evidence of Lucent's plan to replace Visual Insights's older workers. Although it is true that these two employees did assume some of Schuster's former duties, that is not necessarily inconsistent with the company's assertion that the research and development area was ripe for eliminating management overlap and inefficient layering. The elimination of Schuster's position meant the number of executive-level managers at Visual Insights was reduced by one, one of the goals of the restructuring process. It is thus not surprising that some of Schuster's functions were absorbed by Hammond, a lower-level, less experienced (and thus, not surprisingly, younger) employee, and by Eick, creator of Visual Insights's software product, who many believed was "critical" to the success of the venture.

* * *

Schuster next offers proof he says suggests that Lucent's proffered reasons for his termination serve simply as a smokescreen to cover up its age animus and are thus "unworthy of credence." The thrust of Schuster's argument here is that Lucent has changed its account of his termination in ways suggesting that none of its reasons can be considered legitimate. Shifting and inconsistent explanations can provide a basis for a finding of pretext. But the explanations must actually be shifting and inconsistent to permit an inference of mendacity. Even accepting that Lucent may have at times over-defended its decision, we believe that its overall account is substantially consistent with that of a company seeking to reduce costs and restructure in such a way as to attract outside investment.

In support of his inconsistency argument, Schuster notes that Lucent first claimed that Schuster's functions were being eliminated as part of the second RIF, but later acknowledged that some of those functions were transferred to other employees. Lucent also initially claimed that, in deciding whether to include Schuster or Eick in the RIF, it relied on talent profiles prepared for both, which gave Eick a slight advantage, therefore providing an additional age-neutral reason for terminating Schuster over Eick. Later, however, Cogswell stated in deposition testimony, for the first time, that he was concerned about Schuster's "performance" and "management style." By the time it moved for summary judgment, Lucent was relying on the specific issues with Schuster's performance, rather than the admittedly close talent profiles. Schuster argues that Cogswell's specific concerns with his work performance are at odds with the testimony of his supervisor and peers, as well as the high marks (albeit slightly lower than Eick's marks) on his talent profile.

Schuster contends that Lucent changed its story as to who played a role in Schuster's termination. He suggests that Lucent exaggerated Weichel's role in the decision-making process because of his age (while initially failing to note that Weichel opposed Schuster's termination) and minimized Tatelman's role because of his expressed affinity for the work ethic of the 25-year-olds at Microsoft. After initially claiming that Cogswell and Weichel were the decision makers, Lucent later admitted that Tatelman had participated in the decision-making process as well, and further acknowledged that Weichel had disagreed with the decision to terminate Schuster.

Finally, Schuster contends that Lucent attempted to disguise its efforts to remove older workers by including Biernat (age 40) and Burkwald (age 37) in the second RIF, even though those employees had already indicated their intention to leave Visual Insights. Inclusion of these two employees, the argument goes, was necessary since the other three employees included in the second RIF (Schuster, Fyock, and Adler) were all over 50 years old.

To avoid summary judgment in favor of Lucent, Schuster must do more than simply allege that the executives of Visual Insights are lying about their real reason for terminating him—under Rule 56, he must point to specific facts sufficient to cast doubt on the legitimate restructuring and financial reasons offered by Lucent, or which raise doubts as to the credibility of the executives' testimony. He has failed to do so.

* * *

CONCLUSION

Schuster has presented insufficient evidence to raise a genuine issue of material fact as to whether Lucent's reasons for terminating him are merely pretextual. Therefore, summary judgment in favor of Lucent was appropriate, and the judgment of the district court is AFFIRMED.

Case Questions

1. Do you agree that derogatory remarks should not be relevant to the court's decision if they are too removed in point of time from the adverse employment action? How close to the action would you believe remarks should be made to be relevant and considered evidence of pretext?
2. Are you persuaded by the employer's economic reasons for the termination? Do they seem reasonable to you?
3. Which, if any, of Schuster's arguments do you find most persuasive, and why?

Hazen Paper Co. v. Biggins   *507 U.S. 604 (1993)*

The Hazens hired Walter Biggins in 1977 and fired him in 1986 when he was 62 years old. Biggins sued, alleging a violation of the ADEA. The Hazens claimed instead that they terminated him because he did business with their competitors. A jury rendered a verdict for Biggins and the appellate court agreed, relying on evidence that the Hazens really fired him in order to prevent his pension benefits from vesting (which would have happened in the few weeks following his termination). In this case, the Supreme Court determines whether a firing decision based on number of years served is "age-based."

O'Connor, J.

The Courts of Appeals repeatedly have faced the question whether an employer violates the ADEA by

acting on the basis of a factor, such as an employee's pension status or seniority, that is empirically correlated with age. . . . We now clarify that there is no disparate treatment under the ADEA when the factor motivating the employer is some feature other than the employee's age.

* * *

In a disparate treatment case, liability depends on whether the protected trait (under the ADEA, age) actually motivated the employer's decision. The employer may have relied upon a formal, facially discriminatory policy requiring adverse treatment of employees with that trait. Or the employer may have been motivated by the protected trait on an ad hoc, informal basis. Whatever the employer's decision-making process, a disparate treatment claim cannot succeed unless the employee's protected trait actually played a role in that process and had a determinative influence on the outcome.

Disparate treatment, thus defined, captures the essence of what Congress sought to prohibit in the ADEA. It is the very essence of age discrimination for an older employee to be fired because the employer believes that productivity and competence decline with old age.

"Although age discrimination rarely was based on the sort of animus motivating some other forms of discrimination, it was based in large part on stereotypes unsupported by objective fact. . . . Moreover, the available empirical evidence demonstrated that arbitrary age lines were in fact generally unfounded and that, as an overall matter, the performance of older workers was at least as good as that of younger workers."

Thus the ADEA commands that "employers are to evaluate [older] employees . . . on their merits and not their age." The employer cannot rely on age as a proxy for an employee's remaining characteristics, such as productivity, but must instead focus on those factors directly.

When the employer's decision is wholly motivated by factors other than age, the problem of inaccurate and stigmatizing stereotypes disappears. This is true even if the motivating factor is correlated with age, as pension status typically is. Pension plans typically provide that an employee's accrued benefits will become nonforfeitable, or "vested," once the employee completes a certain number of years of service with the employer. On average, an older employee has had more years in the workforce than a younger employee, and thus may well have accumulated more years of service with a particular employer. Yet an employee's age is analytically distinct from his years of service. An employee who is younger than 40, and therefore outside the class of older workers as defined by the ADEA, may have worked for a particular employer his entire career, while an older worker may have been newly hired. Because age and years of service are analytically distinct, an employer can take account of one while ignoring the other, and thus it is incorrect to say that a decision based on years of service is necessarily "age based."

The instant case is illustrative. Under the Hazen Paper pension plan, as construed by the Court of Appeals, an employee's pension benefits vest after the employee completes 10 years of service with the company. Perhaps it is true that older employees of Hazen Paper are more likely to be "close to vesting" than younger employees. Yet a decision by the company to fire an older employee solely because he has nine-plus years of service and therefore is "close to vesting" would not constitute discriminatory treatment on the basis of age. The prohibited stereotype ("Older employees are likely to be—") would not have figured in this decision, and the attendant stigma would not ensue. The decision would not be the result of an inaccurate and denigrating generalization about age, but would rather represent an accurate judgment about the employee—that he indeed is "close to vesting."

We do not mean to suggest that an employer lawfully could fire an employee in order to prevent his pension benefits from vesting. Such conduct is actionable under §510 of ERISA. But it would not, without more, violate the ADEA. That law requires the employer to ignore an employee's age (absent a statutory exemption or defense); it does not specify further characteristics that an employer must also ignore. . . .

We do not preclude the possibility that an employer who targets employees with a particular pension status on the assumption that these employees are likely to be older thereby engages in age discrimination. . . . Finally, we do not consider the special case where an employee is about to vest in pension benefits as a result of his age, rather than years of service, and the employer fires the employee in order to prevent vesting. That case is not presented here. Our holding is simply that an employer does not violate the ADEA just by interfering with an older employee's pension benefits that would have vested by virtue of the employee's years of service.

Case Questions

1. Do you agree with the court that age and years of service are sufficiently distinct to allow for terminations based on years of service and to find no violation of the ADEA where the terminations result

in a greater proportion of older workers being fired?

2. Aren't workers close to vesting more likely to be older workers? And, if so, then do you believe that an employer can use the category "close to vesting" to avoid liability under the ADEA?

3. If an employer did terminate a group of individuals on the basis of their being close to vesting with the intention of getting rid of older workers, what type of evidence would the employees/plaintiffs be able to use to prove the unlawful intent?

There is no consensus in the federal courts on the question of whether there is a "high correlation" between compensation and age in any generic manner that would imply that compensation-based decisions would have a disparate impact on older workers as a general rule. An employer's decision based on salary which disproportionately affected older workers because of the high correlation between age and salary would be actionable age discrimination under a number of federal circuit court decisions.[11] On the other hand, federal courts which have examined the issue more recently, particularly in the wake of *Hazen Paper Co.* v. *Biggins,* have tended to hold that economic decisions do not give rise to liability for age discrimination, despite the disparate impact of such decisions on older workers.[12]

The split among courts of whether economic factors can be considered when terminating older workers can be traced to two fundamentally differing views about the goal of the age discrimination statutes. If the goal of the age discrimination statutes is to preclude decisions based on generalities about older workers which may have no basis as to individuals, then they certainly do not extend to decisions based on relative compensation rates between individual workers. In this view, age discrimination statutes were enacted to prevent employers from assuming that just because an individual attained a certain age, he or she no longer could do the job, or do it as well. This view was best articulated by the dissent in *Metz* v. *Transit Mix, Inc.,* which stated, "The Act prohibits adverse personnel actions based on myths, stereotypes, and group averages, as well as lackadaisical decisions in which employers use age as a proxy for something that matters (such as gumption) without troubling to decide employee-by-employee who can still do the work and who can't."

The other view is that age discrimination statutes were enacted to protect older workers because of their status as older workers, since older workers, generally speaking, face unique obstacles late in their careers. Age discrimination law is thus seen as a kind of protective legislation designed to improve the lot of a people who are vulnerable as a class. If this view is correct, then holding that decisions based solely on salary may contravene laws precluding discrimination based on age makes sense.

Defenses Based on Benefit Plans and Seniority Systems   The ADEA specifically excludes bona fide retirement plans that distinguish based on age but are "not a subterfuge to evade the purpose of [the] Act." "Subterfuge" in this definition denotes those plans that are mere schemes for the purpose of evading the ADEA or the Older

---

[11] See *Caron* v. *Scott Paper Co.,* 834 F. Supp. 33 (D. Me. 1993); *Camacho* v. *Sears, Roebuck de Puerto Rico,* 939 F. Supp. 113 (D. P.R. 1996).

[12] See *Ellis* v. *United Airlines, Inc.,* 73 F.3d 999, 1009 (10th Cir. 1996): "Of those courts that have considered the issue since *Hazen,* there is a clear trend toward concluding that the ADEA does not support a disparate impact claim."

Workers' Benefit Protection Act (discussed below). The effect of the 1978 and 1986 amendments to the ADEA was to completely prohibit involuntary retirement plans when they are imposed on the sole basis of an employee's age.

To qualify as a bona fide voluntary retirement plan allowed by the act, the plan must be truly voluntary. Some employees have contended that there is no voluntary decision when they are given only a short time in which to reach a decision about whether to accept the retirement option. But a short time period in which to reach a decision does not necessarily render the decision involuntary. The determination of what qualifies as a bona fide plan must be made on a case-by-case basis.

It has been held that early retirement plans offered by employers are not bona fide pursuant to the act if a reasonable person would have felt compelled to resign under similar circumstances. However, even after several court decisions relating to the issues of voluntariness, and whether a plan was a subterfuge, employers are left without much direction in terms of the formulation of early retirement programs and other means of providing benefits.

"Same Actor" Defense   A number of appellate courts, including the First, Second, Fourth, Fifth, Sixth, Seventh, Eighth, Ninth, and Eleventh Circuits, have adopted a defense called the "same actor" defense to age discrimination claims. The circuit courts have applied various weights of strength or value of the defense when the hirer and firer are the same actor. These courts have held that when the same "actor" both hires and fires a worker protected by the ADEA, there is a permissible inference that the employee's age was not a motivating factor in the decision. After all, if someone held discriminatory beliefs about older workers, why would that person have hired the worker in the first place? A Fourth Circuit Court reasoned that "claims that the employer animus exists in termination but not in hiring seem irrational. From the standpoint for the putative discriminator, it hardly makes sense to hire workers from a group one dislikes (thereby incurring the psychological costs of associating with them), only to fire them once they are on the job."[13]

Defenses Based on Waivers under the Older Workers' Benefit Protection Act of 1990
In 1990, Congress enacted the Older Workers' Benefit Protection Act (OWBPA), amending section 4(f) of the ADEA. The OWBPA concerns the legality and enforceability of early retirement incentive programs (called "exit incentive programs" in the act) and of waivers of rights under the ADEA, and it prohibits age discrimination in the provision of employee benefits. What this act really deals with are those situations where employees are offered amounts of money through retirement plans as incentives for leaving a company. In that way, the company is not terminating an older worker and, thereby, cannot in theory be held liable under the ADEA.

Many companies also request that an older worker sign a waiver, relinquishing the right to later question the plan by filing an age discrimination action. Once the waiver is signed and the worker accepts the benefits under the plan, the company would like to believe it is safe from all possible claims of discrimination. Where a waiver is valid under the ADEA/OWBPA, the employer can use it as an affirmative defense to an ADEA claim. The burden, however, is on the employer to prove validity. This is not necessarily always the case, as will be discussed.

[13] *Proud v. Stone,* 945 F.2d 796 (4th Cir. 1991).

The OWBPA codifies the EEOC's "equal cost principal," requiring firms to provide benefits to older workers that are at least equal to those provided to younger workers, unless the cost of their provision to older workers *greatly* exceeds the cost of provision to younger workers. Therefore, a firm may only offer different benefits to older and younger workers if it costs a significant amount more to provide those benefits to older workers. This section amends section 4 of the ADEA, which provides that adverse employment actions taken in observance of the terms of a bona fide employee benefit plan are partially exempt from question.

In connection with employee waivers of their rights to file discrimination actions under the ADEA, the OWBPA requires that every **waiver** must be "knowing and voluntary" to be valid. In order to satisfy this requirement, the waiver must meet all of the requirements below:

waiver
The intentional relinquishment of a known right.

1. The waiver must be written in a manner calculated to be understood by an average employee.
2. The waiver must specifically refer to ADEA rights or claims (but may refer to additional acts, such as Title VII or applicable state acts).
3. The waiver only affects those claims or rights that have arisen prior to the date of the waiver (i.e., the employee is not waiving any rights that will be acquired after signing the waiver).
4. The waiver of rights to claims may only be offered in exchange for some consideration in addition to anything to which the individual is already entitled (this usually involves inclusion in an early retirement program).
5. The employee must be advised in writing to consult with an attorney prior to execution of the waiver (this does not mean that the employee must consult with an attorney, but must merely be advised of the suggestion).
6. The employee must be given a period of 21 days in which to consider signing a waiver, and an additional 7 days in which to revoke the signature. Note that where a waiver is offered in exchange for an early retirement plan, as opposed to some other consideration, the individual must have 45 days in which to consider signing the agreement.
7. If the waiver is executed in connection with an exit incentive (early retirement) or other employment termination program, the employer must inform the employee in writing of the exact terms and inclusions of the program.

The waiver may not bar the employee from filing a claim with the EEOC or participating in investigations by the EEOC. Therefore, the employee may testify on another's behalf if requested. The purpose of these provisions is basically to ensure that the employee entered into the agreement that waived her or his rights knowingly and voluntarily based on the "totality of the circumstances."

Based on the court's decision in *Oubre,* below, if an employee signs a defective waiver, the employee is *not* required to tender back any benefits received under the defective waiver. In addition, if the employer offers to individually negotiate the waiver (as opposed to offering a standard form to the employee on a take-it-or-leave-it basis), this may be able to serve as proof to the court that the employee knew what he was doing when he signed the document.

Employers may use general waivers as an attempt to avoid all employment-related liability in contexts other than layoffs. For example, Allstate Insurance decided to transform its 15,200-member sales force from regular employees to independent contractors. To stay on as contractors, the agents were required to sign a release stating that they would not sue Allstate. Those agents who refused to sign the waivers were dismissed. Ninety percent of these agents were over the age of 40. In December 2001, the EEOC filed a suit against Allstate alleging it engaged in age discrimination against its agents.[14]

[14] See "U.S. Sues Allstate over Age Discrimination," Reuters, news.findlaw.com/legalnews/s/20011228/n28194796.html, Dec. 28, 2001.

Oubre v. Entergy Operations, Inc. *118 S. Ct. 838 (1998)*

An employee who received a severance agreement and signed a waiver discharging the employer from all claims later sued the employer for age discrimination. The Court had to determine whether the waiver was effective.

Kennedy, J.

Dolores Oubre worked as a scheduler at a power plant in Louisiana run by her employer, Entergy Operations, Inc. In 1994, she received a poor performance rating. Oubre's supervisor met with her on January 17, 1995, and gave her the option of either improving her performance during the coming year or accepting a voluntary arrangement for her severance. She received a packet of information about the severance agreement and had 14 days to consider her options, during which she consulted with attorneys. On January 31, Oubre decided to accept. She signed a release, in which she "agree[d] to waive, settle, release, and discharge any and all claims, demands, damages, actions, or causes of action . . . that I may have against Entergy. . . ." In exchange, she received six installment payments over the next four months, totaling $6,258.

Oubre filed this suit against Entergy alleging constructive discharge on the basis of her age in violation of the ADEA and state law. She has not offered or tried to return the $6,258 to the employer, nor is it clear she has the means to do so. The lower court agreed with the employer that Oubre had ratified the defective release by failing to return or offer to return the monies she had received. The Court of Appeals affirmed judgment for the employer and we reverse.

* * *

In 1990, Congress amended the ADEA by passing the OWBPA. The OWBPA provides: "An individual may not waive any right or claim under [the ADEA] unless the waiver is knowing and voluntary. . . . [A] waiver may not be considered knowing and voluntary unless at a minimum" it satisfies certain enumerated requirements.

The statutory command is clear: An employee "may not waive" an ADEA claim unless the waiver or release satisfies the OWBPA's requirements. The policy of the Older Workers' Benefit Protection Act is likewise clear from its title: It is designed to protect the rights and benefits of older workers. The OWBPA implements Congress' policy via a strict, unqualified statutory stricture on waivers, and we are bound to take Congress at its word. Congress imposed specific duties on employers who seek releases of certain claims created by statute. Congress delineated these duties with precision and without qualification: An employee "may not waive" an ADEA claim unless the employer complies with the statute. Courts cannot with ease presume ratification of that which Congress forbids.

. . . The statute creates a series of prerequisites for knowing and voluntary waivers and imposes affirmative duties of disclosure and waiting periods. The OWBPA governs the effect under federal law of waivers or releases on ADEA claims and incorporates no exceptions or qualifications. The text of the OWBPA forecloses the employer's defense, notwithstanding how general contract principles would apply to non-ADEA claims.

The rule proposed by the employer (that the employee must first give back monies received before avoiding the release) would frustrate the statute's practical operation as well as its formal command. In many instances a discharged employee likely will have spent the monies received and will lack the means to tender their return. These realities might tempt employers to risk noncompliance with the OWBPA's waiver provisions, knowing it will be difficult to repay the monies and relying on ratification. We ought not to open the door to an evasion of the statute by this device.

Oubre's cause of action arises under the ADEA, and the release can have no effect on her ADEA claim unless it complies with the OWBPA. In this case, both sides concede the release the employee signed did not comply with the requirements of the OWBPA. Since Oubre's release did not comply with the OWBPA's stringent safeguards, it is unenforceable against her insofar as it purports to waive or release her ADEA claim. As a statutory matter, the release cannot bar her ADEA suit, irrespective of the validity of the contract as to other claims.

In further proceedings in this or other cases, courts may need to inquire whether the employer has claims for restitution, recoupment, or setoff against the employee, and these questions may be complex where a release is effective as to some claims but not as to ADEA claims. We need not decide those issues here, however. It suffices to hold that the release cannot bar the ADEA claim because it does not conform to the statute. Nor did the employee's mere retention of monies amount to a ratification equivalent to a valid release of her ADEA claims, since the retention did not comply with the OWBPA any more than the original release did. The statute governs the effect of the release on ADEA claims, and the employer cannot invoke the employee's failure to tender back as a way of excusing its own failure to comply. REVERSED and REMANDED.

Case Questions

1. Do you think the fact that an attorney was consulted before the acceptance of the offer is relevant in this case to determine whether the waiver was knowing and voluntary?

2. As an employer, what should you do to ensure the waiver an individual will be signing is valid?

3. Why do you think an employer must follow such strict guidelines when creating a waiver? Do you think the guidelines are correct? How would you change them?

After the Supreme Court decision in *Oubre,* above, the EEOC issued a notice of proposed rule making to address the issues raised in that case. After receiving comments, the EEOC published its final regulation setting forth its interpretation of the waiver provisions of OWBPA. This regulation became effective on January 10, 2001.[15] The regulation makes clear that employees cannot be required to "tender back" the consideration received under an ADEA waiver agreement before being permitted to challenge the waiver in court. Further, the contract principle of ratification does not apply to ADEA waivers. The EEOC also recognized that covenants not to sue operate as waivers in the ADEA context. Therefore, OWBPA's requirements and these rules apply to such agreements as well.[16]

A firm must be cautious because individual negotiations may lead to slightly different agreements with various employees; and varying benefits among similar employees may constitute a violation of the Employee Retirement Income Security Act (ERISA).

---

[15] 29 CFR 1625.

[16] See Kiren Dosanjh, "Old Rules Need Not Apply: The Prohibition of Ratification and 'Tender Back' in Employees' Challenges to ADEA Waivers," 3 *Journal of Legal Advocacy and Practice* 5 (2001).

The OWBPA also contains the following provisions in connection with early retirement plans, 29 U.S.C. §623:

1. Employers may set a minimum age as a condition of eligibility for normal or early retirement benefits.
2. A benefit plan may provide a subsidized benefit for early retirement.
3. A benefit plan may provide for Social Security supplements in order to cover the time period between the time when the employee leaves the firm and the time when the employee is eligible for Social Security benefits.
4. While severance pay cannot vary based on the employee's age, the employer may offset the payments made by the value of any retiree health benefits received by an individual eligible for immediate pension.

Thus, while an employer may not actually discriminate in the amount of the payments offered by the retirement plan on the basis of age, these provisions actually seem to allow for inconsistent payments to older and younger workers, under certain circumstances.

Note that no provision of the OWBPA prohibits an employer from revoking a retirement offer *while* the employee is considering it. So, for example, a firm could offer an employee a retirement package in a separation agreement; then, while the employee considers it, the firm could revoke it and offer a less attractive package. This could be abused, of course, if it is interpreted as a threat to encourage the worker to decide earlier than the 21-day limit.

Employee's Response: Proof of Pretext

An ADEA case begins as the employee proves the elements of the prima facie claim; then the employer has the chance to justify its decision using any of the above defenses. Now it is again the employee's turn; the employee must show that those reasons or that defense is pretextual. When a claim is pretextual, it means that it is not the true reason for the action, that there is some underlying motivation to which the employer has not admitted. To prove that the offered reason is pretext for an actual case of age discrimination, the employee need not show that age was the *only* factor motivating the employment decision, but only that age was a determining factor.

Where there is direct evidence of discrimination, proof of pretext is not required. This may occur where the employer admits to having based the employment decision on the employee's age, or when a representative of the employer states that the employee is "too old," or that it would be cheaper to hire younger applicants.

The question of what constitutes direct evidence is not always clear. Despite the similarity between statements made by employers, however, statements regarding an applicant's or employee's race are taken more seriously than those about age. For instance, most courts would rule in the employee's favor if it were determined that she was not hired pursuant to the manager's statement, "I don't want any more blacks in my unit." But it is questionable whether this same employer would be held guilty if the manager states, "We need some new ideas in this unit. Let's hire younger analysts." The statement may be viewed as merely descriptive.

An employee can also show pretext by proving that the offered reasons for the adverse employment action have no basis in fact; the offered reasons did not actually motivate the adverse employment action; or the offered reasons are insufficient to motivate the adverse action taken. In addition, in a 2004 case, the First Circuit held that an adverse action taken by a nonbiased decision maker, but based on information from another worker who has a discriminatory motive, still satisfies a prima facie case. In other words, if someone takes an adverse action against an employee based on what appears to be a reasonable factor, the employer will be liable if the basis of that decision is actually grounded in bias and a discriminatory motive.[17] The following case considers a claim involving pretext.

---

[17] *Cariglia v. Hertz Equipment Rental Corporation*, No. 02-2199 (4/5/04).

Pottenger v. Potlatch Corp. *329 F.3d 740 (9th Cir. 2003)*

Pottenger alleged that he was forced to retire at age 60 from his position as Group Vice President of Pulp and Paper at the Potlatch Corporation in violation of the ADEA. Paulson, Potlatch's president, told Pottenger that Potlatch needed to make "real and significant" changes in order to improve its performance. He characterized Pottenger and his team as an "old management team" using an "old business model." Because the company was in financial trouble, and based on his concerns that Pottenger was not capable of bringing about real and significant change, Paulson decided to fire Pottenger. When Pottenger asked Paulson why he was being fired, Paulson stated that he lacked confidence that Pottenger had the commitment to make the hard decisions necessary to make Potlatch successful. Pottenger's replacement was 43 years old. The U.S. District Court for the District of Idaho granted summary judgment to the employer based on a legitimate nondiscriminatory reason, and Pottenger appealed.

William A. Fletcher, Circuit Judge

To prove age discrimination under a disparate treatment theory, Pottenger must show that his age "actually played a role in [Potlatch's decision-making] process and had a determinative influence on the outcome." Pottenger has made out a prima facie case of age discrimination. He was 60 years old; his most recent performance review grade of MR- was not outstanding, but indicated that he was meeting the requirements of the job; he was discharged; and he was replaced by Craig Nelson, then 43 years old, a substantially younger employee with equal or inferior qualifications. Potlatch, in turn, has articulated a legitimate, nondiscriminatory reason for terminating Pottenger: a lack of confidence that Pottenger could make the hard decisions necessary to turn around the ailing Idaho Pulp and Paperboard Division, which he headed. It is undisputed that IPPD (Pottenger's division) lost over $200 million during 1997, 1998, 1999, and the first quarter of 2000. Pottenger may establish pretext through evidence showing that

Potlatch's explanation is unworthy of belief or through evidence showing that discrimination more likely motivated its decision. Pottenger need not rely on only one type of evidence, and he has offered evidence both to cast doubt on Potlatch's credibility and to show a discriminatory motive. At the summary judgment stage, Pottenger's burden is not high. He must only show that a rational trier of fact could, on all the evidence, find that Potlatch's explanation was pretextual and that therefore its action was taken for impermissibly discriminatory reasons. If he does so, then summary judgment for Potlatch is inappropriate.

Pottenger advances several reasons that, in his view, undermine Potlatch's explanation of his discharge. They include positive comments in his performance review, shifting justifications for his dismissal, the brevity of the meeting at which the president and CEO reached their decision to discharge him, and the procedures followed in his termination. Considering all of Pottenger's evidence together, however, we conclude that he has not created a genuine issue of material fact. Pottenger's performance review did contain some positive comments, but it also contained negative comments specifically singling out concerns with his performance in managing IPPD. Potlatch's proffered explanation does not state that Pottenger was incompetent or a generally bad employee; rather, it states that Potlatch lacked confidence that Pottenger could help turn the company around. Instead of casting doubt on Potlatch's explanation, the statements in the performance review are consistent with it. Moreover, although "fundamentally different justifications for an employer's action . . . give rise to a genuine issue of fact with respect to pretext," Pottenger has pointed to no evidence suggesting that Potlatch has ever offered a reason for his dismissal other than doubt about his commitment to making hard decisions to help the company. Finally, the duration of the meeting at which they made the termination decision and the manner of Pottenger's discharge do not create a factual issue regarding the company's credibility. The meeting at which they ultimately made the decision to terminate Pottenger was short, but it obviously came at the end of a much longer process of evaluation and deliberation. There is also little evidence of an established formal or informal company procedure for discharging high-level employees. In fact, when Pottenger himself discharged the then-head of the Idaho Pulp and Paper Division in 1997, he did so in a manner similar to his own discharge. Potlatch's failure to follow some unspecified procedure in its treatment of Pottenger does not cast any doubt on its proffered reason for his termination.

To show discriminatory motive, Pottenger states that Paulson made comments referring to an "old management team," an "old business model," and "deadwood." Remarks can constitute evidence of discrimination. The Supreme Court has held that telling an employee he "was so old [he] must have come over on the Mayflower" and "was too damn old to do [his] job" constituted evidence of age discrimination. We have found a triable issue of material fact when an employee was told upon applying for an executive position that the board "wanted somebody younger for the job," and, in a Title VII case, when an employee was told, during the period that he was otherwise eligible for a university position, that "two Chinks" in the department was "more than enough." These remarks are clearly sufficient to support an inference that the decisionmaker acted in a discriminatory fashion. In other cases, we

have held that some remarks lead to no reasonable inference of discrimination and thus no triable issue of material fact exists. We have found that a supervisor's comment about getting rid of "old timers" because they would not "kiss [his] ass" did not sufficiently support an inference of age discrimination, that a comment that "we don't necessarily like grey hair" constituted "at best weak circumstantial evidence" of discriminatory animus, that the use of the phrase "old-boy network" is generally considered a colloquialism unrelated to age, and that an employer's comment describing a younger employee promoted over an older employee as a "bright, intelligent, knowledgeable young man" did not create an inference of age discrimination.

Paulson's remarks in this case do not sufficiently support an inference of age discrimination so as to create a triable issue of material fact that would defeat summary judgment. In the context of this case, the phrase "old business model," does not support an inference of age discrimination. Similar to the language in *Rose,* the phrase is a colloquialism not generally associated with the target's age. Nor does Paulson's use of the term "old management team" during the same meeting create a triable issue of fact. Similarly, the management committee's use of the term "deadwood" does not suggest age discrimination. The *Oxford English Dictionary* defines "deadwood" as "[a] person or thing regarded as useless or unprofitable; a hindrance or impediment."

* * *

Pottenger also argues discriminatory motive may be inferred from the fact that his replacement was only 43 years old and that shortly before his discharge the company moved a younger employee ahead of him on the successor list for CEO. Evidence that forms part of the prima facie case may also be considered to show that a proffered explanation is pretextual. Without more, however, the fact that Nelson was younger than Pottenger does not create a triable issue of pretext. Nor does the fact that the company moved a younger employee ahead of Pottenger on the CEO successor list suggest that Potlatch acted with any discriminatory motive, for that employee had held a higher position in the company than Pottenger. We have considered all of Pottenger's evidence of pretext and conclude that it does not refute Potlatch's basic rationale for Pottenger's termination—that IPPD was losing money and the company lacked faith that Pottenger was the one to turn IPPD around. Potlatch has leeway to make subjective business decisions, even bad ones. It may have been unfair (and perhaps unwise) for Potlatch to blame Pottenger for IPPD's losses, but it is not surprising that Pottenger's bosses would try to make a change in leadership in a division that was having such consistent trouble. We hold that Pottenger has not created a genuine factual issue of pretext and the district court properly dismissed his disparate treatment claim on summary judgment.

Case Questions

1. Do you think the reasons offered by the employer were pretextual? Why or why not?

2. Do you think that the burden shifting from employee to employer and then back again to the employee is a good system? Why or why not?

3. What can an employer do to insulate itself from terminating individuals for reasons that can be perceived to be pretextual?

In its 2000 decision in *Reeves* v. *Sanderson Plumbing Products,*[18] the U.S. Supreme Court held that a jury may infer discriminatory intent behind an adverse employment action based on the falsity of the employer's explanation. In October 1995, 57-year-old Reeves, who had worked for Sanderson Plumbing for 40 years, was terminated. As a supervisor, Reeves was responsible for keeping attendance records of his employees. After the department reportedly suffered a downturn in productivity due to tardiness and absenteeism, the records were audited. The audit revealed that Reeves and two other managers had made numerous errors in timekeeping. One other manager was discharged along with Reeves. Reeves brought a claim under the ADEA against his former employer, claiming that he had kept accurate attendance records. Further, Reeves argued that the employer's reasons for firing him were merely a pretext for age discrimination that was demonstrated through age-related comments made to him by his supervisor. The U.S. Supreme Court stated in its opinion that once the employer's rationalization has been eliminated, discrimination may well be the most likely alternative explanation for the adverse employment action.[19]

Employee's Prima Facie Case: Circumstances Involving Claims of Disparate Impact

As explained in connection with other forms of discrimination, there are two claims an employee may make against the employer: disparate treatment and disparate impact. The former occurs where an employee is treated differently than other employees because she or he is a member of a protected class. For example, disparate treatment exists where an applicant is not hired because of her age. Disparate impact, on the other hand, exists where a policy or rule of an employer, though not discriminatory on its face, has a different effect on one group than on another. For example, a rule that required all bus drivers to have 20/20 vision may have the effect of limiting the number of older workers who can be bus drivers. Now, this rule is indeed discriminatory, in that it distinguishes between those who have good vision and those who do not. The question is whether the rule is wrongful. In the example, perhaps it is justified by business reasons, and thus perfectly acceptable.

In mid-2005, the Supreme Court reached a decision in *Smith* v. *City of Jackson,* 351 F.3d 183 (2005), that resolved this issue—one that had caused a distinct split in the

---

[18] 530 U.S. 133 (2000).

[19] See "Have Discrimination Cases Gotten More Difficult?" *Texas Lawyer,* Sept. 27, 2000.

circuit courts. In that case, police and public safety officers employed by the city of Jackson, Mississippi, argued that the city had given senior officers lower salary increases than those offered to younger officers. The city had adopted this salary plan "to attract and retain qualified people, provide incentive for performance, maintain competitiveness with other public sector agencies and ensure equitable compensation to all employees regardless of age, sex, race and/or disability." The appellate court held that disparate-impact claims are categorically unavailable under the ADEA.

While holding that disparate impact claims are actionable under the ADEA, the Supreme Court focused a great deal of attention on the provision in the ADEA that allows for different treatment when it is based on reasonable factors other than age (RFOA). "The RFOA provision provides that it shall not be unlawful for an employer 'to take any action otherwise prohibited under [the Act] . . . where the differentiation is based on reasonable factors other than age discrimination . . . .' In most disparate-treatment cases, if an employer in fact acted on a factor other than age, the action would not be prohibited under [the Act] in the first place." The Court explained that the RFOA provision, along with other factors, evidences a *narrower scope* for disparate impact claims under the ADEA compared to Title VII.

In evaluating the city's salary plan, the Supreme Court concluded that reliance on seniority and rank is unquestionably reasonable given the city's goal of raising employees' salaries to match those in surrounding communities. The Court explained again that the analysis in this ADEA case was different from an analysis under Title VII: "While there may have been other reasonable ways for the City to achieve its goals, the one selected was not unreasonable. Unlike the business necessity test, which asks whether there are other ways for the employer to achieve its goals that do not result in a disparate impact on a protected class, the reasonableness inquiry includes no such requirement." The Court therefore decided that the city's decision was based on a "reasonable factor other than age" that responded to the city's legitimate goal of retaining police officers.

Given this decision, cases that arise based on economic justifications may spell some bad news for older workers who were relying on the decision to strengthen their footing with regard to facially neutral termination plans. Often a reduction in force may adversely impact older workers since their seniority may reward them with higher salaries. To reduce costs, a firm may opt to reduce its workforce based in part on salary amounts in order to have the greatest impact. Based on *City of Jackson,* above, it is crucial that the discharges be made on the basis of an objective standard so that the RFOA defense remains available to the employer.

With regard to reductions in force, courts generally absolve the employer from liability where the employer follows a specified procedure for the terminations, where objective criteria are used to determine the individuals to be discharged, and where the entire position is eliminated. In one example of a pre-*City of Jackson* case, the Second Circuit did find that the ADEA allowed disparate impact claims during a reduction in force. Its dicta are relevant as the case offers some insight into the ways in which a court may evaluate such claims in the future.

In 2004, that court upheld a lower court's decision in *Meacham* v. *Knolls Atomic Power Laboratory,* 381 F.3d 56 (2d Cir. 2004), finding that a reduction in force program had a disparate impact on older workers, even though the employer did not intend to discriminate. To state a cause of action, the Second Circuit explained that the employee would need to identify the actual, specific policy that resulted in harm (such as particular selection criteria). Next, the employee would need to show that this policy resulted in a disparity in the retention rates of younger and older employees "sufficiently substantial to raise an inference of causation" (using statistical data, discussed below). The employer is then given the opportunity to explain the business necessity of the challenged employment practice. The burden then shifts back to the employee who may prevail "only if they can show that the employer's explanation was merely a pretext for discrimination." The court suggests that the employee could point to another practice that would achieve the same result at comparable cost without causing a disparate impact on older workers.

In *Meacham,* the Second Circuit found that the employee had satisfied this burden by showing that the selection procedures were extremely imprecise, allowing for excessive subjectivity to impact the results. If an employer seeks to use subjective criteria to make decisions such as these, and if adequate alternative methods exist by which to make the same determination, the court warns that these criteria will need to be validated or audited to ensure that a disparate impact does not result. Employers may instead opt for more effective, job-related, objective criteria when reaching these decisions.

Interestingly, one challenge to stating a claim for discrimination based on a reduction in force is the fourth prong of the traditional prima facie case—where a RIF occurs, no one replaces the employee so there is no one similarly situated. Therefore, in the event of a RIF, age discrimination may be proven where (1) the employer refuses to allow the discharged (or demoted) employee to bump others with less seniority and (2) the employer hires younger workers when the jobs become available after the employee was discharged (or demoted) at the prior salary of the older worker. The question then arises, in an effort not to terminate the employee but to continue to cut costs, can an employer unilaterally reduce the salary of a protected employee to respond to its economic challenges? While this may seem a creative option, Section 4(a)(3) of the ADEA specifically states that it is "unlawful for any employer. . . to reduce the wage rate of any employee in order to comply with this Act." Strangely, though striving to be clear, in light of *City of Jackson,* this prohibition remains vague since an employer may argue that it was not reducing the wage rate to comply with the ADEA but instead for some RFOA such as reducing costs.

Employee's Prima Facie Case: Hostile Environment Based on Age

The Sixth Circuit recognizes a cause of action under the ADEA based on hostile environment age harassment. In *Crawford* v. *Medina General Hosp.,* Crawford claimed hostile environment based on ageist remarks consistently made by her supervisor such as "old people should be seen and not heard" and "I don't think women over 55 should be working." Crawford also alleged that, in addition to the disparaging remarks, the older women are "not included in anything," such as parties, as well as information about minor changes in office procedures, and that the supervisor would customarily call the young people in her office to question them about what the older people were doing "and then she encourages them to go out and confront those people."[20]

---

[20] *Crawford* v. *Medina General Hospital,* 96 F.3d 830 (6th Cir. 1996), at 833.

Though the Sixth Circuit noted that no court had yet to apply the hostile environment context to the ADEA, the court found that it was a "relatively uncontroversial proposition that such a theory is viable under the ADEA."[21] The court then articulated the prima facie case for hostile environment under the act:

1. The employee is 40 years old or older.
2. The employee was subjected to harassment, either through words or actions, based on age.
3. The harassment had the effect of unreasonably interfering with the employee's work performance and creating an objectively intimidating, hostile, or offensive work environment.
4. There exists some basis for liability on the part of the employer.[22]

Though it denied the claim, the Northern District of Illinois also upheld a cause of action under the ADEA for hostile environment age harassment. (*Alexander* v. *CIT Technology Financing Services,* 217 F. Supp. 2d 867 (N.D. Ill., 2002)). The claim will most likely be recognized as well by the Seventh Circuit which stated one year prior "[plaintiff] asserts that he was subjected to a hostile work environment because of his age. This circuit has assumed, without deciding, that plaintiffs may bring hostile environment claims under the ADEA. See *Halloway* v. *Milwaukee County,* 180 F.3d 820, 827 (7th Cir. 1999). We will do likewise here because we conclude that, even if such a hostile work environment claim could be brought under the ADEA, Bennington could not prevail" (*Bennington* v. *Caterpillar Inc.,* 275 F.3d 654 (7th Cir. 2001)). While several other circuits and districts have also so allowed,[23] the remaining courts have refused to expand the ADEA to include a hostile environment claim without express statutory language to the contrary.

Note that, if a hostile environment age harassment claim becomes more universally recognized, the impact may go significant further than a solely age discrimination claim. Consider the impact on constructive discharge. A worker subject to age harassment may be reasonable in quitting, based on the intolerable working condition, which could then give rise to a claim of constructive discharge based on age harassment.

The Use of Statistical Evidence

Courts allow the use of statistical evidence to prove discrimination on the basis of age, though it is generally more useful in disparate impact cases than it is in disparate

---

[21] Ibid. at 834.

[22] Ibid. at 834-35.

[23] *Jones* v. *SmithKline Beecham Corp.,* 309 F. Supp. 2d 343 (N.D.N.Y. 2004); *Lacher* v. *West,* 147 F. Supp. 2d 538 (N.D. Tex. 2001), *Jackson* v. *R.I. Williams & Associates, Inc.,* Civ. A. No. 98-1741, 1998 WL 316090 (E.D. Pa. 1998); *Tumolo* v. *Triangle Pacific Corp.,* 46 F. Supp. 2d 410, 412 (E.D. Pa. 1999); *Burns* v. *AAF-McQuay, Inc.,* 166 F.3d 292, 294 (4th Cir. 1999); *Ricci* v. *Applebee's Northeast, Inc.,* 301 F. Supp. 81 (D. Me. 2004); and *Lacher* v. *Principi,* 2002 WL 1033089 (W.D. Tex. 2002). In addition, while the Tenth Circuit has not expressly recognized a cause of action for hostile work environment under the ADEA, it has decided a case where the plaintiff raised the issue before the district court. See *McKnight* v. *Kimberly Clark Corp.,* 149 F.3d 1125, 1129 (10th Cir. 1998) (deciding a hostile work environment claim under the ADEA, but not addressing the apparent lack of authority for raising such a theory). In light of the *McKnight* case, the Court in *Ellison* v. *Sandia Nat. Laboratories,* 192 F. Supp. 2d 1240 (D. N.M. 2002) assumed without deciding that employee may assert a hostile work environment claim under the ADEA.

treatment cases. However, the court in *Heward* v. *Western Electric Co.* explained the similarities in the application of statistics in disparate impact cases as compared to disparate treatment cases:

> The significance of companywide statistics is heightened in disparate *impact* cases because plaintiffs need only demonstrate statistically that particular companywide practices in actuality operate or have the effect of excluding members of the protected class. However, even in a disparate *treatment* class action or "pattern and practice" suit, only gross statistical disparities make out a prima facie case of discrimination.

In either case, statistical evidence is meticulously examined to ensure that the statistics shed some light on the case. There is a great deal of skepticism relating to statistical evidence in age discrimination cases precisely because of the fact that older workers are likely to be replaced by younger workers, merely as a result of attrition of the workforce. This is not true in cases brought under Title VII based on race or gender discrimination; therefore, statistics may be slightly more relevant to a determination under Title VII, because they may represent pure discrimination.

Where statistics are used to prove discriminatory effect, the Supreme Court has offered some guidance about their use. The Supreme Court has considered percentage comparisons and standard deviation analyses of those comparisons: "As a general rule, . . . if the difference between the expected value and the observed number is greater than two or three standard deviations, then the hypothesis that the [selection process] was random would be suspect." In addition, the Court cautioned that the usefulness or weight of statistical evidence depends on all of the surrounding facts and circumstances, and, specifically, "when special qualifications are required to fill particular jobs, comparisons to the general population (rather than to the smaller group of individuals who possess the necessary qualifications) may have little probative value."

Remedies

The court may award a variety of remedies to a successful employee/plaintiff in an age discrimination action. However, where money damages such as back pay (what the employee would have received but for the violation) or front pay (which includes a reasonable and expected amount of compensation for work that the employee would have performed until the time of her expected retirement) are ascertainable and adequately compensate the employee for damages incurred, the court may *not* grant other **equitable relief**. Compensation for pain and suffering or emotional distress is not available under the ADEA.[24] Forms of equitable relief include reinstatement, promotions, or injunctions.

If an employee-plaintiff proves that the employer-defendant "willfully violated" the ADEA, then the court is also allowed to award **liquidated damages** in an amount equal to unpaid wage liability.[25]

---

equitable relief
Relief that is not in the form of money damages, such as injunctions, reinstatement, promotion. Equitable relief is based on concepts of justice and fairness.

liquidated damages
Liquidated damages limit awards to a predetermined amount. As used in the ADEA, liquidated damages are equal to the unpaid wage and are available in cases involving "willful violations" of the statute.

---

[24] *C.I.R.* v. *Schleier,* 115 S. Ct. 2159 (1995).
[25] U.S.C. §626(b).

EMPLOYEE RETIREMENT INCOME SECURITY ACT

In 1974, Congress passed the Employee Retirement Income Security Act, which regulates private employee benefit plans. While ERISA specifically governs the operation of retirement plan provisions and other benefits, and is therefore relevant to the issue of age discrimination, a complete discussion of its implications is found in Chapter 19.

In short, ERISA's purpose is to protect employees from wrongful denial of all types of benefits, including retirement or pension benefits. Prior to ERISA's enactment, employers were able to discriminate against certain employees in their determination of eligibility for pension benefits and the amount of time one must work for the employer to be eligible for benefits. In addition, many employees suffered from the loss of their benefits when companies underwent management reorganizations, or when the company decided to terminate the plan only a short time before the employees' benefits were to vest. Other employees lost their benefits when they became sick and were forced to quit their job prior to the time at which their pension rights vested.

ERISA prevents such problems as these through its regulation of the determination of who must be covered by pension plans, vesting requirements, and the amount that the employer must invest for the benefit of its employees. In an effort to encourage compliance with this provision, ERISA also requires complete disclosure of the administration of the plan. Further, ERISA stipulates that an employee may not be excluded from a plan on account of age, as long as she or he is at least 21 years of age and is a full-time employee with at least one year of service.

ERISA does have some negative side effects. It has made the provision of benefit plans more costly for employers. In addition, no federal law requires employers to offer retirement plans.

Distinctions among Benefit Plans

Can an employer simply decide to lower the amounts of benefits it offers its employees? Yes, as long as it is in line with requirements of ERISA. However, those reductions must be made across the board; the OWBPA limits the distinctions that an employer may make on the basis of age to only those that are justified by "age-based cost differences."

Many firms also have seniority systems that award benefits on the basis of seniority. Because experience seniority is often balanced in favor of older workers, not as many problems arise as a result of these systems. Those not themselves based in age discrimination are valid. In other words, those systems that disadvantage employees as they age are not protected by the ADEA.

MANAGEMENT CONSIDERATIONS

Generalizations, such as "older people have poorer vision" or "workers over 50 are less motivated than younger workers," may appear to be grounded in fact, based on the experiences of many firms. But adherence to these prejudiced principals during recruitment or retention of employees may cause more problems for the company than it prevents. As with other areas of protection against wrongful discrimination, managers are not precluded by the ADEA from hiring or retaining the most qualified individual; the act specifically requires that the employer do just that.

The employer may be losing a valuable and completely qualified employee simply because it incorrectly believes that all individuals over a certain age are not qualified for the available position. Instead of relying on vague generalizations concerning all individuals of advanced years, employers would do better to reevaluate the true requirements of the position, then test for those characteristics.

For instance, if an employee must have 20/20 vision to safely drive a taxicab, the taxi company will hire the most qualified individuals if it chooses the most competent and experienced from the pool of applicants and subjects these individuals to a vision test. In that way, the employer is sure to locate those workers who are, actually, the most *qualified* for the position, while not excluding an older worker based on a preconceived idea about failing vision. Or, if a position on an assembly line requires great dexterity and speed of movement, the employer should choose the most qualified applicants and allow them to perform the functions required of the position. If the older worker performs adequately, that applicant should be evaluated with no regard to her age.

In addition, employers may inadvertently discriminate against older workers and, in doing so, hurt themselves and their firm by failing to train and develop their older workers. Often older workers are not considered for continuous learning or other development because "they're on their way out, anyway." Managers should pay attention to the basis for decision making and selection in connection with training and development opportunities.

In addition, several problems are unique to the employer's defense of a claim of discrimination as a result of a RIF. These problems arise as a result of the difficulty of complete documentation of employee performance.

First, employers generally do not retain intricate written analyses of performance. Consequently, when asked what are the particular problems associated with the employment of this individual, the employer must rely on the subjective oral reports of its supervisors or managers. The jury is then not only faced with the question of whether the adverse action was justified but also with whether the recollection of the managers is correct or merely fabricated for purposes of the litigation. In addition, the employer should ensure that the performance appraisals that *are* recorded reflect an objective evaluation of the employee's performance at that time. The evaluator must exercise caution in the area of the employee's future potential, because this is an area that may be related to age and comments may be suspect.

Second, managers and supervisors will likely evaluate an employee as compared to other employees. Therefore, a rating of "good" may be the worst rating given in a department. When the RIF later requires that certain employees be discharged, the employer is left with the obligation to justify the termination of an individual who, in fact, never received a poor evaluation. This is not a sympathetic position.

Finally, the employer may make a decision based on some factor other than performance, such as the fact that a retained employee's wife is in the hospital, or that the discharged worker had the opportunity to participate in an early retirement program, while the retained worker could not. Superior care should be exercised in reaching a conclusion regarding terminations where these issues serve as the bases for retention and discharge, because many determining factors could be viewed as age based.

Management Tips

- Any job requirement on the basis of age must be subject to your highest scrutiny. There are extremely few BFOQs allowed on the basis of age alone. Instead, consider what you are actually concerned about and test for that characteristic. For instance, if you are concerned about the eyesight of your applicants or workers, conduct vision tests rather than follow a presumption that older workers will always be disqualified because of their eyesight.

- Reductions in force are prone to problems in connection with age discrimination as a result of higher salaries paid to older and more experienced workers. Review all termination decisions carefully in order to ensure fair and balanced procedures.

- Terminating an older worker and replacing her or him with another worker who is over 40 does *not* protect you from a charge of age discrimination.

- Review all recruiting literature to remove all age-based classifications like "looking for young upstarts to help build growing business."

- You may not terminate an older worker on the basis of age; if you must terminate a worker who is 40 or over, ensuring that you have appropriate documentation to justify dismissal creates a safe harbor.

- In drafting a waiver of discrimination claims for older workers to sign upon termination, review the form to ensure compliance with the OWBPA.

- Employers should neither permit nor encourage age-based remarks, comments, or jokes to avoid liability under the ADEA for age-related harassment. Antiharassment policies and procedures should encompass age and all prohibited factors.

- Employers should be sensitive about the inclination in the past to single out workers over 40 for medical exams.

It is in both the employer's and the employee's interest to ensure that the employee periodically receives an objective, detailed performance appraisal. In this way, the employer protects against later claims that the employee was not informed of the employer's dissatisfaction with her or his work, and the employee can guarantee that the employer may only use valid justifications for its discharge decisions.

Summary

- Employees are protected against discrimination on the basis of their age under the ADEA, unless age is a bona fide occupational qualification.
- To prove a case of age discrimination, the employees must show that:
  1. They are 40 years of age or older.
  2. They suffered an adverse employment decision.
  3. They are qualified for the position (either that they meet the employer's requirements or that the requirements are not legitimate).
  4. They were replaced by someone younger.

- Once the employee has presented this information, the employer may defend its decision by showing that:

  1. Age requirement of a job is a bona fide occupational qualification. This can be done by showing:

     —The age limit is reasonably necessary to the employer's business and

     —All or a substantial number of people over that age are unable to perform the requirements of the job adequately; or

     —Some of the people over that age possess a trait which disqualifies them for the position and it cannot be ascertained except by reference to age.

  2. The decision was made based on some other reasonable factor than age.

  3. The employee was not qualified for the position.

  4. The decision to leave was because of a voluntary retirement plan.

  5. The "same actor" defense may be used in some courts. The presumption is that when the same person hires and fires a worker protected by ADEA, there is a permissible inference that the employee's age was not a motivating factor in the decision to terminate.

- Once the employer presents its defense, the employee will have the opportunity to prove that this defense is mere pretext for the actual discrimination that exists.

- Federal courts are split as to whether an employer can terminate an older employee due to economic considerations.

- Benefit plans and seniority systems cannot be created for the purpose of evading the ADEA or the OWBPA.

- The OWBPA amended section 4(f) of the ADEA and places restrictions where employers offer employees amounts of money through retirement plans as incentives for leaving the company.

- The Employee Retirement Income Security Act (ERISA) regulates private employee benefit plans. It governs the operation of welfare and retirement plan provisions. (See Chapter 19 for a further discussion of ERISA.)

- There is a difference in the circuits whether disparate impact claims are actionable under the ADEA.

- There are a variety of remedies available to those discriminated against due to their age.

- A reduction in force (RIF) occurs when a company is forced to downscale its operations to address rising costs or the effects of a recession. When an individual is terminated pursuant to a bona fide RIF, the employer's actions are protected. In the event of a RIF, age discrimination may be proven when:

  1. The employer refuses to allow a discharged or demoted employee to bump others with less seniority.

  2. The employer hires younger workers when jobs become available.

Chapter-End Questions

1. Calder, age 60, worked as an account executive for TCI Cable, selling advertising time. Calder believed that she had a number of negative experiences at TCI because of her age. She bases this contention on several facts, including several discriminatory comments made by management at TCI. During one of Calder's individual meetings with an executive, he told her that she should walk faster, comparing her to a younger account executive. Another

manager told her that he did not understand why, "at this time in [her] life," she did not want free time to travel. Another referred to a job applicant as "grandma" and hired a younger candidate. Is this evidence of discrimination sufficient to support a claim? [*Calder* v. *TCI Cablevision of Missouri, Inc.,* 298 F.3d 723 (8th Cir. 2002).]

2. Celtec Industries terminated a manager at age 59, who later claimed the termination was based on age discrimination. He attempted to show pretext with evidence that he was fired based on incorrect data (showing a deficit when his unit had actually performed within budget). Is this sufficient? [*Balderston* v. *Fairbanks Morse Engine Division,* 328 F.3d 309 (7th Cir. 2003).]

3. Charles Grubb, 64 years old, was terminated from his laundry manager position at Foote Memorial Hospital. Foote Memorial Hospital had recently purchased the Sisters of Mercy Hospital and was in the process of reorganization when Grubb received his notice. When the hospital decided to eliminate Grubb's position, it made no attempt to determine whether Grubb possessed the skills necessary for other in-house positions and, instead, offered him the position of a truck driver. In addition, when Grubb was informed that his position was eliminated, he was told by his supervisor, "You can call this fired, kicked out, or whatever you want, but old man, you're through." In addition, Grubb's supervisor had told him earlier that he was "too old and set in his ways" and that he ought to retire. Grubb's responsibilities were given to a woman who was 63 years old. Grubb claims that he was terminated as a result of age discrimination. [*Grubb* v. *Foote Memorial Hospital,* 533 F. Supp. 671 (E.D. Mich. 1981); *modified,* 741 F.2d 1486).]

4. Fifty-four-year-old Bennington worked for Caterpillar, Inc. After a series of management changes and actions that Bennington claims made him feel undermined, he retired and filed an age discrimination suit against Caterpillar. The individual who took over Bennington's responsibilities was only five years younger than he was at the time. Is this sufficient to show that they treated this individual more favorably as evidence of age discrimination? [*Bennington* v. *Caterpillar,* 275 F.3d 654 (7th Cir. 2001).]

5. An over-40 employee of the New York Transit Authority is denied a promotion to station supervisor after he refuses to submit to an electrocardiogram (EKG) as part of a physical. The NYTA required the physical, and therefore the EKGs, for all supervisory position candidates who were under 40 and who had problematic medical histories, as well all candidates over 40. The NYTA contended that the examination and test were necessary because of the physical demands of the position. It also argued that people over 40 have an increased risk of heart disease, hence the EKG requirement. How would you determine whether this employee should be required to undergo the test? [*Epter* v. *New York City Transit Authority,* 127 F. Supp. 384 (E.D.N.Y. 2001).]

6. Lyle Ver Planck was the postmaster in Costa Mesa. In 1976, while he was temporarily assigned out of the area, a supervisor position became available. Vincent Limongelli, age 49 and a postal employee since 1944, and five others applied for the position. A three-member advisory panel briefly interviewed each of the applicants. Limongelli was asked about his age and the number of years before he planned to retire. While the panel claims that age and retirement plans had no bearing on its decision, the members unanimously voted to appoint Nathan Ver Planck, Lyle's 39-year-old nephew, as supervisor. Does Limongelli have a basis for a claim? [*Limongelli* v. *Postmaster General of the United States,* 707 F.2d 368 (9th Cir. 1983).]

7. Can an employer be liable under any antidiscrimination statute for refusing to hire someone whom the employer thinks is overqualified? [*Taggart* v. *Time, Inc.,* 924 F.2d 43 (2d Cir. 1991).]

8. The oldest or nearly oldest in each department happened to be the employee chosen by each unit supervisor to be laid off in a cutback. An employee filed suit and the employer claimed that (1) it had the right to terminate the oldest employees because they cost the most to the

company and (2) there was no discrimination or intent to do so because each unit supervisor made her or his own decisions, so there was no concerted effort or decision to get rid of older employees. Are you persuaded by this defense?

9. Since 1975, Featherly had been the production supervisor of the crankshaft department at Teledyne. As a result of a reduction in force in 1987, the crankshaft and the gears departments were combined and Featherly's supervisors determined that he should be laid off because he did not have the versatility to supervise both departments. Consequently, Featherly's duties were given to Gilbert, production manager of the gears department. At the time of his termination, Featherly was 58 years old, with 25 years' seniority; Gilbert was 41 years old, with 12 years of supervisory experience. What does Featherly need to show to be successful on a claim of age discrimination against Teledyne? [*Featherly* v. *Teledyne Industries,* 486 N.W.2d 361 (Mich. 1992).]

10. Fifty-five-year-old Merriweather had worked for 14 years as a benefits coordinator before he was laid off by his employer. The employer contended that it eliminated Merriweather's job for economic reasons. To support its strategic goals, the employer had decided to hire new workers instead of training Merriweather to handle projected additional tasks. The employer chose not to retain an employee who is seven months older than Merriweather as the only full-time benefits coordinator. Two new workers, age 42 and 50, were hired to divide their time between benefits coordination and the added tasks. Merriweather claimed that he was qualified to handle the added responsibilities, but he did not offer evidence to support this claim. You be the judge. Do the employer's actions violate the ADEA? Explain. [*Merriweather* v. *Philadelphia Federation of Teachers Health & Welfare Fund,* 2001 U.S. Dist. LEXIS 18511 (E.D. Pa. 2001).]

Chapter **Twelve**

Disability
Discrimination

Opening Scenarios

SCENARIO 1

1 Scenario

Thekla Tsonis is responsible for filling a vacant position at her firm. The position requires good interpersonal and communication skills and the ability to type, file, and travel on an as-needed basis. An applicant sits before her during an interview for the vacant position. Tsonis is relatively confident that the applicant satisfies the first three criteria. However, Tsonis is concerned about the fourth requirement, traveling on an as-needed basis, because the applicant is bound to a wheelchair due to a muscular disorder that does not affect her cognitive skills or her use of her arms and hands. A second applicant's performance evaluations come from her previous employer and are slightly lower than those received by the first applicant, but the applicant informed Tsonis that she is looking forward to the traveling. Does Tsonis hire the first applicant, even though she believes that the wheelchair will pose a problem with travel and other areas, or does she hire the second?

SCENARIO 2

2 Scenario

A sales manager in a large security systems company was terminated soon after his co-workers learned that he is homosexual and that his life partner has HIV, the virus that causes AIDS. The sales manager himself is HIV-negative. Has the employer violated the Americans with Disabilities Act?

SCENARIO 3

3 Scenario

Marquita applies for a position as a typist, but she has no arms past the elbow. Marquita types 80 words per minute with her toes. How should the employer handle this? Does Marquita have to be hired? If so, how can she be accommodated?

STATUTORY BASIS

Americans with Disabilities Act of 1990, ¶602, §102

No covered entity shall discriminate against a qualified individual with a disability because of the disability of such individual in regard to job application procedures, the hiring, advancement, or discharge of employees, employee compensation, job training, and other terms, conditions, and privileges of employment.

Vocational Rehabilitation Act of 1973, ¶504 §794

No otherwise qualified individual with a disability in the United States . . . shall, solely by reason of her or his disability, be excluded from the participation in, be denied the benefits of, or be subjected to discrimination under any program or activity receiving Federal financial assistance or under any program or activity conducted by any Executive agency.

REMOVING OLD BARRIERS

While Title VII assured certain groups of protection from discrimination in employment decisions, those groups with disabilities continued to face the frustration of physical and attitudinal employment barriers long after the passage of Title VII—employers refused to hire the disabled for fear that they would not be able to perform at the same level as other employees, or employers had fears based on the attitudes of coworkers. Disabled applicants found that they were required to prove themselves and their abilities to a much greater extent than did able-bodied applicants.

Approximately 49.7 million Americans, or almost one in five, have one or more physical or mental disabilities. In 2003, more than a decade after the ADA was signed into law, 60 percent of working age men and 51 percent of working age women with disabilities were employed (10.4 million men and 8.2 million women). Research has shown that the performance of a disabled worker, when properly placed, equals that of an able-bodied worker. It has also been shown that a disabled employee may in fact surpass coworkers as he or she overcomes the effects of his or her disability.

Employers have yet to recognize the potential lost by their underutilization of this valuable resource. Instead, many employment decisions regarding disabled applicants are grounded in naive prejudice. Often, managers reach inaccurate conclusions related to the scope of the disabled applicant's abilities and are apprehensive regarding the perceived costs of employing a disabled person. For instance, an employer who invites an applicant to her office for an interview based on a stellar résumé may be surprised to discover that the applicant is blind.

The employer may immediately jump to the conclusion that this blind applicant is not qualified for the position, which requires a great deal of reading. The employer, however, may be losing an excellent candidate merely because she failed to recognize possible accommodations of this disability, which may allow the applicant to make a meaningful addition to her staff. In fact, many disabled workers are capable of performing the essential requirements of their position with little or no accommodation on the part of their employer.

To ensure that an employer is reaping the greatest benefit from its applicant pool, the employer should be "disability-blind" and evaluate each applicant on the basis of her or his competence. This is true during all stages of employment, including the interview, hiring, employee relations, transfer requests, performance reviews, disciplinary decisions, and termination decisions.

REGULATION

Section 503 of the Rehabilitation Act
Requires affirmative action on the part of federal contractors and agencies to recruit, hire, and train disabled workers.

In an effort to stem the discrimination against disabled employees and applicants, Congress enacted the Vocational Rehabilitation Act of 1973, which applies to the government and any firm that does business with the government. Section 504 of the act prohibits discrimination against otherwise qualified individuals with disabilities by any program or activity receiving federal assistance. The Rehabilitation Act seeks to alleviate the burdens that are specifically confronted by those with disabilities and to ensure that disabled employees or applicants encounter only the burdens that are encountered by those who are not disabled. **Section 503** of the act further requires that, where a federal department or agency enters into a contract that exceeds $10,000 annually, the contractor is required to take affirmative action to employ and promote qualified disabled individuals. Where a contractor or subcontractor has 50 or more employees and contracts of $50,000 or more, it is required to have an affirmative action program at each establishment. Federal contractors, therefore, must take proactive steps to change their hiring policies, recruit disabled employees, train disabled employees so they are likely to advance, and assist in their accommodation should they experience surmountable difficulties in their position.

Exhibit 12.1
Myths about Disability Discrimination

1. A question on an application form about specific disabilities of an applicant is not improper.
2. If an employer would have to alter the working environment to accommodate a disabled applicant or employee, that person is not qualified for the position.
3. Employees with disabilities have many more rights to their jobs than do disabled applicants.
4. Individuals with disabilities generally are incapable of performing the jobs for which they apply.
5. If someone does not have a disability but others believe she or he does, that person is still not protected against discrimination.
6. Individuals with disabilities only create liability for employers and are not good, productive workers.
7. If an applicant with a disability applies for a job, the employer must hire that applicant.
8. HIV status is not a disability under the ADA.
9. Only physical disabilities are protected under the ADA.
10. Employers must give any and all accommodations requested by employees with disabilities.
11. If an applicant needs a reasonable accommodation for a preemployment test, that applicant is not qualified for the job.

Federal employers and contractors have the additional obligation to take steps to employ and to advance disabled workers, pursuant to the Rehabilitation Act's requirement of affirmative action. This may include positive steps to recruit disabled employees; modification of personnel practices to meet the needs of the disabled workforce, such as special training for individuals who will be interviewing disabled applicants; and the training of supervisors and managers to provide the strong internal support and an environment in which a disabled employee would feel welcome.

Unfortunately, since it only applies to the government and federal contractors, the Vocational Rehabilitation Act was insufficient to prevent discrimination against private sector employees and was inconsistently enforced against federal employers. Congress passed other statutes relating to discrimination against the disabled since the Rehabilitation Act, but on a segmented basis. Disabled veterans were protected by one statute, and mine workers who had contracted black lung disease were protected by another; private sector employers remained immune from prosecution in this regard.

Americans with Disabilities Act
Extends Rehabilitation Act protection to employees in the private sector, with few modifications.

Seventeen years after Congress passed the Rehabilitation Act, President George Bush signed into law the **Americans with Disabilities Act (ADA),** which became effective in July 1992. The ADA applied Rehabilitation Act standards to private employers of 25 employees or more until 1994; now the act is enforceable against employers of 15 employees or more. While many employers have complained about the act based on its vague definitions and unclear requirements, the ADA was seen as the "Declaration of Independence" or "Emancipation Proclamation" for the disabled, and the most far-reaching civil rights law to have been passed since the Civil Rights Act of 1964. Even today, however, a majority of employers are unsure about many applications of the act. (See Exhibits 12.1 and 12.2.)

Exhibit 12.2

The following was written prior to the passage of the ADA:

> The employment difficulties of Americans with disabilities deepened during the 1980s, according to new figures from the Census Bureau (www.census.org). This occurred despite the increased efforts and partial successes of Americans with disabilities to assert their rights to equal treatment in transportation, employment, voting, and within society in general. According to the new Census Bureau statistics, workers with disabilities saw their earnings fall further below the income of able-bodied workers as the decade progressed. In 1980, workers with disabilities earned 77% as much as the able-bodied; but, by 1987, they earned only 64%. And a smaller percentage of men with disabilities were working as the decade neared an end than in 1981: 30% in 1981, but only 23% [in 1989]. . . .
>
> Specialists in disability issues are surprised by the negative implications of the new Census Bureau statistics. And they are not certain how to explain the figures, although they offer theories. . . . Philip Calkins, of the President's Committee on Employment of People with Disabilities . . . offers several:

- Health-care costs have really skyrocketed in the 1980s. The costs of health-care, and of health-care insurance, are a major reason why people with disabilities face discrimination in the work force.

- "The number of employees in government at all levels has declined" relative to the U.S. population. "Therefore, the number of places available in those protected areas has declined." With the decline in government jobs, which offer legal protection against discrimination, workers with disabilities increasingly may have been kept in lower paying jobs, experts theorize. This may be a reason for the growing income gap between American workers in general and those with disabilities.

- As America's budget squeeze has tightened during the decade of the 1980s, some of the trims in spending for social programs have cut back on programs that aid people with disabilities, and that help prepare them for employment. [Copyright © 1992 by *Harper's Magazines*. All rights reserved. Reprinted from the May issue by special permission.]

Source: R. Hey, *Christian Science Monitor*, July 16, 1990, p. 8.

In addition, the impact of the ADA has been less than its advocates had hoped. In 1998, the American Bar Association's Commission on Mental and Physical Disability Law reported that the employer-defendant was the successful party in 92 percent of cases brought by allegedly disabled employee-plaintiffs. (However, the study also noted that it excluded the results of settlements since they were so difficult to track.) Also in 1998, the first report of the Presidential Task Force on the Employment of Adults with Disabilities reported on some of the effects of the ADA. Specific to employment, the Task Force concluded that:

> . . . enforcement mechanisms of the ADA have not proven sufficient to begin narrowing the gap in employment rates between people with and without disabilities. Enforcement of existing legislation designed to eliminate disability-based discrimination in all aspects of life, including employment, is clearly inadequate. Enactment of potentially powerful legislative remedies, like the ADA, without commitment of resources to enforcement will not produce desired results. Both

public and private assessments of the ADA suggest that the lack of enforcement, particularly with regard to employment, has diminished the impact that this landmark legislation might otherwise have had.

Although the results seem disappointing, the task force did ask the president to take action on several issues, including:

- Increasing the number of adults with disabilities working for the federal government.
- Increasing employment options for persons with psychiatric disabilities.
- Supporting legislation which allows adults with disabilities to retain Medicare coverage when they return to work.

In an executive order of December 1998, President Clinton supported all these measures and allocated funding for their implementation. In 2004, President Bush established the Workforce Recruitment Program for college students with disabilities in an effort to help employers identify qualified temporary and permanent employees from a variety of fields.

As will be shown later in this chapter, the impact of the ADA has also been limited by recent U.S. Supreme Court decisions. For example, state employees are not able to sue their state employers under the ADA.[1] State employees must depend on state law to protect them against disability discrimination in employment.

To understand the coverage of the act, it is important to understand its scope of protection. The ADA protects the disabled from three types of barriers: intentional discrimination for reasons of social bias against them, neutral standards with disparate impact on the disabled, and discrimination as a result of barriers to job performance that can be fully overcome by accommodation.

Generally, an employer may not reach any employment decision on the basis of the individual's disability; an employer may not classify an applicant or employee because of a disability in a way that adversely affects her or his opportunities or status. Employers may not make presumptions about what a class of disabled individuals may or may not be able to do. Employers may not impose standards or criteria that discriminate against or screen out employees or applicants on the basis of their disability, unless that criteria can be shown to be job-related and consistent with business necessity. Employers may not discriminate against qualified disabled applicants or employees in recruitment, hiring, promotion, training, layoffs, pay, terminations, position assignments, leave policies, or benefits.

How is the protection given to disabled individuals different from that afforded other minorities under Title VII and similar statutes? Under the ADA and the Rehabilitation Act, employers must take *proactive steps* to make their workplaces amenable to the impaired worker, and they may not wait until a problem presents itself. For example, an employer is not merely required to restructure its workplace and job descriptions to allow disabled individuals access as applicants but also to implement mechanisms to retain those disabled workers once hired. This is because Congress has

---

[1] *Board of Trustees of the University of Alabama* v. *Garrett,* 531 U.S. 356.

Signing the Americans with Disabilities Act into Law. Courtesy of the U.S. Department of Labor.

determined that the value of the resources to be provided by the disabled workforce greatly outweighs the costs of their employment.

How do these laws protect the disabled individual, and what must an employer do to ensure that she or he is in compliance? First, it is important to understand that the law merely protects the individual from discrimination based solely on her or his disability. The laws do not require an employer to hire a disabled person who is unable to perform the work required by the position. The operative word, however, is "required." Under the acts, the employer must ascertain the actual components of the position, the elements essential to the employee's performance, and which components are convenient but not essential to be performed by this individual. The employer should ensure that its position descriptions are up to date and job-specific, and that each description specifically outlines every responsibility of the job and discusses the qualifications that may be necessary to satisfy those responsibilities.

ADA and Rehabilitation Act protection
As long as an individual with a disability is otherwise qualified for a position, with or without reasonable accommodation, the employer may not make an adverse employment decision solely on the basis of the disability.

The general policy implemented by the **ADA** and the **Rehabilitation Act** is that, as long as the applicant or employee is otherwise qualified for the position, with or without reasonable accommodation, the acts prohibit any adverse employment decision that is made solely on the basis of the disability. An employer may not terminate an employee, for example, who is able to adequately perform merely because the employee uses a walker to assist in his or her mobility. An employee may be able to claim discrimination on the basis of her or his disability if the employee can prove:

1. That she or he is disabled.
2. That she or he is otherwise qualified for the position.
3. If an accommodation is required, that the accommodation is reasonable.
4. That she or he suffered an adverse employment decision, such as a termination or demotion.

The above analysis is one that is commonly considered to be based on disparate treatment. In a late 2003 decision, *Raytheon Co.* v. *Hernandez*,[2] the Supreme Court held in addition that disparate impact claims are also available to workers based on facially neutral policies that impact qualified individuals with disabilities differently than workers without disabilities. The Court held that, while available, a disparate impact claim would be analyzed according to the legal standards applied to an impact case, rather than a treatment case. Under disparate impact, a facially neutral employment practice may be deemed illegally discriminatory without evidence of an employer's subjective intent to discriminate that is required in a disparate treatment case. In addition, the defense to a disparate impact case is that the facially neutral policy is a business necessity or job-related, while one defense to a disparate treatment case is that there is a legitimate nondiscriminatory reason for the adverse employment action.

Employers should keep in mind that there are state laws as well as the federal laws that protect employees from discrimination. Employees filing claims based on a disability may find greater relief in state courts, applying state laws. In some states, damages are higher for disability discrimination under state laws, and claims are easier to prove than in federal courts applying the federal laws.[3]

"Disability"

disability
A physical or mental impairment that substantially limits one or more of the major life activities of an individual; a record of such impairment; or being regarded as having such an impairment.

A variety of terms are used in the disability discrimination area. What constitutes a disability? The ADA defines **disability** as "(a) a physical or mental impairment that substantially limits one or more of the major life activities of an individual; (b) a record of having such impairment; (c) or being regarded as having such an impairment." A "record" of impairment is discussed in the *Arline* case on page 541. In the third provision, the law protects those persons who are not actually disabled but who are instead *regarded* as having a disability. There is no definitive list of impairments that are considered to be disabilities. Courts are directed to reach determinations based on a case-by-case analysis. This determination is not made on the basis of the name or diagnosis of the employee's impairment but, instead, on the basis of the effect of the impairment on her or his life. Note also that some states even have laws that mandate that certain conditions be considered disabilities, thus eliminating this requirement of the plaintiff's proof. Examples of impairments generally *not* considered to be disabilities include normal pregnancy, predisposition to an illness or disease, personality traits such as a quick temper (unless part of an underlying psychological disorder), or advanced age.

Obesity as a disability has caused confusion among some employers and courts. Morbid obesity, typically defined as being 100 pounds over the normal weight for one's frame, may be considered a disability under the ADA. In addition, obesity may lead to a condition resulting in a disability. State antidiscrimination laws, such as the New Jersey Law Against Discrimination, also treat obesity as an impairment.

[2] *Raytheon Co.* v. *Hernandez,* 124 S. Ct. 513 (2003).
[3] See *City of Moorpark* v. *Ventura County Superior Court,* 959 P.2d 752 (Cal. 1998) and *Dillard's* v. *Beckwith,* 989 P.2d 882 (Nev. 1999).

In one 2002 case, an employee who was morbidly obese due to a genetic condition suffered from related physical problems. The employer fired her after four days of work at its small business in New Jersey, allegedly for having a poor work ethic. A jury awarded the employee a large sum in her discriminatory discharge action, which alleged pretextual reasons for the firing.[4]

This case is not unique. There is instead plenty of evidence that weight discrimination exists throughout all stages of the employment relationship. Title VII protections against discrimination based on gender may be relevant where an overweight woman is subject to different treatment or standards than overweight men. In addition, employers who stereotype the morbidly obese as slovenly or lazy and who then base employment decisions on these unfair assumptions may also be found liable under the ADA. While the mildly obese are not considered impaired, related medical conditions may be considered impairments within the meaning of the ADA. Additionally, if an employer merely regards an overweight employee or applicant as morbidly obese, that individual would be protected from disparate treatment based on that perception.

However, the mere presence of a physical or mental impairment does not lead to protection under the ADA. The impairment must substantially limit one or more of the major life activities (discussed in detail later in this chapter). This leads to the question: What if an employee or applicant can take a medication that mitigates (lessens) the impact of the impairment on daily life? What about medical devices such as hearing aids, prosthetic devices, and eyeglasses?

In June 1999, the Supreme Court released three opinions that articulate and delineate the law in this area, *Sutton* v. *United Air Lines, Murphy* v. *United Parcel Service, Inc.,* and *Albertsons, Inc.* v. *Kirkingburg.* In *Sutton* below, where the plaintiff's uncorrected vision was 20/200 or worse but could be corrected by eyeglasses to 20/20, the Court was asked to determine whether corrective measures should be considered.

---

[4] *Viscik* v. *Fowler Equipment Co., Inc.,* 2002 N.J. LEXIS 360 (March 28, 2002).

Sutton v. United Air Lines, Inc. *119 S. Ct. 2139 (1999)*

The petitioners were severely myopic twin sisters who have uncorrected visual acuity of 20/200 or worse. However, with corrective measures, both function identically to individuals without similar impairments. The sisters applied to United Airlines for positions as commercial airline pilots but were rejected because they did not meet United's minimum requirement of uncorrected visual acuity of 20/100 or better. They filed suit under the ADA. The district court dismissed petitioners' complaint, holding that the sisters were not actually disabled because they could fully correct their visual impairments. The Tenth Circuit affirmed. The Supreme Court reviewed and held that the sisters were not disabled under the ADA.

O'Connor, J.

* * *

The EEOC has issued regulations to provide additional guidance regarding the proper interpretation of [the term "disability"]. After restating the definition of disability given in the statute, the EEOC regulations define the three elements of disability: (1) "physical or mental impairment," (2) "substantially limits," and (3) "major life activities." Under the regulations, a "physical impairment" includes "[a]ny physiological disorder, or condition, cosmetic disfigurement, or anatomical loss affecting one or more of the following body systems: neurological, musculoskeletal, special sense organs, respiratory (including speech organs), cardiovascular, reproductive, digestive, genito-urinary, hemic and lymphatic, skin, and endocrine." The term "substantially limits" means, among other things, "[u]nable to perform a major life activity that the average person in the general population can perform"; or "[s]ignificantly restricted as to the condition, manner, or duration under which an individual can perform a particular major life activity as compared to the condition, manner, or duration under which the average person in the general population can perform that same major life activity." Finally, "[m]ajor [l]ife [a]ctivities means functions such as caring for oneself, performing manual tasks, walking, seeing, hearing, speaking, breathing, learning, and working." . . .

The agencies have also issued interpretive guidelines to aid in the implementation of their regulations. For instance, at the time that it promulgated the above regulations, the EEOC issued an "Interpretive Guidance," which provides that "[t]he determination of whether an individual is substantially limited in a major life activity must be made on a case by case basis, without regard to mitigating measures such as medicines, or assistive or prosthetic devices." The Department of Justice has issued a similar guideline. . .

III

With this statutory and regulatory framework in mind, we turn first to the question whether petitioners have stated a claim under subsection (A) of the disability definition, that is, whether they have alleged that they possess a physical impairment that substantially limits them in one or more major life activities. Because petitioners allege that with corrective measures their vision "is 20/20 or better," they are not actually disabled within the meaning of the Act if the "disability" determination is made with reference to these measures. Consequently, with respect to subsection (A) of the disability definition, our decision turns on whether disability is to be determined with or without reference to corrective measures. Petitioners maintain that whether an impairment is substantially limiting should be determined without regard to corrective measures. They argue that, because the ADA does not directly address the question at hand, the Court should defer to the agency interpretations of the statute, which are

embodied in the agency guidelines issued by the EEOC and the Department of Justice. These guidelines specifically direct that the determination of whether an individual is substantially limited in a major life activity be made without regard to mitigating measures.

Respondent, in turn, maintains that an impairment does not substantially limit a major life activity if it is corrected. It argues that the Court should not defer to the agency guidelines cited by petitioners because the guidelines conflict with the plain meaning of the ADA. The phrase "substantially limits one or more major life activities," it explains, requires that the substantial limitations actually and presently exist. Moreover, respondent argues, disregarding mitigating measures taken by an individual defies the statutory command to examine the effect of the impairment on the major life activities "of such individual." And even if the statute is ambiguous, respondent claims, the guidelines' directive to ignore mitigating measures is not reasonable, and thus this Court should not defer to it.

We conclude that respondent is correct that the approach adopted by the agency guidelines—that persons are to be evaluated in their hypothetical uncorrected state—is an impermissible interpretation of the ADA. Looking at the Act as a whole, it is apparent that if a person is taking measures to correct for, or mitigate, a physical or mental impairment, the effects of those measures—both positive and negative—must be taken into account when judging whether that person is "substantially limited" in a major life activity and thus "disabled" under the Act. . . .

Three separate provisions of the ADA, read in concert, lead us to this conclusion. The Act defines a "disability" as "a physical or mental impairment that *substantially limits* one or more of the major life activities" of an individual. Because the phrase "substantially limits" appears in the Act in the present indicative verb form, we think the language is properly read as requiring that a person be presently—not potentially or hypothetically—substantially limited in order to demonstrate a disability. A "disability" exists only where an impairment "substantially limits" a major life activity, not where it "might," "could," or "would" be substantially limiting if mitigating measures were not taken. A person whose physical or mental impairment is corrected by medication or other measures does not have an impairment that presently "substantially limits" a major life activity. To be sure, a person whose physical or mental impairment is corrected by mitigating measures still has an impairment, but if the impairment is corrected it does not "substantially limi[t]" a major life activity.

The definition of disability also requires that disabilities be evaluated "with respect to an individual" and be determined based on whether an impairment substantially limits the "major life activities of such individual." Thus, whether a person has a disability under the ADA is an individualized inquiry.

The agency guidelines' directive that persons be judged in their uncorrected or unmitigated state runs directly counter to the individualized inquiry mandated by the ADA. The agency approach would often require courts and employers to speculate about a person's condition and would, in many cases, force them to make a disability determination based on general information about how an uncorrected impairment usually affects individuals, rather than on the individual's actual condition. For instance, under this view, courts would almost certainly find all diabetics to be disabled, because if they failed to monitor their blood sugar levels and administer insulin, they would almost certainly be substantially limited in one or more major life activities. A diabetic whose illness does not impair his or her daily activities would therefore be considered disabled simply because he or she has diabetes. Thus, the guidelines approach would create a system in which persons often must be treated as members of a group of people with similar impairments, rather than as individuals. This is contrary to both the letter and the spirit of the ADA.

The guidelines approach could also lead to the anomalous result that in determining whether an individual is disabled, courts and employers could not consider any negative side effects suffered by an individual resulting from the use of mitigating measures, even when those side effects are very severe.

* * *

The dissents suggest that viewing individuals in their corrected state will exclude from the definition of "disab[led]" those who use prosthetic limbs or take medicine for epilepsy or high blood pressure. This

suggestion is incorrect. The use of a corrective device does not, by itself, relieve one's disability. Rather, one has a disability under subsection (A) if, notwithstanding the use of a corrective device, that individual is substantially limited in a major life activity. . . .

Applying this reading of the Act to the case at hand, we conclude that the Court of Appeals correctly resolved the issue of disability in respondent's favor. . . . Accordingly, because we decide that disability under the Act is to be determined with reference to corrective measures, we agree with the courts below that petitioners have not stated a claim that they are substantially limited in any major life activity.

Case Questions

1. Before reviewing this case, would you have considered someone disabled if they had an impairment that could be relieved completely through medication, such that they functioned exactly as a nonimpaired person would function?

2. Would your answer to the above question be the same if the impaired person had lost a limb and now used a prosthetic device? Would that individual be considered "disabled," according to your "gut" instinct? Is that person to be considered any differently in terms of employment than, say, someone with attention deficit disorder who can be completely managed through medication?

3. Assuming it is appropriate for the Court to consider side effects of such corrective measures, as mentioned in the case, how do you propose the Court should balance the side effects versus the correction? In other words, what if the sisters in the above case hated wearing glasses because they didn't like how they looked, or because they claimed they were uncomfortable, or because they claimed they got headaches from the glasses? Would you consider any or all of these effects in determining whether the sisters' disabilities could be corrected and therefore whether they were impaired?

Mental Impairments

The issue of how to handle mental impairments has been a concern for employers and employees alike because of the increased possibility for fraudulent claims (due to the challenge of verification). To address concerns and to offer guidance on the issue, the

EEOC issued its Enforcement Guidance on the Americans with Disabilities Act and Psychiatric Disabilities in April 1997. Three key concepts are addressed in the guidelines. First, the guidelines include "interacting with others" as an example of a major life activity that, if substantially limited by mental impairment, would support a determination of an ADA disability, Second, among the methods for reasonable accommodation of psychiatric disabilities, the guidelines state that employers must consider requests for modified work schedules, individual office space, or changes in supervisory style. The third area on which the guidelines expand relates to an employer's uniformly applied workplace standards for dress, grooming, personal appearance, and behavior. An employee may claim that, due to a mental impairment, he or she cannot conform to certain standards. In this circumstance, the guidelines provide that, in order to avoid fraud, an employer is entitled to document the conduct, verify the disorder, and work toward a reasonable accommodation that will enable the employee to perform the essential functions of the job.

Accordingly, employers should have a process in place to obtain and to evaluate appropriate medical information. The employer can request further information, beyond a doctor's note, from an employee claiming a psychiatric disability by requesting permission from the employee to have the company doctor review his or her medical records. The company can then verify that the accommodation is medically necessary to enable the employee to do the job.

Don Perkl, who was autistic and diagnosed with mental retardation, was hired as a janitor for Chuck E. Cheese restaurant in Madison, Wisconsin. His job duties included mopping floors, cleaning bathrooms, and vacuuming carpets. A district manager fired Perkl after telling one of the store's managers that it was the employer's policy not to hire "those kind of people." Perkl's foster mother described Perkl as "devastated" by the termination. The EEOC brought an action under the ADA on behalf of Perkl. The jury awarded Perkl $70,000 in compensatory damages and $13 million in punitive damages. The judge upheld the jury's verdict, and ordered that Perkl be reinstated to his former position at the restaurant.[5]

Does a mere "inability to get along with others" constitute a disability? The First Circuit originally said that it does not,[6] but the Ninth Circuit later disagreed, contending that a disability exists where the employee can evidence a pattern of withdrawal, consistently high levels of hostility, and failure to communicate when necessary.[7] Amidst this inconsistency among the circuits, the Second Circuit then decided *Jacques* v. *DiMarzio, Inc.,* 386 F.3d 192 (2d Cir. 2004), in which it agreed with the First Circuit that such a determination might be subjective. However, the court also held that a disability exists where the employee is severely limited in the fundamental ability to communicate with others, connect with others, or "go among other people" at the most basic level of activity. Therefore, the court strived to make

[5] *EEOC* v. *CEC Entertainment, Inc.,* 2000 U.S. Dist. LEXIS 13934, 10 Am. Disabilities Cas. (BNA) 1593 (W.D. Wis. 2000).

[6] 105 F.3d 12 (1st Cir. 1997).

[7] 192 F.3d 1226 (9th Cir. 1999).

impairment
"[a]ny physiological disorder or condition . . . affecting one or more of the following body systems: neurological; musculoskeletal; special sense organs; respiratory, including speech organs; cardiovascular; reproductive; digestive; genitourinary; hemic and lymphatic; skin; and endocrine; or any mental or psychological disorder" which substantially limits one of life's major activities. (From the EEOC regulations.)

major life activities
"functions such as caring for one's self, performing manual tasks, walking, seeing, hearing, speaking, breathing, learning and working." (From the EEOC regulations.)

a distinction between a basic "office nuisance" and someone with a more substantial interpersonal limitation.

"Major Life Activity"

Generally, a person who suffers from a serious medical condition is limited in her or his major life activities. Breathing is impaired when one has emphysema; learning is impaired when one suffers from dyslexia. Functioning and procreation are impaired when one is HIV-positive. Other major life activities may include walking, seeing, caring for oneself and working (where one is unable to perform a broad range of jobs, not merely one single job). Employers, however, are offered little guidance by the acts; neither the ADA nor the Rehabilitation Act defines "physical or mental **impairment**" or "**major life activities**." In *Wright* v. *CompUSA, Inc.,* 352 F.3d 472 (1st Cir. 2003), Stephen Wright claimed discrimination on the basis of his attention deficit disorder (ADD). The court disagreed, holding that Wright failed to present evidence that he "could not perform some usual activity compared with the general population, or that he had a continuing inability to handle stress at all times, rather than only episodically." Though Wright claimed limitation in reading, spelling, concentrating, and hearing, among other activities, these impairments only occurred when Wright worked for a manager with a particularly demanding management style. Though these activities, if significantly impaired, would constitute major life activities, Wright's ADD was deemed episodic and therefore not a substantial limitation. (For comparison, see *Moysis* v. *DTG Datanet,* later in this chapter.)[8]

While some employees have argued a "bootstrap" theory of coverage—that if an employer denies a position to an applicant on the basis of his impairment, such denial may be just the act necessary for the employee to prove that the impairment constitutes a disability—this is not accepted by the courts.

In the next case, the U.S. Supreme Court made clear that an impairment must prevent or severely restrict those activities that are of central importance to daily life.

---

[8] A second interesting outgrowth of this case was the court's ruling on Mr. Wright's claim of retaliation based on his request for accommodation. The court ruled that the mere act of requesting an accommodation was "protected activity" under the ADA and therefore remanded the case for trial to determine whether CompUSA's proffered reason for discharge—insubordination—was pretextual.

Toyota Motor Manufacturing, Kentucky, Inc. v. Williams
534 U.S. 184 (2002)

Respondent Williams was employed by the petitioner, Toyota Motor Manufacturing, as an assembly line worker in an automobile manufacturing plant. After being diagnosed with carpal tunnel syndrome, the employee was reassigned to a quality-control inspection job. When her condition worsened, Williams alleged that Toyota refused to accommodate her. Toyota alleged that the worker simply began missing work on a regular basis and that it eventually terminated her based on an allegedly poor attendance record. The trial and appeals courts addressed the issue of whether Williams' impairment substantially limited a major life activity. The Supreme Court determined that an impairment must prevent or severely restrict the individual from doing activities that are of central importance to daily life in order to be considered a disability under the ADA.

O'Connor, J.

I

. . . Respondent began working at petitioner's automobile manufacturing plant in Georgetown, Kentucky, in August 1990. She was soon placed on an engine fabrication assembly line, where her duties included work with pneumatic tools. Use of these tools eventually caused pain in respondent's hands, wrists, and arms. She sought treatment at petitioner's in-house medical service, where she was diagnosed with bilateral carpal tunnel syndrome and bilateral tendinitis. Respondent consulted a personal physician who placed her on permanent work restrictions that precluded her from lifting more than 20 pounds or from "frequently lifting or carrying of objects weighing up to 10 pounds," engaging in "constant repetitive . . . flexion or extension of [her] wrists or elbows," performing "overhead work," or using "vibratory or pneumatic tools."

In light of these restrictions, for the next two years petitioner assigned respondent to various modified duty jobs. Nonetheless, respondent missed some work for medical leave, and eventually filed a claim under the Kentucky Workers' Compensation Act. The parties settled this claim, and respondent returned to work. She was unsatisfied by petitioner's efforts to accommodate her work restrictions, however, and responded by bringing an action in the United States District Court for the Eastern District of Kentucky alleging that petitioner had violated the ADA by refusing to accommodate her disability. That suit was also settled, and as part of the settlement, respondent returned to work in December 1993.

Upon her return, petitioner placed respondent on a team in Quality Control Inspection Operations (QCIO). QCIO is responsible for four tasks: (1) "assembly paint"; (2) "paint second inspection"; (3) "shell body audit"; and (4) "ED surface repair." Respondent was initially placed on a team that performed only the first two of these tasks, and for a couple of years, she rotated on a weekly basis between them. In assembly paint, respondent visually inspected painted cars moving slowly down a conveyor. She scanned for scratches, dents, chips, or any other flaws that may have occurred during the assembly or painting process, at a rate of one car every 54 seconds. When respondent began working in assembly paint, inspection team members were required to open and shut the doors, trunk, and/or hood of each passing car. Sometime during respondent's tenure, however, the position was modified to include only visual inspection with few or no manual tasks. Paint second inspection required team members to use their hands to wipe each painted car with a glove as it moved along a conveyor. The parties agree that respondent was physically capable of performing both of these jobs and that her performance was satisfactory.

During the fall of 1996, petitioner announced that it wanted QCIO employees to be able to rotate through all four of the QCIO processes. Respondent therefore received training for the shell body audit job, in which team members apply a highlight oil to the hood, fender, doors, rear quarter panel, and trunk of passing cars at a rate of approximately one car per minute. The highlight oil has the viscosity of salad oil, and employees spread it on cars with a sponge attached to a block of wood. After they wipe each car with the oil, the employees visually inspect it for flaws. Wiping the cars required respondent to hold her hands and arms up around shoulder height for several hours at a time.

A short while after the shell body audit job was added to respondent's rotations, she began to experience pain in her neck and shoulders. Respondent again sought care at petitioner's in-house medical service, where she was diagnosed with myotendinitis bilateral periscapular, an inflammation of the muscles and tendons around both of her shoulder blades; myotendinitis and myositis bilateral forearms with nerve compression causing median nerve irritation; and thoracic outlet compression, a condition that causes pain in the nerves that lead to the upper extremities. Respondent requested that petitioner accommodate her medical conditions by allowing her to return to doing only her original two jobs in QCIO, which respondent claimed she could still perform without difficulty.

The parties disagree about what happened next. According to respondent, petitioner refused her request and forced her to continue working in the shell body audit job, which caused her even greater physical injury. According to petitioner, respondent simply began missing work on a regular basis. Regardless, it is clear that on December 6, 1996, the last day respondent worked at petitioner's plant, she was placed under a no-work-of-any-kind restriction by her treating physician. On January 27, 1997, respondent received a letter from petitioner that terminated her employment, citing her poor attendance record.

Respondent filed a charge of disability discrimination with the Equal Employment Opportunity Commission (EEOC). After receiving a right to sue letter, respondent filed suit against petitioner in the United States District Court . . . [alleging petitioner had violated the ADA] by failing to reasonably accommodate her disability and by terminating her employment.

Respondent based her claim that she was "disabled" under the ADA on the ground that her physical impairments substantially limited her in (1) manual tasks; (2) housework; (3) gardening; (4) playing with her children; (5) lifting; and (6) working, all of which, she argued, constituted major life *activities* under the Act.

The District Court . . . rejected respondent's arguments that gardening, doing housework, and playing with children are major life *activities*. Although the court agreed that performing manual tasks, lifting, and working are major life *activities,* it found the evidence insufficient to demonstrate that respondent had been substantially limited in lifting or working. The court found respondent's claim that she was substantially limited in performing manual tasks to be "irretrievably contradicted by [respondent's] continual insistence that she could perform the tasks in assembly [paint] and paint [second] inspection without difficulty." The court also found no evidence that respondent had had a record of a substantially limiting impairment, or that petitioner had regarded her as having such an impairment.

[On appeal], the Court of Appeals held that in order for respondent to demonstrate that she was disabled due to a substantial limitation in the ability to perform manual tasks at the time of her accommodation request, she had to "show that her manual disability involved a 'class' of manual *activities* affecting the ability to perform tasks at work." Respondent satisfied this test, according to the Court of Appeals, because her ailments "prevented her from doing the tasks associated with certain types of manual assembly line jobs, manual product handling jobs and manual building trade jobs (painting, plumbing, roofing, etc.)

that require the gripping of tools and repetitive work with hands and arms extended at or above shoulder levels for extended periods of time." In reaching this conclusion, the court disregarded evidence that respondent could "tend to her personal hygiene [and] carry out personal or household chores," finding that such evidence "does not affect a determination that her impairment substantially limited her ability to perform the range of manual tasks associated with an assembly line job." Because the Court of Appeals concluded that respondent had been substantially limited in performing manual tasks and, for that reason, was entitled to partial summary judgment on the issue of whether she was disabled under the Act, it found that it did not need to determine whether respondent had been substantially limited in the major life *activities* of lifting or working, or whether she had had a "record of" a disability or had been "regarded as" disabled.

We . . . consider the proper standard for assessing whether an individual is substantially limited in performing manual tasks. We now reverse the Court of Appeals' decision to grant partial summary judgment to respondent on the issue whether she was substantially limited in performing manual tasks at the time she sought an accommodation.

Merely having an impairment does not make one disabled for purposes of the ADA. Claimants also need to demonstrate that the impairment limits a major life *activity*.

To qualify as disabled, a claimant must further show that the limitation on the major life *activity* is "substantial." The EEOC . . . has created its own definition for purposes of the ADA. According to the EEOC regulations, "substantially limited" means "unable to perform a major life *activity* that the average person in the general population can perform"; or "significantly restricted as to the condition, manner or duration under which an individual can perform a particular major life *activity* as compared to the condition, manner, or duration under which the average person in the general population can perform the same major life *activity*." In determining whether an individual is substantially limited in a major life *activity,* the regulations instruct that the following factors should be considered: "the nature and severity of the impairment; the duration or expected duration of the impairment; and the permanent or long-term impact, or the expected permanent or long-term impact of or resulting from the impairment."

II

Our consideration of this issue is guided first and foremost by the words of the disability definition itself. "Substantially" in the phrase "substantially limits" suggests "considerable" or "to a large degree." See *Webster's Third New International Dictionary* 2280 (1976) (defining "substantially" as "in a substantial manner" and "substantial" as "considerable in amount, value, or worth" and "being that specified to a large degree or in the main"); see also 17 *Oxford English Dictionary* 66–67 (2d ed. 1989) ("substantial": "relating to or proceeding from the essence of a thing; essential"; "of ample or considerable amount, quantity, or dimensions"). The word "substantial" thus clearly precludes impairments that interfere in only a minor way with the performance of manual tasks from qualifying as disabilities.

"Major" in the phrase "major life *activities*" means important. See *Webster's, supra,* at 1363 (defining "major" as "greater in dignity, rank, importance, or interest"). "Major life *activities*" thus refers to those *activities* that are of central importance to daily life. In order for performing manual tasks to fit into this category—a category that includes such basic abilities as walking, seeing, and hearing—the manual tasks in question must be central to daily life. If each of the tasks included in the major life *activity* of performing manual tasks does not independently qualify as a major life *activity,* then together they must do so.

That these terms need to be interpreted strictly to create a demanding standard for qualifying as disabled is confirmed by the first section of the ADA, which lays out the legislative findings and purposes that motivate the Act. When it enacted the ADA in 1990, Congress found that "some 43,000,000 Americans have one or more physical or mental disabilities." If Congress intended everyone with a physical impairment that precluded the performance of some isolated, unimportant, or particularly difficult manual task to qualify as disabled, the number of disabled Americans would surely have been much higher.

We therefore hold that to be substantially limited in performing manual tasks, an individual must have an impairment that prevents or severely restricts the individual from doing *activities* that are of central importance to most people's daily lives. The impairment's impact must also be permanent or long-term.

It is insufficient for individuals attempting to prove disability status under this test to merely submit evidence of a medical diagnosis of an impairment. Instead, the ADA requires those "claiming the Act's protection . . . to prove a disability by offering evidence that the extent of the limitation [caused by their impairment] in terms of their own experience . . . is substantial." . . . That the Act defines "disability" with respect to an individual" makes clear that Congress intended the existence of a disability to be determined in such a case-by-case manner.

* * *

An individualized assessment of the effect of an impairment is particularly necessary when the impairment is one whose symptoms vary widely from person to person. Carpal tunnel syndrome, one of respondent's impairments, is just such a condition. While cases of severe carpal tunnel syndrome are characterized by muscle atrophy and extreme sensory deficits, mild cases generally do not have either of these effects and create only intermittent symptoms of numbness and tingling. Studies have further shown that, even without surgical treatment, one quarter of carpal tunnel cases resolve in one month, but that in 22 percent of cases, symptoms last for eight years or longer.

The Court of Appeals' analysis of respondent's claimed disability suggested that in order to prove a substantial limitation in the major life *activity* of performing manual tasks, a "plaintiff must show that her manual disability involves a 'class' of manual *activities,*" *and that those activities* "affect the ability to perform tasks at work." Both of these ideas lack support.

. . . While the Court of Appeals in this case addressed the different major life *activity* of performing manual tasks, its analysis circumvented *Sutton* by focusing on respondent's inability to perform manual tasks associated only with her job. This was error. When addressing the major life *activity* of performing manual tasks, the central inquiry must be whether the claimant is unable to perform the variety of tasks central to most people's daily lives, not whether the claimant is unable to perform the tasks associated with her specific job. Otherwise, *Sutton*'s restriction on claims of disability based on a substantial limitation in working will be rendered meaningless because an inability to perform a specific job always can be recast as an inability to perform a "class" of tasks associated with that specific job.

. . . [T]he manual tasks unique to any particular job are not necessarily important parts of most people's lives. As a result, occupation-specific tasks may have only limited relevance to the manual tasks inquiry.

In this case, "repetitive work with hands and arms extended at or above shoulder levels for extended periods of time," the manual task on which the Court of Appeals relied, is not an important part of most people's daily lives. The court, therefore, should not have considered respondent's inability to do such manual work in her specialized assembly line job as sufficient proof that she was substantially limited in performing manual tasks.

At the same time, the Court of Appeals appears to have disregarded the very type of evidence that it should have focused upon. It treated as irrelevant "the fact that [respondent] can . . . tend to her personal hygiene [and] carry out personal or household chores." Yet household chores, bathing, and brushing one's teeth are among the types of manual tasks of central importance to people's daily lives, and should have been part of the assessment of whether respondent was substantially limited in performing manual tasks.

The District Court noted that at the time respondent sought an accommodation from petitioner, she admitted that she was able to do the manual tasks required by her original two jobs in QCIO. In addition, according to respondent's deposition testimony, even after her condition worsened, she could still brush her teeth, wash her face, bathe, tend her flower garden, fix breakfast, do laundry, and pick up around the house. The record also indicates that her medical conditions caused her to avoid sweeping, to quit dancing, to occasionally seek help dressing, and to reduce how often she plays with her children, gardens, and drives long distances. But these changes in her life did not amount to such severe restrictions in the *activities* that are of central importance to most people's daily lives that they establish a manual-task disability as a matter of law. On this record, it was therefore inappropriate for the Court of Appeals to grant partial summary judgment to respondent on the issue whether she was substantially limited in performing manual tasks, and its decision to do so must be reversed. . . .

Case Questions

1. Do you agree that "manual tasks unique to any particular job are not necessarily important parts of most people's lives"?

2. What result does the U.S. Supreme Court fear if tasks associated with a specific job were to be considered "major life activities"?

3. By focusing on tasks associated with personal hygiene, household chores, etc., the Court may be encouraging employers to assess whether an employee is limited in performing these tasks. What could an employer do to make such an assessment? Would you advise an employer to take such actions? What impact could this limited definition of "major life activities" have on ADA protections?

Since *Toyota,* courts have used its definitions to guide later decisions. Consider the court's analysis of the definition of disability in the following excerpt and its distinction in the footnote of *Toyota.*

Moysis v. DTG Datanet   *278 F.3d 819 (8th Cir. 2002)*

Moysis worked for Datanet as a systems engineer, which required him to maintain and update systems for Datanet clients. Moysis consistently received high performance reviews, bonuses, and other accolades. While returning from a customer site one day, Moysis was involved in an automobile accident. Following the accident, he was in a coma for six days. Brain scans showed injury to the frontal lobes, which control an individual's personality, emotional responses, impulse control, social abilities, and speech. At the time he was released by his doctor to return to part-time work, increasing to full-time over time, Moysis was terminated, allegedly because of client and coworker complaints. He was told further that Datanet had planned on firing him the day of the accident, but did not do so in order to continue his benefits.

Moysis found a position as a computer systems administrator, but was earning one-third less than he made at Datanet. At trial, Moysis offered testimony from a doctor that, as a result of the accident Moysis had permanent cognitive impairments, which included difficulty with new situations, memory, and reasoning. The impairments adversely affected Moysis' ability to work in unfamiliar surroundings because he "didn't have responses stored away in his brain." The doctor believed Moysis would have fewer problems if he returned to Datanet since he was familiar with the routine, structure, and people.

The jury awarded Moysis $45,993.27 in back pay and $60,000 in compensatory damages on his ADA claim and $200,000 on his intentional infliction of emotional distress claim.

Bright, C.J.

* * *

To prove his ADA claim, Moysis had to show he was disabled, qualified to perform the job, and was terminated because of his disability. Datanet first argues that Moysis presented insufficient evidence of a disability. . . . Moysis was required to show that he had an "impairment that substantially limits one or more of the major life activities." An impairment is substantially limiting if an individual is "[s]ignificantly restricted as to the condition, manner or duration under which . . . the average person in the general population can perform that same major life activity."

Datanet does not challenge that working is a major life activity. Rather, Datanet argues that to be disabled a person must be "precluded from working generally." Its argument is without merit. The Supreme Court has made it clear that the ADA "addresses substantial limitations on major life activities, not utter inabilities." *Bragdon* v. *Abbott*. A person is substantially limited in working if he or she is "significantly restricted in the ability to perform either a class of jobs or a broad range of jobs in various classes as compared to the average person having comparable training, skills and abilities." Because disability is determined on a case-by-case basis, "[a] court must ask whether the particular impairment constitutes for the particular person a significant barrier to employment."

Viewing the evidence in the light most favorable to Moysis, we conclude that he presented sufficient evidence of an actual disability at the time of his December 1996 termination. At that time, Dr. Assam had only released Moysis to work at Datanet on a part-time basis. Both she and Dr. McGrath testified that, although Moysis would be able to work at Datanet, jobs requiring new skills and meeting new people could pose problems. Moysis testified that as a result of the brain injury, he continued to have concentration and short-term memory problems. As the Seventh Circuit has noted in another brain-injury case, "the need for routine," as well as "memory, concentration, and interacting with others [are] activities that feed into the major life activities of learning and working." Moreover, "[t]his is not a case, then, in which plaintiff's condition causes difficulty with a single aspect of a single job position." Rather, Moysis' limitations resulting from his brain injury "translate across a broad spectrum of . . . jobs." Thus, the jury could reasonably find that Moysis' impairments were long-term and substantially limited his "real work opportunities."[1]

Case Question

1. Does the court's footnoted distinction between this case and *Toyota* make sense to you?

[1] This case is clearly distinguishable from the recent Supreme Court case of *Toyota Motor Mfg., Ky., Inc.* v. *Williams,* 534 U.S. 184 (2002). In *Toyota,* the plaintiff suffered from carpal tunnel syndrome, which limited her ability to perform manual tasks. The Court held that "to be substantially limited in performing manual tasks, an individual must have an impairment that prevents or severely restricts the individual from doing activities that are of central importance to most people's daily lives."

"Substantially Limits"

The following case involves an employee who has a contagious disease. The Court was required to determine whether this disease substantially limited the employee's major life activities.

School Bd. of Nassau County v. Arline *107 S. Ct. 1123 (1987)*

Plaintiff, employee Arline, is a teacher who has tuberculosis. In this case, the Supreme Court determined that Arline was disabled pursuant to the definition of the Rehabilitation Act because her disability required hospitalization. The defendant employer argued that Arline was not terminated due to her disease but instead due to the threat that her relapses posed to the health of others. The Court stated that the threat posed to others by one's disability is not distinct from the disability itself; therefore, the employee was considered to be disabled and the employer's actions were subject to scrutiny under the Rehabilitation Act.

Brennan, J.

In determining whether a particular individual is handicapped as defined by the [Rehabilitation] Act, the regulations promulgated by the Department of Health and Human Services are of significant assistance. As we have previously recognized, these regulations were drafted with the oversight and approval of Congress; they provide an important source of guidance on the meaning of section 504.

Within this statutory and regulatory framework, then, we must consider whether Arline can be considered a handicapped individual. According to the testimony of Dr. McEuen, Arline suffered tuberculosis "in an acute form in such a degree that it affected her respiratory system," and was hospitalized for this condition. Arline thus has a physical impairment as that term is defined by the regulations, since she had a "physiological disorder or condition affecting her respiratory system." This impairment was serious enough to require hospitalization, a fact more than sufficient to establish that one or more of her major life activities were substantially limited by her impairment. Thus, Arline's hospitalization for tuberculosis in 1957 suffices to establish that she has a "record of . . . impairment" within the meaning of [the regulations] and is therefore a handicapped individual.

Petitioners concede that a contagious disease may constitute a handicapping condition to the extent that it leaves a person with "diminished physical or mental capabilities," and concede that Arline's hospitalization for tuberculosis in 1957 demonstrates that she has a record of a physical impairment. Petitioners maintain, however, that Arline's record of impairment is irrelevant in this case, since the School Board dismissed Arline not because of her diminished capabilities, but because of the threat that her relapses of tuberculosis posed to the health of others.

We do not agree with petitioners that, in defining a handicapped individual under §504, the contagious effects of a disease can be meaningfully distinguished from the disease's physical effects on a claimant in a case such as this. Arline's contagiousness and her physical impairment each resulted from the same underlying condition, tuberculosis. It would be unfair to allow an employer to seize upon the distinction between the effects of a disease on others and the effects of a disease on a patient and use that distinction to justify discriminatory treatment.

Few aspects of a handicap give rise to the same level of public fear and misapprehension as contagiousness. Even those who suffer or have recovered from such noninfectious diseases as epilepsy or cancer have faced discrimination based on the irrational fear that they might be contagious. The Act is carefully structured to replace such reflexive reactions to actual or perceived handicaps with actions based on reasoned and medically sound judgments: the definition of "handicapped individual" is broad, but only those individuals who are both handicapped *and* otherwise qualified are eligible for relief. The fact that *some* persons who have contagious diseases may pose a serious health threat to others under certain circumstances does not justify excluding from the coverage of the Act all persons with actual or perceived contagious diseases. Such exclusion would mean those accused of being contagious would never have the opportunity to have their condition evaluated in light of medical evidence and a determination made as to whether they were "otherwise qualified." Rather, they would be vulnerable to discrimination on the basis of mythology—precisely the type of injury Congress sought to prevent. We conclude that the fact a person with a record of a physical impairment is also contagious does not suffice to remove that person from coverage under §504.

The remaining question is whether Arline is otherwise qualified for the job of elementary schoolteacher. The basic factors to be considered in conducting such an inquiry are well established. In the context of employment of a person handicapped with a contagious disease, we agree with *amicus* American Medical Association that this inquiry should include: "findings of facts, based on reasonable medical judgment given the state of medical knowledge, about (a) the nature of the risk (how the disease is transmitted), (b) the duration of the risk (how long is the carrier infectious), (c) the severity of the risk (what is the potential to harm third parties), and (d) the probabilities the disease will be transmitted and will cause varying degrees of harm." The next step in the "otherwise qualified" inquiry is for the court to evaluate whether the employer could reasonably accommodate the employee under the established standards for that inquiry.

Because of the paucity of factual findings by the district court, we, like the court of appeals, are unable at this stage to resolve whether Arline is otherwise qualified for her job. We remand the case to the district court to determine whether Arline is otherwise qualified for her position.

Case Questions

1. Consider the similarities between the Court's analysis of the public reaction to contagiousness in *Arline* ("Few aspects of a handicap give rise to the same level of public fear and misapprehension as contagiousness") and the analysis it would have to undergo if Arline had AIDS as opposed to tuberculosis. Any differences? Where do you think any differences might be found in a court's analysis of an employee with HIV? (See *Doe* v. *Kohn Nast & Graf,* later in this chapter.)

2. Is it realistic to think that, as the employer here argued, the contagious aspect of a disease can be divorced from the consideration of the public of having the disease itself? Will an employer always run the risk of being sued in such a situation?

3. What type of policy could you develop that would instruct your managers about how to handle an employee with a contagious disease?

In 1986, the Department of Justice issued an opinion which stated that if fear of contagion is the basis for the termination, the employee is not considered disabled and is not protected under the Rehabilitation Act because the ability to communicate the disease to another is not a disability. The opinion made no distinction based on whether the fear of contagion is reasonable or unreasonable on the part of the employer. However, the Department of Justice opinion was in direct contravention of the Supreme Court's later determination in *Arline,* which specifically stated that chronic contagious diseases are considered to be protected disabilities. The Department of Justice thereafter issued a second memorandum, which reversed its earlier analysis in connection with HIV after Surgeon General Koop informed the Justice Department that physical impairment is almost always present. Do you believe that someone who is contagious due to a congenital disease, but who exhibits no physical impairment, is considered disabled under the act?

Many courts have been faced with the issue of HIV in the workplace and in academic institutions. For instance, in one case, the Court held that the lower court's finding that there was a remote possibility of transmission of HIV from tears, saliva, and urine of an HIV-infected child did not support the segregation of this child from students in a classroom for regularly trainable mentally handicapped children.

Perception of Impairment

The ADA definition of "disability" includes not only an actual impairment but also being *perceived* as having an impairment. Congress included an employee who is perceived as being disabled in the definition of disability because it was concerned with discrimination stemming from simple prejudice, and also from "archaic attitudes and laws" and from "the fact that the American people are simply unfamiliar and insensitive to the difficulties confront[ing] individuals with disabilities."

An employee or applicant is regarded as having an impairment if he or she has a physical or mental impairment that does not substantially limit major life activities, but

substantially limits
"unable to perform a major life activity that the average person in the general population can perform; or significantly restricted as to the condition, manner, or duration under which an individual can perform a major life activity." (From the EEOC regulations.)

which is treated as constituting a limit, as well as an impairment that **substantially limits** major life activities only as a result of the attitudes of others toward such impairment. An example of this type of perceived limitation would involve someone with a disfiguring facial scar that does not limit employment capabilities. If the employer discriminates against this person because of the negative reaction of its customers or clients, "the employer would be regarding the individual as disabled and acting on the basis of that perceived disability." Similarly, HIV-positive employees might be perceived as incapable of functioning while, in fact, no symptoms of the disease are yet manifested or inhibiting. On the other hand, if an employer refuses to hire an applicant merely because the employer believes that person to be ugly, the applicant would probably not be considered disabled and would therefore not be covered by the ADA.

In one particularly interesting case, a telemarketer who was missing 18 teeth was fired from his position after only three days of training. Even though he had generally positive evaluations in the training program, the trainers reported that the gentleman mumbled on the phone. The worker claimed that he did not have a disability and that his missing teeth did not cause him to mumble; he filed an ADA claim based on his employer's *perception* that he was disabled. The district court held that, since the worker did not actually have a disability, he could not sustain a claim that his employer perceived him as disabled. Without finding whether mumbling would be considered a disability, the Seventh Circuit reversed, holding that, "If for no reason whatsoever an employer regards a person as disabled—for example, because of a blunder in reading medical records it imputes to him a heart condition he has never had—and takes an adverse action, it has violated the [ADA]." (Note that, on remand, the district court found that mumbling would not substantially limit a major life activity. Therefore, a decision based on a *perception* of mumbling could not be considered a violation of the ADA.)

The following case explores the issue of whether an employee is "regarded as" having an impairment.

Carruthers v. BSA Advertising, Inc. *57 Fed.R.Serv. 3d 1044 (11th Cir. 2004)*

Carruthers was employed with BSA in the position of art director. In February 2000, Carruthers visited her assigned workers' compensation physician after experiencing pain and swelling in both of her hands. The physician diagnosed her as suffering from a bilateral hand strain/sprain and gave her various work restrictions, which were to be reviewed on a week-to-week basis. Carruthers notified her supervisor of her diagnosis and work restrictions, which included a prohibition on any computer/mouse usage. Subsequent to receiving this notice, BSA placed a classified advertisement for Carruthers' replacement on 5 March 2000 and then fired her in March 2000.

Carruthers filed a complaint alleging that BSA terminated her employment because of a disability or a perceived disability, in violation of the ADA. BSA defended itself claiming that (1) she failed to show that BSA perceived her as having a disability under the ADA and (2) (alternatively) because of her admission that 90 percent of her work was on the computer and because her work restrictions had forbidden any computer usage, she had failed to show that she could perform the essential functions of her job. The district court granted BSA summary judgment and Carruthers appealed.

Per Curiam

* * *

The ADA forbids covered employers from discriminating "against a qualified individual with a disability because of the disability of such individual in regard to . . . discharge of employees." To establish a *prima facie* case of discrimination under the ADA, Carruthers must show that she (1) had, or was perceived to have, a "disability"; (2) was a "qualified" individual; and (3) was discriminated against because of her disability. The ADA defines "disability" as "(A) a physical or mental impairment that substantially limits one or more of the major life activities of such individual; (B) a record of such an impairment; or (C) being regarded as having such an impairment."

In order for any ADA claim to succeed, the claimant must show that her condition of impairment rises to the level of a disability. In Carruthers' case, the sole basis of her contention that she was disabled [was that she was "regarded as" being disabled]. Under the "regarded as" prong, a person is "disabled" if her employer perceives her as having an ADA-qualifying disability, even if there is no factual basis for that perception. As with actual impairments, however, the perceived impairment must be one that, if real, would limit substantially a major life activity of the individual. Carruthers argues that BSA "perceived her as not performing a wide range of jobs." Although Carruthers offers no further description of the specific disability that BSA allegedly perceived her to have, we construe her argument to be that BSA perceived her hand condition as substantially limiting her in the major life activities of working and of performing manual tasks.

The regulations implementing the ADA enumerate several functions that qualify as "major life activities," included among which is the activity of "working." In order for Carruthers to establish that BSA regarded her as substantially limited in the major life activity of working, she must show that BSA perceived her as "significantly restricted in the ability to perform either a class of jobs or a broad range of jobs in various classes as compared to the average person having comparable training, skills, and abilities." See *Sutton* v. *United Air Lines. Inc.*, 527 U.S. 471, 491, 119 S. Ct. 2139, 2151, 144 L.Ed. 2d 450 (1999) ("When the major life activity under consideration is that of working, the statutory phrase 'substantially limits' requires, at a minimum, that plaintiffs allege they are unable to work in a broad class of jobs.")[1] "The inability to perform a single, particular job does not constitute a substantial limitation in the major life activity of working." Thus, an impairment must preclude—or at least be perceived to preclude—an individual from more than one type of job, even if the job foreclosed is the individual's job of choice.

With regard to Carruthers' perceived impairment in performing manual tasks, the Supreme Court recently took up the question of when such an impairment constitutes an ADA disability. *Toyota Motor Mfg., Ky., Inc.* v. *Williams,* 534 U.S. 184, 122 S. Ct. 681, 151 L.Ed. 2d 615 (2002). In rejecting plaintiff's argument that her carpal tunnel syndrome limited her ability to perform a broad class of manual tasks and thus impaired a major life activity, the *Toyota Motor* Court emphasized that both statutory language and congressional intent require that the ADA's "disability" definition be "interpreted strictly to create a demanding standard for qualifying as disabled." The Court highlighted several prerequisites in order for an impairment to the ability to perform manual tasks to qualify as a disability. Specifically, the Court held that the critical inquiry is whether the impairment (a) prevents or severely restricts the performance of (b) activities "of central importance to most people's daily lives." The Court further held that the impairment must have a permanent or long-term impact.

We conclude that no reasonable jury could find that Carruthers' evidence established that BSA perceived her impairment as one that substantially limited the major life activities of working or performing manual tasks. Carruthers herself admitted at trial that BSA's knowledge of her condition was limited to her physician's diagnosis of a bilateral hand strain/sprain and her work restrictions. Aside from BSA's awareness of her initial diagnosis and work restrictions, the only other

---

[1] We do note that the Supreme Court more recently has expressed its reluctance to treat impairment of one's ability to work as an ADA disability. See *Toyota Motor Mfg., Ky., Inc.* v. *Williams,* 534 U.S. 184, 200, 122 S. Ct. 681, 692, 151 L.Ed. 2d 615 (2002) ("Because of the conceptual difficulties inherent in the argument that working could be a major life activity, we have been hesitant to hold as much, and we need not decide this difficult question today"). Previously, however, this circuit has, following the ADA regulations and *Sutton*'s above-quoted language, treated the activity of working as a major life activity. See, e.g., *Cash* v. *Smith,* 231 F.3d 1301, 1306 (2000); *Gordon* v. *E.L. Hamm & Assocs., Inc.,* 100 F.3d 907, 911-12 (11th Cir. 1996). In the absence of a more explicit directive from the Supreme Court, we do not revisit that conclusion here.

support Carruthers offers for her contention that BSA perceived her to be disabled is the fact that (1) BSA informed her that she would be terminated if she could not maintain a full-time schedule and (2) BSA placed an advertisement for her replacement shortly after learning of her inability to perform the basic tasks of her position. Based on this record, we find no indication that BSA regarded, or would have had any reason to regard, Carruthers' condition as rendering her incapable of performing "either a class of jobs or a broad range of jobs in various classes."

Similarly, Carruthers failed to show that BSA perceived her limitations in performing manual tasks as having a permanent or long-term impact and as preventing or severely restricting her from performing activities of central importance to most persons' lives. Indeed, Carruthers admitted at trial that she was able to dress herself, apply her own makeup, and groom herself, albeit with some pain, and that there were no major life activities she could not perform. Moreover, BSA, which was informed that Carruthers' restrictions were to be reviewed on a week-by-week basis, offered to review its staffing situation when Carruthers was ready to return to work. *Cf. Sutton,* 185 F.3d at 1206, 1209 (concluding that court did not err in finding that employer did not perceive employee as having a disability when employee provided employer with doctor's letter stating that he was totally disabled for one month and partially disabled for three weeks thereafter).

. . . Because Carruthers failed to establish the first prong of her *prima facie* case of discrimination in violation of the ADA, we conclude that the district court was correct in granting BSA's motion for judgment as a matter of law. . . . The judgment of the district court is AFFIRMED.

Case Questions

1. Where do you anticipate the "regarded as" arises most often these days in employment contexts?

2. Do you think it is fair to impose the requirement on the worker that she evidence an inability (or perceived inability) to be restricted in performing an entire broad range of jobs rather than simply the one she would naturally choose? Imagine that, for all of your life, you have dreamed of one particular job, and that you were now barred from engaging in that position. Wouldn't you feel as if you were impaired in a major life activity or in something that was "of central importance" to your life?

3. Do you agree with the court's final decision?

"Otherwise Qualified"

The acts state that an employer may not terminate or refuse to hire an employee with a disability who is "otherwise qualified" to perform the essential requirements of his or her position. The determination of a position's essential functions ensures that disabled persons are not disqualified simply because they may have difficulty in performing tasks that bear only a marginal relationship to a particular job. In that way, employers protect themselves from liability and are able to most effectively utilize their human resources.

In one case, the court held that a civilian employee of the Navy failed to establish that she was qualified for her position due to her chronic fatigue syndrome. The court noted that "the accommodation plaintiff seeks is simply to be allowed to work only when her illness permits." The court held that the employee was not otherwise qualified because she was not prepared to pull her full weight. In addition, an employer may not consider the possibility that an employee or applicant will become disabled or unqualified for the position in the future. If the applicant or employee is qualified *at the time the adverse employment action is taken,* the employer has violated the acts.[9]

[9] *Walders v. Garrett,* 765 F. Supp. 303 (D.C. Va. 1991), aff'd 956 F.2d 1163 (4th Cir. Va. 1992).

Direct Threat

Where the claim of disability is based on a disease, the court in the *Arline* case (excerpted earlier in this chapter) held that the determination of whether an individual is "otherwise qualified" should be based on the following factors:

- The nature of the risk (how the disease is transmitted).
- The duration of the risk (how long the carrier is infectious).
- The severity of the risk (potential harm to third parties).
- The probability that the disease will be transmitted and will cause varying degrees of harm.

Scenario

The Supreme Court's decision in the *Arline* case is important because it serves, by implication, as a proclamation that the acts safeguard the rights of employees with HIV or AIDS. Other decisions have echoed or forecasted the determination of the Supreme Court in connection with this definition. This is especially significant, given the high number of HIV-positive employees in the workforce today.

The issue of the level of risk the disabled employee poses to herself or to others is crucial to the determination of whether the applicant is otherwise qualified for the position. The standard for balancing the risk of harm to others against the employer's duties under the acts is whether the employer can show there is a *direct threat* to the health and safety of the potential employee or others. For example, as it has been shown that HIV is not transmitted through casual but only through intimate contact, it is extremely unlikely that a showing of reasonable probability of infection can be made. Therefore, employers who take adverse employment actions based on the unreasonable complaints or fears of coemployees or customers relating to HIV would violate either the Rehabilitation Act or the ADA. Such was the case when the performance company Cirque du Soleil terminated Matthew Cusick, an HIV-positive gymnast, after he concluded preparations for an aerial act in the Las Vegas show, "Mystere." Prior to a later settlement, Renée-Claude Ménard, a Cirque spokesperson, explained "the reasons that motivated our decision have nothing to do with discrimination, but safety," claiming that the company couldn't risk infection of other performers or patrons.[10] However, as this flies in the face of common knowledge about the means of infection discussed above, the parties reached a $600,000 settlement through the EEOC. The settlement included a provision by which Cirque du Soleil agreed to waive confidentiality surrounding the settlement, as well as requirements that Cirque appoint an EEO officer to oversee EEO training of all employees and post a notice about the resolution of this case in its workplace.[11]

In March 1993, the northern district court of Illinois issued the first opinion in this context in connection with a case brought under the ADA, *EEOC* v. *AIC Security Investigations Ltd.* In that case, Charles Wessel, the executive director of AIC, had been diagnosed with an inoperable malignant brain tumor. The evidence in the case suggested that he was still completely able and willing to perform the essential functions of his position. Nevertheless, the employer terminated him because it was concerned

---

[10] Chris Seeley, "HIV Discrimination Looms Large in U.S.," *Southernvoice.com* (11/28/03).

[11] EEOC press release, http://www.eeoc.gov/press/4-22-04.html.

that, as his health declined, he would no longer be able to perform. The jury concluded that since he was otherwise qualified to perform his job, AIC's termination was in violation of the ADA and awarded Wessel $572,000.

This decision was reinforced more recently by the Supreme Court decision in *Chevron USA* v. *Echazabal,*[12] where Chevron refused to employ Echazabal because exposure to toxins at its refinery would have aggravated Echazabal's hepatitis C. Chevron defended itself on the basis of the direct threat that employment would pose to Echazabal's health. The Ninth Circuit disagreed with Chevron, holding that this was an inappropriate inquiry in the context of hiring and was only relevant to the context of ongoing employment?[13] The Supreme Court reversed the Ninth Circuit, rejecting the restrictive language and reaffirming the direct threat defense for the employer. The Court warned employers, however, that the defense is only available where based on "reasonable medical judgment and an individualized assessment" of the circumstances.

The following two cases highlight the factors involved in a court's determination of whether an employee suffers from a disability covered by the ADA and whether the individual remains otherwise qualified for his position.

[12] 536 U.S. 73 (2002).
[13] *Chevron USA* v. *Echazabal,* 226 F.3d 1063 (9th Cir. 2000).

Doe v. Kohn Nast & Graf *862 F. Supp. 1310 (E.D. Pa. 1994)*

Defendant law firm terminated a plaintiff attorney because he had AIDS. Defendant claimed that plaintiff was not covered under the ADA because he was fully capable of performing as an attorney.

Gawthrop, J.

Defendants contend that the plaintiff cannot make out his prima facie case because he is not within the protected class. The thrust of the defense argument is that even though HIV-positive status, most assuredly, is not a happy medical condition with which to be diagnosed, it is not, in fact, disabling. Thus, they say, he is not protected by the statute. The defense argues that plaintiff is able to do just about anything that needs to be done; certainly he is capable of doing that in the context of a law office and courtroom, his chosen line of work, and that here at issue. Occupationally, rather than being disabled, he is perfectly able. To this, the plaintiff responds that his ability to procreate, at least successfully—that is, with uninfected progeny—is impaired irreparably by his malady, and that inability, disability, being a major life activity, brings him within the purview of the statute.

The defense argues that this really is not a relevant concern. Not in any way to be facetious, but plaintiff is not being hired to practice procreation, or to be a professional blood donor, for example. He is being hired to practice law. The defense argues that although he may have some dysfunction in an utterly unrelated area—a dysfunction familiar to millions of Americans, who happen to be sterile, but who nevertheless go about ably living their lives—to hold that that medical problem makes the act applicable to him would be to stretch the language and the purpose of the statute beyond the breaking point.

To analyze this, I must turn first to that language. The statute reads:

The term "disability" means, with respect to an individual—(A) a physical or mental impairment that substantially limits one or more of the major life activities of such individual; (B) a record of such impairment; or (C) being regarded as having such an impairment.

This plain language, although setting forth several specific criteria, provides no express guidance as to whether an HIV-infected person comes within the ambit of the act. In interpreting the meaning of a statute, substantial deference is due the interpretation given its provisions by the agency charged with administering that statute. The agency's interpretation must be given "controlling weight unless it is plainly erroneous or inconsistent with the regulation." Hence, for further guidance, I turn to the regulations defining the components of this statutory provision—(1) physical impairment and (2) substantially limits a major life activity.

Physical Impairment: The Equal Employment Opportunity Commission is the agency charged with administering Title I of the Americans with Disabilities Act, the subchapter proscribing employment discrimination. Its regulations define "physical impairment" as:

Any physiological disorder, or condition, cosmetic disfigurement, or anatomical loss affecting one or more of the following body systems: neurological, musculoskeletal, special sense organs, respiratory (including speech organs), cardiovascular, reproductive, digestive, genitourinary, hemic and lymphatic, skin, and endocrine.

"Physiologic" is defined by *Dorland's Medical Dictionary* (27th ed. 1988) as "characteristic of or conforming to the normal functioning or state of the body or a tissue or organ." A physiological disorder is thus an abnormal functioning of the body or a tissue or organ. One can have one of the statutorily enumerated disabilities without being "disabled" in the usual, common, lay sense of the word. For example, the statute would apply to people who have high blood pressure, that being a hemic disorder, a proclaimed disability. Tens of millions of Americans walk around and live full and active lives, hypertense though they may be. To the lay eye, they hardly seem disabled, yet they have a "disability" within the statutory definition. That lay observation may have a certain common sense ring to it, but my role is not to construe the statute so that it might conform with a lay perception. Rather, I must read with care the definitions of disability that Congress and the EEOC gave us, and decide whether this plaintiff's disease and its symptoms fall within one or more of those express statutory and regulatory definitions, as anomalous as the statutory result might seem to some.

Around the third week of September, 1992, plaintiff developed a fever and a rash. During September through December, 1992, plaintiff's doctor noticed that his patient lost a lot of weight. Towards the end of October and into November, plaintiff's skin became so dry and scaly that at least three people in the firm took note of it.

A skin disorder which is sufficiently noticeable to be remarked upon by several people is classifiable as a cosmetic disfigurement. Further, HIV itself "creates a physiological disorder of the hemic (blood) and lymphatic systems." Dr. Braffman, plaintiff's physician, testified that in late September, 1992, "a few lymph nodes in the neck" were swollen, although not visible to the naked eye. Each of these symptoms fall within the regulatory definition of "physical impairment."

Substantial limits on major life activities: The regulations spell out "major life activities" as:

Functions such as caring for oneself, performing manual tasks, walking, seeing, hearing, speaking, breathing, learning, and working.

The use of the words "such as" indicates that this list is illustrative and is not intended to be exclusive. In construing the statute, trying to figure out just what it means, I deem it significant that the Congress chose to use the broad term "life"—"major life activities." That encompasses a lot. Had the term "work-life," or "work" been used—"major work activities," for example—it would, of course, suggest that the disability would only be deemed relevant in the on-the-job context. Instead, the term "working" appears as just one example of the various major activities embraced within the full scope of one's life. It is clear, therefore, that the language of the statute does not preclude procreating as a major life activity, but may well include it.

A major life activity is substantially limited when an impaired person is:

(i) Unable to perform a major life activity that the average person in the general population can perform; or (ii) Significantly restricted as to the condition, manner or duration under which an individual can perform a particular major life activity as compared to the condition, manner or duration under which the average person in the general population can perform that same major life activity.

Plaintiff argues that because the regulations define a "physical impairment" to include a disorder or condition that affects the "reproductive" system, the ability to procreate is a "major life activity" within the plain meaning of the ADA. The factual record in this case is thin, indeed, as to whether HIV status is a disorder or condition that affects the "reproductive" system. No physicians testified as to that, and the parties seemed content to rely on administrative findings and the rulings of other judges such as that given in *Cain* v. *Hyatt*. That was a case involving a plaintiff with full-blown AIDS, in which Judge Broderick found in dictum that a person who is HIV-infected is substantially limited in a major life activity because of the significant risk of transmitting the HIV infection to a partner or a child, thereby endangering their lives.

The defendants' motion for summary judgment is bottomed largely upon the thesis that plaintiff's illness falls without the types of disability defined, described, and illustrated in the statute and the regulations. Nothing in the record—no evidence, medical or otherwise—counters the above statutory construction, reinforced by administrative and judicial findings, that being HIV-positive places one within the protection of the act. Upon a careful reading of the Act and its interpretive regulations, measured up against the record in this case, I conclude the plaintiff has a physical or mental impairment that substantially limits one or more of his major life activities, and thus has a disability within the meaning of the ADA. Accordingly, plaintiff has met his threshold burden of establishing his prima facie case of disability discrimination.

Case Questions

1. Do you agree with the judge's decision? Is there any problem with the defendant's analysis that if someone is perfectly able to perform her or his job, then there is no disability?

2. The third prong of the definition of disability under the acts includes all of those perceived to be disabled. Should this include all stereotypes, or only those that seem reasonable? For instance, should left-handedness be a protected disability? Height? While an employer's bias against an employee or applicant, which is based on a certain physical or mental trait, may result in an adverse employment action against her, the trait does not necessarily constitute a disability. For example, an employer may have a prejudice against all persons with red hair and may refuse to hire anyone with such hair. This does not mean that a red-haired applicant who is denied a position is disabled; red hair is a characteristic, not a disorder. Can you think of others?

3. How should the courts determine the effect of a societal bias? For instance, if employers generally believe that persons with feet larger than a man's size 10 are clumsy, would a graceful man with size 12 feet be considered disabled? Consider *Blackwell* v. *U.S. Dept. of the Treasury,* in which the district court held that transvestites are disabled under the Rehabilitation Act because many experience strong social rejection in the workplace. Note, however, that the ADA specifically excludes as disabilities transvestism, transsexualism, voyeurism, and gender identity disorders not resulting from physical impairments or other sexual behavior disorders.

Note, however, the Fourth Circuit decided in *Doe* v. *Univ. of Maryland Medical System Corporation,* 50 F.3d 1261 (4th Cir. 1995), that HIV status is relevant to an employee's qualifications in a hospital setting: "The types of procedures in which Dr. Doe is engaged as a neurosurgical resident are not so clearly outside the characteristics of exposure-prone procedures identified by the CDC that we can conclude that deference to public health officials requires us to decide that Dr. Doe does not pose a significant risk." The court in this case decided that, even though the risk of contagion was minimal given Dr. Doe's responsibilities, it could not be eliminated by reasonable accommodation.

However, in the Supreme Court case *Bragdon* v. *Abbott,* which is not an employment case, the Court established guidance for determining when a person has a disability under the ADA and can therefore be applied in employment cases. Sidney Abbott, who was HIV positive, went to her dentist, Bragdon. He refused to treat her unless it was in the hospital due to his fear of her HIV status. Abbott sued claiming Bragdon discriminated against her based on her disability, HIV. The Court considered whether Abbott met the definition of having an "impairment that substantially limits one or more life activities." The Court, relying heavily on medical information, stated she did because an HIV infection is a condition that is inherently disabling. The Court stated, "HIV infection must be regarded as a physiological disorder with a constant and detrimental effect on the infected person's hemic and lymphatic systems from the moment of infection." The Court also noted that HIV substantially limited reproduction, a major life activity. This case challenges many lower court decisions that have held a condition must more or less visibly interfere with the person's public life or economic life on a fairly consistent basis to be a disability under the ADA. However, the Court in *Bragdon* states, in effect, that there are some conditions that are inherent disabilities if they so greatly affect the human biological system, in this case the HIV virus.

Collins v. Blue Cross Blue Shield of Michigan   *579 N.W.2d 435 (Mich. Ct. App. 1998)*

An employee was terminated for expressing homicidal ideas about her supervisor to a psychiatrist while on psychiatric disability leave. The court had to determine if the termination was a violation of the ADA. It determined that it was not.

Holbrook, J.

While employee Collins was on psychiatric disability leave from her employment with Blue Cross Blue Shield, she expressed homicidal ideas regarding her immediate supervisor to a psychiatrist assigned to evaluate her disability claim. Specifically, Collins stated that her supervisor, Jacobson, was "living on borrowed time," that Collins "had killed her a thousand times in her mind," and talked about "taking a .38 and blowing [Jacobson] away." She further indicated that "she had thought of killing her supervisor prior to the company strike and had decided not to when the department was dispersed to other areas." After she returned to work, Collins was terminated as a result of those statements. Collins claimed discrimination under the Americans with Disabilities Act (ADA) and the Michigan Handicappers' Civil Rights Act (HCRA). The matter was submitted to binding arbitration and . . . hearings were held before an arbitrator.

During the hearing, defendant acknowledged that plaintiff's statements to Dr. Wagner were the sole reason for plaintiff's termination. At the hearing, plaintiff testified that she did not recall making most of the statements attributed to her in Dr. Wagner's report, although she did acknowledge calling Jacobson a liar and a bitch. Dr. Wagner testified in a deposition that she would not characterize plaintiff's statements as "threats," but rather as expressions of plaintiff's thoughts. Dr. Wagner also stated that she would defer to the opinion of the treating physician, Dr. Griffin, with respect to whether plaintiff had recovered from her disability or whether she posed any actual threat to Jacobson. Dr. Griffin testified in her deposition that

she never reported plaintiff's homicidal ideation because she did not believe that plaintiff would act on it or that she otherwise posed any threat to Jacobson.

The arbitrator ruled in plaintiff's favor with regard to both claims and ordered that plaintiff be reinstated with back pay to a "comparable, but not identical, position" under a different supervisor and at a different work site if possible. The award added that defendant had the right to satisfy itself that plaintiff did not present a threat to other employees by requiring plaintiff to be examined by another psychiatrist and to continue treatment if necessary.

* * *

The gravamen of this appeal requires us to determine whether the arbitrator committed an error of law in ruling that plaintiff was discharged because of her disability, rather than for her homicidal ideation toward her supervisor. Although we do not dispute the arbitrator's finding of fact that plaintiff's homicidal ideation was a product of her psychiatric condition, we conclude that the arbitrator committed an error of law in ruling that defendant's discharge of plaintiff constituted discrimination under the ADA and the HCRA. We hold that plaintiff failed to establish a prima facie case of discrimination under the ADA or the HCRA because her homicidal ideation left her unqualified for employment with defendant and because defendant did not discharge her because of her disability.

* * *

Defendant argues on appeal that, because plaintiff was discharged for her expressed homicidal ideation regarding her supervisor, not because of her disability, it did not act with discriminatory intent. Our review of the current state of the law regarding this issue supports defendant's argument that a disabled employee may be discharged for misconduct, even where the misconduct is a manifestation of the employee's disability. Recently, in *Palmer* v. *Cook Co. Circuit Court,* the Seventh Circuit Court of Appeals held that an ADA claim failed where the plaintiff had been discharged because of threats she made to her supervisor, not because of her diagnosed major depression/delusional disorder. Chief Judge Posner explained:

> There is no evidence that Palmer was fired because of her mental illness. She was fired because she threatened to kill another employee. The cause of the threat was, we may assume, her mental illness. . . . But if an employer fires an employee because of the employee's unacceptable behavior, the fact that [the] behavior was precipitated by a mental illness does not present an issue under the Americans with Disabilities Act. The Act does not require an employer to retain a potentially violent employee. Such a requirement would place the employer on a razor's edge—in jeopardy of violating the Act if it fired such an employee, yet in jeopardy of being deemed negligent if it retained him and he hurt someone. The Act protects only "qualified" employees, that is, employees qualified to do the job for which they were hired; and threatening other employees disqualifies one.

A qualified individual with a disability is one who satisfies the requisite skill, experience, education, or other work-related requirements of the job and who can perform its essential functions with or without reasonable accommodation. Simply put, the ADA does not cover all disabled persons, but only those who can perform their jobs' essential functions with the aid of reasonable accommodation. Indeed, an express provision of the ADA allows employers to defend against a charge of discrimination by establishing certain employee "qualification standards" that are job-related, consistent with business necessity, and accomplished by reasonable accommodation. "Qualification standards" include "a requirement that an individual shall not pose a direct threat to the health and safety of other individuals in the workplace." "Direct threat" means "a significant risk to the health and safety of others that cannot be eliminated by reasonable accommodation."

Plaintiff argues that defendant impermissibly perceived her as a direct threat to workplace safety, despite the fact that she had never directly threatened her supervisor and despite the opinion of plaintiff's treating psychiatrist that plaintiff would not act on her homicidal ideation. While we acknowledge the distinction between expressing homicidal thoughts to a psychiatrist in the context of a disability benefit determination and directly threatening a co-worker—given that employees are not generally subject to discharge or discipline for mere thoughts or ideas—we are not persuaded that the distinction is controlling on these facts.

* * *

Here, the facts are considerably more compelling. . . . Plaintiff's homicidal thoughts regarding Ms. Jacobson were frighteningly specific and detailed, not vague or isolated. Indeed, plaintiff indicated to Dr. Wagner that her vehement bitterness toward Ms. Jacobson had culminated in a specific plan to kill her, but that plaintiff had decided not to when a strike intervened. We believe it is clear that employers must be afforded wide latitude to ensure a safe workplace for their employees. Where an employee's homicidal thoughts about a co-worker are either expressed in the workplace, or otherwise made known to others in the workplace, the law does not require the employer to establish that the employee would affirmatively act on her homicidal thoughts before discharging her. Thus, we conclude that defendant did not violate the ADA in discharging plaintiff, whom it considered a direct threat to workplace safety.

Finally, we acknowledge that an employer generally has a duty to make "reasonable accommodations" to enable a disabled employee to perform the essential functions of the job, if the employer can do this without "undue hardship." However, the duty of reasonable accommodation applies only where the disabled employee is otherwise qualified for the position. Here, because plaintiff's homicidal thoughts left her unqualified for continued employment with defendant, we need not further address the issue of reasonable accommodation.

Accordingly, because plaintiff has failed to establish a prima facie case under either the ADA or the HCRA, her claims fail. The arbitrator committed substantial legal error in ruling otherwise; therefore, we vacate the circuit court order confirming the arbitrator's award.

The circuit court order confirming the arbitrator's award is VACATED.

Case Questions

1. If you were the employer in this situation, would you have handled this problem the same or differently?

2. Could you think of a situation where a threat would be protected by the ADA when spoken by a person with a disability?

3. Do you think a person with a disability should be held as accountable for their actions as a nondisabled person in the workforce?

"Essential Functions"

essential functions of a position
The employer may not take an adverse employment action against a disabled employee based on the disability where the individual can perform the essential functions of the position: those tasks that are fundamental, not marginal or unnecessary, to the fulfillment of the position's objectives.

For an employer to determine whether one is otherwise qualified for his or her position, the employer must first ascertain what the **essential functions** of that position are. For example, some companies require that all employees have driver's licenses, "in case of emergencies." While this is a meritorious request, the ability to drive is not always a basic requirement of the positions themselves but, instead, is marginal to the objectives of each position. An applicant who cannot drive because of a disability is otherwise qualified for the position, unless the position specifically has driving as its integral purpose, such as a taxi driver or delivery person.

The term "essential" refers to those tasks that are fundamental, and not marginal or unnecessary, to fulfillment of the position objectives. Often this determination depends on whether removing the function would fundamentally change the job. Disabled persons may not be disqualified simply because they may have difficulty in performing tasks that bear only a marginal relationship to a particular job. How does an employer determine what job tasks are considered essential? Employers may not include in their job descriptions responsibilities that are incidental to the actual job or duties that are not generally performed by someone in this position. The employer must look not to the means of performing a function but, instead, to the function desired to be accomplished. Some employers are shocked to find that an individual with disabilities may discover innovative and novel means to accomplish the same task. On the other hand, some individuals cannot perform the essential functions of their jobs no matter what accommodation they might request. For instance, in one case, as a result of his disability, a corrections officer did not have the physical ability to restrain inmates during an emergency. The court held that this ability was an essential function of his position and therefore he was not qualified under the ADA.[14]

Can a job function be *essential* where someone was in the position for 16 years and never performed this task? Is the frequency the function must be performed relevant to determining whether it is essential? In one case, the Fourth Circuit Court of Appeals determined that frequency is just one factor that a manager should look to in determining the essential functions of the position. *Champ* v. *Baltimore County, MD*[15] involved a police officer who sustained an arm injury and was put on light duty. Whole officers were not supposed to remain on light duty for more than 251 days; this officer continued to work in this capacity for 16 years. The Chief of Police then determined that all officers must be able to perform the full duties of a police officer. The court held that this officer could not perform the job's essential functions with or without reasonable accommodation and upheld the officer's termination.

One of the more perplexing issues to have developed since the ADA's inception is attendance. While the EEOC has viewed attendance as being an important but not an

---

[14] *Kees* v. *Wallenstein,* 161 F.3d 1196 (9th Cir. 1998).
[15] 91 F.3d 129 (4th Cir. 1996).

essential function of a job, allowing for a waiver of attendance policies as a reasonable accommodation, some courts have disagreed. In addition, courts have held that employees with erratic, unexplained absences are not protected, even if the attendance issues are due to a disability.[16]

In the next case, the Eighth Circuit Court of Appeals reviews the issue of whether attendance is an essential element of the plaintiff's position and whether a sporadic lack of attendance (whenever the plaintiff's back injury flared up) is sufficient for termination.

[16] *EEOC v. Yellow Freight Systems, Inc.,* 253 F.3d 943 (7th Cir. 2001).

Pickens v. Soo Line Railroad Co. *264 F.3d 773 (8th Cir. 2001)*

Employee Dennis Pickens contends his former employer, Soo Line Railroad (Soo Line) terminated his employment in violation of the ADA after he suffered a back injury. Pickens found upon returning to work that he was only able to sustain full-time employment if he could take off some time when the back injury flared up. He did so on the basis of time off allowed by the collective bargaining agreement but did so in such a manner that it resulted in more than 20 absences in the course of a year. The jury found for Pickens; however, the court ruled in favor of Soo Line as a matter of law.

Hansen, Circuit Judge

* * *

Pickens had worked for the Soo Line from 1973 until 1996 as a railroad conductor. On October 14, 1992, Pickens was injured while on the job. As a result, and after an unsuccessful five-month trial work period, Pickens was unable to continue working for three years. Pickens returned to work in October 1995, but because of medical restrictions limiting his work time to no more than an eight-hour day, he was unable to resume his duties as a conductor. Soo Line offered Pickens a switchman's position to accommodate his medical limitations. Pickens worked as a switchman for three days before concluding the job was too strenuous and refusing to continue working in the position. Because Pickens wished to return to his "road" position as a conductor, he requested that his physician lift his medical restriction to allow for a twelve-hour work day, four days per week—the schedule that the job required. Two months after returning to his duties as a full-time conductor, Pickens found that working four days per week was too strenuous, and he sought another medical restriction. Pickens' physician refused to comply with his request. Consequently, Pickens regularly made himself unavailable for work

by exercising his right to "lay off" under the railroad's collective bargaining agreement.[1]

After he chose to lay off in the spring of 1996, Soo Line required Pickens to obtain a medical status report from his physician prior to returning to work. This was the railroad's policy; however, it was the first time Soo Line had required Pickens to procure a release. One of the questions included in the release asked Pickens' physician whether he was able to return to full-time duty. Although his physician determined Pickens to be incapable of full-time employment, Pickens requested that his physician falsify his condition by answering affirmatively. His physician acquiesced to Pickens' deception of the railroad. Pickens continued his cyclical pattern of routinely laying off, obtaining a medical release, and returning to work when he chose. While waiting for clearance to return to work after a layoff in August 1996, Pickens wrote a letter to Soo Line's claims representative with copies sent to Soo Line's president and chief medical officer, expressing his

[1] The railroad allocates conductors to job assignments based upon a list of employees ranked by seniority. Under the collective bargaining agreement, each employee may withdraw his name from the list or "lay off" if he chooses to use vacation, sick leave, or personal time.

frustration. He wrote in part: "I had my medical restrictions removed to get back to work before and I will do it again if this is required. I will totally disregard safety and common sense if this is required." Concerned both with the possibility that Pickens might act on his threat and that Pickens had misrepresented the status of his health, Soo Line held a hearing pursuant to the collective bargaining agreement and subsequently terminated him on August 16, 1996.

II

* * *

In order to make out a case of discriminatory discharge under the ADA, Pickens must prove that (1) he is disabled within the meaning of the statute; (2) he is a qualified individual; and (3) that he was terminated because of his disability. A qualified individual is one who is able to perform, with or without accommodation, "the essential functions of the employment position that such individual holds or desires." Pickens asserts that he is qualified to perform the essential functions of his job regardless of his excessive absences given the nature of the railroad's scheduling structure. Pickens contends that because the railroad allows an employee to "lay off" of working any day of his choosing, this procedure makes his use of the practice a nonissue. We disagree. This court has consistently held that "regular and reliable attendance is a necessary element of most jobs." Even though the railroad's system of scheduling appears quite flexible, the railroad's policy requires regular, reliable attendance, and Pickens' conductor's job was full-time. Pickens' choice to lay off twenty-nine times from October 1995 to August 1996 is excessive and eviscerates any regularity in his attendance. "An employee who is unable to come to work on a regular basis [is] unable to satisfy any of the functions of the job in question, much less the essential ones."

Pickens' case is similar to *Buckles* v. *First Data Res., Inc.,* 176 F.3d 1098 (8th Cir. 1999). In *Buckles,* a panel of this court reversed the district court's denial of judgment as a matter of law and remanded for entry of judgment in favor of the employer when an employee with acute sinusitis was chronically absent from his job. The employee contended that he was qualified to perform his duties with the accommodation of leaving work any time an air-borne irritant aggravated his condition. Our court disagreed, reasoning that "[u]nfettered ability to leave work at any time is certainly not a reasonable

accommodation," and an employer is not required by the ADA to provide an unlimited absentee policy.

The ADA does cite a part-time or modified work schedule as a reasonable means of accommodation, but we view Pickens' suggested method—that he should be able to work only when he feels like working—as unreasonable as a matter of law. Soo Line accommodated Pickens by assigning him to do the switchman's job where he could work within his medical restrictions for two days per week but be paid for a full five-day work week. This effort proved unsuccessful when Pickens refused to perform as a switchman after only three days on duty. Additionally, he had his physician falsify that he was able to perform full-time work because he did not want to be limited to the part-time list of conductors. Furthermore, as the district court noted, when Pickens applied for disability benefits from the Railroad Retirement Board after Soo Line terminated him, he asserted under penalty of perjury that, as of August 1996, he was completely unable to work in the railroad industry because of his disability. Although Supreme Court precedent mandates that Pickens' admission of a total inability to work is not wholly inconsistent with inclusion under the ADA, this is true only if a reasonable juror could conclude he could perform the essential elements of his job with or without a reasonable accommodation. Our review of the record convinces us that as a matter of law, no reasonable juror could find Pickens to be a qualified individual because he was unable to perform the essential duties of his job with or without a reasonable accommodation.

Case Questions

1. Do you believe that attendance should be considered an essential function of most positions? Under what circumstances?

2. Should it matter that Pickens felt that he had no choice but to "go around" the system because he believed his employer was being unreasonable?

3. The court notes that the ADA does cite a part-time or modified work schedule as a reasonable means of accommodation. However, the court thought that Pickens' suggested method—that he should be able to work only when he feels like working—was unreasonable. If an employee is not sure when his disability will be more prohibitive with regard to work, a part-time schedule might not make sense. How can an employer appropriately accommodate a disabled worker who does not know when her or his disability with require an absence?

The court in *Pickens* was following the lead of several circuits before it. Several years prior, the Seventh Circuit court stated in no uncertain terms that attendance would be an essential function of many, if not most, positions.[17] ". . . We need not go so far as to say that regular attendance is an essential function of *every* job in rendering our decision today, nor do we hold that an individual with erratic attendance can never be a qualified individual with a disability under the ADA . . . However, our review of the entire record in this case supports the District Court's finding that regular attendance is an essential function of the tool and die maker position at (the defendant's workplace)." Similarly, the Seventh Circuit found in a separate case that a request for an unlimited, open-ended number of sick days was not an acceptable accommodation because the plaintiff in that case had failed to show that he could perform the essential functions of his position with that accommodation.[18]

The concept of essential functions under the ADA and the Rehabilitation Act differs slightly from the job-relatedness requirement for selection criteria under Title VII. Under Title VII, an employer has a defense to a claim of discrimination if it can show that the basis for the discrimination was the employee's failure to satisfy job-related requirements.

Under the ADA and the Rehabilitation Act, however, the court will look one step further. The requirement may be job-related, but the court will look to whether that requirement is also consistent with business necessity. In addition, courts disfavor employers who make general exclusions on the basis of business necessity, unless it can be shown that all or substantially all of the individuals who satisfy that category of disability could not do the job, or the exclusion is justified by the high personal or financial risk involved, which cannot be protected against. For example, in *Davis* v. *Bucher,*[19] a categorical exclusion of methadone program participants and those with a history of drug addiction was ruled unlawful, as well as a general prohibition against epileptics in the workforce in *Duran* v. *City of Tampa.*[20]

Of course, this focus on the individual rather than the disability itself may work against an employee with a disability. In *Cowan* v. *MABTSOA,* for example, a superintendent of a bus depot who directed bus maintenance employees was terminated after he used cocaine, refused to participate in a drug treatment program, and stole from his employer. In determining that the employee was not qualified to perform his job, the court recognized that the Rehabilitation Act "does not provide a safe haven in the workplace should they choose to use drugs."[21]

The ADA does not require employers to lower standards or to exclude from their position descriptions functions that are actually required of an employee in that position. It merely dictates that requirements be objectively determined, and not articulated for the purpose of excluding a disabled employee.

---

[17] *Jovanovic* v. *In-Sink-Erator Division of Emerson Electric Co.,* 201 F.3d 894 (7th Cir. 2000).
[18] *EEOC* v. *Yellow Freight Systems, Inc.,* 253 F.3d 943 (7th Cir. 2001).
[19] 451 F. Supp. 791 (E.D. Pa. 1978).
[20] 430 F. Supp. 75 (M.D. Fla. 1977).
[21] 961 F. Supp. 37 (E.D.N.Y. 1997).

How far does the employer have to go for the disabled employee or applicant? The EEOC has defined "reasonable accommodation" in its regulations as follows:

(1) The term "reasonable accommodation" means:

  (i) Any modification or adjustment to a job application process that enables a qualified individual with a disability to be considered for the position such qualified individual desires, and which will not impose an undue hardship on the covered entities business; or

  (ii) Any modification or adjustment to the work environment, or to the manner or circumstances under which the position held or desired is customarily performed, that enables a qualified individual with a disability to perform the essential functions of that position, and which will not impose an undue hardship on the operation of the covered entities business; or

  (iii) Any modification or adjustment that enables a covered entity's employee with a disability to enjoy the same benefits and privileges of employment as are enjoyed by its other similarly situated employees without disabilities, and which will not impose an undue hardship on the operation of the covered entities business.

(2) Reasonable accommodation may include but is not limited to:

  (i) Making facilities used by employees readily accessible to and usable by individuals with disabilities, and

  (ii) Job restructuring; part-time or modified work schedules; reassignment to a vacant position; acquisition or modification of equipment or devices; appropriate adjustment or modification of examinations, training materials or policies; the provision of readers or interpreters; and other similar accommodations for individuals with disabilities.

---

reasonable accommodation
An accommodation to the individual's disability that does not place an undue burden on the employer, which may be determined by looking to the size of the employer, the cost to the employer, the type of employer, and the impact of the accommodation on the employer's operations.

Scenario

"Reasonable Accommodation"

An applicant or employee is otherwise qualified for the position if, with or without *reasonable accommodation,* the worker can perform the essential functions of the position. Reasonable accommodation in this context generally means the removal of unnecessary restrictions or barriers. **Reasonable accommodation** is further defined as what does not place an *undue burden* on the employer. Therefore, as one commentator wrote, "reasonable accommodation is but one side of the coin; undue hardship . . . is the other side." It is generally believed that these types of accommodation expenses are normally quite low, averaging approximately $261 per disabled employee. (See Exhibits 12.3 and 12.4.)

An example of a reasonable accommodation is adapting a work space to the use of a wheelchair. If an employer has two applicants for an open position, one who requires the use of a wheelchair and another who has no disability, the employer may not choose the applicant without a disability solely because of the need to modify the work space for the other applicant (i.e., to provide a reasonable accommodation). But, referring to the hypothetical situation at the introduction of this chapter, what if the wheelchair poses a greater burden than merely adapting a work space?

557

Exhibit 12.4   Cost Guidelines for Reasonable Accommodations

The Job Accommodation Network is a free service of the Office of Disability Employment Policy of the U.S. Department of Labor. The following are examples of possible accommodations for workers with various disabilities.

ATTENTION DEFICIT DISORDER

- A journalist with attention deficit disorder was hyperactive and very sensitive to visual and/or auditory distractions. The employee was provided a cubicle to eliminate distractions. Flextime was also provided, as was additional time to prepare questions in advance. Ear plugs and the use of a tape recorder were also provided. There was no cost for these accommodations.

- An employee with attention deficit disorder and learning disabilities was provided with a personal computer, a personal information manager (PIM), and an environmental sound machine with headphones. In addition, the employee used colored markers and orange sticky dots for color coding, along with yellow mylar sheets for reading and scanning purposes. Cost for these accommodations was $2,350.

- An attorney with attention deficit disorder provided himself with the following accommodations: He exercised on a regular basis to alleviate some of his restless energy, used a software organizer and PIM, utilized colored folders and color coding. In addition, he listened to music when agitated. He purchased a color monitor for his computer (the different colors on the screen were personally effective). He used a word processing program that allowed him to work on more than one task at a time on his screen. Cost for the color monitor and software organizers was $490.

- A worker with attention deficit disorder who worked shift work received a modified work schedule and is now working day work with two days off in a row. This accommodation was at no cost to the employer.

CANCER

- An engineer working for a large industrial company had to undergo treatment for cancer during working hours. She was provided a flexible schedule in order to attend therapy and also continue to work full-time.

- A secretary with cancer was having difficulty working full-time due to fatigue. Her employer accommodated her by allowing her to work part-time and allowing her to take frequent rest breaks while working.

- A psychiatric nurse with cancer was experiencing difficulty dealing with job-related stress. He was accommodated with a temporary transfer and was referred to the employer's employee assistance program for emotional support and stress management tools.

- A lawyer with cancer was experiencing lapses in concentration due to the medication she was taking. Her employer accommodated her by giving her uninterrupted time to work. She was also allowed to work at home two days a week.

CHRONIC PAIN

- An appointment secretary was reprimanded for poor attendance due to chronic pain. She was provided periodic rest breaks when at work and allowed telecommuting part-time.

(continued)

Exhibit 12.4   (continued)

- A human resources manager had chronic pain due to a car accident. The individual was having difficulty getting to work on time. He was accommodated with a flexible schedule to allow more time to access public transit.
- An individual with chronic pain due to a back injury was having difficulty sitting throughout the day. She was accommodated with a reclining workstation.
- An assembly line worker with chronic pain was having difficulty standing for long periods. He was accommodated with a sit-lean stool and anti-fatigue matting.

Source: Reprinted with permission, job Accommodation Network, Office of Disability Employment Policy, U.S. Dept. of Labor, www.jan.wvu.edu.

In that situation, the position for which the disabled applicant applied required a great deal of traveling. Unless there is some reason to believe that the disabled applicant would not be able to travel, the employer must afford her the opportunity. While accommodation may be necessary to allow her to travel, such as a modified schedule to allow her more time to get from one place to another, such accommodation would generally be considered reasonable and required.

Similarly, as in scenario 3, Marquita may need an accommodation to be able to type with her feet. For instance, moving the keyboard to the floor may enable her to perform her job. This may involve little or no expense and would most likely be considered a reasonable accommodation. As for whether the employer must hire Marquita, the employer is not required to hire her if she is not the most qualified individual for the job. However, if she is the best qualified and the accommodation is reasonable, which it appears to be, Marquita may have a claim for disability discrimination.

An accommodation need not be the best possible solution, but it must be sufficient to meet the needs of the individual with the disability. An employee who suffers from a congenital upper respiratory disease may be unable to maintain consistent stamina or a high degree of effort throughout an entire workday. The requirement of reasonable accommodation does not mean that the employer must create a new job, modify a full-time position to create a part-time position, or modify the essential functions of the job. The EEOC's enforcement guidance stipulates, however, that a disabled employee is entitled to reassignment if he or she is qualified to fill a vacant position, *even if he or she can no longer perform the essential functions of her or his own position.* Moreover, the employee does not have to be the *most* qualified person entitled to fill the vacant position—the worker must only be *qualified* in order to be entitled to the position; and the burden is on the employer to notify the worker of open positions for which she or he is qualified. However, the employer does not have to give this employee preference in a reassignment that would be considered a promotion.

In *US Airways* v. *Barnett,*[22] the U.S. Supreme Court held that the ADA does not require a company with a normal seniority system to grant a special assignment to a disabled worker over senior employees. However, "special circumstances" in particular disability cases may override seniority systems.

[22] 535 U.S. 391 (2002).

NEW TOOLS HELP MINNEAPOLIS EMPLOYERS ACCOMMODATE WORKERS WITH DISABILITIES

A central database of accommodations is one tool being used by ADA specialists to bring efficiency to the process of accommodating workers with disabilities. At American Express Financial Advisors in Minneapolis, ADA specialist Michelle Jourdan created a computer database that includes information on any item the company purchased to accommodate somebody with a disability, the item's cost, and how the accommodation is working.

To keep track of legal developments and other resources, Jordan worked with Karen Moore, an accommodation project leader for Northwest Airlines, which is also headquartered in the Minneapolis area, to set up a local business network. The two met at a conference on disability accommodation. They invited other disability compliance specialists to join, and now the group meets once a month for two hours to exchange ideas. All participants have some responsibility for ADA accommodations for their employers.

One effort the network is pursuing is developing a purchasing cooperation with vendors that could provide network members with better deals on devices, such as voice-activated software.

Source: Excerpted from *EEO Review Newsletter,* no. 381, October 1998.

Special circumstances might alter the important expectations created by a seniority system. The plaintiff might show, for example, that the employer, having retained the right to change the system unilaterally, exercises the right fairly frequently, reducing employee expectations that the system will be followed—to the point where the requested accommodation will not likely make a difference. The plaintiff might also show that the system already contains exceptions such that, in the circumstances, one further exception is unlikely to matter. The plaintiff has the burden of showing special circumstances and must explain why, in the particular case, an exception to the seniority system can constitute a reasonable accommodation even though in the ordinary case it cannot. [*US Airways* v. *Barnett,* 535 U.S. 391, 392 (2002).]

In addition, the fact that a proposed accommodation conflicts with an employer's other workplace rules and policies does not necessarily mean that it is not reasonable.

To accommodate an employee, the employer may have to redesign a job and eliminate those tasks not required by the purpose of the position. For instance, an employee who is unable to stand may not be able to reach certain supplies but can otherwise perform the necessary components of her or his position. The employer may be required to accommodate the employee by relocating the supplies to a lower level that is accessible to the employee. On the other hand, the Eighth Circuit found against an employee who sought to use a mobilized cart precisely because she could not prove that she could perform all of her duties from that cart.[23] Other examples of accommodation may include switching a worker's shift time, testing air quality (where a worker has an allergy), or permitting the allergic worker to wear a mask. A blind receptionist might use a light probe to detect which telephone line to answer; deaf employees at a workplace that uses buzzers on equipment would benefit from the use of indicator lights instead. (See Exhibits 12.5 and 12.6.) On the other hand, an employer is not required to

---

[23] *Stafne* v. *Unicare Homes,* 266 F.3d 771 (8th Cir. 2001).

Exhibit 12.6   Examples of Accommodations

Low-technology possibilities:

Lap boards, delivered lunches, telephone amplifiers, computer screen magnifiers, door levers (instead of knobs), walking canes, automatic page turners.

High-technology possibilities:

Robotic devices, screen reading mechanisms, speech synthesizers, telecommunication devices for the deaf, remote control devices, voice-responsive computers.

---

reassign or reallocate *essential* job functions. An accommodation is also unreasonable if it requires a "fundamental alteration" in the nature of the program or imposes financial or administrative costs on the employer. Finally, an, accommodation that constitutes a demotion would violate the ADA, as would segregation of all disabled workers into a different career track.

The following case evaluates the reasonableness of the proposed accommodation— to work from home—in light of its determination of whether physical presence at work is an essential function of the position, as discussed above.

Mason v. Avaya Communications, Inc. *357 F.3d 1114*
(10th Cir. 2004)

Diane Mason sued her former employer Avaya Communications, Inc., claiming that Avaya violated the Americans with Disabilities Act. Prior to working at Avaya, Mason worked as a mail carrier for the United States Post Office in Edmond, Oklahoma, and witnessed the murder of several of her then co-employees in the "Edmond Post Office massacre." After witnessing the event, a doctor diagnosed Mason with post-traumatic stress disorder. Avaya subsequently hired Mason as a "service coordinator." All of Avaya's service coordinators worked at field service administration centers. Mason's job as a service coordinator required her to monitor the current day's queue of repair tickets and to schedule service appointments for technicians working in the field, requiring her to communicate with the various technicians by computer, telephone, and fax.

On March 21, 2000, a Kevin Lunsford, co-employee of Mason, pulled out a knife during a verbal confrontation with another Avaya employee at the Oklahoma City administration center. Mason did not witness the Lunsford incident, but learned of it through her co-employees. After the incident, Avaya suspended Lunsford for a week. While Lunsford was suspended, Mason learned from her co-employees that Lunsford had previously threatened to "go postal," retained a cache of weapons, and compiled a "hit list." When Avaya informed its service coordinators that Lunsford would return to work, they explained it had conducted a fitness-for-duty examination on Lunsford and concluded that he could safely return to the workforce. Upon learning of Lunsford's return, Mason's post-traumatic stress disorder returned, according to her doctors, and she was unable to work in an environment she perceived as unsafe. Among other options, Mason requested Avaya accommodate her disorder by allowing her to work out of her home. Upon investigation, Avaya concluded that Mason could not perform the service coordinator position from her home because physical attendance at the administration center was a function of a service coordinator's job.

Mason alleged that Avaya failed to accommodate her post-traumatic stress disorder by refusing to allow her to work from home. Avaya then terminated Mason because she would not return to work.

The district court granted Avaya's motion for summary judgment, holding Mason was not a qualified individual with a disability under the ADA because (1) Mason's physical attendance in the workplace was an essential function of her job and (2) Mason's request for an at-home accommodation was unreasonable. The Circuit Court affirms.

Baldock, C.J.

* * *

The ADA prohibits discrimination against "a qualified individual with a disability because of the disability of such individual[.]" Discrimination under the ADA includes "not making reasonable accommodations to the known physical or mental limitations of an otherwise qualified individual with a disability who is an . . . employee[.]" . . . Avaya concedes Mason is disabled under the ADA. Thus, we proceed directly to the question of whether Mason is qualified within the meaning of the ADA. Under the second element of the ADA's prima facie case, we employ a two-part analysis to determine whether an individual is qualified: First, the court determines whether the individual can perform the essential functions of the job. . . . Second, *if (but only if)* the court concludes that the individual is unable to perform the essential functions of the job, the court determines whether any reasonable accommodation by the employer would enable h[er] to perform those functions.

On appeal, Mason maintains her disability precludes her from working at Avaya's Oklahoma City administration center while Lunsford is an employee at the center. Mason contends, however, she could perform all the essential functions of her job with a reasonable accommodation. . . . Therefore, we only need to determine whether Mason can perform the essential functions of the service coordinator position; and if not, whether Mason's request to work from home is a reasonable accommodation that would enable her to perform the essential functions of the service coordinator position.

A

The plaintiff bears the burden of showing she is able to perform the essential functions of her job. "Essential functions" are "the fundamental job duties of the employment position the individual with a disability holds or desires." Evidence considered in determining whether a particular function is essential includes: (1) the employer's judgment as to which functions are essential; (2) written job descriptions prepared before advertising or interviewing applicants for the job; (3) the amount of time spent on the job performing the function; (4) the consequences of not requiring the incumbent to perform the function; and (5) the work experience of past incumbents in the job.

The ADA requires us to consider "the employer's judgment as to what functions of a job are essential[.]" The employer describes the job and functions required to perform that job. We will not second guess the employer's judgment when its description is job-related, uniformly enforced, and consistent with business necessity. In short, the essential function "inquiry is not intended to second guess the employer or to require the employer to lower company standards." While we have not previously addressed the question, other circuits have recognized physical attendance in the workplace is itself an essential function of most jobs [citing federal, D.C., third, fourth, fifth, and seventh circuits]. In [one case], the Fifth Circuit concluded that an essential function of a loan analyst's position was physical presence in the office because the position required teamwork. . . . Similarly, in *Tyndall* v. *Nat'l Educ. Centers Inc.*, the Fourth Circuit explained that even when an employee can satisfactorily perform the essential functions of her position, the employee "must be willing to demonstrate these skills by coming to work on a regular basis." The Fourth Circuit reasoned that "a regular and reliable level of attendance is a necessary element of most jobs." As Judge Posner wrote, "[m]ost jobs in organizations public or private involve team work under supervision rather than solitary unsupervised work, and team work under supervision generally cannot be performed at home without a substantial reduction in the quality of the employee's performance." *Vande Zande* v. *Wis. Dep't of Admin.* (7th Cir. 1995).

In this case, Avaya claims Mason could not perform the essential functions of the service coordinator position from home because her physical attendance at the administration center was an essential function of the position. According to Avaya, Mason's physical attendance at the center is an essential function of the service coordination position because the low-level hourly position is administrative in nature and requires supervision. Furthermore, a service coordinator's duties require teamwork. Avaya presented evidence to the district court demonstrating four of the evidentiary factors set forth by the EEOC regulations. Specifically, Avaya presented evidence that (1) it considers attendance at the administration center, supervision, and teamwork as essential functions of the service coordinator position, (2) all of its service coordinators work their entire shift at the administration centers, (3) it has never permitted a service coordinator to work anywhere other than an administration center, and (4) service coordinators cannot be adequately trained or supervised if they are not at the administration center.

Mason responds that her physical attendance at the administration center was not an essential function of the service coordinator position because she can perform all of the essential functions of the job at home using a computer, telephone, and fax machine. In support of her argument, Mason relies on her own first-hand experience: "Ms. Mason testified that she had performed the duties of Service Coordinator for over two (2) years and was well aware of the job functions of that position. She explained, her job consisted of primarily working on the computer through phone and fax lines to coordinate service calls for [Avaya's] customers. . . ." Mason also submits neither supervision nor teamwork are essential functions of a service coordinator position because Avaya's service coordinator job description "makes no mention of 'being supervised' or 'teamwork' as a duty or responsibility." With respect to teamwork, Mason argues her presence at the administration center is not essential because one of the other fourteen service coordinators in her group can perform the "teaming" duties, such as covering for a co-employee on break. With respect to supervision, Mason simply points out that Avaya did not present any evidence indicating it created the service coordinator position so mid-level supervisors would have someone to supervise.

Avaya presented evidence, however, that it could not adequately supervise a service coordinator working from home. Assuming Avaya had the technology to permit Mason to work from home, Avaya established it still could not adequately supervise Mason if she was at home. Although Avaya could tell if Mason was logged into her computer, Avaya's supervisors would not be able to ascertain what she was doing while logged into the computer. Mason could, for example, engage in any number of non-work-related activities while logged into her computer without Avaya's knowledge. The EEOC regulations recognize that "the inquiry into essential functions is not intended to second guess an employer's business judgment with regard to

production standards, whether qualitative or quantitative, nor to require employers to lower such standards." *See* 29 C.F.R. § 1630 App. at 356. At a time when employers are justifiably concerned with productivity at the workplace, we are in no position to second guess Avaya's desire to directly supervise its lower level employees.

Similarly, Avaya presented significant evidence demonstrating teamwork is an essential function of the service coordinator position because the coordinators typically assist and cover for one another in a job even Mason described as "very hectic." Mason's suggestion that teamwork is not an essential function because other service coordinators can pick up the slack in her stead is simply irrelevant in determining whether teamwork is an essential function of the job. As the Seventh Circuit noted in rejecting an argument nearly identical to Mason's: "It is possible that any function, whether or not essential, could be assigned to additional employees. The mere fact that others could do [plaintiff's] work does not show that the work is nonessential." *Basith* v. *Cook County* (7th Cir. 2001). We agree. In fact, Mason's suggestion that the other service coordinators in her group could perform the "teaming" duties for her demonstrates she also considered those duties as functions of the job.

* * *

[T]he district court properly held Mason's physical attendance at the administration center was an essential function of the service coordinator position because the position required supervision and teamwork. . . . Because Mason's disability precludes her from physically attending the Oklahoma City administration center, an essential function of the service coordinator position, we must determine whether Avaya could reasonably accommodate her.

B

* * *

We have not specifically addressed whether working at home may constitute a reasonable accommodation under the ADA. We have consistently held, however, that an employee's request to be relieved from an essential function of her position is not, as a matter of law, a reasonable or even plausible accommodation. In fact, the ADA does not even require an employer to modify an essential function of an existing position in order to accommodate a disabled employee. Several other circuits have likewise recognized that an employer is not obligated by the ADA to eliminate or reallocate the essential functions of the job to accommodate a disabled employee.

Many of our sister circuits have similarly held an employee's request for an at-home accommodation is unreasonable under the ADA. While these decisions have largely collapsed the "essential function" and "reasonable accommodation" analysis, they have all concluded a requested at-home accommodation is unreasonable when the accommodation eliminates an essential function of the job. . . .

The only case to hold a triable issue existed on the reasonableness of an at-home accommodation was one in which the essential functions of the employment position could be performed at home. The Ninth Circuit explained "[w]orking at home is a reasonable accommodation when the essential functions of the position can be performed at home and a work-at-home arrangement would not cause undue hardship for the employer."

* * *

In sum, a request to work at home is unreasonable if it eliminates an essential function of the job; however, summary adjudication may be improper when the employee has presented evidence she could perform the essential functions of her position at home thereby making the at-home accommodation request at least facially reasonable. The Supreme Court has generally eschewed per se rules under the ADA, and we think the determination of whether a request for an at-home accommodation is reasonable must likewise be made on a case-by-case basis. . . .

In this case, Mason's request for an at-home accommodation is unreasonable on its face because it seeks to eliminate an essential function of the service coordinator position. . . . Under the ADA, Avaya is not required to eliminate or change the essential functions of the service coordinator position in order to accommodate Mason's disability. Hence, Mason's request for an at-home accommodation is, as a matter of law, unreasonable.

Case Questions

1. Can you identify positions where physical presence in the workplace is not an essential function of the position?

2. What do you think of the court's rule, articulating the ADA, that it consider "the employer's judgment as to what functions of a job are essential" and not second-guess the employer's judgment? What might be the pros and cons of such a standard?

3. How do you believe the court should balance the worker's firsthand testimony of what her job is like with the employer's evidence of the essential necessities of a position?

Scenario

Scenario 1 presents an issue of reasonable accommodation and concerns the definition of essential functions of a position. If Thekla Tsonis determines that travel is an *essential function* of the position, she may be able to justify "ability to travel" as a qualification for employment. Even if it is a real requirement, the wheelchair-bound applicant may be perfectly able and willing to travel. Tsonis should simply lay out the requirements of the position, then ask both applicants if there is any reason why they would not be able to perform these functions, with or without reasonable accommodation. The wheelchair-bound applicant may need some accommodation, such as assistance getting to and from the airport or travel times that allow her or him to have extra time to arrive at the airport. These would probably be viewed as reasonable accommodations.

Undue Hardship

Undue hardship is not limited to financial difficulty but may also include any accommodation that would be unduly costly, extensive, substantial, or disruptive, or that would fundamentally alter the nature or operation of the business. While employers may also attempt to show that they took an adverse employment action based on their fears relating to future absences or higher insurance costs, an undue hardship, or more than a *de minimis* cost that the employer should not have to bear, these are not acceptable defenses to a claim of discrimination. In fact, courts have gone out of their way to explain the nature of the concept of undue hardship. In *Kilcullen* v. *New York State Dept. of Transp.*,[24] the court explained that it means more than the term "readily achievable," which is used in Title III governing the requirement to alter existing public accommodations. Readily achievable means "easily accomplishable and able to be carried out without much difficulty or expense," the court said. "The duty to provide reasonable accommodation, by contrast, is a much higher standard than the duty to remove barriers in existing buildings (if removing the barriers is readily achievable) and creates a more substantial obligation on the employer." In addition, undue hardship under the ADA is distinct from the duty to provide reasonable accommodation under Title VII in cases of religious discrimination such as *TWA* v. *Hardison,* discussed earlier in Chapter 9. In that case, the court held that accommodations to religious beliefs need not be provided if the cost was more than a *de minimis* expense to the employer. Thus, the court held, "the definition of undue hardship in the ADA is intended to convey a significant, as opposed to a *de minimis* or insignificant, obligation on the part of employers." As an example, in a case dealing with an employer's concern that an obese employee would cost the employer higher health care amounts in the future, the New York high court held that this was not a valid defense even though obese people, as a class, *are* at a greater risk for certain health problems than others. See an additional case on a similar topic below.

---

[24] 33 F. Supp. 2d 133 (N.D.N.Y. 1999), *vac'd on other grounds,* 2000 WL 1038429 (2d Cir. 2000).

Cassidy v. Detroit Edison Company   *138 F.3d 629 (6th Cir. 1997)*

The employee, Cassidy, began suffering allergic reactions to workplace substances after exposure to "stack gas." Over a period of time, the employer attempted accommodations that proved ineffective. The employee was eventually terminated, and she sued under the ADA. The court had to determine whether the employer had reasonably accommodated the employee and found that the employer had done so.

Suhrheinrich, J.

Cassidy worked as an assistant power plant operator at Detroit Edison Company (DEC) until she was exposed to "stack gas" on the job. As a result, she suffered numerous allergic reactions to a multitude of substances. To accommodate her breathing and allergy conditions, the company found an assignment for her in the area with the most filtered and clean air, the computer center. After time, Cassidy experienced more breathing difficulties from exposure in her work environment to cleaning chemicals, diesel fumes, food odors, paint fumes, and smoke. DEC accommodated her by scheduling her for straight day shifts, allowing her to leave when a known allergen would be present, testing the

area to comply with environmental air standards, permitting her to wear a mask and use a breathing machine, and scheduling maintenance when she was not present. DEC also tested its facilities for fungus, bacteria, and mists to find an adequate work environment for her.

Still having breathing problems, Cassidy met with several of her doctors. DEC approved a three-month medical leave on the advice of her doctors. Prior to her return, DEC's chief medical officer requested Cassidy's physicians to specify appropriate restrictions. She submitted a return-to-work statement from one of her physicians stating she could return to a "workstation free of exposure to any agent that may trigger asthma or cause a drop in peak flow and that is well ventilated."

An independent medical examiner examined Cassidy and recommended "a location that is reasonably free of irritants and also an area where she may have some control over the environment through use of desktop air purifiers."

During this time, Defendant's staff continued to assess available positions within the company to accommodate Plaintiff. After the chief medical officer reviewed the restrictions recommended by Cassidy's personal physician he concluded "[u]nder these restrictions there is no position available at Detroit Edison. However, if her physician would possibly modify these restrictions, we might be able to make a position available for her." Upon finding no position available at the company with these restrictions, the company terminated her. Cassidy filed suit, alleging that her termination violated the ADA because the employer had failed to reasonably accommodate her disability. The district court found no genuine issue of material fact, that "[DEC] did all that it possibly could to accommodate [Cassidy] in light of her disability," and granted DEC's motion for summary judgment. Cassidy appealed.

* * *

The employee contends that genuine issues of material fact exist as to whether the employer reasonably accommodated him because the employer did not consider reassignment to a vacant position. The employer responds that it attempted to reasonably accommodate the employee, but that Cassidy proposed only general and vague accommodations, such as a transfer to a position in an allergen-free environment, which did not exist within the company.

* * *

An employee demonstrates disability for purposes of the ADA by showing a substantial limitation on a major life activity, not necessarily the major life activity of working. . . . In the present case, the district court found that Plaintiff was disabled because of her substantial limitation on her major life activity of breathing, not of working.

. . . A disabled employee who claims that he or she is otherwise qualified with a reasonable accommodation "bears the initial burden of proposing an accommodation and showing that [the] accommodation is objectively reasonable." An employer then has the burden of persuasion to show that an accommodation

would impose undue hardship. The reasonableness of an accommodation is a fact issue.

* * *

Under the ADA, an employer need only reassign the employee to a vacant position. Generally, transfer or reassignment of an employee is only considered when accommodation within the individual's current position would pose an undue hardship. An employer may reassign an employee to a lower grade and paid position if the employee cannot be accommodated in the current position and a comparable position is not available. However, a reassignment will not require creating a new job, moving another employee, promoting the disabled employee, or violating another employee's rights under a collective bargaining agreement.

The employer provided several reasonable accommodations, including: initially transferring Plaintiff to the computer department after her first asthmatic attack; allowing Plaintiff to work straight days; scheduling cleaning and maintenance to occur when Plaintiff was gone; allowing Plaintiff to leave when she may be exposed to allergens; allowing Plaintiff to use her prescribed breathing apparatus at work; allowing Plaintiff to use paid and unpaid leave, and testing Plaintiff's work area. The district court noted that based on her physicians' vague recommendations, Plaintiff requested transfers to a vacant position in a well-ventilated and allergen-free workstation that would not "trigger asthma or cause a drop in peak flow." But because Plaintiff did not "identify the precise limitations resulting from the disability and potential reasonable accommodations that could overcome those limitations," the district court concluded that "Defendant did all that it possibly could to accommodate Plaintiff in light of her disability."

We agree with the district court. Plaintiff's proposed accommodation for essentially an allergen-free workplace, which Defendant attempted to locate within the company, was simply too vague to reasonably inform Defendant of a reasonable accommodation, or was otherwise simply unavailable. Defendant attempted numerous accommodations but finally concluded that there was no sufficiently allergen-free work environment within the company in which Plaintiff could perform her job. Plaintiff had the duty to propose an objectively reasonable accommodation. However, Plaintiff simply failed to create a genuine issue of material fact as to Defendant's assertions that no such allergen-free work environment existed within the company for Plaintiff.

Further, Plaintiff also did not demonstrate that there were any vacant positions in such areas.

* * *

Thus, based on Plaintiff's lack of specific proposed accommodation, Defendant's previous attempts to accommodate Plaintiff, and Defendant's conclusion that it did not have a position in the company that satisfied Plaintiff's vague restrictions, there is no genuine issue of material fact that Plaintiff failed to propose or identify an objectively reasonable accommodation. Therefore, Defendant is entitled to judgment as a matter of law. Accordingly, we AFFIRM.

Case Questions

1. Do you believe the employer made a good-faith effort to reasonably accommodate the employee?
2. What do you think about the possibility of the employee working at home, since it did not appear she had breathing problems there? What if this caused animosity among coworkers who wanted to work at home for convenience but could not due to company policy?
3. Cost was not discussed in this opinion, but do you think there should be a dollar limit on the price of a reasonable accommodation?

One example of a job redesign request that was found to be an undue burden on the employer is found in *Guice-Mills* v. *Derwinski*.[25] In that case, the plaintiff, a head nurse at a hospital, suffered from severe depression, which subjected her to feelings of hopelessness, malaise, insomnia, inability to get up in the morning, extreme fatigue, and irritability. As a result of her syndrome, she was unable to arrive at the hospital prior to 10 A.M., while her position required that she arrive at 8 A.M. The employee requested that her position as head nurse be officially changed to allow her to begin work at 10 A.M. The court held that the hospital was not required to accommodate the request because all head nurses were required to begin work at 8 A.M. as a matter of administrative necessity. The court instead found that the hospital's offer to reassign her to a position as a staff nurse so she could work a different shift was a reasonable accommodation.

The Appendix to the EEOC's ADA regulations suggests the following hypothetical situations as examples of the weight to be given to each of the factors in an "undue hardship" determination:

> [A] small day care center might not be required to expend more than a nominal sum, such as that necessary to equip a telephone for use by a secretary with impaired hearing, but a large school district might be required to make available a teacher's aide to a blind applicant for a teaching job. Further, it might be considered reasonable to require a state welfare agency to accommodate a deaf employee by providing an interpreter while it would constitute an undue hardship to impose that requirement on a provider of foster care services.

Where the cost of the accommodation would result in an undue hardship and outside funding is not available, the disabled employee or applicant should be given the option of paying the portion of the cost that constitutes an undue hardship. (See Exhibit 12.7.)

Requests for Accommodation and Employer Responses: Process The EEOC released a lengthy Enforcement Guidance to provide assistance to employers to help them better navigate and understand the EEOC's and the courts' perceptions and expectations

[25] 967 F.2d 794 (2d Cir. 1992).

Exhibit 12.7   Factors in Undue Hardship

In connection with the definition of "undue hardship," the EEOC regulations direct the following:

In determining whether an accommodation would impose an undue hardship on a covered entity, factors to be considered include:

(i) The nature and cost of the accommodation needed under this part;

(ii) The overall financial resources of the facility or facilities involved in the provision of the reasonable accommodation, the number of people employed at such site, and the effect on expenses and resources;

(iii) The overall financial resources of the covered entity, the overall size of the business of the covered entity with respect to the number of its employees, and the number, type, and location of its facilities;

(iv) The type of operation or operations of the covered entity, including the composition, structure, and functions of the workforce of such entity, and the geographic separateness and administrative or fiscal relationship of the site or sites in question to the covered entity; and

(v) The impact of the accommodation upon the operation of the site, including the impact on the ability of other employees to perform their duties, and the impact on the site's ability to conduct business.

concerning the employment of disabled individuals. The guidance clarifies how a disabled individual can request reasonable accommodations and how employers can reasonably accommodate such requests.

According to the Enforcement Guidance, when an ADA situation first arises, the disabled employee must provide notice to the employer of her disability and any resulting limitations. Courts have recognized that an employee has the initial duty to inform his employer of a disability before ADA liability is triggered for failing to provide an accommodation. An employee cannot keep secret his disability and then later sue for failure to accommodate. Nor are employers expected to be clairvoyant. As a general matter, the individual with a disability has the responsibility to inform her employer that an accommodation is needed.

What suffices as a request for an accommodation? A key reasonable accommodation request, according to this guidance, "does not require the employee to speak any magic words . . . the employee need not mention the ADA or even the term accommodation."[26] The courts have also concluded that an employee who merely tells his supervisor that "his pain prevented him from working and that he requested leave under the Family and Medical Leave Act (FMLA)" is protected by the ADA.[27] A request simply asking for continued employment can be a sufficient request for accommodation. Nothing in the ADA requires an individual to use legal terms or to anticipate all of the possible information an employer may need in order to provide a reasonable accommodation. The ADA avoids a formulaic approach in favor of an interactive discussion between the employer and the individual with a disability, after the individual has requested a change

[26] *Schmidt* v. *Safeway Inc.,* 864 F. Supp. 991, 997; 3 AD Cas. (BNA) 1141, 1146–47 (D. Or. 1994).
[27] *McGinnis* v. *Wonder Chemical Co.,* 5 AD Cas. (BNA) 219 (E.D. Pa. 1995).

due to a medical condition. However, some courts have required that individuals initially provide detailed information in order to trigger protection under the act.

In addition, the EEOC encourages employers to be receptive to any relevant information or requests they receive from a third party acting on the disabled individual's behalf because the reasonable accommodation process presumes open communication (in order to help the employer make an informed decision). The essence of the reasonable accommodation concept requires an employer to go out of its way, to maintain a disabled employee's employment. It is an interactive process. It requires participation by both the employee and the employer. As part of that interactive process, once the employer's responsibilities are triggered by appropriate notice from the employee, the employer may want to take the lead. The employer may want to initiate informal discussions about the need for and the scope of any possible accommodation. Communication is essential. The object is to identify the precise limitations resulting from the disability and potential reasonable accommodations that could overcome those limitations.

The EEOC and the courts have been tough on employers who have not been promptly receptive and responsive to disability situations. When determining whether or not there has been an unnecessary delay in responding to ADA situations, the courts consider these relevant factors: (1) the reason(s) for the delay, (2) the length of the delay, (3) how much the individual with a disability and the employer each contributed to the delay, (4) what the employer was doing during the delay, and (5) whether the required accommodation was simple or complex to provide. Employers who do not respond expeditiously to employee's requests tend to suffer greater legal consequences.

Reasonable Accommodation and the Contingent Worker

Employment through staffing firms and temporary agencies offer individuals with disabilities unique opportunities to move into the workforce. During the employee shortage in early 2000, temporary agencies such as Manpower Inc. turned to workers with disabilities to fill its needs.[28] In December 2000, the EEOC issued its Enforcement Guidance "Application of the ADA to Contingent Workers Placed by Temporary Agencies and Other Staffing Firms." Only the staffing firm must provide reasonable accommodations for the application process before any client has been identified as a prospective employer. However, if an employer requests an applicant through the staffing firm, both the staffing firm and the prospective employer must provide reasonable accommodation.

When a staffing firm and its clients are joint employers of an individual with a disability, both are obligated to provide reasonable accommodation at the workplace. Of course, this obligation does not extend to undue hardship. Further, the staffing firm and its clients must have notice of the need for accommodation.

In order to ease the financial burden of providing accommodation, the Internal Revenue Service offers several federal tax incentives to eligible small businesses (those with either 30 or fewer full-time employees or $1 million or less in gross receipts in the preceding tax year) that make these accommodations. First, they can take

---

[28] See Michelle Conlin, "The New Workforce," *Business Week,* Mar. 20, 2000, p. 66.

advantage of the Disabled Access Tax Credit—50 percent of eligible expenditures over $250 (but not over $10,250) made to provide access to the workplace for disabled workers. Second, any business may be eligible for a deduction for removing architectural or transportation barriers to disabled workers in the firm, up to $15,000 per year. (Eligible small businesses can take *both* of these deductions.) Finally, firms that hire workers who are "vocational rehabilitation referrals" certified by local employment agencies will be allowed a tax credit under the Work Opportunity Tax Credit (Internal Revenue Code, sec. 51).

Employee's Responsibility for "Interactive Process": Identification and Request for Reasonable Accommodation

Once an employee learns that she or he will need some form of accommodation in order to perform the essential functions of her or his position, the burden is on the employee to make a request for the accommodation. As mentioned above, except in unusual circumstances, an employee does not have a claim under the ADA for an employer's failure to accommodate unless that employee has made a request for reasonable accommodation that has been denied. Once the employee has made the request for accommodation, she or he has the responsibility to work with the employer to determine the most effective and efficient means by which to meet these needs. "The federal regulations implementing the ADA envision an interactive process that requires participation by both parties."[29] This requirement of interaction would usually include meeting with the worker, obtaining as much information as possible about the condition, discussing alternatives, considering accommodations, and documenting the process.

In one case where an employer requested a medical form from a worker's doctor, the worker refused to provide the form. The worker claimed that she was concerned that the company would misuse the information provided in the form, while the employer asserted that it needed the requested information in order to determine her accommodation needs and to comply with insurance requirements. The Tenth Circuit Court held that the worker's ADA claim was barred because she failed to engage in the interactive process with her employer to determine a reasonable accommodation for her disability: "Even assuming such conduct by Neodata could support a claim under the ADA for failure to provide reasonable accommodation, that claim would only arise after Mrs. Templeton satisfied her duty to notify the employer of the nature of her disability." In another case, an employee's failure to cooperate with the employer's internal job search process prohibited him from claiming that the employer did not fulfill its interactive duty.[30] If the worker refuses or otherwise fails to satisfy the employer's requirements for job transfers, such as qualifying tests or documentation, the employer cannot be held responsible for not interacting with the worker in connection with the identification of a possible accommodation.

In fact, the EEOC's recent Enforcement Guidance on reasonable accommodations specifically states that employers have a right to request medical documentation of

---

[29] *Templeton* v. *Neodata Services, Inc.,* 162 F.3d 617 (10th Cir. 1998).
[30] *Allen* v. *Pacific Bell,* 348 F.3d 1113 (9th Cir. 2003).

disabilities in order to best satisfy their duty to reasonably accommodate. The Enforcement Guidance, however, does not place *too* large a burden on workers for such "interaction." The request [for accommodation] may be in "plain English," and need not explicitly mention the ADA or the term "reasonable accommodation."

Disability Harassment

The ADA prohibits workplace harassment when it creates a hostile environment against disabled workers. While there have not been a great number of cases brought on this basis, there is evidence of a trend toward greater reporting and enforcement of the prohibition. In a federal case in the New Jersey court system, *Lanni* v. *State of New Jersey Dept. of Environmental Protection,* the plaintiff-employee claimed that he was subject to harassment and teasing as a result of his dyslexic learning disability. Coworkers reportedly made faces at Lanni and derogatory sounds when speaking to him, as well as committing some physical abuse. The jury awarded Lanni $277,000, finding an ADA violation.

In another case, in Oregon, a worker who suffered from depression requested that he be separated from the individual who was the source of the harassment. The supervisor refused to separate the two workers, even after the alleged abuser called the plaintiff "mental," "delusional," and "out of his mind," when interviewed by the supervisor. Again, the plaintiff prevailed. Any recovery, however, is limited to the amount of actual damages incurred. Where a plaintiff suffers distress or loss of dignity, damages are recoverable nominally for emotional harm endured.[31]

Intellectual Disabilities

In October 2004, the EEOC published "Questions & Answers about Persons with Intellectual Disabilities in the Workplace and the Americans with Disabilities Act"[32] to address specific issues raised in connection with the 2.5 million people in the United States with an intellectual disability. The guide is essential to employers since it offer examples and information about how to apply the standards discussed in this chapter to situations involving individuals with intellectual disabilities. The EEOC explains that its guidelines follow the model of the President's Committee on Intellectual Disabilities (formerly known as the President's Committee on Mental Retardation) in using this particular terminology. The committee adopted this term to "update and improve the image of people with disabilities who were formerly referred to as people with mental retardation and to help reduce discrimination against these citizens." The committee also "sought to reduce the public's confusion between the terms 'mental illness' and 'mental retardation' and to remove the use of terms that resulted in faulty name-calling."[33]

The EEOC defines intellectual disability as anyone with an IQ of below 70–75, with significant limitations in adaptive skill areas as expressed in conceptual, social, and practical adaptive skills; and with a disability that originated before the

---

[31] *Flowers* v. *Southern Regional Physician Services, Inc.,* 247 F.3d 229 (5th Cir. 2001).

[32] http://www.eeoc.gov/facts/intellectual_disabilities.html.

[33] http://www.acf.hhs.gov/programs/pcpid/index.html.

age of 18. "Adaptive skill areas" refers to basic skills needed for everyday life, including communication, self-care, home living, social skills, leisure, health and safety, self-direction, functional academics (reading, writing, basic math), and work. This is similar to the ADA's concept of major life activities, discussed elsewhere in this chapter. The individual must also meet the traditional requirements of the ADA in that the impairment must limit major life activities, the individual must have had a record of such an impairment, or the individual must be perceived as having such an impairment.

The guidelines offer examples of reasonable accommodations that may be offered to an intellectually disabled applicant or employee, including providing a reader or interpreter, demonstrating what the job requires, replacing a written test with an expanded interview or other measurement technique, restructuring a position, slower-paced training, job coaching, modifying a work schedule, providing modified equipment or relocating a workstation to reduce distractions. Employers are cautioned to be on the lookout for harassment of individuals with intellectual disabilities since about 20 percent of discrimination claims involve this type of concern.

The following are examples of individuals who would be covered under the ADA for intellectual disabilities:

- A person with an intellectual impairment is capable of living on his own, but requires frequent assistance from family, friends, and neighbors with cleaning his apartment, grocery shopping, getting to doctors' appointments, and cooking. He is unable to read at a level higher than the third grade, and so needs someone to read his mail and help him pay bills. This person is substantially limited in caring for himself and therefore has a disability under the ADA.
- A person may have two or more impairments that are not substantially limiting by themselves, but that taken together substantially limit one or more major life activities. In that situation, the person has a disability.
- An employee has a mild intellectual disability and a mild form of ADHD. Neither impairment, by itself, would significantly restrict any major life activity. Together, however, the two impairments substantially limit the employee's ability to concentrate, learn, and work. The employee is a person with a disability.
- A person was erroneously diagnosed as having an intellectual disability that substantially limited his ability to learn when he was attending high school. The applicant has a past record or history of a disability.
- An applicant with a facial deformity that affects her speech applies for a position as a secretary. The applicant is denied employment because the interviewer believes she has an intellectual disability and that the condition will make her unable to communicate with clients effectively. The employer has regarded the applicant as a person with a disability.
- The parent of a child with an intellectual disability applies for a position as an attorney at a law firm and mentions during a discussion with one of her interviewers that she has a child with an intellectual disability. She is denied employment because the employer believes the child's disability will cause her to be absent from work and will affect her productivity. The parent is protected under the ADA.

EFFECT OF REGULATION ON THE ACTIONS OF EMPLOYERS

Potential Responsibility or Liability of Employer

"No Fault" Liability: Workers' Compensation

In addition to liability under the ADA, employer liability with regard to health issues can also arise in connection with workers' compensation. It is important to keep in mind that liability based on workers' compensation is distinct from liability based on the ADA: Just as an injury at work does not necessarily lead to workers' compensation liability, workers' compensation liability does not instantaneously result in an employer's obligation under the ADA. The purpose of the two statutes are distinct, as well. Workers' compensation is a statutory scheme to provide no-fault insurance for lost wages and medical expenses resulting from work-related injuries. The ADA is a federal antidiscrimination statute designed to protect individual rights to equal employment opportunity.

A Remedial History: Purpose of Workers' Compensation   Suppose you work in an office and one morning you come in, turn on the computer, and receive an electrical shock that severely jolts you, nearly knocking you off your chair.

Think of the repercussions of this, financial and otherwise. Now imagine adding this: suing your employer to recover for the losses you suffered as a result of the injury on the job. Among other things, you must find a suitable attorney; find a means of paying the attorney at a time when you are least able, because of your injury; take time away from work to deal with the attorney and your injuries; wait for a court date, which may be a year or more away; and have the attorney gather evidence to support your claim that the employer is responsible for your injury.

When you finally get to court, you are subject to the results of the more formidable resources that the employer can probably afford and also defenses that would prevent the employer from being liable for your injuries. Among other things, the employer may allege it was your **negligence** that caused the injury, or that it was the fault of some other employee.

In the end, after all of your time, energy, and expense, you may lose. Or you may get much less of a judgment than you anticipated. Just when you need it most, you could also lose your job because you sued your employer. You would lose benefits to which your job may entitle you, such as health insurance.

Bleak scenario, isn't it? That is the reason for a system of state and federal workers' compensation statutes. That scenario was the reality in the workplace before such **no-fault** statutes were enacted to address primarily the issues of lost wages and medical expenses incurred in work-related injuries. The main reason for the statutes was to reduce the troublesome scenario the employee had to go through at such a difficult time. But the statutes are not unbalanced. There are benefits for employers also.

With workers' compensation statutes, employees trade off potentially higher damages awarded after litigation against the certainty of smaller benefits provided immediately. Also included in the statutory scheme is the guarantee of protection from employer retaliation for filing workers' compensation claims and the employer's inability to use the usual defenses against the employee to avoid liability for workplace

negligence
Failure to meet the appropriate standard of care for avoiding unreasonable risk of harm to others.

no-fault
Liability for injury imposed regardless of fault.

injuries. The employee gets less in terms of benefits; but the benefits they are allowed are certain if the workers' compensation requirements are met. The employer gains freedom from lawsuits for workplace injuries and the certainty of how much such injuries will cost.

The overall effect is intended to make the workplace more efficient and to assist in the marketplace, since increased accidents mean lost time and lower production. Since workers' compensation statutes are remedial in nature, they are usually broadly construed to permit recovery where possible.

General Statutory Scheme

Workers' compensation plans basically provide compensation for time away from work and medical expenses related to on-the-job injuries. Employers pay into the system, which is administered by a state workers' compensation agent. Each state has a *schedule of benefits,* which tells how long an employee is to receive benefits (generally for a certain number of weeks) and the amount of benefits for a particular injury. The schedules also provide for the employee's death or loss of the use of a limb. Employers usually arrange the payment of their workers' compensation contributions by taking out insurance or self-insuring. Self-insuring involves employers paying into a private fund of their own, while taking out insurance may be done through private or state insurance policies.

The amounts and time periods of benefit coverage vary from state to state. Nonpermanent injury benefit schedule amounts are usually based on some percentage of the employee's weekly wages. There is a limitation on the amount to be received; and, once it is reached, the employer's statutory duty is fulfilled. Generally, in exchange for this immediate nonlitigated payment benefit, the employee does not sue the employer. However, there are states where employees may (under limited circumstances) sue the employer in addition to receiving workers' compensation benefits.

For instance, Florida has determined that, in sexual harassment cases, the workers' compensation statute will not be the exclusive remedy, because of the overwhelming public policy against workplace sexual harassment. In *Ramada Inn Surfside and Adjusto, Inc.* v. *Swanson,*[34] the court, referring to *Byrd* v. *Richardson-Greenshields Securities, Inc.,* stated that "[a]pplying the exclusivity rule of workers' compensation to preclude any and all tort liability effectively would abrogate this policy, undermine the Florida Human Rights Act, and flout Title VII of the Civil Rights Act of 1964."

In concluding that workers' compensation should no longer be the exclusive remedy for workplace sexual harassment injuries, the court noted that:

> workers' compensation is directed essentially at compensating a worker for lost resources and earnings. This is a vastly different concern than is addressed by the sexual harassment laws. While workplace injuries rob a person of resources, sexual harassment robs the person of dignity and self esteem. Workers' compensation addresses purely economic injury; sexual harassment laws are concerned with a much more intangible injury to personal rights. To the extent these injuries are separable, we believe that they both should be, and can be, enforced separately.

[34] 560 So. 2d 300 (Ct. App. Fla., 1st Dist. 1990).

Workers' compensation statutes in some form or another have now been adopted in all states. A small minority of states have made them optional but, in doing so, generally prohibit employers who do not become a part of the state's workers' compensation plan from using the common law defenses if the employer is sued by the employee for negligence.

There is also federal coverage under other legislation, including the Federal Employers' Liability Act of 1908. This act limited the common-law defenses an employer could use, rather than replacing virtually the entire common-law approach to on-the-job injuries with a no-fault system. Later, the Federal Employee's Compensation Act in 1916 provided a workers' compensation scheme for U.S. civil employees. The Longshore and Harbor Workers Service Compensation Act supplements state workers' compensation laws by providing benefits for employees in maritime employment.

"Of or in the Course of" Employment

One of the most frequently litigated areas of workers' compensation is whether the accident injuring an employee arose out of or in the course of employment. An injury that occurs at work is not necessarily work-related. For instance, if a diabetic employee goes into a coma while at work, this may have nothing whatever to do with work except that it occurred there. Though workers' compensation statutes are remedial, and generally an attempt is made to find compensation for injured employees, the statutory requirements must still be met.

"Arising out of or in the course of" employment generally requires the employee's injury be one that has a causal connection with the employee's employment and may involve the time, place, and circumstances of the accident. An employee can be injured off the premises and still have a valid workers' compensation claim if the employee was in the course of employment, just as she may receive an injury on the work premises and not be covered because it did not arise out of employment.

For the most part the system works. However, it is not without flaws. A common problem employers have is that they may routinely respond to inquiries from the workers' compensation office without giving them the closer inspection they deserve. Contributions for larger employers are based on their injury record, so premium contributions, which must be paid by the employer, increase when claims are filed. Without investigation of claims, unwarranted claims slip through, and this unnecessarily increases the employer's contribution. However, it is the experience of the industry as a whole that serves as the basis for premiums; thus, this may not be as crucial for smaller companies. Employer attention to workplace safety can greatly reduce accidents and resulting premiums and claims.

Workers' compensation is big business. An employer must be vigilant about providing a safe workplace and training so preventable workplace accidents are minimized. Some states are taking this very seriously. The California Corporate Criminal Liability Act may impose fines of up to $1 million on corporations for failure to notify employees of a "serious concealed danger" in the workplace. In addition, managers may also be fined and criminally prosecuted if they actually knew of a workplace condition that created a substantial probability of death, great bodily harm, or serious exposure to a hazardous substance. Again, employers should also keep a close watch on claims to ensure that only valid claims are permitted.

Protection of Coworkers

tort

A private (civil) wrong against a person or her or his property.

The employer of an employee with a contagious disability may be liable to coworkers of the employee based on a variety of common-law **tort** theories. While the only remedy available to the employee for common workplace injury is workers' compensation (discussed above), the employer may be additionally liable to its employee for any intentional torts. The employer has both a statutory duty to provide a safe work environment according to federal regulations, as well as a similar common-law duty to refrain from an intentional wrong against the employee. This type of tort liability may arise based on the response of the employer to the news that an employee has a contagious disease. If the employer reacts in a manner that causes the employee severe emotional distress by its outrageous conduct, the employer would be liable in tort. In addition, unwarranted invasions of privacy, breaches of confidentiality, and defamation have been held to be bases for actions against employers. A tortious invasion of privacy occurs where the employer intentionally intrudes into an employee's private affairs, and the court finds that the intrusion would be highly offensive to a reasonable person.

How does this issue arise? Predictably, several cases have been filed by employees who work with HIV-positive employees. Usually, the case will surface after the employee has made requests for additional protections. Pursuant to the Occupational Safety and Health Act, an employer must provide a safe workplace for its employees, free from conditions reasonably believed in good faith to be hazardous. Where an employer knowingly and willfully disregards the safety of its employees, the employer will be liable.

In California, for instance, a group of nurses requested gloves and masks when treating AIDS patients. The nurses were denied protection based on the California Labor Commission's finding that there was no health danger from working in an AIDS ward without protective clothing. The employees' fears must be based on an honest, good faith, and reasonable belief that their safety is threatened. Since the employer is therefore required to protect both the employee, by virtue of the ADA, and the complaining employees, by virtue of the National Labor Relations Act and the Occupational Safety and Health Act, the only answer must be complete education of the workforce to preclude any "good-faith" belief that the employee with AIDS presents a health danger.

Retaliatory Discharge and Remedies Available

The ADA provides for claims of retaliatory discharge based on disability discrimination and allows relief based on Title VII remedies. Congress expanded the remedies available to ADA claimants under the Civil Rights Act of 1991, allowing for the recovery of compensatory and punitive damages in cases of intentional unlawful discrimination. The district courts have been split, however, on whether this expansion of remedies applies to retaliation claims, and no federal court had addressed the matter until recently. The court in *Kramer* v. *Banc of America Securities, LLC,* 355 F.3d 961 (7th Cir. 2004) held that employees suing for retaliatory discharge are limited to those articulated in section (g)(l): "[T]he court may enjoin the respondent from engaging in such unlawful employment practice, and order such affirmative action as may be appropriate, which may include, but is not limited to, reinstatement or hiring of employees, with or without back pay. . . , or any other equitable relief as the court deems appropriate." As a result of its analysis, the court also held that employees are precluded from jury trials in cases of retaliation. Since retaliation claims are common under the ADA, the practical impact of the *Kramer* decision can be far-reaching and is considered something of a windfall to employers, if adopted throughout the circuits.

Disclosure

The issue of whether the employee's co-workers have a right to information related to the employee's condition is an area of hot dispute. You may recall the newspaper stories that explained the American Medical Association was faced with complaints from patients regarding the doctors' responsibility to inform their patients if they have AIDS. The employer may only release information if she or he reasonably believes such disclosure to be necessary.

The EEOC stated in its 1997 guidelines that if employees ask questions about a worker with a disability, the employer must not disclose any medical information in response.

Genetic Testing

Thirty-six railroad workers shared a $2.2 million settlement in the case of *EEOC* v. *Burlington Northern Santa Fe Railroad.* The EEOC alleged that the railroad had secretly conducted genetic tests to determine whether workers' compensation claims based on carpal tunnel syndrome were work-related or the result of a genetic predisposition. In April 2001, two months after the lawsuit was filed, the railroad agreed to stop the testing pending the EEOC's investigation of whether the test violated the ADA. While a court did not rule on the issue, the size of the settlement, which also requires the railroad to update the training of its medical personnel regarding the ADA, indicates that employers engage in genetic testing at their own risk.

Further, at least 26 states have passed laws against genetic discrimination in the workplace. According to an American Management Association 2002 survey, less than 1 percent of the companies polled admitted to engaging in genetic testing. Perhaps employers realize that the potential for liability is too great to support such testing.[35]

In 2003, the Senate passed the Genetic Non-Discrimination Act, which seeks to prohibit discrimination based on genetic information in connection with health insurance or employment. Though it has not yet been passed by the House, the act is significant in that, in addition to its protection against discrimination, it provides a series of privacy provisions that prohibit the collection of genetic information except where health or genetic services are offered by the employer; where an employer needs certain information to comply with the certification provisions of the Family and Medical Leave Act of 1993 or with state family and medical leave laws; where an employer learns the information through publicly available documentation; or where necessary to monitor the effects of toxic substances in the workplace (when authorized by the employee or as required by law).

---

[35] See Darryl Van Duch, "EEOC Goes after Genetic Testing," *National Law Journal,* Apr. 30, 2001.

Family and Medical Leave Act

As discussed in Chapter 6, the Family and Medical Leave Act provides eligible employees with leave based on certain circumstances. The FMLA intersects with the ADA in that both required a covered employer to grant leave based on medical reasons. The ADA's reach is slightly more broad as the ADA applies to private employers of 15 or more employees while the FMLA covers private employers with 50 or more employees.

In addition, the coverage provided by the two acts differs slightly in terms of the circumstances under which each applies. Under the FMLA, an employee may take advantage of the act in connection with a "serious health condition." This is defined as "an illness, injury or physical or mental condition that involves . . . inpatient care . . . or continuing treatment by a health care provider." Of course, those conditions that are covered by this definition might not constitute disabilities under the ADA. The clearest example of this divergence is in the case of pregnancy. Pregnant women qualify for leave under the FMLA but normal circumstances of pregnancy are not considered disabilities under the ADA.

Another distinction between the two acts is the extent of the leave. The FMLA provides for up to 12 weeks of leave per year for covered conditions. The ADA does not identify a specific duration for leaves due to disabilities. In some cases, where leaves for more than 12 weeks would not constitute an undue burden on the employer, a leave for an extended period may be considered to be reasonable accommodation. Under the FMLA, an employee is entitled to return to the same or equivalent position as that which she or he left when taking the leave. Under the ADA, the employee may request additional leave even after an employer informs her or him that their position may no longer be available (or that it would constitute an undue burden to keep it available). If this happens, the employer is obligated to try to find a vacant position for the worker at an equivalent level or, if not available, at a lower level.

MANAGEMENT CONSIDERATIONS

The employer is restricted in its preemployment inquiries related to disabilities. Medical examinations may only be required after the employment offer has been extended, and only where all employees in that position category are subject to similar examinations. Employment may then be conditioned on passing the test. However, as previously stated, where the withdrawal of the offer is based on the discovery of a disability, that disability must be related to adequate performance of the job or business necessity, and there must exist no reasonable accommodation. All information obtained through medical examinations must be kept confidential by the employer. The employer should therefore establish separate files for this information and restrict their access to them.

The ADA apparently treats testing differently based on when the test is given. As mentioned above, no medical testing is allowed preoffer unless if relates specifically to job performance. Once the offer has been made, but prior to employment, some testing might be acceptable. Once hired and employed, employers are far more restricted in

Exhibit 12.8   Preemployment Questions

Examples of questions that *may not* be asked of an applicant for a position:

1. Please list any disabilities.
2. Have you ever filed a workers' compensation claim, and on what basis?
3. Do you have any disability(ies) that may prevent you from performing the requirements of this position?
4. How did you become disabled?
5. How often do you expect to miss work as a result of this disability?

Examples of questions that *may* be asked:

1. This job requires that you [be present for eight hours a day, five days a week], [lift 150-pound bags], [stand for long periods of time]. Can you meet this requirement?
2. If the employer is aware of the disability, the employer may ask how the applicant intends to perform the essential functions of the position with or without accommodation.
3. The employer may request documentation of the need for a requested accommodation.

terms of testing and the decisions that may be based on the results of testing. In one case that found its plaintiff in the middle category where employers have the greatest latitude in testing, the plaintiff alleged that the test violated the ADA. In *Rowles* v. *Automated Production System, Inc.,* the plaintiff was a worker who had been given an offer conditioned on a drug test. The worker, an epileptic, took medication to prevent seizures. Upon learning that this particular medication was on the list of prohibited drugs for which he would be tested, he refused to take the drug test and was fired. Rowles filed a claim under the ADA asserting a violation since the firm prohibited the use of legally prescribed drugs without any showing that testing for these drugs was job related or a business necessity.

The district court judge in *Rowles* held that since the policy prohibited the use of physician-prescribed medication, the policy was in direct violation of the ADA. In so holding, the judge granted partial summary judgment but still required the employee to show that the termination resulted from the illegal policy.

Not all preemployment inquiry issues are so clear. Imagine a situation where the interviewer notices an apparent disability that might interfere with the applicant's job performance. However, when asked if he can perform the essential functions of the position, the applicant replies that he can. The ADA is unclear as to whether the interviewer can inquire further about the applicant's disability given this response. (See Exhibit 12.8.)

Many firms are now adopting educational programs so their managers become more aware of the needs of the disabled. In this way, firms can better prevent problems from arising once the disabled employee joins the workforce. This is of even greater necessity given the ADA's prohibition on preoffer medical examinations. A company may not require a medical examination before an offer has been extended, though it may make a verbal inquiry about whether the applicant is capable of performing the essential functions of the position in question. Only after that time may a company require an examination. Because of this prohibition, many firms employ disabled employees who did not appear to be disabled at the time the offer was extended.

Firms are also developing policies of direct referral of disabled employees to specially designated personnel directors. This director or counselor is aware of job possibilities and would be in the best position to suggest job content modifications and redesign potential. After assignment or reassignment, the counselor usually checks on the employee to ensure that the requirements of the position are appropriate to the needs of the employee and that the employee is satisfying the needs of the firm. In addition, many firms conduct periodic reviews of their position descriptions to ensure that they encompass the essential functions of the position, as well as a review of their job application forms and procedures, facilities, personnel programs, and policies.

Finally, employers should be aware that the Internal Revenue Service offers a Targeted Jobs Tax Credit to employers against five-year wages paid to newly hired workers with disabilities, among others who have difficulty obtaining employment. The program is administered by the U.S. Department of Labor.

Substance Use and Abuse

It is evident that employers must establish cohesive guidelines to ensure their compliance in the area of disability discrimination. (See Exhibit 12.9.) Guidelines have already been established by the courts in connection with claims by alcoholic employees, alleging a disability due to their alcoholism. These guidelines are very tough on employers. In *Rodgers* v. *Lehman,*[36] the court established a five-step directive for the benefit of employers dealing with alcoholic employees:

1. If the employer suspects alcoholism, she must inform the employee of counseling services.
2. If the alcoholism continues, the employer must give the employee a "firm choice" between treatment and discipline.
3. The employer must then provide outpatient treatment.
4. If this is unsuccessful, the employer must provide inpatient treatment.
5. Only if the first four steps fail can the employer legally discharge the employee.

Employers thus have the benefit of a statement by the courts about the proper means of handling such a case under the Rehabilitation Act (and, by inference, the ADA). Employers must follow similar directives in connection with the hiring and retention of employees with other disabilities.

The issue of smoking in the workplace has also become an issue. Many, if not all states have enacted legislation banning smoking in the workplace environment. An employer is forced to balance the rights of smokers without violating the laws intended to protect nonsmokers. But, is nicotine dependence or withdrawal a disability? Does smoking create a physiological or a psychological dependency requiring it to provide a reasonable accommodation for smokers? The answer has not been decided. Congress remains silent on this issue, and the Supreme Court has not had a case on point.

---

[36] 869 F.2d 253 (4th Cir. 1989).

Exhibit 12.9   Self-Audit for ADA Compliance

James Frierson, a professor in the College of Business at East Tennessee State University, suggests that companies conduct a 50-question self-audit in order to identify ADA compliance problem areas and to preclude any potential hazards. Here are some of the questions that Frierson suggests a manager or owner should ask of his or her business:

1. Does the company have a written policy concerning disabled job applicants and employees?

2. Does the company have a system to encourage employees to report their disabilities in order that accommodations can be provided?

3. Has the company notified unions and professional organizations with whom they have a contract of the company's disability policies?

4. Are procedures in place to ensure that all contractors who come into contact with company employees are complying with the ADA?

5. Have all written job descriptions been reviewed and revised to omit outdated or nonessential tasks and, where possible, to describe required job results, rather than methods?

6. Has the company designated individuals to be responsible for making reasonable accommodations? Does the designated individual understand the legal definition of a disabled person? Does the designated individual understand the legal duty of accommodation?

7. How are decisions documented when disabled individuals are not hired, retained, or promoted because the needed accommodation creates an undue hardship?

8. Do all managers who make employment decisions understand the A-B-C-D-E rule? (Frierson contends that disability lawsuits that are settled unfavorably for employers are most likely to occur when people with AIDS, Bad backs, Cancer, Diabetes, and Epilepsy are denied jobs because of a risk of future injury.)

9. Is the company's HR department or any other location where job applicants must go fully accessible to disabled people, including those who use wheelchairs?

10. Have all employment tests and procedures for taking the tests been reviewed to ensure that they accurately measure necessary skills and aptitudes?

11. Has the company created a separate, confidential file for employee health and medical information?

12. Are disabled and nondisabled employees who are in the same job classifications provided with the same fringe-benefit coverage?

Source: James Frierson, "A Fifty-Question Self-Audit on ADA Compliance," *Employment Relations Today* 19, no. 2. Reprinted by permission of John Wiley & Sons, Inc.

Nicotine dependence has been analogized to alcoholism, which has long been recognized as creating a dependency. With the large-scale tobacco litigation, more evidence is coming forward about the dependent nature of nicotine. Further, the American Psychiatric Association's *Diagnostic and Statistical Manual of Mental Disorders,* Fourth Edition (*DSM-IV*), lists nicotine dependence and withdrawal under the heading of nicotine use disorders. In addition, the EEOC's "Enforcement Guidance on the ADA" identifies the *DSM-IV* as a relevant reference for classifying mental disorders. (Note, however, that not all disorders listed in the manual rise to the level of disabilities protected by the ADA.) The EEOC Enforcement Guidance, issued in March 1997, provides more solid support for the position that nicotine withdrawal presents a substantially limiting mental impairment.

Not every smoker would have a claim, however; a claim would only be upheld if the nicotine dependence or withdrawal disabled the claimant in the performance of a major life activity. It has been noted that, in order to make a viable claim under the ADA, the disability must create a "substantial limitation"; that is, it must typically restrict the performance for at least several months. The rights of either recovering or current smokers have not been tested under the ADA.

Drug addiction is also an issue that employers are now facing with regard to disabilities. While current drug use is not protected by the ADA, former illegal drug users, including individuals who either are participating in or have completed a drug rehabilitation program, are not excluded from protection under the ADA. Courts have recognized that, under certain circumstances, drug addiction *may* constitute a disability under the ADA and the Federal Rehabilitation Act. As with all disabilities, the former drug users must demonstrate they have a disability; that is, they must show that the past drug use limits a major life activity and it must have been sufficiently severe to be considered a drug addiction. An employee who is a recovering addict no longer using drugs may use the past drug addiction to argue that he or she has a disability based on a "record of such an impairment."

Interestingly, the advent of state laws permitting the use of marijuana for medicinal purposes may complicate the above discussion. Notwithstanding the fact that the Supreme Court has held that marijuana has no medical benefits worthy of an exception of the Controlled Substances Act,[37] the use of marijuana is allowed under certain circumstances in Alaska, Arizona, California, Colorado, Connecticut, Georgia, Hawaii, Maine, Nevada, Oregon, and Washington. Legislation is pending in Illinois, Massachusetts, Missouri, New York, Ohio, Rhode Island, Vermont, and Wisconsin. In most states where marijuana use is permitted, an employer is not required to accommodate its use in any workplace. However, the definition of "use" remains vague—is an employee "using" if it is in her or his system or only if they actually smoke marijuana while on the job? If the latter, then a worker could smoke marijuana elsewhere and then immediately head for the workplace while still under its influence.

The best an employer can do at this time is to amend its drug and alcohol policies to require disclosure of medical marijuana use in the same way it requires disclosure of the side effects of prescription drugs. Perhaps the worker could also be moved to a position that is less sensitive to its effects. Finally, the employer could grant the worker a leave during the time she or he requires use of the drug. If an employer suspects impairment that could make the worker unqualified for the position, the worker can be tested based on that reasonable suspicion (such as slurred speech, attitude, involvement in an accident, or odor).

It is also important to recall the Supreme Court's decision in *Raytheon Co.* v. *Hernandez,* discussed earlier in this chapter, which held that disparate impact claims are available to workers who test positive for illegal drug use. In that case, the worker

---

[37] *United States* v. *Oakland Cannabis Buyers' Cooperative,* 532 U.S. 483 (2001).

Management Tips

- Never assume the physical or intellectual limitations of a disabled worker or applicant. If you assume that someone can't perform certain functions, you may be creating limitations where none exist.

- Be sure to explore all possible reasonable accommodations for otherwise qualified applicants or employees. Failure to do so might result not only in legal liability but also costs connected with identifying and training alternative candidates. Often, a small accommodation will allow you to retain qualified and experienced disabled individuals.

- Engage in frank and open discussions. Determining the appropriate reasonable accommodation is a collaborative process. Candid communication is the key ingredient leading to successfully handling ADA matters.

- Consult with the employee. Ask questions. Ask the employee to offer suggestions. Asking the employee to provide additional information will lead you to more opportunities for best identifying and handling the accommodation.

- Document that dialogue. These are negotiations. They may or may not lead to litigation. Don't let the employee say that you remained silent once the employee asked for an accommodation. Confirm your efforts to accommodate in writing. This documenta-

tion is one of the best defenses against an employee's memory.

- Be proactive. Reasonable accommodation obligations require action and effort on the employer's part. Flexibility is critical to management's efforts.

- Negotiate. Make counterproposals. Be sure they are fair and reasonable. Remember, an employer is not required to provide the best accommodation, only a reasonable accommodation.

- Review all application materials to ensure that there are no inappropriate questions concerning irrelevant abilities.

- Review all job descriptions to make sure that the job requirements are actually required to complete the job; get rid of extraneous requirements that are not really essential to job performance.

- Since "disability" under the statutes includes someone who is perceived as being disabled, conduct training sessions with all management to educate them regarding what is actually a disability and what is not.

- You are not required to accommodate all disabilities. Consider all costs involved with providing accommodation and consider whether it would be an undue burden under the courts' precedents.

was fired after a positive result on a drug test. The employer had a no-rehire policy, but the court left open the possibility that individuals with disabilities may be entitled to differential treatment under facially neutral policies. Accordingly, recovering drug addicts and/or recovering alcoholics may claim that they should not be covered by such a policy. Based on *Raytheon,* policies may be suspect if they automatically bar reemployment after a positive drug or alcohol test, or for other possible consequences of a covered disability, or if they change the conditions of work for those who have tested positive or exhibit these effects. On the other hand, as long as the employer can justify decisions based on business necessity or job-relatedness, their decisions are more likely to be defensible.

Summary

- Statutory protections against disability discrimination in employment strike a balance between the right of individuals with disabilities to have job opportunities and the need of employers to have an "able" workforce. This balance is achieved by several measures. First, the determination of whether an individual has a disability is made on a case-by-case basis, examining whether the impairment substantially limits one or more of the individual's major life activities. "Major life activities" are defined as activities that have central importance to daily life. "Substantial limitation" is determined by taking into account mitigating measures such as medication and medical devices.

- Not every impairment will lead to protection as a disability. However, those who have a record of such an impairment or have been perceived as having such an impairment are also protected. This prevents employers from defending discriminatory actions on the basis that the individual does not have a current disability.

- The balance between employees' rights and employers' needs is further maintained by the concept of reasonable accommodation. An applicant or employee with a disability, who meets the basic job requirements regarding education, experience, skills, and abilities, may need accommodation to perform the essential job functions. If the accommodation imposes an undue hardship on the employer, the employer is not required to provide it. This determination is also done on a case-by-case basis. Further, if the applicant or employee with a disability poses a direct threat to the health and safety of others that cannot be reasonably accommodated, then that individual is not "qualified" for the position.

- Employers are well advised to ensure that they fairly and equitably analyze these issues in addressing all disability-related situations arising in the workplace.

Chapter-End Questions

1. Den Hartog, who was not disabled, was discharged from his position as headmaster at Wasatch Academy because his adult son, who suffered from bipolar affective disorder and lived with his parents on campus, attacked and threatened several members of the school community. Did his discharge violate the ADA? [*Hartog* v. *Wasatch Academy,* 129 F.3d 1076 (10th Cir. 1997).]

2. Mathews, who was employed as a journey-level mailer at the Denver Post, suffers from epilepsy, including grand mal seizures. He suffered a grand mal seizure that required two days' hospitalization. His doctor told him not to return to work for one month. The employer received a letter from Mathews' physician that stated he was "not comfortable" with Mathews' driving and being near or operating heavy equipment for at least three months. This is a fairly standard guideline generally accepted within the medical community. Operating an insert machine and power dolly were essential functions of Mathews' job. The employee admitted that he could not use the insert machine, but he argued that he was not prohibited from using the power dolly, even though his doctor had specifically mentioned it as posing a danger. The employee and his union representative admitted that even journey-level mailers working on a press line shift were required to use the insert machine and that the press line shifts were required to use the power dolly. Is the employer required to accommodate the employee by modifying or eliminating an essential function of his job? [*Mathews* v. *Denver Post,* 263 F.3d 1164 (10th Cir. 2001).]

3. Davis had been deaf since birth. She applied for a clerk position at the Postal Service. The Postal Service denied her application because she would not be able to answer the telephones, one of the duties of the position. It contended that asking other hearing clerks to take on Davis's telephone duties would lower employee morale and cause bitterness and

dissent. In addition, it claimed that it would be inconvenient to other employees who would need to communicate with someone in the desired position. Is the Postal Service's claim sufficient to satisfy the undue hardship defense? [*Davis* v. *Frank,* 711 F. Supp. 447 (N.D. Ill. 1989).]

4. A disabled employee identifies vacant positions to which he can transfer but fails to formally apply for those positions. Is the employer still responsible for engaging in an interactive process with the worker to identify a reasonable accommodation? [*Shapiro* v. *Township of Lakewood,* 292 F.3d 356 (3d Cir. 2002).]

5. Wood suffered permanent nerve damage at work and could no longer drive a ready-mix concrete truck, though he could drive other trucks. He sought a reassignment but, since his employer didn't have another job for him, he was terminated. He was somewhat limited in walking and in performing certain work functions. He also claimed discrimination based on the fact that his injury resulted in impotence, substantially limiting him in a major life activity. Is he covered? [*Wood* v. *Crown Redi-Mix, Inc.,* 339 F.3d 683 (8th Cir. 2003).]

6. A supervisor returned to work after having a heart attack and found that he had been demoted. His employer regarded him as being substantially limited in his work since he couldn't "handle the pressure" of a supervisory job. Does the employee have a claim under the ADA? [*Cline* v. *Wal-Mart Stores,* 144 F.3d 294 (4th Cir. 1998).]

7. Spangler was an employee in a bank's Demand Services Department. She suffered from dysthymia, a form of depression, along with phobia and bouts of more intense depression. Over several years she was absent from work on a relatively frequent basis. The employer discharged her after continuing absences following two periods of probation for absences from work. She was discharged the day after she had called in that she would be absent because of "depression again." Should Spangler's condition be considered a disability? If so, what, if any, accommodations could have been made for Ms. Spangler? Do you believe her discharge violates the ADA? [*Spangler* v. *Fed. Home Loan Bank,* 278 F.3d 847 (8th Cir. 2002).]

8. A custodian with a mental disability who worked at a large high school submitted a letter from the school psychiatrist stating that he needed to be at a less stressful school. The employer claims that the worker asked only *not* to be at this school and also failed to articulate exactly what kind of accommodation was needed or what type of environment he sought. If an employee seeks an accommodation but does not know what to ask for, is the employer liable for failing to accommodate? [*Bultemeyer* v. *Ft. Wayne Community Schools,* 100 F.3d 1281 (7th Cir. 1996).]

9. A software engineer who needs intravenous fluids on a daily basis and needs to use the bathroom up to 14 times each day as a result of rectal and breast cancer requests accommodation in the form of being allowed to work from home. The employer objects, claiming that the job required teamwork, interactions, and coordination with coworkers. Is this a reasonable accommodation that the employer can provide without experiencing an undue burden? [*Rauen* v. *U.S. Tobacco Mfg. Ltd. Partnership,* 319 F.3d 891 (7th Cir. 2003).]

10. Johnson was diagnosed with paranoid schizophrenia and a bipolar disorder. As long as she took her medication, she was able to function appropriately and effectively in her position. However, when her doctor lowered her dosage and she failed to follow up with necessary outpatient treatment, her behavior became erratic and threatening. In fact, she had an altercation with a coworker after threatening the coworker, and she had to be escorted to the hospital, after which time she was terminated. Johnson claimed discrimination, but her employer argued that, while her condition constituted a mental impairment, it did not necessarily substantially limit any major life activities since she was able to care for herself, study, socialize, and work as long as she took her medication. In addition, they contended

that she was not otherwise qualified since she posed a direct threat. Does Johnson have any argument available to her? [*Johnson* v. *Maynard,* 2003 WL 548754, 25 NDLR P 180 (S.D.N.Y. 2003).]

11. Rossbach was a police officer for the city of Miami, Florida. He was impaired in that he severely injured his arm while apprehending a suspect and had a herniated disc and nerve damage from another on-duty circumstance. Though he could walk, sit, stand, and sleep with his impairments, his abilities in these major life activities were moderately below average and he could not do any of these things for any extended (normal) period of time. Though restricted by the police department to light/limited duty, he applied for additional assignments. He was denied, based on a policy prohibiting any light or limited duty officers from working these particular assignments. The department claimed that Rossbach, though impaired, was not substantially limited in major life activities.

   a. Is Rossbach covered by the ADA?

   b. Is there any argument for coverage based on "being regarded as" disabled?

   c. Is he prevented from performing a class or broad range of jobs?

Part **Three**

Regulation of the Employment Environment

Chapter **Thirteen**

The Employee's Right to Privacy and Management of Personal Information

Chapter Outline

Opening Scenarios

SCENARIO 1

Aravinda has been reading in the news lately of the skyrocketing costs of health care, particularly surrounding the HIV epidemic. She is concerned that her small 10-employee company would suffer a financial disaster if one of its workers contracted the virus since the company's insurance costs would increase. Therefore, she wants to conduct a confidential HIV test of each present employee and future applicant. Aravinda has several concerns. First, what if an individual refuses to take the test based on the grounds of invasion of privacy? Second, if someone tests positive, can Aravinda refuse to hire or can she discharge her or him without violating federal law protecting employees with disabilities? Third, how can she otherwise protect against rising costs? Fourth, if an employee tests negative but Aravinda decides to terminate the employee anyway, is she liable for the *appearance* that the employee is HIV-positive and that Aravinda terminated her or him as a consequence of the test results? How can she ensure that the test results are kept confidential?

SCENARIO 2

Solange receives a "spam" e-mail asking her to go look at a certain Web site. Since she doesn't know who it is from or why she is receiving it, she clicks on the link and finds herself at a website devoted to XXX-rated videos. She is so perturbed by this occurrence that she spends a few moments looking around the website trying to find its site administrator. She intends to send off a message to the administrator asking this person not to send her any more junk mail. After searching for several minutes with no luck, she leaves the Web site and goes back to reading her e-mail. A few days later, she is called into her manager's office and reprimanded for using employer-owned computer equipment for personal interests such as this XXX-rated video site. It seems that her manager was using a program that alerted him any time an employee perused certain inappropriate websites. She tries to explain, but leaves with a written reprimand in her hand and a copy in her files. She is furious, not only at her manager's unwillingness to understand, but also at the invasion of her privacy posed by this computer monitoring. Does her employer have a right to monitor her computer use in this way?

SCENARIO 3

Abraham, a realtor, has three children, two of whom are in college. In order to earn extra money to help with college tuition payments, Abraham (who studied modern dance during his college career) finds a job dancing in a club that caters specifically to women. While not exactly erotic dancing (he keeps all of his clothes on), it isn't ballroom dancing either. Celebrating during a bachelorette party, one of the partners of the real estate firm for which Abraham works catches sight of him dancing. When he arrives at the office the next day, she calls him into her office and orders him to quit his night job. She claims that both clients and potential clients might see him there and he would lose all credibility as a realtor. Does she have a right to require Abraham to do this as a condition of future employment? (Presume that he is an employee and not an independent contractor.)

ARE THERE GUARANTEES IN LIFE?

Philosophers have argued that our society cannot maintain its core values without simultaneously guaranteeing the privacy of the individual. Edward Bloustein writes that "an individual deprived of privacy merges with the mass. His opinions, being public, tend never to be different; his aspirations, being known, tend always to be conventionally accepted ones; his feelings, being openly exhibited, tend to lose their quality of unique personal warmth and to become the feelings of every man. Such a being, although sentient, is fungible; he is not an individual."

Recent inventions and business methods call attention to the next step that must be taken for the protection of the person and for securing to the individual what Judge Cooley calls the right "to be let alone." Instantaneous photographs and newspaper enterprises have invaded the sacred precincts of private and domestic life, and numerous mechanical devices threaten to make good the prediction that "what is whispered in the closet shall be proclaimed from the house-tops."[1]

The concept of privacy as a fundamental right is certainly not limited to the United States or even Western culture. Privacy is protected in the Qur'an[2] and was recognized by Mohammed.[3] Ancient Greece already had laws protecting privacy, and the Jewish Talmud considers privacy an aspect of one's sanctity, providing rules for protecting one's home. In fact, the Talmud contains reference to "harm caused by seeing" (*hezeq re'iyyah*) when one intrudes upon another.

But do employees actually have a "fundamental right to privacy" as many believe? The answer to this question is not as easy as one might presume, given the wide recognition of employee rights in the workplace. The right to privacy may not be as fundamental as employees generally think. This is all the more important in these days of advancing information technology. Computer technology, though largely beneficial, can have a negative effect on employees if the easily obtained information is misused, incorrect, or misleading. Employers now have a greater capacity to invade an employee's privacy than ever before. Among other devices, there are chairs that can sense and record the time an employee spends at his or her desk, computer programs that measure employees' computer keystrokes to ensure they are as productive as they should be, phones that monitor employees' phone calls, and policies related to workplace communication to make sure all communications are work-related.

But perhaps there is presently a greater employer need for seemingly private information. Drug use in American industry costs employers approximately $60 billion per year in absenteeism and attrition; theft of employer property by employees is estimated at $10 billion per year; and failure to perform an intensive reference and background check of an applicant may cost the employer enormous amounts in litigation fees defending claims of negligent hiring.

Finally, in this time of increased competition in the global marketplace, each employee becomes all the more crucial to the workings of the company. An employer has a justified basis for attempting to choose the most appropriate and qualified person for the job; the means by which the employer obtains that information, however, may be suspect.

Since erosion of at-will employment was the dominant issue of the 1980s, scholars have predicted that privacy will be the main theme for the 1990s and beyond. This chapter will address the employee's rights regarding personal information and the employer's responsibilities regarding that information, as well as the employer's right to find out both job-related and nonrelated personal information about its employees. Chapter 3 previously addressed other issues regarding the legality of information

---

[1] Warren and Brandeis, "The Right to Privacy," *Harvard Law Review* 4, no. 193 (1890).

[2] an-Noor 24, pp. 27–28 (Yusufali); al-Hujraat 49, pp. 11–12 (Yusufali).

[3] Vol. 1, Book 10, no. 509 (Sahih Bukhari); Book 31, no. 4003 (Sunan Abu Dawud).

1. Employees have an absolute right to privacy in their workplace.
2. It is a breach of an employee's right to privacy for an employer to ask with whom the employee lives.
3. In the private sector, the Constitution protects employees' right to be free from unreasonable searches and seizures.
4. Without constitutional protection, employees in the private sector are left with no protection against invasions of privacy.
5. Once an employee gives information to an employer, the employer may use it for whatever purpose it desires.

gathering through testing procedures. This chapter will not address issues relating to consumer privacy since they fall outside the scope of the chapter's primary focus.

Background

The U.S. Constitution does not actually speak of privacy, but privacy has been inferred as a necessary adjunct of other constitutional rights we hold. The right to privacy was first recognized by the Supreme Court in *Griswold* v. *Connecticut*, when the Court held that a Connecticut statute restricting a married couple's use of birth control devices unconstitutionally infringed on the right to marital privacy.

fundamental right
A right that is guaranteed by the Constitution, whether stated or not.

The Court held a constitutional guarantee of various zones of privacy as a part of the **fundamental rights** guaranteed by the Constitution, such as the right to free speech and the right to be free from unreasonable searches and seizures. The latter right is that on which many claims for privacy rights are based; the Court has held that under certain circumstances the required disclosure of certain types of personal information should be considered an unreasonable search. It has protected against the mandatory disclosure of personal papers, and it decided in favor of the right to make procreation decisions privately.

While baseless or unjustified intrusions, at first blush, may appear to be completely abhorrent in our society, proponents of the argument that employers can ask whatever they please argue that if an employee does not want to offer a piece of information, there is something the employee is trying to hide. For example, why would an employee refuse to submit to a drug test if that employee is not abusing drugs? Do **private sector** employers have the right to ask their employees any question they choose and take adverse employment actions against the employee if she or he refuses to answer since they are not necessarily constrained by constitutional protections? (See Exhibit 13.1.)

private sector
That segment of the workforce represented by private companies (companies that are not owned or managed by the government or one of its agencies).

Additionally, employees are concerned about the type of information gathered in the course of applying for and holding a job. Who has access to that information? What information may be deemed "confidential," and what does that mean to the employee? Evidently, employers perceive challenging issues among these and others with regard to privacy; as of 2004, there were more than 2,000 chief privacy officers (CPOs) in businesses around the world, more than 10 times the estimate three years ago.[4]

[4] Steve Ulfelder, "CPOs on the Rise?" *Computerworld* (March 15, 2004), http://www.computerworld.com/securitytopics/security/story/0.10801.91166.00.html, quoting Alan F. Westin, president of the nonprofit Privacy & American Business.

PUBLIC SECTOR EMPLOYEE PRIVACY

public sector
That segment of the workforce represented by governmental employers and governmental agency employers. In some situations, this term may include federal contractors.

In regard to the **public sector**, the Constitution protects individuals from wrongful invasions by the state or by an entity acting on behalf of the government. Federal, state, and local employees are therefore protected in their right of privacy from governmental intrusion and excess.

Constitutional Protection

The Fourth Amendment

For the Fourth Amendment's protection against unreasonable search and seizure to be applicable to a given situation, there must first exist a search or seizure. The Supreme Court has liberally interpreted "search" to include the retrieval of blood samples and other bodily invasions, including urinalyses, as well as the collection of other personal information.

For a search to violate the Fourth Amendment, that search must be deemed unreasonable, unjustified at its inception, and impermissible in scope. The Supreme Court in *O'Connor* v. *Ortega* held that a search was justified at its inception where the employer has

> reasonable grounds for suspecting that the search will turn up evidence that the employee is guilty of work-related misconduct, or that the search is necessary for a noninvestigatory work-related purpose such as to retrieve a file.

A search is permissible in scope where

> the measures adopted are reasonably related to the objectives of the search and not excessively intrusive in light of . . . the nature of the misconduct being investigated.

Generally, all searches that are conducted without a judicially issued warrant based on a finding of reasonable cause are held to be *per se* unreasonable. There are several exceptions to this rule, including searches incident to an arrest, some automobile searches, pat-down searches with probable cause to believe the subject is armed, and administrative searches of certain regulated industries.

In *Shoemaker* v. *Handel,* the Supreme Court held that a drug-related urine test of jockeys without a warrant was acceptable because it satisfied the court's two-pronged test. The Court held that (1) where there is a strong state interest in conducting the unannounced warrantless search and (2) where the pervasive regulation of the industry reduces the expectation of privacy, the search does not violate the Fourth Amendment. Similarly, in *Skinner* v. *Railway Labor Executives Ass'n,* 109 S. Ct. 1402 (1989), aff'd 934 F.2d 1096 (9th Cir. 1991), decided three years after *Shoemaker,* the Court again addressed the question of whether certain forms of drug and alcohol testing violate the Fourth Amendment. While this case is discussed in this text in connection with testing, it is relevant here for the Court's analysis of the privacy right challenged. In *Skinner,* the defendant justified testing railway workers based on safety concerns: "to prevent accidents and casualties in railroad operations that result from impairment of employees by alcohol or drugs." The Court held that "[t]he Government's interest in regulating the conduct of railroad employees to ensure safety, like its supervision of probationers or regulated industries, or its operation of a government office, school, or prison, likewise presents 'special needs' beyond normal law enforcement that may justify departures from the usual warrant and probable-cause requirements."

It was clear to the Court that the governmental interest in ensuring the safety of the traveling public and of the employees themselves "plainly justifies prohibiting covered employees from using alcohol or drugs on duty, or while subject to being called for duty." The issue then for the Court was whether the means by which the defendant monitored compliance with this prohibition justified the privacy intrusion absent a warrant or individualized suspicion. In reviewing the justification, the Court focused on the fact that permission to dispense with warrants is strongest where "the burden of obtaining a warrant is likely to frustrate the governmental purpose behind the search," and recognized that "alcohol and other drugs are eliminated from the bloodstream at a constant rate and blood and breath samples taken to measure whether these substances were in the bloodstream when a triggering event occurred must be obtained as soon as possible." In addition, the Court noted that the railway workers' expectations of privacy in this industry are diminished given its high scrutiny through regulation to ensure safety. The Court therefore concluded that the railway's compelling interests outweigh privacy concerns since the proposed testing "is not an undue infringement on the justifiable expectations of privacy of covered employees." Consider the possible implications of this and related decisions on genetic testing in governmental workplaces or in employment in heavily regulated industries such as that involved in *Skinner*.

Finally, the employer may wish to conduct a search of employee lockers. Would this be acceptable? Under what circumstances is an employer allowed to conduct searches? A search may constitute an invasion of privacy, depending on the nature of the employer and the purpose of the search. The unreasonableness of a search is determined by balancing the extent of the invasion and the extent to which the employee should expect to have privacy in this area against the employer's interest in the security of its workplace, the productivity of its workers, and other job-related concerns.

Prior to any search of employer-owned property, such as desks or lockers, employees should be given formal written notice of the intent to search without their consent. Where the employer intends to search personal effects, such as purses or wallets, employees should be forewarned, consent should be obtained prior to the search, and employees should be made well aware of the procedures involved. Consent is recommended under these circumstances because an employee has a greater expectation of privacy in those personal areas. These rights are significantly diminished where the employer is not restrained by constitutional protections.

When an employee is detained during a search, the employer may have a claim for *false imprisonment,* which is defined as a total restraint on freedom to move against the employee's will, such as keeping an employee in one area of an office. The employee need not be "locked" into the confinement to be restrained; but when the employee remains free to leave at any time, there is no false imprisonment.

In the following case, the Supreme Court examines the issue of whether the search of an employee's office violated the Fourth Amendment to the U.S. Constitution.

O'Connor v. Ortega *480 U.S. 709 (1987)*

Respondent, a physician and psychiatrist, was an employee of a state hospital and had primary responsibility for training physicians in the psychiatric residency program. Hospital officials became concerned about possible improprieties in his management of the program, particularly with respect to his acquisition of a computer and charges against him concerning sexual harassment of female hospital employees and inappropriate disciplinary action against a resident. In particular, the officials thought that Dr. Ortega may have misled Dr. O'Connor into believing that the computer had been donated, when in fact the computer had been financed by the possibly coerced contributions of residents. Hospital officials were concerned with charges that Dr. Ortega had sexually harassed two female hospital employees, and that he had taken inappropriate disciplinary action against a resident.

While he was on administrative leave pending investigation of the charges, hospital officials, allegedly in order to inventory and secure state property, searched his office and seized personal items from his desk and file cabinets that were used in administrative proceedings resulting in his discharge. No formal inventory of the property in the office was ever made, and all the other papers in the office were merely placed in boxes for storage. The employee filed an action against the hospital officials under 42 U.S.C. §1983, alleging that the search of his office violated the Fourth Amendment. The trial court found that the search was proper in order to secure state property. The court of appeals held that the employee had a reasonable expectation of privacy in his office, and thus the search violated the Fourth Amendment. The Supreme Court agrees.

O'Connor, J.

This suit under 42 U.S.C. § 1983 presents two issues concerning the Fourth Amendment rights of public employees. First, we must determine whether the respondent, a public employee, had a reasonable expectation of privacy in his office, desk, and file cabinets at his place of work. Second, we must address the appropriate Fourth Amendment standard for a search conducted by a public employer in areas in which a public employee is found to have a reasonable expectation of privacy.

* * *

We granted certiorari and now reverse and remand.

* * *

The Fourth Amendment protects the "right of the people to be secure in their persons, houses, papers, and effects, against unreasonable searches and seizures. . . ." Our cases establish that Dr. Ortega's Fourth Amendment rights are implicated only if the conduct of the Hospital officials at issue in this case infringed "an expectation of privacy that society is prepared to consider reasonable.". . .

Because the reasonableness of an expectation of privacy, as well as the appropriate standard for a search, is understood to differ according to context, it is essential first to delineate the boundaries of the workplace context. The workplace includes those areas and items that are related to work and are generally within the employer's control. At a hospital, for example, the hallways, cafeteria, offices, desks, and file cabinets, among other areas, are all part of the workplace. These areas remain part of the workplace context even if the employee has placed personal items in them, such as a photograph placed in a desk or a letter posted on an employee bulletin board.

Not everything that passes through the confines of the business address can be considered part of the workplace context, however. . . . The appropriate standard for a workplace search does not necessarily apply to a piece of closed personal luggage, a handbag or a briefcase that happens to be within the employer's business address.

* * *

Given the societal expectations of privacy in one's place of work, we reject the contention made by the Solicitor General and petitioners that public employees can never have a reasonable expectation of privacy in their place of work. Individuals do not lose Fourth Amendment rights merely because they work for the government instead of a private employer. The operational realities of the workplace, however, may make some employees' expectations of privacy unreasonable when an intrusion is by a supervisor rather than a law enforcement official. Public employees' expectations of privacy in their offices, desks, and file cabinets, like similar expectations of employees in the private sector, may be reduced by virtue of actual office practices and procedures, or by legitimate regulation. The employee's expectation of privacy must be assessed in the context of the employment relation. An office is seldom a private enclave free from entry by supervisors, other employees, and business and personal invitees. Instead, in many cases offices are continually entered by fellow employees and other visitors during the workday for conferences, consultations, and other work-related visits. Simply put, it is the nature of government offices that others—such as fellow employees, supervisors, consensual visitors, and the general public—may have frequent access to an individual's office. . . .

The undisputed evidence discloses that Dr. Ortega did not share his desk or file cabinets with any other employees. Dr. Ortega had occupied the office for 17 years and he kept materials in his office, which included personal correspondence, medical files, correspondence from private patients unconnected to the Hospital, personal financial records, teaching aids and notes, and personal gifts and mementos. The files on physicians in residency training were kept outside Dr. Ortega's office. Indeed, the only items found by the investigators were apparently personal items because, with the exception of the items seized for use in the administrative hearings, all the papers and effects found in the office were simply placed in boxes and made available to Dr. Ortega. Finally, we note that there was no evidence that the Hospital had established any reasonable regulation or policy discouraging employees such as Dr. Ortega from storing personal papers and effects in their desks or file cabinets, although the absence of such a policy does not create an expectation of privacy where it would not otherwise exist.

On the basis of this undisputed evidence, we accept the conclusion of the Court of Appeals that Dr. Ortega had a reasonable expectation of privacy at least in his desk and file cabinets.

Having determined that Dr. Ortega had a reasonable expectation of privacy in his office, . . . we must determine the appropriate standard of reasonableness applicable to the search. A determination of the standard of reasonableness applicable to a particular class of searches requires "balanc[ing] the nature and quality of the intrusion on the individual's Fourth Amendment interests against the importance of the governmental interests alleged to justify the intrusion." In the case of searches conducted by a public employer, we must balance the invasion of the employees' legitimate expectations of privacy against the government's need for supervision, control, and the efficient operation of the workplace.

✳ ✳ ✳

The governmental interest justifying work-related intrusions by public employers is the efficient and proper operation of the workplace. Government agencies provide myriad services to the public, and the work of these agencies would suffer if employers were required to have probable cause before they entered an employee's desk for the purpose of finding a file or piece of office correspondence. Indeed, it is difficult to give the concept of probable cause, rooted as it is in the criminal investigatory context, much meaning when the purpose of a search is to retrieve a file for work-related reasons. Similarly, the concept of probable cause has little meaning for a routine inventory conducted by public employers for the purpose of securing state property. To ensure the efficient and proper operation of the agency, therefore, public employers must be given wide latitude to enter employee offices for work-related, noninvestigatory reasons.

We come to a similar conclusion for searches conducted pursuant to an investigation of work-related employee misconduct. Even when employers conduct an investigation, they have an interest substantially different from "the normal need for law enforcement." Public employers have an interest in ensuring that their agencies operate in an effective and efficient manner, and the work of these agencies inevitably suffers from the inefficiency, incompetence, mismanagement, or other work-related misfeasance of its employees. Indeed, in many cases, public employees are entrusted with tremendous responsibility, and the consequences of their misconduct or incompetence to both the agency and the public interest can be severe. . . . Public employers have a direct and overriding interest in ensuring that the work of the agency is conducted in a proper and efficient manner. In our view, therefore, a probable cause requirement for searches of the type at issue here would impose intolerable burdens on public employers. The delay in correcting the employee misconduct caused by the need for probable cause rather than reasonable suspicion will be translated into tangible and often irreparable damage to the agency's work, and ultimately to the public interest. Additionally, while law enforcement officials are expected to "schoo[l] themselves in the niceties of probable cause," no such expectation is generally applicable to public employers, at least when the search is not used to gather evidence of a criminal offense. It is simply unrealistic to expect supervisors in most government agencies to learn the subtleties of the probable cause standard. . . .

Balanced against the substantial government interests in the efficient and proper operation of the workplace are the privacy interests of government employees in their place of work which, while not insubstantial, are far less than those found at home or in some other contexts. . . . The employer intrusions at issue here "involve a relatively limited invasion" of employee privacy. Government offices are provided to employees for the sole purpose of facilitating the work of an agency. The employee may avoid exposing personal belongings at work by simply leaving them at home.

. . . We hold . . . that public employer intrusions on the constitutionally protected privacy interests of government employees for noninvestigatory, work-related purposes, as well as for investigations of work-related misconduct, should be judged by the standard of reasonableness under all the circumstances. Under this reasonableness standard, both the inception and the scope of the intrusion must be reasonable:

> Determining the reasonableness of any search involves a twofold inquiry: first, one must consider "whether the . . . action was justified at its inception," second, one must determine whether the search as actually conducted "was reasonably related in scope to the circumstances which justified the interference in the first place."

Ordinarily, a search of an employee's office by a supervisor will be "justified at its inception" when there are reasonable grounds for suspecting that the search will turn up evidence that the employee is guilty of work-related misconduct, or that the search is necessary for a noninvestigatory work-related purpose such as to retrieve a needed file. Because petitioners had an "individualized suspicion" of misconduct by Dr. Ortega, we need not decide whether individualized suspicion is an essential element of the standard of reasonableness that we adopt today. The search will be permissible in its scope when "the measures adopted are reasonably related to the objectives of the search and not excessively intrusive in light of . . . the nature of the [misconduct]."

* * *

On remand, therefore, the District Court must determine the justification for the search and seizure, and evaluate the reasonableness of both the inception of the search and its scope.

Accordingly, the judgment of the Court of Appeals is REVERSED and the case is REMANDED to that court for further proceedings consistent with this opinion.

Case Questions

1. Do you think the standard of the search articulated in this opinion is the correct standard for determining whether a search violates the Fourth Amendment? Think of arguments for both perspectives—the employer and employee.

2. How can an employer protect itself from a claim of an unreasonable search conducted in the workplace? Note the court stated that a policy regarding this issue was not a determinative factor in determining the constitutionality of the search.

3. What could you do as an employee to protect yourself from a company search?

The 5th and 14th Amendments

The 5th and 14th Amendments also protect a government employee's right to privacy in that the state may not restrict one's rights unless it is justified. For instance, the Supreme Court has consistently held that everyone has a fundamental right to travel, free of government intervention. Where the state attempts to infringe on anything that has been determined to be a fundamental right, that infringement or restriction is subject to the *strict scrutiny* of the courts. For the restriction to be allowed, the state must show that the restriction is justified by a *compelling state interest*. Moreover, the restriction must be the least intrusive alternative available.

On the other hand, for those interests not deemed by the courts to constitute fundamental rights, a state may impose any restrictions that can be shown to be *rationally related to a valid state interest,* a much more lenient test.

To determine whether the state may restrict or intrude on an employee's privacy rights, it must first be determined whether the claimed right is fundamental. Two tests are used to make this determination. First, the court may look to whether the right is "implicit in the concept of ordered liberty, such that neither liberty nor justice would exist if [the rights] were sacrificed." Second is whether the right is "deeply rooted in this Nation's history and tradition."

While conception, child rearing, education, and marriage have been held to be within the area of privacy protected by the Constitution, other issues have not yet been addressed or determined by the Court, including the right to be free from mandatory preemployment medical tests. Moreover, the Court has found *no* general right of the individual to be left alone.

The Privacy Act of 1974

Governmental intrusion into the lives of federal employees is also restricted by the Privacy Act of 1974. Much of the discussion in the area of employee privacy is framed by governmental response to the issue, both because of limitations imposed on the government regarding privacy and because of the potential for abuse. The Privacy Act of 1974 regulates the release of personal information about federal employees by federal agencies. Specifically, but for 11 stated exceptions, no federal agency may release information about an employee that contains the means for identifying that employee without the employee's prior written consent. (See Exhibit 13.2.)

There are four basic principles that underly the Privacy Act:

1. Employees should have access to their own personnel files, and there should be some way for them to find out the purposes for which the files are being used.
2. There should be some mechanism by which an employee may correct or amend an inaccurate record.
3. The employee should be able to prevent information from being inappropriately revealed or used without her or his consent, unless such disclosure is required by law.
4. The person who is in charge of maintaining the information must ensure that the files are not falling into the wrong hands and that the information contained within the files is accurate, reliable, and used for the correct reasons.

By affording the employee with these rights, Congress has effectively put the right of disclosure of personal information in the hands of the employee, at least when none of the 11 specified exceptions applies.

When one of the Privacy Act exceptions applies, the act dismisses the employee consent requirement, which gives the agency total control over the use of the file. The right to privacy is not absolute; the extent of protection varies with the extent of the intrusion, and the interests of the employee are balanced against the interests of the employer. Basically, the information requested under either the Privacy Act or the Freedom of Information Act is subject to a balancing test weighing the need to know the information against the employee's privacy interest.

Exhibit 13.2

Privacy Act of 1974

No Agency shall disclose any record which is contained in a system of records by any means of communication to any person, or to another agency, except pursuant to a written request by, or with the prior written consent of, the individual to whom the record pertains, unless disclosure of the record would be

1. To those officers and employees of the agency which maintains the record who have a need for the record in the performance of their duties.
2. Required under section 552 of this title; *(the Freedom of Information Act). (Note that this act does not apply to "personnel, medical, and similar files the disclosure of which would constitute a clearly unwarranted invasion of personal privacy.")*
3. Or a routine use as defined in subsection (a)(7) of this section and described under subsection (e)(4)(D) of this section; *(a purpose that is specifically compatible with the purpose for which the information was gathered).*
4. To the Bureau of the Census for purposes of planning or carrying out a census or survey or related activity. . . .
5. To a recipient who has provided the agency with advance adequate written assurance that the record will be used solely as a statistical research or reporting record, and the record is to be transferred in a form that is not individually identifiable.
6. To the National Archives of the United States as a record which has sufficient historical or other value to warrant its continued preservation by the United States Government, or for evaluation by the Administrator of General Services or his designee to determine whether the record has such value.
7. To another federal agency or to an instrumentality of any government jurisdiction within or under the control of the United States for a civil or criminal law enforcement activity if the activity is authorized by law, and if the head of the agency or instrumentality has made a written request to the agency which maintains the record specifying the particular portion desired and the law enforcement activity for which the record is sought.
8. To a person pursuant to a showing of compelling circumstances affecting the health or safety of an individual if upon such disclosure notification is transmitted to the last known address of such individual.
9. To either House of Congress, or, to the extent of matter within its jurisdiction, any committee or subcommittee thereof, any joint committee or subcommittee of any such joint committee.
10. To the Comptroller General, or any of his authorized representatives, in the course of the performance of the duties of the General Accounting Office.
11. Pursuant to the order of a court of competent jurisdiction.

The Ninth Circuit Court of Appeals has developed guidelines to assist in this balancing test. The court directs that the following four factors be looked to in reaching a conclusion relating to disclosure:

1. The individual's interest in disclosure of the information sought.
2. The public interest in disclosure.
3. The degree of invasion of personal privacy.
4. Whether there are alternative means of getting the information.

Critics of the act suggest that it is enormously weakened as a result of one particular exemption that allows disclosure for "routine use" compatible with the reason the information was originally collected. In addition, certain specific agencies are exempted. For instance, in March 2003, the Department of Justice exempted the National Crime Information Center, which is a resource for 80,000 law enforcement agencies.

The Privacy Act grants employees two options for relief: criminal penalties and civil remedies, including damages and injunctive relief. The act also allows employees who are adversely affected by an agency's noncompliance to bring a civil suit against the agency in federal court.

Privacy Protection Study Commission

The Privacy Protection Study Commission was formed by Congress with the purpose of studying the possibility of extending the Privacy Act to the private sector. In 1977, the commission concluded that the Privacy Act should not be extended to private employers but that private sector employees should be given many new privacy protections. The suggested protections required a determination of current information-gathering practices and their reasons, a limitation on the information that may be collected to what is relevant, a requirement that the employer inform its employees to ensure accuracy, and a limitation on the usage of the information gathered both internally and externally.

The commission further found that certain issues demanded federal intervention and, for this reason, recommended that (1) the use of polygraph tests in employment-related issues be prohibited; (2) pretext interviews be prohibited; (3) the use of arrest or criminal records in employment decisions be prohibited except where otherwise allowed or required by law; (4) employers be required to use reasonable care in selection of their investigating agencies; and (5) the Federal Fair Credit Reporting Act provisions be strengthened. These recommendations have yet to be implemented by Congress, primarily due to private employers' vocal rejection of such an extension of federal law due to the cost of the implementation of the recommendations.

The commission has since established three general policy goals: (1) to attempt to create a balance between what an employee will divulge to the recordkeeping department and what that employee seeks in return for his information; (2) to find a manner by which to ensure fairness to all employees, in that the information that has been processed will not be used against them; and (3) to create and define rules regarding the type of information that may be disclosed and those to whom the information may be given.

Many large corporations have embraced privacy protection programs on their own in accordance with recommendations from the Privacy Commission and in anticipation of federal regulation. In light of this advance implementation, the Privacy Commission recommends that any program guarantee five basic employee procedural rights. The list includes:

- Notice
- Authorization
- Access
- Correction
- Confidentiality

Though the list seems rather specific, the problem lies within the depth and scope of each component.

Federal Wiretapping—Title III

Title III, as amended (particularly by the Electronic Communications Privacy Act of 1986), is codified at Title 18 U.S.C. §§2510–2521. These statutes provide privacy protection for and govern the interception of oral, wire, and electronic communications. Title III covers all telephone communications regardless of the medium, except that it does not cover the radio portion of a cordless telephone communication that is transmitted between the handset and base unit. The law authorizes the interception of oral, wire, and electronic communications by investigative and law enforcement officers conducting criminal investigations pertaining to serious criminal offenses, or felonies, following the issuance of a court order by a judge. The Title III law authorizes the interception of particular criminal communications related to particular criminal offenses. In short, it authorizes the acquisition of evidence of crime. It does not authorize noncriminal intelligence gathering, nor does it authorize interceptions related to social or political views.

Thirty-seven states have statutes permitting interceptions by state and local law enforcement officers for certain types of criminal investigations. All of the state statutes are based upon Title III, from which they derive. These statutes must be at least as restrictive as Title III, and in fact most are more restrictive in their requirements. In describing the legal requirements, we will focus on those of Title III since they define the baseline for all wiretaps performed by federal, state, and local law enforcement agencies. In recent years, state statutes have been modified to keep pace with rapid technological advances in telecommunications. For example, New Jersey amended its electronic surveillance statute in 1993 to include cellular telephones, cordless telephones, digital display beepers, fax transmissions, computer-to-computer communications, and traces obtained through "caller-ID."

Wiretaps are limited to the crimes specified in Title III and state statutes. Most wiretaps are large undertakings, requiring a substantial use of resources. In 1992, the average cost of installing intercept devices and monitoring communications was $46,492. Despite budget constraints and personnel shortages, law enforcement conducts wiretaps as necessary, but obviously, because of staffing and costs, judiciously.

Electronic Communications Privacy Act (ECPA)

At first, Title III was created to combat invasion of the government for eavesdropping in large part due to the Watergate scandal in the 1970s. Originally the federal statutes targeted government eavesdropping on telephone discussion without the consent of the speakers. The federal statute required the government agents to obtain a warrant before they could intercept any oral discussions (though in 2003 no wiretap applications were denied). In late 1986, Congress increased the coverage by broadening the range of electronic communications, resulting in the ECPA.

The ECPA covers all forms of digital communications, including transmissions of text and digitalized images, in addition to voice communications on the telephone. The law also prohibits unauthorized eavesdropping by all persons and businesses, not only

Scenario

the government. In addition, the ECPA prohibits unauthorized access to messages in storage on a computer system, and unauthorized interception of messages in transmission. However, an employer does not violate the ECPA when it opens and reads employee e-mails on its own system.[5]

PRIVATE SECTOR EMPLOYEE PRIVACY

Despite the fact that public and private employers have a similar legitimate need for information about applicants and employees to make informed decisions about hiring, promotion, security, discipline, and termination, privacy rights in the private sector of employment are limited; "the employment relationship generally denies any right to the employee who is arbitrarily treated [by his employer and is] . . . without a union or contract."

The distinction between the treatment of employees in the private and public sectors is one that is created by the constitutional requirement of *state action* as precedent to its application. The Constitution is a limitation made to curb *government* excesses.

Whether there should be a right to privacy in both the public and the private sectors, employers suggest that the employee has three choices when faced with objectionable intrusions by employers: quit, comply, or object and risk termination. Employees argue that they are defenseless because of their economic condition and that their privacy in the private sector is subject to greater abuse precisely because there are no protections and the option to quit is unrealistic.

One explanation offered for the difference between public and private sector privacy protections is compliance-related costs. The implementation of the Privacy Act throughout its agencies costs the government relatively little, because it is conducting self-regulation.

By contrast, ensuring compliance within the private sector requires administration of the compliance and adjudication of violations. The Privacy Protection Study Commission found that requiring an employer to change its manner of maintaining and using records can drastically increase the cost of operation.

These costs include the costs of changing employment recordkeeping practices, removing relevant information from employment decisions, and implementing a social policy of employee privacy protection. These costs are not necessarily "burdensome" to the employer, however. One study found that protecting the rights of employees on a computer system could cost as little as $4 per person. Employers' concern for compliance costs may well be an unrealistic barrier to the development of regulations for privacy rights of private sector employees.

A second distinction between public and private sector employers offered to justify different privacy standards is that more stringent regulation is needed for government employees, because it is common for federal agencies to be overzealous in

---

[5] *Fraser v. National Mutual Insurance,* 352 F.3d 107 (3d Cir. 2003). See also *United States v. Steiger,* 318 F.3d 1039 (11th Cir. 2003); *Konop v. Hawaiian Airlines, Inc.,* 302 F.3d 868 (9th Cir. 2002); and *Steve Jackson Games, Inc. v. U.S. Secret Serv.,* 36 F.3d 457 (5th Cir. 1994).

surveillance and information gathering. Private sector employers, in contrast, do not generally have similar resources and, therefore, are unable to duplicate these invasive activities.

Bases for Right to Privacy in the Private Sector

Private sector employers are not bound by constitutional structures. On a state-by-state basis, however, private sector employees may be afforded protection either by the **common law** or by statute. All but two states provide common-law tort claims to protect individual privacy, such as intrusion into seclusion. Various torts described below have developed to protect individual solitude, the publication of private information, and publications that present personal information in a false light.

common law
Law made and applied by judges, based on precedent (prior case law).

Statutory Claims

State legislatures have responded to the issue of private sector employee privacy in one of four ways:

1. Enacting legislation mirroring federal law regarding the compilation and dissemination of information.
2. Recognizing a constitutional right to privacy under their state constitutions, as in California, Illinois, and Arizona. For example, California appellate courts have found that employees terminated for refusing to submit to drug tests were wrongfully discharged in violation of the state's constitutional guarantee of a right to privacy, which requires employers to demonstrate a compelling interest in invading an employee's privacy. In Pennsylvania, a court held that a drug test violates that state's policy against invasions of privacy where the methods used do not give due regard to the employee's privacy or if the test results disclose medical information beyond what is necessary. Other states that provide constitutional recognition and protection of privacy rights include Alabama, Arizona, Florida, Hawaii, Illinois, Louisiana, Montana, South Carolina, and Washington. However, in all states except California, application of this provision to private sector organizations is limited, uncertain, or not included at all.
3. Protecting employees only in certain areas of employment, such as personnel records or the use of credit information.
4. Leaving private sector employees to fend for themselves while the federal laws and the Constitution afford protection to federal employees and those subject to state action.

Tort Law Protections/Common Law   As mentioned above, courts in almost all states have developed case law, the "common law," which identifies certain torts in connection with private sector invasion of privacy. Georgia was the first jurisdiction whose courts recognized a common law right to privacy. As the court explained in *Pavesich* v. *New England Life Ins. Co.,* 50 S.E. 68 (Ga. 1905), "a right of privacy is derived from natural law, recognized by municipal law, and its existence can be inferred from expressions used by commentators and writers on the law as well as judges in decided cases. The right of privacy is embraced within the absolute rights of personal security and personal liberty." Though some states rely on statutory protections rather than common

tort
Private (civil)
wrong against a
person or her or
his property.

law, only two states—North Dakota and Wyoming—fail to recognize *any* of the four privacy torts discussed in this chapter.[6] A **tort** is a legal wrong, for which the law offers a remedy. The torts of particular interest in this chapter include intrusion into solitude or seclusion, the publication of private information, and publication that places another in a false light. Defamation will also be discussed.

Publication as used in these torts means not only publishing the information in a newspaper or other mass media but generally "bringing it to light" or disseminating the information. In addition, the concept of publication is defined slightly differently depending on the tort. Truth and absence of malice are generally not acceptable defenses by an employer sued for invasion of an employee's privacy. They are acceptable, however, in connection with claims of defamation.

Intrusion into Seclusion   To state a prima facie case for the tort of intrusion into seclusion, the plaintiff employee must show that:

- The defendant employer intentionally intruded into a private area.
- The plaintiff was entitled to privacy in that area.
- The intrusion would be objectionable to a person of reasonable sensitivity.

The intrusion may occur in any number of ways. An employer may:

- Verbally request information as a condition of employment.
- Require that its employees provide information in other ways such as through polygraphs, drug tests, or psychological tests.
- Require an annual medical examination.
- Ask others personal information about its employees.
- Go into private places belonging to the employee.

Any of these methods may constitute a wrongful invasion where it so invades the employee's private sphere that it would be objectionable to a reasonable person. On the other hand, if the employer can articulate a justifying business purpose for the inquiry/invasion, the conduct is more likely to be deemed acceptable.

In *Rogers* v. *Loews L'Enfant Plaza Hotel,* an employee was continually sexually harassed by her supervisor, including bothersome telephone calls to her home, during which he made lewd comments to her about her personal sex life. The sexual harassment evolved into harassment in the workplace, where the supervisor verbally abused her in front of her coworkers, kept important business-related information from her, and refused to include her in meetings. Her employer, refusing to take formal action, suggested that she change positions. The court determined that the telephone calls were not of a benign nature but, instead, were unreasonably intrusive and not normally expected. Further, the harassment constituted an intrusion into a sphere from which the employee could reasonably exclude the defendant. On these bases, the court found in favor of the employee.

In connection with scenario 1, Aravinda's decision in connection with the HIV tests may be governed in part by the law relating to employment testing as discussed in Chapter 14 and in part by the law relating to disability discrimination as

Scenario

---

[6] *Lake* v. *Wal-Mart Stores, Inc.,* 582 N.W.2d 231 (Minn. 1998).

discussed in Chapter 13 (since HIV is considered a disability under the Americans with Disabilities Act). On the other hand, the law relating to intrusion into seclusion would also have application here in terms of disclosure of the test results. If Aravinda discloses the results to anyone or, through her actions, leads someone to a belief about the employee's HIV status, she might be liable under this tort. In addition, it is important to consider that it is highly unlikely that Aravinda has any right to know any employee's HIV status as it is unlikely that the information would be job-related. (Can you imagine what employment position might warrant this type of information? Is HIV status ever considered job related?)

The following case explores the prima facie case for intrusion into seclusion.

Pearson v. Kancilia   *70 P.3d 594 (Colo. App. 2003)*

A chiropractor's employee (Pearson) brought outrageous conduct and invasion of privacy claims against the chiropractor (Kancilia), alleging that he forced her to have sex with him. The district court held that there was sufficient evidence supporting the employee's claim against the chiropractor for unreasonable intrusion upon the seclusion of another.

Dailey, J.

Pearson was subjected by Kancilia to unwanted jokes of a sexual nature, unwanted sexual advances, and unwanted sexual contact. Although she admitted her first sexual encounter was consensual, she related that she thereafter repeatedly told him that she did not want to have sex with him. Nonetheless, he demanded that she continue having sex with him at both her apartment and his office. She maintained she did so because she felt she had no choice in the matter: as his employee, she was afraid of losing her job if she refused him sex. She based her fear upon defendant being the type of person who "if you didn't scratch his back, he wouldn't scratch yours." Defendant made such a remark when Pearson eventually absolutely refused to have sex with him. Thereafter, according to Pearson, defendant fully exposed his penis to her at the office on several occasions.

The jury awarded Pearson $237,685 in compensatory damages on her chiropractic negligence claim, $100,000 in compensatory and punitive damages on her claim for outrageous conduct, and $200,000 in compensatory and punitive damages on her claim for invasion of privacy. Kancilia appeals only that part of the judgment concerning plaintiff's claims for outrageous conduct and invasion of privacy

* * *

B. INVASION OF PRIVACY

Defendant next contends that the trial court erred in submitting Pearson's invasion of privacy claim to the jury. We disagree.

In Colorado, "invasion of privacy" encompasses three separate torts: (1) unreasonable intrusion upon the seclusion of another ("seclusion"); (2) unreasonable publicity given to another's private life ("disclosure"); and (3) appropriation of another's name or likeness ("appropriation").

Here, we are concerned with seclusion. To prevail on such a claim, "a plaintiff must show that another has intentionally intruded, physically or otherwise, upon the plaintiff's seclusion or solitude, and that such intrusion would be considered offensive by a reasonable person."

The absence of a definitive refusal to engage in sex does not defeat as a matter of law a claim for invasion of privacy.

In *Doe* v. *High-Tech Institute. Inc.,* the division adopted the test articulated in *Restatement (Second) of Torts §652B (1981),* namely, that liability is to be imposed "if the intrusion would be highly offensive to a reasonable person." The division further stated, "Although intrusion upon seclusion clearly encompasses an intrusion upon a physical space held in seclusion by a person, the element of seclusion also encompasses intrusions into a person's private concerns based upon a reasonable expectation of privacy in that area."

Pearson based her invasion of privacy claim on evidence that defendant repeatedly came to her apartment early in the morning and demanded to have sex with her. Initially, he arrived with very little advance warning, and he came to her apartment for sex three times a week.

Defendant maintains that he went to Pearson's apartment pursuant to his romantic, sexual relationship with her. However, the jury was free to determine which version of the facts it would accept. As noted by the trial court in denying defendant's motion for directed verdict:

> The facts do establish a reasonable inference that when the Defendant allegedly went to the Plaintiff Pearson's home, [he] went there for the purpose of engaging in sex, and went there purportedly against her will, and she let him in because of the employment relationship and the fear of losing her job; that could amount to a reasonable juror concluding that there has been an intrusion on her solitude.

Pearson's psychologist testified that defendant "now was intruding into her private space" and that "[o]ur homes are our sanctuaries . . . [a]nd now he has demonstrated to her not only can he control her and manipulate and maneuver her during her work hours, but he can now do this in her own residence, her own domicile, her own safe place."

Under the circumstances, we reject defendant's contention that the evidence was insufficient to support the verdict on Pearson's invasion of privacy claim.

Case Questions

1. If the violation occurs where "the intrusion would be highly offensive to a reasonable person," isn't every case of sexual harassment that involves an intrusion into private space an invasion of privacy under this construct?

2. Do you see a distinction where the intrusion is part of a consensual, romantic relationship? Is the inquiry for a privacy violation any different than that of a claim of sexual harassment?

3. What other circumstances could you expect to see a claim upheld for intrusion into seclusion in the workplace context?

Public Disclosure of Private Facts To state a prima facie case for the tort of public disclosure of private facts, the plaintiff employee must show that:

- There was an intentional or negligent public disclosure
- Of private matters, and
- Such disclosure would be objectionable to a reasonable person of ordinary sensitivities.

The information disclosed must not be already publicized in any way, nor can it be information the plaintiff has consented to publish. Therefore, in *Pemberton* v. *Bethlehem Steel Corp.,* publication of an employee's criminal record did not constitute public disclosure of private facts because the criminal record did not contain private facts; it was information that was already accessible by the public.

The public disclosure must be either communication to the public at large or to so many people that the matter must be regarded as substantially certain to become one of public knowledge or one of knowledge to a particular public whose knowledge of the private facts would be embarrassing to the employee. Therefore, publication to all of the employees in a company may be sufficient, while disclosure to a limited number of supervisors may not.

Several states have enacted legislation codifying this common-law doctrine under the rubric of "breach of confidentiality." Connecticut, for instance, has passed legislation requiring employers to maintain employee medical records separate from other personnel records. Other states have limited an employer's ability to disclose personnel-related information or allowed a cause of action where, through the employer's negligent maintenance of personnel files, inaccurate employee information is communicated to a third party.

Yoder v. Ingersoll-Rand Company a.k.a. ARO *31 F. Supp. 2d 565 (W.D. Ohio 1997)*

An employee brings suit against the employer for disclosing to the employee's mother that he had AIDS. The court dismissed this action for invasion of privacy and other claims.

Katz, J.

Lavern Yoder brought an action against his employer to recover for damages he alleged were caused as a result of Defendant's failure to keep his medical records confidential. Lavern Yoder was employed by Defendant as a tow motor driver. Around November 1993, Yoder learned that he was HIV-positive. Yoder made every effort to keep his HIV-positive status confidential from his employer because he was concerned that he might suffer adverse employment consequences if his employer or co-workers learned of his condition. In August 1995, Yoder's doctor recommended that he take a medical leave of absence because of stress-induced asthma. He obtained the necessary disability form. One side required completion by the employee; the other side required completion by the treating physician. After Yoder completed his information, the doctor completed his side but omitted the date of total disability. When the form was returned to Yoder, he forwarded the information to his doctor with an envelope with his employer's address on it. Yoder did not specifically direct it to the hourly disability coordinator, Mary Sullivan.

For reasons unknown to the parties, the envelope was returned to the employer undelivered to the doctor. The firm's procedure for mail without an individual name is for the mail clerk to open it. The mail clerk opened the envelope in order to determine where it should be routed, and read enough of its contents to find Yoder's name. The mail clerk did not read the document further. She replaced the Disability Benefit Request form in the envelope, placed that envelope in a large goldenrod interoffice envelope, put Yoder's name on the interoffice envelope, and routed it to him via his supervisor. Because Yoder was not at work that day, his supervisor received the interoffice envelope. The su-

pervisor noticed that the inner envelope was addressed to the Medical College of Ohio, and thought it might contain urgent information. He did not open the envelope. Since Yoder was not at work, his supervisor gave the envelope to Yoder's mother, who also worked for the firm, and directed her to give to him. Later that day, Yoder's mother opened the envelope and read its contents. She learned from the Physician's Statement that he had AIDS. She had known her son was HIV-positive but did not know he had AIDS. Yoder brought a six-count complaint against the firm for permitting the unauthorized disclosure of his medical condition. Count three alleged the disclosure violated his Fourteenth Amendment right to privacy under the Constitution and count four alleged state common law claim for invasion of privacy. Both sides moved for summary judgment.

* * *

D. FOURTEENTH AMENDMENT PRIVACY RIGHT

In Count III, Plaintiff alleges that the disclosure violated his Fourteenth Amendment right to privacy under the United States Constitution. However, the Fourteenth Amendment applies only to governmental action, and Defendant is not a governmental agency. Defendant's motion for summary judgment on Count III is granted.

E. INVASION OF PRIVACY

In Count IV, Plaintiff brings a common law claim for invasion of privacy. . . .

Ohio courts recognize the tort of invasion of privacy to encompass four distinct types of wrongful acts: (1) intrusion into the plaintiff's seclusion, solitude, or private affairs; (2) public disclosure of private facts about the plaintiff with which the public has no legitimate concern; (3) publicity that places the plaintiff in a false light; and (4) appropriation of the plaintiff's name or likeness for the defendant's advantage.

Yoder alleges an invasion of privacy under the second theory, which is also known as the "publicity" tort. In order successfully to make out a claim under the "publicity" prong, Plaintiff must show five elements:

(1) there must be publicity, i.e., the disclosure must be of a public nature, not private;

(2) the facts disclosed must be those concerning the private life of an individual, not his public life;

(3) the matter publicized must be one which would be highly offensive and objectionable to a reasonable person of ordinary sensibilities;

(4) the publication must have been made intentionally, not negligently; and

(5) the matter publicized must not be a legitimate concern to the public.

Plaintiff can show neither the first nor the fourth element of this test. As to the first element, Plaintiff can prevail only if he shows that the matter has been communicated to "the public at large, or to so many persons that the matter must be regarded as substantially certain to become one of public knowledge." It is not enough to show merely that the matter was communicated by the defendant to a third person. The record evidence indicates that Plaintiff's HIV/AIDS status was actually communicated to only one unauthorized person. Even if the Court accepts Plaintiff's argument that mail clerk Kornrumpf and supervisor Chroninger should be treated as having received the information because they had the opportunity to read Plaintiff's medical report, the information was communicated to three people at most. Three people do not constitute "the public at large." Plaintiff cannot meet the publicity prong of the test.

As to the fourth element, Plaintiff cannot show that Defendant, or its authorized agents, made the disclosure intentionally, even as to Plaintiff's mother. It is undisputed that nothing on the outside of the envelope received in the ARO mail room indicated that it contained a confidential medical record. Kornrumpf's testimony that she did not read the form beyond Plaintiff's name, and did not know that it was a confidential medical record, is undisputed. Chroninger's testimony that he did not read the form, and did not know that it was a confidential medical record, is undisputed. It is a logical impossibility for a party intentionally to disclose information that it does not know it has. Furthermore, the disclosure would not have occurred without Plaintiff's mother's intervening act of opening and reading the medical records without authorization from Defendant. Plaintiff cannot meet the intent prong of the test. Defendant's motion for summary judgment on Count IV is granted.

* * *

Plaintiff's motion for summary judgment is DENIED. Defendant's motion for summary judgment is GRANTED.

Case Questions

1. Do you think Yoder should have prevailed on his state law claim of invasion of privacy? Why or why not?

2. Do you think this case would have been decided differently if the mail clerk and Yoder's supervisor did read the doctor's statements?

3. How many people would have to read a sensitive document such as this to meet the public disclosure requirement for an individual to prevail on his or her claim?

Publication in a False Light   The prima facie case of publication in a false light requires that there was a public disclosure of facts that place the employee in a false light before the public if the false light would be highly offensive to a reasonable person and the person providing the information had knowledge of or recklessly disregarded the falsity or false light of the publication.

Voluntary consent to publication of the information constitutes an absolute bar to a false light action. This type of tort differs from defamation, where disclosure to even one other person than the employer or employee satisfies the requirements. The tort of publicizing someone in a false light requires that the general public be given a false image of the employee. In a false light action, the damage for which the employee is compensated is the inability to be left alone, with injury to one's emotions and mental suffering, while defamation compensates the employee for injury to his or her reputation in the public's perception.

Note that any of the above claims may be waived by the employee if the employee also publishes the information or willingly or knowingly permits it to be published. For example, in *Cummings* v. *Walsh Construction Co.,* the employee complained of public disclosure of embarrassing private facts, consisting of information relating to a sexual relationship in which she was engaged with her supervisor. The court held that, where the employee had informed others of her actions, she waived her right not to have her supervisor disclose the nature of their relationship.

As with defamation, an exception to this waiver exists in the form of compelled self-publication, where an employer provides the employee with a false reason as the basis for termination and the employee is compelled to restate this reason when asked by a future employer the basis of departure from the previous job. Therefore, where the employer intentionally misstates the basis for the discharge, that employer may be subject to liability for libel, because it is aware that the employee will be forced to repeat (or "publish") that reason to others.

Breach of Contract   An employee may also contest an invasion of privacy by her or his employer on the basis of a breach of contract. The contract may be an actual employment contract, collective bargaining agreement, or one found to exist because of promises in an employment handbook or a policy manual.

Defamation   In 1985, it was determined that one-third of all libel suits filed arose from a former employee's claim of bad references by a previous employer. *Libel* refers to defamation in a written document, while *slander* consists of defamation in an oral statement. Either may occur during the course of a reference process. And, while the prima facie case of defamation requires a false statement, even a vague statement that casts doubt on the reputation of an individual by inference can cause difficulties for an employer if it cannot be substantiated.

The elements of a claim for defamation include:

- False and defamatory words concerning employee,
- Negligently or intentionally communicated to a third party without the employee's consent (publication), and
- Resulting harm to the employee defamed.

One cautious solution to this problem area is to request that all employees fill out an exit interview form, which asks, "Do you authorize us to give a reference?" If the applicant answers yes, she or he should be asked to sign a release of liability for the company. One interesting form of defamation has evolved over the past decade. Ordinarily defamation arises from someone other than the defamed employee making defamatory statements about an employee. However, where an employee is given a false or defamatory reason for her or his discharge, the employee is the one who is forced to publicize it to prospective employers.

These circumstances give rise to a cause of action for defamation, termed *compelled self-disclosure,* because the employee is left with no choice but to tell the prospective employer the defamatory reasons for her or his discharge. Barring this result, the employee would be forced to fabricate reasons different from those given by the former employer and run the risk of being reprimanded or terminated for not telling the truth. This cause of action has been recognized, however, only in Colorado, Iowa, Minnesota, Connecticut, and California. (For a more detailed discussion, see Chapter 2.)

An employer may defend against an employee's claim of defamation by establishing the truth of the information communicated. While truth is a complete defense to defamation, it can be difficult to prove without complex paper management.

Employers may also be immune from liability for certain types of statement because of court-recognized privileges in connection with them. For example, an employer is privileged to make statements, even if defamatory, where the statement is made in the course of a judicial proceeding or where the statement is made in good faith by one who has a legitimate business purpose in making the communication (e.g., ex-employer) to one who has a business interest in learning the information (e.g., a prospective employer). This privilege would apply where a former employer offers a good-faith reference to an employee's prospective employer. (See additional discussion of liability for references, below.) "Good faith" means that the employer's statement, though defamatory, is not made with malice or ill will toward the employee.

Love v. University of Cincinnati Hospital *694 N.E.2d 1005 (Ohio Ct. Cl. 1997)*

An employee sued for defamation and breach of contract after a former employer gave a prospective employer details of the employee's termination, despite an agreement that he would not do so.

Gartin, J.

Douglas Love was employed by the employer, University of Cincinnati Hospital, for a little over a year. The parties entered into a settlement agreement when Love resigned which stated that the University records would indicate that Love resigned to seek other employment. The agreement also stated that, in response to requests from outside the University, the University would volunteer only dates of employment, rates of pay, titles of positions held, and accomplishments in favor of Love, provided that such informational requests were directed only to Michael Grodi or Terry White. When Grodi was contacted by an employer considering Love for a position, in response to the question "would you consider rehiring Love if that were to become an option," Grodi informed her that he would not rehire Love because an unprofessional situation had developed between Love and the food service manager. When questioned further, Grodi stated that Love had a difficult time dealing with his coworkers, especially his subordinates. The prospective employer testified that, as a result of Grodi's remarks, she

did not recommend Love for the position for which he was being considered nor did she forward his name to anyone else for consideration. A trial was held before a magistrate on Love's action for breach of a settlement agreement and defamation.

* * *

It is axiomatic that a settlement agreement is a contract designed to terminate a claim by preventing or ending litigation and that such agreements are valid and enforceable by either party. Further, settlement agreements are highly favored in the law.

The words in the settlement agreement must be given their plain meaning. Any negative reference is contrary to the wording utilized in the settlement agreement. The magistrate finds that although [the prospective employer] could not hire plaintiff, she could have recommended him for the contract position; however, as a result of Grodi's comments, she chose not to recommend him for the position. The magistrate finds that Grodi's comments did breach the settlement agreement, since he was to provide only "accomplishments in the favor of Love." Therefore, the magistrate finds that plaintiff's breach of contract claim was proven by a preponderance of the evidence.

As to the defamation claim, defendant proved by a preponderance of the evidence that plaintiff did have trouble getting along with at least two coworkers. Truth is a complete defense to a claim for defamation. [The relevant statute] states that, "[i]n an action for a libel or a slander, the defendant may allege and prove the truth of the matter charged as defamatory. Proof of the truth thereof shall be considered a complete defense." The magistrate finds that defendant was truthful in what was told to [the prospective employer] despite the fact that, pursuant to the settlement agreement, it should not have been communicated. Therefore, defendant

shall prevail on the defamation claim. Based upon the above, judgment is rendered *in favor of plaintiff* on the breach of settlement agreement and *in favor of defendant* on plaintiff's defamation claim.

Case Questions

1. Who do you think "won" in this case?
2. As an employer, would you have handled this situation any differently? Why or why not?
3. Although the employer did not suffer any damages in this suit, can you foresee any problems this conduct could bring in the future?

Regulation of Employee's Off-Work Activities

Employers may regulate the off-work or otherwise private activities of their employees where they believe that the off-work conduct affects the employee's performance at the workplace. This legal arena is a challenging one since, in the at-will environment, employers can generally impose whatever rules they wish. However, as discussed earlier in this chapter, they may then run afoul of common law privacy protections. In addition, some states have enacted legislation protecting against discrimination on the basis of various off-work acts. For instance, New York's lifestyle discrimination statute prohibits employment decisions or actions based on four categories of off-duty activity: legal recreational activities, consumption of legal products, political activities, and membership in a union.

Across the nation, there are other less broad protections of off-work acts. A number of states have enacted protections specifically on the basis of consumption or use of legal products off the job.[7] These statutes originated from the narrower protection for workers who smoked off-duty. Currently, abstention from smoking cannot be a condition of employment in at least 29 states and the District of Columbia (and those states provide antiretaliation provisions for employers who violate the prohibition). In fact, instead of simply identifying the right to use lawful products outside of work, Rhode Island goes further by specifically prohibiting an employer from banning the use of tobacco products while not at work.

On the other hand, employers are not prohibited from making employment decisions on the basis of weight, as long as they are not in violation of the American with Disabilities Act (ADA) when they do so (see Chapter 12). The issue depends on whether the employee's weight is evidence of or due to a disability. If so, the employer will need to explore whether the worker is otherwise qualified for the position, with or without reasonable accommodation, if necessary. If the individual cannot perform the essential functions of the position, the employer is not subject to liability for reaching an adverse employment decision. However, employers should be cautious in this regard since the

---

[7] As of publication, these included Arizona, Connecticut, Washington, D.C., Illinois, Indiana, Kentucky, Louisiana, Maine, Mississippi, New Jersey, New Mexico, Oklahoma, Oregon, Rhode Island, South Carolina, South Dakota, Virginia, West Virginia, and Wyoming. See also John Pearce, Dennis Kuhn, "The Legal Limits of Employees' Off-Duty Privacy Rights," *Organizational Dynamics* 32, no. 4 (2003), pp. 372–383.

ADA also protects workers who are not disabled but who are *perceived* as being disabled, a category into which someone might fall based on their weight.

Laws that protect against discrimination based on marital status exist in just under half of the states. However, though a worker might be protected based on marital *status,* they are not necessarily protected against adverse action based on *the identity of the person* they married. For instance, some companies might have an antinepotism policy under which an employer refuses to hire or terminates a worker based on the spouse working at the same firm, or a conflict-of-interest policy under which the employer refuses to hire or terminates a worker whose spouse works at a competing firm.

A New York decision reaffirms the employer's right to terminate a worker on the basis of romantic involvement. In *McCavitt* vs. *Swiss Reinsurance America Corp.,* 237 F.3d 166 (2d Cir. 2001), the court held that an employee's dating relationship with a fellow officer of the corporation was not a "recreational activity," within the meaning of a New York statute that prohibited employment discrimination for engaging in such recreational activities. The employee contended that, even though "[t]he personal relationship between plaintiff and Ms. Butler has had no repercussions whatever for the professional responsibilities or accomplishments of either" and "Swiss Re . . . has no written anti-fraternization or anti-nepotism policy," he was passed over for promotion and then discharged from employment largely because of his dating. The court agreed with the employer and found that dating was not a recreational activity.

The majority of states protect against discrimination on the basis of political involvement, though states vary on the type and extent of protection. Finally, lifestyle discrimination may be unlawful if the imposition of the rule treats one protected group differently than another. For instance, as discussed elsewhere, if an employer imposes a rule restricting the use of peyote in Native American rituals that take place during off-work hours, the rule may be suspect and may subject the employer to liability. Similarly, the rule may be unlawful if it has a disparate impact on a protected group.

Most statutes or common law decisions, however, provide for employer defenses for those rules that (a) are reasonably and rationally related to the employment activities of a particular employee, (b) constitute a bona fide occupational requirement, or (c) are necessary to avoid a conflict of interest or the appearance of conflict of interest. For example, drug testing in positions that affect the public safety, such as bus driver, would not constitute an unlawful intrusion, because the employer's interest in learning of that information is justified. Where the attempted employer control goes beyond the acceptable realm, courts have upheld an exception to the employment-at-will doctrine based on public policy concerns for personal privacy or, depending on the circumstances, intentional infliction of emotional distress.

Scenario

In connection with scenario 3, does Abraham have to quit his nighttime dancing job? Recall that Abraham is an at-will employee, making the answer somewhat easier. Since he can be terminated for any reason, as long as it is not a wrongful reason, the partner can impose this condition. But consider Abraham's arguments and the ethical, as well as the legal, implications. As long as Abraham can show that his dancing truly has no impact on his work (i.e., that the club is located in a different town from that of his clientele, or that the club has an excellent reputation for beautiful, artistic dancing styles), then he would not have to quit his night job. On the other hand, if Abraham's reputation is soiled by his connection with this club and his boss can show that his work has a negative impact on his ability to perform, then she may be justified in her ultimatum.

Exhibit 13.3

Legal Restrictions on Off-Duty Behavior of Private Employee

Off-Duty Behavior of Private Employee	Business Justification	State Statutory Restrictions on Employer Policy
Illicit drug use	Concern that worker may come to work impaired, jeopardizing the worker's safety and the safety of other workers Quality of work of impaired worker may affect the product or service provided by the company which, in turn, can affect the business' reputation and profitability Conduct is illegal and not deserving of legal protection	46 states allow employers to test for illicit drugs
Alcohol use	Same justifications as applied to those who use illicit drugs, except for the issue of legality	40 states allow employers to regulate off-duty alcohol consumption
Cigarette smoking	Smokers increase employer's health care costs and affect productivity by missing more work due to illness than nonsmokers	22 states allow employers to prohibit off-duty use of tobacco products
Use of weight standards	Same justifications as apply to smokers	49 states allow employers to establish weight standards that do not violate the ADA
Dating between employees	A romantic relationship between employees may affect their productivity The relationship could lead to sexual harassment charges against the employer, especially if one employee is a supervisor of the other Other employees may believe that an involved supervisor is showing favoritism and may then feel that they are victims of discrimination	48 states allow employers to regulate dating between employees
Moonlighting	Working too many hours may impair worker's productivity Working for a competitor could jeopardize privacy of employer information	48 states allow employers to regulate moonlighting
Social relationships with employees of a competitor	Concern that information could be exchanged that would cause harm to the business	48 states allow employers to regulate

Reprinted with permission from John D. Pearce II and Dennis Kuhn, "The Legal Limits of Employees' Off-Duty Privacy Rights," *Organizational Dynamics* 32, no. 4, pp. 372–383, 376 (2003).

In fact, in a case (albeit more extreme) from Arizona, a husband and wife who worked as nurses were fired from a hospital after hospital officials learned that they ran a pornographic Web site when not at work. The couple explained that they engaged in this endeavor in order to save more money for their children's college education. "We thought we could just do this and it really shouldn't be a big deal," said the husband.[8] Though their dismissal attracted the attention of the American Civil Liberties Union for what it considered was at-will gone awry, the nurses had no recourse. In another case, a police office was docked three days' pay when his wife posted nude pictures of herself on the Internet as a surprise to her husband. However, the pay suspension was justified by the department in that case since police officers could arguably be held to a higher standard of conduct than average citizens.

What about the well-intentioned employer who believes that employees who smoke cigarettes will benefit from a "no smoking any time, anywhere" policy? The employer may also be concerned about the financial impact of disease and other health problems related to smoking. The employer may first encounter obstacles in applying this policy in the workplace itself: Some states specifically prohibit discrimination against smokers in employment. Other states regulate smoking in the workplace only in government agencies or public buildings that are also workplaces. Of course, there are other states, like California, that prohibit smoking in all enclosed places of employment and require employers to warn of any toxic substances in the workplace, including tobacco smoke.[9]

The problem in enforcement would grow as the employer tries to encourage or require employees to quit smoking altogether. How would the employer know whether the employees are smoking when not at the workplace? Would the employer's desire to have healthy employees support the intrusion into employees' decisions regarding their own health? Employers who seek to establish an exercise or "healthy eating" program may encounter similar issues. Emphasizing the work-related benefits of such a program and limiting its reach to the workplace (e.g., creating an exercise room at work where employees may take their breaks if they choose) may allow the employer to reach its goal of a healthier workforce. For more information about this issue, see Exhibit 13.3.

---

[8] Mike Brunker, "Cyberporn Nurse: I Feel Like Larry Flynt," MSNBC (July 16, 1999).
[9] CCH Human Resources Workforce Online, *Do Workplace Smoking Laws Regulate Your Business?* www.workforceonline.com/section/03/0005085.htm.

French v. United Parcel Service, Inc.   *2 F. Supp. 2d 128*
(D. Mass. 1998)

Employee brought a claim for wrongful constructive discharge, invasion of privacy, and other torts after his employer kept seeking information about his mental state subsequent to an incident at an off-duty party.

O'Toole, J.

French began employment with UPS in March 1984. During the next fourteen years, he rose through the ranks to become Business Manager of the UPS facility in Chelmsford, Massachusetts. One night after completing his shift, French invited three fellow UPS employees from the Chelmsford facility to attend a beer festival. One of the employees, Daniel DeButts, was a supervisory employee but lower in rank than French. While at French's home, DeButts became intoxicated, emotionally volatile and uncontrollable. When he was left alone in French's garage to "dry out," he lost control, went into a violent rage and caused injury to himself. French and the two other employees found DeButts lying in the garage bleeding. An ambulance was called and DeButts was taken to a local hospital where he was treated and released after twenty-four hours.

Following the incident, French's supervisor, Clark, requested that French report it to his superiors at the Chelmsford facility. Believing that the incident was none of UPS's business, French initially decided not to do so. Clark continued to press French, and later French informed the division manager of operations, his superior, of the incident. French was put on leave pending an investigation. As a result of this suspension, French began treatment for depression. During the next several months while French was still on leave, UPS personnel demanded that French meet with them to discuss the incident. In addition, UPS repeatedly contacted the mental health professionals who were treating French for depression to determine his condition and prognosis for recovery. At the end of the month, French was demoted to the position of supervisor. He returned to work but resigned about five weeks later because of the humiliation he felt in having to perform tasks that had not been his responsibility since the late 1980s. French brought this complaint, alleging four causes of action against UPS: invasion of privacy; reckless infliction of emotional distress; a violation of the Massachusetts Civil Rights Act; and wrongful constructive discharge.

* * *

UPS has moved to dismiss all four counts of French's complaint. . . .

COUNT 1: INVASION OF PRIVACY

The Massachusetts right of privacy statute provides that "[a] person shall have a right against unreasonable, substantial or serious interference with his privacy." To constitute an invasion of privacy, the invasion must be both unreasonable and serious or substantial. French alleges that UPS violated his right to privacy by: (a) insisting that he disclose details concerning an incident that occurred during off-work hours at his home; (b) repeatedly contacting his mental health providers without his consent; and (c) penalizing him, in the form of involuntary leave and demotion, for the incident.

(A) REQUIRING DISCLOSURE ABOUT THE INCIDENT

For purposes of the Massachusetts Privacy Act, "private" facts are not necessarily simply those that are "not public," that is, not generally or widely known. Rather, [the Act] proscribes the "required disclosure of facts about an individual that are of a highly personal or intimate nature." The fact that a fellow employee drank too much at French's house is not a fact about French that is "highly personal or intimate." More importantly, the facts of what happened in the incident were not information that was "private" to French. Three other UPS employees took part in and observed the events, one of whom, Clark, was French's superior in the company hierarchy. Any of these persons was free to describe the incident; none had any apparent relationship with French that imposed some obligation of confidentiality. Indeed, as French's superior, Clark may even have owed UPS a duty to report, sua sponte, what he had observed. Be that as it may, it is surely unlikely that the Massachusetts courts would interpret §1B to give French a right to prohibit Clark (or any one else who was present, including DeButts) from voluntarily disclosing what he had personally observed or done in connection with the incident. In short, the incident was simply not a "private" affair of French alone.

In addition, there are circumstances in which it is legitimate for an employer to know some "personal" information about its employees, so long as the information reasonably bears upon the employees' fitness for, or discharge of, their employment responsibilities. In the employment context "the employer's legitimate interest in determining the employees' effectiveness in their jobs [is] balanced against the seriousness of the intrusion on the employees' privacy." UPS has articulated legitimate business reasons for seeking information about the DeButts incident, including concerns about the soundness of judgment exercised by its supervisory employees in regard to alcohol abuse generally as well as in a particular setting where all participants were UPS employees. In light of these legitimate concerns, the company's questioning him about facts known to several other employees amounted, at most, to a de minimis intrusion into French's privacy, not actionable under the statute.

(B) ATTEMPTED CONTACT OF MENTAL HEALTH CARE PROVIDERS

French also alleges that UPS "repeatedly contacted the mental health professionals who were treating the Plaintiff to determine his condition and prognosis for recovery. UPS made these contacts without the prior consent of the Plaintiff." The complaint does not allege that any private information was actually obtained by UPS. "Whatever unlawful invasion of privacy might have arisen if the defendant[ ] had obtained some of the information sought . . . , the short answer is that. . . . [t]he defendant['s] attempted invasion of privacy . . . failed." The Supreme Judicial Court has twice declined to decide whether the Privacy Act "reaches attempted interference with a person's privacy." The court has suggested that the statute may not reach attempts. Thus, [prior court rulings] rejection of the "failed" invasion as a basis for liability apparently continues to express the law of Massachusetts on this question.

(C) SUSPENSION AND DEMOTION

The employment actions UPS took against French—putting him on involuntary leave and then demoting him—were not themselves an invasion of his privacy within the scope of the statutory cause of action. If these actions were wrongful, it would have to have been for some other reason.

Therefore, French's claim for invasion of privacy must be DISMISSED.

Case Questions

1. Do you agree with the court's decision? Why or why not?
2. Why do you think the court determined the employer had a right to inquire about the incident that occurred off-duty?
3. Why do you think UPS was so concerned about an incident that occurred off-duty?

EMPLOYER'S INFORMATION-GATHERING PROCESS/JUSTIFIED USE/DISCLOSURE OF INFORMATION

The above discussion focused on the scope of the privacy rights of the employee in connection with the dissemination of information. Privacy, however, can be invaded not only by a disclosure of specific types of information but also by the process pursuant to which the information has been obtained. An employer may be liable for its *process* of information gathering, storing, or utilization. Improper retrieval of information may be an invasion where the process of collection constitutes harassment, improper filing or dissemination of the information collected may leave the employer liable for defamation actions, and inappropriate use of data for other purposes than those for which the information was collected may inflict other harms.

The collection or retrieval of information may occur in a variety of ways, depending on the stage of employment and the needs of the employer. For example, an employer may merely make use of the information provided by an applicant on her or his application form, or it may telephone prior employers to verify the data provided by the applicant. One employer may feel confident in an employee's educational background when she sees the employee's diplomas hung on the office wall, while a different employer may feel the need to contact prior educational institutions to verify attendance and actual graduation. On the more lenient end of the spectrum, the employer may rest assured that the employee is all that he states that he is on the application form, while, in more extreme situations, an employer may subject its employees to polygraph analyses and drug tests.

As is covered extensively in other chapters, employers are limited in the questions that may be asked of a potential employee. For example, an employer may not ask an applicant whether she or he is married or plans to have children, or the nature of her or his family's origin. These questions are likely to violate Title VII of the Civil Rights Act because an employer is prohibited from reaching any employment decision on the basis of their answers. In addition, employers are limited in their collection of information through various forms of testing, such as polygraphs or medical tests. These are discussed further in Chapter 3, but employers are constrained by a business necessity and relatedness standard or, in the case of polygraphs, by a requirement of reasonable suspicion. With regard to medical information specifically, employer's decisions are not only governed by the Americans With Disabilities Act but also restricted by the Health Insurance Portability and Accountability Act (HIPAA) (Pub. L. 104-191). HIPAA stipulates that employers cannot use "protected health information" in making employment decisions without prior consent. Protected health information includes all medical records or other individually identifiable health information. (See Exhibit 13.4.)

In connection with the storage of the information collected, employers must be careful to ensure that the information is stored in such a manner that it will not fall into the "wrong" hands. If an improper party has access to the personal information, the employer, again, may be subject to a defamation action by the employee based on the wrongful invasion of her personal affairs. In today's world of advanced computer data storage, new issues arise that have not been previously litigated. For instance, where an item is stored in a computer, it is crucial either to close the file to all but those who have a correct entry code or to delete private information. Access to computer terminals throughout an office creates a problem concerning the dissemination of the private information and the control of access.

The employer offering the reference is responsible for its dissemination only to appropriate parties. A fax machine or postcard would be unacceptable means of transmitting a reference, since this would allow access by innumerable others. Similarly, an employer may get caught wrongfully disclosing information to an inappropriate individual in the case of the telephone reference. Failure to confirm the identity of the caller and purpose of the call may allow disclosure to one who otherwise should have no access to this information.

Electronic Monitoring or Surveillance of Employee Activities

With the dramatic increase in the use of technology in the workplace, several issues have recently developed surrounding the use of e-mail and the Internet. Many state and district courts have dealt with the issues differently or have not faced them at all. On the other hand, 75 percent of companies surveyed for a 2003 report have written policies concerning e-mail use.[10]

---

[10] American Management Association, "2003 Email Rules, Policies and Practices Survey" (2003).

In 1997, the International Labour Organization published a Code of Practice on the Protection of Workers' Personal Data. Though not binding on employers, they serve to help codify ethical standards in connection with the collection and use of employee personal information. The Code includes, among others, the following principles:

5. GENERAL PRINCIPLES

5.1 Personal data should be processed lawfully and fairly, and only for reasons directly relevant to the employment of the worker.

5.2 Personal data should, in principle, be used only for the purposes for which they were originally collected. . . .

5.4 Personal data collected in connection with technical or organizational measures to ensure the security and proper operation of automated information systems should not be used to control the behavior of workers.

5.5 Decisions concerning a worker should not be based solely on the automated processing of that worker's personal data.

5.6 Personal data collected by electronic monitoring should not be the only factors in evaluating worker performance. . . .

5.8 Workers and their representatives should be kept informed of any data collection process, the rules that govern that process, and their rights. . . .

5.10 The processing of personal data should not have the effect of unlawfully discriminating in employment or occupation. . . .

5.13 Workers may not waive their privacy rights.

6. COLLECTION OF PERSONAL DATA

6.1 All personal data should, in principle, be obtained from the individual worker.

6.2 If it is necessary to collect personal data from third parties, the worker should be informed in advance, and give explicit consent. The employer should indicate the purposes of the processing, the sources and means the employer intends to use, as well as the type of data to be gathered, and the consequences, if any, of refusing consent. . . .

6.5 An employer should not collect personal data concerning a worker's sex life; political, religious, or other beliefs; or criminal convictions. In exceptional circumstances, an employer may collect personal data concerning those in named areas above if the data are directly relevant to an employment decision and in conformity with national legislation.

6.6 Employers should not collect personal data concerning the worker's membership in a workers' organization or the worker's trade union activities, unless obliged or allowed to do so by law or a collective agreement.

6.7 Medical personal data should not be collected except in conformity with national legislation, medical confidentiality and the general principles of occupational health and safety, and only as needed to determine whether the worker is fit for a particular employment; to fulfill the requirements of occupational health and safety; and to determine entitlement to, and to grant, social benefits. . . .

6.10 Polygraphs, truth-verification equipment or any other similar testing procedure should not be used.

(continued)

Exhibit 13.4 (continued)

6.11 Personality tests or similar testing procedures should be consistent with the provisions of this code, provided that the worker may object to the testing.

6.12 Genetic screening should be prohibited or limited to cases explicitly authorized by national legislation.

6.13 Drug testing should be undertaken only in conformity with national law and practice or international standards.

11. INDIVIDUAL RIGHTS

11.1 Workers should have the right to be regularly notified of the personal data held about them and the processing of that personal data.

11.2 Workers should have access to all their personal data, irrespective of whether the personal data are processed by automated systems or are kept in a particular manual file regarding the individual worker or in any other file which includes workers' personal data.

11.3 The workers' right to know about the processing of their personal data should include the right to examine and obtain a copy of any records to the extent that the data contained in the record includes that worker's personal data. . . .

11.9 Workers should have the right to demand that incorrect or incomplete personal data, and personal data processed inconsistently with the provisions of this code, be deleted or rectified. . . .

11.11 If the employer refuses to correct the personal data, the worker should be entitled to place a statement on or with the record setting out the reasons for that worker's disagreement. Any subsequent use of the personal data should include the information that the personal data are disputed and the worker's statement.

Little did anyone anticipate what dilemmas would arise as a result of advances in technology over the past few decades. Notwithstanding issues in connection with production, marketing, finance, and other areas of a firm's operations, we now have countless issues that intersect law and ethics with which we were never before confronted. For instance, consider the implications of new technology on the following areas:

- Monitoring usage.
- Managing employee and employer expectations.
- Distinguishing between work use and personal use of technology.
- Managing flextime.
- Maintaining a virtual workplace.
- Protecting against medical concerns for telecommuters.
- Managing/balancing privacy interests.
- Monitoring the use of the Web to spread information and misinformation.
- Managing fair use/disclosure.
- Responding to accessibility issues related to the digital divide.
- Managing temporary workforces.

- Adapting to stress and changing systems.
- Managing liability issues.
- Maintaining proprietary information.
- Measuring performance.

In order to better understand the impact of new technology on these segments of our working environment, it is critical to comprehend the nature of that technology and its capabilities. For instance, though seemingly monumental on the surface, advances in the information-gathering abilities of these technologies are actually merely geometric rather than exponential. Employers have always gathered information about their employees; the only element that has changed in recent decades is how that information is collected rather than the values that underlay the decision to do so.

For instance, Milton Hershey of Hershey's Chocolate used to tour Hershey, Pennsylvania, to see how well his employees maintained their homes. He hired detectives to spy on Hershey Park dwellers in order to learn who threw trash on its lawns. Henry Ford used to condition wages on his workers' good behavior *outside the factory,* maintaining a Sociological Department of 150 inspectors to keep tabs on workers. Technology, therefore, does not present us with new value judgments but, instead, simply presents new ways to gather the information on which to base them. Sorting through these issues is challenging nevertheless. Consider the impact of September 11, 2001 on an employer's decision to share personal employee information with law enforcement. Private firms may be more willing today to share private information than they would have been previously. Consider more particularly the issues raised above and the implications of technology on some of these traditional workplace challenges:

- Technology allows for in-home offices, raising issues of safety as well as privacy concerns; there are now more than 15.7 million U.S. telecommuters. (Recent efforts by OSHA to impose workplace safety standards on home offices received huge flack!)
- Technology allows for greater invasions by the employer but also allows for additional misdeeds by employees.
- Technology blurs the lines between personal and professional lives.
- Technology allows employers to ask more of each employee—each is capable of much greater production.
- What constitutes a "workday"? When is enough enough?
- Should the ability to find something out make it relevant (e.g., off-work activities)?
- Many of the new technologies (e-mail, voice mail) allow for faceless communication.
- Research has shown that excessive exertion of power and authority over employees may actually lead to insecurity, feelings of being overwhelmed and powerless, and doubts about worthiness.[11]

---

[11] Ashley Benigno, "Total Surveillance Is Threatening Your Health," *Asian Labour Update* (Hong Kong: Asia Monitor Resource Center, http://www.amrc.org.hk/Arch/3405.htm, accessed 2/5/02).

Consider the following overview of the implications of the technology economy as reported in the 2001 "World Employment Report," issued by the International Labour Office:

> More and more, boundaries are dissolving between leisure and working time, the place of work and place of residence, learning and working. . . . Wherever categories such as working time, working location, performance at work and jobs become blurred, the result is the deterioration of the foundations of our edifice of agreements, norms, rules, laws, organizational forms, structures and institutions, all of which have a stronger influence on our behavioral patterns and systems of values than we are aware.[12]

Forms of Monitoring

Monitoring in the workplace can take several forms and occurs for numerous reasons. Privacy scholar Colin Bennett identifies four types of surveillance that can specifically impact workers.[13] The first is *surveillance by glitch,* in which information is uncovered by mistake. This occurred, for example, when Microsoft discovered that expired Hotmail accounts retained buddy lists, which were then shared with new subscribers who were given those accounts' e-mail addresses. In the workplace, a glitch could occur when a technician checks to see if a computer's hard drive has been erased by the previous user for use by someone else. That technician might notice inappropriate content on the hard drive. A similar circumstance arose when the dean of Harvard's Divinity School asked a Harvard information management technician to do some work on his Harvard-owned laptop. The technician found inappropriate pornographic materials, and the media frenzy that erupted has only recently subsided. In another example of a glitch or mistake, cheating by a worker in a government agency was discovered when the worker left a copy of a stolen promotion exam in the copying machine. Such glitches may uncover violations of a usage policy even when no systematic monitoring is being conducted.

Bennett's second form of surveillance is *surveillance by default.* This occurs when the default setting is "monitor," whereby all information that is sent through a system is caught and cataloged. An example of this type of monitoring would be the "Cue Cat." A Cue Cat is a mouselike device that was sent to subscribers of certain magazines. They were told that they could scan bar codes in the magazine in order to gather more information on the accompanying topics later through their computers. What these users were not told was that each Cue Cat was individually coded to send subscriber information along with the information request. Therefore, the publishers or advertisers were able to surreptitiously collect data from anyone who used the device at all times. In the workplace, surveillance by default occurs when there is a video camera recording every transaction or activity by default, rather than recording only specific activities. The American Management Association reports that 75 percent of firms surveyed in 2001 regularly record their employees' e-mail transmissions by means of a default setting.[14]

---

[12] U. Klotz, "The Challenges of the New Economy" (Oct. 1999), cited in *World Employment Report 2001: Life at Work in the Information Economy* (International Labour Office: Geneva 2001), p. 145.

[13] Colin Bennett, "Cookies, Web Bugs, Webcams and Cue Cats: Patterns of Surveillance on the World Wide Web," *Ethics and Information Technology* 3, pp. 197–210 (2001).

[14] Dana Hawkins, "Lawsuits Spur Rise in Employee Monitoring," *U.S. News & World Report* (August 13, 2001).

The third form of monitoring is *surveillance by design*, where the entire purpose of the technology is to collect information and, generally, the user is aware of this purpose. Supermarkets often trade discounts on products in exchange for an individual's personal information on the application form for the encoded key chain device that allows the discount. The shopper is fully aware of the exchange when the information is collected, and the entire purpose of the key chain device is to provide information to the store. Often customer service representatives will be notified by an audible "beep" on the telephone that they are being monitored, and they understand that this monitoring will have implications for their performance evaluations. Another type of surveillance by design occurs when firms conduct either random or periodic keyword searches of e-mail or other transmissions. One-quarter of firms surveyed by the American Management Association reported that they perform keyword searches, generally seeking sexual or scatological language to protect themselves from later liability.[15]

Surveillance by possession exists where the employer maintains employee information in a database or some other list. Bennett refers to this form of surveillance as gathering information that could be sold or acquired, such as employee personal information from application forms.

Much of the monitoring that occurs today in American firms is surveillance by design or by default. For instance, an e-mail program that systematically sorts and saves all e-mail that contains certain terms (such as those used in a job search or those that might be considered sexually harassing) would constitute surveillance by default. A monitoring program that tracks Internet accesses and blocks inappropriate websites would be surveillance by design.

How Does Monitoring Work?

Advances in information-gathering technology have allowed monitoring to an extent that was never before possible. Worldwide sales of monitoring technology are estimated at $140 million annually.[16] One example of this new technology is Raytheon's Silentrunner, which allows firms to track everything that occurs on a network, including not only e-mail but also instant messaging (one of the new ways employees thought they had foiled e-mail monitoring).[17] Other products allow trucking firms to track their vehicles across the nation using global positioning[18] or allow managers to test a worker's honesty by using a truth-telling monitor during telephone calls.[19]

The most prevalent Internet-monitoring product in the United States is Websense, with 8.25 million users worldwide. While Websense merely *blocks* certain Web sites,

---

[15] Dana Hawkins, "Lawsuits Spur Rise in Employee Monitoring," *U.S. News & World Report* (August 13, 2001).

[16] Andrew Schulman, "One-Third of U.S. Online Workforce under Internet/Email Surveillance," *Workforce Surveillance Project* (Privacy Foundation) (July 9, 2001), http://www.privacyfoundation.org/workplace/business/biz_show.asp?id=70&ac.

[17] Jeffrey Brenner, "Privacy at Work? Be Serious," *Wired Magazine,* http://www.wired.com/news/business/0,1367,42029,00.html (accessed 2/26/02).

[18] www.omnitracs.com.

[19] www.spyzone.com.

Websense Reporter, an add-on, records all web accesses—not only attempted accesses blocked by Websense but also all nonprohibited Web surfing (70 percent of Websense's customers install Reporter). MIMEsweeper is the most used e-mail monitoring system in the United States, with 6,000 corporate customers and over 6 million ultimate users worldwide. In a less publicized form of monitoring, SWS Security offers a product that allows managers to track the messages a worker receives on a portable paging device so that one could track whether the employee is being distracted by outside messages. Another provider, www.tracingamerica.com, offers the following information at the listed prices:

- Social Security numbers, $25.
- General all-around background search, $39.
- Countywide search for misdemeanors and felonies, $35.
- Whether subject has ever spent time in prison, $25.
- Whether subject has ever served time in a federal prison, $50.
- National search for outstanding warrants for subject, $50.
- Countywide search for any civil filings filed by or against subject, $50.
- Subject's driving record for at least three years back, $30.

The ACLU reports that the number of people subject to surveillance in the workplace rose from 8 million in 1991 to more than 30 million in 1997.[20] Workers believe that something should be done to protect them. In a poll of more than 4,000 people, 90 percent favor legislation that would protect them from technological privacy invasions.[21] These protections are significant when you realize that the average respondent in a professional survey spends one-fourth of the workday on e-mail.

While no related case has yet reached the Supreme Court, these actions have received lower court attention. As early as 1990, Epson America survived a lawsuit filed by a terminated employee who had complained about Epson's practice of reading all employee e-mail.[22] In that case, the court distinguished the practice of *intercepting* an e-mail transmission from storing and reading e-mail transmissions once they had been sent. However, relying on court precedent for protection is a double-edged sword. An employee-plaintiff in one federal action won a case against his employer where the employer had monitored the worker's telephone for a period of 24 hours in order to determine whether the worker was planning a robbery. The court held that the company had gone too far and had insufficient evidence to support its claims.[23] In another action,

[20] American Civil Liberties Union, "New Study on Workplace Surveillance Highlights Lack of Protections, ACLU Says," press release, May 23, 1997.

[21] B. Horovitz, "80% Fear Loss of Privacy to Computers," *USA Today*, Oct. 31, 1995, p. A1. See also Ethics Officer Association, *Technology & Ethics in the Workplace*, 1998 (study of 4,000 workers found that 75 percent believed invasion of privacy issues to be a primary concern).

[22] No. SCW112749, Cal. Sup. Ct., L.A. Cty., 1989, *appeal denied,* Sup. Ct. Cal., 994 Cal. LEXIS 3670 (6/29/94); James McNair, "When You Use Email at Work, Your Boss May Be Looking In," *Telecom Digest,* icg.stwing.upenn.edu/cis500/reading.062.htm, reprinted from the *Miami Herald.*

[23] Winn Schwartau, "Who Controls Network Usage Anyway?" *Network World,* May 22, 1995, p. 71.

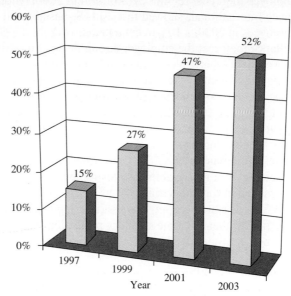

Adapted by authors from data from the American Management Association.

Northern Telecom settled a claim brought by employees who were allegedly secretly monitored over a 13-year period. In this case, Telecom agreed to pay $50,000 to individual plaintiffs and $125,000 for attorneys' fees.[24]

In the American Management Association's 2003 survey, more than half of the respondents reported that they engaged in e-mail monitoring as a result of their concerns for legal liability (Exhibit 13.5). Given the courts' focus in many cases on employer response to claims of sexual harassment or unethical behavior, among other complaints, firms believe that they need a way to uncover these inappropriate activities. More than 10 percent of firms reported receiving a subpoena for employee e-mail, and 22 percent of the firms reported firing employees for inappropriate e-mail.[25] Without monitoring, how would companies know what occurs? Moreover, as courts maintain the standard in many cases of whether the employer "knew or should have known" of wrongdoing, the state-of-the-art definition of "should have known" becomes all the more vital. If most firms use monitoring technology to uncover such wrongdoing, the definition of "should have known" will begin to include an expectation of monitoring.

Employee theft has led both public and private employers to monitor their employees by using video surveillance. According to the National Retail Security Survey,

[24] Bureau of National Affairs, "Northern Telecom Settles with CWA on Monitoring," *Individual Employment Rights,* Mar. 10, 1992, p. 1.

[25] American Management Association, "2003 Email Rules, Policies and Practices Survey" (2003).

employee theft cost retailers $15 billion in 2000. Another study conducted in 2001, by Hayes International, showed that 30 U.S.-based retail chains caught 73,326 dishonest employees in 2000, a 10 percent increase over the 1999 figure. Nevertheless, video surveillance may cost the employer through loss of morale. "Would you like to work in an environment where every time you blow your nose . . . it's on videotape?" asks Lewis Maltby, president of the National Workrights Institute in Princeton, New Jersey.[26]

Courts have supported reasonable monitoring of employees in open areas as a method of preventing and addressing employee theft. For example, in *Sacramento County Deputy Sheriff's Ass'n* v. *County of Sacramento*,[27] a public employer placed a silent video camera in the ceiling overlooking the release office countertop in response to theft of inmate money. The California Court of Appeals determined that the county had engaged in reasonable monitoring, because employee privacy expectations were diminished in the jail setting.[28]

While, as stated earlier, there is little legislation that actually relates to these areas specifically, there is some statutory protection from overt intrusions, though the statute does not apply in all circumstances. The federal wiretapping statute, Title III of the Omnibus Crime Control and Safe Streets Act of 1968, as amended by the Electronic Communications Privacy Act of 1986 (18 U.S.C. §§2510–2520), protects private and public sector employees from employer monitoring of their telephone calls and other communications without a court order.

There are two exceptions to this general prohibition. First, interception is authorized where one of the parties to the communication has given prior consent. Second, the "business extension" provision creates an exception where the equipment used is what is used in the ordinary course of business. An employer must be able to state a legitimate business purpose and there must be minimal intrusions into employee privacy, such that they would not be objectionable to a reasonable person. The ECPA is explored more fully with regard to its application to e-mail communications in the *Fraser* case at the end of this chapter.

Why Do Firms Monitor Employee Internet Use?

Web access at work may allow employees to be more creative and productive, but it also creates great risks. A September 2000 survey by the Web site Vault.com found that 90 percent of employees surf non-work-related Web sites while at work.[29] (See Exhibit 13.6) Wasted time, overclogged networks, and inappropriate material seeping into the workplace are all reasons why employers may seek to limit employees' Internet use at work. Of the employers surveyed, 42 percent reported that they restrict or monitor employees' Internet use.[30]

---

[26] Karen Robinson-Jacobs, "Retailers Taking Aim at Employee Pilferage," *Los Angeles Times,* Feb. 16, 2002, p. C1.

[27] 59 Cal. Rptr. 2d 834 (Cal. Ct. App. 1996).

[28] See Ted Clark, "Legal Corner: Monitoring Employee Activities: Privacy Tensions in the Public Workplace," *NPLERA Newsletter,* June 1999, www.seyfarth.com/practice/labor/articles/ll_1393.html.

[29] Cohen, op. cit., p. 70.

[30] Ibid.

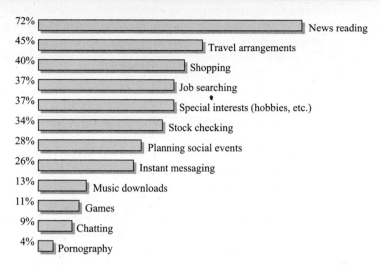

72%	News reading
45%	Travel arrangements
40%	Shopping
37%	Job searching
37%	Special interests (hobbies, etc.)
34%	Stock checking
28%	Planning social events
26%	Instant messaging
13%	Music downloads
11%	Games
9%	Chatting
4%	Pornography

Source: Alan Cohen, "Worker Watchers: Want to Know What Your Employees Are Doing Online? You Can Find Out without Spooking Them," *Fortune/CNET Technology Review,* Summer 2001, pp. 72, 70–80, based on Vault.com's Second Annual Survey of Internet Use in the Workplace, September 2000.

As mentioned above, monitoring is made simpler through an employee's use of a computer. Employers now customarily provide many employees with personal computers that are linked either to the Internet or, at least, to an internal network. Employers can monitor the computer user's activities. As to the type of information that can be gathered, the Privacy Demonstration Page of the Center for Democracy and Technology can feed back to viewers information that it finds out merely because one has accessed the page. For instance, the page tells one individual viewer the type of computer that the viewer is using, the browser the individual is using, the server from which the viewer is operating, and some of the pages the viewer has recently visited. While this information may not necessarily seem personal to some, consider the facts of scenario 2. The employer in that case seems to be within its rights to monitor the use of its computers.

2
Scenario

The need to monitor employees' usage becomes clear when one focuses on five areas of potential employer liability: defamation, copyright infringement, sexual harassment, discrimination, and obscenity.

As discussed previously in this chapter, the guidelines that apply to a general defamation claim also apply to issues surrounding the Internet. However, some contend that the opportunity for harm is far greater. This is because employees and employers can easily disseminate information to a wide range of media. Not only can employers be subject to defamation claims by their own employees, but the far greater threat is the liability a company faces when an employee, as a representative of the employer, defames another individual using the Internet (with access provided by the employer) as the medium.

Further, firms are concerned about inappropriate use of web software, such as occurs when an employee downloads program files without compensating the creator or when employees use copywritten information from the Web without giving credit to the original author, thereby exposing the firm to potentially significant copyright infringement liability. Finally, when an employee downloads software programs from the Web, the computer systems within the firm have the potential to be compromised by viruses or even unauthorized access.

Sexual harassment and discrimination by employees via the Web are governed by the same general guidelines that were previously discussed in the chapters addressing sexual harassment and discrimination. However, many employees believe that once an e-mail message is deleted, it is permanently removed from the system. This is not the case. Because of this, e-mail sent on company time, with contents that constitute sexual harassment, that might create a hostile working environment, or that contain other forms of discrimination, may easily be discovered, both by the employer and by opposing parties to litigation against the employer. In fact, in 2003 14 percent of companies in the American Management Association Survey had been ordered by a court to produce employee e-mail. For example, female warehouse employees alleged that a hostile work environment was created in part by inappropriate e-mail, and they sought $60 million in damages in federal court. The case settled out of court.[31] E-mail is discussed in greater detail in the next section. Finally, obscenity becomes a critical issue, and the company may be placed at risk when employees download pornographic images while at the workplace.

Moreover, a firm might be concerned about the impression created when an employee visits various sites. Consider these scenarios: A customer service representative at an electronics store is surfing the Internet using one of the display computers. She accesses a website that shows graphic images of a crime scene. A customer in the store who notices the images is offended. Another customer service representative is behind the counter, using the store's computer to access a pornographic site, and starts to laugh. A customer asks him why he is laughing. He turns the computer screen around to show her the images that are causing him amusement.

Certainly, the employer would be justified in blocking employees' access to such websites. But what about sites of activist groups regarding sensitive issues such as abortion: Should an employer be allowed to block or restrict access to such sites? If such access may be restricted in order to promote efficiency and professionalism, then should employers be allowed to limit access to such innocuous sites as eBay or ESPN.com? The Vault.com survey mentioned above revealed that over half of employees who make personal use of the Internet at work restrict their surfing to less than half an hour a day. By limiting or restricting access to websites, the employer may be creating an environment in which employees do not feel trusted and perhaps feel inhibited about using the Internet for creative, work-related purposes because they fear being reprimanded for misusing access.[32]

Employers seem to have business justification for other types of monitoring: "If [the employer] sees you doing something on the screen that they think you can do in a

---

[31] *Harley* v. *McCoach,* 928 F. Supp. 533, E.D. Pa. 1996, cited in "Cyberliability: An Enterprise White Paper," Elron Software, www.internetmanager.com.

[32] Cohen, op. cit., p. 76.

quicker way, they can tell you. They can even tell you ways to talk to people, or they can tell you ways to do things quicker to end your [customer service] call quicker," says Kathy Joynes, a travel agent for American Express who works out of her home, but whose supervisor can shadow her computer screen at any time.[33]

Because of the overall potential liability for their employees' actions, employers should develop a formal policy or program regulating employee usage of the Internet. In addition to having a formal policy, employers may choose to establish a process of monitoring their employee's Internet usage. This may involve tracking Web sites visited and the amount of time spent at each site with software programs designed for that specific purpose. However, employers need to consider the employees' rights to free speech and privacy when developing such policies and systems. (See Exhibits 13.7 and 13.8.)

Employee E-Mail Usage

Employers' needs to monitor e-mail must be weighed against the employees' right to privacy. The employer is interested in ensuring that the e-mail system is not being used in ways that offend others, to harm morale, or for disruptive purposes. Likewise, an employer may choose to review e-mail in connection with a reasonable investigation of possible employee misconduct. Also, companies that maintain sensitive data may be concerned about disclosure of this information by disloyal or careless employees, apparently justifying this type of intrusion.

Problems with e-mail abuse may extend beyond the end of the employment relationship. After an employee was fired by Intel Corporation, he began to air grievances about the company via e-mail. He repeatedly flooded his former employer's e-mail system with mass e-mails that its security department was unable to block. Intel sought and obtained an injunction on the theory of trespass to chattels. A California appellate court rejected the former employee's appeal that the injunction violated free speech principles.

While monitoring e-mail transmissions over telephone lines is forbidden by the ECPA, communications within a firm do not generally go over the phone lines and therefore may be legally available to employers. In addition, there are numerous exceptions to the ECPA's prohibitions, including situations where one party to the transmission consents, where the provider of the communication service can monitor communications, or where the monitoring is done in the ordinary course of business. In order to satisfy the ECPA consent exception, however, the employer's interception must not exceed the scope of the employee's consent. Employers must be aware, as well, that an employee's knowledge that the employer is monitoring certain communications is insufficient to be considered implied consent. To avoid liability, employers must specifically inform employees of the extent and circumstances under which e-mail communications will be monitored.

Despite the failure of legislative attempts to require employers to notify employees that their e-mail is being monitored, such as the proposed Notice of Electronic Monitoring Act, employers should provide such notification, as described below.[34] In addition,

---

[33] Dan Charles, "High-Tech Equipment in the Workplace," *All Things Considered,* National Public Radio, Apr. 1, 1996.

[34] Christopher A. Weals, "Workplace Privacy," *Legal Times,* Mar. 6, 2002.

WHY DO FIRMS MONITOR TECHNOLOGY USAGE?

- Managing the workplace:
  —Ensuring compliance with affirmative action.
  —Administering workplace benefits.
  —Placing workers in appropriate positions.
- Ensuring effective, productive performance:
  —Preventing loss of productivity to inappropriate technology use.
  —Recent reports evidence a rise in personal use of technology, with 85.6 percent of employees admitting sending or receiving personal e-mails at work, 55.1 percent of employees admitting to having received politically incorrect or offensive e-mails at work, and 62 percent of firms finding employees accessing sex sites during the workday.[*]
  —13 percent of employees spend over two hours a day surfing nonbusiness sites.[†]
  —A recent survey in the U.K. reports that, of the workers surveyed, 53 percent behave "immorally" in e-mail; 38 percent have used e-mail in the pursuit of political gain within their company, at the expense of others; and 30 percent admit to having sent racist, pornographic, sexist, or otherwise discriminatory e-mails while at work.[‡]
- Protecting information and guarding against theft.
- Protecting investment in equipment and bandwidth.
- Protecting against legal liability, including possible:
  —Perceptions of hostile environments.
  —Violations of software licensing laws.
  —Violations regarding proprietary information or trade secrets.
  —Inappropriate gathering of competitive intelligence.
  —Financial fraud.
  —Theft.
  —Defamation/libel.
  —Discrimination.
- Maintaining corporate records (including e-mail, voice mail, and so on).
- Investigating *some* personal areas. (Consider Infoseek executive Patrick Naughton's pursuit of a tryst with an FBI agent posing as a 13-year-old girl in a chat room.)

WHY SHOULD FIRMS LIMIT MONITORING?

- Monitoring may create a suspicious and hostile workplace.
- Monitoring constrains effective performance (employees claim that lack of privacy may prevent "flow").
- It may be important to conduct *some* personal business at the office, when necessary.
- Monitoring causes increased workplace stress and pressure, negatively impacting performance.
- Employees claim that monitoring is an inherent invasion of privacy.
- Monitoring does not always allow for workers to review and correct misinformation in the data collected.
- Monitoring constrains the right to autonomy and freedom of expression.
- Monitoring intrudes on one's right to privacy of thought. ("I use a company pen; does that mean the firm has a right to read my letter to my spouse?")

[*] Elron Software, "Guide to Internet Usage and Policy" (2001), pp. 7, 17.
[†] Alan Cohen, "Worker Watchers," *Fortune/CNET Technology Review* (Summer 2001), pp. 70, 76.
[‡] Institute for Global Ethics, "U.K. Survey Finds Many Workers Are Misusing Email," *Newsline* 5, no. 10 (3/11/02).

Exhibit 13.8

Allowable Monitoring

Telephone calls	Monitoring is permitted in connection with quality control. Notice to the parties to the call is often required by state law, though federal law allows employers to monitor work calls without notice. If the employer realizes that the call is personal, monitoring must cease immediately.
E-mail messages	Under most circumstances, employers may monitor employee e-mails. Even in situations where the employer claims that it will not, its right to monitor has been held to persist. However, where the employee's reasonable expectation of privacy is increased (such as a password-protected account), this may impact the court's decision.
Voice mail system messages	Though not yet completely settled, appears to be similar analysis as e-mail messages.
Internet use	Where the employer has provided the equipment and/or the access to the Internet, the employer may track, block, or review Internet use.

some states have now imposed notice requirements before monitoring, including Delaware and Connecticut.

Computer Usage Policies

An employer can meet its business necessity to monitor e-mail, protect itself from liability, and, at the same time, respect the employees' legitimate expectation of privacy in the workplace in numerous ways. Employers should develop concise written policies and procedures regarding the use of company computers, specifically e-mail. The Society for Human Resource Management strongly encourages companies both to adopt policies that address employee privacy and to ensure that employees are notified of such policies. Any e-mail policy should be incorporated in the company policies and procedures manuals, employee handbooks, and instruction aids to ensure that the employee receives consistent information regarding the employer's rights to monitor employee e-mail. Additionally, a company could display a notice each time an employee logs on to a company computer indicating the computers are to be used only for business-related communication or explaining that the employee has no reasonable expectation of privacy in the electronic messages. Employers can also periodically send memos reminding employees of the policy. For a sample e-mail, voice mail, and computer systems policy, see Exhibit 13.9.

"An employer has a strong defense to a potential invasion of privacy claim by an employee if the employer implements an e-mail policy that is both written and communicated to the employee, thereby stating that e-mail is for business purposes only and the employer may access the e-mail both in the ordinary course of business and if business

Exhibit 13.9   Sample E-Mail, Voice Mail, and Computer Systems Policy

Subject: **E-Mail, Voice mail and Computer Systems Policy**

Purpose: To prevent employees from using the Company computer and voice-mail systems for harassing, defamatory, or other inappropriate communications. To preserve the Company's right to monitor and retrieve employee communications. To prohibit excessive personal use of the company's electronic systems.

Related Policies: Other related policies are: Harassment Prevention, Rules of Conduct, Confidentiality of Company Information, Solicitations.

Background: Inappropriate employee use of Company computer, e-mail, and voice-mail systems can subject the Company to significant legal exposure. Due to the effervescent nature of computer communications, employees will often say things in e-mail that they would never put in writing. Thus, it is important that all employers have a policy which strongly prohibits the inappropriate use of the Company's electronic systems, and puts employees on notice that the employer reserves the right to monitor such use.

Policy: The Company provides its employees with access to Company computers, network, Internet access, internal and external electronic mail, and voice mail to facilitate the conduct of Company business.

Company Property: All computers and data, information and software created, transmitted, downloaded, or stored on the Company's computer system are the property of Company. All electronic mail messages composed, sent, and received are and remain the property of Company. The voice mail system and all messages left on that system are Company property.

Business Use and Occasional Personal Use: The Company's computers, network, Internet access, electronic mail, and voice mail systems are provided to employees to assist employees in accomplishing their job responsibilities for the Company. Limited occasional personal use of such facilities is acceptable, provided such use is reasonable, appropriate, and complies with this policy. If you have any questions as to whether a particular use of such facilities is permissible, check with your supervisor before engaging in such use. The use of Company's computers, network, Internet access, electronic mail, and voice mail for personal use does not alter the facts that the foregoing remain Company property, and that employees have no reasonable expectation of privacy with respect to such use.

Privacy: Employees shall respect the privacy of others. Except as provided below, messages sent via electronic mail are to be read only by the addressed recipient or with the authorization of the addressed recipient. The data, information and software created, transmitted, downloaded, or stored on the Company's computer system may be accessed by authorized personnel only. Employees should understand that the confidentiality of electronic mail cannot be ensured. Employees must assume that any and all messages may be read by someone other than the intended recipient. Personal passwords are not an assurance of confidentiality. *There is no reasonable expectation of privacy in any e-mail, voice mail, and/or other use of Company computers, network, and systems.*

Exhibit 13.9   (continued)

Prohibited Conduct:

- Employees may not use the Company's computers, network, Internet access, electronic mail, or voice mail to conduct illegal or malicious activities.

- Employees may not transmit or solicit any threatening, defamatory, obscene, harassing, offensive, or unprofessional material. Offensive content would include, but not be limited to, sexual comments or images, racial slurs, gender-specific comments or any comments that would offend someone on the basis of his or her race, religion, color, national origin, ancestry, disability, age, sex, marital status, sexual orientation, or any other class protected by any federal, state, or local law.

- Employees may not create, transmit, or distribute unwanted, mass, excessive or anonymous e-mails, electronic vandalism, junk e-mail, or "spam."

- Employees may not access any Web site that is sexually or racially offensive or discriminatory.

- Employees may not display, download, or distribute any sexually explicit material.

- Employees may not violate the privacy of individuals by any means, such as by reading private e-mails or private communications, accessing private documents, or utilizing the passwords of others, unless officially authorized to do so.

- Employees may not represent themselves as being someone else, or send anonymous communications.

- Employees may not use the e-mail, voice mail, or computer systems to solicit for religious causes, outside business ventures, or personal causes.

- Employees may not transmit any of Company's confidential or proprietary information including (without limitation) customer data, trade secrets, or other material covered by Company's policy re: Confidentiality of Company information.

- Employees may not install, run, or download any software (including entertainment software or games) not authorized by the Company.

- Employees may not disrupt or hinder the use of the Company computers or network, or infiltrate another computer or computing system.

- Employees may not damage software or propagate computer worms or viruses.

Only authorized employees may communicate on the Internet on behalf of the Company.

Monitoring: Company maintains the right to monitor and record employee activity on its computers, network, voice mail and e-mail systems. Company's monitoring includes (without limitation) reading e-mail messages sent to received, files stored or transmitted, and recording Web sites accessed.

(continued)

Exhibit 13.9 (continued)

Archiving: It is Company's practice to archive (i.e., make backup copies) of all electronic documents, files, and e-mail messages incident to the Company's normal back-up procedures. Employees should therefore understand that even when a document, file, or message is deleted, it may still be possible to access that message. Management and law enforcement agencies have the right to access these archives.

Copyright Laws: Any software or other material downloaded into the Company's computers may be used only in ways consistent with the licenses and copyrights of the vendors, authors, and owners of the material. No employee shall make illegal or unauthorized copies of any software or data.

Violations of this Policy: Any violation of this policy may result in disciplinary action up to and including immediate termination. Any employee learning of any violation of this policy should notify his or her _____ [e.g., immediate supervisor] immediately.

Dates: Be sure to date policies when they become effective. Hang on to old policies and be sure to change the date on revised versions.

Source: Lee T. Paterson, ed., *Sample Personnel Policies,* Professionals in Human Resources Association (PIHRA), 2002.

---

reasons necessitate. Thus, an employer protects itself from lawsuits when it adopts an e-mail policy, notifies the employees of the policy, and faithfully adheres to it."[35]

Kevin Conlon, district counsel for the Communication Workers of America, suggests these additional guidelines that may be considered in formulating an accountable process for employee monitoring.

1. There should be no monitoring in highly private areas, such as restrooms.
2. Monitoring should be limited to the workplace.
3. Employees should have full access to any information gathered through monitoring.
4. Continuous monitoring should be banned.
5. All forms of *secret* monitoring should be banned. Advance notice should be given.
6. Only information relevant to the job should be collected.
7. Monitoring should result in the attainment of some business interest.

As early as 1970, the U.S. Department of Health, Education and Welfare developed principles along these same lines for a Code of Fair Employment Practices (CFEP), which includes five points. A review of these principles evidences attention to fundamental philosophical concerns such as a respect for individual autonomy and a congruent respect for business needs, as well as accountability.

[35] Michael Traynor, "How Extensively Can an Employer Monitor Messages?" *National Law Journal,* Jan. 31, 1994, at S2, S3, citing *Bourke* v. *Nissan Motor Corp. in U.S.A.,* No. B068705 (Cal. App. 2d) Div. 5 (July 26, 1993).

The first CFEP principle is *openness,* meaning that maintenance or collection of personal information must be disclosed to the subject. The second principle is *disclosure.* A subject should be informed of not only the fact that information is to be collected but also the contents of that information and the purposes for which it will be used. The third principle is the concept of *secondary usage,* which requires that information collected for one purpose may not be used for a second purpose. Fourth, the CFEP mandates that individuals have the right to *correction* of erroneous personal information. The fifth principle directs that firms maintain appropriate *security* surrounding the information collected in order to protect against misuse.

Similarly, Doug Rollyson, senior technical advisor of Superior Consultant Corporation, advises that employers take the following five steps in designing a computer usage policy:

1. Conduct an audit of existing information systems. For example, how is e-mail and Internet usage integrated into the organization's business objectives? Who has access to sensitive data? How much time do employees spend on the Internet? What sites can they visit?

2. Develop the elements of the Computer Usage Policy (CUP) based on the results of the audit. Involve the Information Technology and Legal Departments. Specify in the policy what is and is not acceptable computer usage behavior. Give concrete, specific examples of prohibited actions.

3. Develop a set of standard consequences to violations of the CUP. Be sure to consistently execute the organization's stated responses to violations.

4. Communicate the CUP to employees. This should be done in writing and through mandatory training sessions.

5. Enforce the CUP. Invest in the proper software tools.[36]

Failure to adhere to any of the above-stated principles may result in a violation of corporate integrity or a lack of accountability to those affected by the monitoring. If a manager consistently reviews all of her or his subordinate's e-mails with no notice to the individual workers and without regard to the business-relatedness of the particular missives, the manager may acquire information that is completely unrelated to the person's job but that affects the way in which the manager treats the employee. For instance, through review of e-mail, a manager might find out that a worker is a member of a far-right Republican organization. The manager, a staunch Democrat, may allow this division between them to impact how she or he treats the worker. In the end, this result would be unprofitable for the business as a whole.

As is apparent from the above discussion, it is possible to implement a monitoring program that is true to the values of the firm and accountable to those it impacts—the workers. Appropriate attention to the nature and extent of the monitoring, the notice given to those monitored, and the ethical management of the information obtained will ensure a balance of employer and employee interests.

---

[36] Doug Rollyson, "Five Steps to Designing a Computer Usage Policy," Superior Consultant Holdings Corporation, 2000, webmd-practice.medcast.com/Z/Channels/3119/article151.

Michael A. Smyth v. The Pillsbury Company *914 F. Supp. 97* (E.D. Pa. 1996)

Michael Smyth worked for the Pillsbury Company. Pillsbury installed an electronic mail (e-mail) system in order to "promote internal communications between its employees." Pillsbury told its employees that e-mail transmissions were confidential and would not be intercepted or used by Pillsbury against its employees as grounds for termination. Smyth exchanged e-mails with his supervisor which were, in fact, intercepted by Pillsbury management. Three months later, Smyth was terminated for transmitting what it deemed to be "inappropriate and unprofessional comments" over its e-mail system. (The e-mails contained threats to "kill the backstabbing bastards" in discussions of management and referred to the company holiday party as the "Jim Jones Kool Aid affair.")

Weiner, J.

Pennsylvania is an employment at-will jurisdiction and an employer "may discharge an employee with or without cause, at pleasure, unless restrained by some contract."

However, in the most limited of circumstances, exceptions have been recognized where discharge of an at-will employee threatens or violates a clear mandate of public policy. A "clear mandate" of public policy must be of a type that "strikes at the heart of a citizen's social right, duties and responsibilities."

Plaintiff claims that his termination was in violation of "public policy which precludes an employer from terminating an employee in violation of the employee's right to privacy as embodied in Pennsylvania common law." In support for this proposition, plaintiff directs our attention to a decision by our Court of Appeals in *Borse v. Piece Goods Shop, Inc.* In *Borse,* the plaintiff sued her employer alleging wrongful discharge as a result of her refusal to submit to urinalysis screening and personal property searches at her work place pursuant to the employer's drug and alcohol policy. After rejecting plaintiff's argument that the employer's drug and alcohol program violated public policy encompassed in the United States and Pennsylvania Constitutions, our Court of Appeals stated "our review of Pennsylvania law reveals other evidence of a public policy that may, under certain circumstances, give rise to a wrongful discharge action related to urinalysis or to personal property searches. Specifically, we refer to the Pennsylvania common law regarding tortious invasion of privacy."

The Court of Appeals in *Borse* observed that one of the torts which Pennsylvania recognizes as encompassing an action for invasion of privacy is the tort of "intrusion upon seclusion." As noted by the Court of Appeals, the Restatement (Second) of Torts defines the tort as follows:

> One who intentionally intrudes, physically or otherwise, upon the solitude or seclusion of another or his private affairs or concerns, is subject to liability to the other for invasion of his privacy, if the intrusion would be highly offensive to a reasonable person.

Liability only attaches when the "intrusion is substantial and would be highly offensive to the 'ordinary reasonable person.'" Although the Court of Appeals in *Borse* observed that "the Pennsylvania courts have not had occasion to consider whether a discharge related to an employer's tortious invasion of an employee's privacy violates public policy," the Court of Appeals predicted that in any claim where the employee claimed that his discharge related to an invasion of his privacy "the Pennsylvania Supreme Court would examine the facts and circumstances surrounding the alleged invasion of privacy. If the court determined that the discharge was related to a substantial and highly offensive invasion of the employee's privacy, [the Court of Appeals] believe that it would conclude that the discharge violated public policy." In determining whether an alleged invasion of privacy is substantial and highly offensive to a reasonable person, the Court of Appeals predicted that Pennsylvania would adopt a balancing test which balances the employee's privacy interest against the employer's interest in maintaining a drug-free workplace. Because the Court of Appeals in Borse could "envision at least two ways in which an employer's drug and alcohol program might violate the public policy protecting individuals from tortious invasion of privacy by private actors" the Court vacated the district court's order dismissing the plaintiff's complaint and remanded the case to the district court with directions to grant Borse leave to amend the Complaint to allege how the defendant's drug and alcohol program violates her right to privacy.

Applying the Restatement definition of the tort of intrusion upon seclusion to the facts and circumstances of the case *sub judice,* we find that plaintiff has failed to state a claim upon which relief can be granted. In the first instance, unlike urinalysis and personal property searches, we do not find a reasonable expectation of privacy in e-mail communications voluntarily made by an employee to his supervisor over the company e-mail system notwithstanding any assurances that such communications would not be intercepted by management. Once plaintiff communicated the alleged unprofessional comments to a second person (his supervisor) over an e-mail system which was apparently utilized by the entire company, any reasonable expectation of privacy was lost. Significantly, the defendant did not require plaintiff, as in the case of a urinalysis or personal property search, to disclose any personal information about himself. Rather, plaintiff voluntarily communicated the alleged unprofessional comments over the company e-mail system. We find no privacy interests in such communications.

In the second instance, even if we found that an employee had a reasonable expectation of privacy in the contents of his e-mail communications over the company e-mail system, we do not find that a reasonable person would consider the defendant's interception of these communications to be a substantial and highly offensive invasion of his privacy. Again, we note that by intercepting such communications, the company is not, as in the case of urinalysis or personal property searches, requiring the employee to disclose any personal information about himself or invading the employee's person or personal effects. Moreover, the company's interest in preventing inappropriate and unprofessional comments or even illegal activity over its e-mail system outweighs any privacy interest the employee may have in those comments.

In sum, we find that the defendant's actions did not tortiously invade the plaintiff's privacy and, therefore, did not violate public policy. As a result, the motion to dismiss is GRANTED.

Case Questions

1. Do you agree with the court's conclusion that, even if Smyth had a reasonable expectation of privacy of his transmissions, an interception would not be highly offensive to a reasonable person?

2. Are you sympathetic to an employer's reasons for wanting to intercept e-mail such as that involved in this case?

3. The court seems to be saying that, even though Pillsbury stated that it would not intercept e-mail, the employee should not have relied on this promise. Do you agree with this conclusion?

Fraser v. Nationwide Mut. Ins. Co.   *352 F.3d 107 (3d Cir. 2003)*

Richard Fraser, an at-will independent insurance agent for Nationwide Mutual Insurance Company, was terminated by Nationwide. The parties disagree on the reason for Fraser's termination. Fraser argues Nationwide terminated him because he filed complaints regarding Nationwide's allegedly illegal conduct; for criticizing Nationwide to the Nationwide Insurance Independent Contractors Association; and for attempting to obtain the passage of legislation in Pennsylvania to ensure that independent insurance agents could be terminated only for "just cause." Nationwide argues, however, that it terminated Fraser because he was disloyal. It points out that Fraser drafted a letter to two competitors—Erie Insurance Company and Zurich American Insurance —expressing Contractors Association members' dissatisfaction with Nationwide and seeking to determine whether Erie and Zurich would be interested in acquiring the policyholders of the agents in the Contractors Association. (Fraser claims that the letters only were drafted to get Nationwide's attention and were not sent.) When Nationwide learned about these letters, it claims that it became concerned that

Fraser might also be revealing company secrets to its competitors. It therefore searched its main file server—on which all of Fraser's e-mail was lodged—for any e-mail to or from Fraser that showed similar improper behavior. Nationwide's general counsel testified that the e-mail search confirmed Fraser's disloyalty. Therefore, on the basis of the two letters and the e-mail search, Nationwide terminated Fraser's Agreement. It is this search of his e-mail that gives rise to Fraser's claim for damages under the Electronic Communications Privacy Act of 1986 ("ECPA") and a parallel Pennsylvania statute.

Ambro, C.J.

* * *

B. ECPA CLAIMS AND PARALLEL STATE LAW CLAIMS

Fraser argues that, by accessing his e-mail on its central file server without his express permission, Nationwide violated Title I of the ECPA, which prohibits "intercepts" of electronic communications such as e-mail.[1] The statute defines an "intercept" as "the aural or other acquisition of the contents of any wire, electronic, or oral communication through the use of any electronic, mechanical, or other device." Nationwide argues that it did not "intercept" Fraser's e-mail within the meaning of Title I because an "intercept" can only occur contemporaneously with transmission and it did not access Fraser's e-mail at the initial time of transmission.

On this matter of statutory interpretation which we review *de novo,* we agree with Nationwide. Every circuit court to have considered the matter has held that an "intercept" under the ECPA must occur contemporaneously with transmission. The first case to do so, *Steve Jackson Games,* noted that "intercept" was defined as contemporaneous in the context of an aural communication under the old Wiretap Act, and that when Congress amended the Wiretap Act in 1986 (to create what is now known as the ECPA) to extend protection to electronic communications, it "did not intend to change the definition of 'intercept.'" Moreover, the Fifth Circuit noted that the differences in definition between "wire communication" and "electronic communication" in the ECPA supported its conclusion that stored e-mail could not be intercepted within the meaning of Title I. A "wire communication" under the ECPA was (until recent amendment by the USA Patriot Act[2]) "any aural transfer made in whole or in part through the use of facilities for the transmission of communications by the aid of wire, cable, or other like connection between the point of origin and the point of reception . . . *and such term includes any electronic storage of such communication."* By contrast, an electronic communication is defined as "any transfer of signs, signals, writing, images, sounds, data, or intelligence of any nature transmitted in whole or in part by a wire, radio, electromagnetic, photoelectronic or photooptical system . . . but does *not include . . . any wire or oral communication."* Thus, the Fifth Circuit reasoned that because "wire communication" explicitly included electronic storage but "electronic communication" did not, there can be no "intercept" of an e-mail in storage, as an e-mail in storage is by definition not an "electronic communication."

Subsequent cases, cited above, have agreed with the Fifth Circuit's result. While Congress's definition of "intercept" does not appear to fit with its intent to extend protection to electronic communications, it is for Congress to cover the bases untouched. We adopt the reasoning of our sister circuits and therefore hold that there has been no "intercept" within the meaning of Title I of ECPA.

2. Title II

Fraser also argues that Nationwide's search of his e-mail violated Title II of the ECPA. That Title creates civil liability for one who "(1) intentionally accesses without authorization a facility through which an electronic communication service is provided; or

---

[1] As noted, Fraser also argues that Nationwide has violated the Pennsylvania counterpart to ECPA Title 1, *18* Pa. Cons. Stat. § 5702, et seq. Because this statute is interpreted in the same way as the ECPA, the analysis and conclusions in the text apply equally to this state-law claim, which Fraser also does not analyze separately.

[2] The USA Patriot Act § 209, Pub. L. No. 107-56, §209(1)(A), 115 Stat. 272, 283 (2001), amended the definition of "wire communication" to eliminate electronic storage from the definition of wire communication.

(2) intentionally exceeds an authorization to access that facility; and thereby obtains, alters, or prevents authorized access to a wire or electronic communication while it is in electronic storage in such system." The statute defines "electronic storage" as "(A) any temporary, intermediate storage of a wire or electronic communication incidental to the electronic transmission thereof; and (B) any storage of such communication by an electronic communication service for purposes of backup protection of such communication."

The District Court granted summary judgment in favor of Nationwide, holding that Title II does not apply to the e-mail in question because the transmissions were neither in "temporary, intermediate storage" nor in "backup" storage. Rather, according to the District Court, the e-mail was in a state it described as "post-transmission storage." We agree that Fraser's e-mail was not in temporary, intermediate storage. But to us it seems questionable that the transmissions were not in backup storage—a term that neither the statute nor the legislative history defines. Therefore, while we affirm the District Court, we do so through a different analytical path, assuming without deciding that the e-mail in question was in backup storage.

[The ECPA] excepts from Title II seizures of e-mail authorized "by the person or entity providing a wire or electronic communications service." There is no circuit court case law interpreting this exception.

However, in *Bohach* v. *Citv of Reno,* a district court held that the Reno police department could, without violating Title II, retrieve pager text messages stored on the police department's computer system because the department "is the provider of the 'service'" and "service providers [may] do as they wish when it comes to accessing communications in electronic storage." Like the court in *Bohach,* we read [the ECPA] literally to except from Title II's protection all searches by communications service providers. Thus, we hold that, because Fraser's e-mail was stored on Nationwide's system (which Nationwide administered), its search of that e-mail falls within the exception to Title II.

* * *

Case Questions

1. Before reviewing the court's decision, but after reading the facts of this case, did you believe the employer was justified in monitoring the employee's e-mail and then terminating him?

2. Do you agree with the district court's analysis of the ECPA's treatment of e-mail and e-mail transmissions? Doesn't it simply mandate that employers monitor moments after an e-mail is sent?

3. What is the implication of the court's, final decision with regard to the *Bohach* exception?

WAIVERS OF PRIVACY RIGHTS

search
A physical invasion of a person's space, belongings, or body.

waiver
The intentional relinquishment of a known right.

On occasion, an employer may request that an employee waive her or his privacy rights as a condition of employment. This condition could be a **search**. A **waiver** would exempt the employer from liability for claims the employee may have as a result of privacy issues. While a valid waiver must be voluntarily given, requiring a waiver as an employment condition is a questionable approach. Employers maintain a superior bargaining position from which to negotiate such an arrangement, so voluntariness is questionable.

Waivers exist at all stages of employment, from preemployment medical screenings to a waiver of age discrimination claims when being bought out of one's job at an old age. Courts are not consistent in their acceptance of these waivers; but one common link among those that are approved is that there exists some form of consideration in which the employee receives something in return for giving up rights.

It has thus been held that the waiver at least be accompanied by an offer of employment. No waiver that is given by an applicant prior to a job offer would be considered valid and enforceable. Other requirements articulated by the courts include that the waiver be knowingly and intelligently given, and that it be clear and unmistakable, in writing, and voluntary.

PRIVACY RIGHTS SINCE SEPTEMBER 11, 2001

The United States implemented widespread modifications to its patchwork structure of privacy protections since the terror attacks of September 11, 2001. In particular, proposals for the expansion of surveillance and information gathering authority were submitted and many, to the chagrin of some civil rights attorneys and advocates, were enacted.

The most public and publicized of these modifications was the adoption and implementation of the Uniting and Strengthening America by Providing Appropriate Tools Required to Intercept and Obstruct Terrorism United States (USA PATRIOT) Act of 2001, Pub. L. No. 107-56. The USA PATRIOT Act expanded states' rights with regard to Internet surveillance technology, including workplace surveillance and amending the Electronic Communications Privacy Act in this regard. The act also grants access to sensitive data with only a court order rather than a judicial warrant, among other changes, and imposes or enhances civil and criminal penalties for knowingly or intentionally aiding terrorists. In addition, the new disclosure regime increased the sharing of personal information between government agencies in order to ensure the greatest level of protection.

Title II of the act provides for the following enhanced surveillance procedures, among others, that have a significant impact on individual privacy and may impact an employer's effort to maintain employee privacy:

- Expanded authority to intercept wire, oral, and electronic communications relating to terrorism and to computer fraud and abuse offenses.
- Provided roving surveillance authority under the Foreign Intelligence Surveillance Act of 1978 (FISA) to track individuals. (FISA investigations are not subject to Fourth Amendment standards but are instead governed by the requirement that the search serve "a significant purpose").
- Allowed nationwide seizure of voice mail messages pursuant to warrants (i.e., without the previously required wiretap order).
- Broadened the types of records that law enforcement may obtain, pursuant to a subpoena, from electronic communications service providers.
- Permitted emergency disclosure of customer electronic communications by providers to protect life and limb.
- Offered nationwide service of search warrants for electronic evidence.

Pursuant to these provisions, the government is now allowed to monitor anyone on the Internet simply by contending that the information is "relevant" to an ongoing

Management Tips

- Public sector employees are subject to protection by the Constitution and the Privacy Act; private sector employees are instead protected by common law and state-by-state restrictions on invasions of privacy.

- As an employer, you may search your employees' property where the employee does not have any expectation of privacy; the difficulty comes in determining where that expectation exists.

- Since many privacy protections exist on a state-by-state level, be sure to investigate the specific protections for which you are responsible in the states in which you do business.

- While it may appear reasonable for you to want to regulate certain off-work activities of your employees, be wary of overrestricting, since courts do not look on these regulations positively.

- You are less likely to find problems with a waiver of privacy rights where the waiver is accompanied by an offer of employment.

- When you do collect personal information about your employees, be sure to regulate access to this information, since unwarranted disclosure might constitute an invasion of privacy even where the original collection of information is allowed.

criminal investigation. In addition, the act provides anti–money laundering provisions designed to combat money laundering activity or the funding of terrorist or criminal activity through corporate activity or otherwise. All financial institutions must now report suspicious activities in financial transactions and keep records of foreign national employees, while also complying with antidiscrimination laws discussed throughout this text. It is a challenging balance, claim employers.

Though some of its surveillance and information–sharing provisions are set to expire (or "sunset") in 2005, the USA PATRIOT Act was not the only legislative response. By September 2002, the Office of Management and Budget had recorded 58 new regulations responding to terrorism[37] and both federal and state agencies have passed a number of new pieces of legislation. Not everyone is comfortable with these new protections. Out of concern for the USA PATRIOT Act's new permitted investigatory provisions, some librarians now warn computer users in their libraries that their computer use could be monitored by law enforcement agencies. *The Washington Post* reports that some are even ensuring privacy by destroying records of sites visited, books checked out, and logs of computer use[38] The American Civil Liberties Union reports that a number of communities have passed Anti-USA PATRIOT Act resolutions.[39]

[37] Office of Management and Budget, "Stimulating Smarter Regulation: 2002," *Report to Congress on the Costs and Benefits of Regulations and Unfunded Mandates on State, Local, and Tribal Entities* (March 2003).

[38] Rene Sanchez, "Librarians Make Some Noise over Patriot Act," *The Washington Post* (April 10, 2003, p. A20.

[39] http://www.aclu.org/SafeandFree/SafeandFree.cfm?ID=11256&c=206.

Employers have three choices in terms of their response to a governmental request for information. They may:

1. Voluntarily cooperate with law enforcement by providing, upon request (as part of an ongoing investigation), confidential employee information.

2. Choose not to cooperate and ask instead for permission to seek employee authorization to release the requested information.

3. Request to receive a subpoena, search warrant, or FISA order from the federal agency before disclosing an employee's confidential information.[40]

Summary

Basic rules that, if followed, may preclude employer liability for invasions of privacy are:

- First, conduct an information audit for the purpose of determining those areas of the company's practices and procedures that have the potential for invasion, including what type of information is collected, how that information is maintained, the means by which the information is verified, who has access to the information, and to whom the information is disclosed. The audit should cover all facets of the organization's activities, from recruitment and hiring to termination. In addition, it may be helpful to ascertain what type of information is maintained by different sectors of the organization.

- Second, in connection with sensitive areas where the company maintains no formal policy, develop a policy to ensure appropriate treatment of data. It is recommended that a policy and procedure be maintained in connection with the acquisition of information, the maintenance of that information, the appropriate contents of personnel files, the use of the information contained therein, and the conduct of workplace investigations. For instance, in connection with the maintenance of personnel files and the accumulation of personal information about company employees, the employer should request only information justified by the needs of the firm and relevant to employment-related decisions.

- Third, the information collected should be kept in one of several files maintained on each employee: (1) a personnel file, which contains the application, paperwork relating to hiring, payroll, and other nonsensitive data; (2) medical file, which contains physicians' reports and insurance records; (3) evaluation files, which contain any evidence of job performance including, but not limited to, performance appraisals; and (4) confidential file, which contains data relating to extremely sensitive matters that should not be disclosed except with express and specific authority, such as criminal records or information collected in connection with workplace investigations.

- Fourth, information should be gathered from reliable sources, rather than sources of questionable repute, such as hearsay, lie detector tests, and subjective indicators. Irrelevant or outdated material should periodically be expunged from these records as well.

- Fifth, publicize privacy policies and procedures, and educate employees regarding their rights as well as their responsibilities.

---

[40] Vance Knapp, "The Impact of the Patriot Act on Employers," http://www.rothgerber.com/newslettersarticles/le0024.asp (2003).

Chapter-
End
Questions

1. Can a government employee state a claim for a violation of the constitutional right to privacy when she was required, as a job applicant, to sign an affidavit stating that she had not used tobacco products for one year prior to the application date?

2. A homosexual employee files a claim of invasion of privacy against his employer who shared with coworkers the fact that the employee's male partner was listed on his insurance policy and pension plan as his beneficiary. Does he have a claim?

3. Young, an employee with the Grand Gulf Nuclear Power Station, entered the hospital for unknown reasons. Her coworkers speculated that she was suffering from radiation exposure. To discourage concern regarding radiation, the employer informed the employees that Young's illness was related to a recent hysterectomy. Young sues for an invasion of privacy. Does she win? [*Young* v. *Jackson,* 572 S.2d 378 (Miss. 1990).]

4. Bodewig was a part-time checker for a Kmart store. During one particular sale, she and a customer, Golden, had a disagreement about the "sale" price of a particular item; the customer left her merchandise at the counter and went to check the listed price on the shelf. While waiting for the customer to return, Bodewig voided that sale and put the merchandise aside to continue helping the other customers in line. When Golden returned, she accused Bodewig of taking $500 that she had left on the counter with her merchandise. Bodewig denied even seeing the money. The store manager searched Bodewig's coat pockets and did not find any money. He then balanced her cash drawer, and it balanced perfectly. Golden was still convinced that Bodewig had taken her money and continued to cause a loud scene. The store manager asked a female employee to accompany Bodewig to the washroom to strip-search her for the money. Bodewig was asked to strip down to her briefs, and there was no sign of any money. Golden claimed that she had between $500 to $600 in her purse; she wouldn't count it out, but she maintained her belief that Bodewig had stolen her money. Bodewig quit her job soon after this incident and filed charges based on invasion of privacy with the effect of emotional distress. Kmart claims that it did what was necessary to take care of the irate customer, and Bodewig did not resist the search at the time. Is Kmart's defense sufficient? [*Bodewig* v. *Kmart, Inc.,* 635 P.2d 657 (Or. 1981).]

5. David Patton, a merchandising manager for J.C. Penney Company, was having an intimate relationship with a coworker. The store manager, McKay, told Patton that if he did not cease this relationship with a coemployee, his job would be in danger. Patton refused to break off his relationship, claiming that he did not socialize with this woman at work, and the relationship did not have an adverse effect on his performance as evidenced by his awards "Merchant of the Month" and "Merchant of the Year," both earned while dating this coemployee. The company had no specific written policies about dating coworkers; however, McKay maintained that dating coworkers was not allowed and continued to threaten Patton's job. Finally, Patton asked for a transfer to another department because McKay threatened to discharge him for unsatisfactory performance. McKay denied the transfer and discharged him for unsatisfactory performance. Patton filed charges against the company and McKay that his discharge was outrageous conduct that violated his privacy. Did it? [*Patton* v. *J.C. Penney Co.,* 719 P.2d 854 (Or. 1986).]

6. The employer of an over-the-road trucker customarily rented and then paid for the trucker's hotel room during business travel. When a permit book went missing, the employer searched the trucker's hotel room without authorization from the employee. Does the trucker have a reasonable expectation of privacy in that hotel room? [*Sowards* v. *Norbar Inc.* 605 N.E. 2d 468 (Ohio Ct. App. 1992).]

7. Carol Kobeck, a night-shift worker for Nabisco, Inc., brought suit against the company on the grounds that the company's violation of her privacy was the cause of her husband

committing suicide. Kobeck's husband had called her at work one night and was told that she was not working that night. The next day, he went into the store because she had not yet come home. The assistant personnel manager, Carmical, confirmed that Kobeck had not worked the night before or for several other nights, when she had told her husband that she would be working, from which he deduced that she was having an affair with another man. Kobeck's husband confronted her that night and accused her of cheating. She denied the accusation, but that night her husband committed suicide and left a note, saying he killed himself because he loved her and wanted her to be happy. Kobeck charges Nabisco with violating her privacy by disclosing her schedule and attendance records to her husband without her knowledge or approval. [*Kobeck v. Nabisco, Inc.,* 305 S.E.2d 183 (Ga. App. 1983).]

8. Kristine Naragon was a graduate assistant for Louisiana State University at Baton Rouge's School of Music. She mainly had teaching responsibilities and was often praised for her work and dedication. When the university discovered that she was a lesbian and was involved with a student, the school of music renewed her yearly contract but revoked teaching responsibilities and replaced them with purely research-oriented responsibilities. Naragon claims that her privacy rights and her freedom of association rights were violated because she is a lesbian, and she wants her teaching privileges restored. The university maintains that there was no obligation to renew Naragon's contract as it stood, and the university felt that her conduct with a student, lesbian or not, warranted less contact with the students. Naragon defends her conduct by showing that this student was not and never had been a student in her class. Was there an invasion of privacy by the employer? Why or why not? [*Naragon v. Wharton,* 572 F. Supp. 1117 (1983).]

9. Marriott Resorts had a formal company party for more than 200 employees. At one point during the party, they aired a videotape that compiled employees' and their spouses' comments about a household chore that they hated. However, as a spoof, the video was edited to make it seem as if they were describing what it was like to have sex with their partner. One employee's wife sued Marriott for intrusion into seclusion and publication in a false light. Does she have a claim? [*Stein v. Marriott,* 944 P.2d 374 (Utah Ct. App. 1997).]

10. Swenson worked as a rural route mail carrier for the U.S. Postal Service in California. In October 1985, she wrote letters to her representative and senator claiming that her postmaster deliberately undercounted rural route mail boxes, qualifying him for bonus and merit awards while forcing his workers to work off the clock. After the congressmen contacted the Postal Service, it responded with two letters, which form the basis of Swenson's Privacy Act claim. They disclosed private facts about her employment status, explaining that she had filed charges of sex discrimination as well as two grievances in response to warnings from her employer. Swenson claims that the disclosure of the information to the congressmen constituted a violation of the Privacy Act. Is she right? [*Swenson v. U.S. Postal Service,* 890 F.2d 1075 (9th Cir. 1989).]

11. As fire marshall for a town in Texas, Joe had his own office in which he had a computer but no Internet. In Joe's absence, Smith, the city's network administrator, entered Joe's office to install the city network on his computer. Smith discovered that Joe had installed a password, without which Smith could not access the computer's hard drive to complete his task. Smith notified Joe's supervisor, who called Joe at home to get his password. After resuming work on the computer, Smith noticed the presence of newsgroups. Smith knew that no one was permitted to have newsgroups on his or her computer, but the policy had not been communicated to the fire station employees, including Joe. Looking at the newsgroups, Smith noticed three titles suggesting the presence of pornography. He clicked on one newsgroup title, alt.erotica.xxx.preteen, and saw that about 25 of the approximately 60 files had been

read. The city's public safety director, Keller, instructed Smith and Fire Chief Ure to get what was needed from Joe's office to view the contents of his computer, as well as any zip disks or drives. The material taken from Joe's office revealed explicit child pornography. Joe was convicted for possession of child pornography. Did the collection of evidence from Joe's office violate his Fourth Amendment rights? Explain. [*United States* v. *Slanina,* 283 F.3d 670 (5th Cir. 2002).]

12. A college provided its security officers with a locker area in which to store personal items. The security officers occasionally used the area as a dressing room. After incidents of theft from the lockers and reports that the employees were bringing weapons to campus, the college installed a video surveillance camera in the locker area. Did the employees have a reasonable expectation of privacy that was violated by the video surveillance? Explain. [*Thompson* v. *Johnson County Community College,* 930 F. Supp. 501 (D. Kan. 1996) aff'd 108 F.3d 1388 (10th Cir. 1997).]

Chapter **Fourteen**

Labor Law

Opening Scenarios

STATUTORY BASIS

Employees shall have the right to self-organization, to form, join, or assist labor organizations, to bargain collectively through representatives of their own choosing, and to engage in other concerted activities for the purpose of collective bargaining or other mutual aid or protection, and shall also have the right to refrain from any or all such activities. [National Labor Relations Act of 1935, 29 U.S.C. §151-169, §157, Section 7.]

COMING TOGETHER ON ISSUES

The NBA "avoids the apocalypse" by reaching a labor agreement, thereby narrowly avoiding a walkout; the National Hockey League loses its season to labor disputes, angering thousands of loyal fans; baseball lockouts threaten to cost revenues and crowds; disgruntled private sector lawyers unionize over pay and working conditions for the first time; non-members paying union fair-share fees are determined to be entitled to a formal, independent audit of the union; United Airlines aircraft mechanics reject a long-term deal agreed on during negotiations that would reduce benefits and cut pay 5 percent, only to have a bankruptcy judge grant United's request to temporarily cut mechanics' pay by 10 percent, instead; US Airways, struggling to avoid bankruptcy, gets the OK to throw out their labor contracts for 8,500 workers; the U.S. Department of Defense proposes slowing Lockheed Martin's production of the F/A-22 Raptor and the C-130J Hercules planes and eliminating them by 2008, and the machinists union walks off the job on strike, rejecting a three-year contract the company proposed to adjust wage and benefit issues; workers are increasingly threatened by outsourcing jobs to other countries whose wages are extremely low and have no unions; building trade unionists, traditionally opposed to curbing development for fear of losing jobs, team up with those opposed to urban sprawl, convinced that doing so will hold potential for more and better jobs. Though they have lost much of the numbers and clout that they once had, perhaps maybe even because they have done their job too well, as you can see from these recent issues, unions are still an important part of the American workplace landscape. (See Exhibit 14.1.)

collective bargaining
Negotiations and agreements between management and labor about wages, hours, and other terms and conditions of employment.

Labor law is actually a very different and discrete part of the law from employment law, but given its far-reaching impact on the workplace, it is important to be familiar with its basic history and provisions in order to have a more complete knowledge of issues in the workplace environment. Labor law involves **collective bargaining** between employers and employees about issues in the workplace. Rather than each employee striking his or her own deal with the employer, the law now permits employees to do so in an organized and collective way. This was not always so. The agrarian nature of the economy in the United States was such that until the middle of the 18th century, the majority of working Americans worked on farms. In 1820, only about 12 percent of workers were employed in manufacturing. By 1860, that number increased to about 18 percent, and the location of manufacturing had shifted from private homes to factories. As this trend continued to grow so did the size of the labor class, and the basis for modern labor problems was created. Compounding the competitive nature of industry during this time was the simultaneous improvement of the transportation system. This served to allow products from other markets to compete with local products, thus decreasing the local demand and the profit margin of production. This was often offset by decreasing the wage of the worker. It was in this atmosphere that the earliest strikes took place.

A Historical Accounting

Labor law has a long and somewhat acrimonious history in this country. Central to an understanding of the struggle between labor and management is understanding the role the courts played in shaping labor policy before the United States Congress enacted legislation that forms the basis for labor relationships today. There were four weapons of choice that business used to control early unionizing efforts: criminal conspiracy laws, injunctions, antitrust laws, and constitutional challenges. A brief examination of these early antiunion efforts helps to explain how the balance between workers' rights and management's rights was ultimately reached.

Criminal Conspiracy Laws

In the 1800s, many courts considered activity by workers such as striking and picketing to be common law criminal conspiracies. Workers were convicted for trying to improve working conditions through union efforts. As early as 1806, employers in the shoemaking industry in Philadelphia discovered that they could enlist the aid of the courts by charging their unionized employees with criminal conspiracy. Thus, if a group of employees attempted to exert pressure on an employer to increase wages, they would be charged with criminal conspiracy and, if convicted, subject to imprisonment. Generally, the penalties imposed were fines rather than jail, but along with them came the threat of harsher sentences upon subsequent convictions. This acted to discourage and even eliminate union activity. This practice continued until 1842 when the landmark case of *Commonwealth* v. *Hunt* severely criticized the use of criminal conspiracy theory to discourage unionization.

Exhibit 14.1   Interesting Union Factoids

According to the 2004 report of the U.S. Department of Labor's Bureau of Labor Statistics, released in January 2005:

- There are 15.5 million union members in the United States.
- 12.5 percent of wage and salary workers are union members, down from 12.9 in 2003.
- The median weekly earning for union members is $781; for nonunion workers, $612.
- Men are more likely to be union members (13.8 percent) than women (11.1 percent); when records were first kept in 1983, the gap between men and women was 10 points, but men's union membership declined more rapidly than women's and narrowed the gap.
- Blacks are more likely to be in a union (15.1 percent) than whites (12.2 percent), Asians (11.4 percent), or Hispanics (10.1 percent).
- Older workers, 45 to 54, were more likely to be union members (17 percent) than younger workers, 16 to 24 (4.7 percent).
- Full-time workers are more likely to be union members (13.9 percent) than part-time workers (6.4 percent).
- All states in the Middle Atlantic and Pacific divisions had membership rates above the national average.
- All states in the East South Central and West South Central have rates below the national average, with the Mountain Division at or below the national average.
- The largest numbers of union members live in California (2.4 million) and New York (2 million).
- About half (7.8 million) of the country's union members live in just six states (California, New York, Michigan, Illinois, Pennsylvania, and Ohio).
- The two states with that have had the lowest union membership rates since records have been kept are North Carolina (2.7 percent) and South Carolina (3 percent); Arkansas and Mississippi each have 4.8 percent, the next lowest rate.
- The four states that have had the highest rate every year since data has become available are New York (25.3 percent), Hawaii (23.7 percent), Michigan (21.6 percent), and Alaska (20.1 percent).
- Union membership rate has steadily declined from a high of 20.1 percent in 1983, the first year the data was available.
- 8 percent of private industry is union (half of what it was in 1983), but 36 percent of government workers.
- Two occupational groups have the highest unionization rates (37 percent): (1) education, training, and library occupations and (2) protective service occupations such as police and firefighters.
- In the private sector, transportation and utilities have the highest rate (24.9 percent), followed by telecommunications (22.4 percent), construction (14.7 percent), information industries (14.2 percent), and manufacturing (12.9 percent). Financial activities were lowest at 2 percent union membership.

Source: *Union Members Summary,* U.S. Department of Labor, Bureau of Labor Statistics, http://www.bls.gov/news.release/union2nr0.htm.

Commonwealth v. Hunt   *45 Mass. (4 Metc.) 111 (Mass. 1842)*

A lower court found a group of seven shoemakers who belonged to a union guilty of conspiracy because they refused to work for an employer who hired a shoemaker who was not a member of their union. The Supreme Judicial Court of Massachusetts, in reversing the convictions, found not only that it was not an unlawful activity to unionize but that the object of unions may be "highly meritorious and public spirited."

Shaw, J.

Without attempting to review and reconcile all the cases, we are of opinion, that as a general description, though perhaps not a precise and accurate definition, a conspiracy must be a combination of two or more persons, by some concerted action, to accomplish some criminal or unlawful purpose, or to accomplish some purpose, not in and of itself criminal or unlawful, by criminal or unlawful means. We use the terms criminal or unlawful, because it is manifest that many acts are unlawful, which are not punishable by indictment or other public prosecution; and yet there is no doubt, we think, that a combination by numbers to do them would be an unlawful conspiracy, and punishable by indictment.

Several rules upon the subject seem to be well established, to wit, that the unlawful agreement constitutes the gist of the offence, and therefore that it is not necessary to charge the execution of the unlawful agreement.

Another rule is a necessary consequence of the former, which is, that the crime is consummate and complete by the fact of unlawful combination, and, therefore, that if the execution of the unlawful purpose is averred, it is by way of aggravation, and proof of it is not necessary to conviction; and therefore the jury may find the conspiracy, and negative the execution, and it will be a good conviction.

And it follows, as another necessary legal consequence, from the same principle, that the indictment must—by averring the unlawful purpose of the conspiracy, or the unlawful means by which it is contemplated and agreed to accomplish a lawful purpose—set out an offense complete in itself; and that an illegal combination, imperfectly and insufficiently set out in the indictment, will not be aided by averments of acts done in pursuance of it.

From this view of the law respecting conspiracy, we think it an offence which especially demands the application of that wise and humane rule of the common law, that an indictment shall state, with as much certainty as the nature of the case will admit, the facts which constitute the crime intended to be charged. This is required, to enable the defendant to meet the charge and prepare for his defence, and, in case of acquittal or conviction, to show by the record the identity of the charge, so that he may not be indicted a second time for the same offence. It is also necessary, in order that a person, charged by the grand jury for one offence, may not be substantially convicted, on his trial, of another.

From these views of the rules of criminal pleading, it appears to us to follow, as a necessary legal conclusion, that when the criminality of a conspiracy consists in an unlawful agreement of two or more persons to compass or promote some criminal or illegal purpose, that purpose must be fully and clearly stated in the indictment; and if the criminality of the offence, which is intended to be charged, consists in the agreement to compass or promote some purpose, not of itself criminal or unlawful, by the use of fraud, force, falsehood, or other criminal or unlawful means, such intended use of fraud, force, falsehood, or other criminal or unlawful means, must be set out in the indictment.

We are here carefully to distinguish between the confederacy set forth in the indictment, and the confederacy or association contained in the constitution of the Boston Journeymen and Bootmakers' Society, as stated in the little printed book, which was admitted as evidence on the trial. Because, though it was thus admitted as evidence, it would not warrant a conviction for anything not stated in the indictment. It was proof, as far as it went to support the averments in the indictment. If it contained any criminal matter not set forth in the indictment, it is of no avail.

Now, it is to be considered, that the preamble and introductory matter in the indictment—such as unlawfully and deceitfully designing and intending unjustly to extort great sums, etc.—is mere recital, and not traversable, and therefore cannot aid an imperfect averment of the facts constituting the description of the offence. The same may be said of the concluding matter, which follows the averment, as to the great damage and oppression not only of their said masters, employing them in said art and occupation, but also of divers other workmen in the same art, mystery and occupation, to the evil example, &c. If the facts averred constitute the crime, these are properly stated as the legal inferences to be drawn from them. If they do not constitute the charge of such an offence, they cannot be aided by these alleged consequences.

Stripped then of these introductory recitals and alleged injurious consequences, and of the qualifying epithets attached to the facts, the averment is this: that the defendants and others formed themselves into a society, and agreed not to work for any person, who should employ any journeyman or other person, not a member of such society, after notice given to discharge such workman.

The manifest intent of the association is to induce all those engaged in the same occupation to become members of it. Such a purpose is not unlawful. It would give them a power which might be exerted for useful and honorable purposes, or for dangerous and pernicious ones. If the latter were the real and actual object, and susceptible of proof, it should have been specially charged. Such an association might be used to afford each other assistance in times of poverty, sickness and distress; or to raise their intellectual, moral, and social condition; or to make improvement in their art; or for other proper purposes. Or the association might be designed for purposes of oppression and injustice. But in order to charge all those, who become members of an association, with the guilt of a criminal conspiracy, it must be averred and proved that the actual, if not the avowed object of the association, was criminal. An association may be formed, the declared objects of which are innocent and laudable, and yet they may have secret articles, or an agreement communicated only to the members, by which they are banded together for purposes injurious to the peace of society or the rights of its members. Such would undoubtedly be a criminal conspiracy, on proof of the fact, however meritorious and praiseworthy the declared objects might be. The law is not to be hoodwinked by colorable pretenses. It looks at truth and reality, through whatever disguise it may assume. But to make such an association, ostensibly innocent, the subject of prosecution as a criminal conspiracy, the secret agreement, which makes it so, is to be averred and proved as the gist of the offence. But when an association is formed for purposes actually innocent, and afterwards its powers are abused by those who have the control and management of it, to purposes of oppression and injustice it will be criminal in those who thus misuse it, or give consent thereto, but not in the other members of the association.

Nor can we perceive that the objects of this association, whatever they may have been, were to be attained by criminal means. The means which they proposed to employ, as averred in this count, and which, as we are now to presume, were established by the proof, were, that they would not work for a person, who, after due notice, should employ a journeyman not a member of their society. Supposing the object of the association to be laudable and lawful, or at least not unlawful, are these means criminal? The case supposes that these persons are not bound by contract, but free to work for whom they please, or not to work, if they so prefer. On this state of things, we cannot perceive, that it is criminal for men to agree together to exercise their own acknowledged rights, in such a manner as best to subserve their own interests.

Suppose a baker in a small village had the exclusive custom of his neighborhood, and was making large profits by the sale of his bread. Supposing a number of those neighbors, believing the price of his bread too high, should propose to him to reduce his prices, or if he did not, that they would introduce another baker; and on his refusal, such other baker should, under their encouragement, set up a rival establishment, and sell his bread at lower prices; the effect would be to diminish the profit of the former baker, and to the same extent to impoverish him. And it might be said and proved, that the purpose of the associates was to diminish his profits, and thus impoverish him, though the ultimate and laudable object of the combination was to reduce the cost of bread to themselves and their neighbors. The same thing may be said of all competition in every branch of trade and industry; and yet it is through that competition, that the best interests of trade and industry are promoted. It is scarcely necessary to allude to the familiar instances of opposition lines of conveyance, rival hotels, and the thousand other instances, where each strives to gain custom to himself, by which he may lessen the price of commodities, and thereby diminish the profits of others.

We think, therefore, that associations may be entered into, the object of which is to adopt measures that may have a tendency to impoverish another, that is, to diminish his gains and profits, and yet so far from being criminal or unlawful, the object may be highly meritorious and public spirited. The legality of such an association will therefore depend upon the means to be used for its accomplishment. If it is to be carried into effect by fair or honorable and lawful means, it is, to say the least, innocent; if by falsehood or force, it may be stamped out with the character of conspiracy. REVERSED.

Case Questions

1. Why do you think it was necessary to dissolve the relationship between criminal conspiracy and the labor movement? What was the relationship given between criminal acts and employees' rights to control their environment at work?

2. Why do you think the court found that there was some good in organizing to affect the employer's policies? Explain.

3. Do you agree with the court's analysis in this case? Explain.

Despite *Commonwealth* v. *Hunt,* the criminal conspiracy trials retained some vitality until the 1890s. During this time, conspiracy trials were losing steam because of difficulty in getting juries to side with employers. Another method of discouraging unions was being developed which would prove equally difficult for labor.

Injunctions

injunction
A court order requiring individuals or groups of persons to not perform certain acts that the court has determined will do irreparable harm.

Employers sought the use of **injunctions** to gain immediate relief from workers' attempted collective bargaining activities. This legal action was encouraged and proliferated after 1895. In that year, the U.S. Supreme Court issued a decision that upheld the constitutionality of the labor injunction.[1] Armed with this potent legal support, judges were quick to apply this remedy to quash strikes and protests. Judges often committed abuses by wielding their power in personal ways. For example, when an injunction was sought, a judge would have to decide whether a union's objectives were lawful or unlawful. Judges outlawed many union activities this way. This was not always an issue of improper motivation; Judges were left without legislative directives, and in their absence were free to use their own beliefs, attitudes, and prejudices to reach conclusions. Given the antilabor sentiment among the business class, which was the background of a good many judges of this period, the result was overwhelmingly against labor's attempt to organize.

yellow dog contract
Agreement employers require employees to sign stating they do not belong to a union and will not join one. Now illegal.

This method came to a head in the case of *Hitchman Coal Company* v. *Mitchell,*[2] in which the Supreme Court declared that a labor injunction could be used to enforce a **yellow dog contract**. The yellow dog contract was a device used by anti-union employers to stop the progress of the union movement. It was the promise of a worker not to join a labor union while in the hire of an employer. Yellow dog contracts, used sparingly before *Hitchman,* proliferated afterward. Employees, often faced with no alternative employment options, were forced to sign yellow dog contracts. Later, if their employer was faced with a unionizing campaign, the employer could receive an injunction that would restrain anyone from encouraging these workers to join a union. This decision's hostile view toward organized labor dealt a harsh blow to workers seeking to organize. Its effects were felt until 1932, when yellow dog contracts were ended by Congress.

Antitrust Attacks

The early part of the 20th century saw declining competition and mammoth growth of industrialization. By 1930, nonagricultural occupations accounted for about 80 percent of the labor force. Business leaders saw the advantage of cooperation and began to

[1] *In re Debs,* 158 U.S. 564 (1895).
[2] 245 U.S. 229 (1917).

establish price agreements, trusts, pools, and trade associations. These devices were intended to stamp out competition between rivals. Elimination of competition meant growth of huge and powerful corporations whose purpose was to monopolize an area. Once competition was eliminated, it was easy to control prices and make them whatever the corporation wanted them to be. Of course, this was a disaster for consumers who were at the mercy of the monopolies. Congress enacted the Sherman Antitrust Act in 1890 to eliminate monopolistic control of the nation's economy. After its passage, labor unions learned that the law limited a variety of their activities. Unions were prosecuted under various provisions which were interpreted to include them under the provisions that prohibited "every contract, combination . . . or conspiracy, in restraint of trade. . . ." When unions challenged the application of the Sherman Antitrust Act to their activities, the Supreme Court, in 1908,[3] held that the Sherman Act applied to labor unions, giving business a new weapon to combat unionism. In addition, the case held that individual union members were responsible for the actions of its officers, making the rank and file liable for judgments against the union, and outlawed **secondary boycotts**. In response, unions organized themselves into a strong political force and in 1912 helped to elect Woodrow Wilson (who had pledged his support to the American Federation of Labor) as well as other democratic candidates. The Democratic Party soon fulfilled its promise to organized labor, and in October 1914 the Clayton Act became law. Section 6 of that act provided that "nothing contained in the antitrust laws shall be construed to forbid the existence and operation of labor organizations" nor shall labor unions be held to be "illegal combinations or conspiracies in restraint of trade under the antitrust laws."

More importantly, the Clayton Act regulated the procedure by which a federal court could issue an injunction against labor. Some of the most important gains from labor's perspective were the requirement that an injunction not be issued without notice to the union, absent emergency circumstances; a jury trial for those members who were charged with a violation under the injunction; the requirement that a bond be posted by the party seeking the injunction and indemnifying the union if they were found to have acted lawfully; and the requirement that specific acts be enjoined and not just the activity of the union wholesale.

Constitutional Challenges to Early Congressional Enactments

Early efforts by federal and state legislators to support organized labor were thwarted by the courts as a whole. Many state laws were declared unconstitutional by state supreme courts. Congress continued to recognize the rights of labor organizations and in 1898 passed the Erdman Act. The objective of the act was to set up a procedure by which conflicts in the railroad industry could be handled. Among other rights, it gave the railroad workers the right to self-organization and collective bargaining and outlawed the yellow dog contract. At this time Congress targeted railroad workers for protection largely because of the Pullman strike, which had disrupted service in 1894. Feeling the need to ensure against further disruptions that had the effect of paralyzing the nation's transportation system, Congress thought it found a way to make this issue one of constitutional dimension by making it one of interstate commerce. However, when confronted with the issue of whether Congress could

secondary boycott
A work stoppage by employees who are not directly involved in the labor dispute, done to show union solidarity.

[3] *Loewe v. Lawlor* (a.k.a. the *Danbury Hatters* case), 208 U.S. 274 (1908).

regulate industry by regulating employer–employee relations in this way, the Supreme Court held that Congress could not and struck down this critical law. The Court was not partial to any laborers in particular. In 1918 and 1923, the Court struck down congressional laws that would have controlled the use of child laborers and legislation that would have given women a minimum wage when employed in industry.

Out of Necessity Comes Change

The start of World War I saw the first real movement away from antiunion sentiment. The need for uninterrupted production and for preventing wartime strikes was seen as critical for the greater national interest. President Woodrow Wilson formed the National War Labor Board for the purpose of peacefully resolving labor disputes. This precursor of the National Labor Relations Board (NLRB) embodied many of the tenets that were eventually adopted by the NLRB. While the war acted to create a moratorium on attacks on organized labor, it also served to show that peaceful efforts aimed at resolving labor disputes were possible. After World War I the National War Labor Board was dismantled, but the unmistakable effect was that it was a stepping stone toward recognition of the organized labor movement.

Congress continued to enact piecemeal legislation aimed at limited pockets of laborers, but in 1932, responding to the harsh effects of the Depression, Congress enacted the National Industrial Recovery Act (NIRA). This law put business in charge of regulating prices and production. Because the regulation of the market in this way was a clear violation of the Sherman Antitrust Act, the NIRA exempted any price control measure (called "codes") from the reach of the Sherman Act. In addition, the NIRA established a minimum wage and gave workers collective bargaining and other rights. Under the NIRA, the ranks of organized labor began to increase. It was under the umbrella of the NIRA that President Roosevelt created the National Labor Board in 1933 and bolstered its enforcement provisions in 1934. Both the NIRA and the Board operated successfully until a dispute with the automobile industry, which it could not settle, undermined labor's confidence in the Board to such an extent that it was effectively dismantled. In 1935, the NIRA was declared unconstitutional by the Supreme Court because, the Court held, neither the president of the United States nor any private group (such as the business entities given the power under the NIRA to control prices) had the constitutional authority to do what was required of them under the act.

It is against this backdrop that the modern labor movement was born. After this, Congress was able to successfully enact legislation that has formed the basis of what we know as organized labor. Through a series of enactments that have shifted the balance of power first to the unions and then to employers, the balance that has been created is subject today only to refinement. (See Exhibits 14.2 and 14.3.)

At one point, labor unions enjoyed great popularity in the United States. According to the U.S. Department of Labor's Bureau of Labor Statistics, in 2004, about 12.5 percent of the workforce (about 15.5 million) was unionized, a decrease from former years, such as 1983, the first year for which comparable union data are available, when the number was 20.1 percent.

Due in part to such factors as the reduction in the labor force of traditionally heavily unionized industries, such as steel manufacturing, international competition,

Chronology

1940s-1960s *The postwar economic boom establishes the model for middle-class Americans' expectations of ever-rising earnings and job security.*

1956
William H. Whyte Jr. describes the emerging ethos of the corporate employee in his best-selling book, *The Organization Man.* According to an often-unspoken pledge of reciprocal loyalty, the company offered job security, rising earnings and generous fringe benefits in return for the employee's commitment to stay with the firm for his entire career.

1970s *Rising labor costs and growing competition from overseas suppliers prompt U.S. corporations to step up automation and set up plants in low-cost countries.*

1973
The steady rise in workers' earnings that has marked the postwar period comes to a halt after the first of a series of oil crises sparks inflation and slows economic growth.

1979
In the first phase of corporate restructuring, manufacturers begin cutting production jobs. General Motors, Ford and Chrysler will eliminate 350,000 jobs over the next decade.

1980s *Corporations eliminate millions of blue-collar jobs in an attempt to "restructure" their operations to become more competitive with foreign producers.*

1981-82
The worst recession since the Great Depression of the 1930s takes its greatest toll on the manufacturing industries of the Midwest, pushing unemployment among blue-collar workers to double-digit levels.

1985
IBM — hurt by mounting competition from foreign computer makers — begins cutting its work force.

1989
A wave of bank consolidations and closures begins, resulting in the loss of more than 100,000 jobs in that sector to date.

1990s *Restructuring begins to cut into white-collar employment as corporations eliminate many middle-management positions.*

July 1990
Recession begins, accelerating the pace of layoffs. While blue-collar workers continue to bear the brunt of unemployment, companies are for the first time cutting out entire layers of middle management to reduce labor costs and make their operations more flexible to changing economic conditions. As a result, white-collar unemployment spreads throughout U.S. industry.

August 1990
Sears, the nation's third-largest retailer, begins a cost-reduction program that will cut about 33,000 positions by the end of 1991.

1991
Restructuring accelerates. U.S. corporations announce more than a half million permanent staff cuts affecting both production and white-collar workers.

Nov. 26, 1991
IBM announces it will cut 20,000 jobs next year.

Dec. 18, 1991
General Motors says it will close 21 of its 125 North American plants and pare 74,000 positions, or 18 percent of its work force, over the next four years.

Jan. 7, 1992
Sears announces it will eliminate an additional 7,000 positions by automating customer-service tasks.

Jan. 21, 1992
United Technologies Corp. announces it will cut 13,900 jobs in its defense and civilian industries.

Feb. 4, 1992
Congress approves legislation providing an additional 13 weeks of unemployment compensation. President Bush, who blocked or vetoed two similar measures in 1991, signs the bill into law Feb. 7.

Feb. 24, 1992
General Motors names the first 12 of 21 plants to be closed in the U.S. and Canada. GM also posts a $4.45 billion loss for 1991 — the largest in American corporate history.

2000s *The global marketplace continues to transform American employment patterns.*

2005
According to the Labor Department, most of the 24.6 million new jobs that will be added to the U.S. economy over the 15-year period ending in 2005 will be high-skill positions requiring more training than most of the jobs they will replace.

Source: *Congressional Quarterly Researcher* 2, no. 8 (Feb. 28, 1992), p. 171.

Exhibit 14.3   Union Role in Services Expanding

Many experts say that, following a sharp decline in clout and membership in the 1980s, labor unions will need to evolve into providers of social and financial services if they are to survive. One example would be the addition of alcohol and drug abuse prevention services to union employee assistance plans. Some unions have already begun offering bargain financial services to their members in the form of reduced-fee credit cards and checking accounts.

There are some bright spots on the horizon for labor unions. The failure of union-busting as a management tool is reason for optimism. Still, private sector union membership and union influence have weakened labor's bargaining position for workers' economic benefits. The AFL-CIO has sought new recruits by creating a new membership category called an "associate member." It also aired the "Union, yes" television advertising campaign to attract workers. Many labor experts are guardedly optimistic about these revitalization attempts and say that the scales of power still appear to be tilted in favor of management.

Source: Copyright © 1990 by the New York Times Company. Reprinted by permission.

aggressive nonunionizing campaigns by employers, union concessions during downturns in the economy, and loss of jobs to other countries with cheaper labor, the percentage has steadily decreased since the 70s. (See Exhibit 14.4.)

Yet with over 15 million members, labor unions remain an important part of the workplace. With the 2004 median weekly income of full-time wage and salary union members being $781 compared with $612 for nonunion employees (although union membership does not totally account for the difference), we can see at least some of why unions may still play an important part in the workplace landscape. In this chapter, we will discuss the basic laws addressing collective bargaining and what the laws require.

LABOR LAWS

Four main federal laws comprise the statutory basis for labor law and unionization. The legislation initiating a move toward collective bargaining in the United States began with restricting court responses to union activity and establishing the right of employees to form labor organizations and to be protected against unfair labor practices at the hands of employers.

Until the Norris-LaGuardia Act of 1932 and the Wagner Act of 1935 (generally referred to as the National Labor Relations Act of 1935), employers had held virtually all the power. However, once that right to bargain collectively was created and unions established, the matter took on some rather sinister twists. Unions started feeling their power and often went overboard in using it.

This resulted in two other legislative measures to address the evolution of collective bargaining. The Taft-Hartley Act (also known as the Labor Management Relations Act) amended the Wagner Act in 1947 to establish unfair *union* practices, and the Landrum-Griffin Act of 1959 gave certain civil rights to union members and addressed corruption of union officials.

Exhibit 14.4   Maquiladoras: Mexico's Cheap Labor Lures Firms

See an example of why labor complains about managements' moving jobs out of the United States:

U.S. COMPANIES TAKE JOBS SOUTH

History—Mexico introduced maquiladoras in 1965. There are about 2,100 plants providing 500,000 jobs. More than 80 American companies have built assembly plants—among them, General Motors and Zenith Electronics.

How it works—U.S. companies deliver raw materials and parts to the maquiladoras and receive finished goods, paying no taxes, and only a duty on the cost of labor. Workers are paid $5 to $7 a day. In the United States, the same jobs pay $8 to $15 an hour.

Results—The foreign exchange earnings, about $4 billion a year, are second only to the state-run oil industry.

Conditions—Some plants provide employees with cheap lunches, food coupons, health services, and housing aid, but many others are sweatshops that expose workers to toxic chemicals without protective gear or adequate ventilation.

Management—American companies say the flight south is a matter of survival. "Over the past 20 years, the U.S. television industry has been under siege by foreign competitors," Zenith spokesman John Taylor said. "If we didn't have operations in Mexico, we would have been out of business years ago."

Labor—Mark Anderson of the AFL-CIO in Washington estimates 400,000 jobs that either existed in the United States or would have been created have moved to Mexico. "American companies don't advertise the fact they're closing their plants in the United States and moving to Mexico," he said. "We have gone from 10,000 jobs in 1975 to about 6,000," said Fred Gross, president of the United Auto Workers Local 292 in Kokomo, Indiana. "Based on what we've experienced . . . it's [the North American Free Trade Agreement being negotiated by the United States, Mexico, and Canada] going to send more jobs to Mexico."

Source: S. Hayward, "Mexico's Cheap Labor Lures Firms," *State*, May 17, 1992, p. 1H.

THE NORRIS-LAGUARDIA ACT

The Norris-LaGuardia Act was the first major labor law statute enacted in the United States. The opening section of the Norris-LaGuardia Act established that government recognized that the job to a worker is more important than a worker is to a corporation. It recognized that the only real power workers had was in impacting employers through numbers. An employer may not be disturbed when one worker walks out, but most certainly will be when all or most workers do so. The Norris-LaGuardia Act endorsed collective bargaining as a matter of public policy. To implement this policy, Congress sharply curbed the power of the courts to intervene in labor disputes, including curtailing use of the injunction. Norris-LaGuardia did not give labor unions any new legal rights; rather, it allowed them more freedom to operate free from court control and interference. This greatly facilitated labor unions acting as effective collective bargaining agencies.

Section 4 of the act declares that no federal court has the power to issue any form of injunctive relief in any case involving a labor dispute if that injunction would prohibit any person who was participating in such a dispute from doing certain acts. Judges cannot restrain any strike, regardless of its objective, and cannot restrain picketing activities. A labor union can provide relief funds to its strikers and publicize its labor disputes, and workers could urge other employees to join the conflict. Norris-LaGuardia allows a union to act in defense of a person prosecuted for his or her actions or to prosecute an action under the worker's contract. A union can conduct meetings to promote the interests of workers. Norris-LaGuardia protected any "labor dispute" even though parties did not stand as employer–employee with each other, further encouraging collective bargaining.

Most importantly, while it did not directly outlaw yellow dog contracts, the act declared that yellow dog contracts were inconsistent with U.S. public policy and not enforceable in any court in the United States. Later, the NLRB held that an employer engaged in an unfair labor practice if it demanded that an employee execute such an agreement.

The act also had significant impact in curbing prosecution under the antitrust laws. In its statement of purpose, Congress claimed that the intent of the act was to give labor what it thought it had received under the Clayton Act. Given the broadly stated purpose of the act, the Supreme Court has broadly construed it, providing unions with the opportunity to engage in activities calculated to effect the collective bargaining process. When Norris-LaGuardia limited the enforcement of yellow dog contracts and removed the impediments of workers to organize in a concerted fashion, the way was paved for enactment of the National Labor Relations Act three years later.

THE WAGNER/NATIONAL LABOR RELATIONS ACT

Of the four pieces of seminal labor legislation, it is the National Labor Relations Act (NLRA) that most people consider to be the mainstay of union activity, since it established the right of employees to form unions, to bargain collectively, and to strike. Recall that at one time it had been illegal—in fact, criminal—for employees to join together in an effort to collectively bargain with employers.

The National Labor Relations Act

In order to avoid the unconstitutional delegation of legislative power, Congress, in enacting the NLRA, placed the administration of the act in the hands of the National Labor Relations Board (NLRB), an independent federal administrative agency, rather than in the hands of an industrial group; set up standards to govern the exercise of power delegated to that administrative agency; and provided for the judicial enforcement of the orders of that agency. The board was empowered to issue remedial orders, enforceable in the courts, to prevent commission of unfair labor practices. Five such unfair practices were outlined in Section 8 of the act. Under this section, it is an unfair labor practice to:

- Interfere with, restrain, or coerce employees in the exercise of their rights.
- Interfere with the formation of a labor organization.

- Discriminate in the hiring or tenure of employment or discourage membership in a labor organization.
- Retaliate for filing charges or testifying under the act.
- Refuse to bargain with the representatives of the employees.

Notably absent from this act are unfair labor practices that might be committed by unions, although there were unfair labor practices listed that might be committed by employers. In the political climate that prevailed in 1935, the government placed its weight on the side of laborers because of the imbalance between corporate power and the labor market. The act was government's attempt to guarantee them the right to organize so they would be able to bargain on a more equal basis with employers.

As you can imagine, given the history we discussed, creation of the NLRB did not rest well with business. For the first few years of its existence the board survived a well-organized and concerted attack challenging its constitutionality and the scope of its authority. Finally, in 1937 and 1938, the U.S. Supreme Court brought the avalanche of injunction suits against the NLRB to a halt in a series of rulings that found the authority of the board to determine whether an employer had engaged in an unfair labor practice was exclusive, subject only to subsequent judicial review after the board had issued its decision, and detailing the scope of the NLRB's legal powers. These decisions form the foundations of the NLRB that are still effective today.

With the constitutionality of the NLRB settled and the injunctions halted, the judicial proceedings during the third year of the board's existence concerned the correctness of the NLRB's decisions and the power of the board to fashion remedies. Certain principles of law were established, including that employees on strike were still employees; that employees striking because of an unfair labor practice are entitled to reinstatement, even if reinstatement makes it necessary to discharge employees hired to replace them; and that threatened economic loss does not justify the commission of an unfair labor practice. From 1935 to 1947 the courts developed a vast body of law dealing with labor issues.

The National Labor Relations Board

community of interests
Factors employees have in common for bargaining purposes.

The NLRB is the independent federal agency that enforces labor laws in the private sector. Once sufficient interest has been indicated by the employees (usually by signing union authorization cards), the NLRB conducts elections to determine what union, if any, will represent the employees in collective bargaining. The NLRB also decertifies unions that employees no longer wish to have represent them, issues labor regulations, hears unfair labor practice cases at the agency level, and otherwise administers the NLRA.

bargaining unit
The group of employees in a workplace that have the legal right to bargain with the employer.

In collective bargaining, employees with a **community of interests**—that is, similar workplace concerns and conditions—come together as a **bargaining unit** that the union will represent. The community of interests is based on such factors as similarity of the jobs the employees perform, similar training or skills, and so on. While the general rule is that at least two employees must be in a bargaining unit, an employer may agree to a one-person unit, such as for an on-site craftworker (e.g., a carpenter who belongs to a carpenter's union being employed at a worksite as the only carpenter).

Employees may unionize either by signing a sufficient number of authorization cards, by voting in a union during a union representation election, or, in some cases, by the NLRB ordering the employer to bargain with a union. NLRB supervises the union election and certifies the results. The employer cannot interfere in any way with the employees' efforts to form a union, as done in opening scenario 1.

Concerted Activity

Section 7 of the NLRA guarantees employees the right to engage in concerted activities for mutual aid or protection. Typical protected concerted activities include union organizing, the discussion of unionization among employees, and the attempt by one employee to solicit union support from another employee. But concerted activity need not involve a union. Activities by groups of employees unaffiliated with a union to improve their lot at their workplace are deemed protected concerted activities.

Concerted activity also covers activity by a single employee, even if no other employee joins him or her. The reasoning is that the protected status of such activity should not turn on whether another employee decides to join the activity. Not all concerted activity is protected, however. Acts or threats of violence are not protected.

shop steward
Union member chosen as intermediary between the union and employees.

collective bargaining agreement
Negotiated contract between labor and management.

industrial union
Union with branches at particular workplaces.

business agent
The representative of a union, usually craft.

craft unions
Unions composed of skilled craftworkers not situated at any one workplace.

Unions

Unions are composed of nonsupervisory or nonmanagerial employees, including part-time workers. Specifically excluded from the NLRA are agricultural and domestic workers, independent contractors, and those employed by their spouse or parent.

The union's **shop steward**, elected by the members, is the intermediary generally between the union and the employer. He or she may collect dues and recruit new workers, and, if a union member feels the **collective bargaining agreement** has been violated in some way, or an unfair labor practice has been committed, the shop steward is usually the first to contact the employer and discuss the issue, hopefully having it resolved.

Many unions are formed with employees of a particular plant who may be part of a larger union network. For instance, the employees who process meat at a meat processing plant may organize and become the local branch or affiliate of an international meat processing labor organization, an **industrial union**. Rather than being organized at a particular workplace, unions also may be organized around a particular craft, totally detached from a particular workplace. In such cases, the **business agent** of the **craft union** (e.g., carpenters) represents the union craftworker's interest at a given jobsite. Employers will often contact the craft union when they need the type of employees represented by that union.

An interesting phenomenon in the past decade or so has been the unionization or attempted unionization of groups traditionally nonunion. For instance, since the early 1990s, registered nurses across the country have been seeking to unionize and have been doing so in record numbers. Before that time, nurses had considered unions to be for blue-collar workers, while nurses were considered professionals. One of the first projects President Clinton undertook when he came into office was to ask his wife, Hillary Rodham Clinton, to head up efforts to make health care more accessible and affordable to all. The health industry's response was unprecedented restructuring, and the resulting downsizing, among other things, displaced registered nurses. Registered nurses' perception of unions as being only for blue-collar workers changed, and they began to seek a collective voice purportedly to protect their profession and patient safety.

Even private attorneys are getting into the act. District attorneys had for some time been unionized in the public sector, but in 2003, in what is believed to be a first in the private legal profession, lawyers at the Phoenix office of the Los Angeles law firm of Parker Stanbury, which subcontracts with Pre-Paid Legal Service to provide easily accessible legal services, voted to unionize. Citing a lack of response by their employer to their complaints about low pay, few research materials, no law library, limited Internet access, hourly performance quotas, and even working in open cubicles, they voted in representation by the local Teamsters union which also represents truckers, grocery companies, bakery drivers, and UPS employees. There were allegations that management frequently tried to block the organizing effort, but the unionized lawyers say they have been contacted by several other private attorneys interested in exploring unionizing.

There have also been organizing efforts for other nontraditional groups such as graduate students, college football players, medical interns and residents, and congressional researchers.

We cannot leave the area of organizing efforts without touching on another topic important to that area: the rise of the use of labor management consulting firms to thwart efforts at unionization. These organizations (often known as "union busters") arose in the 1970s as primarily only a handful of law firms. Today, such firms have grown into a very sophisticated, billion-dollar industry. By 1989, employers hired antiunion consultants in 76 percent of all union organizing campaigns. To the extent that employers can stop organizing efforts by hiring help regarding how to discourage employees from voting to have union representation, they would consider the money paid as well worth the price.

mandatory subject of bargaining Wages, hours, and other conditions of employment, which, by law, must be negotiated between labor and management.

The consulting firms' efforts may be successful in keeping unions out, but the employers may pay in other ways. For instance, in February 2000, the nurses at Long Beach Memorial Hospital ran an organizing campaign to have the nurses join the California Nurses Association. A consulting firm was brought in to help keep the union out. The vote was eventually 591 to 581 to not have the nurses represented by a union, but the NLRB issued a complaint against the hospital alleging 26 violations of federal labor law. Many tactics are used to thwart unions during organizing efforts, some legal and some not (Exhibit 14.5). The best tactic is to have a workplace in which employees feel no need for a union because their needs are taken care of by the employer. However, if employers choose to make use of management consulting firms to keep unions out of the workplace, they should keep in close touch with the consultants and their tactics in order to avoid being left holding the bag when the NLRB comes calling with allegations of unfair management practices.

permissive subjects of bargaining Nonmandatory subjects that can be negotiated between labor and management.

Good-Faith Bargaining

Under the NLRA, an employer is required to bargain in good faith with union representatives about wages, hours, and terms and conditions of employment. These are **mandatory subjects of bargaining**. While employers may actually bargain about other matters (**permissive subjects**), only a refusal to bargain about

Exhibit 14.5   Antiunionizing Tactics

Below is a list of tactics used by employers over the years, both legal and illegal, to keep their employees from voting for union representation. Of course, this is an extremely creative process, so the list is not exhaustive.

- Utilize scare tactics, including additional security guards and guard dogs, to create an atmosphere of fear and intimidation.
- Direct managers to disseminate misinformation about the union.
- Direct managers to disseminate antiunion flyers—one company passed out over 100 different flyers!
- Run newspaper ads against the union.
- Create antiunion videos and deliver them to employees' homes.
- Offer enticements such as improved working conditions and pay increases, and imply that they will not come about if the union is voted in.
- Plead for more time to try to make things better.
- Have supervisors interrogate employees to find out how they intend to vote.
- Pressure supporters not to talk to other employees about the union.
- Place managers in employee hangouts, such as lounges, cafeterias, or break rooms, to inhibit employees' discussion of the union vote.
- Have supervisors write letters to individual employees telling them things like the supervisor will lose his or her job if the union is voted in.
- Ignore and isolate pro-union employees.
- Use ethnicity as a wedge between various ethnic groups.
- Have supervisors call daily mandatory meetings.
- Have supervisors engage employees in one-on-one conversations about the union as much as possible.
- Disseminate antiunion buttons, flyers, posters, videos, bumper stickers, and T-shirts.
- Have an antiunion website.
- Install locked, glass-covered bulletin boards all over the workplace and post antiunion material on them.
- Make supervisors think they will lose their jobs if they do not get the employees to vote against the union.
- Have a few employees run an antiunion campaign.
- Spring last-minute surprises on employees, such as rumors of possible workplace shutdown, bonuses, or pay raises.
- Have payroll send out checks with an amount equal to union dues taken out, tell employees this is what their paychecks will look like if the union is voted in, and then put the money back in their next paychecks.
- Shut down part or all of operations and allege that the shutdown is because of union costs.

mandatory subjects of bargaining may form the basis of an unfair labor practice. (See Exhibit 14.6.)

At times, management and labor may differ on whether a particular matter is a mandatory subject of bargaining. If this disagreement is legitimate, it can form the

Wages—including cost-of-living increases, production increases, learners' and apprentices' overtime.

Benefits—including vacations, sick pay, holidays, insurance.

Hours—including overtime and determinations about assignment.

Seniority—setting forth how employee seniority is determined and used.

Management security—employers may make their own decisions about how to run the business as long as they are not contrary to the collective bargaining agreement or law.

Union security—the union's legal right to exist and to represent the employees involved.

Job security—how employees will maintain employment, including procedures for layoffs, downsizing, work sharing, and so on.

Dues checkoff—right of a union to have the employer deduct union dues from employees' wages and turn them over to the union.

Union shop—requires all employees to join the union within a certain time of coming into the bargaining unit.

Modified union shop—requires that all new employees must join the union after an agreement becomes effective, as must any employees who were already union members; but those already working, who were not union members and do not wish to join, need not do so.

Maintenance-of-membership—employees who voluntarily join a union may leave only during a short window period prior to agreement expiration.

Agency shop—requires all employees of the bargaining unit to pay union dues, whether union members or not.

Grievances—sets forth the basis for grievances regarding conflicts over the meaning of the collective bargaining agreement and procedures for addressing them.

Exclusive representation—the union representative will be the only party who can negotiate with the employer about matters affecting bargaining unit employees.

Arbitration—the matters which cannot be otherwise resolved will be submitted to arbitration to be resolved by a neutral third party whose decision is usually binding.

Midterm negotiations—permits agreed-on topics to be reopened to negotiation prior to contract expiration.

No-strike, no lockout—parties agree that the employees will not strike or will only do so under limited circumstances and that employers will not engage in lockouts. Instead, the grievance procedure will be used to handle labor disputes.

---

basis of an unfair labor practice—for instance, a union may allege management has committed an unfair labor practice by refusing to bargain over a mandatory subject of bargaining such as wage increases. In the *HHS* case, for example, the union demanded negotiations on the issue of the agency's new smoking ban.

closed shop
Employer hires only union members.

    If the matter proposed for negotiation is illegal, such as a proposal to have a **closed shop**, it is bad-faith bargaining even to bring it up as a proposal, and management's refusal to bargain cannot be the basis of an unfair labor practice.

The law requires only that the parties bargain in good faith about appropriate matters, not that one party necessarily agree with the other's position and include it in the collective bargaining agreement. The intent is to prevent management from unilaterally instituting workplace policies that closely affect workers without at least getting employee input and negotiating the matter. The fact that one side or the other does not receive what it wants in the contract is not just cause for an unfair labor practice. As long as good-faith bargaining takes place, there has been compliance with the statute.

An example of bargaining in bad faith might occur when, for instance, management comes to the bargaining table and denies a raise to employees without offering any evidence whatever as to why, and simply continues to reject the union's wage proposals. It could also occur if one side rejects proposals out of hand without making counterproposals to the other side. Missing negotiation sessions and setting forth unsupported proposals could support an unfair labor practice charge. Of course, failing to show up for negotiations or refusing to sign the written agreement to which the parties orally agreed would also be bad-faith bargaining. The cases below demonstrate several ways in which employers failed to bargain in good faith.

National Labor Relations Board v. Beverly Enterprises, Inc.
174 F.3d 12 (1st Cir. 1999)

Employer unilaterally instituted a wage decrease and a $5 fee for lost time cards. The union believed management should have negotiated these issues with them. The court agreed.

Bownes, J.

Beverly operates a nursing home in Plymouth, Massachusetts. Historically, Beverly had given its employees annual wage increases on the anniversaries of their respective starting dates with the company. On March 23, 1993, the NLRB certified the Hospital Workers Union, Local 767, Service Employees International Union (the union), as the exclusive bargaining representative of all full-time and part-time service and maintenance employees at Beverly's Plymouth facility.

Beginning in June 1993, the union and the company engaged in contract negotiations. The parties disagreed as to the amount of wage increases the employees would receive. In October 1994, the union told the company that it would be difficult to persuade its unit members to accept an annual increase of less than 4 percent. At the parties' final negotiating session, on December 13, 1995, Beverly responded to the union's earlier proposal of 4 percent by proposing a 2 percent annual wage increase. The union expressed shock at the newly lowered offer and did not immediately make a counteroffer. The parties went on to discuss an unrelated dispute and

tempers flared. The union spokesperson stated that he needed to check with his attorney on the bargaining unit issue.

While these negotiations were taking place, Beverly continued to provide its employees with wage increases on their employment anniversaries, and continued to award a maximum wage increase of 4 percent to the overwhelming majority of them. This practice changed in 1996, however. That year, the company gave to approximately 90 percent of the company's unit employees a maximum wage increase of 3 percent. Beverly did not provide notice to the union that it would lower the maximum wage increase from 4 percent to 3 percent, nor did Beverly bargain with the union over the issue. Instead, Beverly unilaterally announced the change to the union in a letter, dated March 14, 1996. The letter described the imposition of the 3 percent. maximum wage increase as a "compromise" between the parties' negotiating positions.

In approximately January 1996, Beverly changed its system of keeping track of its employees' work time. It replaced its system of paper timecards with a system using plastic timecards that contained a magnetic strip. Included in its new system was a new policy requiring unit employees to pay a five-dollar fee for lost timecards. In making these changes, Beverly neither gave notice to nor bargained with the union. As of the date of the NLRB hearing on April 15, 1997, the company had collected the five-dollar lost-timecard fee on at least seventeen occasions. Between January and June 1996, the union contacted Beverly on several occasions and requested that it remedy its unilateral changes and that the parties resume bargaining.

An employer's duty to bargain with its employees' chosen representatives is an essential element of our national labor policy. The object of the NLRA was to insure that employers and their employees could work together to establish mutually satisfactory conditions of employment. The basic theme of the Act was that through collective bargaining the passions, arguments, and struggles of prior years would be channeled into constructive, open discussions leading, it was hoped, to mutual agreement. The duty to bargain is part and parcel of that policy's preference for resolving labor disputes peacefully, through good faith collective bargaining, rather than by means of industrial strife which has a destructive effect on the economy.

Because of these policy considerations, Section 8(a)(5) of the NLRA, as amplified by Section 8(d), requires an employer to bargain collectively with its employees' representatives over "wages, hours, and other terms and conditions of employment." Section 8(a)(5) makes it an unfair labor practice for an employer "to refuse to bargain collectively with the representatives of [its] employees." That section is also violated if an employer unilaterally changes any term or condition of employment without affording the union representing its employees a meaningful opportunity to negotiate "in fact." In addition, "it is generally unlawful for an employer to withdraw recognition of the union as a means of refusing to bargain."

A pay system in which the employer does not exercise discretion in the timing or the amount of the wage increase awarded is a mandatory subject of bargaining. This means, with respect to the anniversary wage increases, that an employer cannot unilaterally change the status quo, as Beverly did here, without bargaining with the union. Even during negotiations, an employer must maintain the "dynamic status quo" pertaining to employees' wages. Therefore, by unilaterally changing the amount of a fixed wage increase without bargaining with the certified representative of its employees, an employer violates Section 8(a)(5) of the Act. It is important to our national labor policy that companies not act unilaterally on subjects of mandatory bargaining; doing so defeats the whole purpose of that policy's preference for peaceful negotiation of disputes rather than industrial strife.

The second unfair labor practice found by the Board was Beverly's unilateral imposition of a five-dollar charge for lost timecards. The company does not dispute that it implemented a new policy requiring all employees to pay a five-dollar charge for lost timecards, nor that it undertook this new policy without notice to or bargaining with the union. Beverly characterizes the change as a mere "change to time-clock procedure," and argues that it therefore does not rise to the level of a change in terms and conditions of employment.

But Beverly mischaracterizes the issue: the union did not argue that Beverly had to bargain with the union about a purely mechanical change to its "time-clock procedure." The company's charging of a fee to employees for lost timecards—not the procedure that management required workers to follow to record their time—constituted a change in a term or condition of employment, and therefore Beverly's unilateral change in such terms or conditions without first pursuing collective bargaining violated the NLRA.

The imposition of a replacement fee qualifies as a "material, substantial, and significant" change in the terms and conditions of employment. Beverly argues that the five-dollar charge simply reflected Beverly's passing along its cost to replace a card. But how Beverly derived its five-dollar fee is not the issue. It may be perfectly fair, but the problem is that the fee constitutes a change in the terms and conditions of employment and Beverly must bargain with the union over such issues, not unilaterally impose them unless impasse is reached.

The only legitimate question Beverly raises is whether the size of the replacement fee is so small that Beverly could impose it without having to negotiate with the union at all. Our national labor policy prefers employers and employees to bargain collectively over terms and conditions of employment, rather than to take unilateral action that can lead to industrial strife. Under that labor policy, the presumption is in favor of a duty to bargain, and against an exception to that duty on the ground that the unilateral action is allegedly de minimis. The Board's order is ENFORCED.

Case Questions

1. Do you understand why the court said the issue of the new time card system must be negotiated? Explain.

2. Why do you think the employer decided to grant the employees a raise that was smaller than the one the employer usually gave?

3. Do you agree with the employer that the 3 percent raise was a "compromise" wage?

> If agreement is not reached with the union after good-faith bargaining is conducted, the union may then be free to advance to other alternatives it can exercise, up to and including strikes. Unions are also capable of engaging in refusals to bargain or bargaining in bad faith. These are not activities exclusive to management.

Duty of Fair Representation

Frequently when union members do not like the contract that results from collective bargaining negotiations, they will allege the union has breached its duty of fair representation. This duty, not formally defined in the statute and often used as a catchall allegation, requires the union to represent all employees fairly and nondiscriminatorily. If employees feel that one group has come out better than another in a contract, they will use the duty of fair representation as a basis for challenging the contract. The U.S. Supreme Court speaks to this issue in the following case.

Air Line Pilots Association, Int'l. v. O'Neill *499 U.S. 65 (1991)*

There was a bitter strike between the Air Line Pilots Association, International (ALPA), and Continental Airlines, Inc., after Continental filed for reorganization under Chapter 11 of the Bankruptcy Code and repudiated its collective bargaining agreement with ALPA. The strike went on for over two years, during which time Continental hired replacement workers and many pilots crossed the picket lines to go to work for Continental. Eventually the union negotiated a deal with Continental that allowed some of the striking pilots to return to work. However, the terms of the settlement were less favorable than a complete surrender to Continental would have been, particularly as it related to seniority for the striking pilots, which was the basis of their duty assignment system. The striking pilots did not like the deal which was struck between the union and management and alleged that in reaching the agreement, the union breached its duty of fair representation. The U.S. Supreme Court held that a union has done its job as long as the union's settlement with the employer is not "wholly irrational or arbitrary."

Stevens, J.

ALPA's central argument is that the duty of fair representation requires only that a union act in good faith and treat its members equally and in a nondiscriminatory fashion. The duty, the union argues, does not impose any obligation to provide *adequate* representation. The District Court found that there was no evidence that ALPA acted other than in good faith and without discrimination.

The union maintains, not without some merit, that its view that courts are not authorized to review [whether] the rationality of good-faith, nondiscriminatory union

decisions is consonant with federal labor policy. The Government has generally regulated only "the *process* of collective bargaining," . . . but relied on private negotiations between the parties to establish "their own character for the ordering of industrial relations," . . . As we have previously stated, "Congress intended that the parties should have wide latitude in their negotiations, unrestricted by any governmental power to regulate the substantive solution of their differences."

There is, however, a critical difference between governmental modification of the terms of a private agreement and an examination of those terms in search of evidence that a union did not fairly and adequately represent its constituency. Our decisions have long recognized that the need for such an examination proceeds directly from the union's statutory role as exclusive bargaining agent. Just as fiduciaries owe their beneficiaries a duty of care as well as a duty of loyalty, a union owes employees a duty to represent them adequately as well as honestly and in good faith.

ALPA suggests that a union need owe no enforceable duty of adequate representation because employees are protected from inadequate representation by the union political process. ALPA argues that employees "do not need protection against representation that is inept but not invidious" because if a "union does an incompetent job its members can vote in new officers who will do a better job or they can vote in another union."

[W]e have repeatedly identified three components of the duty [of fair representation], including a prohibition against "arbitrary" conduct. Writing for the Court in the leading case in this area of the law, Justice White explained:

> The statutory duty of fair representation was developed over 20 years ago in a series of cases involving alleged racial discrimination by unions certified as exclusive bargaining representatives under the Railway Labor Act, . . . and was soon extended to unions certified under the N.L.R.A. . . . under this doctrine, the exclusive agent's statutory authority to represent all members of a designated unit includes a statutory obligation to serve the interests of all members without hostility or discrimination toward any, to exercise its discretion with complete good faith and honesty, and to avoid arbitrary conduct.

Congress did not intend judicial review of a union's performance to permit the court to substitute its own view of the proper bargain for that reached by the union. Any substantive examination of a union's performance, therefore, must be highly deferential, recognizing the wide latitude that negotiators need for the effective performance of their bargaining responsibilities. For that reason, the final product of the bargaining process may constitute evidence of a breach of duty only if it can be fairly characterized as so far outside a "wide range of reasonableness," that it is wholly "irrational" or "arbitrary."

For purposes of decision, we may assume that the Court of Appeals was correct in its conclusion that, if ALPA had simply surrendered and voluntarily terminated the strike, the striking pilots would have been entitled to reemployment in the order of seniority. Moreover, we may assume that Continental would have responded to such action by rescinding its assignment of all the bid positions to working pilots. After all, it did rescind about half of those assignments pursuant to the terms of the settlement. Thus, we assume that the union made a bad settlement—one that was even worse than a unilateral termination of the strike.

Nevertheless, the settlement was by no means irrational. A settlement is not irrational simply because it turns out *in retrospect* to have been a bad settlement. Viewed in light of the legal landscape at the time of the settlement, ALPA's decision to settle rather than give up was certainly not illogical. At the time of the settlement, Continental had notified the union that all of the . . . bid positions had been awarded to working pilots and was maintaining that none of the strikers had any claim on any of those jobs.

The suggestion that the "discrimination" between striking and working pilots represented a breach of the duty if fair representation fails. REVERSED and REMANDED

Case Questions

1. Do you agree that the Court should not look into the substance of complaints about the union's duty of fair representation?

2. For the striking pilots who feel they were discriminated against, what are the drawbacks of the union?

3. Considering that the union had been on strike for over two years and management had hired replacement workers and nonstriking employees, what sort of position do you think that management was in when negotiating with the union?

Collective Bargaining Agreements

If all goes well, bargaining between labor and management results in a collective bargaining agreement. This is the term for the contract that is reached between the employer and the union about workplace issues. There is no set form that this

Exhibit 14.7

Management Unfair Labor Practices

- Trying to control the union or interfering with union affairs, such as trying to help a certain candidate get elected to a union office.
- Discriminating against employees who join a union or are in favor of bringing in a union or who exercise their rights under the law (e.g., terminating, demoting, or giving poor working schedules to such employees).
- Interfering with, coercing, or restraining employees exercising their rights under the labor law legislation (e.g., telling employees they cannot have a union or they will be terminated if they do).
- Refusal to bargain or refusal to bargain in good faith.

management security clause
Parties agree that management has the right to run the business and make appropriate business decisions as long as applicable laws are complied with.

midterm negotiations
Collective bargaining negotiations during the term of the contract.

agreement must take, and it may be any length and contain any provisions the parties decide. (See Exhibit 14.6.) Job and union security is the main issue for employees, while freedom from labor strife, such as strikes, slowdowns, and work stoppages, is paramount for employers. Management will often wish to include a **management security clause**, stating that it has the power to run its business and make business decisions as long as it is not in violation of the collective bargaining agreement or the law.

Toward that end, in addition to wages and hours, collective bargaining agreements often also contain provisions regarding strikes, arbitration of labor disputes, seniority, benefits, employment classifications, and so on. Because things change, the agreement is in effect only for a specified period. Prior to expiration of that period, the parties will negotiate a new contract, to take effect when the old one ends.

The collective bargaining agreement may also include a clause permitting **midterm negotiations**. These are negotiations during the life of the contract, rather than immediately prior to its expiration, about matters on which the parties have agreed they will permit interim negotiations. The parties may not be able to agree on a particular provision and, rather than allow it to hold up the entire contract, will agree to come back together later to negotiate it. Alternatively, the parties may agree to midterm negotiations because the contract may cover a fairly long period and the provision subject to midterm negotiation is one that may change quickly and need to be reviewed before the contract's expiration date.

Unfair Labor Practices

Refusal to bargain in good faith is not the only unfair labor practice that an employer can commit. Others include engaging in activities that would tend to attempt to control or influence the union, or to interfere with its affairs, and discriminating against employees who join or assist unions. Actual interference by the employer need not be proved for it to be considered an unfair labor practice. Rather, the question is whether the activity tends to interfere with, restrain, or coerce employees who are exercising rights protected under the law. (See Exhibit 14.7.) The following case indicates the extent of possible unfair labor practices. It is the basis for opening scenario 2.

Scenario

Columbia Portland Cement Co. v. National Labor Relations Board *979 F.2d 460 (6th Cir. 1992)*

The employer engaged in unfair labor practices that eventually led employees to engage in an unfair labor practice strike. After the union gave an unconditional request for reinstatement to the employer, the employer refused to reinstate them, and also unilaterally gave a wage increase without consulting the union. The court found both to be unfair labor practices by the employer.

Contie, J.

Petitioner, Columbia Portland Cement Company (the "Company"), operates a limestone shale quarry and cement production facility in Zanesville, Ohio. Since at least September 1, 1984, Local Lodge D24 of the Cement, Lime, Gypsum & Allied Workers Division of the International Brotherhood of Boilermakers, Iron Shipbuilders, Blacksmiths, Forgers and Helpers, AFL-CIO (the "Union"), has represented the Company's employees. The most recent collective-bargaining contract between the Union and the Company's predecessor expired on May 1, 1984, but the predecessor company and the Union agreed to extend that contract during negotiations for a new contract.

The Company purchased the facility from the predecessor on August 28, 1984. The Company notified the Union on August 29, 1984, that it intended to terminate the extended contract and desired to negotiate a new one. The parties failed to reach agreement on a new contract, however, and on October 28, 1984, the Company unilaterally implemented the last offer it had made. On May 8, 1985, the employees went out on strike.

By letter dated April 29, 1987, the Union made an offer to return to work on behalf of the striking employees. The letter stated that the employees "unconditionally offer to return to work immediately." In response, the Company sent a letter dated May 7, 1987, informing the Union that, "with regard to [the] unconditional offer to return to work," the Company would not reinstate the striking employees. The Company contended that some of the employees had been lawfully terminated, and that the remainder were permanently replaced economic strikers who would be kept on a list for future vacancies.

On April 20, 1988, the Company offered reinstatement, without back pay, to 62 of the striking employees; 33 eventually returned to work.

"A strike which is caused in whole or in part by an employer's unfair labor practices *is* an unfair labor practice strike." Employees who go out on strike in response to an employer's unfair labor practices may not be permanently replaced by other employees. Unfair labor practice strikers are entitled to immediate reinstatement by the employer upon their unconditional offer to return to work. Refusing to reinstate striking employees after their unconditional offer to return to work violates section 8(a)(3) and (1) of the Act.

The Company granted employees a wage increase of 20 cents per hour; replaced the retirement plan with a 401(k) plan; and changed the grievance procedure to by-pass the union and deal directly with the grievant. These actions all violate the employer's duty to bargain with the employees' exclusive bargaining agent in contravention of section 8(a)(5) and (1). Accordingly, the Board's decision must be AFFIRMED.

Case Questions

1. Why do you think the employer refused to rehire the strikers after they gave an unconditional promise to return?

2. Do you think it is fair that employees striking because of an unfair labor practice are entitled to reinstatement? Explain.

3. Do you think the new owner of the business took this hard line in dealing with the union in order to try to initially establish its dominance over the union? Explain.

As mentioned previously, some employers are more aggressive in interfering with their employees' unionizing efforts.

Davis Supermarkets, Inc. v. National Labor Relations Board
2 F.3d 1162 (D.C. Cir. 1993)

The owners of a supermarket whose employees at one of its outlets wanted to vote in a union interfered with the employees' organizing efforts and terminated several employees. The company was found by the NLRB to have committed unfair labor practices, and the company vehemently disagreed. The court upheld the NLRB's decision and found in favor of the employees.

Mikva, C. J.

In March 1986, Local 23 launched a concerted organizing campaign in the Hempfield store, which employed more than one hundred men and women. Over the next few months, Donald Porter, an organizer for Local 23, met with various employees on and off the store's premises, urging them to sign authorization cards for Local 23. Some of the employees that he successfully recruited solicited authorization cards from other employees.

By April 19, 1986, a total of thirteen employees had signed authorization cards for Local 23. On that day, the Company summarily laid off eight workers, six of whom had signed authorization cards. In May, the Company fired or constructively fired two other employees who had signed cards. In July, the Company constructively discharged Linda Kunkle, who had also signed a card for Local 23.

On May 1, at two separate meetings with various employees of the Hempfield store, Bob Davis, the chairman of the Company's board of directors, told the assembled workers that he wanted them to sign authorization cards for the Steelworkers. After one of the meetings, a Steelworkers representative from the Greensburg store and an official of that union handed out Steelworkers contracts and authorization cards to the employees. Following the other meeting, two Steelworkers representatives from the Greensburg facility distributed Steelworkers contracts and cards.

The Company challenges the findings of unfair labor practices as to the firings, and the aiding of the Steelworkers at the Hempfield facility. The Board found the April 19 layoffs to be violations of section 8(a)(1) and 8(a)(3) of the Act. Section 8(a)(1) states, "It shall be an unfair labor practice for an employer . . . to interfere with, restrain, or coerce employees in the exercise of [self-organization and collective bargaining] rights guaranteed in section 157 of this title." 29 U.S.C. 158(a)(1). Section 8(a)(3) makes it an unfair labor practice for an employer "by discrimination in regard to hire or tenure of employment or any term or condition of employment to encourage or discourage membership in any labor organization." 29 U.S.C. 158(a)(3).

The Company alleges that it fired the six employees for a variety of valid reasons, including "attitude problems," poor performance and consolidation in response to slow business. The Board did not find these explanations believable, in light of the shifting reasons offered for the dismissals, the lack of evidence of performance and attitude problems, the absence of prior warnings to the employees supposedly fired for such problems, and the quick replacement of the workers allegedly laid off for economic reasons with employees from the Greensburg store. The Board found instead that the firings were part of a strategy to suppress Local 23's organizing campaign.

Despite the Company's assertions, there is considerable direct evidence that it knew of or suspected the pro-union sympathies of at least some of the workers. For example, about a year before she was fired, Shotts asked two managers about getting a union in the store, and the managers warned her not to talk about it any further. Also, on March 25, 1986, Welsh's immediate supervisor interrogated her about a Local 23 meeting that she had attended. As for the other employees, however, there is, as the Company maintains, scant direct evidence that the Company was aware they were union supporters when it discharged them.

The lack of direct evidence does not, however, necessarily render the Board's findings of anti-union motivation inadequate. The Board found substantial circumstantial evidence that the Company knew of the employees' union activities, and "although the Board may not base its decision on mere conjecture, the element of knowledge may be shown by circumstantial evidence from which a reasonable inference may be drawn." "Similarly, the Board may infer discriminatory motive from circumstantial evidence." Among the factors on which the Board may base such inferences are "the timing of the discharges in relation to the union activity [and] the simultaneous nature of otherwise unconnected dismissals."

Both the timing and the nature of the discharges in this case suggest anti-union motivations. The firings occurred just as Local 23's campaign was picking up steam, and the employees, who worked in various different departments, were all dismissed on the same day for entirely disparate reasons. Furthermore, of the eight employees laid off, six were union supporters, and this occurred at a time when only thirteen out of more than one hundred employees had signed cards. In light of the summary and targeted nature of the dismissals and the Company's failure to come up with plausible legitimate reasons for them, there was probably sufficient evidence to find that the six firings were violations of the Act.

Nonetheless, there is a somewhat troubling lack of evidence that the Company even had the opportunity to learn of the union advocacy of several of the fired workers. Hilty and Garris, in particular, seem to have performed very few union-related actions on store premises within the sight of other people.

There is, however, an alternative and less problematic manner in which to assess the legality of these six layoffs. Although the General Counsel ordinarily must show that the employer was aware of the pro-union sentiments of a dismissed employee in order to establish an 8(a)(3) violation, he does not have to make such a showing if the dismissal is part of a mass layoff "for the purpose of discouraging union activity."

The Board's finding of an unlawful mass layoff is clearly supported by substantial evidence. A supervisor told Defibaugh on April 19, the day of the firings, that "they heard the union was getting close to the number they needed for an election and they were getting rid of the troublemakers and the people with attitude problems."

We thus hold that the first part of the *Wright Line* test, requiring a showing that firings were motivated by anti-union animus, is satisfied under the mass discharge theory. According to the second part of the test, the employer can overcome the showing of anti-union motivation only by establishing, by a preponderance of the evidence, that "the discharge would have occurred in any event and for valid reasons."

Because the Board's findings were clearly reasonable, we see no basis for overturning its conclusions. We therefore uphold the Board's determination that the six April 19 layoffs constituted unfair labor practices in violation of sections 8(a)(1) and 8(a)(3) of the Act.

In addition to the six April 19 firings, the Board also found three discharges or constructive discharges that occurred in later months to be violations of sections 8(a)(1) and 8(a)(3). Because the dismissals of Larry Miller, Charles Miscovich, and Linda Kunkle occurred on three different dates ranging from May to July, the mass discharge theory does not apply. In order to establish anti-union animus, the General Counsel was therefore required to establish that the Company was aware that each of the three employees supported Local 23.

Miller was discharged on May 14, 1986. The Company alleges that it fired Miller, a bagger and stockboy, because, while on break, he ate food that he had stolen from the store. The Board found, however, that the store manager who fired Miller never even asked him whether he had paid for the items. Moreover, neither of the two employees with whom Miller had been eating were similarly discharged. In light of the fact that Miller repeatedly spoke to Porter, Local 23's organizer, in the parking lot of the Hempfield store, and that the store manager once told Porter to leave Miller alone, there is substantial evidence that the Company knew of Miller's support of Local 23 and fired him for this reason.

Miscovich worked a day shift at the Hempfield store because he also had a night job at a gas station. In mid-May, shortly after Miscovich signed a Local 23 authorization card, the store manager began scheduling him for night shifts. When Miscovich reminded the manager of his situation, he responded that Miscovich had to work when told to or not work at all. After that, Miscovich was never able to work at the store again.

There is no doubt that the Company was aware of Miscovich's pro-union stance, for he was called to a May 12 meeting where Bob Davis, the chairman of the Company, told the assembled workers that he knew they had all signed authorization cards. There is substantial evidence to support the Board's conclusion that the Company constructively discharged Miscovich in violation of sections 8(a)(1) and 8(a)(3).

On July 26, Kunkle quit her job, after suffering through three weeks of inexcusable treatment. The Company transferred her from an office job to the meat department, reduced her hours, required her to stay in a back room and wrap meat, and forbade other employees to talk to her about anything except meat.

There is no doubt that the Company was aware of Kunkle's pro-union activities. Kunkle was an active and public Local 23 supporter who had signed an authorization card, solicited cards from other employees, and picketed the store to protest its unfair labor practices. The Company apparently photographed her picketing. Moreover, she was one of the employees present at the May 12 meeting where Bob Davis told the assembled workers that he knew they had all signed authorization cards. We uphold the Board's finding that Kunkle was unlawfully constructively discharged. Unfair labor practices ruling UPHELD.

Case Questions

1. Do the employer's violations seem clear to you? Why do you think the employer did not think they were so clear?

2. If you were the employer in a similar situation, and had read this case, what would you do when your employees wanted to unionize?

3. Think about the 3 employees terminated outside the mass layoffs. How would you have handled these situations as a manager?

In another decision, what may have appeared to a company to be legitimate employee–management negotiations with nonunion employees was held to violate the NLRA. It is the basis for opening scenario 3.

Scenario

Electromation v. National Labor Relations Board *35 F.3d 1148* *(7th Cir. 1993)*

A nonunion company negotiated with its workers to resolve labor issues through "employee participation" or "employee–management" focus groups rather than a union. The court held that these committees constituted labor organizations and were dominated by the employer, thus constituting an unfair labor practice.

Will, J.

At the time of the events which gave rise to this suit, Electromation's approximately 200 employees, most of whom were women, were not represented by any labor organization. To minimize the financial losses it was experiencing at the time, the company in late 1988 decided to cut expenses by revising its employee attendance policy and replacing the 1989 scheduled wage increases with lump sum payments based on the length of each employee's service at the company.

In January 1989, the company received a handwritten request signed by 68 employees expressing their dissatisfaction with and requesting reconsideration of the revised attendance bonus/wage policy. After meeting with the company's supervisors, the company President, John Howard, decided to meet directly with employees to discuss their concerns. Accordingly, on January 11, 1989, the company met with eight employees—three randomly selected high-seniority employees, three randomly selected low-seniority employees, and two additional employees who had requested that they be included—to discuss a number of matters, including wages, bonuses, incentive pay, tardiness, attendance programs, and bereavement and sick leave policy, all normal collective bargaining issues.

Following this meeting, Howard met again with the supervisors and concluded that management had "possibly made a mistake in judgment in December in deciding what we ought to do" . . . [and] "that the better course of action would be to involve the employees in coming up with solutions to these issues." The company determined that "action committees" would be an appropriate way to involve employees in the process. Accordingly, on January 18, 1989, the company met again with the same eight employees and proposed the creation of action committees to "meet and try to come up with ways to resolve these problems; and that if they came up with solutions that we believed were within budget concerns and they generally felt would be acceptable to the employees, that we would implement these suggestions or proposals." At the employees' suggestion, Howard agreed that, rather than having a random selection of employee committee members, sign-up sheets for each action committee would be posted.

On the next day, the company posted a memorandum to all employees announcing the formation of the following five action committees: (1) Absenteeism/Infractions; (2) No Smoking Policy; (3) Communication Network; (4) Pay Progression for Premium Positions; and (5) Attendance Bonus Program. Sign-up sheets were also posted at this time.

On February 13, 1989, the International Brotherhood of Teamsters, Local Union No. 1049 (the "union") demanded recognition from the company. Until then, the company was unaware that any organizing efforts had occurred at the plant. In late February, Howard informed Employee Benefits Manager Loretta Dickey of the union's demand for recognition. Upon the advice of counsel, Dickey announced at the next meeting of each committee that, due to the union demand, the company could no longer participate in the committees, but that the employee members could continue to meet if they so desired.

Finally, on March 15, 1989, Howard formally announced to the employees that "due to the union's campaign, the Company would be unable to participate in the [committee] meetings and could not continue to work with the committees until after the [union] election." The union election took place on March 31, 1989; the employees voted 95 to 82 against union representation. On April 24, 1989, a regional director of the Board issued a complaint alleging that Electromation had violated the Act.

Section 2(5) of the Act defines a labor organization as:

> any organization of any kind, or any agency or employee representation committee or plan, in which employees participate and which exists for the purpose, in whole or in part, of dealing with employers concerning grievances, labor disputes, wages, rates of pay, hours of employment, or conditions of work.

Under this statutory definition, the action committees would constitute labor organizations if: (1) the Electromation employees participated in the committees; (2) the committees existed, at least in part, for the purpose of "dealing with" the employer; and (3) these dealings concerned "grievances, labor disputes, wages, rates of pay, hours of employment, or conditions of work."

With respect to the first factor, there is no question that the Electromation employees participated in the action committees. Turning to the second factor, which is the most seriously contested on appeal, the Board found that the activities of the action committees constituted "dealing with" the employer. We agree with the

Board that the action committees can be differentiated only in the specific subject matter with which each dealt. Each committee had an identical relationship to the company: the purpose, structure, and administration of each committee was essentially the same. We note, in addition, that even if the committees are considered individually, there exists substantial evidence that each was formed and existed for the purpose of "dealing with" the company. It is in fact the shared similarities among the committee structures which compels unitary treatment of them for the purposes of the issues raised in this appeal.

Given the Supreme Court's holding that "dealing with" includes conduct much broader than collective bargaining, the Board did not err in determining that the Electromation action committees constituted labor organizations within the meaning of Sections 2(5) and 8(a)(2) of the Act.

Finally, with respect to the third factor, the subject matter of that dealing—for example, the treatment of employee absenteeism and employee bonuses—obviously concerned conditions of employment. We further agree with the Board that the purpose of the action committees was not limited to the improvement of company efficiency or product quality, but rather that they were designed to function and in fact functioned in an essentially representative capacity. Accordingly, given the statute's traditionally broad construction, there is substantial evidence to support the Board's finding that the action committees constituted labor organizations.

Section 8(a)(2) declares that it shall be an unfair labor practice for an employer: to dominate or interfere with the formation or administration of any labor organization or contribute financial or other support to it: Provided, that subject to rules and regulations made and published by the Board pursuant to Section 6, an employer shall not be prohibited from permitting employees to confer with him during working hours without loss of time or pay. Section 8(a)(1) provides that it shall be an unfair labor practice for an employer: to interfere with, restrain or coerce employees in the exercise of the rights guaranteed in section 157 of this title. Section 7 in turn provides that: [e]mployees shall have the right to self-organization, to form, to join, or assist labor organizations, to bargain collectively through representatives of their own choosing, and to engage in other concerted activities for the purpose of collective bargaining or other mutual aid or protection, and shall also have the right to refrain from any and all such activities except to the extent that such right may be affected by an agreement requiring membership in a labor organization as a condition of employment as authorized in section 158(a)(3) of this title.

Electromation argues that the Board's ruling in this case implies that an employer violates Section 8(a)(2) whenever it proposes a structure whereby the employees and employer "cooperate," or meet together to discuss topics of mutual concern. The company thus asserts that the Board may find a violation of Section 8(a)(2) only where it finds that the employer has actually undermined the free and independent choice of the employees.

The company played a pivotal role in establishing both the framework and the agenda for the action committees. Electromation unilaterally selected the size, structure, and procedural functioning of the committees; it decided the number of committees and the topic(s) to be addressed by each. The company unilaterally drafted the action committees' purposes and goal statements, which identified from the start the focus of each committee's work. Also, as was pointed out during oral argument, despite the fact that the employees were seriously concerned about the lack of a wage increase, no action committee was designated to consider this specific issue. In this way, Electromation actually controlled which issues received attention by the committees and which did not. Although the company acceded to the employees' request that volunteers form the committees, it unilaterally determined how many could serve on each committee, decided that an employee could serve on only one committee at a time, and determined which committee certain employees would serve on, thus exercising significant control over the employees' participation and voice at the committee meetings. Also, although it never became a significant issue because so few employees signed up for the committees, the initial sign up sheets indicated that the employer would decide which six employees would be chosen as committee members where more than six expressed interest in a particular committee. Ultimately, the company limited membership to five and determined the five to serve. Also, the company designated management representatives to serve on the committees. Employee Benefits Manager Dickey was assigned to coordinate and serve on all committees. In the case of the Attendance Bonus Program Committee, the management representative—Controller Mazur—reviewed employee proposals, determined whether they were economically feasible, and further decided whether they would be presented to higher management. This role of the management committee members effectively put the employer on both sides of the bargaining table, an avowed proscription of the Act.

Finally, the company paid the employees for their time spent on committee activities, provided meeting space, and furnished all necessary supplies for the committees' activities. While such financial support is clearly not a violation of Section 8(a)(2) by itself, in the totality of the circumstances in this case such support may reasonably be characterized to be in furtherance of the company's domination of the action committees. We therefore conclude that there is substantial evidence to support the Board's finding of unlawful employer domination and interference in violation of Section 8(a)(2) and (1). NLRB ORDER ENFORCED.

Case Questions

1. Did the employer seem to intentionally violate the law? Explain.

2. What do you think would motivate an employer to prefer to deal directly with an employee participation group rather than a union?

3. Do you think it's harmful to put the employer on "both sides of the bargaining table"? Explain the pros and cons.

In Exhibit 14.5 we listed many of the antiunion organizing tactics that have been used by management over the years to thwart union efforts to organize, and in Exhibit 14.7 we listed management unfair labor practices. In Exhibit 14.8 we list some specific acts employers can and cannot engage in during organizing efforts. It would be wise for employers to use these lists as guides in order to avoid unfair labor practice complaints.

Exhibit 14.8   Cans and Can'ts during Union Campaigns

Often referred to as "NO TIPS" (threats, interrogation promises, or spying, along with several other things an employer cannot do), during a unionizing campaign, the employer *can't*:

- Threaten to fire an employee for joining a union.
- Try to help the employees form a union.
- Lay off or terminate employees who support the union.
- Allow employees to copy antiunion leaflets at work and pass them out.
- Let employees hold antiunion meetings at work.
- E-mail, post, or circulate threatening or intimidating letters or leaflets.
- Try to question employees about their support of (or opposition to) the union.
- Terminate, discipline, transfer, or reassign union supporters to less desirable shifts, duties, or locations without some legitimate business cause other than their union support.
- Ask about union meetings or union activities.
- Spy on union activities or union supporters.
- Isolate all union supporters so that they cannot speak with other employees.
- Promise wage increases or other benefits if employees don't join the union.
- Threaten to take away job benefits if employees vote in a union.
- Ban pro-union buttons if such things are generally permitted.

During a unionizing campaign, an employer *can:*

- Send letters to employees' homes.
- Establish a suggestion box or complaint process.
- Give pay raises or benefits overall, not just to union supporters. (This can be limited after the union applies for its certificate or gives notice to bargain its first agreement.)
- Hold meetings in an effort to address or solve problems it becomes aware of.
- Tell employees how good the company is.
- Tell employees how good the company's benefits and working conditions are.
- Address issues that it may become aware of during the unionizing process.

Strikes and Lockouts

The NLRA permits certain strikes by employees as a legitimate form of protest. (See Exhibit 14.9.) When a union strikes, union members do not work but, instead, generally gather outside the employer's place of business and carry signs about the nature of the strike (**picketing**) and chant slogans. Engaging in such activity is for purposes of pressuring management to concede, bringing attention to the strikers' demands, gathering support, and discouraging others who may support the employer. For instance, a picket line may encourage shoppers going into a grocery store not to patronize the store where the clerks are on strike because wages are too low.

Legitimate strikes may be called by the union either for economic reasons or because of unfair labor practices. For instance, the employees may strike when a collective bargaining agreement expires or if the employees are attempting to force economic

picketing
The carrying of signs, which tell of an unfair labor practice or strike, by union members in front of the employer's business.

673

Exhibit 14.9

Types of Strikes

- *Economic strike*—used to exert pressure on the employer regarding economic issues. Also used for strikes resulting from any other reason than an unfair labor practice. Protected activity.
- *Unfair labor practice strike*—called by union because of an employer's unfair labor practice. Protected activity.
- *Sympathy strike*—employees of struck employer refuse to cross picket line. Whether protected depends on circumstances.
- *Sitdown strike*—employees illegally take possession of workplace during strike. Not protected activity.
- *Wildcat strike*—strike not authorized by union. Generally not protected activity, but may be.
- *Intermittent strike*—strikes that occur from time to time and are not announced. Not protected activity.
- *Slowdown*—employees remain on the job and generally do not produce as much. Unprotected activity.

concessions from the employer. If employees strike for legally recognized reasons, their actions are protected under the NLRA and they retain their status as employees. Strikes not authorized by the union are called "**wildcat strikes**" and are illegal if they force the employer to deal with the employees, rather than the union, or impose the will of the minority, rather than the majority. They have been found not to be unlawful if they are merely to make a statement.

wildcat strike
A strike not sanctioned by the union.

If the employer replaces the strikers with new employees, then once the strike is over, the strikers have a right to reinstatement if they offer an unconditional offer to return to work. If their jobs are occupied by replacement workers, then unfair labor practice strikers are entitled to be reinstated, but economic strikers are not.

lockout
Management does not allow employees to come to work.

Just as employees can stop working if they feel the need to strike to make their point, the employer can close the premises to employees and engage in a **lockout**. In a lockout, the employer curtails employment by either shutting down the plant or by bringing in temporary nonunion employees after laying off striking workers. Under the NLRA, the employer may engage in lockouts not as a way of avoiding bargaining or unionizing but, rather, as with strikes, to bring pressure to bear on the other side for legitimate purposes.

no-strike, no-lockout clause
Labor and management agree that labor will not strike and management will not stage a lockout.

Many collective bargaining agreements contain **no-strike, no-lockout clauses**, which either prohibit or limit the availability of this action and, instead, call for the use of the grievance process to handle issues. In 2002, baseball commissioner Bud Selig pledged not to lock out players throughout the season and the World Series. His statement left open the possibility that team owners would come up with new work rules after that. Because the players' union had been working without a labor contract since November 7, 2001, they interpreted the commissioner's statement as a "veiled threat" to impose vast economic changes as soon as the postseason ended. In 1994, in its eighth walkout since 1972, the baseball players' union struck in order to fight management's plan to implement changes that included a salary cap. The walkout lasted 232 days and resulted in the cancellation of the World Series for the first time since 1904. In 2002, after fighting for months over changes imposed by club owners, the players entered into a new contract on August 30, avoiding the strike deadline by only hours.

More recently, we saw the unfortunate National Hockey League fiasco where differences between the owners and players, primarily over the issue of salary caps, resulted in a five-month lockout by the owners and, eventually, cancellation of the entire season by the NHL commissioner. It was the first time a major North American professional sports league lost an entire season to a labor dispute. Want to hear a coincidence? The last time the Hockey League's Stanley Cup was not awarded was in 1919, because of a flu epidemic. The year before, the Boston Red Sox had won the World Series. This time around, when the cup wasn't awarded because of labor disputes canceling the season, the Red Sox had once again, after over 80 years, won the World Series the year before. Wow!

In the case below, the court discusses legitimate purposes for which an employer can stage a lockout and what happens if the workers are replaced with temporary employees during the lockout.

Local 825, Int'l Union of Operating Engineers v. National Labor Relations Board *829 F.2d 458 (3d Cir. 1987)*

Management engaged in a lockout and hired temporary employees to fill in during the lockout period. The union charged that the hiring of temporary employees was an unfair labor practice. The court disagreed.

Mansmann, J.

Harter Equipment, Inc. (Harter), is a New Jersey corporation engaged in the sale, distribution and service of construction and lawn maintenance equipment. The union represents a unit of the company's employees, including parts and service department mechanics, "parts men"; a truck driver and a painter. Negotiations to renew the contract began on October, 1981. From the beginning, the company made it clear that it needed substantial cost concessions because it was operating at a loss. On the day the contract expired (December 1, 1981), the company submitted a "final" proposal providing, among other things, for certain wage reductions and a union security clause. The union rejected the proposal but indicated that the employees desired to continue working without a contract. Harter then refused to permit the employees to punch in or work. On December 4, the employees began picketing the company with signs stating they had been locked out.

Harter and the union continued to negotiate on the union security issue. However, after the withdrawal of

proposals made by the union which had been accepted by the company, Harter decided to hire temporary replacements to complete service work already in the shop.

After temporary employees were hired, the parties continued to bargain but no final contract was consummated. The company continued to hire temporary replacements and the union continued to picket until April 1, 1982, when the unfair labor practice charge was filed by the union.

The National Labor Relations Board held that absent specific proof of anti-union animus, an employer does not violate §8(a)(3) by hiring temporary replacements in order to engage in business operations during an otherwise lawful lockout, including a lockout initiated for the sole purpose of bringing economic pressure to bear in support of a legitimate bargaining position. This petition for review followed.

The Board's findings of fact are conclusive if supported by substantial evidence on the record considered as a whole, which we find it is. We turn now to an examination of whether the use of temporary replacements by

Harter is inherently destructive of employee rights. The Court has defined conduct which is inherently destructive of employee rights as conduct which carries with it unavoidable consequences which the employer not only foresaw but which he must have intended. In that respect, the conduct would bear its own indicia of intent. We bear in mind that §8(a)(3) proscribes action impinging on the employees' rights to bargain collectively, strike, or engage in union activities.

In this case, the Company made it clearly known from the beginning of the negotiating sessions that while it desired an amicable renegotiation of its contract, it could not afford major wage concessions because of its declining economic fortunes. Indeed, many of the proposals suggested to the union contained less favorable terms than had been incorporated in the agreement due to expire. It was the company's intention to return the regular employees to work when the negotiations were completed, even though the advertisements for the temporary help did not state that the positions were temporary.

We cannot find that such use of temporary employees was inherently destructive of the employees' right to bargain collectively, strike, or engage in union activities. The use of the replacements during the lockout was a tactic chosen by the employer obviously to put pressure upon the union. Such pressure, however, affects the realities of the union's bargaining positions rather than any right as such to bargain collectively, strike or engage in other concerted activity. As the Supreme Court has noted for example, in respect to a strike, vis-à-vis lockouts, the union has no right to determine exclusively the timing and duration of all work stoppages.

The pressure Harter brought to bear in this case also was not destructive of the employees' rights due to the use of temporary employees. The court has previously noted three considerations in evaluating whether the use of temporary replacements had an inherently destructive or comparatively slight effect on employee rights. The court considered the duration of temporary employment and whether a definite date of termination had been communicated to the union and employees, and found that a definite date of duration for the temporary hires had been communicated. Second, the court noted that the option of returning to work was available to the employees upon their acceptance of the employer's terms, and third, the employer had agreed to continue in effect the union-security clause from the old contract.

In this case, although the advertisements for the replacement workers did not state that the positions were temporary, it was indeed the company's intention to return the regular employees to work at the conclusion of the dispute. In regard to the second factor, the union could have returned its members to work on terms less profitable than desired. As for the union-security clause, the company had agreed to the latest of a series of union proposed security clauses, only to have it withdrawn by the union. Thus, the company in effect had agreed to such a clause.

Under these circumstances, we do not believe that the company's conduct was inherently destructive of employee rights. The "balance of power" between the union and the company may have tilted toward the company through the use of this type of pressure tactic, but as the Board noted, replacing the employees with temporary workers had no greater adverse effect on the right to bargain collectively than did the concededly lawful lockout.

Given this finding, "if the adverse effect of the discriminatory conduct on employee rights is 'comparatively slight' an anti-union motivation must be proved to sustain the charge if the employer has come forward with evidence of legitimate and substantial business justifications for the conduct." Thus, the "slight" impact on employee rights (to organize, etc.) which the conduct at issue arguably had, is negated if the employer has established a legitimate and substantial business justification for his conduct.

Here, that standard has been met. The Company was in financial straits and the union was aware of its financial problems. Moreover, no temporary replacements were hired until six weeks after the commencement of the lockout, during which period no unit work was performed. We find that a legitimate business justification existed in this case and that no violation of §8(a)(1) or §8(a)(3) occurred. DENY the union's petition for review.

Case Questions

1. Do you agree with the court that this was legitimate pressure on the union?

2. What is the significance, to you, of the employer waiting six weeks before bringing in temporary replacements?

3. Is there an inherent imbalance between the relative positions of labor and management making a lockout more pressure-laden than a strike?

Exhibit 14.10

Union Unfair Labor Practices

- Refusal to bargain or bargaining in bad faith—that is, not attending bargaining sessions, not providing proposals, not providing necessary information.
- Coercing or restraining employees in exercising their rights to join (or not join) a union. This is not a problem if the union and employer have a provision in their collective bargaining agreement that states a nonunion member coming into the bargaining unit must join the union within a certain amount of time.
- Charging discriminatory or very high dues or entrance fees for admittance into the union.
- Threatening, encouraging, or influencing employees to strike in an effort to pressure the employer to join an employer organization, to get the employer to recognize an uncertified union, or to stop doing business with an employer because of the employer not doing so.
- Influencing employers to discriminate against, or otherwise treat differently, employees who do not belong to the union or are denied union membership for some other reason than nonpayment of union dues or fees.

THE TAFT-HARTLEY ACT

With the enactment of the NLRA and the subsequent gains made in unionism, the Taft-Hartley Act in 1947 was enacted as an amendment to the NLRA to curb excesses by unions. Most importantly, the Taft-Hartley Act changed the policies of the NLRA. No longer were all employers legislatively determined to be frustrating the organizational rights of their employees. Congress recognized that unions had grown so strong and powerful over the years that their activities required federal regulation. As such, unions were to have certain limitations placed on their activity. Congress wanted employers, employees, and labor organizations to recognize one another's legitimate rights and made the rights of all three subordinate to the public's health, safety, and interest.

right-to-work laws Permits employees to choose not to become a part of the union.

Section 7 was rewritten to recognize the right of an employee to refrain from concerted activity, including union activity. Like section 8 of the Wagner Act, which enumerates unfair labor practices that could be committed by employees, section 8 of the Taft-Hartley Act spells out six unfair labor practices that could be committed by organized labor (see Exhibit 14.10), thereby bringing unions under the regulation of the federal law. Under this section, it is an unfair labor practice for unions to

union shop Union and management agree that employees must be a member of the union.

1. Restrain or coerce employees in the exercise of their rights or employers in the selection of their representatives for collective bargaining.
2. Cause an employer to discriminate against an employee.
3. Refuse to bargain with an employer.
4. Engage in jurisdictional or secondary boycotts.
5. Charge excess or discriminatory initiation fees or dues.
6. Cause an employer to pay for goods or services that are not provided.

union shop clause Provision in a collective bargaining agreement allowing a union shop.

Before closed shops (where the employee must become a member of the union in order to obtain a job) were outlawed by the Taft-Hartley Act, states enacted right-to-work

677

Exhibit 14-11

Right-to-Work States

According to the U.S. Department of Labor, the following states had right-to-work laws in effect as of January 1, 2005:

Alabama	Nevada
Arizona	North Carolina
Arkansas	North Dakota
Florida	Oklahoma
Georgia	South Carolina
Idaho	South Dakota
Iowa	Tennessee
Kansas	Texas
Louisiana	Utah
Mississippi	Virginia
Nebraska	Wyoming

Indiana has a policy in effect, but it only applies to school employees.

agency shop clause
Requires nonunion members to pay union dues without having to be subject to the union rules.

free riders
Bargaining unit employees who do not pay dues but whom the union is still obligated to represent.

laws. This was done in response to the use of closed shops by unions to control dissenters by severing their union membership, without which they could not work in a closed shop. The NLRA permits states to have **right-to-work laws,** and as of 2005, 22 of them do. Oklahoma became the 22nd state on October 1, 2001. In a right-to-work state, employment cannot be conditioned on union membership. Despite some employees' nonparticipation in the union, and thus their not being required to pay union dues, the union must still represent these employees as a part of the bargaining unit. If a state is not a right-to-work state, the union and employer may have as a part of their collective bargaining agreement union security device a provision for a **union shop.** This provision, called a **union shop clause,** requires the employer to have all members or potential members of the bargaining unit agree that they will join the union within a certain amount of time (not less than 30 days) after becoming employed.

It is also permissible for the collective bargaining agreement to contain an **agency shop clause,** which requires nonunion members to pay to the union the usual union dues and fees without joining the union and thereby becoming subjected to union rules. Some right-to-work laws do not allow this and, instead, permit nonunion employees of the bargaining unit to be **free riders**—that is, to receive union benefits without having to pay union dues or fees. In the case below, the court addressed pro football players who did not want to pay union dues.

National Football League Players Ass'n v. Pro Football, Inc.
857 F. Supp. 71 (D.D.C. 1994)

The NFL Players Association (NFLPA) brought suit to force the Redskins' management and Management Council to enforce an arbitrator's award requiring them to suspend Redskin team players who did not pay their union dues. The court had to determine whether the arbitrator's decision was enforceable, and that depended on the location of the players' predominant place of work: the place where the players primarily practiced—Virginia, which is a right-to-work state—or the place where they played most of their games—Washington, D.C., which is not. The court held that the primary site was Virginia, where the players practiced, and since that is a right-to-work state, the nonunion players were not required to pay dues to the union.

Hogan, J.

NFLPA and the NFL Management Council signed a collective bargaining agreement ("CBA") on May 6, 1993, that governs the employment of professional football players. In executing the CBA, the NFLPA acted as the sole and exclusive representative of the individuals who play football for NFL teams and the Management Council acted as the sole and exclusive representative of the NFL teams that employ these football players.

Article V of the agreement contains a standard agency shop provision that requires NFL players to pay union dues or an equivalent service fee within 30 days of employment. The agreement states that this provision is applicable "wherever and whenever legal." If, after written notification to the NFL Management Council that a player has not paid the proper fees, the matter is not resolved within seven days, the agreement indicates that the player should be suspended without pay. Additionally, Article V states that "[a]ny dispute over compliance with, or the interpretation, application or administration of this Article" will be resolved through arbitration. The resulting arbitration decision "will constitute full, final and complete disposition of the dispute, and will be binding on the player(s) and Club(s) involved and the parties to this agreement."

Although §8(a)(3) of the National Labor Relations Act, 29 U.S.C. §158(a)(3), permits employers to establish agency shops, §14(b) of the Act, 29 U.S.C. §164(b), allows states and territories to exempt themselves from §8(a)(3) by enacting laws prohibiting agency shops. Such laws are commonly referred to as right-to-work laws. Virginia has enacted such a law.

The arbitrator ordered the Redskins to comply with the agreement and to suspend players who failed to pay their dues or fees. Interpreting the Supreme Court's decision in *Oil, Chemical, and Atomic Workers, International Union v. Mobil Oil Corp.,* 426 U.S. 407 (1976), the arbitrator found that the District of Columbia, not Virginia, was the players' predominant job *situs* because the Redskins play more games there (at RFK stadium) than anywhere else. Although the players spend the majority of their time practicing in Virginia, the arbitrator found that the team's games are the *"raison d'etre"* of the players' employment and produce the team's revenues. The arbitrator also relied on the fact that players' compensation is related to the number of games for which they appear on the Redskins roster. Therefore, the arbitrator issued an award that required the Redskins to suspend any players who failed to pay the proper fees.

It is true that the Redskins would not exist if the team did not play its games in the District of Columbia and elsewhere. The team's revenue comes primarily from playing games, not practicing. However, to adopt an economic-based *raison d'etre* test would potentially create difficulties in application. Professional athletes, musicians, actors, and others who may spend most of their time in one place practicing, but earn their revenue based upon a limited number of performances, would face the possibility that the application of agency shop provisions may vary from year to year depending on the location of their performances in a given year. Further, the Redskins themselves may be presented with situations where players are under contract but do not play in the District of Columbia at all because of injuries or some other concerns. If a player does not participate in a single game in the District of Columbia (e.g.—Terry Orr), the player could possibly be subject to Virginia's right-to-work laws, because the *raison d'etre* would be different. This could create the anomalous situation in which players on the same team would be covered by the labor laws of different jurisdictions. This is not the type of situation envisioned by the Supreme Court when it adopted the job *situs* test.

The Court's primary concern must be with predictability. The NFLPA may have some legitimate equitable arguments about the financial significance of the games that are played in the District of Columbia, as opposed to the practices that occur in Virginia. Nevertheless, when the Redskins players get up in the morning to go to work, they usually go to Redskins Park, not RFK stadium. Practices, conditioning, and meetings are an integral part of game preparation. Since the players spend most of their time working in Virginia, *Mobil Oil* indicates that Virginia law should apply to them. Regardless of the intuitive appeal of the arbitrator's decision, it does not conform with the current state of the law. Carving out exceptions to *Mobil Oil* for the Redskins (and eventually others) would limit the predictability and usefulness of *Mobil Oil.*

Because the arbitrator in this case clearly erred in interpreting *Mobil Oil,* he placed the Redskins in the unenviable position of being ordered to violate the law and public policy of Virginia. Although the Court is ordinarily quite reluctant to act as a Monday morning quarterback and second-guess an arbitrator, public policy mandates that the Court step in and act in this particular case. The Court finds that the arbitrator's decision violated the law and public policy of Virginia

and therefore cannot stand. Thus, although the team has struggled recently on the gridiron, the Redskins have won a surprising come-from-behind victory here in the judicial arena. DISMISSED.

Case Questions

1. Do you agree with the court's decision about where the Redskins' main place of business is? Explain.

2. What do you think of the right-to-work laws? Discuss.

3. As a manager, what are the advantages and disadvantages of being in a right-to-work state? Explain.

A frequent bone of contention with union members is the use of union dues for activities with which the members do not agree. This is a particularly interesting question when it involves the agency shop, since employees who do not want to belong to the union must still pay to the union an amount equal to the union dues (often called a *service fee*). This is, of course, to prevent the problem of free riders who benefit from union activity but do not contribute to the union's resources. In the case that follows, the U.S. Supreme Court addressed the issue of what the union could use this money for.

Lehnert v. Ferris Faculty Association *500 U.S. 507 (1991)*

Several members of a bargaining unit objected to the way their service fee funds were used, even though they were not members of the union in this agency shop. The Court addressed several different ways in which the money could and could not be spent.

Blackmun, J.

Michigan's Public Employment Relations Act (Act) provides that a duly selected union shall serve as the exclusive collective-bargaining representative of public employees in a particular bargaining unit. The Act, which applies to faculty members of a public educational institution in Michigan, permits a union and a government employer to enter into an "agency-shop" arrangement under which employees within the bargaining unit who decline to become members of the union are compelled to pay a "service fee" to the union.

Respondent Ferris Faculty Association (FFA), an affiliate of the Michigan Education Association (MEA) and the National Education Association (NEA), serves, pursuant to this provision, as the exclusive bargaining representative of the faculty of Ferris State College in Big Rapids, Michigan. Ferris is a public institution established under the Michigan Constitution and is funded by the State.

The bargaining, agreement required all employees in the bargaining unit who did not belong to the FFA to pay a service fee equivalent to the amount of the dues required of a union member. Of the $284 service fee for 1981–1982, the period at issue, $24.80 went to the FFA, $211.20 to the MEA, and $48 to the NEA.

Petitioners were members of the Ferris faculty during the period in question and objected to certain uses by the unions of their service fees. Petitioners instituted this action, claiming that the use of their fees for purposes other than negotiating and administering a collective-bargaining agreement with the Board of Control violated rights secured to them by the First and Fourteenth Amendments to the United States Constitution.

The Court's decisions in this area prescribe a case-by-case analysis in determining which activities a union constitutionally may charge to dissenting employees, and set forth several guidelines to be followed in making such determinations. Chargeable activities must (1) be "germane" to collective-bargaining activity;

(2) be justified by the government's vital policy interest in labor peace and avoiding "free riders," and (3) not significantly add to the burdening of free speech that is inherent in the allowance of an agency or union shop.

In arguing that these principles exclude the charges here, employees propose two limitations on the use by public-sector unions of dissenters' contributions. First, they urge that they may not be charged over their objection for lobbying activities that do not concern legislative ratification of, or fiscal appropriations for, their collective-bargaining agreement. Second, as to nonpolitical expenses, employees assert that the local union may not utilize dissenters' fees for activities that, though closely related to collective bargaining generally, are not undertaken directly on behalf of the bargaining unit to which the objecting employees belong. We accept the form proposition but find the latter to be foreclosed by our prior decisions.

We turn to the union activities at issue in this case.

The Court of Appeals found that the union could constitutionally charge employees for the costs of a Preserve Public Education (PPE) program designed to secure funds for public education in Michigan, and that portion of the MEA publication, the *Teacher's Voice,* which reported these activities. Employees argue that, contrary to the findings of the courts below, the PPE program went beyond lobbying activity and sought to affect the outcome of ballot issues and "millages" or local taxes for the support of public schools. Given our conclusion as to lobbying and electoral politics generally, this factual dispute is of little consequence. None of these activities was shown to be oriented toward the ratification or implementation of employees' collective-bargaining agreement. We hold that none may be supported through the funds of objecting employees.

Employees next challenge the Court of Appeals' allowance of several activities that the union did not undertake directly on behalf of persons within employees' bargaining unit. This objection principally concerns NEA "program expenditures" destined for States other than Michigan, and the expenses of the *Teacher's Voice* listed as "Collective Bargaining" and "Litigation." Our conclusion that unions may bill dissenting employees for their share of general collective-bargaining costs of the state or national parent union is dispositive as to the bulk of the NEA expenditures. The District Court found these costs to be germane to collective bargaining and similar support services and we decline to disturb that finding. No greater relationship is necessary in the collective-bargaining context.

This rationale does not extend, however, to the expenses of litigation that does not concern the dissenting employees' bargaining unit or, by extension, to union literature reporting on such activities. While the union is clearly correct that precedent established through litigation on behalf of one unit may ultimately be of some use to another unit, we find extraunit litigation to be more akin to lobbying in both kind and effect.

Moreover, union litigation may cover a diverse range of areas from bankruptcy proceedings to employment discrimination. When unrelated to an objecting employee's unit, such activities are not germane to the union's duties as exclusive bargaining representative. We hold that the Amendment proscribes such assessments in the public sector.

The Court of Appeals determined that the union constitutionally could charge employees for certain public relations expenditures. In this connection, the court said: "Public relations expenditures designed to enhance the reputation of the teaching profession . . . are, in our opinion, sufficiently related to the unions' duty to represent bargaining unit employees effectively so as to be chargeable to dissenters." We disagree. Like the challenged lobbying conduct, the public relations activities at issue here entailed speech of a political nature in a public forum. More important, public speech in support of the teaching profession generally is not sufficiently related to the union's collective-bargaining functions to justify compelling dissenting employees to support it. Expression of this kind extends beyond the negotiation and grievance-resolution contexts and imposes a substantially greater burden upon First Amendment rights that do the latter activities.

Nor do we accept the Court of Appeals' comparison of these public relations expenses to the costs of union social activities chargeable to dissenters. We have held that the communicative content of union social activities, if any, derives solely from the union's involvement in them. "Therefore, the fact that the employee is forced to contribute does not increase the infringement of his First Amendment rights already resulting from the compelled contribution to the union." The same cannot be said of the public relations charges upheld by the Court of Appeals which covered "informational picketing, media exposure, signs, posters and buttons."

The District Court and the Court of Appeals allowed charges for those portions of the *Teachers' Voice* that concern teaching and education generally, professional development, unemployment, job opportunities, award programs of the MEA, and other miscellaneous matters. Informational support services such as these are neither political nor public in nature. Although they do not directly concern the members of employees' bargaining unit, these expenditures are for the benefit of all and we discern additional infringement of First Amendment rights that they might occasion. In short, we agree with the Court of Appeals that these expenses are comparable to the *de minimis* social activity charges.

The Court of Appeals ruled that the union could use the fees of objecting employees to send FFA delegates to the MEA and the NEA conventions and to participate in the 13E Coordinating Council, another union structure. The employees challenge that determination and argue that the meetings were those of affiliated parent unions rather than the local, and therefore do not relate exclusively to the employees' unit.

We need not determine whether employees could be commanded to support all the expenses of these conventions. The question before the Court is simply whether the unions may constitutionally require employees to subsidize the participation in these events of delegates from the local. We hold that they may. That the conventions were not solely devoted to the activities of the FFA does not prevent the unions from requiring employees' support. We conclude above that the First Amendment does not require so close a connection. Moreover, participation by members of the local in the formal activities of the parent is likely to be an important benefit of affiliation.

The chargeability of expenses incident to preparation for a strike which all concede would have been illegal under Michigan law is a provocative question. At the beginning of the 1981–1982 fiscal year, the FFA and Ferris were engaged in negotiating a new collective-bargaining agreement. The union perceived these efforts to be ineffective and began to prepare a "job action" or, in more familiar terms, to go out on strike. These preparations entailed the creation by the FFA and the MEA of a "crisis center" or "strike headquarters."

Had the FFA actually engaged in an illegal strike, the union clearly could not have charged the expenses incident to that strike to dissenters. We can imagine no legitimate governmental interest that would be served

by compelling objecting employees to subsidize activity that the State has chosen to disallow. Similarly, one might expect the State to prohibit unions from using dissenters' funds to threaten or prepare for such conduct. The Michigan Legislature, however, has chosen not to impose such a restriction, and we do not find the First Amendment to require that limitation.

The employees can identify no determination by the State of Michigan that mere preparation for an illegal strike is itself illegal or against public policy, and we are aware of none. Further, we accept the rationale provided by the Court of Appeals in upholding these charges that such expenditures fall "within the range of reasonable bargaining tools available to a public sector union during contract negotiations." The District Court expressly credited trial testimony by an MEA representative that outward preparations for a potential strike serve as an effective bargaining tool and that only one out of every seven or eight "job action investigations" actually culminates in a strike.

In sum, these expenses are substantially indistinguishable from those appurtenant to collective-bargaining negotiations. The District Court and the Court of Appeals concluded, and we agree, that they aid in those negotiations and inure to the direct benefit of members of the dissenters' unit. Further, they impose no additional burden upon First Amendment rights. The union may properly charge employees for those costs.

AFFIRMED in part and REVERSED in part, and REMANDED.

Case Questions

1. Do you agree with the Court's decision regarding funds spent for activities preparatory to a strike that could not legally take place? Does the Court's position make sense to you? Explain.

2. As an employer who has a unionized workplace, how would you feel about this decision?

3. Does the agency shop provision requiring nonunion members to contribute a service fee equal to the union dues make sense to you?

THE LANDRUM-GRIFFIN ACT

Also known as the Labor Management Reporting and Disclosure Act, this legislation was enacted in response to congressional investigations into union corruption from 1957 to 1959. After finding evidence of such corruption, the legislation was passed.

Exhibit 14.12   Union Members' Bill of Rights

Among other things, the Landrum-Griffin Act provides that:

- Union members have the right to attend union meetings, vote on union business, and nominate candidates for union elections.
- Members may bring an agency or court action against the union after exhausting union procedures.
- Certain procedures must be followed before any dues or initiation fee increases.
- Except for the failure to pay dues, members must have a full and fair hearing when being disciplined by the union.

Based on the investigative findings, the purpose of the law is to establish basic ways of unions operating to ensure a democratic process, to provide union members with a minimum bill of rights attached to union membership, and to regulate the activities of union officials and the use of union funds. (See Exhibit 14.12.)

The act provides a bill of rights for union members. Looking at some of the provisions of the bill of rights, one might think that they are so simplistic as to be taken as givens for an organization. However, keep in mind that the bill of rights was enacted in response to union abuses actually found during the two-year congressional investigation.

The Landrum-Griffin Act also set forth specific procedures to be followed when unions hold elections, including voting for officers by secret ballot, holding elections at least every three years (other times for different levels of the union, such as international officers), candidates being able to see lists of eligible voters, and procedures for having an election declared improper. Provisions were also enacted to safeguard union funds. Under the act, unions cannot use union funds for anything except benefiting the union or its members. Funds cannot be used to support union office candidates, and union officials, agents, employees, and so on cannot acquire financial interests that conflict with the union's. The law made stealing or embezzling union funds a federal crime.

LABOR RELATIONS IN THE PUBLIC SECTOR

Much of what has been discussed relates to the private sector. Of more recent vintage is the matter of collective bargaining in the public sector.

Federal Employees

Historically, there has been little legislation affecting the labor relations of public employees (federal, state, and local government employees). The NLRA has always exempted these employees. There is yet no uniform federal policy on public labor–management relations. Currently, however, over half of the 50 states and the District of Columbia have collective bargaining statutes covering most, if not all, public employees.

Over time, federal employees formed associations, but only postal workers were not powerless to influence their workplace. In 1962, President Kennedy established the right of federal employees to form and join unions. Since that time union ranks have increased among this sector.

Federal restrictions prevent federal unions from conducting direct bargaining over wages and benefits and from striking. The Civil Service Reform Act of 1978 established the Federal Labor Relations Authority (FLRA) to administer federal sector labor law. This agency may be thought of as the federal counterpart to the private sector's National Labor Relations Board (NLRB).

State, County, and Municipal Public Employees

Most public employee organizations at the state, county, and municipal levels can be divided into three major categories—professional associations, craft unions, and industrial-type unions. *Professional associations* are composed of a wide variety of professionals. One of the largest segments of this population belongs to the National Education Association (NEA). This organization of public school teachers has over 1 million members, and in addition to teachers, consists of principals, administrators, and other school specialists. The Fraternal Order of Police does not consider itself a union, but many local lodges engage in collective bargaining, handle grievances, and represent the interests of their members to their employers.

Craft unions consist of such workers as the International Association of Firefighters (IAFF), which is an affiliate of the AFL-CIO. Another teachers union that considers itself part of the craft union is the American Federation of Teachers (AFT), which limits its membership to classroom teachers only. While craft unions are too numerous to count, many of them are familiar and have been in existence for nearly a century, such as the United Mine Workers and International Brotherhood of Electrical Workers.

The union that dominates the *industrial-type union* is the American Federation of State, County, and Municipal Employees (AFSCME), an affiliate of the AFL-CIO. These local unions may represent an entire city or county, or they may represent a smaller unit of government, such as a department or a group of employees that cuts across many departments.

The AFL-CIO assists public workers' unions who affiliate with it through its Public Employees Department. This department, formed in 1974, has 33 affiliated unions which represent millions of federal, state, and local government employees. These unions represent workers as diverse as schools, courts, regulatory agencies, hospitals, transportation networks, police, and firefighters. The AFL-CIO believes that state and local employees are the only workers in the United States who do not enjoy the basic right to enter into collective bargaining agreements with their employers. That is, there is no national legislation that gives these workers the right to enter into collective bargaining agreements. If they have the right, it is because the state in which they operate has enacted state legislation that permits it.

To many, the most important difference between the public and private collective bargaining is that the federal government and most state statutes do not contain the right of public employees to strike. This prohibition is grounded in the need to protect public health and safety (i.e., to prevent police officers or firefighters from being out on strike while crime rises or buildings burn), as well as the sovereignty doctrine deeming striking against a governmental employer as inconsistent with the government being the sovereign or highest authority.

State and federal employees have not always honored the prohibition on striking. While many ignored the prohibition, probably the most famous example occurred when the federal air traffic controllers, represented by the Professional Air Traffic Controllers Organization (PATCO), went on strike in 1981. One of the reasons the strike was so memorable was undoubtedly because newly elected President Ronald Reagan took a hard line and terminated 11,000 striking employees.

United States v. Professional Air Traffic Controllers Organization *653 F.2d 1134 (7th Cir. 1981)*

PATCO Local No. 316 at Chicago's O'Hare Airport demanded an upgrade of the airport and a tax-free bonus of $7,500 for each air traffic controller. The Federal Aviation Administration refused to meet the demand. In response, from August 6 to 15, 1980, PATCO conducted a unified slowdown of airport traffic which resulted in several delays. The United States sought an injunction on August 18, 1980, and the action was dismissed. The United States appealed from the district court's decision holding that only the Federal Labor Relations Authority, not the district court, had the authority to enjoin such a strike.

Swygert, J.

Title VII of the Civil Service Reform Act of 1978 was enacted to provide a comprehensive statutory scheme for the regulation of federal labor–management relations. The statute created a new, independent agency, the Federal Labor Relations Authority (FLRA), which was to be primarily responsible for carrying out the purposes of Title VII. When Congress enacted Title VII, it adopted the language of section 19(b)(4) of the Executive Order [Executive Order 11491, as amended, which regulated federal labor–management relations prior to enactment of the Civil Service Reform Act] making it an unfair labor practice for a union "to call, or participate in, a strike, work stoppage, or slowdown." The reason for Congress's prohibition of strikes by federal employees was reiterated during the congressional debates on Title VII:

> The primary reason for Government services is to supply the public with certain essentials of life which cannot reasonably be supplied by the average citizen himself, or to him by private enterprise. Because these services are essential to the health, welfare and safety of the public, it becomes intolerable that they be interrupted.

Dismissing or indicting the air traffic controllers involved in the slowdown would not be a viable remedy for the Government. First, terminating a substantial number of controllers would seriously impair the FAA's ability to provide the public with this essential service; this is precisely the sort of result that the statutory provisions were intended to prevent. Second, indicting or terminating the controllers after a strike does nothing to prevent the strike and the serious consequences that would surely follow. Thus, the only remedy available to the Government that can prevent a strike is an injunction we conclude that an injunction is an available remedy. REVERSED and REMANDED.

Case Questions

1. In your opinion, based on the *PATCO* decision, should public employees have the right to strike?

2. Do you agree with Congress's assessment of why that right is not provided to public employees?

3. Given the court's language about the perils of terminating the air traffic controllers, why do you think President Reagan did so? What would you have done differently, if anything?

There are also differences between the private and public sector about what may be negotiated. While the U.S. postal workers may do so, generally federal employees cannot bargain over wages, hours, or benefits. On the other hand, they can bargain about the numbers, types, and grades of positions, procedures for performing work or exercising authority, the use of technology, and alternatives for employees harmed by management decisions.

Management Tips

Dealing with unions can be a sticky business. The very idea is antithetical to many business owners who feel the business is theirs and that they should have full control. Giving over any control to employees through the unions and the collective bargaining process is not easy for them. Collective bargaining, is, however, the law. Following the tips below can help avoid problems:

- If employees decide they wish to unionize, do not try to negatively influence the decision.
- Do not assume any employee you speak to for the purpose of persuading employees not to unionize will keep the conversation confidential.
- Know the kinds of things the employer can legally do to influence the unionizing decision, and do only those things that are permissible.
- Once the union is in place, conduct all negotiations only with the union representatives. Avoid making side deals with individual employees.

- Treat the collective bargaining process as one would any business activity. Do not invite unfair labor practice charges by engaging in activity that could be deemed a refusal to bargain in good faith.
- Know what the law requires—the employer need not do any more than the law requires in permitting the union to conduct its business. Know well what the employer can and need not do.
- Keep the lines of communication open between labor and management.
- Try to keep the "us versus them" mentality from having a negative impact on the collective bargaining process. It can be difficult to avoid, but if you can, it helps negotiations stay on an even keel, without letting egos get in the way.
- Play hard ball without setting management up for an unfair labor practice charge.

Summary

- The four main labor law statutes form a framework within which employers and employees may address workplace issues with some modicum of predictability.
- Laws paved the way for unionism by preventing courts from prohibiting union activity. They also provided a statutory basis, with the Wagner or National Labor Relations Act, and they fine-tuned and addressed union abuses, with the Taft-Hartley Act and the Landrum-Griffin or Labor Management Recording and Disclosure Act.
- Private employers and employees are free to negotiate upon mandatory as well as permissive terms of bargaining to determine matters of wages, hours, and other terms and conditions of employment.

Chapter-End Questions

1. After a bitter strike and boycott that included the use of "scabs" to replace workers in the walnut industry and strike-related violence, a returning worker who had been a quality control supervisor prior to the strike was placed in a seasonal packing position, a job with less status, because the employer was afraid that the replacement workers, some of whom were still on the job, would try to instigate violence against the returning workers. The workers claimed that the employer refused to place them in their prior positions because of retaliation for striking. Does the employer have an obligation to place workers in a position where

there might be violence aimed at them? [*Diamond Walnut Growers* 1075 (D.C. Cir. 1997).]

2. Bloom was hired to perform clerical work for Group Health Incorpor— fessional Employees International Union Local 12. Group Health had tive bargaining agreement that contained a union security clause that sta— be "members in good standing," which Bloom interpreted as requiring that he pay union dues. Upon filing a grievance with the NLRB, what is the likely outcome? [*Bloom* v. *NLRB,* 30 F.3d 1001 (8th Cir. 1994).]

3. C. Tyler Williams Co. set up a committee called the Employee-Owners' Influence Council (EOIC). All employees were encouraged to become members. Of 150 employees who applied, 30 of Tyler Williams' 8,000 employees were selected by the company. They discussed such issues as medical insurance benefits, the Employee Stock Ownership Plan, and family and medical leave. Is this type of employee–management team in violation of the NLRA? [*Polaroid* v. *NLRB,* 329 NLRB No. 47 (Oct. 6, 1999).]

4. In its employee handbook, an employer stated that it would do "*everything possible* to maintain the company's union-free status for the benefit of both our employees and [the Company]." Is this an unfair labor practice under the NLRB? [*Aluminum Casting & Engineering Co.* v. *NLRB,* 328 NLRB No. 2 (Apr. 9, 1999).]

5. A truck driver who refused to drive a truck because he "smelled fumes" informed his coworker of this fact. When the employee was disciplined for refusing to take the truck, he alleged that he was engaged in "concerted activity." What basis does he have for alleging this? [*NLRB* v. *PALCO,* 1998 U.S. App. LEXIS 3521 (Dec. 21, 1998).]

6. An employer was hiring employees after a strike. On employment applications, they asked the potential employees whether they belonged to a union. Was the employer engaged in an unfair labor practice? [*Mathews Readymix, Inc.* v. *NLRB,* 165 F.3d 74 (D.C. Cir. 1999).]

7. The employer engaged in the practice of photographing an employee engaged in picket line activity. Is this illegal surveillance, even though the activity was "open and obvious," no action was taken against the employee, and the employer was preparing a defense regarding potential illegal secondary activity? [*Clock Electric, Inc.* v. *NLRB,* 162 F.3d 907 (6th Cir. 1998).]

8. What are the most important differences between public and private sector collective bargaining?

9. During contract negotiations, employer and union exchange information on the union's proposal for pay raises. The employer rejects the proposal. The employer is adamant and refuses to agree to the raises. The union alleges that this is an unfair labor practice in that the employer is not bargaining in good faith. Is it?

10. The union strikes the employer in an effort to receive higher wages. The employer brings in workers to replace the striking employees. Agreement is finally reached between the employer and employees. Must the employer dismiss the replacement workers?

Chapter **Fifteen**

Occupational Safety and Health

Opening Scenarios

SCENARIO 1

Scenario

Jessie Caterez owns and operates a general construction business. He recently was successful in obtaining a bid to build a new athletic facility. Although his company can do most of the work, he needs to hire other contractors to do parts of the job, such as cement contractors and welders to lay the foundation of the building. He selects Cem-Steel as the subcontractor to lay the foundation and the steel work. During the cement work, Jane Sprint, an employee of Cem-Steel, is hospitalized due to the large number of cement particles she has inhaled. Her employer, Cem-Steel, had not provided protective mouth masks. The Occupational Safety and Health Administration (OSHA) cites Caterez for violation of its regulation about protective gear requirements. Is Caterez liable or Cem-Steel?

SCENARIO 2

Donna is the supervisor at a construction worksite. The company for which she works has a rule that employees cannot ride on the side of equipment vehicles because of the potential for physical harm. Donna posts signs about this and cautions her workers, but they still hitch rides on any available vehicle. Shelly and Jack are on break and too tired to walk back to the main area of the worksite. So, Shelly jumps on one of the single-person forklift vehicles and Jack climbs aboard the side rails. Halfway back to the central area of the worksite, Jack falls off and is injured. The Occupational Safety and Health Administration (OSHA) cites the company for violation of its regulation about riding on vehicles. Is the employer liable?

SCENARIO 3

Paul Kibler has worked for New England Bell Telephone for 11 years when he discovers he has AIDS. While the telephone company agrees to let him continue working, his co-workers refuse to pick up their assignments in the same office as Paul, and they demand that someone from the phone company walk out to their trucks to deliver assignments. When the phone company refuses, the employees walk off the job, claiming that they are being subjected to unsafe working conditions in violation of the general duty clause. What is the employer's duty?

SCENARIO 4

Hubert Steloik has recently created a new, promising business—Chemical Corp. He has found a niche in the market due to the recent desire of companies to recycle plastic. One chemical needed for this process was tphycioligycic, and not many chemical companies are providing the chemical. The company has been up and running for approximately one year. Several of the employees handling tphycioligycic complained to the Director of Safety that their throats burned after working with the chemical for long periods of time. Because not all of the employees handling the chemical have complained about such side effects, the director has not take any action. Several weeks ago, one of the workers died due to breathing complications. OSHA investigates and issues a violation to Chemical Corp. for violating the general duty clause of the Occupational Safety and Health Act. The director later finds out that the other chemical companies have not provided the chemical due to the chemical's hazardous nature, which was cited in one of the major industry publications two years ago. Steloik does not feel he should be liable because he was unaware of such risks. Will the violation stand?

STATUTORY BASIS

Occupational Safety and Health Act

§654 (§5) Duties
(a) Each employer—
(1) shall furnish to each of his employees employment and a place of employment which are free from recognized hazards that are causing or are likely to cause death or serious physical harm to his employees;

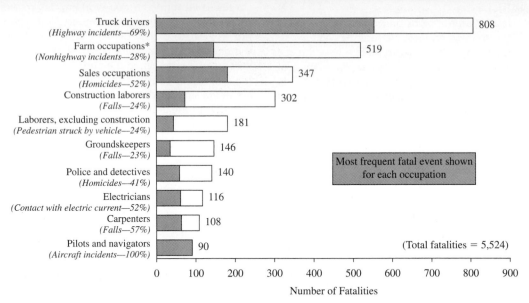

*Farm occupations include the following: Nonhorticultural farmers, nonhorticultural farm managers, farm workers, and farm worker supervisors.

Source: U.S. Department of Labor, Bureau of Labor Statistics, Census of Fatal Occupational Injuries, 2002. Graph courtesy of Athena Research Corporation.

(2) shall comply with occupational safety and health standards promulgated under this Act.

(b) Each employee shall comply with occupational safety and health standards and all rules, regulations and orders issued pursuant to this Act which are applicable to his own actions and conduct.

SAFETY AT WORK

contributory negligence
A defense to a negligence action based on the injured party's failure to exercise reasonable care for her or his own safety.

Workplace safety seems like it might not be such a big deal—that is, of course, until you slip on a banana peel in the cafeteria at work and break your sacroiliac and you're laid up for 10 weeks with no income. Or you slip on spilled salad dressing in the kitchen of the restaurant for which you work and you can't continue to pay your tuition. Or you turn on your computer at the office and receive a severe shock that fries your nervous system and puts you in the hospital for weeks. Workplace safety is often perceived as the bailiwick of angry-looking union reps or blue-collar "working stiffs" who carry lunch pails to work. But it is a workplace issue that affects us all. *Each year* 6,000 Americans die from workplace injuries, another 50,000 workers die from illnesses caused by workplace exposure, and 4.7 million suffer nonfatal workplace injuries costing businesses over $170 billion (as of 2002). (See Exhibits 15.1 and 15.2.)

Exhibit 15.2   The Manner in Which Workplace Fatalities Occurred, 2002

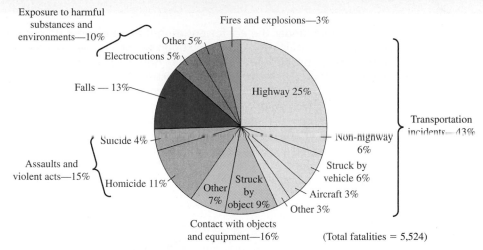

Exposure to harmful substances and environments—10%
Fires and explosions—3%
Other 5%
Electrocutions 5%
Falls — 13%
Highway 25%
Suicide 4%
Non-highway 6%
Transportation incidents—43%
Struck by vehicle 6%
Assaults and violent acts—15%
Homicide 11%
Struck by object 9%
Aircraft 3%
Other 7%
Other 3%
Contact with objects and equipment—16%
(Total fatalities = 5,524)

Note: Totals for major categories may include subcategories not shown separately. Percentages may not add to totals because of rounding.

Source: US Department of Labor, Bureau of Labor Statistics, Census of Fatal Occupational Injuries, 2002. Graph courtesy of Athena Research Corporation.

assumption of risk
A defense to a negligence action based on the argument that the injured party voluntarily exposed herself or himself to a known danger created by the other party's negligence.

fellow servant rule
An employer's defense to liability for an employee's injury where the injury occurred on the job and was caused by the negligence of another employee.

To further complicate matters, until fairly recently there was no comprehensive requirement that employers provide for the safety of workers on their premises toiling for them. Prior to the enforcement of the Occupational Safety and Health Act in 1970, employers were only bound by the common law to provide employees with a safe place to work. However, employers also had the benefit of three common-law defenses that allowed them to escape from liability in connection with 85 to 90 percent of industrial accidents: contributory negligence, assumption of risk, and the fellow servant rule.

Contributory negligence allows the employer to defend against the employee's injury suit by claiming that the employee contributed to the injury through his or her own negligence. The **assumption of risk** defense precludes the employee from recovering when the employee knows of a risk involved in the workplace, chooses to chance not being injured, and is in fact injured. The **fellow servant rule** permits the employer to escape liability when the negligence was the fault of an employee rather than the employer. The injured worker, consequently, did not find much protection from the requirement that the employer provide a safe working environment.

While most states enacted occupational safety and health laws, these were not generally enforced. As an example of this lack of enforcement, one commentator cites that in 1970 there were only 1,600 inspectors ensuring compliance with state laws. Since there were three times as many fish and game wardens as safety inspectors, trout and quail were better protected than working men and women. In addition, workers' compensation statutes attempted to compensate the worker once the injury was sustained.

691

Responsibility under the act for ensuring that employees do not put themselves into any unsafe position rests ultimately upon each employer, not the employees, and employers may not shift their responsibility onto their employees. *Caterpillar Inc.* v. *Occupational Safety and Health Review Commission*, 122 F.3d 437 (7th Cir. 1997).

The act's broad remedial scope is designed to "assure as far as possible every working man and woman in the Nation safe and healthful working conditions." As courts have determined, the act's legislative history suggests that its primary focus was making places of employment, rather than specific employees, safe from work related hazards. This implies that "once an employer is deemed responsible for complying with OSHA regulations, it is obligated to protect every employee who works in its workplace." *United States* v. *Pitt-Des Moines, Inc.*, 168 F.3d 976 (7th Cir. 1999).

It is important to note that most of these statutes severely limit the recovery of the employee to medical expenses and only to a portion of lost wages. Under OSHA, although workers are still limited in their financial recovery to what they can obtain under workers' compensation laws, they may now obtain relief from hazardous situations in the form of correction of the circumstances by the employers.

State legislation regarding protection against hazards varied from state to state, so stringent legislation in one state merely pushed the employer to relocate to a more permissive state. No answer was left but to provide national standards. On December 29, 1970, President Richard Nixon signed into law the Occupational Safety and Health Act, attempting to ensure safe and healthful working conditions for all employees and to preserve the human resources of the United States. Since 1971, OSHA claims that the act has helped to cut workplace fatalities by more than 60 percent and injury/illness rates by 40 percent.

The act covers 115 million workers at more than 7.1 million workplaces. The act is clear regarding which employers are subject to its requirements—any employer that has employees and is in a business affecting commerce (most employers!). The act is slightly less clear, however, about which employees are covered. (See Exhibit 15.3.)

Section 5(a) of the act imposes two basic requirements on employers to accomplish the goal of a safer workplace. First, the employer must comply with all the safety and health standards dictated by the Department of Labor, generally called the "compliance" requirements. Second, the employer must "furnish to each of [its] employees employment and a place of employment which are free from recognized hazards that are causing or are likely to cause death or serious physical harm." This broad requirement is called the "general duty" clause, and traditional employer defenses are not often available.

Many employers contend that the mere breadth of the act is overwhelming and unnecessary. (See Exhibit 15.4.) The standards promulgated under the act are often burdensome and, the employers argue, overcautious. Consequently, many argue that the act has not satisfied its stated purpose but has, instead, needlessly increased the cost of doing business. In response to such criticism, OSHA has increased its commitment to assist small businesses and to include all stakeholders in its efforts.

1. There is no need for OSHA because of workers' compensation.
2. OSHA requirements are always costly.
3. Anyone working for an employer is covered under the act.
4. Once an employer trains its employees regarding the use of a product, piece of equipment, and so on, the responsibility of that employer is concluded.
5. If there is no specific mention of a certain situation in the act, then the act does not cover that situation.

The act has, in fact, made a difference. Since 1970, when Congress created the Occupational Safety and Health Administration (OSHA), which administers the act, fatality rates have dropped—the overall workplace death rate has been cut in half. More than 100,000 workers who might have died on the job did not because of improved safety and health.

The following case addresses the issue of whom the act covers; does the language in Section 5(a), which reads, "furnish to each of *its* employees . . . ," limit the liability of the employer to only those individuals who are actually employees of the cited employer?

United States v. Pitt-Des Moines, Inc.   *168 F.3d 976 (7th Cir. 1999)*

In this case, the court addresses a waiver of OSHA liability for worker injuries or death when work has been subcontracted out. The court determined that the subcontractee was liable also, even though the injured employee was employed by another.

Flaum, J.

In the construction of a postal facility, the USPS (United States Postal Service) hired Hyman/Power (HP) as the general contractor who, in turn, hired Pitt-Des Moines, Inc. (PDM) to fabricate and erect the structural steel for the project. PDM, in turn, subcontracted out part of the steel erection work to MA Steel. (In other words, USPS hired HP, who hired PDM, who hired MA Steel.) During part of the construction, steel beams were joined together and then hoisted to form the skeleton of the building. Under OSHA regulations, two bolts were required when joining the beams together before they could be hoisted. In the processes of hoisting steel beams a beam dropped killing two workers: one worker from PDM and one worker from MA Steel.

Although PDM received previous warnings about this OSHA regulation from Turner/Ozanne (a company hired to oversee the project), PDM did not alter their procedures. Rather, the company stated they were using a higher quality bolt and thus only one was required. When the Turner/Ozanne representative asked OSHA about this one-bolt process, they said that they were unaware of such practice and confirmed the representative's belief that two bolts were required. It was later determined by OSHA examiners that the cause of the beams falling was the lack of the two bolts. A jury consequently found PDM guilty of willfully violating OSHA safety standards resulting in the death of "any employee," namely Newsome of PDM and Thormeyer of MA Steel, and willfully violating an OSHA rule, known as the "training rule," requiring employers to instruct each of their employees in the safety regulations applicable to a given worksite. The counts were based on the violations that directly resulted in the death of the workers. PDM now appeals.

* * *

The original indictment alleged that both Newsome and Thormeyer were employed by PDM. Prior to trial,

693

the district court ruled that under the "multi-employer doctrine" the government only needed to prove that Thormeyer was an employee at the worksite; it did not need to prove that he was PDM's employee to establish a violation of OSHA. Following this ruling the government issued a superseding information containing the same charges as the indictment, but claiming that Thormeyer was employed at the worksite, but not by PDM.

* * *

MULTI-EMPLOYER DOCTRINE

Applying the multi-employer doctrine, the district court held that PDM could be liable for the death of Thormeyer without proof that he was PDM's employee so long as the government could show that he was an employee of the worksite exposed to the risk created by the contractor's safety violations. PDM now challenges this decision, claiming that the doctrine is inconsistent with the plain language of the Act and the purposes of the Act. However, none of PDM's objections to the district court's use of the doctrine are convincing. . . .

The doctrine holds that on multi-employer worksites, an employer who creates a safety hazard can be liable under the Act regardless of whether the employees threatened are its own or those of another employer on the site. Courts which have adopted the doctrine cite for statutory support the duties imposed on employers by Section 654(a) of the Act. These duties are two-fold:

> Each employer—
> (1) Shall furnish to each of his employees employment and a place of employment which are free from recognized hazards that are causing or are likely to cause death or serious physical harm to his employees.
> (2) Shall comply with Occupational Safety and Health standards promulgated under this chapter.

The first duty requires employers to protect their own employees from obvious hazards even when those hazards are not covered by specific safety regulations imposed by the Act. This duty is considered general because it asks employers to protect employees from all kinds of serious hazards, regardless of the source. Although general, the words "his employees" indicates that the duty imposed by 654(a)(1) is limited to an employer's own employees. Section 654(a)(2), on the other hand, contains no such limiting language. Courts have interpreted this provision as imposing a specific burden on employers to comply with and carry out the

Act's safety standards regardless of whom in a given workplace is threatened by noncompliance. Unlike Section 654(a)(1), which imposes a general duty to a specific class, 654(a)(2) implies a specific duty to a more general class. Thus, courts have held that when an employer on a worksite violates a safety regulation, it can face liability under the Act regardless of whether those exposed to the resulting danger were the employer's own employees or those of another.

While Section 654(a)(2) provides the statutory basis for the multi-employer doctrine, courts garner additional support for it from the underlying purpose of the Act. The Act's broad remedial scope is designed "to assure as far as possible every working man and woman in the Nation safe and healthful working conditions." As courts have determined, the Act's legislative history suggests that its primary focus was making places of employment, rather than specific employees, safe from work related hazards. This implies that "once an employer is deemed responsible for complying with OSHA regulations, it is obligated to protect every employee who works in its workplace." Therefore, the combination of Section 654(a)(2)'s broad language and the goal of safer workplaces have led courts to conclude that the multi-employer doctrine is fully consistent with the Act.

* * *

Next, while we are aware of no explicit authorization in the legislative history for the imposition of liability under the multi-employer doctrine, we have found none precluding it. As this court has observed, the congressional record relating to multi-employer job sites is sparse: "In enacting this law, Congress apparently gave little thought to the unique relationship which arises when employees of a number of different employers work in and around the same job site and are subject to the hazards which may exist at that site." In the absence of specific guidance, this court must attempt to render an interpretation of the Act which best fulfills the "stated congressional purpose in an equitable manner." Without the doctrine, employers could avoid OSHA liability for the hazardous conditions they create merely because the threatened or harmed workers— although their presence was entirely foreseeable and they are covered by the Act—happen to be on the payroll of another. Indeed this would be true even when, as here, the violating employer was the only one on the site who could reasonably have prevented the harm. We do not believe that this is the result Congress intended by enacting Section 654(a). We consider the multi-employer doctrine to be more consistent with the Act's broadly remedial purpose.

* * *

While we consider this an appropriate basis for establishing an employer's potential liability, we emphasize that multi-employer liability has limits. While the Act seeks to create safer working environments, "it is clear that the Act is not nor could it be designed to eliminate all occupational accidents. Rather it is designed to require 'a good faith effort to balance the need of workers to have a safe and healthy work environment against the requirement of industry to function without undue interference.'" Because construction sites often entail different employees being exposed to hazards created by more than one employer, the affected employees on a worksite should be afforded the full protection of the Act regardless of their employer. Yet the class of employees who will trigger liability under the multi-employer doctrine should be limited to those with regular access to the areas controlled or directly impacted by the employer accused of violating a safety regulation. Although the logical class is composed of those on a given worksite, it may in certain circumstances be narrower. The doctrine is limited to exposure by the employees of the violating employer "or those of other employers engaged in a common undertaking." While we need not decide the exact contours of the doctrine here, it is enough to emphasize that at a minimum it excludes exposure by a "passerby or unrelated third persons."

This limitation, however, is not exceeded here, and it was appropriate for the district court to hold that PDM could be liable for the death of Thormeyer under the multi-employer doctrine. Thormeyer was employed as an ironworker on the Post Office worksite. His job was to follow PDM's raising gang and bolt up the connections they made. He belonged on the site and regularly worked within the zone of danger created by any unsafe connections. Thormeyer was an entirely foreseeable victim of any willful safety violations PDM may have committed and thus easily fell within the multi-employer doctrine. AFFIRMED.

Case Questions

1. How far do you think this opinion goes? What would you do to protect your company from unexpected liability as a result of the exposure of another employer's employees to hazards at a worksite where your employees were working?

2. Would this opinion extend liability to individuals who were present at a worksite but not working?

3. The review commission, in a separate opinion, concluded that an employer at a multiemployer worksite is not responsible for safety hazards to its own or other's employees where:

   a. Those hazards have been created by another employer.

   b. The employer did not create and does not control the hazard.

   c. The employer does not have the expertise to correct or even to recognize the hazard.

   d. The employer has taken reasonable measures to protect its own employees from the hazards.

   Is this a reasonable solution?

1 Scenario   In scenario 1, Caterez could be found liable due to the multiemployer doctrine. An employer is liable as long as the government can show that the employee at a worksite was exposed to the risk by the contractor's safety violations. An employer that creates a safety hazard can be liable under the act regardless of whether the employees threatened are its own or those of another employer on the site. Courts have held that when an employer on a worksite violates a safety regulation, it can face liability under the act regardless of whether those exposed to the resulting danger were the employer's own employees or those of another. In scenario 1, if it can be shown that Jane Sprint was exposed to the cement dust due to the contractor's safety violation of not providing the mask, Caterez can be held liable and would be the responsible party to handle the OSHA violation.

PROCEDURE FOR ENFORCEMENT

Responsibility for enforcing the acts rests with the Occupational Safety and Health Administration (OSHA) under the auspices of the Department of Labor. The administration provides for inspections of the workplace by OSHA compliance officers, either as a result of complaints from employees, grievances filed by other sources, or reports of fatal or multiple injuries. Routine inspections in certain high-risk industries are also conducted by the officers. The act protects from retaliation against employees who file complaints, in that it prohibits an employer from discharging or discriminating against any employee who exercises any right afforded by the act.

Employers can challenge a citation or penalty imposed by appealing to the Occupational Safety and Health Review Commission (OSHRC), an independent federal agency created to decide contests of citations or penalties resulting from OSHA inspections of American workplaces. The review commission, therefore, functions as an administrative court, with established procedures for conducting hearings, receiving evidence, and rendering decisions by its administrative law judges (ALJs).

To ensure that the inspectors are viewing the workplace in the same condition as that experienced by the employees, inspections are conducted without prior notice to an employer. In fact, anyone giving unauthorized advance notice of the inspection to the employer can be punished by a fine of up to $1,000. The officer will arrive at the worksite, ask to see the safety and accident records of the employer, conduct a "walk around" to visually inspect the site, and conclude by discussing with the employer any violations or concerns, as well as possible solutions to the problems. Because OSHA cannot inspect all 7 million worksites covered by the act, it has established an inspection priority system in order to have the most significant impact. Under this system, the agency inspects situations of imminent danger, catastrophes and fatal accidents, employee complaints involving serious harm, referrals, or planned inspections.

Penalties

Penalties and "abatement orders" are assessed in connection with the officer's report. A nonserious or a serious violation may require payment of a penalty ranging from $0 to $7,000, while repeated and/or willful violations have a price tag of up to $70,000 per violation or up to $500,000 plus prison time if the violation was willful and involved a fatality. Criminal sanctions and even higher fines are also possible where the employer acts willfully and causes the death of an employee. Congress is currently contemplating raising these fines.

Once imposed, some OSHA fines may appear to be minimal in light of the harm or potential for harm caused by the violation. However, it is important to realize that OSHA penalties are based on violations of standards and failure to comply, rather than the number or severity of injuries. While death may be the result of one violation of one OSHA provision, minor physical harm may result from a group of violations. The latter would likely result in a larger fine. In fact, if no willfulness can be shown, the maximum penalty for any violation is $7,000.

"Willfulness"

The question of "willfulness" is one that remains somewhat open in the courts. It is an important one to answer as fines can be significantly increased where willfulness is shown. Such was the case against Tyson Foods, Inc., when an employee inhaled a poisonous gas while repairing equipment leaks. The gas, which eventually killed the worker, was created by decaying chicken feathers and the company was fined $436,000.[1] OSHA defines a "willful" violation in a 2003 publication, "All about OSHA," as "a violation that the employer intentionally and knowingly commits or a violation that the employer commits with plain indifference to the law. The employer either knows that what he or she is doing constitutes a violation, or is aware that a hazardous condition existed and made no reasonable effort to eliminate it." However, its decisions indicate that the Occupational Safety and Health Review Commission seems to consider a "willful" violation as one about which the employer knew or should have known. Either definition is somewhat unclear.

In a 2003 case, the Occupational Safety and Health Review Commission held that a willful violation is one "committed with intentional, knowing or voluntary disregard for the requirements of the Act, or with plain indifference to employee safety" and differentiated a willful violation from others by "an employer's heightened awareness of the illegality of the conduct or conditions and by a state of mind, i.e., conscious disregard or plain indifference for the safety and health of employees."[2] The court did provide an affirmative defense to employers in that an employer's good faith reasonable belief that it was not required to comply with the cited standard "may negate willfulness provided the employer's belief was objectively reasonable under the circumstances."[3] Unfortunately, by using terms such as "reasonable" and "should have known," the concept of willful violations seemed to edge closer to negligence.

In mid-2003, however, the D.C. circuit court tried to narrow this definition to provide employers with a bit more guidance on the matter. In *American Wrecking Corp.* v. *Secretary of Labor,* No. 02-1379 (D.C. Cir. 2003), the court held that that an employer that commits an OSHA violation through negligence has not committed a "willful" violation. In that case, the administrative law judge originally found willfulness because a certain unsafe condition was "so obvious" as to render "unreasonable" the employer's belief in its safety. The court found, however, that "this reasoning is patently flawed." The court warned that to find willfulness because the employer should have known of hazardousness "would erase the distinction between violations that are willful and those that are not." Instead, the court held that "a distinction between serious and willful violations exists *only if willfulness means knowledge that the conditions violate the statute or regulations—actual rather than imputed knowledge,* for otherwise we are back to negligence" (emphasis added). The commission reaffirmed this conclusion in a 2004 case, *Froedtert Memorial Lutheran Hospital Inc.,* OSHRC Docket No. 97-1839 (2004).

---

[1] Tom Parsons, "Tyson Foods Fined," Softcom.com/Associated Press (4/9/04).

[2] *Secretary of Labor* v. *Capeway Roofing Systems, Inc.,* OSHRC Docket No. 00-1986 (2003), citing *Falcon Steel Co.,* 16 BNA OSHC 1179, 1181, 1993-95 CCH OSHD ¶ 30,059, p. 41,330 (No. 89-2883, 1993) (consolidated).

[3] *Secretary of Labor* v. *Capeway Roofing Systems, Inc.,* OSHRC Docket No. 00-1986 (2003), citing *General Motors Electro-Motive Div.,* 14 BNA OSHC 2064, 2068,1991-93 CCH OSHD ¶ 29,240, p. 39,168 (No. 82-630,1991).

Standards

So, how does OSHA determine what standards to apply? The act provides for the creation of the National Institute for Occupational Safety and Health (NIOSH), which is the research arm of the Occupational Safety and Health Administration. The purpose of NIOSH is to conduct research in workplace health and safety and to formulate and make recommendations to the secretary of labor. If those recommendations are approved, then they may become the standards of conduct in connection with a certain industry.

For instance, NIOSH recently conducted a great deal of research in connection with the ergonomic and radiation hazards of computers in the workplace. This has become a significant area of worker concern, since more than 600,000 workers are injured on the job each year from repetitive motion injuries alone. In August 1992, NIOSH developed and recommended standards for employers to follow with regard to that segment of their workforce that may be at risk from ergonomic hazards. The administration then issued an Advance Notice of Proposed Rulemaking and requested comments on the proposed rules regarding ergonomics safety and a health management standard. When asked what were the reasons for the delay in moving forward with the standards, NIOSH responded that the reason for such long delays is the "numerous checks and balances" in the legal system for enacting regulations: "Research is certainly one of the issues. Research quality is always a subject of debate. NIOSH is doing its best to provide the research support, but it is a slow and deliberate process which is costly." (Until the standards are approved, workers *may* be able to recover under the general duty clause; see p. 700.)

Interestingly enough, ergonomics became a controversial political issue amidst the hotly contested 2000 presidential election. In 1999, the Clinton administration's OSHA released proposed ergonomics standards, which business lobbies sought to prevent from becoming final. On November 13, just days after Election Day 2000, the Clinton administration's OSHA released the final ergonomics standards, causing a political fury on Capitol Hill between Democrats and the business interests' Republican allies.

Under the Congressional Review Act of 1996, federal legislators may rescind regulations through a process that ensures quick action. If regulations are rescinded under this statute, then the agency is forbidden from ever enacting rules that are "substantially similar" to those that were voted down. In March 2001, Congress voted to repeal OSHA's ergonomics regulations.[4]

Managerial Liability

Courts have ruled that when a corporate officer in a position of authority supervises the acts that resulted in an OSHA violation, she or he could be held individually criminally liable for the offense. However, the Department of Justice has been reluctant to enforce claims against individual decision makers, prosecuting only 4 out of 30 criminal cases referred to it by OSHA.[5]

---

[4] See Deirdre Davidson and Tatiana Boncompagni, "The Swift Demise of OSHA Rules," *Legal Times,* Mar. 14, 2001.

[5] Marsha Katz, "Managerial Liability for Health and Safety: Is It a Crime?: A Review of Court Cases," unpublished manuscript, p. 3.

COMPLIANCE PROVISIONS

Specific Regulations

Certain specific regulations seem to apply across the board to all types of employment environments. First, a number of specific requirements involve the physical layout of the worksite. Adequate safety measures must be taken, such as proper ventilation where necessary, adequate means of emergency exit if the need arises, safety nets, guard rails, and so on. Second, employees must be trained and informed (through classes, labels, signs) regarding protective measures, for everything from wearing protective devices, such as masks, to the proper use of chemicals. Third, medical examinations must be provided by the employer where an employee has been exposed to toxic substances.

In connection with the development of specific standards, OSHA can begin standards setting procedures on its own initiative or in response to petitions from other parties. If it is determined that a specific standard is needed, any of several advisory committees may be called upon to develop specific recommendations. Recommendations for standards also may come from NIOSH, which conducts research on various safety and health problems, provides technical assistance to OSHA, and recommends standards for OSHA's adoption. Once OSHA has developed plans for a standard, it publishes these intentions in the *Federal Register* as a "Notice of Proposed Rulemaking." One example of this process surrounds the development of OSHA's recommendations for poultry processing facilities to reduce the number and severity of work-related musculoskeletal disorders. In preparing the recommendations, OSHA reviewed existing practices and programs as well as available scientific information on ergonomics and then solicited comments from representatives of trade and professional associations, labor organizations, individual firms, and other interested parties. The final recommendations were announced in September 2004.

Interestingly, the General Accounting Office found in 2004 that OSHA's voluntary compliance programs have been significantly effective in reducing the number of workplace injuries and illnesses. "By many accounts, OSHA's voluntary compliance strategies have improved employers' safety and health practices by allowing the agency to play a collaborative, rather than a policing, role with employers." The report also stated that according to participants, the programs "have considerably reduced their rates of injury and illness" and have fostered "better working relationships with OSHA, improved productivity, and decreased worker compensation costs to their involvement in the voluntary compliance programs."[6] Some current areas of OSHA inquiry include workplace ergonomics, methylene chloride, nursing homes, silica tuberculosis, and workplace violence.

One of the most burdensome requirements on employers is the **continual-training requirement** in connection with the communication of workplace hazards. OSHA requires that employers adopt a program of continual training of their employees regarding safety in the workplace. Every time an employee is hired or transferred into a new

continual-training requirement OSHA requires that the employer provide safety training to all new employees and to all employees who have been transferred into new positions.

[6] General Accounting Office, Report to the Chairman, Subcommittee on Workforce Protections, Committee on Education and the Workforce, House of Representatives, "OSHA's Voluntary Compliance Strategies Show Promising Results, but Should Be Fully Evaluated before They Are Expanded," GAO-04-378 (March 2004).

position, even for just a day, the employer is required to provide safety training to that employee. A violation of this requirement is generally the most frequently cited type of violation on an annual basis. As a result, OSHA has made some effort to simplify the requirement and now supplies employers with material safety data sheets regarding various types of chemicals and the surrounding hazards associated with them.

Emergency Temporary Standards

emergency temporary standards
These standards are imposed by OSHA without immediately going through the typical process where an employee is exposed to grave danger from exposure to substances and the standards are necessary to protect employees from the danger.

Section 6(a) of the act provides that the secretary of labor may establish **emergency temporary standards** that will be effective immediately on publication in the *Federal Register* without having to go through the lengthy rule-making process otherwise required by the act. The secretary is allowed to do so where he or she "determines (a) that employees are exposed to grave danger from exposure to substances or agents determined to be toxic or physically harmful or from new hazards, and (b) that such emergency standard is necessary to protect employees from such danger." The emergency standard is effective until regular standards are approved through the regular procedures or for six months, whichever is shorter.

Generally, the standard expires prior to the completion of the formal rule-making process. In addition, courts hesitate to enforce temporary standards to the extent they enforce formal standards because there may be insufficient notice given to the employers and there has been little opportunity for any critique or comment regarding the temporary standard. As a matter of fact, while some emergency temporary standards are put into place without opposition, every temporary standard that has been contested in court (whether for lack of proof, for insufficient danger, or for lack of proof of necessity) has been rejected by the courts.

GENERAL DUTY CLAUSE

general duty clause
A provision of the act requiring that employers furnish to each employee employment and a place of employment free from recognized hazards that cause or are likely to cause death or serious physical harm to the employee.

There was much discussion in Congress prior to the passage of the act relating to the act's **general duty clause**. The clause protects employees against certain hazards in the workplace, *where no other OSHA standard would address the condition.* Many representatives were concerned that the phrase as first proposed (merely that the employer must provide a safe and healthful workplace) was too vague to inform employers of what their actual obligations were, that it violated due process requirements, and that it did not have a mandatory penalty provision.

As a result, the House of Representatives proposed a more narrowly construed version: Employers were to provide a workplace free from any hazards that are readily apparent and are causing or are likely to cause death or serious physical harm. The proposal also contained a provision for mandatory penalties for an initial citation under the clause. The clause, as passed, reads: "Each employer . . . shall furnish to each of his employees employment and a place of employment which are free from recognized hazards that are causing or are likely to cause death or serious physical harm to his employees."

Under the general duty clause, once it is found that a certain chemical used in an employer's manufacturing process causes reproductive harm, or perhaps damage to the employees' skin, for example, the employer must take steps to protect the employees and to provide a workplace free from these hazards. It is the employer's responsibility to be aware of these workplace hazards and to ensure that all employees are equally protected.

Recognizable Hazards

One of the most serious concerns of employers is determining what constitutes a "recognized" hazard. Imagine the employer's apprehension that a court some day in the future will rule that the effect of secondhand smoke in offices is a recognized hazard to other nonsmokers in that office. If that were the case, an employer may be liable to a nonsmoker who suffers a smoke-related injury because the employer did not provide a smoke-free environment in which to work.[7] In anticipation of such a situation, many states have regulations on the provision of smoke-free working conditions.

A similar situation arose several years ago in connection with Johns-Manville and the exposure of its workers and others to the hazards of asbestos. A court held Johns-Manville, manufacturer of the asbestos, liable for the harms that resulted from the exposure.

On the other hand, during the discussion prior to the passage of the general duty clause by Congress, Representative Steiger made the following remarks:

> However, this requirement [general duty clause] is made realistic by its application only to situations where there are recognized hazards which are likely to cause or are causing serious injury or death. Such hazards are the type that can readily be detected on the basis of basic human senses. Hazards which require technical or testing devices to detect them are not intended to be within the scope of the General Duty requirement.

Governor Pyle, in his testimony on the clause, defined "recognized" as "obvious and admitted by all concerned." In the end, it appears that the definition most often adopted is that of Representative Daniels. Daniels claimed that a recognized hazard may take the form of actual knowledge when the employer actually knows of the hazard or the form of constructive knowledge if the industry recognizes the hazard even if the employer doesn't actually know of the hazard.

Scenario

When does an employer have "actual" knowledge? This can be shown in one of two ways. First, it can be shown through past safety practices or policies of the employer that evidence the employer knew there might be a hazard. For example, if an employer has issued a rule that all employees working in a certain area must wear a mask to prevent inhaling fumes from the chemicals with which they work, the rule might evidence the employer's actual knowledge that inhalation of the chemicals posed a risk. Second, actual knowledge may be shown where the hazard is so obvious that anyone would be aware of it. For instance, these days we are acutely aware that working with asbestos can be hazardous to one's health. Consequently, where a position requires asbestos exposure, that hazard may be so obvious that anyone would be aware of it.

One of the problems that has arisen in connection with the first example above is that an employer may be extra careful with its employees and protect them against any possible risk, rather than any known risk. In doing so, the employer may set standards higher than those necessary to protect the worker. If, however, the employer's standards

---

[7] However, note that, though permitted in some states, many states do not allow a tort action on the basis of an OSHA violation (see, for example, *Morocco* v. *Rex Lumber Co.*, No. AC21931 (Conn. Ct. App. 2002)).

and regulations are going to be held against it when the time comes to evaluate what hazards the employer was aware of, perhaps there would be less incentive to establish high standards in the first place.

The Occupational Safety and Health Review Commission, however, discounts this concern by contending that few employers would abandon their safety procedures merely to avoid citation for a violation. What do you think? If you knew that your safety procedures may some day be used against you to prove that you were aware of a hazard, would you *ever* set a safety standard to protect against an unknown risk?

Barring actual knowledge, the employer may also be held responsible for knowledge of those hazards of which its entire industry is aware. An employer's knowledge may be inferred from an OSHA regulation that is issued to an industry about a certain hazard or from an industry publication citing a potential problem area, or a voluntary industry standard may be used against a specific employer that claims it was not aware of the risk.

Scenario 1

In 2003, OSHA began to issue its first recommendations or guidelines with regard to the prevention of ergonomic (musculoskeletal) injuries in specific professions, such as nursing, grocery stores, and the poultry industry. Until specific regulations are issued for most industries, however, violations with regard to ergonomic risks are most often covered by the general duty clause. As of June 2004, OSHA had issued 13 general duty clause violations for ergonomic hazards and has more cases under evaluation. Pepperidge Farm learned how to manage these challenges the hard way when OSHA inspectors identified 175 instances of ergonomic injuries caused by employee repetitive motion activities at its Downington, Pennsylvania, plant.[8] While an administrative law judge found that the injuries were directly caused by the repetitive action of employees who assembled, packaged, and packed cookies at the plant, the judge found that OSHA had not proven that the ergonomics program that Pepperidge Farm had set up to prevent those injuries was inadequate and dismissed the charges. The Occupational Health and Safety Review Commission affirmed the ruling, holding that the company had taken reasonable steps to reduce the injuries. The court held that

> The Secretary has failed to establish that the process engaged in by Pepperidge to abate the ergonomics hazards at Downington was insufficient. Further the Secretary has not shown that the additional steps not taken by Pepperidge were feasible and that their efficacy in reducing the hazard was so compelling that the failure to have implemented them by the time of the inspection rendered Pepperidge's process inadequate.[9]

The importance of this case is to serve as a warning for employers who do not pay attention to these ergonomic issues. If a firm does not respond to these challenges in a reasonable manner, it may be held liable under OSHA's general duty clause, notwithstanding the lack of specific standards in this emerging arena.

---

[8] *Secretary of Labor* v. *Pepperidge Farm, Inc.,* OSHRC Dkt. No. 89-0265, 17 OSHA Cas. (BNA) 1993 (1997), http://www.oshrc.gov/decisions/pdf_1997/89-0265.pdf.

[9] Ibid. at 114.

Likely to Cause Serious Physical Harm or Death

What does the term "likely" mean in connection with those risks that an employer must protect against? If there is a chance that 1 person in 1,000 may be harmed, does that mean that the risk is likely, or must 5 people out of 10 be at risk for harm to be likely? The Review Commission has stated that the harm need not be likely but possible. In fact, the commission has said that "the proper question is not whether an accident is likely to occur, but whether, if an accident does occur, the result is likely to be death or serious physical harm."

HIV/AIDS

Where a problem has recurred in the workplace, but no new OSHA standards have yet been developed to deal with this problem, employees are left to seek relief from the risk through the general duty clause. Think about areas of questionable risk that have been in the news lately. One area that has received a great deal of attention because of its fatal repercussions is HIV exposure. Individual employees have expressed concern regarding the safety of their exposure to HIV-positive co-workers or exposure to unsafe conditions where transmission may occur. There is no OSHA standard that directly addresses exposure to blood-borne pathogens, such as HIV, so the general duty clause may apply.

Scenario 3

While the hazard of contracting HIV is a recognized hazard in general, within the workplace there are few situations where an employee may be at risk of transmission from a co-worker. Consequently, an employee's claim that an unsafe environment exists merely due to the presence of an HIV-positive co-worker has little credence.

A second area of rising concern for employers is the potential for ergonomic injuries in various occupations. Work-related musculoskeletal disorders (WMSDs) occur as a result of a repetitive motion that causes discomfort and sometimes the loss of use of the worker's arms, hands, wrists, knees, or some other limb or joint. WMSDs may result, for instance, where a computer word processor is not given sufficient break time away from the computer. Newspaper writers have complained of the inability to use their hands to type because of the pain that now results. WMSDs account for 34 percent of all lost-workday injuries and illnesses, according to the Bureau of Labor Statistics. Roger Stevens, chief ergonomist at OSHA, claims that WMSDs account for almost 50 percent of all worker compensation claims. OSHA has responded to this growing cry for protection from WMSDs in the workplace.

John Morrell & Company, a large meat-packing company, was fined $4.3 million by OSHA for poor conditions in its plants, including the repetitive requirements of its labor force. As a partial settlement of an OSHA claim, the firm has agreed to hire a neurologist and an ergonomist to oversee medical treatment at the plants. In a separate case regarding a newspaper office in Fresno, California's state OSHA office ordered that the employer comply with such specific standards as increased knee room for computer operators, more available work space at each workstation, foot rests and arm rests, and adjustable terminals.

Other claims, however, have not been so successful. The probability of relief in any given case may turn upon the interpretation of "serious physical harm." Some interpreting the clause claim that intermittent pain or pain that fluctuates in severity or duration may not be sufficient to meet the serious physical harm standard.

TELECOMMUTING

Recent surveys show that approximately 8 million American workers now telecommute full time.[10] In a February 2000 directive, OSHA stated that it will not hold employers liable for their employee's home offices. However, if an employee works out of a car, then the employer is responsible for that "virtual worksite."

Nevertheless, in July 2000 OSHA issued an advisory letter stating that employers who must keep OSHA injury and illness records should record injuries and illnesses that occur in home-based work sites, as long as they are work-related and otherwise subject to the recording requirement.[11]

REFUSAL TO WORK

Where an employee or a group of employees believes that the employer has violated its general duty to provide a safe working environment, the employees may refuse, without fear of retaliation, to work in that environment or to perform a given task. The employees' refusal must be based on a reasonable apprehension of death or serious injury, coupled with a reasonable belief that no less drastic alternative is available. If an employee chooses not to perform an assigned task as a result of this apprehension, the act prohibits an employer from discharging or discriminating in any other way against that employee.

In *Whirlpool Corporation* v. *Marshall,*[12] the U.S. Supreme Court upheld an OSHA regulation protecting employees against retaliation for refusing to work under dangerous conditions. Two employees at a Whirlpool plant refused to perform maintenance work that would require them to walk on elevated mesh screens less than two weeks after a coworker fell to his death through the screens. The employees were sent home and written reprimands were placed in their personnel files. The Court held that Whirlpool had illegally retaliated against the employees.

VIOLENCE IN THE WORKPLACE

In 2002, 609 homicides occurred at the workplace, equivalent to three deaths daily.[13] The most vulnerable positions included cashiers and managers of food service and lodging establishments (a total of 165 homicides out of 609). Of course, workplace violence can range from threats and verbal abuse to physical assaults and homicide. OSHA reports that approximately 2 million Americans are victims of workplace violence each year. Workers who have extensive contact with the public, who work alone or in small groups, at night, or in high-crime areas, are at a greater risk. Moreover, for the past four years, an annual study of Fortune 1000 corporate security professionals

---

[10] See Stephen A. Fuchs, "Do you Know Where Your Employees Are?" *New Jersey Law Journal,* Jan. 3, 2002.

[11] Ibid.

[12] 445 U.S. 1 (1980).

[13] Associated Press, "American Workplace Deaths, Homicides Decline Again," *USA Today,* (9/18/03).

- Establish a zero-tolerance policy regarding workplace violence against or by employees.
- Provide safety education for employees to inform them of standards of conduct, what to do if they witness or are subjected to workplace violence, and how to protect themselves.
- Secure the workplace with appropriate measures such as video surveillance, extra lighting, alarm systems, guards, electronic keys, and identification badges.
- Provide drop safes to limit the amount of cash on hand.
- Equip field staff with cellular phones and hand-held alarms and require them to keep a contact person informed of their location throughout the day. Keep employer-provided vehicles properly maintained.
- Instruct employees not to enter any location where they feel unsafe. Provide an escort service at night.
- Investigate and remedy all workplace violence claims promptly.

Source: Adapted from "OSHA Fact Sheet on Workplace Violence," 2002.

---

conducted by Pinkerton Consulting and Investigations found that workplace violence is the number-one security concern facing American business.[14]

What can an employer do to protect employees from workplace violence? A zero-tolerance policy toward workplace violence and a prevention program are key elements of protection. Although OSHA does not have rules on violence in the workplace (as of June 2004), it does offer guidelines for employers seeking to prevent workplace violence. (See Exhibit 15.5.) Employers who do not take reasonable steps to prevent or abate a recognized violence hazard in the workplace may be found to be in violation of the general duty clause. However, failure to implement the specific suggestions offered by OSHA is not in itself a violation of the general duty clause.

Domestic violence may intrude upon the workplace. Abusers may attack, stalk, or harass their partners at work. Under new OSHA regulations,[15] employers are not exempt from reporting workplace injuries due to assaults by family members or ex-spouses as part of their recordkeeping requirements.[16]

EMPLOYER REPORTING RESPONSIBILITIES AND EMPLOYEE RIGHTS

Reporting Requirements

Accidents do not "just happen"—they are caused; and it is the goal of OSHA's reporting requirements that the causes are properly identified so future accidents will be prevented.

[14] Pinkerton Consulting and Investigations, "Fortune 1000 Rate Workplace Violence Top Security Threat," www.pinkertonagency.com/news/prIST6.4.html, June 4, 2002.

[15] 29 C.F.R.1904.5, effective January 1, 2002.

[16] NOW Legal Defense and Education Fund, *Employment Rights for Survivors of Abuse: Safety Planning in the Workplace: Protecting Yourself and Your Job,* June 2001. For more information, see www.nowldef.org.

Any employer covered by the act, with the exception of those with 11 or fewer employees, must maintain certain records for OSHA compliance. Where the injury or illness is work-related and meets the general recording criteria or falls into specific categories, reporting is mandated. The records must contain the following information, must be reported on Form 200 produced by the Department of Labor, and must be posted for the employees to see each year from February 1 to March 1 (i.e., it need not be filed with the government but, instead, must be kept throughout the year and compiled for the February posting):

1. Incident date.
2. Category of illness, if applicable.
3. Description of incident.
4. Identification of affected employee.
5. Extent of illness or injury.
6. If incident was an illness, whether the employee was eventually transferred or terminated.

Within six days of an incident reported on Form 200, an additional record containing more complete information (Form 101) must be made and filed with OSHA. In addition, an incident involving fatalities or the hospitalization of five or more employees must be reported to the administration within 48 hours of the incident.

The determination of whether to report an illness or injury is relatively complicated. If the injury or illness does not result from a work-related cause, no report need be made. If the injury or illness is work-related, then it must be reported as long as it is an illness, a death, or an injury that involves (1) medical treatment, (2) loss of consciousness, (3) restriction of work or motion, or (4) transfer to a different position. If the injury does not fit into one of these four categories, then no report needs to be made.

An illness or injury is considered work-related if (1) it occurred on the employer's premises, (2) it occurred as a result of work-related activities, (3) the employee was required to be there by the employer, or (4) the employee was traveling to work or to a place he or she was required to be by the employer. If the activity does not fit into one of these categories, then it was not work-related and no report needs to be made.

Because of their low risk of hazards, employers in certain industries are not required to file Forms 200 and 101. Among others, these industries include auto dealers, apparel stores, eating and drinking places, insurance offices, motion picture companies, legal offices, and educational services.

Employee Rights

To ensure the efficacy of the act, the act affords certain rights to employees. These rights are identified on OSHA poster 2203, which may be placed in the workplace. While employees must be informed of their OSHA rights by their employer, displaying this poster is not mandatory. Employee rights include requesting and participating in inspections, notice of an employer's violations or citations, access to monitoring procedures and results, and access to medical information. In addition, employees who provide information to OSHA are protected from discharge and/or discrimination by the employer in retaliation for the reporting. If any negative employment action is taken as a result of the employee's report or other provision of information, the worker may file a complaint with OSHA.

EMPLOYER DEFENSES

Reckless Behavior

If hazardous circumstances occur at the employer's place of business, is the employer liable for any harm that results, no matter what? Would this be a fair rule? There are some rules in law that provide that where an employer knew or should have known of a certain situation, then the employer is liable for the harm that results from that situation. For instance, in connection with a sexual harassment case, an employer is liable for the harassment where the employer knew of the harassing behavior or hostile environment or where the employer *should have known* of the situation. Therefore, even if the employer did not know because it refused to see the problem, sometimes called the "ostrich defense," the employer will still be liable.

How does this apply to OSHA violations? If the employer had a stellar safety record, had gone for years without an incident or violation, had conducted on-the-job group safety meetings, had issued written handouts regarding the safety instructions and the requirements of the act, but *still* suffered an incident, do any of the previous precautionary measures lessen the employer's chances of being held liable for the resulting harm? Courts generally respond that employers may use prior precautions as a means to minimize their liability. If they did not allow this defense, OSHA would instead impose "strict liability" on employers—that is, liability no matter what steps the employer takes to prevent it, liability merely because it happened at the employer's worksite.

In *Horne Plumbing and Heating* v. *OSHRC,* the employer had done precisely what we just mentioned above in terms of precautionary measures; yet, when two men ignored the employer's instructions, as well as warnings from coworkers, and worked in an unsafe area of the site, they were killed. The court noted: "A hazard consisting of conduct by employees, such as equipment riding, cannot be totally eliminated. A willfully reckless employee may on occasion circumvent the best conceived and most vigorously enforced safety regime. Congress intended to require elimination only of preventable hazards." The court found that the employer did everything possible to ensure compliance with the law, short of remaining at the worksite and directing the operations itself. Was this final effort required? The court responded that [citing a separate case]:

> While close supervision may be required in some cases to avoid accidents, it is unrealistic to expect an experienced and well-qualified [worker] to be under constant scrutiny. Such a holding by the Commission, requiring that each employee be constantly watched by a supervisor, would be totally impractical and in all but the most unusual circumstances, an unnecessary burden.

So, according to *Horne Plumbing,* the rule is that, where an employer takes all reasonable steps to prevent a hazard, but an employee's **reckless** disregard for the precautions causes him or her harm, the employer is relieved of liability for that harm. Instead, an employer will be held liable only for the foreseeable, plausible, and therefore preventable acts of its employees.

Also, note that companies with adequate safety programs in place are much less likely to be held responsible for the acts of their employees, whether reckless or merely

recklessness Conscious disregard for safety; conscious failure to use due care.

Scenario 2

negligent. On the other hand, where no safety program is in place, an employer is much more likely to be liable for injuries resulting from preventable accidents, even if it makes a good-faith attempt to comply with the standard.

Physical or Economic Impossibility of Compliance

Perhaps the most difficult safety standards to enforce are those that command the greatest opposition from the employees. While the safety basis for most specific standards *is* apparent from the standard itself, and most employees adhere because of the potential hazards that would exist if they did not, there are some standards that employees contest. These standards would be those where the employees believe that the burden of complying is greater than the danger prevented by the compliance. Consequently, even though employers have rules about complying with that standard, it would be difficult to enforce without "policing" the employees.

In this situation, contrary to the above, noncompliance with the standard by the employees *is* foreseeable and predictable. The employer could not use the defense that the employees' actions were not expected or preventable. For example, in *Atlantic & Gulf Stevedores* v. *OSHRC,* the safety standard in question was an OSHA requirement that employees wear protective hard hats while on the job. The problem arose because only a small number of the longshoremen were willing to wear the hats. In addition, the longshoremen's unions opposed the hard hat requirement, so the secretary of labor had imposed a moratorium on the enforcement of the requirement for several years. Employers were threatened with wildcat strikes or walkouts if they attempted to fire those who did not comply. As a result, when Atlantic & Gulf Stevedores was cited for a violation of this OSHA requirement, it defended itself by claiming that compliance with the standard was not achievable.

The court compared this case to another where it concluded that the economic feasibility of a standard is relevant to its validity. An economically impossible standard would prove unenforceable, the court said, and the burden of policing a regulation uniformly ignored by a majority of industry members would prove to be overwhelming.

However, since the purpose of OSHA is to look for improvement in the techniques of industrial safety, many times its prescriptions for remedy are not appealing to those who must adhere to them. To remove this requirement would be akin to agreeing to an unsafe workplace, something that would be patently against the aims of OSHA. Therefore, the court held that the safety of the workforce is of greater importance than the burden of dealing with work stoppages. The employer should negotiate with the unions to be allowed to terminate those workers who do not comply and offer concessions in exchange for compliance. Barring agreement, the employer could apply to the secretary for a variance from the standard that would allow this employer to be free from compliance based on the specific situation at its worksite. A *variance* is a right given to the employer not to comply with the standard, either permanently or on a temporary basis, if the employer's work environment is at least as safe as if the employer had complied.

OSHA directs that employees comply with its requirements, but OSHA contains no penalty or fine provisions to use against an employee who does not comply. The responsibility to ensure employee compliance is left to the employer through discipline or termination.

Employee Reduction of Risk

While employees are obligated under OSHA to "comply with occupational safety and health standards and all rules, regulations, and orders," are they responsible to take extra measures to ensure their own safety?

In a case that preceded *Johnson Controls,* the court of appeals for the District of Columbia addressed the OSHA implications of fetal protection policies. Similar to *Johnson Controls,* in *Oil, Chemical, and Atomic Workers Int'l Union* v. *American Cyanamid Co.* the company had a fetal protection policy that prohibited fertile women from certain positions. The women sued claiming that, instead of making the workplace safe, the employer had attempted to get around the requirements of the act by requiring that the female employees undergo surgical sterilization so the worksite no longer presented a hazard to them. The issue in the case was whether such a requirement for the position was a violation of the act.

The court found that, where the situation could not be remedied (i.e., the company could not reduce the lead concentrations to a level that posed an acceptable risk to fetuses), the sterilization option was an appropriate alternative. The company was not attempting to pass on to the employees the cost of maintaining an environment more hazardous than that allowed by law, but it was making an attempt to permit the employees to mitigate costs to them imposed by unavoidable physiological facts. Since the workplace could not be made safe, employees had the choice of either not working in that workplace or undergoing the sterilization to make it safe for them. Note that this is different from the fetal protection policy in the gender chapter where the employer required females to show proof of infertility in order to be able to work there, but had no such requirement for men.

In order to better understand the court's thought process in this case, consider its actual language, included below.

Oil, Chemical, and Atomic Workers Int'l Union v. American Cyanamid Co. *741 F.2d 444 (D.C. Cir. 1984)*

In the case that follows, the court discusses fetal protection policies and whether they violate the OSHA act.

Bork, J.

. . . This, essentially, was the reasoning of the Review Commission. The Commission pointed out that the Act does not define the term "hazard" and turned to the legislative history for guidance. "Congressional floor debates, committee reports, and individual and minority views . . . are replete with discussions of air pollutants, industrial poisons, combustibles and explosives, noise, unsafe work practices and inadequate training and the like." From this, and other evidence of a similar nature, the Commission concluded that "Congress conceived of occupational hazards in terms of processes and materials which cause injury or disease by operating directly upon employees as they engage in work or work-related activities." The fetus protection policy, by contrast, does not affect employees while they are engaged in work or work-related activities. The decision to be sterilized "grows out of economic and social factors which operate primarily outside the workplace," and hence the fetus protection policy "is not a hazard within the meaning of the general duty clause." Id. We agree with this conclusion. Were we to decide otherwise, we would have to adopt a broad principle of unforeseeable scope: any employer policy which, because of employee economic incentives, left open an option exercised outside the workplace that might be harmful would constitute a "hazard" that made the employer liable under the general duty clause. It might be possible to legislate limitations upon such a principle but that is a task for Congress rather than courts. As it now stands, the Act should not be read to make an employer liable for every employee reaction to the employer's policies. There must be some limit to the statute's reach and we think that limit surpassed by petitioners' contentions. The kind of "hazard" complained of here is not, as the Commission said, sufficiently comparable to the hazards Congress had in mind in passing this law.

We are not prepared to speculate that, although Congress was thinking only about tangible hazards such as chemicals, it would, had it considered the subject, have decided that any employer-offered choice which leads to injury rather than discharge is a violation of the Act. That conclusion would have required a great deal of thought about unforeseen liabilities for employers and how far to let employees decide what is in their own best interest. It is not possible to say that, in all circumstances imaginable, Congress would have made employers liable for giving employees an option where the only feasible alternative was discharge. It seems to us safer, therefore, to confine the term "hazards" under the general duty clause to the types of hazards we know Congress had in mind.

Petitioners' argument may reveal a degree of uneasiness about the implications of their position. It is clear that American Cyanamid had to prevent exposure to lead of women of childbearing age, and, furthermore, that the company could not have been charged under the Act if it had accomplished that by discharging the women or by simply closing the Department, thus putting all employees who worked there, including women of childbearing age, out of work. The company was charged only because it offered the women a choice. Perhaps uncomfortable with the position that it was the offering of a choice

that made the company liable, counsel for OCAW stated at oral argument that there would have been no violation if the company had simply stated that "only sterile women" would be employed in the Department because there would then have been no "requirement" of sterilization. We agree that such an announcement would not have involved a violation of the general duty clause, but we fail to see how that policy differs under the statute from the policy American Cyanamid adopted. An "only sterile women" announcement would also have given women of childbearing age the option of surgical sterilization. The only difference between this case and the hypothetical is that here the company pointed out the option and provided information about it. As petitioners frame the issue, therefore, violation of the general duty clause depends on the explicitness with which an employer phrases an option made available by its policy. It cannot be that the employer is better shielded from liability the less information it provides. It would, in any event, be difficult to find that distinction in the words of the general duty clause.

The case might be different if American Cyanamid had offered the choice of sterilization in an attempt to pass on to its employees the cost of maintaining a circumambient lead concentration higher than that permitted by law. But that is not this case. The company could not reduce lead concentrations to a level that posed an acceptable risk to fetuses. The sterilization exception to the requirement of removal from the Inorganic Pigments Department was an attempt not to pass on costs of unlawful conduct but to permit the employees to mitigate costs to them imposed by unavoidable physiological facts.

The women involved in this matter were put to a most unhappy choice. But no statute redresses all grievances, and we must decide cases according to law. Reasoning from precedent, congressional intent, and the unforeseeable consequences of a contrary holding, we conclude that American Cyanamid's fetus protection policy did not constitute a "hazard" within the meaning of the OSHA Act.

Unlike *UAW* v. *Johnson Controls, Inc.,* in Chapter 6, *Oil, Chemical, and Atomic Workers Int'l Union* v. *American Cyanamid Co.* dealt with the issue of whether OSHA can consider the company policy as a hazard to an employee's health. The court found that "[t]he decision to be sterilized 'grows out of economic and social factors which operate primarily outside the workplace,' and hence the fetus protection policy is not a hazard within the meaning of the general duty clause." Therefore, although these may appear to be contradictory rulings, the issues the courts were resolving were separate and distinct.

Where an employer cannot on its own make a workplace safe for its employees, but through the acts of its employees the workplace can be made safe, the employer is allowed to require those acts for anyone that chooses to work there. Instead of not offering the opportunity at all (taking away an option for the employees), the employer is merely allowing only those employees for whom the workplace would be safe to work there. There is no true requirement to undergo a sterilization process in the above case, but merely the offer that anyone who does or who can prove that she cannot bear children may work in that position. In the *Donovan* case below, the U.S. Supreme Court takes a look at the economic argument made by the employer.

American Textile Manufacturers Institute, Inc. v. Donovan
452 U.S. 490 (1981)

In this case, the U.S. Supreme Court dealt with the issue of whether OSHA must consider whether the cost of the standard it develops bears a reasonable relationship to its benefits. It determined that it does not have to have a reasonable relationship.

Brennan, J.

Congress enacted the Occupational Safety and Health Act of 1970 (Act) "to assure so far as possible every working man and woman in the Nation safe and healthful working conditions. . . ." The Act authorizes the Secretary of Labor to establish, after notice and opportunity to comment, mandatory nationwide standards governing health and safety in the workplace. In 1978, after much input, the Secretary, acting through OSHA, promulgated a standard limiting occupational exposure to cotton dust. Cotton dust is an airborne particle byproduct of the preparation and manufacture of cotton products, exposure to which induces a "constellation of respiratory effects" known as "byssinosis" or, in its more serious manifestations, "brown lung." This disease was one of the expressly recognized health hazards that led to passage of the Act.

Byssinosis is a serious and potentially disabling respiratory disease primarily caused by the inhalation of cotton dust. Byssinosis is a "continuum . . . disease," that has been categorized into four grades. In its least serious form, byssinosis produces both subjective symptoms, such as chest tightness, shortness of breath, coughing, and wheezing, and objective indications of loss of pulmonary functions. In its most serious form,

byssinosis is a chronic and irreversible obstructive pulmonary disease, clinically similar to chronic bronchitis or emphysema, and can be severely disabling. At worst, as is true of other respiratory diseases including bronchitis, emphysema, and asthma, byssinosis can create an additional strain on cardiovascular functions and can contribute to death from heart failure. ("There is an association between mortality and the extent of dust exposure".)

Cotton manufacturers challenged the validity of the "Cotton Dust Standard." They contend that the Act requires OSHA to demonstrate that its Standard reflects a reasonable relationship between the costs and benefits associated with the Standard. The Secretary of Labor counters that Congress balanced the costs and benefits in the Act itself, and that the Act should therefore be construed not to require OSHA to do so. They interpret the Act as mandating that OSHA enact the most protective standard possible to eliminate a significant risk of material health impairment, subject to the constraints of economic and technological feasibility. We granted certiorari, to resolve this important question.

The principal question presented in these cases is whether the Act requires the Secretary, in promulgating a standard pursuant to the Act, to determine that the costs of the standard bear a reasonable relationship to its benefits. The cotton manufacturers urge not only that OSHA must show that a standard addresses a significant risk of material health impairment, but also that OSHA must demonstrate that the reduction in risk of material health impairment is significant in light of the costs of attaining that reduction. The Secretary, on the other hand, contends that the Act requires OSHA to promulgate standards that eliminate or reduce such risks "to the extent such protection is technologically and economically feasible." To resolve this debate, we must turn to the language, structure, and legislative history of the Act.

The starting point of our analysis is the language of the statute itself. The Act provides: "The Secretary, in promulgating standards dealing with toxic materials or harmful physical agents under this subsection, shall set the standard which most adequately assures, to the extent feasible, on the basis of the best available evidence, that no employee will suffer material impairment of health or functional capacity even if such employee has regular exposure to the hazard dealt with by such standard for the period of his working life."

Although their interpretations differ, all parties agree that the phrase "to the extent feasible" contains the critical language in the Act for purposes of these cases. The plain meaning of the word "feasible" supports the Secretary's interpretation of the statute. According to Webster's *Third New International Dictionary of the English Language 831* (1976), "feasible" means "capable of being done, executed, or effected." Thus, the Act directs the Secretary to issue the standard that "most adequately assures . . . that no employee will suffer material impairment of health," limited only by the extent to which this is "capable of being done." In effect then, Congress itself defined the basic relationship between costs and benefits, by placing the "benefits" of worker health above all other considerations save those making attainment of this "benefit" unachievable. Any standard based on a balancing of costs and benefits by the Secretary that strikes a different balance than that struck by Congress would be inconsistent with the command set forth in the Act. Thus, cost-benefit analysis by OSHA is not required by the statute because feasibility analysis is.

When Congress has intended that an agency engage in cost-benefit analysis, it has clearly indicated such intent on the face of the statute. Certainly in light of its ordinary meaning, the word "feasible" cannot be construed to articulate such congressional intent. We

therefore reject the argument that Congress required cost-benefit analysis in the statute.

Even though the plain language of the Act supports this construction, we must still decide whether the general definition of an occupational safety and health standard, either alone or in tandem with the Act, incorporates a cost-benefit requirement for standards dealing with toxic materials or harmful physical agents. Section 3(8) of the Act, 29 U.S.C. §652(8) provides: "The term 'occupational safety and health standard' means a standard which requires additional requirements for issuance of a subcategory of occupational safety and health standards dealing with toxic materials and harmful physical agents: it required that those standards be issued to prevent material impairment of health to the extent feasible."

Congress could reasonably have concluded that health standards should be subject to different criteria than safety standards because of the special problems presented in regulating them. Not only does the legislative history confirm that Congress meant "feasible" rather than "cost-benefit" when it used the former term, but it also shows that Congress understood that the Act would create substantial costs for employers, yet intended to impose such costs when necessary to create a safe and healthful working environment. Congress viewed the costs of health and safety as a cost of doing business. Senator Yarborough, a cosponsor of the Williams bill, stated: "We know the costs would be put into consumer goods but that is the price we should pay for the 80 million workers in America."

When Congress passed the Act in 1970, it chose to place pre-eminent value on assuring employees a safe and healthful working environment, limited only by the feasibility of achieving such an environment. We must measure the validity of the Secretary's actions against the requirements of that Act. Accordingly, we AFFIRM IN PART, and VACATE IN PART.

Case Questions

1. Do you think OSHA's standard is fair? Unfair? Explain.
2. Given the standard, what do you think an employer can do to limit liability?
3. Do you think it is possible that the standard adopted by the Court may have had something to do with the fact that the hazard was one that was the basis for passing the act in the first place?

Exhibit 15.6   OSHA Publications

The Occupational Safety and Health Administration produces many publications to offer guidance and direction to employers concerned about safety and health. The following are but a sampling of the many available by contacting the OSHA regional office in your area:

All about OSHA, OSHA Publication 2056.
How to Prepare for Workplace Emergencies, OSHA Publication 3088.
Hazard Communications Guidelines for Compliance, OSHA Publication 3111.
Hazardous Waste and Emergency Response, OSHA Publication 3114.

greater hazard defense
An employer may use the greater hazard defense to an OSHA violation where the hazards of compliance are greater than the hazards of noncompliance, where alternative means of protection are unavailable, and where a variance was not available.

"Greater Hazard" Defense

Employers may contend that compliance with a health or safety standard would subject the employees to a **greater hazard** than what is prevented by the compliance. For example, in one case, a citation was issued because a construction company failed to install a cable railing on the perimeter of the top of a building it was constructing. The employer presented evidence that the risk involved in constructing the railing would subject its employees to a greater risk than if the railing were not there. To assert this defense, however, an employer must show:

- The hazards of compliance with the standard are greater than the hazards of noncompliance.
- Alternative means of protection are unavailable.
- A variance from the secretary of labor was unavailable or inappropriate.

GUIDANCE?

The Occupational Safety and Health Act of 1970 makes employers responsible for the safety of the workplace. While OSHA regulates certain known hazards and industries under the general duty clause, the employer may be held liable for workplace hazards even if specific regulations do not exist. There are reporting requirements under the act, as well as enforcement procedures and penalties. Where employees reasonably believe that there is an immediate danger presented by a workplace hazard, they have the right to refuse to expose themselves to the hazard. Current problem areas that are not presently regulated but that present significant workplace hazards include ergonomic considerations as well as workplace violence. While some areas are very specific about their regulatory requirements, it is most helpful if the employer maintains a commonsense and comprehensive approach to workplace safety and health issues. (See Exhibit 15.6.)

So how does a manager ensure that her or his company is not violating OSHA? There are, of course, a variety of practices that a manager can implement to protect the company from liability:

- There should be a standard procedure for investigating and recording accidents. If a standard procedure is in place, any employee who is involved in an incident will

Management Tips

- The purpose of OSHA is to provide a safe workplace; much of the act is commonsense protection against harm for the employees.
- Remember: Complying with OSHA is cheaper than paying fines for noncompliance.
- Beware: Just because a situation is not specifically mentioned by the act, this doesn't mean that the situation is not covered by OSHA. The general duty clause provides protection for employees from many hazards that are not covered by specific regulations.
- If you are accused of a willful violation based on a determination that you "should have known" that something constituted a violation or that you were unreasonable in believing that something was safe or did not constitute a violation, you should explore the basis for that determination and ensure that the willfulness of the violation is not based on mere negligence.
- Since employee misuse is no defense to a safety violation, the best way to prevent these types of violations is to conduct exceptional training for all employees on all equipment.

- Employees have the right to refuse to work based on their reasonable concern about death or serious injury. Don't let a situation get to this point; take precautions in advance to allay concerns or to provide for a safe environment.
- In connection with economic impossibility of compliance as a defense to a violation, make sure that you have sufficient documentation to support the claim of impossibility.
- OSHA provides protection from liability for voluntary actions that an employee might take in order to help a coworker in need of emergency physical help. In these situations, the employer will normally not be cited for its failure to train employees who perform "good samaritan" acts. However, an employer might be held liable if the "good samaritan" was an employee designated to perform this type of assistance by the employer or if life-threatening accidents would be reasonably foreseeable in the employee's position and he or she has not been instructed on how to respond.

have guidance about the proper method of handling the incident. Without standard procedures, employees may do what they think is best, which may not always be in line with OSHA requirements.

- When an incident is investigated properly, perhaps the investigation will uncover the unsafe condition that led to the incident. In this way, the unsafe conditions can be remedied and additional accidents may be prevented.
- The manager should answer the following questions regarding any investigation and report: What happened and why? How might this be prevented in the future? To make sure that the actions of the employees or investigators are most effective, it is recommended that the company draft a form for the accident investigation report. The employer is then certain that all of the necessary information will be obtained.
- Once all the information has been compiled and recorded, the manager must determine what action will be taken in response to the report. The action that led to the injury or accident may be eliminated from the workplace.

- Implement training or educational programs to teach employees about proper usage of materials or machines to prevent accidents.
- Determine whether more safety measures must be put in place to adequately protect the employees involved in that operation.

As the administration has found that safety programs and policies that establish standard procedures regarding safety issues significantly reduce the number of incidents and violations at a work site, the Occupational Safety and Health Administration has issued voluntary program guidelines. The guidelines include the following recommendations:

1. An effective safety program should include provisions for the systematic identification, evaluation, and prevention or control of general workplace hazards, specific job hazards, and potential hazards that may arise from foreseeable conditions.
2. An effective safety program should look beyond legal requirements toward addressing all potential hazards.
3. An effective safety program will include the following four elements:
   a. Management commitment and employee involvement.
   b. Worksite analysis to identify present and potential hazards.
   c. Hazard prevention and control.
   d. Safety and health training.

Summary

- Due to the lack of state legislation protecting employees against hazards, national standards were put into place through the Occupational Safety and Health Act. The act was passed to provide employees with a safe place to work with uniform standards. Since its passage over 100,000 fatalities have been prevented, due in part to OSHA efforts.
- Enforcing the act rests with the Occupational Safety and Health Administration (OSHA) under the authority of the Department of Labor. Penalties and abatement orders can be assessed in connection with an OSHA violation. The penalties range from $0 to $70,000 and may include criminal sanctions and higher fines up to $500,000 where an employer acted willfully and caused an employee's death.
- The process for determining standards is lengthy. OSHA can begin the standards-setting procedure on its own initiative or in response to petitions from other parties. Advisory committees may be called upon to develop specific recommendations. There are two standing advisory committees, the National Advisory Committee on Occupational Safety and Health (NACOSH) and the Advisory Committee on Construction Safety and Health. Recommendations may also come from the National Institute for Occupational Safety and Health (NIOSH), which conducts research on various safety and health problems, provides technical assistance to OSHA, and recommends standards of OSHA's adoption. Once standards are proposed, OSHA publishes these intentions in the *Federal Register,* and, in some cases, information will be solicited from interested parties on the proposal. A public hearing may be held on the proposal. After the comment period and public hearing, if one is held, OSHA will publish the full, final text of the standard in the *Federal Register* including the reasoning and rationale behind the standard. Due to the many steps involved, the process, as can be assumed, is time consuming.
- There are differing types of regulations, specific regulations and the general duty clause of the act. Specific regulations generally apply across the board of all types of employers, such

as adequate safety measures and the continual training requirement. The general duty clause of the act is broader and protects employees against certain hazards in the workplace where no other OSHA standard would address the condition. The clause states, "[e]ach employer . . . shall furnish to each of his employees employment and place of employment which are free from recognized hazards that are causing or likely to cause death or serious physical harm to his employees."

- Most employers, except for those with 11 or fewer employees, must maintain certain records for OSHA compliance. Employers in certain industries, due to their low risk of hazards, are not required to maintain such records.

- Employers may have certain defenses to OSHA violations. The first, reckless behavior on the part of the employee, may be a defense when an employer took all reasonable steps to prevent a hazard but the employee's own reckless conduct created the accident. Physical or economic impossibility of compliance may be a defense to an OSHA regulation when a variance is issued by OSHA to allow the employer's noncompliance. Employee reduction of risk could be a defense where an employer cannot on its own make a workplace safe for its employees, but through the acts of its employees the workplace can be made safe. Lastly, the "greater hazard" defense applies where the safety standard would subject the employees to a greater hazard than what is prevented by the compliance.

Chapter-End Questions

1. A number of producers of benzene and benzene-containing products asked the OSHA Review Commission to review a new health standard, which limited occupational exposure to benzene to one part benzene per million parts of air and required employers to assure that no employee comes into physical contact with it. The Occupational Safety and Health Administration instituted the standard because benzene is a carcinogen (may be cancer-producing) for which there is no known safe level of exposure. The benzene producers contest the standard, arguing that the best available evidence does not show that the reduction of the permissible exposure level from 10 parts per million to 1 part per million is reasonably necessary or appropriate to provide safe or healthful employment. OSHA responds that its policy is to limit employee exposure to carcinogens to the lowest feasible level. How should this matter be reviewed? [*American Petroleum Institute* v. *OSHA,* 581 F.2d 493 (5th Cir. 1978, affirmed 448 U.S. 607).]

2. Titanium Metals produces titanium ingots in Nevada. Titanium is a highly flammable substance during processing and can be ignited by heat, sparks, friction, or striking other small particles. To minimize dust accumulation, the company installed a collecting tube on its machines and periodically washed the entire area surrounding the machines. One day, while a machine operator was using the machine in the normal way, an explosion and fire erupted and another employee was burned to death. The company was served with two OSHA violations: (1) for failure to provide nonsparking tools and equipment and (2) for allowing flammable accumulations of titanium. The company claims that the hazard posed by the metal is not a *recognized hazard,* which would trigger the employer's general duty. The titanium industry is still in its infancy (less than 30 years old) and no precise standards exist respecting the appropriate levels of dust accumulation. Also, never in its eight-year history has the company had such an explosion, so it was unprepared and it would have never expected death or serious injury. Are these acceptable defenses? [*Titanium Metals Corp. of Amer.* v. *Usery,* 579 F.2d 536 (9th Cir. 1978).]

3. Lactos Laboratories is an interstate manufacturer of animal feed concentrates. In the course of its manufacturing process, the company uses fish parts, which are treated with sulfuric

acid when packaged. One night, a truck delivering the fish parts deposited the mixture into a Lactos tank, which overflowed into an adjacent room in the basement and filled it to a depth of 31 inches. The company used a pump to get rid of most of the overflow but ordered the employees to enter the room when the level had decreased 3 to 4 inches to clean up the remaining debris and to repair some pumps. The employees who entered were almost immediately overcome by hydrogen sulfide gas (caused when the sulfur came into contact with iron sulfide particles which had fallen from the ceiling), as were those who tried to help them. Lactos had no emergency equipment available and had taken no safety precautions to cope with accumulations of the gas. In the end, three employees died, and two were seriously injured.

Lactos defended itself against violations cited by OSHA by claiming that the sulfide gas was an unforeseeable hazard. Do you agree? [*Brennan* v. *OSHA Review Commission,* 494 F.2d 460 (8th Cir. 1974).]

4. In 1971, at a motel construction site operated by National Realty, Smith, a foreman with the company rode the running board of a front-end loader driven by one of his subordinates, Williams. The loader stalled while going down a ramp and swerved off the ramp. Smith jumped from the loader but was killed when it toppled off the ramp and fell on him. National Realty had a policy at the time against equipment riding, but Williams did not order Smith off the vehicle because Smith was his superior. National Realty was later cited by OSHA, "in that an employee was permitted to stand as a passenger on the running board of a loader while the loader was in motion." National Realty claims that it did not permit Smith to ride the machine. What does NR need to prove to show that it did not permit this type of behavior? [*National Realty & Construction Co.* v. *OSHRC,* 489 F.2d 1257 (D.C. Cir. 1973).]

5. Employees at Whirlpool worked beneath an overhead conveyor transport. To protect employees from objects that continually fell from the conveyors, Whirlpool installed a wire mesh guard screen 20 feet above the plant floor. Maintenance employees spent several hours each week cleaning objects that fell from the conveyors onto the wire mesh. To perform this duty, the employees usually stood on the wire frames, but sometimes found it necessary to stand on the screen mesh itself. While the company's policy admonished the employees to stand only on the frames, several employees did not and fell through the mesh, sustaining injuries. Keller, an employee stationed in this position, refused to continue to clean the mesh, claiming that he had reason to believe such work would be dangerous. Is he allowed to stop his work? [*Whirlpool* v. *Marshall,* 100 S. Ct. 883 (1980).]

6. No employer intends to harm its employees. How would you define the term "willful" that would give rise to penalties of up to $70,000?

7. Worcester Polytechnic Institute (WPI) hired Francis Harvey & Sons as general contractor. SGH, an engineering firm, was hired to do certain structural engineering services in connection with the project. After a Harvey employee expressed concern to SGH via a telephone call about a potentially dangerous structural defect in the concrete flooring, he was told to continue his work. Later, the flooring collapsed and five workers were hurt. No SGH employees were working at the worksite. After a complaint was filed against SGH, SGH defended, claiming that the worksite was not a "place of employment" of the structural engineering firm and, consequently, OSHA did not apply. Do you agree? [*Reich* v. *Simpson, Gumpertz & Heger, Inc.,* 1993 WL 310699 (1st Cir. 1993).]

8. General Dynamics manufactures M-1 Abrams tanks for the Department of Defense. The tanks have internal hydraulics that leak during assembly so the workers use a solvent called Trichloro to clean up spills. In its gaseous state, the solvent may cause serious illness or death. The manner in which the tank repairers performed the cleanups was essentially a

matter of the cleaning team's discretion, except that the tanks be ventilated when using more than one pint of solvent, since all tank repairmen were highly skilled. After a plant employee was overcome by fumes, and another died, OSHA issued a citation, claiming that General Dynamics violated the general duty clause. General Dynamics defended against the citation because it was acting in complete conformance with a separate OSHA section, which specifically set forth the limitations of employee exposure to Trichloro. Is General Dynamics free from responsibility under the general duty clause where it is in compliance with a more specific proscription? [*International Union, UAW* v. *General Dynamics Land Systems Division,* 815 F.2d 1570 (D.C. Cir. 1987).]

9. Morello Brothers is a roofing company that has done business with the federal government for years. In 1984, Morello began to perform roofing services on a building that housed OSHA offices. Several OSHA employees noticed a variety of violations and issued citations. Morello attempted to remedy the situation. One month later, similar citations were again issued for noncompliance. Finally, on a third visit, OSHA found compliance insufficient and issued a citation for willful violation. Morello argues that there was no evidence of willfulness, even though similar violations went continually uncorrected. Is it correct? [*Brock* v. *Morello Bros. Construction,* 809 F.2d 161 (1st Cir. 1987).]

10. What is required to prove a section 5(a) violation of the general duty clause?

Chapter **Sixteen**

Employee Retirement Income Security Act

Chapter Outline

Opening Scenarios

SCENARIO 1

Scenario

Travis, the manager of operations at a large manufacturing firm, walks into his office on Monday morning to find his assistant Beth apparently upset. She informs him that she was recently diagnosed with hepatitis and filed a claim for medical costs with the company's insurer. She then found that, since the time of her diagnosis and after having informed the human resources division of that diagnosis, the company reduced its medical coverage and placed a cap of $2,000 on certain claims, including those for hepatitis. Beth contends that she is being discriminated against and that the company should not be able to reduce coverage just to avoid having to pay her present and future claims. Is she right?

SCENARIO 2

Scenario

Kimberly's supervisor, Gordon, continually hounds and threatens Kimberly by saying, "If you don't work more hours, I'll have to fire you and you'll lose all of your pension benefits!" She doesn't want to lose her job but feels that this type of harassment is completely inappropriate. In fact, the added stress that Gordon has imposed on Kimberly at the workplace by his constant threats about her financial future has landed her in therapy. Kimberly wants to file a claim against Gordon and the firm for which she works, claiming intentional infliction of emotional distress. When she tells Gordon, however, he just laughs in her face, saying that he and their employer are both immune from this claim since it is preempted by ERISA. Is he right, and what does this preemption mean to Gordon and the firm in terms of defenses and the costs of liability?

INTRODUCTION

Enron. The name of this Texas-based energy corporation conjures up images of accountants shredding documents, corporate executives testifying before Congress, and other snapshots of corporate scandal. Perhaps the most disturbing pictures are of the current and former Enron employees who lost their retirement savings in their employer's collapse. These employees had retirement plans that were invested heavily in Enron stock. There are many others who never worked for Enron but whose retirement plans are also affected. For example, the University of California lost $145 million when Enron's stock collapsed, while the Florida State Board of Administration and New York City pension funds lost a combined $444 million.[1]

While Enron may seem unique, there are many other large corporations where the retirement savings of the employees depend on the market performance of the employer's stock. In a recently published survey of 401(k) plans sponsored by 200 of the nations' largest publicly held corporations, 25 had more than 60 percent of their total assets invested in the employer's stock. Coca-Cola Co. had 81 percent of its 401(k) plan assets invested in company stock, and McDonald's Corporation had 74 percent of its plan's assets invested in its stock. As stock values of such large corporations decline, the employees' retirement savings are at risk.[2]

[1] See Maureen Milford, "UC Takes Charge of Enron Suit," *National Law Journal,* Mar. 7, 2002.
[2] See Mark L. Silow, "Investments in Employer Stock: The Enron Legacy," *The Legal Intelligencer,* Feb. 18, 2002.

Could "Enron" happen at other companies? In the wake of Enron, additional legislation has been called for. However, at the time of this writing, the momentum for changes affecting 401(k) retirement plans has ebbed.[3] Still, Enron's troubles continue. Along with the negative publicity, Enron faces a shareholders' class action and a creditors committee entirely composed of ex-Enron employees in its bankruptcy proceedings.[4]

While legislative reform may be stalled, employers should not wait for regulations to implement the lessons learned from Enron. Strict compliance with statutory protections is an important step toward avoiding the fallout of the Enron collapse. This chapter explores the statutory protections for retirement plan participants that are designed to prevent such catastrophes.

BACKGROUND

Although not required to provide such benefits, once an employee begins full-time employment, and in some cases part-time employment, many firms offer her or him the benefit of investing in the company's retirement plan. Employees take a portion of their salary and invest it through their employer in a plan that provides funding for the employee's retirement. But if the employer goes bankrupt, or the employee switches jobs, what happens to all of this money the employee paid into that plan? Or assume an employee has excellent medical benefits with his present company, benefits of which he often takes advantage; is he tied to that company and discouraged from leaving because he is concerned that he will not find those benefits on his own or elsewhere? What about an employee who pays into a retirement fund through her employer, only to find there are insufficient funds for her to receive the benefits when she retires?

In 1974, as a result of concerns regarding the protection of pension benefits of workers who lost their jobs prior to retirement, Congress enacted the Employee Retirement Income Security Act (ERISA), a federal law that governs certain administrative aspects of employee benefit and retirement plans. Congress had been concerned about the millions of employees and their dependents who were affected by employee benefit plans. Congressional findings reported that, to provide for the general welfare of employees, disclosure rules should be stronger and safeguards should be provided with respect to the establishment, operation, and administration of such plans (although ERISA does not require employers to provide any particular benefits). The findings further stated that, despite the enormous growth of employee benefit plans, many employees with long years of employment were losing anticipated retirement benefits due to the lack of vesting provision in the plans and the inadequacy of current minimum standards. Since employees and their beneficiaries were being deprived of anticipated benefits, Congress felt the need to establish minimum standards to ensure the equitable character of such plans and their financial soundness. The underlying purpose of

---

[3] See Ronald Brownstein, "Prospects Dimming for Post-Enron Reform Legislation," *Los Angeles Times,* May 28, 2002, p. A17.

[4] See Matthew Hagman, "Ex-Enron Employees Get Creditors Committee," *Miami Daily Business Review,* Feb. 20, 2002.

Exhibit 16.1

Myths about ERISA

1. Your pension plans are not protected against the trustees who administer them.
2. No matter what, if you put money into a retirement plan, it will be there when you retire.
3. No matter what, if you put money into a retirement plan, it will not be there when you retire.
4. ERISA applies only to retirement or pension funds.

ERISA is to protect the interests of individuals participating in employee benefit plans. (See Exhibit 16.1.)

ERISA therefore was designed to encourage cautious, careful management of retirement funds by employers who were receiving tax benefits for doing so. As we will see in the next section, ERISA coverage is not restricted to merely retirement plans but covers many types of promised employee benefits. ERISA is a complex act that is multifaceted. There are courses focusing solely on ERISA. Therefore, this chapter will focus on the basics of the ERISA statute to give the reader a general understanding of the statute.

STATUTORY BASIS

Employee Retirement Income Security Act

§1132. Civil Enforcement.
(a) A civil action may be brought—
(1) By a participant or beneficiary—
(B) to recover benefits due to him under the terms of his plan, to enforce his rights under the terms of the plan, or to clarify his rights to future benefits under the terms of the plan.

§1140. Interference with protected rights.
It shall be unlawful for any person to discharge, fine, suspend, expel, discipline, or discriminate against a participant or beneficiary for exercising any right to which he is entitled under the provisions of an employee benefit plan, or for the purpose of interfering with the attainment of any right to which such participant may become entitled under the plan.

WHO IS COVERED

An employer that offers welfare benefits (e.g., health, life, disability, or accident insurance) or retirement plans to its employees is subject to certain requirements under ERISA. (See below for further explanation of types of plans.) ERISA covers most private sector employee benefit plans. In general, ERISA does not cover plans established or maintained by governmental entities or churches. ERISA does not cover plans maintained outside the United States primarily for the benefit of nonresident aliens. ERISA does not cover plans maintained for nonemployees such as a director or independent contractors.

TYPES OF PLANS TO WHICH ERISA APPLIES

employee benefit plans
A plan, fund, or program that has been established by an employer to cover benefits for its employees relating to medical or hospital care, death, unemployment, or vacation benefits.

defined contribution plans
A plan that defines the amount of the employee contribution, without a specific amount to be recovered at retirement.

defined benefit plan
A plan that defines in advance the amount to be recovered on retirement.

ERISA technically applies to **employee benefit plans** and covers two basic types of plans. The first type of plan ERISA covers is welfare plans. A *welfare plan* is any plan, program, or fund that the employer maintains to provide the following: medical, surgical, or hospital care; benefits for sickness, accident, disability, or death; unemployment benefits; vacation benefits; apprenticeship and training programs; day care centers; scholarship funds; prepaid legal services; or severance pay. However, payroll practices from the employer's general assets are not welfare benefit plans covered by ERISA.

The other type of plan ERISA covers is retirement or pension plans. There are two general forms of *pension plans:* those with **defined contributions** and those with **defined benefits**. The former involves plans in which each employee has her or his own account and the benefits received at retirement are based solely on the principal and income contributed. Contributions and defined contribution plans can come from employees, the employer, or both. Defined benefit plans comprise all other plans but generally refer to plans where the amount the employee receives at retirement is specifically designated at the time the employee enters the plan. Contributions to defined benefit plans generally only come from the employer, although some old plans also allow employee contributions. In defined contribution plans, the security comes from knowing the amount of principal that will be invested, while the security in defined benefit plans comes from knowing exactly how much will be paid in the end.

Requirements of a Tax Qualified Plan

In order for a retirement or pension plan to be qualified for tax purposes—and thus the contributions are not taxable to the employee and deductible by the employer—it must satisfy some general requirements. First, the plan must be permanent; that is, it cannot have a planned, definite expiration date. Although the employer can change or terminate the plan, evidence that the plan was not a bona fide program from its inception will disqualify the plan. Second, the plan must be in writing and communicated to all employees in a language they will understand within 90 days after the employee opts in or 120 days after the plan is established. Third, the plan assets must be held in trust by one or more trustee(s). Fourth, the plan must be for the exclusive benefit of the employees and their beneficiaries. There can be no reversion of the trust's assets to the employer, except when all liabilities of the plan have been satisfied. Fifth, the plan may not favor highly compensated employees over nonhighly compensated employees. Sixth, the plan must satisfy certain minimum participation, vesting, and distribution requirements. Lastly, the plan must be established and maintained by the employer. Funding the program can result from employer or employee contributions or both.

ERISA REGULATIONS

ERISA sets uniform minimum standards to ensure that employee benefit plans are created and maintained in a fair and financially sound manner. Also, employers must provide promised benefits and satisfy ERISA's requirements for managing and administering pension and welfare plans. There are two main important issues arising from ERISA compliance: reporting and disclosure, and fiduciary duties. The Department of Labor (DOL) has the authority to enforce ERISA.

Reporting and Disclosure

ERISA requires the employer or plan administrator to provide information to each participant and beneficiary about retirement plans and welfare plans; this information must also be provided to the federal government under certain circumstances. The required information includes a summary plan description (SPD), identifying in understandable terms (1) the plan participants' and beneficiaries' rights, (2) benefits, and (3) responsibilities under the plan. Plan changes must also be addressed in the summary plan description or a summary of material modifications. The SPD is required to be furnished to each participant eligible for benefits under the plan, as well as other beneficiaries. The SPD is not required to be filed with the DOL, but it must be furnished when requested. Additionally, an annual report must be filed with the DOL containing financial and other information concerning the operation of the plan. Plan administrators must also furnish participants and beneficiaries with a summary of the information contained in the annual report. Certain plans may be exempt for the annual report requirement. For instance, the reporting and disclosures laws do not apply to welfare plans with fewer than 100 participants.

The Sarbanes-Oxley Act of 2002 was passed in response to the perceived abuses in corporate governance of Enron, WorldCom, and others. One such abuse addressed by Sarbanes-Oxley was to add a new disclosure requirement to ERISA. ERISA now requires that participants in individually directed account plans must be notified in advance of any period in which they will be prohibited from trading in their plan accounts, or so called "blackout" periods. Additionally, Sarbanes-Oxley added a right of action under the federal securities laws against corporate officers to require them to return any profits they receive from buying or selling compensatory company stock during a pension blackout period.

Fiduciary Duty

Prior to the enactment of ERISA, plan coordinators routinely abused the funds entrusted to them, often at the expense of the employees. For instance, the funds may have been offered as loans to selected people, with little or no interest in return and little or no security for the loans, thereby interfering with employees' ability to earn income from the otherwise proper investment of funds.

fiduciary
One who holds funds in trust for another; one who holds a position of trust and confidence.

ERISA established a number of requirements, called *fiduciary standards,* to prevent these abuses. Those authorized to make decisions about the placement and investment of the pension plan or those who offer the plan investment advice are considered **fiduciaries** and are subject to the following fiduciary requirements:

- *Loyalty*—Fiduciaries must discharge their duties *solely in the interests of plan participants.* Although a fiduciary may have other concerns, they must ignore those concerns when making fiduciary decisions. They must have undivided loyalty to the participants in the plan.
- *Exclusive purpose*—Fiduciaries when making decisions must make them with the *exclusive purpose* of providing benefits under the plan and defraying the reasonable

expenses under the plan. Accordingly fiduciaries may not act for their personal benefit or for the benefit of their employer or any other party.

- *Prudence*—A fiduciary must exercise the care and judgment one would expect from a prudent person pursuing similar objectives under the same circumstance. In some instances this requires a fiduciary to rely on the judgment of advisors, provided that such advisors are prudently selected and supervised. Prudence is determined at the time the investment decision is made and not retroactively with 20/20 hindsight.
- *Diversification*—When investing plan assets a fiduciary must do so in a diversified manner so as to avoid large losses. This *diversification* standard is intended to limit the investment risk of a plan. The *prudence* standard generally would require that a fiduciary managing the investments of a plan maintain a diversified portfolio. However, the *diversification* standard in effect creates a presumption that an undiversified portfolio is not prudent.
- *Compliance with plan documents*—A fiduciary is required to administer the plan in a manner that is *consistent with its governing documents*.

Difficult questions often arise under these duties, however, such as how much risk the plan manager should assume when investing the plan assets or what types of investments might be otherwise appropriate. The answers to these questions have different impacts, depending on whether the fund is a defined contribution plan or a defined benefit plan. In the former, the amount of the contribution is set, but the amount that the individual receives upon retirement depends on the investment strategy of the plan manager. It is the plan manager, after all, who invests the contributions, and the employee who receives what is amassed over the years.

In a defined benefit plan, the amount the employee will receive on retirement is a set amount generally based on a formula. If the fund manager makes poor decisions, it is the fund and the employer that will suffer; if the manager invests wisely and the fund does better than expected, it is the employer who benefits because the necessity for employer contributions to attain the level of the benefit defined may decrease.

If fiduciaries of retirement plans are required to diversify the plan's assets and act prudently, why did Enron, like other large corporations, have such a significant concentration of plan assets in the company's stock? ERISA provides an exception to the fiduciary requirements for "individual account plans" that allow participants to direct the investment of their accounts. Individual account plans are defined contribution plans like popular 401(k) plans. However, the fiduciary is still responsible for selecting the menu of investment alternatives and providing adequate information concerning these choices. One such investment is often the employer's stock. Whether the employer's stock should be an investment and whether the amount of investment in employer stock should be limited is a question of prudence and diversification, as Enron has proved.

Employers may match employee contributions to their retirement plans with company stock over which employees may or may not have the ability to direct investment. After the Enron collapse, proposals were made in Congress to restrict employers' right to match employee contributions with company stock. However, after employers threatened to end matching if they could not use their own shares, support for these restrictions faded.[5] If employees are not allowed to direct investment of employer matching contributions, such as by selling the shares, continued investment in employer stock will be subject to the general fiduciary requirements of ERISA.

Certain transactions between an employee benefit plan and "parties in interest," which include the employer, fiduciaries, and others who may be in a position to exercise improper influence over the plan, are prohibited by ERISA and may suffer penalties. Most of these types of transactions are also prohibited by the tax code. However, there are some statutory exemptions from the prohibited transaction rules, and the DOL and IRS can authorize such exemptions through regulatory and individual exemptive procedures.

[5] See Lee Walczak et al., "Let the Reforms Begin," *Business Week,* July 22, 2002, pp. 26–31, 29.

Varity Corp. v. Howe *116 S. Ct. 1065 (1996)*

At the time employer Varity Corporation transferred its money-losing divisions in its subsidiary Massey-Ferguson, Inc., to Massey Combines, a separate firm (it called the transfer "Project Sunshine"), it held a meeting to persuade its employees of these failing divisions to change benefit plans. Varity conveyed the impression that the employees' benefits would remain secure when they transferred. In fact, Massey Combines was insolvent from the day it was created and, by the end of its receivership, the employees who had transferred lost all of their nonpension benefits. The employees sued under ERISA, claiming that Varity breached its fiduciary duty in leading them to withdraw from their old plan and to forfeit their benefits. The district court held for the employees, and the court of appeals affirmed.

Breyer, J.

. . . The second question—whether Varity's deception violated ERISA-imposed fiduciary obligations—calls for a brief, affirmative answer. ERISA requires a "fiduciary" to "discharge his duties with respect to a plan solely in the interest of the participants and beneficiaries." To participate knowingly and significantly in deceiving a plan's beneficiaries in order to save the employer money at the beneficiaries' expense, is not to act "solely in the interest of the participants and beneficiaries." As other courts have held, "[l]ying is inconsistent with the duty of loyalty owed by all fiduciaries and codified in section 404(a)(1) of ERISA."

Because the breach of this duty is sufficient to uphold the decision below, we need not reach the question of whether ERISA fiduciaries have any fiduciary duty to disclose truthful information on their own initiative, or in response to employee inquiries.

We recognize, as mentioned above, that we are to apply common-law trust standards "bearing in mind the special nature and purpose of employee benefit plans." But we can find no adequate basis here, in the statute or otherwise, for any special interpretation that might insulate Varity, acting as a fiduciary, from the legal consequences of the kind of conduct (intentional misrepresentation) that often creates liability even among strangers.

We are aware, as Varity suggests, of one possible reason for a departure from ordinary trust law principles. In arguing about ERISA's remedies for breaches of fiduciary obligation, Varity says that Congress intended ERISA's fiduciary standards to protect only the financial integrity of the plan, not the individual beneficiaries. This intent, says Varity, is shown by the fact that Congress did not provide remedies for individuals harmed by such breaches; rather, Congress limited relief to remedies that would benefit only the plan itself. This argument fails, however, because, in our view, Congress did provide remedies for individual beneficiaries harmed by breaches of fiduciary duty.

Case Questions

1. What should Varity have done in order to avoid liability under ERISA?

2. How can an employee ensure that she or he knows all of the facts relevant to a question such as the one present in this case?

3. Why do you think Varity handled this in the way that it did?

Eligibility and Vesting Rules

ERISA requires that all employees of age 21 or over who have completed one year of employment must be covered by their employer's pension plan.

vesting
Acquiring a right or an interest that is irrevocable by the donor.

Vesting means acquiring rights. For instance, assume that Margaret tells Dianne that she will leave her home to Dianne in her will. Is Dianne's interest in Margaret's home vested? No, not until Dianne has acquired the rights to the home on the death of Margaret, when the will becomes effective. On the other hand, if Margaret leaves Dianne her home through an irrevocable trust, where Margaret has the right to use the home during her life, but the trust irrevocably gives the right to Dianne on Margaret's death, Dianne's right to the home is vested as soon as the trust is put into place and is irrevocable. Dianne's right may be vested, though she does not have an actual ownership interest yet or any right to use the home until Margaret's death.

In connection with pension plans, the concept of vesting is much the same. ERISA provides that an employee's right to her or his pension benefit becomes 100 percent nonforfeitable after five years of employment or gradually nonforfeitable over seven years (20 percent per year beginning in the third year). In either case, the employee's right is vested, but the employee may not obtain the money or use it until retirement. Once an employee's rights in the plan are vested, the employee cannot lose the pension benefits, even if she or he switches employers. Regardless of vesting schedules, employees are 100 percent vested and have the right to their own contributions at all times.

Funding Requirements for Defined Benefit Plans

To ensure that adequate funds are available to the employees on their retirement under defined benefit plans, ERISA dictates how those plans should be funded throughout the years. Employers must fund the normal costs of the plan each year and amortize their employees' liabilities from previous service over not more than 40 years and from formation of new plans over 30 years.

In addition, employers with defined benefit plans must purchase insurance from the Pension Benefit Guarantee Corporation (PBGC) to cover potential losses of benefits on the termination of a plan. The PBGC was established by ERISA. The PBGC is similar to the FDIC in that it acts to insure pensions to a certain guaranteed limit in the event that the plan and the employer are unable to pay all promised benefits: The pensions of retired workers generally are insured for the full amount owed, while the pensions of vested but still employed workers are covered only to the extent that their vested interests have accrued at the time the plan terminates, but only to a level guaranteed by the PBGC. Accordingly, workers can lose promised and accrued benefits.

Modification of Benefit Plans

When a firm considers modifying a retirement plan for its employees, it must be wary since the employees may have been making decisions in reliance on the original benefit plan. Even if a proposed plan offers greater benefits than those originally included, an employer has a fiduciary duty to notify all employees of the changes that might take effect once the employer gives the proposal "serious consideration." Consider the perspective of someone who is about to retire but who might have greater benefits if she simply waits a month or two until a new plan is implemented. She would prefer to know about the possibility, wouldn't she?

"Serious consideration" exists where the employer has a specific proposal under consideration, where it is being discussed by senior management with the authority to implement the changes, and where senior management is actually discussing it for purposes of implementation. A discussion by an employer is not deemed serious consideration where it represents simply gathering data or formulating strategies, commissioning studies, or interacting with senior management regarding possible plan designs or where it is being discussed in the abstract rather than in terms of practicalities.[6]

Where a plan is being given serious consideration, managers must truthfully and forthrightly offer the information to all employees. If notice of the possible changes are not given to employees, the firm should make eligibility for plan participation retroactive to the date of serious consideration. See Exhibit 16.2 for a discussion of interpretation of fiduciary responsibilities in the Enron case and Exhibit 16.3 for an overview of benefit plans.

[6] *McAuley International Business Machines Corp.,* 165 F.3d 1038 (6th Cir. 1999).

Exhibit 16.2   The Impact of Enron on ERISA Litigation

The collapse of Enron in a mire of fraud and scandal served as a trigger for a wide-ranging series of legal and regulatory reforms in the area of corporate governance. But the ripple effects of the Enron crisis have spread to other legal issues, too. A lawsuit involving Enron's retirement plans, which were partially destroyed by the company's collapse, addresses many of the most disputed issues involving ERISA—and so far, the plaintiffs have won most of the early battles in court.

The ERISA piece of the Enron debacle involves the company's three retirement plans: a 401(k) savings plan, an ESOP (Employee Stock Ownership Plan), and a cash balance plan. The defendants are Enron, the Administrative Committees for the plans, the individual members of the Administrative Committees, Ken Lay, and certain other officers and directors of Enron. The suit also asserts claims against Northern Trust in its role as "directed trustee" and record-keeper of the plans. In a nutshell, the suit alleges that the defendants breached their fiduciary duties by:

- Allowing the 401(k) Plan and the ESOP to continue to acquire and hold Enron stock after the defendants knew or should have known it was an imprudent investment;
- Failing to disclose to plan participants facts that would have enabled them to make an informed judgment regarding their continued acquisition and holding of Enron stock;
- Affirmatively inducing participants to continue to invest their 401(k) contributions in Enron stock after the defendants knew or should have known it was an imprudent investment;
- "Locking down" the 401(k) (i.e., prohibiting any transfers among investment options) during the switch to a new trustee and record-keeper, at a time when the defendants knew or should have known of facts that made such a lockdown imprudent; and
- Calculating the offset under the Cash Balance Plan using the artificially inflated price of Enron stock.

Exhibit 16.2   (continued)

The defendants filed multiple motions to dismiss, which were addressed by the Court in late September 2003 in a 327-page ruling. That ruling favored the plaintiffs on most of the ERISA issues.

CORPORATE VERSUS PERSONAL LIABILITY

Like many benefit plans, Enron's plans gave fiduciary responsibility to entities—the company and Administrative Committees appointed by the company—rather than to individuals. Traditionally, employees acting within the scope of their employment have not been held personally liable for the actions they take on behalf of the corporation. Nonetheless, the plaintiffs in the *Enron* litigation are seeking money damages from the individual members of the Administrative Committees and from the company's officers and directors named as defendants in the suit.

Some courts have followed the traditional rule in ERISA cases. In *Confer* v. *Customer Engineering Co.,* for example, the Third Circuit held that: "when an ERISA plan names a corporation as a fiduciary, the officers who exercise discretion on behalf of the corporation are not fiduciaries within the meaning of [ERISA] unless it can be shown that these officers have individual discretionary roles as to plan administration." This seems like a sensible rule, since sophisticated employees won't want to serve in a capacity that puts their personal assets at risk—and those who don't understand the risks probably would not make good fiduciaries!

However, some courts have held individuals personally liable in ERISA cases, and that is the position taken by the Department of Labor, which has the responsibility for enforcing ERISA.

That was enough for the Court in the *Enron* case, which chose to impose personal liability on the individual defendants. The Court wrote: "In view of the broad language [and] the functional and flexible definition of 'fiduciary' . . . this Court agrees with those courts which reject a per se rule of nonliability for corporate officers acting on behalf of the corporation and instead make a functional, fact-specific inquiry to assess 'the extent of responsibility and control exercised by the individual with respect to the Plan' to determine if a corporate employee . . . has exercised sufficient discretionary authority and control to be deemed an ERISA fiduciary and thus personally liable for a fiduciary breach."

DUTY TO DISCLOSE

ERISA includes elaborate rules describing specific plan information that must be disclosed to plan participants. However, courts have since taken these specific responsibilities and crafted a much broader and more amorphous duty to disclose information in certain circumstances.

For example, the Supreme Court has ruled, not unreasonably, that it is a breach of fiduciary duty to lie to plan participants about their benefits. But it has not yet addressed whether fiduciaries have an affirmative duty to disclose certain truthful information. Lower courts, however, have faced a flood of cases alleging a "breach of duty to disclose," arguing that any damage to the plaintiff could have been avoided if the fiduciary had simply provided more or better information. Some courts have imposed a broad affirmative duty to disclose information whenever the fiduciary knows or should know that silence might be harmful.

The *Enron* Court took a middle path, holding that an affirmative duty to disclose does exist—but only when there are "special circumstances" with a potentially "extreme impact" on the "plan as a whole." (In other words, in situations like *Enron.)*

(continued)

Exhibit 16.2   (continued)

The plaintiffs in *Enron* also came up with a unique and untested theory in an attempt to impose personal fiduciary liability "up the chain" in the organization. They allege that Enron's board had the power to appoint members of the Administrative Committees, which makes the board members fiduciaries, with the duty to disclose to the committee members any information they needed to do their job. In other words, they contend that Ken Lay and any other board members who were aware of alleged fraud had a duty to relay that information to the Administrative Committees, who then similarly had a duty to act to protect the plans and disclose the information to plan participants so they could protect themselves.

Some defendants argued that they could not make such disclosures because selective release of information to the Administrative Committees and/or plan participants would have violated federal securities laws. But the Court was not entirely persuaded. The *Enron* Court held that insiders could have disclosed the damaging information to the public at large (therefore not violating the law) and then could have sold the plans' stock after the market had reacted to that information. That would not have avoided the entire loss, but it would have avoided some of the loss. Similarly, the Court noted that the decision not to purchase stock can be based on inside information, so the Committees could have eliminated Enron stock as a future investment option and thereby minimized the losses for plan participants. In other words, the *Enron* Court treated the insider-trading defense as a limitation on damages rather than a complete bar to liability.

RESPONSIBILITY OF DIRECTED TRUSTEES

Given the complexity of modern retirement plans, it is not surprising that multiple entities wind up in a position of fiduciary responsibility. ERISA specifically allows a trustee to take actions on behalf of the plan according to the instructions of another fiduciary. But ERISA states that a directed trustee can only follow "proper" directions that are not in violation of ERISA.

What constitutes "proper" directions? And what liability attaches to the directed trustee if things go wrong, even if the trustee was just following orders? The law is vague on this topic. There are three possibilities:

1. The directed trustee is liable whenever the fiduciary who gave the instructions was breaching its duty, regardless of whether the directed trustee knew or should have known about the breach.
2. The directed trustee is only liable if it had actual knowledge of the breach. It has no duty to inquire or investigate.
3. The directed trustee can safely follow directions unless it knows or should have known that the directing fiduciary was breaching its duty, and has a duty to conduct a "reasonable" investigation.

The *Enron* Court chose the third option, rejecting the "actual knowledge" argument and establishing a broad basis for liability. This is in keeping with the rest of its approach to fiduciary responsibilities. But in its dicta, the Court went even further, stating that in any ERISA retirement plan holding company stock, whenever there are significant red flags regarding a company's financial statements, it is an issue of fact whether the directed trustee had a fiduciary duty to investigate the advisability of purchasing the company's stock for the plan. This assessment of responsibility by the directed trustee goes beyond even the allegations raised by the plaintiffs in their complaint. It also runs counter to ERISA's legislative history, as well as the decisions of several other courts.

Exhibit 16.2 (continued)

REMEDIES

But the plaintiffs did lose one round in the *Enron* Court, with regard to the issue of remedying the damages they alleged.

Under ERISA, plaintiffs can bring a claim of breach of fiduciary duty under two sections of the law: § 502(a)(2), in which individual participants can sue on behalf of the plan as a whole and obtain broad relief, including money damages; and § 502(a)(3), in which individual participants can sue on their own behalf but can obtain only "appropriate equitable relief," not money damages.

The plaintiffs tried to get around this last restriction by arguing that it did not apply because they were suing fiduciaries. If a trustee committed a breach of trust, they argued, then forcing the trustee to make the plaintiffs whole from his or her own resources would be a form of "appropriate equitable relief," not money damages.

But the Court, while acknowledging that the argument was "artfully pled," concluded that if a claim walks and talks like a duck, it must be a duck. The Court held that claims of this type seeking money from a fiduciary are claims for compensatory damages—and are prohibited under § 502(a)(3).

CONCLUSION

Obviously, the *Enron* Court's decision denying most of the defendants' initial motions to dismiss was a significant victory for the plaintiffs. The actions of one lower court on a motion to dismiss, of course, do not necessarily signal a fundamental shift in how higher courts—including the Supreme Court—will ultimately decide many of these key issues under ERISA. But as is so often the case, bad facts (which aren't hard to find in the *Enron* case) often encourage courts to broaden the law in order to punish bad behavior. Hopefully, defendants in subsequent litigation won't end up paying the price.

Reprinted with permission of the authors, partners in the law firm of Faegre & Benson, LLP (www.faegre.com). Copyright 2004 Faegre & Benson LLP. All rights reserved.

Source: Steven L. Severson and Paul W. Heiring.

Consolidated Omnibus Budget Reconciliation Act of 1985 (COBRA)

The promise of temporarily continued health care coverage when someone stops working was established by the Consolidated Omnibus Budget Reconciliation Act of 1985 ("COBRA") and was codified in ERISA. The COBRA provisions apply to group health plans provided by employers with 20 or more employees on a typical working day in the previous calendar year. COBRA gives participants and beneficiaries the right to maintain, at their own expense, coverage under their health plan that would be lost due to a change in circumstance, such as termination of employment or divorce.

If the employee is legally terminated or loses benefit coverage due to a reduction in hours, COBRA requires that employers extend employee health insurance coverage for up to 18 months at 102 percent of the rates originally charged while the individual was

Exhibit 16.3   Employee Benefit Plans Overview

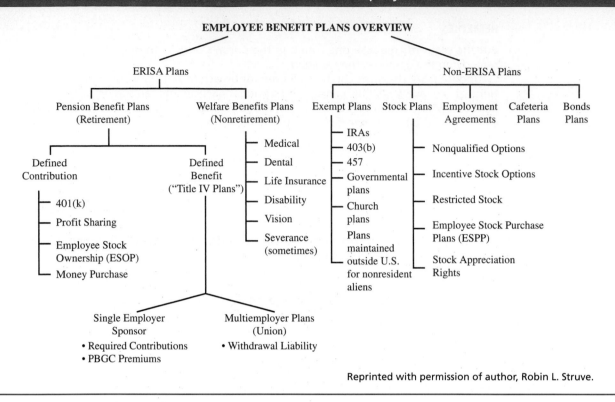

EMPLOYEE BENEFIT PLANS OVERVIEW

ERISA Plans — Non-ERISA Plans

ERISA Plans:
- Pension Benefit Plans (Retirement)
  - Defined Contribution
    - 401(k)
    - Profit Sharing
    - Employee Stock Ownership (ESOP)
    - Money Purchase
  - Defined Benefit ("Title IV Plans")
    - Single Employer Sponsor
      - Required Contributions
      - PBGC Premiums
    - Multiemployer Plans (Union)
      - Withdrawal Liability
- Welfare Benefits Plans (Nonretirement)
  - Medical
  - Dental
  - Life Insurance
  - Disability
  - Vision
  - Severance (sometimes)

Non-ERISA Plans:
- Exempt Plans
  - IRAs
  - 403(b)
  - 457
  - Governmental plans
  - Church plans
  - Plans maintained outside U.S. for nonresident aliens
- Stock Plans
  - Nonqualified Options
  - Incentive Stock Options
  - Restricted Stock
  - Employee Stock Purchase Plans (ESPP)
  - Stock Appreciation Rights
- Employment Agreements
- Cafeteria Plans
- Bonds Plans

Reprinted with permission of author, Robin L. Struve.

still working for the employer. In this way, while the coverage is paid for by the employee, COBRA provides guaranteed coverage for an employee who leaves employment for a relatively short time where that person may have difficulty obtaining coverage. General notice informing the covered individuals must be given informing them of their rights under COBRA and describing the law.

The Health Insurance Portability and Accountability Act

Statutory Basis

The Health Insurance Portability and Accountability Act (HIPAA) is a federal law that amended ERISA in 1996 to promote standardization and efficiency in the health care industry.[7] Title I of the act relates to *health insurance reform*. This prong of the act provides rights and protections for participants and beneficiaries enrolled in group health plans. HIPAA essentially protects individuals from discrimination based on their health status because it restricts exclusion from coverage due to preexisting medical conditions. Due to HIPAA regulations, employers are prohibited from denying coverage or charging more for coverage based on an individual's past or present poor health. Other

[7] Health Insurance Portability and Accountability Act of 1996, Pub. Law. No. 104-191 (Aug. 21, 1996).

REPORTING AND DISCLOSURE

Participants

- *Summary Plan Descriptions* (SPD)—Within 90 days after employee becomes participant in plan, or 120 days after plan becomes subject to ERISA. Updated SPD must be provided every 5 years if amendments made to plan or 10 years if no amendments made. Note: The Pension Welfare Benefits Administration has become the Employee Benefits Security Administration.
- *Summary of Material Modifications*—210 days after the end of the plan year in which the modification or change was adopted.
- *Summary Annual Reports*—Within 9 months after the close of the plan year. Model notice available.
- *Notice to Participants of Underfunded Plans*—Defined benefit plans that are less than 90% funded. 2 months after the deadline for filing Form 5500 for such plan. Model notice available.
- *COBRA Notices.*
- *Blackout Period Notices*—30 day advance notice, with limited exceptions.
- Plan documents upon request.

IRS/DOL

- Form 5500.

PBGC

- Premiums—defined benefit plans only.

Penalties

- Daily penalties for failure to file required reports or provide required disclosure.
- Penalties for failure to provide required participant disclosure—generally $110/day per participant.
- DOL/IRS penalties range from $25 per day to $110 per day for delinquencies.
- Criminal penalties can apply.
- DOL delinquent filer program available with reduced set penalties.

FIDUCIARY DUTIES

- Plan assets held exclusively for the purposes of providing benefits to participants and beneficiaries.
- Prudent person rule.
- Investment diversification.
- Must abide by plan document.
- Participant-directed accounts.
- Plan assets must be invested as soon as possible, but no later than 15 business days after the end of the month in which payroll withholding occurs.

(continued)

Exhibit 16.4   (continued)

- Prohibited Transactions:
  - —Loans.
  - —Sales/purchases.
  - —Providing services.
  - —Using plan assets for own account.
- Breach of fiduciary duty is a personal liability. Make sure to have indemnification!

GENERAL WELFARE PLAN ISSUES

- *Severance Plans*—ERISA plans if they have an "administrative scheme." If not, then no.
- *Cafeteria Plans*—Not ERISA plans but still subject to IRS Form 5500 reporting (waived at this time). Cafeteria plan contributions not subject to FICA.
- *Disability*—When is an employee no longer "employed" once on disability? ADA concerns.

GENERAL PENSION PLAN ISSUES

- *401(k) Plans*—Nondiscrimination/plan operation issues.
- *Cash Balance Plans*—Age discrimination and funding issues.
- *Defined Benefit Pension Plans*—Funding and cost of administration issues.

Source: Reprinted with permission of Robin L. Struve, "What Everyone Should Know About ERISA."

HIPAA protections relate to the portability of medical coverage by individuals who experience a job loss or job change. When such an event occurs, HIPAA may increase the ability to obtain or maintain health coverage for oneself or one's dependent's if the election is made within a certain time frame.

Title II of HIPAA is the *administrative simplification* prong, which targets the security and privacy of health information. The administrative simplification rules are intended to create a uniform system for processing, retaining, and securing health care information by encouraging the use of electronic technology, mandating standardization of health-related transactions, and promoting security precautions to maintain the privacy of health information.[8]

Administrative Simplification Compliance

In establishing the administrative simplification provisions, Congress recognized that, though efficient, the use of electronic technology also heightened the potential for misuse of health information. Consequently, Congress delegated responsibility for developing and implementing the administrative simplification provisions of HIPAA to the U.S. Department of Health and Human Services (HHS) and mandated the adoption of privacy protections to address this issue. These complex privacy protections ultimately became collectively known as the Privacy Rule.[9]

---

[8] Sections 261 through 264 of HIPAA require the Secretary of HHS to publicize standards for the electronic exchange, privacy, and security of health information. Collectively these are known as the *administrative simplification provisions*.

[9] 45 CFR §160 and §164 ("Privacy Rules") (Aug. 14, 2002).

Exhibit 16.5   Compliance Deadlines

ADMINISTRATIVE SIMPLIFICATION COMPLIANCE DEADLINES

October 16, 2002	Electronic Heath Care Transactions and Code Sets (if no extension field)
April 14, 2003	Implementation of Privacy Standards to Protect PHI—all covered entities (except small health plans)
April 16, 2003	Electronic Heath Care Transactions and Code Sets (start software/systems testing)
October 16, 2003	Electronic Heath Care Transactions and Code Sets
April 14, 2004	Implementation of Privacy Standards to Protect PHI—small health plans
July 30, 2004	Employer Identifier Standard
April 20, 2005	Security Standards—all covered entities (except small health plans)
August 1, 2005	Employer Identifier Standard—small health plans
April 20, 2006	Security Standards—small health plans
May 23, 2007	National Provider Identifier—all covered entities (except small health plans)
May 23, 2008	National Provider Identifier—small health plans

In response to Congress's mandate, HHS issued its final regulations in the form of the Privacy Rule in late 2000. The rule became effective on April 14, 2001, with a mandatory compliance date of April 14, 2003 (April 14, 2004, for small health plans). (See Exhibit 16.5 for more compliance dates).

HIPAA Privacy Rule

The Privacy Rule specifically addresses the permitted and prohibited use(s) and disclosure(s) of health information by organizations subject to it.[10] A covered entity is generally permitted (but not required) to use and disclose protected health information, *without* an individual's authorization, for the following purposes or situations:

- To the individual for "treatment," "payment," and "health care operations" as defined in the rule.
- To certain governmental authorities if abuse, neglect, or domestic violence is at issue for many law enforcement activities pursuant to court orders and/or subpoenas.
- To funeral directors, coroners, or medical examiners to identify a deceased person or to determine the cause of death.
- To HHS when it is undertaking a compliance investigation, review, or enforcement action.

---

[10] Though certain information may be released pursuant to permitted uses and disclosures, the amount of released information should be limited to the "minimum necessary" that is needed to accomplish the intended purpose of the use, disclosure, or request, as defined in the rules.

Generally, covered entities may use or disclose protected health information only if the use or disclosure is permitted or required by the Privacy Rule.[11] In very general terms, a group health plan may use protected health information internally or disclose it externally only under the limited circumstances and for the specific purposes articulated in the Privacy Rule. Otherwise, group health plans may use or disclose protected health information only with the specific permission of the individual who is the subject of the protected health information. Such permission is manifested in the form of a signed, valid authorization form.

According to the Privacy Rule, authorization forms must be written in plain language and they must include a number of elements, including the following:[12]

- A description of the protected health information to be used and disclosed.
- The person(s) authorized to make the use or disclosure.
- The person(s) to whom the covered entity may make the disclosure.
- An expiration date or event.
- The purpose for which the information may be used or disclosed.
- A notice of the individual's right to revoke the authorization.

Further, in some circumstances, it may be necessary to include additional information for the authorization to be valid. There are special rules, for instance, that apply to psychotherapy notes and the use of health information for marketing purposes. The validity of an authorization may also be subject to various state laws and may be further varied depending on the subject of the health information that is being used or disclosed. Additional privacy requirements may be imposed by state law in jurisdictions where the state law provides greater protections for health information.

The Privacy Rule attempts to strike a balance between permitting important uses of information and protecting the privacy of people who seek medical treatment. The rule is supposedly flexible and comprehensive enough to cover the variety of uses and disclosures that need to be addressed while still promoting high quality health care.

The Privacy Rule protects all "individually identifiable health information" held or transmitted by a covered entity or its business associates, in any form or media, whether electronic, paper, or oral. "Individually identifiable health information" is information, including demographic data, that relates to:

- The individual's past, present, or future physical or mental health or condition.
- The provision of health care to the individual.
- The past, present, or future payment for the provision of health care to the individual.

and that identifies the individual or for which there is a reasonable basis to believe *can be* used to identify the individual.

Individually identifiable health information includes many common identifiers such as the individual's name, address, birth date, and/or Social Security Number. The Privacy Rule calls this information *protected health information* (PHI).

Common examples of documents that may contain PHI are accident/injury reports, investigative reports, physician certification forms for medical leaves of absences,

---

[11] See 45 CFR §164.502(a).

[12] See 45 CFR §164.508.

hospital admission forms, workers' compensation claim forms, death certificates, correspondence regarding the health status of an employee, legal papers, interoffice correspondence, and other common forms that are used by companies in the normal course of their business. For example, when an employee comes into an employer's benefits office and enrolls in the employer's group health plan, the form that they complete with their name and their choice of plan is considered PHI.

The Privacy Rule applies to any entity that is:

- A health care provider that conducts certain transactions in electronic form.
- A health care clearinghouse.
- A health plan.

The Privacy Rule refers to entities that fall within one or more of the above categories as *covered entities.* Many varied organizations (in addition to hospitals) *may* be considered a covered entity due to the activities they conduct. For instance, a university might be considered a covered entity if it has a student health center or a mental health center that provides health care. A grocery store may be considered a covered entity if it has a group health plan managed by the benefits office for its employees.

General Obligations of Covered Entities

In general, the Privacy Rule requires covered entities to notify patients of their privacy rights and to explain how their personal health information can be used or disclosed by the organization or its business associates. To this end, they must prepare and distribute a Notice of Privacy Practices to their patients or employees depending on the activities that they regularly conduct.

Further, covered entities are required to adopt and implement privacy policies and procedures. These policies should be widely publicized and distributed to all individuals within the organization. Individuals who work closely with health information or who are responsible for securing this information should receive detailed training on the organization's established policies and procedures.

All covered entities should make an effort to prevent unauthorized viewing or access to (electronic and paper) health records in their care. To this end, administrative, physical, and technical safeguards should be implemented. Specific protective steps may include the establishment of regular and ongoing training sessions for new and current employees who handle health information; documentation of office procedures for managing health information; creating firewalls between departments to shield those departments that maintain health information from, for example, individuals who make human resources decisions; adding locks to file cabinets that house medical information; and using passwords and timed screen savers on all computers of individuals whose jobs require them to regularly come into contact with health information.

Organizations must also designate a privacy officer who has responsibility for ensuring that the above steps are adopted and followed, and that complaints regarding privacy violations are addressed through the organization's established procedures. The Privacy Officer should use a monitoring plan to randomly check on the effectiveness of the organization's privacy practices. (See Exhibit 16.6 for a sample monitoring plan.)

Exhibit 16.6
Sample Monitoring Plan

Specific Risk (1)	Operating Control (2)	Monitoring Control (3)	Evidence of Control	Oversight Control (4)	Evidence of Oversight Control
Complaint of inappropriate use/disclosure of their PHI.	HIPAA policy forbids this action by personnel.	Violations of HIPAA policy are subject to disciplinary action.	Policy that supports disciplinary action for violation of HIPAA policy.	Complaint procedure, as outlined in university HIPAA policy.	Periodic check by component areas of complaints logged by privacy office.
New employees in component areas are not trained on HIPAA protocol.	Policy officials within each component area should train new employees in their respective areas.	Written training procedures developed by departments that handle PHI.	Training attendance forms signed by training participants once training is completed.	Training attendance forms are returned to privacy officer once training has been completed.	Training attendance forms are filed in privacy office.
Notice of privacy practices is not distributed in accordance with HIPAA.	Component areas set up procedures that govern the designated times and manner when notice is to be distributed.	Random (annual), periodic auditing/monitoring by privacy office of organization's privacy practices.	Schedule of random/periodic monitoring.	Complaint procedure, as outlined in university HIPAA policy.	Periodic check by component areas of complaints logged by privacy office.
"Business associates" are not bound by agreement with the organization before they access PHI.	Component areas identify vendors and any others who may have access to PHI and provide this information to privacy officer.	Privacy officer contacts vendor and memorializes terms of agreement.	Business associate agreements.	Business associate agreements are cataloged in organization's database.	Random audits of database.
PHI is not protected by administrative, physical, and technical safeguards.	Component areas set up procedures that determine the minimum necessary disclosures to make pursuant to valid requests; in addition, component areas have to identify physical safeguards to protect PHI locks on file cabinets, passwords on computers.	Review departmental procedures and establish random, periodic auditing/monitoring by privacy officer.	Schedule of random/periodic monitoring.	Complaint procedure, as outlined in HIPAA policy.	Periodic check by component areas of complaints logged by privacy office.

Enforcement of the Privacy Rule

HHS delegated responsibility for enforcing the Privacy Rule to the HHS Office for Civil Rights (OCR). The Privacy Rule does not provide a private right of action for individuals to sue covered entities for alleged violations. However, covered entities may be subject to private lawsuits borne under tort or other legal theories. For example, individual state laws may offer relief that can be invoked by private plaintiffs. Further, some situations may be governed by ERISA, which would allow participants and beneficiaries to sue for enforcement of the applicable plan document, including, perhaps, the amendments required by the Administrative Simplification Rules.

HIPAA violations are subject to civil and criminal sanctions enforced by the Department of Justice. For instance, HHS may impose civil monetary penalties on a covered entity of $100 per failure to comply with a Privacy Rule requirement. In addition, a person who knowingly obtains or discloses individually identifiable health information in violation of HIPAA faces a fine of $50,000 and up to one year of imprisonment. The criminal penalties increase to $100,000 and up to $250,000 and up to 10 years of imprisonment if the wrongful conduct involves the intent to sell, transfer, or use individually identifiable health information for commercial advantage, personal gain, or malicious harm.

The Privacy Rule does not preempt all state privacy laws. Furthermore, there are no provisions in the Privacy Rule that exempt an employer from complying with other federal laws such as ERISA, ADA, and FMLA. In jurisdictions where the state privacy laws are more stringent than HIPAA, those laws or the relevant portions thereof are preserved and should be applied instead of HIPAA:[13] Therefore, a state privacy law that provides more privacy protections or greater individual rights than provided by the federal Privacy Rule will generally govern the situation.

Accordingly, employers should initially determine whether and to what extent they are required to follow state law (including local statutes and regulations) instead of the requirements of the Privacy Rule. The HHS Web site http://www.hhs.gov contains numerous links and technical assistance on HIPAA-related topics.

ENFORCEMENT OF ERISA

ERISA is enforced by the Department of Labor and the Internal Revenue Service (IRS) of the Department of the Treasury. The IRS is responsible for the requirements surrounding vesting, participation, and funding by removing tax-exempt status for those retirement plans that violate vesting and participation standards and by taxing the deficiencies in compliance with funding standards. The Department of Labor, on the other hand, administers the provisions with relation to disclosure, reporting, and fiduciary responsibilities. As discussed above, fiduciaries may be removed by the department for failure to act with due care or for engaging in an inappropriate conflict of interest.

---

[13] For instance, Illinois has more stringent requirements regarding use and disclosure of genetic health information. See 410 ILCS 513/15, et seq.—the Genetic Information Privacy Act—regarding the use and disclosure of mental health information. See 740 ILCS 110/1, et seq., the Mental Health and Developmental Disabilities Confidentiality Act.

Individual plaintiffs may file actions based on ERISA violations. ERISA preempts all state laws that relate to employee benefit plans, whether or not the situation contemplated by the state law is actually covered specifically in ERISA. Accordingly, state tort claims for tortious interference with employee benefit plans, state claims for intentional or negligent infliction of emotional distress in connection with the handling of disability benefits, and actions for unjust enrichment, for fraud, and for conversion are preempted by ERISA. The only form of relief for these types of injuries would be ERISA; state common-law claims would not be appropriate. This is more of a burden on the employee than the employer:

1. "Bad faith" becomes a nonissue under ERISA, while it may be critical to a common law claim.
2. Certain defendants, such as the plan sponsor or claims review agents (unless a fiduciary), cannot be sued.
3. There is no such thing as compensatory or punitive damages against the employer under ERISA, though they are available under tort law.
4. The process for a claim is slower.
5. There is no jury trial under ERISA as there would be under tort law.
6. Attorneys' fees and costs are recoverable.

Scenario

In an effort to prevent subversion of the act's requirements, ERISA provides that an employee who is terminated "for the purpose of interfering with the attainment of any right to which the employee may become entitled" under ERISA has a claim based on section 510 of the act. That is, ERISA prohibits employers from discharging employees merely to prevent their rights from vesting or to prevent them from receiving other benefits under the act.

Employers have the right to reduce or modify employee benefits (unless prohibited by contractual obligations), as long as similarly situated plan participants are treated alike. For instance, the employer may not reduce benefits for one full-time employee without similarly reducing the benefits for all similar employees. In order to prevail on a claim of a violation of section 510 of the act, in the case of discharge, the employee must prove that the employer terminated her or his employment with the "specific intent" to interfere with her or his benefit rights.

In *Owens v. Storehouse, Inc.,* 984 F.2d 394 (11th Cir. 1993), the court was asked to consider the employer's (Storehouse) choice to limit coverage for specific types of claims, a choice that could adversely impact certain employees. Specifically, the employer's insurance company notified Storehouse that it intended to cancel the firm's policy because of the high incidence of AIDS in the retail industry generally, and among Storehouse's employees specifically (five employees had AIDS at the time). Eventually, Storehouse convinced the company to continue the contract, but there was now a $75,000 deductible for AIDS-related claims, while other coverage began at $25,000. As it looked for another insurer, Storehouse considered placing a $25,000 lifetime cap on all AIDS-related claims. Owens, an employee, sued claiming that this modification lowering the cap violated ERISA. The court held that there is no "vested" interest in the type of coverage an employer provides, even once someone begins to take advantage of that coverage, as long as the employer reserves the right to change or terminate its terms. As there was no specific intent to violate ERISA (i.e., denial of coverage in retaliation for exercising an ERISA right), the employer prevailed. (Note: This type of arrangement would now be prohibited by the ADA as it would be discriminatory against someone with a disability.)

In an interesting twist, a 2004 case found that an employer is allowed to amend a plan in order to benefit one individual but is not in violation of ERISA if it refuses to amend the plan to benefit another. In *Coomer* v. *Bethesda Hosp., Inc.,* 370 F.3d 499 (6th Cir. 2004), the employer amended its pension plan to allow a lump sum cash-out in excess of $5,000 (the maximum allowed under the plan and the IRS) for one former employee. Several years later, other employees requested similar treatment and were denied. The court said that the hospital's actions were allowed under ERISA. ERISA does not prohibit all forms of discrimination, just those that are taken because someone takes advantage of an ERISA right or interference with the attainment of any ERISA right to which that person would be otherwise entitled. Therefore, the court held that the employer's actions, though by definition "discriminated" between individuals, were not in violation of ERISA.

In the following case, the Supreme Court evaluated a similar claim with regard to the amendment of a pension plan that expanded the definition of disqualifying employment and resulted in a suspension of early retirement benefits to some participants, in possible violation of ERISA's prohibition against reducing an accrued right or benefit under a pension plan (the "anticutback" rule), an issue not addressed in *Owens* because those benefits were welfare benefits not protected by ERISA's accrual rule.

Central Laborers' Pension Fund v. Heinz *124 S. Ct. 2230 (2004)*

Retirees who had been receiving early retirement benefits from a multiemployer pension fund sued the fund under ERISA's anticutback rule after their plan was amended to expand which types of postretirement employment triggered suspension of such benefits. Heinz understood that, if he were to work as "a union or non-union construction worker" ("disqualifying employment'), his pension would be suspended during that time. However, he also understood that they would not be suspended if he chose to work in a supervisory capacity. Heinz therefore took a job in central Illinois in 1996 as a construction supervisor after retiring, and the plan continued to pay out his monthly benefit.

In 1998, the plan's definition of disqualifying employment was expanded by amendment to include any job "in any capacity in the construction industry (either as a union or non-union construction worker)." The plan took the amended definition to cover supervisory work and warned Heinz that if he continued on as a supervisor, his monthly pension payments would be suspended. Heinz kept working, and the plan stopped paying.

Heinz sued to recover the suspended benefits on the ground that applying the amended definition of disqualifying employment so as to suspend payment of his accrued benefits violated ERISA's anticutback rule. The District Court granted judgment for the plan, only to be reversed by a divided panel of the Seventh Circuit, which held that imposing new conditions on rights to benefits already accrued was a violation of the anticutback rule. The Supreme Court granted certiorari in order to resolve the resulting Circuit Court split and affirms the Seventh Circuit in favor of the retirees.

Souter, J.

With few exceptions, the "anti-cutback" rule of the Employee Retirement Income Security Act of 1974

(ERISA) prohibits any amendment of a pension plan that would reduce a participant's "accrued benefit." The question is whether the rule prohibits an amendment expanding the categories of postretirement employment that triggers suspension of payment of early retirement benefits already accrued. We hold such an amendment prohibited.

* * *

II

A

There is no doubt about the centrality of ERISA's object of protecting employees' justified expectations of receiving the benefits their employers promise them. "Nothing in ERISA requires employers to establish employee benefits plans. Nor does ERISA mandate what kind of benefits employers must provide if they choose to have such a plan. ERISA does, however, seek to ensure that employees will not be left empty-handed once employers have guaranteed them certain benefits. . . .[W]hen Congress enacted ERISA, it 'wanted to . . . mak[e] sure that if a worker has been promised a defined pension benefit upon retirement—and if he has fulfilled whatever conditions are required to obtain a vested benefit—he actually will receive it.'"

ERISA's anti-cutback rule is crucial to this object, and (with two exceptions of no concern here) provides that "[t]he accrued benefit of a participant under a plan may not be decreased by an amendment of the plan. . . ." After some initial question about whether the provision addressed early retirement benefits, a 1984 amendment made it clear that it does. Now § 204(g) provides that "a plan amendment which has the effect of . . . eliminating or reducing an early retirement benefit . . . with respect to benefits attributable to service before the amendment shall be treated as reducing accrued benefits."

Hence the question here: did the 1998 amendment to the Plan have the effect of "eliminating or reducing an early retirement benefit" that was earned by service before the amendment was passed? The statute, admittedly, is not as helpful as it might be in answering this question; it does not explicitly define "early retirement benefit," and it rather circularly defines "accrued benefit" as "the individual's accrued benefit determined under the plan. . . ." Still, it certainly looks as though a benefit has suffered under the amendment here, for we agree with the Seventh Circuit that, as a matter of common sense, "[a] participant's benefits cannot be understood without reference to the conditions imposed on receiving those benefits, and an amendment placing materially greater restrictions on the receipt of the benefit 'reduces' the benefit just as surely as a decrease in

the size of the monthly benefit payment." Heinz worked and accrued retirement benefits under a plan with terms allowing him to supplement retirement income by certain employment, and he was being reasonable if he relied on those terms in planning his retirement. The 1998 amendment undercut any such reliance, paying retirement income only if he accepted a substantial curtailment of his opportunity to do the kind of work he knew. We simply do not see how, in any practical sense, this change of terms could not be viewed as shrinking the value of Heinz's pension rights and reducing his promised benefits.

B

The Plan's responses are technical ones, beginning with the suggestion that the "benefit" that may not be devalued is actually nothing more than a "defined periodic benefit the plan is legally obliged to pay," so that § 204(g) applies only to amendments directly altering the nominal dollar amount of a retiree's monthly pension payment. A retiree's benefit of $100 a month, say, is not reduced by a post-accrual plan amendment that suspends payments, so long as nothing affects the figure of $100 defining what he would be paid, if paid at all. Under the Plan's reading, §204(g) would have nothing to say about an amendment that resulted even in a permanent suspension of payments. But for us to give the anti-cutback rule a reading that constricted would take textual *force majeure,* and certainly something closer to irresistible than the provision quoted in the Plan's observation that accrued benefits are ordinarily "expressed in the form of an annual benefit commencing at normal retirement age."

The Plan also contends that, because §204(g) only prohibits amendments that "eliminat[e] or reduc[e] an early retirement benefit," the anti-cutback rule must not apply to mere suspensions of an early retirement benefit. This argument seems to rest on a distinction between "eliminat[e] or reduc[e]" on the one hand, and "suspend" on the other, but it just misses the point. No one denies that some conditions enforceable by suspending benefit payments are permissible under ERISA: conditions set before a benefit accrues can survive the anti-cutback rule, even though their sanction is a suspension of benefits. Because such conditions are elements of the benefit itself and are considered in valuing it at the moment it accrues, a later suspension of benefit payments according to the Plan's terms does not eliminate the benefit or reduce its value. The real question is whether a new condition may be imposed after a benefit has accrued; may the right to receive certain money on a certain date be limited by a new condition narrowing that right? In a given case, the new condition may or may not be invoked to justify an actual suspension of benefits, but at the moment the new condition is imposed, the accrued benefit becomes less valuable, irrespective of any actual suspension.

* * *

This is not to say that § 203(a)(3)(B) does not authorize some amendments. Plans are free to add new suspension provisions under § 203(a)(3)(B), so long as the new provisions apply only to the benefits that will be associated with future employment. The point is that this section regulates the contents of the bargain that can be struck between employer and employees as part of the complete benefits package for future employment.

The judgment of the Seventh Circuit is AFFIRMED Justice Breyer, with whom the Chief Justice, Justice O'Connor, and Justice GINSBURG join, CONCURRING.

Case Questions

1. Notwithstanding the law as applied, do you believe an employer should be able to change the terms of pension plan qualifications once individuals have begun to avail themselves of the benefits? Can you think of *any* circumstances where you might be persuaded that the employer should be able to modify the plan in this regard?

2. The Court does not seem to be persuaded at all by the Plan's arguments, though the District Court found in its favor. Are you persuaded by *any* of the Plan's arguments?

It should be noted that some ERISA claims under section 510 may also be asserted under the Age Discrimination in Employment Act (ADEA). For instance, since benefits are more likely to become vested as a worker gains seniority and as seniority may be more likely with advancing age, employers attempting to avoid paying benefits may be more likely to terminate older workers, giving rise to a claim under both ERISA and the ADEA.

Management Tips

- ERISA is a complicated statute that contains many specific regulations regarding the establishment, maintenance, and investment of employee benefit plans and their assets. Don't assume compliance; maintain consistent review.

- You do not *have* to provide retirement or welfare benefits (health, life, disability) to your employees. If you *do,* however, ERISA applies.

- Since ERISA preempts most state laws relating to employee benefit plans, don't consider a state safe harbor where it is not in compliance with ERISA.

- While ERISA does not currently prevent employers from allowing their employees who participate in individual retirement account plans like 401(k) plans to invest all or a large portion of their retirement savings in their company's

stock, Enron has shown the dangers of such an investment strategy.* If possible, don't match employee contributions with company stock, especially if the employee has opted to invest heavily in company stock under his or her retirement plan. Or, if the company matches in company stock, consider allowing diversification out of the stock.

- Monitor who is a fiduciary under the plan. Fiduciary status should be clearly established. Corporate officers and directors should not have discretionary authority over plan assets unless they are clearly fiduciaries.

- Stay abreast of legislation affecting the administration of employees' retirement plans.

* See Mark Silow, "Investments in Employer Stock: The Enron Legacy," *The Legal Intelligencer,* Feb. 18, 2002.

Summary

Concerns that management must address in considering the management implications of ERISA are:

- First, when organizing and implementing an employee benefit plan, the employer must ensure the plan meets the requirements for qualification as to participation, vesting, nondiscrimination, and funding.
- Second, the employer must determine who will be a fiduciary under the plan and ensure that only such fiduciaries have responsibility for administration and investments under the plan.
- Third, the employer should seek competent legal, accounting, and financial advisors to assist in compliance with the terms of ERISA, the tax code, and other laws affecting employee benefit plans.

Chapter-End Questions

1. Leigh and Dusek are beneficiaries of the Reliable Corporation Employee Profit Sharing Trust and former owners of the Reliable Corporation. The trust was originally created by the company as an employees' profit-sharing trust that, until March 1978, held all its funds in fixed-income money market investments. In late March, the trust invested approximately 30 percent of its assets in the stock of three companies; the trust administrators also held large personal interests in each of these three companies. The trust lost no money on the challenged transactions and in fact gained a return on the investment of 72 percent. However, the beneficiaries contest the transaction, claiming that the administrators violated their fiduciary duties by investing in companies where they, the administrators, would reap a personal benefit. In doing so, the beneficiaries argue, the administrators were acting in *their* interests and not necessarily in the best interests of the trust. The administrators made money, which they would not have otherwise made had they been making trust investments solely on the basis of what was best for the trust.

   Note that the applicable ERISA section reads that "if ERISA fiduciaries breach their duties by risking trust assets for their own purposes, beneficiaries may recover the fiduciaries' profits made by misuse of the plan's assets." Decide the beneficiaries' claim in this case. What other information would you need? [*Leigh* v. *Engle,* 727 F.2d 113 (7th Cir. 1984).]

2. What is the difference between a defined contribution plan and a defined benefit plan?

3. Northwest Airlines decided to limit the benefit accruals of pilots once they became 60 years old. Seventeen pilots who were over 60 filed an action against the airline, alleging that the company's plan violated ERISA because pilots under 60 were to accrue benefits faster than pilots over 60. Are they correct? [*Atkins* v. *Northwest Airlines,* 967 F.2d 1197 (9th Cir. 1992).]

4. Does a plan violate ERISA if it refuses to allow same-sex unmarried couples to participate in the company-sponsored benefit plan?

5. A trustee of a pension plan is the owner and principal officer of the employer who sponsors the plan—a construction company. The trustee contracted with his own company to build a restaurant on the land leased by the plan from an independent third party. The trustee caused the plan to pay additional fees to the company and himself that were not stated in the contract. Is this a violation of ERISA? [*Marshall* v. *Kelly,* 465 F. Supp. 341 (W.D. Okla. 1978).]

6. A trustee of a plan, who was also a participant, denied a discretionary payment of a lump sum accrued benefit to a participant who had terminated employment. What would be the argument that this was self-dealing? [*Fine* v. *Semet,* 514 F. Supp. 34 (S.D. Fla. 1981).]

7. Four individuals collectively owned an investment management company, an investment banking company, and a registered broker-dealer company. The investment management

company managed assets for pension plans. Under agreements to raise capital for several unrelated companies, the investment banking company and the broker-dealer invested plan assets in exchange for a commission. Is this a prohibited receipt of consideration by a fiduciary in connection with transactions involving plan assets? [*Lowen* v. *Tower Asset Management Inc.,* 829 F.2d 1209 (2d Cir. 1987).]

8. Should an employee's salary, for purposes of profit sharing plan contributions, include bonuses in addition to base salary? [*Lowry* v. *Bankers Life and Casualty Retirement Plan,* 871 F.2d 522 (5th Cir. 1989).]

9. If an employer is reorganizing and the liability on its severance benefits plan will result as soon as the transfer of interest is made, can the corporation modify its benefits program to avoid that liability? [*Sulton* v. *Weirton Steel Division,* 724 F.2d 406 (4th Cir. 1983).]

10. Feinberg is a bookkeeper who had worked for Pfeiffer Company for 37 years at the time the board decided to pass a resolution in her favor. The resolution stated that "she be afforded the privilege of retiring from active duty in the corporation at any time she may elect to see fit to do so on retirement pay of $200 per month for the rest of her life." She worked for two more years, then retired. She was paid $200 per month for seven years; then the employer cut back when legal counsel advised the board that the money was a gift, rather than a legal obligation. Feinberg sued for breach of contract. What result? [*Feinberg* v. *Pfeiffer Co.,* 322 S.W.2d 163 (Mo. Ct. App. 1959).]

11. A Washington State statute provided that upon divorce, designation of a spouse as a beneficiary of a nonprobate asset was revoked automatically. Two months after divorcing his wife, Mr. Egelhoff died. He had not left a will and had not changed his pension plan's designation of his former wife as the beneficiary. Children of the late Mr. Egelhoff sought to recover benefits of his pension plan, arguing that under state law, the benefits should pass to them because their father's former wife was not a qualified beneficiary. The ex-wife of the decedent argued that ERISA preempts the state law. Should the benefits pass to the children of Mr. Egelhoff? [*Egelhoff* v. *Egelhoff,* 532 U.S. 141 (2001).]

Chapter **Seventeen**

Fair Labor Standards Act

Chapter Outline

Opening Scenarios

SCENARIO 1

Fourteen-year-old Shamika wants to earn money to save toward college. She decides to deliver newspapers. Her mother objects, telling Shamika that she considers the job too dangerous and that, anyway, Shamika at 14 is underage for employment. Is Shamika's mom correct?

SCENARIO 2

When asked to work overtime, Chad tells his boss that, under the law, he is not required to work over 40 hours per week and declines the overtime. Is Chad correct?

SCENARIO 3

Drake, a new MBA graduate, is hired into a management job. It is Drake's first job as a professional. After several months, Drake finds he is leaving work later and later. Drake begins to resent that he works late, putting in more and more hours, and is not receiving any more than the originally agreed upon salary. He is contemplating legal action against his employer for violation of the Fair Labor Standards Act. Will it be worth his while to pursue this?

STATUTORY BASIS

Every employer shall pay to each of his employees who in any workweek is engaged in commerce or in the production of goods for commerce, or is employed in an enterprise engaged in commerce or in the production of goods for commerce, wages at the following rates: . . . not less than $5.15 an hour beginning September 1, 1997. Sec. 6(a), Fair Labor Standards Act of 1938, as amended, 29 USC 201, et seq.

. . . No employer shall employ any of his employees for a workweek longer than forty hours unless such employee receives compensation for his employment in excess of the hours above specified at a rate not less than one and one-half times the regular rate at which he is employed. Sec. 7(a)(1), Fair Labor Standards Act of 1938, as amended, 29 USC 201, et seq.

SHOW ME THE MONEY!

Face it. If we were all rich and didn't have to work, many of us would not do so. If we *do* have to work, we want to make sure that we get all that is coming to us. We don't want to have to work for whatever meager wages our employer wants to pay us. We don't want to have to compete with 10-year-olds for our job—even if they *are* qualified! We don't want to have to work whatever number of hours our employer decides he or she wants us to work, just to get the most out of us. In many parts of the world, this is precisely how things are. In fact, it is also the reason many manufacturers have their goods manufactured elsewhere. While things may be changing because of world pressure being brought to bear on the issue, it is still true that much of the world operates without these rules. Just as the United States once did.

It may seem strange to us now, but there was a time when children eight and nine years old and even younger were made to work until midnight and beyond to keep the wheels of the industrial revolution turning. There were no laws to regulate the maximum number of hours a child could be required to work, or how much employees were required to be paid by their employer. Under the broad constitutional powers that

Congress has to regulate interstate commerce, in 1938 it passed a law to regulate pay and hours worked.

The law, now amended several times, is called the Fair Labor Standards Act (FLSA). The act set standards for the minimum age for workers, **minimum wages** they can make, and the rate at which they must be paid if they work over a certain amount of time during a workweek. The act also prohibits pay differentials based solely on gender.

minimum wages
The least amount a covered employee must be paid in hourly wages.

The purpose of the minimum wage laws is to ensure that all workers, especially those at the lower end of the pay scale, maintain at least a minimum standard of living that keeps them from poverty. On the other hand, FLSA has been criticized as causing poverty in certain sectors of the workforce—for example, with unskilled minority teenagers, whom employers will not hire even at minimum wage, because it is deemed too high a price to pay for the contributions of this group, whose unemployment rate can run as high as 50 percent. A training wage of 85 percent of the minimum wage for certain groups is provided in an effort to encourage employment, but employment of certain groups remains low. (See Exhibit 17.1.)

According to the American Bar Association, in 2001, for the first time, class action lawsuits seeking overtime pay surpassed class action lawsuits seeking relief from workplace discrimination. Just in the past couple of years, lawsuits for violations of the Fair Labor Standards Act have resulted in several significant settlements or judgments: $18 million for Starbucks employees, nearly $30 million for Tandy Corporation employees at Radio Shack, $5.1 million for Cingular Wireless customer service representatives, $3 million for Tyson Food employees, and in the largest class action overtime pay lawsuit ever tried in the United States, more than a whopping $200 million for Farmers Insurance Exchange claims representatives. Legal issues are as diverse as employers not allowing slaughterhouse employees to be on the clock (and thus, be paid) for the time it takes to change into their work attire and walk to their work area, to employers intentionally misclassifying employees so that they will not qualify for time-and-a-half pay for the hours worked over 40; from Wal-Mart allowing underage employees to operate hazardous equipment, to not paying employees requested by the employer to begin work before they were scheduled to do so and end work after their scheduled quitting time. The federal government recovered more than $196 million in back wages in 2004 alone.

FLSA underwent a major regulatory revision effective August 2004. The goal of the new rules promulgated under FLSA' s regulatory rule-making authority was to simplify the rules for applying FLSA's "white collar" exemptions for employees in executive, administrative, professional, and outside sales jobs. This chapter will discuss the basic requirements of the Fair Labor Standards Act, the recent changes in the regulations, and how FLSA's requirements impact the workplace and the nearly 110 million employees covered by the law.

GENERAL PROVISIONS

FLSA is administered by the U.S. Department of Labor's Wage and Hour Division, which has authority to investigate, gather information, issue regulations, and enforce FLSA provisions. States also have wage and hour provisions administered by comparable state agencies. In addition to regulating child labor, wages, and hours, FLSA also requires employers

Though published in 1989, this is still a timely and interesting piece that provides you with insight about a matter dear to the hearts of many of you: work-study jobs and how an increase in the minimum wage impacts them. It makes for interesting reading and gives you something to think about the next time the perennial debate of raising the minimum wage arises.

Congress and the White House have spent an inordinate amount of time wrangling over increasing the minimum wage. While the chief sticking point has been over the level the new minimum would be set at, insufficient attention has been paid to the key question: "How will the new minimum wage affect the American economy?"

There are a number of institutions facing fixed budgets as far as part-time help is concerned. Most colleges have work-study programs with which they are able to hire students to help professors. Academic departments have a fixed operating budget from which they must cover all of their expenses plus the hiring of work-study students. Another class of employees used is that of temporary service workers.

If there is an increase in the minimum wage, the limited budget cannot be expanded, so fewer students will be able to be hired with the fixed amount of funds available. Many of these students, in order to save money, are going to colleges which are supported by state governments. Will the state legislature add enough money to the schools' budgets so they can increase the departmental budgets, enabling these students to be hired?

More likely, a number of jobs which had been available to aid students suddenly will be gone. Some students who rely on that extra money to help them through the school year will have to drop out, and we will have lost an individual who might have been able to contribute a great deal to our world.

Businesses other than schools will also feel the crunch. Fast-food chains rely on part-time employees, generally high school students. To pay the higher wages, when there is no increase in the amount of output per worker, will mean the prices of their product will have to be increased to meet the added expense. This adds to the levels of inflation already present and does not satisfy the main aim of the increase, which is to raise the buying power of the individual. Meanwhile, the minimum wage will not affect those already earning above that level, except to lower the buying power of the dollars available to them.

The increase in these wages could affect our economic position overseas as well. The trade imbalance is fueled by wages which are higher than comparable salaries in other developed countries for jobs requiring similar skills. The minimum wage increase will tend to force other salaries above it higher in order to keep "equity" in the labor market. The higher wages will be reflected in prices, causing consumers to cut back on their demand for domestic products over nondomestic goods and resulting in a further increase in the U.S. trade deficit.

Government is like the camel which sticks its nose into a tent. After a while, the camel is the only one in the tent, and the other occupants have had to vacate. The minimum wage is becoming another of the inflationary aspects of the economy. Coupled with the savings and loan bailouts, the level of all debt, and low productivity, it well could be the act which pushes us into a recession.

Source: Reprinted from *USA Today Magazine*, July 1989, copyright 1989 by the Society for the Advancement of Education Inc.

to keep records on wages and hours, though there is no particular form in which such records must be kept. Violations, if willful, are crimes punishable by fines of up to $10,000, with second convictions resulting in possible imprisonment. Child labor violations carry civil penalties. FLSA contains antiretaliation provisions to protect employees who use FLSA, such as filing a complaint or participating in an FLSA proceeding. The federal regulations of the Wage and Hour Division can be found at 29 C.F.R. Part V.

If FLSA is violated by the employer underpaying employees, employees may recover back wages. There is a two-year statute of limitations, which stretches to three for willful violations. In the case below, the issue of willfulness arose regarding a claim for overtime compensation under the act.

Alabama A&M University v. King et al. *119 Lab. Cas. ¶ 35,538 (Ala. Civ. App. 1991)*

Nine employees of Alabama A&M University who worked as residence hall counselors in female dormitories on campus alleged that they were due overtime pay for working 60-hour weeks for a two-and-a-half-year period. While FLSA requires payment of overtime for work in excess of 40 hours per week, executive, administrative, or professional employees are exempt from this provision. The university argued that the employees were administrative. The jury found for the employees, who then requested damages, which would be greater if it was found that the university's actions were willful violations of FLSA.

Russell, J.

In the present action the trial court's initial instructions to the jury on the issue of willful violation of the FLSA included the following language:

> Unless you are reasonably satisfied from the evidence that the defendant university in failing to pay these plaintiffs overtime knew it was violating the statute, or that the defendant university in failing to pay these plaintiff's overtime showed reckless disregard for the matter of whether its failure to pay them overtime was a violation of the statute, then you cannot find that any violation which may have occurred was willful.
>
> If you are reasonably satisfied from the evidence that the plaintiffs were non-exempt employees, and that Alabama A&M either knew or showed reckless disregard to the matter of whether its conduct was prohibited by the Fair Labor Standards Act as to the plaintiffs, you would then find Alabama A&M guilty of willful violation of the Fair Labor Standards Act.

In a supplemental charge the trial court said that the reckless disregard standard requires an employer to make a reasonable effort to determine whether the plan it is following would constitute a violation of the law.

Alabama A&M alleges the trial court's supplemental instruction to the jury that the university was required "to make a reasonable effort" to determine its compliance with the law was legally incorrect and unquestionably prejudicial in that it allowed the jury to invoke too lenient of a standard in finding willful conduct.

The imposition of a duty upon Alabama A&M to "make a reasonable effort" to determine whether it was violating the requirements of the FLSA is contrary to the standard established by the U.S. Supreme Court. We find the jury charge was legally incorrect and prejudicial to the university. REVERSED AND REMANDED.

Case Questions

1. Should a high standard be imposed to find that the employer willfully violated the statute? Why or why not?

2. How should willfulness be established?

3. Does it make sense to you that an employer and an employee may differ over what type of employee the employer categorizes the employee as? Why or why not?

COVERED EMPLOYEES

Since FLSA was enacted pursuant to the powers of Congress to regulate interstate commerce, that requirement forms, in part, a basis for determining coverage. Actually, there are two types of coverage in FLSA: individual coverage and enterprise coverage. If the individual employee's job involves interstate commerce directly, such as an over-the-road truck driver traveling from state to state, or moving or preparing goods for interstate commerce, including phoning and using the mail, then the individual is covered. For enterprise coverage, all employees of a business will be covered if the business is engaged in interstate commerce or in producing goods for interstate commerce and meets a minimum gross annual income requirement of $500,000. The law applies to both part-time and full-time employees. Federal, state, and local employees are also covered by the law, though there are some specific provisions for certain state and local employees.

If an employee works for certain types of businesses, then the $500,000 minimum does not apply. That is, employees will be covered even if their employer does not make at least $500,000 per year. These organizations include hospitals and other institutions primarily engaged in the care of the sick, aged, mentally ill, or disabled who reside on the premises; schools for children who are mentally or physically disabled or gifted; preschools, elementary, and secondary schools and institutions of higher education; and federal, state, and local government agencies. The law also covers domestic service workers, such as day workers, housekeepers, chauffeurs, cooks, or full-time babysitters, if they receive at least $1,400 (2004) in cash wages from one employer in a calendar year, or if they work a total of more than eight hours a week for one or more employers. State laws may also apply and when both cover a situation, the law setting the higher standards must be the one used.

FLSA contains exemptions from these rules for several groups, which vary depending on the area of FLSA being addressed. They will be discussed under the relevant sections.

As you can see from the case below, even the threshold decision as to who is covered by the act is not always an easy one. The court was faced with deciding whether topless dancers who only received tips were, in fact, employees for purposes of the Fair Labor Standards Act provisions on minimum wages, overtime, and recordkeeping requirements.

Reich v. Circle C Investments, Inc.   *998 F.2d 324*
(5th Cir. 1993)

The court analyzes whether topless nightclub dancers who received no compensation except tips from customers are employees subject to FLSA or "business women renting space, stages, music, dressing rooms and lights from the club," not subject to the law. The court determined that they were, in fact, employees for FLSA purposes.

Reavley, J.

The secretary of labor alleges that a topless nightclub has improperly compensated its dancers, waitresses, disc jockeys, bartenders, doormen, and "housemothers," and has failed to keep accurate records of the hours worked by its employees. The district court determined that the topless dancers and other workers are "employees" under the FLSA and that the club willfully violated its minimum wage, overtime and record-keeping provisions.

The dancers receive no compensation from the club. Their compensation is derived solely from the tips they receive from customers for performing on stage and performing private "table dances" and "couch dances." At the end of each night, the dancers must pay the club a $20 "tip-out," regardless of how much they make in tips. The club characterizes this tip-out as stage rental and argues that the dancers are really tenants. According to the club, the dancers are neither employees nor independent contractors, but are business women renting space, stages, music, dressing rooms, and lights from the club.

To determine employee status under the FLSA, we focus on whether the alleged employee, as a matter of economic reality, is economically dependent upon the business to which she renders her services, or in business for herself. To make this determination, we must analyze five factors.

The first factor is the degree of control exercised by the alleged employer. The district court found that the club exercises a great deal of control over the dancers. They are required to comply with weekly work schedules, which the club compiles with input from the dancers. The club fines the dancers for absences or tardiness. It instructs the dancers to charge at least $10 for table dances and $20 for couch dances. The dancers supply their own costumes, but the costumes must meet standards set by the club. The dancers can express a preference for a certain type of music, but they do not have the final say in the matter. The club has many other rules concerning the dancers' behavior; for example, no flat heels, no more than 15 minutes at one time in the dressing room, only one dancer in the restroom at a time, and all dancers must be "on the floor" at opening time. The club enforces these rules by fining infringers.

The club attempts to de-emphasize its control by arguing that most of the rules are directed at maintaining decorum or keeping the club itself legal. The club explained that it publishes the minimum charge for table and couch dances at the request of the dancers to prevent dancers from undercutting each others' prices. Finally, it stresses the fact that it does not control the dancers' routines. We believe, however, that the record fully supports the district court's findings of significant control.

The second factor is the extent of relative investments of the worker and alleged employer. The district

court found that a dancer's investment is limited to her costumes and a padlock. The amount spent on costumes varies from dancer to dancer and can be significant. The club contends that we should also consider as an investment each dancer's nightly tip-out, which it characterizes as rent. The district court rejected this argument, and so do we. It is the economic realities that control our determination of employee status.

Third, we must look at the degree to which the workers' opportunity for profit and loss is determined by the alleged employer. Once customers arrive at the club, a dancer's initiative, hustle and costume significantly contribute to the amount of her tips. But the club has a significant role in drawing customers. Given its control over determinants of customer volume, the club exercises a high degree of control over a dancer's opportunity for "profit." Dancers are far more closely akin to wage earners toiling for a living than to independent entrepreneurs seeking a return on their risky capital investments.

The fourth factor is the skill and initiative required in performing the job. Many of the dancers did not have any prior experience with topless dancing before coming to work at the club. They do not need long training or highly developed skills to dance at the club. A dancer's initiative is essentially limited to decisions involving costumes and dance routines. This does not exhibit the skill or initiative indicative of persons in business for themselves.

Finally, we must analyze the permanency of the relationship. The district court found that most dancers have short-term relationships with the club. Although not determinative, the impermanent relationship between the dancers and the club indicates non-employee status.

Despite the lack of permanency, on balance, the five factors favor a determination of employee status. A dancer has no specialized skills and her only real investment is in her costumes. The club exercises significant control over a dancer's behavior and the opportunity for profit. The transient nature of the workforce is not enough here to remove the dancers from the protections of the FLSA. AFFIRMED.

Case Questions

1. Does any of the case surprise you? Explain.
2. If you were the club owner and did not want the dancers to be employees, after receiving this decision, how would you change things?
3. Do you think the dancers should have been considered employees? Why or why not?

MINIMUM WAGES

When unions were legalized during the Great Depression, they immediately attempted to bargain for higher wages. John L. Lewis, the well-known president of the United Mine Workers (UMW), left the American Federation of Labor (AFL) and formed the Congress of Industrial Organizations (CIO) and the UMW struck for higher wages. The two organizations later linked up to form the AFL-CIO, and wages have always been an extremely important item on the collective bargaining agenda.

After World War II, the minimum wage law was established in hopes that it would avoid another depression. The advocates of the law, primarily unions and other workers, thought that a minimum wage would accomplish this by providing everyone with enough money on which to live without causing economic harm to business owners.

Under FLSA, employers are required to pay covered employees a certain minimum hourly wage. Since September 1, 1997, the wage has been $5.15. In 1938, when FLSA was enacted, it was 25 cents per hour.

State wage laws may have higher minimums than the federal law. For example, Washington, D.C., has a minimum wage of $6.60 per hour, Massachusetts, $6.75 per hour, and New York's minimum wage increased to $6.00 per hour on January 1, 2005, with scheduled increases to $6.75 on January 1, 2006 and $7.15 on January 1, 2007.

In addition to minimum wages, covered employees working over 40 hours per week are entitled to overtime pay of at least time and a half—at least one and one-half times the covered employee's regular hourly wage rate.

Wage rates may be lower if, in accordance with appropriate regulations, an industry wage order makes them so in Puerto Rico, the Virgin Islands, or American Samoa. If the covered employee is an apprentice, learner, or disabled worker, then, under certain circumstances, she or he may receive less than the minimum wage if the employer obtains a certificate issued by the Department of Labor's wage and hour administrator.

Examples of subminimum wage employees include, for instance, student-learners (vocational education students); full-time students in retail or service establishments, agriculture, or institutions of higher education; employees whose earning or productive capacity is impaired by a physical or mental disability, including those related to age or injury, for the work to be performed. Payment of a subminimum wage encourages employers to hire these groups of employees although they would not otherwise be willing to pay regular minimum wage to them. In order to pay less than minimum wage, however, the employer must receive a certificate from the Wage and Hour Division.

Tipped employees (defined in the regulations as those who regularly receive more than $30 a month in tips) may be paid direct wages of $2.13 per hour, rather than $5.15, but the employer must make up the difference if the tips do not equal the usual minimum wage. Employees under age 20 may be paid $4.25 per hour (rather than the usual $5.15) during the first 90 days of employment. After that, they must be paid regular minimum wage. Employees may be paid on a piece-rate rather than an hourly rate, as long as they receive the equivalent of the minimum wage. (See Exhibits 17.3 and 17.4 for wage and overtime exemptions.)

Exhibit 17.2 discusses one aspect of the issue of low wages. *Kilgore* demonstrates that there may be problems with something as simple as even determining who receives minimum wages.

Exhibit 17.2   Discrimination and Low-Wage Workers

EEOC Addresses Discrimination against Low-Wage Earners at Historic Public Meeting in Houston:

In its second public forum outside the nation's capital this year, the U.S. Equal Employment Opportunity Commission (EEOC) held its monthly meeting in Houston on Tuesday, June 22, 1999, to hear testimony from expert witnesses on discrimination as it affects low-wage workers—particularly immigrants, minorities, and women.

The day-long meeting, held at Texas Southern University's Thurgood Marshall School of Law, attracted an outpouring of approximately 300 people, including community and business leaders, civil rights advocates and educators, state and local government officials, over a dozen print and electronic media outlets, as well as the public at large. The historic gathering marked another step in EEOC's ongoing effort to reach out to agency stakeholders, especially under-served communities, and expand its presence at the grassroots level.

"We left the Washington Beltway to listen carefully to experts and advocates at the local level who have first-hand knowledge about the problems facing low-wage workers," said EEOC Chairwoman Ida L. Castro. "The information we gathered will provide us with a solid foundation to develop our work plan so that together we can focus on these important issues."

During the meeting, three expert panels, including one affected individual, shared their experiences and insights on how best to break down the barriers to equal employment opportunity for low-wage earners. The Commission heard testimony from representatives of the following organizations: AFL-CIO; Asian Law Caucus; NAACP; Mexican American Legal Defense and Education Fund; Houston Immigration and Refugee Coalition; Texas Rural Legal Aid; Refugee Services Alliance; Wage and Hour Division, U.S. Department of Labor; and the Institute for Rehabilitation and Research. Also participating in the panel discussions were esteemed faculty members from the University of Texas.

Panelists discussed a number of issues affecting low-wage earners including wage bias, worker exploitation, industry trends, demographic and population changes, challenges faced by immigrants and undocumented employees, the role of organized labor, welfare-to-work programs, temp services and contingent workers, low job classification, and limited job opportunities for older workers and persons with disabilities.

In addition to the expert witnesses, the Commission heard testimony from Francisco Javier Guevera, a Mexican construction worker from Houston, who provided personal insights about his employment as a low-wage immigrant worker. The meeting "opened a whole new world" he said, because he previously had no knowledge about the laws enforced by EEOC, nor did he understand how to utilize the agency's complaint process.

"Due to a lack of education, cultural differences, and language barriers, too many low-wage workers are unaware of their rights, unfamiliar with EEOC's charge processing procedures, and unable to get a fair shot at the American dream," said Ms. Castro.

Among the recommendations made by the panelists were to increase enforcement attention to the agricultural, poultry, meat packing, construction, and restaurant industries; survey employees under the H-2A temporary farm worker program to ensure that employers are complying with the EEO laws; and monitor public works construction projects to safeguard against workplace bias.

"Too many employers continue to abuse and take advantage of low-wage earners because they are vulnerable to threats of retaliation and fear deportation," Ms. Castro

Exhibit 17.2 (continued)

said. "EEOC will enhance collaboration with stakeholders and provide more strategic enforcement to root out the bad actors and remedy egregious discrimination wherever and whenever it exists."

Under Chairwoman Castro's leadership, the Commission has made several major enforcement reforms which have increased the efficiency and effectiveness of agency operations. These include enhancing outreach, education, and technical assistance to stakeholders with a special emphasis on small and mid-sized employers as well as underserved communities; and revamping the agency Web site to make information more accessible in a user-friendly format.

Source: EEOC, June 24, 1999, www.eeoc.gov/press/6-24-99.html. Used with permission.

Exhibit 17.3 Exemptions from Both Minimum Wage and Overtime Pay

- Executive, administrative, and professional employees (including teachers and academic administrative personnel in elementary and secondary schools), outside sales employees, and employees in certain computer-related occupations (as defined in Department of Labor regulations).
- Employees of certain seasonal amusement or recreational establishments, employees of certain small newspapers, seamen employed on foreign vessels, employees engaged in fishing operations, and employees engaged in newspaper delivery.
- Farm workers employed by anyone who used no more than 500 "man-days" of farm labor in any calendar quarter of the preceding calendar year.
- Casual babysitters and persons employed as companions to the elderly or infirm.

Source: http://www.dol.gov/esa/whd.

Kilgore v. Outback Steakhouse of Florida, Inc. *160 F.3d 294 (6th Cir. 1998)*

Employee servers who were required to pool their tips and have them redistributed to other types of employees who were not paid minimum wage challenge this practice as a violation of the minimum wage provision of the FLSA. The court permitted the arrangement.

Kennedy, J.

Outback's tip pooling arrangement requires its servers to contribute a share of their tips to a tip pool, which the restaurant distributes to hosts, bus persons, and bartenders. The servers' mandated contribution is three percent of their "total gross sales," which includes not only food and beverages, but also gift certificates and

755

merchandise such as steak knives and T-shirts sold to customers at a server's assigned tables.

The restaurant paid its hosts and servers $2.125 per hour—one half the minimum wage at the time in question—with the required minimum wage difference made up through the tip pool arrangement. It was undisputed that hosts and servers never received less than the minimum wage for a workweek under this arrangement. Servers testified, however, that customer tips often fell short of the fifteen percent industry standard, and that Outback's tip pool requirement "routinely" required them to "tip out" more than thirty-five percent of the tips they actually received.

The FLSA, at 29 U.S.C. §203(m), permits employers to use a tip credit to account for up to fifty percent of the minimum wage but only with respect to "tipped" employees. The statute defines a "tipped employee" as "any employee engaged in an occupation in which he customarily and regularly receives more than $30 a month in tips." 29 U.S.C.§203(t). Section 203(m) also states that use of the tip credit this way "shall not be construed to prohibit the pooling of tips among employees who customarily and regularly receive tips."

Employee servers and hosts allege that the required tip-out amount was impermissibly excessive, and, therefore, not "customary and reasonable" as required under Labor Department interpretations of the relevant statutory sections. They also contended that Outback's use of the tip credit to calculate the minimum wage was unlawful with respect to hosts because they did not qualify as "tipped employees."

Even though Outback prohibits hosts from accepting tips, they receive more than $30 a month in tips if tip pool receipts are included. Employees who receive tips from a tip pool are employees who 'receive tips' according to Department of Labor regulations, case law, and Department of Labor practices. Accordingly, the hosts meet the qualifications of Sections 203(t) and 203(m).

The hosts perform services to customers—greeting and seating, giving out menus, and sometimes "enhancing the wait" by serving food. These activities constitute sufficient interaction with customers in an industry where undesignated tips are common. Accordingly, the hosts are engaged in an occupation in which tips are customarily and regularly received and thereby qualify as tipped employees. AFFIRMED.

Case Questions

1. Do you consider the restaurant's pool tipping policy to be fair to the servers who received the tips? Explain.
2. Does the court's analysis make sense to you, that if hosts receive tips from the tip pot, then they are employees who routinely receive tips? Explain.
3. Why do you think the employer uses this method of payment?

As mentioned, FLSA has exemptions, so not everyone is covered under the statute. At least 41 states provide coverage for employees exempted under FLSA, with about 16 states setting limits above those of the federal law.

Sometimes the rate of pay is not so clear cut. In *Casserly,* the court had to deal with whether employees on call should be able to receive overtime pay when their on-call time goes beyond their regular 40-hour week.

Casserly v. Colorado *844 P.2d 1275 (Colo. App. 1992)*

Employees, physician assistants for the state correctional facility, argued that they should be able to collect time-and-a-half overtime pay for the time over 40 hours that they are on call away from their jobs at the facilities. They make nearly $18 per hour as base pay, and the employer wants to pay them $1.75 per hour for "on-call time" rather than the time and a half that FLSA requires. The court agreed with the employees.

Metzger, J.

Plaintiff employees were employed as physician assistants at the State Correctional Facility at Canon City,

Colorado. Each employee was assigned to a single facility for full-time duties requiring not less than 40 hours per week. In addition, on a rotating basis, each employee was required to provide emergency medical services to inmates after regular working hours. Employees were compensated at one and one-half their regular rate of pay for those hours they were physically present at a facility responding to a call.

Before November 1988, the employees were not paid for the time spent waiting for calls. After that time, defendants paid employees at a rate of $1.75 per hour as "on-call" pay.

During on-call periods, employees were required to respond to any of seven facilities covering an 8-mile radius within 20 minutes of receiving a call for services (if they determined that the call necessitated a physical response to a facility and could not be handled by telephone). The number and frequency of calls received during any on-call shift were not predictable.

The need to respond immediately to medical calls required employees to maintain a constant state of readiness. They did not engage in recreational activities during these hours, nor did they use this time for their own personal purposes. Employees testified that they did not shower, walk for recreation, cook meals, eat in restaurants, entertain guests, perform yard work, or attend sporting events during their on-call hours. Some employees rented motel rooms in Canon City in order to meet the response time requirements rather than going home during these shifts.

Employees claimed their time spent waiting for calls constituted hours worked pursuant to 29 U.S.C. 201-219 (1988), the Federal Fair Labor Standards Act (FLSA), and that they should be compensated at a rate of time and one-half for all hours spent on-call in excess of their regular 40 hours per week.

The employees filed a formal grievance with defendants in March 1988 for overtime pay and supplied copies of state fiscal rules incorporating the provisions of the FLSA and affidavits detailing the restrictions imposed upon their lives while on-call. The grievance was denied.

The defendants contend the trial court erred in failing to follow the terms of an agreement alleged to exist between the Department of Corrections and the employees regarding compensation for waiting time. They further contend the court erred in finding that this agreement was against public policy. We find no error.

Defendants assert that, in March 1988, the Department of Corrections officials and the employees had agreed that time spent waiting for calls would be compensated at $1.75 per hour, and time spent when employees physically traveled to a facility responding to a call would be compensated at time and one-half. Thus, they argue, the trial court erred in refusing to consider the impact of this agreement on employees' FLSA claims. We reject this contention.

The trial court found that any agreement by the employees to provide on-call services for the Department of Corrections was not an agreement to perform those services without the compensation required by law. It correctly determined that, as a matter of law, an agreement entered into in good faith cannot supersede the FLSA or be used as a defense against employees' claims.

The FLSA's overtime requirement, 29 U.S.C. 207 (1988), has two purposes: (1) to encourage employers to hire additional workers rather than employ fewer workers for longer hours; and (2) to compensate employees who do work overtime for the burden of having to do so. The Act "forbids pay plans that have the effect of reducing the pay for overtime to less than one and one-half times the employees' regular rate, even though the plans may be acceptable to the employees involved."

Given the nature of the demands on the employees during their waiting time, we conclude, as did the trial court, that any agreement to pay them $1.75 per hour (well below their average salary of nearly $18 per hour) would be contrary to the purpose of the FLSA and thus would violate public policy.

Defendants next argue the trial court erred in awarding overtime compensation to the employees for the time spent waiting for calls. We find no error.

The FLSA requires the payment of time and one-half of an employee's regular rate of pay for each hour worked in excess of 40 hours in any workweek. 29 U.S.C. 207(a)(1) (1988).

"An employee who is required to remain on call on the employer's premises or so close thereto that he cannot use the time effectively for his own purposes is working while 'on call.'" 29 C.F.R. 785.17 (1991). Whether "waiting time" is "working time" depends on the particular case and is a question of fact to be resolved by the trial court.

The test is whether the time is spent predominately for the employer's benefit or for the employee's benefit. If the time spent is predominately for the employer's benefit, the employee is "engaged to be waiting" and is entitled to compensation.

Renfro v. *City of Emporia,* 948 F.2d 1529 (10th Cir. 1991), illustrates the on-call standard under the FLSA. In *Renfro,* the Court of Appeals affirmed a summary judgment entered on behalf of firefighters who had alleged their "on-call" time was compensable. The City of Emporia had two fire stations and each station maintained a separate on-call list. Firefighters employed with the City were regularly scheduled to work six shifts of 24 hours each in a 19-day cycle, for a total of 144 hours. Each firefighter also appeared on a mandatory callback list for each 24-hour period following a regularly scheduled tour of duty. During this callback period, the firefighters were not required to remain at the station house premises. However, they were required to carry pagers and to return to work within 20 minutes if called or be subject to discipline. The number of callbacks firefighters received ranged from zero to 13 per day but averaged approximately four to five per day.

The firefighters argued that the on-call policy greatly restricted their personal activities. They asserted that, because of the 20-minute time constraint and the large number of callbacks, they could not go out of town, could not do simple things such as change oil or do other work on their cars, could not go to a movie or out to dinner for fear of being called back, could not be alone with their children unless they had a babysitter "on-call," could not drive anywhere with anyone when on call (i.e., they would have had to take separate cars in case of a callback), and could not participate in group activities for fear of being called away. The appellate court concluded that the trial court's findings were supported by the record and that its application of the FLSA was appropriate in determining that the firefighters were due overtime compensation for their "on-call" time.

Here, the trial court made ample findings to support its conclusion that the employees could not use on-call time effectively for their own purposes, and the evidence in the record fully supports this determination.

This evidence included the high number of calls received (ranging from 10 to 12 calls per weekday shift, up to 24 calls on a weekend shift), the number of facilities (7) and geographical radius (8 miles) involved, and the 20-minute response time required. The employees testified, as noted above, concerning the severe restrictions placed on their personal activities by the on-call status. Indeed, one physician assistant testified that he remained partially dressed and slept on a couch near the telephone rather than going to bed at night.

There is overwhelming evidence in the record demonstrating that waiting time was not spent in ways the employees would have chosen had they been free to do so. Hence, we will not disturb the trial court's finding that the employees could not use the time effectively for their own purposes and, thus, were "working" for purposes of the FLSA.

AFFIRMED as to the employer's liability.

Case Questions

1. Why do you think the employer thought the employees were not entitled to time-and-a-half pay for being on call over 40 hours?

2. Is there any way you can think of that the employer can get around paying time and a half to the employees? Explain.

3. The employer agreed to pay the employees $1.75. Can you think of why an employer would do this?

The following are the primary exemptions from both the wage and the overtime provisions of FLSA. Note that under FLSA some employees are exempt from the overtime provisions but not the minimum wage provisions (see Exhibit 17.4).

1. Outside salespeople, executive, administrative, and professional employees, including teachers and academic administrative employees in elementary and secondary schools. (This is why it would not be worth Drake's time to pursue a claim in opening scenario 3).

Exhibit 17.4

Other FLSA Exemptions

As you can see from the list below, there are many exemptions to the FLSA provisions. These do not include state exemptions that may exist.

(MW = minimum wage; OT = overtime; CL = child labor)

Aircraft salespeople—OT

Airline employees—OT

Amusement/recreational employees in national parks/forests/wildlife refuge system—OT

Babysitters on a casual basis—MW & OT

Boat salespeople—OT

Buyers of agricultural products—OT

Companions for the elderly—MW & OT

Country elevator workers (rural)—OT

Disabled workers—MW

Domestic employees who live in—OT

Farm implement salespeople—OT

Federal criminal investigators—MW & OT

Firefighters working in small (less than five firefighters) public fire departments—OT

Fishing—MW & OT

Forestry employees of small (less than nine employees) firms—OT

Fruit & vegetable transportation employees—OT

Homeworkers making wreaths—MW, OT, & CL

Houseparents in nonprofit educational institutions—OT

Livestock auction workers—OT

Local delivery drivers and drivers' helpers—OT

Lumber operations employees of small (less than nine employees) firms—OT

Motion picture theater employees—OT

Newspaper delivery—MW, OT, & CL

Newspaper employees of limited circulation newspapers—MW & OT

Police officers working in small (less than five officers) public police departments—OT

Radio station employees in small markets—OT

Railroad employees—OT

Seamen on American vessels—OT

Seamen on other than American vessels—MW & OT

Sugar processing employees—OT

Switchboard operators—MW & OT

Taxicab drivers—OT

Television station employees in small markets—OT

Truck and trailer salespeople—OT

Youth employed as actors or performers—CL

Youth employed by their parents—CL

Source: http://www.dol.gov/elaws/esa/flsa/screen75.asp.

2. Employees of certain individually owned and operated small retail or service establishments not part of a covered enterprise.
3. Employees of certain seasonal amusement or recreational establishments, messengers, full-time students, employees of certain small newspapers, switchboard operators of small telephone companies, sailors employed on foreign vessels, employees engaged in fishing operations.
4. Farm workers employed by anyone who used more than 500 person-days of farm labor in any calendar quarter of the preceding calendar year.
5. Casual babysitters and people employed as companions to the elderly.

As mentioned in the beginning of the chapter, the FLSA overtime regulations underwent a major overhaul in August 2004 regarding their exemption for white-collar professionals; that is, primarily those in executive, administrative, and professional jobs. This matter had been debated for years and was accomplished under President Bush. These rules are extremely important since they determine who must be paid overtime for working more than 40 hours per week. The general rule was that white-collar employees in the above categories were not entitled to overtime pay. Determinations as to who fit into these categories were made using a salary test and a duties test.

In an effort to restore the overtime protections originally afforded by the law and reflect current workplace conditions, for the first time employers would be required to pay overtime to as many as 1.3 million lower-income workers who work over 40 hours per week. Before passage of the new regulations, it was estimated that about 640,000 white-collar professionals who were required to receive overtime (i.e., some engineers and pharmacists) would lose the right to receive overtime. Though survey results indicated most employers would not take away overtime pay from employees, an Economic Policy Institute analysis concluded that more than 6 million workers could lose their overtime pay. It was estimated that another 10.7 million whose pay status was uncertain regarding the payment of overtime would receive clarification. While the changes were projected to cost employers up to $375 million in additional annual payroll and $739 million in one-time implementation costs, the government estimated that the rules would reduce FLSA violations and save businesses an additional $252 million per year.

Prior to the rule change, the salary levels used in the wage and hour rules had not been updated for nearly 30 years. Under the old rules, FLSA exempted from overtime pay workers who made more than $155 per week, or $8,060 per year, and who met certain other requirements that had been complained of as convoluted and confusing. For instance, the employee also had to devote at least 80 percent of his or her time to "exercising discretion" or other "intellectual" tasks that cannot be "standardized in . . . a given period of time." The new rules were designed to simplify application of the regulations to white-collar exemptions.

Under the new regulations, which require businesses to review their existing pay levels and jobs to make sure employees are being paid correctly under the new rules, employees earning up to $23,660 per year, or $455 per week, are automatically entitled to overtime pay, regardless of whether they are hourly or annual salaried employees. That is, regardless of the classification of the job, if the salary is at or below a certain level ($23,660 per year or $455 per week), the employee is entitled to overtime pay. For the most part, executive employees would be exempt if they manage two or more employees, have hiring, firing, and promotion authority or significant input, or if they have advance degrees or similar training and work in a specialized field or the operations, finance, and auditing areas of a business. It was speculated that the jobs that would be most affected by the new overtime regulations would be assistant managers in stores, restaurants, and bars. Under the new regulations, an employer could boost salaries (that is, pay an employee more than $23,660) in order to avoid the new rules requiring overtime to be paid to those who earn up to $23,660.

Employees who earn at least $100,000 per year and perform some executive, professional (either learned or creative), or administrative job duties are automatically exempt from the overtime provisions of FLSA. Government officials speculated that an estimated 107,000 white-collar employees earning $100,000 or more who had been eligible for overtime under the old regulations would lose it under the new rules.

A "safe harbor" provision allows employers to address improper deductions from an employee's salary instead of automatically losing an exemption for making a mistake. Under the safe harbor provision, an employer will not lose an otherwise valid white-collar exemption if the employer has written policies and does not repeatedly or willfully violate the regulations or continue to make deductions after receiving a complaint. The employer's written policy, which should actually be implemented and enforced, should explain how employees are paid and allow employees to register complaints for violations of the employer's written policy. If there is no such policy, the employer runs the costly risk of losing the exemption not only for the employee against whom the improper deductions were made, but also for all employees in the same job classification who worked for the same manager for the entire time period. The goal is to have employers institute and enforce written policies that allow them to take prompt remedial action on complaints (including restoring any incorrect salary deductions) without exposing the employer to potential liability from litigation.

As with the prior regulations, the Department of Labor can collect back wages for overtime violations and companies not in compliance run the risk of costly lawsuits by employees. Retaliation against employees filing claims or reporting an employer's violations is a separate violation of the law. Since FLSA class action lawsuits have increased by 70 percent since 2000, and the new regulations may change many employees' status from what it was before the new regulations, it is a safe bet that this is an area to which an employer would do well to give considerable attention. Exhibit 17.5 provides a side-by-side comparison of the new and old regulations.

In the following *Newspapers of New England* case, you will see how detailed the inquiry must be in order to determine whether an employee is exempt. While the rules for journalists were left intact by the new regulations, it is these sorts of cases that the new regulations were promulgated to decrease. The goal of the new regulations was to provide employers with more guidance as to who was exempt and who was not, so that there would be less of a need for litigation to make such determinations. Due to the wide variance among journalists and their duties, the analysis in the case is still necessary.

Exhibit 17.5   Overtime Security for the 21st Century Workforce

Comparing the Tests for Executive Employees

	Short Test Before 08/23/2004	Standard Test Effective 08/23/2004
Salary Level	**$250 per week**	**$455 per week**
Duties	Whose primary duty consists of the management of the enterprise in which the employee is employed or of a customarily recognized department or subdivision thereof; and Includes the customary and regular direction of the work of two or more other employees therein.	Whose primary duty is management of the enterprise in which the employee is employed or of a customarily recognized department or subdivision thereof; Who customarily and regularly directs the work of two or more other employees; and Who has the authority to hire or fire other employees or whose suggestions and recommendations as to the hiring, firing, advancement, promotion, or any other change of status of other employees are given particular weight.

Comparing the Tests for Administrative Employees

	Short Test Before 08/23/2004	Standard Test Effective 08/23/2004
Salary Level	**$250 per week**	**$455 per week**
Duties	Whose primary duty consists of the performance of office or nonmanual work directly related to management policies or general business operations of the employer or the employer's customers; and Which includes work requiring the exercise of discretion and independent judgment.	Whose primary duty is the performance of office or nonmanual work directly related to the management or general business operations of the employer or the employer's customers; and Whose primary duty includes the exercise of discretion and independent judgment with respect to matters of significance.

Comparing the Tests for Professional Employees

	Short Test Before 08/23/2004	Standard Test Effective 08/23/2004
Salary Level	**$250 per week**	**$455 per week**
	Whose primary duty consists of the performance of work requiring knowledge of an advanced type in a field of science or learning	Whose primary duty is the performance of work requiring knowledge of an advanced type (defined as work which is

Exhibit 17.5   (continued)

Duties	customarily acquired by a prolonged course of specialized intellectual instruction and study; and Which includes work requiring the consistent exercise of discretion and judgment; or Whose primary duty consists of the performance of work requiring invention, imagination, or talent in a recognized field of artistic endeavor.	predominantly intellectual in character, and which includes work requiring the consistent exercise of discretion and judgment) in a field of science or learning customarily acquired by a prolonged course of specialized intellectual instruction; or Whose primary duty is the performance of work requiring invention, imagination, originality, or talent in a recognized field of artistic or creative endeavor.

Comparing the Tests for Computer Employees

	Short Test Before 08/23/2004	Standard Test Effective 08/23/2004
Salary Level	$250 per week *or, if paid hourly,* $6^1/_2 \times \$4.25$ (i.e., $27.63 an hour)	$455 per week *or* $27.63 an hour
Duties	Primary duty of performing work that requires theoretical and practical application of highly specialized knowledge in computer systems analysis, programming, and software engineering, and employed and engaged in these activities as a computer systems analyst, computer programmer, software engineer, or other similarly skilled worker in the computer software field, as provided in § 541.303, which includes work requiring the consistent exercise of discretion and judgment. §541.303(b): Whose primary duty consists of one or more of the following: (1) The application of systems analysis techniques and procedures, including consulting with users, to determine hardware, software, or system functional specifications; (2) The design, development, documentation, analysis, creation, testing, or modification of computer systems or programs, including prototypes, based on and	Computer systems analysts, computer programmers, software engineers or other similarly skilled workers in the computer field are eligible for exemption, but only if the employee's primary duty consists of: (1) The application of systems analysis techniques and procedures, including consulting with users, to determine hardware, software, or system functional specifications; (2) The design, development, documentation, analysis, creation, testing, or modification of computer systems or programs, including prototypes, based on and related to

(continued)

Exhibit 17.5 (continued)

related to user or system design specifications;
(3) The design, documentation, testing, creation, or modification of computer programs related to machine operating systems; or
(4) A combination of the aforementioned duties, the performance of which requires the same level of skills.

user or system design specifications;
(3) The design, documentation, testing, creation, or modification of computer programs related to machine operating systems; or
(4) A combination of the aforementioned duties, the performance of which requires the same level of skills.

Comparing the Tests for Outside Sales Employees

	Short Test Before 08/23/2004	Standard Test Effective 08/23/2004
Salary Level	**No minimum salary required**	**No minimum salary required**
Duties	Who is employed for the purpose of and who is customarily and regularly engaged away from the employer's place or places of business in making sales; or obtaining orders or contracts for services or for the use of facilities for which a consideration will be paid by the client or customer; and	Whose primary duty is making sales or obtaining orders or contracts for services or for the use of facilities for which a consideration will be paid by the client or customer; and
	Who does not devote more than 20 percent of the hours worked in the work week by nonexempt employees of the employer to activities that are not incidental to and in conjunction with the employee's own outside sales or solicitations.	Who is customarily and regularly engaged away from the employer's place or places of business in performing such primary duty.

Source: http://www.dol.gov/esa/regs/compliance/whd/fairpay/fairpayprintpage2.asp?REF=side-by-side_PF.htm.

Reich v. Newspapers of New England, Inc. *44 F.3d 1060 (1st Cir. 1995)*

In this case the court determines whether reporters who do general reporting for a small local newspaper are subject to the FLSA overtime pay requirements.

Torruella, J.

The Monitor is an award-winning small-city newspaper with a daily circulation in excess of 4,000 copies. Its reporters are assigned to tasks ranging from writing features to covering legislative, municipal, and town governments and agencies. The reporters work essentially unsupervised, have authority and discretion over what they do and write, and decide how their assignments should be executed. Most of their time, however, is spent on "general assignment" work, and their writing is mainly focused on "hard news."

Even though its reporters work extended hours, management at *The Monitor* discourages overtime. Rather, it prefers that its employees seek compensatory time. The secretary of labor asserts that *The Monitor's* overtime policy violates the FLSA, and seeks a permanent injunction and back pay for the employees. *The Monitor* responds that the employees are exempt professionals.

The FLSA's overtime compensation provisions do not apply to professionals. The specific requirements of the exemption are not set forth in the statute. Rather, they are articulated in Department of Labor regulations and interpretations.

The regulation enumerates several types of professional exemptions, but only the "artistic professional" exemption, which applies to professionals working in a "recognized field of artistic endeavor," applies here. The regulation outlines both a short and long test for determining whether an employee qualifies as an artistic professional. The long test is applied to employees who earn weekly salaries of at least $170 but less than $250. Both tests demand that the employee's "primary duty" consist of work requiring "invention, imagination, or talent." The long test also requires that the employee's primary duty consist of "[w]ork that is original and creative in character." 29 CFR 541.3(a)(2).

The Monitor maintains that the district court erroneously applied the long test to three reporters whose weekly salary qualified them for analysis under the short test. This issue is not dispositive, however, because we believe the employees are exempt under either test.

The relevant portion of the short test requires us to determine (1) the employee's "primary duty," and (2) whether the performance of that duty requires "invention, imagination, or talent." Because the secretary stipulated that writing was the primary duty of these employees, the only issue remaining is whether their writing required "invention, imagination, or talent."

The day-to-day duties of the three reporters consisted primarily of "general assignment" work. Among other things, their stories covered public utility commission hearings; criminal and police activity; city and state legislative proceedings; business events, including compiling a list of people who had been promoted; and local art events. Rarely were they asked to editorialize about or interpret the events they covered. Rather, in the words of one of the employees, the focus of their writing was "to tell someone who wanted to know what happened . . . in a quick and informative and understandable way." Thus, these reporters were like the majority of reporters in that their work "depends primarily on intelligence, diligence, and accuracy." They were not performing duties that would place them in that minority of reporters whose work depends primarily on invention, imagination, or talent. Although some of their work product demonstrated creativity, invention, imagination, and talent, their writing did not exhibit these qualities on a day-to-day basis.

Our decision should not be read to mean that all journalism work is non-exempt. The determination of whether the exemption applies to a given employee depends on the specific duties and characteristics required by the position rather than its actual title. AFFIRMED.

Case Questions

1. Are you surprised by this decision?
2. Does this decision make sense to you?
3. Why do you think the employer chose to interpret the regulation as it did?

MAXIMUM HOURS

Scenario

Actually, FLSA does not limit the hours employees work but, rather, sets standards for the hours constituting a normal workweek for wage purposes. The statute then sets wage rates for hours worked over and above the normal week. The 40-hour workweek and wage rate were discussed previously in the minimum wage section, as were the exemptions. That is why, in opening scenario 2, Chad is incorrect in telling his boss that the law says he does not have to work over 40 hours per week. The law doesn't dictate hours, but merely states that, if Chad does work over 40 hours, he must be paid time and a half for the time he worked in excess of 40 hours. In the *Sherwood* case, the court analyzes whether a creative reporter is exempt from the overtime provisions of FLSA.

Sherwood v. Washington Post *871 F. Supp. 1471*
(D.D.C. 1994)

A newspaper reporter whose primary duties required invention, imagination, and talent is found to be exempt from the overtime requirement of the FLSA.

Johnson, J.

A former reporter for the *Washington Post* contends that the paper violated the FLSA by refusing to pay overtime for all hours worked in excess of 40 hours per week. The reporter's primary duty for the paper was to gather news and present it to readers in a clear, fair, balanced and expert fashion. He was also required to originate story ideas, piece together seemingly unrelated facts, analyze facts and circumstances, and present his stories in an engaging style. His fact gathering thus involved more than passively writing down what others told him. He was required to cultivate sources, utilize his imagination and other skills in seeking information, and continually develop his finely tuned interviewing skills. The reporter was required to advise his editors when he believed that particular topics might be newsworthy, and was expected to originate ideas for stories.

He was the one primarily responsible for producing story ideas and following through on their investigation. The court finds that the duties of originating story ideas, and getting information to shape and develop stories, required invention, imagination and talent by the reporter. JUDGMENT FOR DEFENDANT.

Case Questions

1. Do you understand the difference between this case and the *Newspapers of New England* case? Explain.
2. Do you think there should be a distinction in FLSA between those who use their imagination, talent, and invention and those who do not, though they do the same thing, such as work as reporters for a newspaper?
3. How would you change this FLSA scheme, if you could?

comp time
Compensatory time. Time off given to an employee who works over a certain amount of hours. Given in lieu of overtime pay, generally to those who do not qualify for such pay.

In *Moreau,* the U.S. Supreme Court wrestled with the issue of whether sheriffs could receive **comp time** rather than time and a half for overtime worked. This has become an increasingly heated topic for exempt employees who would not otherwise be entitled to overtime pay but wish to receive some form of compensation for working more than 40 hours per week. (See Exhibit 17.6 for exemptions and partial exemptions from overtime pay.)

Exhibit 17.6

Full and Partial Overtime Pay Exemptions

EXEMPTIONS FROM OVERTIME PAY ONLY

Certain commissioned employees of retail or service establishments; auto, truck, trailer, farm implement, boat, or aircraft salesworkers; or parts-clerks and mechanics servicing autos, trucks, or farm implements who are employed by nonmanufacturing establishments primarily engaged in selling these items to ultimate purchasers.

Employees of railroads and air carriers, taxi drivers, certain employees of motor carriers, seamen on American vessels, and local delivery employees paid on approved trip rate plans.

Announcers, news editors, and chief engineers of certain nonmetropolitan broadcasting stations.

Domestic service workers living in the employer's residence.

Employees of motion picture theaters.

Farmworkers.

PARTIAL EXEMPTIONS FROM OVERTIME PAY

Partial overtime pay exemptions apply to employees engaged in certain operations on agricultural commodities and to employees of certain bulk petroleum distributors.

Hospitals and residential care establishments may adopt, by agreement with their employees, a 14-day work period instead of the usual 7-day workweek, if the employees are paid at least time and one-half their regular rates for hours worked over 8 in a day or 80 in a 14-day work period, whichever is the greater number of overtime hours.

Employees who lack a high school diploma, or who have not attained the educational level of the 8th grade, can be required to spend up to 10 hours in a workweek engaged in remedial reading or training in other basic skills without receiving time and one-half overtime pay for these hours. However, the employees must receive their normal wages for hours spent in such training and the training must not be job specific.

Source: http://www.dol.gov/esa/wpd.

Moreau v. Klevenhagen *508 U.S. 22 (1993)*

A group of sheriffs wanted to be paid time and a half rather than comp time for overtime under the FLSA. They alleged the statute allowing for comp time did not apply to them; thus, they should be paid overtime rather than comp time. The Supreme Court held that under FLSA they could lawfully be compensated with comp time rather than time and a half for the overtime worked.

Stevens, J.

Because the text of the FLSA Amendments of 1985, 99 Stat. 70, codified at 29 U.S.C. 207(o) provides the framework for our entire analysis, we quote the most relevant portion at the outset. Subsection 7(o)(2)(A) states:

(2) A public agency may provide compensatory time [in lieu of overtime pay] only—

(A) pursuant to—

(i) applicable provisions of a collective bargaining agreement, memorandum of understanding, or any other agreement between the public agency and representatives of such employees; or

(ii) in the case of employees not covered by subclause (i), an agreement or understanding arrived at between the employer and employee before the performance of the work. . . .

Petitioners are a group of employees who sought, unsuccessfully, to negotiate a collective FLSA compensatory time agreement by way of a designated representative. The narrow question dispositive here is whether petitioners are "employees not covered by subclause (i)" within the meaning of subclause (ii), so that their employer may provide compensatory time pursuant to individual agreements under the second subclause.

Petitioner Moreau is the president of the Harris County Deputy Sheriffs Union, representing approximately 400 deputy sheriffs in this action against the County and its sheriff, respondent Klevenhagen. For several years, the Union has represented Harris County deputy sheriffs in various matters, such as processing grievances and handling workers' compensation claims, but it is prohibited by Texas law from entering into a collective-bargaining agreement with the County. Accordingly, the terms and conditions of petitioners' employment are included in individual form agreements signed by each employee. These agreements incorporate by reference the County's regulations providing that deputies shall receive one and one-half hours of compensatory time for each hour of overtime work.

The employees filed this action, alleging, inter alia, that the County violated the Act by paying overtime work with comp time, rather than overtime pay, absent an agreement with their representative authorizing the substitution. Employees contended that they were "covered" by subclause (i) of subsection 7(o)(2)(A) by virtue of their union representation, and that the County therefore was precluded from providing comp time pursuant to individual agreements (or pre-existing practice) under subclause (ii).

Employers find the language of the statute perfectly clear. In their view, subclause (ii) plainly authorizes individual agreements whenever public employees have not successfully negotiated a collective-bargaining agreement under subclause (i). Employees, on the other hand, contend that ambiguity in the statute itself justifies resort to its legislative history and the DOL regulations, and that these secondary sources unequivocally preclude individual comp time agreements with employees who have designated a representative. We begin our analysis with the relevant statutory text.

At least one proposition is not in dispute. Subclause (ii) authorizes individual comp time agreements only "in the case of employees not covered by subclause (i)." Our task, therefore, is to identify the class of "employees" covered by subclause (i). This task is complicated by the fact that subclause (i) does not purport to define a category of employees, as the reference in subclause (ii) suggests it would. Instead, it describes only a category of agreements—those that (a) are bargained with an employee representative, and (b) authorize the use of comp time.

Respondents read this shift in subject from "employees" in subclause (ii) to "agreement" in subclause (i) as susceptible of just one meaning: employees are covered by subclause (i) only if they are bound by applicable provisions of a collective-bargaining agreement. Under this narrow construction, subclause (i) would not cover employees who designate a representative if that representative is unable to reach agreement with the employer, for whatever reason; such employees would remain "uncovered" and available for individual comp time agreements under subclause (ii).

We find this reading unsatisfactory. First, while the language of subclauses (i) and (ii) will bear the interpretation advanced by respondents, we cannot say that it will bear no other. Purely as a matter of grammar, subclause (ii)'s reference to "employees" remains unmodified by subclause (i)'s focus on "agreement," and "employees . . . covered" might as easily comprehend employees with representatives as employees with agreements.

Second, employer's reading is difficult to reconcile with the general structure of subsection 7(o). Assuming designation of an employee representative, employer's theory leaves it to the employer to choose whether it will proceed under subclause (i), and negotiate the terms of a collective comp time agreement with the representative, or instead proceed under subclause (ii), and deal directly with its employees on an individual basis. If the employer is free to choose the latter course (as most employers likely would), then it need only decline to negotiate with the employee representative to render subclause (i) inapplicable and authorize individual comp time agreements under subclause (ii). This permissive interpretation of subsection 7(o), however, is at odds with the limiting phrase of subclause (ii) at issue here. Had Congress intended such an open-ended authorization of the use of comp time, it surely would have said so more simply, forgoing the elaborate subclause structure that purports to restrict use of individual agreements to a limited class of employees. Employer's broad interpretation of the subsection 7(o) exception is also in some tension with the well-established rule that "exemptions from the [FLSA] are to be narrowly construed."

At the same time, however, we find equally implausible a reading of the statutory text that would deem employees "covered" by subclause (i) whenever they select a representative, whether or not the representative has the ability to enter into the kind of agreement described in that subclause. If there is no possibility of reaching an agreement under subclause (i), then that subclause cannot logically be read as applicable. In other words, "employees . . . covered by subclause (i)" must, at a minimum, be employees who conceivably could receive comp time pursuant to the agreement contemplated by that subclause.

The most plausible reading of the phrase "employees . . . covered by subclause (i)" is, in our view, neither of the extreme alternatives described above. Rather, the phrase is most sensibly read as referring to employees who have designated a representative with the authority to negotiate and agree with their employer on "applicable provisions of a collective bargaining agreement" authorizing the use of comp time. This reading accords significance to both the focus on the word "agreement" in subclause (i) and the focus on "employees" in subclause (ii). It is also true to the hierarchy embodied in subsection 7(o), which favors subclause (i) agreements over individual agreements by limiting use of the latter to cases in which the former are unavailable.

This intermediate reading of the statutory text is consistent also with the DOL regulations, interpreted most reasonably. It is true that 29 CFR 553.23(b), read in isolation, would support the employees' view that selection of a representative by employees—even a representative without lawful authority to bargain with the employer—is sufficient to bring the employees within the scope of subclause (i) and preclude use of subclause (ii) individual

agreements. So interpreted, however, the regulation would prohibit entirely the use of comp time in a substantial portion of the public sector. It would also be inconsistent with the Secretary's statement that "the question . . . whether employees have a representative for purposes of FLSA section 7(o) shall be determined in accordance with State or local law and practices." This clarification by the Secretary convinces us that when the regulations identify selection of a representative as the condition necessary for coverage under subclause (i), they refer only to those representatives with lawful authority to negotiate agreements.

Thus, under both the statute and the DOL regulations, employees are "covered" by subclause (i) when they designate a representative who lawfully may bargain collectively on their behalf—under the statute, because such authority is necessary to reach the kind of "agreement" described in subclause (i), and under the regulation, because such authority is a condition of "representative" status for subclause (i) purposes. Because we construe the statute and regulation in harmony, we need not comment further on the employees' argument that the Secretary's interpretation of the 1985 Amendments is entitled to special deference.

The employees' in this case did not have a representative authorized by law to enter into an agreement with their employer providing for use of comp time under subclause (i). Accordingly, they were "not covered by subclause (i)," and subclause (ii) authorized the individual agreements challenged in this litigation. AFFIRMED.

Case Questions

1. Why do you think the employer wanted to pay comp time rather than time and a half?

2. Do you agree with the Court's assessment of the statutory language permitting the comp time? Explain.

3. Do you think that since this was a public employer the Court was more sensitive to the issue of public finances, accountability to the public, the need for containing costs, and the potential for abuse in overtime when the public's welfare is at issue? Explain.

CHILD LABOR LAWS

FLSA sets minimum age standards for allowing children to work. Under the law, most cannot work before age 16, with 18 being the minimum age for hazardous jobs. The Department of Labor publishes a list of such occupations. Children between the ages

Exhibit 17.7   Nonfarm FLSA Rules for Employees under 18

According to the Department of Labor, in nonfarm work, the permissible jobs and hours of work, by age, are as follows:

Youths 18 years or older may perform any job, whether hazardous or not, for unlimited hours.

Youths 16 and 17 years old may perform any nonhazardous job, for unlimited hours.

Youths 14 and 15 years old may work outside school hours in various nonmanufacturing, nonmining, nonhazardous jobs under the following conditions: no more than 3 hours on a school day, 18 hours in a school week, 8 hours on a nonschool day, or 40 hours in a nonschool week. Also, work may not begin before 7 A.M., nor end after 7 P.M., except from June 1 through Labor Day, when evening hours are extended to 9 P.M. Under a special provision, youths 14 and 15 years old enrolled in an approved Work Experience and Career Exploration Program (WECEP) may be employed for up to 23 hours in school weeks and 3 hours on school days (including during school hours).

Fourteen is the minimum age for most nonfarm work. However, at any age, youths may deliver newspapers; perform in radio, television, movie, or theatrical productions; work for parents in their solely owned nonfarm business (except in manufacturing or on hazardous jobs); or gather evergreens and make evergreen wreaths.

Source: http://www.dol.gov/esa/regs/compliance/whd/hrg.htm#6.

Scenario 1

of 14 and 16 may work at certain types of jobs that do not interfere with their health, education, or well-being, such as the traditional newspaper deliverer set forth in opening scenario 1. (See Exhibit 17.7 for an overview of the rules.) Certain agricultural work is permitted also. States may have child labor laws even stricter than the federal, and, if so, they override federal law. Exhibit 17.8 indicates not only how important an issue this can become but also how divided.

Labor Secretary Robert Reich's announcement last week that he was moving to suspend restrictions on the hours that 14- and 15-year-olds may work as baseball bat boys and girls runs counter to a recommendation by an advisory panel established to review the child labor laws.

Reich's position accords with that of former Vice-President Dan Quayle, who unsuccessfully worked to lift the ban during his tenure in the Senate. Quayle had sought to amend the Fair Labor Standards Act after the Labor Department said bat boys and girls must be at least 16 years old because 14- and 15-year-olds may not work beyond 9:00 P.M. during the summer and 7:00 P.M. while school is in session.

Reich said last May 27 he was suspending enforcement of the DOL regulation for the remainder of the baseball season. "After a preliminary review, the current child labor policy, as it has been applied to batboys and batgirls, seems off base," he said.

Exhibit 17.8   (continued)

Reich's move was prompted by the Savannah Cardinals' firing of Tommy McCoy, a bat boy under the age of 16. The Labor Department had alerted the team that McCoy's employment might pose a problem. The investigation had not proceeded any further before Reich decided to suspend enforcement while examining the rule.

Reich said an examination of whether "the child labor regulation in such a case is truly necessary" is "[c]onsistent with the current efforts to reinvent government, to make it more responsive and efficient." McCoy has since gone back to work for the Cardinals. It is "not the intent of the law to deny young teenagers employment opportunities, so long as their health and well-being are not impaired," Reich said.

Reich's move runs counter to the position adopted by the now-defunct independent Child Labor Advisory Committee. In 1989, the panel recommended and the Labor Department agreed that there should be no exception for hours and times of work for 14- and 15-year-olds working as bat boys and girls in professional baseball.

Linda Golodner, co-chair of the Child Labor Coalition, criticized Reich's move, voicing concern that it sets a precedent for other changes in the child labor regulations. Golodner, who headed the advisory panel, told BNA May 28 the coalition opposes any exceptions to allowing 14- and 15-year-olds to work longer hours, no matter how "glamorous" the industry.

Source: Reprinted with permission from *Daily Labor Reports,* no. 103 (June 15, 1993), pp. A-13–A-14. Copyright 1993 by the Bureau of National Affairs, Inc. (800-372-1033), www.bna.com.

Lynnville Transport, Inc. v. Chao *316 F. Supp. 2d 790* (*S.D. Iowa, CD 2004*)

The Department of Labor fined the employer for, among other things, allowing minors to operate certain equipment deemed to be too dangerous for their age, in violation of the child labor regulations. The employer argued that the minors did not operate the part of the equipment that presented the greatest danger, but the court sided with DOL and deemed any use of the equipment by minors to be a violation of the regulations.

Gritzner, J.

Lynnville, a closely held corporation located in Sully, Iowa, is a livestock hauling firm. The work that is the subject of this case involved the cleaning of the trailers used for hauling livestock. Between January 1996 and January 1998, this work was being performed in part by minor-aged children. The minor employees set their own work schedule and never worked at a time that interfered with their school or extracurricular activities. The parents of the children were aware of their children's schedules and the nature of the work they performed.

The minors occasionally used a New Holland LX 865 Skid Loader ("skid loader") to push manure into a pit and to pull a wagon to transport slats between the trucks and the washing shed. When used for this purpose, it was not necessary to, and the minors did not, raise the shovel of the skid loader from its lowest level.

In January 1998, Ronald Mease, an investigator for the Wage and Hour Division, conducted an investigation of Lynnville. During this investigation, the investigator found that Lynnville employed nine minors under the age of 18 to clean trailers. Of the nine minors, seven were under the age of 16, and three were 13 years old when they began working at Lynnville. At least five of the minors used the skid loader as part of their job duties, including two under age 14, and one additional child under age 16.

The issue here is whether the Agency correctly construed the applicable law, i.e., the applicable statutes

771

and regulations. The FLSA is a remedial statute, enacted in the public interest. The courts have found there is a particularly compelling public interest in protecting the health and well-being of working children. The child labor provisions of the FLSA were enacted to ensure that the children's employment will not physically harm them or interfere with their schooling.

The FLSA prohibits the employment of oppressive child labor in commerce, in the production of goods for commerce, or in any operation that qualifies as an "enterprise" under the Act. 29 U.S.C. §212(c). "Oppressive child labor" is defined in the Act as a condition of employment under which (1) any employee under the age of sixteen years is employed by an employer . . . in any occupation, or (2) any employee between the ages of sixteen and eighteen years is employed by an employer in any occupation which the Secretary of Labor shall find and by order declare to be particularly hazardous for the employment of children between such ages or detrimental to their health or well being. . . . The Secretary of Labor shall provide by regulation or by order that the employment of employees between the ages of fourteen and sixteen years in occupations other than manufacturing and mining shall not be deemed to constitute oppressive child labor if and to the extent that the Secretary of Labor determines that such employment is confined to periods which will not interfere with their schooling and to conditions which will not interfere with their health and well-being. 29 U.S.C. §203(1).

In accordance with this statutory provision, the Secretary of Labor has promulgated Hazardous Occupations ("HO") orders which prohibit or strictly regulate certain activities by minors. See 29 C.F.R. §570, subpart e ("Occupations Particularly Hazardous for the Employment of Minors Between 16 and 18 Years of Age or Detrimental to Their Health or Well-Being"). The regulation at issue here is HO Order No. 7. See 29 C.F.R. §570.58.

Use of the skid loader by the minor employees was found to violate HO Order No. 7 for "occupations involved in the operation of power-driven hoisting apparatus." 29 C.F.R. §570.58(a). In the regulation, the "work of operating [a] . . . hoist, or high-lift truck" is listed as one of the occupations particularly hazardous and violative of the FLSA. 29 C.F.R. §570.58(a) (l). The regulation further provides the following, in relevant part:

> (4) The term hoist shall mean a power-driven apparatus for raising or lowering a load by the application of a pulling force that does not include a car or platform running in guides. The term shall include all types of hoists, such as base mounted electric, clevis

suspension, hook suspension, monorail, overhead electric, simple drum and trolley suspension hoists. (5) The term high-lift truck shall mean a power-driven industrial type of truck used for lateral transportation that is equipped with a power-operated lifting device usually in the form of a fork or platform capable of tiering loaded pallets or skids one above the other. Instead of a fork or platform, the lifting device may consist of a ram, scoop, shovel, crane, revolving fork, or other attachments for handling specific loads. The term shall mean and include high lift trucks known under such names as fork lifts, fork trucks, fork-lift trucks, tiering trucks, or stacking trucks, but shall not mean low-lift trucks or low-lift platform trucks that are designed for the transportation of but not the tiering of material. 29 C.F.R. §570.58(b)(4)-(5).

Lynnville argues the issue is whether the simple use of a device that has the capacity to hoist or high lift is enough to meet the requirements of the regulations. The evidence in the record indicates that while some minors occasionally used the skid loader, the hoist or high-lift features were never used. Indeed, the Government accepts this contention.

The ALJ found "it is the mere *use* of the skid loader by minors that is precluded by Section 570.58(a)(l) . . . even if the minors' use of the equipment was consistent with that normally performed by low-lift trucks" (emphasis added). In so finding, the ALJ reasoned that "although the minors testified that they did not lift the shovel of the skid loader to high levels in performing their duties, the fact that they had the opportunity to do so, either intentionally or unintentionally, by moving the levers, placed the minors and other minors in the area in a potentially hazardous position." According to the ALJ, to find otherwise "would allow the employers and/or the minors to make the decision as to how the hazardous equipment should be operated to preclude a hazardous condition," a result certainly not allowed under the statute or regulations. The operation of a high-lift truck by a minor is a *per se* violation of the regulations and the operation of such a truck by minors is precluded by the hazardous order even if the minors' use of the equipment was consistent with that normally performed by low-lift trucks.

The Court finds the Agency's construction of the HO regulation concerning the skid loader did not contradict the statute or the plain language of the regulation. Therefore, the Court affirms the Agency's interpretation of 29 C.F.R. §570.58 as applied to Lynnville in the present action.

The law applies equally to the employer who acts with the best of intentions as it does to the employer who would subject minor laborers to dangerous and abusive conditions. Under the circumstances of this case, the frustration expressed in the record by management at Lynnville Transport is not surprising. The record indicates a benevolent effort to provide work opportunities to young people, without significant interference to their education, under the watchful attention of their parents, and with potential, but not actual, peril. The task of this Court, however, is to apply the law, not offer social commentary. Therefore, under the facts of the case, applicable law, and the narrow scope of this Court's review of agency action, the Court finds the decision of the Agency is supported by substantial evidence and was not clearly erroneous or an abuse of discretion. The decision of the Agency is AFFIRMED [and] the case is DISMISSED.

Case Questions

1. Do you agree with the court's decision? Explain.

2. Do you think it protects minors to have the rule applied this way (that is, making it a violation even if the minor does not use the part of the equipment that is dangerous)? Explain.

3. If you were an employer, what would you have done regarding minors after the court's decision?

Management Tips

As you have seen, there are several unexpected ways in which an employer can unwittingly violate the Fair Labor Standards Act. Becoming familiar with the requirements of the law and knowing its limitations proves helpful, as do the following tips:

- Whenever an employee is not an adult, check to make sure the employee is working only in ways authorized by law and hours dictated by law. Do not make exceptions.

- The purpose of time-and-a-half pay is to encourage employers to bring on extra employees when needed, rather than using present employees to take on extra duties or work extra hours. Keep this in mind when there is a pattern of excessive overtime pay. It may well indicate the need for additional employees.

- Be familiar with the employees exempted from wage and hour requirements so that wages are not paid out unnecessarily.

- Conduct periodic audits of the workplace to make sure employees are working as efficiently as possible so that overtime is limited only to what is necessary.

- Use the resources of the wage and hour offices if you run into a situation that seems unclear. You can access the office at http://www.dol.gov/esa/whd.

Summary

- FLSA is a comprehensive piece of legislation that governs wages, hours, and the employment of minors in the workplace and requires equal pay for both genders.

- While its coverage is far-reaching, it does provide exemptions.

- Employers are required to pay covered employees at least the minimum wage.

- Covered employees must be compensated at a rate of time and one-half their normal rate of pay for hours worked over 40 in one week.

- Children are prohibited from working if they are below a certain age, with exceptions.

- Be familiar with both the provisions of coverage and the exemptions, because violations may result in civil and criminal liability.

- Under the new regulations, in general, employees making under $23,660 are automatically considered to qualify for overtime pay, and those over $100,000 are automatically considered exempt from overtime pay.

Chapter-End Questions

1. A Christmas tree grower used seasonal help to assist in harvesting Christmas trees and did not pay them overtime wages since the growers deemed the employees as engaged in agriculture, which is exempted from the overtime provisions. DOL argued that the planting, fertilizing, and all other tasks relevant to growing the trees was performed by others who were agricultural workers exempted from the overtime provisions. However, they argued, since the seasonal employees only harvested the trees, they were not engaged in agriculture, but rather in forestry and lumbering, which requires the payment of overtime wages. Which view prevails? [*DOL* v. *N.C. Tree Growers Ass'n., Inc.,* 377 F.3d 345 (4th Cir. 2004).]

2. An employment placement agency employed Ursula as a staffing coordinator. Ursula received pay at straight-time rates for working any hours over 40. After resigning, Ursula claimed that the placement agency failed to pay her overtime wages as required by law. The agency claimed Ursula was an administrative employee who was exempt from overtime pay laws. Should Ursula receive the overtime pay? [*Tift* v. *Professional Nursing Serv., Inc.,* 886 P.2d 1158 (Wash. App. Div. 1, 1995).]

3. A manufacturer agreed with the union to allow it to have its union representatives (president and vice president) work on union matters full time and be paid by the manufacturer. The manufacturer agreed to pay the employees for 40 hours per week plus an amount based on the average overtime worked by employees in their departments. The employees handled grievances and workers' compensation claims but performed no work for the manufacturer. The employees demanded time and a half for overtime pay for hours worked over 40, rather than the amount based on the average overtime worked by their department coworkers. The manufacturer refused to pay. Should the employees receive what they asked for, under FLSA? [*Douglas* v. *Argo-Tech Corp.,* 113 F.3d 67 (6th Cir. 1997).]

4. An ambulance service scheduled employees in 24-hour shifts, but only paid them for 13 or 14 hours of work. They deducted 8 hours for sleep and 3 hours for meals, even though they counted as little as 30 minutes as a meal break. The employees challenged this practice. Will they win? [*Bayles* v. *American Medical Response of Colorado, Inc.,* 950 F. Supp. 1053 (D. Colo. 1996).]

5. A nonprofit religious organization derived most of its income from the operation of commercial businesses staffed by its "associates." These people, former drug addicts and criminals, received no cash salaries but were provided with food, clothing, shelter, and other benefits. Are these "associates" subject to the FLSA? [*Tony and Susan Alamo Foundation* v. *Secretary of Labor,* 471 U.S. 290 (1985).]

6. Truck drivers employed by a freight company were required to conduct safety inspections on their trucks and take them in for repair if they failed the inspections. They were not paid by the employer for doing this Does FLSA require that they be paid? [*Barrentine* v. *Arkansas-Best Freight System,* 450 U.S. 728 (1981).]

7. Can an employer be imprisoned for violating the FLSA? Explain.

8. Allbright finds that Benito, Juana, and Lao Tsu, three of his employees, were the cause of the discovery of FLSA violations. As a result, he terminates them. Do the employees have any recourse? Explain.

9. Thomas, an elementary school teacher, is resentful of the time he has to spend before and after school correcting papers, copying work sheets for students, and creating interesting and stimulating classroom bulletin boards for the children. Janella, an hourly employee at the local toy factory, tells Thomas that he should file a claim against his employer for violating the FLSA because when she works over a certain number of hours per week she is paid overtime, and Thomas should be too. What should Thomas do?

10. Sasha is employed as the Winstons' babysitter when they must occasionally stay over in town because of their jobs. Sasha is becoming increasingly discontented with her wages, which are below minimum wage. What relief does the FLSA provide for Sasha?

Glossary

A

ADA and Rehabilitation Act protection   As long as an individual with a disability is otherwise qualified for a position, with or without reasonable accommodation, the employer may not make an adverse employment decision solely on the basis of the disability.

adverse employment action   Any action or omission that takes away a benefit, opportunity, or privilege of employment from an employee.

affinity orientation   Whom one is attracted to for personal and intimate relationships.

affirmative action   Intentional inclusion of women and minorities in the workplace based on a finding of their previous exclusion and/or underrepresentation.

affirmative action plan   A government contractor's plan containing placement goals for inclusion of underrepresented or excluded women and minorities in the workplace and timetables for accomplishing the goals.

Age Discrimination in Employment Act   Prohibits discrimination in employment on the basis of age for individuals who are at least 40 years old.

agency shop clause   Requires nonunion members to pay union dues without having to be subject to the union rules.

706 agency   State agency that handles EEOC claims on the basis of a work-sharing agreement with the EEOC.

AIDS   Acquired immune deficiency syndrome, a syndrome in which the individual's immune system ceases to function properly and during which the individual is susceptible, in most cases fatally, to opportunistic diseases. AIDS is not transmitted through casual contact; to transmit the disease, there must be an exchange of fluids. The disease may be transmitted through sexual contact, during which there is an exchange of bodily fluids; needle sharing; or an exchange of blood.

Americans with Disabilities Act   Protects from employment discrimination those who are disabled but can still perform a job, with or without the need for reasonable accommodation that does not cause the employer undue hardship.

antiretaliation provisions   Provisions making it illegal to treat an employee adversely because the employee pursued his or her rights under Title VII.

arbitration   The selection of a neutral or third party to consider a dispute and to deliver a binding or nonbinding decision.

assumption of risk   A defense to a negligence action based on the argument that the injured party voluntarily exposed herself or himself to a known danger created by the other party's negligence.

at-will employment   An employment relationship where there is no contractual obligation to remain in the relationship and either party may terminate the relationship at any time, for any reason as long as the reason is not prohibited by law, such as for discriminatory purposes.

availability   Minorities and women in a geographic area who are qualified for a particular position.

B

back pay   Money awarded for time employee was not working (usually due to termination) because of illegal discrimination.

bargaining unit   The group of employees in a workplace that have the legal right to bargain with the employer.

BFOQ   Bona fide occupational qualification reasonably necessary to the employer's particular business. Legalized discrimination.

bi-gender affinity orientation   Someone attracted to both genders.

bona fide occupational qualification (BFOQ) Permissible discrimination if legally necessary for employer's particular business.

business agent   The representative of a union, usually craft.

business necessity   Defense to a disparate impact case based on the employer's need for the policy as a legitimate requirement for the job.

C

claimant or charging party   The person who brings an action alleging violation of Title VII.

closed shop   Employer hires only union members.

collective bargaining   Negotiations and agreements between management and labor about wages, hours, and other terms and conditions of employment.

collective bargaining agreement   Negotiated contract between management and the union representing employees covering wages, hours, and other terms and conditions of employment.

common law   Law made and applied by judges, based on precedent (prior case law).

community of interests   Factors employees have in common for bargaining purposes.

comp time   Compensatory time. Time off given to an employee who works over a certain amount of hours. Given in lieu of overtime pay, generally to those who do not qualify for such pay.

comparable worth   A Title VII action for pay discrimination based on gender, in which jobs held mostly by women are compared with comparable jobs held mostly by men who are paid more than the women, to determine if there is gender discrimination.

compelled self-publication   Occurs when an ex-employee is forced to repeat the reason for her or his termination and thereby makes a claim for defamation.

compensatory damages   Money awarded to compensate the injured party for direct losses.

conciliation   Attempting to reach agreement on a claim through discussion, without resort to litigation.

constructive discharge   Occurs when the employee is given no reasonable alternative but to terminate the employment relationship because of (usually) illegal activity toward the employee; considered an involuntary act on the part of the employee.

continual-training requirement   OSHA requires that the employer provide safety training to all new employees and to all employees who have been transferred into new positions.

contributory negligence   A defense to a negligence action based on the injured party's failure to exercise reasonable care for her or his own safety.

corporate management compliance evaluation   Evaluations of mid- and senior-level employee advancement.

covenant of good faith and fair dealing   Implied contractual obligation to act in good faith in the fulfillment of each party's contractual duties of employment.

craft unions   Unions composed of skilled craftworkers not situated at any one workplace.

D

debar   Prohibit a federal contractor from further participation in government contracts.

defamation   An intentional tort involving the publication of false statements about another.

defendant   One against whom a case is brought.

defined benefit plan   A plan that defines in advance the amount to be paid to retiree on retirement.

defined contribution plans   A plan that defines the amount of the employee contribution, without a specific amount to be paid at retirement.

de novo review   Complete new look at administrative case by the reviewing court.

disability   A physical or mental impairment that substantially limits one or more of the major life activities of an individual; a record of such impairment; or being regarded as having such an impairment.

disparate treatment   Treating similarly situated employee differently because of prohibited Title VII factors.

disparate/adverse impact   Effect of facially neutral policy is deleterious for Title VII group.

duty to reasonably accommodate   The employer's duty to try to find a way to avoid conflict between workplace policies and an employee's religious practices or beliefs or disability.

E

EEO investigator   Employee of EEOC who reviews complaints for merit.

eligibility testing   Tests an employer administers to ensure that the potential employee is capable and qualified to perform the requirements of the position.

emergency temporary standards   These standards are imposed by OSHA without immediately going through the typical process when an employee is exposed to grave danger from exposure to substances and the standards are necessary to protect employees from the danger.

employee benefit plans   A plan, fund, or program that has been established by an employer to cover benefits for its employees relating to medical or hospital care, death, unemployment, or vacation benefits.

equitable relief Relief that is not in the form of money damages, such as injunctions, reinstatement, promotion. Equitable relief is based on concepts of justice and fairness.

essential functions of a position Under the ADA, those tasks that are fundamental, not marginal or unnecessary, to the fulfillment of the job's objectives.

exhaustion of administrative remedies Going through the established EEOC administrative procedure before being permitted to seek judicial review of an agency decision.

F

face validity A test that looks well suited to its purpose.

facially neutral policy Workplace policy applies equally to all appropriate employees.

fellow servant rule An employer's defense to liability for an employee's injury where the injury occurred on the job and was caused by the negligence of another employee.

fetal protection policies Policies an employer institutes to protect the fetus or reproductive capacity of employees.

fiduciary One who holds funds in trust for another; one who holds a position of trust and confidence.

four-fifths rule Minority must do at least 80 percent or four-fifths as well as majority on screening device or presumption of disparate impact arises, and device must then be shown to be job related.

free riders Bargaining unit employees who do not pay dues but whom the union is still obligated to represent.

front pay Money awarded for time a claimant would have been in a job had illegal discrimination not occurred to keep him or her out.

fundamental right A right that is guaranteed by the Constitution.

G

gender dysphoria The psychological condition of a person's physical gender being at odds with his or her emotional/psychological gender.

"gender-plus" discrimination Employment discrimination based on gender and some other factor such as marital status or children.

gender/sexual reassignment surgery The surgery required to change a person's gender.

gender stereotypes The assumption that most or all members of a particular gender must act a certain way.

general duty clause A provision of the OSHA law requiring that employers furnish to each employee employment and a place of employment free from recognized hazards that cause or are likely to cause death or serious physical harm to the employee.

genetic testing Investigation and evaluation of an individual's biological predispositions based on the presence of a specific disease-associated gene in his or her chromosomes.

greater hazard defense Employer's defense to an OSHA violation where the hazards of compliance are greater than the hazards of noncompliance, where alternative means of protection are unavailable, and where a variance was not available.

Guidelines on Discrimination Because of Religion or National Origin Federal guidelines that apply only to federal contractors or agencies and that impose on these employers an affirmative duty to prevent discrimination.

H

HIV Human immunodeficiency virus, the virus that causes AIDS.

hostile environment sexual harassment Sexual harassment in which the harasser creates an abusive, offensive, or intimidating environment for the harassee.

I

impairment "[a]ny physiological disorder or condition . . . affecting one or more of the following body systems: neurological; musculoskeletal; special sense organs; respiratory, including speech organs; cardiovascular; reproductive; digestive; genitourinary; hemic and lymphatic; skin; and endocrine; or any mental or psychological disorder" which substantially limits one of life's major activities. (From the EEOC's ADA regulations.)

implied contract A contract that is not expressed, but, instead, is created by conduct of the parties involved.

independent contractor Generally, a person who contracts with a principal to perform a task according to her or his own methods, and who is not under the principal's control regarding the physical details of the work.

industrial union   Union with branches at particular workplaces.

injunction   A court order requiring individuals or groups of persons to not perform certain acts that the court has determined will do irreparable harm.

IRS test   List of 20 factors to which the IRS looks to determine whether someone is an employee or an independent contractor.

J

job analysis   Information regarding the nature of the work associated with a job and the knowledge, skills, and abilities required to perform that work.

job group analysis   Combines job titles with similar content, wage rates, and opportunities.

judicial affirmative action   Affirmative action ordered by a court, rather than arising from Executive Order 11246.

judicial review   Court review of an agency's decision.

L

liquidated damages   A predetermined amount of damages. As used in the ADEA, liquidated damages are equal to the unpaid wage and are available in cases involving "willful violations" of the statute.

lockout   Management does not allow employees to come to work.

M

major life activities   "functions such as caring for one's self, performing manual tasks, walking, seeing, hearing, speaking, breathing, learning and working." (From the EEOC's ADA regulations.)

make-whole relief   Attempts to put claimant in the position he or she would have been in had there been no discrimination.

management security clause   Parties agree that management has the right to run the business and make appropriate business decisions as long as applicable laws are complied with.

mandatory arbitration agreements   Agreement an employee signs as a condition of employment, requiring that any workplace disputes be arbitrated rather than litigated.

mandatory retirement   Employee must retire upon reaching a specified age. Deemed illegal by the 1986 amendments to the ADEA, with few exceptions.

mandatory subject of bargaining   Wages, hours, and other conditions of employment, which, by law, must be negotiated between labor and management if there is a union representing employees.

midterm negotiations   Collective bargaining negotiations during the term of the contract rather than when the contract expires.

minimum wages   The least amount a covered employee must be paid in hourly wages.

N

national origin discrimination protection   It is unlawful for an employer to limit, segregate, or classify employees in any way on the basis of national origin that would deprive them of the privileges, benefits, or opportunities of employment.

national origin   Individual's or her or his ancestor's place of origin (as opposed to citizenship), or physical, cultural, or linguistic characteristics of an origin group.

negligence   Failure to meet the appropriate standard of care for avoiding unreasonable risk of harm to others.

no reasonable cause   EEOC finding that no reasonable basis for illegal discrimination exists.

no-fault   Liability for injury imposed regardless of who was at fault.

noncompete agreement   An agreement signed by the employee agreeing not to disclose the employer's confidential information or enter into competition with the employer for a specified period of time and/or within a specified region.

no-strike, no-lockout clause   Clause in a collective bargaining agreement that labor and management agree that labor will not strike and management will not stage a lockout.

O

organizational profile   Staffing patterns showing organizational units, relationship to each other, and gender, race and ethnic composition. Generally for affirmative action plan purposes.

P

performance appraisal   Periodic assessment of an employee's performance, usually completed by her or his immediate supervisor and reviewed, at times, by others in the workplace.

permissive subjects of bargaining   Nonmandatory subjects that can be negotiated between labor and management but are not required to be.

picketing   The carrying of signs, which tell of an unfair labor practice or strike, by union members in front of the employer's business.

placement goal   Percentage of women and/or minorities to be hired to correct underrepresentation, based on availability in the geographic area under an affirmative action plan.

plaintiff   One who brings a civil action.

polygraph   A device that measures biological reactions to individuals when questioned to determine if they are telling the truth; lie detector.

preemployment testing   Testing that takes place before hiring, or sometimes after hiring but before employment, in connection with such qualities as integrity, honesty, drug and alcohol use, HIV, or other characteristics.

prima facie case   Alleging facts that fit each requirement of a cause of action.

private sector   Companies that are not owned or managed by the government or one of its agencies.

public policy   A legal concept intended to ensure that no individual lawfully do that which has a tendency to be injurious to the public or against the public good.

public sector   That segment of the workforce represented by governmental employers and governmental agency employers. In some situations, this term may include federal contractors.

punitive damages   Money damages over and above compensatory damages, designed to punish flagrant wrongdoers and to deter them and others from engaging in similar conduct in the future.

Q

qualified for the position   Able to meet the employer's legitimate job requirements.

quid pro quo sexual harassment   Sexual harassment in which the harasser requests sexual activity from the harassee in exchange for workplace benefits.

R

reasonable accommodation   An accommodation to the individual's disability that does not place an undue burden on the employer, as determined by size of the employer, cost to the employer, type of employer, and impact of the accommodation on the employer's operations.

reasonable cause   EEOC finding that basis for illegal discrimination exists.

reasonable person standard   Viewing the harassing activity from the perspective of a reasonable person in society at large (generally tends to be the male view).

reasonable victim standard   Viewing the harassing activity from the perspective of a reasonable person experiencing the harassing activity.

recklessness   Conscious disregard for safety; conscious failure to use due care.

recordkeeping and reporting requirements   Title VII requires that certain documents must be maintained and periodically reported to the EEOC.

respondent or **responding party**   Person to whom an EEOC claim is directed, usually the employer.

retroactive seniority   Seniority that dates back to the time the claimant was treated illegally.

reverse discrimination   Lawsuit or claim brought by majority member who feels adversely affected by the use of an affirmative action plan.

right-to-sue letter   Letter given by EEOC to claimants, permitting them to pursue their claim in court.

right-to-work laws   Permits employees to choose not to become a part of the union.

S

screening device   Factor used to weed out applicants from the pool of candidates.

search   A physical invasion of a person's space, belongings, or body by someone (usually in authority) looking for something.

secondary boycott   Work stoppage by employees who are not directly involved in the labor dispute. Done to show union solidarity.

section 503 of the Rehabilitation Act   Requires affirmative action on the part of federal contractors and agencies to recruit, hire, and train disabled workers.

severe and pervasive activity   Harassing activity that is more than an occasional act or is so serious that it is the basis for liability.

shop steward   Union member chosen as intermediary between the union and employees.

substantially limits   "unable to perform a major life activity that the average person in the general population can perform; or significantly restricted as to the condition, manner, or duration under which an individual can perform a major life activity." (From the EEOC's ADA regulations.)

T

tort   Private (civil) wrong against a person or her or his property.

transsexual/transgender   Someone who undergoes an operation to change from one gender to another.

U

under color of state law   Government employee is illegally discriminating against another during performance of his or her duties.

underrepresentation or **underutilization**   Significantly fewer minorities or women in the workplace than relevant statistics indicate are available.

undue hardship   Burden imposed on an employer, by accommodating an employee's religious conflict or disability, that would be too onerous for the employer to bear.

union shop   Union and management agree that employees must be a member of the union.

union shop clause   Provision in a collective bargaining agreement allowing a union shop.

V

validation   Evidence that shows a test evaluates what it says it evaluates.

valuing diversity   Learning to accept and appreciate those who are different from the majority and value their contributions to the workplace rather than view them as a negative.

vesting   Acquiring a right or an interest that is irrevocable by the donor.

vicarious liability   The imposition of liability on one party for the wrongs of another. Liability may extend from an employee to the employer on this basis if the employee is acting within the scope of her or his employment at the time the liability arose.

W

waiver   The intentional relinquishment of a known right.

wildcat strike   Strike not sanctioned by the union.

Y

yellow dog contract   Agreement employer requires employee to sign stating employee does not belong to a union and will not join one. Now illegal.

Case Index

General Index